ACCOUNTING
Information for
Business Decisions

Billie M. Cunningham
University of Missouri–Columbia

Loren A. Nikolai
University of Missouri–Columbia

John D. Bazley
University of Denver

THE DRYDEN PRESS
Harcourt Brace College Publishers

Fort Worth   Philadelphia   San Diego   New York   Orlando   Austin   San Antonio
Toronto   Montreal   London   Sydney   Tokyo

Publisher: Mike Roche
Acquisitions Editor: Bill Schoof
Market Strategist: Charles Watson
Developmental Editor: Jennifer Langer
Project Editor: Jim Patterson
Art Director: Biatriz Chapa
Production Manager: Darryl King

Credits appear on page 1011, which constitutes a continuation of the copyright page.
Cover illustration: Bill Brammer

ISBN: 0-03-022429-2
Library of Congress Catalog Card Number: 99-60960

Address for orders:
The Dryden Press
6277 Sea Harbor Drive
Orlando, FL 32887-6777
1-800-782-4479

Address for editorial correspondence:
The Dryden Press
301 Commerce Street, Suite 3700
Fort Worth, TX 76102

Web site address:
http://www.hbcollege.com

The Dryden Press, Dryden, and the Dryden Press logo are registered trademarks of Harcourt Brace & Company.

Printed in the United States of America

9 0 1 2 3 4 5 6 7 8   048   9 8 7 6 5 4 3 2 1

The Dryden Press
Harcourt Brace College Publishers

The Dryden Press Series in Accounting

Principles of Accounting
Integrated Financial/Managerial

Cunningham, Nikolai, and Bazley
ACCOUNTING: Information for Business Decisions

Technology Components

Guided Exploration, LLC
Interactive Decision Cases for Financial Accounting

Bell, Kirby, and Gantt
Guide to Understanding and Using Annual Reports

Davis
*OMAR (Online Multimedia Accounting Review:
The Accounting Cycle)*

Communication

McKay and Rosa
*The Accountants Guide to Professional
Communication: Writing and Speaking the Language
of Business*

Financial

Hanson and Hamre
Financial Accounting
Eighth Edition

Porter and Norton
Financial Accounting: The Impact on Decision Makers
Second Edition

Porter and Norton
Financial Accounting: The Impact on Decision Makers
Alternate Second Edition

Stickney and Weil
*Financial Accounting: An Introduction to Concepts,
Methods, and Uses*
Ninth Edition

Knechel
The Monopoly Game Practice Set

Managerial

Maher, Stickney, and Weil
*Managerial Accounting: An Introduction to Concepts,
Methods, and Uses*
Sixth Edition

Intermediate

Williams, Stanga, and Holder
Intermediate Accounting
Fifth Edition
1998 Update

Advanced

Pahler and Mori
Advanced Accounting: Concepts and Practice
Seventh Edition

Financial Statement Analysis

Stickney and Brown
Financial Statement Analysis: A Strategic Perspective
Fourth Edition

Auditing

Guy, Alderman, and Winters
Auditing
Fifth Edition

Rittenberg and Schwieger
Auditing: Concepts for a Changing Environment
Second Edition

Theory

Bloom and Elgers
*Foundations of Accounting Theory and Policy:
A Reader*

Bloom and Elgers
Issues in Accounting Policy: A Reader

Governmental and Not-For-Profit

Douglas
*Governmental and Nonprofit Accounting:
Theory and Practice*
Second Edition

Reference

Bailey and Miller
Miller Comprehensive GAAS Guide
College Edition

Williams and Miller
Miller Comprehensive GAAP Guide
College Edition

CAUTION: This textbook has a number of themes that revolve around candy, and this preface is no exception. While this book has a lot of the great accounting ingredients you are used to (and all that you will need), it also "breaks the mold" as it incorporates a number of phrases and terms well known to candy lovers (and we believe that includes accountants). Our intent is that you will get a number of cravings while reading this preface, not the least of which is the desire to devour this book and to share its great taste with your colleagues and your students.

Two Great Courses that Make One Great Text . . .

You may recall hearing different food or beverage products promoting how natural and good they are for you by using the phrases "No artificial colors. No artificial sweeteners." Well, we would like to paraphrase those slightly to convey a similar message that is the initial premise as to why this text for the elementary accounting sequence is natural and good for you: "No artificial separation!"

In the real-world, today's students will face an accounting environment where managment accounting and financial accounting issues are integrated everyday. The traditional — and artificial— separation of these topics in textbooks tends to lead students to a perception that the two areas are unrelated. We also believe that traditional and highly technical "preparer-oriented" accounting textbooks (1) isolate accounting from general business decisions, (2) lose students' interest, and (3) reinforce a common misconception that accounting is best left only to accountants. Therefore, such a separation misses the big picture of an integrated accounting system that provides economic information to all users—which is what the overwhelming majority of your students in introductory accounting will be. This textbook thoroughly integrates management accounting and financial accounting topics in a way that is more reflective of the world students will face outside of the classroom.

Sometimes You Feel Like a Debit, Sometimes You Don't . . .

A major focus of this textbook is on *using* management accounting and financial accounting information in various business settings. Therefore, we wrote this book at a "nontechnical" level for *all* business and non-business students—not just those intending to be accounting majors. But, because two of us are heavily involved in teaching intermediate accounting and write an intermediate accounting textbook, we are also aware of the needs of your accounting majors. So we also discuss *accumulating* and *reporting* accounting information. We take a non-procedural approach by explaining transactions in terms of the accounting equation and the use of T-accounts rather than debits and credits. But, we realize there is a need in many situations to teach procedures. To that end, we have provided a full chapter-length appendix (Appendix B) on recording, storing, summarizing, and reporting accounting information. This appendix covers the accounting cycle, from journal entries (using debits and credits) through the post-closing trial balance. We designed it so that you may use it anywhere you see fit in the process of teaching from this book. We assure you that our accounting majors who have used this elementary accounting text are well-prepared to enter our intermediate accounting classes.

In addition, The Dryden Press offers OMAR: Online Multimedia Accounting Review, a CD-ROM and/or Web-based review/course on the accounting cycle. OMAR may be used to supplement the elementary accounting sequence, as an independent study for accounting majors, or as a first part of the intermediate accounting course. Recent focus groups have indicated such a review is helpful regardless of the textbook or orientation used in the first course and have praised the development of this learning tool.

KEY FEATURES OF THIS TEXT

An Introduction to Business Approach

Chapters 1 and 10 take an "introduction to business" approach to orient students to the business environment—that is, the operations of a company, the different functions of business, managers' responsibilities, and the types of information, management reports, and financial statements the company's integrated accounting system provides for use in internal and external decision making. These chapters provide students with a basic understanding of business so they can more effectively envision the context in which accounting information is collected and used, and the types of decisions users make in this context. This approach allows students to see the "big picture" more clearly.

Creative and Critical Thinking

Chapter 2 is unique for accounting textbooks and we integrate that uniqueness into the rest of the book. It introduces students to creative and critical thinking and how they are used in decision making and problem solving. Our entire book emphasizes the type of analytical thinking that successful accountants and other business people use in a world that is constantly changing and becoming more complex. We believe that as you use analytical thinking in your decision process regarding this textbook, you will not only decide to adopt the book but will also be able to use it in a way that will foster your students' growth.

In keeping with Chapter 2, the remaining chapters introduce students to various aspects of accounting, and are designed to help them develop their thinking skills. "STOP" questions throughout the textbook (identified by a "stop light") ask students to take a break from reading, and to think about an issue and/or consider the outcome of a situation. We also ask them *why* they think what they think. The end-of-chapter (EOC) materials include both structured and unstructured questions and problems that emphasize the use of creative and critical thinking skills by the students. Therefore, some of the questions and problems do not have a "correct" answer. The focus is on the approach or process that students use to solve them. With the increasing complexity of business activities, we think our inclusion of creative and critical thinking materials will better prepare students to understand the substantive issues involved in new or unusual business practices.

The Simpler Things

Earlier we mentioned a "non-technical" approach. Although we explain identification, measurement, recording, and reporting of economic information, we discuss these activities at a basic level (increases and decreases in account balances) and do not include a discussion of debit and credit rules and journal entries in the main body of the text. We do emphasize the double-entry accounting system through the use of the accounting equation (Assets = Liabilities + Owners' Equity) and its linkage to the income equation (Income = Revenues − Expenses). We use T-accounts to record transactions, but we explain the increases or decreases in relation to the accounting equation rather than as debits and credits. We chose this approach to better help students gain an understanding of the logic of the accounting system and its interrelationships, without getting them "bogged" down in the mechanics of the system. We also emphasize the effects of transactions on a company's financial statements, and the impact they have on analysis of the company (e.g., its risk, liquidity, financial flexibility, operating capability). For those wanting to incorporate the mechanics of the system, as we mentioned earlier, we do provide a thorough coverage of debits, credits, and journal entries in Appendix B.

Because You've Kept Us Apart for Too Long...

We also mentioned earlier that this book integrates management accounting and financial accounting topics in a way that is more reflective of the world students will face outside of the classroom. In blending our discussion of management accounting and financial accounting, we address several management accounting topics prior to discussing specific financial accounting topics. In large part, a company must plan its activities before it communicates its plans to external users, and it must operate and evaluate its operations (internal decision making) before it communicates the results of its operations to external users. Therefore, in keeping with the "introduction to business" theme and the logical sequencing of business activities, we discuss accounting for planning first, and then for operating and evaluating (controlling)—discussing management accounting and financial accounting where they logically fit into this framework.

For instance, Chapter 3 covers cost-profit-volume (CVP) analysis for planning purposes. After students have an understanding of cost and revenue relationships, we introduce them to budgeting in Chapter 4. The discussion of the master budget includes projected financial statements, which links the coverage back to the financial statements we mentioned in Chapter 1. Chapter 5 then introduces the measurement of, and accounting for, the operations of a company. Chapters 6 through 9 then describe a company's major financial statements and discuss how external users would use these statements to analyze the company.

Besides integrating management accounting and financial accounting topics, this book also integrates business issues and values and international issues, where appropriate, throughout the text. This approach reinforces the idea that societal and global issues are not topics that can and should be dealt with separately from the other issues, bur rather are an integral and significant part of business in today's world.

Building Block Approach

This textbook also uses a building-block approach. It begins with starting and operating a small retail candy store—a sole proprietorship—and then progresses through the operations of a more complex company in the form of a candy manufacturer—a corporation. This allow students to learn basic concepts first and then later to broaden and reinforce those concepts in a more complex setting. Several of the same topics reemerge, but each time they are refined or enhanced by a different company structure, a different type of business, or a different user perspective. For example, because of its location at the beginning of the semester, the Chapter 3 discussion of CVP analysis is simple. We cover it again in greater depth in Chapter 11, after students have a better understanding of costs in a manufacturing setting. Each time we revisit an issue, we discuss the uses of accounting information for both internal and external decision-making as appropriate.

Likewise, we use a building-block approach to arranging the end-of-chapter materials according to levels of learning. To indicate these levels, we have divided the homework into sections on Testing Your Knowledge, Applying Your Knowledge, and Making Evaluations. These categories are arranged so that the answers to questions require students to use increasingly higher-order thinking skills as they move from one category of questions to the next. The *Testing Your Knowledge* section includes questions that test students' knowledge of specifics—terminology, specific facts, concepts and principles, classifications, and so forth. The *Applying Your Knowledge* section includes questions, problems, and situations that test students' abilities to translate, interpret, extrapolate, and apply their knowledge. The *Making Evaluations* section includes questions, problems, and cases that test students' abilities to apply their knowledge, but also their abilities to analyze elements, relationships, and principles, to synthesize a variety of information, and to make judgements based on evidence and accounting criteria.

Real-World/World-Wide/Total World: http://www.dryden.com/account/cunningham/

Life is not a "textbook case." That's why we not only integrate management accounting and financial accounting topics, but also include information about real-world companies as examples for many of these topics. And, we include analyses of the financial information of some of these companies in the text and in the homework materials of many chapters. In conjunction with our Web site, our "Summary Surfing" section of each chapter gives students the opportunity to connect to some of these companies via the World Wide Web for further evaluation. The Web site also features links to home pages and Yahoo! Profiles of companies found in the text, as well as a collection of useful accounting links for students and instructors. It will be continually updated.

HOW TO USE THIS TEXT

". . . a well thought out and very well-planned text. The explanations are easy to read and follow. I could teach myself from this book."—Rebe Herling, Student

Since we (and others) have class tested this book, we thought you might appreciate hearing what we have learned from this experience:

1. *Faculty Preferences:* For years, Hershey's made the Kiss only in plain chocolate. Although they had put almonds in a chocolate bar, they couldn't perfect doing so with a Kiss. Nonetheless, they kept trying, and as you know, succeeded several years ago. It's been a great success since then. You, too, can succeed in integrating the financial and managerial accounting areas for the best taste. For financial accounting faculty, the textbook is so well written (see student quote above) that the management accounting material is not difficult to teach. For the management accounting faculty, the book leads with management accounting material and there is much less financial procedure than in traditional ones, so it is not difficult to teach either. Although change doesn't occur without some effort, we have tried to make this change as easy as possible for both of you by providing a great support package that will help you step into the classroom with minimum effort. Rather than having to completely rewrite your course notes, check out the *PowerPoint Slides* or the *Instructor's Resource Kit.* Rather than having to develop new activities for your students to engage in during class, try some that we have provided in the Instructor's Resource Kit. Instead of having to develop completely new exam questions and solutions, try out the supporting *Test Bank.*

2. *The Transfer Issue:* This book is not an Oreo cookie. It is not designed so that you can split up the parts and eat them separately. So, given that most transfer students will check out the receiving school's policies first, we suggest that receiving schools using our book advise transfer students that they should take their entire accounting sequence at one school or the other, but not half and half. To sending schools using our book, we suggest you give your students similar advice. For your course sequence, we suggest that you devote sufficient time to coverage of Appendix B (the accounting cycle, including debits and credits) so that your students who transfer have an adequate foundation in accounting procedures.

3. *Pedagogy:* We designed the pedagogical features of this book with the purpose of guiding the readers through it in a way that will help them learn the material in the

book. Opening introductory questions for each chapter highlight the major topics and pique the students' interest as well as guide their reading. In support of these questions, as we mentioned earlier, "STOP" questions throughout each chapter ask students to pause and answer a question related to what they have just read and primes them for what comes next. Each question encourages reflection, critical thinking, and understanding while students read the chapter, and helps them build on their previous experience while learning accounting. We have found these questions to be useful for stimulating class discussions because, for the most part, there is no one correct answer to these questions. The Summary at the end of each chapter briefly answers the opening introductory questions, but also encourages students to use their creative and critical thinking skills to expand on the key points of the chapter, to develop more complete answers to the opening introductory questions, and to determine what other questions they have that might lead them to learn more about the issues introduced in the chapter.

We include the financial section of General Mills annual report in Appendix C, and we have homework assignments at the ends of many chapters that ask students questions about the financial information in this annual report. In addition, the real-world company names that we use in the book are highlighted in hypertext and their web addresses are listed nearby in the margin. Students either can use these addresses to directly access the companies' web sites, or look them up on the book's web site. This feature encourages students to "search out" available information about companies on the Internet and also to see the range of information about companies that is available on the Internet. We have also found that these sites are great resources for making additional assignments and for use in class discussion. The Summary Surfing section at the end of each chapter provides assignments on the web and gives students the opportunity to retrieve and evaluate information on the Internet.

4. *How to use the end-of-chapter materials:* The book is constructed in a "building block" approach and so is the homework. We suggest you assign it in the same manner: ask students to test their knowledge first, then apply their knowledge, and finally, after building a strong base of understanding, make evaluations. Each chapter has a Dr. Decisive problem that asks students to apply their new knowledge in a situation closer to one they might currently experience, making accounting a little more personal and relevant for them. In a "Dear Abby" format, students are asked to answer a "problem" mailed in by a reader. We have found it to be a fun way for students to work on teams, where the team constructs an answer to the question or evaluates another team's answer to the question.

5. *Snickers:* ". . . by chuckling at the joke, the accounting concept it illustrated was planted firmly in my mind." Lisa Mitchell, Student. The cartoons and photographs in the book are not just for levity. They provide visual enhancements of ideas, as well as humor, and help students apply their knowledge by interpreting cartoons and photos.

6. *Alternative Course:* We wrote this book for the elementary accounting sequence, but the very nature of its design has led to its successful use in MBA and Executive MBA/Small Business Programs.

CLASS TESTED

We know there is always a concern about First Editions, but you might have noted that two of us teach in Missouri—the "show-me" state. Having a need to "show ourselves" that the book works, we class-tested it at the University of Missouri—Columbia for eight semesters, and faculty members at other institutions class-tested this book more recently. At the end of each semester, we used student and instructor feedback to make the book even better. Here is what we found, and it has been confirmed by other class testers:

- Students liked reading this book.
- The writing style is "user friendly" so that the topics are very understandable .
- The end-of-chapter homework is tied well to the topical coverage in the chapters.
- The solutions manual is very clean.
- Instructors found the book to be clear and easy to teach from.

Furthermore, to assure ourselves that the homework and solutions are error-free, we wrote and checked all the homework items and solutions ourselves. In addition, all the solutions were accuracy-checked by graduate students and teaching assistants.

USER FEEDBACK

We would love to list all the positive quotes here that we've received from students and instructors who class-tested the book, but our editors say that would add significantly to the page count and thus to the cost of the book (which our marketing manager advises would result in negative comments from the students). So, we've listed one of each. This should help prove our point as well as illustrate that we have listened to the input of others in all stages of the development of this text.

"[Early in the first semester] I've had three students already tell me that they are really enjoying reading the text!! Wanted to let you know that I've been teaching accounting for 11 years and this is the first time I've ever heard any students make that comment. You should be very proud." Instructor, Winthrop University, September 1998.

"I enjoyed studying out of the book because it was written in a manner that is clear and easy to understand. The fact that the examples (Sweet Temptations, Unlimited Decadence) were used throughout the text was very helpful." Nathan Troup, student, November 1998.

ANCILLARY PACKAGE

Solutions Manual with Check Figures for Selected Questions
Written by Loren Nikolai, Billie Cunningham, and John Bazley

A comprehensive manual containing all the solutions to the end-of-chapter homework items contained in the student text.

Instructor's Resource Kit
Written by Wanda DeLeo and Angela LeTourneau both of Winthrop University

Prepared by users of **Accounting: Information for Business Decisions**, this manual contains lecture outlines, classroom activities, and chapter quizzes. The Instructor's Resource Kit was also created hand-in-hand with the PowerPoint lecture slides to provide a cohesive and seamless package for you.

Test Bank
Written by Richard File of the University of Nebraska at Omaha

The test bank contains over 2,400 questions to help you evaluate your students' performances. The test bank, continuing on the text's vision of teaching critical thinking skills, contains questions which require students to evaluate accounting information using tools provided in the chapters. Question formats included in this test bank are multiple choice, fill-in-the-blank, exercises, and problems that include "what if" analysis. This test bank is also available in a computerized version by ExaMaster for Windows.

Study Guide
Written by Janet Cassagio of Nassau Community College and Diane Sturek of William Woods University

Designed to engage students further into class material, the study guide encourages students to practice what they have learned. Janet Cassagio and Diane Sturek have written a manual with not only practice problems for students to evaluate what they have learned, but with more activities designed to enhance their learning and communication skills by applying chapter concepts to various situations.

Lecture Software in Microsoft PowerPoint™
Written by Marilyn Maus of Moorhead State University

The essential instructor tool for lecturing, provides an outline with examples corresponding to text chapters. The slides also contain several selected end-of-chapter homework items which you can use within a lecture as additional examples, or to go over homework selections with students in class.

Student PowerPoint™ Notes

We have provided a complete set of student notes in a manual so that it is less necessary for you to cover all topics in class. Furthermore, students can focus their attention in class on the material you are covering, rather than being distracted by trying to write down *everything* you say. They can simply add to the lecture information in a space provided next to the corresponding slide. We have a comprehensive package designed to include valuable exhibits from the text for class lectures. Furthermore, the solutions to end-of-chapter questions in the Applying Your Knowledge, Making Evaluations, and the Dr. Decisive exercises are provided to aid in classroom review.

Overhead Transparencies
Web Site (http://www.dryden.com/account/cunningham/)
Contains links to companies featured throughout the text and "Summary Surfing" questions.

"Kit"-Kat:

You may wish your students to purchase some of the above ancillaries. Your Dryden Press/Harcourt Brace representative can add value to your selections by creating a "kit" with the main text for a discounted price. Contact him or her for more information.

KUDOS!

This book is a work in process, and we will appreciate your feedback and suggestions for improvement as it evolves into the second edition. But it wouldn't have progressed this far without the help, creative ideas, encouragement, and hard work of numerous individuals, including the following:

Reviewers

Frank Beigbeder— Rancho Santiago College
Susan Borkowski— LaSalle University
Judith Cadle—Tarleton State University

Terri Gutierrez—University of Northern Colorado
Bonnie Hairrell—Birmingham Southern College
John Hartwick—Bucks County Community College
Matthew Monippallil—Eastern Illinois University
Jacqueline Sanders—Mercer County Community College
Marlane Sanderson—Moorhead State University
Philip Siegel—Long Island University
Leon Singleton—Santa Monica College

Class Testers and Preliminary Edition Users
Wanda DeLeo—Winthrop University
Debbie Luna—El Paso Community College
Angie Letourneu—Winthrop University
Marilyn Maus—Moorhead State University
Judy McLean—Moorhead State University
Sandy Devona—Northern Illinois University

Teaching Assistants/Class Testers at the University of Missouri—Columbia

Jaime Bierk	Tim Koski	Mike Richey
Marcia Bunten	Lee Kraft	Andrea Romi
Cassi Costner	Shannon Lee	Robbie Schoonmaker
Rachel Davis	Jennifer Liesmann	Jennifer Seeser
Carrie Duff	Aaron Meinert	Ken Smith
Gwen Ernst	Holly Monks	Dessie Stafford
John Faries	Shannon Mudd	Tom Stauder
Katrinka Goldberg	Lynn Nelson	Diane Sturek
Stacy Gower	Margaret Ofodile	Aaron Thorne
Dave Gusky	Susan Parker	Robyn Vogt
Mark Gutwein	Cindy Patterson	Kelly Ward
Mike Hart	Matt Peters	Michael Weiss
Melissa Kahmann	Katrina Pon	Lisa Wright

Others who made invaluable contributions along the way:

Robin Roberts, University of Central Florida, and James Stallman, University of Missouri—Columbia, for significant contributions to earlier versions of several chapters in this book

Tom Schmidt for his insightful (and inciteful) comments on Chapter 2

Scott Summers and Vairam Arunachalam, University of Missouri—Columbia for their advice on certain technical issues

Jennifer Seeser and Diane Sturek for the solutions they developed to the end-of-chapter homework

Cassi Costner and Emily Reinkemeyer for their accuracy checks of these solutions

Nathan (N8) Troup for his assistance in the development of certain aspects of the text and ancillaries

Donna Hetzel, Western Michigan University for her accuracy checks of the test bank

Dana Cunningham for her Chapter 8 photograph

Bob Hammerschmidt for his Chapter 8 quote

Anita Blanchar for her meticulous typing of various ancillaries

Karen Staggs for typing parts of the manuscript

The thousands of students who endured the class testing of previous editions, especially those students who noticed and reported errors, inconsistencies, and typos in previous versions.

Those who made conscientious efforts toward the production of this book:

Mike Reynolds, Bill Schoof, Jessica Fiorillo, Jennifer Langer, Laura Hayes, Charles Watson, Jim Patterson, Bill Brammer, Biatriz Chapa, Linda Blundell, Darryl King, Kimberly Powell, Kimberly Samuels, Barrett Lackey, Teddy Diggs, Kathleen Lindstrom, Don Grainger, and Kathy Jones.

And thank you to all of the Dryden sales people for their observations, suggestions, and colossal past and *future* efforts to make this book known to those who dare to change.

About the Authors

Billie M. Cunningham

Billie Cunningham is an Adjunct Assistant Professor in the School of Accountancy at the University of Missouri—Columbia (MU). She has received several awards for outstanding teaching, including the *1995 Exemplary Accounting Educator Award* from the Missouri Association of Accounting Educators. While teaching at Collin County Community College (CCCC) in Plano, Texas, she received the CCCC District nomination for the national *1990 CASE Professor of the Year*, the CCCC *1987-88 Outstanding Faculty Award*, and the CCCC District nomination for the state *1987-88 Minnie Stevens Piper Award*. In addition, she received a *1989 National Teaching Excellence Award* from the National Institute for Staff and Organizational Development and was the co-recipient of the *1997 Holstein Creativity Award*. She also has taught at Texas Christian University. She received her B.B.A., M.B.A. and Ph.D. from the University of North Texas. Professor Cunningham has conducted numerous workshops around the country on the use of writing exercises in accounting classes and on incorporating creative and critical thinking strategies into the accounting classroom. She was a coauthor of three previous books: *Accounting: Principles and Applications*, Fifth Edition (1986); *Financial Accounting: Principles and Applications*, Fifth Edition (1986); and *Accounting: Basic Principles,* Fifth Edition (1986); and a contributing author on *Cost Accounting: Principles and Applications*, Fourth Edition (1984) (all with McGraw-Hill Publishing Company).

Professor Cunningham has published articles in professional journals, including *Journal of Accounting Education, Issues in Accounting Education, Accounting Education: A Journal of Theory, Practice and Research, The CPA Journal, Research in Accounting Regulation, Management Accounting, Essays in Economic and Business History, The Community/Junior College Quarterly of Research and Practice Special Edition on College Teaching and Learning,* and *The Community/Junior College Quarterly of Research and Practice*. She has received the Outstanding Article Award from the Two-Year College Section of the American Accounting Association. In addition, she serves on the Editorial Review Board of *Advances in Accounting Education*, and has served as an ad hoc reviewer for *Issues in Accounting Education* and *Journal of Accounting Education*. Professor Cunningham is the faculty advisor for the Association of Accountancy Students at MU. She is a member of the American Accounting Association (AAA), in which she was Chair of the Two-Year College Section and Chair of the Teaching and Curriculum Section, served on the AAA Accounting Education Advisory Committee, and as Vice-President and member of the Executive Committee of the AAA. Professor Cunningham has chaired or served on numerous Federation of Schools of Accountancy committees. She is married and has one adult child. Her family has two bunnies. She sings in her car, dances in her living room, and is an aerobics enthusiast and avid golfer (and we use that term loosely).

Loren A. Nikolai

Loren Nikolai is the Ernst & Young Professor in the School of Accountancy at the University of Missouri—Columbia (MU). He received his B.A. and M.B.A. from St Cloud State University and his Ph.D. from the University of Minnesota. Professor Nikolai has taught at the University of Wisconsin at Platteville and at the University of North Carolina at Chapel Hill. Professor Nikolai has received the University of Missouri system-wide *1999 Presidential Award for Outstanding Teaching*, the MU College of Business and Public Administration *1999 Teacher of the Year Award*, the MU Alumni Association *1996 Faculty Award*, the MU College of Business and Public Administration *1994 Accounting Professor of the Year Award*, the Missouri Society of CPAs *1993 Outstanding Accounting Educator of the Year Award*, the MU *1992 Kemper Fellowship for Teaching Excellence*, the St. Cloud State University *1990 Distinguished Alumni Award*, and the Federation of Schools of Accountancy *1989 Faculty Award of Merit*, and was the co-recipient of the *1997 Holstein Creativity Award*. He holds a CPA certificate in the state of Missouri and previously worked for the 3M Company. Professor Nikolai is the lead author of *Intermediate Accounting*, Eighth Edition (2000, South-Western Publishing

Company). He was the lead author of two previous textbooks: *Principles of Accounting*, Third Edition (1990) and *Financial Accounting*, Third Edition (1990; PWS-Kent Publishing Company), and was the coauthor of *Financial Accounting: Concepts and Uses*, Third Edition (1995; South-Western Publishing Company).

Professor Nikolai has published numerous articles in *The Accounting Review, Journal of Accounting Research, The Accounting Educator's Journal, Journal of Accounting Education, The CPA Journal, Management Accounting, Policy Analysis, Academy of Management Journal, Journal of Business Research,* and other professional journals. He was also lead author of a monograph published by the National Association of Accountants. Professor Nikolai has served as an ad hoc reviewer for *The Accounting Review* and *Issues in Accounting Education*. He has made numerous presentations around the country on curric-

ular and pedagogical issues in accounting education. Professor Nikolai is the Faculty Vice President of the Beta Alpha Psi chapter at MU. He is a member of the American Accounting Association, the American Institute of Certified Public Accountants (AICPA), and the Missouri Society of CPAs (MSCPA). He has served on the AICPA's Accounting and Auditing Practice Analysis Task Force Panel and the Accounting Careers Subcommittee; he has also served on the MSCPA's Relations with Educators, Accounting Careers, and Accounting and Auditing Committees. Professor Nikolai has chaired or served on numerous Federation of Schools of Accountancy (FSA) and American Accounting Association (AAA) committees, was AAA Director of Education for 1985-1987, and was President of the FSA for 1994. Professor Nikolai is married and has two adult children and one grandson. His family has four cats, and he is an avid basketball player and sprinter (100m and 200m).

John D. Bazley

John D. Bazley, Ph.D., CPA, is Professor of Accountancy in the School of Accountancy of the Daniels College of Business at the University of Denver where he has received the University *1990 Distinguished Teaching Award*, the *Vernon Loomis Award for Excellence in Advising*, the *Alumni Award for Faculty Excellence*, the *Jerome Kesselman Endowment Award for Excellence in Research,* and the *1995 Cecil Puckett Award* of the Daniels College of Business. Professor Bazley earned a B.A. from the University of Bristol in England and an M.S. and Ph.D. from the University of Minnesota. He has taught at the University of North Carolina at Chapel Hill and holds a CPA certificate in the state of Colorado. He has taught national professional development classes for a major CPA firm and was consultant for another CPA firm. Professor Bazley is the coauthor of *Intermediate Accounting*, Eighth Edition (2000, South-Western Publishing Company). He was the lead author of *Financial Accounting: Concepts and Uses,* Third

Edition (1995; South-Western Publishing Company) and the co-author of two previous books: *Principles of Accounting*, Third Edition (1990) and *Financial Accounting*, Third Edition (1990; PWS-Kent Publishing Company).

Professor Bazley has published articles in professional journals, including *The Accounting Review, Management Accounting, Accounting Horizons, Practical Accountant, Academy of Management Journal, The Journal of Managerial Issues,* and *The International Journal of Accounting,* and was a member of the Editorial Boards of *Issues in Accounting Education* and the *Journal of Managerial Issues.* He was also a coauthor of a monograph on environmental accounting published by the National Association of Accountants. He has served on numerous committees of The Federation of Schools of Accountancy (including chair of the Student Lyceum Committee), the American Accounting Association, and the Colorado Society of CPAs (including the Continuing Professional Education Board). Professor Bazley is a member of the American Institute of Certified Public Accountants, the Colorado Society of CPAs, and the American Accounting Association. He is married and has two young children. His family has four cats, and he enjoys skiing, playing golf, and car racing.

Brief Contents

Contents

PART 1

OVERVIEW: BUSINESS, ACCOUNTING, AND THE ROLE OF CREATIVE AND CRITICAL THINKING

This section consists of two chapters

which introduce you to business and

accounting, and discuss the role of

creative and critical thinking in

business decisions. After reading

these chapters, you will be able to:

▸ *understand the role of accounting information in business*

▸ *describe the planning, operating, and evaluating activities of managing a company*

▸ *know the difference between management accounting and financial accounting*

▸ *identify internal and external accounting reports*

▸ *explain the meaning of creative and critical thinking*

▸ *apply creative and critical thinking in business decisions*

CHAPTER 1

INTRODUCTION TO BUSINESS AND ACCOUNTING

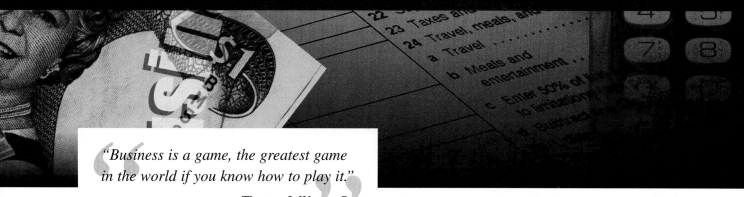

"*Business is a game, the greatest game in the world if you know how to play it.*"
—Thomas J. Watson Sr.

1 Why is it necessary to have an understanding of business before trying to learn about accounting?

2 What is the role of accounting information within the business environment?

3 What is private enterprise, and what forms does it take?

4 What types of regulations do companies face?

5 What activities contribute to the operations of a company?

6 Are there any guidelines for reporting to company managers?

7 Are there any guidelines for financial reporting in the United States?

8 What role does ethics play in the business environment?

1 *Why is it necessary to have an understanding of business before trying to learn about accounting?*

What are you planning to do when you graduate from college—maybe become an accountant, a veterinarian, work your way up to marketing manager for a multinational company, manage the local food bank, or open a sporting goods store? Regardless of your career choice, you will be making business decisions, both in your personal life and at work. We have oriented this book to students like you who are interested in business and the role of accounting in business. You will see that accounting information, used properly, is a powerful tool for making good business decisions. People inside a business use accounting information to help determine and manage costs, set selling prices, and control the operations of the business. People outside the business use accounting information to help make investment and credit decisions about the business. Just what kinds of businesses use accounting? All of them! So let's take a little time to look at what *business* means.

Business affects almost every aspect of our lives. Think for a moment about your normal daily activities. How many businesses do you usually encounter? How many did you directly encounter today? Say you started the day with a quick trip to the local convenience store for milk and eggs. While you were out, you noticed that your car was low on fuel, so you stopped at the corner gas station. On the way to class, you dropped some clothes off at the cleaners. After your first class, you skipped lunch so that you could go to the bookstore and buy the calculator you need; after buying a candy bar for sustenance, you headed to your next class. In just half a day, you already interacted with four businesses: the convenience store, the gas station, the cleaners, and the bookstore.

 Actually, you encountered a fifth business, your school. Why would you describe your school as a business?

Although you were directly involved with four businesses, you were probably *affected* by hundreds of them. For example, two different businesses manufactured the calculator and the candy bar you purchased at the bookstore. Suppose that Unlimited Decadence Corporation manufactured the candy bar that you purchased. As we illustrate in Exhibit 1-1, Unlimited Decadence purchased the candy bar ingredients from many other businesses *(suppliers)*. Each supplier provided Unlimited Decadence with particular ingredients. Shipping businesses *(carriers)* moved the ingredients from the suppliers' warehouses to Unlimited Decadence's factory. Then, after the candy bars were manufactured, a different shipper carried them from Unlimited Decadence to the bookstore. Making and shipping the calculator would follow the same process. You can see that many businesses are involved with manufacturing, shipping, and selling just two products. Now think about all the other products that you used during the morning and all the businesses that the manufacture and delivery of each product might have involved. Before leaving your house, apartment, or dorm this morning, you could easily have been affected by more than one hundred businesses.

2 *What is the role of accounting information within the business environment?*

Products and services affect almost every minute of our lives, and businesses provide these products and services to us. As you will soon see, accounting plays a vital role in both businesses and the business environment by keeping track of a business's economic resources and economic activities, and then by reporting the business's financial position and the results of its activities to people who are interested in how well it is doing. (This is similar to the way statistics are gathered and reported for baseball players and other athletes.)

Accounting focuses on the resources and activities of individual businesses. However, we will begin our study of accounting by first looking at private enterprise and the environment in which businesses operate. Our discussion will include the types and forms of business and some of the regulatory issues associated with forming and operating a business. Then we will discuss the activities of managers within a business. Next we will introduce the role of accounting information within a business and in the business environment. Finally, we will discuss the importance of ethics in business and accounting.

Exhibit 1-1 Businesses Involved with the Manufacture and Sale of Candy Bars

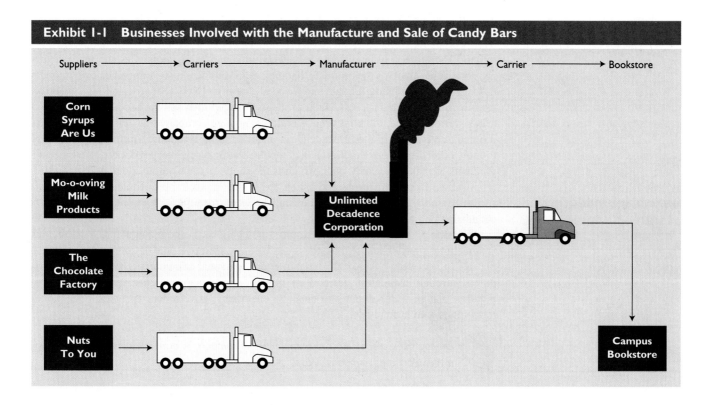

Suppliers ⟶ Carriers ⟶ Manufacturer ⟶ Carrier ⟶ Bookstore

Corn Syrups Are Us

Mo-o-oving Milk Products

The Chocolate Factory

Nuts To You

Unlimited Decadence Corporation

Campus Bookstore

Private Enterprise and Capitalism

Businesses in the United States and most other countries operate in an economic system based on *private enterprise.* In this system, individuals (people like us, rather than public institutions like the government) own companies that produce and sell services and/or goods for a profit. These companies generally fall into three categories: service companies, merchandising companies, and manufacturing companies.

3 *What is private enterprise, and what forms does it take?*

Service Companies

Service companies perform services or activities that benefit individuals or business customers. The dry cleaning establishment where you dropped off your clothes this morning provides the service of cleaning and pressing your clothes for you. Companies like A Great Cut, Midas Muffler Shops, Mighty Maids, and UPS, and professional practices such as accounting, law, architecture, and medicine, are all service companies. Other companies in the private enterprise system produce or provide goods, or tangible, physical products. These companies can be either *merchandising companies* or *manufacturing companies.*

www.agreatcut.com
www.midas.com
www.metropark.com/
   mightymaids
www.ups.com

Merchandising Companies

Merchandising companies purchase goods (sometimes referred to as merchandise or products) for resale to their customers. Some merchandising companies, such as the bookstore where you bought your calculator and candy bar or the convenience store where you bought your milk and eggs, are *retailers.* Retailers sell their goods directly to the final customer or consumer. JCPenney, Toys 'R' Us, and Circuit City are retailers. Other examples of retailers include shoe stores and grocery stores. Some merchandising companies, such as plumbing supply stores, electrical suppliers, or beverage distributors, are *wholesalers.* Wholesalers primarily sell their goods to retailers or other commercial users.

www.jcpenney.com
www.toysrus.com
www.circuitcity.com

Manufacturing Companies

Manufacturing companies make their products and then sell these products to their customers. Therefore, a basic difference between merchandising companies and manufacturing companies involves the products that they sell. Merchandising companies *buy* products that are physically ready for sale and then sell these products to their customers, whereas manufacturing companies *make* their products first and then sell the products to their customers. For example, the bookstore is a merchandising company that sells the candy bars it purchased from Unlimited Decadence, a manufacturing company. Unlimited Decadence, though, purchases (from suppliers) the chocolate, corn syrup, dairy products, and other ingredients to make the candy bars, which it then sells to the Campus Bookstore and other retail stores. General Motors and Black & Decker are examples of manufacturing companies. Exhibit 1-2 shows the relationship between manufacturing companies and merchandising companies.

The line of distinction between service, merchandising, and manufacturing companies is sometimes blurry because a business can be more than one type of company. For example, Dell Computer Corporation manufactures personal computers, services those computers (through installation, technology transition, and management), and sells the computers it manufactures directly to business customers, government agencies, educational institutions, and individuals.

 Do you think a supplier to a manufacturing company is a merchandising company or a manufacturing company? Why?

Whether a company is a service, merchandising, or manufacturing company (or all three), for it to succeed in a private enterprise system, it must be able to obtain cash to begin to operate and then to grow. As we will discuss in the next sections, companies have several sources of cash.

Entrepreneurship and Sources of Capital

Owning a company involves a level of risk, along with a continuing need for **capital.** Although *capital* has several meanings, we use the term here to mean the funds a company needs to operate or to expand operations. In the next two sections we will discuss the risk involved with owning a company and possible sources of capital.

www.gm.com
www.blackanddecker.
com

www.dell.com

Do you think this is a service company, a merchandising company, or a manufacturing company? Why?

ZIGGY © 1983 ZIGGY AND FRIENDS, INC. Dist. by UNIVERSAL PRESS SYNDICATE. Reprinted with permission.
All rights reserved.

Entrepreneurship

Companies in a private enterprise system produce and sell services and goods for a profit. So, profit is the primary objective of a company. Profit rewards the company's owner or owners for having a business idea and for following through with that idea by investing time, talent, and money in the company. The company's owner hires employees, purchases land and a building (or signs a lease for space in a building), and purchases (or leases) any tools, equipment, machinery, and furniture necessary to produce or sell services or goods, *expecting, but not knowing for sure, that customers will buy what the company provides.* An individual who is willing to risk this uncertainty in exchange for the reward of earning a profit (and the personal reward of seeing the company succeed) is called an **entrepreneur.** Entrepreneurship, then, is a combination of three factors: the company owner's idea, the willingness of the company's owner to take a risk, and the abilities of the company's owner and employees to use capital to produce and sell goods or services. But where does the company get its capital?

Sources of Capital

One source of capital for a company is the entrepreneur's (or company owner's) investment in the company. An entrepreneur invests money "up front" so that the company can get started. The company uses the money to acquire the resources it needs to function. Then, as the company operates, the resources, or capital, of the company increase or decrease through the profits and losses of the company.

When an entrepreneur invests money in a company, he or she hopes to eventually get back the money he or she contributed to the company (a return of the contribution). Furthermore, the entrepreneur hopes to periodically receive additional money above the amount he or she originally contributed to the company (a return *on* the contribution). The entrepreneur would like the return *on* the contribution to be higher than the return that could have been earned with that same money on a different investment (such as an interest-bearing checking or savings account).

Borrowing is another source of capital for a company. To acquire the resources necessary to grow or to expand its product lines, a company may have to borrow money from institutions like banks (called *creditors*). This occurs when the cash from the company's profits, combined with the company owner's contributions to the company, is not large enough to finance its growth. But borrowing by a company can be risky for the owner or owners. In some cases, if the company is unable to pay back the debt, the owner must personally assume that responsibility.

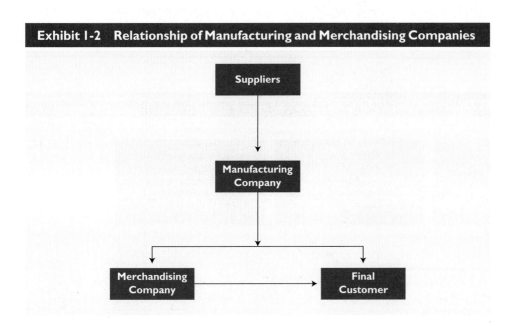

Exhibit 1-2 Relationship of Manufacturing and Merchandising Companies

Borrowing can also be risky for a company. If the company cannot repay its debts, it will soon find itself unable to continue operating. In addition to earning a profit, then, another objective of a company is to remain solvent. Remaining **solvent** means that the company can pay off its debts.

The terms *service, merchandising,* and *manufacturing* describe what companies do (perform services, purchase and sell goods, or make and sell products). We next discuss the forms that companies take, or how companies are organized.

The Forms That Companies Take

Several types of organizations use accounting information in their decision-making functions but do not have profit-making as a goal. These organizations are called not-for-profit organizations and include many educational institutions, religious institutions, charitable organizations, municipalities, governments, and some hospitals. Since making a profit is not a goal of these organizations, some aspects of accounting for these organizations' activities are unique and beyond the scope of this book.

In this book we emphasize *business* organizations. These business organizations, or *companies,* are a significant aspect of the U.S. and world economies. As Exhibit 1-3 shows, a company may be organized as a (1) sole proprietorship, (2) partnership, or (3) corporation.

Sole Proprietorships

A **sole proprietorship** is a company owned by one individual who is the sole investor of capital into the company. Usually the sole owner also acts as the manager of the company. Small retail stores and service firms often follow this form of organization. The sole proprietorship is the most common type of company because it is the easiest to organize and simplest to operate. In 1996, about 76 percent of all companies were sole proprietorships.[1]

Partnerships

A **partnership** is a company owned by two or more individuals (sometimes hundreds of individuals) who each invest capital, time, and/or talent into the company and share in the profits and losses of the company. These individuals are called partners, and their responsibilities, obligations, and benefits are usually described in a contract called a **partnership agreement.** Accounting firms and law firms are examples of partnerships. In 1996, just under 7 percent of all companies were partnerships.[2]

 If you and a friend decide to become business partners, do you think you need a formal partnership agreement? Why, or why not?

Exhibit 1-3   Types of Business Organizations (Companies)

Sole Proprietorships	Partnerships	Corporations
• Single owner-manager	• Two or more owners (partners)	• Stockholders have separate identity from company
• Small companies	• Partnership agreement	• Capital stock
• Most common type of business organization		• Greatest volume of business

---

[1]U.S. Treasury Department, Internal Revenue Service, *Statistics of Income Bulletin*, Fall 1998, 258, 259, 261.
[2]Ibid.

Corporations

A **corporation** is a company organized as a separate legal entity, or body (separate from its owners), according to the laws of a particular state. In fact, the word *corporation* comes from the Latin word for body *(corpus)*. In 1996, over 17 percent of all companies were corporations.[3]

By being incorporated, a company can enter into contracts, own property, and issue stock. A company issues shares of *capital stock* to owners, called *stockholders,* as evidence of the owners' investment of capital into the corporation. These shares are transferable from stockholder to stockholder, and each share represents part-ownership of the corporation. A corporation may be owned by one stockholder or by many stockholders (these stockholders are called *investors*). In fact, many large corporations have thousands of stockholders. For example, in their 1997 annual reports, The Gap and Intel Corporation indicated that their stockholders owned 393,133,028 and 1,628,000,000 shares of stock, respectively!

www.gap.com
www.intel.com

The organization and legal structure of a corporation are more complex than that of a sole proprietorship or a partnership. Although sole proprietorships are the most common type of company, corporations conduct the greatest volume of business in the United States. In 1996, sole proprietorships earned nearly 6 percent, partnerships close to 6 percent, and corporations just under 89 percent of all business sales in the United States.[4]

Since most of what we discuss in this text applies to all types of companies, we will use the general term *company* to apply to any company, regardless of structure. If the topic relates only to a specific type of company, we will identify the type of company.

The Regulatory Environment of Business

Companies affect each of us every day, but they also affect each other, the economy, and the environment. Just as individuals must abide by the laws and regulations of the cities, states, and countries in which they live and work, all companies, regardless of type, size, or complexity, must deal with regulatory issues.

4 *What types of regulations do companies face?*

Think again about that candy bar you had as a snack today. When Unlimited Decadence Corporation was formed, the company had to do more than build a factory, purchase equipment and ingredients, hire employees, find retail outlets to sell the candy bar, and begin operations. It also had to deal with the regulatory issues involved with opening and operating even the smallest of companies. Furthermore, its managers must continue to address regulatory issues as long as they continue to operate the company.

 Suppose a company is about to open a factory down the street from your house. What concerns do you have? What regulations might help reduce your concerns?

Many different laws and authorities regulate the business environment, covering issues such as consumer protection, environmental protection, employee safety, hiring practices, and taxes. Companies must comply with different sets of regulations depending on where their factories and offices are located. We discuss these sets of regulations next.

Local Regulations

City regulations may involve zoning (parts of the city in which companies may operate), certificates of occupancy, and for some companies, occupational licenses and pollution control. Counties are concerned with issues such as the following: health permits for companies that handle, process, package, and warehouse food; registration of the unique name of each company; and control of pollution to air, land, or water.

---

[3]Ibid.
[4]Ibid.

State Regulations

States also regulate the activities of companies located within their borders. Most states require corporations to pay some form of state tax, usually an income tax (a tax on profit), a franchise tax (a fee for the privilege of conducting corporate business in the state), or both. New companies (regardless of form) in most states must apply for sales tax numbers and permits. Each state has unemployment taxes that companies operating within that state must pay.

Practicing professionals, such as doctors, lawyers, and accountants, must get a license for each state in which they practice. Finally, states regulate companies that conduct certain types of business. For example, in Texas, companies that sell, transport, or store alcoholic beverages must obtain licenses from, and pay fees to, the state of Texas. Massachusetts regulations ban selling fireworks, whereas New Hampshire allows the sale of fireworks.

Federal Regulations

The federal government has a variety of laws and agencies that regulate companies and the business environment. These laws and agencies relate to specific aspects and activities of companies, regardless of the city or state in which the companies are located.

Internal Revenue Service

All companies have some dealings with the Internal Revenue Service (IRS). Each company must withhold taxes from its employees' pay and send these taxes to the IRS. Furthermore, the IRS taxes the profits of the companies themselves. The type of company determines who actually pays the taxes on profits, though. Corporations must pay their own income taxes to the IRS because from a legal standpoint, they are viewed as being separate from their owners. Sole proprietorships and partnerships, however, do not pay taxes on their profits. Rather, owners of these types of companies include their share of the company profits along with their other taxable income on their personal income tax returns. This is because the tax law does not distinguish the owners of sole proprietorships and partnerships from the companies themselves.

Laws and Other Government Agencies

A variety of laws and government departments and agencies (other than the IRS) regulate companies. Federal departments and agencies oversee the administration of laws governing areas such as competition (the Federal Trade Commission and the Department of Justice), fair labor practices (the Department of Labor), safety (the Occupational Safety and Health Administration), workplace discrimination (the Equal Employment Opportunity Commission), control of pollution to air, land, or water (the Environmental Protection Agency), and the like.

International Regulations

When a company conducts business internationally, it also must abide by the laws and regulations of the other countries in which it operates. These laws and regulations address such issues as foreign licensing, export and import documentation requirements, tax laws, multinational production and marketing regulations, domestic ownership of company property, and expatriation of cash (how much of the company's cash can leave the country). Of course, these laws and regulations differ from country to country, so a company operating in several countries must abide by many laws and regulations. Exhibit 1-4 lists some of the more common regulatory issues facing companies operating in different jurisdictions.

 Suppose that as a manager of a manufacturing company, you have the opportunity to have many parts of your product manufactured in another country where the labor is much cheaper and the environmental regulations are less stringent. What are the pros and cons of taking advantage of this opportunity?

Exhibit 1-4	Common Regulatory Issues Companies Face		
City and County Issues	**State Issues**	**Federal Issues**	**International Issues**
zoning	state tax	federal taxes	foreign licensing
certificate of occupancy	sales tax	competition	exports and imports
occupational license	unemployment taxes	labor standards	taxes
environmental regulations	professional licenses	working conditions	multinational production and
health permit	industry-specific regulations	workplace discrimination	marketing
company name and registration			property ownership
			cash restrictions

Integrated Accounting System

A company is responsible to many diverse groups of people, both inside and outside the company. For example, its managers and employees depend on the company for their livelihood. Customers expect a dependable product or service at a reasonable cost. The community expects the company to be a good citizen. Owners want returns on their investments, and creditors expect to be paid back. Governmental agencies expect companies to abide by their rules.

People in all of these groups use accounting information about the company. This information comes from an integrated accounting system. An **integrated accounting system** is a means by which accounting information about a company's activities is identified, measured, recorded, and retained so that it can be communicated in an accounting report. A company's integrated accounting system provides much of the information used by the many diverse groups of people outside the company (these are sometimes called **external users**), as well as by the managers within the company (these are sometimes called **internal users**). Two branches of accounting, management accounting and financial accounting, use the information in the integrated accounting system to produce reports for different groups of people. Management accounting provides vital information about a company to internal users; financial accounting gives information about a company to external users.

Management Accounting Information

Management accounting information helps managers plan, operate, and evaluate a company's activities. Managers must operate in a changing environment. They need information to help them compete in a world market in which technology and methods of production are constantly changing. Moreover, in a world exploding with new information, managers must manage data in a way that will let them use it more efficiently and effectively. Accounting is one of the critical tools of information management.

Since management accounting helps managers inside the company, it is free from the restrictions of regulatory bodies interested in reporting to external users. Therefore, management accounting information can be expressed in whatever form is useful for managers, such as in dollars, units, hours worked, products manufactured, numbers of defective units, or service agreements signed. The integrated accounting system produces information about segments of the company, products, tasks, plants, or individual activities, depending on what information is important to the manager who is using the information.

Financial Accounting Information

Financial accounting information is organized for the use of interested people outside of the company. External users analyze the company's financial reports as one source of financial information about the company. For these financial reports to be useful to external users, companies reporting to outsiders follow specific guidelines, or rules, known as *generally accepted accounting principles,* which we will discuss later in this chapter.

Financial accounting information developed by the integrated accounting system is expressed in dollars in the United States and in different currencies (such as yen, euros, and pesos) in other countries. This information emphasizes the whole company and sometimes important segments of the company.

Both internal and external users need accounting information to make decisions about a company. Since external users want to see the reported results of management activities, we discuss these activities next. Then we will discuss how accounting information supports management activities and external decision-making.

Management Activities

5 *What activities contribute to the operations of a company?*

Managers play a vital role in a company's success—by setting goals, making decisions, committing the resources of the company to achieving these goals, and then by achieving these goals. To help ensure the achievement of these goals and the success of the company, managers use accounting information as they perform the activities of planning the operations of the company, operating the company, and evaluating the operations of the company for future planning and operating decisions. Exhibit 1-5 shows these activities.

Planning

Management begins with planning. A clear plan lays out the organization of, and gives direction to, the operating and evaluating activities. **Planning** establishes the company's goals and the means of achieving these goals. Managers use the planning process to identify what resources and employees the company needs in order to achieve its goals. They also use the planning process to set standards, or "benchmarks," against which they later can measure the company's progress toward its goals. Periodically measuring the company's progress against standards or benchmarks helps managers identify whether the company needs to make corrections to keep itself on course. Because the business environment changes so rapidly, plans must be ongoing and flexible enough to deal with change before it occurs or as it is happening.

Managers of companies operating in more than one country have more to consider in their planning process than do those operating only in the United States. Managers of multinational companies must also consider such factors as multiple languages, economic systems, political systems, monetary systems, markets, and legal systems. In such companies, managers must also encourage the communication between and among branches in several countries.

Operating

Operating refers to the set of activities that enable the company to conduct its business according to its plan. For Unlimited Decadence, these are the activities that ensure that

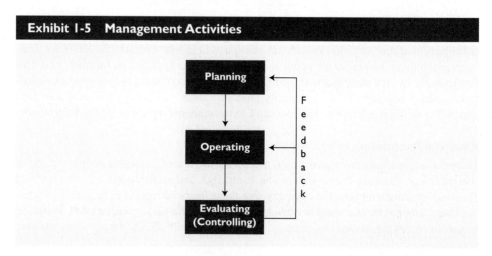

Exhibit 1-5   Management Activities

candy bars get made and sold. They involve gathering the resources and employees necessary to achieve the goals of the company, establishing organizational relationships among departments and employees, and working toward achieving the goals of the company. In operating the company, managers and work teams must make day-to-day decisions about how best to achieve these goals. For example, accounting information gives them valuable data about a product's performance. With this information, they can decide which products to continue to sell and when to add new products or drop old ones. If the company is a manufacturing company, managers and work teams can decide what products to produce and whether there is a better way to produce them. With accounting information, managers can also make decisions about how to set product selling prices, whether to advertise and how much to spend on advertising, and whether to buy new equipment or expand facilities. These decisions are ongoing and depend on managers' evaluations of the progress being made toward the company's goals and on changes in the company's plans and goals.

Evaluating

Evaluating is the management activity that measures actual operations and progress against standards or benchmarks. It provides feedback for managers to use to correct deviations from those standards or benchmarks, and to plan for the company's future operations. Evaluating is a continuous process that attempts to prevent problems or to detect and correct problems as quickly as possible.

As you might guess, the more countries in which a company operates, the more interesting the evaluating activity becomes. Because of cultural and other differences, evaluation methods and feedback used in some countries may have little meaning in other countries. For example, it would be difficult to convince employees of the importance of high quality if these employees are used to standing in long lines for whatever quality and quantity of merchandise is available in their country. Managers must pay particular attention to the cultural effects of evaluation methods and feedback in order to achieve effective control.

 Even coaches of professional sports teams perform the activities of planning, operating, and evaluating. If a team's goal is to win the Super Bowl, how would the head coach implement each of these activities?

Planning, operating, and evaluating all require information about the company. The company's accounting system provides much of the quantitative information managers use.

Do you think these people are engaged in planning activities, operating activities, or evaluating activities? Why?

Accounting Support for Management Activities

Management accounting involves the identification, measurement, recording, accumulation, and communication of economic information about a company for internal users in management decision-making. Internal users include individual employees, work groups or teams, departmental supervisors, divisional and regional managers, and "top management." Management accountants, then, provide information to internal users for planning the operations of the company, for operating the company, and for evaluating the operations of the company. With the help of the management accountant, managers use this information to help them make decisions about the company.

The reports that result from management accounting can help managers *plan* the activities and resources needed to achieve the goals of the company. These reports may provide revenue (amounts charged to customers) estimates and cost estimates of planned activities and resources, and an analysis of these cost estimates. By describing how alternative actions might affect the company's profit and solvency, these estimates and analyses help managers plan.

In *operating* a company, managers use accounting information to make day-to-day decisions about what activities will best achieve the goals of the company. Management accounting helps managers make these decisions by providing timely economic information about how each activity might affect profit and solvency.

Accounting information also plays a vital role in helping managers *evaluate* the operations of the company. Managers use the revenue and cost estimates generated during the planning and decision-making process as a benchmark, and then evaluate the company's actual revenues and costs against that benchmark.

Since managers are making decisions about their own company, and since each company is different, the information the management accountant provides must be "custom fitted" to the information needs of the company. This involves selecting the appropriate information to be reported, presenting that information in an understandable format (interpreting the information when necessary), and providing the information when it is needed for the decisions being made.

Management accounting responsibilities and activities thus vary widely from company to company. Furthermore, these responsibilities and activities continue to evolve as management accountants respond to the need for new information, a need caused by the changing business environment.

In response to this changing business environment, the Institute of Management Accountants (IMA) publishes guidelines for management accounting called Statements on Management Accounting (SMAs).

Statements on Management Accounting

6 *Are there any guidelines for reporting to company managers?*

SMAs serve as guidelines for management accountants to use in fulfilling their responsibilities. The SMAs are nonbinding (they are not rules that must be followed), but because they are developed by professional accountants, leaders in industry and colleges and universities, management accountants turn to SMAs for help when faced with new situations.

Framework for Management Accounting

The responsibility for identifying issues to be addressed by SMAs lies with an IMA committee called the Management Accounting Practices Committee. One of the first activities this committee undertook was to develop a framework for the work it was assigned to do. The "Framework for Management Accounting" developed by this committee defines the scope of the SMAs, including a statement of the objectives of management accounting and a description of the activities and responsibilities of management accountants.[5]

---

[5]Institute of Management Accountants, *Statements on Management Accounting: Objectives of Management Accounting,* Statement No. 1B, June 17, 1982.

Company-specific responsibilities and unique elements of a company's internal reports may change, but the underlying goals of management accounting remain the same:

▶ To inform people inside and outside the company about past or future events or circumstances that affect the company

▶ To interpret information from inside and outside the company and to communicate the implications of this information to various segments of the company

▶ To establish planning and control systems that ensure using the company's resources in accordance with company policy

▶ To develop information systems (create manual or computer systems that contain, process, and manage accounting data)

▶ To implement the use of modern equipment and techniques to aid in identifying, gathering, analyzing, communicating, and protecting information

▶ To ensure that the accounting system provides accurate and reliable information

▶ To develop and maintain an effective and efficient management accounting organization

In order to see how a company's accounting information helps managers in their planning, operating, and evaluating activities, briefly consider three key management accounting reports prepared with these goals in mind.

Basic Management Accounting Reports

Budgets, cost analyses, and manufacturing cost reports are examples of management tools the accounting system provides. Exhibit 1-6 illustrates the relationships between management activities and these reports.

 Suppose you are the manager of your company's sales force. What type of information would you want to help you do your job?

Budgets

Budgeting is the process of quantifying managers' plans and showing the impact of these plans on the company's operating activities. Managers present this information in a *budget* (or *forecast*). Once the planned activities have occurred, managers can evaluate the results of the operating activities against the budget to make sure that the actual operations

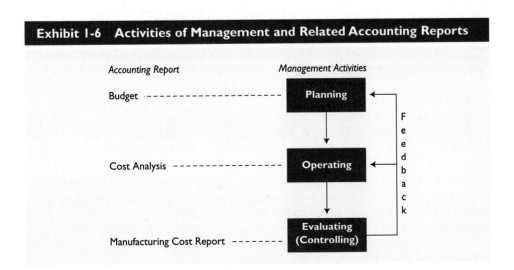

Exhibit 1-6   Activities of Management and Related Accounting Reports

Accounting Report   *Management Activities*

Budget - - - - - - - - - - - - - - - - - Planning

Cost Analysis - - - - - - - - - - - - - Operating

Manufacturing Cost Report - - - - - - - Evaluating (Controlling)

Feedback

of the various parts of the company achieved the established plans. For example, Unlimited Decadence might report a budget showing how many boxes of candy bars it plans to sell during the first three months of 2000. Later, when actual sales have been made, managers will compare the results of these sales with the budget to determine if their forecasts were "on target" and, if not, to find out why differences occurred. We will discuss budgets further in Chapters 4 and 12.

Cost Analyses

Cost analysis, or cost accounting, is the process of determining and evaluating the costs of specific products or activities within a company. Managers use cost analysis when making decisions about these products or activities. Unlimited Decadence might use a cost analysis to decide whether to stop or to continue making the Divinely Decadent candy bar. The cost analysis might show that the candy bar is profitable because it earns more than it costs to make. The fact that this candy bar makes a profit will be one factor in the managers' decisions. If the candy bar does not make a profit, the company's managers would have to resolve the ethical issue of whether to lay off the employees who produced the candy bar. (Can you think of an alternative to a layoff?)

 Suppose you are a manager of a company that makes a food product thought to create major health problems after long-term use. What facts would you consider in trying to decide whether the company should drop the product or continue producing it?

We will discuss cost analysis reports again in Chapter 15.

Manufacturing Cost Reports

As we mentioned above, managers must monitor and evaluate a company's operations to determine if its plans are being achieved. Accounting information can highlight specific "variances" from plans, indicating where corrections to operations can be made if necessary.

A manufacturing cost report might show that total actual costs for a given month were greater than total budgeted costs. However, it might also show that some actual costs were greater than budgeted costs while others were less than budgeted costs. The more detailed information will be useful for managers as they analyze why these differences occurred. We will discuss manufacturing cost reports again in Chapter 17.

Accounting Support for External Decision-Making

 Say you have been offered a job at Unlimited Decadence. What economic information concerning Unlimited Decadence would you want to know about to help you decide whether to accept the job offer?

Management accounting gives people inside a company vital business information, but companies must provide business information about their performances to current and potential investors and creditors, too. Many other people outside of the company are also interested in this information. **Financial accounting** involves the identification, measurement, recording, accumulation, and communication of economic information about a company for external users to use in their various decisions. External users are people and groups outside the company who need accounting information to decide whether or not to engage in some activity with the company. These users include individual investors, stockbrokers and financial analysts who offer investment assistance, consultants, bankers, suppliers, labor unions, customers, and local, state, and federal governments and governments of countries in which the company does business.

The accounting information that helps external users make a decision (for example, whether or not to extend a bank loan to a company) may be different from the information a manager within the company needs. Thus the accounting information prepared for the external user may differ from that prepared for the internal user. However, some of the accounting information the internal user needs also helps the external user and vice versa. For example, Unlimited Decadence may not continue to produce and sell the new candy bar unless there is enough money to do so. In weighing the likelihood of getting a loan from the bank, company managers will probably want to evaluate the same financial information that the bank evaluates. On the other hand, in deciding whether to make a loan to Unlimited Decadence, the bank will consider the likelihood that Unlimited Decadence will repay the loan. Since this likelihood may depend on current and future sales of the candy bar, the bank may want to evaluate the sales budget that Unlimited Decadence's managers developed as part of the planning process.

Many external users evaluate the accounting information of more than one company, and need comparable information from each company. For example, a bank looks at accounting information from all of its customers who apply for loans, and must use comparable information in order to decide to which customers to make loans. This need for comparability creates a need for guidelines or rules for companies to follow when preparing accounting information for external users. Over the years, because of the activities of several professional accounting organizations, a set of broad guidelines for financial accounting has evolved in the United States. These guidelines are referred to as generally accepted accounting principles.

Generally Accepted Accounting Principles

Generally accepted accounting principles, or **GAAP,** are the currently accepted principles, procedures, and practices that are used for financial accounting in the United States. These principles, or "rules," must be followed in the external reports of all companies that sell capital stock to the public in the United States and by many other companies as well. GAAP cover such issues as how to account for inventory, buildings, income taxes, and capital stock, how to measure the results of a company's operations, and how to account for the operations of companies in specialized industries, such as the banking industry, the entertainment industry, and the insurance industry. Without these agreed-upon principles, external users of accounting information would not be able to understand the meaning of this information. (Imagine if we all tried to communicate with each other without any agreed-upon rules of spelling and grammar!)

Several organizations contribute to GAAP through their publications (called "pronouncements" or "standards"). The three most important organizations that develop GAAP in the United States are the Financial Accounting Standards Board (FASB), the Securities and Exchange Commission (SEC), and the American Institute of Certified Public Accountants (AICPA). The FASB is a seven-member full-time board of professional accountants and businesspeople; it issues *Statements of Financial Accounting Standards.* The SEC is a branch of the U.S. government; it issues *Financial Reporting Releases.* The AICPA is the professional organization of all certified public accountants (CPAs); it issues *Statements of Position.*[6]

Accounting is less standardized worldwide than in the United States because of cultural, legal, economic, and other differences among countries. However, several organizations have made progress in developing worldwide accounting standards. Most notably, the International Accounting Standards Committee (IASC) has issued over 30 standards covering issues such as accounting for inventories, property and equipment, and the results of a company's operations. Although compliance with these standards is voluntary, most of the more than 100 accountancy organizations represented on this committee have

7 *Are there any guidelines for financial reporting in the United States?*

---

[6]Each of these organizations issues other documents that influence and establish GAAP, but they are too numerous to mention here.

agreed to eventually require the *International Accounting Standards* as part of their countries' generally accepted accounting standards.

Many GAAP pronouncements are complex and very technical in nature. In this book, we will introduce only the basic aspects of the generally accepted accounting principles that apply to the issues we discuss. It is important to recognize, however, that these principles do change; they are modified as business practices and decisions change, as better accounting techniques are developed.

Basic Financial Statements

Companies operate to achieve various goals. They may be interested in providing a healthy work environment for their employees, in reaching a high level of pollution control, or in making contributions to civic and social organizations and activities. However, to meet these goals, a company must first achieve its two primary objectives: *earning a satisfactory profit* and *remaining solvent*. If a company fails to meet either of these objectives, it will not be able to achieve its various goals and will not be able to survive in the long run.

Profit (commonly referred to as *net income*) is the difference between the cash and credit sales of a company and its total costs *(expenses)*. **Solvency** is a company's long-term ability to pay its debts as they come due. As you will see, external users analyze the *financial statements* of a company to determine how well the company is achieving its two primary objectives.

Financial statements are accounting reports used to summarize and communicate financial information about a company. A company's integrated accounting system produces three major financial statements: the income statement, the balance sheet, and the cash flow statement. Each of these statements summarizes specific information that has been identified, measured, recorded, and retained during the accounting process.

Income Statement

A company's **income statement** summarizes the results of its operating activities for *a specific time period* and shows the company's profit for that period. It shows a company's revenues, expenses, and net income (or net loss) for that time period, usually one year. Exhibit 1-7 shows what kind of information appears in a company's income statement. **Revenues** are the prices charged to a company's customers for the goods or services the company provides to them. **Expenses** are the costs of providing the goods or services. These amounts include the costs of the products the company has sold (either the cost of making these products or the cost of purchasing these products), the costs of conducting business (called operating expenses), and the costs of income taxes, if any. The **net income** is the excess of revenues over expenses, or the company's profit; a **net loss** arises when expenses are greater than revenues. We will discuss the income statement further in Chapter 6 and throughout the book.

Exhibit 1-7 What a Company's Income Statement Shows

Revenues

Here's where the company shows what it charged customers for the goods or services provided them during a specific time period.

Expenses

Here's where the company lists the costs of providing the goods and services during that period.

Net Income

This is the difference between revenues and expenses.

Exhibit 1-8 What a Company's Balance Sheet Shows

Assets

Here's where the company lists its economic resources, such as cash, inventories of its products, and equipment it owns.

Liabilities

Here's where the company lists its obligations to creditors, such as suppliers, employees, and banks.

Owner's Equity

Here's where the company lists the owner's current investment in the assets of the company (the contributions of the owner plus the cumulative earnings left in the company).

Balance Sheet

A company's **balance sheet** summarizes its financial position *on a given date.* It is also called a *statement of financial position.* Exhibit 1-8 shows what kind of information appears on a balance sheet. A balance sheet lists the company's assets, liabilities, and owner's equity on the given date. **Assets** are economic resources that a company owns and that it expects will provide future benefits to the company. **Liabilities** are the company's economic obligations (debts) to its creditors—people outside the company such as banks and suppliers—and employees. The **owner's equity** of a company is the owner's current investment in the assets of the company, which includes the owner's original contribution to the company and any earnings (net income) that the owner leaves in the company. A corporation owner's equity is called **stockholder's equity.** We will discuss the balance sheet further in Chapter 7 and throughout the book.

Cash Flow Statement

A company's **cash flow statement** summarizes its cash receipts, cash payments, and net change in cash for a specific time period. Exhibit 1-9 shows what kind of information appears in a cash flow statement. The cash receipts and cash payments for operating activities, such as products sold or services performed and the costs of producing the products or services, are summarized in the *cash flows from operating activities* section of the statement. The cash receipts and cash payments for investing activities are summarized in the *cash flows from investing activities* section of the statement. Investing activities include the purchases and sales of assets such as buildings and equipment. The cash receipts and cash payments for financing activities, such as money borrowed from and repaid to banks, are summarized in the *cash flows from financing activities* section of the statement. We will discuss the cash flow statement further in Chapters 8 and 19, and throughout the book.

Exhibit 1-9   What a Company's Cash Flow Statement Shows

Cash Flows from Operating Activities

Here's where the company lists the cash it received and paid in selling products or performing services for a specific time period.

Cash Flows from Investing Activities

Here's where the company lists the cash it received and paid in buying and selling assets such as equipment and buildings.

Cash Flows from Financing Activities

Here's where the company lists the cash it received and paid in obtaining and repaying bank loans and from contributions and withdrawals made by the company's owners.

A company may publish its income statement, balance sheet, and cash flow statement, along with other related financial accounting information, in its **annual report.** Many companies (mostly corporations) do so. We will discuss the content of an annual report in Chapter 10.

Ethics in Business and Accounting

8 *What role does ethics play in the business environment?*

Business and accounting exist in an environment in which many issues and events cannot be interpreted as absolutely right or wrong. Every decision or choice has pros and cons, costs and benefits, and people or institutions who will be affected positively or negatively by the decision. In a setting where many issues and events fall between the extremes of right and wrong, it is very important that accountants and businesspeople maintain high ethical standards. Several groups have established codes of ethics addressing ethical behavior to help accountants and their business associates work their way through the complicated ethical issues associated with business issues and events. These groups include the American Institute of Certified Public Accountants (AICPA), the Institute of Management Accountants (IMA), the International Federation of Accountants (IFAC), and most large companies.

Professional Organizations' Codes of Ethics

The members of the AICPA adopted a code of professional conduct that guides them in their professional work.[7] It addresses such issues as self-discipline, honorable behavior, moral judgments, the public interest, professionalism, integrity, and technical and ethical standards. The IMA has a code of conduct that is similar to the AICPA's code.[8] It addresses competence, confidentiality, integrity, objectivity, and resolution of ethical conflict.

The IFAC is an independent, worldwide organization. Its stated purpose is to "develop and enhance a coordinated worldwide accountancy profession with harmonized standards." As part of its efforts, it has developed a code of ethics for accountants in each country to use as the basis for founding their own codes of ethics.[9] Because of the wide cultural, language, legal, and social diversity of the nations of the world, the IFAC expects professional accountants in each country to add their own national ethical standards to the code to reflect their national differences, or even to delete some items of the code at their national level. The code addresses objectivity, resolution of ethical conflicts, professional competence, confidentiality, tax practice, cross-border activities, and publicity. It also addresses independence, fees and commissions, activities incompatible with the practice of accountancy, clients' money, relations with other professional accountants, and advertising and solicitation.

Ethics at the Company Level

Many companies have codes or statements of company and business ethics. Texas Instruments Incorporated (TI), which manufactures microchips, calculators, and other electronic equipment, has several documents containing guidelines for ethical decision-making. It even has an ethics committee and a director of ethics! The most important ethics document at TI is called *Ethics in the Business of TI.* It was originally published in 1961 and has been periodically revised since then.

The spirit of TI's code of ethics is described by the president and chief executive officer on the inside cover of the publication. "Texas Instruments will conduct its business in accordance with the highest ethical and legal standards. . . . We will always place integrity before shipping, before billings, before profits, before anything. If it comes down to a

---

[7]American Institute of Certified Public Accountants, *Code of Professional Conduct,* as amended January 14, 1992 (New York: AICPA, 1992).

[8]Institute of Management Accountants, *Statements on Management Accounting: Standards of Ethical Conduct for Management Accountants,* Statement No. 1C, June 1, 1983.

[9]International Federation of Accountants, *Code of Ethics for Professional Accountants* (New York: IFAC, 1992).

choice between making a desired profit and doing it right, we don't have a choice. We'll do it right."[10] The code addresses the marketplace, gifts and entertainment, improper use of corporate assets, political contributions, payments in connection with business transactions, conflict of interest, investment in TI stock, TI proprietary information, trade secrets and software of others, transactions with governmental agencies, and disciplinary action, among other subjects.

In our society, we expect each other to behave within a range of civilized standards. This expectation allows our society to function with minimal confusion and misunderstanding. In both our personal and our business lives, ethics and integrity are our "social glue."

Framework of the Book

Now that you have been introduced to business and accounting, it is almost time to begin a more in-depth study of the use of accounting information in the business environment. But first we will take a chapter to discuss the types of thinking necessary for one to survive in this environment. Chapter 2 describes creative and critical thinking, the types of thinking done by successful people in accounting and business. In each succeeding chapter you will see examples of creative and critical thinking and will be given the opportunity to practice them.

Beginning in Chapter 3 we will discuss, in more depth, accounting and its use in the management activities of planning, operating, and evaluating, starting with a simple company. Then, in later chapters, we will progress through more complex companies. We will also discuss the use of accounting by decision-makers outside the company.

As you read through the book, you will begin to notice the same topics reemerging; but note that each time, a topic will be refined or enhanced by a different company structure, a different type of business, or a different user perspective. You will also notice that we continue to discuss ethical considerations. That's because ethical considerations exist in all aspects of business and accounting.

You will also notice that international issues appear again and again. Many companies operating in the United States have home offices, branches, and subsidiaries in other countries or simply trade with companies in foreign countries. Managers must know the implications of conducting business in foreign countries and with foreign companies. External users of accounting information also must know the effects of these business connections.

Summary

At the beginning of the chapter we asked you several questions. During the chapter, we asked you to STOP and answer some additional questions to build your knowledge about specific issues. Be sure you answered these additional questions. Below are the questions from the beginning of the chapter, with a brief summary of the key points relating to the answers. Use your thinking skills to expand on these key points to develop more complete answers to the questions and to determine what other questions you have that might lead you to learn more about the issues.

1 Why is it necessary to have an understanding of business before trying to learn about accounting?

Accounting involves the identification, measurement, recording, accumulation, and communication of economic information about a company for decision-making. It focuses on the resources and ac-

---

[10]Texas Instruments Incorporated, *Ethics in the Business of TI* (1990).

tivities of companies. Therefore, you need to understand companies, and the business environment in which they exist, before trying to learn how to account for their resources and activities.

2 What is the role of accounting information within the business environment?

Accounting information helps people inside and outside companies make decisions. It supports management activities by providing managers with quantitative information about their company to aid them in planning, operating, and evaluating the company's activities. Accounting information supports external decision-making by providing people outside of the company, such as investors, creditors, stockbrokers, financial analysts, bankers, suppliers, labor unions, customers, and governments, with financial statements containing economic information about the performance of the company.

3 What is private enterprise, and what forms does it take?

Companies in the private enterprise system produce goods and services for a profit. These companies can be service, merchandising, or manufacturing companies. Entrepreneurs, or individuals, invest money in companies so that the companies can acquire resources, such as inventory, buildings, and equipment. The companies then use these resources to earn a profit. The three types of business organization are (1) the sole proprietorship, owned by one individual, (2) the partnership, owned by two or more individuals (partners), and (3) the corporation, incorporated as a separate legal entity and owned by numerous stockholders who hold capital stock in the corporation.

4 Why must the activities of companies be regulated? What types of regulations do companies face?

All companies, regardless of type, size, or complexity, must contend with regulatory issues. Numerous laws and authorities regulate companies on issues ranging from environmental protection to taxes. Each city, county, state, and country has its own regulations. Owners of companies must learn and comply with the regulations issued by the governments where the companies are located and in the areas in which the companies conduct business.

5 What activities contribute to the operations of a company?

Managers strive to make their company successful through setting and achieving the goals of their company, making decisions, and committing the resources of the company to the achievement of these goals. Planning provides the organization and direction for the other activities. Operating involves gathering the necessary resources and employees and implementing the plans. Evaluating measures the actual progress against standards or benchmarks so that problems can be corrected.

6 Are there any guidelines for reporting to company managers?

The Institute of Management Accountants publishes a broad set of nonbinding guidelines for management accountants to use in fulfilling their responsibilities. These guidelines provide help for management accountants when they are faced with new situations.

7 Are there any guidelines for financial reporting in the United States?

So that external users can understand the meaning of accounting information, companies follow agreed-upon principles in their external reports. The FASB, the SEC, and the AICPA contribute to the development of generally accepted accounting principles, the standards or "rules" that many companies must follow.

8 What role does ethics play in the business environment?

Since the world is a complex place, where issues are not always clear, decisions must be made in an ethical context with the best available information. Accounting information can be relied on only if it is generated in an ethical environment. Many groups have established codes of ethics.

Key Terms

annual report *(p. 20)*	**cash flow statement** *(p. 19)*
assets *(p. 19)*	**corporation** *(p. 9)*
balance sheet *(p. 19)*	**cost analysis or cost accounting** *(p. 16)*
budgeting *(p. 15)*	**entrepreneur** *(p. 7)*
capital *(p. 6)*	**evaluating** *(p. 13)*

expenses *(p. 18)*
external users *(p. 11)*
financial accounting *(p. 16)*
financial statements *(p. 18)*
generally accepted accounting principles
   (GAAP) *(p. 17)*
income statement *(p. 18)*
integrated accounting system *(p. 11)*
internal users *(p. 11)*
liabilities *(p. 19)*
manufacturing companies *(p. 6)*
merchandising companies *(p. 5)*
net income *(p. 18)*

net loss *(p. 18)*
owner's equity *(p. 19)*
partnership *(p. 8)*
partnership agreement *(p. 8)*
planning *(p. 12)*
profit *(p. 18)*
revenues *(p. 18)*
service companies *(p. 5)*
sole proprietorship *(p. 8)*
solvency *(p. 18)*
solvent *(p. 8)*
stockholders' equity *(p. 19)*

Here is an opportunity to gather information on the Internet about real-world issues related to the topics in this chapter. Go to http://www.dryden.com/account and click on the Cunningham, Nikolai, and Bazley book cover. Click on Summary Surfing, then click on this chapter number, and answer the following questions.

▶ Click on **OSHA** (U.S. Occupational Safety and Health Administration). Click on *About OSHA*, and then click on *Mission Statement*. What is the mission of OSHA? Now click on *Occupational Safety and Health Act of 1970*, and then click on *Section 4-Applicability of This Act*. To whom does this act apply? Go back and click on *Section 8-Inspections, Investigations, and Recordkeeping*. According to this act, what is the secretary allowed to do?

▶ Click on **TI** (Texas Instruments). In the *Quick Search box,* type "ethics," and click *Go.* Then click on *Ethics at Texas Instruments*. What are the three primary functions of the TI Ethics Office? Now click on *Ethics Organization at Texas Instruments*. What does the TI Ethics Committee do?

SUMMARY SURFING

Integrated Business and Accounting Situations

Answer the Following Questions in Your Own Words

Testing Your Knowledge

I-I How would you describe private enterprise?

I-2 What distinguishes a service company from a merchandising or manufacturing company?

I-3 How is a merchandising company different from a manufacturing company? How are the two types of company the same?

I-4 What is entrepreneurship?

I-5 Suppose you were an entrepreneur. Where might you go for business capital?

I-6 What distinguishes a corporation from a partnership and a sole proprietorship?

I-7 What types of regulations must companies comply with in different jurisdictions?

I-8 What is the purpose of an integrated accounting system?

I-9 Given what you have learned from this chapter, how would you define *accounting*?

I-10 How would you describe the similarities and differences between management accounting and financial accounting? Why are they different, and why are they similar?

I-11 How do management accounting reports help managers with their activities?

I-12 What is the purpose of Statements on Management Accounting (SMAs)?

I-13 What are generally accepted accounting principles?

I-14 How do financial accounting reports help external users?

I-15 Why have various business groups found it necessary to establish codes of ethics?

Applying Your Knowledge

www.aa.com
www.toyota.com

I-16 How is American Airlines an example of a service company? How is Toyota Motor Corporation an example of a manufacturing company?

I-17 How might knowledge of a company's cash receipts and payments affect a bank's decision about whether to loan the company money? What financial statement would the loan officer want to look at to begin to understand the company's cash receipts and payments?

I-18 What factors would you consider in deciding whether to operate your company as a sole proprietorship, a partnership, or a corporation?

I-19 Suppose you are Ichabod Cook, CEO of Unlimited Decadence Corporation, maker of candy bars. Unlimited Decadence currently operates in the northeastern United States, and you are considering opening a factory and sales office in California. What questions do you want answered before you proceed with this idea?

I-20 Refer to I-19. Suppose, instead, that you are considering opening a factory and sales office in Tokyo. What questions do you want answered before proceeding with *this* idea? How do you explain the similarities and differences in these two sets of questions?

I-21 What are some examples of company information in which both internal and external users have an interest?

I-22 Suppose you are a manager of The Foot Note, a small retail store that sells socks. Give an example of information that would help you in each of the management activities of planning, operating, and evaluating the operations of the store.

I-23 What are generally accepted accounting principles, and how do they affect the accounting reports of companies in the United States? Why might the owner or owners of a company be concerned about a proposed new accounting principle?

I-24 A friend of yours, Timorous ("Tim," for short) Ghostly, who has never taken an accounting course, has been assigned a short speech in his speech class. In this speech, Tim must describe the financial statements of a company. Tim has come to you for help (with his professor's permission). He says, "Please describe what financial statements are, what the major financial statements are, and what each financial statement includes." Prepare a written response to Tim's request.

I-25 How do codes of ethics help businesspeople make decisions?

Making Evaluations

1-26 Your friend, Vito Guarino (an incredible cook!), plans to open a restaurant when he graduates from college. One evening, while extolling the virtues of linguini to you and some of your other friends, he glances down at your accounting textbook, which is open to Exhibit 1-2. "What kind of a company is a restaurant?" he asks. "How would a restaurant fit into this exhibit?" Everyone in the room waits with great anticipation for your answer and the rationale behind your answer. What are you going to say?

1-27 You and your cousin, Harvey, have decided to form a partnership and open a landscaping company in town. But before you do, you and Harvey would like to "iron out" a few details about how to handle various aspects of the partnership and then write a partnership agreement outlining these details. What specific issues would you like to see addressed in the partnership agreement before you begin your partnership with Harvey?

1-28 Suppose you are thinking about whether presidents of companies should be allowed to serve on the FASB. What do you think are the potential benefits of allowing them to serve? What do you think are the potential problems?

1-29 Read a daily newspaper for the next week. What evidence do you find that supports the need for business codes of ethics?

1-30 You just nabbed a plum job joining a team of consultants writing an advice column, "Dear Dr. Decisive," for the local newspaper. Yesterday, you received your first letter:

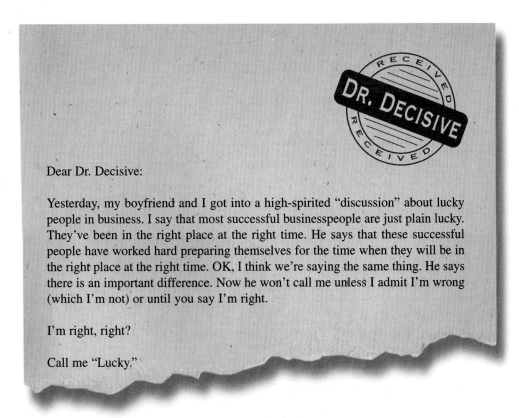

Dear Dr. Decisive:

Yesterday, my boyfriend and I got into a high-spirited "discussion" about lucky people in business. I say that most successful businesspeople are just plain lucky. They've been in the right place at the right time. He says that these successful people have worked hard preparing themselves for the time when they will be in the right place at the right time. OK, I think we're saying the same thing. He says there is an important difference. Now he won't call me unless I admit I'm wrong (which I'm not) or until you say I'm right.

I'm right, right?

Call me "Lucky."

Required: Meet with your Dr. Decisive team and write a response to "Lucky."

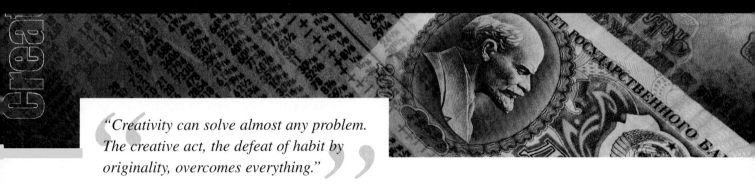

CHAPTER 2

CREATIVE AND CRITICAL THINKING, PROBLEM-SOLVING, AND THEIR ROLES IN BUSINESS AND ACCOUNTING

"Creativity can solve almost any problem. The creative act, the defeat of habit by originality, overcomes everything."

—George Lois

1 *What factors are causing the business environment and the role of accounting within that environment to change?*

2 *What skills can people develop to better prepare themselves for problem-solving and decision-making in the rapidly changing business environment?*

3 *How can people learn to think creatively and critically?*

4 *How can creative and critical thinking help people make better business decisions?*

5 *What are the logical stages in problem-solving and decision-making?*

Have you ever heard the phrase "creative accounting"? People sometimes use it to describe a form of accounting that "sidesteps" generally accepted accounting principles or manipulates accounting information, legally or not. (This type of "accounting" is also sometimes jokingly referred to as "cooking the books.") In this context, "creative accounting" might generate accounting reports that benefit the company or division doing the reporting, mislead the reader of the reports, lead to bad decisions, and perhaps result in a substantial fine or jail sentence for the "creative accountant." According to another, more amusing interpretation, this phrase is an oxymoron—a person cannot be creative and also be an accountant. This reading of the phrase is based on caricatures and stereotypes of accountants that are usually not appropriate.

 Compare how a movie might portray a photographer, doctor, or lawyer versus how it might portray an accountant.

We like to think more positively of creative accounting, to see it as searching for and using innovative solutions to complex management accounting and financial accounting problems. In a constantly evolving business environment, businesspeople, including accountants, face complex, ambiguous, dynamic, and difficult-to-interpret economic events that can cause challenges for which no guidelines, or only sketchy guidelines, exist. These situations present opportunities for companies to grow and change, so accountants and other businesspeople try to anticipate changes in the business environment and to address the associated challenges even before they occur. But finding creative solutions is just the start in wrestling with the challenges associated with today's economic events. Smart businesspeople must also develop and use their critical thinking skills to identify the *best* solutions to these problems and to make optimum decisions. In fact, recognizing a crucial need for people with more of these skills, accounting firms and other companies are actively recruiting "the best and the brightest" creative and critical thinkers.

The Changing Business Environment

1 *What factors are causing the business environment and the role of accounting within that environment to change?*

Why is the business environment changing so rapidly? As Exhibit 2-1 illustrates, a combination of many interwoven factors in this environment contributes to its complexity and excitement.

One contributor to the rapidly evolving business environment is the *information explosion.* More information is being generated than ever before, and this information is available to more people than ever. On the information superhighway, networks such as the Internet make available an almost endless list of information that includes library listings, books, journal articles, corporation's financial reports, catalogs, and directories of companies, organizations, and people with similar interests. Since it is impossible to use, let alone understand, all the available information, businesspeople must be able to filter it to select what is timely and relevant for making decisions. Furthermore, new discoveries can quickly make old information obsolete or invalid. Because of the amount and accessibility of information, and because new information may replace existing information, company managers must be able to use their creative and critical thinking skills to evaluate and manage this information to their advantage. We will discuss this idea more thoroughly later in the chapter.

Consider how *technological advances* have affected the transmittal of information. Many businesspeople have extended their workday by using cellular phones to conduct business during commuting time. Fax machines and e-mail now allow us to transmit documents across the world instantly. Computer networks facilitate information transmittal to and from multiple computers. Huge databases, such as airline flight schedules and rate structures, are now stored in computer files and accessed by millions of users around the world. Satellites allow global audiovisual communication. Rather than traveling to other cities to attend conferences, for example, many businesspeople attend satellite-facilitated

Exhibit 2-1	Factors Affecting the Complexity of the Business Environment

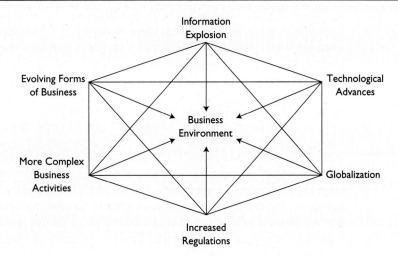

teleconferences, sometimes staying in their own offices. Telephone-answering machines now allow messages to be played at "fast-forward" speed so that the listener can hear them in less time! These technological advances allow virtually instant access to current events and up-to-date information.

Technological advances affect not only the products we use and the way business is conducted but also the way the products are manufactured. For example, advanced technologies have allowed the production process to become automated. In many of our factories, computers are used to plan, operate, and monitor manufacturing processes and to make adjustments to these processes as needed. The Saab factory, for example, is fully automated and capable of manufacturing automobiles without human intervention. Robots are now common workers on many production lines.

The *globalization* of business activities and economies is providing more opportunities for companies to conduct business by creating a larger, more diverse marketplace. At the same time, it is providing new business challenges. For example, when companies begin to sell their products in other countries, they must translate their product names and advertising slogans into different languages. This type of translation is not as straightforward as it might first appear. Consider the dilemma <u>Kentucky Fried Chicken</u> faced when it tried to translate its slogan "finger-lickin' good" into Taiwanese. The literal translation was, "Eat your fingers off."[1]

Businesspeople not only must hurdle language barriers (imagine translating "Extra Super-Duper Complete and Pure Decadence Candy Bar") but also must translate transactions involving foreign currencies (for example, Japanese yen to U.S. dollars). Furthermore, as we discussed in Chapter 1, they must learn to negotiate other cultures, economies, laws, and ways of conducting business.

As we also discussed in Chapter 1, another factor adding to the complexity of the business environment is the *increased regulations* that companies must address. Not only are there a growing number of regulations affecting companies in the United States (candy bars probably have a hundred or more regulations affecting them in the United States), but when companies operate in other countries, the number of regulations they face increases substantially with each country in which they conduct their business. This issue has caused many countries to draft agreements among themselves to minimize barriers to free trade. Examples of these agreements include the European Union (EU) of 15 European

Do you think this behavior is acceptable in all cultures? Why, or why not?

[1]Harry Berkowitz, "Top Firm Slogan Translations a Disaster," *Montreal Gazette,* September 1, 1994.

nations, the North American Free Trade Agreement (NAFTA) among Canada, Mexico, and the United States, and the General Agreement on Tariffs and Trade (GATT), a 124-nation pact that created a World Trade Organization to referee trade disputes among its members.

More complex business activities also contribute to the changing business environment. For example, business owners and managers are finding more creative methods of financing their activities, new outlets for investing their excess cash, a larger variety of alternatives for compensating their employees, and more complicated tax laws with which they must comply.

Finally, *evolving forms of business* are cropping up in the new business environment. For example, numerous variations of the simple business organizations that we discussed in Chapter 1 (sole proprietorships, partnerships, and corporations) now exist. These variations developed in response to the more complex business environment and include such exotic-sounding organizations as general partnerships, limited partnerships, domestic corporations, foreign corporations, nonprofit corporations, professional corporations, business corporations, limited liability companies, and Subchapter S corporations. Each of these forms of organization has legal advantages and disadvantages that the others don't have, and each addresses a particular aspect of the business environment. A company owner chooses the form of business that most closely meets the company's needs.

The factors discussed above not only contribute to the complexity and excitement of the business environment but also challenge the assumptions on which companies and their employees operate. For example, the assumption that a college graduate will go out into the world, pursue a lifelong career, and never return to college is no longer valid. People now change careers several times before they retire. Often, in order to make a change, they return to college between careers to "retool," or to expand their education to include new skills. Even people who stay in the same career expand their education (through continuing professional education, short courses, conferences, and seminars) to improve their knowledge and abilities.

It is easy to see that a person entering or remaining in this dynamic environment must be dynamic also. In the following sections, we will discuss the characteristics, attitudes, and skills that help people succeed in the business world. While reading these sections, keep in mind that these are attributes and abilities that people learn over a period of time and continue to develop for the rest of their lives (similar to the way athletes learn and improve their athletic skills).

The Successful Businessperson

Imagine a successful businessperson. Perhaps the person, with sleeves rolled up and hands dirty, is working hard on some project. Or maybe he or she, business-suited and with briefcase in hand, is heading for a meeting. You may have a picture of what this businessperson looks like, but what really determines success is harder to see. It's more a matter of approach than of image.

The successful businessperson thrives on change, seeing it as an opportunity rather than an obstacle. However, treating change as an opportunity is more than just a matter of attitude (more than simply seeing the glass as "half full"). It also involves being *prepared* for the opportunity; the successful businessperson is both willing and *able* to change. Therefore, this person is devoted to lifelong learning, realizing that continuous learning is the only way to keep up with and be prepared for the fast-paced change we described earlier.

To be able to adapt to change (or "go with the flow"), the successful businessperson develops certain other qualities as well. He or she welcomes others' viewpoints, appreciates differences among people, takes educated and thoughtful risks, anticipates environmental trends and identifies the potential problems and opportunities associated with these trends, and willingly abandons old plans if new information, or technology, makes them less workable. This doesn't mean that the successful businessperson is a chameleon, changing colors every time the business environment changes, but it does mean that he or she is flexible and adaptable.

The Accountant of the 21st Century

The accountant, as a businessperson in the 21st century, will have the characteristics we mentioned above but also will have the skills and knowledge advanced by the largest accounting firms[2] and later championed by the Accounting Education Change Commission (AECC).[3] These skills include the communication, interpersonal, and intellectual skills needed not only by accountants to effectively practice accounting in a changing environment but also by other businesspeople as well.

2 *What skills can people develop to better prepare themselves for problem-solving and decision-making in the rapidly changing business environment?*

Communication Skills

An accountant's job involves both collecting and communicating information. A key part of collecting information is knowing where to look for it. Although some information may be located in routine places, such as checkbook registers and sales invoices, the accountant has to be ready to look beyond the routine. Information may appear in written form (such as documents, written procedures, reports, journals, and reference materials) or in verbal form (such as conversations or presentations).

To gather information from both written and verbal sources, then, an accountant must be a proficient reader and listener. In this case, reading and listening mean more than they appear to at first glance. To be useful, the information gathered must be *relevant* to the decision at hand. The accountant must be able to interpret information, decide whether it is relevant, and then filter out everything else. This means that the accountant cannot be just a casual reader or listener. Rather, the accountant must *analyze* the information he or she reads or hears, actively trying to understand it by considering both its context and its source. Context includes such aspects as how the perspective or bias of the source influenced the information, how the information was developed, and what assumptions were made in developing the information. To gain this understanding, the accountant must use critical thinking skills, which we will discuss later in the chapter.

Accountants also communicate information. They must be able to present their ideas coherently to people at different levels of the company (all the way up to the chair of the board of directors) and also to people outside the company who have different interests and backgrounds, as well as various levels of accounting and business understanding. These ideas may be presented formally or informally, in written or oral form. An accountant, then, also must be an effective speaker and writer.

Interpersonal Skills

Although working with numbers may be the most familiar aspect of an accountant's job (have you ever heard accountants referred to as "number crunchers" or "bean counters"?), working with people is just as important. Accountants collect information from some people and communicate it to others. They work on team projects, act as leaders within a department, and also serve on teams that span the entire company. Since accountants advise managers and board members, they have to possess the same interpersonal skills that a competent manager or board member possesses. These skills include the ability to lead and influence others, to motivate others, to withstand and resolve conflict, and to organize and delegate tasks.

[2]Arthur Andersen & Co., Arthur Young, Coopers & Lybrand, Deloitte Haskins & Sells, Ernst & Whinney, Peat Marwick Main & Co., Price Waterhouse, and Touche Ross, *Perspectives on Education: Capabilities for Success in the Accounting Profession* (New York, 1989).

[3]Accounting Education Change Commission, *Objectives of Education for Accountants,* Position Statement No. 1, September 1990.

Intellectual Skills

The large accounting firms and the AECC recognized that gathering information, interpreting it, and effectively communicating it to others relies on the businessperson's ability to think creatively and critically. Creative thinking and critical thinking are necessary and complementary skills for successful, efficient problem-solving and decision-making. However, these skills do not necessarily come naturally. You might be an extremely creative thinker but not a good critical thinker. Similarly, you might be a very capable critical thinker but not a very creative thinker. Or perhaps you're somewhere between "extremely good" and "just awful" in both skills. Luckily, though, you can continue to improve your creative and critical thinking skills. We will spend the second half of this chapter introducing you to specific creative and critical thinking skills, and we will illustrate their use in solving accounting-related problems throughout the book.

Creative problem-solving and critical thinking skills are extremely important for the accountant in the rapidly changing business environment. However, these skills alone are not sufficient. Accountants must also have a knowledge base that supports these skills. This knowledge base is grouped into three categories.[4] The first category, **general knowledge,** encompasses knowledge about history and cultures; an ability to interact with people who have dissimilar ideas; a sense of the contrasting economic, political, and social forces in the world and of the magnitude of world issues and ideas; and experience in making value judgments. The second category, **organizational and business knowledge,** includes an understanding of the effects of economic, social, cultural, and psychological forces on businesses; an understanding of how businesses work; an understanding of methods and strategies for managing change; and an understanding of how technology helps organizations. The third category, **accounting and auditing knowledge,** includes the ability to construct accounting data, as well as the ability to use this data to make decisions, to exercise judgments, to evaluate risks, and to solve problems. According to the largest public accounting firms, then, the accountant must be an analytical thinker and must be able to apply creative and critical thinking to problem-solving and decision-making within the business world.

Creative and Critical Thinking

3 *How can people learn to think creatively and critically?*

Have you ever tried a sport and performed dreadfully but then, after practice and perseverance, found that your skills gradually improved for that sport? Improvement begins with awareness; you need to be conscious of your performance, make an effort to improve it, and focus your efforts on an image of what constitutes good performance. A serious tennis player studies tennis. She not only practices but also compares her performance and form with an ideal or with her last game; she reads books and newspaper columns on tennis and tennis form and visualizes herself playing in the different situations they describe; she watches better tennis players as they play, and she improves by playing against tennis players who are better at the game than she is.

Exhibit 2-2 shows a tennis lesson from a series of syndicated lessons appearing in newspapers around the country. Designed to help tennis players improve their games, each lesson gives instructions in a specific skill (or even in one small aspect of a skill). Have you seen lessons designed to help thinkers improve their thinking? When we talk about improving our minds, we tend to refer to gaining more knowledge rather than to improving our thinking performance and form. Most of us spend little time monitoring our thinking and comparing it with an ideal. Perhaps this is either because we do not know how to think about thinking or because we do not know what the ideal is.

Most of us tend to consider thinking, like breathing, to be a natural function. We all do it. (After all, isn't thinking supposed to distinguish us from other animals?) However, *creative*

---

[4]Arthur Andersen & Co. et al., *Perspectives on Education,* 7, 8.

Exhibit 2-2   Evaluating Your Tennis Game

STAN SMITH'S TENNIS CLASS

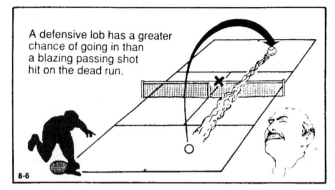

©1992 Stan Smith's Tennis Class, distributed by King Features Syndicate, Inc. Reprinted with special permission.

From this description, do you think using a defensive lob is the result of creative or critical thinking?

and *critical* thinking takes practice, just like tennis. Few people expect to be good at tennis their first time on the court. At first, *bad* tennis seems to be the norm. But with practice aimed at improving and at learning new forms and specific techniques, *better* tennis comes more naturally. In the same way, practicing creative and critical thinking, including new "forms and techniques," makes it more natural. Awareness of our current thinking patterns helps us recognize our strengths and weaknesses; this knowledge gives us a starting point for modifying and improving our thinking performance. We will spend the remainder of the chapter discussing and analyzing the processes (or "forms and techniques") and ideals of creative and critical thinking.

Creative Thinking

Creative thinking is the process of actively generating new ideas to discover solutions to a problem. Effective creative thinking begins with learning to be spontaneous. Letting your thoughts flow freely opens the door to new ideas. Not all of these ideas will be great, but don't try to make that judgment right away. What matters now is generating lots of ideas. Let yourself be spontaneous; you may be surprised at what comes through the door. Like learning a sport, learning to be a creative thinker means developing and nurturing some new skills and attitudes.

Characteristics of the Creative Thinker

Although some people believe that creativity is a talent that people are born with, some characteristics of creative thinking can be developed. One of these characteristics is *inquisitiveness,* or a questioning attitude. Inventions and innovations arise from inquisitive people. If you accept, without question, the way things are, it is difficult to recognize problems, and of course, if you do not recognize the existence of a problem, it is difficult to get creative about the solution to that problem. In this sense, creative thinkers are "problem finders." That is, they tend to explore alternative problems before deciding which problem should be addressed. For example, 3M's Post-it notes solved a problem but not the one its inventor started out to address. The problem the inventor was initially trying to solve was how to make a superpermanent adhesive, but each attempt produced an adhesive that didn't stick very well. By using the relatively nonsticky adhesive to solve a different problem—how to attach, to objects and paper, notes that would peel off easily without damaging either—the inventor and his product became an instant success. A good start toward creativity, then, includes an attitude of healthy skepticism that questions existing approaches, practices, techniques, and even the original statement of the problem. If you feel uncomfortable asking questions, remember that no one has all the answers, no matter what anyone may tell you.

www.3M.com

Creative individuals strive for both fluency and flexibility in their thinking. **Fluency** refers to the *number* of ideas generated or solutions proposed by the problem-solver. **Flexibility** refers to the *spectrum* of ideas generated. When a problem-solver is flexible, he or she will probably develop a broad array of ideas for solving a problem, and some of these ideas may be very unconventional.

Suppose your boss has asked you, the marketing manager, to develop some ideas that will increase sales of a sugarless, fat-free candy bar. Without censoring yourself, how many ideas can you come up with in the next two minutes?

Creative thinkers are willing to express ideas that are different from everyone else's ideas. They don't censor themselves and their ideas because of what someone else might think (allowing for both fluency and flexibility in their thought processes). They also have patience in their search for solutions to problems. Rather than accept the first workable solution they encounter (limiting their fluency and flexibility), they continue to generate workable solutions. Whereas the desire to find a quick solution often limits fluency and flexibility, patience and relaxation seem to have the opposite effect. In fact, some of the most creative thinking occurs at the least-expected times, such as when people are in the shower or on vacation.

Remember, you can develop and improve the creative thinking characteristics we have just discussed. Exhibit 2-3 lists some questions you can ask yourself when you are trying to think creatively; these questions will help you progress as a creative thinker.

Strategies of the Creative Thinker

Have you heard of a process called **brainstorming?** It's an example of creative thinking in a group. If you look up *brainstorm* in the dictionary, you will see that one of the definitions refers to "a harebrained idea."[5] Brainstorming generates plenty of these, but it also generates many reasonable ideas, some of which began as "harebrained ideas." In the process of brainstorming, members of a group try to generate as many solutions as possible to a particular problem. For example, maybe your company is trying to cut costs. Brainstorming is one way to generate numerous cost-cutting ideas (probably many more ideas than could be generated by one person thinking alone). In the interest of not inhibiting or censoring anyone in the group, any idea counts during a brainstorming session, no matter how ridiculous (or "harebrained") it may seem on the surface (and participants must be supportive, not judgmental). This guideline improves the spontaneity of the ideas. Remember, even the most ridiculous idea will generate other ideas, some of which may be outstanding. The generation of ideas from other ideas is sometimes called **piggybacking.** The group continues this process until everyone runs out of ideas or until a reasonable amount of time has passed.

Exhibit 2-3   Questions for Creative Thinkers to Ask Themselves
What is it about this idea that stimulates my curiosity?
Can I come up with more ideas?
Can I come up with a greater variety of ideas?
Do I develop ideas independently and not eliminate them from consideration because of social influences?
Do I consider several alternatives before acting?

---

[5]*Webster's Ninth New Collegiate Dictionary,* s.v. "brainstorm."

Another creative thinking strategy is to draw analogies. **Drawing analogies** involves making connections among facts, ideas, or experiences that are normally considered separately. Discovering these connections often leads to creative solutions to problems; the creative thinker often sees innovative ways of applying a similar solution to two seemingly dissimilar problems. Say, for example, that on your first job, you are asked to design a system for keeping track of the company's cash expenditures. You might use your experience keeping track of your own personal expenditures as a starting point for solving this problem, looking for similarities and differences between the company's and your own cash expenditures.

 How many similarities and differences can you think of between how a company might spend its cash and how you spend your cash?

While brainstorming about these similarities and differences, you might use a creative thinking strategy called **attribute listing,** which involves listing the characteristics of an object or idea to gain insights into its possible usefulness. The spontaneous, uncensored listing of an object's characteristics can help you do away with preconceived notions that may limit your ability to think creatively. For example, suppose you are asked to list all the possible uses you can think of for your calculator. If you list only mathematical functions, you have not considered all the attributes of the calculator. Did you include its weight, shape, color, hardness, and size? Given these attributes, can you think of other uses for your calculator (maybe a doorstop, a paperweight, a projectile, or even a stalling device that keeps the remote-control addicts in your household from changing stations on the television—until they discover they are holding a calculator)?

Now that you've seen how to generate ideas using creative thinking strategies, we will look at ways of using these ideas to solve problems. This is where critical thinking comes into play.

Critical Thinking

Critical thinking is the process that evaluates the ideas generated by creative thinking. Critical thinking determines if any of the ideas will work, what types of problems they might have, whether they can be improved, and which ones are better than others. To be a successful critical thinker, you have to be in the right frame of mind, use the thought processes and actions necessary for thinking critically, and constantly watch and monitor your thinking (much as the tennis player watches her game).

Characteristics of the Critical Thinker

Above all, the critical thinker values truth rather than the *appearance* of truth. As you will see, the emotional state, thought processes, and activities involved in thinking critically all help the critical thinker sort out the truth. For example, in looking for the truth, critical thinkers must be independent and objective. Being **independent** means that in the process of evaluating ideas, the critical thinker must rely on his or her own conclusions rather than those of others. This doesn't mean that the critical thinker is a know-it-all—just that he or she doesn't accept the beliefs of others without questioning where those ideas came from, what evidence supports them, and what assumptions were made in developing the ideas.

Objectivity, the quality of being unbiased, is a very difficult characteristic to achieve but one that critical thinkers must have if they value truth. All people select, organize, and interpret information based on their own perceptions, beliefs, and past experiences. Even when we are trying very hard to understand someone else's point of view, we tend to say to ourselves, "Here is how I would feel if I were in that situation . . . therefore, he must feel the same way." We tend to unconsciously impose our own perceptions, beliefs, and past experiences on our understanding of information, ideas, and other people. For this reason, information and understanding are almost automatically biased. Besides being willing to consider new ideas and information, critical thinkers know that they may have limitations that keep them from true understanding. They not only recognize that they may have biases and prejudices but also watch for and try to eliminate these biases from their thinking. By realizing that their viewpoints are a product of their unique experiences, critical thinkers are better able to really listen to and understand other viewpoints.

As part of their search for truth and their continual striving toward independent, objective thinking, critical thinkers develop openness to new and different ideas, as well as empathy for other points of view. Have you ever encountered a "know-it-all"? Do you remember feeling frustrated that this person did not listen to your perspective or to your contributions to the conversation? As you have probably experienced, a "know-it-all" assumes that there is no more to learn about a subject. Unfortunately, this assumption blocks that person's receptivity to new information and new perspectives about the subject. How much more could the "know-it-all" learn by keeping an open mind? Furthermore, could this person make better decisions by acknowledging the limits of his or her own knowledge and by making use of all available relevant information?

Critical thinkers also *tolerate ambiguity* and willingly *defer judgment* until they can collect more information and consider and evaluate other solutions. Many problems involve complex issues with multiple interpretations and numerous good solutions. Critical thinkers, like creative thinkers, do not accept the first solution generated as necessarily being the best solution. Rather, they gather multiple solutions and evaluate them against predetermined values or criteria. As you learn about accounting, you will also learn about some of the values and criteria that accountants use for evaluating information and ideas. Critical thinkers also recognize that "good" ideas are often relative rather than absolute (for example, "higher quality," "more probable," and "more objective"). So even though many ideas may satisfy the critical thinker's values and criteria, some ideas may be better than others.

Finally, critical thinkers *have grit.* Have you ever had an idea that you *knew* was right (after analyzing and evaluating other ideas and viewpoints), but nobody else agreed with you? Grit is what kept you from caving in to the majority opinion. Grit keeps you going when the going gets tough. As we said before, many problems in business are complex and multifaceted. Identifying problems, finding solutions, and overcoming all the obstacles and frustrations along the way takes perseverance.

Just as with creative thinking characteristics, you can develop and improve the critical thinking characteristics we have just discussed. Exhibit 2-4 lists some questions you can ask yourself when you are trying to think critically; these questions will help you improve your critical thinking.

Strategies of the Critical Thinker

To make sense of the world, to develop solutions to complex problems, to deal with ambiguous issues, and to make decisions, the critical thinker must apply a variety of thinking and reasoning strategies to the thought process. First, the critical thinker must be able to define, clearly and precisely, the problem or issue at hand. Without a clear and precise definition of the problem, it is almost impossible to generate the best solution—how could you identify the relevant information for solving it?

Exhibit 2-4   Questions for Critical Thinkers to Ask Themselves

If an issue is controversial, do I accept my first reaction to it, or do I debate the issue in my head first?

Do I tend to reject new evidence that contradicts my current opinion on a subject, or do I evaluate the new evidence and then decide whether to accept it or reject it?

When I am trying to solve a problem, do I usually accept the first solution that "works," or do I generate multiple solutions and then choose the best one?

When others disagree with me, do I usually listen to them with an open mind and critically evaluate their ideas, or do I try to defend my own ideas?

Language and clear thinking are directly related. To test thinking for clarity, a critical thinker can ask the following questions about the language used in the reasoning process. Is it specific? Is it precise? Is it accurate? If the language used is not specific, precise, and accurate, chances are that the thinking behind the words is not clear. Consider the following two problem definitions.

1. "Unlimited Decadence Corporation has a problem with high costs."

2. "Many employees at Unlimited Decadence Corporation think their departments must spend as much as they budgeted for this year or else their departments will be allocated less money to spend next year."

Which of the problem definitions do you think would generate more-focused solutions? Why? Perhaps you chose the second definition because it is clearer and more precise than the first definition. The first problem definition might even lead you down the wrong path. For example, you might spend time looking for overpriced expenditures when the problem at hand is that departments are making *too many* expenditures. We will look more closely at the process of recognizing and defining problems later in this chapter.

After the decision-maker recognizes and defines the problem, he or she must identify, gather, and then evaluate the data relevant to the problem at hand. The decision-maker must use creative thinking skills to determine what is known about the problem. To make this determination, he or she must first develop ideas about where to locate the data. Sources of data include people familiar with the problem and written material such as reports, documents, memos, and books that contain information about the problem.

Next, the decision-maker uses creative thinking skills to determine what additional information and support is needed and is available to solve the problem. After collecting the relevant data and before using it for problem-solving and decision-making, the decision-maker must use critical thinking skills to analyze the data for faulty logic, unsupported assumptions, and emotional appeal. For example, consider the following statement made by a rather disgruntled employee of Unlimited Decadence: "All programmers should have to work regular hours, from 8:00 A.M. to 5:00 P.M. just like everybody else. It isn't fair that the computer programmers can come in late. Sure, they come in during the middle of the night to fix programs when the computer crashes, and they program on into the night when they are 'on a roll,' but we all know it's just a party up there. Mortimer, one of the programmers, is a major party animal. I've been to several parties with him."

Faulty logic can cause you to arrive at a conclusion that isn't warranted. In evaluating the information, the critical thinker must consider the nature of evidence supporting it. How true are the supporting reasons? Do these reasons support the conclusion? In the above example, the decision-maker might ask if it is true that night work is just a "party." An untrue assertion can lead a decision-maker to the wrong decision, so it is vital to determine, with evidence, that the assertion is valid. The critical thinker also must evaluate the relevance of the evidence used to support arguments or solutions. Does the assertion that Mortimer is a "party animal" at a party necessarily mean that he is a "party animal" at work?

 In this situation, what other questions might a decision-maker ask?

Besides evaluating the relevance (or appropriateness) of the information, the decision-maker must also evaluate the credibility of its sources. What do we know about the disgruntled employee? Is he a habitual complainer whose allegations typically don't "hold water"? Is he responsible and normally "on target" with his observations? Is the information provided by this one employee enough to support his own assertion? (By the way, have you checked out the credentials of the authors of this book? Are these credentials relevant to the decision involving whether or not to believe what the authors have written?) Finally, the disgruntled employee has thrown in a dose of emotional appeal: "It isn't *fair. . . .*" Although critical thinkers do not ignore the emotional effects of alternatives, they must consider the alternatives objectively and not be unduly swayed by emotional appeals.

 Do you see any other faulty logic, unsupported assumptions, or emotional appeal in the employee's statement?

Evidence and reasoning must not only be relevant to the arguments, solutions, and decisions they support but also *consistent* with them. If it is true that the night shift parties all night, does it make sense to have the programmers maintain regular work hours? Would that solve the problem *and* get the work of the company done? If programmers maintained regular working hours, would they be available to fix programs in the middle of the night, and would they be willing to continue a programming streak even though it's 5:00 P.M.? Might another solution work better?

Information and events do not exist in a vacuum. Rather, each of these factors influences and is influenced by the others. Therefore, the critical thinker must synthesize all relevant information, combining it with insights and knowledge to form meaningful patterns in order to gain understanding. Physicians synthesize information when diagnosing an illness based on a patient's symptoms and other information that the physician knows or learns. In business and accounting, the critical thinker also uses symptoms to "diagnose" a problem. The ability to recognize similarities and differences among symptoms and to use other insights and knowledge helps the business decision-maker develop meaningful patterns that are useful in synthesizing information.

Critical thinkers use a variety of thinking skills in the problem-solving process. Among these skills is the ability to use logic. **Inductive logic** is reasoning that moves from the specific to the general—from an observation or assumption to a generalized conclusion. An example of a conclusion reached through inductive logic is the following statement: "A recent employee poll reveals that 97 percent of employees think the company should provide a fitness center for employee use." In arriving at this conclusion, the company surveyed a sample of employees. The results of the survey of *specific* employees were used to generalize about the opinions of *all* the employees.

Conversely, **deductive logic** is reasoning that moves from a general statement or assertion to a specific conclusion. Consider the following example of a conclusion reached through deductive logic: "All Unlimited Decadence employees are paid on Fridays. Penelope is an Unlimited Decadence employee. Therefore, Penelope is paid on Fridays." As long as the first two sentences are true, the conclusion is necessarily true. Exhibit 2-5 illustrates the difference between inductive and deductive logic.

Is the future rock star trying to use inductive or deductive logic? How did you decide? Do you see any flaws in his logic?

ZITS

©1997 ZITS, by Jerry Scott & Jim Borgman. Reprinted with special permission.

Exhibit 2-5   Inductive and Deductive Logic

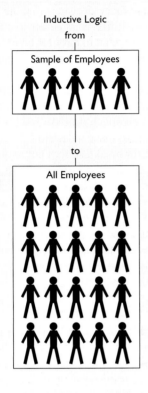

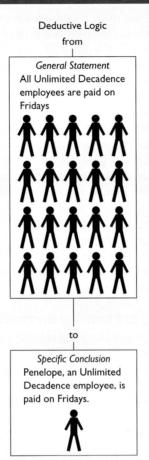

Evidence must be relevant for and consistent with arguments, solutions, and decisions, but it must also be logical when it stands alone (without considering the argument, solution, or decision to which it applies). For instance, think back to the example of deductive reasoning regarding Penelope's pay. Try changing the last line of that example so that the reasoning reads: "All Unlimited Decadence employees are paid on Fridays. Penelope is an Unlimited Decadence employee. Therefore, all Unlimited Decadence employees are Penelope." How would you rate the logic of that reasoning on the continuum from logical to illogical? If you ranked it closer to illogical than to logical, does it make sense to use it as evidence supporting a decision about when Penelope is paid?

Finally, in evaluating information, a critical thinker must be sure, within reason, that he or she has considered all relevant information, all points of view, and all workable solutions. Incomplete information leads to less than optimal reasoning, problem-solving, and decision-making.

A critical thinker measures ideas and problem solutions against ideals or goals closely related to the critical thinking characteristics we described above. Most thinking falls somewhere on a continuum between ideal and imperfect, and many arguments are made and positions defended through the use of thought processes that do not measure up to the ideals. Unfortunately, an unwary thinker may be persuaded by ideas or solutions that are less than ideal.

Applying Creative and Critical Thinking to Business Decisions

4 *How can creative and critical thinking help people make better business decisions?*

Every day of our lives, we must solve problems and make decisions ranging from minor issues, like what to have for breakfast, to major issues, like what career to choose. Think about your breakfast decision this morning. To choose what to have for breakfast, you had to gather certain information, such as what type of food you had available to eat, how *much* of this food was available (did you ever pour a bowl of cereal only to find that there wasn't enough milk in the refrigerator?), what type of food you could tolerate in the morning, when your next meal would be, what activities you had planned for the day, the nutritional content of the food, what dishes were clean, and how much time the food would take to prepare. After evaluating all the facts, you were able to make a decision.

5 *What are the logical stages in problem-solving and decision-making?*

A simple problem like choosing what to have for breakfast does not require complex analysis (you may need just a quick shower, first, to wake you up). However, many business problems can involve a jumble of information, opinions, considerations, risks, and alternatives. A systematic method, including creative and critical thinking, is necessary to organize the problem-solving approach and to decide on a solution to the problem. Exhibit 2-6 illustrates the four stages in decision-making and the particular impact of creative and critical thinking on each stage. Notice that creative thinking is more important in the earlier stages, while critical thinking is more important in the later stages. We will discuss these stages of decision-making in the next four sections.

Recognizing and Defining the Problem

The first stage in solving a problem is the recognition and definition of the problem for which a decision must be made. As we suggested earlier in the chapter, the chances of arriving at a successful solution to a problem are considerably reduced if the decision-maker does not have a clear understanding of the problem. An incorrectly defined problem will lead to an unproductive course of action at best and could actually create new problems or make the current problem worse. To fully understand the problem, the decision-maker needs to gather the facts surrounding the problem, identify the objectives that would be achieved by solving the problem, and clearly state the problem.

For example, consider the situation facing Basil Doowright, a manager at Unlimited Decadence Corporation. Basil's newly health-conscious boss, Graham Wheatley, has asked if it is possible to manufacture and sell a new, fat-free, sugarless candy bar to be called "Empty Decadence." Basil doesn't want to make a hasty decision, so he uses creative thinking skills to brainstorm a list of questions he has about the idea. Basil's first list looks like this:

1. Why does Wheatley want us to manufacture this new candy bar?

2. When must a decision be made?

3. Who inside the company would be affected by a decision to manufacture and sell this new candy bar? How would they be affected?

Exhibit 2-6 Creative and Critical Thinking and Four Stages in Problem-Solving and Decision-Making

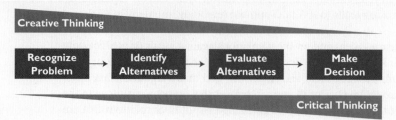

4. Who outside the company would be affected by a decision to manufacture and sell this new candy bar? In what ways would they be affected?

5. How can I break this decision down into smaller parts?

6. What additional information do I need to solve the problem?

7. Where can I find additional information?

 Why do you think it is important to know who will be affected by a business decision and how they will be affected?

Answers to these questions will no doubt lead to further, more probing questions such as the following:

8. Can we manufacture an outstandingly delicious, sugarless, fat-free candy bar that meets the company's standards of excellence?

9. How long would it take to develop, market, and manufacture this new candy bar?

10. Who would buy this new candy bar?

11. Will people quit purchasing the popular Pure Decadence candy bar and instead buy the new Empty Decadence candy bar? Or will people who typically avoid buying candy bars be tempted by the fat-free, sugarless qualities of the Empty Decadence, leaving the sales of the Pure Decadence candy bar virtually unaffected, thereby increasing total customers and total sales?

12. What kind of competition would this new candy bar face?

13. At what price could the company sell the new candy bar?

14. What resources would the company have to acquire in order to manufacture this new candy bar? Are these resources available?

15. What would the additional costs be? Does Unlimited Decadence have access to additional financing, if necessary?

16. Would additional people have to be hired? What skills and talents should these people have? What is the probability of finding people with these skills and talents?

17. Would production of the new candy bar cause Unlimited Decadence to have to comply with additional government regulations?

18. Would any of the ingredients, such as sugar substitutes or flavorings, pose health risks?

 In trying to decide whether or not it is possible to manufacture an outstandingly delicious, sugarless, fat-free candy bar that meets the company's standards of excellence, what else might you ask?

Now that Basil has an initial list of questions, he brainstorms about where he might find answers to them. In this case, Basil's list of sources of information would include such people as suppliers, customers and potential customers (through market surveys), marketing managers, production managers, the chief financial officer and accountants, environmental control managers, distribution managers, and human resources managers. As we mentioned earlier in our discussion of critical thinking, Basil would have to analyze information from these sources for faulty logic, unsupported assumptions, and emotional appeal and would have to determine the credibility of the sources of information and the nature of evidence supporting the information. Basil would then have to synthesize the information received from separate sources into an understandable "whole," or a clear statement of the problem.

In identifying the objectives that would be achieved by solving the problem, Basil would have to determine the results that should occur if a decision is made to manufacture and sell the new candy bar. In other words, what is it that his boss would like to achieve by having Unlimited Decadence manufacture the Empty Decadence candy bar? Basil surmises that Wheatley wants to:

1. Satisfy customers who have a need for sweets but not the accompanying calories,

2. Enhance Unlimited Decadence's reputation for being an industry leader and an innovator,

3. Increase the market share (that is, get a greater percentage of all candy sales, perhaps by bringing in people who have a sweet tooth but who haven't been buying Unlimited Decadence products because of the fat and sugar), and

4. Increase profit for the company.

After using creative and critical thinking skills to gather, analyze, and synthesize the facts about the problem and the results that could be achieved by solving the problem (from all perspectives), Basil should have a better understanding of the problem. This understanding will allow Basil to state the problem more clearly and in more detail than he did in the original problem statement, perhaps even allowing for a division of the problem into subproblems. Exhibit 2-7 shows the memo that Basil wrote to Wheatley outlining the problem.

Exhibit 2-7   Basil's Memo Outlining the Problem

September 11, 2000

TO: Graham Wheatley

FROM: Basil Doowright *BD*

SUBJECT: Empty Decadence

You asked me if it is possible to manufacture and sell a new, fat-free candy bar to be called "Empty Decadence." I have thought about this for several days and would like to know whether I completely understand the assignment. I presume that you would like Unlimited Decadence to manufacture and sell a new candy bar while at the same time achieving the following objectives:

1. Satisfy customers who have a need for sweets without the accompanying calories,

2. Enhance our reputation as an innovator and industry leader,

3. Increase our market share, and

4. Increase our profit.

Am I on target? I will appreciate your response in the next day or two. Thanks.

Identifying Alternative Solutions

After the problem has been clearly defined and stated, the problem-solver, using both creative and critical thinking, identifies alternative solutions. Generating numerous alternative solutions makes it more likely that at least one will be workable.

Discussing the problem and possible solutions with other people can help identify alternative solutions. By talking with people who are uninvolved with or unaffected by the problem or its solution, Basil is likely to get a more objective assessment of the problem or perhaps an entirely new perspective on it. Brainstorming with a group would generate plenty of ideas from which to choose workable solutions. Basil decides to call a meeting, inviting several people from all areas of the company to join a brainstorming team.

After generating a list of ideas, the team must critically evaluate them to identify potentially workable solutions. To be workable, the solutions must fit within the boundaries or limits of the company. For instance, the chief financial officer tells the brainstorming team that the company can borrow only $400,000 to launch the new product; the purchasing officer lists for the team all the available suppliers of ingredients; the production manager reminds the team that Valentine's Day orders will keep managers so preoccupied and production employees so swamped that work on the new product cannot begin until after February 14; and the cleaning crew supervisor informs the team that because the company uses only pure mountain spring water to clean the machines every day, the factory must be located in the mountains. Given this new information, the team comes up with several workable alternatives:

1. Don't manufacture or sell the new candy bar, and stay with the status quo. (This may be workable, but it may not achieve Wheatley's objectives.)

2. Manufacture and sell only a small number of new candy bars to test-market the concept before beginning full-scale production.

3. Manufacture and sell a large number of new candy bars (without test-marketing the concept).

4. Drop the Decadent Thunderbolt candy bar product line (which many customers stopped purchasing because it kept them awake at night), and convert the production resources so they can be used for manufacturing the Empty Decadence candy bar.

 Can you think of other possible alternatives for solving this problem?

Weighing the Advantages and Disadvantages of Each Solution

After the team identifies potential workable solutions, Basil must evaluate each of them. Although creative thinking and critical thinking are both useful in developing a list of the advantages and disadvantages of each solution, critical thinking becomes paramount in this stage.

In this example, accounting information is useful in evaluating each solution because each is likely to have different economic effects. Accounting information that is relevant to Basil in weighing the advantages and disadvantages of each solution includes information about the solution's effect on the company's costs, profits, and related income taxes, as well as its effect on the timing of cash receipts and payments. Furthermore, if the Decadent Thunderbolt product line is dropped, Basil must also consider the accompanying change in profits caused by dropping this product line, as well as the change in profits caused by the movement of the Decadent Thunderbolt customers to other candy bars.

After gathering accounting and other information for each alternative, Basil can list the advantages and disadvantages of each alternative. For example, Exhibit 2-8 shows Basil's list of advantages and disadvantages for alternative 2: "Manufacture and sell only a small number of new candy bars to test-market the concept before beginning full-scale

Exhibit 2-8	Basil's List of Advantages and Disadvantages for Manufacturing and Selling Only a Small Number of New Candy Bars

Advantages	Disadvantages
This alternative will require a smaller initial investment in factory equipment and personnel than would the full-scale production alternative.	A market failure could damage the reputation of the company.
With this alternative, Unlimited Decadence has less to lose if the Empty Decadence candy bar does not sell as predicted than it would lose if the full-scale production alternative is implemented and the sales of the Empty Decadence candy bars are less than predicted.	The cost of additions to the factory and personnel could outweigh the money brought into the company through the sale of the Empty Decadence candy bar.
	Company employees assigned to produce the Empty Decadence candy bar would be spending time that would otherwise be contributing to the production and sale of well-established candy bars.
Feedback from the test market can be used to improve the Empty Decadence candy bar before it is marketed nationally.	While Unlimited Decadence is test-marketing the Empty Decadence candy bar, the company's competitors could launch a successful full-scale market blitz with a similar candy bar.
Positive market response to the Empty Decadence candy bar might open up new sources of financing for further expansion of the factory.	
A new group of customers might be tapped because of the sugarless, low-fat nature of the Empty Decadence candy bar.	

production." Basil should evaluate the advantages and disadvantages of each workable solution in this way in order to fully understand each alternative solution.

 Can you think of advantages and disadvantages of not manufacturing and selling the new candy bar?

Choosing a Solution

The first three stages of the problem-solving process break down the problem in a systematic and detailed manner so that Basil becomes completely familiar with the problem and its possible solutions. After these first three stages, Basil must choose the best solution from among the alternative workable solutions. Basil makes the product decision based, to a great extent, on the accounting information gathered in the previous stage, in which he evaluated the alternatives. However, even after the advantages and the disadvantages of each alternative have been listed and quantified (when possible), the choice of a solution can be difficult. This is because individual advantages and disadvantages weigh differently in the decision and are hard to compare. Not all advantages are equally desirable, and not all disadvantages are equally undesirable. One technique that is useful in ordering the alternatives is to rank them based on their effectiveness in achieving the desired results, and then also to rank them based on their desirability in terms of the company's value system. For example, suppose the company values an innovative image more than one of stability. In this case, the last three alternatives would rank higher than the first. Another technique that is useful in choosing a solution is to combine the best features of multiple alternative solutions while eliminating some of the disadvantages that each alternative would have if it alone was selected.

Notice that creative and critical thinking are used throughout the problem-solving and decision-making process, although not evenly throughout the process. As we illustrated in Exhibit 2-6, some stages of the process require more of one kind of thinking than the other.

The decision-making process is similar for people who are outside the company and are making decisions about the company. For example, assume Unlimited Decadence applies for a three-year bank loan of $400,000. When this request is made, the banker recognizes that a decision must be made about granting the loan. For the banker, there are many alternatives, including refusing the bank loan, granting a loan of a smaller or greater amount for a shorter or longer time, or granting the loan as requested. The banker must have information concerning the cash in Unlimited Decadence's checking and savings accounts, the cash Unlimited Decadence must spend to pay its bills and the amount it expects to collect from its customers, the timing of these payments and collections, and the way in which the bank loan would be used. By gathering the related accounting information, the banker can evaluate whether Unlimited Decadence needs the bank loan, the appropriate amount and length of time of the loan, and the likelihood that Unlimited Decadence will repay the loan. The banker makes the loan decision, to a great extent, on the basis of accounting information provided by Unlimited Decadence.

Accounting Information and Decision-Making

The role of accounting information in the decision-making process is further illustrated in Exhibit 2-9. As this exhibit illustrates, the accounting information system and decision-making are interactive in nature; that is, an accountant collects information about a company (locates, gathers, interprets, and organizes relevant information) and communicates this information to both internal and external users to assist them in making decisions. These decisions have an impact on the company's activities, which then have an impact on the company's resulting accounting information (as is reflected when the accounting information accumulation and communication process is repeated again).

For the bank loan and product decisions, you can see that the decisions made by both the internal and the external users will affect the accounting information accumulated and communicated about the company. Before either decision is reached, the information accumulated and communicated will be the information needed to make the decisions, as we discussed earlier. After the decisions are made, regardless of the alternative chosen (whether or not the bank grants a loan to Unlimited Decadence and whether or not Unlimited Decadence manufactures and sells the Empty Decadence candy bar), the result of the decision will affect Unlimited Decadence's future activities and, in turn, result in different accounting information about the company.

Creative and Critical Thinking Orientation of the Book

In the rapidly changing business environment, the businessperson has to interpret, evaluate, synthesize, and apply new information and technology. With this new information and technology come new problems, many of which have several reasonable solutions and many of which may not have obvious solutions or any solutions. In this environment,

Exhibit 2-9 Accounting Information and Decision-Making

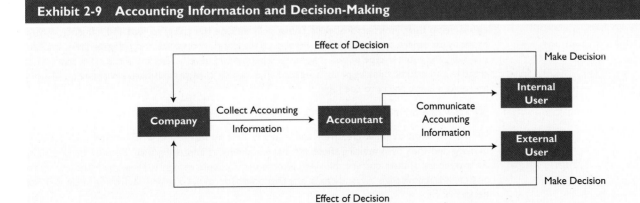

businesspeople and accountants are not operating in a "textbook world," where there are clear-cut, right and wrong answers and where the relevant facts for making decisions are neatly laid out. Therefore, to help you prepare for this challenging environment, throughout this book we will illustrate the use of creative and critical thinking for solving accounting-related problems. Then, in the Integrated Business and Accounting Situations at the ends of the chapters, we will give you the opportunity to enhance your own creative and critical thinking skills. In addition to solving problems that have specific "correct" solutions, we will ask you to make decisions and to solve problems that may have several reasonable solutions or obscure solutions. We will also ask you to interpret, evaluate, and synthesize information and to apply new information to new and different situations. In other words, we are asking you to think creatively and critically.

Summary

At the beginning of the chapter we asked you several questions. During the chapter, we asked you to STOP and answer some additional questions to build your knowledge about specific issues. Be sure you answered these additional questions. Below are the questions from the beginning of the chapter, with a brief summary of the key points relating to the answers. Use your creative and critical thinking skills to expand on these key points to develop more complete answers to the questions and to determine what other questions you have that might lead you to learn more about the issues.

1 What factors are causing the business environment and the role of accounting within that environment to change?

The business environment is dynamic and is becoming increasingly complex. More information is being generated than ever before, and this information is available to more people than ever before. Technology is advancing at a rapid rate, affecting not only the products we use but also the way the products are manufactured and the way business is conducted. Business activities and economies are becoming globalized, the number of regulations is escalating, business transactions are becoming more complex, and new forms of business are emerging. Because of this dynamic and complex business environment, the successful businessperson must be able to take change in stride, be devoted to lifelong learning, be open to other viewpoints, be tolerant of differences, be willing to take educated and thoughtful risks, be able to anticipate environmental trends and identify the potential problems and opportunities associated with these trends, and be ready to abandon old plans and to change course in light of new information.

2 What skills can people develop to better prepare themselves for problem-solving and decision-making in the rapidly changing business environment?

Besides being willing to change, businesspeople can develop skills that better prepare them for problem-solving and decision-making in this environment. Businesspeople can become broadly proficient in all forms of communication: speaking, writing, listening, and reading. Businesspeople can also develop their interpersonal skills. These skills include the ability to lead and influence others, to motivate others, to withstand and resolve conflict, and to organize and delegate tasks. Intellectual skills are another type of skill that businesspeople can develop. Beyond these skills, a variety of creative and critical thinking skills is needed in a rapidly changing business environment. Among these skills is the ability to use logic.

3 How can people learn to think creatively and critically?

People can learn to think creatively and critically first by learning new forms and techniques of thinking and then by practicing these techniques, aiming at improving their decision-making skills. An awareness of their current thinking patterns helps people recognize their strengths and weaknesses; this knowledge gives them a starting point for modifying and improving their thinking performance.

4 **How can creative and critical thinking help people make better business decisions?**

The ideas generated by creative thinking provide the raw materials of the decision-making process. Critical thinking helps decision-makers analyze decision alternatives for faulty logic, unsupported assumptions, and emotional appeal. Furthermore, it helps decision-makers evaluate the relevance of evidence used to support decision alternatives, the credibility of the sources of evidence, and the consistency of the evidence with the decision alternatives it supports. Finally, creative thinking and critical thinking help decision-makers be sure that all relevant information, all points of view, and all workable solutions have been considered.

5 **What are the logical stages in problem-solving and decision-making?**

Many business problems are difficult and complicated. A systematic approach is necessary to organize the problem and to decide on a solution to the problem. The four stages in problem-solving and decision-making are (1) recognize the problem, (2) identify alternatives, (3) evaluate the alternatives, and (4) make the decision. The accounting information system plays a big part in the business decision-making process.

Key Terms

accounting and auditing knowledge *(p. 32)*
attribute listing *(p. 35)*
creative thinking *(p. 33)*
critical thinking *(p. 35)*
deductive logic *(p. 38)*
drawing analogies *(p. 35)*
flexibility *(p. 34)*

fluency *(p. 34)*
general knowledge *(p. 32)*
independent *(p. 35)*
inductive logic *(p. 38)*
objectivity *(p. 35)*
organizational and business knowledge *(p. 32)*
piggybacking *(p. 34)*

Here is an opportunity to gather information on the Internet about real-world issues related to the topics in this chapter. Go to http://www.dryden.com/account and click on the Cunningham, Nikolai, and Bazley book cover. Click on Summary Surfing, then click on this chapter number, and answer the following questions.

▶ Click on **cthink** (Critical Thinking). Click on *college & university*. Scroll down, and click on *Library*, and then, under *Fundamentals of Critical Thinking*, click on *Helping Students Assess Their Thinking*. Identify the eight guidelines helpful to students in developing their reasoning abilities. List two activities under each guideline. Which guideline(s) seems especially helpful to you?

▶ Click on **Creativity Web.** Click on *Creativity Basics*, and then click on *Obstacles to Creativity*. What are some obstacles to creativity? Go back and click on *What can I do to increase my creativity?* What are some of the suggestions given to overcome these obstacles?

SUMMARY SURFING

Integrated Business and Accounting Situations

Answer the Following Questions in Your Own Words

Testing Your Knowledge

2-1 Describe the factors affecting the business environment and the impact of each of these factors.

2-2 Think of a recent discovery, technological innovation, world event, regulation, or other factor affecting the business environment (one not mentioned in the chapter). What effect has this factor had on the business environment? What future effect do you think this factor will have on the business environment?

2-3 What does it mean to be prepared for an opportunity?

2-4 What are the broad skills, as outlined by the largest public accounting firms, that are necessary for practicing accounting and for effectively conducting business?

2-5 What is the difference between thinking and critical thinking?

2-6 How do the creative thinking characteristics of fluency and flexibility complement each other?

2-7 What are the "ground rules" for brainstorming?

2-8 How does piggybacking work during a brainstorming session?

2-9 What is the difference between being independent and being objective?

2-10 What is the advantage of deferring judgment when making a decision?

2-11 Why is it important to evaluate the credibility of a source of information?

2-12 What is the difference between inductive logic and deductive logic?

2-13 What is the difference between creative thinking and critical thinking? How is each used in decision-making and problem-solving? How do creative thinking and critical thinking complement each other?

2-14 How do general knowledge and organizational and business knowledge support creative and critical thinking?

2-15 Describe the stages of problem-solving. What pitfalls might you encounter at each stage?

2-16 Describe how accounting information is used in each of the stages of problem-solving.

Applying Your Knowledge

2-17 Suppose you are a manager at Unlimited Decadence Corporation and you receive the following memo from your boss, Max Armstrong: "The results of a survey that I just received indicate that American teenagers will flock to the stores to buy a sugarless, fat-free candy bar. Can we manufacture this type of candy bar? When could we have this product ready for the market?"

Required: Before you begin the extensive research necessary for your response to his questions, what would you like to know about the survey? How would the answers to these questions affect what you do next?

2-18 Consider the following arguments:
  (a) "I went over to our supplier's warehouse today and talked with the secretary, who was unbelievably rude! Since he is the only representative of our supplier that I have met, my only conclusion is that everyone who works there must be rude."
  (b) "Lyle Biggerstaff, CEO of a large corporation, was able to avoid a lawsuit brought by a customer because he had taped a previous telephone conversation in which the customer both requested unsafe changes in the product and promised not to hold the corporation liable for the consequences of those changes. Given his experience, our company should tape all telephone conversations."
  (c) "All purchases over $100 must originate with a purchase order form. Last week, the data-processing manager purchased a $4,000 computer. Therefore, there must have been a purchase order form."

(d) "Almost everyone in the accounting department is a member of the AICPA—the few who are not members either are not ambitious or are careless."

Required: For each argument, indicate whether it is sound and why, or why not. If it is not sound, what would make it sound?

2-19 Consider the following opposing sides of an issue:
(a) All companies, even those in other countries, should have to follow generally accepted accounting principles.
(b) All companies should not have to follow generally accepted accounting principles.

Required: Identify reasons that support each side of the issue.

2-20 Suppose that your job is beginning to eat into your personal time. During the last six months you have noticed that you have been taking files home with you to work on after supper and on the weekends. Even so, you are having trouble keeping up. After explaining this to your boss, she suggests that you find a way to work more efficiently. Furthermore, she points out that there are many people who would be glad to take over your job.

Required: (1) What are some alternative ways to approach your boss? What reasons, information, and evidence might support your point of view?
(2) What reasons, information, and evidence might support your boss's point of view? In what ways might these reasons affect the approach you take in presenting your problem to your boss?

2-21 You have just landed your dream job working for a gourmet food importer and distributor. Your new boss wants your opinion about whether to open a new branch office in El Paso, Texas. You desperately want to make a good impression on your first assignment and want to be sure you have a good grasp of the situation before you form your opinion.

Required: What questions do you want answered before you offer your opinion to your boss? Where might you find the answers to your questions?

2-22 Suppose your boss has asked you to design a system to keep track of your company's cash expenditures.

Required: (1) Before designing this system, what might you want to know that would help you define the problem?
(2) List as many ideas as you can for the design of this system.
(3) What are the advantages and disadvantages of each of your design ideas?

2-23 Suppose that your brother, the owner of The Last Custard Stand (a specialty dessert shop), has asked you for a substantial loan to help him expand his business.

Required: What would you like to know about The Last Custard Stand before you make a decision about whether to loan the company money? How could the answers to each of your questions affect your decision? What accounting information could your brother provide you that could affect your decision?

2-24 Refer to 2-23. At your request, your brother provides you with the following information:

Revenues for 2000	$60,000
Expenses for 2000	(55,000)
Profit for 2000	$ 5,000

Required: How could this information be presented differently to make it more meaningful for you in reaching your loan decision? What could be added to this particular information to make it more meaningful for you?

2-25 The office copier has just quit working and is beyond repair. The big question now is what to do with it. Your boss is offering a cash prize for each of the following:
(a) The longest list of ideas for what to do with the copier
(b) The most unusual idea
(c) The widest variety of ideas

Required: See if you can win all the cash by providing a written list of your ideas.

2-26 Your new co-worker just came in and made the following statement: "Every Friday is casual day around here; people wear casual clothes to work on Fridays. Jan, over there, is wearing jeans and a T-shirt today. It must be Friday. TGIF!!!"

Required: What's wrong with your co-worker's logic?

Making Evaluations

2-27   In this chapter, we discussed the following statement made by a rather disgruntled employee of Unlimited Decadence:

"All programmers should have to work regular hours, from 8:00 A.M. to 5:00 P.M. just like everybody else. It isn't fair that the computer programmers can come in late. Sure, they come in during the middle of the night to fix programs when the computer crashes, and they program on into the night when they are 'on a roll,' but we all know it's just a party up there. Mortimer, one of the programmers, is a major party animal. I've been to several parties with him."

Required: Suppose you are this employee's boss. How would you evaluate and respond to this statement? (What faulty logic, unsupported assumptions, or emotional appeals do you see in the statement? Does the employee make any valid points?)

2-28   Is a business suit the most appropriate article of clothing to wear to a business meeting?

Required: Answer the question based on what you believe to be true (answer either "yes," "no," or "not sure"). Explain why you answered the way you did. Now give the reasons and evidence that you believe support your answer (authorities, references, facts, personal experience).

2-29   Consider, again, the plight of the manager at Unlimited Decadence Corporation, whose boss wants to manufacture and sell the new Empty Decadence candy bar, perhaps using it to replace the Decadent Thunderbolt candy bar. Suppose the accounting department has projected that profit per candy bar will be $0.10 higher for the Decadent Thunderbolt than for the Empty Decadence candy bar. The marketing department predicts that Unlimited Decadence can sell 100,000 Empty Decadence candy bars the first year and then more each year for the next ten years if it drops the Decadent Thunderbolt candy bar. During that same time period, the marketing department forecasts that sales of the Decadent Thunderbolt will be 80,000 candy bars the first year, with sales decreasing slightly after that if the company does not produce the Empty Decadence candy bar. However, if the company produces both candy bars, predicted sales for Empty Decadence will be reduced to 70,000 candy bars the first year, with a slow and steady increase in sales over the next ten years. Predicted sales for the Decadent Thunderbolt will decrease to 65,000 during the first year and decrease slightly each year for the next ten years.

The production department has determined that the new candy bar is possible to manufacture and that the factory can be reconfigured to accommodate the new candy bar while continuing to produce the old candy bar. If Unlimited Decadence drops the Decadent Thunderbolt candy bar, it can convert the equipment so that it can be used to produce the Empty Decadence candy bar. The human resources department is confident that numerous qualified people are available to work if the company wants to produce both candy bars. If the company drops the Decadent Thunderbolt candy bar, those people currently working on the Decadent Thunderbolt candy bar can be easily retrained to work on the Empty Decadence candy bar. The chief financial officer has arranged for financing, if it is needed.

Required: (1) Based on the above information, what are the advantages and disadvantages of (a) dropping the Decadent Thunderbolt product line and producing the Empty Decadence candy bar, (b) continuing production of the Decadent Thunderbolt and not producing the Empty Decadence candy bar, (c) producing both the Decadent Thunderbolt and the Empty Decadence candy bars, or (d) producing neither candy bar? How would you decide which alternative is best?

(2) What additional information would make your decision easier?

(3) What other alternative solutions can you think of?

2-30   The changing business environment provides many challenges for today's businessperson but also opportunities.

Required: What opportunities do you see that result from this environment? How would you prepare yourself to take full advantage of these opportunities?

2-31   Yesterday, you received the letter shown on the following page for your advice column in the local paper:

Dear Dr. Decisive:

Last night my girlfriend and I got into an argument at the Cracked Cuticles concert. I told her that the Cracked Cuticles had to be making money because one of the large ticket outlets was sponsoring them and ticket outlets don't sponsor groups that don't make money. We just studied inductive and deductive logic in class, so she commented that I had just used deductive logic. I patiently explained to her that, no, I had just used inductive logic. Now she won't speak to me, let alone go to another concert with me, until you settle this. Help!

Call me "Mr. Right."

Required: Meet with your Dr. Decisive team and write a response to "Mr. Right."

CHAPTER OUTLINE

PART 2

PLANNING IN AN ENTREPRENEURIAL ENVIRONMENT

This section includes two chapters which discuss planning for a small company. After reading these chapters, you will be able to:

▶ *describe what a business plan is and what it contains*

▶ *prepare various parts of a business plan*

▶ *understand the differences between variable and fixed costs*

▶ *use cost-volume-profit analysis in business decisions*

▶ *prepare a master budget for a retail company*

▶ *use a master budget in evaluating a company's performance*

CHAPTER 3

DEVELOPING A BUSINESS PLAN: COST-VOLUME-PROFIT ANALYSIS

> *"He who every morning plans the transaction of the day, and follows out that plan, carries a thread that will guide him through the maze of the most busy life. But where no plan is laid, where the disposal of time is surrendered merely to the chance of incidence, chaos will soon reign."*
>
> —Victor Hugo

1 *Since the future is uncertain and circumstances are likely to change, why should a company bother to plan?*

2 *What should a company include in its business plan?*

3 *How does accounting information contribute to the planning process?*

4 *What do decision-makers have to be able to predict in order to estimate profit at a given sales volume?*

5 *How can decision-makers predict the sales volume necessary for estimated revenues to cover estimated costs?*

6 *How can decision-makers predict the sales volume necessary to achieve a target profit?*

7 *How can decision-makers use accounting information to evaluate alternative plans?*

1 *Since the future is uncertain and circumstances are likely to change, why should a company bother to plan?*

Suppose your sister Anna has hired you, as an employee-advisor, to help her open and run a candy store. Anna, who earned her B.B.A. degree last year with a major in marketing, has an insatiable sweet tooth and has always "hungered" to own a candy store. After long and lively discussions with you about the name of the company, Anna decides to name it "Sweet Temptations." You and Anna arrange to obtain retail space, to purchase display fixtures, supplies, and candy, to hire an employee to sell candy, and to advertise in the newspaper. Now you are ready to open for business. But whoa! Not so fast. Have you thought of everything? If you and Anna want Sweet Temptations to succeed, there are other issues that you must consider before you open your company. Instead of rushing into business when the idea is fresh, first you would be smart to develop a detailed business plan that addresses these issues.

Planning in a New Company

2 *What should a company include in its business plan?*

A **business plan** describes a company's goals and its plans for achieving those goals. The business plan is used by both internal and external users. A business plan typically includes

1. a description of the company,

2. a marketing plan,

3. a description of the operations of the company, and

4. a financial plan.

We will discuss each of these parts in later sections.

A business plan has three main purposes. First, it helps an entrepreneur to visualize and organize the company and its operations. Remember from Chapter 2 how Basil tested the strengths and weaknesses of the proposal to make the Empty Decadence candy bar? Similarly, thinking critically about your hopes for the business and putting a plan on paper will help you and Anna imagine how the plan will work and will help you evaluate the plan, develop new ideas, and refine the plan. By looking at the plan from different points of view, such as those of managers who have responsibility for marketing the company's products or purchasing its inventory of products, you can discover and correct flaws before implementing the plan. Then "paper mistakes" won't become real mistakes!

Second, a business plan serves as a "benchmark," or standard, against which the entrepreneur can later measure the actual performance of a company. You and Anna will be

DILBERT® BY SCOTT ADAMS

able to evaluate differences between the planned performance of Sweet Temptations, as outlined in its business plan, and its actual performance. Then you will be able to use the results of your evaluation to adjust Sweet Temptations' future activities. For instance, suppose in its first month of business, sales are higher than you and Anna predicted. If you decide that sales will continue at this level, you can use this information to increase Sweet Temptations' future candy purchases.

Third, a business plan helps an entrepreneur obtain the financing that new and growing companies often need. When Anna starts looking for additional funding for Sweet Temptations, potential investors and creditors may request a copy of the company's business plan to help them decide whether or not to invest in Sweet Temptations or to loan it money. For example, as part of its loan-making decisions, Central Trust Bank in Jefferson City, Missouri, routinely evaluates the business plans of companies that apply for business loans at the bank.

Investors and creditors, such as Central Trust Bank, have two related concerns when they are making investment and credit decisions. One concern is the level of risk involved with their decisions. **Risk** usually refers to how much uncertainty exists about the future operations of the company. The other concern is the **return,** or money back, that they will receive from their investment and credit decisions. A thorough business plan will provide useful information for helping investors and creditors evaluate their risk and potential return. Now let's look at the parts of a business plan.

Description of the Company

A business plan usually begins with a description of the company and its basic activities. Details of this description include information about the organization of the company, its product or service, its current and potential customers, its objectives, where it is located, and where it conducts its business.

For example, Sweet Temptations is a new retailing company located in a "high-growth" suburb north of a major metropolitan area. Initially, Sweet Temptations will sell only one kind of candy—boxes of chocolates. You and your sister Anna will expand the "product line" to include other kinds of candy as the company grows. After the sale of chocolates is "up and running," and after you graduate, you plan to join Anna full-time as a partner in the company. You and Anna are eager to begin marketing and operating the company but are waiting to do so until after you finish writing the company's business plan and obtain financing. You realize that writing the plan is helping you to think through the various aspects of the business so that you don't "miss something" important in planning your activities. Exhibit 3-1 illustrates how you might describe Sweet Temptations in its business plan.

The organization of a company and its personnel can have a major influence on the success of a company. Therefore, the description of the company also includes a listing of the important people and the major roles they will play in the company. This listing can include the individuals responsible for starting the company, significant investors who also are providing expertise and direction to the company, and influential employees and consultants who have a strong impact on the company. Exhibit 3-2 shows some highlights of how you might discuss Sweet Temptations' organization in its business plan. Notice how this part of the plan highlights the combination of your major in business and Anna's degree in marketing. This part may also contain the company's policies or strategies for selecting, training, and rewarding employees. These issues are particularly important for the long-term success of the company.

Marketing Plan

The marketing section of a business plan shows how the company will make sales and how it will influence and respond to market conditions. This section receives a lot of attention from investors and creditors because the company's marketing strategy and its ability to implement that strategy can be very important to the company's success.

The marketing section provides evidence of the demand for the company's products or services, including any market research that has been conducted. This section also describes the current and expected competition in the market, as well as relevant

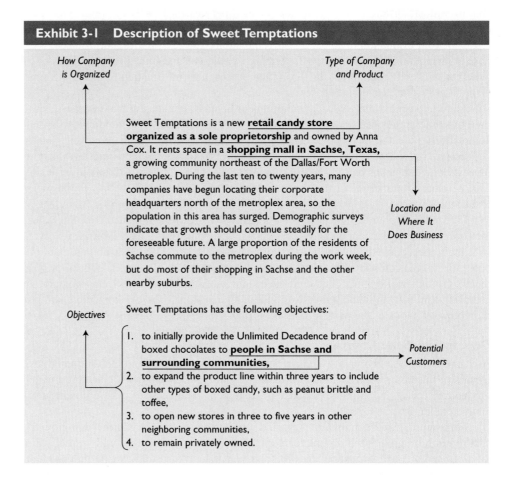

Exhibit 3-1 Description of Sweet Temptations

How Company is Organized

Type of Company and Product

Sweet Temptations is a new **retail candy store organized as a sole proprietorship** and owned by Anna Cox. It rents space in a **shopping mall in Sachse, Texas,** a growing community northeast of the Dallas/Fort Worth metroplex. During the last ten to twenty years, many companies have begun locating their corporate headquarters north of the metroplex area, so the population in this area has surged. Demographic surveys indicate that growth should continue steadily for the foreseeable future. A large proportion of the residents of Sachse commute to the metroplex during the work week, but do most of their shopping in Sachse and the other nearby suburbs.

Location and Where It Does Business

Objectives

Sweet Temptations has the following objectives:

1. to initially provide the Unlimited Decadence brand of boxed chocolates to **people in Sachse and surrounding communities,**
2. to expand the product line within three years to include other types of boxed candy, such as peanut brittle and toffee,
3. to open new stores in three to five years in other neighboring communities,
4. to remain privately owned.

Potential Customers

government regulations. The marketing section describes how the company will promote, price, and distribute its products (the company's "marketing strategy"), as well as the predicted growth, market share, and sales of its products (its "sales forecast") by period. This information is helpful to the entrepreneur as a starting point for thinking about the company's other activities related to sales, such as timing the purchase of its inventories. The marketing section is also helpful to people outside the company, such as bank loan officers, because it shows how well the entrepreneur has thought through the company's sales potential and how the company will attract and sell to customers.

Sweet Temptations' business plan may be an inch thick! We don't have room to show each part of its plan, so in the next sections we will ask you to think about what to include. The following is a brief description of Sweet Temptations' market conditions. Initially, Sweet Temptations will have a temporary marketing advantage. Currently, community members must drive at least 30 miles to purchase boxes of Unlimited Decadence chocolates (and they actually make the drive!). After evaluating the community's available retail space (and plans for building retail space), you and Anna believe that there will be very little competition during the next several years. However, you eventually expect competing stores to open in the community. In the meantime, part of your marketing plan is to build a reputation for friendly service and quality products. Your advertising will focus on the quality ingredients used in the chocolates. Furthermore, your initial advertising "punch" will include the fact that Unlimited Decadence now produces, and Sweet Temptations sells, mini-versions of "everyone's favorite candy bars" in boxed form. You believe Sweet Temptations has a distinct advantage in selling Unlimited Decadence chocolates because of the already established good reputation and popularity of the Unlimited Decadence candy bars.

Exhibit 3-2 Organization of Sweet Temptations

The team at Sweet Temptations is composed of four people, one of whom is a financial consultant. The members of this team are as follows:

Anna Cox	Owner	
(Your name)	Employee/adviser	*Listing of Important People and the Roles They Will Play*
Jaime Gonzales	Employee	
Joe Smiley	Consultant	

Each of these individuals brings special skills to Sweet Temptations. Anna Cox graduated last year with a B.B.A. in marketing from State U. She has already earned a reputation for her marketing and business skills. While in school, she won the National Student Marketing Association's prestigious Student Marketer of the Year Award and the coveted Small Business Institute's Rising Star Award. She graduated with highest honors. While in school, Anna worked for three retail stores, two of which were start-up companies. One of the start-up companies was a candy store.

(Your name) is an honors business student at State U. and will be graduating in two years. (Your first name) has worked twenty hours per week "keeping the books" at a local candy store for the past two years. Prior to that, (your first name) worked summers and part time during the school year doing miscellaneous jobs at the same candy store.

Qualifications of Important People

Jaime Gonzales is an honors business student at State U. Jaime has worked summers at several restaurants in Sachse.

Joe Smiley is a partner in the management advisory services area of (name of company), a large public accounting firm in Dallas. His firm specializes in consulting with start-up companies.

 What information about market conditions facing Sweet Temptations would you include in the marketing section of its business plan?

Description of Company Operations

Since a company is organized to deliver a product or service to a market, the business plan must address how the company will develop and enhance its products or services. The company operations section of a business plan includes a description of the relationships between the company, its suppliers, and its customers, as well as a description of how the company will develop, service, protect, and support its products or services. This section also includes any other influences on the operations of the company. The company operations section of the business plan is important because it helps the entrepreneur think through the details of making the idea work. Also, it helps outside users evaluate the entrepreneur's ability to successfully carry out the idea.

Here is a brief description of Sweet Temptations' operations. Sweet Temptations has a ready supply of chocolates. Unlimited Decadence has no sales agreements with any other candy stores within a 30-mile radius of Sweet Temptations. Furthermore, you know of other potential suppliers—candy manufacturers who have high production standards, quality ingredients, and good reputations in the candy industry. In fact, Anna is now talking with representatives of these companies and visiting their kitchens so that she will have identified and selected other suppliers by the time Sweet Temptations is ready to sell other types of candy.

 What information about Sweet Temptations' operations would you include in its business plan?

Other influences on the operations of the company might also be described in this section. These other influences might include the availability of employees, concerns of special-interest groups, regulations, the impact of international trade, and the need for patents, trademarks, and licensing agreements.

 If Sweet Temptations' major supplier of chocolates was a company in Brussels, Belgium, rather than Unlimited Decadence Corporation, what additional issues do you think should be included in this section of the business plan? What else do you think managers, owners, creditors, and investors would like to know?

Financial Plan

Since Sweet Temptations is a new company, it has no credit history or recent financial statements. Therefore, Anna should also provide a detailed, realistic financial plan in Sweet Temptations' business plan. The purpose of the financial plan section is to identify the company's capital requirements and sources of capital, as well as to describe the company's projected financial performance. For a new company, this section also highlights the company's beginning financial activities, or "start-up" costs.

Here is some information about Sweet Temptations' start-up costs:

> Anna has decided that she will invest $15,000 of her own money as capital to run Sweet Temptations. Based on the rent charged for space in the shopping mall, she has determined that it will cost $1,000 per month to rent store space in the mall. When Sweet Temptations signs a rental contract for the store in December 1999, it will pay six months' rent in advance, totaling $6,000. Based on a supplier's cost quotation, Anna has determined that Sweet Temptations can buy store equipment for $1,800. The supplier will allow Sweet Temptations to make a $1,000 down payment and to sign a note (a legal document, referred to as a *note payable*) for the remaining amount, to be paid later. Based on the purchases budget (which we will discuss in Chapter 4), Sweet Temptations will purchase 360 boxes of chocolates for "inventory" in December 1999 at a cost of $1,620 from Unlimited Decadence. Unlimited Decadence has agreed to allow Sweet Temptations to pay for this inventory in January 2000. Sweet Temptations will also purchase $700 of supplies in December 1999, paying for the supplies at that time.

 What information about Sweet Temptations' start-up costs would you include in the financial section of its business plan?

Identifying Capital Requirements

Most companies eventually need additional funding, or **capital.** The financial section of a business plan should include a discussion of the company's capital requirements and potential sources of that capital. For new companies and small companies, this discussion can be the most important part of the business plan. As you may have noticed while reading the business section of your local newspaper, if a company does not have enough capital and sources of capital, it will have a difficult time surviving.

Significant "start up" costs for a company.

An entrepreneur can determine a company's capital requirements by analyzing two major issues. First, the entrepreneur should decide what resources the company needs, such as buildings, equipment, and furniture. Then, the entrepreneur can estimate how much capital the business will need in order to acquire those resources. Cost quotations, appraisals, and sales agreements are a good starting point for this estimate. Next, the entrepreneur should analyze the company's projected cash receipts and payments to determine whether it will have enough cash to buy the resources and, if not, how much cash the company will need to borrow. Planning capital requirements involves projections, not guarantees, so the entrepreneur must expect and provide for reasonable deviations from plans. Suppose, for example, that cash sales for the month turn out to be less than expected. For "surprises" like this, the entrepreneur should plan to have a "cash buffer," which is extra cash on hand above the projected short-run cash payments of the company. One purpose of this buffer is to protect the company from differences between actual cash flows and projected cash flows, and also from unanticipated problems such as having to replace a refrigerated display case sooner than expected. A cash buffer lets the company operate normally through downturns without having to look for financing. It also lets the company take advantage of unexpected opportunities that require cash.

 Can you think of an example of an unexpected opportunity for which an entrepreneur or manager might find a cash buffer to be handy?

Sources of Capital

Once the entrepreneur knows the company's capital requirements, potential sources of capital can be identified. Here, the entrepreneur must know both the length of time that the company plans to use the capital before paying it back to creditors or returning it to investors, and the availability of short- and long-term sources of capital. The entrepreneur can determine how long the company will need to use the capital by analyzing the company's projected cash receipts and payments. We will discuss the tools of this analysis more thoroughly in Chapter 4.

Short-term capital will be repaid within a year or less. Short-term capital can come from two sources. First, suppliers provide short-term capital to some of their customers through what is called "trade credit." Trade credit involves allowing a customer to purchase inventory "on credit" if the customer agrees to pay soon, usually within 30 days. You and Anna have an arrangement with Unlimited Decadence that will allow Sweet Temptations to buy boxed chocolates on credit and pay Unlimited Decadence 30 days later.

If Sweet Temptations took longer than 30 days, on the average, to sell its inventory of chocolates, do you think its arrangement with Unlimited Decadence would be valuable? What other questions would you like answered to help you determine the answer to this question?

www.sba.gov

Second, financial institutions, such as commercial banks, provide loans to companies, many of which are "backed" by government agencies such as the U.S. Small Business Administration. These institutions require a more formal agreement with a company than do issuers of trade credit. Also, they charge interest on these short-term loans. At some point, Anna may talk with her banker to arrange a small line of credit for Sweet Temptations. A **line of credit** allows a company to borrow money "as needed," with a pre-arranged, agreed-upon interest rate and a specific payback schedule. We discuss short-term capital more in Chapter 9.

Long-term capital will be repaid to creditors or returned to investors after more than a year. Initially, as we mentioned in Chapter 1, companies obtain capital from the owner and from bankers. Sweet Temptations obtained its initial capital from Anna, who invested money from her savings account. Other sources of long-term capital can include friends and relatives, commercial banks, and leasing companies. Many loans are guaranteed by the Small Business Administration or the state's economic-development agency. For example,

www.frostyfactory.com

after being turned down for a bank loan, the owner of Frosty Factory of America, a Ruston, Louisiana company that manufactures slush machines for making sorbets and frozen drinks, took his company's business plan to the Louisiana State Economic Development Corporation. After reviewing the plan, the state agency agreed to guarantee 50 percent of the loan. The bank reconsidered and loaned the company $325,000.[1]

All institutions require a formal agreement with the company about payment dates and interest rates. But suppose Sweet Temptations borrows money from Anna's and your friends and relatives. Do you think it is necessary to have a formal written agreement between these friends and relatives and Sweet Temptations? Why or why not?

Eventually, as a company grows too large to be financed by the owner and these other sources, it may offer private placements or public offerings. Private placements are securities that are sold directly to private individuals or groups (called *investors*). Public offerings involve issuing stocks or bonds to the public (investors) through securities firms or investment bankers. We will discuss stocks and bonds as a source of long-term capital in Chapters 22 and 24.

For the near future, several of Anna's and your friends and relatives have agreed to lend Sweet Temptations specific amounts of money, as needed. Anna and these friends and relatives have agreed that the interest rate on these loans will match the market interest rate at the time of each loan. Sweet Temptations includes this information in its financial plan.

Projected Financial Performance

This section of the financial plan projects the company's financial performance. Suppose Anna has assigned you the responsibility of preparing this section of Sweet Temptations' financial plan. Although projecting a company's financial performance involves uncertainty, if you follow some guidelines, the financial performance information will be more dependable.

First, the data that you use should be as reliable as possible. Since Sweet Temptations is a new company, you don't have historical data to use for planning purposes. When you have sketchy data (or no data at all), industry averages found in such sources as *Moody's, Standard & Poor's,* and *Robert Morse Associates* can serve as a guide.

---

[1]Pete Weaver, "Need a Loan? See Your State," *National Business,* April 1995, 51R.

If you use Moody's, Standard & Poor's, or Robert Morse Associates for industry information, you must be able to identify the industry in which Sweet Temptations is operating. What are some key words that you could use to identify the industry?

Second, because predicting a company's financial performance is uncertain, you should consider several scenarios. "What if" questions are useful for this type of planning. What if we sell only 800 boxes of chocolates? What if we sell 1,300 boxes of chocolates? The scenarios should be realistic and perhaps should consider the best case, the worst case, and the most probable case.

Third, you should revise your projection as more facts become available. Finally, it is important that the financial plan is consistent with the information in the other sections of the business plan. For example, since the marketing section of Sweet Temptations' business plan refers to the advertising that you plan to do, the financial plan section must show advertising costs.

The financial performance section of the financial plan includes projected financial statements,[2] supported by cost-volume-profit analysis and budgets. Budgets include reports on such items as estimated sales, purchases of inventory, and expenses, as well as estimated cash receipts and payments. In the remainder of this chapter we will discuss cost-volume-profit analysis and its relationship to the projected income statement. In Chapter 4, we will discuss budgets and how they fit into a company's financial plan.

In summary, you have just learned that the business plan shows the direction a company will be taking during the next year. You have also learned that the business plan includes a description of the company, a marketing plan, a description of company operations, and a financial plan. Accountants are most involved with the financial plan, which includes an analysis of predicted costs, sales volumes, and profits. We thus will spend the remainder of this chapter discussing cost-volume-profit analysis and its use in planning.

Cost-Volume-Profit (C-V-P) Planning

Determining if a company will be profitable is difficult before it begins operations. This uncertainty is part of the risk that the entrepreneur takes in starting a business. Although it can be scary, it is also part of the fun. Uncertain profit does not mean that the entrepreneur should disregard any type of analysis before beginning the operations of a company, however. It is possible to take educated risks based on estimations of costs, sales volumes, and profits. The financial plan should include an analysis of these factors. One type of analysis that uses these three factors is called cost-volume-profit analysis.

3 *How does accounting information contribute to the planning process?*

Cost-Volume-Profit Analysis

Cost-volume-profit (C-V-P) analysis shows how profit will be affected by changes in sales volume, selling prices of products, and the various costs of the company. C-V-P analysis sometimes is called "break-even analysis." Entrepreneurs use C-V-P analysis to help them understand how the plans they make will affect profits. This understanding can produce more-informed decisions during the planning process.

C-V-P analysis is based on a simple profit computation involving revenues and costs. This computation can be shown in an equation or in a graph. Although equations provide precise numbers, C-V-P graphs provide a convenient visual form for presenting the analysis to decision-makers. However, to understand a C-V-P equation or graph, decision-makers also must understand how costs behave.

---

[2]The financial plan usually includes a projected balance sheet, but to simplify the discussion in this chapter, we won't discuss the projected balance sheet until Chapter 12.

Cost Behavior

A careful cost analysis considers the activity level of the operation that causes the cost. For example, Unlimited Decadence, a manufacturing company, might measure its activity by using the number of cases of chocolate bars produced or the number of hours worked in producing these cases of chocolate bars. On the other hand, Sweet Temptations, a retail company, might measure its activity by using the number of boxes of chocolates *sold.* The activity level (the number of boxes of candy bars sold) is often referred to as **volume.** The relationship between an activity's cost and its volume helps us determine the cost's behavior pattern.

To understand what C-V-P equations and graphs reveal about a company's profitability, let's first look at two cost behavior patterns that describe how most costs behave. These are called fixed costs and variable costs.

Fixed Costs

Fixed costs are constant in total; they are *not* affected by changes in volume. Managers' salaries are usually fixed costs, for instance. For another example, think about the $1,000 monthly rent that Sweet Temptations will pay for its retail space. Sweet Temptations' activity level is its sales volume—the number of boxes of chocolates sold. The rent cost of the retail space will not change as a result of a change in the sales volume, assuming you have planned carefully and have leased enough retail space. Since the rent cost does not change as volume changes, it is a fixed cost. The graph in Exhibit 3-3 illustrates the relationship between the rent cost and the sales volume. As you can see, the rent cost will be $1,000 whether Sweet Temptations sells 500 boxes of chocolates or 1,000 boxes.

Note in Exhibit 3-3 that we show a fixed cost as a horizontal straight line on the graph, indicating that the cost will be the same (fixed) over different volume levels. It is important not to be misled about fixed costs. Saying that a cost is "fixed" does not mean that it cannot change from one time period to the next. In the next period, Sweet Temptations could rent more retail space if needed or the landlord could raise the rent when the lease is renewed, causing the rent cost to be higher. To be fixed, a cost must remain constant for a time period in relation to the volume attained *in that same time period.* For example, most companies consider the costs of using their buildings, factories, office equipment, and furniture—called *depreciation*[3]—to be fixed. That is, depreciation costs within a specific time period will not change even if volume changes within that time period.

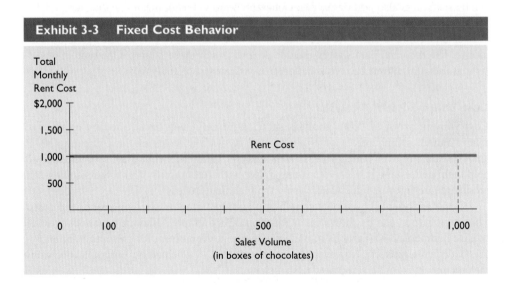

Exhibit 3-3   Fixed Cost Behavior

---

[3]We will discuss in Chapters 5 and 21 how a company determines its depreciation cost. We include a brief discussion here because most companies have some depreciation costs to consider in evaluating their operations.

You have estimated that Sweet Temptations' monthly fixed costs will include the $1,000 rent cost plus $2,050 total salaries for you and Jaime Gonzales (the employee Anna hired to sell candy), $200 consulting costs, $305 advertising costs, $30 supplies costs, $15 depreciation of the store equipment, and $250 telephone and utility costs.[4] Sweet Temptations' total fixed costs will be the sum of the individual fixed costs, or $3,850.

 What would the graph look like for Sweet Temptations' $3,850 total fixed costs? Why?

Decision-makers sometimes state fixed costs as a dollar amount *per unit,* computed by dividing total fixed costs by the volume in units. This can be misleading and should be avoided. For instance, at a sales volume of 500 boxes of chocolates, Sweet Temptations' fixed cost per box of chocolates will be $7.70 ($3,850 fixed costs ÷ 500 boxes of chocolates). At a sales volume of 1,000 boxes of chocolates, the fixed cost per box of chocolates will only be $3.85 ($3,850 fixed costs ÷ 1,000 boxes of chocolates). Comparing $7.70 with $3.85, you might think that total fixed costs decrease as sales volume increases. This is not true! Sweet Temptations' total fixed costs will be $3,850 regardless of the sales volume.

Variable Costs

A **variable cost** is constant *per unit*, and changes in total in direct proportion to the change in volume. For instance, Sweet Temptations' cost of purchasing chocolates from Unlimited Decadence is a variable cost. You have estimated that it will cost $4.50 for each box of chocolates that Sweet Temptations purchases from Unlimited Decadence. The total cost of purchasing boxes of chocolates varies in proportion to the number of boxes purchased. If Sweet Temptations sells 500 boxes of chocolates in January, the total variable cost of these boxes of chocolates sold will be $2,250 (500 boxes of chocolates × $4.50 per box). If the volume doubles to 1,000 boxes of chocolates, the total variable cost of boxes of chocolates sold will also double to $4,500 (1,000 boxes of chocolates × $4.50 per box). It is important to remember that the total variable cost increases in proportion to volume because each unit has the same variable cost.

Exhibit 3-4 shows the estimated total variable costs of boxes of chocolates sold by Sweet Temptations at different sales volumes. Note that a variable cost is shown by a straight line sloping upward from the origin of the graph. If no boxes of chocolates are sold, the total variable cost will be $0. The slope of the line is the rate at which the total variable cost will increase each time Sweet Temptations sells another box of chocolates. This rate is the variable cost per unit of volume, or $4.50 per each additional box of chocolates sold.

 How could rent be a variable cost? If it were a variable cost, how do you think it would affect Sweet Temptations' variable costs line in Exhibit 3-4?

Because graphs are easy to see, we used them to show Sweet Temptations' fixed and variable costs in Exhibits 3-3 and 3-4. For C-V-P analysis, however, it is often better to use equations because they show more precise numbers. For instance, the equation for the total amount of a variable cost is

Total variable cost = vX
where:
v = variable cost per unit sold, and
X = sales volume.

---

[4]Some supplies, telephone, and utility costs may have minimum charges, but their total costs are affected by changes in the volume of usage. These costs are called *mixed costs* which we will discuss in Chapter 11. For simplicity, here we assume they are fixed costs.

Exhibit 3-4 Variable Cost Behavior

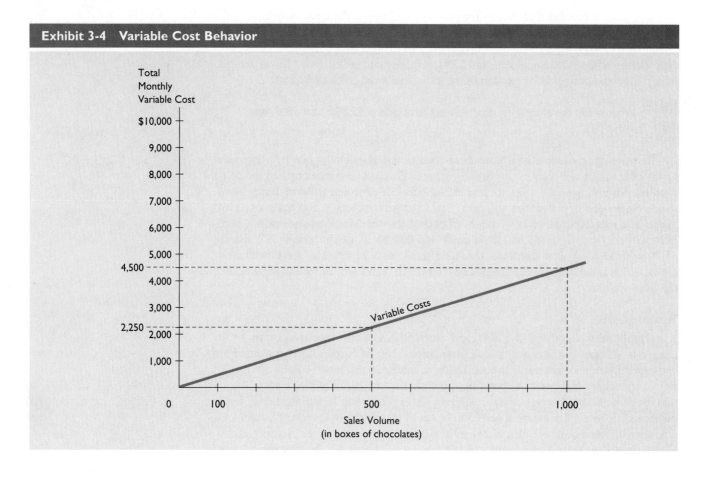

The equation for the variable cost line in Exhibit 3-4 is

> Total variable cost of boxes of chocolates sold = $4.50X
> where:
> $\quad$ X = sales volume.

Total Costs

Total costs at any volume are the sum of the fixed costs and the variable costs at that volume. For example, at a sales volume of 500 boxes of chocolates, Sweet Temptations' estimated fixed costs are $3,850 and its estimated variable costs are $2,250 (500 × $4.50), for an estimated total cost of $6,100 at that volume. At a sales volume of 1,000 boxes of chocolates, estimated fixed costs are $3,850, estimated variable costs are $4,500 (1,000 × $4.50), and the estimated total cost is $8,350. Exhibit 3-5 illustrates the total cost in relation to sales volume. Notice that if no boxes of chocolates are sold, the total cost will be equal to the fixed costs of $3,850. As sales increase, the total cost will increase by $4.50 per box, the amount of the variable cost per box.

$\quad$ The equation for the total cost is

> Total cost = $f + vX$
> where:
> $\quad f$ = total fixed costs,
> $\quad v$ = variable cost per unit sold, and
> $\quad X$ = sales volume.

The equation for the total cost line in Exhibit 3-5 is

Exhibit 3-5 Total Cost Behavior

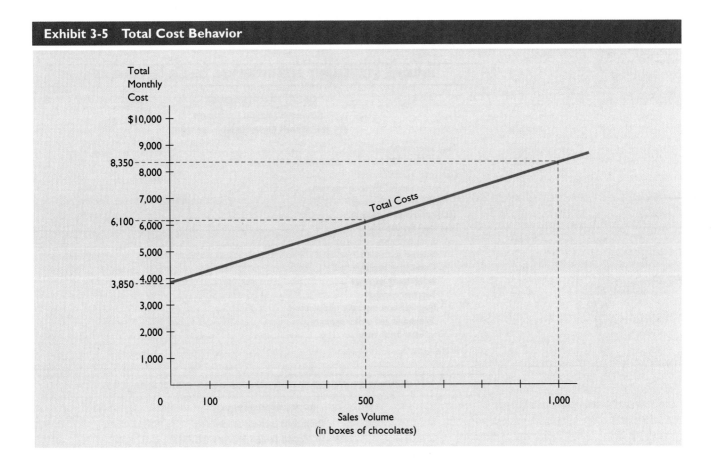

Total cost of boxes of chocolates sold = $3,850 + $4.50X$
where:
X = sales volume.

Now that you understand the relationships of volume, fixed costs, and variable costs to the total cost, we can use C-V-P analysis to estimate profit.

Profit Computation

According to the marketing plan, Sweet Temptations expects to sell 720 boxes of chocolates at $10 each in January. The top part of Exhibit 3-6 shows Sweet Temptations' projected income statement for internal decision-making, as it might appear in the business plans.[5] The projected income statement for internal users shows expenses as fixed and variable. With this arrangement, the internal decision-maker can perform C-V-P analysis.

The income statement may be rearranged for external decision-makers, as we show in the lower part of Exhibit 3-6. External decision-makers find this format understandable and use this form of income statement for their investment and credit decisions. This income statement results from the following equation:

$$\text{Net Income (Profit)} = \text{Revenues} - \text{Expenses}$$

In this equation, revenues include cash and credit sales, and expenses include the cost of boxes of chocolates sold and the expenses to operate the business. It is important to keep in

---

[5] In a business plan, a company would more likely show a projected income statement for a quarter (three months) of a year. We will discuss this in Chapter 4.

Exhibit 3-6   Projected Income Statements: Internal and External Users

INCOME STATEMENT FOR INTERNAL DECISION-MAKERS

SWEET TEMPTATIONS
Projected Income Statement
For the Month Ended January 31, 2000

Total sales revenues:		$7,200
($10 × 720 boxes of chocolates)		
Less total variable costs:		
Cost of boxes of chocolate sold		(3,240)
($4.50 × 720 boxes)		
Total contribution margin		$3,960
Less total fixed costs:		
Rent expense	$1,000	
Salaries expense	2,050	
Consulting expense	200	
Advertising expense	305	
Supplies expense	30	
Depreciation expense: display cases	15	
Telephone and utility expense	250	
Total fixed costs		(3,850)
Profit		$ 110

INCOME STATEMENT FOR EXTERNAL DECISION-MAKERS

SWEET TEMPTATIONS
Projected Income Statement
For the Month Ended January 31, 2000

Revenues:		
Sales revenues		$7,200
Expenses:		
Cost of boxes of chocolates sold:	$3,240	
Rent expense	1,000	
Salaries expense	2,050	
Consulting expense	200	
Advertising expense	305	
Supplies expense	30	
Depreciation expense: display cases	15	
Telephone and utility expense	250	
Total expenses		(7,090)
Net income		$ 110

mind that although we presented the information in the lower part in an order different from that used in the top part, the two formats will result in the same profit (net income) amount.

Profit Graph

One way of graphing a company's net income (profit) is to show both its revenues and its costs (expenses) on the same graph. Recall that the graph of a company's total costs includes its fixed costs and its variable costs, as we illustrated in Exhibit 3-5 for Sweet Temptations. The graph of a company's revenues is shown by a straight line sloping upward from the origin of the graph. The slope of the line is the rate (selling price per unit) at which the total revenues increase each time the company sells another unit.

The graph in Exhibit 3-7 shows the estimated total revenue line and the estimated total cost line for Sweet Temptations. Note that the total revenue line crosses the total cost line at 700 boxes of chocolates. At this point, the total revenues will be $7,000, and the total costs will be $7,000, so there will be zero profit. The unit sales volume at which a

Exhibit 3-7 Profit Graph for Sweet Temptations

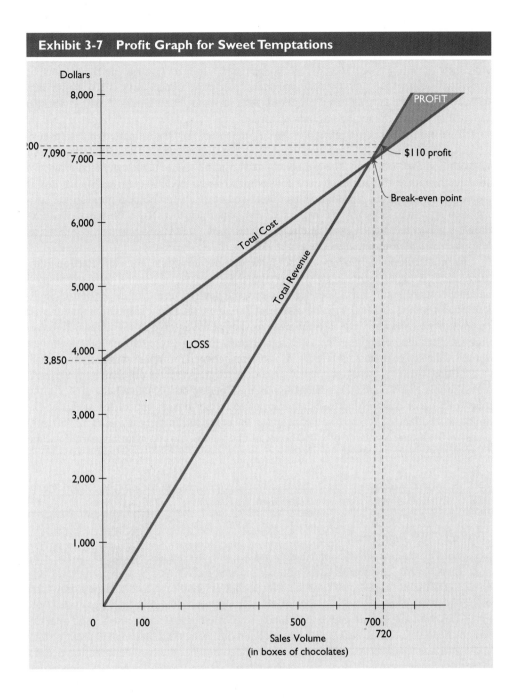

company earns zero profit is called the **break-even point.** Above the break-even unit sales volume, the total revenues of the company are more than its total costs, so there will be a profit. Below the break-even point, the total revenues are less than the total costs, so there will be a loss. For instance, at a sales volume of 720 boxes of chocolates, the graph in Exhibit 3-7 shows that Sweet Temptations will earn a profit of $110 (as we computed in the income statement in Exhibit 3-6), the difference between the $7,200 estimated total revenue and $7,090 estimated total cost at this volume. Although some decision-makers use this type of graph, many others prefer to use a different graph that shows a company's contribution margin, as we discuss next.

Contribution Margin

To estimate profit at different volume levels, the entrepreneur needs C-V-P information in a form that relates the estimated revenues and estimated variable costs to the estimated fixed

Farcus by David Waisglass
Gordon Coulthart

**"Duffy sure has a way
with visual aids."**

FARCUS® is reprinted with permission
from Laughing Stock Licensing Inc.,
Ottawa, Canada. All major reserved.

costs. In the top part of Exhibit 3-6, Sweet Temptations first calculates its estimated sales revenue ($7,200) by multiplying the number of boxes of chocolates it expects to sell (720) by the selling price per box ($10). Sweet Temptations determines the total estimated variable costs of selling the 720 boxes of chocolates ($3,240) by multiplying the number of boxes it expects to sell (720) by the variable cost per box of chocolates ($4.50). These total variable costs are then subtracted from total sales revenue. The $3,960 ($7,200 − $3,240) difference is called the total contribution margin.

The **total contribution margin** is the difference between the estimated total sales revenue and the estimated total variable costs. It is the amount, at a given sales volume, that will contribute to "covering" the estimated fixed costs. To compute the estimated profit, we subtract the total estimated fixed costs for the month from the total contribution margin. If the contribution margin is more than the total fixed costs, there will be a profit. If the contribution margin is less than the total fixed costs, there will be a loss. The top part of Exhibit 3-6 shows that Sweet Temptations' estimated profit is $110 ($3,960 total contribution margin − $3,850 total fixed costs).

The contribution margin may also be shown on a per-unit basis. The **contribution margin per unit** is the difference between the estimated sales revenue per unit and the estimated variable costs per unit. For Sweet Temptations, the contribution margin per unit is $5.50 ($10 sales revenue − $4.50 variable costs). At 720 units, the total contribution margin will be $3,960 (720 × $5.50), which is the same as shown on the top part of Exhibit 3-6. Later, you will see that computing the total contribution margin (by either method described above) is the key to understanding the relationship between profit and sales volume.

Exhibit 3-8 shows what the total contribution margin will be at different unit sales volumes. In this graph, since the contribution margin of one box of chocolates is $5.50, the total contribution margin increases at a rate of $5.50 per box of chocolates sold. For example, at a volume of 500 boxes of chocolates, the contribution margin will be $2,750 (500 boxes × $5.50). At a volume of 1,000 boxes of chocolates, the contribution margin will be $5,500 (1,000 boxes × $5.50).

 If variable costs were higher per unit, would you expect the contribution margin line in Exhibit 3-8 to be steeper or flatter than it is? Why?

Showing C-V-P Relationships

Now that you understand the contribution margin and fixed costs, we can show the estimated profit or loss at different sales volumes in a graph. Exhibit 3-9 shows how sales volume affects the estimated profit (or loss) for Sweet Temptations. Two lines are drawn on this graph. One line shows the estimated total contribution margin at different sales volumes. It is the same line as shown in Exhibit 3-8. The other line shows the $3,850 total estimated fixed costs. The vertical distance between these lines is the estimated profit or loss at the different sales volumes. Remember, estimated profit is the total contribution margin minus the estimated total fixed costs. Note that this graph shows that Sweet Temptations will earn $0 profit if it sells 700 boxes of chocolates; this is its break-even point. Above the break-even unit sales volume (such as at a volume of 1,000 boxes), the total contribution margin ($5,500) is more than the total estimated fixed costs ($3,850), so there would be a profit ($5,500 − $3,850 = $1,650). Below the break-even point (such as at a volume of 500 boxes), the total contribution margin ($2,750) is less than the total estimated fixed costs, so there would be a loss ($2,750 − $3,850 = −$1,100).

 If fixed costs were greater, would you expect Sweet Temptations to break even at a lower sales volume or a higher sales volume? Why?

Profit Computation (Equation Form)

In Exhibit 3-9, we show a graph of the C-V-P relationships for Sweet Temptations. Graphs are usually a helpful tool for an entrepreneur (and students!) to see a "picture" of these relationships. Sometimes, however, an entrepreneur (or student) does not need a picture to

Exhibit 3-8 Relationship between the Total Contribution Margin and the Unit Sales Volume

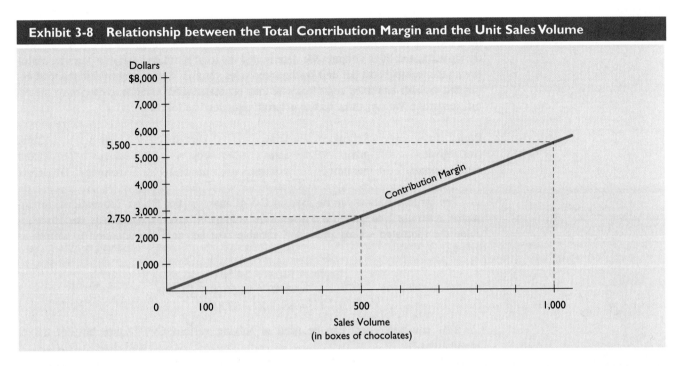

Exhibit 3-9 Cost-Volume-Profit Relationships for Sweet Temptations

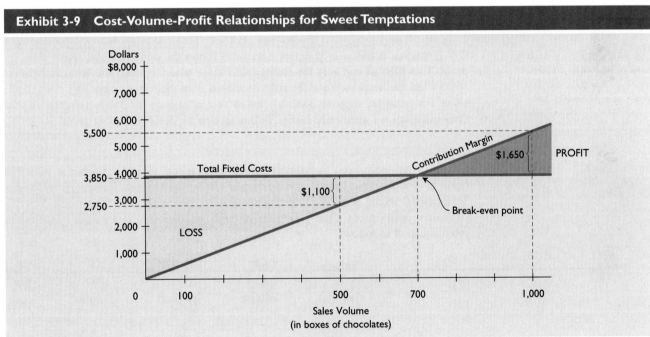

understand the relationships. In this case, using equations may be a better and faster way to understand C-V-P relationships. (You may have already thought of these equations as you studied Exhibit 3-9.) In this section, we look at how to use equations for C-V-P analysis to answer the following questions:

1. How much profit will the company earn at a given unit sales volume?

2. How many units must the company sell to break even?

3. How many units must the company sell to earn a given amount of profit? (The given amount is usually a desired profit that the company uses as a goal.)

In the following discussion, we use Sweet Temptations' revenue and cost information from the projected income statement for internal decision-makers, in the top part of Exhibit 3-6. We determined the total sales revenue by multiplying the selling price per unit by the estimated sales volume. We determined the total estimated variable costs by multiplying the variable cost per unit by the same sales volume. And we subtracted the total estimated variable and fixed costs from the total estimated sales revenue to determine the estimated profit. We can show this in a "profit equation" as follows:

$$\text{Profit (for a given sales volume)} = \left[\begin{array}{c}\text{Selling}\\\text{price}\\\text{per unit}\end{array} \times \begin{array}{c}\text{Unit}\\\text{sales}\\\text{volume}\end{array}\right] - \left[\begin{array}{c}\text{Variable}\\\text{cost}\\\text{per unit}\end{array} \times \begin{array}{c}\text{Unit}\\\text{sales}\\\text{volume}\end{array}\right] - \begin{array}{c}\text{Total}\\\text{fixed}\\\text{costs}\end{array}$$

The profit equation can be used in C-V-P analysis. For Sweet Temptations, for instance, if we use X to stand for a given sales volume of boxes of chocolates, and if we include the estimated selling price and variable cost per unit, the equation is written as follows:

$$\begin{aligned}\text{Profit} &= \$10X - \$4.50X - \$3,850\\&= (\$10 - \$4.50)X - \$3,850\\&= \$5.50X - \$3,850\end{aligned}$$

This equation, then, can be used in solving various C-V-P questions for Sweet Temptations.[6]

Using C-V-P Analysis

4 *What do decision-makers have to be able to predict in order to estimate profit at a given sales volume?*

C-V-P analysis is useful in planning because it shows the impact of alternative plans on profit. This analysis can help the entrepreneur make planning decisions and can help investors and creditors evaluate the risk associated with their investment and credit decisions. For instance, suppose Anna has asked you to answer, for Sweet Temptations, the three questions we mentioned earlier. In this section we describe how to do so.

Estimating Profit at Given Unit Sales Volume

Suppose Anna wants you to estimate Sweet Temptations' monthly profit if it sells 750 boxes of chocolates (i.e., a unit sales volume of 750 boxes) a month. Remember that Sweet Temptations' selling price is $10 per unit and its variable cost is $4.50 per unit. You can estimate monthly profit when 750 boxes of chocolates are sold in a month by using the profit equation as follows:

$$\text{Profit} = \left[\begin{array}{c}\text{Selling}\\\text{price}\\\text{per unit}\end{array} \times \begin{array}{c}\text{Unit}\\\text{sales}\\\text{volume}\end{array}\right] - \left[\begin{array}{c}\text{Variable}\\\text{cost}\\\text{per unit}\end{array} \times \begin{array}{c}\text{Unit}\\\text{sales}\\\text{volume}\end{array}\right] - \begin{array}{c}\text{Total}\\\text{fixed}\\\text{costs}\end{array}$$

$$\begin{aligned}&= (\$10 \times 750) - (\$4.50 \times 750) - \$3,850\\&= \$7,500 - \$3,375 - \$3,850\\&= \underline{\$275}\end{aligned}$$

Thus, you can tell Anna that Sweet Temptations will make a monthly profit of $275 if it sells 750 boxes of chocolates a month.

---

[6]Note in the last line of the equation that the $5.50 is the contribution margin per unit. This can come in handy as a "shortcut" when using the profit equation, so that the equation becomes:

$$\text{Profit (for a given sales volume)} = \left[\begin{array}{c}\text{Contribution}\\\text{margin}\\\text{per unit}\end{array} \times \begin{array}{c}\text{Unit}\\\text{sales}\\\text{volume}\end{array}\right] - \begin{array}{c}\text{Total}\\\text{fixed}\\\text{costs}\end{array}$$

Finding the Break-Even Point

Suppose Anna wants you to estimate how many boxes of chocolates Sweet Temptations must sell to break even each month. Recall that the break-even point is the unit sales volume that results in zero profit. This occurs when total sales revenue equals total costs (total variable costs plus total fixed costs). To find the break-even point, we start with the profit equation. Remember that the contribution margin per unit is the difference between the sales revenue per unit and the variable costs per unit. With this in mind, we can rearrange the profit equation[7] into a break-even equation as follows:

$$\frac{\text{Unit sales volume}}{\text{(to earn zero profit)}} = \frac{\text{Total fixed costs}}{\text{Contribution margin per unit}}$$

So for Sweet Temptations, you can tell Anna that the break-even point is 700 boxes of chocolates, computed using the break-even equation as follows (letting X stand for the unit sales volume):

$$\frac{\text{Unit sales volume}}{\text{(to earn zero profit)}} = \frac{\$3,850 \text{ total fixed costs}}{(\$10 \text{ selling price} - \$4.50 \text{ variable cost}) \text{ per unit}}$$

$$X = \frac{\$3,850}{\$5.50}$$

$$X = \underline{700} \text{ boxes of chocolates}$$

You can verify the break-even sales volume of 700 boxes of chocolates with the following schedule:

Total sales revenue (700 boxes of chocolates @ $10.00 per box) $7,000
Less: Total variable costs (700 boxes of chocolates @ $4.50 per box) .... (3,150)
Total contribution margin (700 boxes of chocolates @ $5.50 per box) $3,850
Less: Total fixed costs .... (3,850)
Profit.. $ 0

Finding the Unit Sales Volume to Achieve a Target Profit

Finding the break-even point gives the entrepreneur useful information. However, most entrepreneurs are interested in earning a profit that is high enough to satisfy their goals and the company's goals. A company often states its profit goals at amounts that result in a satisfactory return on the average total assets used in its operations. Since this is an introduction to C-V-P analysis, we will wait to discuss what is meant by "satisfactory return" and "average total assets" until Chapter 11. Here we will assume an amount of profit that is satisfactory. Suppose Anna's goal is that Sweet Temptations earn a profit of $110 per month. How many boxes of chocolates must Sweet Temptations sell per month to earn $110 profit? To answer this question, we slightly modify the break-even equation.

5 *How can decision-makers predict the sales volume necessary for estimated revenues to cover estimated costs?*

6 *How can decision-makers predict the sales volume necessary to achieve a target profit?*

---

[7]For those of you who want "proof" of this break-even equation, since the contribution margin per unit is the selling price per unit minus the variable cost per unit, we can substitute the total contribution margin per unit into the profit equation as follows:

$$\text{Profit} = \left[\begin{array}{c} \text{Contribution} \\ \text{margin} \\ \text{per unit} \end{array} \times \begin{array}{c} \text{Unit} \\ \text{sales} \\ \text{volume} \end{array} \right] - \begin{array}{c} \text{Total} \\ \text{fixed} \\ \text{costs} \end{array}$$

Since break-even occurs when profit is zero, we can omit the profit, move the total fixed costs to the other side of the equation, and rewrite the equation as follows:

$$\text{Total fixed costs} = \left[\begin{array}{c} \text{Contribution} \\ \text{margin} \\ \text{per unit} \end{array} \times \begin{array}{c} \text{Unit} \\ \text{sales} \\ \text{volume} \end{array} \right]$$

Finally, we can divide both sides of the equation by the contribution margin per unit to derive the break-even equation:

$$\frac{\text{Total fixed costs}}{\text{Contribution margin per unit}} = \frac{\text{Unit sales volume}}{\text{(to earn zero profit)}}$$

The break-even point is the sales volume at which the total contribution margin is equal to, or "covers," the total fixed costs. Therefore, each additional unit sold above the break-even sales volume increases profit by the contribution margin per unit. Hence, to find the sales volume at which the total contribution margin "covers" both total fixed costs *and* the desired profit, we can modify the break-even equation simply by adding the desired profit to fixed costs, as follows:

$$\text{Unit sales volume (to earn a desired profit)} = \frac{\text{Total fixed costs} + \text{Desired profit}}{\text{Contribution margin per unit}}$$

So, if we let X stand for the unit sales volume, Sweet Temptations needs to sell 720 boxes of chocolates to earn a profit of $110 a month, computed as follows:

$$X = \frac{\$3,850 + \$110}{\$5.50 \text{ per box of chocolates}}$$

$$X = \underline{\underline{720}} \text{ boxes of chocolates}$$

You can verify the $110 profit with the following schedule:

Total sales revenue (720 boxes of chocolates @ $10.00 per box)	$7,200
Less: Total variable costs (720 boxes of chocolates @ $4.50 per box)	(3,240)
Total contribution margin (720 boxes of chocolates @ $5.50 per box)	$3,960
Less: Total fixed costs	(3,850)
Profit	$ 110

Since Anna had included the desired profit of $110 per month in Sweet Temptations' business plan, the income statement for internal decision-makers shown in the top part of Exhibit 3-6 is an expanded version of the preceding schedule.

Summary of the C-V-P Analysis Computations

Exhibit 3-10 summarizes the equations that we used in our discussion of C-V-P analysis. Although it may be tempting to try to memorize them, you should strive to understand how these equations relate to one another.

Exhibit 3-10 Summary of Cost-Volume-Profit Computations

$$\text{Profit (for a given sales volume)} = \left[\text{Selling price per unit} \times \text{Unit sales volume} \right] - \left[\text{Variable cost per unit} \times \text{Unit sales volume} \right] - \text{Total fixed costs}$$

or

$$= \left[\text{Contribution margin per unit} \times \text{Unit sales volume} \right] - \text{Total fixed costs}$$

$$\text{Unit sales volume (to earn zero profit)} = \frac{\text{Total fixed costs}}{\text{Contribution margin per unit}}$$

$$\text{Unit sales volume (to earn a desired profit)} = \frac{\text{Total fixed costs} + \text{Desired profit}}{\text{Contribution margin per unit}}$$

Other Planning Issues

Providing answers to the previous three questions showed how C-V-P analysis is useful in planning. There are many other planning issues for which C-V-P analysis provides useful information. For instance, suppose you and Anna are considering alternative plans for Sweet Temptations to raise its monthly profit. These plans include:

7 *How can decision-makers use accounting information to evaluate alternative plans?*

1. Raising the selling price of the boxes of chocolates to $11 per box. With this alternative, the variable costs per box of chocolates and the total fixed costs do not change.

2. Purchasing a premium line of chocolates rather than the superior line, thus increasing the variable costs to $4.60 per box. You and Anna are considering this alternative because the improvement in the quality of the chocolate may cause the sales volume of boxes of chocolates to increase. With this change, neither the selling price per unit nor the total fixed costs change.

3. Increasing the total fixed costs by spending $110 more on advertising. With this alternative, the selling price per unit and the variable costs per unit do not change, but the additional advertising may cause an increase in sales volume.

 How would you modify the graph in Exhibit 3-9 to provide information for Plan #1?

We do not show C-V-P analysis for these three issues at this time because we will discuss similar issues in Chapter 11. We raise these issues here to get you to think about how to use the C-V-P equations or graphs to provide helpful information. The C-V-P analysis for these three alternative plans, however, does not provide all the information you need to make a decision. It is a helpful tool, but it is most effective when used with critical thinking. You must think about the effects each of the alternatives has on your customers.

For instance, each of the alternatives is likely to affect the number of boxes of chocolates that Sweet Temptations can sell. A change in selling price would certainly affect your customers' decisions to purchase boxes of chocolates. A decrease in selling price would bring the boxes of chocolates into the spending range of more people (probably increasing the number of boxes of chocolates you could sell), whereas an increase in selling price may make the boxes of chocolates too expensive for some customers (possibly decreasing the number of boxes of chocolates you could sell). Selling a higher quality of chocolates may attract a different, or additional, group of customers, thus affecting sales volume. Increasing advertising may make more people aware of, and may attract more customers to, Sweet Temptations. Before you make a decision, you should consider how it will affect customers' interest in your product and estimate the probable unit sales volume for each alternative. Then, for whatever sales volume you expect, the analysis can provide a more realistic profit estimate.

Business Issues and Values: Waste Not, Want Not

C-V-P accounting information is one factor that influences business decisions, but entrepreneurs also need to consider the nonfinancial effects of their decisions. For example, if the managers of a company are thinking about lowering the company's total costs by omitting toxic waste cleanup around the factory, they must ask questions such as the following: What will be the impact on the environment? What health effects might the employees suffer later? What might be the health impact on the company's neighbors? Legally, can we even consider not cleaning up the toxic waste? Although omitting toxic waste cleanup may reduce total costs dramatically, these managers might consider the other, more-difficult-to-measure costs to be too high. Therefore, after weighing all the factors sur-rounding the alternatives, the managers may choose a more socially acceptable alternative that results in a less favorable profit.

Summary

At the beginning of the chapter we asked you several questions. During the chapter, we asked you to STOP and answer some additional questions to build your knowledge about specific issues. Be sure you answered these additional questions. Below are the questions from the beginning of the chapter, with a brief summary of the key points relating to the answers. Use your creative and critical thinking skills to expand on these key points to develop more complete answers to the questions and to determine what other questions you have that might lead you to learn more about the issues.

1 Since the future is uncertain and circumstances are likely to change, why should a company bother to plan?

A business plan helps the owners or managers of a company organize the company, serves as a benchmark against which they can evaluate actual company performance, and helps the company obtain financing. The business plan consists of a description of the company, a marketing plan, a description of the company's operations, and a financial plan. Accounting information contributes to the planning process by providing information for C-V-P analysis and by including in the financial plan the effects that estimated revenues, variable costs, and fixed costs have on the company's profits.

2 What should a company include in its business plan?

A business plan should include a description of the company, a marketing plan, a description of the operations of the company, and a financial plan. The description should include information about the organization of the company, its products or services, its current and potential customers, its objectives, where it is located, and where it conducts business. The marketing plan shows how the company will make sales and how it will influence and respond to market conditions. The company operations section includes a description of the relationships between the company, its suppliers, and its customers, as well as a description of how the company will develop, service, protect, and support its products or services. The financial plan identifies the company's capital requirements and sources of capital, and describes the company's projected financial performance.

3 How does accounting information contribute to the planning process?

Accountants determine how revenues, variable costs, and fixed costs affect profits based on their observations of how costs "behave" and on their estimates of future revenues and costs. By observing cost behavior patterns, accountants are able to classify the costs as fixed or variable, and then to use this classification to predict the amounts of the costs at different activity levels. Accounting information, then, can help decision-makers evaluate alternative plans by using C-V-P analysis to show the profit effect of each plan. C-V-P analysis is a tool that helps managers think critically about the different aspects of each plan.

4 What do decision-makers have to be able to predict in order to estimate profit at a given sales volume?

To estimate profit at a given sales volume, decision-makers must be able to predict the product's selling price, the costs that the company will incur, and the behavior of those costs (whether they are fixed or variable costs). The fixed costs will not change because of sales volume, but the variable costs will change directly with changes in sales volume.

5 How can decision-makers predict the sales volume necessary for estimated revenues to cover estimated costs?

To predict the sales volume necessary for estimated revenues to cover estimated costs, decision-makers must rearrange the profit equation into the break-even equation. Using what they know about the product's selling price and the behavior of the company's costs, the decision-makers can determine the contribution margin per unit of product by subtracting the estimated variable costs per unit from the product's estimated selling price. Then they can substitute the contribution margin and the estimated fixed costs into the equation and solve for the necessary sales volume.

6 How can decision-makers predict the sales volume necessary to achieve a target profit?

Predicting the sales volume necessary to achieve a target profit is not very different from predicting the sales volume necessary for estimated revenues to cover estimated costs. The only difference is that the decision-makers must modify the break-even equation by adding the desired profit to the estimated fixed costs. Then, after substituting the contribution margin and the estimated fixed costs plus the desired profit into the equation, they can solve for the necessary sales volume.

7 How can decision-makers use accounting information to evaluate alternative plans?

Decision-makers can determine how changes in costs and revenues affect the company's profit. Based on accounting information alone, the alternative that leads to the highest profit will be the best solution. However, decision-makers should also consider the nonfinancial effects that their decisions may have.

Key Terms

break-even point *(p. 69)*
business plan *(p. 56)*
capital *(p. 60)*
contribution margin per unit *(p. 70)*
cost-volume-profit (C-V-P) analysis
  (p. 63)
line of credit *(p. 62)*
long-term capital *(p. 62)*

return *(p. 57)*
risk *(p. 57)*
short-term capital *(p. 61)*
total contribution margin *(p. 70)*
total costs *(p. 66)*
variable cost *(p. 65)*
volume *(p. 64)*

Here is an opportunity to gather information on the Internet about real-world issues related to the topics in this chapter. Go to http://www.dryden.com/account and click on the Cunningham, Nikolai, and Bazley book cover. Click on Summary Surfing, then click on this chapter number, and answer the following questions.

S U M M A R Y
S U R F I N G

▶ Click on **SBA** (U.S. Small Business Administration). Click on *Learn about SBA,* and then click on *Strategic Plan.* What are the mission and goals of the SBA? Go back and click on *Message from the Administrator.* What percent of the gross national product do small businesses generate? How much technological innovation do small businesses invent? Go back to *Learn about SBA,* click on *Profile,* and then click on *Lending.* What percent of a loan amount up to $750,000 can the SBA guarantee? What is the maximum interest rate allowed? What is the function of the Women's Prequalification Loan? What is the function of the Minority Prequalification Loan?

▶ Click on **SBA** (U.S. Small Business Administration). Scroll down, and click on *Starting;* then, on the left side, click on *Business Plans.* In "Business Plan Outline," what are the three elements (identified by roman numerals) of a business plan? Identify a few components under each section. In "The Business Plan: What It Includes," what are the four distinct sections? How do these compare with what we discussed in the chapter?

Integrated Business and Accounting Situations

Answer the Following Questions in Your Own Words

Testing Your Knowledge

3-1 Since the future is uncertain and circumstances are likely to change, why should the managers and owners of a company bother to plan?

3-2 Describe the three main functions of a business plan.

3-3 Describe the components of a business plan. How does each of these components help an investor, a creditor, and a manager or owner make decisions about a company?

3-4 Why is it important for a company to have a cash buffer on hand?

3-5 How can an entrepreneur determine a company's capital requirements?

3-6 What is the difference between short-term and long-term capital?

3-7 Explain what cost-volume-profit analysis is.

3-8 How does cost-volume-profit analysis help entrepreneurs develop their companies' business plans?

3-9 How can you tell whether a cost is a variable cost or a fixed cost?

3-10 What is a contribution margin?

3-11 Explain what it means when a company breaks even.

3-12 Indicate the effect (increase, decrease, no change, or not enough information) that each of the following situations has on break-even unit sales. If you answer "not enough information," list the information that you need in order to be able to determine the effect.

(a) A retail company purchases price tags to use in place of the stickers it has used in the past.

(b) An athletic equipment store leases more retail space.

(c) A bakery increases its advertising expense.

(d) A merchandiser plans to increase the selling price of its product. To counter potential decreases in sales, the merchandiser also plans to increase the amount of per-product commission that the sales staff earns.

(e) An accounting firm plans to increase its billing rate per hour.

(f) A retail company has found a supplier that will provide the same merchandise its old supplier provided, but at a lower price.

(g) A private college in the Northwest installs air conditioning in its dormitories.

(h) A retail company reduces advertising expenses and increases the commissions of its sales force.

(i) Instead of having its office building cleaned by a cleaning service, a company plans to hire its own cleaning crew.

3-13 If the total variable cost per unit increases while the selling price per unit, the fixed costs, and the sales volume remain the same, how would you expect the change in variable costs to affect profit? the break-even point?

3-14 If total fixed costs increase while the selling price per unit, the variable costs per unit, and the sales volume remain the same, how would you expect the change in fixed costs to affect profit? the break-even point?

3-15 How does the income statement shown in the top portion of Exhibit 3-6 help internal decision-makers perform cost-volume-profit analysis?

Applying Your Knowledge

3-16 Imagine that you are going to start your own company. Think about the concept for a minute.

Required: What will you call your company? What kind of product or service will you sell? What price will you charge for your product or service? Why? What variable costs and what fixed costs do you think you will incur?

3-17 Suppose you want to start a company that sells sports equipment.

Required: Go to the reference section of your library. What type of information can you find in *Moody's* or *Standard & Poor's* to help you prepare projected financial statements for your company?

3-18 TLC Company sells a single product, a food basket (containing fruit, cheese, nuts, and other items) that friends and family can purchase for college students who need a little extra TLC. This product, called the Exam-O-Rama, sells for $10 per basket. The variable cost is $7 per basket, and the total fixed cost is $24,000 per year.

Required: (1) Draw one graph showing TLC's (a) total revenues and (b) total costs as volume varies. Locate the break-even point on the graph.
   (2) What is TLC's profit equation in terms of units sold?
   (3) What is TLC's break-even point in units?

3-19 Bathtub Rings Company sells shower-curtain rings for $1.60 per box. The variable cost is $1.20 per box, and the fixed cost totals $30,000 per year.

Required: (1) What is Bathtub Rings' profit equation in terms of boxes of shower-curtain rings sold?
   (2) Draw a graph of Bathtub Rings' total contribution margin and total fixed cost as volume varies. Locate the break-even point on this graph.
   (3) What is Bathtub Rings' break-even point in units?
   (4) What would total profits be if Bathtub Rings sold 500,000 boxes of shower-curtain rings?
   (5) How many boxes of shower-curtain rings would Bathtub Rings have to sell to earn $50,000 of profit?

3-20 Go Figure Company sells small calculators for $12 each. This year, Go Figure's fixed cost totals $110,000. The variable cost per calculator is $8.

Required: (1) Compute the break-even point in number of calculators.
   (2) Compute the number of calculators required to earn a profit of $70,000.
   (3) If the total fixed cost increases to $150,000 next year,
      (a) what will Go Figure's break-even point be in number of calculators?
      (b) what profit (or loss) will Go Figure have if it sells 30,000 calculators?
      (c) how many calculators will Go Figure have to sell to earn a profit of $70,000?

3-21 Silencer Company sells a single product, mufflers for leaf blowers. The company's profit computation for last year is shown here:

Sales revenue (2,000 units @ $25)	$50,000
Less variable costs	(16,000)
Contribution margin	$34,000
Less fixed costs	(22,000)
Profit	$12,000

Silencer has decided to increase the price of its product to $30 per muffler. The company believes that if it increases its fixed advertising (selling) cost by $3,400, sales volume next year will be 1,800 mufflers. Variable cost per muffler will be unchanged.

Required: (1) Using the above income statement format, show the computation of expected profit for Silencer's operations next year.
   (2) How many mufflers would Silencer have to sell to earn as much profit next year as it did last year?
   (3) Do you agree with Silencer's decision? Explain why or why not.

3-22 Rapunzel Company currently sells a single product, shampoo, for $4 per bottle. The variable cost per bottle is $3. Rapunzel's fixed cost totals $10,000.

Required: (1) Compute the following amounts for Rapunzel Company:
      (a) Contribution margin per bottle of shampoo
      (b) Break-even point in bottles of shampoo
      (c) The profit that Rapunzel will earn at a sales volume of 25,000 bottles of shampoo

(d) The number of bottles of shampoo that Rapunzel must sell to earn a profit of $16,000

(2) Rapunzel is considering increasing its total fixed cost to $12,000 and then also increasing the selling price of its product to $5. The variable cost per bottle of shampoo would remain unchanged. Repeat the computations from (1), using this new information. Will this decision be a good one for Rapunzel? Why or why not?

(3) Draw a graph with four lines to show the following:

(a) Total contribution margin earned when Rapunzel sells from 0 to 10,000 bottles of shampoo at a selling price of $4 per bottle

(b) Total contribution margin earned when Rapunzel sells from 0 to 10,000 bottles of shampoo at a selling price of $5 per bottle

(c) Rapunzel's fixed cost total of $10,000

(d) Rapunzel's fixed cost total of $12,000

(e) Rapunzel's break-even point in bottles of shampoo before and after the selling price and fixed cost changes

(4) Does the graph support your conclusion in (2) above? If so, how does it support your conclusion? If not, what new or different information did you get from the graph?

3-23 The Body Shop Equipment Company sells a small, relatively lightweight multipurpose exercise machine. This machine sells for $700. A recent cost analysis shows that The Body Shop's cost structure for the coming year is as follows:

Variable cost per unit..$ 325
Total annual fixed costs.. 125,000

Required: (1) Draw a graph that clearly shows (a) total fixed cost, (b) total cost, (c) total sales revenue, and (d) total contribution margin as the sales volume of exercise machines increases. Locate the break-even point on the graph.

(2) Compute the break-even point in number of machines.

(3) How many machines must the Body Shop sell to earn $30,000 of profit per year?

(4) How much profit would be earned at a sales volume of $420,000?

(5) Sean McLean, the owner of the Body Shop Equipment Company, is considering traveling a circuit of gyms and fitness centers around the United States each year to demonstrate the exercise machine, distribute information, and obtain sales contracts. He estimates that this will cost about $6,000 per year. How many additional exercise machines must the company sell per year to cover the cost of this effort?

3-24 Lady MacBeth Company sells bottles of dry cleaning solvent (spot remover) for $10 each. The variable cost for each bottle is $4. Lady MacBeth's total fixed cost for the year is $3,600.

Required: (1) Answer the following questions about the company's break-even point.

(a) How many bottles of spot remover must Lady MacBeth sell to break even?

(b) How would your answer to (1a) change if Lady MacBeth lowered the selling price per bottle by $2? What if, instead, it raised the selling price by $2?

(c) How would your answer to (1a) change if Lady MacBeth raised the variable cost per bottle by $2? What if, instead, it lowered the variable cost by $2?

(d) How would your answer to (1a) change if Lady MacBeth increased the total fixed cost by $60? What if, instead, Lady MacBeth decreased the total fixed cost by $60?

(2) Answer the following questions about the company's profit.

(a) How many bottles must Lady MacBeth sell to earn $4,800 profit?

(b) How would your answer to (2a) change if Lady MacBeth lowered the selling price per bottle by $2?

(c) Suppose that for every $1 the selling price per bottle decreases below its current selling price of $10 per bottle, Lady MacBeth predicts sales volume will increase by 325 bottles. Assume that before lowering the selling price, Lady MacBeth predicts that it can sell exactly 1,400 bottles. Can Lady MacBeth earn $4,800 profit by lowering the selling price per bottle by $2? Explain why or why not.

(d) Suppose that for every $1 the selling price per bottle increases above its current selling price of $10 per bottle, Lady MacBeth predicts sales volume will decrease by 200 bottles. Assume that before raising the selling price, Lady MacBeth predicts that it can sell exactly 1,400 bottles. Can Lady MacBeth earn $4,800 profit by raising the selling price per bottle by $2? Explain why or why not.

(e) How would your answer to (2a) change if Lady MacBeth raised the variable cost per bottle by $2? What if, instead, it lowered the variable cost per bottle by $2?

(f) How would your answer to (2a) change if Lady MacBeth raised the total fixed cost by $60? What if, instead, Lady MacBeth lowered the total fixed cost by $60?

3-25 The Brickhouse Company is planning to lease a delivery van for its northern sales territory. The leasing company is willing to lease the van under three alternative plans:
Plan A—Brickhouse would pay $0.34 per mile and buy its own gas.
Plan B—Brickhouse would pay $320 per month plus $0.10 per mile and buy its own gas.
Plan C—Brickhouse would pay $960 per month, and the leasing company would pay for all gas.
The leasing company will pay for all repairs and maintenance, insurance, license fees, and so on. Gas should cost $0.06 per mile.

Required: Using miles driven as the units of volume, do the following:
(1) Write out the cost equation for the cost of operating the delivery van under each of the three plans.
(2) Graph the three cost equations on the same graph (put cost on the vertical axis and miles driven per month on the horizontal axis).
(3) At what mileage per month would the cost of Plan A equal the cost of Plan B?
(4) At what mileage per month would the cost of Plan B equal the cost of Plan C?
(5) Compute the cost, under each of the three plans, of driving 3,500 miles per month.

3-26 The Mallory Motors Company sells small electric motors for $1.60 per motor. Variable costs are $1.20 per unit, and fixed costs total $60,000 per year.

Required: (1) Write out Mallory's profit equation in terms of motors sold.
(2) Draw a graph of Mallory's total contribution margin and total fixed cost as volume varies. Locate the break-even point on this graph.
(3) Compute Mallory's break-even point in units.
(4) What total profit would Mallory expect if it sold 500,000 motors?
(5) How many motors would Mallory have to sell to earn $50,000 profit?

3-27 The Campcraft Company is a small manufacturer of camping trailers. The company manufactures only one model and sells the units for $2,500 each. The variable costs of manufacturing and selling each trailer are $1,600. The total fixed cost amounts to $180,000 per year.

Required: (1) Compute Campcraft's contribution margin per trailer.
(2) Compute Campcraft's profit (or loss) at a sales volume of 160 trailers.
(3) Compute the number of units that Campcraft must sell for it to break even.
(4) Compute the number of units that Campcraft must sell for it to earn a profit of $31,500.

3-28 This year Babco's fixed costs total $110,000. The company sells babushkas for $12 each. The variable cost per babushka is $8.

Required: (1) Compute the break-even point in number of babushkas.
(2) Compute the number of babushkas that Babco must sell to earn a profit of $70,000.

(3) If the total fixed cost increases to $150,000 next year,
    (a) what will be Babco's break-even point in babushkas?
    (b) what profit (or loss) will Babco have if it sells 30,000 babushkas?
    (c) how many babushkas will Babco have to sell to earn a profit of $70,000?

3-29 The Cardiff Company sells a single product for $40 per unit. Its total fixed cost amounts to $360,000 per year, and its variable cost per unit is $30.

Required: (1) Compute the following amounts for the Cardiff Company:
    (a) Contribution margin per unit
    (b) Break-even point in units
    (c) The number of units that must be sold to earn $30,000 profit
    (2) Repeat all computations in (1), assuming Cardiff decides to increase its selling price per unit to $45. Assume that the total fixed cost and the variable cost per unit remain the same.

Making Evaluations

3-30 Suppose your wealthy Aunt Gert gave you and your cousins $10,000 each. Assume for a moment that you are not associated with Sweet Temptations and that you are considering loaning the $10,000 to Sweet Temptations.

Required: From the information included in Sweet Temptations' business plan so far, do you think this would be a wise investment on your part? Why or why not? What else would you like to know before making a decision (you don't have to limit your thinking to Sweet Temptations)?

3-31 Refer to 3-30. What if Aunt Gert instead gave you $100,000 and you were interested in investing it in Sweet Temptations?

Required: Would this change your answers to 3-30? Why or why not?

3-32 Joe Billy Ray Bob's Country and Western Company sells a single product—cowboy hats—for $20 per hat. The total fixed cost is $180,000 per year, and the variable cost per hat is $15.

Required: (1) Compute the following amounts for Joe Billy Ray Bob's Country and Western Company:
    (a) Contribution margin per hat
    (b) Break-even point in hats
    (c) The numbers of hats that must be sold to earn $15,000 of profit
    (2) Repeat all computations in (1), assuming Joe Billy Ray Bob's decides to increase its selling price per hat to $25. Assume that the total fixed cost and the variable cost per hat remain the same.
    (3) Do you agree with Joe Billy Ray Bob's decision to increase its selling price per hat? What other factors should the managers consider in making this decision?

3-33 The Vend-O-Bait Company operates and services bait vending machines placed in gas stations, motels, and restaurants surrounding a large lake. Vend-O-Bait rents 200 machines from the manufacturer. It also rents the space occupied by the machines at each location where it places the machines. Arnie Bass, the company's owner, has two employees who service the machines. Monthly fixed costs for the company are as follows:

Machine rental
    200 machines × $100 per month... $20,000
Space rental
    200 locations × $60 per month 12,000
Employee wages
    2 employees × $800 per month 1,600
Other fixed costs 2,400
Total $36,000

Currently, Vend-O-Bait's only variable costs are the costs of the night crawlers, which it purchases for $1.20 per pack. Vend-O-Bait sells these night crawlers for $1.80 per pack.

Required: (1) Answer the following questions:

    (a) What is the monthly break-even point (in packs sold)?

    (b) Compute Vend-O-Bait's monthly profit at monthly sales volumes of 52,000, 56,000, 64,000, and 68,000 packs, respectively.

(2) Suppose that instead of paying $60 fixed rent per month, Arnie Bass could arrange to pay $0.20 for each pack of night crawlers sold at each location to rent the space occupied by the machines. Repeat all computations in (1).

(3) Would it be desirable for Arnie Bass to try to change his space rental from a fixed cost ($60 per location) to a variable cost ($0.20 per pack sold)? Why or why not?

3-34 Refer to 3-24. Suppose your boss at Lady MacBeth is considering some alternative plans and would like your input on the following three independent alternatives:

(a) Increase the selling price per bottle by $3

(b) Decrease the variable cost per bottle by $2 by purchasing an equally effective, but less "environmentally friendly," solvent from your supplier

(c) Decrease the total fixed cost by $1,260.

Assume again that Lady MacBeth currently sells bottles of dry cleaning solvent for $10 each, the variable cost for each bottle is $4, and the total fixed cost for the year is $3,600.

Required: (1) How many bottles would Lady MacBeth have to sell to break even under each of the alternatives? Using this accounting information alone, write your boss a memo in which you recommend an alternative.

(2) Maybe your boss would like to earn a profit of $4,320. How many bottles would Lady MacBeth have to sell to earn a profit of $4,320 under each of the alternatives? Which of the three alternatives would you recommend to your boss? Is this consistent with your recommendation in (1)? Why or why not? What other issues did you consider when making your recommendation?

3-35 Cameron Balloons manufactures hot-air balloons in Ann Arbor, Michigan. After a wildly successful decade of operations, Cameron's production dropped to a little more than half of its normal production level because of the recession that occurred in the early 1990s. To remain competitive, Cameron decided to cut costs by "letting go" eight of its employees.[8]

Required: (1) What effect did the decision have on Cameron's break-even point? on the number of balloons Cameron would have to sell to earn a desired profit?

(2) What nonfinancial issues do you think the owners of Cameron Balloons had to resolve in order to make this decision?

(3) What questions do you think the owners had to answer in order to resolve these issues?

3-36 Suppose you work for the Miniola Hills Bus Company. The company's 10 buses made a total of 80 trips per day on 310 days last year, for a total of 350,000 miles. Another year like last year will put the company out of business (and you out of your job!). Your boss has come to you for help. Last year, the company lost $102,000, as shown here:

Revenue from riders (496,000 @ $0.50)		$248,000
Less operating costs:		
Depreciation on buses	$100,000	
Garage rent	20,000	
Licenses, fees, and insurance	40,000	
Maintenance	15,000	
Drivers' salaries	65,000	
Tires	20,000	
Gasoline and oil	90,000	(350,000)
Loss		($102,000)

Your boss is considering the following two plans for improving the company's profitability:

(a) Plan A—change the bus routes and reduce the number of trips to 60 per day in order to reduce the number of miles driven

---

[8]Tucker Comstock, "How One Company Sustained Its Lift," *Nation's Business,* April 1995, 6.

(b) Plan B—sell bus tokens (five for $1.00) and student passes ($2.50 to ride all week) in order to increase the number of riders

Required: (1) Write your boss a memo discussing the effect that each of these plans might have on the costs and revenues of the bus company. Identify in your memo any assumptions you have made.

(2) If you were making this decision, what questions would you like answered before making the decision?

3-37 Yesterday, you received the following letter for your advice column in the local paper:

Dear Dr. Decisive:

What do you think about this situation? My boyfriend refuses to meet me for lunch until I admit I am wrong about this, which I'm NOT. The other day, when we went to lunch at Subs and Floats on campus, he noticed that they had raised the price of BLT subs. He got mad because he thinks the only reason they raised the price was to increase their profit. I told him that, first of all, their profit might not increase and that, second, he was basing his conclusion on some assumptions that might not be true and that if he would just *open up his mind,* he might see how those assumptions are affecting his conclusion. Well, *then* he got mad at *me.* I'm really upset because I know I'm right and because now I have to buy my own lunch. Will you please explain why I'm right? I know he'll listen to you (he reads your column daily). Until you answer, I'll be

"Starving."

Required: Meet with your Dr. Decisive team and write a response to "Starving."

DEVELOPING A BUSINESS PLAN: BUDGETING

"Adventure is the result of poor planning."
—Colonel Blatchford Snell

1 *How does a budget contribute toward helping a company achieve its goals?*

2 *Do the activities of a company have a logical order that drives the organization of a budget?*

3 *What is the structure of the budgeting process, and how does a company begin that process?*

4 *What are the similarities and differences between a retail company's master budget and a service company's master budget?*

5 *After a company begins the budgeting process, is there a strategy it can use to complete the budget?*

6 *How can a manager use a budget to evaluate a company's performance and then use the results of that evaluation to influence the company's plans?*

85

Unless you have been lucky enough to win the lottery, you probably have to budget your money. (Even if you *have* won the lottery, you probably want to budget your money.) Think for a minute about where you get your money. Do you receive cash from a job, a scholarship, financial aid, your parents, or some combination of these sources? Now think about where you spend your money. Most likely you spend it on day-to-day living expenses such as food, rent, utilities, and miscellaneous items, as well as on college-related costs such as tuition, fees, and books. Budgeting helps you to estimate when—and how much—cash will come in, and also helps you figure out when—and how much—cash you will need to pay out. With these estimates, you can plan your activities so that you have enough cash to pay for them.

 Suppose in budgeting your future cash payments, you realize that unless something changes, you will not have enough cash to pay your next car insurance bill. What alternatives do you have to solve this problem?

Companies have to budget their resources too. For most companies, **budgeting** is a formal part of the planning process and results in a set of related reports called budgets. A **budget** is a report that gives a financial description of one part of a company's planned activities. For example, a budget might show how many products the company plans to sell, the dollar amount of these sales, and when the company will collect the cash from these sales. Another budget might show how much cash a company plans to spend renting business space, employing workers, and advertising its products, and when the company plans to incur these costs.

Why Budget?

I *How does a budget contribute toward helping a company achieve its goals?*

Budgeting improves the planning, operating, and evaluating processes by helping an entrepreneur

▶ add discipline, or order, to the planning process,

▶ recognize and avoid potential operating problems,

▶ quantify plans, and

▶ create a "benchmark" for evaluating the company's performance.

Budgeting Adds Discipline

Companies survive or fail because of the financial results of their activities. Therefore, *before implementing planning decisions,* effective entrepreneurs carefully think about what will happen as a result of these decisions. That's where budgeting comes in; the more complete and detailed the planning process is, the easier it is for an entrepreneur to foresee what might happen. Budgets add discipline because of their orderliness and detail.

Budgeting Highlights Potential Problems

Using budgeting to describe a company's plans allows the entrepreneur to uncover potential problems before they occur and to spot omissions or inconsistencies in the plans. For example, you and Anna may plan for Sweet Temptations to sell more boxes of chocolates in February than during other months because of expected Valentine's Day sales. Through the budgeting process, you may discover that unless something changes, Sweet Temptations will not have enough boxes of chocolates on hand in February to fill the expected customer orders. By seeing this problem ahead of time, you and Anna can adjust your purchase plans, perhaps preventing disappointed customers from having to go elsewhere to buy candy.

If you and Anna decide to purchase more chocolates in January and February because of expected increases in sales, Sweet Temptations will also have a higher bill from

THE FAR SIDE By GARY LARSON

Early business failures

©1985. Far Works, Inc./Distributed by Universal Press Syndicate. Reprinted with permission.

How do you think a business plan could have helped this company?

Unlimited Decadence. You and Anna will have to plan to have enough cash on hand to pay the bill when it is due. This plan will show up in the part of the budget that shows expected *purchases.* The budgeting process helps the entrepreneur see and evaluate how changes in plans affect different parts of a company's operations.

Budgeting Quantifies Plans

Business plans include the operating activities needed to meet the company's goals. A budget quantifies, or expresses in numbers, these operating activities and goals. For example, most companies have a goal of earning a specific profit for the budget year. This is stated in their business plans. Recall from Chapter 3 that Sweet Temptations included in its business plan a goal of earning a profit of $110 per month, or $1,320 ($110 × 12) during the coming year. The C-V-P analysis included in the business plan in Chapter 3 indicates that to earn this profit, Sweet Temptations must have monthly sales averaging 720 boxes of chocolates, so during the year it must sell at least 8,640 boxes (720 × 12) of chocolates. Sweet Temptations' budget will indicate how many boxes of chocolates it plans to sell each month of the year to meet its profit goal and how many boxes it must purchase each month to support its projected sales.

Budgeting also quantifies the resources that the company expects to use for its planned sales and purchasing activities. For example, if Sweet Temptations must purchase 900 boxes of chocolates to cover its expected sales for any given month, the budget will indicate how much (and when) Sweet Temptations expects to pay for these chocolates.

Budgeting Creates Benchmarks

Since budgets help quantify plans, an entrepreneur also uses budgets as "benchmarks." The entrepreneur periodically compares the results of the company's actual operating activities with the related budget amounts. These comparisons measure the company's progress toward achieving its goals and help the entrepreneur evaluate how efficiently the company is using its resources. The comparisons also help the entrepreneur focus on what changes should be made, if any, to bring the company's operating activities more in line with its goals. To save time and effort, the entrepreneur uses a management principle known as **management by exception.** Under this principle, the entrepreneur focuses on improving the activities that show significant differences (or exceptions) between budgeted and actual results. These activities have the greatest potential for positively influencing the company's operations.

Operating Cycles

Earlier, we referred to the operating activities of a company. The operating activities of a company depend on whether it is a retail, service, or manufacturing company because each of these different types of companies has a different operating cycle. In budgeting, a company quantifies its planned activities in relation to its operating cycle. This process is similar to when you prepare your personal budget for the semester. Before we get into the details of budgeting, we will briefly discuss the operating cycles of retail and service companies. We will discuss the operating cycle of a manufacturing company in Chapter 12.

2 *Do the activities of a company have a logical order that drives the organization of a budget?*

The Operating Cycle of a Retail Company

A **retail company's operating cycle** is the average time it takes the company to use cash to buy goods for sale (called inventory), to sell these goods to customers, and to collect cash from its customers. Sweet Temptations' operating cycle is the time it takes to pay cash to purchase boxes of chocolates from Unlimited Decadence, to sell these chocolates to customers, and to collect the cash from the customers. Unlimited Decadence allows Sweet Temptations to "charge" its purchases of boxes of chocolates. From Sweet Temptations' point of view, these are called *credit purchases* and result in *accounts payable.* Similarly, although most of Sweet Temptations' sales are cash sales, it also allows some of its customers to "charge" their purchases of chocolates. (These purchases are made on "charge accounts" set up directly between the customers and Sweet Temptations; they are not made on charge cards such as VISA or Discover.) From Sweet Temptations' point of view, sales to these customers are called *credit sales* and result in *accounts receivable.*

 From the customers' point of view, what do you think Sweet Temptations' credit sales to them are called?

Sweet Temptations will pay cash for its accounts payable to Unlimited Decadence within 30 days of the purchases. Similarly, Sweet Temptations will collect cash from customers' accounts receivable within a few days after their purchases of chocolates. We will talk more about how a company decides to extend credit to customers later in this chapter and in Chapter 9.

Exhibit 4-1 shows Sweet Temptations' operating cycle. As you will see later, Sweet Temptations' budgeting process quantifies its operating cycle and its other activities.

The Operating Cycle of a Service Company

Service companies have a budgeting process that is very similar to that of retail companies. One major difference between these two types of companies, however, involves their operating cycles. A **service company's operating cycle** is the average time it takes the company to use cash to acquire supplies and services, to sell the services to customers, and to collect cash from its customers.

Exhibit 4-2 shows the operating cycle of Hasty Transfer Company, a shipping company hired by Unlimited Decadence to ship its chocolates to Sweet Temptations and other retail companies around the country. This operating cycle may be shorter than that of a retail company because there is no inventory to purchase.

The operating cycle for some service companies can be much longer than the cycle for most retail companies because for these service companies, one service, or job, can take months or years. For example, think about the life of some of the advertising campaigns you have observed recently. For instance, the Energizer Bunny (batteries) and Tony the Tiger (cereal) have been around for years. Many service companies with long jobs try to shorten their operating cycles by periodically collecting payments from their customers for completed segments of the work. Hasty Transfer's operating cycle, on the other hand,

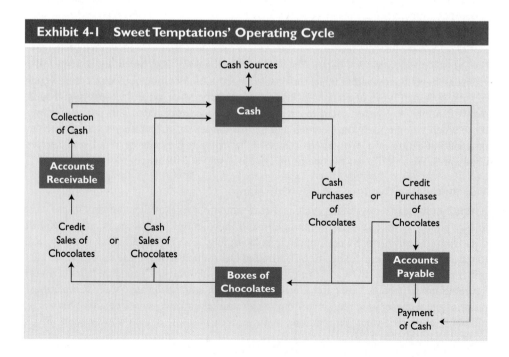

Exhibit 4-1   Sweet Temptations' Operating Cycle

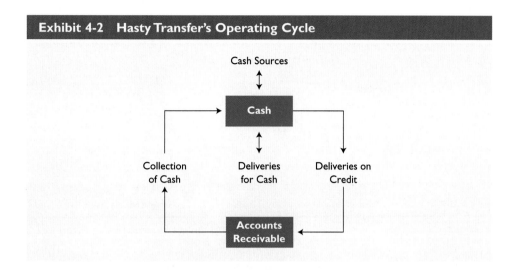

Exhibit 4-2   Hasty Transfer's Operating Cycle

could average only two or three days, since it delivers perishable candy to companies in the same city in which Unlimited Decadence's factory is located and also to companies around the country. The length of Hasty Transfer's operating cycle depends on Hasty's collection policies and when it expects to be paid by its customers. Like Sweet Temptations, Hasty Transfer quantifies its operating cycle and other activities in a budget.

 How long do you think a university's or college's operating cycle is? What are the components of its operating cycle?

The Budget as a Framework for Planning

Budgeting is most useful in decision-making when it is organized to show different aspects of operations. The master budget is the overall structure a company uses to organize its budgeting process. A **master budget** is a set of interrelated reports (or budgets) showing the relationships among a company's (1) goals to be met, (2) activities to be performed in its operating cycle, (3) resources to be used, and (4) expected financial results. A company includes the master budget with the C-V-P analysis in the financial plan section of its business plan.

The individual budgets in the master budget may be different from company to company. These differences are due to the number of different products each company sells, the varying sizes and complexities of the companies, operations, and whether the companies are retail, service, or manufacturing companies. Regardless of the differences, each master budget describes the relationships between a company's goals, activities, resources, and results.

A master budget for a retail company usually includes the following budgets and projected financial statements:

3 *What is the structure of the budgeting process, and how does a company begin that process?*

1. Sales budget

2. Purchases budget

3. Selling expenses budget

4. General and administrative expenses budget

5. Cash budget

6. Projected income statement

7. Projected balance sheet

The "Tony the Tiger" advertising campaign has been around for decades. Do you think the agency's operating cycle is *that* long?

4 *What are the similarities and differences between a retail company's master budget and a service company's master budget?*

www.jcpenney.com

A service company's master budget does not include a purchases budget and usually combines the expenses budgets. A manufacturing company's master budget includes additional budgets related to its manufacturing activities. A company prepares its master budget for a year or more into the future. It breaks the master budget down by each budget period—generally a quarter (three-month period). Within each quarter, it shows the budget information on a monthly basis. Some companies develop budgets for each department which they then combine to form a master budget. For example, JCPenney might develop budgets for apparel, for housewares, for bed and bath accessories, for optical departments, and for styling salons.

Exhibit 4-3 shows (with arrows) the important relationships among the reports in Sweet Temptations' master budget. We will discuss the nature and the relationships of Sweet Temptations' budgets to illustrate how a retail company plans and describes its operating activities. Since Sweet Temptations is a small company, the illustrations will be simple. The larger a company is, the more complex and detailed its budget reports must be to be useful. Often, though, managers of large companies prepare summaries similar to the simpler budgets that we use in this chapter.

When you look at the budgets for Sweet Temptations, try to understand the logic of their development and how they interrelate. As you study the budgets, remember the following "start-up" information from Chapter 3. During December 1999 Anna plans to

▶ invest $15,000 in Sweet Temptations,

▶ rent store space for $1,000 per month, paying $6,000 in advance for six months' rent,

▶ buy $1,800 of store equipment by making a $1,000 down payment and signing a note payable for the remaining amount,

▶ order 360 boxes of chocolates from Unlimited Decadence for $1,620, to be paid for in January 2000,

▶ purchase and pay for $700 of supplies.

For each budget, we will also briefly discuss the similar budget for Hasty Transfer, a service company.

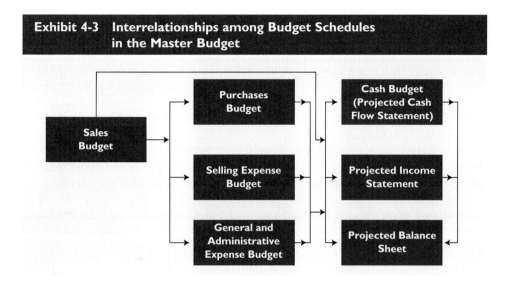

Exhibit 4-3 Interrelationships among Budget Schedules in the Master Budget

The Sales Budget

The budgeting process begins with the sales budget because product sales or service contracts affect all the other operating activities of a company. (Without sales of chocolates, why would Sweet Temptations be in business? Without arrangements with Unlimited Decadence and other companies to ship chocolates and other goods, why would Hasty Transfer exist?) A retail company without sales would not need employees, inventory, retail space, store equipment, supplies, advertising, or utilities. As you will soon see, the same is true for a service company. For this reason, the sales budget affects all of the other budgets.

The Retail Company's Sales Budget

For a retail company, the **sales budget** shows the number of units of inventory that the company expects to sell each month, the related monthly sales revenue, and in which months the company expects to collect cash from these sales. To estimate the number of units of inventory it will sell in each month, a company gathers various types of information, such as past sales data, industry trends, and economic forecasts. If Sweet Temptations were an older company, you and Anna might analyze Sweet Temptations' past sales trends to get an idea about what sales level to expect for the future. However, you should also consider the current economic conditions or circumstances that affect the candy industry.

For example, if the economy has worsened and people are struggling to get food on the table, customers may view the purchase of chocolates as a luxury, and sales may drop, regardless of the level of past sales. On the other hand, if the economy is improving, people may have extra income to spend (extra disposable income), and sales of candy may increase. New findings and breakthroughs also can affect sales. For example, in 1995, Ross-Abbott Labs manufactured and helped test a cholesterol-lowering candy bar called a Cardiobar. Volunteers who tested the cardiobars, which come in chocolate and raspberry flavors, lowered their cholesterol level by 33 points! Those who ate look-alike candy bars had no significant change in their cholesterol levels. When the candy bars "hit the market," their sales may affect the sales of other candy bars already on the market.[1]

5 *After a company begins the budgeting process, is there a strategy it can use to complete the budget?*

www. abbott.com

 How do you think a well-publicized discovery that sugar is actually good for people would affect your prediction of candy sales for next year?

---

[1]"Anti-Cholesterol Cardiobar Takes the Hard out of Arteries," *Columbia Missourian*, November 14, 1995, 2A.

Market analysts or consultants are another source of information about the estimated number of products to be sold. Although Anna has a marketing degree, she is busy getting the company "up and running." Therefore, she has hired Joe Smiley (see Exhibit 3-2) to study the market for boxed chocolates in the area north of the metroplex and provide an analysis, including a report on the effect that different prices would have on potential sales of the chocolates. Joe's research should help Anna predict sales during Sweet Temptations' first year of operations. Large companies have additional sources of market information, including their sales forces as well as marketing and advertising specialists. We will discuss the sources in Chapter 12.

After a company has estimated the amount of inventory it expects to sell, it determines its estimated sales revenue by multiplying the number of units of inventory it expects to sell by the unit selling price. After computing its monthly estimated sales revenue, the company determines how much cash it expects to collect each month from sales. If all sales are cash sales, the cash to be collected each month is equal to the sales revenue of that month. For most companies, however, a portion (sometimes substantial) of their sales are credit sales. If a company allows credit sales, its cash collections of accounts receivable will lag behind its sales revenues.

 What do you think is the difference between cash sales and sales revenue? Are they the same thing?

The credit-granting policy of a company can have a great impact on the length of time between the sale of its product and the collection of cash from that sale. You and Anna would certainly not grant credit to a customer with a poor credit history because there would be a good chance that the customer either will pay you a long time after the sale, pay you only part of the bill, or not pay you at all. Many companies spend a lot of time and effort studying the paying habits of their customers and deciding on an appropriate credit-granting policy. The goal is to shorten the time between sales and collections of cash, and reduce the risk of not being able to collect from their customers. At the same time, companies don't want an overly restrictive credit policy that discourages customers from buying on credit.

 What information about a customer do you think would be helpful in Sweet Temptations' decision of whether or not to grant the customer credit?

Anna has decided to grant credit to a few nearby companies, hoping they will make numerous purchases. To start, Anna estimates that these credit sales will be about 5 percent of total sales. She has also decided to give these credit customers terms of n/10 ("net 10"), which means that they will pay Sweet Temptations within ten days of when they make credit purchases. Anna selected n/10 because Sweet Temptations is a new company and she does not think it should wait more than ten days to receive cash from its credit customers. Because of this policy, Sweet Temptations will collect roughly two-thirds of each month's credit sales in the month of the sales and the remaining one-third of the credit sales in the following month.

Exhibit 4-4 shows the relationship between Sweet Temptations' January credit sales and its cash collections from these sales. This diagram shows that the sales revenue is earned at the time of the credit sale. However, the cash collection from the credit sale occurs ten days after the sale takes place. As you can see in the exhibit, cash collections from January credit sales occur partly in January and partly in February. For instance, the cash collections from the January 1 credit sales occur on about January 11, and the cash collections from the credit sales on January 31 occur on about February 10.

Exhibit 4-5 shows the sales budget of Sweet Temptations for the first quarter of 2000. The sales amounts are based on Joe Smiley's market analysis. Notice that it shows budgeted sales for each month both in units (boxes of chocolates) and in dollars of sales revenue, and that the monthly sales amounts are added across to show the quarter totals (2,460 units; $24,600 sales revenue). Also notice that the sales budget divides total sales each month between cash sales and credit sales.

Exhibit 4-4 Relationship between Credit Sales and Cash Collections

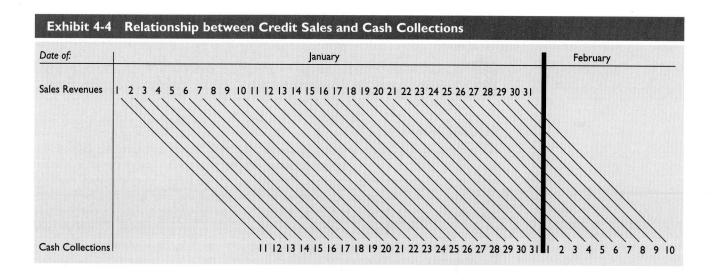

Exhibit 4-5 Sales Budget

Sweet Temptations
Sales Budget
First Quarter 2000

	January	February	March	Quarter
Budgeted total unit sales				
(boxes of chocolates)	720	1,200	540	2,460
Budgeted selling price per box	$ 10	$ 10	$ 10	$ 10
Budgeted total sales revenue	$7,200	$12,000	$5,400	$24,600
Budgeted cash sales				
(95% of total sales revenue)	$6,840	$11,400	$5,130	$23,370
Budgeted credit sales				
(5% of total sales revenue)	360	600	270	1,230
Budgeted total sales revenue	$7,200	$12,000	$5,400	$24,600
Expected cash collections:				
From cash sales	$6,840	$11,400	$5,130	$23,370
From January credit sales	240[a]	120[a]		360
From February credit sales		400[a]	200[a]	600
From March credit sales			180[a]	180
Total cash collections	$7,080	$11,920	$5,510	$24,510

[a]Sweet Temptations estimates that it will collect two-thirds of each month's credit sales during the month of sale. It will collect the remaining one-third in the month following the sale.

 How do you think dividing total monthly sales between cash sales and credit sales helps in the creation of the rest of the sales budget?

The Service Company's Sales Budget

The sales budget of a service company is very similar to the sales budget of a retail company, except that the former is selling services rather than products. When Hasty Transfer budgets its sales, it is budgeting sales of delivery services. Expected cash collections from customers depend on Hasty's collection policies. For example, Hasty may expect to be paid by its customers when it picks up merchandise the customers want to ship. On the other hand, Hasty may expect to be paid by its customers only after it delivers the customers' merchandise. Furthermore, Hasty may grant credit to some of its customers—a policy that also will affect the timing of its cash receipts.

 A new airline called Air South began flying from Jacksonville, Florida, to Atlanta, Georgia, in January 1995. The fare for the trip at that time was $19 plus a 32-cent stamp. How do you think Air South budgeted its cash receipts? How do you think Air South is doing now?

Seasonal Sales

Some companies' sales occur evenly throughout the year. Other companies experience *seasonal sales.* That is, these companies' customers purchase the inventory or services more often in some months than in others. The sale of ski apparel is an example of seasonal sales. Although ski shops sell some ski apparel throughout the year, most of their sales occur right before and during ski season. A company offering skiing lessons (a service) may not even be open during the summer. The sale of candy is not as extreme, but it does have some seasonality. For Sweet Temptations, monthly sales differences during its first quarter reflect an expected increase in sales as Valentine's Day approaches.

 What other seasonal effects would you expect for Sweet Temptations?

The Retail Company's Purchases Budget

Once a company has estimated (budgeted) its unit sales for each month of the quarter, it can determine the best approach for purchasing the needed inventory. Sweet Temptations expects to sell 2,460 boxes of chocolates this quarter (from the sales budget in Exhibit 4-5). You may be wondering how many of those boxes Sweet Temptations should be ordering now. In making this purchase decision, you should consider several factors.

First, there are the costs of keeping the company's money invested in inventory (rather than investing it somewhere else), of storing and handling inventory, and of paying for insurance and taxes on inventory. Higher inventory levels also increase the risk of theft, damage, and obsolescence. If Sweet Temptations holds too many boxes of chocolates, you and Anna risk either selling chocolates that are not fresh and losing future customers, or having to throw away old chocolates. (Or, with more chocolates around, you may be more tempted to eat the inventory!) Also, there is a physical limit to the number of boxes you can stock in the candy store. For these reasons, some companies use "just-in-time" (JIT) inventory systems, in which they purchase inventory a day before they need it. We will discuss JIT inventory systems in Chapter 18.

On the other hand, it also can be very expensive not to carry enough inventory. For example, if Sweet Temptations starts running low on chocolates, it may have to pay Hasty Transfer higher shipping costs for rush orders or pay Unlimited Decadence higher costs per box for smaller, last-minute orders. You may also risk alienating customers if you run out of inventory. Every company must plan its own inventory levels, considering the costs of both carrying and not carrying inventory and trying to keep the combined total at the lowest possible amount. We will discuss this planning decision more fully in Chapter 15. Even though the purchases budget does not address all of the above factors, it will help you and Anna make the best purchase decision.

The **purchases budget** shows the purchases (in units) required in each month to make the expected sales (from the sales budget) in that month and to keep inventory at desired levels. It also shows the costs of these purchases and the expected timing and amount of the cash payments for these purchases.

Frequently, companies set desired end-of-month inventory levels at either a constant percentage of the following month's budgeted unit sales or at large enough levels to meet future sales for a specified time. Since many companies base their purchase orders on sales *estimates,* they want to have extra inventory available to sell in case they have underestimated their sales or in case their next shipment of inventory arrives later than expected.

Anna plans to order chocolates from Unlimited Decadence once every month. She has also decided that during any month, Sweet Temptations should have enough candy on hand to cover that month's candy sales and also to maintain an ending inventory large enough to cover one-half of the next month's sales. For example, projected sales for the first quarter of 2000 (from the sales budget in Exhibit 4-5) and for April (from projections for the second quarter) are as follows:

	January	February	March	April
Budgeted total unit sales (boxes of chocolates)	720	1,200	540	900

Based on Anna's purchasing policy, Sweet Temptations must have enough inventory during January to equal budgeted sales for January plus one-half of budgeted sales for February, or 1,320 boxes of chocolates [720 boxes + ½ (1,200)]. (Then, if Sweet Temptations sells 720 boxes during January, it will have inventory at the end of January equal to half of February's budgeted sales.) Since Sweet Temptations will start business in January with the 360 boxes of chocolates purchased in December (½ of the 720 January budgeted sales), January purchases must be 960 boxes (1,320 total boxes needed −360 boxes already on hand). Sweet Temptations uses the same calculations to determine each month's purchases of boxes of chocolates. Exhibit 4-6 illustrates how budgeted purchases and budgeted sales are linked together for the first quarter of the year.

 What do you think are the advantages of Anna's plans to order chocolates once per month rather than more often?

Normally, Sweet Temptations will make purchases during the first week of each month and will receive delivery of the purchases at the beginning of the second week of the month. However, since Sweet Temptations will open for business in January, it must purchase 360 boxes of chocolates in mid-December so that they will be available to sell on the first day of business in January. No sales of chocolates will occur in December, so the amount of chocolates that Sweet Temptations purchases in December will still be in Sweet Temptations' inventory at the end of December (and at the beginning of January).

Exhibit 4-7 shows the purchases budget of Sweet Temptations for the first quarter of 2000. Remember that Sweet Temptations wants to purchase enough boxes of chocolates each month to meet budgeted sales during the month and to have enough boxes left at the end of the month to cover one-half of the next month's sales. These boxes must come from the inventory on hand at the beginning of the month and from any purchases that the

---

Exhibit 4-6   The Link between Budgeted Purchases and Budgeted Sales

	December	January	February	March	April
		First Quarter 2000			
Budgeted Sales[a]		720 boxes	1,200 boxes	540 boxes	900 boxes
		× ½ × ½	× ½ × ½	× ½ × ½	× ½
		360 360	+ 600 600	+ 270 270	+450
Budgeted Purchases	360 boxes	960 boxes	870 boxes	720 boxes	
	December	January	February	March	April
		First Quarter 2000			

[a]From Exhibit 4-5, except April which was estimated as part of second quarter projections.

Exhibit 4-7 Purchases Budget

Sweet Temptations
Purchases Budget
First Quarter 2000

	January	February	March	Quarter
Budgeted total unit sales (boxes of chocolates)	720	1,200	540	2,460
Add: Desired ending inventory of boxes of chocolates[a]	600	270	450[b]	450[c]
Total boxes of chocolates required	1,320	1,470	990	2,910
Less: Beginning inventory of boxes of chocolates[d]	(360)[e]	(600)	(270)	(360)[f]
Budgeted purchases of boxes of chocolates	960	870	720	2,550
Purchase price per box of chocolates	$ 4.50	$ 4.50	$ 4.50	$ 4.50
Cost of purchases	$4,320	$3,915	$3,240	$11,475
Cash payments for purchases	$1,620[e]	$4,320	$3,915	$ 9,855

[a] The desired ending inventory is 1/2 of next month's budgeted sales.
[b] April's budgeted sales are 900 boxes of chocolates.
[c] The desired ending inventory at the end of the quarter is the same as the desired ending inventory at the end of March (which is the end of the quarter).
[d] The beginning inventory is the same as the previous month's ending inventory.
[e] 360 boxes of chocolates, at a total purchase price of $1,620, ordered in December 1999 to prepare for the start of business.
[f] The quarter's beginning inventory is the same as December's ending inventory (January's beginning inventory).

company makes during the month. By subtracting the budgeted beginning inventory from the total inventory required for any given month, you can determine how many purchases (in boxes) to budget for that month. Since purchases are a *variable* cost, the cost of boxes of chocolates purchased is determined by multiplying the number of boxes by $4.50 per unit. Since Sweet Temptations has an agreement with Unlimited Decadence to pay for its purchases within 30 days after the purchases, the payment for each month's purchase is budgeted for the following month. For instance, the budgeted January purchase of 960 boxes of chocolates costing $4.50 per box amounts to a total purchase cost of $4,320, which is budgeted to be paid in February.

Companies that purchase their inventories from suppliers in other countries sometimes pay for their purchases in the other countries' currencies (yen or pesos rather than dollars, for example). These companies should budget their purchases in dollars, however. Suppose, for example, that Sweet Temptations purchased boxes of chocolates from a Belgian company instead of from Unlimited Decadence. Since Belgium is a member of the European Union that uses a currency called a *euro,* Sweet Temptations would have to convert euros to dollars when preparing its purchases budget.

Remember that budgets represent a company's *plans* and are based on estimates. As new information becomes available, the company sometimes changes its plans.

 Suppose that January sales turn out to be 1,010 boxes of chocolates. Should Sweet Temptations change its plans for February and March? What questions should you ask before deciding whether the plans should change, which part of the plans should change, and by how much?

The Retail Company's Selling Expenses Budget

To sell its inventory, a retail company must engage in selling activities. The **selling expenses budget** shows the expenses and related cash payments associated with planned selling activities. Examples of selling expenses include salespeople's salaries and commissions, store rent, and advertising. Each of these expenses directly relates to sales.

A selling expenses budget is developed by reviewing past selling expenses (if they are available) and then adjusting them for current plans. It is important for the entrepreneur to understand prior cost behavior patterns when creating a selling expenses budget because some selling expenses are *variable* and change directly with the amount of inventory sold whereas some remain *fixed* regardless of the sales volume. By applying these behavior patterns, the entrepreneur can predict what each selling expense will be at a given estimated sales volume. Sales commissions are an example of variable selling expenses, since total sales commissions increase in direct proportion to increases in sales. Store rent and advertising, on the other hand, are fixed selling expenses, in many cases, because total rent and advertising expenses stay the same as sales increase during the period. In developing a selling expenses budget, the entrepreneur should also be able to distinguish selling expenses from general and administrative expenses. Sometimes fixed expenses must be allocated on a reasonable basis between the two types of expenses.

Exhibit 4-8 shows the selling expenses budget for Sweet Temptations for the first quarter of 2000. The January expenses are the same items listed in Exhibit 3-6 in Chapter 3. These expenses are all *fixed* expenses, so Sweet Temptations expects them to be the same in all three months. (Remember, though, that selling expenses also can be variable expenses.) Not all the *amounts* from Exhibit 3-6 are related to selling activities, however. You and Anna have estimated that three-fourths of each of the following expenses is tied directly to selling activities. The other one-fourth of each expense is tied to the administrative activities of Sweet Temptations and will be included in the general and administrative expenses budget. These expenses are allocated to the selling expenses budget as follows:

Exhibit 4-8   Selling Expenses Budget

	Sweet Temptations *Selling Expenses Budget* *First Quarter 2000*			
	January	February	March	Quarter
Budgeted selling expenses:[a]				
Rent expense	$ 750.00	$ 750.00	$ 750.00	$2,250.00
Salaries expense	1,537.50	1,537.50	1,537.50	4,612.50
Consulting expense	150.00	150.00	150.00	450.00
Advertising expense	305.00	305.00	305.00	915.00
Supplies expense	22.50	22.50	22.50	67.50
Depreciation expense:				
Store equipment	15.00	15.00	15.00	45.00
Telephone and utility				
expense	187.50	187.50	187.50	562.50
Total budgeted selling				
expenses	$2,967.50	$2,967.50	$2,967.50	$8,902.50
Budgeted cash payments for				
selling expenses[b]	$2,180.00	$2,180.00	$2,180.00	$6,540.00

[a]Exhibit 3-6 shows Sweet Temptations' projected expenses for the month of January. Since these are *fixed* expenses, they are expected to be the same for February and March.

[b]The $787.50 ($2,967.50 − $2,180) difference between the total budgeted selling expenses and budgeted cash payments for selling expenses each month occurs because the expenses for rent, supplies, and depreciation ($750 + $22.50 + $15) relate to Sweet Temptations' planned December expenditures for rent, supplies, and equipment. They are not counted again as cash payments.

Rent	$1,000 × 3/4 = $ 750.00
Salaries	$2,050 × 3/4 = $1,537.50
Consulting	$ 200 × 3/4 = $ 150.00
Supplies	$ 30 × 3/4 = $ 22.50
Telephone and utilities	$ 250 × 3/4 = $ 187.50

Like the purchases budget, the selling expenses budget includes a schedule of budgeted cash payments for each month in the budget period. The company's payment policies and how they apply to the individual expenses determine the budgeted cash payments.

For now, Sweet Temptations' payment policy is to pay for all of its expenses (except rent, supplies, and depreciation) in the month in which they occur. However, if its policy were to make payments in the month following the expenses, the cash payment schedule of the selling expenses budget would resemble the cash collection schedule illustrated in the sales budget in Exhibit 4-5. Notice that there is a $787.50 ($2,967.50 − $2,180) difference between the budgeted total selling expenses each month and the budgeted monthly cash payments for these expenses. This is because Sweet Temptations expects to pay cash in advance for six months' rent, purchase supplies with cash, and make a cash down payment to buy store equipment in December 1999 to get ready to open for business. The $787.50 ($750 rent expense + $22.50 supplies expense + $15 depreciation expense) monthly expenses related to these planned December cash expenditures are not counted again as planned cash payments in January, February, or March.

The Retail Company's General and Administrative Expenses Budget

For a retail company, the **general and administrative expenses budget** shows the expenses and related cash payments associated with expected activities other than selling. Examples of general and administrative expenses are secretaries' salaries, consulting charges, and the cost of renting office space. To prepare the general and administrative expenses budget, the entrepreneur reviews past expenses (if they are available), identifies them as fixed or variable, and adjusts them for current plans.

Exhibit 4-9   General and Administrative Expenses Budget

Sweet Temptations
General and Administrative Expenses Budget
First Quarter 2000

	January	February	March	Quarter
Budgeted general and administrative expenses[a]:				
Rent expense	$ 250.00	$ 250.00	$ 250.00	$ 750.00
Salaries expense	512.50	512.50	512.50	1,537.50
Consulting expense	50.00	50.00	50.00	150.00
Supplies expense	7.50	7.50	7.50	22.50
Telephone and utilities expense	62.50	62.50	62.50	187.50
Total budgeted general and administrative expenses	$ 882.50	$ 882.50	$ 882.50	$2,647.50
Budgeted cash payments for general and administrative expenses[b]	$ 625.00	$ 625.00	$ 625.00	$1,875.00

[a]Exhibit 3-6 shows Sweet Temptations' projected expenses for the month of January. Since these are fixed expenses, Sweet Temptations expects them to be the same for February and March.
[b]The $257.50 ($882.50 − $625) difference between the total budgeted general and administrative expenses and the budgeted cash payments for these expenses each month occurs because the monthly expenses ($250 + $7.50) related to the planned December cash expenditures for rent and supplies are not counted again as cash payments.

Exhibit 4-9 shows the general and administrative expenses budget for Sweet Temptations for the first quarter of 2000. These expenses are all *fixed* expenses, although general and administrative expenses can also be variable expenses. As we discussed earlier, Sweet Temptations allocates the total of certain monthly expenses between selling activities and general and administrative activities. Recall that you and Anna estimated that one-fourth of each of the expenses is tied directly to administrative activities. The other three-fourths of each is tied to sales activities and appears on the selling expenses budget. These expenses are allocated to the general and administrative expenses budget as follows:

Rent	$1,000 × 1/4 = $250.00
Salaries	$2,050 × 1/4 = $512.50
Consulting	$ 200 × 1/4 = $ 50.00
Supplies	$ 30 × 1/4 = $ 7.50
Telephone and utilities	$ 250 × 1/4 = $ 62.50

Like the selling expenses budget, the general and administrative expenses budget includes a schedule of budgeted cash payments for each month in the budget period. These cash payments are determined according to the company's payment policies. Sweet Temptations plans to pay for all the expenses listed on the general and administrative expenses budget in the month they occur except for rent and supplies, which it paid for in December.

The Service Company's Expenses Budget

Service companies do not have a purchases budget for inventory, since they are selling a service rather than a product. Also, they usually do not divide their budgeted expenses into two different budgets, one for selling expenses and one for general and administrative expenses. Instead, in budgeting expenses, service companies simply prepare an "operating expenses" budget.

Remember that our discussion of cost behaviors in Chapter 3 noted that variable costs vary in total in direct proportion to volume. "Volume" can refer to a variety of activities. One measure of volume used by retail companies is number of unit sales. Because they are selling a service, though, service companies are very labor-intensive. Salaries are a major expense for these companies, and many of their other expenses vary with the number of hours that the employees work. Therefore, many service companies use the number of hours that employees work as a measure of volume. Regardless, service companies have many of the same fixed expenses that retail companies have, such as rent and advertising.

Cash Management and the Cash Budget

The way a company manages its cash can make the difference between success and failure. Cash management involves keeping an eye on the company's cash balance to make sure that

1. there is enough cash on hand to pay for planned operations during the current period,

2. there is a "cash buffer" on hand, and

3. there is not too much cash on hand.

An insufficient cash balance can cause a problem for a company. Without enough cash, a company will have trouble operating at a normal level and paying its bills. In the most extreme case, an entrepreneur will not be able to operate the company at all because it will have gone out of business. Therefore, a good entrepreneur is always looking for long- and short-term financing sources, such as lines of credit at a bank that allow the company to borrow money "as needed" and loan guarantees from government agencies such as the U.S. Small Business Administration. A good entrepreneur also watches the company's cash balance to determine when to pay back the financing. We will discuss short-term financing again in Chapter 14 and long-term financing in Chapter 22.

www.sba.gov

A cash buffer means having some extra cash on hand (or available through a line of credit) to cover normal, but unexpected, events. For example, an unexpected surge in candy sales would cause Sweet Temptations to have to purchase more inventory than planned. A cash buffer would help cover that purchase. A company's insurance policy would usually cover abnormal and unexpected events such as natural disasters or fires.

Too much cash on hand may seem like an odd problem to have because almost everyone would like to have more cash. An excessive cash balance is a problem for a company, though, because this cash balance is not productive. That is, cash earns nothing for the company unless the company invests it internally in profitable projects, or externally in an interest-bearing account or in government or business securities that earn dividends or interest. Therefore, a successful entrepreneur continually watches for good investment opportunities—even short-run opportunities. We will discuss short-term and long-term investments in Chapter 23.

The Retail Company's Cash Budget

The **cash budget** shows the company's expected cash receipts and payments, and how they affect the company's cash balance. The cash budget is very important in cash management. It helps the entrepreneur anticipate cash shortages, thus avoiding the problems of having too little cash on hand to operate and to pay its bills. This budget also helps the company avoid having excess cash that could be better used for profitable projects or investments.

Besides helping the entrepreneur anticipate cash shortages and excesses, the cash budget can also help external users. For example, a potential lender (such as a bank) may want to evaluate the company's cash budget to see how the company plans to use the borrowed cash and to anticipate when the company will have enough cash to repay the loan.

A cash budget is similar in many respects to the cash flow statement we discussed in Chapter 1. However, the cash budget shows the cash receipts (inflows) and cash payments (outflows) that the company *expects* as a result of its plans, whereas the cash flow statement reports the company's *actual* cash receipts and payments. Like the cash flow statement (see Exhibit 1-9), a cash budget may have three sections: it always has an *operating activities* section, and if the company plans for investing or financing activities, the cash budget will have separate *investing activities* and *financing activities* sections.

The **operating activities section** of the cash budget summarizes the cash receipts and payments the company expects as a result of its planned operations. These expected cash flows come from the sales, purchases, and expenses budgets we discussed earlier. This section also shows the net cash inflows (excess of cash receipts over cash payments) or the net cash outflows (excess of cash payments over cash receipts) expected from operations. Adding the net cash inflows to the beginning cash balance (or subtracting the net cash outflows) results in the expected cash balance from operations at the end of the budget period.

The **investing activities section** of the cash budget—if needed—shows the cash payments and receipts the company expects from planned investing activities. A company's investing activities include, for instance, purchases or sales of land, buildings, and equipment, or investments in the stocks and bonds of governments or other companies.

 Why do you think cash receipts from the sale of land, buildings, and equipment, as well as from dividends received on investments, are included in the investing section of the cash budget?

Although investing activities can occur at any time, companies usually have policies about investing cash balances on hand in excess of a predetermined amount. For instance, based on planned operating activities, Anna has decided that Sweet Temptations should invest any cash on hand in excess of $15,000 in any month.

The **financing activities section** of the cash budget—if needed—shows the cash receipts and payments the company expects from planned financing activities. A company's financing activities include borrowings and repayments of loans, investments by owners, and withdrawals by owners. The cash budget helps a manager decide when financing activities will be necessary. Anna, for example, in considering the need for a cash buffer, has decided that Sweet Temptations will begin financing activities when its cash balance drops below $7,000.

Exhibit 4-10 shows Sweet Temptations' cash budget for the first quarter of 2000. Notice that Sweet Temptations' cash budget summarizes the receipts and payments that you saw in the budgets we discussed earlier. The cash receipts amounts come from the sales budget, and the cash payments amounts come from the purchases budget, the selling expenses budget, and the general and administrative expenses budget. The $7,300 beginning cash balance for January (and the quarter) is Sweet Temptations' cash balance at the end of December, assuming preparations for the start of business go according to plan. The ending cash balance for each month is also the beginning cash balance for the next month.

Sweet Temptations has no investment activities planned for this quarter since the expected cash balances in the first three months of 2000 are not more than $15,000. Also, none of the monthly cash balances during the quarter are less than $7,000, so no financing activities are planned during this quarter. Thus, Sweet Temptations' cash budget does not include an investing activities or a financing activities section. We will discuss planned cash flows from both investing and financing activities in Chapter 12.

The Service Company's Cash Budget

The cash budget of a service company is similar to that of a retail company except that the service company reports cash flow information that is obtained from fewer budgets. In Sweet Temptations' cash budget, information came from the sales, purchases, selling expenses, and general and administrative expenses budgets. A service company's cash budget information, on the other hand, would be obtained from its sales budget and its operating expenses budget. Information from these budgets would be used in the same way that a retail company uses its information to prepare the projected financial statements we discuss in the next sections.

Exhibit 4-10 Cash Budget

Sweet Temptations
Cash Budget
First Quarter 2000

	January	February	March	Quarter
Cash flow from operating activities:				
Cash receipts from sales[a]	$7,080.00	$11,920.00	$ 5,510.00	$24,510.00
Cash payments for:				
Purchases[b]	1,620.00	4,320.00	3,915.00	9,855.00
Selling expenses[c]	2,180.00	2,180.00	2,180.00	6,540.00
General and administrative expenses[d]	625.00	625.00	625.00	1,875.00
Total payments	$4,425.00	$ 7,125.00	$ 6,720.00	$18,270.00
Net cash inflow (outflow) from operations	$2,655.00	$ 4,795.00	($ 1,210.00)	$ 6,240.00
Add: Beginning cash balance	7,300.00	9,955.00	14,750.00	7,300.00
Ending cash balance from operations	$9,955.00	$14,750.00	$13,540.00	$13,540.00

[a]From sales budget (Exhibit 4-5)
[b]From purchases budget (Exhibit 4-7)
[c]From selling expenses budget (Exhibit 4-8)
[d]From general and administrative expenses budget (Exhibit 4-9)

The Projected Income Statement

A **projected income statement** summarizes a company's expected revenues and expenses for the budget period, assuming the company follows its plans. Note that the projected income statement is *not* the same as the cash budget. In Exhibit 4-4, we showed the relationship between sales revenues from credit sales and cash collections from sales. If a company has credit sales, cash receipts occur later than the related sales. The same thing can happen with expenses. Many times, the cash payment for an expense occurs later than the activity that causes the expense. For example, usually employees work before being paid. If the work occurs late in March, the company may not pay the employees until early in April. The projected salaries expense will appear on the projected income statement for the quarter that ends in March (since the work occurred in March), but the projected cash payment will appear on April's cash budget. In other words, timing differences between the operating activities and the related cash receipts and payments cause the differences between the projected income statement and the cash budget. The projected income statement reports on the company's planned operating activities, whereas the cash budget reports on the expected cash receipts and payments related to those activities.

The projected income statement is important because it shows what the company's profit will be if the company follows its plans. At this point in the budgeting process, if the expected profit for the budget period is not satisfactory, the entrepreneur may revise the company's plans to try to increase the profit. In Chapter 3 we discussed how a company uses C-V-P analysis to estimate how some changes in plans will affect its profit. If, as a result of this analysis, the entrepreneur changes the company's plans, then the budgets are changed according to these revised plans.

 What changes do you think an entrepreneur might make in a company's plans to increase its expected profit?

Exhibit 4-11 shows Sweet Temptations' projected income statement for the first quarter of 2000. Sweet Temptations includes this income statement in its business plan. There are three differences between this statement and the income statement[2] for internal decision-makers that we showed in the top part of Exhibit 3-6. First, the income statement in Exhibit 4-11 is for the first *quarter* of 2000. To keep the discussion simple, we showed only the income statement for January in Exhibit 3-6. (If Sweet Temptations had chosen to show an income statement for each month of the first quarter in Exhibit 4-11, the January profits of Exhibits 4-11 and 3-6 would be identical.) Second, in Exhibit 4-11 we group the fixed costs into two categories—selling expenses and general and administrative expenses. In Exhibit 3-6 we listed each expense separately and did not attempt to categorize them. Finally, in Exhibit 4-11 we do not list all the separate expenses because they are shown in the selling expenses and general and administrative expenses budgets.

Notice that the amounts of most of the revenues and expenses in the projected income statement in Exhibit 4-11 come from the budgets we discussed earlier. The variable cost of boxes of candy sold, however, is computed by multiplying the budgeted number of boxes *sold* during the quarter (2,460, from the sales budget in Exhibit 4-5) by Sweet Temptations' cost per box ($4.50, from the purchases budget in Exhibit 4-7). So the cost of boxes of chocolates *sold* that Sweet Temptations listed on its projected income statement is different from the cost of boxes of chocolates *purchased* that Sweet Temptations listed on its purchase budget. This is because the number of boxes sold is different than the number of boxes purchased.

The Projected Balance Sheet

In Chapter 1, we indicated that a balance sheet is a basic financial statement of a company. A balance sheet shows a company's financial position on a particular date. It lists the

---

[2]We could rearrange this income statement so that it would look similar to the income statement for external users that we show in the lower part of Exhibit 3-6. To save space, we do not include the rearranged income statement in Exhibit 4-11.

Exhibit 4-11   Projected Income Statement

Sweet Temptations
Projected Income Statement
For the Quarter Ended March 31, 2000

Total sales revenue		$24,600[a]
Less total variable costs		
Cost of boxes of chocolates sold		(11,070)[b]
Total contribution margin		$13,530
Less total fixed costs:		
Selling expenses	$8,902.50[c]	
General and administrative expenses	2,647.50[d]	
Total fixed costs		(11,550)
Profit		$ 1,980

[a]From the sales budget (Exhibit 4-5).
[b]The 2,460 budgeted total sales in number of boxes (Exhibit 4-5) times the $4.50 cost per box (Exhibit 4-7).
[c]From the selling expenses budget (Exhibit 4-8).
[d]From the general and administrative expenses budget (Exhibit 4-9).

company's assets, liabilities, and owner's equity. In the same way, a **projected balance sheet** summarizes a company's expected financial position at the end of a budget period, assuming the company follows its plans. Usually, a company includes a projected balance sheet in its master budget. Because preparing a projected balance sheet can be complex, we will wait until Chapter 12 to show one. If we did include a projected balance sheet for Sweet Temptations, it would show what resources (assets) Sweet Temptations expects to have, how much it expects to owe its creditors (liabilities), and what it expects Anna's investment (owner's equity) in the assets of the company to be at the end of the quarter.

Using the Master Budget in Evaluating the Company's Performance

Managers of all types of companies use budgets as planning tools. Budgeting is also a valuable tool for *evaluating* how a company, division, department, or team actually performed. By analyzing differences between a company's budgeted results and its actual results, a manager can determine where plans went wrong and where to take corrective action next time.

6 *How can a manager use a budget to evaluate a company's performance and then use the results of that evaluation to influence the company's plans?*

Finding Differences between Actual and Budgeted Amounts

Comparing budgeted amounts to actual results is an important part of the budgeting process. By using the budgets discussed in this chapter as benchmarks, a manager can evaluate the differences between the actual performance of the company and its planned performance. By understanding *why* the differences occurred, a manager can decide what actions to take for future time periods. For example, Exhibit 4-12 shows a comparison (called a **cost report**) between Sweet Temptations' budgeted and actual expenses for the first quarter of 2000. A large company would usually divide its cost report into selling expenses and general and administrative expenses, and also by division, department, manager, product, or some other identifiable unit. This breakdown is not necessary for Sweet Temptations' cost report because it has only a few items.

With a quick glance at this cost report, you can see that Sweet Temptations' actual expenses were $70 greater than budgeted expenses in the first quarter of 2000. You can even see that the negative difference between total planned and actual expenses occurs because the telephone and utility expense as well as the supplies expense were more than expected. However, knowing that there are differences is not enough information for a manager to

Exhibit 4-12 Comparison of Actual vs. Budgeted Amounts

Sweet Temptations Company
Cost Report
For the Quarter Ended March 31, 2000

	Budgeted	Actual	Favorable (Unfavorable) Difference
Rent expense	$ 3,000	$ 3,000	—
Salaries expense	6,150	6,150	—
Consulting expense	600	600	—
Advertising expense	915	915	—
Supplies expense	90	110	$(20)
Depreciation expense	45	45	—
Telephone and utility expense	750	800	(50)
	$11,550	$11,620	$(70)

use in explaining the differences and in planning the next time period's activities. It is at this point in the evaluation process that a manager must use creative and critical thinking skills. A manager can learn about the causes of the differences by asking questions and investigating further. As we discussed in Chapter 2, the answers to these questions will generally lead to additional questions. The cost report gives the manager a starting point from which to begin an investigation.

Learning Why Differences Occur

While analyzing the difference between the budgeted and the actual telephone and utility expense, Anna might ask herself questions such as the following:

1. Which of the monthly telephone and utility bills were higher or lower than expected?

2. Why were these bills different from what was expected? Was there a difference because Sweet Temptations has just begun operations and Anna had no previous experience to use in estimating what the expenses would be?

3. Did the difference occur because of selling activities or because of general and administrative activities (or both)?

4. What other explanations are there for the differences?

    After formulating the questions she wants answered, Anna can devise a strategy to find the answers. Looking for answers will require Anna's creative thinking skills. Suppose she decides to start her investigation by first looking at the monthly telephone and utility bills. If she finds minor differences between planned and actual expenses for all the bills except for the electricity bill, these minor differences can be attributed to her use of estimates. Minor differences from estimates are to be expected, so there would be no need to plan any correcting activities for the future. Suppose, however, that in looking at the electricity bill, Anna discovers that the electric company raised its rate 10 percent since she created the budget. Before planning for the next quarter, Anna must ask another question: Will the same increase be in effect next quarter? If so, Anna will use this information in her future planning and budgeting activities, and the next master budget will include the 10 percent increase in Sweet Temptations' planned electricity expenses.

 What questions do you think Anna should ask about the difference between planned and actual supplies expenses?

A manager can use information from the master budget to help identify the causes of differences between budgeted and actual expenses, and then to decide what to change in the future. As you just saw, an analysis of the causes of these differences may lead an owner or manager to make changes in future budgets. On the other hand, the same analysis may lead the owner or manager to change future activities rather than future budgets. For example, suppose packaging workers at Unlimited Decadence are working overtime repackaging boxes of chocolates because of a sudden decrease in the quality of purchased packaging materials. Because of this unplanned problem, the actual salary expense for Unlimited Decadence will be higher than its budgeted salary expense. An analysis of the cause of this salary difference may lead the packaging manager to look for a new supplier of packaging materials.

Differences between planned and actual expenses can also be positive differences. For example, Sweet Temptations' telephone and utility expense could have been less than the budgeted expense. Suppose Anna based Sweet Temptations' budgeted telephone and utility expense on a well-publicized planned increase in utility rates. If the state Public Utility Commission later turns down the rate increase, Sweet Temptations' actual expense will be less than the budgeted expense. Anna will use this rate information, which she noticed because of her analysis of the difference between the planned and the actual expenses, for her future planning activities. Unless circumstances change between this budget period and the next budget period, Anna will use the old rate to budget Sweet Temptations' utility expense.

At other times, differences between planned and actual results can have both positive and negative consequences. For instance, in 1997 Burger King introduced its "Big King" sandwich as competition against McDonald's "Big Mac" sandwich. In its sales budget, Burger King had estimated that it would sell 1.8 million Big Kings a day. The good news was that the sandwich was so popular that Burger King sold nearly 3 million per day—about 70 percent more than it had expected! The bad news was that since Burger King had budgeted and then made its purchases based on anticipated sales, the *un*anticipated sales quickly caused shortages in Big King sandwiches in many cities causing Burger King to "miss out" on the additional sales.

Do you think Burger King's estimate of Big King sales affected its estimate of sales of french fries?

www.burgerking.com
www.mcdonalds.com

Business Issues and Values

The accounting information included in budgets affects and is affected by business decisions. In using this information for decision-making, entrepreneurs must also consider other, nonfinancial issues. For example, suppose a small new airline has entered a market dominated by a large well-established airline. To effectively compete, the new company determines that it must cut costs. A look at the budget shows that one of the largest costs, and an easy one to reduce, is maintenance costs on the fleet. When making the decision about whether to reduce maintenance costs, the entrepreneur would have to consider whether reducing these costs now would drive up future maintenance costs. But more importantly, the entrepreneur would have to consider the safety of the passengers and crew. In this case, the safety concern may outweigh the financial gain resulting from reducing the maintenance costs.

Summary

At the beginning of the chapter we asked you several questions. During the chapter, we asked you to STOP and answer some additional questions to build your knowledge about specific issues. Be sure you answered these additional questions. Below are the questions from the beginning of the chapter, with a brief summary of the key points relating to the answers. Use your creative and critical thinking skills to expand on these key points to develop more complete answers to the questions and to determine what other questions you have that might lead you to learn more about the issues.

1 How does a budget contribute toward helping a company achieve its goals?

A budget helps a company by giving a financial description of the activities planned by the company to help it achieve its goals. It also helps by adding order to the planning process, by providing an opportunity to recognize and avoid potential operating problems, by quantifying plans, and by creating a "benchmark" for evaluating the company's performance.

2 Do the activities of a company have a logical order that influences the organization of a budget?

Yes, the operating activities of the company make up what is called the company's operating cycle. A company's operating cycle is the average time it takes the company to use cash to buy goods and services, to sell these goods to or perform services for customers, and to collect cash from these customers. The order of activities, and the cash receipts and payments associated with these activities, influence how a company organizes its budget.

3 What is the structure of the budgeting process, and how does a company begin that process?

The master budget is the overall structure used for the financial description of a company's plans. It consists of a set of budgets describing planned company activities, the cash receipts or payments that should result from these activities, and the company's projected financial statements (what the financial statements should look like if the planned activities occur). The budgeting process begins with the sales budget because product or service sales affect all other company activities. By gathering various types of information, such as past sales data, knowledge about customer needs, industry trends, economic forecasts, and new technological developments, a company estimates the amount of inventory (or employee time) to be sold in each budget period. Cash collections from sales are planned by examining the company's credit-granting policies. Cash payments for expenses are planned by examining the company's payment policies.

4 What are the similarities and differences between a retail company's master budget and a service company's master budget?

For a retail company, the master budget usually includes a sales budget, a purchases budget, a selling expenses budget, a general and administrative expenses budget, a cash budget, a projected income statement, and a projected balance sheet. A service company does not have a purchases budget, and it usually has one operating expenses budget.

5 After a company begins the budgeting process, is there a strategy it can use to complete the budget?

Yes. For example, a retail company follows a strategy similar to the following. After budgeting sales, the company plans the amount and timing of inventory purchases. To budget purchases, the company examines the costs associated with inventory purchases and storage as well as the costs of not carrying enough inventory. It also considers its policy on required inventory levels. After budgeting purchases, the company plans the cash payments for inventory purchases by reviewing its payment agreements with suppliers. To budget expenses, the company must first determine the behaviors of these expenses. It budgets fixed expenses by evaluating previous fixed expenses and then adjusting them (if necessary) according to the plans for the coming time period. It budgets variable expenses by first observing what activity causes these expenses to vary and then computing the total expenses by multiplying the cost per unit of activity by the budgeted activity level. For a retail company, the activity level is usually sales. The company budgets the cash payments for these expenses by reviewing the company's policy on the payment of expenses. The information for developing the cash budget comes from the other previously prepared budgets, as does the information for creating the projected income statement.

6 How can a manager use a budget to evaluate a company's performance and then use the results of that evaluation to influence the company's plans?

A manager uses a master budget to evaluate a company's performance by comparing the information in the various budgets with the results that occur after the planned activities are implemented. The manager identifies the differences between budgeted and actual results, and learns about the causes of these differences by asking questions and investigating further. Based on these investigations, a manager may adjust the company's activities and plans, as well as its future budgets.

Key Terms

budget *(p. 86)*

budgeting *(p. 86)*

cash budget *(p. 100)*

cost report *(p. 103)*

financing activities section *(p.100)*

general and administrative expenses budget *(p. 98)*

investing activities section *(p. 100)*

management by exception *(p. 87)*

master budget *(p. 89)*

operating activities section *(p.100)*

projected balance sheet *(p. 103)*

projected income statement *(p. 102)*

purchases budget *(p. 94)*

retail company's operating cycle *(p. 87)*

sales budget *(p. 91)*

selling expenses budget *(p. 97)*

service company's operating cycle *(p. 88)*

Here is an opportunity to gather information on the Internet about real-world issues related to the topics in this chapter. Go to http://www.dryden.com/account and click on the Cunningham, Nikolai, and Bazley book cover. Click on Summary Surfing, then click on this chapter number, and answer the following questions.

▶ Click on **CSB** (Canada/British Columbia Business Service Center). Under *Planning Fundamentals,* click on *Preparing a Cash Flow Forecast.* What is a cash flow forecast, and how does it compare with the cash budget that we discussed in the chapter? What are the three steps involved in preparing a cash flow forecast? How would preparing the budgets discussed in the chapter help an entrepreneur in preparing a cash flow forecast?

S U M M A R Y
S U R F I N G

Integrated Business and Accounting Situations

Answer the Following Questions in Your Own Words

Testing Your Knowledge

4-1   What is it about budgeting that adds discipline to the planning process?

4-2   If a problem comes to light during the budgeting process, what is the manager likely to do?

4-3   "Budgeting serves as a benchmark for evaluation." Explain what that means.

4-4   Describe a master budget. Why might a master budget be different from one company to another?

4-5   How are the master budgets of a retail company and a service company similar to each other? How are they different from each other?

4-6   Describe the operating cycle of a retail company. How are the operating cycles of a retail company and a service company similar to and different from each other?

4-7   Why must the sales budget be developed before any of the other budgets? Where does information for sales forecasts come from?

4-8   If you just finished budgeting sales for next year, what information would you need to be able to budget cash collections from sales?

4-9 How does knowing forecasted sales help a manager develop a purchases budget? What else besides forecasted sales would a manager have to know to complete the purchases budget?

4-10 When developing a selling expenses budget and a general and administrative expenses budget, why do you have to know how expenses behave?

4-11 Why must you complete all the other budgets before you can develop the cash budget?

4-12 Why is it important to know about anticipated cash shortages ahead of time?

4-13 What is a "cash buffer" and what is an example of a circumstance where a company could use a cash buffer?

4-14 Why is having too much cash on hand a problem?

4-15 On the cash budget, why is the beginning cash balance for January the same as the beginning cash balance for the first quarter of the year? Why is the March ending cash balance the same as the first quarter's ending cash balance? How do you determine the first quarter's cash receipts from sales?

4-16 How is the cash budget similar to a cash flow statement? How are they different from each other?

4-17 Why is the cash budget not the same as the projected income statement? What items included on the projected income statement are not included on the cash budget?

4-18 In evaluating a company's performance, why do managers or owners need to learn the causes of differences between actual and budgeted amounts?

Applying Your Knowledge

4-19 Jaime's Hat Shop sells hats with college logos on them; the hats sell for $22 each. This year, Jaime expects to sell 350 hats in May, 300 in June, 420 in July, 800 in August, 1,040 in September, and 750 in October. On average, 25 percent of his customers purchase on credit. Jaime allows those customers to pay for their purchases the month after they have made their purchases.

Required: Prepare a sales budget for Jaime's Hat Shop for the third quarter of this year.

4-20 Refer to 4-19. Company policy is to plan to end each month with an ending inventory equal to 20 percent of the next month's projected sales. Jaime's pays $8 for each hat that it purchases. Jaime and his supplier have an arrangement that allows Jaime's Hat Shop to pay for each purchase 60 days after the purchase.

Required: Prepare a purchases budget for the third quarter of this year for Jaime's Hat Shop.

4-21 Refer to 4-19. Jaime's ended the second quarter of this year with 60 hats on hand.

Required: (1) Notice that Jaime's ended the second quarter with less than 20 percent of projected sales for July. What do you think accounts for the difference?
(2) How many hats should Jaime's purchase in July?

4-22 Refer to 4-19. Jaime's Hat Shop expects to incur the following expenses for each month of the third quarter of this year:

Rent (30% general and administrative, 70% selling)	$1,200
Utilities (30% general and administrative, 70% selling)	600
Advertising	400
Salaries (30% general and administrative, 70% selling)	5,000
Commissions (for each hat sold)	2

In January, Jaime had prepaid the rent for the whole year. Jaime plans to pay for all the other expenses in the month they occur.

Required: (1) Prepare a selling expenses budget for the third quarter of this year.
(2) Prepare a general and administrative expenses budget for the third quarter of this year.

4-23 Refer to 4-19 through 4-22. Jaime's Hat Shop ended June with a cash balance of $10,343.

Required: Prepare a cash budget for the third quarter of this year.

4-24 Refer to 4-19 through 4-22.

Required: Prepare a projected income statement for the third quarter of this year.

4-25 Mark and Lawanda are partners in a new executive search company called Executive Lost and Found. Executive Lost and Found, which begins operations in December, matches the skills of displaced executives (executives who have been laid off) with the needs of companies looking for top managers. Mark estimates that the employees of Executive Lost and Found will spend 1,000 hours in December, 1,400 hours in January, 1,200 hours in February, and 1,450 hours in March working on filling executive positions for Lost and Found's clients. Executive Lost and Found will bill each of its clients at the end of the month, charging $400 per hour spent working for that client during the month. On average, 50% of the billings for any month will be collected during the following month, 30% during the second month following the billing, and 20% during the third month following the billing.

Required: Prepare a sales budget for Executive Lost and Found for the quarter (January through March).

4-26 Butler Company sells a single product for $5 per unit. Sales estimates (in units) for the last four months of the year are as follows:

	Units
September	40,000
October	45,000
November	35,000
December	40,000

All of Butler's sales are credit sales, and it expects to collect each account receivable 15 days after the related sale. Assume that all months have 30 days.

Required: Prepare a sales budget for the last three months of the year, including estimated collections of accounts receivable.

4-27 The sales budget for Merita Medallion Company shows budgeted sales (in medallions) for December and the first four months of next year:

	Medallions
December	100,000
January	40,000
February	90,000
March	150,000
April	50,000

Required: Prepare a budget for the number of medallions Merita needs to purchase in the first three months of next year for each of the following two *independent* situations:

(1) The company's policy is to have inventory on hand at the end of each month equal to 25% of the following month's sales requirement.

(2) The company's policy is to keep each month's ending inventory to a minimum without letting it fall below 5,000 medallions. Assume that the December 1 inventory has 5,000 medallions and that the company's only supplier is willing to sell a maximum of 125,000 medallions to the company per month.

4-28 Top Dog Pet Store sells dog food in 20-pound bags for $10 per bag, which it buys from its supplier for $6 per bag. Top Dog estimates that its sales of bags of dog food for the second quarter of the year will be as follows:

April	1,200 bags
May	1,400
June	1,500

Top Dog's policy is to have bags of dog food on hand at the end of each month equal to 10% of the next month's budgeted sales (bags). It expects to have 120 bags of dog food on hand at the end of March and expects to sell 1,650 bags in July. Top Dog expects its cost of purchases to be $6,660 in March; it pays for its purchases in the following month.

Required: (1) Prepare a purchases budget for bags of dog food for the second quarter of this year for Top Dog

(2) How many bags of dog food did Top Dog expect to sell in March?

4-29 Blanchar Business Machines estimates its monthly selling expenses as follows:

Advertising	$22,000 per month
Sales salaries	$18,000 per month
Sales calls on customers	$35 per machine
Commissions paid to sales personnel	$50 per machine
Delivery	$20 per machine

Assume that Blanchar pays selling expenses in the month after they are incurred. Based on current plans of Blanchar's sales department, monthly sales estimates are as follows: March—70 units, April—90 units, May—100 units, June—110 units.

Required: Prepare a selling expense budget for the *second* quarter for Blanchar Business Machines.

4-30 That Fat Cat Company sells cat food in ten-pound bags for $6.20 per bag. Sales estimates for the first three months of the year are as follows:

January	40,000 bags
February	35,000 bags
March	30,000 bags

December sales were 30,000 bags of cat food. That Fat Cat's desired ending inventory of cat food each month is 30% of the next month's sales estimate (in bags). All sales are cash sales. That Fat Cat purchases bags of cat food at $5.20 per bag and pays for them the month *after* the purchase. General and administrative expenses total $35,000 per month (including $20,000 depreciation), and That Fat Cat pays for these expenses (except for depreciation) in the same month they are incurred. January's current liabilities (all to be paid in January) total $71,500. The company's cash balance on January 1 is $75,000.

Required: Prepare a cash budget for each of the first two months of the year.

4-31 Refer to 4-30.

Required: Prepare a projected income statement for February. How do you explain the differences between the income statement and the cash budget?

Making Evaluations

4-32 Suppose you are a banker, and the controller of a small company asks you for a short-term $10,000 loan, due in 120 days. Interest on the loan would be 12%, due when the loan is paid back. To support his request, he gives you the following information from his company's cash budget for the next quarter:

	January	February	March	Quarter
Cash flow from operations:				
Cash receipts from sales	$20,000	$14,400	$13,600	$48,000
Cash payments for				
Purchases	$15,000	$10,800	$10,200	$36,000
Selling expenses	3,300	3,300	3,300	9,900
General and administrative expenses	1,650	650	650	2,950
Total payments	$19,950	$14,750	$14,150	$48,850
Net cash inflow (outflow) from operations	$ 50	($ 350)	($ 550)	($ 850)
Cash flow from investments:				
Cash receipt from sale of equipment	———	3,000	———	3,000
Net cash inflow (outflow) from operations and investments	$ 50	$ 2,650	($ 550)	$ 2,150
Add: Beginning cash balance	4,880	4,930	7,580	4,880
Ending cash balance from operations and investments	$ 4,930	$ 7,580	$ 7,030	$ 7,030

Required: (1) What is your first reaction?
(2) Before making your decision, what else would you like to know about this company? Can any of what you would like to know be found in any of the company's other budgets or financial statements? What other budgets or

statements would you like the owner to provide for you? What information would you hope to get from each of these budgets or statements?

(3) What other information would help you make your decision?

(4) Can you think of any circumstances in which it would be a good idea to loan this company $10,000?

(5) Depending on the information you are able to get, what other alternatives are there to loaning or not loaning this company $10,000?

4-33 Joe, Billy, Ray, and Bob are business partners who own Joe Billy Ray Bob's Country and Western Wear. Joe Billy Ray Bob's arrangement with all of its clothing suppliers allows it to pay for its merchandise purchases one month after the purchases have been made. About 15% of their customers make purchases on credit. These customers pay for their purchases one month after they have made their purchases. All the partners agree that a bank loan would allow Joe Billy Ray Bob's to revamp the storefront (perhaps causing more customers to want to come inside and shop). The partners are having a disagreement, however, about the cash budget that they plan to include in their loan application package. Joe, Billy, and Bob believe that the budget should be revised to present the bank with the most positive projected cash flows. To accomplish this revision, they are suggesting that on the cash budget, payments for purchases be shown *two* months after the purchases have been made, rather than one month as agreed to by Joe Billy Ray Bob's suppliers. Joe, Billy, and Bob are also suggesting that cash receipts from credit customers be budgeted in the same month as the related sales rather than one month later, even though they expect these customers to wait a month before paying for their purchases. Ray thinks the budget should reflect the partners' actual expectations. The partners have come to you for advice.

Required: (1) What ethical issues are involved in this decision?

(2) If the partners make the revisions, what effect will the revisions have on the sales budget? on the purchases budget? on the cash budget?

(3) Who stands to gain and who stands to lose by this budget revision? Is the gain or loss temporary or permanent, short-term or long-term?

(4) How might the bank be hurt by the changed budget? How might the company be hurt by the changed budget?

(5) Since the budget represents a plan of action, how might the changed budget affect the activities of the company during the budget period?

(6) Are there other alternatives to choose from besides changing the budget or not changing the budget?

(7) What do you recommend that the partners do?

4-34 Assume that a company collects two-thirds of its sales revenue in the month of sale and the remaining one-third in the following month.

Required: How much revenue has the company actually earned in the month of the sale? Should the company record revenue on the income statement in the month when it collects the cash or when the work was done to earn the revenue? What reasons do you have for choosing one alternative over the other? (What are your reasons for not choosing the other alternative?)

4-35 The airline industry is very competitive—management is under constant pressure to improve company profits. Ideas that could improve profits include the following:

(a) Increasing the price of tickets

(b) Reducing the number of flight attendants

(c) Reducing the number of flights on which meals are served

(d) Serving smaller meals or serving snacks instead of meals

(e) Limiting the size of—or eliminating—raises

(f) Reducing the number of baggage handlers

Required: For each of these ideas, describe the effect the idea would have on each of the budgets and on the projected financial statements. What other issues should management consider in deciding whether to implement any of these ideas?

4-36 Bill Morgan is the manager of the sales department of Rise & Shine Company, which sells deluxe bread makers. At the beginning of each month, Bill estimates the total cost of operating the department for the month. At the end of the month he compares the total estimated costs to the total actual costs to determine the "difference." If the difference is "small," he doesn't investigate any further because he prefers to spend his time on "more important" issues.

At the beginning of April, Bill estimated that the total operating costs of the sales department would be $60,500. For April, the actual operating costs were $60,400. At the end of April, Bill says "The sales department is doing pretty well. We came in $100 under budget for the month."

Alice Hoch, the president of the company, has come to you for help. She says "I am concerned that we are not doing enough analysis of our costs, and I need your help. Start with the sales department and prepare for me a 'cost report' to help me review the costs for April. You can have whatever information you need."

Upon investigation, you find the sales department was expected to sell 500 units (bread makers) in April. Based on these projected sales, its budgeted fixed costs were as follows: advertising, $18,000 and salaries, $25,000, while its budgeted variable costs were $25 commission per unit sold and $10 delivery cost per unit sold. You determine that, during April, 500 units were sold and the sales department spent $19,300 for advertising and $22,600 for salaries. It also paid the $25 commission per unit sold and paid $6,000 for delivering the 500 units.

Required: Write a report to the president that (a) includes a cost report for the sales department that compares the budgeted costs to the actual costs for April, (b) identifies the questions you think the president should ask to analyze any differences you find, and (c) suggests some potential answers to the questions.

4-37   Joe Collagen is the president of a small retail company that sells a skin-smoothing lotion and that has been operating for several years. He keeps meticulous records of his actual operating activities, including monthly sales, purchases, and operating expenses, as well as the related cash receipts and payments. However, Joe has never prepared a master budget for the company. He comes to you for help and says, "My profits have been slowly decreasing and I don't know why. Also, sometimes when I least expect it, the company runs short of cash and I have to invest more into it. I've heard that preparing a master budget is a good thing to do, but I don't know what is involved or where to begin."

Required: Prepare a report to the president that explains (a) what budgets and projected financial statements are included in a master budget, and (b) clearly specifies how he would use the information from his previous actual operating activities to develop each of these budgets and the projected income statement.

4-38   Steve and Tammy are thinking of opening a fitness center with facilities for aerobics, weight training, jogging, and lap swimming as well as diet and injury consultation. They plan to buy land and build their facility near the new shopping mall. They want to employ a director, an assistant director, experts to supervise members in each fitness area, and numerous consulting dietitians and sports medicine professionals. They hope to have the entire facility, including an outdoor all-weather track and an indoor swimming pool, completed by the end of the year. They also believe that it will be important to have the facility fully equipped and staffed before they begin taking memberships. Although their estimates indicate that the fitness center can be profitable if they can establish a growing membership over the first five or six years, many small businesses in town have failed because of "cash flow problems" (excess of cash payments over cash receipts). Before committing themselves to this venture, Steve and Tammy have come to you for advice and for help in preparing a cash budget.

Required: Write Steve and Tammy a memo explaining why they might have cash flow problems during their early periods of operations. Show them how they can identify these cash flow problems through careful cash budgeting. Make a few suggestions that might help them reduce such problems if they do decide to open the fitness center.

4-39   Yesterday, you received the following letter for your advice column in the local paper:

Dear Dr. Decisive:

Please help my overly compulsive girlfriend, who even reads your column compulsively. She is on the New Housing Committee of her sorority. (They are planning to build a new house.) Last night, after a great movie, she was telling me that her sorority had to take a budget to the bank in order to get a loan. Then she told me about their budget, and I can't BELIEVE how "nit-picky" it is—and I told her so in those words. Well, the movie was terrific, but the evening turned out to be a disaster. We got into a MAJOR fight, and now she says she doesn't want to go out with me next weekend (not that I want to go out with someone so COMPULSIVE next weekend). Here are the details of what I told her:

1. It doesn't matter that her sorority has a problem collecting dues and rent from its members. The members always pay eventually, and that's all the bank needs to know.

2. It doesn't matter that the electric company plans to raise the utility rate it charges. That's the future—this is now. Her sorority should budget costs that are real (costs they have already experienced), not costs based on the plans of the electric company.

Please explain to her why you agree with me and why these issues will not affect the bank's decision. Maybe she will realize that her compulsion is EXTREME and then we will be able to go out next weekend. I'm just

"Laid Back."

Required: Meet with your Dr. Decisive team and write a response to "Laid Back."

CHAPTER OUTLINE

PART 3

OPERATING, REPORTING, AND EVALUATING IN AN ENTREPRENEURIAL ENVIRONMENT

This section consists of five chapters

which introduce you to a small

company's accounting system and

its financial statements, and how to

use these financial statements for

business decisions. After reading

these chapters, you will be able to:

▶ *understand how a company's accounting system is designed*

▶ *explain the concepts, principles, and terms used in accounting*

▶ *account for various business transactions of a company*

▶ *prepare and use an income statement, balance sheet, and cash flow statement for a company*

▶ *use ratio analysis to evaluate a company's operating capability, financial flexibility, and profitability*

▶ *describe how to manage and control a company's working capital*

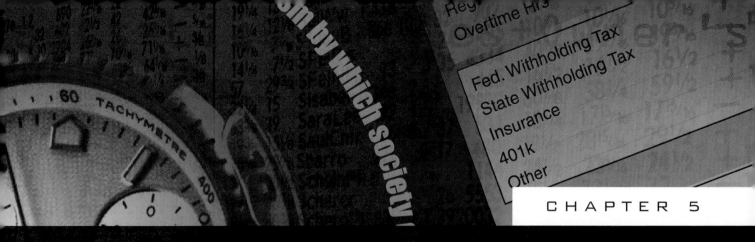

CHAPTER 5

ACCOUNTING FOR THE OPERATIONS OF A COMPANY

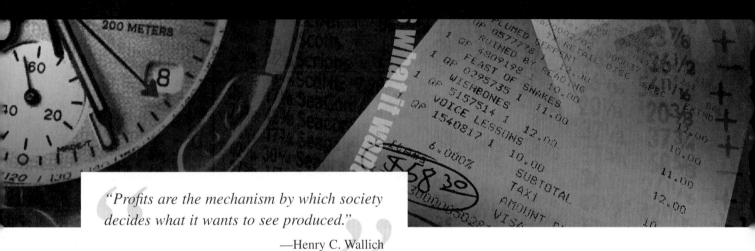

"Profits are the mechanism by which society decides what it wants to see produced."

—Henry C. Wallich

1 *Why do managers, investors, creditors, and others need information about a company's operations?*

2 *What are the basic concepts and terms that help identify the activities that a company's accounting system records?*

3 *What do users need to know about the accounting equation for a company?*

4 *Why are at least two effects of each transaction recorded in a company's accounting system?*

5 *What are revenues and expenses, and how is the accounting equation expanded to record these items?*

6 *What are the accounting principles and concepts related to net income?*

7 *Why are end-of-period adjustments necessary?*

Accounting methods such as C-V-P analysis and budgeting help managers carry out the planning, operating, and evaluating activities of a company. However, managers must also *keep track of* the company's operations in order to evaluate its performance (and also their own performance as managers). Managers develop and use an accounting system for this purpose. For example, a company's accounting system shows managers whether the company sold as many goods as it expected and whether it stayed within its budgets.

Managers are not the only people interested in the operations of a company. External users need information about the company's operations to help them decide whether to do business with a company. In this chapter we discuss the role of financial accounting in decision-making and explain the basics of the financial accounting process.

Financial Accounting Information and Decision-Making

Let's return to our discussion of Unlimited Decadence Corporation, the candy bar manufacturer, to see why external users need accounting information. As you can imagine, it takes lots of sugar to make candy bars. Suppose for a moment that you are the president of Sugar Supply Company and that Unlimited Decadence Corporation is considering a purchase of sugar. Unlimited Decadence wants to make bulk purchases on credit and pay for them 30 days later when it has collected money from its candy bar customers.

 As president of Sugar Supply Company, how would you initially react to this request? Why? What facts may change your mind?

Although your immediate response may be to sell the sugar to Unlimited Decadence, you should think carefully before agreeing to the credit arrangement. Certainly, companies like to make sales. However, increasing sales by extending credit is a good decision only if you are reasonably sure that your credit customers will pay their bills. If Unlimited Decadence doesn't pay its bills, Sugar Supply Company will have given up some of its resources and have nothing to show for it.

The four-step problem-solving process we discussed in Chapter 2 provides an excellent framework for analyzing this credit decision. You already did the first step—recognizing that the problem is to decide whether to sell sugar to Unlimited Decadence Corporation on credit. You now can take the second step—identifying your company's alternatives. You might decide not to extend credit to Unlimited Decadence, to extend credit under more strict or more lenient terms, or to agree to the original request.

Why do managers, investors, creditors, and others need information about a company's operations?

The third step, evaluating each alternative by weighing its advantages and disadvantages, helps you decide which alternative best helps your company meet its goals of remaining solvent and earning a satisfactory profit. The alternative that you choose will depend, in part, on your company's ability to extend credit and on its existing credit policies. When you perform this step, financial accounting information about Unlimited Decadence plays a big role, helping you determine how good a customer Unlimited Decadence will be.

Exhibit 5-1 shows a simplified income statement and a simplified balance sheet for Unlimited Decadence for the first quarter of 2000.[1] When you analyze these financial statements, you learn from the income statement that during the quarter, Unlimited Decadence earned $18,100,000 of revenues from selling candy bars and made $720,000 net income. From the balance sheet, you learn that on March 31, 2000, Unlimited Decadence had $1,200,000 cash in the bank, inventories of $1,300,000 , and other assets (e.g., trucks, factory, etc.) totaling $16,800,000, and that it owed $3,000,000 to suppliers and $2,000,000 to the bank. Each of these items should affect the specific credit terms, if any, that you are willing to offer. After evaluating the alternatives, you are ready to make a decision about Unlimited Decadence's credit request.

---

[1]For simplicity, we assume here that Unlimited Decadence sells only one type of candy bar. We will relax this assumption in later chapters. Furthermore, Unlimited Decadence Corporation's actual financial statements have many more items, which we don't show here because you have not studied them yet. We will show more complete financial statements in later chapters.

Exhibit 5-1 Income Statement and Balance Sheet

UNLIMITED DECADENCE
Income Statement
For Quarter Ended March 31, 2000

(in thousands of dollars)

Revenues:		
Sales revenue		$18,100
Expenses:		
Cost of candy bars sold	$11,500	
Selling expenses	3,460	
General and administrative expenses	1,940	
Total expenses		(16,900)
Income before income taxes		$ 1,200
Income tax expense		(480)
Net Income		$ 720

UNLIMITED DECADENCE
Balance Sheet
March 31, 2000

(in thousands of dollars)

Assets		Liabilities	
Cash	$ 1,200	Accounts payable (suppliers)	$ 3,000
Inventories	1,300	Notes payable (bank)	2,000
Other assets	16,800	Total Liabilities	$ 5,000
		Stockholders' Equity	
		Total Stockholders' Equity	$14,300
		Total Liabilities and	
Total Assets	$19,300	Stockholders' Equity	$19,300

This is just one example of how financial accounting information can help external decision-makers choose whether or not to do business with a company. Another example is when a banker studies a company's financial statements to decide the conditions for granting a loan. Businesspeople routinely make decisions like these. In each case, financial statements provide information that is important in solving business problems.

Making good decisions based on information in financial statements assumes that there is agreement about what is included in those statements and how the amounts are measured. Without agreement on what accounting information the balance sheet, income statement, and cash flow statement should contain, the statements would be essentially useless. If every company defined and measured financial statement items such as assets, liabilities, revenues, and expenses differently, there would be no way to compare one company's information with another's.

 What difficulties do you think would be caused if each state defined traffic laws differently (e.g., laws stipulating on which side of the road to drive) and used different traffic signs?

The "generally accepted accounting principles" (GAAP) that we mentioned in Chapter 1 were developed to overcome this problem by setting rules for companies to follow when they prepare financial statements. Thus, if you know that a company's financial statements are prepared according to GAAP and you know what rules are included in GAAP, you can confidently use the information in its financial statements for your decision-making. The rest of this chapter will give you a basic understanding of the financial accounting process. This process provides the information a company needs for preparing financial statements according to GAAP. Once you have learned some fundamental concepts, we will discuss how the accounting process accumulates and reports information about a company's activities.

Basic Concepts and Terms Used in Accounting

2 *What are the basic concepts and terms that help identify the activities that a company's accounting system records?*

Several basic concepts and terms help us identify the activities that a company's accounting process records:

1. Entity concept

2. Transactions

3. Source documents

4. Monetary unit concept

5. Historical cost concept

Each of these items is important for understanding the process of accumulating and reporting information about a company's activities.

Entity Concept

As you saw in Chapter 1, there are three broad forms of companies—sole proprietorships, partnerships, and corporations. Regardless of a company's form, its accounting records must remain separate from those of its owner, or owners. Even though Anna Cox is the sole proprietor of Sweet Temptations, she doesn't consider her personal assets as belonging to Sweet Temptations, nor does she consider Sweet Temptations' assets to be hers. If Anna owns all or part of several companies, she will keep separate records for each of them. This separation is the basis of the entity concept. An **entity** is considered to be separate from its owners and from any other company. Thus, each company is an entity and has its own accounting system and accounting records. An owner's personal financial activities are *not* included in the accounting records of the company unless this activity has a *direct* effect on the company. For instance, if Anna Cox buys a car only for personal use, its purchase would *not* affect Sweet Temptations' accounting records. On the other hand, if Anna uses personal funds to buy a delivery van to be used in the company, the purchase *would* affect the company's records.

 Why do you think it is important to treat each entity separately?

Combining company-related items and personal items makes it hard to tell which items are intended for business purposes and which items are for personal use. External users interested in a company's activities would gain little information if you gave them financial statements that included the combined items. With a separate accounting system for a company, it is much easier to identify, measure, and record company activities and to prepare financial statements for the company. Therefore, the financial statements provide more useful information to managers and external users for evaluating the effectiveness of the company's operations.

Transactions

Recall from Chapter 1 that accounting involves the identification, measurement, recording, accumulation, and communication of a company's economic information for use in decision-making. The accounting process usually begins with a business transaction. A **transaction** is an exchange of property or service by a company with another entity. For example, when Unlimited Decadence Corporation purchases sugar, it exchanges cash (or the promise to pay cash) for the ingredients needed to make candy. Many events or activities of a company may be described as transactions. Someone, such as the company's accountant or owner, initially records these transactions based on information from source documents.

Source Documents

A **source document** is a business record used as evidence that a transaction has occurred. A source document may be a company check, a sales receipt, a bill from a supplier, a bill sent to a customer, a payroll time card, or a log of the miles driven in the company's delivery truck. Although a company's accounting process begins when a transaction occurs, the identification, measurement, and recording of information are based on an analysis of the related source document. For instance, the check that Unlimited Decadence writes to pay for a bulk purchase of sugar shows the date of the transaction, the dollar amount, the name of the company to whom the check was written (called the *payee*), and possibly the reason for the check. Several source documents may be used as evidence of a single transaction. In addition to the canceled check, source documents for Unlimited Decadence's sugar purchase include the sales invoice from the sugar supplier and the report from the loading dock stating that the sugar arrived at Unlimited Decadence's factory.

Monetary Unit Concept

The source documents for transactions show the value of the exchange in terms that both internal and external users agree on and understand. Since the purpose of recording and analyzing a company's transactions is to understand the company's financial activities, it makes sense to record transactions in terms of money. This idea is known as the **monetary unit concept.** In the United States the monetary unit is the dollar, and therefore U.S.-based companies show their financial statements in dollars. The monetary unit used depends on the national currency of the company's country. For example, Sony uses the Japanese yen, while Volkswagen and Benetton use the European Union euro.

www.world.sony.com
www.vw.com
www.benetton.com

www.jaguarcars.com
www2.ford.com

 If a company does business in several countries, what currency do you think it uses to prepare its financial statements? Why? Since Jaguar is owned by Ford, do you think its financial statements are prepared in British pounds or U.S. dollars?

If Unlimited Decadence purchases a Volkswagen from this dealership in Germany, do you think this candy maker should record the purchase in dollars or euros? Why?

Historical Cost Concept

As we all know, the value of every country's currency changes as a result of inflation. Also, the values of particular goods and services change in the marketplace as supply and demand change. So a company has to decide whether to adjust the recorded amounts to include these types of changes. Under generally accepted accounting principles in the United States, companies generally do *not* record the change in the value of either the currency or the individual goods and services. Instead, they use the historical cost concept or, simply, the cost concept. The **historical cost concept** states that a company records its transactions based on the dollars exchanged (the cost) at the time the transaction occurred. The related source documents show this cost, and the company's accounting records continue to show the *cost* involved in each transaction regardless of whether the *value* of the property or service owned increases (or decreases) or whether the *value* of the currency changes over time. For instance, suppose that a company acquires land for $100,000 and that a year later the value of the land has increased to $130,000. Under the historical cost concept, the company continues to show the land in its accounting records at $100,000, the acquisition cost. However, later in the book you will see that companies do adjust some assets for changes in their values.

 Why do you think most accountants wouldn't want to change the recorded value for the land from $100,000 to $130,000? Why might some want to change?

In Exhibit 5-2 we combine the entity concept, the monetary unit concept, and the historical cost concept to develop Unlimited Decadence Corporation's balance sheet that we showed in Exhibit 5-1. In this balance sheet, we (a) separate company items from personal items according to the *entity concept*, and (b) use the *monetary unit concept* and the *historical cost concept* to show dollar values for each company-related item.

These three concepts are the foundation of what the accounting process shows. With this in mind, you can see how that process functions. The accountant, or the owner, uses the *entity concept* to separate the activities of a company from the owner's activities, which are not related to the company. The company's *transactions* are identified by analyzing *source documents*. The accountant or owner then enters the transactions into the company's accounting records using *monetary units* based on the *costs* involved in its activities. Every time a company activity occurs, the accountant or owner uses these concepts to help decide the proper way to record that activity. After the economic information about a company's activities is recorded and accumulated, the ultimate goal of the accounting process is to communicate this information in the company's balance sheet, its income statement, and its cash flow statement, each prepared according to GAAP.

Components of the Accounting Equation

We can now begin to discuss how the **accounting system** works—the process used to identify, measure, record, and retain information about a company's activities so that the company can prepare its financial statements. This process is based on the three sections of a balance sheet: the asset, liability, and owner's equity sections. Every time a company records the exchange of property or services with another party, the transaction affects at least one of the sections of the balance sheet. So before moving on, consider the following expanded definitions of assets, liabilities, and owner's equity.

Assets

Assets are a company's economic resources that will provide future benefits to the company. A company may own many assets, some of which are physical in nature—such as land, buildings, supplies to be used, and inventory that the company expects to sell to its customers. Other assets do not have physical characteristics but are economic resources because of the legal rights (benefits) they convey to the company. These assets include

Exhibit 5-2 Unlimited Decadence's Assets and Liabilities and Balance Sheet

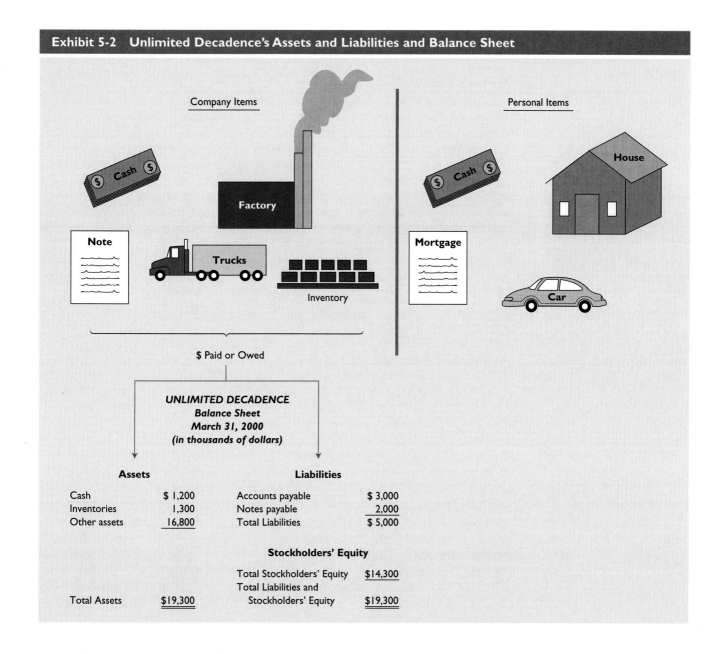

UNLIMITED DECADENCE
Balance Sheet
March 31, 2000
(in thousands of dollars)

Assets		Liabilities	
Cash	$ 1,200	Accounts payable	$ 3,000
Inventories	1,300	Notes payable	2,000
Other assets	16,800	Total Liabilities	$ 5,000
		Stockholders' Equity	
		Total Stockholders' Equity	$14,300
		Total Liabilities and	
Total Assets	$19,300	Stockholders' Equity	$19,300

amounts owed by customers to the company (**accounts receivable**), the right to insurance protection (**prepaid insurance**), and investments made in other companies.

 Can you think of more examples of assets? How do each of these examples meet the definition of assets?

Liabilities

Liabilities are the economic obligations (debts) of a company. The external parties to whom a company owes the debts are referred to as the **creditors** of the company. Liabilities include amounts owed to suppliers for credit purchases (**accounts payable**) and amounts owed to employees for work they have done (**wages and salaries payable**). Legal documents are often evidence of liabilities. These documents establish a claim (**equity**) by the creditors (the **creditors' equity**) against the assets of a company.

Can you think of more examples of liabilities? How do each of these examples meet the definition of liabilities?

Owner's Equity

The **owner's equity** of a company is the owner's current investment in the assets of the company. (A partnership's balance sheet would refer to **partners' equity,** and a corporation's balance sheet would call this **stockholders' equity**, as you saw in Exhibits 5-1 and 5-2.) The capital invested in the company by the owner, the company's earnings from operations, and the owner's withdrawals of capital from the company all affect owner's equity. For a sole proprietorship, the balance sheet shows the owner's equity by listing the owner's name, the word *capital,* and the amount of the owner's current investment in the company. As you will see later, partners' equity and stockholders' equity appear slightly differently. Owner's equity is sometimes referred to as **residual equity** because creditors have first legal claim to a company's assets. Once the creditors' claims have been satisfied, the owner is entitled to the remainder (residual) of the assets. Sometimes the total of the liabilities (creditors' equity) is combined with the owner's equity, and the result is referred to as the **total equity** of the company.

Using the Accounting Equation

3 *What do users need to know about the accounting equation for a company?*

In summary, accountants use the term *assets* to refer to a company's economic resources, and they use the terms *liabilities* and *owner's equity* to describe claims on those resources. All of a company's economic resources are claimed by either creditors or owners. Therefore, the financial accounting system is built on a simple equation:

$$\text{Economic Resources} = \text{Claims on Economic Resources}$$

Using the accounting terms you have learned, we can restate the equation:

$$\text{Assets} = \text{Liabilities} + \text{Owner's Equity}$$

This mathematical expression is known as the basic **accounting equation**. The equality of the assets to the liabilities plus owner's equity is the reason a company's statement of financial position is called a *balance* sheet: the monetary total for the economic resources (assets) of the company must always be *in balance* with the monetary total for the claims (liabilities + owner's equity) on the economic resources. Like the components of any other equation, the components of this equation may be transposed. Another way of showing the equation is as follows:

$$\text{Assets} - \text{Liabilities} = \text{Owner's Equity}$$

In this form of the equation, the left-hand side (i.e., assets minus liabilities) is referred to as **net assets.** This form of the equation also stresses that owner's equity may be thought of as a residual amount. Regardless of what form the equation takes, it must always balance. Because a transaction normally begins the accounting process, a company must record each transaction in a way that maintains this equality. Keeping this equality in mind will help you understand other aspects of the accounting process.

The Dual Effect of Transactions

4 *Why are at least two effects of each transaction recorded in a company's accounting system?*

To keep the accounting equation in balance, *a company must make at least two changes in its assets, liabilities, or owner's equity* when it records each transaction. This is called the **dual effect of transactions**. For instance, when an owner invests $20,000 in a company, assets (cash) are increased by $20,000 and owner's equity (owner's capital) is increased by $20,000. This transaction causes two changes—one change in the asset section of the balance sheet and one change in the owner's equity section of the balance sheet. Because the left-hand side *and* the right-hand side both increase by the same amount, the accounting equation (assets = liabilities + owner's equity) stays in balance.

The fact that transactions always have a dual effect does not mean that every transaction will affect both sides of the equation—or even two components of the equation. A transaction may affect only one side, by increasing one asset and decreasing another asset by the same amount. For example, assume a company buys office equipment for $400 cash. In this case, the asset Office Equipment increases by $400 and the asset Cash decreases by $400. The accounting equation still balances after the company records this transaction because the transaction does not affect the right side of the equation and because the *total* for the asset (left) side of the equation is not changed.

To understand how the accounting equation and the dual effect of transactions provide structure to a company's accounting system, think about these concepts as describing a company's "transaction scales." Exhibit 5-3 shows a set of "transaction scales." Instead of measuring the weight of various objects, using ounces or pounds as measuring units, these scales measure transactions, using dollars (historical cost monetary units). Suppose a company currently has assets of $100,000, liabilities of $25,000, and owner's equity of $75,000. Assume that the company's accountant or owner "places" the company's current economic resources (assets of $100,000) on the left side of the scales and "places" current claims on those resources (liabilities of $25,000 + owner's equity of $75,000) on the right side of the scales. Remember, after each transaction the scales must balance. The dual effect of transactions provides a way to keep the scales in balance as company activities are placed (recorded) on the scales. Note that in Exhibit 5-3 the left side of the scales holds $100,000 in total assets and the right side holds $25,000 in liabilities and $75,000 in owner's equity. The scales balance according to the accounting equation:

$$\textbf{Assets} = \textbf{Liabilities} + \textbf{Owner's Equity}$$
$$\$100,000 = \$25,000 + \$75,000$$

As we stated earlier, regardless of the type of transaction that occurs, the accounting equation, like our set of transaction scales, must always balance. Exhibits 5-4 and 5-5 use the scales to illustrate two more transactions. In Exhibit 5-4, you can see what happens

Exhibit 5-3   Illustration of the Dual Effect of Transactions: "Transactions Scales"

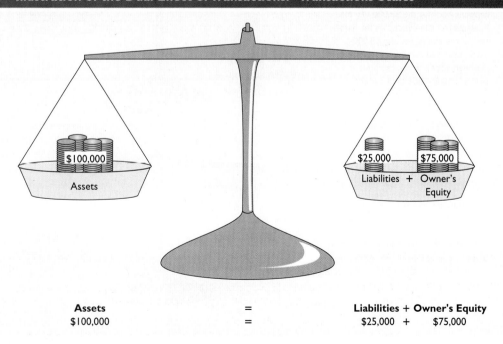

Assets	=	**Liabilities + Owner's Equity**
$100,000	=	$25,000 + $75,000

when the company's owner deposits $5,000 *from personal funds* into the company's bank account. The first frame shows the accounting equation in balance before the owner's deposit. The second frame shows the equation *out of balance* because only one change, the $5,000 increase in company assets on the left side of the equation, has been recorded. In the last frame, the scales again balance, showing that the $5,000 owner's equity increase on the right side of the equation has been recorded. After this transaction, the accounting equation is as follows:

Assets = Liabilities + Owner's Equity
$105,000 = $25,000 + $80,000

Exhibit 5-5 shows what happens when the company writes a check to the bank for $20,000 to pay off a bank loan. The accounting equation stays in balance because assets and liabilities decrease by the same amount:

Exhibit 5-4 "Transaction Scales": Increase in Assets and Owner's Equity

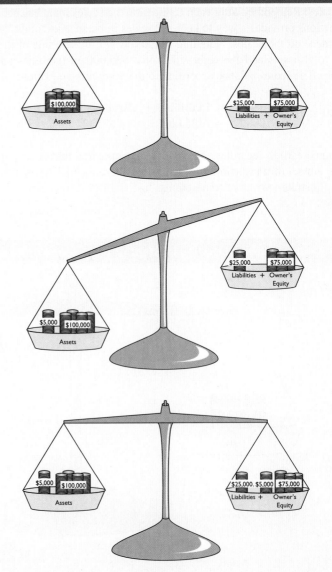

The "transaction scales" balance in this frame because the company's assets ($100,000) equal the company's liabilities ($25,000) plus owner's equity ($75,000).

In this frame, the "transaction scales" are out of balance. This happens because the $5,000 increase in assets has been added to the asset side of the scales, but the $5,000 increase in owner's equity has not yet been added to the liabilities and owner's equity side of the scales.

The "transaction scales" are in balance again once the $5,000 increase in owner's equity has been added to the liabilities and owner's equity side of the scales.

$$\text{Assets} = \text{Liabilities} + \text{Owner's Equity}$$
$$\$85,000 = \$5,000 + \$80,000$$

 Do you think that companies in other countries use this same structure? Why or why not?

Accounting for Transactions to Start a Business

In Chapters 3 and 4 you saw how managers use accounting information to develop a business plan to show potential investors. Managers also use accounting information for internal decision-making. C-V-P analysis and budgeting provide accounting information that helps managers answer questions such as the following: How much money do we need to have on hand to start the business? How much inventory should we have available? How much money can

Exhibit 5-5 "Transaction Scales": Decrease in Assets and Liabilities

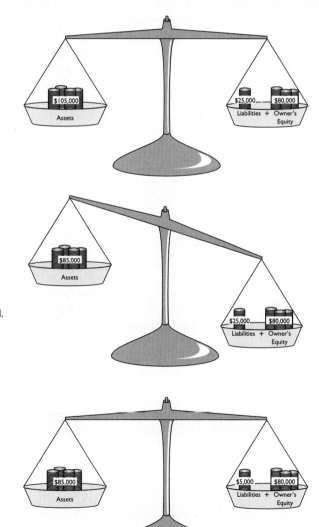

The "transaction scales" balance in this frame because the company's assets ($105,000) equal the company's liabilities ($25,000) plus owner's equity ($80,000).

The "transaction scales" do not balance in this frame because, although the $20,000 decrease in assets has been taken off the scales, the liabilities have not yet been changed.

The "transaction scales" are in balance again once the $20,000 decrease in liabilities is removed from the liabilities and owner's equity side of the scales.

we spend to advertise the grand opening of the business? These initial transactions are undertaken for one purpose—so that managers can pursue the goal of earning a satisfactory income (profit) for the owners. The profit goal is met by selling goods or services to customers at prices that are higher than the costs of providing the goods or services.

Once a company starts operating, it uses financial statements to report to external users about its operations. To prepare these financial statements, the company's accountant or owner identifies transactions and records them in the accounting system. This analysis uses the accounting equation and recognizes the dual effect of transactions.

 If you loaned money to a company, how often would you want the company to report on its operations? Why?

The transactions recorded in the accounting system are the basis for the internal and external reports that the company issues. Therefore, it is very important that the transactions are entered correctly, since they "live on" in the system, sometimes for many years.

With the accounting equation (and the dual effect of transactions) in mind, watch Anna Cox as she analyzes and records the transactions involved in starting her business, Sweet Temptations. Note how Anna uses accounting concepts, the accounting equation, and the dual effect of transactions to build an effective accounting system.

Investing Cash

Anna Cox starts her business on December 15, 1999, by writing a $15,000 personal check and depositing it in a checking account she opened for Sweet Temptations. Anna wants to open the candy store to customers on January 2, 2000, so that she can build some customer traffic before people start buying their Valentine candy. This company checking account is separate, of course, from her personal account because of the entity concept.

Anna decides to establish a simple accounting system on a sheet of paper by listing assets, liabilities, and owner's equity as headings of separate columns that she divides into subcolumns for specific kinds of assets, liabilities, and owner's equity. She records each transaction by entering the amounts in the appropriate columns. Anna uses the receipt issued by Sweet Temptations for her check and the bank deposit slip she used to open the company's bank account as source documents for the first transaction. Exhibit 5-6 shows how she records this first transaction.

 Does Anna Cox's personal check serve as a source document for Sweet Temptations? Why or why not?

As a result of the first transaction, Sweet Temptations now has an asset, Cash, recorded at the transaction amount of $15,000, and owner's equity, A. Cox, Capital, showing Anna's $15,000 investment. Note that Anna makes two entries to record the dual effect of the transaction—one to an asset and one to owner's equity—and that the accounting equation balances because she increases both sides of the equation by the same amount.

Exhibit 5-6 Anna Invests Cash in Sweet Temptations

Trans	Date	Assets		=	Liabilities	+	Owner's Equity
		Cash					A. Cox, Capital
(1)	12/15/99	+ $15,000					+ $15,000
		$15,000		=			$15,000

Prepaying Rent

To open Sweet Temptations at the Westwood Mall, Anna signed, in the company's name, a rental agreement with the mall's manager on December 16, 1999. The monthly rent is $1,000, and the agreement requires that rent for six months be paid in advance. Since the space is empty, the mall manager agrees to let Anna begin setting up her business immediately but not to start charging her rent until January 1, 2000. This arrangement works well for Anna because now she can begin purchasing store equipment, supplies, and inventory.

So, on December 16, Anna writes a company check for $6,000 ($1,000 × 6 months) to the Westwood Mall. Sweet Temptations' check and the signed rental agreement are the source documents for the transaction. Exhibit 5-7 shows how Anna records this second transaction.

The benefit of using the mall space for six months to conduct business represents an economic resource, or asset, to Sweet Temptations. As a result, Anna records $6,000 as an increase in a new asset—Prepaid Rent. Because cash is paid out, she decreases the asset Cash by the total amount paid, $6,000. She subtracts this amount from the previous amount of Cash to show a new amount, $9,000. After recording the transaction, she checks the accounting equation to see that it remains in balance. She does this by adding the assets ($9,000 + $6,000) and comparing this $15,000 amount with the total of the liabilities ($0) plus owner's equity ($15,000). As you can see, the equation still balances.

 How many changes did Anna make in the accounting equation to record this transaction? Why?

Purchasing Supplies with Cash

On December 17, 1999, Sweet Temptations purchases $700 of office and store supplies from City Supply Company by writing a check for $700. Anna receives an *invoice* that lists the items purchased, the cost of each item, and the total cost. She uses the invoice as the source document to record this third transaction, as we show in Exhibit 5-8. Because the supplies will be used to conduct business, Anna records them as an asset, Supplies, of $700. Because the purchase is made with cash, she reduces the asset Cash by $700. Note that the changes in these two assets offset each other on the left side of the accounting equation, which thus remains in balance.

Purchasing Inventory on Credit

On December 20, 1999, Sweet Temptations purchases $1,620 of candy (360 boxes of candy for $4.50 each) on credit from Unlimited Decadence Corporation. Sweet Temptations agrees to pay for the candy within 30 days of purchase. An invoice from Unlimited Decadence is the source document for the transaction. Exhibit 5-9 shows how Anna records this fourth transaction. Sweet Temptations needs a way to keep track of the cost of the candy that it buys from manufacturers and has on hand to sell to retail candy customers. Anna thus adds a subcolumn to assets to record Inventory. She increases Inventory by the

Exhibit 5-7   Sweet Temptations Prepays Rent

Trans	Date	Cash	+	Prepaid Rent	Assets	=	Liabilities	+	Owner's Equity A. Cox, Capital
(1)	12/15/99	+ $15,000							+ $15,000
(2)	12/16/99	− $ 6,000		+ $6,000					
		$ 9,000	+	$6,000		=			$15,000

Exhibit 5-8   Sweet Temptations Purchases Supplies with Cash

Trans	Date	Cash	+	Prepaid Rent	+	Supplies	=	Liabilities	+	Owner's Equity A. Cox, Capital
(1)	12/15/99	+ $15,000								+ $15,000
(2)	12/16/99	− $ 6,000		+ $6,000						
(3)	12/17/99	− $ 700				+ $700				
		$ 8,300	+	$6,000	+	$700	=			$15,000

cost of the candy, $1,620, but does not reduce Cash because none was paid out. Since Sweet Temptations agrees to pay for the inventory later, it incurs a debt, or a liability. Anna calls the liability Accounts Payable because it is an amount to be paid by the company, and she increases Accounts Payable by $1,620. Note that Unlimited Decadence Corporation, not Anna Cox, finances this increase in Sweet Temptations' assets (economic resources). Unlimited Decadence is now Sweet Temptations' creditor because it has a claim on $1,620 of the candy store's assets. The $1,620 increase in economic resources matches the $1,620 increase in the claims on those resources. So, the left side of the accounting equation and the liability component of the right side both increase by $1,620. The accounting equation balances after the transaction is recorded.

Purchasing Store Equipment with Cash and Credit

On December 29, 1999, Sweet Temptations purchases store equipment from Ace Equipment Company at a cost of $2,200. It pays $1,000 down and signs a note agreeing to pay the remaining $1,200 (plus interest of $24) at the end of three months. Anna uses the invoice, the check, and the note to record this fifth transaction, as we show in Exhibit 5-10. Because the store equipment is an economic resource to be used in the business, Anna increases the asset Store Equipment by the total cost of $2,200. She decreases the asset Cash by the amount paid, $1,000. Since Sweet Temptations incurs a $1,200 liability and issues a legal note, Anna increases the liability Notes Payable by this amount. She does not record any interest now because interest accumulates as time passes, and no time has passed since Sweet Temptations issued the note. This transaction affects two assets and a liability, but the accounting equation remains in balance.

Selling Extra Store Equipment on Credit

Sweet Temptations obtained a special price on the store equipment by buying a "package," which included an extra computer desk that the company did not need. So on December 30,

Exhibit 5-9   Sweet Temptations Purchases Inventory on Credit

Trans	Date	Cash	+	Prepaid Rent	+	Supplies	+	Inventory	=	Accounts Payable	+	Owner's Equity A. Cox, Capital
(1)	12/15/99	+ $15,000										+ $15,000
(2)	12/16/99	− $ 6,000		+ $6,000								
(3)	12/17/99	− $ 700				+ $700						
(4)	12/20/99							+ $1,620		+ $1,620		
		$ 8,300	+	$6,000	+	$700	+	$1,620	=	$1,620	+	$15,000

Exhibit 5-10   Sweet Temptations Purchases Store Equipment with Cash and Credit

Trans	Date	Cash	+	Prepaid Rent	+ Supplies	+ Inventory	+ Store Equipment =	Accounts Payable	+ Notes Payable +	Owner's Equity A. Cox, Capital
(1)	12/15/99	+ $15,000								+ $15,000
(2)	12/16/99	− $ 6,000		+ $6,000						
(3)	12/17/99	− $ 700			+ $700					
(4)	12/20/99					+ $1,620		+ $1,620		
(5)	12/29/99	− $ 1,000					+ $2,200		+ $1,200	
		$ 7,300 +		$6,000 +	$700 +	$1,620 +	$2,200 =	$1,620 +	$1,200 +	$15,000

1999, Sweet Temptations sells the desk, which cost $400, for that same amount to The Hardware Store, another store in the mall. The Hardware Store agrees to pay for the desk on January 7. Exhibit 5-11 shows how Anna records this sixth transaction. Because Sweet Temptations sells one of its economic resources, Anna decreases the asset Store Equipment by $400, the cost of the desk. Because the amount to be received from The Hardware Store in January is an economic resource for Sweet Temptations, Anna also records an increase of $400 in the asset Accounts Receivable. Again, note the equality of the accounting equation.

Expanding the Accounting Equation

Until now, we have focused on how a company records transactions that occur when it is preparing to open for business. You have learned how the accounting equation changes as the company uses its accounting system to record an owner's investment, the purchases of assets with cash and on credit, and the sale of equipment. After the company opens for business, internal and external users of financial statements need income information to evaluate how well the company has been operating. By recording the transactions of its day-to-day operations, a company develops this income information. As you continue reading, keep the accounting equation and the dual effect of transactions in mind.

Anna had no problem using the basic accounting equation to record the start-up transactions in the balance sheet columns. However, she needs to modify the accounting system to record the income-producing transactions, such as sales to customers; these transactions do not fit easily into the equation as it is currently stated.

5 *What are revenues and expenses, and how is the accounting equation expanded to record these items?*

Exhibit 5-11   Sweet Temptations Sells Extra Store Equipment on Credit

Trans	Date	Cash	+	Prepaid Rent	+ Supplies	+ Inventory	+ Store Equipment	+ Accounts Receivable =	Accounts Payable	+ Notes Payable +	Owner's Equity A. Cox, Capital
(1)	12/15/99	+ $15,000									+ $15,000
(2)	12/16/99	− $ 6,000		+ $6,000							
(3)	12/17/99	− $ 700			+ $700						
(4)	12/20/99					+ $1,620			+ $1,620		
(5)	12/29/99	− $ 1,000					+ $2,200			+ $1,200	
(6)	12/30/99						− $ 400	+ $ 400			
		$ 7,300 +		$6,000 +	$700 +	$1,620 +	$1,800 +	$ 400 =	$1,620 +	$1,200 +	$15,000

If you were Anna, how would you expand Sweet Temptations' accounting system so that you could record revenue and expense transactions? What column headings would you add to the accounting system?

To modify the accounting system, Anna separates the Owner's Equity part of the equation into two sections. The first, Owner's Capital, lets her record transactions relating to her investments and withdrawals of capital from the company. The second lets her record net income (revenues and expenses). For recording both types of transactions, the equality of the accounting equation is maintained because of the dual effects of transactions. The expanded accounting equation is as follows:

$$\text{Assets} = \text{Liabilities} + \overbrace{\text{Owner's Capital} + \underbrace{\text{Net Income}}_{\text{Revenues} - \text{Expenses}}}^{\text{Owner's Equity}}$$

Recall from Chapter 1 that the income of a company is commonly referred to as net income. **Net income** is the excess of revenues over expenses *for a specific time period*. Net income is sometimes called *net profit*, *net earnings*, or simply *earnings*. **Revenues** are the prices a company charged to its customers for goods or services it provided during a specific time period. **Expenses** are the costs of providing the goods or services to customers during the time period.

Anna records revenue and expense transactions by expanding the columns in the simple accounting system she uses. To find out how much net income Sweet Temptations earned over a specific time period (e.g., the month of January), she subtracts the total in the expense column from the total in the revenue column.

Accounting Principles and Concepts Related to Net Income

6 *What are the accounting principles and concepts related to net income?*

Earlier in the chapter we explained several basic concepts and terms used in accounting. Before you learn how a company records its daily transactions to determine net income, it is helpful to know several additional accounting principles and concepts that are part of GAAP.

Accounting Period

A company typically operates for many years. The company's owner (internal user) needs information about its net income on a regular basis to make operating decisions. External users of financial statement information also need to know about the company's net income on a regular basis to make timely business decisions. Suppliers need this information for granting credit, creditors need this information for renewing bank loans, and investors need this information for providing additional capital.

Given that both internal and external users benefit when a company routinely reports its net income, the question is: How often should a company do so? Earlier we said that net income is the excess of revenues over expenses for a specific time period. An **accounting period** is the time span for which a company reports its revenues and expenses. Most companies base their financial statements on a twelve-month accounting period called a *fiscal year* or a *fiscal period*. The fiscal year is often the same as the *calendar year;* however, a company whose operations are seasonal may use a year that corresponds more closely to its *operating cycle*. For instance, a retail company (such as Wal-Mart) may use January 31, 2000 through January 31, 2001 for its fiscal year so that its accounting period will include the purchase and sale of inventory that peaks for the December holiday season. Many companies also compute and report their net income on a quarterly basis. These accounting periods (and others shorter than a year) are referred to as *interim* periods. In

"Well, gentlemen, Christmas is over."

Lou Myers © 1997 from the New Yorker Collection. All Rights Reserved.

Do you think this company uses a calendar year or a fiscal year as its accounting period? Why?

this book we often present simplified examples that use one month as the accounting period.

Earning and Recording Revenues

Revenues result from a company's operating activities that contribute to its earning process. Broadly speaking, every activity of a company contributes to its earning process. More specifically, a company's **earning process** includes purchasing (or producing) inventory, selling the inventory (or services), delivering the inventory (or services), and collecting and paying cash. Although a company *earns* revenues continuously during this process, it generally *records* revenues near or at the end of the earning process.[2] This is because (1) the earning process is complete (the company has made the sale and delivered the product or performed the service) and (2) the prices charged to customers are collectible (accounts receivable) or collected. So we can say that a company **records revenues** during the accounting period in which they are earned and are collectible (or collected).

Matching Principle

Expenses are subtracted from revenues to calculate net income. Another way of saying this is that the costs used up are *matched* against the prices charged to customers to determine

---

[2]Construction companies sometimes take several years to complete a project (e.g., an office building). To more fairly report their yearly net income, these companies record a portion of their total revenues each year based on the amount earned during the year.

net income. The **matching principle** states that to determine its net income for an accounting period, a company computes the expenses involved in earning the revenues of the period and deducts the total expenses from the total revenues earned in that period. By matching expenses against revenues, a company has a good idea of how much better off it is at the end of an accounting period as a result of its operations during that period.

Accrual Accounting

Accrual accounting is related to both the recording of revenue and the matching principle. When a company uses **accrual accounting**, it records its revenue and related expense transactions in the same accounting period that it provides goods or services (in the period in which it *earns* the revenue), regardless of whether it receives or pays cash in that period. To accrue means to accumulate. Accrual accounting makes accounting information helpful to external users because it does not let cash receipts and cash payments distort a company's net income. Otherwise, the amount of revenues the company earned during an accounting period could be distorted because the company may have received cash earlier or later than it sold goods or provided services. The amount of expenses could be distorted because the company may have paid cash earlier or later than it incurred (or used up) the related costs.

 Do you think that, by requiring accrual accounting to be used in the preparation of income statements, GAAP implies that a company's cash receipts and payments are not important? Why or why not?

Under accrual accounting, a company must be certain that it has recorded in each accounting period all revenues that it earned during that period, even if it received no cash during the period. Similarly, at the end of each accounting period, the company must be certain that it has matched all expenses it incurred during the period against the revenues it earned in that same period even if it paid no cash during the period.

Summary. How do these concepts relate to a company's accounting system? A company sets up and uses its accounting system based on the *accounting equation* and the *dual effect of transactions*. A company, which is a separate *entity* from its owners, analyzes *source documents* to record its *transactions*. It records the transactions in the accounting system in *monetary units* based on the *historical costs* involved in the company activity. In keeping with *accrual accounting*, a company records its revenue transactions when the revenues are *earned and collectible*, and it records expenses when it incurs the costs. The *matching* principle ensures that all expenses are matched with the revenues they helped earn so that the company can calculate its net income for each *accounting period*.

Recording Daily Operations

Here's how Anna uses the expanded accounting equation to record the day-to-day operations of the Sweet Temptations candy store at the Westwood Mall.

Cash Sale

On January 2, 2000, Anna Cox opens Sweet Temptations for business. Sweet Temptations sells a total of 30 boxes of candy at $10 a box for cash. For each sale, the cash register tape lists the date, the type and number of boxes of candy sold, and the total dollar amount of the sale. Anna uses the cash register tape as the source document for the 30 cash sales, which total $300. At the end of the day, Anna increases the Revenues section of Owner's Equity by $300. She also increases Cash by this amount. Of course, Sweet Temptations had to give customers 30 boxes of candy in order to make the $300 in sales. By checking the purchasing records, Anna knows that the candy originally cost Sweet Temptations $135 ($4.50 × 30 boxes) when purchased from Unlimited Decadence Corporation. Because Sweet Temptations no longer owns the candy, Anna decreases Inventory by $135. In addition, because the cost of the candy is a cost of providing the goods that were sold to customers, she increases Expenses by $135.

Exhibit 5-12 shows Sweet Temptations' accounting equation at the close of its first business day, assuming no other transactions occur. The first line in Exhibit 5-12 shows Sweet Temptations' total assets, liabilities, and owner's equity at the *start* of its first business day. These totals came from the transactions that Anna recorded in December as she prepared for business (see the totals in Exhibit 5-11). The next line shows how Anna records the cash sale on January 2. Note on this line that Anna shows that the increase in Expenses causes a decrease in Net Income (and therefore Owner's Equity) by putting a minus sign in the column before the increased amount [i.e., $|-|$ + $135] in the Expense column. Note also how the accounting equation remains in balance because of the dual effect of the cash sales transaction. Cash sales will take place every day that Sweet Temptations is open. Although Anna would record these cash sales transactions every day as they occur, to keep things simple in Exhibit 5-20 (later in the chapter), we include a transaction to represent *all* of the cash sales (770 boxes) that took place from January 3, 2000 through January 31, 2000. These sales total $7,700 ($10 × 770 boxes), so Anna increases both Revenues and Cash by that amount. She also increases Expenses by $3,465 ($4.50 × 770 boxes) and decreases Inventory by that same amount.

 Do you think it is typical to have customers purchase 30 boxes of candy from a small retail store on its first day of business? How could you verify your opinion?

Payment for Credit Purchase of Inventory and Additional Inventory Purchase

Recall that Sweet Temptations purchased its beginning inventory on credit from Unlimited Decadence Corporation on December 20, 1999. Anna recorded this transaction as a $1,620 increase in Inventory and a $1,620 increase in Accounts Payable. On January 3, 2000, Anna writes a Sweet Temptations check to Unlimited Decadence as payment for the December 20, 1999, purchase. An invoice from Unlimited Decadence is the source document for the transaction. To show the results of this transaction, Anna decreases the asset Cash by $1,620. Because the company no longer owes Unlimited Decadence for its purchase, she also decreases the liability Accounts Payable by $1,620.

On January 4, 2000, Sweet Temptations purchases 960 boxes of chocolates (at $4.50 per box) on credit from Unlimited Decadence for $4,320. As a result of the purchase, Anna increases Inventory by $4,320, and because the purchase is made on credit, she also increases Accounts Payable by the same amount. Exhibit 5-13 shows the changes in the accounting equation resulting from these two transactions.

 Does this purchase correspond to the expected purchase noted in Sweet Temptations' purchases budget for January, as we discussed in Chapter 4?

Credit Sale

On January 6, 2000, Sweet Temptations sells 10 boxes of candy for $100 on credit to Bud Salcedo, owner of Bud's Buds flower shop, next door to Sweet Temptations. The sales invoice lists the date, the type of candy sold, the flower shop's name and account number, and the total dollar amount of the sale. Anna assigns each of Sweet Temptations' credit customers a unique account number to help her identify transactions the company has with each of these customers. (This will be particularly useful as the number of credit customers grows.) Having the account number on the sales invoice lets Sweet Temptations keep track of the money each customer owes.

Anna increases the Revenues section of Owner's Equity by $100. Because Sweet Temptations sold the candy on credit instead of receiving cash, Anna increases the asset Accounts Receivable by $100. Remember, Sweet Temptations has to dip into its candy inventory to make the $100 sale. By checking the purchasing records, Anna knows that the

Exhibit 5-12 Sweet Temptations Makes Cash Sales

		Assets						=	Liabilities		+	Owner's Equity		
			Prepaid			Store	Accounts		Accounts	Notes		Owner's Capital / A. Cox, Capital	Net Income	
Trans	Date	Cash	Rent	Supplies	Inventory	Equipment	Receivable		Payable	Payable		Capital	Revenues	Expenses
	1/1/00	$7,300	$6,000	$700	$1,620	$1,800	$400	=	$1,620	$1,200	+	$15,000		
(1)	1/2/00	+$300			−$135								+$300	+$135
		$7,600	$6,000	$700	$1,485	$1,800	$400	=	$1,620	$1,200	+	$15,000	$300	$135

Exhibit 5-13 Sweet Temptations Pays for Credit Purchases and Makes Additional Credit Purchase of Inventory

		Assets						=	Liabilities		+	Owner's Equity		
Trans	Date	Cash	Prepaid Rent	Supplies	Inventory	Store Equipment	Accounts Receivable		Accounts Payable	Notes Payable		A. Cox, Capital	Revenues	Expenses
	1/1/00	$7,300	$6,000	$700	$1,620	$1,800	$400	=	$1,620	$1,200	+	$15,000		
(1)	1/2/00	+$300			−$135								+$300	+$135
(2)	1/3/00	−1,620							−1,620					
(3)	1/4/00				+$4,320				+$4,320					
		$5,980	$6,000	$700	$5,805	$1,800	$400	=	$4,320	$1,200	+	$15,000	$300	$135

Exhibit 5-14 Sweet Temptations Sells Candy on Credit

		Assets						=	Liabilities		+	Owner's Equity		
Trans	Date	Cash	Prepaid Rent	Supplies	Inventory	Store Equipment	Accounts Receivable		Accounts Payable	Notes Payable		A. Cox, Capital	Revenues	Expenses
	1/1/00	$7,300	$6,000	$700	$1,620	$1,800	$400	=	$1,620	$1,200	+	$15,000		
(1)	1/2/00	+$300			−$135								+$300	+$135
(2)	1/3/00	−1,620							−1,620					
(3)	1/4/00				+$4,320				+$4,320					
(4)	1/6/00				−$45		+$100						+$100	+$45
		$5,980	$6,000	$700	$5,760	$1,800	$500	=	$4,320	$1,200	+	$15,000	$400	$180

boxes originally cost $45. Because the company no longer owns the candy, Anna decreases Inventory by $45. In addition, because the cost of the candy is a cost of providing the goods sold, she increases Expenses by $45. Exhibit 5-14 shows the four changes in the accounting equation from this transaction. The accounting equation remains in balance.

Receipt of Payment for Credit Sale of Extra Store Equipment

Sweet Temptations receives a check for $400 from The Hardware Store on January 7, 2000. The check is to pay for the store equipment that Sweet Temptations sold on credit to The Hardware Store on December 30, 1999. As you can see in Exhibit 5-15, Anna reduces the asset Accounts Receivable by $400 because The Hardware Store has settled its account and no longer owes Sweet Temptations any money. She increases the asset Cash by $400 to show the receipt of the check.

Withdrawal of Cash by Owner

On January 20, 2000, Anna Cox withdraws $50 cash from the business for personal use, writing a $50 check to herself from the Sweet Temptations bank account. She then deposits the check in her personal bank account. The check is the source document for the transaction. A **withdrawal** is a payment from the company to the owner. Thus, it is a disinvestment of assets by the owner. Therefore, as we show in Exhibit 5-16, Anna records a decrease in Cash and a decrease in Owner's Equity by the amount of the withdrawal ($50).

 What do you think Anna would record if she took ten boxes of candy instead of cash?

We will discuss withdrawals in more detail in Chapter 6.

 Can you think of any possible ethical issues involved in withdrawals?

Payments for Consulting and Advertising

To prepare for a Valentine's Day grand opening sale, Sweet Temptations hires the Dana Design Group to produce an advertisement. The design group charges $200 and presents the ad on January 25, 2000. Sweet Temptations writes a check for the full amount that day. The receipt received from Dana Design is the source document. As a result of this transaction, Anna increases Expenses by $200 and decreases Cash by $200.

Also on January 25, 2000, Sweet Temptations pays for the advertisement to be published in Westwood Mall's end-of-January promotional flyer. The quarter-page advertisement cost $300. The bill from Westwood Mall's management office is the source document for the transaction. As we show in Exhibit 5-17, to record this transaction, Anna increases Expenses by $300 and decreases Cash by the same amount. Note that the accounting equation remains in balance after these transactions are recorded.

 If Cash was mistakenly decreased by only $100 when the last transaction was recorded, how would you find out that an error was made?

Acquisition of Store Equipment

On January 29, 2000, Sweet Temptations purchases an additional candy display case. Sweet Temptations pays $200 in cash by writing a check. As you can see in Exhibit 5-18, Anna increases Store Equipment by $200 and decreases Cash by the same amount.

Payment of Salaries and of Telephone and Utility Bills

Sweet Temptations employs two people (you and Jaime Gonzales) to help stock and sell candy. On January 31, 2000, you both receive checks, totaling $2,050, as payment for your services during January. Your time cards, wage rate schedules, and paychecks are the

Exhibit 5-15 Sweet Temptations Receives Payment from Credit Sale of Extra Store Equipment

| | | Assets | | | | | | = | Liabilities | | + | Owner's Equity | | |
| | | | | | | | | | | | | Owner's Capital | Net Income | |
Trans	Date	Cash	+ Prepaid Rent	+ Supplies	+ Inventory	+ Store Equipment	+ Accounts Receivable	=	Accounts Payable	+ Notes Payable	+	A. Cox, Capital	+ Revenues	− Expenses
(1)	1/1/00	$7,300	$6,000	$700	$1,620	$1,800	$400		$1,620	$1,200		$15,000		
(2)	1/2/00	+$ 300			−$ 135								+$300	+$135
(3)	1/3/00	−$ 1,620							−$1,620					
(4)	1/4/00				+$4,320				+$4,320					
	1/6/00				−$ 45		+$100						+$100	+$ 45
(5)	1/7/00	+$ 400					−$400							
		$6,380	+ $6,000	+ $700	+ $5,760	+ $1,800	+ $100	=	$4,320	+ $1,200	+	$15,000	+ $400	− $180

Exhibit 5-16 Anna Withdraws Cash from Sweet Temptations

| | | Assets | | | | | | = | Liabilities | | + | Owner's Equity | | |
| | | | | | | | | | | | | Owner's Capital | Net Income | |
Trans	Date	Cash	+ Prepaid Rent	+ Supplies	+ Inventory	+ Store Equipment	+ Accounts Receivable	=	Accounts Payable	+ Notes Payable	+	A. Cox, Capital	+ Revenues	− Expenses
(1)	1/1/00	$7,300	$6,000	$700	$1,620	$1,800	$400		$1,620	$1,200		$15,000		
(2)	1/2/00	+$ 300			−$ 135								+$300	+$135
(3)	1/3/00	−$ 1,620							−$1,620					
(4)	1/4/00				+$4,320				+$4,320					
	1/6/00				−$ 45		+$100						+$100	+$ 45
(5)	1/7/00	+$ 400					−$400							
(6)	1/20/00	−$ 50										−$ 50		
		$6,330	+ $6,000	+ $700	+ $5,760	+ $1,800	+ $100	=	$4,320	+ $1,200	+	$14,950	+ $400	− $180

Exhibit 5-17 Sweet Temptations Pays for Consulting and Advertising

		Assets						=	Liabilities		+	Owner's Equity		
												Owner's Capital	Net Income	
Trans	Date	Cash	Prepaid Rent	Supplies	Inventory	Store Equipment	Accounts Receivable	=	Accounts Payable	Notes Payable	+	A. Cox, Capital	Revenues −	Expenses
(1)	1/1/00	$ 7,300	$6,000	$700	$1,620	$1,800	$400		$1,620	$1,200		$15,000		
(2)	1/2/00	+$ 300			−$ 135								+$300 −	+$135
(3)	1/3/00	−$ 1,620							−$1,620					
(4)	1/4/00				+$4,320				+$4,320					
(5)	1/6/00				−$ 45		+$100						+$100 −	+$ 45
(6)	1/7/00	+$ 400					−$400							
(7)	1/20/00	−$ 50										−$ 50		
(8)	1/25/00	−$ 200												+$200
	1/25/00	−$ 300												+$300
		$ 5,830 +	$6,000 +	$700 +	$5,760 +	$1,800 +	$100	=	$4,320 +	$1,200	+	$14,950 +	$400 −	$680

Exhibit 5-18 Sweet Temptations Purchases Another Display Case

		Assets						=	Liabilities		+	Owner's Equity		
												Owner's Capital	Net Income	
Trans	Date	Cash	Prepaid Rent	Supplies	Inventory	Store Equipment	Accounts Receivable	=	Accounts Payable	Notes Payable	+	A. Cox, Capital	Revenues −	Expenses
(1)	1/1/00	$ 7,300	$6,000	$700	$1,620	$1,800	$400		$1,620	$1,200		$15,000		
(2)	1/2/00	+$ 300			−$ 135								+$300 −	+$135
(3)	1/3/00	−$ 1,620							−$1,620					
(4)	1/4/00				+$4,320				+$4,320					
(5)	1/6/00				−$ 45		+$100						+$100 −	+$ 45
(6)	1/7/00	+$ 400					−$400							
(7)	1/20/00	−$ 50										−$ 50		
(8)	1/25/00	−$ 200												+$200
	1/25/00	−$ 300												+$300
(9)	1/25/00	−$ 200				+$ 200								
		$ 5,630 +	$6,000 +	$700 +	$5,760 +	$2,000 +	$100	=	$4,320 +	$1,200	+	$14,950 +	$400 −	$680

Do you think Sweet Temptations' location next to Bud's Buds will improve its sales of Valentine candy? Why, or why not?

source documents for the transactions. As you can see in Exhibit 5-19, Anna decreases the asset Cash by $2,050. Because paying an employee's salary is a cost of providing goods and services to customers, she also increases Expenses by the same amount.

On January 31, 2000, Sweet Temptations pays its telephone bill and its utility bill (heat, light, and water) for January. The two checks are written for $60 and $190, respectively. Anna records each transaction separately, using the bills and checks as the source documents. As you can see in Exhibit 5-20, she decreases Cash and increases Expenses for both transactions.

Exhibit 5-20 also shows the summary transaction, that we discussed earlier, of all the cash sales from January 3 through January 31.

 How many additional boxes of candy did Sweet Temptations sell for cash during January? Why were Expenses increased by $3,465?

End-of-Period Adjustments

7 *Why are end-of-period adjustments necessary?*

Remember, revenues are the prices charged to a company's customers for goods or services it provided during the accounting period, and expenses are the costs of providing those goods or services during the period. The net income is the excess of revenues over expenses for the period. To calculate net income for a month, for example, a company counts the dollar totals for all the revenue and expense transactions of that specific month and subtracts the expense total from the revenue total. That is, it matches the expenses against the revenues for the month.

To calculate a company's net income under accrual accounting, the company must make sure that all its revenues and expenses for the accounting period are included in the totals. For Sweet Temptations, Anna can easily verify that the revenue total is correct because every sale is listed on a source document (a sales invoice or a cash register tape), which she used to record each sales transaction. Anna can verify that *most* of Sweet Temptations' expenses are correct because they also have source documents (invoices, utilities bills, and time cards).

Exhibit 5-19   Sweet Temptations Pays Salaries

		Assets						=	Liabilities		+	Owner's Equity		
												Owner's Capital	Net Income	
Trans	Date	Cash	Prepaid Rent	Supplies	Inventory	Store Equipment	Accounts Receivable		Accounts Payable	Notes Payable		A. Cox, Capital	Revenues	Expenses
	1/1/00	$7,300	$6,000	$700	$1,620	$1,800	$400		$1,620	$1,200		$15,000		
(1)	1/2/00	+$300			–$135								+$300	+$135
(2)	1/3/00	–$1,620							–$1,620					
(3)	1/4/00				+$4,320				+$4,320					
(4)	1/6/00				–$45		+$100						+$100	+$45
(5)	1/7/00	+$400					–$400							
(6)	1/20/00	–$50										–$50		
(7)	1/25/00	–$200												+$200
(8)	1/25/00	–$300												+$300
(9)	1/25/00	–$200				+$200								
(10)	1/30/00	–$2,050												+$2,050
		$3,580	$6,000	$700	$5,760	$2,000	$100		$4,320	$1,200		$14,950	$400	$2,730

Exhibit 5-20   Sweet Temptations Pays Telephone and Utility Bills and Records Sales for January 3–January 31

		Assets						=	Liabilities		+	Owner's Equity		
												Owner's Capital	Net Income	
Trans	Date	Cash	Prepaid Rent	Supplies	Inventory	Store Equipment	Accounts Receivable		Accounts Payable	Notes Payable		A. Cox, Capital	Revenues	Expenses
	1/1/00	$7,300	$6,000	$700	$1,620	$1,800	$400		$1,620	$1,200		$15,000		
(1)	1/2/00	+$300			–$135								+$300	+$135
(2)	1/3/00	–$1,620							–$1,620					
(3)	1/4/00				+$4,320				+$4,320					
(4)	1/6/00				–$45		+$100						+$100	+$45
(5)	1/7/00	+$400					–$400							
(6)	1/20/00	–$50										–$50		
(7)	1/25/00	–$200												+$200
(8)	1/25/00	–$300												+$300
(9)	1/25/00	–$200				+$200								
(10)	1/31/00	–$2,050												+$2,050
(11)	1/31/00	–$60												+$60
	1/31/00	–$190												+$190
	1/3/00 thru 1/31/00	+$7,700			–$3,465								+$7,700	+$3,465
		$11,030	$6,000	$700	$2,295	$2,000	$100		$4,320	$1,200		$14,950	$8,100	$6,445

Do you think it sometimes may be difficult to identify when a sale has occurred? Why?

It is more difficult, however, for a company to make sure that *all* of the expenses it incurred during the month are included in the net income calculation because some of the costs of providing goods or services occur without a source document. Since these expense transactions don't have source documents, there is no "automatic trigger" for recording the transactions. Before calculating its net income, then, a company must analyze its unique expenses (and a few unique revenues, which we will briefly discuss later) to see if it needs to adjust (increase) the total expenses (or revenues) to include those without source documents. These adjustments are called **end-of-period adjustments**.

 What types of expenses can you think of that occur without source documents?

In general, end-of-period adjustments involve assets that a company had at the beginning of the accounting period but that it used during the period to earn revenues. As assets lose their potential for providing future benefits, they are changed to expenses. Anna must analyze Sweet Temptations' assets to see what additional expenses to record. As you will see, the end-of-period adjustments may also include liabilities that a company owes because of expenses that must be recorded. Let's take a look at the four end-of-period adjustments that Anna makes (which we show later in Exhibit 5-21) before calculating Sweet Temptations' net income for January 2000, its first month of operations.

Supplies Used

Recall that on December 17, 1999, Sweet Temptations purchased $700 of supplies from City Supply Company. At this time, Anna increased the asset Supplies by $700 to show the cost of this new asset. Sweet Temptations thus purchased the pens, paper, blank sales invoices, and other items it needed to operate the business.

Because Sweet Temptations operated during January, it used some of these supplies. Thus, at January 31, 2000, the $700 original amount of Supplies is not correct. Anna must adjust the amount to show that since some of the supplies were used, they now are an expense, and only part of the $700 of supplies is still an asset. Anna determines that the office supplies used during January amount to $30. She makes an end-of-period adjustment to increase Expenses by $30 and decrease the asset Supplies by $30. When she subtracts the $30 from the $700 original amount, the $670 ending amount is the cost of supplies the company still owns at the end of January.

 How do you think Anna determined the amount of supplies used up?

Expired Rent

Recall that Sweet Temptations wrote a check for $6,000 to the Westwood Mall on December 16, 1999, to pay in advance for six months' rent starting on January 1, 2000. At that time Anna recorded a $6,000 asset, Prepaid Rent, to show that Sweet Temptations had purchased the right to use space in the Westwood Mall for six months (January through June) at a price of $1,000 per month. At the end of January, Sweet Temptations has used up one month of Prepaid Rent—for January—because the business occupied the mall space for that entire month. Therefore, Anna must include the cost of the mall space as an expense in the calculation of Sweet Temptations' net income.

Since Sweet Temptations made the $6,000 payment on December 16, 1999, no other source documents relating to the rental of the mall space exist. Although Sweet Temptations has used up one of its six months of rent, the amount listed for Prepaid Rent is still $6,000.

Anna must adjust the Prepaid Rent amount to show that only five months of prepaid rent remain. To do so, she increases Expenses for January by $1,000 and reduces Prepaid Rent by the same amount. Now Prepaid Rent shows the correct amount of $5,000 ($1,000 × 5) for the remaining five months.

 What adjustment do you think Anna would make at the end of January if Sweet Temptations occupied the rental space for January but did not pay for any rent until February?

Depreciation of Store Equipment

At the beginning of January the amount for the asset Store Equipment was listed at the cost of $1,800. Sweet Temptations purchased the store equipment because it would help earn revenue. The equipment includes, for instance, display cases, a cash register, and a moving cart. Although Sweet Temptations doesn't expect any equipment to wear out completely after one month or even one year, it does not expect it all to last indefinitely. At some point in the future the display cases will become outdated, the cash register will quit working, and the moving cart will fall apart. At that time the company will decide to sell or dispose of the equipment.

The store equipment provides benefits to the company every period in which it is used. Because Sweet Temptations used the store equipment in January to help earn candy revenue and because the store equipment has a finite life, a portion of the cost of the store equipment is included as an expense in the January net income calculation. **Depreciation** is the part of the cost of a physical asset allocated as an expense to each time period in which the asset is used.

The simplest way to compute depreciation is to divide the cost by the estimated life of the asset. For now, assume that the depreciation for the store equipment is $15 a month. Anna makes an end-of-period adjustment for January's depreciation by increasing Expenses by $15 and decreasing the asset Store Equipment by $15.[3] Now store equipment shows the $1,985 remaining cost (called its "book value"). As Sweet Temptations uses the store equipment in each future month, it will record an additional $15 depreciation which will reduce the book value of the equipment. Therefore, at any point in time the difference between the original cost and the book value is the "accumulated depreciation" to date. We will discuss the methods used to calculate depreciation in Chapter 21.

Accrual of Interest

At the end of December 1999, Sweet Temptations purchased store equipment by signing a $1,200 note payable to be paid at the end of three months. Generally, all notes payable also involve the payment of interest for the amount borrowed. This interest is an expense of doing business during the time between the signing of the note and the payment of the note. Sweet Temptations agreed to pay $24 total interest for the note, so that at the end of the three months Sweet Temptations will pay $1,224 ($1,200 + $24). Interest accumulates (*accrues*) over time until it is paid. Since Sweet Temptations owed the note during all of January, Anna must record one month of interest on the note as an expense of doing business during January. Because Sweet Temptations will not pay the interest until it pays the note, it records the January interest as an increase in a liability. For now, assume that the interest is $8 per month ($24 ÷ 3). Anna makes an end-of-period adjustment for the January interest by increasing Expenses by $8 and increasing the liability Notes Payable by $8. We will discuss how to compute interest later in the book.

Exhibit 5-21 shows how these end-of-period adjustments affect Sweet Temptations' accounting equation. Note that each adjustment maintains the equality of the equation and has a dual effect on the equation.

---

[3]Sweet Temptations also purchased $200 of additional store equipment late in January. Sweet Temptations will include the depreciation on this store equipment as an expense in later months as it uses the equipment.

Exhibit 5-21 Sweet Temptations Makes End-of-Period Adjustments

		Assets						=	Liabilities		+	Owner's Capital	+	Net Income		
Trans	Date	Cash	+ Prepaid Rent	+ Supplies	+ Inventory	+ Store Equipment	+ Accounts Receivable	=	Accounts Payable	+ Notes Payable	+	A. Cox, Capital	+	Revenues	−	Expenses
	1/31/00	$11,030	$6,000	$700	$2,295	$2,000	$100		$4,320	$1,200		$14,950		$8,100	−	$6,445
(1)	1/31/00			−$ 30											−	+$ 30
(2)	1/31/00		−$1,000												−	+$1,000
(3)	1/31/00					−$ 15									−	+$ 15
(4)	1/31/00									+$ 8					−	+$ 8
	1/31/00	$11,030	+ $5,000	+ $670	+ $2,295	+ $1,985	+ $100	=	$4,320	+ $1,208	+	$14,950	+	$8,100	−	$7,498

End-of-Period Revenue Adjustments

There are a few end-of-period adjustments that a company may need to make to ensure that its revenues are correct for the accounting period. Here, we briefly discuss two. First, a company may have a note receivable (asset) that earns interest that the company will collect when it collects the note. At the end of the accounting period, the company must record any interest that has accumulated *(accrued)* by increasing Revenues and increasing the asset Notes Receivable. Second, a company might collect cash in advance from a customer for sales of merchandise that it will deliver or services that it will perform for the customer later in the current accounting period or in the next accounting period. In this case, the company has not earned the revenue at the time of the cash collecton. Therefore, it records the receipt by increasing Cash and increasing a liability (sometimes called *Unearned Revenue*). Then, at the end of the current accounting period the company must decrease the Unearned Revenue and increase Revenues for the amount of revenue it has earned during the period. We will discuss end-of-period revenue adjustments more completely in later chapters.

 At the end of January, 2000, what adjustment would Ace Equipment Company make for the $8 interest it has earned on the $1,200 note it received from Sweet Temptations at the end of December, 1999?

Net Income and the Balance Sheet

After recording the results of all the transactions and end-of-period adjustments (shown in Exhibit 5-21), Anna calculates Sweet Temptations' net income for January:

$$\textbf{Net Income} = \textbf{Revenues} - \textbf{Expenses}$$
$$\$602 \quad = \quad \$8,100 \quad - \quad \$7,498$$

A company will normally prepare an income statement that lists the various types of revenues and expenses included in net income. For simplicity, in this chapter we use a simple accounting system, which does not help in the preparation of a detailed income statement. In the next chapter we will expand the accounting system to make it easier to prepare an income statement. Anna can, however, compare the actual net income amount for January with the projected net income that she calculated when she planned Sweet Temptations' operations. In Chapter 3, she calculated a projected net income for Sweet Temptations of $110 for January 2000. Anna should be pleased; by achieving an actual net income of $602, Sweet Temptations has done better than she expected. Later in the book, we will discuss how internal and external users analyze the financial statements of a company to understand how well it did for a specific time period.

To prepare the January 31, 2000 balance sheet for Sweet Temptations, Anna uses the end-of-the-month amounts for each asset, liability, and owner's equity item listed in Exhibit 5-21. Exhibit 5-22 shows Sweet Temptations' balance sheet at January 31, 2000.

You should be able to trace the asset and liability amounts directly to the ending amounts listed on Exhibit 5-21. The assets on the balance sheet are rearranged, however, to show them in the order of their *liquidity*, or how quickly the assets can be used up or converted to cash. We will discuss liquidity more in later chapters. Also notice that Anna must calculate the balance sheet amount for Owner's Equity (A. Cox, capital) at the end of January. It is the sum of all of the owner's equity items included in Exhibit 5-21:

A. Cox, capital	$14,950
Revenues	+ 8,100
Expenses	− 7,498
Owner's Equity	$15,552

Expressed another way, it is the sum of A. Cox, capital and net income ($14,950 + $602).

Exhibit 5-22 Sweet Temptations' Balance Sheet

SWEET TEMPTATIONS
Balance Sheet
January 31, 2000

Assets		**Liabilities**	
Cash	$11,030	Accounts payable.................................	$4,320
Accounts receivable	100	Notes payable.....................................	1,208
Inventory.................................	2,295	Total Liabilities...................................	$5,528
Supplies...................................	670		
Prepaid rent...........................	5,000	**Owner's Equity**	
Store equipment....................	1,985	A. Cox, capital	$15,552[a]
		Total Owner's Equity............................	$15,552
		Total Liabilities	
Total Assets	$21,080	and Owner's Equity...........................	$21,080

[a]$14,950 + $8,100 − $7,498; from Exhibit 5-21.

Since Anna is the owner, the net income (revenues minus expenses) is included in her capital amount on the January 31, 2000 balance sheet. Using the total amounts for the asset, liability, and owner's equity sections of Sweet Temptations' balance sheet, we can state the accounting equation on January 31, 2000 as follows:

$$\textbf{Assets = Liabilities + Owner's Equity}$$
$$\$21,080 = \$5,528 + \$15,552$$

Because Anna properly recorded Sweet Temptations' transactions, the company's accounting equation is in balance at January 31, 2000.

Just as we expanded the accounting equation to record revenue and expense transactions, we will discuss other changes in the accounting system throughout the book. The changes make it easier to keep track of company activities and increase the usefulness of the accounting system. We will also introduce additional accounting concepts to help you understand why companies make changes to the accounting system. In the next three chapters, we will take a detailed look at three very important outputs of the accounting process—the income statement, the balance sheet, and the cash flow statement. We will also continue to answer questions concerning what accounting is, how accounting works, why accounting is performed, and how accounting information is used for problem-solving and decision-making. We will also discuss how to minimize errors which, among other things, can cause major embarrassments, as we discuss below.

Business Issues and Values: A Billion Here, a Billion There

www.fid-intl.com

In one year, Fidelity Investments estimated that it would make a year-end distribution of $4.32 per share to shareholders in its *Magellan Fund*. The company then admitted to an error. Included in a letter sent to shareholders was the following statement: " . . . The error occurred when the accountant omitted the minus sign on a net capital loss of $1.3 billion and incorrectly treated it as a net capital gain on (a) separate spreadsheet. This meant that the dividend estimate spreadsheet was off by $2.6 billion." The error had no effect on the fund's results or on the shareholders' taxes but was clearly an embarrassment to the company's management!

Summary

At the beginning of the chapter we asked you several questions. During the chapter, we asked you to STOP and answer some additional questions to build your knowledge about specific issues. Be sure you answered these additional questions. Below are the questions from the beginning of the chapter, with a brief summary of the key points relating to the answers. Use your creative and critical thinking skills to expand on these key points to develop more complete answers to the questions and to determine what other questions you have that might lead you to learn more about the issues.

1 Why do managers, investors, creditors, and others need information about a company's operations?

Internal and external users need information about a company's operations to evaluate alternatives. For instance, a manager needs this information to decide which alternative best helps the company meet its goals of remaining solvent and earning a satisfactory profit. A banker also needs this information to decide the conditions for granting a loan.

2 What are the basic concepts and terms that help identify the activities that a company's accounting system records?

The basic concepts and terms that help identify the activities that a company's accounting system records are the entity concept (each company is separate from its owners), transactions (exchanges between a company and another entity), source documents (business records as evidence of transactions), the monetary unit concept (transactions are recorded in monetary terms), and the historical cost concept (transactions are recorded based on dollars exchanged).

3 What do users need to know about the accounting equation for a company?

Users need to know the accounting equation: Assets = Liabilities + Owner's Equity. They need to know that assets are a company's economic resources, liabilities are a company's debts, and owner's equity is the owner's current investment in the assets of the company.

4 Why are at least two effects of each transaction recorded in a company's accounting system?

A company's accounting system is designed so that two effects of each transaction are recorded in order to maintain the equality of the accounting equation. Under the dual effect of transactions, recording a transaction involves at least two changes in the assets, liabilities, and owner's equity of a company.

5 What are revenues and expenses, and how is the accounting equation expanded to record these items?

Revenues are the prices a company charged its customers for goods or services provided during an accounting period. Expenses are the costs of providing the goods or services during the period. Net income is the excess of revenues over expenses for the period. The accounting equation is expanded as follows to record revenues and expenses: Assets = Liabilities + [Owner's Capital + (Revenues − Expenses)].

6 What are the accounting principles and concepts related to net income?

The accounting principles and concepts related to net income are the accounting period, earning and recording revenues, the matching principle, and accrual accounting. The accounting period is the time span used by a company to report its net income. A company records revenues during the accounting period in which they are earned and collectible. The matching principle states that a company matches the total expenses of an accounting period against the total revenues of the period to determine its net income. Accrual accounting means that a company records its revenues and expenses in the accounting period in which it provides goods or services, regardless of whether it receives or pays cash.

7 Why are end-of-period adjustments necessary?

End-of-period adjustments are necessary to record any expenses that a company has incurred (or any revenues that the company has earned) during the accounting period but that it has not yet recorded. Adjustments ensure that these expenses (and revenues) are included in the company's net income calculation.

Key Terms

accounting equation *(p. 124)*	**liabilities** *(p. 123)*
accounting period *(p. 132)*	**matching principle** *(p. 134)*
accounting system *(p. 122)*	**monetary unit concept** *(p. 121)*
accounts payable *(p. 123)*	**net assets** *(p. 124)*
accounts receivable *(p. 123)*	**net income** *(p. 132)*
accrual accounting *(p. 134)*	**owner's equity** *(p. 124)*
assets *(p. 122)*	**partners' equity** *(p. 124)*
creditors *(p. 123)*	**prepaid insurance** *(p. 128)*
creditors' equity *(p. 123)*	**records revenues** *(p. 133)*
depreciation *(p. 143)*	**residual equity** *(p. 124)*
dual effect of transactions *(p. 124)*	**revenues** *(p. 132)*
earning process *(p. 133)*	**source document** *(p. 121)*
end-of-period adjustments *(p. 142)*	**stockholders' equity** *(p. 124)*
entity *(p. 120)*	**total equity** *(p. 124)*
equity *(p. 123)*	**transaction** *(p. 120)*
expenses *(p. 132)*	**wages and salaries payable** *(p. 123)*
historical cost concept *(p. 122)*	**withdrawal** *(p. 137)*

Integrated Business and Accounting Situations

Answer the Following Questions in Your Own Words

Testing Your Knowledge

5-1 Why do external users need financial accounting information about a company? How can financial statements help these external users?

5-2 Why is it important for external users to know that a company's financial statements are prepared according to GAAP?

5-3 Name and briefly define five concepts and terms that you need to understand to identify the activities that a company's accounting system records.

5-4 What is the entity concept? How does it affect the accounting for a specific company?

5-5 What is a transaction? Why is it important in accounting?

5-6 What is a source document? Why does a company need to prepare source documents?

5-7 What are the monetary unit and historical cost concepts? How do they affect the recording of transactions?

5-8 Define assets. Give four examples.

5-9 Define liabilities. Give two examples.

5-10 Define owner's equity. What items affect owner's equity?

5-11 Why is a company's statement of financial condition called a balance sheet?

5-12 What are a company's net assets? How do they relate to owner's equity?

5-13 What is meant by the dual effect of transactions? How does it relate to the accounting equation?

5-14 How is the accounting equation used to set up a simple accounting system? Use the accounting equation to record a $500 cash purchase of equipment on July 1.

5-15 Define revenues, expenses, and net income. How is the accounting equation expanded to record income-related transactions?

5-16 Name and briefly define four principles and concepts relating to net income.

5-17 What is an accounting period? What is the usual length of an accounting period?

5-18 What is a company's earning process, and when does the company record revenues?

5-19 What is the matching principle? Why is it useful to a company?

5-20 What is accrual accounting, and why is it important?

5-21 How do the accounting concepts, principles, and terms discussed in the chapter relate to the accounting system of a company?

5-22 What are end-of-period adjustments? Why are they needed?

Applying Your Knowledge

5-23 Each of the following cases is independent of the others:

Case	Assets	Liabilities	Owner's Equity
1	A	$24,000	$56,000
2	$79,000	B	$42,000
3	$98,000	$17,000	C

Required: Determine the amounts for A, B, and C.

5-24 At the beginning of the year, the Thomas Lighting Company had total assets of $89,000 and total liabilities of $22,000. During the year, the total assets increased by $16,000. At the end of the year, owner's equity totaled $84,000.

Required: Determine (1) the owner's equity at the beginning of the year and (2) the total liabilities at the end of the year.

5-25 At the end of the year a company's total assets are $75,000, and its total owner's equity is $48,000. During the year the company's liabilities decreased by $11,000 while its assets increased by $7,000.

Required: Determine the company's (1) ending total liabilities, (2) beginning total assets, and (3) beginning owner's equity.

5-26 The following transactions are taken from the records of Phantom Security Company:

$$\text{Assets} = \text{Liabilities} + \text{Owner's Equity}$$

(a) Rex Simpson, the owner, invested $12,000 cash in the business.

(b) Phantom paid $6,000 cash to acquire security equipment.

(c) Phantom received a $7,000 cash loan from Story County Bank.

Required: Determine the overall effect of each transaction on the assets, liabilities, and owner's equity of Phantom Security Company. Use the symbols *I* for increase, *D* for decrease, and *N* for no change. Also show the related dollar amounts.

5-27 On August 31, 2000, the Hernandez Engineering Company's accounting records contained the following items (listed in alphabetical order):

Accounts payable	$3,700
Accounts receivable	4,000
Cash	5,200
L. Hernandez, capital	?
Notes payable	6,000
Office equipment	7,500
Office supplies	600
Prepaid insurance	800

Required: Prepare a balance sheet for the Hernandez Engineering Company at August 31, 2000. Insert the correct amount for L. Hernandez, capital.

5-28 Listed below, in random order, are all the items included in the Ridge Rental Company balance sheet at December 31, 2000:

Land	$ 2,200
Accounts receivable	3,500
Cash	?
Supplies	900

Accounts payable	4,600
Building	19,000
A. Ridge, capital	?
Rental equipment	5,600
Notes payable	5,700

Total assets on December 31, 2000 are $32,600.

Required: Prepare a balance sheet for the Ridge Rental Company on December 31, 2000. Insert the correct amounts for Cash and for A. Ridge, capital.

5-29 In the chapter, we stated that a transaction is an exchange of property or service by a company with another entity. We also explained that in the recording of a transaction, at least two changes must be made in the assets, liabilities, or owner's equity of a company.

Required: In each case below, describe a transaction that will result in the following changes in the contents of a company's balance sheet:

(a) Increase in an asset and increase in a liability
(b) Decrease in an asset and decrease in a liability
(c) Increase in an asset and decrease in another asset
(d) Increase in an asset and increase in owner's equity
(e) Increase in an asset and increase in revenues
(f) Increase in expenses and decrease in an asset

5-30 Recall from the chapter that we defined a source document as a business record used by a company as evidence that a transaction has occurred.

Required: Name the source documents you think a company would use as evidence for each of the transactions listed below.

(a) Receipt of cash from the owner for additional investment in the company
(b) Payment by check to purchase office equipment
(c) Purchase of office supplies on credit
(d) Sale of office equipment at its original purchase price to a local CPA
(e) Purchase of fire and casualty insurance protection
(f) Sale of inventory on credit

5-31 During October the Wilson Company incurred the following costs:
(a) At the beginning of the month, the company paid $600 to an insurance agency for a two-year comprehensive insurance policy on the company's building.
(b) The company purchased office supplies costing $970 on credit from Bailey's Office Supplies.
(c) The company paid the telephone company $110 for telephone service during October.
(d) The owner withdrew $1,200 for personal use.
(e) The company found that of the $970 of office supplies purchased in (b), only $900 remained at October 31.

Required: For each of the preceding items, identify whether it would be recorded as an asset or an expense by the Wilson Company for October. List the dollar amount and explain your reasoning.

5-32 Gertz Rent-A-Car is in the business of providing customers with quality rental cars at low rates. The company engaged in the following transactions during March:
(a) J. Gertz deposited an additional $1,900 of his personal cash into the company's checking account.
(b) The company collected $1,500 in car rental fees for March.
(c) The company borrowed $7,000 from the 1st National Bank to be repaid in one year.
(d) The company completed arrangements to provide fleet service to a local company for one year, starting in April, and collected $18,000 in advance.

Required: For each of the preceding transactions, identify which would be recorded as revenues by Gertz Rent-A-Car for March. List the dollar amount and explain your reasoning.

5-33 The Slidell Auto Supply Company entered into the following transactions during the month of July:

Date	Transaction
7/1	Joan Slidell, the owner, deposited $10,000 in the company's checking account.
7/11	Slidell Auto Supply purchased $800 of office supplies from Jips Paper Company, agreeing to pay for half of the supplies on July 31 and the rest of the supplies on August 15.
7/16	Slidell Auto Supply purchased a three-year fire insurance policy on a building owned by the company, paying $600 cash.
7/31	Slidell Auto Supply paid Jips Paper Company half the amount owed for the supplies purchased on July 11.

Required: Using the basic accounting equation that we presented in this chapter, record the preceding transactions. Use subheadings for the specific kinds of assets, liabilities, and owner's equity. Set up your answer in the following form:

Date   *Assets*   =   *Liabilities*   +   *Owner's Equity*

5-34 Amy Dixon opened the Dixon Travel Agency in January, and the company entered into the following transactions during January:

(a) On January 2, Amy deposited $25,000 in the company's checking account.

(b) To conduct its operations, the company purchased land for $3,000 and a small office building for $15,000 on January 3, paying $18,000 cash.

(c) On January 5, the company purchased $700 of office supplies from City Supply Company, agreeing to pay for half of the supplies on January 15 and the remainder on February 15.

(d) On January 12, the company purchased office equipment from Ace Equipment Company at a cost of $3,000. It paid $1,000 down and signed a note, agreeing to pay the remaining $2,000 at the end of one year.

(e) On January 15, the company paid City Supply Company half the amount owed for the supplies purchased on January 5.

(f) On January 28, Amy decided that the company did not need a desk it had purchased on January 12 for $400. The desk was sold for $400 cash to Chris Watson, an insurance agent, for use in his office.

(g) On January 30, the company collected $900 of commissions for travel arrangements made for customers during January.

(h) On January 31, the company paid Frank Jones $500 for secretarial work done during January.

(i) On January 31, the company received its utilities and phone bill, totaling $120 for January. It will pay for this bill in early February.

(j) On January 31, Amy withdrew $400 from the company for her personal use.

Required: (1) Using the accounting equation format we developed in the chapter, record the preceding transactions.

(2) Prove the equality of the accounting equation at the end of January.

(3) List the source documents that you would normally use in recording each of the transactions.

5-35 Parsons Fashion Designers was started on June 1. The following transactions of the company occurred during June:

(a) E. Parsons started the business by investing $28,000 cash.

(b) Land and an office building were acquired at a cost of $5,000 and $18,000, respectively. The company paid $6,000 down and signed a note for the remaining balance of $17,000. The note is due in two years.

(c) Design equipment was purchased. The cash price of $2,600 was paid by writing a check to the supplier.

(d) Office supplies totaling $250 were purchased on credit. The amount is due in 30 days.

(e) A one-year fire insurance policy was purchased for $800.

(f) Fashion design commissions (fees) of $1,200 were collected for June.

(g) An assistant's salary of $600 was paid for June.

(h) E. Parsons withdrew $500 from the company for personal use.

(i) Utility bills totaling $150 for June were received and will be paid in early July.

Required: (1) Using the accounting equation format shown in the chapter, record the preceding transactions.

(2) Prove the equality of the accounting equation at the end of June.

(3) List the source documents that you would normally use in recording each of the transactions.

5-36 L. Snider, a young CPA, started Snider Accounting Services on September 1, 2000. During September, the following transactions of the company took place:

(a) On September 1, Snider invested $7,000 to start the business.

(b) On September 1, the company paid $3,000 for one year's rent of office space in advance.

(c) On September 2, office equipment was purchased at a cost of $5,000. A down payment of $1,000 was made, and a $4,000, one-year note was signed for the balance owed.

(d) On September 5, office supplies were purchased for $600 cash.

(e) On September 18, $1,000 was collected from clients for accounting services performed.

(f) On September 28, a $500 salary was paid to an accounting assistant.

(g) On September 29, Snider withdrew $800 for personal use.

(h) On September 30, the company billed clients $1,200 for accounting services performed during the second half of September.

(i) On September 30, the September utility bill of $100 was received; it will be paid in early October.

(j) On September 30, Snider recorded the following adjustments:

1. Rent expense of $250
2. Depreciation of $60 on office equipment
3. Interest expense of $40 on note payable
4. Office supplies used of $50

Required: (1) Using the accounting equation format shown in the chapter, record the preceding items.

(2) Prove the equality of the accounting equation at the end of September.

(3) Calculate the net income of the company for September.

(4) Prepare a balance sheet for the company on September 30, 2000.

5-37 The Johnson Drafting Company was started on March 1, 2000 to draw blueprints for building contractors. The following transactions of the company occurred during March:

Date	Transactions
3/1	M. Johnson, the owner, started the business by investing $15,000 cash.
3/2	Land and a small office building were purchased at a cost of $4,000 and $20,000, respectively. A down payment of $8,000 was made, and a note for $16,000 was signed. The note is due in one year.
3/3	Cash of $4,800 was paid to purchase computer drafting equipment.
3/8	Drafting supplies totaling $850 were purchased on credit. The amount is due in early April.
3/15	The company collected $1,500 from contractors for drafting services performed.
3/28	M. Johnson withdrew $1,000 for personal use.
3/29	The company received a $110 utility bill for March, to be paid in April.
3/30	The company paid $600 in salary to a drafting employee.
3/30	The company billed contractors $2,000 for drafting services performed during the last half of March.
3/31	The company recorded the following adjustments:
	(a) Depreciation of $80 on the office building
	(b) Depreciation of $100 on computer drafting equipment
	(c) Interest of $160 on note payable
	(d) Drafting supplies used of $150

Required: (1) Using the accounting equation format shown in the chapter, record the preceding transactions.

(2) Prove the equality of the accounting equation at the end of March.

(3) Calculate the net income of the company for March.

(4) Prepare a balance sheet for the company on March 31, 2000.

5-38 The five transactions that occurred during June, the first month of operations for Brown's Gym, were recorded as follows:

		Assets					=	Liabilities		+	Owner's Equity
Trans	**Date**	**Cash**	**+ Gym Supplies**	**+ Land**	**+ Building**	**+ Gym Equipment**	**=**	**Accts. Payable**	**+ Notes Payable**	**+**	**Tom Brown, Capital**
(a)	6/01/00	+ $25,000									+ $25,000
(b)	6/05/00	− 8,000		+ $5,000	+ $23,000				+ $20,000		
(c)	6/07/00	− 270	+ $270								
(d)	6/17/00	− 4,000				+ $10,000			+ 6,000		
(e)	6/26/00		+ 480					+ $480			
Balances	6/30/00	$12,730 +	$750 +	$5,000 +	$23,000 +	$10,000	=	$480 +	$26,000	+	$25,000

Required: (1) Describe the five transactions that took place during June.
(2) Prepare a balance sheet on June 30, 2000.

5-39 The following transactions were recorded by the Sutton Systems Design Company for May, its first month of operations:

		Assets					=	Liabilities		+	Owner's Equity
Trans	**Date**	**Cash**	**+ Office Supplies**	**+ Land**	**+ Building**	**+ Office Equipment**	**=**	**Accts. Payable**	**+ Notes Payable**	**+**	**Steve Sutton, Capital**
(a)	5/01/00	+ $55,000									+ $55,000
(b)	5/02/00	− 8,000		+ $6,000	+ $18,000				+ $16,000		
(c)	5/08/00	− 3,500				+ $7,500			+ 4,000		
(d)	5/10/00		+ $1,100					+ $1,100			
(e)	5/22/00	+ 300				− 300					
Balances	5/31/00	$43,800 +	$1,100 +	$6,000 +	$18,000 +	$7,200	=	$1,100 +	$20,000	+	$55,000

Required: (1) Describe the five transactions that took place during May.
(2) Prepare a balance sheet at May 31, 2000.

5-40 At the beginning of July 2000, Patti Dwyer established PD Company by investing $25,000 cash in the business. On July 5, the company purchased land and a building, making a $6,000 down payment (which was 10% of the purchase price) and signing a 10-year mortgage for the balance owed. The land was 20% of the cost, and the building was 80% of the cost. On July 17, the company purchased $3,800 of office equipment on credit, agreeing to pay half the amount owed in 10 days and the remainder in 30 days. On July 27, the company paid the amount due on the office equipment. On July 31, the company sold $900 of the office equipment that it did not need to another company for $900. That company signed a note requiring payment of the $900 at the end of one year.

Required: Based on the preceding information, prepare a balance sheet for PD Company on July 31, 2000. Show supporting calculations.

Making Evaluations

5-41 Your friend Maxine plans to supplement her job salary by running her own company at night and on the weekends. When the company earns enough money so that she can pay for a vacation home in the Caribbean, she plans to pay the bills of the company, sell the company's remaining assets, withdraw all the company's cash, and shut down the company. Since she will be extremely busy with her regular job and with running her new company, she plans to wait until she is ready to shut down the company to prepare a balance sheet, income statement, and cash flow statement. You think this is a bad idea.

Required: Do your best to convince Maxine that she should prepare financial statements more often, giving her examples of how doing this can help her and her company.

5-42 Chris Schandling is a loan officer at the First National Bank in Rochester, Minnesota. One day Nathan Wooten, who owns KidzLand (an indoor playground for young children), comes to the bank to see Chris about getting a $50,000 loan.

Required: (1) What types of questions do you think Chris will ask Mr. Wooten? Come up with at least three types of questions.

(2) What types of financial information do you think Chris will ask Mr. Wooten to provide? If Mr. Wooten asks Chris why this financial information is needed, how should Chris respond?

(3) Is it important that KidzLand's financial statements follow GAAP? Why or why not?

5-43 Andrew Poist works for Nilakanta and Company, a public accounting firm in Florence, South Carolina. On October 4, 2000, Sydney Langston, who started selling decorative, carved-wood duck decoys out of a booth at Cypress Court Mall during the first week in September, comes to see Andrew for some accounting help.

Mr. Langston walks into Andrew's office carrying a small cardboard box. He tells Andrew the following:

"After I retired, I decided I needed something to help keep me busy. I started this little business, "The Woodshed," a month ago. It is open only on Fridays when the mall has its Craft Day. I leased the booth for one year. So, every Friday until September 1, 2001, I will display my ducks in the booth and sell them.

I know I should have come to see you before I got started. I just kept putting it off. So, here's what I did. Throughout the month of September I tossed everything having to do with the Woodshed's finances into this box. It has all kinds of documents in it. I have all of my bank deposits for the month, checks I wrote that were paid by my bank, the receipts for the woodworking supplies I bought the day I started, etc. I sorted out some items, like checks I wrote to the grocery store and the electric company. Anyway, it's the first part of October, and I can't figure out how well the Woodshed did in September. Can you?"

"Of course I can," replies Andrew. "I'll have something for you in a couple of days."

Mr. Langston leaves, and Andrew opens the small box. Inside is a small pile of documents:

(a) Five deposit slips from Mr. Langston's checking account. They total $2,200. Andrew notices that on four of the deposit slips, Mr. Langston wrote "Craft Sales." Each one of the deposit dates corresponds to each of the four Fridays in September. On the other deposit slip, which is for $1,300, Mr. Langston wrote "Social Security."

(b) Six canceled checks from Mr. Langston's checking account. They total $3,350. Four checks written to Miranda's Woodworking Supplies Company total $600. One check for $350 was written to Circuit City, and one check for $2,400 was written to Cypress Court Mall Management.

(c) A handwritten schedule that reads as follows:

Mallard	$ 60	sold
Grey Goose	$100	sold
Baby Duck	$ 40	sold
Swan	$200	
Donald Duck	$ 70	sold
Large Mallard	$130	sold

Required: (1) Using the information Mr. Langston supplied to Andrew, calculate your best estimate of the revenues, expenses, and net income for the Woodshed for September 2000.

(2) How could your calculations of revenues, expenses, and net income be misstated? When Andrew meets with Mr. Langston to discuss the Woodshed's operating results for September, what questions should he ask concerning the information Mr. Langston supplied?

5-44 In this assignment, we are going to chronicle the changes in value and ownership of one asset—a one-acre plot of land on the corner of Cedar Springs Road and McKinney Avenue in Dallas, Texas—from January 1999 through December 2001. Here are the significant events that happened to that plot of land during this time period:

January 4, 1999:	The land is purchased for $450,000 by Dalton Realty Company.
April 25, 2000:	Dalton Realty receives a tax assessment notice from the city of Dallas stating that the city now values the land at $510,000 for local tax purposes.
December 12, 2000:	The land is sold by Dalton Realty Company to Park Cities Development Company for $515,000. Park Cities pays in cash.
May 22, 2001:	Using the land as collateral (meaning that if Park Cities fails to repay its loan, the bank may get ownership of the land), Park Cities borrows $550,000 from North Carolina National Bank.
June 14, 2001:	Park Cities rents the land to The Crescent Court office complex for six months. The Crescent Court will store construction equipment on the land while making renovations to its office space.
December 31, 2001:	Park Cities sells the land to The Crescent Court for $590,000.

Required: When business closes for each day listed below, state (1) which company shows this land in its accounting records as an asset, and (2) at what dollar amount the land is shown in that company's accounting records.

Date	Company showing the land as its asset	Dollar amount shown
1-4-99		
4-25-00		
12-12-00		
5-22-01		
6-14-01		
12-31-01		

5-45 Five years ago, Linda Monroe became the sole owner of LM Electronics. LM Electronics sells home entertainment centers, car audio equipment, and computers. LM advertises that it sells only the best brands, purchasing its inventory from well-known manufacturers in Japan, Germany, Norway, and the United States. Before opening this company, Linda was the accountant for The Music Warehouse. She understands accounting extremely well and maintains LM Electronics' accounting records according to generally accepted accounting principles.

On Friday morning, September 12, one of Linda's best customers, Sandy Wheeler, purchased a German-made CD player for $600. Linda was excited about making the sale because LM had only recently started carrying this particular brand. Linda filled out the sales invoice, collected the money, and helped Sandy carry the CD player out to her car.

Later that same day, Linda's friend Chris Tucker came into the store, also wanting to purchase a CD player. After browsing through the store, Chris started to leave. Linda stopped him and asked, "Chris, didn't you find a CD player that you would like to own?" Chris responded: "Well, Linda, I saw several items I would love to own, but I hadn't realized how expensive the equipment was. I guess I really can't afford to buy a new CD player."

Except for the deposit of the day's cash sales in the bank, no other activity took place that day at LM Electronics. After the store closed, Linda began thinking about Chris's comment. Early that evening Linda telephoned Chris and said: "Chris, I know you were wanting a new CD player, but if you are interested in saving a bunch of money, I would like to sell you the CD player I use at home. It is about two years old, and it is in great shape. I would sell it to you for $100."

Chris was very excited about Linda's offer. He drove over to Linda's house that same night, gave Linda $100 in cash, and took the CD player home. Linda immediately deposited the $100 in the bank night depository.

Required: Given the facts presented above and the information you learned in the chapter, (1) indicate whether you agree or disagree with the following statements, and (2) explain each answer (this is the most important part, so think through the following statements carefully).

(a) Linda Monroe sold two CD players on September 12.

(b) LM Electronics sold two CD players on September 12.

(c) LM Electronics should record CD player sales of $700 on September 12.

(d) Linda Monroe should deposit $700 in the bank on September 12.

5-46 Paul Jenkins is the sole owner of Friendly Pawn Shop. Friendly Pawn Shop buys and sells jewelry, musical instruments, televisions, telephones, and small kitchen appliances. Paul has owned the pawn shop for almost one year, and the shop has developed a reputation as an honest, reliable place for families to buy or sell their used items.

Up until now, Friendly Pawn Shop has bought and sold goods only from retail customers. Paul believes that Friendly Pawn Shop is overstocked with jewelry, and he thinks the shop does not have enough musical instruments to meet the demand that will occur after the new school year starts. Paul believes that the pawn shop needs to sell some jewelry, which cost about $1,500, and replace it with several trumpets, trombones, and flutes.

Friendly Pawn Shop advertises in the newspaper when it wants to buy particular types of used items. This way Paul has the opportunity to inspect the goods before they are purchased, and he has the opportunity to discuss the history of each item with its current owner. In the present situation, however, Paul is considering making a merchandise trade with a wholesale pawnbroker. Although Paul is almost convinced that the trade will be the best way for his company to obtain the musical instruments, he has two major concerns.

First, Paul is concerned about maintaining Friendly Pawn Shop's reputation for reliable merchandise. He knows almost all of his customers, and he has earned their trust. Because Paul does not know where the wholesaler's musical instruments were purchased, he worries that he will be trading good jewelry for inferior-quality musical instruments. He would not find out that the instruments are inferior until the customers told him of their dissatisfaction. Second, Paul does not know how to record the trade in Friendly Pawn Shop's accounting records. He knows that the jewelry he plans to trade cost $1,500 and that he was going to try to sell the jewelry for $4,000. Paul does not know how much the wholesaler paid for the musical instruments or what price to charge his customers for each item.

Required: (1) Using the four-step approach you learned earlier in this book, discuss how you think Paul should solve this business problem.

(2) Assuming Friendly Pawn Shop trades the jewelry for the musical instruments owned by the wholesale pawnbroker, discuss how you think this transaction should be recorded in the accounting records. Be sure to include references to the accounting concepts introduced in this chapter.

5-47 Your friend Jim Wilson is about to prepare the January 31 balance sheet for his new company, Cheap Fun Video Arcade. This is Cheap Fun's first month of operation, and Jim is also going to calculate the first month's net income. He needs to prepare the balance sheet and calculate net income so he can pass the information along to his parents. They loaned him $5,000 so that he could start Cheap Fun.

Although Jim thinks that business is booming, he has a big problem. He does not know enough about accounting to prepare the balance sheet or calculate January's net income. As a matter of fact, Jim had never heard the words "balance sheet" and "net income" until his parents asked him to promise to furnish these statements to them every month before they would agree to loan Jim the $5,000.

Luckily, Jim saves every piece of paper associated with Cheap Fun. He kept copies of all of the business agreements he signed. He deposited all of the money Cheap Fun earned in the company's bank account and retained copies of every deposit slip. Jim also paid every company bill with a check and saved all of the related documents.

Required: Assume Jim wants to prepare Cheap Fun's January 31 balance sheet and January's income statement according to generally accepted accounting principles. Describe to Jim, in your own words, how he should organize the information about Cheap Fun's January transactions so that he can prepare a balance sheet and an income statement and keep his promise to his parents.

5-48 Samson Construction Company is a small company that constructs buildings. Normally, the time for Samson to complete the construction of a building is about six months.

Recently, Samson signed a contract to build a three-story office building at a price of $900,000. Samson expects that it will take two years to complete the construction, at a cost of $600,000.

Bill Samson, the owner, has come to you for advice. He says: "Normally, my company records the revenue and related expenses for a project when it is completed. However, this new project will take much longer than usual. My construction crews will be working on the project for two years. My company will have to pay for their salaries plus all the materials, etc., so a lot of money will be tied up in the contract and won't be recovered until the selling price is collected when the building is completed. How and when should my company record the revenue and expenses on this project?"

Required: Prepare a written answer to Bill Samson's question.

5-49   Yesterday, you received the following letter for your advice column at the local paper:

Dear Dr. Decisive:

My girlfriend went with me and my family to Hawaii last month, and we had a great time. But we have a question that we hope you will answer. Suppose a company has accumulated frequent flier miles (which it hasn't used yet) from plane tickets that it purchased for business trips taken by its employees. Are the company's frequent flier miles an asset or an expense? My girlfriend says they're an asset, but I think they're an expense. We have a bet on your answer. If I lose, I have to take hula lessons. If she loses, she has to take sumo wrestling lessons.

Please help!! I don't look good in a grass skirt.

"Wrestling Fan"

Required: Meet with your Dr. Decisive team and write a response to "Wrestling Fan."

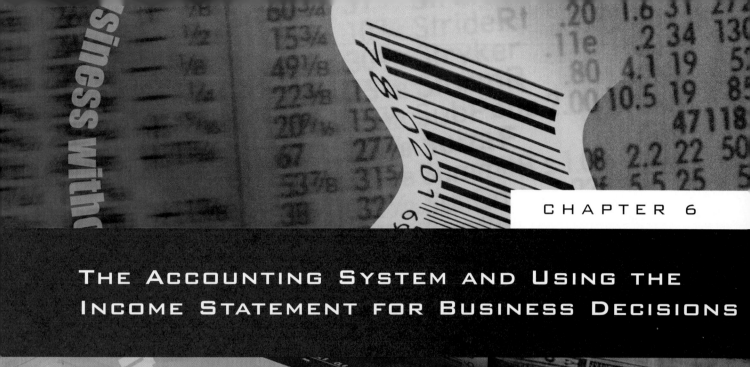

CHAPTER 6

THE ACCOUNTING SYSTEM AND USING THE INCOME STATEMENT FOR BUSINESS DECISIONS

"Business without profit is not business any more than a pickle is candy."

—Charles F. Abbott

1 *Why is a company's income statement important?*

2 *How are changes in a company's balance sheet and income statement accounts recorded in its accounting system?*

3 *What are the parts of a retail company's classified income statement, and what do they contain?*

4 *What is inventory and cost of goods sold, and what inventory systems may be used by a company?*

5 *What are the main concerns of external decision-makers when they use a company's income statement to evaluate its performance?*

6 *What type of analysis is used by external decision-makers to evaluate a company's profitability?*

In Chapter 5 we looked at the fundamentals of the financial accounting process. You saw how basic accounting concepts, such as the entity concept, the accounting equation, and accrual accounting, provide the framework for the accounting system that a company uses to record its day-to-day activities. The system provides internal users with valuable information that helps managers in their planning, operating, and evaluating activities. The revenue and expense transactions are also the basis of a company's income statement, which shows external users the company's profit (income) for the accounting period.

In this chapter, we discuss the importance of the income statement, introduce and explain how to use T-accounts to record accounting information, describe and present a classified income statement, and show how the income statement helps managers and external users make business decisions.

Why the Income Statement Is Important

1 *Why is a company's income statement important?*

A company's income statement plays a key role in the decision-making of the users by communicating the company's revenues, expenses, and net income (or net loss) for a specific time period. A company earns income by selling inventory (goods) or by providing services to customers during an accounting period. Recall that revenues are the prices a company charges its customers for the goods or services. Expenses are the costs of providing the goods or services during the period. An income statement is based on the equation we showed in Chapter 5:

Net Income = Revenues − Expenses

www.apple.com
www.att.com
www.avon.com
www.blackanddecker.
   com
www.kodak.com
www.rmcfusa.com

Companies may use different titles for their income statements, including *statement of income* (Apple Computer, AT&T, Avon Products), *statement of earnings* (Black & Decker, Eastman Kodak), or *statement of operations* (Rocky Mountain Chocolate Factory, Inc., Bird). You may also hear the income statement referred to as a *profit and loss (P&L) statement*.

Recall from Chapter 4 that a company prepares a "projected" income statement for *internal* use as part of its master budget. Exhibit 6-1 shows how internal users (managers) use a company's *projected* income statement and actual income statement in their decision-making, as well as how *external* users use a company's actual income statement to make economic decisions. We explain the impact of the income statement on users' decisions in the rest of this section.

The income statement summarizes the results of a company's operating activities for a specific accounting period. These operating activities stem from the planning and operating decisions that managers made during the period. Hence, a company's income statement shows the relationship between managers' decisions and the results of those decisions. This information helps both internal and external users evaluate how well the company's managers have "managed" during the period. By comparing a company's income statement information from period to period, users also can evaluate managers' ability over the longer run.

Let's first look at how managers use the income statement for making comparisons. Remember from Chapter 5 that a company keeps track of its activities by using an accounting system based on the accounting equation (Assets = Liabilities + Owner's Equity) and the dual effect of transactions. The accounting system provides the information that managers need to compare actual results with the expected (budgeted) results and to prepare external financial statements. At the end of an accounting period (e.g., one year), a company's income statement will show how well many of its managers' business decisions worked out.

For example, the revenue and expense information shows the results of manager's cost-volume-profit (C-V-P) analysis and budgeting decisions. In Chapter 3, you saw how Anna Cox used C-V-P analysis to develop her business plan. C-V-P analysis showed her how Sweet Temptations could break even and how it could earn a satisfactory profit. Anna

Exhibit 6-1   Uses of a Company's Income Statement

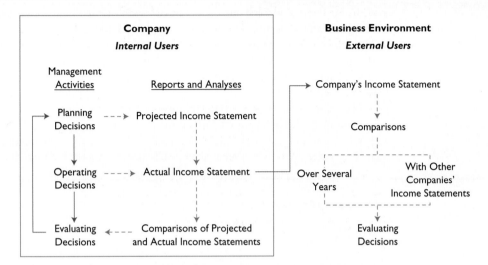

calculated that Sweet Temptations needed to sell 700 boxes of candy for $10 a box for the company to break even. In addition to helping managers predict a company's break-even point, C-V-P analysis improves managers' operating decisions such as estimating how much inventory to purchase, what sales price to charge, and what effect on profit to expect from price changes. We determined that if Sweet Temptations was able to sell 720 boxes, it would earn a profit of $110.

Consider the decision that managers must make about what sales price to charge. If Anna sets the price too high, Sweet Temptations risks not selling enough boxes to break even. If she sets the price too low, Sweet Temptations may sell many boxes of candy but may not earn high enough revenues to cover the costs of selling the candy. Later, when the accounting system keeps track of every sale, it records those sales at the prices that the customers actually paid. (Remember that every sale generates a sales invoice to document the transaction and the amount of the sale.) If Anna did a good job of assessing the market and establishing an appropriate price, Sweet Temptations will make sales, will earn revenues high enough to cover its expenses, and will make a profit that it will report on its income statement.

In Chapter 4, we discussed how budgets help managers make plans, control company expenses, and evaluate company performance. If you were the manager of Sweet Temptations, budgeting would allow you to compare your expectations for revenue and expense amounts (reported in the projected income statement) with the actual amounts (reported in the actual income statement). If sales were higher or expenses lower than expected, you could find out what you did right and keep doing it. If, on the other hand, sales were lower or expenses higher than expected, you could analyze your mistakes and try to improve.

 How do you think a company's decision to decrease the price of its product will affect the revenues that it reports on its income statement? How will this decision affect its expenses?

As valuable as C-V-P analysis and budgets are for internal decision-making, companies do not report to external decision-makers much of the information they provide. For one thing, companies don't want to reveal specific cost or budget information to their competitors. For another, many companies prepare internal accounting reports daily, so external users may be more confused than helped by the sheer volume of information.

External users need accounting information that lets them compare a company's actual operating performance over several years or with other companies. Suppliers, for example, do not have the resources to grant credit to all customers. A supplier can compare its customers' income statements to determine which ones might be the best credit risks. Generally accepted accounting principles (GAAP) ensure that all companies calculate and publish financial statement information in a similar, and thus comparable, manner. Thus, understanding GAAP is important to the accountant who prepares financial statements and to the external decision-maker who uses these statements to make business decisions.

In Chapter 5 we introduced a simple accounting system, as well as several concepts and terms that form the foundation of GAAP. In this chapter we modify that accounting system, expand on our discussion of GAAP as it relates to the income statement, and begin to explain how external users evaluate income statement information for decision-making.

Accounting System for Recording and Retaining Information

2 *How are changes in a company's balance sheet and income statement accounts recorded in its accounting system*

In Chapter 5 we kept track of Sweet Temptations' transactions using the accounting equation to set up columns for recording amounts for assets, liabilities, and/or owner's equity. We then expanded the accounting equation to include revenue and expense transactions. Adding revenue and expense columns let us keep track of these transactions separate from owner investments and withdrawals. In this simple accounting system, the column method worked well. However, real companies need to keep more-detailed records of their transactions, so the column method doesn't work. From this point on, we will discuss an accounting system that uses what are called "T-accounts" to keep track of a company's activities.

Limitations of the Column Method of Recording Transactions

To set the stage for our use of T-accounts, let's briefly look at the major limitation of the column method. The income statement includes the total amounts for several different types of revenues and expenses for the accounting period. For instance, as you will see later, Sweet Temptations' income statement shows total expense amounts for the cost of the candy sold, rent, depreciation, salaries, and utilities, to name a few. Real companies have many (sometimes hundreds!) different types of expenses (and many types of revenue). Imagine how wide the paper used in recording transactions would have to be to have columns for hundreds of expenses, plus all of the specific types of assets, liabilities, equities, and revenues. The use of T-accounts avoids this limitation. As you will see, the flexibility of using T-accounts lets a company record and retain many different types of detailed accounting information in its accounting system to help internal users make good business decisions and prepare useful and complete financial statements for external users.

The Need to Record Income Information Separately

Before we use T-accounts, you need to understand why a company has to record its net income information separately. As we discussed in Chapter 5, net income affects owner's equity, so a company's accounting system records all revenues as increases in owner's equity and records all expenses as decreases in owner's equity. Remember, however, that a company reports only the ending amounts for its assets, liabilities, and owner's equity on its balance sheet. Reporting the ending amount in owner's equity may be useful for certain purposes, but it does not help users understand the company's net income. A good accounting system is able to identify, measure, record, retain, and report the amounts for a company's revenue, expense, and owner investment and withdrawal transactions, as well as the amounts for its assets, liabilities, and owner's capital. This gives managers detailed net income and financial position information that can help their internal decision-making and that can be used in preparing both an income statement and a balance sheet.

The T-Account Method

The T-account method is a simple way of recording transactions. Under this method, the transactions for individual types of assets, liabilities, and owner's equity are recorded (entered) in **T-accounts** (or simply **accounts**), so called because each account looks like a capital **T**. The account title (e.g., Cash, Accounts Receivable, Accounts Payable) appears across the top of the T. A T-account looks like this:

Account Title

| Left side | Right side |

All of the increases in the account are recorded on one side of the T, and all of the decreases in the account are recorded on the other side. At any point in time, the *balance* of an account is the difference between the amounts recorded in the left and the right sides of the T-account.

 Think back to the "transaction scales" in Chapter 5. If a company keeps a separate T-account for each asset, liability, and owner's equity item (revenue or expense), how do you think it keeps its "scale" in balance for a particular transaction?

Why use T-accounts instead of columns? First, using T-accounts eliminates having to work with lots of account columns. Each account can be kept separately on individual computer files (or sheets of paper). Second, using one side of the T for increases and the other for decreases makes it much easier to calculate the total monetary increases and decreases for a particular asset, liability, revenue, or expense. Finally, as you will see, the design of the T-account helps ensure that the accounting equation remains in balance after every transaction.

Using T-Accounts for Assets, Liabilities, and Owner's Equity

Now that you know that all increases related to a particular account are recorded on one side of the T-account and all decreases on the other, you are probably wondering which side is for increases and which is for decreases. Which side is used for each relates to the accounting equation and depends on what the T-account is recording. Remember that assets are on the left side of the accounting equation, and liabilities and owner's equity are on the right side. Increases in assets are recorded on the left side of their T-accounts; decreases in asset accounts are recorded on the right side. For liability and owner's equity accounts, though, increases are recorded on the right side of their T-accounts, and decreases are on the left side, as we show below:

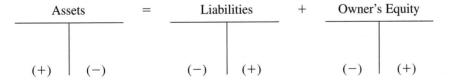

So, again, assets are on the left side of the equation; increases in assets are recorded on the left sides of their T-accounts. Liabilities and owner's equity are on the right side of the equation; increases in liabilities and owner's equity accounts are recorded on the right side of their T-accounts.

You may now have a question such as, "How will the T-account method help me keep the accounting equation in balance and follow the dual effect of transactions rule?" This is a very important question. If you understand the answer completely, you will have a much easier time learning how the accounting system keeps track of transactions and generates financial statements.

Showing the Dual Effect of Transactions

Before you learn the answer to the question, let's refresh your memory about the accounting equation and the dual effect of transactions. You know that the accounting equation, Assets = Liabilities + Owner's Equity, must always remain in balance. Recall from Chapter 5 that the dual effect of transactions means that when a transaction is recorded, at least two changes must be made in the assets, liabilities, or owner's equity of a company. The T-account method helps meet these requirements because of a basic rule: For every transaction recorded, *the total dollar amount of the changes on the left sides of the T-accounts must equal the total dollar amount of the changes on the right sides of the T-accounts.* Regardless of which type of asset, liability, or owner's equity account is involved in a transaction (or how many accounts are involved), following this rule makes it much easier to keep a company's accounting equation in balance and maintain the dual effect of transactions. Then, at the end of the company's accounting period, the balance of each asset, liability, and owner's capital account can be determined and a balance sheet can be prepared.

Using T-Accounts for Revenues and Expenses

The T-account method also makes it easier to record information about specific revenues and expenses. For example, instead of having only one column to record expense transactions, a company uses separate T-accounts for each different type of expense, such as advertising, salaries, supplies, or utilities.

By keeping separate T-accounts for each revenue and expense, the company can use the balances in these accounts to prepare an income statement at the end of each accounting period. Because revenue and expense T-accounts are used to record net income transactions *for only one accounting period*, they are called **temporary accounts.** Asset, liability, and owner's equity T-accounts are called **permanent accounts** because they are used *for the life of the company* to record balance sheet transactions.

After a company prepares its income statement for an accounting period, it transfers the ending balances from the temporary revenue and expense T-accounts into the permanent T-account for the owner's capital. This way, when a new accounting period starts, (1) the revenue and expense T-accounts (temporary accounts) no longer contain the amounts of any transactions from previous periods, (2) the accounting system keeps the revenue and expense transactions of the current period separate from the revenue and expense transactions of other periods, and (3) the permanent (balance sheet) accounts are up-to-date (net income has been added to the previous balance of the owner's capital T-account).

Using T-accounts to record revenue and expense transactions does not violate any of the concepts, principles, and rules that we have already discussed for an accounting system. Recall that the right side of the accounting equation includes the owner's equity (capital) account. When using T-accounts, a company records increases in owner's equity on the right side of the T-account. Since revenues increase owner's equity, all increases in revenues are recorded on the right side of their T-accounts. Expenses, however, decrease owner's equity. Thus increases in all expenses are recorded on the left side of their T-accounts. Because withdrawals also decrease owner's equity, they too are recorded on the left side of a Withdrawals T-account. The Withdrawals T-account is also a temporary account, used to accumulate the total amount of withdrawals made by the owner during the accounting period.

Summary of Rules for Recording Transactions

Before we go on, let's quickly review how to record accounting information in the permanent T-accounts for assets, liabilities, and owner's equity (capital), and in the temporary T-accounts for revenues, expenses, and withdrawals:

1. **Record increases in assets on the left side of their T-accounts (and record decreases on the right side of their T-accounts).**

2. **Record increases in liabilities on the right side of their T-accounts (and record decreases on the left side of their T-accounts).**

3. **Record increases in permanent owner's equity (capital) on the right side of this T-account and record decreases on the left side of this T-account. Owner's equity temporary T-accounts have the following rules:**
   (a) **Record increases in revenues on the right side of their T-accounts (and record decreases on the left side of their T-accounts).**
   (b) **Record increases in expenses on the left side of their T-accounts (and record decreases on the right side of their T-accounts).**
   (c) **Record increases in withdrawals on the left side of this T-account (and record decreases on the right side of this T-account).**

Remember that the T-account method is applied using the accounting equation and dual effect of transactions rules that we introduced in Chapter 5. In Exhibit 6-2 we show how the accounting equation and the T-account method are related.

 What would be the consequences if the original inventor of the T-account method had decided to reverse the increases and decreases in accounts (e.g., to record increases in assets on the right-hand side of asset accounts)?

In accordance with the accounting equation and T-account rules, then, a company creates and uses a T-account for each asset, liability, owner's capital, owner's withdrawal, revenue, and expense. In the company's accounting system, all of the accounts are stored together in one location, called a general ledger. A **general ledger** is the entire set of accounts for a company and might be stored on a computer disk or in a three-ring binder.

Exhibit 6-2 How the Accounting Equation and the T-Account Method Are Related

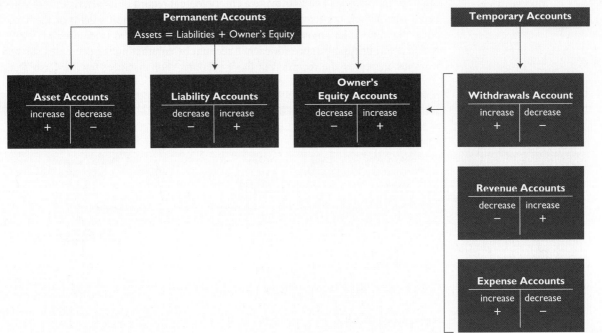

Examples of Using T-Accounts

Let's use the T-account method to record the December 1999 transactions for Sweet Temptations, the same transactions that we showed in column form in Chapter 5. We illustrate balance sheet transactions here and then show revenue and expense transactions later in the chapter.

Recording the Investment of Cash

Anna Cox started her retail candy store, Sweet Temptations, on December 15, 1999, by writing a $15,000 personal check and depositing the money in a separate checking account for Sweet Temptations. This transaction increased the asset Cash by $15,000 and increased the owner's equity item A. Cox, Capital by $15,000. Exhibit 5-6 in Chapter 5 showed how Anna used the accounting equation as a basis for recording this transaction in two columns. The top part of Exhibit 6-3 shows these columns, and the bottom part shows how Anna would record them using T-accounts instead. Both methods keep the accounting equation in balance and maintain the dual effect of transactions.

When using the T-accounts, Anna would record the date of the transaction and the $15,000 increase in Cash on the left side of its T-account. This is called "making an entry" in the T-account. She would record the date and the $15,000 increase in A. Cox, Capital on the right side of its T-account. Making these two entries keeps the accounting equation in balance because the assets increase by $15,000 and the owner's equity also increases by $15,000. (Also, the total dollar amount of the changes on the left sides of the T-accounts equals the total dollar amount of the changes on the right sides of the T-accounts.) Recording the transaction in this manner maintains the dual effect of transactions because it makes at least two changes in Sweet Temptations' assets, liabilities, or owner's equity.

Recording Various Transactions

Now that you have seen how to record one transaction, let's look at how to record all of Sweet Temptations' transactions for December 1999. The upper part of Exhibit 6-4 shows the columns from Exhibit 5-11, and the lower part shows how Anna would record these transactions using the T-accounts. For comparison purposes, we number the T-account entries in the lower part to correspond to the transaction numbers in the upper part. Normally, a company enters the date of a transaction in the respective T-account to help keep track of all the transactions and to provide a chronological record of its activities. For each numbered transaction, the total dollar amounts recorded on the left side(s) of the T-accounts equal the total dollar amounts recorded on the right side(s). On December 31, 1999, Anna would determine the balance for each T-account by subtracting the decreases she recorded from the increases she recorded in the T-account.[1] For instance, for the Cash T-account,

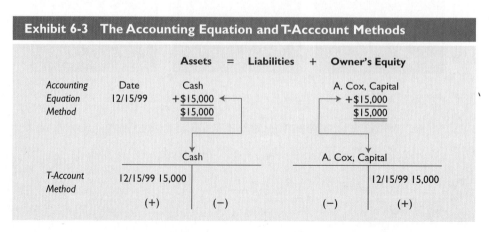

Exhibit 6-3   The Accounting Equation and T-Acccount Methods

[1]For simplicity, in later chapters we will include the date in a T-account entry and/or the balance of a T-account only when it is critical to the discussion.

Exhibit 6-4 Detailed Comparison of the Column and T-Account Recording Methods

Column Method for Recording Six Transactions

		Assets						=	Liabilities		+	Owner's Equity
Trans	Date	Cash	Prepaid Rent	Supplies	Inventory	Store Equipment	Accounts Receivable		Accounts Payable	Notes Payable		A. Cox, Capital
(1)	12/15/99	+$15,000										+$15,000
(2)	12/16/99	−$ 6,000	+$6,000									
(3)	12/17/99	−$ 700		+$700								
(4)	12/20/99				+$1,620				+$1,620			
(5)	12/29/99	−$ 1,000				+$2,200				+$1,200		
(6)	12/30/99					−$ 400	+$400					
	12/31/99	$ 7,300 +	$6,000 +	$700 +	$1,620 +	$1,800 +	$400	=	$1,620 +	$1,200	+	$15,000

Accounting equation balances after the six transactions are recorded using the column method.

$17,820 = $2,820 + $15,000

T-account Method for Recording the Same Six Transactions

Cash	
(1) 15,000	6,000(2)
	700(3)
	1,000(5)
7,300	

Prepaid Rent	
(2)6,000	
6,000	

Supplies	
(3)700	
700	

Inventory	
(4)1,620	
1,620	

Store Equipment	
(5)2,200	400(6)
1,800	

Accounts Receivable	
(6)400	
400	

Accounts Payable	
	1,620(4)
	1,620

Notes Payable	
	1,200(5)
	1,200

A. Cox, Capital	
	15,000(1)
	15,000

Accounting equation balances after the six transactions are recorded using the T-account method.

$17,820 = $2,820 + $15,000

Anna would subtract the total decreases of $7,700 ($6,000 + $700 + $1,000) from the $15,000 increase to determine the $7,300 ending balance. Notice that both the column and the T-account methods result in the same ending balances for each asset, liability, and owner's equity account; therefore, the accounting equation remains in balance.

 Now try your hand at using T-accounts by recording two of Sweet Temptations' January 2000 transactions. Record the January 3 payment of the $1,620 accounts payable and the January 7 collection of the $400 accounts receivable.

The Retail Company's Income Statement

3 *What are the parts of a retail company's classified income statement, and what do they contain?*

As we discussed earlier in the chapter, the income statement is an important part of the decision-making process for both internal and external users. It is an expansion of the income equation that we presented earlier:

$$\text{Net Income} = \text{Revenues} - \text{Expenses}$$

Revenues may be thought of as the "accomplishments" achieved by a company during an accounting period. Revenues are the prices charged to customers and *result in increases in assets (cash or accounts receivable) or decreases in liabilities (unearned revenues).* Expenses may be thought of as the "efforts" or "sacrifices" made by a company during an accounting period to earn revenue. Expenses are the costs of providing goods and services and *result in decreases in assets or increases in liabilities.*

Keep these definitions in mind while we discuss how a company provides revenue and expense information to external users in its "classified" income statement. Let's return to Sweet Temptations to see how Anna records and reports the results of her first month of operations. To reinforce your understanding of the T-account method, we will show how to record a few revenue and expense transactions. We will also show Sweet Temptations' classified income statement. As you look at this income statement, focus on understanding the income statement sections but also think about how Anna recorded the individual revenue and expense transactions.

The classified income statement of a retail company like Sweet Temptations has two parts: an "operating income" section and an "other items" section. **Operating income** includes all the revenues earned and expenses incurred in the primary operating activities of the company. The operating income section has three subsections: (1) revenues, (2) cost of goods sold, and (3) operating expenses. **Other items** include any revenues and expenses that are not directly related to the primary operations of the company, items such as interest revenue and interest expense. Exhibit 6-5 shows Sweet Temptations' classified income statement for January 2000.

In the next sections, we will discuss various issues related to recording and reporting revenues and expenses. We refer to Exhibit 6-5 to show how Sweet Temptations reports certain items.

Revenues

A retail company sells goods to customers either for cash or on credit. When goods are sold on credit, some retail companies offer an incentive for prompt payment. Whether the sales are for cash or on credit, customers sometimes return the goods they purchased. Let's see how companies record these aspects of sales.

Sales Revenue

Whether a customer buys goods for cash or on credit, retail companies use a Sales Revenue, or simply Sales, T-account to record the transaction. Recall from Chapter 5 that the source document for a sale is a sales invoice or simply an invoice. Some companies that

Exhibit 6-5 Sweet Temptations' Classified Income Statement

SWEET TEMPTATIONS
Income Statement
For the Month Ended January 31, 2000

Sales revenues (net)	$ 8,100
Cost of goods sold	(3,645)
Gross profit	$ 4,455
Operating expenses (see Exhibit 6-7):	
Selling expenses ... $2,961	
General and administrative expenses ... 884	
Total operating expenses	(3,845)
Operating income	$ 610
Other item:	
Interest expense	(8)
Net Income	$ 602

(handwritten: 59 300; 40 200; 18,600; $22,200; 600; 21 600)

sell only a few products or have a computerized accounting system may use a cash register tape or a credit card receipt as the source document. Exhibit 6-6 shows the sales invoice that Sweet Temptations used for one of its sales. This invoice shows you that on January 6, 2000, Sweet Temptations sold 10 boxes of milk chocolate candy for $10 per box, totaling to a $100 sale. Notice that the invoice also tells you that the invoice number was 0001, that the boxes of milk chocolate had an inventory identification number (ID #) of 0036, that it was a credit sale, and that the credit sale was made to Bud's Buds. It is important that the invoice includes all of the sales information needed to record this transaction.

Anna used the following T-accounts in Sweet Temptations' accounting system to record this transaction:

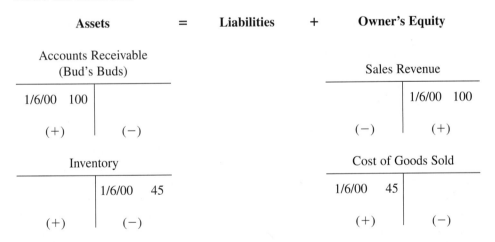

Exhibit 6-6 Sweet Temptations' Sales Invoice

Invoice #0001	SWEET TEMPTATIONS			Cash____	Credit X
	Sales Invoice				

Date	Description	ID #	# of Boxes	Unit Price	Total
1/6/00	milk chocolate	0036	10	$10	$100

Sold To: __Bud's Buds__   Acct # __0103__

Notice that four T-accounts are involved because both a revenue and an expense are recorded. Anna recorded the sale by increasing the Accounts Receivable T-account on the left side and increasing the Sales Revenue T-account on the right side for $100. Anna used the inventory identification number from the boxes of candy that Sweet Temptations sold to determine the cost of the candy ($45: 10 boxes at $4.50 per box). Then Anna recorded the cost of the sale by decreasing the Inventory T-account on the right side and increasing the Cost of Goods Sold (an expense) T-account on the left side. Notice that the accounting equation stays in balance because the total dollar amount recorded on the left sides of the T-accounts ($100 increase in Accounts Receivable and the $45 increase in Cost of Goods Sold) equals the total dollar amount recorded on the right sides of the T-accounts ($100 increase in Sales Revenue and the $45 decrease in Inventory). Anna recorded each sales transaction for January in the same way (except that she recorded cash sales in the Cash T-account rather than the Accounts Receivable T-account). At the end of the accounting period, she calculated the $8,100 balance in the Sales Revenue T-account and reported it as revenue on Sweet Temptations' income statement for January. She calculated the $3,645 balance in the Cost of Goods Sold T-account and reported it as an expense on the income statement.

How Sales Policies Affect Income Statement Reporting

Companies may have several policies related to the sales of their goods or services. There are three types: discount policies, sales return policies, and sales allowance policies. Companies want to encourage customers to buy their merchandise or services, and sales policies help them do this. A retail company's specific policies will also have an impact on its net sales—the net dollar amount of sales reported on the income statement—because its revenues for an accounting period should include only the prices actually charged to customers for goods sold during the period. In the following sections, we will discuss each of these sales-related policies.

Discounts

Have you ever taken advantage of a two-for-one special, paid a lower price because you bought a larger quantity of the same item, or used a coupon to get three dollars off the price of your pizza? If so, the company you bought from offered you a discount. A **quantity** (or trade) **discount** is a reduction in the sales price of a good or service because of the number of items purchased or because of a sales promotion.

Companies use discounts to attract customers and increase sales. Suppose that in early February, Sweet Temptations puts in its front window a sign that reads, "Valentines Day Special—Buy four or more boxes of chocolates and receive a 10% discount." By using this sales promotion, Sweet Temptations hopes that people walking by will notice the sign, come into the store, and buy candy. In addition, the company hopes that customers who had planned to buy only one or two boxes will instead buy four so that they can get the discount. Anna also hopes the policy will encourage repeat customers.

Before deciding to start a specific quantity discount policy, Sweet Temptations uses C-V-P analysis to determine the discount that will most likely improve company profits. Once a quantity discount policy is set, the company keeps track of the impact the policy has on sales, costs, and profits. However, the company does *not* record quantity discounts in its accounting system.

A company also may decide to offer a discount for early payment on credit sales. A **sales discount** is a percentage reduction of the invoice price if the customer pays the invoice within a specified period. A sales discount is frequently called a **cash discount** because when taken by a customer, the discount reduces the cash received. The sales invoice shows the terms of payment. These terms vary from company to company, although most competing companies have similar credit terms.

Sales (cash) discount terms might read 2/10, n/30 ("two ten, net thirty"). The first number is the percentage discount (2%), and the second number (10) is the number of days in the discount period. The discount period is the time, starting from the date of the

The ultimate in quantity discounts!

invoice, within which the customer must pay the invoice to get the sales discount. The term n/30 means that the total invoice price is due within 30 days of the invoice date. Thus 2/10, n/30 is read as "a 2% discount is allowed if the invoice is paid within 10 days; otherwise, the total amount of the invoice is due within 30 days." If Sweet Temptations makes a $50 sale on credit with terms 2/10, n/30 and the customer pays the invoice within 10 days, the customer would pay $49 [$50 − (0.02 × $50)], and $1 would be the sales discount taken. Sometimes companies offer cash discounts by charging a lower price for cash sales (rather than credit sales). Some gas stations have this policy. A company's accounting system keeps track of sales (cash) discounts by reducing sales revenue by the amount of sales discounts taken.

 How do you think a sales discount taken by a credit customer when paying the account receivable is recorded in the customer's accounting system?

Sales Returns and Allowances

When a customer buys merchandise, both the company and the customer assume that it is not damaged and is acceptable to the customer. Occasionally, on checking the merchandise after the purchase, the customer may find that it is damaged, is of inferior quality, or simply is the wrong size or color. Most retail companies have a policy allowing customers to return merchandise. For example, The Limited, Inc.'s Express store prints its return policy on all its price tags. A **sales return** occurs when a customer returns previously purchased merchandise. The effect of a sales return is to cancel the sale.

www.limited.com

Have you ever returned merchandise to a company? Did the company ask to see your sales receipt? Did you or the salesperson fill out additional source documents? Why?

If a customer discovers that merchandise is damaged, a company may offer the customer a sales allowance. A **sales allowance** occurs when a customer agrees to keep the merchandise, and the company refunds a portion of the original sales price.

Although this transaction is not part of our ongoing analysis of Sweet Temptations, assume that one of its customers, Roger Leslie, purchased four boxes of chocolates for $10 per box and paid cash. Remember, each box of candy costs Sweet Temptations $4.50. The transaction increased both Sweet Temptations' Cash and its Sales Revenue by $40 (4 × $10), increased Cost of Goods Sold (an expense) by $18 (4 × $4.50), and decreased Inventory by $18. Anna recorded this transaction in Sweet Temptations' T-accounts as follows:

| | **Assets** | **=** | **Liabilities** | **+** | **Owner's Equity** | |

Assets = Liabilities + Owner's Equity

Cash

40	
(+)	(−)

Sales Revenue

	40
(−)	(+)

Inventory

	18
(+)	(−)

Cost of Goods Sold

18	
(+)	(−)

What would have happened if later that day when Roger opened the candy, he noticed that half of it was melted? If he returned to the store, Anna might have asked him if he wanted to exchange the candy for new boxes, return the candy for a refund, or accept a $20 sales allowance and keep the candy. If the candy still tasted fine, Roger might have decided to accept the sales allowance.

Because Roger paid for the candy with cash, Sweet Temptations would have granted the sales allowance by refunding him $20 cash. Anna would have recorded this sales allowance transaction in Sweet Temptations' T-accounts as follows:

Assets = Liabilities + Owner's Equity

Cash

	20
(+)	(−)

Sales Revenue

20	
(−)	(+)

If Roger originally purchased the candy on credit, Sweet Temptations would have granted the sales allowance by decreasing Roger's Account Receivable balance, instead of the Cash balance, by $20.

 If Roger returned the candy for a refund, how would you record the transaction?

Whether a company grants a sales return or a sales allowance, it prepares a source document called a credit memo. (Remember that a source document serves as evidence that a transaction has occurred.) A **credit memo** is a business document that lists the information for a sales return or allowance. It includes the customer's name and address, how the original sale was made (cash or credit), the reason for the sales return or allowance, the items that were returned or on which the allowance was given, and the amount of the return or allowance. The credit memo is the source document used to record the return or allowance. As we will discuss in Chapter 18, it is also the document used to keep track of "external failure costs," a measure of customer dissatisfaction. The effect of recording sales discounts, sales returns, and sales allowances is to reduce sales revenue (as we will discuss in the next section).

 How can a company's sales return policy help increase profits? Do you think a sales return policy ever can hurt more than it helps? How?

Net Sales

At the end of the accounting period, the balance of a company's Sales Revenue T-account is determined by subtracting the total of the left side from the total of the right side. The amounts recorded on the right side of the T-account are the total sales. The amounts recorded on the left side are the sales returns and allowances, and the sales (cash) discounts taken. The balance of the Sales Revenue account is called Sales Revenue (net), or Net Sales, and is reported on the company's income statement.

In January 2000 Sweet Temptations did not allow any cash discounts and did not have any customers return their purchases or ask for an allowance. The company thus reports total sales revenue of $8,100 on its income statement, as we show in Exhibit 6-5. It seems that Sweet Temptations' customers were satisfied with the quality of the candy they bought. In general, the amounts that a company records as sales returns and allowances (and sales discounts) provide useful information about the quality of the company's products (and the effect of its cash discount policy).

 Do you think a company should report to its managers a single net sales amount or both the total sales and the sales returns, allowances, and discounts? To external users? Why?

Expenses

An old business phrase says, "You have to spend money to make money." But, a company should understand that planning and controlling its expenses is an important part of running a business. In the previous section you saw how Sweet Temptations, a retail company, recorded and reported its revenues. In this section we focus on expenses.

Cost of Goods Sold

One of the major expenses of a retail company is the cost of the goods (merchandise) that it sells during the accounting period. A classified income statement shows this expense as the **cost of goods sold**.

Although all retail companies report their costs of goods sold, *how* a retail company calculates the amount depends on the type of inventory system it uses. Remember, **inventory** is the merchandise a retail company is holding for resale. A company uses an inventory system to keep track of the inventory it purchases and sells during an accounting period and, thus, the inventory it still owns at the end of the period. Companies use either a perpetual inventory system or a periodic inventory system. Because the type of inventory system that a company uses affects its managers' decisions and the income statement calculations, we briefly discuss the cost of goods sold under each type of system.

4 *What is inventory and cost of goods sold, and what inventory systems may be used by a company?*

Perpetual Inventory System

A **perpetual inventory system** keeps a continuous record of the cost of inventory on hand and the cost of inventory sold. Under the perpetual inventory system, when a company purchases an item of inventory, it increases the asset Inventory by the invoice cost of the merchandise plus any freight charges (sometimes called *transportation-in*) it paid to have the inventory delivered. When the company sells merchandise, it records the sale in the usual way. It also reduces Inventory and increases Cost of Goods Sold by the cost of the inventory that it sold. (We illustrated this earlier for one of Sweet Temptations' sales.) So, the company has Inventory and Cost of Goods Sold T-accounts that are perpetually up-to-date, and the company always knows the physical quantity of inventory it should have on hand.

 Do you think perpetual inventory records could be wrong? What could cause the records to show either too much or too little inventory?

Because of computer technology, many retail stores use a perpetual inventory system. When you buy something in a store, if the salesperson uses a scanner to record your purchase, the company is using a perpetual inventory system. Computers help stores record sales transactions and keep their perpetual inventory records. For instance, a grocery store uses an optical scanner to read a bar code and record the price of the item into the cash register. The store's computer simultaneously increases Cash (or Accounts Receivable) and Sales Revenue for the item's sales price, reduces Inventory and increases Cost of Goods Sold by the amount of that item's cost, and updates the count of the quantity of inventory on hand. Most department stores use a perpetual inventory system, as do most retail stores that sell a relatively small number of very expensive items, such as automobiles and jewelry.[2]

Whether a company sells expensive jewelry or generic grocery items, the company's perpetual inventory system keeps up-to-date amounts for both Inventory and Cost of Goods Sold. This information helps managers with decisions about day-to-day operations. By monitoring the daily changes in inventory amounts, managers can decide when to make inventory purchases, thus making sure that inventory items are always in stock. Because the cost of goods sold information is current, managers can also compare the revenues and costs of recent sales and estimate the company's profitability. However, managers should evaluate the costs of computerized equipment, employee training, and the other support needed to operate a perpetual inventory system before deciding to use this type of system. In some cases, the benefits may not justify the added costs of keeping perpetual records. As computer technology becomes more affordable and as competition increases, an increasing number of companies are finding that perpetual systems are worth the costs.

At the end of an accounting period, a company includes the balance of its Inventory T-account on its balance sheet. The company includes the balance of its Cost of Goods Sold T-account on its income statement. As we illustrated earlier, Sweet Temptations uses a perpetual inventory system. At the end of January 2000, its Inventory T-account has a balance of $2,295, and its Cost of Goods Sold T-account has a balance of $3,645 from all the purchases and sales transactions recorded in January. We show these T-accounts below (the amounts are the same as those listed in Exhibit 5-20):

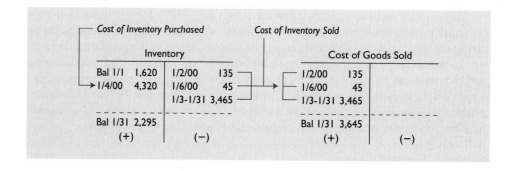

[2]In Chapter 9 we will discuss accounting for inventory in more detail. Accounting systems may keep track only of inventory quantities, instead of inventory costs, on a perpetual basis.

What do you suppose is on the woman's clipboard?

The $3,645 cost of goods sold is reported on the income statement shown in Exhibit 6-5. The $2,295 ending inventory is reported on the balance sheet shown in Exhibit 5-22. We will discuss perpetual inventory systems in more detail in Chapter 9.

Periodic Inventory System

A **periodic inventory system** does not keep a continuous record of the inventory on hand and sold, but determines the inventory at the end of each accounting period by physically counting it. Because a periodic inventory system does *not* reduce the Inventory T-account each time a sale occurs, the *only* time the company knows the cost of its inventory on hand is when it counts the inventory.

Why would a company choose not to keep perpetual inventory records? There are two common reasons. First, many companies that use a periodic inventory system are small enough that they can manage their inventory without perpetual records. Second, many companies sell a high volume of similar, inexpensive goods. Because the items are not expensive, perpetual records are not as important for keeping day-to-day physical control over the inventory. For these reasons, a company may decide that the costs of a perpetual system (i.e., recordkeeping costs, computer hardware and software costs) are not worth the benefits.

Because a company using a periodic system does not keep perpetual records, it must physically count its inventory at year-end. Physically counting the inventory is the only way for the company to determine an accurate inventory amount to be reported in the company's ending balance sheet. Therefore, a company usually counts its inventory immediately after the last working day of its fiscal year.[3] This is a difficult and time-consuming task. Thus, most companies time their fiscal year to end when inventory levels are likely to be low and business is slow. For example, most department stores take their inventory following the "after Christmas" sales, whereas a ski shop might count its inventory in June.

---

[3]A company using a perpetual inventory system also physically counts its inventory at year-end. Even though its accounting records show what should be in the inventory, the company takes a physical count to test the accuracy of the accounting records and to estimate the amount of lost or stolen inventory.

Perhaps you have noticed a company's advertisement that says something like the following:

This company is reducing its prices to sell more goods so that it will not have to spend as much time counting inventory. Near the end of the year it is not unusual for a company to close temporarily, so that it can count its inventory. If you saw the company's sign (like the one in the picture on this page) and peeked in the window, you would see people moving from one aisle to the next, counting the merchandise on each shelf.

How does a company using a periodic system know its cost of goods sold? Since the company does not record the cost of the goods sold when each sales transaction takes place, it must *calculate* its cost of goods sold for an accounting period as follows:

$$\text{Cost of Goods Sold} = \underbrace{\underbrace{\text{Cost of Beginning Inventory}}_{} + \underbrace{\text{Cost of Net Purchases}}_{}}_{\text{Cost of goods available for sale}} - \underbrace{\underbrace{\text{Cost of Ending Inventory}}_{}}_{\text{Cost of goods \textbf{not} sold}}$$

A company knows the cost of its beginning inventory because the beginning inventory for a new accounting period is the same as the ending inventory for the previous accounting period. A company's cost of net purchases is the dollar amount it recorded during an accounting period for the merchandise it bought for resale. The term **net purchases** is used because the amount of merchandise purchases (invoice cost and transportation-in) is adjusted (reduced) for purchases returns, allowances, and discounts. (These adjustments are similar to the net sales adjustments that we discussed earlier.) A company's **cost of ending inventory** is the dollar amount of merchandise on hand, based on the physical count, at the end of the accounting period.

Cost of Goods Sold and Gross Profit

Because cost of goods sold is usually a retail company's largest expense, many companies subtract cost of goods sold from net sales to determine **gross profit.** Gross profit is the amount of revenue that a company has "leftover" (after recovering the cost of the products it sold) to cover its operating expenses. Sweet Temptations subtracts its $3,645 cost of goods sold from its $8,100 sales revenue (net) to get its $4,455 gross profit, as we showed in Exhibit 6-5.

 Do you think Anna Cox is pleased with Sweet Temptations' gross profit? Why or why not?

Operating Expenses

Of course, the cost of goods sold is not the only expense that a retail company incurs. Activities such as having a sales staff, occupying building space, or running advertisements in the newspaper also cost money. These types of expenses are called operating expenses. **Operating expenses** are the expenses (other than cost of goods sold) that a company incurs in its day-to-day operations.

A company records its operating expenses in T-accounts according to the rules we discussed earlier. For instance, when Sweet Temptations paid $300 for advertising on January 25, 2000, Anna recorded the transaction as follows:

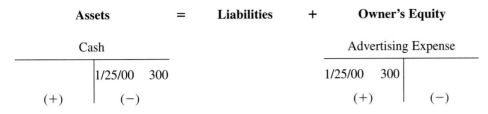

Likewise, on January 31, 2000 when Anna prepared the end-of-period adjustments of $1,000 for rent and $15 for depreciation, she recorded the expenses as follows:

Assets = **Liabilities** + **Owner's Equity**

Prepaid Rent

	1/31/00 1,000
(+)	(−)

Rent Expense

1/31/00 1,000	
(+)	(−)

Store Equipment

	1/31/00 15
(+)	(−)

Depreciation Expense

1/31/00 15	
(+)	(−)

Companies refer to the recording of end-of-period adjustments as making **adjusting entries.**

A company may divide its operating expenses section of the income statement into two parts, one for selling expenses and the other for general and administrative expenses. **Selling expenses** are the operating expenses related to the sales activities of a company. Sales activities are activities involved in the actual sale and delivery of merchandise to customers. Selling expenses include such items as sales salaries expense, advertising expense, and delivery expense (sometimes called *transportation-out*) for merchandise sold. **General and administrative expenses** are the operating expenses related to the general management of a company. They include such items as office salaries expense, insurance expense, and office supplies expense.

 Why do you think that companies may report selling expenses separately from general and administrative expenses?

Some operating expenses involve both sales activities and the general management of a company. Consider utilities, for example. A company keeps telephones at sales desks and office desks, and both sales areas and office spaces are provided with electricity. In these cases, a company allocates part of the total expense to selling expenses and the remainder to general and administrative expenses based on an estimate of how much is used for each activity, as we discussed in Chapter 4.

Exhibit 6-7 shows a detailed schedule of Sweet Temptations' operating expenses for January 2000. Anna developed this schedule from the balances in Sweet Temptations' expense T-accounts at the end of January. These balances are based on all the expense transactions Anna recorded in the T-accounts during January. Although we do not show these expense T-accounts here, the amounts she recorded are the same as those in the Expenses column in Exhibits 5-20 and 5-21. Most of Sweet Temptations' operating expenses are selling expenses. However, Anna estimates that one-quarter of each total for rent ($1,000), salaries ($2,050), consulting ($200), supplies ($30), telephone ($60), and utilities ($190) expenses are general and administrative expenses.[4] Sweet Temptations includes the $2,961

---

[4]For simplicity, the salaries, supplies, and utilities expense allocations are rounded to the nearest dollar.

Exhibit 6-7   Sweet Temptations' Operating Expenses

SWEET TEMPTATIONS
Schedule 1: Operating Expenses
For Month Ended January 31, 2000

Selling expenses

Rent expense	$ 750	
Sales salaries expense	1,537	
Consulting expense	150	
Advertising expense	300	
Sales supplies expense	22	
Depreciation expense	15	
Sales telephone expense	45	
Sales utilities expense	142	
Total selling expenses		$2,961

General and administrative expenses

Rent expense	$ 250	
Office salaries expense	513	
Consulting expense	50	
Office supplies expense	8	
Office telephone expense	15	
Office utilities expense	48	
Total general and administrative expenses		$ 884

total selling expenses and the $884 total general and administrative expenses on its income statement in Exhibit 6-5. The detailed schedule of expenses is included with its income statement so that users interested in specific types of expenses can get the information they need.

Operating Income, Other Items, and Net Income

On a company's income statement, the total operating expenses are deducted from gross profit to determine **operating income**. In Exhibit 6-5, Anna adds the total selling expenses to the total general and administrative expenses to determine the $3,845 total operating expenses. She deducts the total operating expenses from the $4,455 gross profit to determine Sweet Temptations' operating income of $610.

The **other items** (sometimes called the *nonoperating income*) section of a company's income statement includes items that are not related to the primary operations of the company. Reported in this section are revenues and expenses related to investing activities or to financing the company's operations (e.g., interest revenue and interest expense), revenues and expenses (called gains and losses) related to selling property and equipment assets, and incidental revenues and expenses (e.g., miscellaneous rent revenue, losses due to theft or fire). We will discuss these items more fully later in the book. Sweet Temptations includes interest expense of $8 in its other items section. This interest expense relates to the note payable that it owed for the entire month of January.

The total amount of the "other items" (nonoperating income) section is added to (or subtracted from) the operating income to determine a company's net income. The net income of Sweet Temptations for the month ended January 31, 2000 is $602, determined by subtracting the $8 other item (interest expense) from the $610 operating income.

Uses of the Income Statement for Evaluation

To help you understand *how* internal and external decision-makers use income statements, we will first briefly review *why* companies prepare financial statements and *what* the statements show. Recall that accounting information helps managers plan, operate, and evaluate company activities. Managers use accounting information on a day-to-day basis to help make decisions (e.g., what type of sales return policy to use or how much inventory to order) to achieve their objective of earning a profit and thereby increasing the company's value. At the end of a specific time period, managers prepare financial statements to report to external users the cumulative results of their day-to-day decisions. By analyzing a company's financial statements, external users can evaluate how well managers' decisions worked and decide whether to do business with the company.

If you are a creditor, a company's financial statements help you decide whether to loan money to the company and, if so, under what loan arrangements (e.g., the interest rate to charge, the amount of time to allow before the loan must be repaid, the restrictions to place on the company's ability to borrow additional money). If you are an investor, a company's financial statements help you estimate the return you may expect on your investment and whether you want to become or continue to be an owner.

 Who else do you think is interested in a company's financial statements? Why?

Investors use the income statement to help judge their return on investment, and creditors use it to help make loan decisions. On what do these users base their evaluations? To make their business decisions, financial statement users evaluate a company's risk, operating capability, and financial flexibility. Although these may sound like complicated terms, once we have explained them you will see that they describe the main concerns of most investors and creditors.

When investors or creditors use the income statement to evaluate a company's risk, they are estimating the chances that the company will *not* earn a satisfactory profit or that it will earn a higher-than-expected profit. So **risk** is the uncertainty about the future earnings potential of a company. The greater the chances are that a company will earn a satisfactory profit or will earn a higher-than-expected profit, the less risk there is in investing in that company. As the chances decrease that a company will earn a satisfactory profit or the chances increase that it will earn a lower-than-expected profit, the risk of investing in that company increases. A company's "risk factor" affects the expected investment return that is needed to attract investors and affects the interest rate that creditors charge on that company's loans. The greater the risk, the higher will be the required rate of return and the interest rate.

External users evaluate a company's operating capability and financial flexibility because these factors help determine a company's level of risk. **Operating capability** refers to a company's ability to continue a given level of operations. For example, by comparing a company's current set of financial statements with those of prior years, external users can learn about the company's ability to earn a stable stream of operating income. If the statements show that the company can do this, chances are good that the company will be able to maintain its current level of operations.

Financial flexibility refers to a company's ability to adapt to change. External users want to see evidence of financial flexibility because this means that a company can take advantage of business opportunities, such as introducing a new product or building a new warehouse. As you would expect, investors want the company to grow, so they prefer companies that have financial flexibility.

 Do you think your personal financial flexibility is high or low? Why?

Business Issues and Values

Have you ever had a part-time job? If so, then you know that many companies depend on part-time employees in their operations. For some companies, part-time employees make up a large percentage of their employee group. By using part-time employees, these companies may significantly enhance their financial flexibility because they can hire and lay off employees quickly. They also avoid having to pay for items such as health insurance

5 *What are the main concerns of external decision-makers when they use a company's income statement to evaluate its performance?*

NEEDED: Part-time receptionist and technician. Office hours 12 noon–8p.m. Apply in person. NO telephone calls. Horton Animal Hospital–Forum Blvd.

and retirement benefits, which companies normally pay for full-time employees. Other companies, though still using some part-time employees to help the companies improve their financial flexibility, have a different view regarding their commitment to their employees. They believe that it is part of their social responsibility to hire, train, and retain full-time employees. Although these companies may have less financial flexibility than those that depend more on part-time employees, some investors and creditors feel that a commitment to full-time employees offsets this limitation.

For example, consider Malden Mills, a Lawrence, Massachusetts manufacturer of Polar tec and Polar fleece (fabrics in demand by such retailers as Eddie Bauer and L.L. Bean). When it burned to the ground just before Christmas in 1995, the owner gave every employee a $275 Christmas bonus. Then he announced that all employees would continue to receive full pay and benefits for at least 90 days. His decision was based on the philosophy that "Loyalty and profit go hand in hand! Superior employees produce a superior product, and loyal customers and loyal employees are cut from the same fabric."[5]

www.eddiebauer.com
www.llbean.com

6 *What type of analysis is used by external decision-makers to evaluate a company's profitability?*

Ratios

To evaluate a company's operating performance, managers and external users may perform ratio analysis. **Ratio analysis** consists of computations in which an item on the company's financial statements is divided by another, related item. Although individual users may compute ratios themselves, groups that specialize in financial analysis compute and publish ratios for many companies and industries. The ratios are "benchmarks" used to compare a company's performance with that of previous periods and with that of other companies. There are many commonly computed ratios, which we will discuss in later chapters. As an introduction, here we discuss two that relate to profitability, since profitability affects risk, operating capability, and financial flexibility.

Profit Margin

One ratio is the profit margin, which is usually expressed as a percentage. A company's **profit margin** is calculated as follows:

$$\text{Profit Margin} = \frac{\text{Net Income}}{\text{Net Sales}}$$

If a company's profit margin is higher than that of previous years or higher than that of other companies, it usually means that the company is doing a better job of controlling its expenses in relation to its sales.

The profit margin of Sweet Temptations for January 2000 is calculated as follows, based on the information in Exhibit 6-5:

$$7.43\% = \frac{\$602}{\$8,100}$$

This means that, on average, 7.43 cents of every sales dollar is profit (net income) for Sweet Temptations. Since this is Sweet Temptations' first month of operations, we cannot compare the 7.43% profit margin for January with the profit margin of previous months. However, this profit margin during initial operations is a positive sign.

Gross Profit Percentage

A second ratio is the gross profit percentage (sometimes called the *gross profit margin*), which relates a company's gross profit to its net sales. The **gross profit percentage** is calculated as follows:

[5]"Mill Owner Keeps Faith with Workers," *Columbia Daily Tribune*, December 22, 1996, sec. A, 1.

$$\text{Gross Profit Percentage} = \frac{\text{Gross Profit}}{\text{Net Sales}}$$

A retail company's gross profit generally ranges from 20% to 60% of net sales depending on the types of products it sells. The gross profit percentage of Sweet Temptations for January 2000 is calculated as follows:

$$55\% = \frac{\$4,455}{\$8,100}$$

This means that, on average, 55 cents of every sales dollar (after the cost of goods sold is subtracted) is left to cover operating expenses and other expenses, and to increase Sweet Temptations' net income. Again, we cannot make comparisons with previous months, but this 55% gross profit margin for January is within the range of a retail company's usual gross profit. This is another positive sign of Sweet Temptations' successful initial operating capability. The managers of a retail company keep a close watch on the company's gross profit because changes in gross profit typically result in large changes in net income.

Profitability Ratios of Actual Companies

To illustrate ratio analysis, we will use information from the financial statements of two retail companies, JCPenney Company Inc. (JCPenney) and Sears Roebuck and Co. (Sears). Their profit margins[6] for 1997 were as follows:

www.jcpenney.com
www.sears.com

	JCPenney	Sears
Profit Margin	1.9%	3.3%

When we compare these two ratios, it is clear that Sears was more successful at generating net income from its sales than was JCPenney, since Sears made over 1.7 times more profit from each dollar of sales.

Would you expect Sears' gross profit percentage also to be more than 1.7 times higher than JCPenney's? Why or why not?

Now let's compare the gross profit percentages for the two companies.

	JCPenney	Sears
Gross Profit Percentage	27.8%	26.4%

Notice that Sears had a *lower* gross profit margin than JCPenney, even though it had a *higher* profit margin. Based on a comparison of these ratios, we can say that JCPenney was more efficient than Sears in controlling the costs of merchandise but that Sears was more efficient than JCPenney in controlling operating expenses.

How else might you explain the differences in the ratios of the two companies?

We will expand the discussion of operating capability and financial flexibility in Chapter 7, adding new ratios for analysis. We also will continue our comparison of JCPenney and Sears.

---

[6]We use well-known corporations in this illustration because the financial statements of most small entrepreneurial companies are not publicly available. For simplicity, we do not show the calculations of the ratios, although the numbers were taken from each company's financial statements. For instance, we calculated JCPenney's profit margin by dividing its net income of $566 million by its net sales of $29,618 million. We calculated Sears' profit margin by dividing its net income of $1,188 million by its net sales of $36,371 million.

DILBERT® reprinted by permission of United Features Syndicate, Inc.

Statement of Changes in Owner's Equity

A company's owner's equity is affected by the owner's investments and withdrawals, as well as by the company's revenue and expense transactions. Although an income statement and its supporting schedules help external users understand the results of revenue and expense activities, the statement and schedules do not include all the activities that affect owner's equity. A company prepares a supplementary schedule, called a statement of changes in owner's equity, for this purpose. The **statement of changes in owner's equity** summarizes the transactions that affected owner's equity during the accounting period. A company presents this statement to "bridge the gap" between its income statement and the amount of owner's capital it reports on the balance sheet.

   The schedule begins with the balance in the owner's capital T-account at the beginning of the accounting period. Then, the total amount of the owner's investments for the accounting period is added because this amount increases the owner's claim on the company's assets. Next, the amount of the company's net income is added because this amount also increases the owner's claim on the company's assets as a result of its operating activities for the accounting period. Finally, the amount of withdrawals that the owner made during the accounting period is subtracted. The final amount is the owner's capital balance at the end of the accounting period. The company reports this amount on its ending balance sheet.

 Do you think withdrawals by an owner are expenses? Why or why not?

   By summarizing all the transactions affecting the owner's equity of a company, the statement of changes in owner's equity helps to complete the picture of the company's financial activities for the accounting period. External users find this information helpful in evaluating the changes in the claims on the company's assets, changes that have an impact on its risk, operating capability, and financial flexibility.

 If you saw a large amount of withdrawals reported in a company's statement of changes in owner's equity, how would that affect your evaluation of its risk? Why?

   Exhibit 6-8 shows Sweet Temptations' statement of changes in owner's equity for the month ended January 31, 2000. The $15,000 beginning amount of owner's capital comes from the A. Cox, Capital T-account (shown in Exhibit 6-4). Anna made no additional

Exhibit 6-8 Sweet Temptations' Statement of Changes in Owner's Equity

SWEET TEMPTATIONS
Statement of Changes in Owner's Equity
For Month Ended January 31, 2000

A. Cox, capital, January 1, 2000	$15,000
Add: Net income..	602
	$15,602
Less: Withdrawals..	(50)
A. Cox, capital, January 31, 2000	$15,552

investments during the accounting period, so the next item is net income. The $602 net income comes from the income statement in Exhibit 6-5. The $50 of withdrawals comes from the A. Cox, Withdrawals T-account in Sweet Temptations' accounting records, as we will illustrate in the next section. The $15,552 ending amount for A. Cox, Capital is the amount reported as owner's equity in Sweet Temptations' January 31, 2000 balance sheet (shown in Exhibit 5-22).

Managers and external users know that a company's income statement and statement of changes in owner's equity do not provide all of the financial information needed for business decisions. Information that is not reported on the company's income statement can have a big impact on its ability to earn profits in the future. In the next chapter, we will discuss how managers, investors, and creditors use the balance sheet in conjunction with the income statement to make business decisions.

Withdrawals Entries

Earlier in the chapter we noted that to record an increase in an owner's withdrawals T-account, the company makes an entry in the left side of the account. To record a decrease, the company makes an entry in the right side of the account. To illustrate, recall that Anna Cox withdrew $50 from Sweet Temptations on January 20, 2000. Anna recorded this withdrawal as follows:

Assets	**=**	**Liabilities**	**+**	**Owner's Equity**
Cash				A. Cox, Withdrawals
	1/20/00 50			1/20/00 50	
(+)	(−)			(+)	(−)

Notice that in this entry, Anna increased the A. Cox, Withdrawals T-account by recording $50 on the left side of the account, and she decreased the Cash T-account by recording $50 on the right side of the account. We will illustrate how to record a decrease in an owner's withdrawals account in the next section.

Closing Entries

Earlier in the chapter we discussed how revenue, expense, and withdrawals T-accounts are *temporary accounts* used to accumulate a company's net income and withdrawals amounts for the accounting period. We noted that a company transfers the amounts (balances) in these T-accounts to the permanent T-account for the owner's capital at the end of the accounting period. As a result, at the beginning of the new accounting period, each revenue, expense, and withdrawals T-account has a zero balance, so the company can accumulate the net income and withdrawals amounts for that period. Also at the beginning of the new accounting period, the amount (balance) of the permanent T-account for the owner's capital is up-to-date.

To focus on the content of the income statement, we did not discuss the process used to transfer the revenue, expense, and withdrawals amounts to the owner's capital T-account. This is done through the process of preparing "closing entries." **Closing entries** are entries made by a company at the end of an accounting period to create a zero balance in each revenue, expense, and withdrawals T-account, and to "update" the owner's equity by transferring the balances in the revenue, expense, and withdrawals T-accounts to the T-account for owner's capital. A company prepares closing entries after it prepares its financial statements.

The balances of the revenue and expense T-accounts are not transferred directly to the owner's capital T-account. Instead, a company first transfers them to an "income summary" T-account. An **Income Summary** T-account is an account used in the closing process to accumulate the amount of net income (or net loss) before transferring it to the T-account for owner's capital.

We illustrate the closing entry process for Sweet Temptations at the end of January 2000 in Exhibit 6-9. In this illustration, Sweet Temptations uses a month as its accounting period; normally a company would have a longer accounting period (such as a year). In Exhibit 6-9, we use the revenue, expense, and withdrawals T-accounts (the temporary accounts) of Sweet Temptations for the month of January 2000. Normally, Sweet Temptations would obtain the January 31, 2000 balance in each of these T-accounts from its accounting records. Since we do not show all the T-accounts in this chapter, you should refer to Exhibit 6-5 for the sales revenue, cost of goods sold, and interest expense amounts, Exhibit 6-7 for the other operating expenses (remember that in this exhibit, the total amount for several of the expenses is separated into selling expenses and general and administrative expenses), and Exhibit 6-8 for the withdrawals amount.

In its closing entry process, on January 31, 2000, Sweet Temptations first closes its Sales Revenue (net) T-account. Since there is an $8,100 balance in the right side of this T-account on this date, Sweet Temptations makes a closing entry (labeled *cl*) of $8,100 in the left side of this account. At the same time, it transfers the $8,100 sales revenue amount to the right side of the Income Summary T-account, as we show by the arrow. After this closing entry, the Sales Revenue (net) account has a zero balance.

Next, Sweet Temptations closes each of its expense accounts. For example, let's look at Cost of Goods Sold (an expense). There is a $3,645 balance in the left side of this T-account at the end of January. So Sweet Temptations makes a $3,645 closing entry in the right side of this account. It follows the same procedure for each of the other expense accounts. Then, Sweet Temptations totals the amounts of the closing entries to each of the expense T-accounts and transfers the $7,498 *total* amount of the expenses to the left side of the Income Summary account, as we show by the arrow.[7] After these closing entries, all of the expense accounts have zero balances.

Now, $8,100 (the total revenue) is recorded in the right of the Income Summary T-account, and $7,498 (the total expenses) is recorded in the left side. The difference, $602 ($8,100 − $7,498), is the net income of Sweet Temptations for January 2000 (see Exhibit 6-5). Sweet Temptations makes a closing entry for $602 in the left side of the Income Summary T-account and transfers this net income amount to the right side of the A. Cox, Capital T-account (the permanent account), as we show by the arrow. After this closing entry, the Income Summary account has a zero balance, and the A. Cox, Capital account is larger by the amount of Sweet Temptations' net income.

[7]If a company has more than one revenue account, it would use the same procedure for transferring the *total* revenues to the right side of the Income Summary account.

Exhibit 6-9 Closing Entries at the End of January 2000

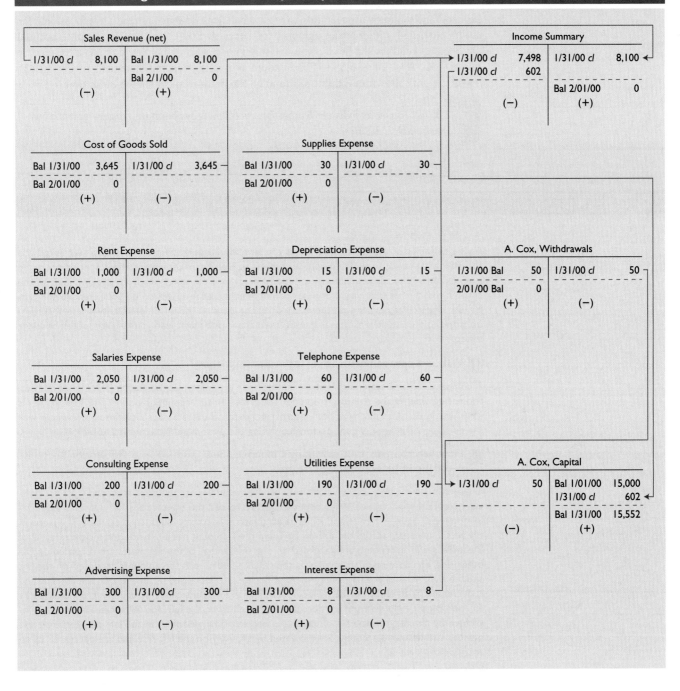

 What would Sweet Temptations' Income Summary T-account look like if it had a net loss instead of a net income? What closing entry would Sweet Temptations make to transfer this net loss to the A. Cox, Capital T-account?

Finally, Sweet Temptations closes the withdrawals account. There is a $50 balance in the left side of the A. Cox, Withdrawals T-account at the end of January—the amount that Anna Cox withdrew from the business during January. So Sweet Temptations makes a $50 closing entry in the right side of this account and transfers this amount to the left side of the A. Cox, Capital T-account, as we show by the arrow. After this closing entry, the A. Cox, Withdrawals account has a zero balance, and the A. Cox, Capital account is smaller by the amount of Anna's withdrawals.

At this point, Sweet Temptations has completed its closing process. All of the revenue, expense, and withdrawals accounts have zero balances, so they are ready to accumulate the net income (and withdrawals) amounts for February 2000. The A. Cox, Capital account has been updated for the net income and the withdrawals of January and has a balance on January 31, 2000 of $15,552. This amount is reported on the statement of changes in owner's equity shown in Exhibit 6-8 (and on the balance sheet shown in Exhibit 5-22).

 Which accounts in Sweet Temptations' accounting system have nonzero balances on February 1, 2000?

Summary

At the beginning of the chapter we asked you several questions. During the chapter, we asked you to STOP and answer several additional questions to build your knowledge about specific issues. Be sure you answered these additional questions. Below are the questions from the beginning of the chapter, with a brief summary of the key points relating to the answers. Use your creative and critical thinking skills to expand on these key points to develop more complete answers to the questions and to determine what other questions you have that might lead you to learn more about the issues.

1 Why is a company's income statement important?

A company's income statement is important because it summarizes the results (revenues, expenses, and net income) of the company's operating activities for an accounting period. This information is useful in the decision-making of both internal and external users because it helps to show how well the company's management has performed during the period and from period to period.

2 How are changes in a company's balance sheet and income statement accounts recorded in its accounting system?

Changes in a company's balance sheet and income statement accounts are recorded in its accounting system using T-accounts. A T-account is used to record the transactions for individual asset, liability, owner's equity, revenue, and expense accounts. A T-account looks like a capital T. The name of the account appears across the top of the T, and the T-account has a left side and a right side. All of the increases in an account are recorded on one side, and all of the decreases are recorded on the other side. The balance of an account is the difference between the amounts recorded on the left and the right sides of the T-account. An asset T-account is increased by an entry on the left side and is decreased by an entry on the right side. Liability and owner's capital T-accounts are increased by an entry on the right side and are decreased by an entry on the left side. A revenue T-account is increased by an entry on the right side and is decreased by an entry on the left side. Expense and owner's withdrawals T-accounts are increased by an entry on the left side and are decreased by an entry on the right side.

3 What are the parts of a retail company's classified income statement, and what do they contain?

The classified income statement of a retail company includes two parts, an operating income section and an other items section. The operating income section includes revenues, cost of goods sold, and operating expenses subsections related to a company's primary operating activities. The other items section includes any revenues or expenses that are not directly related to the company's primary operations.

4 What is inventory and cost of goods sold, and what inventory systems may be used by a company?

Inventory is the merchandise a retail company is holding for resale. Cost of goods sold is the cost to the company of the merchandise that it sells during the accounting period. A company may use either a perpetual inventory system or a periodic inventory system. A perpetual inventory system keeps a continuous record of the cost of inventory on hand and the cost of inventory sold. A periodic inventory system does not keep a continuous record of the inventory on hand and sold, but uses a physical count to determine the inventory on hand at the end of the accounting period.

5 **What are the main concerns of external decision-makers when they use a company's income statement to evaluate its performance?**

When external decision-makers use a company's income statement to evaluate its performance, they are concerned about the company's risk, operating capability, and financial flexibility. Risk is uncertainty about the future earnings potential of the company. Operating capability refers to the company's ability to continue a given level of operations. Financial flexibility refers to the company's ability to adapt to change.

6 **What type of analysis is used by external decision-makers to evaluate a company's profitability?**

Ratio analysis is used by external users to evaluate a company's profitability. Ratio analysis involves computations in which an item on the company's financial statements is divided by another, related item. The ratios are compared with the company's ratios in previous periods or with other companies' ratios. The ratios used to evaluate a company's profitability include the profit margin (net income divided by net sales) and the gross profit percentage (gross profit divided by net sales).

Key Terms

adjusting entries *(p. 177)*
cash discount *(p. 170)*
closing entries *(p. 184)*
cost of ending inventory *(p. 176)*
cost of goods sold *(p. 173)*
credit memo *(p. 172)*
financial flexibility *(p. 179)*
general and administrative expenses
  (p. 177)
general ledger *(p. 165)*
gross profit *(p. 176)*
gross profit percentage *(p. 180)*
income summary *(p. 184)*
inventory *(p. 173)*
net purchases *(p. 176)*
operating capability *(p. 179)*
operating expenses *(p. 176)*

operating income *(p. 168, 178)*
other items *(p. 168, 178)*
periodic inventory system *(p. 175)*
permanent accounts *(p. 164)*
perpetual inventory system *(p. 173)*
profit margin *(p. 180)*
quantity discount *(p. 170)*
ratio analysis *(p. 180)*
risk *(p. 179)*
sales allowance *(p. 172)*
sales discount *(p. 170)*
sales return *(p. 171)*
selling expenses *(p. 177)*
statement of changes in owner's equity
  (p. 182)
T-accounts *(p. 163)*
temporary accounts *(p. 164)*

Here is an opportunity to gather information on the Internet about real-world issues related to the topics in this chapter. Go to http://www.dryden.com/account and click on the Cunningham, Nikolai, and Bazley book cover. Click on Summary Surfing, then click on this chapter number, and answer the following questions.

▶ Click on **JCPenney.** Find the company's income statements. Compute the profit margin and the gross profit percentage for the most current year. How do these results compare with the 1997 ratios we discussed in this chapter?

▶ Click on **Sears.** Find the company's income statements. Compute the profit margin and the gross profit percentage for the most current year. How do these results compare with the 1997 ratios we discussed in this chapter?

SUMMARY
SURFING

Integrated Business and Accounting Situations

Answer the Following Questions in Your Own Words

Testing Your Knowledge

6-1   Write out the income statement equation, and explain its components.

6-2   Explain how managers use a company's income statement for decision-making.

6-3   Identify the major limitation of the column method for recording transactions.

6-4   Draw a T-account, and identify its parts.

6-5   Explain the relationship between the accounting equation and increases and decreases in T-accounts.

6-6   What rule is used in recording transactions in T-accounts to keep the accounting equation in balance and to maintain the dual effect of transactions?

6-7   What is the difference between "temporary" and "permanent" accounts?

6-8   Explain the rules for recording increases and decreases in revenue and expense T-accounts.

6-9   Identify the parts and subsections of a retail company's classified income statement. What is included in each part?

6-10   Explain the difference between a quantity discount and a sales (cash) discount.

6-11   Explain the difference between a sales return and a sales allowance.

6-12   What is a perpetual inventory system? How is a company's cost of goods sold determined under this system?

6-13   What is a periodic inventory system? How is a company's cost of goods sold determined under this system?

6-14   What are operating expenses? Explain the difference between selling expenses and general and administrative expenses.

6-15   Explain the meaning of the terms *risk, operating capability,* and *financial flexibility.*

6-16   What is ratio analysis, and what is it used for?

6-17   Explain how to compute a company's profit margin. What is this ratio used for?

6-18   Explain how to compute a company's gross profit percentage. What is this ratio used for?

6-19   Explain what is included in a statement of changes in owner's equity and how the statement is used.

Applying Your Knowledge

6-20   On August 1 of the current year, Judy Kimberly started the Nu-Way Advertising Agency, and the company engaged in the following transactions during August:

Date	Transactions
Aug. 1	Judy Kimberly deposited a $9,000 personal check into the agency's checking account
2	Nu-Way acquired land and an office building at a cost of $2,000 and $22,000, respectively. A down payment of $4,000 was made, and a one-year note was signed for the balance.
14	Nu-Way purchased several pieces of office equipment at a total cost of $1,500. The entire amount is due September 15.
26	Nu-Way purchased office supplies at a cost of $850 cash.

Required: (1) Prepare T-accounts for the following items: Cash, Land, Building, Office Equipment, Office Supplies, Accounts Payable, Notes Payable, and J. Kimberly, Capital.

(2) Enter the preceding transactions into the T-accounts from (1) and compute the August 31 cash balance.

(3) List the source documents normally used in recording each of the transactions.

6-21   On June 1 of the current year, Jody Weis started the Weis Company. The company engaged in the following transactions during June:

Date	Transactions
June 1	Jody Weis deposited $17,000 cash in the company's checking account.
3	The company purchased land and an office building for $6,000 and $33,500, respectively, paying $9,500 down and signing a 10-year mortgage for the balance owed.
18	The company purchased $2,000 of office equipment, paying $1,000 down and agreeing to pay the remaining $1,000 in 30 days.
24	The company purchased office supplies for $1,600 cash.

Required: (1) Prepare T-accounts for the following items: Cash, Land, Building, Office Equipment, Office Supplies, Accounts Payable, Mortgage Payable, and Jody Weis, Capital.

(2) Enter the preceding transactions into the T-accounts from (1) and compute the June 30 cash balance.

(3) List the source documents normally used to record each of the transactions.

6-22 On July 1, Drexel's Appliance purchased $5,000 of goods for resale. On July 15, it sold $2,600 of these goods to customers at a selling price of $4,000. The company uses a perpetual inventory system, and all transactions were for cash.

Required: Prepare T-account entries to record this information.

6-23 On April 6, Piper Model Shop made a cash sale of $127 in merchandise to a customer. The company uses a perpetual inventory system; the merchandise had cost Piper $88. On April 8, the customer was given a sales allowance of $25 cash for a defective model that the customer chose to keep.

Required: (1) Prepare T-account entries to record this information.

(2) What source documents would be used to record each transaction?

6-24 The Riles Landscaping Service entered into the following transactions during March:

Date	Transactions
Mar. 1	Provided landscaping service for customer, collecting $975 cash.
2	Paid three months' rent in advance at $270 per month on storage/office building.
5	Purchased $50 of repair parts on credit from LT's, a small-engine service company, to be used immediately in repairing several of the company's mowers.
10	Provided landscaping service for a customer, with the customer agreeing to pay the contract price of $2,450 in 15 days.
15	Paid $50 due to LT's for repair parts purchased on March 5.
25	Collected $2,450 from customer for service provided on March 10.
31	Paid $40 for March utilities bill.
31	Paid $1,800 to employees for March salaries.
31	Received $82 March telephone bill, to be paid in early April.

Required: (1) Record the preceding transactions in appropriately titled T-accounts.

(2) List the source documents normally used to record these transactions.

6-25 Stevel Stor-All rents storage facilities to customers. It entered into the following transactions during April:

Date	Transactions
Apr. 1	S. Stevel, owner, invested $1,000 cash into the company.
2	Purchased a three-year insurance policy on the company's building for $480 cash.
6	Purchased office supplies on credit at a cost of $94.
14	Paid $30 on account for supplies purchased on April 6.
15	Collected storage fees totaling $720 for the first half of April.
30	Paid April telephone bill of $82.
30	Collected storage fees totaling $750 for the last half of April.
30	Paid $600 to employee for April salary.
30	Received $98 April utility bill, to be paid in early May.

Required: (1) Record the preceding transactions in appropriately titled T-accounts.

(2) List the source documents normally used to record these transactions.

6-26 The following information is available for the Arnhold Horn Company for the year:

Beginning inventory	$ 43,000
Ending inventory	50,000
Purchases	102,000
Purchases returns and allowances	4,000

Required: Prepare a schedule that computes the cost of goods sold for the year.

6-27 The income statement information of the Weeden Furniture Company for 2000 and 2001 is as follows:

	2000	2001
Cost of goods sold	$ (a)	$59,300
Interest expense	500	0
Selling expenses	(b)	10,800
Operating income	20,800	(d)
Sales (net)	97,000	(e)
General expenses	7,900	(f)
Net income	(c)	21,600
Interest revenue	0	600
Gross profit	39,000	40,200

Required: Fill in the blanks lettered (a) through (f). All the necessary information is listed. (*Hint:* It is not necessary to find the answers in alphabetical order.)

6-28 The following information is taken from the T-accounts of the Harburn Hobby Shop for the month of October of the current year.

Cost of goods sold	$53,000
Sales revenue (net)	88,000
Selling expenses	5,000
Interest expense	1,000
General and administrative expenses	12,000

Required: (1) Prepare a classified income statement for Harburn.
(2) Compute Harburn's profit margin.

6-29 The following information is taken from the T-accounts of Foile's Music Store for the current year ended December 31.

Depreciation expense: office equipment	$ 1,600
Interest revenue	725
Sales salaries expense	8,200
Rent expense	1,800
Depreciation expense: store equipment	2,400
Sales revenue (net)	95,100
Office salaries expense	4,000
Interest expense	250
Office supplies expense	600
Cost of goods sold	59,400
Advertising expense	360

Of the rent expense, 5/6 is applicable to the store and 1/6 is applicable to the office.

Required: (1) Prepare a classified income statement for Foile's Music Store for the current year.
(2) Compute the profit margin.
(3) Compute the gross profit percentage. Does this percentage fall near the high or the low end of the range of typical retail companies' gross profit percentages?

6-30 The December 31, 2000, income statement accounts and other information of Lyon's Hardware are shown below:

Advertising expense	$ 4,300
Depreciation expense: store equipment	1,600
Depreciation expense: building (store)	3,700
Depreciation expense: office equipment	2,300
Depreciation expense: building (office)	1,100
Interest revenue	1,700
Interest expense	900
Cost of goods sold	63,900
Insurance expense	350
Sales (net)	102,000
Office supplies expense	480
Store supplies expense	800
Sales salaries expense	5% of net sales

Office salaries expense	2,600
Utilities expense (store)	1,500
Utilities expense (office)	400

Required: (1) Prepare a classified 2000 income statement for Lyon's Hardware.

(2) Compute the profit margin for 2000. If the profit margin for 1999 was 12.5%, what can be said about the 2000 results?

6-31 The Jardine Tax Services Company was established on January 1 of the current year to help clients with their tax planning and with the preparation of their tax returns. During January, the company entered into the following transactions:

Date		Transactions
Jan.	2	D. Jardine set up the company by investing $5,000 in the company's checking account.
	3	The company paid $2,400 in advance for one year's rent of office space.
	4	Office equipment was purchased at a cost of $6,000. A down payment of $1,000 was-made, and a $5,000 note payable was signed for the balance owed. The note is due in one year.
	7	Office supplies were purchased for $800 cash.
	16	Fees of $1,700 were collected from clients for tax services provided during the first half of January.
	29	A salary of $700 was paid to the office secretary.
	30	Jardine withdrew $900 for personal use.
	31	The January utility bill of $120 was received; it will be paid in early February.
	31	Clients were billed $2,300 for tax services performed during the second half of January.
	31	Jardine recorded the following adjustments:
		a. Rent expense for the month
		b. Depreciation of $45 on office equipment
		c. Interest expense of $50 on the note payable
		d. Office supplies used (the office supplies on hand at the end of the month cost $720)

Required: (1) Record the preceding transactions in appropriate T-accounts.

(2) Prepare a classified income statement for the company for January.

(3) Prepare a balance sheet for the company on January 31.

(4) Briefly comment on how well the company did during January.

6-32 The Salanar Answering Service Company was started on April 1 of the current year to answer the phones of doctors, lawyers, and accountants when they are away from their offices. The following transactions of the company occurred and adjustments were made during April:

Date		Transaction
Apr.	1	P. Salanar started the business by investing $3,000 cash.
	2	The company paid cash of $900 in advance for six months' rent of office space.
	3	The company purchased telephone equipment costing $5,500, paying $1,500 down and signing a $4,000 note payable for the balance owed.
	6	Office supplies totaling $450 were purchased on credit. The amount is due in early May.
	15	The company collected $800 from clients for answering services performed during the first half of April.
	28	P. Salanar withdrew $600 for personal use.
	29	The April $110 utility bill was received; it is to be paid in May.
	30	The company paid $300 salary to a part-time employee.
	30	Clients were billed $900 for answering services performed during the last half of April.
	30	Salanar recorded the following adjustments:
		a. Rent expense for April
		b. Depreciation of $42 on telephone equipment
		c. Interest of $40 on the note payable
		d. Office supplies used of $58

Required: (1) Record the preceding transactions in appropriate T-accounts.

(2) Prepare a simple income statement for the company for April.

(3) Prepare a balance sheet for the company on April 30.

(4) Briefly comment on how well the company did during April.

6-33 The Steed Art Supplies Company sells various art supplies to local artists. The company uses a perpetual inventory system, and the balance of its inventory of art supplies at the beginning of August was $2,500. Its cash balance was $800, and the J. Steed, capital balance was $3,300 at the beginning of August. Steed entered into the following transactions during August:

Date	Transactions
Aug. 1	J. Steed invested another $1,000 cash into the company.
2	Purchased $400 of art supplies for cash.
4	Made a $900 sale of art supplies on credit to P. Tarlet, with terms of n/15; the cost of the inventory sold was $550.
6	Purchased $700 of art supplies on credit from the Rony Company, with terms of n/20.
10	Returned, for credit to its account, $100 of defective art supplies purchased on August 6 from the Rony Company.
12	Made cash sales of $250 to customers; the cost of the inventory sold was $160.
13	Granted a $25 allowance to a customer for damaged inventory sold on August 12.
15	Received payment from P. Tarlet of the amount due for inventory sold on credit on August 4.
25	Paid balance due to the Rony Company for purchase on August 6.

Required: (1) Record the preceding transactions in appropriate T-accounts.
(2) Determine the balance in the Cash and Inventory accounts at the end of August.
(3) Compute the gross profit and the gross profit percentage for August.

6-34 The Kerem Heater Company sells portable heaters and related equipment. The company uses a perpetual inventory system, and its inventory balance at the beginning of November was $2,600. Its cash balance was $1,500, and the B. Kerem, capital balance was $4,100 at the beginning of November. Kerem entered into the following transactions during November:

Date	Transactions
Nov. 1	B. Kerem invested another $900 cash into the company.
2	Made $480 cash sales to customers; the cost of the inventory sold was $280.
3	Purchased $1,700 of heaters for cash from Jokem Supply Company.
5	Received $250 cash allowance from Jokem Supply Company for defective inventory purchased on November 3.
6	Paid $210 for parts and repaired defective heaters purchased from Jokem Supply Company on November 3.
8	Made a $1,500 sale of heaters on credit to Arvin Nursing Home, with terms of 2/10, n/20; the cost of the inventory sold was $850.
15	Purchased $1,100 of heaters on credit from Duwell Supplies, with terms of n/15.
18	Received amount owed by Arvin Nursing Home for heaters purchased on November 8, less the cash discount.
30	Paid for the inventory purchased from Duwell Supplies on November 15.

Required: (1) Record the preceding transactions in appropriate T-accounts.
(2) Determine the balance in the Cash and Inventory accounts at the end of November.
(3) Compute the gross profit and the gross profit percentage for November.

6-35 Four independent cases related to the owner's equity account of the Cox Company follow:

Case	L. Cox, Capital May 1	Net Income for May	Withdrawals in May	L. Cox, Capital May 31
1	$ A	$2,700	$1,000	$26,700
2	37,000	B	1,720	40,250
3	28,200	900	C	24,800
4	34,000	1,820	1,500	D

Required: Determine the amounts of A, B, C, and D.

6-36 The beginning balance in the R. Barnum, Capital account on October 1 of the current year, was $20,000. For October, the Barnum Company reported total revenues of $3,000 and total expenses of $1,250. In addition, R. Barnum withdrew $1,200 for his personal use on October 25.

Required: Prepare a statement of changes in owner's equity for October for the Barnum Company.

6-37 The revenue, expense, and withdrawals T-account balances of the Swartz Furniture Company on December 31, 2000 are as follows:

Sales	$98,000
Advertising expense	12,700
Depreciation expense	3,100
Cost of goods sold	31,600
B. Swartz, withdrawals	8,000
Salaries expense	27,500
Utilities expense	3,500
Rent expense	6,000

Required: (1) What is the company's net income for 2000?

(2) Using T-accounts, prepare the company's closing entries at the end of 2000 (assume the B. Swartz, Capital T-account had a balance of $29,400 on January 1, 2000).

6-38 Refer to 6-29. Combine the two depreciation expense amounts, and combine the two salaries expense amounts. Assume that D. Foile withdrew $7,200 from the company during the current year and that the D. Foile, Capital T-account had a $58,500 balance on January 1 of the current year.

Required: Using T-accounts, prepare closing entries for Foile's Music Store on December 31.

Making Evaluations

6-39 A company engages in many types of activities.

Required: For each of the following sets of changes in a company's accounts, give an example of an activity that the company could engage in that would cause these changes and explain why you think the activity would cause these particular changes:

(1) Increase in an asset and decrease in another asset
(2) Increase in an asset and increase in a liability
(3) Increase in an asset and increase in owner's equity
(4) Increase in an asset and increase in a revenue
(5) Decrease in an asset and increase in an expense
(6) Decrease in an asset and decrease in a liability

6-40 A friend of yours in this accounting class is confused and says: "I just don't understand revenues and expenses. I learned earlier in this chapter that assets are increased by entries on the left side of the T-accounts and liabilities are increased by entries on the right side. Then I read later that expenses are increased by entries on the left side of the T-accounts and revenues are increased by entries on the right side. So the way I look at it, expenses must be assets, and revenues must be liabilities. And if that isn't confusing enough, my teacher says that not all increases in assets are the result of revenues and not all decreases in assets result in expenses. Wow! Does this make sense to you?"

Required: Prepare a written explanation for each issue raised by your friend. Use examples where needed.

6-41 During the current accounting period, the bookkeeper for the Nallen Company made the following errors in the year-end adjustments:

			Effect of Error on:			
Error	Revenues	Expenses	Net Income	Assets	Liabilities	Owner's Equity
Example: Failed to record $200 of salaries owed at the end of the period	N	U $200	O $200	N	U $200	O $200
1. Failed to adjust prepaid insurance for $400 of expired insurance						
2. Failed to record $500 of interest expense that had accrued during the period						

3. Inadvertently recorded $300 of annual depreciation twice for the same equipment

4. Failed to record $100 of interest revenue that had accrued during the period

5. Failed to reduce unearned revenues for $600 of revenues that were earned during the period

Required: Assuming that the errors are not discovered, indicate the effect of each error on revenues, expenses, net income, assets, liabilities, and owner's equity at the end of the accounting period. Use the following code: O = Overstated, U = Understated, and N = No effect. Include dollar amounts. Be prepared to explain your answers.

6-42 Suppose you own a retail company and are considering whether to allow your customers to have quantity discounts, sales discounts, and sales allowances.

Required: How do you think quantity discounts, sales discounts, and sales allowances would affect the results of a company's C-V-P analysis and its budgets? Explain what the effects would be. If a company gives quantity discounts, sales discounts, and sales allowances, what information would it need in order to conduct C-V-P analysis and develop budgets? (What questions would you have to ask?)

6-43 Your friend Allison is planning to open an automobile parts store and has come to you for advice about whether to use a perpetual or a periodic inventory system.

Required: Before you advise her, list the questions you would like to ask her. How would the answer to each question help you advise her? Explain to her the advantages and disadvantages of each system.

6-44 Cara Agee owns a hairstyling shop, Air Hair Company. It is now November 2000, and Cara thinks she might need a bank loan. Her bank has asked Cara to prepare a "projected" income statement and to compute the "projected" profit margin for next year. Although she has never developed this information before, she understands that to do so, she must make a "best guess" of her revenues and expenses for 2001 based on past activities and future estimates. She asks for your help and provides you with the following information.

(a) Styling revenues for 2000 were $80,000. Cara expects these to increase by 10% in 2001.

(b) Air Hair employees are paid a total "base" salary of $30,000 plus 20% of all styling revenues.

(c) Styling supplies used have generally averaged 15% of styling revenues; Cara expects this relationship to be the same in 2001.

(d) Air Hair recently signed a two-year rental agreement on its shop, requiring payments of $400 per month, payable in advance.

(e) The cost of utilities (heat, light, phone) is expected to be 25% of the yearly rent.

(f) Air Hair owns styling equipment that cost $12,000. Depreciation expense for 2001 is estimated to be 1/6 of the cost of this equipment.

Required: Prepare a projected income statement for Air Hair Company for 2001 and compute its projected profit margin. Show supporting calculations.

6-45 The Gray Service Company had a fire and lost some of the accounting records it needed to prepare its 2000 income statement. Stan Gray, the owner, has been able to determine that his capital in the business was $32,000 at the beginning of 2000 and was $33,000 at the end of 2000. During 2000 he withdrew $14,000 from the business. Stan has also been able to remember or determine the following information for 2000.

(a) Cash service revenues were twice the amount of net income; credit service revenues were 40% of cash service revenues.

(b) Rent expense was $250 per month.

(c) The company has one employee, who was paid a salary of $14,000 plus 10% of the service revenues.

(d) The supplies expense was 15% of the total expenses.

(e) The utilities expense was $100 per month for the first nine months of the year and $200 per month during the remaining months of the year due to the cold winter.

Stan also knows that the company owns some service equipment, but he cannot remember the cost or the amount of depreciation expense.

Required: Using the preceding information, prepare Gray Service Company's 2000 income statement. Show supporting calculations.

6-46   Your boss has given you last year's income statements of two companies and asked you to recommend one in which your company should invest. The income statements include the following information (in thousands):

	Amalgamated Snacks	Gourmet Goodies
Net sales	$1,360,000	$2,000
Cost of goods sold	884,000	1,360
Selling expenses	205,294	312
General and administrative expenses	114,541	110
Net income	156,165	218

Required: Based on this information alone, which company would be the better investment choice? Explain your answer. What other information would you like to have in order to make a more informed decision? How would this information help you recommend the one in which you think your company should invest?

6-47   A paragraph accompanying recent financial statements of <u>Dillard's Department Stores Inc.</u> begins: "Advertising, selling, administrative and general expenses increased as a percentage of sales in [the current year] compared to [last year]. This occurred because of the slower growth rate of sales during the year as compared to prior years."

www.dillards.com

Required: How does the second sentence explain the first? Explain in more detail how this could happen.

6-48   On January 3, 2001, Ken Harmot agreed to buy the Ace Cleaning Service from Janice Steward. They agreed that the purchase price would be five times the 2000 net income of the company. To determine the price, Janice prepared the following condensed income statement for 2000.

Revenues	$ 48,000
Expenses	(36,000)
Net Income	$ 12,000

Janice said to Ken: "Based on this net income, the purchase price of the company should be $60,000 ($12,000 × 5). Of course, you may look at whatever accounting records you would like." Ken examined the accounting records and found them to be correct, except for several balance sheet accounts. These accounts and their December 31, 2000 balances are as follows: two asset accounts—Prepaid Rent, $2,400; and Equipment, $3,600; and one liability account—Unearned Cleaning Service Revenues, $0.

Ken gathered the following company information related to these accounts. The company was started on January 2, 1998. At that time, the company rented space in a building for its operations and purchased $4,800 of equipment. At that time, the equipment had an estimated life of 8 years, after which it would be worthless. On July 1, 2000, the company paid one year of rent in advance at $200 per month. On September 1, 2000, customers paid $600 in advance for cleaning services to be performed by the company for the next 12 months. Ken asks for your help. He says: "I don't know how these items affect net income, if at all. I want to pay a fair price for the company."

Required: (1) Discuss how the 2000 net income of the Ace Cleaning Service was affected, if at all, by each of the items.
(2) Prepare a corrected condensed 2000 income statement.
(3) Compute a fair purchase price for the company.

6-49   The bookkeeper for Powell Import Service Agency was confused when he prepared the following financial statements.

Powell Import Service Agency
Profit and Expense Statement
December 31, 2000

Expenses:

Salaries expense	$ 21,000
Utilities expense	3,400
Accounts receivable	1,600
C. Powell, withdrawals	20,000
Office supplies	1,500
Total expenses	$(47,500)

Revenues:

Service revenues	$ 47,000
Accounts payable	1,100
Accumulated depreciation: office equipment	1,800
Total revenues	$ 49,900
Net Revenues	$ 2,400

Powell Import Service Agency
Balancing Statement
For Year Ended December 31, 2000

Liabilities		Assets	
Mortgage payable	$27,000	Building	$44,000
Accumulated depreciation:		Depreciation expense:	
building	6,400	building	1,600
Total Liabilities	$33,400	Office equipment	9,700
		Depreciation expense:	
C. Powell, capital[a]	27,000	office equipment	900
Total Liabilities and		Cash	4,200
Owner's Equity	$60,400	Total Assets	$60,400

[a]$24,600 beginning capital + $2,400 net revenues

C. Powell asks for your help. He says: "Something is not right! My company had a fantastic year in 2000; I'm sure it made more than $2,400. I don't remember much about accounting, but I do recall that 'accumulated depreciation' should be subtracted from the cost of an asset to determine its book value." You agree. After examining the financial statements and related accounting records, you find that, with the exception of office supplies, the *amount* of each item is correct even though the item might be incorrectly listed in the financial statements. You determine that the office supplies used during the year amount to $800 and that the office supplies on hand at the end of the year amount to $700.

Required: (1) Review each financial statement and indicate any errors you find.
(2) Prepare a corrected 2000 income statement, statement of changes in owner's equity, and ending balance sheet.
(3) Compute the profit margin for 2000 to verify or refute C. Powell's claim that his company had a fantastic year.

6-50 Yesterday, the letter shown on the following page arrived for your advice column in the local paper.

Dear Dr. Decisive:

I can't believe I am writing to you. In the past, I have always tried to solve my own problems, but now I have one I can't solve on my own. My roommate and I are taking an accounting course together. One night, or maybe I should say very early one morning, we were debating where a bank's interest expense goes on its income statement. I think it should go in the "other items" section, but my roommate thinks it should go in "operating expenses." We could argue about this forever, but neither one of us is willing to give in. My roommate agrees that we will accept your answer. If I win, I don't have to pay my roommate interest on the money I owe him.

"Interested"

Required: Meet with your Dr. Decisive team and write a response to "Interested."

CHAPTER 7

USING THE BALANCE SHEET
FOR BUSINESS DECISIONS

"There are but two ways of paying a debt: increase income, or increase thrift."

—Thomas Carlyle

1 *Why is a company's balance sheet important?*

2 *What do users need to know about a company's classified balance sheet?*

3 *What is a company's liquidity, and how do users evaluate it?*

4 *What is a company's financial flexibility, and how do users evaluate it?*

5 *Why and how do users evaluate a company's profitability?*

6 *What is a company's operating capability, and how do users evaluate it?*

In Chapter 6 you saw how a company's income statement provides managers and external users with important information about its activities. By describing the revenues, expenses, and net income (or net loss) for an accounting period, the income statement helps show whether a company is earning a satisfactory profit. A company's net income (net loss) for an accounting period is the increase (decrease) in owner's equity that resulted from the operating activities of that period. An income statement prepared according to generally accepted accounting principles (GAAP) also enables users to compare financial results from period to period or across companies.

Although the income statement provides useful information for business decision-making, managers and external users don't use it alone. They also study the balance sheet. In this chapter, we discuss the importance of the balance sheet. First, we look at the principles, concepts, and accounting methods related to the balance sheet. Second, we describe and present a classified balance sheet. Finally, we explore how managers and external users use a balance sheet to help them make business decisions.

Why the Balance Sheet Is Important

1 *Why is a company's balance sheet important?*

A balance sheet provides information that helps internal and external users evaluate a company's ability to achieve its primary goals of earning a satisfactory profit and remaining solvent. You may recall that the income statement provides information that is used for similar purposes. The income statement and the balance sheet provide different yet related types of information.

An income statement presents a summary of a company's operating activities for an accounting period: revenues earned, expenses incurred, and the net income that resulted. So, the income statement reports on a company's actions *over a period of time* or, as some say, the "flow of a company's operating activities." The income statement answers questions such as the following: "How much sales revenue did the company earn last year?" "What was the cost of advertising for the year?"

In contrast, a balance sheet presents a company's financial position *on a specific date,* allowing users to "take stock" of a company's assets, liabilities, and owner's equity on that date. Managers and external users need this "financial position" information in order to make business decisions. By examining the balance sheet, users can answer questions such as the following: "What types of resources does the company have available for its operations?" "What are the company's obligations?" They can find out how much money customers owe the company (accounts receivable), see the total dollar amount of the inventory on hand at year-end, and discover how much money the company owes its creditors (accounts payable).

 Some people say that the balance sheet is a "snapshot" of a company's assets, liabilities, and owner's equity on a given date. What do they mean? Do you agree? Why or why not?

Why Users Need Both the Balance Sheet and the Income Statement

Remember the creative thinking strategies we discussed in Chapter 2? Let's try a couple of analogies to understand why internal and external users need both the income statement and the balance sheet. You will get the most out of these analogies if you read them actively. In other words, every time you see a question, don't just read ahead, but try to come up with your own answers first. Making analogies really will help you understand accounting—we promise!

Let's say that you want to predict whether your friend Chuck can bake a delicious loaf of bread. What do you need to know to increase your chances of making an accurate prediction? We think you need to know three related pieces of information. First, before baking delicious bread, Chuck must have all of the cooking equipment and the ingredients for the bread on hand: flour, butter, yeast, salt, sugar, bread pans, an oven, etc. So, your first question should be, "Does Chuck have everything he needs to bake the bread?" However, even if he has all of the necessary equipment and ingredients, does that mean he can bake delicious bread? Certainly not! The second question you would ask is, "Has he baked delicious bread before?" If the answers to both these questions are yes, it is likely that he can bake a delicious loaf of bread. If the answer to either of these questions is no, then you are much less sure about his ability to bake. Do you agree? The third question (and probably the most important question if you plan on eating his bread) is not as easy to answer. That question is, "Does he still know how to bake?" You won't know the answer to this question until you taste his next loaf out of the oven.

You would follow a similar strategy if you were trying to determine whether a company can earn a satisfactory profit. You want to know if the company has the assets, liabilities, and owner's equity (does it have the "ingredients"?) needed to earn a satisfactory profit (to bake a delicious loaf of bread). You also need to know if the company has been able to use its resources in the past to earn such a profit (has it baked delicious bread before?). Because a company's balance sheet and income statement provide this financial information, analyzing both statements helps you make an informed decision about the company's ability to earn a satisfactory profit (can it still "bake"?). If either financial statement is missing, it is much more difficult to predict how well the company will perform.

For example, to estimate a company's sales revenue for 2000, it is important to know the amount of cash and the amount of inventory available for sale at the beginning of 2000, and the amount of sales revenues in 1999. You would look at the beginning balance sheet to see if the company has sufficient cash to pay for expenses such as advertising, rent, and salaries and whether it has enough inventory to meet customers' demands for its product. Last year's sales revenue gives an indication of how well a company will perform in the current period. You look at the income statement to find that amount.

Now let's try a sports analogy. Suppose you want to estimate how long it will take a friend, Barb, to run a marathon. What questions would you want answered? You would probably want information about her physical characteristics—things like her age, her height, or her muscle development. These physical characteristics will help you understand her potential running ability. Equally important is information about how well she has used her physical attributes—how long it took her to run her last marathon, when she last ran, and how often she exercises.

When you ask about Barb's physical characteristics, you are "taking stock" of her physical resources, much as an investor analyzes a balance sheet to take stock of a company's

How do you think these legs would be listed on a marathoner's balance sheet?

financial resources. By learning how well she has used her physical attributes, you are getting information about her past activities that can help you predict her ability to run a fast race. Running a fast race is to sports what earning a satisfactory profit is to business.

 Can you think of any other analogies? What are the goals of the activities in your analogies? What information can help you predict whether the goal will be attained?

The lesson to be learned from our analogies is this: whenever you try to estimate if a goal can be reached—whether the goal is baking a delicious loaf of bread, running a marathon in a certain amount of time, or earning a satisfactory profit—many different types of related information are helpful. A company's balance sheet is one important source of unique and valuable information for predicting the company's financial performance.

Cost-Volume-Profit Analysis, Budgeting, and the Balance Sheet

In Chapter 6, we discussed the relationship between cost-volume-profit (C-V-P) analysis, budgeting, and the income statement. Remember that a company's income statement reports on the results of many of its managers' operating decisions. At least in part, the revenue and expense information shows the results of past C-V-P analysis and budgeting decisions.

Balance sheet information also summarizes the results of managers' decisions. For instance, in Chapter 4 we saw how Anna Cox used a sales budget to help her decide how much inventory Sweet Temptations should keep on hand. A company also uses the sales budget to decide how often to purchase inventory and how many units to order. The accounting system keeps track of inventory balances to help the company evaluate these budgeting decisions and report the inventory as an asset on the balance sheet. If the amount of inventory on hand grows at a faster rate than sales from year to year, the company probably overestimated both sales and its need to make inventory purchases. If the amount of inventory on hand is decreasing as a proportion of sales from year to year, the company may have underestimated sales and the need to make additional inventory purchases.[1]

 What other balance sheet information helps you evaluate the budgeting decisions of a company's managers?

Remember that financial statements help external users decide if they want to do business with a company. External users are interested in a company's assets, liabilities, and owner's equity because, as we explained in the previous section, these items describe a company's financial characteristics. Because external users may be trying to decide *which* company to do business with, companies prepare balance sheets according to GAAP. Since U.S. companies follow the same set of accounting rules when preparing their financial statements, external users can reliably compare the financial positions of any of these companies as part of their decision-making processes. In the sections that follow, we will briefly review the basic accounting principles that underlie the balance sheet and we will discuss the components of a classified balance sheet.

The Accounting Equation and the Balance Sheet

Recall from Chapter 5 that the financial accounting process is based on a simple equation:

Economic Resources = Claims on Economic Resources

Using accounting terminology, we restated the equation as follows:

Assets = Liabilities + Owner's Equity

---

[1] Some companies intentionally minimize the amount of inventory they keep on hand. These companies buy their inventory "just-in-time" to meet their sales. We will discuss this just-in-time philosophy more in Chapter 18.

Remember that this mathematical expression is known as the basic **accounting equation** and that the equality of the assets to the liabilities plus owner's equity is the reason a company's statement of financial position is often called a *balance* sheet. The monetary total for the economic resources (assets) of a company must always be *in balance* with the monetary total for the claims to the economic resources (liabilities + owner's equity).

 Do you remember the "transactions scales" we showed in Chapter 5? How did they work?

The **balance sheet** is a financial statement that reports the types and the monetary amounts of a company's assets, liabilities, and owner's equity on a specific date. A company prepares a balance sheet at the end of each accounting period, although it can prepare a balance sheet at any other time to give a current "snapshot" of the company's financial position. Before preparing a balance sheet, though, the company must be certain that the monetary totals for each of its assets and liabilities and the monetary total for owner's equity are correct. By "correct," we mean that since the date of the last balance sheet, all of the company's transactions and events have been recorded in the accounting records according to GAAP. As we discussed in Chapter 6, we also mean that the balances of the revenue, expense, and owner's withdrawals accounts at the end of the accounting period have been transferred to the owner's capital account.

Exhibit 7-1 shows Sweet Temptations' balance sheet accounts in its accounting system on January 31, 2000. The T-accounts include the correct balance for each of Sweet Temptations' assets, liabilities, and owner's capital (after including the revenue, expense, and withdrawals amounts for January) accounts.

Exhibit 7-2 shows Sweet Temptations' January 31, 2000 balance sheet. By comparing Exhibit 7-2 with Exhibit 7-1, you can see how the balances in the T-accounts provide the information needed to prepare a balance sheet. Notice that the balance sheet shows the balance for each account. Also notice that the liability and owner's equity items are listed below the assets. This format is called a *report form* of balance sheet (as compared with the *account form,* shown in Exhibit 5-22, which lists the components in an accounting

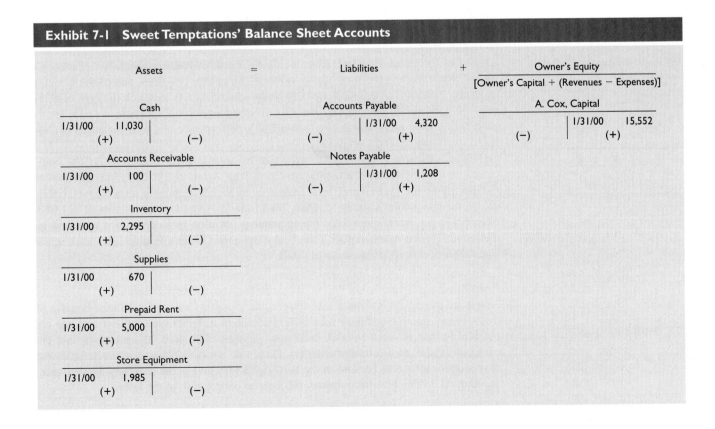

Exhibit 7-1 Sweet Temptations' Balance Sheet Accounts

Exhibit 7-2 Classified Balance Sheet

Sweet Temptations
Balance Sheet
January 31, 2000

Assets

Current Assets
Cash	$11,030	
Accounts receivable	100	
Inventory	2,295	
Supplies	670	
Prepaid rent	5,000	
Total current assets		$19,095

Property and Equipment
Store equipment (net)	$ 1,985	
Total property and equipment		1,985
Total Assets		$21,080

Liabilities

Current Liabilities
Accounts payable	$ 4,320	
Note payable	1,208	
Total current liabilities		$ 5,528
Total Liabilities		$ 5,528

Owner's Equity

A. Cox, capital	$15,552
Total Liabilities and Owner's Equity	$21,080

equation format—assets on the left and liabilities and owner's equity on the right). The report form of balance sheet is common because it is easier to show the accounts vertically on a standard sheet of paper.

2 *What do users need to know about a company's classified balance sheet?*

Sweet Temptations' balance sheet is called a **classified balance sheet.** By "classified," we mean that the balance sheet shows subtotals for assets, liabilities, and owner's equity in related groupings. A company decides on the classifications based on the type of business it is in. Later in the chapter, you will see that these groupings make it easier for financial statement users to evaluate a company's performance and to compare its performance with that of other companies.

Notice the way Sweet Temptations organizes its classified balance sheet. The company adds together the asset groupings to report Total Assets of $21,080 and adds together the liability groupings to report Total Liabilities of $5,528. Finally, it adds the total liabilities to the total owner's equity to report Total Liabilities and Owner's Equity of $21,080. Because Sweet Temptations kept the accounting equation in balance as it recorded its transactions, Total Assets equals Total Liabilities plus Owner's Equity. Let's look at the balance sheet classifications in more detail.

Assets

Assets are a company's economic resources that it expects will provide future benefits to the company. A large company may own hundreds of different types of assets. Some are physical in nature—such as land, buildings, supplies to be used, and inventory that the company expects to sell to its customers. Others do not have physical characteristics but are economic resources because of the legal rights they give to the company. For instance, accounts receivable give the company the right to collect cash in the future.

Think about the different types of assets owned by the grocery store where you shop. We would need several pages to present a complete list, but here are a few examples: cash, accounts receivable, cleaning supplies, grocery carts, storage shelves, forklifts, refrigerators, freezers, bakery equipment, cash registers, the building, the parking lot . . . whew! We'll stop there, but notice that we did *not* even mention any inventory items (groceries).

 If you work, list the types of assets owned by the company for which you work. If you don't work, talk with someone who does, and find out what types of assets are owned by the company for which he or she works.

Because Sweet Temptations started with a very small amount of capital, it has only a few assets. This small-company example makes it easier for you to see the basic framework that a company uses in accounting for and reporting its resources. When presenting a classified balance sheet, a small retail candy store, a large grocery store, or almost any other type of retail company uses the same classifications for its assets. Look at the balance sheet for a large retail company, and you will likely find subtotals for current assets, long-term investments, and property and equipment.

Current Assets

Current assets are cash and other assets that the company expects to convert into cash, sell, or use up within one year.[2] Current assets include (1) cash, (2) marketable securities, (3) receivables, (4) inventory, and (5) prepaid items. The current assets section presents these items in the order of their liquidity—that is, according to how quickly they can be converted into cash, sold, or used up. Because companies need cash to pay currently due liabilities, grouping current assets together helps financial statement users evaluate a company's ability to pay its current debts.

Cash includes cash on hand (i.e., cash kept in cash registers or the company's safe) and in checking and savings accounts. *Marketable securities,* sometimes called *temporary investments* or *short-term investments,* are items such as government bonds and capital stock of corporations in which the company has temporarily invested (and which the company expects to sell within a year). A company usually makes these short-term investments because it has cash it does not need immediately for purchasing inventory or paying liabilities. Instead of just keeping the cash in the bank, the company purchases the marketable securities to earn additional revenue through interest or dividends. Investment companies such as PaineWebber, Merrill Lynch, and Charles Schwab help other companies (and individual investors) buy and sell marketable securities.

www.painewebber.com
www.ml.com
www.schwab.com

Receivables include accounts receivable (amounts owed by customers) and notes receivable (and related interest). *Inventory* is goods held for resale. *Prepaid items* such as insurance, rent, office supplies, and store supplies will not be converted into cash but will be used up within one year. Note in Exhibit 7-2 that the current assets for Sweet Temptations on January 31, 2000 total $19,095, consisting of cash ($11,030), accounts receivable ($100), inventory ($2,295), supplies ($670), and prepaid rent ($5,000). Remember, the amount for each current asset listed on Sweet Temptations' balance sheet comes from the related account balance in its accounting system.

Assets that are not classified as current assets are called noncurrent assets. The balance sheet shows noncurrent assets, such as long-term investments and property and equipment, in separate categories.

Long-Term Investments

Long-term investments include items such as notes receivable, government bonds, bonds and capital stock of corporations, and other securities. Sometimes these are called

---

[2]As we discussed in Chapter 4, some companies, such as lumber, distillery, and tobacco companies, have operating cycles of longer than one year, so they use their operating cycle to define current assets.

noncurrent marketable securities. A company must *intend* to hold the investment for more than one year to classify it in the long-term investments section of the balance sheet.

Why would a company purchase a corporation's stock? A company makes investments for many reasons, which we will discuss in more detail later. The most basic reason, however, is because the company believes the investment will increase the company's profit. For example, a company may invest in the stock of a corporation because it expects the price of that stock to increase. If that happens, when the company sells the stock later, it will have a gain, which will increase its net income.

Sweet Temptations has not made any long-term investments. At this early stage of the company's life, Sweet Temptations uses its cash to replenish inventory and meet other basic business needs such as paying salaries, rent, and advertising. Therefore Sweet Temptations shows no long-term investments on its January 31, 2000 balance sheet.

Property and Equipment

Property and equipment includes all the physical, long-term assets used in the operations of a company. Often these assets are referred to as *fixed assets* or *operating assets* because of their relative permanence in the company's operations. Assets that have a physical existence, such as land, buildings, equipment, and furniture, are listed in this category. Land is listed on the balance sheet at its original cost. The remaining fixed assets are listed at their book values. The **book value** of an asset is its original cost minus the related accumulated depreciation. **Accumulated depreciation** is the total amount of depreciation expense recorded over the life of an asset to date; thus, it is the portion of the asset's cost that has been "used up" to earn revenues to date. The book values for fixed assets change from period to period as the company sells and/or buys these assets and as accumulated depreciation increases. The balance sheet thus helps report on related budgeting and operating decisions made by the company's managers. We will discuss accumulated depreciation in detail in Chapter 21.

You may be wondering how to reconcile the historical cost concept with the reported book value of a company's property and equipment. As a company uses up assets other than property or equipment, the assets that have *not* been used remain on its balance sheet at their historical cost. The assets that *have* been used no longer exist in the company. But when the company uses property or equipment, the asset still exists in the company until the company has finished using it. Every year, the company uses a portion of the asset, but the entire asset still continues to physically exist in the company. What the company reports (the book value) on its balance sheet represents the portion of the property or equipment that the company has not yet used.

Notice in Exhibit 7-2 that Sweet Temptations' store equipment is classified as property and equipment on its balance sheet. Also notice that the store equipment is listed at $1,985 (net). The "(net)" tells the reader that accumulated depreciation has been deducted from the cost (the $1,985 book value consists of the $2,000 cost less $15 accumulated depreciation, as we discussed in Chapter 5). Sweet Temptations does not include any amounts for land or buildings because it rents space in the Westwood Mall and thus does not own such items.

 Sometimes a company has difficulty deciding how to classify its assets. For example, do you think the cars owned by a rental car company are classified as inventory or equipment? Why? Can you think of more examples that present a dilemma?

Liabilities

Liabilities are the economic obligations (debts) of a company. The external parties to whom the company owes the economic obligations are the company's *creditors.* Legal documents often serve as evidence of liabilities. These documents establish a claim *(equity)* by the creditors (the *creditors' equity*) against the assets of the company.

Companies have many different types of liabilities. For instance, consider the claims that creditors may have on the grocery store's assets we listed earlier. The grocery store probably borrowed money from a bank (by signing a mortgage) to finance its purchases of land and a building. The company also could have obtained the funds used to purchase refrigerators, freezers, baking equipment, and other types of equipment from a bank by signing a long-term (e.g., ten-year) note payable. Most likely, it purchased grocery items from suppliers on credit, resulting in accounts payable. Generally, a company has two types of liabilities—current and noncurrent.

Current Liabilities

Current liabilities are obligations that the company expects to pay within one year by using current assets. Current liabilities include (1) accounts payable and salaries payable, (2) unearned revenues, and (3) short-term notes (and interest) payable. Like current assets, current liabilities are usually listed in the order of their liquidity—that is, how quickly they will be paid.

Accounts payable (amounts owed to suppliers) and *salaries payable* (amounts owed to employees) are common examples of obligations to pay for goods and services.

Unearned revenues are advance collections from customers for the future delivery of goods or the future performance of services. For instance, if a customer pays a company in advance for rent or for some service, the company owes the customer the future use of the rental space or the service, and it records the liabilities as unearned rent or unearned fees.

Short-term *notes payable* (and related interest owed) are obligations that arise because a company signs a note (legal document) that it will pay within one year. The portion of noncurrent liabilities (discussed next) that the company will pay during the next year is also included in current liabilities.

In Exhibit 7-2, Sweet Temptations' current liabilities total $5,528. Sweet Temptations has two kinds of current liabilities—accounts payable ($4,320) and a short-term note payable ($1,208, which includes the $1,200 borrowed plus $8 accrued interest, as we discussed in Chapter 5). Remember that the amount for each current liability comes from the related account balance in the company's accounting system.

Noncurrent Liabilities

Noncurrent liabilities are obligations that a company does not expect to pay within the next year. Noncurrent liabilities are also called *long-term* liabilities because a company usually won't pay them for several years. This category includes such items as long-term notes payable, mortgages payable, and bonds payable (we will look at these in Chapter 22 when we discuss corporations). In most cases, a company incurs a long-term liability when it purchases property or equipment because it "finances" the purchase by borrowing the money to buy the item, and then pays back the amount borrowed over a period longer than a year.

The noncurrent liabilities section shows the past financing decisions of the company's managers. The balance sheet for Sweet Temptations in Exhibit 7-2 does not include a noncurrent liabilities section because the company has not yet incurred any long-term debt.

 Is the fact that Sweet Temptations has no long-term liabilities good or bad? Why?

Owner's Equity

Owner's equity is the owner's current investment in the assets of the company. It is the company's assets less its liabilities. For a sole proprietorship, such as Sweet Temptations, the balance sheet lists the total ending owner's equity in a single *capital* account. The balance sheet shows the owner's equity by listing the owner's name, the word *capital,* and the amount of the current investment. The balance sheets of a partnership and corporation show the owner's equity slightly differently, as we will discuss later in the book. *Residual equity* is a term sometimes used for owner's equity because creditors have first legal claim to a company's assets. Once the creditors' claims have been satisfied, the owner is entitled to the remainder (residual) of the assets.

The ending balance in the account for the owner's capital is affected by the owner's additional investments or withdrawals and by net income. As we discussed in Chapter 6, the company prepares a separate schedule, the statement of changes in owner's equity, to report these items. It also makes closing entries to update the owner's capital account. We show the statement of changes in owner's equity for Sweet Temptations for January 2000 in Exhibit 7-3. Note that we show the $15,552 ending amount of A. Cox, Capital on the balance sheet in Exhibit 7-2. The $21,080 total liabilities and owner's equity ($5,528 total liabilities + $15,552 owner's equity) is equal to the $21,080 total assets.

Using the Balance Sheet for Evaluation

Remember our bread-baking analogy? We said that without the proper equipment and ingredients, your friend Chuck will have difficulty making delicious bread, no matter how skilled he is. We also noted that the balance sheet informs users of a company's "financial ingredients." Company managers, investors, and creditors are very interested in this information. Without enough resources ("ingredients"), a company will have difficulty remaining solvent and earning a satisfactory profit, no matter how skilled its managers.

However, just having the necessary baking ingredients for the baker is not sufficient. The ingredients have to be mixed in the proper proportions at the proper times to improve the chances of baking good bread. Likewise, a company can manage its mix (i.e., types and amounts) of assets, liabilities, and owner's equity to improve its chances of remaining solvent and earning a profit.

A manager is concerned with the company's balance sheet because it is used to evaluate his or her own performance. Also, since external users make investment and credit decisions based in part on balance sheet information, a manager knows that the company's balance sheet affects its ability to get a bank loan or attract new investors.

External users analyze a company's balance sheet to determine whether the company has the right amount and mix of assets, liabilities, and owner's equity to justify making an investment in the company. What they look at in a balance sheet depends on the type of investment they are considering. Short-term creditors are mostly interested in a company's short-term liquidity—whether it can pay current obligations as they are due. Long-term creditors are concerned about whether their interest income is safe and whether the company can continue to earn income and generate cash flows to meet its financial commitments. Investors are concerned about whether they will receive a return on their investment, and how much of a return they will receive. Some potential investors are interested in "solid" companies, that is, companies whose financial statements indicate stable earnings (and, therefore, a steady return). Others want to invest in newer companies that may earn higher income (and, therefore, a higher return) but have more risk.

Notice that in describing the information that external users need from financial statements, we use the words *short-term, long-term, liquidity, stability,* and *risk.* Balance sheet items are classified in a way that help address these needs.

Exhibit 7-3 Statement of Changes in Owner's Equity

Schedule A

Sweet Temptations
Statement of Changes in Owner's Equity
For Month Ended January 31, 2000

A. Cox, capital, January 1, 2000	$15,000
Add: Net income	602
	$15,602
Less: Withdrawals	(50)
A. Cox, capital, January 31, 2000	$15,552

Remember from Chapter 2 that decision-making consists of four stages—recognizing the problem, identifying the alternatives, evaluating the alternatives, and making the decision itself. Financial accounting information becomes especially useful when managers and external users want to evaluate the alternatives they have identified. In the next sections, we will discuss a few of the main financial characteristics ("financial ingredients") that managers and external users study when making business decisions. In addition, we will discuss the types of analyses that they use to evaluate a company's performance. Some of these analyses include calculating and evaluating financial statement ratios, which we introduced in Chapter 6. The ratios are "benchmarks" against which decision-makers compare a company's performance with its performance in prior periods and with the performance of other companies.

Evaluating Liquidity

Liquidity is a measure of how quickly an asset can be converted into cash or a liability can be paid. It is an important financial characteristic because to remain solvent, a company must have cash to pay its liabilities as they become due. The need for adequate liquidity is a major reason a company prepares a cash budget.

3 *What is a company's liquidity, and how do users evaluate it?*

External users assess how well a company manages its liquidity by studying its working capital. **Working capital** is a company's current assets minus its current liabilities. The term "working capital" is used because this excess is the dollar amount of liquid resources a company has to "work with" after it pays all of its short-term debts. Often, users make slightly different computations for the same purpose. The current ratio and the quick (acid-test) ratio are two common indicators of a company's liquidity.

 Given the definition of liquidity, do you think working capital is a good measure of a company's ability to pay its liabilities? Why or why not?

Current Ratio

The **current ratio** shows the relationship between current assets and current liabilities and is probably the most commonly used indicator of a company's short-run liquidity. It is calculated as follows:

$$\text{Current Ratio} = \frac{\text{Current Assets}}{\text{Current Liabilities}}$$

When we refer to water as "liquid" and a company as "liquid," do we mean the same thing? How are the meanings similar?

The current ratio is more useful than working capital for measuring a company's liquidity because the current ratio allows comparisons of different-sized companies.

In the past, as a "rule of thumb," users thought a current ratio of 2.0, or 2 to 1 (signifying that a company has twice the amount of current assets as current liabilities) was satisfactory. If a company's current assets were twice its current debt, creditors generally believed that even if an emergency arose requiring an unexpected use of cash, the company could still pay its short-term debts.

Today, however, users pay more attention to (1) industry structure, (2) the length of a company's operating cycle, and (3) the "mix" of current assets. The mix is the proportion of different items that make up the total current assets. This mix has an effect on how quickly the current assets can be converted into cash. For instance, if a company has a high proportion of prepaid items within its current assets, it may be in a weak liquidity position because prepaid assets are used up rather than being converted into cash. Also, if a company has too *high* a current ratio compared with the ratios of similar companies in the same industry, this may indicate poor management of current assets. For example, maybe the company keeps too much cash on hand rather than investing its excess cash. Finally, the shorter a company's operating cycle, the less likely it is to need a large amount of working capital or as high a current ratio to operate efficiently.

 How do you think the length of a company's operating cycle would affect the amount of working capital it needs or the size of its current ratio?

Sweet Temptations has working capital of $13,567, calculated by subtracting the $5,528 total current liabilities from the $19,095 total current assets, shown in Exhibit 7-2. The company's current ratio is 3.45 ($19,095 total current assets divided by $5,528 total current liabilities), which would be high for an older company. Because Sweet Temptations is a new company, a high current ratio is good because it indicates a strong ability to pay current debts. Anna Cox will want to keep track of this ratio as she makes decisions about future credit purchases.

Quick Ratio

The **quick ratio** is a more convincing indicator of a company's short-term debt-paying ability. Short-term lenders often use this ratio when deciding whether to extend credit. The quick ratio uses only the current assets that may be easily converted into cash—referred to as quick assets. *Quick assets* consist of cash, short-term marketable securities, accounts receivable, and short-term notes receivable. The quick ratio excludes inventory because it may not be sold soon and it may be sold on credit; in both cases, inventory cannot be turned into cash as quickly. The quick ratio also excludes prepaid items because they are not convertible into cash. This is why the ratio is sometimes called the *acid-test* ratio. Thus, the quick ratio is calculated as follows:

$$\text{Quick (Acid-test) Ratio} = \frac{\text{Quick Assets}}{\text{Current Liabilities}}$$

The quick ratio shows potential liquidity problems when a company has a poor mix of current assets. For instance, the quick ratio will show that a company with a lot of inventory has less liquidity than indicated by its current ratio. The current ratio won't show this because it includes inventory in the numerator. A quick ratio of 1.0, or 1:1 (showing that a company's quick assets and current liabilities are equal) has generally been considered satisfactory, but users also consider the industry structure as well as the length of the company's operating cycle.

 Suppose a company has a quick ratio of 0.5. What do you think of its liquidity? Does your opinion change if you learn that unearned rent revenue amounts to 60 percent of the company's current liabilities? Why or why not?

Sweet Temptations' quick ratio is 2.01, calculated by dividing Sweet Temptations' $11,130 total quick assets ($11,030 cash + $100 accounts receivable) by its $5,528 total current liabilities. Again, it seems that Sweet Temptations is in a good short-term financial position. Note that Sweet Temptations' quick ratio is about two-thirds of its current ratio because the quick ratio calculation excludes the inventory, supplies, and prepaid rent.

 Why do you think words like "liquid" and "quick" are used in reference to a company's current assets and current liabilities?

Liquidity Ratios of Actual Companies

To illustrate ratio analysis, we continue our evaluation, which we began in Chapter 6, of JCPenney Company Inc. and Sears Roebuck and Co. The companies' current ratios and quick ratios at the end of 1997 were as follows:

www.jcpenney.com
www.sears.com

	JCPenney	Sears
Current Ratio	1.87	1.94
Quick Ratio	0.84	1.56

Both the current ratio and the quick ratio of Sears were higher than those of JCPenney. While Sears' current ratio was slightly below the 2.0 "rule of thumb," its quick ratio was considerably higher than the 1.0 "rule of thumb." On the other hand, both the current ratio and the quick ratio of JCPenney were below the respective norms. This means that JCPenney is more likely to have short-term liquidity concerns than Sears.

Evaluating Financial Flexibility

Recall from Chapter 6 that **financial flexibility** is the ability of a company to adapt to change. It is an important financial characteristic because it enables a company to increase or reduce its operating activities as needed. For example, a company with financial flexibility can revise its purchasing plan to take advantage of temporary reductions in wholesale inventory prices. The current ratio and the acid-test ratio can be used to assess short-term financial flexibility.

4 *What is a company's financial flexibility, and how do users evaluate it?*

Managers, owners, and creditors are also interested in a company's ability to take advantage of major, long-term business opportunities. For a company to be able to purchase additional retail stores, build another manufacturing plant, or adopt new information technologies, it must have enough available resources or must be able to raise additional resources. To assess long-term financial flexibility, financial statement users evaluate a company's debt levels. To do this, they calculate a company's debt ratio.

Debt Ratio

The **debt ratio** shows the percentage of total assets provided by creditors and is calculated as follows:

$$\text{Debt Ratio} = \frac{\text{Total Liabilities}}{\text{Total Assets}}$$

This ratio is subtracted from 100% to show the percentage of total assets contributed by the owner. The desired mix between debt and owner's equity depends on the type of business and the country in which the company is located. For example, in Japan, historically investors have preferred a higher debt ratio than is typical for U.S. companies. This is true primarily because Japanese creditors and investors have worked together more closely. (However, in Japan's current economic environment, this relationship may change.) In the United States, creditors prefer that a company have a lower debt ratio because if business declines, a lower debt ratio indicates that the company is more likely to be able to pay the interest it owes as well as its other fixed costs. Up to a point, *owners* prefer a higher debt ratio, particularly when the return earned on assets purchased by the company with the borrowed money is higher than the interest the company has to pay to its creditors. We will discuss this in more detail later.

 Debt ratios vary from industry to industry. What economic factors do you think would account for these differences?

Sweet Temptations has a debt ratio of 0.26 ($5,528 total liabilities divided by $21,080 total assets). Its debt ratio indicates that most of its assets (74%) are financed by owner's equity. Because Sweet Temptations is new and has no long-term debts, the debt ratio and the current ratio show that it has no immediate problems with solvency or liquidity—that is, it has financial flexibility. If Sweet Temptations decides to expand, creditors will like the fact that, so far, it has relied on Anna's investments and short-term liabilities to finance its operations.

Debt Ratios of Actual Companies

The debt ratios of JCPenney and Sears at the end of 1997 were as follows:

	JCPenney	Sears
Debt Ratio	68.7	84.9

Because of its lower proportion of debt, we can conclude that JCPenney relied less on creditors to finance its assets. Therefore, JCPenney had higher financial flexibility because borrowing more money would be easier for the company. JCPenney may also be able to borrow money at a lower interest rate because the lenders may think it has a lower level of risk.

Relationship between the Income Statement and the Balance Sheet

Although decision-makers find the ratios we just presented—the current ratio, the quick ratio, and the debt ratio—to be very helpful, these ratios do have one limitation: they use only balance sheet information. *It is very important for you to know that many significant business questions can be answered only by analyzing a company's income statement and balance sheet together.* This is the only way to determine whether a company has made a "satisfactory" profit and to calculate other measures of its "operating capability" (which we will discuss later).

 Do you think creditors always need to evaluate a company's balance sheet and income statement before granting a loan? Why or why not?

Say, for instance, that on its income statement, a company reports that net income for the accounting period is $5 million. Five million dollars may sound like a lot, but did the company earn a satisfactory profit? You can't tell without comparing the $5 million with the dollar amount of resources the company used to earn the income (and with the income it earned in each of the last few years). The $5 million may or may not be satisfactory depending on the size of the company (and how well it has done in prior periods).

Let's say the company reports $50 million of total assets on its balance sheet at the end of the accounting period. We can divide the company's net income for the period by its total assets (a net income to total assets ratio) and calculate the company's rate of return on assets. Using the dollar amounts given, this company earned a 10% return on assets ($5 million ÷ $50 million). Just how satisfied a company's managers, investors, and creditors are with a 10% return on assets depends on how well similar types of companies performed, and on whether this return met or exceeded their expectations. Financial statements work as a *set* of information because as we noted in the example above, external

Exhibit 7-4   Relationships among Financial Statements

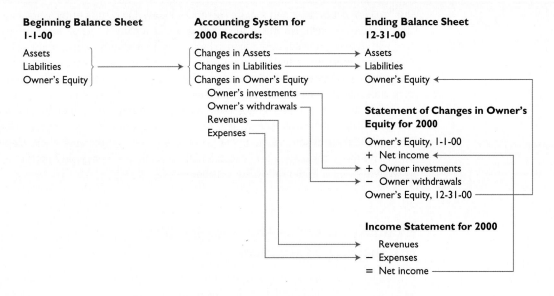

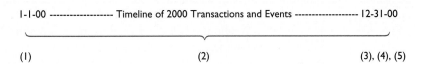

(1)   (2)   (3), (4), (5)

Activities

(1) The beginning balance sheet lists the resources and claims on resources at the start of 2000.

(2) During 2000, the accounting system records all 2000 transactions and events according to GAAP.

(3) An income statement for the period ending 12-31-00 is prepared and net income is calculated.

(4) A statement of changes in owner's equity is prepared that shows how net income and owner investments and withdrawals affected the 12-31-00 owner's equity amount.

(5) A balance sheet is prepared that shows the assets, liabilities, and owner's equity amounts for 12-31-00.

users need both the income statement and the balance sheet to evaluate a company's performance and financial position.

Exhibit 7-4 illustrates the relationships among the financial statements.[3] Here we show a balance sheet for January 1, 2000 on the far left of the exhibit. This balance sheet reports the resources and claims on resources of a company on the first day of January. It shows the mix of "financial ingredients" that the company had available to work with when starting the accounting period. During the accounting period (2000), the company had many transactions and events affecting assets, liabilities, and owner's equity (owner's investments and withdrawals, revenues and expenses), and all of these transactions and events were recorded in its accounting system. At the end of the accounting period, the company

---

[3]The cash flow statement is also a useful financial statement, along with the balance sheet and the income statement. We will discuss this statement in Chapter 8, so we have not included it in our present discussion.

prepares its financial statements. Take some time to study Exhibit 7-4 carefully before you move on; it contains some very important concepts.

The 2000 income statement summarizes how the company used its financial "ingredients" to earn net income and remain solvent. It shows the results of the operating decisions the company's managers made to improve the company's financial position (e.g., how much advertising it used, how much salary expense it incurred, how many sales it made). The year's operating activities, owner's investments, and owner's withdrawals all affect the company's mix of financial resources and the claims to its resources. The 2000 ending balance sheet shows the effects of the net changes.

With the financial information contained in the beginning and ending balance sheets, along with the income statement, you can see what resources the company started with, how it used those resources, and what resources it owns at the end of the accounting period. With this information, you can calculate liquidity, solvency, and performance ratios, as we will discuss in the following section.

Evaluations Using the Balance Sheet and the Income Statement

A company's managers, investors, and creditors use information from its income statement and balance sheet to calculate ratios for measuring the company's financial success. The numerator of each ratio is an income statement amount showing the "flow" into or out of the company (e.g., net income, net credit sales, cost of goods sold) *during* the accounting period. The denominator of each ratio is a balance sheet amount showing the "resources" used to obtain the "flow." Some of these ratios use an *average* figure for the denominator. This is because balance sheet amounts are measured at a *point in time* (the beginning and the end of the accounting period). By using an average amount for the accounting period (average total assets, average owner's equity, average inventory) in the denominator, the balance sheet amount "covers" the same time period as the income statement amount. To determine the average amount, add the beginning and the ending amounts together and then divide by 2. We will discuss some common ratios and their calculations in the following sections.

Evaluating Profitability

5 *Why and how do users evaluate a company's profitability?*

Decision-makers use profitability ratios to evaluate how well a company has met its profit objectives in relation to the resources invested. Two of these profitability ratios are the return on total assets ratio and the return on owner's equity ratio.

Return on Total Assets

A company's managers have the responsibility to use the company's assets to earn a satisfactory profit. The amount of net income earned compared with total assets shows whether a company used its economic resources efficiently. A company's **return on total assets** is calculated as follows:

$$\text{Return on Total Assets} = \frac{\text{Net Income} + \text{Interest Expense}}{\text{Average Total Assets}}$$

The net income is obtained from the company's income statement. If a company reports any interest expense on its income statement, decision-makers using this ratio add the amount back to net income in the numerator. They make this adjustment because the interest expense is a financial cost paid to creditors and not an operating expense of earning revenue. (The company could have earned the same income before interest expense if the owner had contributed assets rather than financing them through creditors.) Because the company uses its assets to earn net income over the entire accounting period, decision-makers use the *average* total assets for the period as the denominator.

When comparing one company's return on total assets with that of another company, you should consider the age of the assets of each company. With increasing prices today, a company using recently purchased assets (at higher prices) will show a lower return on these assets. Also, older assets have higher amounts of accumulated depreciation and therefore lower book values.

 Do you think companies' liabilities affect how their return on total assets ratios are interpreted? Why or why not?

Let's calculate Sweet Temptations' return on total assets for January 2000. Listed below is the information needed to make the calculation (we took the information from its financial statements):

Net income for January 2000:	$ 602
Interest expense for January 2000	8
Total assets, January 1, 2000	17,820
Total assets, January 31, 2000	21,080

The return on total assets ratio of Sweet Temptations for January 2000 is calculated as follows:

$$3.14\% = \frac{\$602 + \$8}{[(\$17,820 + \$21,080)/2]}$$

Although this 3.14% return on assets for Sweet Temptations seems low, remember that it is for one month and not for an entire year, as is typical. (Multiplying the ratio by 12 [months] gives an estimate of Sweet Temptations' ratio for the year.) If Sweet Temptations can keep up January's level of income for the rest of the year, it is likely to earn a satisfactory rate of return on its assets for 2000.

Return on Owner's Equity

A company's managers also have the responsibility to earn a satisfactory return on the owner's investment in the company. Dividing net income by the *average* owner's equity shows the company's return (in percentage terms) to the owner—resulting from all of the company's activities during the accounting period. A company's **return on owner's equity** is calculated as follows:

$$\text{Return on Owner's Equity} = \frac{\text{Net Income}}{\text{Average Owner's Equity}}$$

Note that in contrast to the return on total assets ratio, the return on owner's equity ratio does not add interest expense back to net income. This is because net income is a measure of a company's profits available to owners *after* incurring the financial cost related to creditors.

We can calculate Sweet Temptations' return on owner's equity for January 2000 by taking the information listed below from its financial statements:

Net income for January 2000	$ 602
A. Cox, capital, January 1, 2000	15,000
A. Cox, capital, January 31, 2000	15,552

The return on owner's equity ratio of Sweet Temptations for January 2000 is calculated as follows:

$$3.94\% = \frac{\$602}{[(\$15,000 + \$15,552)/2]}$$

DILBERT® reprinted by permission of United Features Syndicate, Inc.

How do you think Ernie's plan would boost his company's return-on-assets ratio? Do you think it is a good idea? Why or why not?

Sweet Temptations' 3.94% return on owner's equity for January 2000 is low, but again it is for only one month. (Multiplying the ratio by 12 gives an estimate of Sweet Temptations' ratio for the year.) Also, Sweet Temptations' return on owner's equity is higher than its return on total assets. This shows users that the company has benefited from using debt to help finance its assets.

Profitability Ratios of Actual Companies

The ratios used to evaluate the profitability of JCPenney and Sears for 1997 were as follows:

	JCPenney	Sears
Return on Total Assets	5.0%	6.9%
Return on Owners' Equity	8.5%	22.0%

Based on Sears' higher return on total assets and its higher return on owners' equity, we can say that it used its assets more efficiently and earned a more satisfactory profit for its owners than did JCPenney.

Evaluating Operating Capability

6 *What is a company's operating capability, and how do users evaluate it?*

Recall from Chapter 6 that **operating capability** refers to a company's ability to sustain a given level of operations. Information about a company's operating capability is important in evaluating how well it is maintaining its operating level, and in predicting future changes in its operating activity. The current ratio helps predict a company's ability to continue to purchase inventory. If a company's current ratio is less than 2.0, investors may worry that the company's operations won't generate enough cash to replenish inventory. The debt ratio helps evaluate whether a company has the resources to replace property and equipment.

In this section we discuss how evaluating the level of a company's activities can provide insights into its operating capability. This is done through activity ratios, used to show the length of the parts of the company's operating cycle. This knowledge lets users evaluate the liquidity of selected current assets. Recall that a retail company's operating cycle is the length of time it takes to invest cash in inventory, make credit sales, and convert the receivables into cash. Two common activity ratios are the (1) inventory turnover and (2) accounts receivable turnover.

Inventory Turnover

A company purchases, sells, and replaces inventory throughout its accounting period. Dividing the company's cost of goods sold (from its income statement) for the period by the average inventory (from its beginning and ending balance sheets) shows the number of times the company *turns over* (or sells) the inventory during that period. A company's **inventory turnover** is calculated as follows:

$$\text{Inventory Turnover} = \frac{\text{Cost of Goods Sold}}{\text{Average Inventory}}$$

As a general rule, the higher the inventory turnover, the more efficient the company is in its purchasing and sales activities and the less cash it needs to invest in inventory. A company with a higher turnover generally purchases its inventory more often and in smaller amounts than it would if it had a lower inventory turnover. It is also less likely to have obsolete inventory (because it holds on to its inventory for only a short time before selling it). These efficiencies "free up" a company's cash—it needs less cash and can invest excess cash in other earnings activities. However, a company's inventory turnover can be too high. If a company's inventory turnover is too high, the company may not be keeping enough inventory on hand to meet customer demand, and it may be missing out on additional sales.

Let's calculate Sweet Temptations' inventory turnover for January 2000. Listed below is the information needed to make the calculation (we took the information from its financial statements):

Cost of goods sold for January 2000	$3,645
Inventory, January 1, 2000	1,620
Inventory, January 31, 2000	2,295

We can calculate Sweet Temptations' inventory turnover ratio for January 2000 as follows:

$$1.86 \text{ times} = \frac{\$3,645}{[(\$1,620 + \$2,295)/2]}$$

This ratio shows that Sweet Temptations turned over its inventory almost two times in January. (To estimate Sweet Temptations' inventory turnover for the year, assuming every month has the same rate of turnover, multiply the January turnover by 12.) Since Sweet Temptations is a candy store, this turnover is a good sign that Sweet Temptations is operating efficiently (who wants to buy old candy?). Over the next few months Anna should continue to monitor Sweet Temptations' inventory turnover to see if she needs to make any changes in its purchasing budget.

Users sometimes want a different measure of how efficient a company is in its inventory activities—how long it takes a company to sell its inventory. This measure is called the **number of days in the selling period.** Dividing the number of operating days in a company's business year (a company that does business seven days a week has 365 days in its business year) by its inventory turnover shows the number of days in its selling period, as follows:

$$\text{Number of Days in Selling Period} = \frac{\text{Number of Days in Business Year}}{\text{Inventory Turnover}}$$

This ratio estimates the average time (in days) it takes the company to sell its inventory. Because we are calculating these ratios for Sweet Temptations for only one month, we use 30 days (the number of days Sweet Temptations was open in January, excluding New Year's Day) as the numerator. With that in mind, the number of days in its selling period is calculated as follows:

$$16.13 \text{ days} = \frac{30}{1.86}$$

This ratio tells us that in January, Sweet Temptations sold its inventory about every 16 days. To evaluate how well it is managing its inventory, we should compare these results with how long a box of candy stays "fresh," with Sweet Temptations' ratio in previous years (if it were not a new company), and with other companies' performances.

 What do you think Anna should do if a box of candy stays "fresh" about 2 weeks?

Accounts Receivable Turnover

If a company sells inventory on credit, it must collect the accounts receivable from the sales to complete its operating cycle. Dividing a company's net credit sales for the period (from its income statement) by its average accounts receivable (from its beginning and ending balance sheets) shows how many times the average receivable turns over (is collected) each period. A company's **accounts receivable turnover** is calculated as follows:

$$\text{Accounts Receivable Turnover} = \frac{\text{Net Credit Sales}}{\text{Average Accounts Receivable}}$$

The accounts receivable turnover measures how efficiently a company collects cash from its credit customers. Users prefer to see a higher turnover, which shows that the company has less cash tied up in accounts receivable, collects this cash faster, and usually has fewer customers who don't pay.

The amount of net *credit* sales is the best amount to use as the numerator. This is the number that managers use when making this calculation. However, since companies don't give a breakdown between credit and cash sales on their income statements, external users must calculate the ratio using total net sales. Because using total net sales increases the numerator (unless all sales are credit sales), this calculation will overestimate the number of times a company's accounts receivable turns over.

Users often divide a company's accounts receivable turnover into the number of days in the business year to show the **number of days in the collection period,** as follows:

$$\text{Number of Days in Collection Period} = \frac{\text{Number of Days in Business Year}}{\text{Accounts Receivable Turnover}}$$

The number of days in a company's collection period is the average time it takes the company to collect its accounts receivable. By comparing a company's average collection period with the days in its credit terms (i.e., 2/10, n/30), a user can see how aggressive the company is in collecting overdue accounts. The user can also compare this number with with the ratios for past years and with those of other companies. Because Sweet Temptations made only one credit sale in January, we do not calculate these accounts receivable ratios here. To estimate the number of days in a company's operating cycle, a user can add together the number of days in the company's selling period and the number of days in its collection period.

 Is a company's operating cycle always the same, or can a company control the length of its operating cycle? What, if anything, can be done to control the length of the operating cycle?

Operating Capability Ratios of Actual Companies

The ratios used to evaluate the operating capability of JCPenney and Sears for 1997 were as follows:

	JCPenney	Sears
Inventory Turnover	3.6	5.5
Accounts Receivable Turnover	7.0	1.9

Sears' higher inventory turnover shows that it took less time to sell its inventory than did JCPenney, indicating that Sears was more efficient in managing its inventory. However, JCPenney was more efficient in collecting its cash from credit customers than was Sears, as shown by its higher accounts receivable turnover.[4]

Limitations of the Income Statement and the Balance Sheet

In Chapters 5 and 6 you saw that a company's accounting system is based on several important accounting concepts and principles. The concepts and principles were created to ensure that companies' accounting systems provide useful, reliable, and relevant information to their managers and other interested parties.

 The key concepts and principles are the entity concept, the monetary unit concept, the historical cost concept, the accounting period concept, the matching principle, and accrual accounting. In your own words, describe why each of these is important.

These concepts and principles guide accountants as they analyze company activities, record transactions, make adjustments, and prepare a company's income statement and balance sheet. Yet even though we have seen how concepts and principles help to build a useful accounting system, they also set limits on the types of information the financial statements provide. These limits restrict the usefulness of the information. For example, the historical cost concept requires that the asset Land be reported on a company's balance sheet at its original cost. So if a company purchased land in 1975 for $10,000, its 2000 ending balance sheet will list "Land $10,000," no matter how much the land is currently worth. In 2000, the land may be worth much more than $10,000. Thus, the balance sheet doesn't always show each asset's current value. But if the company has no intention of selling an asset, the current value may not be relevant.

Another limitation of the income statement and the balance sheet is that they do not provide much information about a company's cash management because they are based on accrual accounting. Hence, investors and creditors also need a financial statement that provides a summary of a company's cash flows during an accounting period. Thus, a company prepares and reports a third financial statement—the cash flow statement, and we will discuss it in Chapter 8.

 What do a company's balance sheet and income statement reveal about its management of cash? What else would an investor or creditor want to know?

Business Issues and Values

Recall that assets are a company's economic resources that it expects will provide future benefits to the company. As we mentioned above, in accordance with GAAP, companies record assets at their historical cost and do not change these amounts for changes in their values. One of the major economic resources of many companies is their employees. A company that has a loyal, well-trained employee group has a valuable "asset" that may increase in value over time because of additional training and job satisfaction. This employee group makes very important contributions to the company's ability to earn profits. (Do you continue to shop at a store where the employees are rude?) But because of the historical

---

[4]However, Sears' accounts receivable turnover may have been lower in part because it encourages its credit customers to extend the payments on their "revolving charge" accounts, for whch Sears charges these customers interest.

cost concept, the company cannot report this economic resource as an asset on the balance sheet it issues to external users. However, some companies that take pride in the quality of their employees do prepare internal reports that include measures of their employees' values; their managers use these reports for internal decision-making.

 Does "investing" in its employees worsen a company's reported performance in the current year?

Summary

At the beginning of the chapter we asked you several questions. During the chapter, we asked you to STOP and answer some additional questions to build your knowledge about specific issues. Be sure you answered these additional questions. Below are the questions from the beginning of the chapter, with a brief summary of the key points relating to the answers. Use your creative and critical thinking skills to expand on these key points to develop more complete answers to the questions and to determine what other questions you have that might lead you to learn more about the issues.

1 Why is a company's balance sheet important?

A company's balance sheet is important because this statement provides internal and external users with information to help evaluate the company's ability to achieve its primary goals of earning a satisfactory profit and remaining solvent. A balance sheet provides information about a company's economic resources and the claims on those resources (its financial position) on a specific date.

2 What do users need to know about a company's classified balance sheet?

Users need to know that a company's classified balance sheet shows important subtotals, in related groupings, for the assets, liabilities, and owner's equity of the company. The groupings include current assets and noncurrent assets, as well as current liabilities and noncurrent liabilities. Current assets are cash and other assets that a company expects to convert into cash, sell, or use up within one year. Current assets include cash, marketable securities, receivables, inventory, and prepaid items. Noncurrent assets are assets other than current assets; these include items such as long-term investments, as well as property and equipment. Current liabilities are obligations that a company expects to pay within one year by using current assets. Current liabilities include accounts payable and salaries payable, unearned revenues, and short-term notes (and interest) payable. Noncurrent liabilities are obligations that a company does not expect to pay within the next year; these include items such as long-term notes payable, mortgages payable, and bonds payable.

3 What is a company's liquidity, and how do users evaluate it?

A company's liquidity is a measure of how quickly its current assets can be converted into cash to pay its current liabilities as they become due. Users evaluate a company's liquidity by studying its working capital (current assets minus current liabilities), current ratio (current assets divided by current liabilities), and quick (acid-test) ratio (quick assets divided by current liabilities).

4 What is a company's financial flexibility, and how do users evaluate it?

A company's financial flexibility is its ability to adapt to change. Measures of a company's financial flexibility are used to assess whether the company can increase or reduce its operating activities as needed. Users study a company's current ratio and quick ratio to evaluate its short-term financial flexibility. They study a company's debt ratio (total liabilities divided by total assets) to evaluate its long-term financial flexibility.

5 Why and how do users evaluate a company's profitability?

Users evaluate a company's profitability to determine how well it has met its profit objectives in relation to the resources invested. They study a company's return on total assets ([net income plus interest expense] divided by average total assets) and return on owner's equity (net income divided by average owner's equity) ratios to evaluate a company's profitability.

6 **What is a company's operating capability, and how do users evaluate it?**

A company's operating capability is its ability to sustain a given level of operations. Measures of a company's operating capability are used to assess how well the company is maintaining its operating level and to predict future changes in its operating activity. Users study a company's activity ratios to determine the length of the parts of the company's operating cycle. These ratios include the inventory turnover (cost of goods sold divided by average inventory) and the accounts receivable turnover (net credit sales divided by average accounts receivable).

Key Terms

accounting equation *(p. 203)*
accounts receivable turnover *(p. 218)*
accumulated depreciation *(p. 206)*
assets *(p. 204)*
balance sheet *(p. 203)*
book value *(p. 206)*
classified balance sheet *(p. 204)*
current assets *(p. 205)*
current liabilities *(p. 207)*
current ratio *(p. 209)*
debt ratio *(p. 211)*
financial flexibility *(p. 211)*
inventory turnover *(p. 217)*
liabilities *(p. 206)*

liquidity *(p. 209)*
long-term investments *(p. 205)*
noncurrent liabilities *(p. 207)*
number of days in the collection period *(p. 218)*
number of days in the selling period *(p. 217)*
operating capability *(p. 216)*
owner's equity *(p. 207)*
property and equipment *(p. 206)*
quick ratio *(p. 210)*
return on owner's equity *(p. 215)*
return on total assets *(p. 214)*
working capital *(p. 209)*

Here is an opportunity to gather information on the Internet about real-world issues related to the topics in this chapter. Go to http://www.dryden.com/account and click on the Cunningham, Nikolai, and Bazley book cover. Click on Summary Surfing, then click on this chapter number, and answer the following questions.

▶ Click on **JCPenney.** Find the appropriate financial statement(s). Compute the current ratio, quick ratio, debt ratio, return on owners' equity, and inventory turnover for the most current year. How do these results compare with the 1997 ratios we discussed in this chapter?

▶ Click on **Sears.** Find the appropriate financial statements. Compute the current ratio, quick ratio, debt ratio, return on owners' equity, and inventory turnover for the most current year. How do these results compare with the 1997 ratios we discussed in this chapter?

**S U M M A R Y
S U R F I N G**

Integrated Business and Accounting Situations

Answer the Following Questions in Your Own Words

Testing Your Knowledge

7-1 What is a balance sheet, and what types of questions can a user answer by studying the balance sheet?

7-2 What is the accounting equation, and how does it relate to the balance sheet of a company?

7-3 What is the difference between an account form and a report form of balance sheet?

7-4 Explain what is meant by a "classified" balance sheet, and identify the major groupings of assets and liabilities.

7-5 Explain the meaning of "current assets."

7-6 Identify and briefly explain the major current assets.

7-7 What are long-term investments? Give several examples.

7-8 What is property and equipment? At what amount is each item of property and equipment listed on the balance sheet?

7-9 Explain the meaning of "current liabilities."

7-10 Identify and briefly explain the major current liabilities.

7-11 What are noncurrent liabilities? Give several examples.

7-12 What is owner's equity, and why is it sometimes called "residual equity"?

7-13 What is meant by "liquidity," and why is it important?

7-14 Explain how to compute the current ratio and what it is used for.

7-15 Explain how to compute the quick ratio and what it is used for.

7-16 What is meant by "financial flexibility," and why is it important?

7-17 Explain how to compute the debt ratio and what it is used for.

7-18 Explain how to compute a company's return on total assets and what it is used for.

7-19 Explain how to compute a company's return on owner's equity and how it relates to the return on total assets.

7-20 What is meant by a company's "operating capability," and why is information about it important?

7-21 Explain how to compute a company's inventory turnover. Is a high inventory turnover good or bad? Why?

7-22 Explain how to compute a company's accounts receivable turnover. What is a "good" accounts receivable turnover? Why?

Applying Your Knowledge

7-23 In each of the following situations, the total increase or decrease for one component of the accounting equation is missing:
(a) Assets increased by $9,400; liabilities increased by $3,200.
(b) Liabilities decreased by $2,000; owner's equity increased by $10,000.
(c) Assets decreased by $6,200; owner's equity decreased by $12,500.
(d) Owner's equity increased by $27,500; liabilities decreased by $5,715.
(e) Assets increased by $12,600; owner's equity decreased by $25,750.

Required: Using Assets: $60,000 = Liabilities: $20,000 + Owner's Equity: $40,000 as the beginning accounting equation, for each of the preceding situations determine (1) the total increase or decrease for the missing component of the equation, and (2) the amount of each component in the *ending* accounting equation. Treat each situation independently.

7-24 The total increase or decrease for one component of the accounting equation is missing in each situation that follows:
(a) Assets decreased by $12,000; liabilities decreased by $6,500.
(b) Owner's equity decreased by $15,750; assets decreased by $7,500.
(c) Liabilities increased by $1,000; owner's equity decreased by $5,000.
(d) Owner's equity increased by $20,000; assets increased by $9,650.

Required: Using Assets: $45,000 = Liabilities: $15,000 + Owner's Equity: $30,000 as the beginning accounting equation, for each of the preceding situations determine (1) the total increase or decrease for the missing component of the equation, and (2) the amount of each component in the *ending* accounting equation. Treat each situation separately.

7-25   Listed below are the balances of selected accounts of the Watson Company at the end of the current year:

Equipment	$18,500
Prepaid insurance	3,600
Notes payable (due in 30 days)	7,100
Cash	2,900
Land	11,700
Accounts receivable (net)	8,200
Inventory	24,400
Mortgage payable (due next year)	33,000
Notes receivable (due in 60 days)	4,000
Marketable securities (short-term)	6,300
Buildings (net)	74,000
Notes receivable (due in 2 years)	5,600

Required: Prepare the current assets section of the Watson Company's balance sheet.

7-26   Listed below are the balances of selected accounts of the Chriswat Company at the end of the current year:

Notes receivable (due in 3 years)	$14,200
Accounts payable	18,300
Bonds payable (due in 5 years)	46,000
Land	13,500
Marketable securities (short-term)	6,400
Salaries payable	5,700
Notes payable (due in 6 months)	8,000
Mortgage payable (due next year)	3,600
Unearned rent revenue (6 months)	2,400
Notes payable (due in 2 years)	10,000
Mortgage payable (due in 5 years)	18,000

Required: Prepare the current liabilities section of the Chriswat Company at the end of the current year.

7-27   A classified balance sheet contains the following sections:
A. Current assets   D. Current liabilities
B. Long-term investments   E. Noncurrent liabilities
C. Property and equipment   F. Owner's equity

Required: The following is a list of accounts. Using the letters A through F, indicate in which section each account is shown.

_____ 1. Land
_____ 2. Accounts payable
_____ 3. A. Smith, capital
_____ 4. Cash
_____ 5. Bonds payable
_____ 6. Equipment
_____ 7. Accounts receivable
_____ 8. Unearned revenue
_____ 9. Mortgage payable (due in 4 years)
_____ 10. Salaries payable
_____ 11. Marketable securities (short-term)
_____ 12. Notes receivable (due in 2 years)
_____ 13. Buildings
_____ 14. Notes payable (due in 9 months)
_____ 15. Prepaid insurance
_____ 16. Inventory

7-28   The following is an alphabetical list of the accounts of Swenson Stores on December 31, 2000:

Accounts payable	General expenses
Accounts receivable	Interest expense
Administrative expenses	Interest payable (current)
Bonds payable (due 2010)	Interest receivable (current)
Buildings (net)	Interest revenue
Cash	Inventory
Cost of goods sold	Investment in government bonds (due 2011)
Equipment (net)	Land
Mortgage payable (10 equal annual payments)	Prepaid insurance

Notes payable (due in 6 months)	Salaries payable
Notes payable (due in 4 years)	Sales
Notes receivable (due in 8 months)	Selling expenses
Notes receivable (due in 3 years)	T. Swenson, capital
Office supplies	Temporary investments in securities

Required: Prepare a December 31, 2000 classified balance sheet (without amounts) for Swenson Stores.

7-29 The financial statement information of the Leon Appraisal Company for 2000 and 2001 is as follows:

	2000	2001
Assets, 12/31	(a)	$308,900
Expenses	$ 47,400	51,600
Net income	(b)	39,700
Liabilities, 12/31	153,500	(e)
Leon, capital, 1/1	(c)	117,200
Revenues	82,600	(f)
Leon, withdrawals	24,000	(g)
Leon, capital, 12/31	(d)	126,900

Required: Fill in the blanks lettered (a) through (g). All the information is listed. (*Hint:* It is not necessary to calculate your answers in alphabetical order.)

7-30 The financial statement information of the Charles Adjusting Company for 2000 and 2001 is as follows:

	2000	2001
Charles, capital, 12/31	$ 83,500	(d)
Charles, withdrawals	(a)	$ 24,000
Revenues	(b)	65,000
Charles, capital, 1/1	69,400	(e)
Liabilities, 12/31	(c)	116,800
Net income	24,100	(f)
Charles, additional investments	8,000	(g)
Expenses	35,200	39,800
Assets, 12/31	184,500	211,500

Required: Fill in the blanks lettered (a) through (g). All the information is listed. (*Hint:* It is not necessary to calculate your answers in alphabetical order.)

7-31 The balance sheet information at the end of 2000 and 2001 for the Decatur Medical Equipment Company is as follows:

	2000	2001
Current assets	(a)	$ 25,000
Noncurrent liabilities	(b)	34,900
Long-term investments	$ 19,200	22,500
Davis, capital	81,900	(d)
Total liabilities	(c)	(e)
Current liabilities	14,500	12,300
Total assets	132,200	(f)
Property and equipment (net)	85,700	93,100

Required: Fill in the blanks labeled (a) through (f). All the necessary information is provided. (*Hint:* It is not necessary to calculate your answers in alphabetical order.)

7-32 The balance sheet information at the end of 2000 and 2001 for Columbia Electronics is as follows:

	2000	2001
Bevis, capital	$ 83,500	$ 88,700
Current liabilities	(a)	9,800
Property and equipment (net)	(b)	87,500
Current assets	18,500	(e)
Long-term liabilities	(c)	30,200
Total assets	(d)	(f)
Working capital	9,300	10,200
Long-term investments	23,700	(g)
Total liabilities	38,100	(h)

Required: Fill in the blanks labeled (a) through (h). All the necessary information is provided. (*Hint:* It is not necessary to calculate your answers in alphabetical order.)

7-33 The following items and their corresponding amounts appeared in the accounting records of the Office Equipment Specialists Company on December 31, 2000:

Accounts receivable	$ 3,900
Accounts payable	2,900
Building (net)	24,000
Cash	1,400
Delivery equipment (net)	10,000
Inventory	7,500
J. Jenlon, capital	34,700
Mortgage payable (due 9/1/2002)	29,000
Marketable securities	2,000
Notes payable (due 10/1/2001)	10,000
Office supplies	2,300
Land	6,000
Notes receivable (due 12/31/2002)	7,000
Office equipment (net)	6,400
Prepaid insurance	1,700
Notes payable (due 12/31/2004)	11,000
Interest payable (due 10/1/2001)	1,000
Unearned revenue	3,000
Investment in government bonds (due 12/31/2009)	20,000
Salaries payable	600

Required: (1) Prepare a classified balance sheet for the Office Equipment Specialists Company on December 31, 2000.

(2) The Office Equipment Specialists Company is applying for a short-term loan at a local bank. If you were the banker, would you grant the company a loan? Explain your decision using what you learned in this chapter about evaluating a company's liquidity.

7-34 The following accounts and account balances were listed in the accounting records of the Rigons Lighting Company on December 31, 2000:

Salaries payable	$ 1,100
Accounts receivable	11,300
Investment in government bonds (due 12/31/2004)	30,000
Accounts payable	7,700
Unearned revenue	1,000
Building (net)	37,000
Interest payable (due 9/1/2001)	200
Cash	6,100
Notes payable (due 12/31/2002)	15,000
Store equipment (net)	14,000
Prepaid insurance	900
Office equipment (net)	9,600
Inventory	13,200
Notes receivable (due 12/31/2003)	8,000
P. Rigons, capital	84,300
Land	4,000
Mortgage payable (due 7/1/2002)	22,500
Office and store supplies	2,700
Marketable securities	2,000
Notes payable (due 9/1/2001)	7,000

Required: (1) Prepare a classified balance sheet for the Rigons Lighting Company on December 31, 2000.

(2) The Rigons Lighting Company is applying for a $2,000 short-term loan at a local bank. If you were the banker, would you grant a loan to the company? Explain your decision using what you learned in this chapter about evaluating a company's liquidity.

7-35 Taylor Machines Company has the following condensed balance sheet on December 31, 2000:

Current assets ....$ 12,400		Current liabilities ....$ 5,800	
Noncurrent assets 91,200		Noncurrent liabilities 36,700	
		Total Liabilities................................$ 42,500	
		T. Taylor, capital................................ 61,100	
		Total Liabilities and	
Total Assets................................$103,600		Owner's Equity $103,600	

The company's quick assets are 60% of its current assets.

Required: Compute the company's working capital and its current, quick, and debt ratios at the end of 2000.

7-36 Simpson Company reported net income of $78,200 for 2001. Interest expense of $4,800 was deducted in the calculation of this net income. The following schedule shows other information about the company's capital structure:

	12/31/2000	12/31/2001
Total Assets	$670,000	$730,000
Total Owner's Equity	415,000	465,000

Required: (1) Compute the return on total assets for 2001.
(2) Compute the return on owner's equity for 2001.
(3) Compute the debt ratio at the end of 2001. How does this compare with the debt ratio at the end of 2000?

7-37 Parket Company began 2000 with accounts receivable of $32,000 and inventory of $40,000. During 2000, the company made total net sales of $500,000, of which 70% were credit sales. The company's cost of goods sold averaged 60% of total net sales during 2000. Parket was open for business each day of the year, and at the end of the year it had accounts receivable of $36,000 and inventory of $60,000.

Required: (1) Compute the inventory turnover and the number of days in the selling period for 2000.
(2) Compute the accounts receivable turnover and the number of days in the collection period for 2000.
(3) What is your estimate of the number of days in the company's operating cycle during 2000?

Making Evaluations

7-38 A friend of yours makes this statement: "Accumulated depreciation and depreciation expense are the same thing, since they both measure the portion of the cost of an asset that has been 'used up' to earn revenues."

Required: Do you agree or disagree with your friend's statement? Support your answer.

7-39 Many long-term loans are payable over a period of time. For example, when a company takes out a mortgage to finance a building, it pays off a fraction of that mortgage every month.

Required: What criteria would you use to decide whether to classify the mortgage as a current liability or a long-term liability, and how would you classify the mortgage?

7-40 In this chapter, we said that the quick ratio is a better measure of liquidity than is the current ratio because the quick ratio includes only those current assets that may be easily converted to cash.

Required: What is the quick ratio? Do you think this is the best-possible measure of liquidity? If so, defend your answer. If not, design a better measure and defend it.

7-41 On March 8, 2000, Peter Bailey started his own company by depositing $10,000 in the Bailey Company checking account at the local bank. On March 14, 2000, the Bailey Company checkbook was stolen. During that period of time, the Bailey Company had entered into several transactions, but unfortunately it had not set up an accounting system for recording the transactions. Bailey did save numerous source documents, however, which had been put into an old shoebox.

In the shoebox is a fire insurance policy dated March 13, 2000, on a building owned by the Bailey Company. Listed on the policy was an amount of $300 for one year of insurance. "Paid in Full" had been stamped on the policy by the insurance agent. Also included in the box was a deed for land and a building at 800 East Main. The deed was dated March 10, 2000, and showed an amount of $40,000 (of which $8,000 was for the land). The deed indicated that a down payment had been made by the Bailey Company and that a mortgage was signed by the company for the balance owed.

The shoebox also contained an invoice dated March 14, 2000, from the Ace Office Equipment Company for $600 of office equipment sold to the Bailey Company. The invoice indicates that the amount is to be paid at the end of the month. A $34,000 mortgage, dated March 10, 2000, and signed by the Bailey Company, for the purchase of land and a building is also included in the shoebox. Finally, a 30-day, $4,000 note receivable is in the shoebox. It is dated March 15, 2000, and is issued to the Bailey Company by the Ret Company for "one-half of the land located at 800 East Main."

The Bailey Company has asked for your help in preparing a classified balance sheet as of March 15, 2000. Peter Bailey indicates that company checks have been issued for all cash payments. Bailey has called its bank. The bank's records indicate that the Bailey Company's checking account balance is $9,500, consisting of a $10,000 deposit, a $200 canceled check made out to the Finley Office Supply Company, and a $300 canceled check made out to the Patz Insurance Agency.

You notice that the Bailey Company has numerous office supplies on hand. Peter Bailey states that a company check was issued on March 8, 2000, to purchase the supplies but that none of the supplies had been used.

Required: Based on the preceding information, prepare a classified balance sheet for the Bailey Company on March 15, 2000. Show supporting calculations.

7-42 The following items appear (in thousands) on the January 31, 1998 and February 1, 1997 financial statements of Dillard Department Stores Inc.:

www.dillards.com

	January 31, 1998	February 1, 1997
Accounts receivable	$1,158,682	$1,130,504
Inventory	1,784,765	1,556,958
Sales	6,631,752	6,227,585
Cost of goods sold	4,393,291	4,124,765

Suppose Dillard's wants to arrange with its supplier to pay for merchandise 90 days after the purchase.

Required: Based on the above information, would you, as a supplier, feel confident about Dillard's' ability to pay you in 90 days? Justify your answer. If you were making the decision to grant Dillard's credit, what other information would you like to know about Dillard Department Stores Inc.?

7-43 Bart Brock is thinking about starting his own company, BB's. At the beginning of October 2000, he plans to invest $15,000 into the business. During October the company will purchase land, a small building to house the business, some office equipment, and some supplies. Bart has found land and a building that would be suitable for the company. The purchase price of both the land and the building is $50,000. Bart estimates that the cost of the land is 15% of the total price and the building is 85% of the total price. Bart wants the company to "finance" this purchase through its bank. The bank would require BB's to make a 20% down payment and would also require the company to sign a mortgage for the balance. Bart has determined that there is too much land, however, so that if BB's purchased the land and building, it would sell one-quarter of the land to another company to use as a parking lot. The other company has agreed to buy the land at a price equal to the cost paid by BB's and to sign a note requiring payment of this cost at the end of two years. Bart has found some used office equipment that could be purchased by BB's for $2,500 on credit, to be paid in 60 days. He also expects that BB's will need $800 of office supplies, which the company would purchase with cash. Before the bank will lend BB's the money to buy the land and building, it has requested a "projected" balance sheet for the company, along with a "projected" current ratio and debt ratio as of October 31, 2000, based on the preceding plans. Bart Brock has asked for your help.

Required: (1) Using the preceding information, prepare a projected balance sheet, current ratio, and debt ratio for BB's as of October 31, 2000. Show supporting calculations.

(2) Basing your decision solely on this information, if you were the banker would you give BB's the loan? What other information would help you make your decision?

7-44 Today is January 1, 2001. Last night you were at a New Year's Eve party at which you ran into a long-lost friend, Art Washet, who is the owner of Washet Company. In a conversation, Art mentioned that his company would like to borrow $5,000 from you now and repay you $6,000 at the end of two years. You told him to stop by your house today with his financial records. He has just dropped off the following balance sheet, along with his accounting records:

Washet Company

Balance Sheet

For Year Ended December 31, 2000

Working capital.....................	$ 11,100	Noncurrent liabilities..................	$ 9,400
Other assets..........................	93,900	Owner's equity.............................	95,600
Total.......................................	$105,000	Total	$105,000

Your analysis of these items and the accounting records reveals the following information (the amounts in parentheses indicate deductions from each item):

(a) Working capital consists of the following:

Equipment (net)	$ 14,000
Land	10,000
Accounts due to suppliers	(28,000)
Inventory, including office supplies of $3,700	34,700
Salaries owed to employees...	(2,600)
Note owed to bank (due June 1, 2001)	(17,000)
	$ 11,100

(b) Other assets include the following:

Cash...	$ 6,000
Prepaid insurance...	1,900
Buildings (net)...	46,000
Long-term investment in government bonds................	30,000
A. Washet, withdrawals...	10,000
	$ 93,900

(c) Noncurrent liabilities consist of the following:

Mortgage payable (due March 1, 2005).........................	$ 33,000
Accounts due from customers...	(16,600)
Notes receivable (due December 31, 2003)................	(7,000)
	$ 9,400

(d) Owner's equity includes the following: *[handwritten: marketable sec.]*

A. Washet, capital...	$104,900
Securities held as a temporary investment...................	(11,000)
Interest payable (due with note on June 1, 2001)	1,700
	$ 95,600

Required: (1) Using your analysis, prepare a properly classified December 31, 2000 balance sheet (report form) for Washet Company.

(2) Compute the current ratio and the quick ratio for the company on December 31, 2000. Basing your decision solely on this information, would you loan $5,000 to the company?

7-45 Ray Young owns and operates a repair service called Ray's Rapid Repairs. It is the end of the year, and his bookkeeper has recently resigned to move to a warmer climate. Knowing only a little about accounting, Ray prepared the following financial statements, based on the ending balances in the company's accounts on December 31, 2000:

Ray's Rapid Repairs
Income Statement
For Year Ended December 31, 2000

Repair service revenues		$ 29,000
Operating expenses:		
Rent expense	$ 3,800	
Salaries expense	9,900	
Utilities expense	1,100	
R. Young, withdrawals	16,000	
Total operating expenses		(30,800)
Net Loss		$ (1,800)

Ray's Rapid Repairs
Balance Sheet
December 31, 2000

Assets		Liabilities and Owner's Equity	
Cash	$ 1,600	Accounts payable	$ 2,600
Repair supplies	2,300	Note payable (due 1/1/03)	10,000
Repair equipment	15,000	Total Liabilities	$12,600
		R. Young, capital^a	6,300
		Total Liabilities and	
Total Assets	$18,900	Owner's Equity	$18,900

^aBeginning capital − net loss

Ray is upset and says to you: "I don't know how I could have had a net loss in 2000. Maybe I did something wrong when I made out these financial statements. Could you help me? My business has been good in 2000. In these times of high prices, people have been getting their appliances and other items repaired by me instead of buying new ones. I used to have to rent my repair equipment, but business was so good that I purchased $15,000 of repair equipment at the beginning of the year. I know this equipment will last 10 years even though it won't be worth anything at the end of that time. I did have to sign a note for $10,000 of the purchase price, but the amount (plus $1,200 annual interest) will not be due until the beginning of 2003. I still have to rent my repair shop, but I paid $3,800 for two years of rent in advance at the beginning of 2000, so I am OK there. And besides, I just counted my repair supplies, and I have $1,000 of supplies left from 2000 which I can use in 2001."

He continues: "I'm not too worried about my cash balance. I know that customers owe me $700 for repair work I just completed in 2000. These are good customers and always pay, but I never tell my bookkeeper about this until I collect the cash. I am sure I will collect in 2001, and that will also make 2001 revenues look good. In fact, it will almost offset the $600 I just collected in advance (and recorded as a revenue) from a customer for repair work I said I would do in 2001. I still have to write a check to pay my bookkeeper for his last month's salary, but he was my only employee in 2000. In 2001 I am going to hire someone only on a part-time basis to keep my accounting records. You can have the job, if you can determine whether the net loss is correct and, if not, what it should be and what I am doing wrong."

Required: (1) Set up T-accounts (including the balances shown in the financial statements) for the following accounts: Repair Service Revenues, Rent Expense, Salaries Expense, Repair Supplies, Repair Equipment, and Note Payable.

(2) Using the T-accounts from (1) plus whatever other T-accounts you need, prepare any year-end adjustments you think are appropriate for 2000. Show any supporting calculations.

(3) Prepare a corrected 2000 income statement, statement of changes in owner's equity, and ending classified balance sheet (report form).

(4) Write a brief report to Ray Young, summarizing your suggestions for improving his accounting practices.

7-46 The following are a condensed 2000 income statement and a December 31, 2000 balance sheet for Murf Company:

Murf Company
Income Statement
For Year Ended December 31, 2000

Sales (net).................................	$152,200
Cost of goods sold	(91,300)
Gross profit.............................	$ 60,900
Operating expenses................	(47,300)
Interest expense......................	(2,800)
Net Income...............................	$ 10,800

Murf Company
Balance Sheet
December 31, 2000

Cash...	$ 3,000
Marketable securities (short-term).....................	2,100
Accounts receivable...	6,350
Inventory	9,650
Property and equipment (net)	97,900
Total Assets...	$119,000
Current liabilities..	$ 12,400
Note payable (due 12/31/05)...............................	35,000
Total Liabilities...	$ 47,400
S. Murf, capital...	71,600
Total Liabilities and Owner's Equity...................	$119,000

On January 1, 2000, the accounts receivable were $6,050, the inventory was $10,950, the total assets were $110,000, and the owner's capital was $62,600. The company makes 60% of its net sales on credit and operates on a 300-day business year. At the end of 1999, the following ratio results were computed, based on the company's financial statements for 1999:

(a)	Current	2.0
(b)	Quick	1.0
(c)	Debt	43.3%
(d)	Inventory Turnover	8.5 times (35.3 days)
(e)	Accounts Receivable Turnover	14 times (21.4 days)
(f)	Gross Profit Percentage	39.2%
(g)	Profit Margin	6.8%
(h)	Return on Total Assets	10.9%
(i)	Return on Owner's Equity	15.0%

The company has hired you to update its ratio results and compare its performance in 2000 with that in 1999.

Required: (1) Compute the preceding ratios for 2000.

(2) Write a short report that compares the company's performance in 2000 with that in 1999 regarding its liquidity, financial flexibility, operating capability, and profitability.

7-47 Yesterday, you received the letter shown on the following page for your advice column in the local paper:

Dear Dr. Decisive:

I always read your column and think you do a good job settling squabbles. Here's one for you. I took my accounting book home over the break, and one of my parents (let's just call him "Dad") started to look through it. Soon he encountered a statement he didn't agree with, and the squabble began. Here's the statement: "If a company has a higher return on owner's equity than its return on total assets, this shows users that the company has benefited from using debt to help finance its assets." Dad says that a company will always have a higher return on owner's equity than it will have on total assets because owner's equity is always going to be smaller than total assets. I say that Dad is not correct. I think that sometimes a company can have a return on owner's equity that is lower than its return on total assets. His logic doesn't take into account the fact that when a company has debt, it also has interest, and that interest expense affects the company's return on assets but not its return on owner's equity. But when I challenge Dad, we always end up arguing. And every time we talk, the same subject comes up. Please help, and please show us with numbers! I need some peace and quiet.

"Enough Already"

Required: Meet with your Dr. Decisive team and write a response to "Enough Already."

Proceeds from borrowings
Repayment of debt
Proceeds from NMG public offering
...of Common Stock
...from receivables securitiz...

CHAPTER 8

USING THE CASH FLOW STATEMENT FOR BUSINESS DECISIONS

"The use of money is all the advantage there is in having it."
—Benjamin Franklin

1 *Why is a company's cash flow statement important?*

2 *What are the types of transactions that may cause cash inflows and cash outflows for a company?*

3 *What do users need to know about a company's cash flow statement?*

4 *How are the cash flows from the operating activities of a company reported on its cash flow statement under the direct method?*

5 *How do users combine the changes in a company's current assets and current liabilities with its revenues and expenses for the accounting period to determine the company's operating cash flows?*

6 *Why do internal and external users study a company's cash flow statement in conjunction with its income statement and balance sheet?*

7 *What cash flow ratios are used to evaluate a company's performance?*

In Chapters 6 and 7 we studied two major financial statements: the income statement, which summarizes the results of a company's operating activities during an accounting period, and the balance sheet, which shows the financial position of a company on a specific date. Together, these statements provide managers, investors, and creditors with information about a company's operating performance and financial condition.

However, as we mentioned in Chapter 7, there are some limits to how well a company's income statement and balance sheet can measure and report its activities and financial position. In this chapter we discuss how a company uses a third financial statement, the cash flow statement, to summarize its cash activities during an accounting period. More specifically, we (1) discuss why the cash flow statement is important, (2) define the components of the cash flow statement, (3) describe how the cash flow statement is used in evaluating a company, and (4) analyze the relationships between the cash flow statement and the cash budget, the income statement, and the balance sheet.

There are many issues involving the cash flow statement. In this chapter we focus on the basics. We will discuss other, more advanced topics in later chapters.

Why the Cash Flow Statement Is Important

A cash flow statement shows the changes in a company's cash during an accounting period by listing the cash inflows and outflows from its operating, investing, and financing activities during the period. The cash flow statement primarily provides information about a company's ability to remain solvent (meet its obligations) and to grow. It summarizes the "flow" of *cash* activities during an accounting period and provides information that cannot be obtained by studying the company's income statement or balance sheet. So, analyzing the cash flow statement provides answers to the following questions: "How much cash was provided or used by the company's operating activities?" "How much cash did the company receive or spend in investing or financing activities?" Managers and others study a company's cash flows because the company cannot survive if it does not have enough cash to operate on a day-to-day basis and if it does not pay its debts when they are due.

 What do a company's balance sheet and income statement show about its management of cash? What else do you think an investor or creditor would want to know?

Understanding Cash Flow Transactions

To use a company's cash flow statement for evaluating its performance, you first must understand how the company's accounting system provides the cash flow information. Remember that a company's accounting system records all its transactions and is based on the *accrual* accounting concept.

A company's **cash flow statement** shows the inflows (receipts) and outflows (payments) of cash during an accounting period, explaining how its beginning cash balance changed to its ending cash balance because of transactions that resulted in increases and decreases in cash. A company's beginning cash balance is the amount of cash listed on its balance sheet at the end of the last accounting period (which is also the balance sheet for the beginning of the current period). A company's ending cash balance is the amount of cash listed on its balance sheet at the end of the current accounting period. "*Cash inflows*" is another way of saying "transactions that resulted in *increases* in cash." "*Cash outflows*" is another way of saying "transactions that resulted in *decreases* in cash." Without a cash flow statement, all that external users would know about a company's cash would be the beginning and ending cash balances.

Thus the balance sheet and the cash flow statement are related. The equation below shows this relationship and uses Sweet Temptations as an example:

What do you think this button means?

1 *Why is a company's cash flow statement important?*

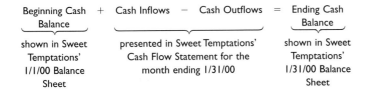

Beginning Cash + Cash Inflows − Cash Outflows = Ending Cash
Balance   Balance

shown in Sweet | presented in Sweet Temptations' | shown in Sweet
Temptations' | Cash Flow Statement for the | Temptations'
1/1/00 Balance | month ending 1/31/00 | 1/31/00 Balance
Sheet | | Sheet

Recall that in Chapters 5 and 6, you learned how a company uses its accounting system to record increases and decreases in cash (as well as in other assets, liabilities, and owner's equity). In Exhibit 8-1 we show that the basic information needed to create a cash flow statement is located in the Cash account. All increases in cash are listed on the left side of the T-account, and all decreases are listed on the right side. So, every cash transaction that occurred during an accounting period is shown in this T-account. An internal manager can look at this account and see all the transactions that caused inflows and outflows of cash. However, not all managers have the desire (or need) to look at detailed records. And the external user, of course, cannot look at the company's T-accounts. Therefore, both need the cash flow statement.

Cash Inflows and Outflows

To understand the cash flow statement, you need to know the kinds of transactions that cause a company's cash inflows and outflows. Inflows of cash occur, for example, when a company sells inventory for cash or issues a note payable for cash or when an owner invests cash in the company. So, we can say that a company's cash inflows are caused by certain decreases in assets (other than cash), increases in liabilities, and increases in owner's equity during an accounting period.

2 *What are the types of transactions that may cause cash inflows and cash outflows for a company?*

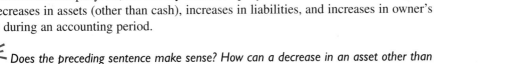

Does the preceding sentence make sense? How can a decrease in an asset other than cash cause a cash inflow?

Outflows of cash occur, for example, when a company purchases inventory for cash or pays a note payable or when the owner withdraws cash from the company. So, we can say that a company's cash outflows are caused by certain increases in assets (other than cash), decreases in liabilities, and decreases in owner's equity during the accounting period. We summarize these cash inflows and outflows in Exhibit 8-2. We show the categories in a Cash account to remind you that these activities are recorded in the accounting system.

Exhibit 8-1 Cash Account and Cash Flows

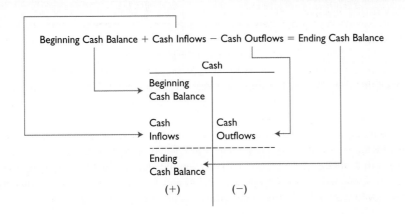

Exhibit 8-2   Balance Sheet Accounts and Cash Flows

	Cash	
Beginning Cash Balance		
Cash Inflows		*Cash Outflows*
1. Decreases in assets other than cash		1. Increases in assets other than cash
2. Increases in liabilities		2. Decreases in liabilities
3. Increases in owner's equity		3. Decreases in owner's equity
Ending Cash Balance		
(+)		(−)

In the following two sections we will discuss the types of transactions that may result in either a cash inflow or a cash outflow. To illustrate these transactions, we provide six examples for a hypothetical company. (We will discuss Sweet Temptations' cash transactions later in the chapter.) For these examples, we assume the company has a beginning cash balance of $2,000. By analyzing the changes in the cash balance, you can better understand how each transaction affects cash.

Inflows of Cash

There are three types of transactions that may cause a company's cash inflows. One type of transaction that may cause cash inflows involves *decreases in assets other than cash*. A decrease in an asset (other than cash) causes an inflow (increase) of cash when cash is received in exchange for the asset. This type of cash inflow occurs when a company collects an account receivable or sells property and equipment.

For example, assume that the company's account balances for Cash and Accounts Receivable are $2,000 and $800 respectively. If the company collects $200 from a customer for a previous credit sale, it enters this transaction into its accounting system, using the T-account approach as follows:

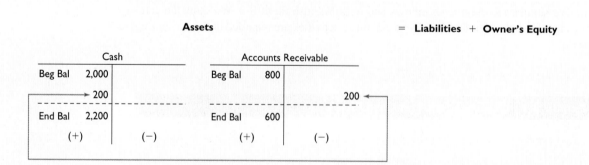

Notice that the $200 decrease in the asset Accounts Receivable resulted in a $200 increase in cash. Also, if a company sells property or equipment for cash, Property and Equipment decreases and Cash increases.

A second type of transaction that may cause cash inflows involves *increases in liabilities*. An increase in a liability causes an inflow (increase) of cash when a company receives cash in exchange for the liability. For example, assume that the company's account balances for Cash and Notes Payable are $2,200 and $1,500, respectively. If the company borrows $4,000 from a bank, this transaction results in the following:

Assets	=	Liabilities	+	Owner's Equity

Cash

Beg Bal	2,200
	→ 4,000
End Bal	6,200
(+)	(−)

Notes Payable

	Beg Bal	1,500
		4,000 ←
	End Bal	5,500
(−)		(+)

The cash balance increases from \$2,200 to \$6,200 as a result of the \$4,000 increase in a liability.

A third type of transaction that may cause cash inflows involves *increases in owner's equity*. Owner's equity increases mainly because of additional investments by owners and net income. An additional investment causes an inflow (increase) of cash because the owner has used cash from personal sources to increase his or her investment in the company. Net income is slightly more complicated because the cash inflows and outflows for operating activities are usually not equal to the revenues and expenses included in net income. This is because net income is based on the accrual concept, whereas here we are concerned with cash flows. We will discuss revenues, expenses, and net income, and their effects on cash flows later in the chapter, and again in Chapter 19.

In this example, assume the company's account balances for Cash and Owner's Capital are \$6,200 and \$50,000, respectively. If the owner invests an additional \$1,000 in the company, this transaction is entered into its accounting system as follows:

Assets	= Liabilities +	**Owner's Equity**

Cash

Beg Bal	6,200
	→ 1,000
End Bal	7,200
(+)	(−)

Owner, Capital

	Beg Bal	50,000
		1,000 ←
	End Bal	51,000
(−)		(+)

The cash balance increases from \$6,200 to \$7,200 as a result of the \$1,000 increase in owner's equity.

 Stop and think of additional examples of each type of transaction that causes cash inflows. How would these transactions affect the company's T-accounts?

Outflows of Cash

There also are three types of transactions that may cause a company's cash outflows. Instead of separately showing the T-accounts to explain each type, in this section we

Exhibit 8-3   Outflows of Cash

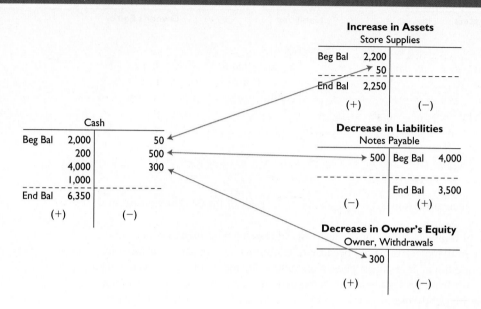

discuss the transactions. After our discussion, we show the results of these transactions in Exhibit 8-3.

One type of transaction that may cause cash outflows involves *increases in assets other than cash.* An increase in an asset (other than cash) causes an outflow (decrease) of cash when a company pays cash for the asset. When the company makes a $50 cash purchase of store supplies, this type of transaction occurs.

A second type of transaction that may cause cash outflows involves *decreases in liabilities.* A decrease in a liability causes an outflow (decrease) of cash when a company uses cash to pay the debt. When the company pays $500 to reduce its note payable, this type of transaction occurs.

A third type of transaction that may cause cash outflows involves *decreases in owner's equity.* For example, owner's equity decreases because of the owner's withdrawals. When the owner withdraws $300 from the company, this type of transaction occurs.

Exhibit 8-3 lists the T-accounts and shows how each type of transaction is recorded in the accounting system, reducing the cash balance.[1]

 Think of additional examples of each type of transaction that causes cash outflows. How would each of these transactions affect the company's T-accounts? If you're having trouble, don't move on. You need to understand this before you continue.

The Organization of the Cash Flow Statement

3 *What do users need to know about a company's cash flow statement?*

Now that you know where to find information about cash transactions, you also need to know the best way to present this information in a company's cash flow statement. This is a challenging task. Think about trying to develop a report that summarizes the cash you received and paid out during the last month or year!

[1]For illustrative purposes, we do not show the T-accounts under the accounting equation. Note that the $300 amount in the owner's withdrawals account will be closed to the owner's capital account at the end of the accounting period, as we discussed in Chapter 6.

How would you summarize your cash flows for last month? Imagine getting out your checkbook and summarizing all of the deposits and payments in a useful manner. Were any of the deposits related to student loans? Did you buy any durable goods (a television or a telephone)?

The cash flow statement shows a company's cash flows in three sections according to the *type* of activity that caused the increase or decrease in cash. The three sections are (1) cash flows from operating activities, (2) cash flows from investing activities, and (3) cash flows from financing activities. **Operating activities** include the primary activities of buying, selling, and delivering goods for sale, as well as providing services. They also include the activities that support the primary activities, such as administrative activities. **Investing activities** include lending money and collecting on the loans, investing in other companies, and buying and selling property and equipment. **Financing activities** include obtaining capital from the owner and providing the owner with a return on the investment, as well as obtaining capital from creditors and repaying the amounts borrowed. Exhibit 8-4 lists examples of the cash inflows and cash outflows from each type of activity.

For each type of cash activity, notice that the *net* cash flow provided by that type of activity is calculated by subtracting the cash outflows from the cash inflows. So, we can restate the link between the cash balances shown in a company's beginning and ending balance sheets and its cash flow statement as follows:

	Beginning Cash Balance (1/1/00)
+/−	Net Cash Flows From Operating Activities
+/−	Net Cash Flows From Investing Activities
+/−	Net Cash Flows From Financing Activities
=	Ending Cash Balance (1/31/00)

Exhibit 8-4 Examples of Cash Flows

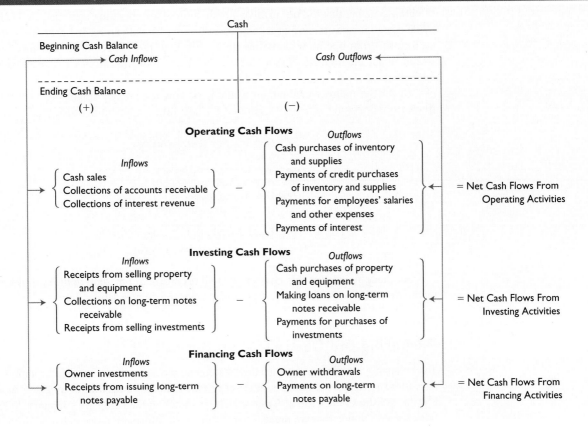

Net Cash Flows from Operating Activities

4 *How are the cash flows from the operating activities of a company reported on its cash flow statement under the direct method?*

There are two methods of calculating and reporting a company's net cash flows from operating activities. One method is called the direct method. The other is called the indirect method. A company using the **direct** method subtracts the operating cash outflows from the operating cash inflows to determine the net cash provided by (or used in) operating activities. Under the direct method, a company may report operating cash inflows in as many as three categories: (1) collections from customers, (2) collections of interest, and (3) other operating receipts. It may report operating cash outflows in as many as four categories: (1) payments to suppliers, (2) payments to employees, (3) payments of interest, and (4) other operating payments. Using this method, a company organizes the cash flows from operating activities section of its cash flow statement as follows:

Cash Flows From Operating Activities
Cash Inflows:
   Collections from customers
   Collections of interest
   Other operating receipts
     Cash inflows From operating activities
Cash Outflows:
   Payments to suppliers
   Payments to employees
   Payments of interest
   Other operating payments
     Cash outflows for operating activities
Net cash provided by operating activities

Under the **indirect** method, a company adjusts its net income to compute the net cash flow from operating activities. That is, it lists net income first and then makes adjustments (additions or subtractions) to net income. It makes these adjustments for two reasons: (1) to eliminate expenses, such as depreciation expense, that were included in the calculation of net income but that did not involve a cash outflow for operating activities, and (2) to include those changes in current assets (other than cash) and current liabilities that affected cash flows from operating activities differently than they affected net income. In other words, under the indirect method, income flows are converted from an *accrual* basis to a *cash* basis.

Under the indirect method, an example of how a company might organize the cash flows from operating activities section of its cash flow statement is as follows:

Cash Flows from Operating Activities
Net income
Adjustments for differences between net income
  and cash flows from operating activities:
   Add: Depreciation expense
     Increase in accounts payable
     Increase in salaries payable
   Less: Increase in accounts receivable
Net cash provided by operating activities

For the remainder of this chapter, we will use the *direct* method in the cash flow statement. We will discuss the indirect method further in Chapter 19.

Preparing the Cash Flow Statement

To explain how to prepare the cash flow statement, we now turn to Sweet Temptations' January 2000 activities. This is the same set of transactions we used in Chapters 5, 6, and 7. Exhibit 8-5 shows the Cash account, which kept track of the company's January 2000 cash transactions. Notice that we present two columns of information on each side of the Cash

Exhibit 8-5 Sweet Temptations' Cash T-Account

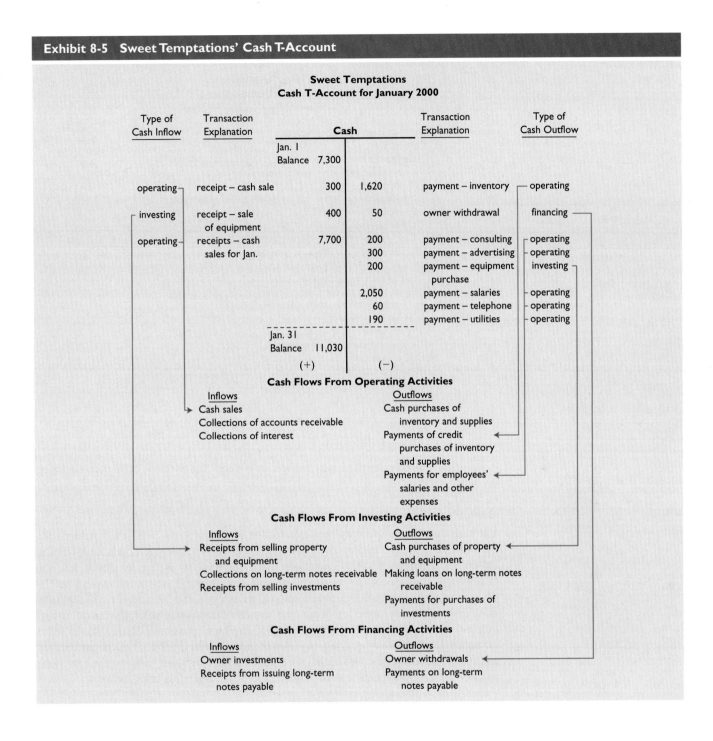

Sweet Temptations
Cash T-Account for January 2000

Type of Cash Inflow	Transaction Explanation	Cash		Transaction Explanation	Type of Cash Outflow
		Jan. 1 Balance 7,300			
operating	receipt – cash sale	300	1,620	payment – inventory	operating
investing	receipt – sale of equipment	400	50	owner withdrawal	financing
operating	receipts – cash sales for Jan.	7,700	200	payment – consulting	operating
			300	payment – advertising	operating
			200	payment – equipment purchase	investing
			2,050	payment – salaries	operating
			60	payment – telephone	operating
			190	payment – utilities	operating
		Jan. 31 Balance 11,030			
		(+)	(−)		

Cash Flows From Operating Activities

Inflows	Outflows
Cash sales	Cash purchases of inventory and supplies
Collections of accounts receivable	Payments of credit purchases of inventory and supplies
Collections of interest	Payments for employees' salaries and other expenses

Cash Flows From Investing Activities

Inflows	Outflows
Receipts from selling property and equipment	Cash purchases of property and equipment
Collections on long-term notes receivable	Making loans on long-term notes receivable
Receipts from selling investments	Payments for purchases of investments

Cash Flows From Financing Activities

Inflows	Outflows
Owner investments	Owner withdrawals
Receipts from issuing long-term notes payable	Payments on long-term notes payable

account. The inside columns provide a brief explanation of each transaction recorded in the account. We then use the explanations to classify the items according to the type of cash flow activity. The outer columns label each item as an operating, investing, or financing cash inflow or cash outflow. As Exhibit 8-5 shows, we determined each item's type of cash flow activity by comparing the item explanations with the more general descriptions of activities that we presented in Exhibit 8-4.

Exhibit 8-6 shows Sweet Temptations' cash flow statement for the month ending January 31, 2000. The statement shows a summary of the company's cash flows by category of activity. In the following two sections, we will use Sweet Temptations' Cash account to

Exhibit 8-6 Sweet Temptations' Cash Flow Statement

Sweet Temptations
Cash Flow Statement
For Month Ended January 31, 2000

Cash Flows From Operating Activities
    Cash Inflows:
        Collections from customers .... $ 8,000
        Cash inflows from operating activities .... $ 8,000
    Cash Outflows:
        Payments to suppliers .... $(1,620)
        Payments to employees .... (2,050)
        Other operating payments .... (750)
        Cash outflows for operating activities .... (4,420)
    Net cash provided by operating activities .... $ 3,580
Cash Flows From Investing Activities
        Sale of store equipment .... $ 400
        Purchase of store equipment .... (200)
    Net cash provided by investing activities 200
Cash Flows From Financing Activities
        Withdrawals by owner .... $ (50)
    Net cash used for financing activities .... (50)
Net Increase in Cash .... $ 3,730
Cash, January 1, 2000 7,300
Cash, January 31, 2000 .... $11,030

explain the information that each section of Sweet Temptations' cash flow statement provides.

Cash Flows From Operating Activities

The cash flows from operating activities section of a company's cash flow statement provides financial statement users with information about its ability to obtain cash from its day-to-day activities. Sweet Temptations' operating cash *inflow* for January is listed as "Collections from customers" and totals $8,000. In Exhibit 8-7 we show that the $8,000 is the sum of two items in the Cash account: (1) a cash sale of $300 and (2) a $7,700 summary cash sale that we used for all the other January cash sales. The $4,420 operating cash *outflows* consist of the following: (1) a $1,620 inventory purchase, (2) $2,050 for salary payments, (3) $200 for consulting, (4) $300 for advertising, (5) $60 for telephone charges, and (6) $190 for utilities. Notice that we combined the consulting, advertising, telephone, and utilities cash payments into an "other" category of operating cash outflows.

 Why do you think we combined the consulting, advertising, telephone, and utilities payments? In summarizing your personal cash flows, would you combine certain categories of items? Why or why not?

Sweet Temptations' net cash flows from operating activities totals $3,580. We arrive at this amount by subtracting the $4,420 total operating cash outflows from the $8,000 total operating cash inflows.

Cash Flows from Investing and Financing Activities

Exhibit 8-8 shows that Sweet Temptations' $200 net cash provided by investing activities during January 2000 consisted of two items. A $400 investing cash *inflow* resulted from the sale of store equipment. A $200 investing cash *outflow* resulted from a purchase of

Exhibit 8-7 Explanation of Cash Flow Statement (Operating Activities)

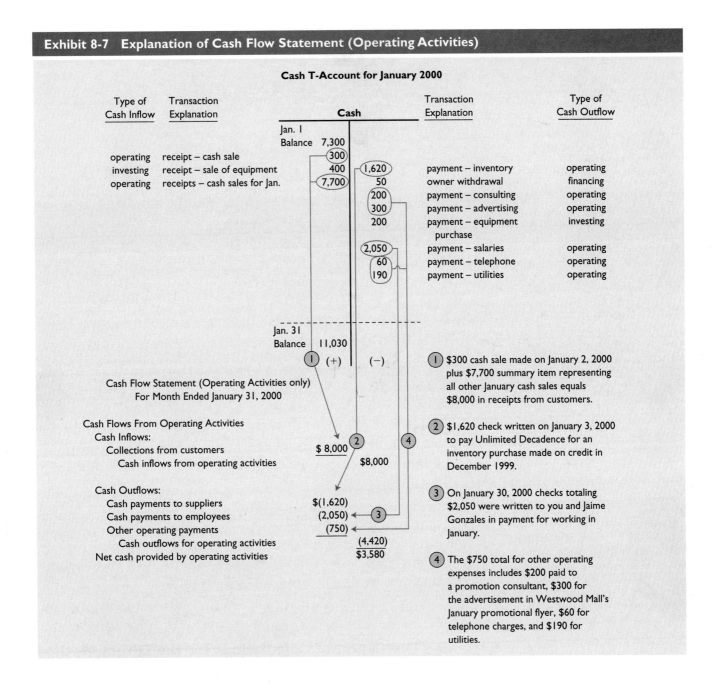

store equipment. Sweet Temptations' $50 net cash outflow for financing activities consisted of one item, Anna Cox's $50 withdrawal.

Reconciliation of Cash Balances

At the bottom of Exhibit 8-8, we also show the net increase in cash, and we "reconcile" the beginning cash balance to the ending cash balance. The $3,730 net increase in cash is determined by adding the $3,580 net cash provided by operating activities and the $200 net cash provided by investing activities, and subtracting the $50 net cash used for financing activities. We add this $3,730 increase in cash to the $7,300 January 1, 2000 cash balance to show the $11,030 January 31, 2000 cash balance. This $11,030 cash balance is the same amount we showed in Sweet Temptations' January 31, 2000 balance sheet in Exhibit 5-22 of Chapter 5.

Exhibit 8-8   Explanation of Cash Flow Statement (Investing and Financing Activities)

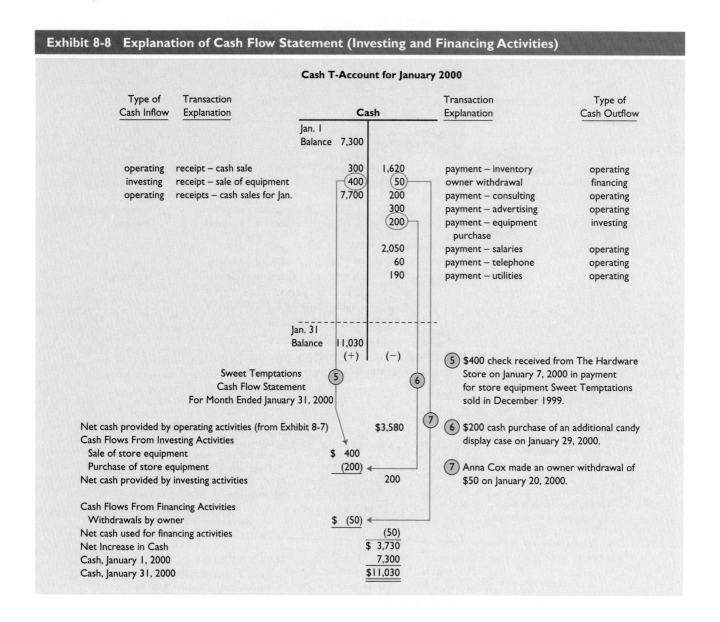

Cash T-Account for January 2000

Expanded Discussion of Calculations for the Direct Method

A company does not always prepare its cash flow statement each month. Many times the company will prepare its cash flow statement each quarter or each year. When a cash flow statement is not prepared for a long time, the company may have hundreds of entries in its Cash T-account. In this case, it is very time-consuming to analyze each entry to see whether it involved a cash inflow or outflow from an operating, investing, or financing activity. Furthermore, sometimes an external user (e.g., bank) evaluating a company's performance may have the company's income statement and balance sheet but not its cash flow statement. In these cases the company or external user may use a "shortcut" approach to preparing a cash flow statement. This approach involves analyzing the company's income statement amounts and the changes in its balance sheet amounts to determine the change in cash. In later chapters, we will study how to analyze the changes in balance sheet amounts to determine the cash inflows and cash outflows from investing and financing activities. In this chapter we focus on determining the cash inflows and cash outflows from operating activities.

To understand how to determine a company's operating cash flows, remember how a company operates. To begin its operations, a company buys inventory for cash or on credit (increasing accounts payable). When a company makes cash or credit sales during the current accounting period, it increases cash or accounts receivable and revenues, and increases cost of goods sold and reduces inventory. It increases other expenses and either decreases cash or increases liabilities (e.g., salaries payable) for the expenses. When the company collects its accounts receivable, it increases cash and decreases accounts receivable. When it pays its accounts payable, it decreases cash and decreases accounts payable. This collec-tion of accounts receivable and payment of accounts payable may occur weeks or even months later in the next accounting period. When the company records all of these transactions, it always keeps the accounting equation in balance and maintains the dual effect of transactions.

To determine its cash inflows and outflows from operating activities, a company can analyze its income statement accounts and the changes in its balance sheet accounts related to its day-to-day operations. The reason a company does this analysis relates to accrual accounting, that we discussed in Chapter 5. Under **accrual accounting,** a company records its revenue and related expense transactions in the same accounting period that it provides goods or services, regardless of whether it receives or pays cash in that period. Thus, the analysis for the operating cash flows involves "converting" accrual accounting information to operating cash flow information. From our earlier discussion, recall that a company must report several types of cash inflows and outflows from operating activities. To keep this discussion simple, we will focus on determining the collections from customers, the payments to employees, and the payments to suppliers. These are the major operating cash flows.

5 *How do users combine the changes in a company's current assets and current liabilities with its revenues and expenses for the accounting period to determine the company's operating cash flows?*

Collections from Customers

To determine a company's collections from customers during the accounting period, recall that it can make sales for cash or for credit. So its Sales Revenue account includes both cash and credit sales. Its Accounts Receivable account (an asset) includes increases due to the credit sales and decreases due to collections of accounts receivable. So, if the Accounts Receivable account balance *decreases* during the accounting period, this means that *more* cash was collected (from current and previous credit sales) than the amount of current credit sales that were made. Or, if the Accounts Receivable account balance *increases* during the accounting period, this means that *less* cash was collected than the amount of credit sales. By taking the balance in its Sales Revenue account and adding to it the decrease in Accounts Receivable (or subtracting the increase in Accounts Receivable), a company can determine its cash collections from customers during the accounting period.

The upper part of Exhibit 8-9 shows how to calculate a company's cash collected from customers. In this example, assume that a company made cash sales of $30,000 and credit sales of $40,000 during its *first* year of operations and collected $35,000 of the related accounts receivable. At the end of the year its Sales Revenue account shows a balance of $70,000, and its Accounts Receivable account shows an increase of $5,000 above its balance at the beginning of the year. The $65,000 cash collected from customers is determined by subtracting the $5,000 increase in Accounts Receivable from the $70,000 in Sales Revenue. (You can confirm the $65,000 cash collected by adding the cash sale of $30,000 to the accounts receivable collection of $35,000.)

Payments to Employees

To determine a company's payments to employees, recall that its Salaries Expense account includes the amount of salaries earned by employees during this period. This amount includes both salaries that were paid to employees and salaries that were recorded as owed to employees at the end of the period for work they did during the accounting period. The Salaries Payable account (a liability) includes increases due to salaries owed

Exhibit 8-9 Calculations for Major Operating Cash Flows

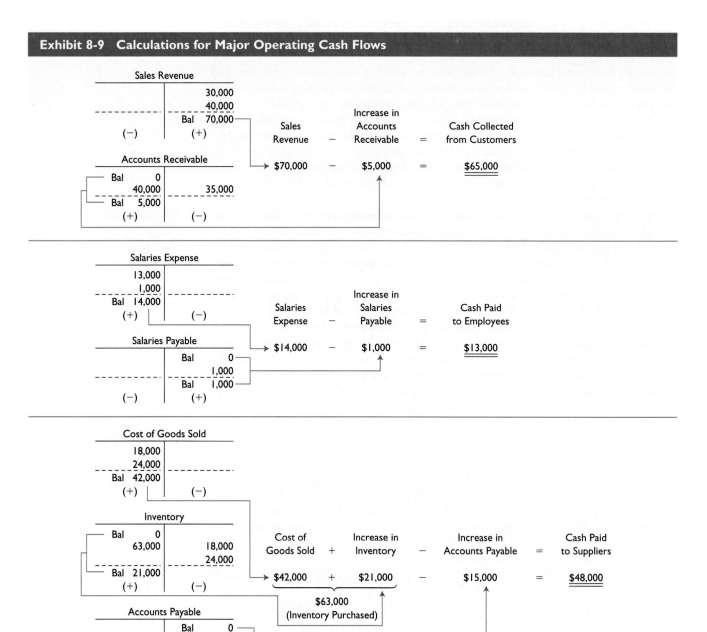

to employees at the end of the current accounting period and decreases due to payments of employees' salaries from the previous accounting period. So, if the Salaries Payable account balance *decreases* during the period, this means that *more* cash was paid this period for salaries than employees earned this period. Or, if the Salaries Payable account balance *increases* during the period, this means that *less* cash was paid this period for salaries than employees earned this period. By taking the balance in the Salaries Expense account and adding the decrease in Salaries Payable (or subtracting the increase in Salaries Payable), a company can determine the cash it paid to employees during the accounting period.

The middle part of Exhibit 8-9 shows how to calculate the cash payments to employees. In this example, assume that the company paid salaries of $13,000 and recorded salaries owed of $1,000 at the end of its first year of operations. At year-end, the Salaries Expense account shows a balance of $14,000, and its Salaries Payable account shows an increase of $1,000. The $13,000 cash paid to employees is determined by subtracting the $1,000 increase in Salaries Payable from the $14,000 in Salaries Expense.

 Using this analysis, how would you determine the amount of interest that was paid during the year?

Payments to Suppliers

The calculations of the cash collected from customers and paid to employees each involved one income statement account and one balance sheet account. The calculation of the cash paid to suppliers is slightly more complicated because it involves one income statement account and two balance sheet accounts. To determine a company's payments to suppliers, recall that its Cost of Goods Sold account includes the cost of inventory sold to customers during the accounting period. The Inventory account includes entries for both the purchase and the sale of inventory. So, if the Inventory account increases during the accounting period, this means that more inventory was purchased than sold. If it decreases, more inventory was sold than purchased. The inventory was purchased either by paying cash or using credit. The Accounts Payable account (a liability) includes increases due to credit purchases of inventory and decreases due to payments of accounts payable. So, if the Accounts Payable account balance *decreases* during the accounting period, this means that *more* cash was paid (for current and previous credit purchases) than the amount of credit purchases of inventory that were made during the current period. Or, if the Accounts Payable account balance *increases* during the period, this means that *less* cash was paid than the amount of credit purchases of inventory.

Because the cost of inventory (both cash and credit) "flows" into the Inventory account at the time of purchase and flows out at the time of sale (and into the Cost of Goods Sold account), two calculations must be made to determine the cash paid to suppliers for inventory. First, the total amount of inventory purchased must be determined. This is done by adding the increase in the Inventory account to (or subtracting the decrease from) the balance in the Cost of Goods Sold account. Then, the impact of the credit purchases must be eliminated. This is done by adding the decrease in Accounts Payable to (or subtracting the increase in Accounts Payable from) the total amount of inventory purchased. The end result is the cash paid to suppliers during the accounting period.

The lower part of Exhibit 8-9 shows how to calculate the cash paid to suppliers. In this example, assume that the cost of goods sold related to the cash sales and credit sales were $18,000 and $24,000, respectively, so that the Cost of Goods Sold account shows a balance of $42,000. The Inventory account shows an increase of $21,000 during the year. The Accounts Payable account shows an increase of $15,000. The $63,000 total amount of inventory purchased is determined by adding the $21,000 increase in Inventory to the $42,000 in Cost of Goods Sold. The $48,000 cash paid to suppliers is determined by subtracting the $15,000 increase in Accounts Payable from the $63,000 total amount of inventory purchased.

For the sake of discussion, we used a simple example that had only a few numbers in each balance sheet account. To some of you, it may appear that our analysis could have been shortened even more. In reality, balance sheet accounts may have many numbers in them, and for external users, only the balances (from the beginning and ending balance sheets) are known. So, the method we explained will work under complex or simple circumstances. We also explained how to calculate only three operating cash flows. The analysis used for calculating other operating cash flows is the same. We show a diagram of the calculations for all operating cash flows in Exhibit 8-10.

Exhibit 8-10   Calculations for All Operating Cash Flows

Income Statement Amounts	Adjustments	Cash Flows From Operating Activities	Net Operating Cash Flows
Sales revenue	+ Decrease in accounts receivable or − Increase in accounts receivable	= Collections from customers	
Interest revenue and dividend revenue	+ Decrease in interest receivable or − Increase in interest receivable	= Interest and dividends collected	Cash Inflows From Operating Activities
Other revenues	+ Increase in unearned revenues[a] or − Decrease in unearned revenues[a]	= Other operating receipts	
Cost of goods sold	+ Increase in inventory or − Decrease in inventory + Decrease in accounts payable or − Increase in accounts payable	= Payments to suppliers	
Salaries expense	+ Decrease in salaries payable or − Increase in salaries payable	= Payments to employees	Cash Outflows For Operating Activities
Interest expense	+ Decrease in interest payable or − Increase in interest payable	= Payments of interest	
Other expenses	+ Increase in prepaid expenses or − Decrease in prepaid expenses − Depreciation[b]	= Other operating payments	

[a]Unless related to normal sales; then the adjustment is made to sales revenue
[b]Unless listed as separate item on income statement

Analysis of the Cash Flow Statement

Financial statement users think that cash flows are a critical part of a company's ability to remain solvent. A comment from a bank executive sums up why evaluating a company's cash flows is important: "A bank lends cash to its customers, collects interest from them, and requires the customers to repay the loan in cash. It's all about cash."[2]

By reviewing a company's cash flow statement, external users can see how a company obtained and used its cash. Because a company summarizes its cash flows by operating, investing, and financing activities, users can compare the amounts in each section of the statement to see if important changes have occurred. External users can evaluate the company's need for additional cash to pay for its existing operations or for the expansion of its operations. They can also evaluate the ability of the company to make interest payments and to pay off debt when it comes due. A comparison with the cash flows of other companies also can show, for instance, that the company is obtaining a greater proportion of its cash from investing activities than are similar companies. This situation may indicate a problem with the company's net cash flows from operating activities. One possible explanation is that the company is selling a relatively large portion of its assets to get the cash

---

[2]R. A. (Bob) Hammerschmidt Jr., Chairman, Central Missouri Region, *Commerce Bank*, October 31, 1997.

it needs for operations. If it does not replace the assets, the company may hamper its ability to obtain cash from operations in the future. For example, suppose you owned a lawn-mowing business, and because your company was short on cash, you sold several of the company's lawn mowers for cash. Would the company be able to mow as many lawns after the sale as it could before the sale?

Managers are able to use the information in the cash flow statement in much the same way as do external users. They can determine whether the net cash flow from operating activities is large enough to finance existing operations, whether excess cash from operating activities may be sufficient to finance expansion projects, or whether additional cash must be obtained from external parties.

In addition, both managers and external users use the cash flow statement in conjunction with the balance sheet and the income statement to help evaluate a company. All three financial statements help users analyze three important company characteristics: (1) liquidity and solvency, (2) ability to make property and equipment purchases, and (3) cash flow returns (which we discuss later).

Financial statement users assess a company's *liquidity* and *solvency* to see whether a company is generating enough cash to pay its debts. Recall from Chapter 7 that liquidity refers to how quickly a company can convert its assets to cash to pay its short-term debts as they come due. In that chapter, we showed you how decision-makers use the current assets and current liabilities sections of the balance sheet to calculate the current ratio and the acid-test ratio. Solvency refers to a company's ability to pay its long-term debts as they come due. The debt ratio is calculated from balance sheet information to help assess solvency.

These balance sheet ratios are important in assessing a company's liquidity and solvency. However, they focus on the relationship between a company's assets and liabilities without regard for a company's ability to generate the cash needed to pay its debts. By showing a company's sources and uses of cash, the cash flow statement provides additional information about a company's management of cash.

In addition to paying its debts, a company must have enough property and equipment to continue earning a satisfactory profit. For example, Sweet Temptations may need to have cash available to buy additional equipment. If, for instance, an Unlimited Decadence frozen candy bar becomes quite popular, Sweet Temptations must be able to purchase refrigerated display cases. Assessing a company's ability to make these types of purchases helps decision-makers determine how well a company can continue to perform.

6 *Why do internal and external users study a company's cash flow statement in conjunction with its income statement and balance sheet?*

What are this student's operating cash flows from his lawn mowing activities?

It is unlikely that a company can continue to be successful unless it can obtain most of its cash from its operating activities. Thus, financial statement users want to know whether or not the cash the company received from selling goods or services is more than the cash it paid to provide the goods or services. External users can compare the company's net cash flow from operating activities for a given year with that year's income from operations to assess how well its operating activities provide cash.

A company's ability to generate enough cash to remain in business and earn a satisfactory profit can also be studied by computing its **cash flow returns.** By "cash flow returns," we mean the company's cash flows divided by the dollar amount of its assets or owner's equity. This is similar to the return on total assets or the return on owner's equity calculations we discussed in Chapter 7. We will discuss each of these evaluations in the following sections.

Relationship between the Cash Flow Statement and the Cash Budget

Remember from Chapter 4 that a cash budget gives a description of the company's planned cash activities. Also recall that one purpose of a budget is to provide a benchmark for the evaluation of a company's performance. One way managers evaluate their company's operating performance for an accounting period is by comparing the information from the operating activities section of the company's cash flow statement with the projected operating cash flows in its cash budget.

Listed below is a comparison of the January 2000 cash budget information for Sweet Temptations (from Exhibit 4-10 of Chapter 4) and the actual cash flow from operations information for January.

Item	Budget	Actual	Effect of Difference on Cash Balance
Cash receipts from sales	$7,080	$8,000	+$920
Cash paid to suppliers	(1,620)	(1,620)	0
Cash paid to employees	(2,050)	(2,050)	0
Cash paid for other operating items	(755)	(750)	+ 5
Net cash provided by operations	$2,655	$3,580	+$925

As you can see, Sweet Temptations did an excellent job of following its January operating cash budget. Cash receipts from sales were $920 greater than budgeted, and cash paid for other operating items was $5 less than budgeted. Hence, Sweet Temptations ended January with $925 more cash than it expected. Because Sweet Temptations is so small, it was able to anticipate its operating cash outflows (payments) almost exactly. More difficult to anticipate, however, is the amount of operating cash inflow for January. The cash flow information for sales reinforces our conclusion that Sweet Temptations had a successful first month of operations.

 How do you think this comparison will affect the cash budget for the next period? Why?

In the remainder of this chapter, we will discuss some additional, more specific ways that managers and external decision-makers use the cash flow statement to evaluate a company's performance.

Relationship between the Cash Flow Statement and the Income Statement

The income statement and the cash flow statement are related because both report on a company's activities during an accounting period. The difference between the two is that the income statement reports on activities using accrual accounting whereas the cash flow statement reports only on cash activities. Because of the differences in the way these statements measure income and cash flows and because of the type of information that results from these differences, managers, investors, and creditors are interested in both measures of operating performance.

Operating Cash Flow Margin

In Chapter 6, we explained that a company's profit margin (net income ÷ net sales) is an important measure of profitability. Information from the cash flow statement is used to calculate an additional profitability (and liquidity) measure. The operating cash flow margin is calculated as follows:

7 *What cash flow ratios are used to evaluate a company's performance?*

$$\text{Operating Cash Flow Margin} = \frac{\text{Net Cash Flow Provided by Operating Activities}}{\text{Net Sales}}$$

This ratio describes how much net cash the company generated from each dollar of net sales. It is similar to a profit margin measure, but in this case the higher the ratio, the better the company is at generating cash from operating activities and the greater is its liquidity.

For example, Exhibit 8-6 shows that in January, Sweet Temptations' net cash provided by operating activities was $3,580. Its net sales for January were $8,100 (see Exhibit 5-21). Therefore, its operating cash flow margin was 0.44 ($3,580 ÷ $8,100). This means that Sweet Temptations generated $0.44 net cash for each dollar of its net sales.

 What do you think causes the difference between the amount of Sweet Temptations' net sales and the net amount of cash it generated from its net sales?

Operating Cash Flow Margins of Actual Companies

To illustrate ratio analysis, we continue our evaluation of JCPenney Company Inc. and Sears Roebuck and Co., discussed in Chapters 6 and 7. The companies' operating cash flow margins for 1997[3] were as follows:

www.jcpenney.com
www.sears.com

	JCPenney	Sears
Operating Cash Flow Margin	4.1%	(1.5)%

Notice that JCPenney was more efficient than Sears at generating cash from sales, indicating that JCPenney had more liquidity in 1997.

 In Chapter 6, Sears' profit margin was higher than that of JCPenney. Why do you think there was an opposite difference between the two companies' operating cash flow margins?

Relationship between the Cash Flow Statement and the Balance Sheet

The balance sheet is related to the cash flow statement in much the same way as it is related to the income statement. Recall from Chapter 7 that a company's balance sheet shows the "stock" of its resources at a specific date and that the company's income statement shows the "flow" of its operating activities for an accounting period. Further, remember that a company's income statement and balance sheet are used together to assess how well the company performed given its level of resources. Because net cash flow from operating activities provides an alternative measure ("flow") of company performance, it also can be used with balance sheet information to assess how well a company performed given its resources.

---

[3]Sears had a negative operating cash flow margin because it had a *negative* cash flow from operating activities in 1997.

Cash Return Ratios

Two ratios used to assess a company's cash flow performance in relation to its resources are (1) the cash return on total assets, and (2) the cash return on owner's equity. These ratios are calculated as follows:

$$\text{Cash Return on Total Assets} = \frac{\substack{\text{Net Cash Flow Provided by} \\ \text{Operating Activities}} + \substack{\text{Interest} \\ \text{Paid}}}{\text{Average Total Assets}}$$

$$\text{Cash Return on Owner's Equity} = \frac{\substack{\text{Net Cash Flow Provided by} \\ \text{Operating Activities}}}{\text{Average Owner's Equity}}$$

A company's cash return on total assets measures how well the company is using its resources to generate net cash from operating activities. Interest payments are added back in the numerator because they are returns to the creditors who loan the company money to purchase some of the assets, and are not operating cash outflows. Exhibit 8-6 shows that in January, Sweet Temptations' net cash provided by operating activities was $3,580. Its average total assets for January were $19,450. ([$17,820 total assets on January 1 + $21,080 total assets on January 31] divided by 2—see Exhibit 5-22.) Therefore, its cash return on total assets was 18.4 percent ($3,580 ÷ $19,450). Notice that we did not add back interest payments in the numerator because Sweet Temptations made no interest payments in January. A cash return on total assets of 18.4 percent means that every dollar Sweet Temptations had invested in assets in January generated net cash from Sweet Temptations' operating activities of 18.4 cents.

A company's cash return on owner's equity measures how much net cash from operating activities the company generated with each dollar of owner's capital. Sweet Temptations' average owner's equity during January was $15,276. ([$15,000 owner's equity on January 1 + $15,552 owner's equity on January 31] divided by 2—see Exhibit 5-22.) Its cash return on owner's equity was 23.4 percent ($3,580 net cash flow from operating activities ÷ $15,276). This means that each dollar of Anna Cox's capital generated net cash from operating activities of 23.4 cents.

The two cash return ratios are used much the same as are the return on total assets and return on owner's equity ratios discussed in Chapter 7. These cash return ratios help managers and external users assess whether or not the company is generating enough cash from its operating activities.

Cash Return Ratios of Actual Companies

The ratios used to evaluate the cash returns of JCPenney and Sears for 1997 were as follows:

	JCPenney	Sears
Cash Return on Total Assets	7.8%	2.3%
Cash Return on Owners' Equity	18.3%	(10.3)%

These ratios indicate that JCPenney generated more cash for each dollar of assets and much more cash for each dollar of owners' equity than did Sears (which had a *negative* cash return on owner's equity). The differences seen in these cash flow ratio comparisons are not consistent with the return on total assets and return on owner's equity ratios we discussed in Chapter 7.

 Explain why you think the cash return ratios for JCPenney and Sears are not consistent with their ratios that we discussed in Chapter 7. What additional information do you need to evaluate this inconsistency?

We have only scratched the surface regarding how managers, investors, and creditors use accounting information to make business decisions. In Chapter 9 we will discuss specific uses of accounting information for cash management, inventory control, and debt management, just to name a few topics.

Business Issues and Values

As the end of an accounting period approaches, an entrepreneur may notice that unless something changes, the company's net cash flows for the period will not be as high as planned. In an effort to remedy this less-than-happy realization, the owner may postpone payments to the company's suppliers and employees. The effect is to reduce the cash payments from operations for the period and, therefore, to increase the company's net cash flows from operating activities. The company's operating cash flow margin, cash return on total assets, and cash return on owner's equity will all be higher than they would have been if the company had not postponed payments to suppliers and employees. But although this action may make the company "look better" in the short run, it has some negative effects. External users of the company's cash flow statement might think that the company is more liquid (and healthier) than it really is, perhaps leading them to make ill-informed decisions about the company. A more immediate effect is the reduced cash flows of the suppliers and employees. In deciding whether to take actions such as this, managers and owners must look "beyond the numbers" and consider all the "stakeholders" in the decision. In other words, managers must consider who will be affected by the different decision alternatives (in this case the company, the external users, the employees, and the suppliers, at a minimum) and how the alternatives will affect these people.

Summary

At the beginning of the chapter we asked you several questions. During the chapter, we asked you to STOP and answer some additional questions to build your knowledge about specific issues. Be sure you answered these additional questions. Below are the questions from the beginning of the chapter, with a brief summary of the key points relating to the answers. Use your creative and critical thinking skills to expand on these key points to develop more complete answers to the questions and to determine what other questions you have that might lead you to learn more about the issues.

1 Why is a company's cash flow statement important?

A company's cash flow statement is important because it summarizes the changes in the company's cash by listing the cash inflows and cash outflows from its operating, investing, and financing activities during an accounting period. This information cannot be obtained from the company's income statement or balance sheet. The information is useful to decision-makers in evaluating the company's solvency and liquidity.

2 What are the types of transactions that may cause cash inflows and cash outflows for a company?

The types of transactions that may cause cash inflows for a company are decreases in its assets other than cash, increases in its liabilities, and increases in its owner's equity. The types of transactions that may cause cash outflows for a company are increases in its assets other than cash, decreases in its liabilities, and decreases in its owner's equity.

3 What do users need to know about a company's cash flow statement?

Users need to know that a company's cash flow statement shows its cash inflows and cash outflows according to the type of activity that caused the increase or decrease in cash. There are three sections: the cash flows from operating activities, the cash flows from investing activities, and the cash flows from financing activities. The net cash flows from each section are summed, and the total increase (decrease) in cash is added to (subtracted from) the beginning cash balance to determine the ending cash balance.

4 How are the cash flows from the operating activities of a company reported on its cash flow statement under the direct method?

Under the direct method, a company reports its cash flows from operating activities in two parts: operating cash inflows and operating cash outflows. A company may report as many as three categories of operating cash inflows (e.g., collections from customers) and as many as four categories of operating cash outflows (e.g., payments to suppliers).

5 How do users combine the changes in a company's current assets and current liabilities with its revenues and expenses for the accounting period to determine the company's operating cash flows?

The change in accounts receivable is combined with the sales revenue to determine the collections from customers. The change in salaries payable is combined with the salaries expense to determine the payments to employees. The change in inventory and the change in accounts payable are combined with the cost of goods sold to determine the payments to suppliers.

6 Why do internal and external users study a company's cash flow statement in conjunction with its income statement and balance sheet?

Internal and external users study a company's cash flow statement in conjunction with its income statement and balance sheet to evaluate the company's liquidity and solvency, its ability to purchase property and equipment, and its cash flow returns.

7 What cash flow ratios are used to evaluate a company's performance?

The operating cash flow margin (net cash flow from operating activities divided by net sales) is used to evaluate a company's profitability (and liquidity). The cash return on total assets ([net cash flow from operating activities + interest paid] divided by average total assets) and the cash return on owner's equity (net cash flow from operating activities divided by average owner's equity) are used to evaluate a company's performance in relation to its available resources.

Key Terms

accrual accounting *(p. 245)*	**financing activities** *(p. 239)*
cash flow returns *(p. 250)*	**indirect** *(p. 240)*
cash flow statement *(p. 234)*	**investing activities** *(p. 239)*
direct *(p. 240)*	**operating activities** *(p. 239)*

SUMMARY SURFING

Here is an opportunity to gather information on the Internet about real-world issues related to the topics in this chapter. Go to http://www.dryden.com/account and click on the Cunningham, Nikolai, and Bazley book cover. Click on Summary Surfing, then click on this chapter number, and answer the following questions.

▶ Click on **ABM.** What kinds of services does ABM provide its customers? Find ABM's statements of cash flows. How much cash did ABM receive from customers for the most current year? How much cash did ABM pay to suppliers and employees during the most current year? Find ABM's balance sheets. What is ABM's cash return on owners' (stockholders') equity for the most current year?

Answer the Following Questions in Your Own Words

Testing Your Knowledge

8-1 What is a cash flow statement, and what types of questions can a user answer by studying a company's cash flow statement?

8-2 Write out a cash flow equation that links the beginning and the ending cash balances.

8-3 What three types of transactions related to balance sheet items may cause cash inflows? Give an example of each.

8-4 What three types of transactions related to balance sheet items may cause cash outflows? Give an example of each.

8-5 Identify the three sections of a company's cash flow statement, and briefly explain what is included in each section.

8-6 How is the net cash provided by operating activities determined under the direct method?

8-7 What are the three categories of operating cash inflows under the direct method?

8-8 What are the four categories of operating cash outflows under the direct method?

8-9 Describe how to compute a company's collections from customers during an accounting period, based on an analysis of its income statement and its beginning and ending balance sheets.

8-10 Describe how to compute a company's payments to employees during an accounting period, based on an analysis of its income statement and its beginning and ending balance sheets.

8-11 Describe how to compute a company's payments to suppliers during an accounting period, based on an analysis of its income statement and its beginning and ending balance sheets.

8-12 How is the operating cash flow margin of a company computed, and what does it describe?

8-13 How is the cash return on total assets of a company computed, and what does it measure?

8-14 How is the cash return on owner's equity of a company computed, and what does it measure?

Applying Your Knowledge

8-15 The following are several transactions and activities of a company:
(a) Receipt from sale of building
(b) Withdrawal by owner
(c) Decrease in accounts receivable
(d) Payment for purchase of investment
(e) Receipt from issuance of long-term note payable
(f) Payment for purchase of inventory

Required: Indicate in which section of the company's cash flow statement each of the preceding items would appear. Also indicate whether each would be an inflow or an outflow.

8-16 The following are several transactions and activities of a company:
(a) Cash sales
(b) Decrease in accounts payable
(c) Payment for purchase of equipment
(d) Investment by owner
(e) Payment of long-term note payable
(f) Receipt from selling investment

Required: Indicate in which section of the company's cash flow statement each of the preceding items would appear. Also indicate whether each would be an inflow or an outflow.

8-17 The following is selected information taken from the Cash T-account of the Wilson Book Company for May:
- (a) Cash sales, $10,000
- (b) Payment of interest, $600
- (c) Payment for inventory, $1,000
- (d) Collection of accounts receivable, $3,000
- (e) Payments to employees, $5,000
- (f) Collection of interest, $500

Required: Prepare the cash flows from operating activities section of the Wilson Book Company's cash flow statement for May.

8-18 Rocky Shoe Company has the following information in its Cash T-account for August:
- (a) Paid employees, $4,500
- (b) Paid suppliers, $2,000
- (c) Made cash sales of $12,000
- (d) Collected $800 interest
- (e) Paid $500 interest
- (f) Collected $5,000 of accounts receivable

Required: Prepare the cash flows from operating activities section of Rocky Shoe Company's cash flow statement for August.

8-19 The following is a list of items to be included in the cash flow statement of the Brockman Lawn Sprinklers Company for the current year:
- (a) Payment for purchase of trenching equipment, $6,000
- (b) Payments to suppliers, $3,200
- (c) Receipt from sale of land, $1,000
- (d) Collections from customers, $15,800
- (e) Withdrawals by owner, $2,500
- (f) Receipt from issuance of note payable, $4,000
- (g) Payments to employees, $5,600
- (h) Beginning cash balance, $1,200

Required: (1) Prepare the company's cash flow statement.
   (2) If net sales were $69,000, compute the company's operating cash flow margin.

8-20 The items to be included in the Garcia Hardware Company's cash flow statement for the current year are as follows:
- (a) Investment by owner, $3,000
- (b) Payments to employees, $8,100
- (c) Receipt from sale of investments, $1,300
- (d) Ending cash balance, $7,300
- (e) Payments for inventory, $6,000
- (f) Cash collected from customers, $17,400
- (g) Withdrawals by owner, $1,800
- (h) Payment for purchase of warehouse, $9,200
- (i) Payment of interest, $500

Required: (1) Prepare the company's cash flow statement.
   (2) If the average owner's equity was $15,500, compute the company's cash return on owner's equity.

8-21 An analysis of the Toney Company's Cash T-account for September shows the following entries:
- (a) Beginning cash balance, $800
- (b) Collections from customers, $21,300
- (c) Payment for purchase of storage shed, $8,500
- (d) Investment by owner, $5,000
- (e) Payment to suppliers, $12,400
- (f) Collection of interest, $600
- (g) Receipt from sale of equipment, $2,100
- (h) Payments of employees' salaries, $4,500
- (i) Payment of interest on loan, $700
- (j) Ending cash balance, $3,700

Required: Prepare the company's cash flow statement for September.

8-22 The Leone Company's Cash T-account shows the following entries for June:
  (a) Beginning cash balance, $400
  (b) Receipt from issuance of note, $10,000
  (c) Payment of interest on loan, $900
  (d) Payment for purchase of sales fixtures, $1,800
  (e) Collections from customers, $33,400
  (f) Owner withdrawal, $4,000
  (g) Payment of employees' wages, $7,000
  (h) Payment for delivery van, $12,000
  (i) Payments to suppliers, $16,200
  (j) Ending cash balance, $1,900

  Required: Prepare the company's cash flow statement for June.

8-23 Among other items, the Kelly Company's income statement for the year shows sales revenue of $77,500, cost of goods sold of $46,300, and salaries expense of $21,200. An analysis of its beginning and ending balance sheets for the year shows an increase in accounts receivable of $2,900, a decrease in inventory of $7,100, a decrease in accounts payable of $5,600, and a decrease in salaries payable of $2,800.

  Required: Determine the company's collections from customers, payments to suppliers, and payments to employees for the year.

8-24 While reviewing the Taber Company's income statement for the year, you find that it had sales of $81,600, cost of goods sold of $50,000, and wages expense of $30,200. A review of its beginning and ending balance sheets shows a decrease in accounts receivable of $3,400, an increase in inventory of $4,500, an increase in wages payable of $3,300, and an increase in accounts payable of $7,800.

  Required: Determine the company's collections from customers, payments to suppliers, and payments to employees for the year.

8-25 Frey Company's 2000 cash flow statement, as developed by its bookkeeper, is as follows:

Frey Company
Cash Flow Statement
December 31, 2000

Cash Inflows:
    Receipt from sale of equipment.................................$ 1,500
    Collections from customers 50,800
    Receipt from issuance of note payable......................   5,800
        Total inflows $58,100
Cash Outflows:
    Payments to employees...$24,300
    Withdrawals by owner.. 5,000
    Payment to purchase land.. 8,000
    Payments to suppliers.. 19,600
        Total outflows... 56,900
Increase in Cash...$ 1,200
Cash, January 1, 2000..   4,400
Cash, December 31, 2000 ....$ 5,600

  You determine that the *amounts* of the items listed on the statement are correct but are incorrectly classified.

  Required: Prepare a correct 2000 cash flow statement for Frey Company.

8-26 The cash flow statement information of the Fairview Flowers Shop for 2000 is as follows:

Net cash provided by operating activities	$17,000
Cash, January 1, 2000	8,500
Receipt from sale of equipment	6,300
Owner withdrawals	25,000
Net cash used for investing activities	(a)
Cash paid to employees	9,200
Cash, December 31, 2000	(b)
Cash received from customers	44,300
Receipt from issuance of note payable	(c)

Net cash used for financing activities	5,000
Cash paid to suppliers	(d)
Payment to purchase building	23,000
Net decrease in cash	(e)

Required: Fill in the blanks lettered (a) through (e). All the necessary information is listed. (*Hint:* It is not necessary to calculate your answers in alphabetical order.)

8-27 The cash flow statement information of the Bray Tire Company for 2000 is as follows:

Net increase in cash	$ (a)
Cash received from customers	60,200
Receipt from sale of land	5,000
Cash, January 1, 2000	(b)
Net cash used for investing activities	7,800
Cash paid to suppliers	25,900
Net cash provided by operating activities	(c)
Cash, December 31, 2000	11,000
Payment to purchase equipment	(d)
Cash paid to employees	19,100
Net cash used for financing activities	(e)
Receipt from issuance of note payable	10,000
Owner withdrawals	16,000

Required: Fill in the blanks labeled (a) through (e). All the necessary information is listed. (*Hint:* It is not necessary to calculate your answers in alphabetical order.)

8-28 Welch Raskits Company has asked for your assistance in preparing its cash flow statement for 2000. Among other items, its 2000 income statement shows sales revenue of $65,500, cost of goods sold of $36,000, and salaries expense of $18,400. You analyze its 2000 beginning and ending balance sheets and find a beginning cash balance of $8,100, an increase in accounts receivable of $4,800, an increase in inventory of $2,200, an increase in accounts payable of $4,600, and a decrease in salaries payable of $2,100. Further investigation shows that the owner withdrew $12,000 and that the company sold land for $5,300, issued a note payable for $8,000, and purchased a van for $14,800.

Required: (1) Using your findings, prepare the company's 2000 cash flow statement.
(2) Compute the company's 2000 operating cash flow margin.

8-29 You have been hired by Seeser Flappits Company to prepare its cash flow statement. The company provides you with its 2000 income statement as follows:

Sales		$56,400
Cost of goods sold		(31,400)
Gross profit		$25,000
Salaries expense	$19,200	
Depreciation expense	2,800	
Other expenses (all cash)	1,000	
Total operating expenses		(23,000)
Net Income		$ 2,000

You determine that these numbers are correct. You review the company's 2000 beginning and ending balance sheets and find that the cash balance was $1,800 on January 1, 2000, and $4,700 on December 31, 2000. In addition, you find the following changes:

Accounts receivable	$4,100 decrease
Inventory	5,600 decrease
Accounts payable	2,500 decrease
Salaries payable	1,200 increase

Furthermore, you determine that during 2000, the company sold equipment for $4,800, purchased land for $13,000, and issued a note payable for $7,500, all for cash. The owner also withdrew $9,600. After all these changes, the company had average total assets of $74,000 for 2000.

Required: (1) Using your findings, prepare the company's 2000 cash flow statement.
(2) Compute the company's 2000 cash return on total assets.

8-30 In 2000, Franklin Fibers Company had net cash provided by operating activities of $8,600. A review of its 2000 financial statements shows that the company had net income of

$9,000, average total assets of $93,800, and average owner's equity of $50,000. Included in the net income were sales of $77,000 and interest expense (all cash) of $600.

Required: Using the preceding information, for 2000 compute the company's (1) operating cash flow margin, (2) cash return on total assets, and (3) cash return on owner's equity.

8-31 Nibbets Baskets Company had net cash provided by operating activities of $4,200 for 2000. The company's income statement showed sales (net) of $40,000, interest expense of $400, and net income of $4,000. Its 2000 beginning balance sheet listed total assets of $42,000 and owner's equity of $18,000, and its 2000 ending balance sheet listed total assets of $48,000 and owner's equity of $22,000. Interest payable decreased by $100 during the year.

Required: Using the preceding information, compute the company's (1) operating cash flow margin, (2) profit margin, (3) cash return on total assets, (4) return on total assets, (5) cash return on owner's equity, and (6) return on owner's equity.

Making Evaluations

8-32 Now that you have begun studying accounting, it seems as though *everyone* is coming to you for advice. Just yesterday, your mother's friend Juanita asked you to explain the following sentences that appear in the notes to recent financial statements of <u>Dillard Department Stores</u>: "[This year], the Company generated $299.1 million in cash from operating activities, as compared to $395.3 million [last year] and $314.5 million [the year before that]. The primary reason for the decrease [this year] was an increase in merchandise inventories." Since you didn't have time to explain it then (or to get your thoughts together), you asked Juanita if you could mail her an explanation.

www.dillards.com

Required: Write Juanita that note, being careful to use language that she can understand (since she has never had an accounting course).

8-33 The owner of Roadkill Recycling Company (a company that publishes "kitchen-tested" recipes) has come to your bank for a loan. He states: "In each of the last two years our cash has gone down. This year we need to increase our cash by $7,000 so that we have a $20,000 cash balance at year end. We have never borrowed any money on a long-term basis and are reluctant to do so. However, we definitely need to purchase some new, more advanced equipment to replace the old equipment we are selling this year. We also want to invest in the stock market. Given our expected net income and the money we will receive from our depreciation expense, I estimate we will have to borrow $12,000, based on the following schedule."

Schedule of Cash Flows for the Year 2001

Inflows of cash:	
Collections from customers	$ 33,000
Collections of interest	2,000
Other operating receipts	4,000
Receipt from sale of old equipment	8,000
Depreciation expense	6,000
Bank loan (estimated)	12,000
Total inflows	$ 65,000
Outflows of cash:	
Purchase of equipment	$(20,000)
Salaries	(28,000)
Other operating payments	(3,000)
Payments to suppliers	(7,000)
Total outflows	(58,000)
Increase in Cash	$ 7,000

The owner explains that the company will purchase $5,000 of office furniture from him. The payment of $5,000 from the company to him for the office equipment was not included in the schedule of cash flows because it would involve only a transaction between the company and him and would be of no interest to "outsiders." The owner also states that if his figures are "off a little bit," the most the company wants to borrow is $16,000. You determine that the amounts he has listed for each item are correct, except the bank loan.

Required: (1) Prepare a projected cash flow statement that shows the necessary bank loan for Roadkill Recycling Company to increase cash by $7,000.

(2) Explain to the president why his $12,000 estimate of the bank loan is incorrect.

(3) Suggest ways to reduce the necessary bank loan and still increase cash.

(4) Make a list of questions you would like the owner to answer before you decide whether or not to make a loan to Roadkill Recycling Company.

8-34 Your friend Basil Nutt has come to you for advice. He says: "I don't understand it. My company, Nutts and More, had a net income of $4,300 in 2000, so I expected the balance in the company's cash account to go up. But the cash went down from $8,000 to $600! The company is almost broke, and it didn't buy any equipment, and I didn't make any withdrawals. The company used its cash only for operating activities. Help me figure out what is going on."

You study the company's accounting records and find that it prepared an income statement and a balance sheet. The company's 2000 income statement is as follows:

Sales...		$72,300
Cost of goods sold...		(40,000)
Gross profit...		$32,300
Salaries expense	$18,000	
Depreciation expense......................................	4,100	
Other expenses (all cash)...............................	5,900	
Total operating expenses		(28,000)
Net Income		$ 4,300

You determine that the income statement is correct. You also find that during 2000, the company's accounts receivable increased by $6,300, its inventory increased by $7,500, its accounts payable decreased by $3,000, and its salaries payable increased by $1,000.

Required: Prepare for Basil Nutt a report that explains why his company's cash decreased during 2000.

8-35 The following are pairs of ratios related to the income statement, the cash flow statement, and the balance sheet:

(1) Profit Margin	*and*	Operating Cash Flow Margin
(2) Return on Total Assets	*and*	Cash Return on Total Assets
(3) Return on Owner's Equity	*and*	Cash Return on Owner's Equity

Required: For each of the preceding pairs of ratios, explain the similarities and the differences between the two ratios in the pair. In your discussion, be sure to include an explanation of the *interpretation* of each ratio.

8-36 Suppose, at a party last weekend, your friend LaQuinta mentioned to you, in confidence, that her company was in the middle of a big scandal. It seems that the company needed a loan in order to enter into a top-secret marketing effort. In preparing the financial statements necessary for securing the loan, the company's bookkeeper noticed that cash flows from operations had been declining over the past five years, although total cash flows had been increasing. Apparently afraid that the bank would turn down the company's request for a loan if it saw the company's decreasing trend in cash flows from operations, he decided to reclassify cash receipts from the sale of equipment as collections from customers.

Required: (1) What do you think the bookkeeper hoped to accomplish by making the reclassification?

(2) Who do you think might be affected by this decision, and how might they be affected?

(3) If you were the company's owner, how would you have reacted to the bookkeeper's "help"?

8-37 On January 1, 2000, Paula Randolph opened a boutique called P.R.'s Boutique. At that time she deposited $30,000 cash in the company's checking account. Paula then immediately wrote company checks to purchase $7,000 of inventory and $16,000 of store equipment, and to pay two years' rent in advance for store space. Paula estimated that the store equipment would last ten years and would then be worthless. During the year, the boutique appeared to operate successfully. Paula did not know anything about accounting, although she did keep an accurate company checkbook. The company checkbook showed the following summarized items on December 31, 2000:

Payment for store equipment	$16,000
Payment for two years' rent of store space	2,400
Payments for purchases of inventory*	23,000
Receipts from cash sales	38,000
Payments for operating expenses	12,000
Withdrawals of cash for personal use	11,000

*Including $7,000 beginning inventory

On December 31, 2000, Paula asks for your assistance. She says: "The ending cash balance in the company checkbook is $3,600. Since my initial investment was $30,000, the company seems to have had a net loss of $26,400. Something must be wrong. I am sure the company did better than that. Please find out what the company's earnings were for 2000, why the cash went down so much during 2000, and what its financial position is at the end of 2000. Also, for what the company sold in 2000, how does its profit percentage compare with its operating cash intake percentage?"

You agree to help Paula. She tells you that the company used a periodic inventory system during 2000, that she has just finished "taking inventory," and that the cost of the 2000 ending inventory is $9,000. She has kept copies of invoices made out to customers who purchased merchandise on credit. These uncollected invoices total $12,000. Paula also has a file of unpaid invoices from suppliers for purchases of inventory. These unpaid invoices add up to $8,000. Just as you begin your calculations, Paula says: "Oh yes, $10,000 of the payments for operating expenses were employees' salaries. I also owe my employees $700 of salaries that they have earned this week."

Required: (1) Prepare a 2000 income statement, a 2000 cash flow statement, and a December 31, 2000 balance sheet for P.R.'s Boutique. Include explanations for all amounts shown.

(2) Answer Paula's question about the comparison of the "profit percentage" with the "operating cash intake percentage."

8-38 Jay Ryan owns "Jay's Skate Board Shop," which he opened on April 1, 2000. At that time Jay invested $20,000 cash into the company. With this money, the shop immediately purchased store equipment for $8,000. Jay estimated that this equipment would last ten years and would have no value after that time. The shop also purchased $6,000 of inventory for cash and paid $1,800 for one year of store rent in advance. During the year, the shop was open for business six days a week. Over the nine-month period in 2000, Jay withdrew $1,000 per month for his personal expenses. He used a periodic inventory system, employed one part-time helper, and paid the shop's bills by company check. For most of the year the shop made only cash sales and paid for purchases before the goods were shipped from the shop's supplier. However, near the end of the year the shop began to sell items on credit to a few "responsible customers." Jay kept a small notebook of the amounts of these credit sales. They totaled $3,000 at the end of 2000, and none had been collected yet. Because the shop was such a good customer, its suppliers allowed the shop to purchase $4,000 of inventory on credit near the end of 2000. The shop had not yet paid for these purchases at the end of 2000. At the end of 2000, Jay wanted to know how well the shop was doing, so he prepared the following "income statement."

Income Statement for 2000

Cash receipts:		
Cash sales		$40,000
Cash payments:		
Salary to part-time help	$ 3,200	
Cash purchases of inventory	20,000	
Rent expense	1,800	
Utilities expense	1,300	
Withdrawals	9,000	(35,300)
Net Income		$ 4,700

Jay did not feel comfortable with this information and came to you, a small-business consultant, for help. He said: "The shop shows net income of $4,700, but there is $16,700 in the company's checking account, so cash went down by $3,300. I don't understand. I just 'took inventory,' and it amounts to $5,000 (including the credit purchases), but the shop owes $400 of salary to my employee. I want to know how much the shop earned in 2000, what were its cash flows in 2000, and where the shop stands financially at the end of 2000. I also am interested in the return ratios on my investment in the company over the last nine months. Finally, I need a recommendation about my accounting system. Please prepare a report for me that answers these questions."

Required: Prepare for Jay a report that includes an income statement and a cash flow statement for the nine months ended December 31, 2000, and a balance sheet on December 31, 2000 for his shop. Include explanations for all amounts shown, as well as a discussion that answers Jay's questions and that recommends an accounting system.

8-39 Ava Mendleson operates a small fabric shop. She has been earning a satisfactory profit but is short of cash. Following is an accurate but unclassified balance sheet of the store on December 31, 1999.

Mendleson's Fabric Shop
Balance Sheet
December 31, 1999

Cash	$ 2,500
Store equipment (net)	6,400
Inventory	9,500
Accounts receivable	3,000
Total Assets	$21,400
Accounts payable	$ 4,500
Ava Mendleson, capital	16,900
Total Liabilities and Owner's Equity	$21,400

On January 2, 2000, Ava went to her bank to get a loan for her company. The bank agreed to loan her $5,000 under the following conditions. First, the note payable would be a three-year note, so that the company would repay $5,000 plus $1,500 interest on December 31, 2002. Second, she must prepare a "forecasted" classified income statement for 2000 that shows that the company expects to earn a net income of at least $11,000 and that it will have "satisfactory" profit margin and return ratios. Third, she must prepare a "forecasted" cash flow statement for 2000 that shows that the company expects to have cash on hand at the end of 2000 of at least $10,000 (including the cash from the bank loan) and that it will have "satisfactory" operating cash flow ratios. Finally, she must prepare a "forecasted" classified balance sheet as of December 31, 2000 that shows a current ratio of at least 3.0 and a debt ratio of no more than 40%.

Ava has never prepared any forecasted financial statements. She understands, however, that they are prepared using the best estimates she can make, based on the store's previous operations and her future expectations. Ava has come to you for help, having gathered the following information:

(a) Sales for 2000 are expected to be $80,000. Of these, half will be cash sales, and half will be credit sales. There are no cash discounts. Of the credit sales, 10% will not be collected until 2001. The accounts receivable on December 31, 1999 will be collected in 2000.

(b) Purchases of inventory for 2000 are expected to be $50,000. All purchases are on credit; there are no cash discounts. Of the purchases, 12% will not be paid until 2002. The accounts payable on December 31, 1999 will be paid in 2000.

(c) Sales returns and purchases returns are expected to be insignificant.

(d) The company's gross profit percentage has been 40% of sales, and this rate is expected in 2000.

(e) The store rents space in a local mall. The rent is $200 per month; the rent for the whole year is due on January 6, 2000.

(f) The store equipment that originally cost $8,000 has a 10-year estimated life, after which it is expected to have no value.

(g) Ava pays her one salesperson a basic salary of $7,000 per year, plus 10% of gross sales. The total salary for 2000 will be paid in cash by the end of the year.

(h) Ava expects to withdraw $8,000 during 2000 to cover her personal living expenses.

(i) Other operating expenses are expected to be $1,600 in 2000; these will be paid in cash by the end of the year.

You determine that the information Ava has gathered is "reasonable" and includes her best estimates.

Required: (1) Prepare a forecasted classified income statement for 2000. Show supporting calculations.

(2) Prepare a forecasted cash flow statement for 2000. Show supporting calculations.

(3) Prepare a forecasted classified balance sheet as of December 31, 2000. Show supporting calculations.

(4) Compute the applicable ratios and briefly discuss whether the company has met the bank's conditions.

8-40 Yesterday, you received the following letter for your advice column in the local paper:

Dear Dr. Decisive:

My mom and I haven't had a major disagreement since I was 16, but now we can't see eye-to-eye (and it isn't even about my social life!). It all started from a comment that her friend made when visiting us the other day. The comment was something like this: "I don't know how to interpret the financial reports my accountant gave me the other day for my shop. I do know this—the shop had a huge profit last year, but it ended up with less cash this year than it did last year." Well, of course, that led to a discussion between my mom and her friend, but I just couldn't leave well enough alone. I thought they were "barking up the wrong tree," so I had to interject my two cents. Here's the issue: is it possible for a company to have a positive cash flow from operations in the same year that it has a net loss or to have a negative cash flow from operations in the same year that it has a net income? I think it isn't possible. Income and cash flows may be different, but they will both be either positive or negative. Mom disagrees. In fact, she disagrees so strongly that she says if you say I am right, she will raise the amount of the monthly check she sends me. In the meantime, I am . . .

"Knowledge Rich, But Cash Poor"

Required: Meet with your Dr. Decisive team and write a response to "Knowledge Rich, But Cash Poor."

CHAPTER 9

MANAGING AND REPORTING WORKING CAPITAL

> "*Most people have wrong-minded ideas about why companies fail. They think it's because of a lack of money. In most cases, it has very little to do with that.*"
>
> —Michael E. Gerber, author and business consultant

1 *What is working capital, and why is its management important?*

2 *How can managers control cash receipts in a small company?*

3 *How can managers control cash payments in a small company?*

4 *What is a bank reconciliation, and what are the causes of the difference between a company's cash balance in its accounting records and its cash balance on its bank statement?*

5 *How can managers control accounts receivable in a small company?*

6 *How can managers control inventory in a small company?*

7 *How can managers control accounts payable in a small company?*

According to Michael E. Gerber, accounting issues are the basis for three of the top-ten reasons why small companies fail. These three are (1) a lack of management systems, such as financial controls, (2) a lack of financial planning and review, and (3) an inadequate level of financial resources.[1] The third reason can be interpreted to mean "a lack of money." The first two reasons, however, focus on managing a company's financial resources.

Often, it is difficult for a new company to keep an adequate amount of financial resources. Because so many companies start with very little cash, a relatively new term, called "bootstrapping," describes how these companies operate under such tight financial constraints. The term is taken from an old phrase about being self-reliant: these companies are "pulling themselves up by their bootstraps." Some very successful companies, for example Dell Computer Corporation and Joe Boxer Company, started business with very limited resources. These companies were able to manage their resources effectively and grow into sizable businesses.

In this chapter, we build on the knowledge you gained in previous chapters. We take a closer look at how companies manage and report four important balance sheet items: cash, accounts receivable, inventory, and accounts payable. As you will learn, how a company manages these items affects its cash flows, financial performance, and financial reporting. More specifically, we define *working capital,* discuss its importance, examine its major components, and explain how managers and external users evaluate it. We believe that through proper short-term financial management, many small companies can increase their likelihood of success.

www.del.com
www.joeboxer.com

Working Capital

1 *What is working capital, and why is its management important?*

A company's **working capital** is the excess of its current assets over its current liabilities. That is, working capital is current assets minus current liabilities.

Why do you think this man is wearing a life vest?

"Gentlemen, I'm afraid I have some rather unfortunate news about our little company."

Frank Model ©1982 from The New Yorker Collection. All Rights Reserved.

[1]Interview with Michael E. Gerber by Maria Shao, *Des Moines Register,* February 14, 1994, 15-B.

Why do you think this amount is called "working" capital? Why do you think a company is concerned with its working capital?

Recall that the current asset section of a company's balance sheet includes assets that the company expects to convert into cash, sell, or use up within one year. The current liability section includes liabilities that it expects to pay within one year by using current assets. The term *working capital* represents the *net* resources that managers have to *work with* (manage) in the company's day-to-day operations. Exhibit 9-1 shows Sweet Temptations' balance sheets for December 31, 2001, and December 31, 2000. We have assumed that Sweet Temptations has operated for two years and has recorded all its transactions correctly. We highlight the current sections of the balance sheet and calculate Sweet Temptations' working capital at the bottom of Exhibit 9-1. Note that the amount of the current liabilities (accounts payable) is subtracted from the total amount for the current assets (cash, accounts receivable, and inventory) to calculate working capital. Changes in any of these four items affect Sweet Temptations' working capital. Decisions that managers make regarding any of these items are considered part of *working capital management*. Other terms for working capital management are *operating capital management* and *short-term financial management*.

 How much working capital do you need in your personal life? Why?

Exhibit 9-1   Sweet Temptations' Balance Sheets

Sweet Temptations
Comparative Balance Sheets
December 31, 2001 and 2000

Assets	December 31, 2001		December 31, 2000	
Current Assets				
Cash	$ 5,818		$ 5,014	
Accounts receivable (net)	7,340		8,808	
Inventory	1,570		1,300	
Total current assets		$14,728		$15,122
Property and Equipment				
Store equipment (net)	$13,500		$10,420	
Total property and equipment		13,500		10,420
Total Assets		$28,228		$25,542
Liabilities				
Current Liabilities				
Accounts payable	$ 7,540		$ 7,731	
Total current liabilities		$ 7,540		$ 7,731
Noncurrent Liabilities				
Notes payable	$ 5,000		$ 5,000	
Total noncurrent liabilities		5,000		5,000
Total Liabilities		$12,540		$12,731
Owner's Equity				
A. Cox, capital		$15,688		$12,811
Total Liabilities and Owner's Equity		$28,228		$25,542

Working Capital = Current Assets − Current Liabilities
12/31/2001 Working Capital = $14,728 − $7,540 = $7,188
12/31/2000 Working Capital = $15,122 − $7,731 = $7,391

Companies manage working capital because they want to keep an appropriate amount on hand. But what is an *appropriate* amount of working capital for a company? An appropriate amount is enough working capital to finance its day-to-day operating activities plus an extra amount in case something unexpected happens. For instance, the extra amount may enable the company to buy inventory when it is offered at a reduced price or to cover the lost cash when a customer doesn't pay its account. If a company has too little working capital, it risks not having enough liquidity. If it has too much, the company risks not putting its resources to their best use. In summary, companies manage working capital to keep an appropriate balance between (1) having enough working capital to operate and to handle unexpected needs for cash, inventory, or short-term credit and (2) having so much excess cash, inventory, or available credit that profitability is reduced.

Keeping the right amount of working capital requires careful planning and monitoring. For instance, the timing of inventory purchases usually does not coincide with the timing of sales. Thus, at any given time a company may find itself with either too little or too much inventory. Cash receipts usually do not coincide with the company's need to use its cash. So, a company may have excess cash sitting idly in its checking account, or it may need additional short-term financing.

The fact that customers have some control over when they make their payments affects a company's management of cash collections from its accounts receivables. The longer customers take to pay, the longer the company has to wait between the time when it purchased inventory and the time when it receives cash from the sale. The company can manage this aspect of working capital by setting policies that encourage early payment of accounts receivable.

On the other hand, the company must also manage the payments of its obligations. It should make these payments on time, as well as take advantage of purchases discounts available from its suppliers.

Managing working capital affects all aspects of a company's operating activities. Exhibit 9-2 shows a time line of Sweet Temptations' (ST) operating activities. The top half of the exhibit shows Sweet Temptations' transactions with its supplier, Unlimited Decadence (UD). These consist of Sweet Temptations purchasing boxes of chocolates (increasing inventory) on credit (increasing accounts payable), paying the invoices as they come due (decreasing cash and accounts payable), and monitoring inventory to determine when to restock (not shown).

 Why do you think Sweet Temptations waits until almost the invoice due date to process its cash payment to Unlimited Decadence?

The bottom half of Exhibit 9-2 shows Sweet Temptations' transactions with its customers. These consist of Sweet Temptations making candy sales (decreasing inventory) on credit (increasing accounts receivable) or for cash (not shown), and of credit customers mailing payments based on the credit terms of the sales (decreasing accounts receivable). When Sweet Temptations receives customers' payments, it deposits the checks in the bank (increasing cash). These deposits are then available to make cash payments.

Managers control each aspect of the operating cycle to ensure that operating activities are performed in accordance with company objectives. As you will see, they do this by establishing an internal control structure. An **internal control structure** is a set of policies and procedures that directs how employees should perform a company's activities.

The reporting by a company of the amount of each current asset and current liability on its balance sheet provides external users with information about the company's ability to keep an appropriate level and mix of working capital. In turn, this reporting helps managers and users evaluate the company's liquidity.

To put this another way, working capital is to a company what water is to a plant. If the plant does not have enough water, it will not grow. Eventually, it will wither and die. If the plant receives too much water, it will drown. Just as plants need the right amount of water in order to grow, companies need the right amount of working capital to achieve de-

Exhibit 9-2 Working Capital Flows

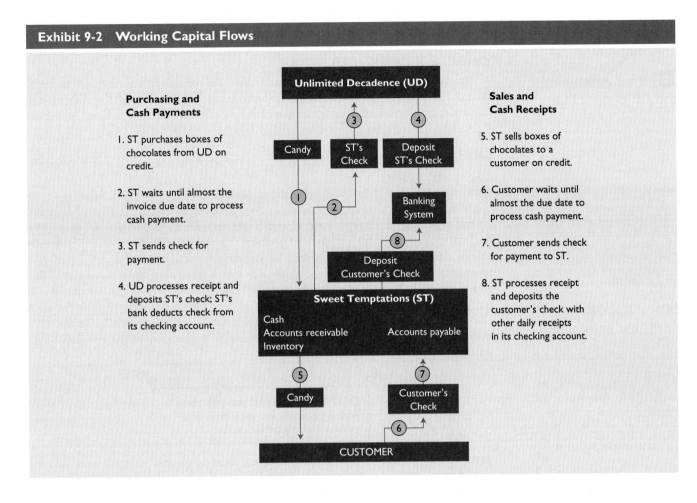

Purchasing and Cash Payments

1. ST purchases boxes of chocolates from UD on credit.

2. ST waits until almost the invoice due date to process cash payment.

3. ST sends check for payment.

4. UD processes receipt and deposits ST's check; ST's bank deducts check from its checking account.

Sales and Cash Receipts

5. ST sells boxes of chocolates to a customer on credit.

6. Customer waits until almost the due date to process cash payment.

7. Customer sends check for payment to ST.

8. ST processes receipt and deposits the customer's check with other daily receipts in its checking account.

sired levels of profitability and liquidity. In the following sections we will discuss how a company manages, controls, and reports its working capital items—cash, accounts receivable, inventory, and accounts payable.

Cash

A company's **cash** includes money on hand, deposits in checking and savings accounts, and checks and credit card invoices that it has received from customers but not yet deposited. A simple rule is that cash includes anything that a bank will accept as a deposit.

In addition to being an integral part of a business, cash is also the most likely asset for employees and others to steal or for the company to misplace. For example, cash received from customers in a retail store has no identification marks that have been recorded by the store. Therefore, when cash is "missing" it is very difficult to prove the cash was stolen or who stole it. Also, cash that is illegally transferred from a company bank account involves no physical possession of the cash by the thief, and if the thief can conceal or destroy the records, the theft of the money may not be traceable. Although internal control procedures are necessary for all phases of a company's business, they are usually most important for cash.

Simple Cash Controls

For any size company, the best way to prevent both intentional and unintentional losses is to hire competent and trustworthy personnel and to establish cash controls. Next, we discuss two categories of simple cash controls. These are internal controls over (1) cash receipts and (2) cash payments. These controls apply to all cash transactions except those dealing with a company's petty cash fund, which we will discuss later in the chapter.

Controls over Cash Receipts

 2 *How can managers control cash receipts in a small company?*

A company uses internal control procedures for cash receipts to ensure that it properly records the amounts of all cash receipts in the accounting system and to protect them from being lost or stolen. Cash receipts from a company's operating activities result from cash sales and from collections of accounts receivable mailed in by its customers.

How might an employee steal from his or her employer when working at a company's cash register?

For cash sales, a company should use three control procedures. The most important control procedure is the proper use of a cash register. Managers should make sure that a prenumbered sales receipt is completed for every sale and that the salespeople ring up each sale on the register. In most companies, the cash register produces the receipt as well as a tape containing a chronological list of all sales transactions rung up on the register. This step is important because it is the first place that sales get entered into the accounting system. The fact that customers expect to receive a copy of the receipt helps ensure that each sale is entered. As a customer, you may have been part of a company's cash controls without even knowing it. At many **Sbarro Pizza** franchises, for example, there is a sign near the cash register that reads,

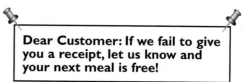

Dear Customer: If we fail to give you a receipt, let us know and your next meal is free!

This added control increases the likelihood that salespeople will enter all sales into the cash register, and it signals to company employees the importance of this activity.

 Could an employee at Sbarro's still take money from the company? How?

Second, when a check is accepted for payment, the salesperson should make sure that the customer has proper identification in order to minimize the likelihood that the check will "bounce." Even this procedure is not always adequate. For instance, in Vail, Colorado (and in other ski areas), retail and service companies must be especially careful in accepting checks at the end of the ski season because some customers close out their accounts when they leave.

Third, at the end of each salesperson's work shift, the employee should match the total of the amounts collected (cash plus checks and credit card sales) against the total of the cash register tape and report any difference between the two totals to a supervisor.

www.quiktrip.com

Some companies (e.g., QuikTrip) use a fourth control procedure for cash sales. These companies remove the "big bills" from cash registers even during one employee's shift. For example, if more than five 20-dollar bills are in the register, the employee inserts the excess bills through a slot into a locked safe that is kept behind the counter. Only the store manager knows the combination to the safe.

A company should use three control procedures to safeguard collections of cash from accounts receivable. First, either the owner-manager or an employee who does not handle accounting records should open the mail. This control procedure is called *separation of duties*. Separating the duties of handling accounting records and opening the mail prevents an employee from stealing undeposited checks *and* covering up the theft by making a fictitious entry in the accounting records. Second, immediately after opening the mail, the employee should list all of the checks received. Later, if a customer claims to have previously paid a bill, the company can review the list. You may be wondering what happens if the customer *did* pay the bill but the receipt is not listed because the employee stole the undeposited check. In this case, the customer's canceled check (from the customer's bank) may help the company discover that its employee stole the check. Third, while opening the mail, the employee should restrictively endorse each incoming check for deposit in the company's bank account. At Sweet Temptations, this is done by stamping "for deposit only—Sweet Temptations" on the back of each check. If a check is lost or stolen, the endorsement makes it more difficult to cash the check illegally.

 Why do you think an owner might be interested in not recording all cash receipts?

Finally, a company should adopt one additional procedure to help it safeguard the cash collected from both its cash sales and its accounts receivable. It should deposit all cash receipts intact daily. This means that at the end of the day, the company should take all of its cash (everything included in our definition of cash), fill out a deposit slip, and make a bank deposit. These daily bank deposits aid in two ways. First, keeping a substantial amount of cash at the company overnight is taking an unnecessary risk of theft. By depositing all cash receipts on a daily basis, the company does not leave cash unattended overnight. Second, the bank's deposit records show the company's cash receipts for each day. When the company receives its monthly bank statement, the company can check the daily bank deposits listed in the bank statement against its Cash account to determine that it deposited all its recorded cash receipts in the bank and that it properly recorded all bank deposits in its Cash account.

Controls over Cash Payments

 Why do you think an employee might want to deceive the company about its cash payments?

The basic rule for good internal control over cash payments is to have all payments made by check. A very small company that the owner operates may have little need for any additional internal control procedures. The owner purchases items, signs checks for payment, and pays employees by check. As the company grows, two more controls over cash payments can provide added security over cash. First, the company should pay only for approved purchases that are supported by proper documents. The proper documents generally include an approved copy of the company's purchase order providing evidence that the company actually ordered the items (which we will discuss in detail later in the chapter), a freight receipt showing evidence that the company received the items it ordered, and the supplier's invoice. This procedure reduces the chances that the company will pay either for items that it did not want to purchase or for items that it has not received. Second, immediately after writing the check for payment, the owner should stamp "PAID" on the supporting documents. Canceling the documents in this way prevents the company from paying for items more than once.

3 *How can managers control cash payments in a small company?*

 Why do you think an owner might be interested in not recording all cash payments?

Bank Reconciliation

Despite all of the procedures used to control the receipts and payments of cash, errors in a company's records can still occur. Since the bank also keeps a record of the company's cash balance, the company can use both sets of records to determine what its correct cash balance should be. However, the time when the company records its receipts and payments differs from the time when the bank records them. Therefore, a company uses a bank reconciliation to determine the accuracy of the balance in its Cash account. In this section, we discuss what a bank reconciliation is, why it is necessary, and how it is performed.

 Do you reconcile your bank statement every month? What risks do you take if you don't reconcile the statement?

A company's bank independently keeps track of the company's cash balance. Each month the bank sends the company a **bank statement** that summarizes the company's banking activities during the month. In most cases, the bank returns the company's deposit slips and canceled checks (or photos of these items) along with the bank statement. A company uses its bank statement and returned items, along with its cash records, to prepare a bank reconciliation.

When a company uses the internal control procedures of depositing daily receipts and paying only by check, the ending balance in its Cash T-account should be the same as the bank's ending cash balance for the company's checking account, except for a few items. (We will discuss the various causes of the difference between the two balances below.) A company prepares a **bank reconciliation** to analyze the difference between the ending cash balance in its accounting records and the ending cash balance reported by the bank in the bank statement. Through this process, the company learns what changes, if any, it needs to make in its Cash account balance. This enables the company to report the correct cash balance on its balance sheet.

4 *What is a bank reconciliation, and what are the causes of the difference between a company's cash balance in its accounting records and its cash balance on its bank statement?*

Exhibit 9-3 Causes of Difference in Cash Balances

1. *Deposits in Transit.* A **deposit in transit** is a cash receipt that the company has added to its Cash account but that the bank has not included in the cash balance reported on the bank statement. When a company receives a check, it records an increase to its Cash account. As illustrated in Exhibit 9-2, a short period of time may pass before the company deposits the check and the bank records it. At the end of each month the company may have deposits in transit (either cash or checks) that cause the deposits recorded in the company's Cash account to be greater than deposits reported on the bank statement.

2. *Outstanding Checks.* An **outstanding check** is a check that the company has written and deducted from its Cash account but that the bank has not deducted from the cash balance reported on the bank statement because the check has not yet "cleared" the bank. As illustrated in Exhibit 9-2, a period of time is necessary for the check to be received by the payee (the company to whom the check is written), deposited in the payee's bank, and forwarded to the company's bank for subtraction from the company's bank balance. Therefore, at the end of each month a company usually has some outstanding checks that cause the cash payments recorded in its Cash account to be more than the cancelled checks itemized on the bank statement.

3. *Deposits Made Directly by the Bank.* Many checking accounts earn interest on the balance in the account. For these accounts, the bank increases the company's cash balance in the bank's records by the amount of interest the company earned on its checking account; the bank lists this amount on the bank statement. This causes deposits listed on the bank statement to be greater than the deposits listed in the company's Cash account. The company is informed of the amount of interest when it receives the bank statement.

4. *Charges Made Directly by the Bank.* A bank frequently imposes a service charge for a depositor's checking account and deducts this charge directly from the bank account. Banks also charge for the cost of printing checks, according to an agreed price, and for the cost of stopping payment on checks. The company is informed of the amount of the charge when it receives the bank statement, which includes a document stating the amount of the deduction.

   When the company receives a customer's check, it adds the amount to its Cash account and deposits the check in its bank account for collection. The company's bank occasionally is unable to collect the amount of the customer's check. That is, the customer's check has "bounced." A customer's check that has "bounced" is called an **NSF (not sufficient funds) check.** Because the bank did not receive money for the customer's check, it lists the check as an NSF check on the bank statement. Although the bank usually informs the company immediately of each NSF check, there may be some NSF checks that are included in the bank statement and that the company has not recorded.

   At the end of the month, the bank lists any service charges and NSF checks as deductions on the bank statement—deductions not yet listed in the company's Cash account.

5. *Errors.* Despite the internal control procedures established by the bank and the company, errors may arise in either the bank's records or the company's records. The company may not discover these errors until it prepares the bank reconciliation. For example, a bank may include a deposit or a check in the wrong depositor's account or may make an error in recording an amount. Or, a company may record a check for an incorrect amount or may forget to record a check.

Exhibit 9-3 summarizes the causes of the difference between the ending cash balance listed on the bank statement and the ending cash balance listed in the company's records. The causes include (1) deposits in transit, (2) outstanding checks, (3) deposits made directly by the bank, (4) charges made directly by the bank, and (5) errors.

 Which of the five listed items are most important when you reconcile your bank account?

The Structure of a Bank Reconciliation

Exhibit 9-4 shows a common way to structure a bank reconciliation. Notice that the reconciliation has two sections: an upper section starting with the bank's record of the company's ending cash balance, and a lower section starting with the company's record of its cash balance. It is logical to set up these two sections because the purpose of the bank reconciliation is to determine the company's correct ending cash balance. By adjusting the cash balance in each section for the amounts that either are missing or are made in error, the company is able to determine its reconciled (correct) ending cash balance.

For example, in the upper section, a deposit in transit is added to the ending cash balance from the bank statement because this deposit represents a cash increase that the bank has not yet added to the company's checking account. In the lower section, a service charge made by the bank is subtracted from the ending balance in the company's Cash account because this charge represents a cash decrease that the company has not yet recorded.

The bank reconciliation is complete when the ending reconciled cash balances calculated in these two sections are the same. This ending reconciled cash balance is the correct cash balance that the company includes in its ending balance sheet. This form of bank reconciliation acts as another type of internal control over cash because it enables a company to identify errors in its cash-recording process and to know its correct cash balance at the end of each month.

Preparing a Bank Reconciliation

When you prepare a bank reconciliation, keep in mind that you are doing it to determine the correct ending cash balance to be shown on the company's balance sheet. The cash balance at the end of the month is correct if it includes *all* of the company's transactions and events that affected cash. As you work through the upper section of the reconciliation, ask yourself, "What cash transactions (e.g., checks written and deposits made) have taken place that the bank doesn't know about?" In the lower section ask yourself, "What is not included in calculating the company's ending cash balance but should be (e.g., bank service charges, interest earned)?" Keep these questions in mind as you work through the reconciliation until the reconciled balances are the same.

Exhibit 9-4 Structure of a Bank Reconciliation

Company Name
Bank Reconciliation
Date for Cash Balance Being Reconciled

	Ending Cash Balance from the Bank Statement	
+	Deposits in Transit	
−	Outstanding Checks	
+/−	Errors Made by the Bank	
=	Ending Reconciled Cash Balance	←
	Ending Cash Balance from Company Cash Account	Must be the Same
+	Deposits Made Directly by the Bank	the Same
−	Charges Made Directly by the Bank	
+/−	Errors Made by the Company	
=	Ending Reconciled Cash Balance	←

To prepare a bank reconciliation, you need two sets of items: (1) the bank statement for the month being reconciled, along with all of the items returned with the statement, and (2) the company's cash records. With these items, you can work through a reconciliation in a step-by-step manner. Exhibit 9-5 summarizes the eight steps to follow in preparing a bank reconciliation.

In the following section, we illustrate the reconciliation process by preparing Sweet Temptations' December 31, 2001 bank reconciliation.

Sweet Temptations' Bank Reconciliation

Exhibit 9-6 shows several documents: Sweet Temptations' Cash account for December, the December bank statement the company received from First National Bank, and the

Exhibit 9-5　Steps in Preparing a Bank Reconciliation

1. *Set up the proper form for the bank reconciliation.* Fill in the information you already know (e.g., ending unadjusted cash balances from the bank statement and the Cash account).

2. *Look for deposits in transit.* Compare the increases in cash listed in the company's Cash account with the deposits shown on the bank statement. Check to see if any increase in the company's Cash account is not listed as a deposit on the bank statement. For any deposit in transit, add the amount to the ending cash balance from the bank statement listed on the reconciliation.

3. *Look for outstanding checks.* Compare the decreases in cash listed on the company's Cash account with the checks shown on the bank statement. Identify any decrease that is shown in the company's Cash account during the month but that is not matched with a corresponding check deduction on the bank statement. Starting from the company's records, trace each decrease to its check listing on the bank statement. Subtract the amounts of the outstanding checks from the ending cash balance from the bank statement listed on the bank reconciliation.

4. *Identify any deposits that were made directly by the bank but that are not included as increases in the company's Cash account.* Look through the bank statement for bank deposits that the company has not recorded as increases in its Cash account. Usually, these deposits are for interest earned on the company's checking account balance. Add these deposits to the balance of the company's Cash account listed on the bank reconciliation.

5. *Identify any charges that were made directly by the bank but that are not included as decreases in cash on the company's records.* Look through the bank statement for bank charges that the company has not recorded as decreases in its Cash account. Usually, these charges result from bank services such as printing checks or handling the company's own NSF checks. Deduct these charges from the balance of the company's Cash account listed on the bank reconciliation.

6. *Determine the effect of any errors.* While completing steps 1 through 5, you may discover that the bank or the company (or both) made an error during the processing of the cash transactions. If you find a bank error, contact the bank to get the error corrected in the company's checking account, and correct the amount of the error in the upper section of the bank reconciliation. If the company made an error, correct the amount of the error in the lower section of the reconciliation.

7. *Complete the bank reconciliation.* After you have finished steps 1 through 6, complete the reconciliation. Include the date and amount for any deposit in transit, and list the check numbers for any outstanding checks. This improves documentation and makes the reconciliation easier for others to understand. Describe any bank charges or error corrections in sufficient detail so that these activities can be recorded properly in the company's accounting records. At this point, the reconciled (correct) cash balances in both sections of the reconciliation should be the same. If not, trace back through the process carefully to locate any mistakes (e.g., outstanding checks you failed to include, math errors, etc.).

8. *Adjust the balance of the company's Cash account to agree with the corrected cash balance.* The lower section of a completed reconciliation answers the question "What is not included in the company's ending cash balance but should be?" The last step in preparing a reconciliation is to record these items in the company's Cash account (and the other related accounts). This recording changes the company's cash balance from the amount listed at the top of the lower section of the bank reconciliation to the correct ending amount.

completed bank reconciliation. Exhibit 9-6 also summarizes Steps 1 through 7 from Exhibit 9-5 that Anna Cox followed to prepare the reconciliation. We use an arrow and a number to trace each step on the documents.

In step 8, Anna entered the reconciling items listed in the lower section of Sweet Temptations' bank reconciliation (interest earned, bank service charge, and correction of error) into the company's accounting records on December 31, 2001, as follows:

Assets	=	Liabilities	+	Owner's Equity

Cash		Accounts Payable		Interest Revenue	
12.25	15	27			12.25
	27				
(+)	(−)	(−)	(+)	(−)	(+)

Banking Expense	
15	
(+)	(−)

Exhibit 9-7 shows that after Anna recorded the reconciling items, Sweet Temptations' Cash account balance is the correct amount: $5,783. Anna will add this amount to the total amount in the petty cash fund (discussed later) and will show the combined total as "Cash" on Sweet Temptations' December 31, 2001 balance sheet.

Additional Controls over Cash

Two other steps in preparing a bank reconciliation help a company keep control over its cash. First, the company should make sure that any deposit in transit listed on the bank reconciliation for the *previous* month is listed as a deposit on the current bank statement. If it is not listed, the company should investigate to determine what happened to the deposit. It may be that the deposit was misplaced or even stolen. Second, the company should investigate any outstanding check from the *previous* month that is still outstanding for the current month. It may be that the check was misplaced or was lost in the mail. Sweet Temptations has neither of these situations. The $101 deposit recorded by the bank on December 1 was a deposit in transit at the end of November. And check #938 for $21 paid by the bank on December 1 was an outstanding check at the end of November.

Petty Cash Fund

Although paying for all items by check is excellent internal control, it can be inconvenient. So, to make it easier for employees to make small, but necessary, purchases, a company may set up a petty cash fund. A **petty cash fund** is a specified amount of money that is under the control of one employee and that is used for making small cash payments for the company. A company uses a petty cash fund because some payments can be made only with "currency" or because writing checks for small amounts (e.g., for postage) would be cumbersome. There is less control over these expenditures, but the amounts involved are so small that an employee probably will not be tempted to steal.

 What items do you always pay for with "currency"?

To start a petty cash fund, a company gives an employee an amount of money, say $50, to be kept at the company. Usually the employee keeps the money locked in his or her desk drawer. Each time a payment is made from the fund, the employee makes a record of the payment and keeps a written receipt. At any time, the total of the receipts plus the remaining cash should equal the amount (in this case, $50) that was originally given to the employee. When the fund gets low or on the date of its balance sheet, the company

Exhibit 9-6 Sweet Temptations' Bank Reconciliation

Cash

Beg Bal. 12/1/2001 $3,238.48

Date	Amount		Date	Ch#	Amount
Dec. 1	$142.25		Dec. 1	#939	$287.94
Dec. 3	155.21		Dec. 3	#940	34.51
Dec. 3	142.15		Dec. 3	#941	26.79
Dec. 4	154.45		Dec. 8	#942	136.00
Dec. 5	198.00		Dec. 8	#943	593.15
Dec. 6	98.66		Dec. 10	#944	385.00
Dec. 8	190.23		Dec. 10	#945	190.12
Dec. 10	163.65		Dec. 14	#946	489.57
Dec. 10	187.04		Dec. 24	#947	452.18
Dec. 11	156.55		Dec. 24	#948	347.00
Dec. 12	177.91		Dec. 28	#949	1,904.78
Dec. 13	217.87		Dec. 29	#950	121.00
Dec. 15	313.57				
Dec. 15	293.32				
Dec. 17	336.58				
Dec. 18	387.22				
Dec. 19	441.10				
Dec. 20	457.16				
Dec. 22	451.82				
Dec. 22	591.78				
Dec. 24	458.25				
Dec. 27	287.35				
Dec. 28	335.76				
Dec. 29	418.43				
Dec. 31	786.00				

End Bal. 12/31/2001
Before
Reconciliation $5,812.75

SWEET TEMPTATIONS
WESTWOOD MALL #117
SACHSE, TX 75665-0117

First National Bank
7th and Grand
Sachse, TX 75662-3443
Phone (214) 353-9800
Member FDIC

NO. 137-187-8
Beginning balance December 1, 2001 $ 3,158.48
Deposits and other additions:
Deposits:

Dec. 3	$101.00		
Dec. 3	142.25	Dec. 17	$313.57
Dec. 3	155.21	Dec. 17	293.32
Dec. 3	142.15	Dec. 17	336.58
Dec. 4	154.45	Dec. 19	387.22

Steps to Complete Bank Reconciliation

Step 1. Anna transferred the $5,465 cash balance from the bank statement and the $5,812.75 balance from Sweet Temptations' Cash account to the reconciliation. Next, she completed the upper section of the reconciliation.

Step 2. Anna compared the increases in the Cash account with the bank deposits and found that the December 31 increase of $786.00 was not listed on the bank statement. She entered $786.00 on the reconciliation as a deposit in transit.

Step 3. Anna compared the bank statement's listing of checks and Sweet Temptations' record of decreases in its Cash account and found that all but two of the decreases (check #948 for $347.00 and check #950 for $121.00) were deducted on the current month's bank statement. She subtracted these outstanding checks from the ending cash balance of the bank statement in the reconciliation. After completing the upper section of the bank reconciliation, Anna calculated the reconciled ending cash balance to be $5,783.00.

Step 4. Anna began completing the lower section of Sweet Temptation's reconciliation. Anna reviewed the deposits listed in the bank statement and found that Sweet Temptations had not recorded a $12.25 bank deposit for interest earned as an increase in its Cash account. She added the $12.25 deposit to the company's ending balance on the reconciliation.

Step 5. Anna reviewed the charges on the bank statement and found that Sweet Temptations had not recorded a $15.00 bank service charge (for printed checks) as a decrease in its Cash account. She subtracted the $15.00 charge from the company's ending cash balance on the reconciliation.

Step 6. When Anna compared the decreases in Sweet Temptations' Cash account with the bank statement in step three, she also found that Sweet Temptations had incorrectly recorded check #942 (in payment of an account payable) in its records for $136 instead of $163. Because the amount that Sweet Temptations should have recorded is $27.00 more than the amount that it did record ($163.00 − $136.00), Anna subtracted $27.00 from the company's ending cash balance on the reconciliation.

Step 7. After completing the lower section of the reconciliation, Anna calculated the reconciled ending cash balance to be $5,783.00. Anna also observed that the reconciled balances shown in the upper and lower sections of the bank reconciliation are the same. This indicates that she completed the bank reconciliation properly.

Exhibit 9-6—*continued*

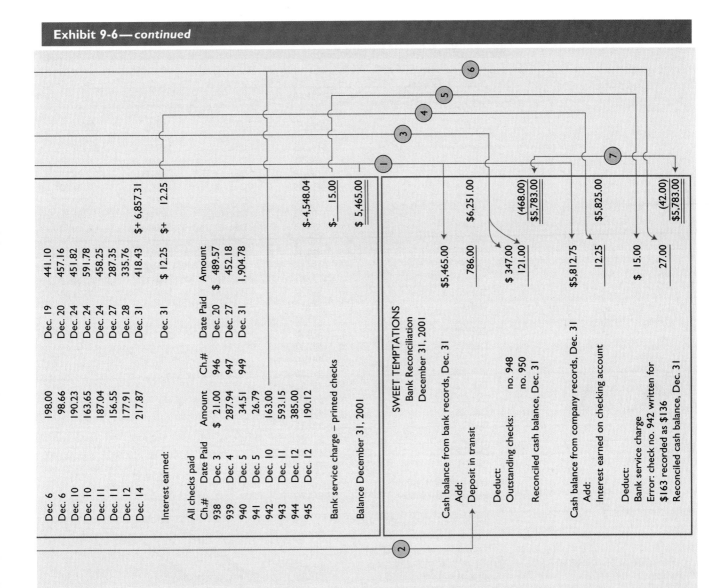

Dec. 6	198.00		Dec. 19	441.10
Dec. 6	98.66		Dec. 20	457.16
Dec. 10	190.23		Dec. 24	451.82
Dec. 10	163.65		Dec. 24	591.78
Dec. 11	187.04		Dec. 24	458.25
Dec. 11	156.55		Dec. 27	287.35
Dec. 12	177.91		Dec. 28	335.76
Dec. 14	217.87		Dec. 31	418.43	$+ 6,857.31

Interest earned: Dec. 31 $ 12.25 $+ 12.25

All checks paid

Ch.#	Date Paid	Amount		Ch.#	Date Paid	Amount
938	Dec. 3	$ 21.00		946	Dec. 20	$ 489.57
939	Dec. 4	287.94		947	Dec. 27	452.18
940	Dec. 5	34.51		949	Dec. 31	1,904.78
941	Dec. 5	26.79				
942	Dec. 10	163.00				
943	Dec. 11	593.15				
944	Dec. 12	385.00				
945	Dec. 12	190.12				

Bank service charge – printed checks   Dec. 31 $ 12.25 $- 4,548.04

$- 15.00

Balance December 31, 2001 $ 5,465.00

SWEET TEMPTATIONS
Bank Reconciliation
December 31, 2001

Cash balance from bank records, Dec. 31		$5,465.00
Add:		
Deposit in transit		786.00
		$6,251.00
Deduct:		
Outstanding checks: no. 948	$ 347.00	
no. 950	121.00	(468.00)
Reconciled cash balance, Dec. 31		$5,783.00
Cash balance from company records, Dec. 31		$5,812.75
Add:		
Interest earned on checking account		12.25
		$5,825.00
Deduct:		
Bank service charge	$ 15.00	
Error: check no. 942 written for $163 recorded as $136	27.00	(42.00)
Reconciled cash balance, Dec. 31		$5,783.00

Exhibit 9-7 Adjustments from Bank Reconciliation

Cash

Beg Bal. 12/1/2001 $3,238.48

Date	Amount	Date	Ch#	Amount
Dec. 1	$142.25	Dec. 1	#939	$ 287.94
Dec. 3	155.21	Dec. 3	#940	34.51
Dec. 3	142.15	Dec. 3	#941	26.79
Dec. 4	154.45	Dec. 8	#942	136.00
Dec. 5	198.00	Dec. 8	#943	593.15
Dec. 6	98.66	Dec. 10	#944	385.00
Dec. 8	190.23	Dec. 10	#945	190.12
Dec. 10	163.65	Dec. 14	#946	489.57
Dec. 10	187.04	Dec. 24	#947	452.18
Dec. 11	156.55	Dec. 24	#948	347.00
Dec. 12	177.91	Dec. 28	#949	1,904.78
Dec. 13	217.87	Dec. 29	#950	121.00
Dec. 15	313.57			
Dec. 15	293.32			
Dec. 17	336.58			
Dec. 18	387.22			
Dec. 19	441.10			
Dec. 20	457.16			
Dec. 22	451.82			
Dec. 22	591.78			
Dec. 24	458.25			
Dec. 27	287.35			
Dec. 28	335.76			
Dec. 29	418.43			
Dec. 31	786.00			

Ending Bal.12/31/2001
Before Reconciliation $5,812.75

Adjustments to company records based on bank reconciliation:

Interest earned	12.25	Bank service charge		15.00
		Correct error for check no. 942		27.00

Reconciled Cash Bal
12/31/2001 $5,783.00

             (+)   (−)

replenishes the fund to the original amount and uses the receipts to record the various cash transactions in its accounting system. For each receipt, the company records an increase in the related expense (or asset) T-account (e.g., postage expense, office supplies) and a decrease in its Cash T-account. This ensures that all of the petty cash payments are included in the amounts reported in the company's financial statements.

Sweet Temptations keeps a petty cash fund totaling $35. As we will discuss next, Anna adds this amount to Sweet Temptations' ending reconciled cash balance for its checking account so that Sweet Temptations shows its total cash on its balance sheet.

Reporting the Cash Balance on the Balance Sheet

Cash is usually the first asset listed on the balance sheet because it is the most liquid current asset. Recall that Cash includes money on hand, deposits in checking and savings accounts, and checks and credit card receipts that a company has received but not yet deposited. As we discussed in the previous sections, a company's accounting system keeps track of these items separately. When reporting Cash on its balance sheet, a company must combine the balances of each of these items.

Sweet Temptations' total cash balance at December 31, 2001, consists of two items:

1. The December 31 reconciled cash balance in its checking account	$5,783.00
2. The amount in its petty cash fund	35.00
Total cash balance on December 31, 2001	$5,818.00

Notice that Sweet Temptations shows this amount as Cash on its December 31, 2001 balance sheet in Exhibit 9-1.

A company that sells on credit cannot manage its cash without managing its accounts receivable. We will discuss the management of accounts receivable next.

 Have you ever applied for credit? What steps did you have to go through? Why do you think you had to go through that process in order to get credit?

Accounts Receivable

Accounts receivable are the amounts owed to a company by customers from previous credit sales. The company intends to collect these amounts in cash. Companies make sales on credit for two basic reasons. The first reason is that selling on credit may be more convenient than selling for cash. For example, when a company is selling goods that have to be shipped, it is common for the purchaser to pay for the goods after receiving them. Between the time that the purchaser receives the goods and the time that the seller collects the payment, the seller has extended credit to the purchaser. The second reason a company makes credit sales is that managers believe that offering credit will encourage customers to buy items that they might not otherwise purchase. This is common in retail sales, when the customer may not have enough cash to make the purchase.

 Do credit card sales result in accounts receivable? Some? All? None?

Credit sales using accounts receivable are not the same as "credit card sales." If you use a credit card to pay for goods that are sold to you, it is the credit card company (e.g., VISA,

www.visa.com

©1996. The Family Circus, by Bil Keane, Inc. Dist. by COWLES SYNDICATE, INC. Reprinted with special permission of King Features Syndicate, Inc.

www.mastercard.com
www.discover.com

Mastercard, Discover) that is extending credit to you, not the company that sold you the goods. A retail store deposits its credit card receipts into its checking account just as it does its cash receipts. Because of this, credit card sales receipts are sometimes referred to as "instant cash."

The Decision to Extend Credit

If accounts receivable increase a company's sales, why not automatically decide to grant all customers credit? The decision is not automatic because accounts receivable also have two disadvantages. One disadvantage of credit sales is that having accounts receivable requires significant management effort. Managers must make credit investigations, prepare and send bills, and encourage payments from the customers. All of these activities involve a cost to the company in money and in employee time. The second disadvantage is that when a company makes credit sales, there is always the chance that the purchaser will not pay. However, just because a company has some uncollectible accounts ("bad debts"), it does not mean that the company should not make credit sales. If, given the additional revenues and costs of managing accounts receivable, the company's profits are increased by extending credit, then credit sales help the company achieve its goals. A company uses a form of C-V-P analysis for this evaluation. We will explain more about a company's decision to extend credit in Chapter 13. In this chapter, we focus on managing and reporting the accounts receivable for a small company.

Simple Controls over Accounts Receivable

 Has anyone ever asked to borrow money from you? If they did, what factors affected your decision? Will you deal with the next situation in the same way? Why or why not?

5 *How can managers control accounts receivable in a small company?*

Accounts receivable provide a greater increase in profit if credit sales are monitored properly. Internal controls over accounts receivable focus on procedures that help maximize the increase in profit from granting credit. For a small company, such as Sweet Temptations, three control procedures should be used with accounts receivable.

First, before extending credit, a company should determine that a customer is likely to pay. The risk of not collecting customers' accounts is greatly reduced if a company extends credit only to customers who have a history of being financially responsible. But how does a company decide if a customer is creditworthy? And how much credit should a company extend?

 Some companies grant credit "on the spot" with no credit checks. Why would a company do this? What problems could the company later encounter?

To answer these questions, a company asks each potential credit customer to complete a credit application (similar to the one you would fill out for a car loan). Normally, a credit application requests that the applicant provide the following information: (1) the name of the applicant's employer and the applicant's income, (2) the name of the applicant's bank, his or her bank account numbers, and the balances in his or her accounts, (3) a list of assets, (4) credit card account numbers and amounts owed, and (5) a list of other debts. The company will contact the applicant's employer, bank, and credit card companies to verify the application information and ask questions about the applicant's credit history. If the applicant has been financially responsible (i.e., earns a minimum level of income, has not issued many NSF checks, and has made bank and credit card payments in a timely manner), the company approves the application. The amount of credit that it approves depends on the applicant's income, amounts of other debt, and the specific results of the company's investigation. Credit sales should be made only to customers whose credit it has approved.

Second, a company should monitor the accounts receivable balances of its customers. Recall from Chapter 6 that credit customers agree to accept certain payment terms. Common credit terms are "2/10, net/30." Under this arrangement the customer agrees that a

2 percent cash discount will be granted if it makes payment within 10 days and that, if it does not make payment then, the full amount is due in 30 days. To monitor customer credit effectively, a company needs to have an accounting system that is able to keep track of each customer's credit activity. The company also needs to have an organized collection effort. It should mail monthly statements to customers and should consider payments not received in 30 days (in this case) to be past due. It should send personalized letters to customers whose accounts become past due and should deny them additional credit until it collects the past-due amounts. If accounts become very overdue, say 90 days or more, the company can use telephone calls to encourage payments. At some point, it may consider an overdue account to be uncollectible and may decide not to make any further effort to collect the account or to turn it over to a collection agency.

Third, a company should monitor its total accounts receivable balance. If the balance increases, the company should investigate the reasons for the increase. If the increase resulted from an increase in credit sales from creditworthy customers, the company will continue with its standard collection efforts. However, if the increase resulted from a slowdown in cash collections, the company should reexamine its credit and collection policies to try to solve the problem.

Regardless of the collection effort made by a company, it can expect that some of its accounts receivable will not be collectible. The point of the collection effort is to improve the percentage of accounts receivable that *are* collected. Most financial statement users know that some of a company's accounts receivable are not collectible. In the next section, we will discuss how a company includes this information when reporting the amount of its accounts receivable on its balance sheet.

 Would you rather know the amount you are owed or the amount you expect to receive? Why?

Accounts Receivable Balance

The amount of accounts receivable that a company reports on its balance sheet is the amount of cash it expects to receive from customers as payments for previous credit sales. The words "expects to receive" reflect the fact that the company may not collect all of its accounts receivable. So, the amount a company shows on its balance sheet as accounts receivable is the total owed by customers (the "gross" amount) less an amount that it expects to be uncollectible. GAAP refers to this amount as the *net realizable value* of accounts receivable.

A company shows its accounts receivable at their net realizable value because, as part of an analysis of its liquidity, financial statement users are concerned with the company's ability to turn accounts receivable into cash. As you learned in Chapter 8, predicting a company's cash flows helps external users make business decisions.

The gross amount of the total accounts receivable at year-end is calculated by adding all of the individual customers' balances. However, the dollar amount of accounts receivable that are uncollectible requires an estimate. This is because the company doesn't know which customers won't pay. (If, at the time of the credit sale, the company thought a particular customer would not pay for the goods, it would not have granted the credit!)

Given the uncertainties of collecting accounts receivable, how does a company estimate the amount that it expects will be uncollectible? In general, a company bases this estimate on its past experience with collections. Using the company's history as a guide, it either calculates the estimate as a percentage of credit sales (e.g., 1 percent of credit sales) or bases the estimate on an "aging analysis" of the accounts receivable (i.e., the older a receivable is, the more likely it is to be uncollectible). We will discuss specific types of estimation methods in Chapter 13.

To inform financial statement users that a company is showing its accounts receivable at the net realizable value, the company places the word "net" after accounts receivable on the balance sheet: Accounts receivable (net).

Sweet Temptations shows its accounts receivable on its December 31, 2001 balance sheet (Exhibit 9-1) as follows:

Accounts receivable (net) $7,340

To determine this net amount, Sweet Temptations calculated its dollar estimate of uncollectible accounts receivable and subtracted it from the total amount of accounts receivable listed in the accounting records. Assuming Sweet Temptations' gross accounts receivable are $7,874 (the company's accounting system keeps track of this amount), we can determine that its estimated uncollectible accounts receivable at December 31, 2001 are $534 ($7,874 − $7,340).

Many companies generate accounts receivable by selling inventory. We will discuss inventory management in the next section.

Inventory

 Why do companies sometimes sell their goods for 50 percent off the retail price? Why do they advertise that they are having an inventory reduction sale? Should this affect the way they account for their inventory?

A company's **inventory** is the merchandise being held for resale. In Chapter 6, we discussed how a company uses either a perpetual inventory system or a periodic inventory system to keep track of its merchandise. That discussion focused on the calculation of a company's cost of goods sold. Remember that the cost of goods sold is the cost a company has incurred for the merchandise (goods) it has sold to customers during the accounting period. The company includes the cost of goods sold as an expense on its income statement. In this section, we focus on the calculation of a company's ending inventory.

Accounting for, controlling, and reporting on inventory are important for several reasons. First, selling inventory is the primary way a retail or manufacturing company gets cash from operating activities (and earns a profit). If the amount of inventory is too low, the company could have future difficulties providing the cash it will need for operations. Second, a company usually expects to turn over its inventory (purchase it, sell it, and replace it with newly purchased inventory) several times during the year. If inventory sales slow down, investors and creditors may become concerned about the company's ability to continue to sell the inventory at a satisfactory profit. Finally, inventory can be stolen and/or can become obsolete. For these reasons, a company must effectively account for, control, and report on its inventory.

Simple Inventory Controls

6 *How can managers control inventory in a small company?*

A company should establish several simple internal controls that will help safeguard its inventory and improve record-keeping. First, it should control the ordering and acceptance of inventory deliveries. In a small company, the owner is usually the only person who places orders for inventory. But even in a small company, the owner should place orders using a purchase order. A **purchase order** is a document authorizing a supplier to ship the items listed on the document at a specific price. It is signed by an authorized person in the company. Use of purchase orders helps ensure that purchasing activities are efficient and that no unauthorized person can purchase inventory.

A company should keep a list of the purchase orders or copies of the purchase orders where employees can have access to them. Employees receiving inventory need to know what has been ordered because they should accept only approved orders. In addition, employees should check the quantity and condition of every order received. If, on further inspection, an employee finds that the order was not filled properly (e.g., the wrong boxes of chocolates are received) or that the goods are damaged (e.g., the chocolates melted), the supplier should be notified immediately.

Think about the last time you went shopping. What physical controls over inventory did you notice?

Second, a company should establish physical controls over inventory while the inventory is being held for sale. One physical control involves restricting access to inventory. You have probably seen signs on certain company doors that state:

FOR EMPLOYEES ONLY

Companies post the signs to help keep customers out of storage areas. Other controls include locked display cases, magnetic security devices, and camera surveillance systems.

Finally, to make sure that inventory records are accurate, a company should periodically take a physical count of its inventory. Whether a company uses a perpetual or a periodic inventory system (discussed in Chapter 6), by physically counting inventory the company can determine the accuracy of its inventory records and can estimate losses from theft, breakage, or spoilage. Almost all companies count inventory at least once a year. Many companies count inventory after closing on the date of their year-end balance sheet. By counting inventory at the end of the fiscal year, a company can use the inventory count to help determine the dollar amount of inventory that it will show on its balance sheet and the cost of goods sold that it will show on its income statement.

Recall that Sweet Temptations uses a perpetual inventory system, so it keeps a running balance of its inventory and cost of goods sold in its accounting records. To verify the accuracy of these balances, Anna Cox and an employee spent two hours counting the boxes of chocolates in Sweet Temptations' inventory after it closed on December 31, 2001. When they were finished, Anna calculated that Sweet Temptations owned 274 boxes of Unlimited Decadence chocolates at year-end.

Why do you think a doctor's office would control access to patient records?

Determining the Cost of Ending Inventory

A company shows its inventory on its ending balance sheet as a *dollar amount*. So, after the company has counted the number of units in its ending inventory, it must determine the appropriate unit *cost* for each item. How does a company figure out the cost of each inventory item? To answer that question, we need to explain two things: (1) the relationship among cost of goods available for sale, cost of goods sold, and year-end inventory, and (2) the concept of cost flows.

Cost of Goods Available for Sale, Sold, and Held in Inventory

At the start of any month, a company has a certain number of inventory items available for sale—its beginning-of-the-month inventory. For example, say Sweet Temptations starts the month of December 2001 with 590 boxes of chocolates. During the month, a company like Sweet Temptations sells some of its inventory and makes purchases to restock for additional sales. Ideally, at the end of the month, one of two things has happened to all of the items that were available for sale during the month. Either the goods were sold *or* the goods remain in inventory. If Sweet Temptations purchases an additional 300 boxes of chocolates during December and sells 616 boxes, 274 boxes remain in inventory on December 31. Remember that the year-end physical count of inventory was 274 boxes. These calculations for the month of December can be summarized as follows:

	Beginning inventory for December	590 boxes
+	December purchases	300 boxes
=	Goods available for sale during December	890 boxes
−	Goods sold during December	(616) boxes
=	Goods in inventory on December 31, 2001	274 boxes

As we discussed in earlier chapters, when Sweet Temptations prepares its financial statements for the month, it includes the *cost* of the goods sold during the month in the monthly income statement and the *cost* of the ending inventory in the month-end balance sheet, based on its perpetual inventory records. For December, Sweet Temptations' Cost of Goods Sold account shows a balance of $3,399.75, and its Inventory account shows an ending balance of $1,570.25. To arrive at these amounts, Sweet Temptations converted the number of boxes of candy purchased, sold, and on hand to dollar amounts. Sweet Temptations recorded these dollar amounts in its Inventory and Cost of Goods Sold T-accounts, as we illustrated in Chapter 6.

Exhibit 9-8 shows the December inventory information for Sweet Temptations.[2] Notice that Sweet Temptations' beginning inventory cost $5.50 per box. The purchase it made on December 13 cost $5.75 per box. Since the unit costs of the inventory changed during the month, Sweet Temptations had to decide which cost to assign to the boxes it sold and which cost to assign to the boxes left in inventory. For example, should it assign all of the boxes a cost of $5.50 or all a cost of $5.75? Or should it use both costs and, if so, to which boxes should it assign $5.50 and to which ones $5.75? Or should it use the average of both costs?

A company must have a *method* for deciding how to calculate the dollar amounts for inventory and cost of goods sold, and it may use one of several methods to determine these dollar amounts. However, the company should use its chosen method consistently from year to year, unless a different method would better reflect the company's operations, so that users of its financial statements can compare its performance from year to year. Here, we discuss the specific identification method. We will discuss other methods in Chapter 19.

Specific Identification Method

The **specific identification method** allocates costs to cost of goods sold and to ending inventory by assigning to each unit sold and to each unit in ending inventory the cost to the company of purchasing that particular unit. Under this method a company keeps track of the cost of each inventory item separately. Usually, it does this tracking through a computer system or through an inventory coding system. For example, on every box of chocolates that Sweet Temptations receives from Unlimited Decadence, the date the chocolates were made is stamped on the bottom. Because Unlimited Decadence sends its chocolates out freshly made, Sweet Temptations can use this date to tell which shipment a box came from and the exact cost of the box.[3] Many companies have *point of sale* cash register systems that scan the inventory codes to keep track of the costs of inventory sold and inventory on hand.

For example, say that on December 21 a customer purchases three boxes of chocolates for $12 per box and pays in cash. As Anna rings up the sale, she notes on the sales receipt that two boxes are dated 11-29-2001 and one box is dated 12-13-2001. From Exhibit 9-8 we can see that the boxes dated 11-29-2001 cost $5.50 per box and the box dated 12-13-2001 cost $5.75. When she records this sale, Anna increases the Sales and Cash accounts

---

Exhibit 9-8   Sweet Temptations' Inventory Information

Beg. Inventory, Dec. 1	590 boxes @ $5.50 per box = $3,245
December 13, purchase	300 boxes @ $5.75 per box = 1,725
Cost of goods available for sale	890 boxes $4,970
Sales during December	(616) boxes
End. Inventory, Dec. 31	274 boxes

---

[2]Normally, when a company takes a physical inventory at the end of its fiscal year, it calculates its units and costs of goods available for sale for the entire year. For simplicity, we illustrate Sweet Temptations' inventory information for only one month.

[3]Although we did not mention it in Chapter 6, we used the specific identification method in our earlier inventory discussion.

by \$36 (\$12 × 3 boxes). She decreases the Inventory account and increases the separate expense account—Cost of Goods Sold—by \$16.75, the exact cost of the items sold (\$5.50 + \$5.50 + \$5.75).

The inventory amount that Sweet Temptations shows on its December 31, 2001 balance sheet is calculated from the results of the physical inventory count. (This amount should be the same as the amount that it shows in its accounting records.) Recall that 274 boxes remained in inventory on December 31. Under the specific identification method, in addition to counting the inventory, Anna and her employee must keep track of the boxes according to the stamped dates. Exhibit 9-9 shows Anna's inventory count instructions, the results of the count, and the year-end inventory and cost of goods sold calculations.

 As a manager, would you "allow" customers to select any box of chocolates from the shelves?

Because Sweet Temptations' physical inventory count of 274 boxes is the same as the calculation of its ending inventory from its inventory records of beginning inventory, purchases, and sales shown earlier, the \$1,570.25 cost of the ending inventory calculated in Exhibit 9-9 is the same as the amount in its Inventory account. Furthermore, the \$3,399.75 cost of goods sold calculated in Exhibit 9-9 is the same as the amount in its Cost of Goods Sold account. So, by taking a physical count, Sweet Temptations has verified that the amounts in its accounting records are correct.

Now suppose that Anna and her employee counted 253 boxes of chocolates dated 12-13-2001 but only 17 boxes dated 11-29-2001. In this case, 4 boxes of chocolates are

---

Exhibit 9-9 Sweet Temptations' Year-End Inventory Calculation

The Inventory Count

After Sweet Temptations closes on the evening of December 31, 2001, Anna and one employee spend two hours counting the company's inventory. Anna tells her employee how the count will work: "You and I will count all of the items independently of each other. I will follow along right behind you. We will count one section of the store at a time. Both of us will mark our findings on inventory count sheets, noting separately the number of boxes dated 11-29-2001 and the number dated 12-13-2001. We have to count these boxes separately because we purchased them at different prices and we value inventory using the specific identification method. After we finish each section of the store, we will compare our results to see that we agree on the count. If the numbers don't match, we will recount the section. After we count all of the inventory, we will compute a total for the number of boxes dated 11-29-2001 and 12-13-2001."

The Results of the Inventory Count

Sweet Temptations' inventory count ran smoothly. After compiling all of the inventory count sheets, Anna concluded that the year-end inventory consisted of the following:

253 boxes of chocolates dated 12-13-2001
21 boxes of chocolates dated 11-29-2001

December 31, 2001 Inventory Calculation

253 boxes @ \$5.75 =	\$1,454.75
21 boxes @ \$5.50 =	115.50
Ending inventory	\$1,570.25

December Cost of Goods Sold Calculation

Cost of goods available for sale (Exhibit 9-8)	\$4,970.00
− Ending inventory	(1,570.25)
Cost of goods sold	\$3,399.75

missing, and the cost of the ending inventory is $1,548.25 [(253 × $5.75) + (17 × $5.50)]. Anna should try to find out why these boxes are missing. For instance, they may have been given away as "free samples," stolen (or eaten by the employees), or thrown away because they were stale. Whatever the reason, she should adjust the accounting records by increasing the Cost of Goods Sold account and decreasing the Inventory account by $22 (4 × $5.50) for the missing boxes.

 Suppose that the year-end count of inventory is less than the accounting records show as ending inventory because Anna threw away stale boxes of chocolates. How might this information affect Anna's future decisions?

Accounts Payable

As we explained earlier in the chapter, companies often sell on credit to customers. These credit sales result in accounts receivable. Similarly, companies often make purchases on credit, which result in the liability accounts payable. **Accounts payable** are the amounts that a company owes to its suppliers for previous credit purchases of inventory and supplies. The reasons for purchasing on credit are similar to the reasons for selling on credit. The first reason is that purchasing on credit is often more convenient than purchasing with cash. The second reason for purchasing on credit is to delay paying for purchases and, by doing so, to obtain a short-term "loan" from the supplier. Many companies, particularly small companies, are often short of cash and find it difficult to pay for their purchases immediately. Managers of these companies, therefore, try to delay payment until their companies receive the cash from the eventual sale of their products; they then use this cash to pay the amounts their companies owe. This delay is the reason many suppliers offer their customers cash discounts for prompt payment.

Simple Controls over Accounts Payable

7 *How can managers control accounts payable in a small company?*

A company's accounts payable represent promises to pay the amounts due to other businesses. As is the case with accounts receivable, a company needs controls over accounts payable. Controls over accounts payable should focus on three primary concerns. The first concern involves the ability of employees to obligate the company to an account payable. Giving too many employees the authority to place orders for company purchases makes it more difficult for managers to coordinate and monitor credit purchases, and makes it easier for untrustworthy employees to obligate the company for personal expenditures. In response to this concern, a company should limit the number of employees who have the authority to make company purchases. In a small company, this authority may be given only to the owner. Larger companies usually have a purchasing department that controls all company purchases.

Second, once a company incurs an account payable, the company is concerned that it makes each payment at the appropriate time and that the *supplier* records each payment properly. A company monitors the timeliness of its payments by having an employee keep track of the credit terms of each account payable. If cash discounts are available, the company should take advantage of the cash savings by making the payment within the cash discount period. A company makes sure that the supplier records its payments properly by checking the supplier's monthly statements. If the payment is not recorded properly, an employee should investigate the discrepancy and perhaps contact the supplier.

Finally, managers, investors, and creditors are concerned about a company's total dollar amount of accounts payable because, in the very near future, the company will need to use its cash to pay these liabilities. If the accounts payable are large relative to the company's current assets, the company may experience liquidity problems.

Managers will investigate relatively large increases in accounts payable. If the increase is a result of planned increases in inventory, they assume that increased sales will provide the cash needed to pay the liabilities. If the increase is a result of cash flow problems, managers may postpone purchases of inventory and/or property and equipment, or may contact suppliers to try to arrange an extension of the credit terms.

Accounts Payable Balance

The amount of accounts payable that a company owes on the balance sheet date is listed in the current liabilities section of the ending balance sheet. A company calculates this amount by summing the accounts payable owed to individual suppliers. As Exhibit 9-1 shows, on December 31, 2001, Sweet Temptations' accounts payable total $7,540.

Business Issues and Values

 Has anyone ever forgotten to repay you for money that he or she borrowed? Has it ever been difficult for you to pay off a debt? How should a company handle these situations? What factors should it consider when developing policies concerning late payments by its customers or to its suppliers?

We started the chapter by stating that managing working capital effectively is an important part of financial management. This is especially true for new companies that have a relatively small amount of capital and may be prone to liquidity problems. But how aggressive should a company be in managing its working capital? When trying to collect accounts receivable payments, some companies repeatedly telephone customers at their offices and homes. On the other hand, when trying to hold off paying their own debts, some companies continue to tell suppliers that "the check is in the mail" when it really is not.

The ethics of aggressive working capital management has been questioned by some business leaders and critics. Instead of being seen as conscientious, a company that uses aggressive collection efforts can be viewed as intimidating and harassing. A company that signs a purchase agreement, even though it knows that it will make suppliers wait an additional 30 or 60 days before paying for the goods, can be viewed as untrustworthy, not as a shrewd financial planner. What do you think? We will continue to discuss these types of issues in future chapters when we examine corporations.

Summary

At the beginning of the chapter we asked you several questions. During the chapter, we asked you to STOP and answer some additional questions to build your knowledge about specific issues. Be sure you answered these additional questions. Below are the questions from the beginning of the chapter, with a brief summary of the key points relating to the answers. Use your creative and critical thinking skills to expand on these key points to develop more complete answers to the questions and to determine what other questions you have that might lead you to learn more about the issues.

1 What is working capital, and why is its management important?

Working capital is current assets minus current liabilities. A company needs to manage its working capital so that it keeps an appropriate balance between having enough to conduct its operations and to handle unexpected needs, and having too much so that profitability is reduced.

2 How can managers control cash receipts in a small company?

Managers can control cash receipts by requiring the proper use of a cash register, separating the duties of receiving and processing collections of accounts receivable, and depositing receipts every day.

3 **How can managers control cash payments in a small company?**

Managers can control cash payments by paying all bills by check, paying only for approved purchases supported by source documents, and immediately stamping "paid" on the supporting documents after payment.

4 **What is a bank reconciliation, and what are the causes of the difference between a company's cash balance in its accounting records and its cash balance on its bank statement?**

A bank reconciliation is an analysis that a company uses to resolve the difference between the cash balance in its accounting records and the cash balance reported by the bank on its bank statement. The causes of the difference are deposits in transit, outstanding checks, deposits made directly by the bank, charges made directly by the bank, and errors.

5 **How can managers control accounts receivable in a small company?**

Managers can control accounts receivable by evaluating a customer's ability to pay before extending credit, monitoring the accounts receivable balance of each customer, and monitoring the total accounts receivable balance.

6 **How can managers control inventory in a small company?**

Managers can control inventory by establishing policies for ordering and accepting inventory, establishing physical controls over inventory being held for sale, and taking a periodic physical count of the inventory.

7 **How can managers control accounts payable in a small company?**

Managers can control accounts payable by coordinating and monitoring credit purchases, making payments at the appropriate time, and monitoring the total accounts payable balance.

Key Terms

accounts payable *(p. 286)*

accounts receivable *(p. 279)*

bank reconciliation *(p. 272)*

bank statement *(p. 272)*

cash *(p. 269)*

deposit in transit *(p. 272)*

internal control structure *(p. 268)*

inventory *(p. 282)*

NSF (not sufficient funds) check *(p. 272)*

outstanding check *(p. 272)*

petty cash fund *(p. 275)*

purchase order *(p. 282)*

specific identification method *(p. 284)*

working capital *(p. 266)*

S U M M A R Y
S U R F I N G

Here is an opportunity to gather information on the Internet about real-world issues related to the topics in this chapter. Go to http://www.dryden.com/account and click on the Cunningham, Nikolai, and Bazley book cover. Click on Summary Surfing, then click on this chapter number, and answer the following questions.

▶ Click on **UACPA** (Utah Association of CPAs). Scroll to the bottom of the page, and click on *Small Business*. Scroll down, and click on *Watching Your Cash Flow*. What are some of the suggested cash management procedures regarding employees, accounts receivable, banking practices, and accounts payable?

Integrated Business and Accounting Situations

Answer the Following Questions in Your Own Words

Testing Your Knowledge

9-1 What is a company's "working capital," and what is included in its two components?

9-2 Why does a company manage its working capital?

9-3 Define "cash" for a company.

9-4 Briefly discuss the controls over cash sales.

9-5 Briefly discuss the controls over collections of cash from accounts receivable.

9-6 Briefly discuss the controls over cash payments.

9-7 What is a bank reconciliation?

9-8 Identify the causes of the difference between the ending cash balance in a company's records and the ending cash balance reported on its bank statement.

9-9 Briefly explain what is meant by "deposits in transit" and "outstanding checks."

9-10 Briefly explain what are included in deposits made directly by the bank and charges made directly by the bank.

9-11 Prepare an outline of a bank reconciliation for a company.

9-12 Briefly explain what a petty cash fund is and how it works.

9-13 Why do companies make sales "on credit"?

9-14 Briefly discuss the controls over accounts receivable.

9-15 Briefly explain how a company reports its accounts receivable on its ending balance sheet.

9-16 Why is accounting for and reporting of inventory important?

9-17 Briefly discuss the controls over inventory.

9-18 Briefly explain how the specific identification method works for determining inventory costs.

9-19 Evaluate this statement: "My company uses a perpetual inventory system so it doesn't need to take a periodic physical inventory."

9-20 Briefly discuss the controls over accounts payable.

Applying Your Knowledge

9-21 The following are several internal control weaknesses of a small retail company in regard to its cash receipts and accounts receivable:
  (a) Sales invoices are not prenumbered.
  (b) Receipts from daily sales are deposited every Tuesday and Thursday evening.
  (c) One employee is responsible for depositing customer checks from collections of accounts receivable and for recording their receipt in the accounts.
  (d) For credit sales on terms of 2/10 net/30, customers are allowed, for convenience, the discount if payment is received within 20 days.
  (e) A money box is used instead of a cash register to store both the sales invoices and the cash from the sales.
  (f) Credit sales of a large dollar amount can be approved by any sales employee.
  (g) When customers write checks for payment, only the identification of customers who look "untrustworthy" is verified.

  Required: (1) For each internal control weakness, explain how the weakness might result in a loss of the company's assets.
  (2) For each internal control weakness, explain what action should be taken to correct the weakness.

9-22 The following are several internal control weaknesses of a retail company in regard to its cash payments, accounts payable, and inventory:
  (a) The inventory of gold jewelry for sale is kept in unlocked display cases.

(b) One employee is responsible for ordering inventory and writing checks.

(c) Some purchases are made by phone, and no purchase order is written up.

(d) The company takes a physical inventory every two years.

(e) Employees are allowed to bring coats, bags, and purses into working areas.

(f) Inventory received at the loading dock is rushed immediately to the sales floor before it is counted.

(g) When inventory is low, any sales employee can prepare a purchase order and mail it to the supplier.

(h) For efficiency, the company pays invoices on credit purchases once a month, even if it has to forgo any cash discounts for prompt payment.

Required: (1) For each internal control weakness, explain how the weakness might result in a loss of the company's assets.

(2) For each internal control weakness, explain what action should be taken to correct the weakness.

9-23 A company is preparing its bank reconciliation and discovers the following items:

(a) Outstanding checks

(b) Deposits in transit

(c) Deposits made directly by the bank

(d) Charges made directly by the bank

(e) The bank's erroneous underrecording of a deposit

(f) The company's erroneous underrecording of a check it wrote

Required: Indicate how each of these items would be used to adjust (1) the company's cash balance or (2) the bank balance to calculate the reconciled cash balance.

9-24 At the end of March, the Elbert Company records showed a cash balance of $6,943. When comparing the March 31 bank statement with the company's Cash account, the company discovered that deposits in transit were $725, outstanding checks totaled $862, bank service charges were $28, and NSF checks totaled $175.

Required: (1) Compute the March 31 reconciled cash balance of the Elbert Company.

(2) Compute the cash balance listed on the March 31 bank statement.

9-25 At the end of September, the Bross Bicycle Company's records showed a cash balance of $3,496. When comparing the September 30 bank statement, which showed a cash balance of $1,860, with the company's Cash account, the company discovered that outstanding checks were $462, bank service charges were $23, and NSF checks totaled $89.

Required: (1) Compute the September 30 reconciled cash balance of the Bross Bicycle Company.

(2) Compute the September deposits in transit.

9-26 The following five situations (columns 1-5) are independent:

	1	2	3	4	5
Ending balance in the company's checking account	(a)	$2,000	$4,000	$12,000	$3,000
Deposits made directly by the bank	$ 200	(b)	300	450	200
Deposits in transit	600	800	(c)	500	900
Outstanding checks	450	1,200	600	(d)	1,000
Ending cash balance from bank statement	6,000	3,000	4,100	12,000	(e)

Required: Compute each of the unknown amounts, items (a) through (e).

9-27 An examination of the accounting records and the bank statement of the Evans Company at March 31, 2000 provides the following information:

(a) The Cash account has a balance of $6,321.96.

(b) The bank statement shows a bank balance of $3,901.81.

(c) The March 31 cash receipts of $3,260.95 were deposited in the bank at the end of that day but were not recorded by the bank until April 1.

(d) Checks issued and mailed in March but not included among the checks listed as paid on the bank statement were as follows:

Check No. 706	$869.38
Check No. 717	212.00

(e) A bank service charge of $30 for March was deducted on the bank statement.

(f) A check received from a customer for $185 in payment of his account and deposited by the Evans Company was returned marked "NSF" with the bank statement.

(g) Interest of $10.42 earned on the company's checking account was added on the bank statement.

(h) The Evans Company discovered that Check No. 701, which was correctly written as $562 for the March rent, was recorded as $526 in the company's accounts.

Required: (1) Prepare a bank reconciliation on March 31, 2000.

(2) Record the appropriate adjustments in the company's T-accounts. Compute the ending balance in the Cash T-account.

9-28 You have been asked to help the Rancher Company prepare its bank reconciliation. You examine the company's accounting records and its bank statement at May 31, 2000, and find the following information:

(a) The Cash account has a balance of $7,801.24.

(b) The bank statement shows a bank balance of $3,831.04.

(c) The May 31 cash receipts of $4,926.18 were deposited in the bank at the end of that day but were not recorded by the bank until June 1. → deposit in transit

(d) Checks issued and mailed in May but not included among the checks listed as paid on the bank statement were as follows:

Check No. 949	$518.65 } checks outstanding
Check No. 957	699.95

(e) A bank service charge of $27 for May was deducted on the bank statement. → charge by bank

(f) A check received from a customer for $241 in payment of her account and deposited by the Rancher Company was returned marked "NSF" with the bank state- → charge from NFS from bank ment.

(g) Interest of $25.18 earned on the company's checking account was added on the bank statement. → deposit by bank

(h) The Rancher Company discovered that Check No. 941, which was correctly written as $647.21 for the May utility bill, was recorded as $627.41 in the company's error by (19.80) accounts.

Required: (1) Prepare a bank reconciliation on May 31, 2000.

(2) Record the appropriate adjustments in the company's T-accounts. Compute the ending balance in the Cash T-account.

9-29 The Huron Company keeps a petty cash fund of $80. On June 30 the fund contained cash of $36.87 and the following petty cash receipts:

Office supplies	$10.00
Postage	27.48
Miscellaneous	5.65

Required: (1) If the company's fiscal year ends June 30, should the petty cash fund be replenished on June 30? Why?

(2) How much cash is needed to replenish the petty cash fund?

(3) Prepare entries in the company's T-accounts to record the petty cash payments.

9-30 On December 31, 2000, the Bighorn Condominium Management Company had a balance of $70 in its petty cash fund, a reconciled balance of $1,283 in its checking account, and a $4,672 balance in its savings account.

Required: Show how the company would report its cash on its December 31, 2000 balance sheet.

9-31 The Snow-Be-Gone Company sells one type of snowblower and uses the perpetual inventory system. At the beginning of January, the company had a balance in its Cash account of $2,100 and an inventory of 8 units (snowblowers) costing $100 each. During January, it made the following purchases and sales of inventory:

Jan. 5	Purchases	5 units @ $102 per unit
12	Sales	11 units @ $150 per unit
18	Purchases	12 units @ $104 per unit
25	Purchases	6 units @ $103 per unit
29	Sales	13 units @ $150 per unit

All purchases and sales were for cash. The company uses "bar codes" to verify each sale. For the sales on January 12, 8 were units from the beginning inventory, and 3 were units purchased on January 5. For the sales on January 29, 9 were units purchased on January 18, and 4 were units purchased on January 25.

Required: (1) Record the beginning balances in the Cash and Inventory T-accounts. Using T-accounts, record the purchases and sales transactions during January and compute the ending balances of all the accounts you used.

(2) Assume that the company counted its inventory at the end of January and determined that it had 7 snowblowers on hand. Prove that the ending balance in the Inventory account that you computed in (1) is correct.

(3) Compute the company's gross profit.

9-32 The Kvam Lawn Mower Store sells one type of lawn mower at a price of $200 per unit. On June 1, it had an $800 accounts receivable balance and a $600 accounts payable balance, as well as an inventory of 10 mowers costing $120 each. During June, its purchases and sales of mowers were as follows:

	Purchases	**Sales**
June 8	5 mowers @ $125 each	
15		11 mowers
21	6 mowers @ $121 each	
26	4 mowers @ $124 each	
30		8 mowers

All purchases and sales were on credit. No payments or collections were made during June. The company has a perpetual inventory system and uses "bar codes" to verify each sale. For the sales on June 15, 8 were mowers from the beginning inventory, and 3 were mowers purchased on June 8. For the sales on June 30, 2 were mowers from the beginning inventory, 5 were mowers purchased on June 21, and 1 was a mower purchased on June 26.

Required: (1) Record the beginning balances in the Accounts Receivable, Inventory, and Accounts Payable T-accounts. Using T-accounts, record the purchases and sales transactions during June and compute the ending balances of all the accounts you used.

(2) Assume that the company counted its inventory at the close of business on June 30 and determined that it had 6 mowers in stock. Prove that the ending balance in the Inventory account that you computed in (1) is correct.

(3) Compute the company's gross profit percentage for June. How does this compare with its gross profit percentage of 40.8% for May? What might account for the difference?

9-33 The Bugs-Be-Gone Company sells two types of screen doors. Model A, which sells for $30, is the basic screen door, and Model B, which sells for $50, is the deluxe screen door that features removable glass panels so that it can be turned into a storm door during the winter. At the beginning of July, the company had a balance in its Cash account of $1,600 and an inventory consisting of 12 units of Model A costing $20 each and 15 units of Model B costing $35 each. During July, it made the following purchases and sales of inventory:

		Model A	**Model B**
July 6	Sales	8 units @ $30 each	10 units @ $50 each
13	Purchases	9 units @ $19 each	10 units @ $36 each
20	Sales	10 units @ $30 each	12 units @ $50 each
24	Purchases	7 units @ $21 each	6 units @ $37 each
29	Sales	7 units @ $30 each	3 units @ $50 each

All purchases and sales are for cash. The company has a perpetual inventory system, using "bar codes" to verify each sale. For the sales on July 20, 3 units of Model A were from the beginning inventory, and 7 were units purchased on July 13; 5 units of Model B were from the beginning inventory, and 7 were units purchased on July 13. For the sales on July 29, 1 unit of Model A was purchased on July 13, and 6 were units purchased on July 24; 1 unit of Model B was purchased on July 13, and 2 were units purchased on July 24.

On July 31, the company counted its inventory and determined that it had 3 units of Model A and 6 units of Model B on hand. However, 1 of the 3 units of Model A was run over by a customer's truck and had to be thrown away. This unit had been in the beginning inventory.

Required: (1) Record the beginning balances in the Cash and Inventory T-accounts. Using T-accounts (use one account for inventory), record the purchases and sales transactions during July and compute the ending balances of all the accounts you used.

(2) Record the disposal of the damaged unit and prove the accuracy of the ending balance in the Inventory account.

(3) Compute the gross profit percentage. How was this affected by the damaged inventory?

(4) Do you think your work would have been easier if you had used two inventory accounts in (1)? How do you think a company with many items of inventory keeps track of these items under a perpetual inventory system?

Making Evaluations

9-34 Your brother, always bursting with curiosity, recently purchased a fishing rod from a catalog. While he was filling out the order form, he noticed the warning: "Don't Send Cash!" So, after pointing it out to you, he asked, "Does it seem odd to you that a company wouldn't appreciate receiving cash? You're taking accounting. Don't they teach you in there that companies need cash? Why would they say such a thing?"

Required: Tell your brother why you think the company puts this warning in its catalogs, give him some examples of what might happen if customers paid for their purchases with cash, and explain how checks and credit cards might prevent this from happening.

9-35 Sam Lewis has been operating a service station for several years. Although he occasionally has employed students part-time, he has collected the cash and checks for gas and service work himself. He now has decided to open a second service station and put himself more in the role of a manager. He will hire employees to run the service stations and to pump gas and do repair work.

Required: How should Sam Lewis implement internal control procedures over cash receipts for the service stations?

9-36 Your dad's friend Frank was over for dinner the other night, and discussion turned to his business, Frank's Franks, which is responsible for street-corner vending of hotdogs, pretzels, beer, and soda. It's a small company, with an office downtown and four vending carts located in different areas of downtown. When you asked Frank what kind of internal controls his company has in place, Frank said: "We don't have a formal system of internal controls—don't need them. My employees are family members and friends, and I trust them completely! Now when the business grows, and I have to hire strangers, then I'll think about those controls. But now, the company's profitable, and I'm happy." After Frank left, you talked to your dad about what you had learned in accounting, and asked whether he thought Frank would appreciate hearing about it. Your dad assured you that Frank would be open to your suggestions.

Required: Write a letter to Frank explaining how you think his company would benefit from a system of internal controls, even though he trusts his employees. Also describe specific controls that Frank could use in his particular business.

9-37 Your friend Ruby Johnson works as a cashier in an upscale restaurant located in a business center that includes a bank. She works the late shift, and since the restaurant caters to the convention crowd, she generally doesn't leave work until 2:00 or 2:30 in the morning. One day, when you were having lunch with her, she began complaining about one aspect of her job: "My boss is a real stickler for procedures. Even though it's really late when the last customer leaves, and even though we are exhausted, we still have to follow *procedure*. Before the host and I can leave, we have to count the money in the register and match it against the register tape and match both amounts against the dollar total of the checks the customers paid. And, as if that's not enough, we have to make sure that every check number is accounted for. Every night the manager writes down the numbers of the checks each waitperson has been given to use that night for taking customer orders. At the end of the night, the waitpeople give the cashier all the checks they didn't use. If any money is missing, guess who takes the blame and has to make up the difference? Anyway, after we count the money, we have to put the money and the tape in a deposit bag, walk it across the parking lot to the bank, and deposit it in the bank's night-deposit box, *even though there is a safe right under the cash register!* Like we're not sitting ducks for anybody who wants to rob us. I don't understand why she would risk our lives like that. Furthermore, the boss unlocks the part of the register that contains a copy of the tape that we took to the bank, and uses that tape to enter the day's cash receipts amount into the accounting system. Like she really trusts me so much that she has to keep the tape copy under lock and key. What a jerk!" Now that you are taking accounting, you have a little better insight into why the boss is so interested in these procedures.

Required: Explain to Ruby what's going on before she does something rash, like quit her job.

9-38 The Anibonita Company is a retail store with three sales departments. It also has a small accounting department, a purchasing department, and a receiving department. All inventory is kept in the sales departments. When the inventory for a specific item is low, the manager of the sales department that sells the item notifies the purchasing department, which then orders the merchandise. All purchases are on credit. Anibonita pays the freight charges on all its purchases after being notified of the cost by the freight company. When the inventory is delivered, it is inspected and checked in by the receiving department and then sent to the sales department, where it is placed on the sales shelves. After notification that the ordered inventory has been received, the accounting department records the purchase. Upon receipt of the supplier's invoice or the freight bill, the accounting department verifies the invoice (or freight bill) against the purchase order and the receiving report before making payment.

Required: Briefly explain the internal controls that the Anibonita Company uses for its purchasing process. Include in your discussion what source documents it probably uses.

9-39 The JeBean Company makes only sales on credit. All JeBean's customers order through the mail. The company has a small accounting department, a credit department, an inventory department, and a shipping department. After approval of an order by the credit department, the merchandise is assembled in the inventory department and then sent to the shipping department. The shipping department packs the merchandise in cardboard boxes; then it is picked up by the freight company and shipped to the customer. The JeBean Company pays for freight charges on all items shipped to customers after being notified of the cost by the freight company. After verification of shipment, the accounting department mails an invoice to the customer and records the sale. On receipt of the customer's check, the accounting department records the collection.

Required: Briefly explain the internal controls that the JeBean Company uses for its sales process. Include in your discussion what source documents it probably uses.

9-40 Oliver Bauer, owner of Bauer's Retail Store, has been very careful to establish good internal control over inventory purchases for his store. The store has several employees, and since Ollie cannot devote as much time as he would like to running the store, he has entrusted a longtime employee with the task of purchasing inventory. This employee has worked for Ollie for 15 years and knows all of the store's suppliers. Whenever inventory must be purchased, the employee prepares a purchase order and mails it to the supplier. When a rush order is needed, the employee occasionally calls in the order and does not prepare a purchase order. This procedure is acceptable to the suppliers because they know the employee. When the merchandise is received from the supplier, this employee carefully checks in each item to verify the correct quantity and quality. This job is usually done at night after the store is closed, thus allowing the employee to help with sales to customers during regular working hours. After checking in the items, the employee initials the copy of the supplier invoice received with the merchandise, staples the copy to the purchase order (if there is one), records the purchase in the company's accounts, and prepares a check for payment. Oliver Bauer examines the source documents (purchase order and initialed invoice) at this point and signs the check, and the employee records the payment. Ollie has become concerned about the store's gross profit, which has been steadily decreasing even though he has heard customers complaining that the store's selling prices are too high. He has a discussion with the employee, who says: "I'm doing my best to hold down costs. I will continue to do my purchasing job as efficiently as possible (even though I am overworked). However, I think you should hire another salesperson and spend more on advertising. This will increase your sales and, in turn, your gross profit."

Required: Why do you think the gross profit of the store has gone down? Prepare for Oliver Bauer a report that summarizes any internal control weaknesses existing in the inventory purchasing procedure and explain what the result might be. Make suggestions for improving any weaknesses you uncover.

9-41   In the chapter, we mentioned that if Sweet Temptations came up short four boxes of candy, it should increase its Cost of Goods Sold account and decrease its Inventory account by the cost of those boxes. Suppose Anna wanted to keep a record of candy shortages in the accounting system.

Required: Design a way that Sweet Temptations' accounting system could be changed to accommodate Anna's request.

9-42   Suppose that one of your company's largest customers has written an NSF check for $9,734 and your boss has just found out about it. This morning he comes flying into your office (with smoke coming out of his ears) and demands to know how this NSF check will affect specific accounts in the company's financial statements. You examine the bank statement that came in the morning's mail and notice that, not only has the customer written an NSF check, but the bank has charged you a fee of $75 for processing this check.

Required: List the accounts that will be affected by this turn of events, and indicate by how much they will be affected. What do you think should happen next?

9-43   You are a consultant for several companies. The following are several independent situations you have discovered, each of which may or may not have one or more internal control weaknesses. The names of the companies have been changed to protect the innocent.

(a)   In Company A, one employee is responsible for counting and recording all the receipts (remittances) received in the mail from customers paying their accounts. Customers usually pay by check, but they occasionally mail cash. Every day, after the mail is delivered, this employee opens the envelopes containing payments by customers. She carefully counts all remittances and places the checks and cash in a bag. She then lists the amount of each check or cash received and the customer's name on a sheet of paper. After totaling the cash and checks received, she records the receipts in the company's accounts, endorses the checks in the company's name, and deposits the checks and cash in the bank.

(b)   Company B has purchased several programmable calculators for use by the office and sales employees. So that these hand calculators will be available to any employee who needs one, they are kept in an unlocked storage cabinet in the office. Anyone who takes and uses a calculator "signs out" the calculator by writing his or her name on a sheet of paper posted near the cabinet. When the calculator is returned, the employee crosses out his or her name on the sheet.

(c)   Company C owns a van for deliveries of sales to customers. No mileage is kept of the deliveries, although all gas and oil receipts are carefully checked before being paid. To advertise the store, Company C printed two signs with the store's name and hung one on each side of the van. These signs are easily removable so that the van can be periodically cleaned without damaging the signs. The company allows employees to borrow the van at night or on the weekends if they need the van for personal hauling. No mileage is kept of the personal hauling, but the employee who borrowed the van must fill the gas tank before returning the van.

(d)   Employee Y is in charge of employee records for Company D. Whenever a new employee is hired, the new employee's name, address, salary, and other relevant information are properly recorded. Every payday, all employees are paid by check. At this time Employee Y makes out each employee's check, signs it, and gives it to each employee. After distributing the paychecks, Employee Y makes an entry in the company's accounts, increasing Salaries Expense and decreasing Cash for the total amount of the salary checks.

(e) To reduce paperwork, Company E places orders for purchases of inventory from suppliers by phone. No purchase order is prepared. When the goods arrive at the company, they are immediately brought to the sales floor. An employee then authorizes payment based on the supplier's invoice, writes and signs a check, and mails payment to the supplier. Another employee uses the paid invoice to record the purchase and payment in the company's accounts.

(f) All sales made by Company F, whether they are for cash or on account, are "rung up" on a single cash register. Employee X is responsible for collecting the cash receipts from sales and the customer charge slips at the end of each day. The employee carefully counts the cash, preparing a "cash receipts" slip for the total. Employee X sums the amount on the cash receipts slip and the customer charge slips, and compares this total with the total sales on the cash register tape to verify the total sales for the day. The cash register tape is then discarded, and the cash is deposited in the bank. The cash receipts slip and the customer charge slips are turned over to a different employee, who records the cash and credit sales in the company's accounts.

Required: (1) List the internal control weakness or weaknesses you find in each of the preceding independent situations. If no weakness can be found, explain why the internal control is good.

(2) In each situation in which there is an internal control weakness, describe how you would remedy the situation to improve the internal control.

9-44 Yesterday, you received the letter shown on the following page for your advice column in the local paper:

Dear Dr. Decisive:

Well, this takes the cake! I thought my boss was a little on the shady side, and now I'm pretty convinced, but some of my friends think I'm wrong. What do you think? Here's some background. My company uses the specific identification method to assign costs to inventory and cost of goods sold. Well, this year our inventory consisted of two batches of goods. We paid $6.00 per unit for each inventory item in the old batch and $6.75 for each item in the batch we purchased this year. As it turned out, most of the inventory items we sold this year came out of the new batch (the $6.75 ones). The effect was that our cost of goods sold for the year is higher than it would have been if we had sold the old batch of items before we sold items from the new batch. (Are you following me?) So my attitude is, "Well, que sera sera." Well, that's not my boss's attitude. This morning he came into my office and actually asked me to "recost" the inventory and cost of goods sold assuming that we sold the items in the old batch first and then sold items from the new batch. But we didn't!! Of course, his method would make the cost of goods sold that we report in our income statement lower and our net income higher. So the company would look better. But something about this really galls me. My friends say: "So what? What difference does it make?" Help! You can call me

"Ethical Ethyl" (or not)

Required: Meet with your Dr. Decisive team and write a response to "Ethical Ethyl."

CHAPTER OUTLINE

PART 4

PLANNING IN A CORPORATE ENVIRONMENT

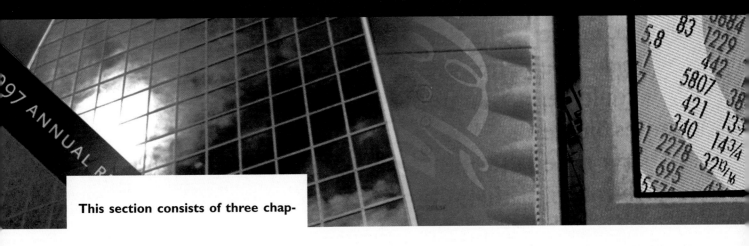

This section consists of three chapters which introduce you to corporations, and how planning in large companies differs from planning in small companies. After reading these chapters, you will be able to:

▶ *explain the organizational structure of a corporation*

▶ *describe the unique features of a corporation's financial statements*

▶ *understand the differences between variable, fixed, and mixed costs*

▶ *use multiple product cost-volume-profit analysis in business decisions*

▶ *prepare a master budget for a manufacturing company*

▶ *use a master budget in the evaluation of a large company's responsibility centers*

CHAPTER 10

INTRODUCTION TO CORPORATIONS:
STRUCTURES, REPORTS, AND ANALYSES

"When something goes wrong in a large corporation, you blame the bureaucracy. When something goes wrong in your small company, there is no one to blame but yourself."

—Unknown

1 *What are the three most common forms of business organizations and their basic characteristics?*

2 *What are the qualities that make accounting information about large corporations useful for decision-making?*

3 *What do users need to know about the stockholders' equity section of a corporation's balance sheet and about its income statement?*

4 *How does a corporation provide information to external users?*

5 *How do users perform intracompany and intercompany analyses?*

6 *What is percentage analysis, and what are its three types?*

Starting with this chapter, we begin to study how accounting information helps managers, investors, and creditors of larger companies make business decisions. There are many similarities in how small and large companies operate. Both use cost-volume-profit (C-V-P) analysis, budgeting, and a GAAP-based accounting system. But, in part because large companies are more complex, there are many differences in the ways these companies make decisions and use accounting information. Large companies have a more formal and well-defined organizational and decision-making structure. In a small company, the owner-manager decides when to order additional inventory, to which customers to extend credit, or how to get the resources needed to expand. A large company usually has entire departments that deal with each of these issues. Large companies also usually have a complex ownership structure.

As we mentioned in Chapter 1, there are three main forms of business organizations: sole proprietorships, partnerships, and corporations. Corporations generally are larger than sole proprietorships or partnerships. In fact, although less than 20 percent of U.S. companies are corporations, they make 90 percent of all U.S. sales.

Most large retail or manufacturing companies are corporations. As a result of incorporating, companies must follow additional laws and regulations. And although companies of all sizes face complicated business decisions, such as determining whether to rent or buy equipment, larger companies are more likely to do so.

In this chapter, we introduce several aspects of the environment in which larger corporations operate. First, we explain the legal forms and characteristics of different business organizations. Second, we discuss the structure of large corporations. Third, we discuss the qualities that make accounting information about large corporations useful for decision-making. Fourth, we focus on the unique aspects of financial reporting for large corporations. Finally, we discuss what financial information about corporations external decision-makers use and how they use it.

1 *What are the three most common forms of business organizations and their basic characteristics?*

www.atitech.com

www.daytons.com

www.ey.com

www.equuscap.com

www.deltaca.com

www.generalmills.com

www.ul.com

Forms of Business Organizations

Think about the following names of companies:

ATI Technologies, Incorporated

Dayton Hudson Corporation

Ernst & Young LLP

Equus Capital Partners, LP

Delta Electronics, Incorporated

General Mills Corporation

Underwriters Laboratories Incorporated

Did you notice several words the names have in common? Five of the companies include either "corporation" or "incorporated" in their name. Two companies include the letters "LP" or "LLP" in their title. Why do companies include these designations in their names? These designations reveal a company's form of organization. The word *corporation,* or *incorporated,* indicates that the company is a separate legal entity known as a corporation. The "P" in LP and LLP stands for partnership. (We will discuss the L and LL later.)

Choosing a company's legal form is an important decision for the company's owners to make. For example, as a company owner, this decision determines how laws and regulations affect your personal responsibility to pay the company's debts. When choosing among legal forms, you need to know the characteristics and advantages and disadvantages of each. Once you select a legal form and start operating your company, laws and regulations specific to your type of company will affect some of your business decisions. In this section we discuss the three most common forms of business organizations: sole proprietorships, partnerships, and corporations. In addition, we explain how some aspects of these forms have been combined to create three other forms: limited partnerships, limited liability partnerships, and Subchapter S corporations.

Sole Proprietorships

A **sole proprietorship** is a company owned by one person who is the sole investor of capital into the company. Because Anna Cox is the only investor in Sweet Temptations, this company is an example of a sole proprietorship. In general, sole proprietorships are small companies that focus either on selling merchandise or on performing a service. Many of the small shops you see downtown are sole proprietorships.

Usually, the owner of a sole proprietorship also manages the company. The owner makes the company's important decisions, such as when to purchase equipment, how much debt to incur, and to which customers to extend credit. In the United States, tax laws and regulations require each owner of a sole proprietorship to report and pay taxes on his or her company's taxable income. The company's taxable income is included in the owner's individual income tax return; there is no separate income tax return for a sole proprietorship. So, the owner adds the income from the sole proprietorship to his or her other sources of income, such as wages earned from other jobs and interest received from bank deposits. In the case of Sweet Temptations, Anna Cox includes with her personal income tax return a schedule that reports Sweet Temptations' taxable income. She includes this amount in her total personal taxable income. Anna calculates her personal income tax liability based on all her sources of income. In addition to income taxes, individuals who operate a sole proprietorship must pay self-employment taxes. These taxes are similar to social security taxes, and the owner also calculates and reports them on his or her individual tax return.

U.S. laws state that an owner of a sole proprietorship must assume personal responsibility for the debts incurred by the company. This requirement is referred to as **unlimited liability.** Unlimited liability may be a problem for the owner of a sole proprietorship because if the company cannot pay its debts, the company's creditors may force the owner to use his or her personal assets to pay them. So, if the sole proprietorship becomes insolvent, the owner may lose *more than* the amount of capital he or she invested in the company. Thus, unlimited liability adds additional financial risk for the owner of a sole proprietorship.

The life of a sole proprietorship is linked directly to its individual owner. Basically, a sole proprietorship ceases to exist when the owner decides to stop operating as a sole proprietor. If the owner of a sole proprietorship decides to sell the company, the owner's sole proprietorship dissolves, and the new owner or owners must choose the new company's form of business organization. Because of these characteristics, a sole proprietorship is said to have a **limited life.**

Partnerships

 Have you ever shared the purchase and use of an item with someone? Maybe you share a computer or an apartment. How do you decide how much money each contributes? How do you split the costs of software, rent, or insurance?

By definition, a sole proprietorship is owned by only one person. What if two or three people come up with a great business idea and want to start a company? What if the owner of a sole proprietorship wants someone else to invest in her company? One option is for the individuals to operate their company as a partnership. A **partnership** is a company owned by two or more individuals who each invest capital into the company.

Individuals must make many decisions before starting a partnership. These decisions include the following:

1. The dollar amount each partner will invest

2. The percentage of the partnership each individual will own

3. How to allocate and distribute partnership income to each partner

4. How business decisions will be made

5. The steps to be taken if a partner withdraws from the partnership or if a new partner is added

To limit disagreements, partners should always sign a contract, called a **partnership agreement,** before their company begins operations. This is a good idea even if partners are best friends or close relatives. This agreement specifies the terms of the formation, operation, and termination of the partnership. It defines the nature of the business, the types and number of partners, the capital contributions required of each partner, the duties of each partner, the conditions for admission or withdrawal of a partner, the method of allocating income to each partner, and the distribution of assets when the partnership is terminated.[1]

Characteristics of Partnerships

 What concerns would you have about joining a partnership? Why?

Partnerships have many characteristics that are similar to those of sole proprietorships. Each partner is required by tax laws and regulations to report his or her share of the partnership's income on his or her individual income tax return. Laws and regulations regarding unlimited liability also apply to partnerships. In addition, a partnership has a **limited life.** It terminates whenever the partners change (i.e., when a partner leaves the partnership or when a new partner is added).

Of course, there is a basic difference between partnerships and sole proprietorships in that a partnership requires two or more owners. Several partnership characteristics relate to the co-ownership feature. To understand these characteristics, assume that Anna Cox invites her friend, Sanjeev Patal, to form Sweet Temptations as a partnership. If Sanjeev is like most other people, the first thing he would think is "What would I be getting myself into?" Because of a partnership's legal and business characteristics, he may be getting into more than he thinks. One important characteristic to know is that all the partners jointly own all the assets owned by a partnership; this is called **joint ownership.** Therefore, if Sanjeev contributes his property to the partnership, it no longer belongs to him alone.

Before entering a partnership, you should also know that each partner is an agent of the partnership. An **agent** is a person who has the authority to act for another. Thus a partner has the power to enter into and bind the partnership—and, therefore, all the partners—to any contract within the scope of the business. For example, either Anna or Sanjeev can bind the partnership to contracts for purchasing inventory, hiring employees, leasing a building, purchasing fixtures, or borrowing money. All of these activities are within the normal scope of a retail candy business.

The fact that each partner can obligate the partnership to honor contracts affects the unlimited liability requirements. **Unlimited liability** for a partnership means that each partner is liable for *all* the debts of the partnership. A creditor's claim is on the partnership, but if there are not enough assets to pay the debt, each partner's personal assets may be used to pay the debt. The only personal assets that are excluded are a partner's assets protected by bankruptcy laws, such as a personal residence. If one of the partners uses personal assets to pay the debts of the partnership, that partner has a right to claim a share of the payment from the other partners.

---

[1]If a partnership does not have a formal agreement about how to operate, its partners resolve any disputes by referring to the Uniform Partnership Act. The Uniform Partnership Act, a set of laws adopted by most states, governs the formation, operation, and liquidation of a partnership in the absence of a partnership agreement.

Given the partnership characteristics we just discussed, if you were about to form a partnership, what specific items would you want to include in your partnership agreement?

Partnership Equity

Accounting for the owners' equity of a partnership differs from accounting for the owner's equity of a sole proprietorship (and a corporation). Company transactions that do not affect owners' equity are recorded in the same way regardless of the organizational form. But because a partnership's ownership is divided among the partners, its accounting system has a *Capital* account for each partner.

A partnership's net income is computed in the same way as is the net income for a sole proprietorship. However, because there is more than one owner in a partnership, the net income must be allocated to each partner. Before their company begins operations, the partners need to decide how to split the partnership's net income among themselves and list this allocation in the partnership agreement. Two factors that usually affect the distribution of income among partners are (1) the dollar amount of capital contributed by each partner, and (2) the dollar value of the time each partner spends working for the partnership. These factors are important because the portion of net income allocated to each partner represents the return on his or her investment of capital or time. A partnership includes a schedule at the bottom of its income statement that shows how, and how much, net income is allocated to each partner.

In addition to keeping track of each partner's capital, a partnership's accounting system also has a *Withdrawals* account for each partner. When a partner makes a withdrawal, his or her specific withdrawal account is increased by the amount of that withdrawal.

Corporations

Recall that Unlimited Decadence is a corporation that manufactures candy bars and sells them to companies like Sweet Temptations. Although a corporation is made up of individual owners, the law treats it as a separate "being." A **corporation** is a separate legal entity that is independent of its owners and is run by a board of directors. Hence, it has a *continuous* life beyond that of any particular owner. Therefore, it has a number of advantages. Because of the legal separation of the owners and the company, ownership in a corporation may be easily passed from one individual to another. Briefly, here's how it works. In exchange for contributing capital to the corporation, owners of a corporation receive shares of the corporation's *capital stock*. Hence, they are called **stockholders.** These shares of stock are the "ownership units" of the corporation and are *transferable.* That is, the current stockholders can transfer or sell their shares to new owners. As we discuss later, the capital stock of many corporations sells on organized stock markets such as the New York Stock Exchange, the American Stock Exchange, the Tokyo Stock Exchange, and the London Stock Exchange. So stockholders of these corporations can sell their shares to new owners more easily.

www.nyse.com
www.amex.com
www.tse.or.jp
www.londonstockex.
  co.uk

Because a corporation is a separate legal entity, a stockholder has no personal liability for the corporation's debts. Therefore each stockholder's liability is limited to his or her investment. Corporations tend to be larger than sole proprietorships and partnerships, so to operate, they need more capital invested by owners. Since transferring ownership is easy and since stockholders have *limited liability,* corporations can usually attract a large number of *diverse investors* and the large amounts of capital needed to operate. Corporations also can attract *top-quality managers* to operate the different departments, so stockholders are not involved in the corporations' operating decisions.

There also are several disadvantages of a corporation. As a separate legal entity, a corporation must pay federal and state income taxes on its taxable income. It reports this income on an income tax return for corporations. The maximum federal income tax rate for corporations is currently 35 percent, but since many of them also pay state income taxes, it is not unusual for the combined income taxes to be more than 40 percent of a corporation's taxable income. If some, or all, of the after-tax income of the corporation (the other

60 percent of the corporation's taxable income) is distributed to stockholders as dividends, the stockholders again may be taxed on this personal income. This is referred to as **double taxation.**

 Why do you think this is called double taxation? Is the stockholder taxed twice? Why or why not?

As we discussed earlier in this chapter, for a sole proprietorship or a partnership, the owners may have to use personal assets to pay the company's debts. However, since the owners (stockholders) of a corporation have limited liability, a corporation (particularly a smaller one) may find it more difficult to borrow money. Since the creditors can't go to the owners for payment, they may think there is more risk of not being paid.

Corporations also are subject to *more government regulation.* For instance, the federal and state governments have laws to protect creditors and owners. For example, the laws of the state in which it is incorporated usually limit the payment of dividends by a corporation. Since creditors cannot go to the owners of a corporation for payment of its debts, limiting the corporation's dividend payments is a way of protecting creditors—the corporation may have more resources with which to pay its debts. In addition, if a corporation's capital stock is traded in the stock market, the corporation must file specified reports with the Securities and Exchange Commission.

However, the advantages of a corporation usually exceed the disadvantages when a business grows to a reasonable size. Exhibit 10-1 summarizes the characteristics of each type of business organization.

Other Legal Forms of Business Organizations

Remember the company names we listed at the start of this section? Two companies had the letters LP or LLP in their names (Equus Capital Partners, LP and Ernst & Young LLP). The initials "LP" stand for "limited partnership," and the initials "LLP" stand for "limited liability partnership." Both types of partnerships were created by law to reduce the unlimited liability of partners.

Exhibit 10-1   General Characteristics of Each Form of Business Organization

Characteristics	Sole Proprietorships	Partnerships	Corporations
Number of owner(s)	Single owner	Two or more owners (partners)	Usually many owners (stockholders)
Size of businesses	Small	Most are small; some professional partnerships (e.g., law firms) have several hundred partners.	Many are very large; some may have stock traded on an exchange.
Examples of businesses that typically have this legal form	Small retail shops; local service or repair shops; single practitioners such as CPAs, lawyers, doctors	Law firms; CPA firms; real estate agencies; family-owned businesses	Manufacturing companies; multinational companies; retail store chains; fast-food chains
Who makes business decisions	Owner	Depends on partnership agreement. Small partnerships will have all partners involved in business decisions; large partnerships will have managing partners. Partners are agents.	Decided by board of directors. Large corporations are managed by business professionals who often own little or no stock.
Liability of Owner(s)	Unlimited	Unlimited	Limited
Life of Organization	Limited	Limited	Continuous

Why should the government pass laws limiting a partner's liability? In the case of limited partnerships, the laws were enacted to protect partners who are not active in the management of a large partnership, so that they won't lose more money than they invested. In a limited partnership only certain partners (usually the partners who originally set up the partnership) have unlimited liability. These partners are called "general partners." Other investors (called "limited partners") in a limited partnership do not have unlimited liability. Instead of having all their personal assets at risk, limited partners may lose only the amount of money they invested in the limited partnership.

In recent years, laws have been passed that allow large public accounting firms and other types of partnerships to become limited liability partnerships. The CPA profession actively lobbied the U.S. Congress and state legislatures to enact legislation allowing limited liability partnerships. These types of partnerships limit, to a prescribed amount, *each* partner's risk of losing his or her personal assets as a result of ownership in an LLP.

Another form of business organization, a Subchapter S corporation, is available to small businesses. A Subchapter S corporation maintains the attractive features of corporate ownership. The distinctive feature of these corporations is that the owners—not the corporation—pay income taxes on corporate income. Thus, owners of a Subchapter S corporation are not subject to double taxation.

In the sections that follow, we will make general statements about the characteristics of corporations. Because corporations are subject to state laws, which may differ, these general statements may not always be entirely accurate. However, the general overview will help you understand what you need to know for later discussions.

Starting a Corporation

To operate as a corporation in the United States, a company must be incorporated in one of the states. **Incorporation** is the process of filing the required documents and obtaining permission from a state to operate as a corporation. The state-approved documents are called **articles of incorporation.**

After the state approves the incorporation, the individuals who filed for incorporation meet to complete several important tasks. First, they distribute among themselves the first issuance of capital stock. (As holders of the company's stock, these individuals have the right to vote on major corporate policies and decisions.) Then they (the stockholders) decide on, among other things, (1) a set of rules (bylaws) to regulate the corporation's operations, (2) a board of directors to supervise the corporation's ordinary business activities, and (3) a team of people to serve in top management positions.

Not all corporations are huge companies like General Motors or Exxon. Some corporations are small companies that are owned by one person or a few people. The owners of small companies set them up as corporations because the owners want the legal benefits of incorporation, primarily limited liability. If a corporation is owned by a small number of investors, it is called a **closely-held corporation.** The stock of a closely-held corporation may not be purchased by the general public, and the board of directors places restrictions on the selling of stock by current stockholders. Generally, closely-held corporations are relatively small, although some, such as Hallmark Corporation (the company that makes Hallmark greeting cards) and Mars Inc. (the company that manufactures M&Ms, the Milky Way candy bar, Kal Kan pet food, and Uncle Ben's rice), are very large multinational companies.

www.gm.com
www.exxon.com

www.hallmark.com
www.mars.com

Publicly-held corporations sell their stock to the general public, and generally there are no restrictions on the selling of stock by current stockholders. After a corporation sells its stock to the public in what is called an **initial public offering** (or IPO), the stock begins to trade in a secondary equity market. The **secondary equity market** is where investors buy the stock of corporations from other investors rather than from the corporations. This means that the corporations have already issued this stock. In these secondary markets, the stock is traded between new and current stockholders, so the corporation is not involved in the trade.

A typical trading day on the New York Stock Exchange.

Today, the secondary equity market is well established and plays an important role in the global economy. The New York, American, Tokyo, and London Stock Exchanges are just a few of the national organizations in the secondary equity market, and they trade the stocks of thousands of corporations. For example, on an average day, the New York Stock Exchange (NYSE) trades over 670 million shares of stock.[2] By contacting a stockbroker, you can purchase stock in companies such as Hershey's or Matsushita Electric.

 Assume you plan to invest $1,000. Think of three publicly-held corporations. Which would you invest in? Why? What factors would influence your decision?

The Organizational Structure of Large Corporations

 Do you think the size of a company affects how it interacts with its customers? employees? suppliers? If so, why?

After the incorporation process is completed, a corporation begins operations. Recall that companies are created to achieve two specific goals: to earn a satisfactory profit by providing services or products to customers and to remain solvent. To accomplish these goals, each company must be organized into a structure that makes clear the jobs and working relationships of the employees of that company. This structure shows who is responsible for each task, whether it is an individual or a work team, and who reports to whom.

In a small company, the structure may be simple. The owner makes all of the important business decisions, and all of the company's employees report directly to the owner. This is consistent with our discussion in Chapter 9 of working capital controls. However, as a company grows (e.g., hires more employees, opens additional stores, uses more suppliers), the owner will have more difficulty managing all of the company's activities. Also, the owner may not have the desire, or ability, to manage a larger organization. Eventually, the owner delegates some of these responsibilities to other managers. At this point, the small company starts to become a large company and may incorporate.

---

[2]*NYSE Quick Reference Sheet* (New York: NYSE, November 30, 1998).

The organizational structure of a large corporation can be divided logically in a number of ways, such as by type of customer, by type of product, by geographical location, or by function. Whatever the organization, however, almost all large companies have functional areas involving marketing, production, human resources, finance, and distribution. All large companies also have an information technology component, but its personnel generally work in each functional area. In most companies, the **marketing** function identifies consumer needs, analyzes consumer behavior, evaluates customer satisfaction, and promotes the company's products. The **production** function is a manufacturing activity that uses people and equipment to convert materials, components, and parts into products that the company will sell to customers. The **human resources** function is responsible for managing the company's employee-related activities, such as recruiting, hiring, training, and compensating employees, as well as providing a safe workplace. The **finance** function plans the company's capital requirements for both the short and the long term. This involves locating sources of capital and investing excess cash inside or outside of the United States. This unit is also responsible for accounting activities. The **distribution** function makes products available to customers through physical distribution systems. Exhibit 10-2 summarizes the responsibilities within each function. The management of a corporation uses accounting information to identify, estimate, control, and report the costs of the marketing, production, human resources, finance, and distribution functions.

Enterprise Resource Planning Systems

In Chapter 1, we discussed an *integrated accounting system* in which accounting information about a company's activities is identified, measured, recorded, and retained so that it can be communicated in an accounting report. We pointed out that the managers of a company use the information in the accounting reports from the integrated accounting system to help them make decisions. Many corporations are now "reengineering" their operations by installing **enterprise resource planning (ERP) systems,** of which the integrated accounting system is one part. An ERP system involves computer software that is "multi-functional." That is, the software records and stores many different types of data (e.g., units, quantities, times, prices, names, pay rates, and addresses, to name a few) in a *data warehouse.* The software is "integrated" so that a manager who is in the process of making a decision can perform *data mining* to extract useful information from the data warehouse. Companies like SAP, Oracle, and PeopleSoft are developing and improving ERP systems to help the managers in a corporation's marketing, production, human resources, finance, and distribution functions use this computer technology to improve their decisions. We will discuss how corporations are reengineering various aspects of their operations relating to accounting in later chapters.

www.sap.com
www.oracle.com
www.peoplesoft.com

Qualities of Useful Accounting Information

Given the size, complexity, and wide dispersion of ownership of large corporations, summarizing and reporting useful accounting information to internal and external users is a

Exhibit 10-2 Business Functional Units

Marketing	Production	Human Resources	Finance	Distribution
Identifying consumer needs	Converting materials into products	Recruiting, hiring, training, terminating employees	Locating cash resources	Moving products from company to customer
Analyzing consumer behavior	Overseeing purchasing	Compensating employees	Investing excess cash	Moving products within company
Evaluating customer satisfaction	Controlling production	Providing safe working conditions	Accounting	Protecting inventory
Promoting products				Processing orders

challenging task. In later chapters, we will discuss how managers develop and use tools such as C-V-P analysis and master budgeting for internal decision-making in large corporations. In the remainder of this chapter, we focus on financial reporting for external decision-making. Two of the major advantages of the corporate form of organization—the ease of transferring ownership and the ability to attract large amounts of capital—have a significant effect on financial reporting.

As a small sole proprietorship, Sweet Temptations uses its financial reporting to provide information to Anna Cox and to the bank that makes loans to Sweet Temptations. A large corporation has many external users who also are interested in its financial information. They include individual investors, stockbrokers, and financial analysts who offer investment assistance. They also include consultants, bankers, suppliers, employees, labor unions, and local, state, and federal governments. In this section we discuss many of the qualities that accounting information should have in order to be useful to these external decision-makers.

 Suppose you are a banker trying to decide whether to grant a loan to a company. When the company provides its financial information to you for your decision, what qualities would you want that information to have?

Conceptual Framework and Decision Usefulness

As an aid in establishing GAAP for financial reporting, the Financial Accounting Standards Board (FASB) has developed a **conceptual framework.** This framework is a set of concepts that provides a logical structure for financial accounting and reporting. Under this conceptual framework, the general objective of financial reporting is to provide useful information for external users in their decision-making. Therefore, in the United States, *improving external decision-making* is the primary purpose of financial accounting information. Other countries may have other objectives for financial accounting information, such as satisfying government requirements for computing income taxes, demonstrating compliance with the government's economic plan, or monitoring social responsibility activities.

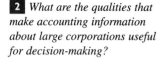 **2** *What are the qualities that make accounting information about large corporations useful for decision-making?*

To be useful for external decision-making, financial accounting information must be relevant and reliable. Closely related to relevance and reliability are materiality and validity. We show these qualities of useful information in Exhibit 10-3. Although these concepts apply to financial reporting, they are equally applicable to management accounting information used for internal decision-making.

Relevant Accounting Information

Accounting information is **relevant** when it has the capacity to influence a user's decision. For example, suppose Second National Bank is considering whether to loan Unlimited Decadence money to be used for the purchase of new production equipment. The amount of cash in Unlimited Decadence's checking and savings accounts and the

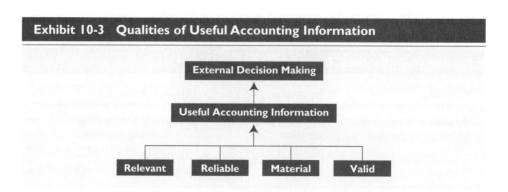

Exhibit 10-3 Qualities of Useful Accounting Information

cash it expects to collect from sales and to pay its suppliers are relevant for the banker's decision.

 If you were buying a new car, what information about the car would be relevant to you?

Reliable Accounting Information

Even if information is relevant, users must have confidence that the information they are using for decision-making is reliable. Accounting information is **reliable** when it is capable of being verified. Reliability does not always mean certainty. For example, Unlimited Decadence may be able to reliably *estimate* how many of its credit sales will not be collectible if there has been a uniform pattern of uncollectibility in the past. Source documents such as invoices, cash receipts, and canceled checks play an important part in verifying the reliability of accounting information.

 If you have a checking account, how do you verify the ending balance on your monthly bank statement? Do you consider the information reliable? Why or why not?

Materiality

Materiality is like relevance because both concepts relate to influencing a user of accounting information. Accounting information is **material** when the monetary amount is large enough to make a difference in a user's decision. Only material accounting information should be accumulated and communicated to users. Materiality is relative, however. A $1,000 purchase may be material to you but may be only a "drop in the bucket" to someone like Celine Dion or Michael Jordan. Similarly, what is material accounting information for Sweet Temptations may not be material for a company like Unlimited Decadence because of their different sizes.

Many users consider that an item *is not* material if its dollar amount is less than 5% and *is* material if the dollar amount is more than 10%. But the question here is, 5% or 10% of what? If an item is related to the income statement, then a user could use net income, gross profit, or some other summary amount (or even a single item) as the basis for comparison. So, for instance, if an income statement item is 12% of a company's net income, a user would generally consider the item to be material relative to net income. If another item is 3% of sales, the user would generally consider the item to be immaterial relative to sales. If an item is related to the balance sheet, then a user could use total assets, total liabilities, total owners' equity, or a summary amount such as current assets or working capital (or even a single item) as a basis for comparison. Furthermore, a user has to decide whether an amount between 5% and 10% is, or is not, material. So you should understand that materiality is a concept that involves significant judgment and critical thinking.

 How much would you consider as a material difference in prices in purchasing a new mountain bike? a new car?

Valid Accounting Information

Validity is closely related to reliability. Accounting information is **valid** when it shows a realistic picture of what it is meant to represent. To be valid, accounting information must realistically portray the results of a company's activities and financial position. Valid accounting information is like a good videotape or snapshot from a camera that does not distort the real picture (unlike your driver's license photo).

Keep these qualities in mind as you consider how to accumulate and use financial and management accounting information. We now turn to financial reporting for large corporations.

Unique Features of a Corporation's Financial Statements

3 *What do users need to know about the stockholders' equity section of a corporation's balance sheet and about its income statement?*

Financial statements for corporations follow the same structure that we discussed in earlier chapters and illustrated with Sweet Temptations. A corporation's balance sheet shows the dollar amounts of its assets, liabilities, and owners' equity on a specific date. Its income statement reports revenues, expenses, and net income for a specific period of time. The cash flow statement shows the corporation's cash receipts and payments from operating, investing, and financing activities for a specific period. Like Sweet Temptations, corporations prepare these financial statements according to GAAP.

However, the size and complexity of large corporations requires additional information. Some of this information relates to two aspects of a corporation's financial statements: (1) the equity section of its balance sheet, and (2) the presentation of earnings on its income statement.

Equity in a Corporation

The laws of each state apply to companies incorporated in that state. Various state laws require special accounting procedures for the owners' equity of a corporation. States passed these laws to help protect the absentee owners of a corporation (those not directly involved in the management of the company) as well as its creditors.

Corporate Capital Structure

The owners' equity of a corporation is called **stockholders' equity** because the owners of a corporation are called stockholders. Usually there are many stockholders of a corporation, and frequent changes in ownership can occur; as a result, maintaining separate capital accounts for each owner would be impractical. Instead, the stockholders' equity on a corporation's balance sheet is usually separated into two sections: contributed capital and retained earnings.[3] This division of stockholders' equity is required by state laws.

The **contributed capital** section shows the total investments made by stockholders in the corporation. As we will discuss in the next section, this section usually consists of two parts—capital stock and additional paid-in capital. The **retained earnings** reports the corporation's total lifetime net income that has been reinvested in the corporation and not distributed to stockholders as dividends.

Capital Stock and Legal Capital

Capital stock refers to the ownership units in the corporation. There are two types of capital stock: common stock and preferred stock. If a corporation issues only one type of stock, this is called **common stock.** If a corporation also issues another type of stock, that stock is called **preferred stock.** The differences between common stock and preferred stock involve stockholders' rights, and we will discuss these differences in Chapter 24. Here we focus on common stock.

A corporation may issue common stock for cash. It also may trade stock for an asset such as land or equipment. When an investor buys stock from the corporation, the corporation records the issuance (selling) price using both a Common Stock account and an Additional Paid-in Capital account. To protect creditors, state laws require corporations to keep in the company a minimum amount of the capital contributed by the owners. This is called legal capital. Usually, **legal capital** is a monetary amount per share of common stock, called the **par value.** The par value is stated in the articles of incorporation and is printed on each stock certificate. The par value of a share of common stock is often set very low—perhaps $10, $2, or even less per share—and has *no* relationship to the value of the stock. The total legal capital of a corporation is determined by multiplying the par value per share by the number of shares issued. Generally, states require companies to keep track

---

[3] A corporation may also have a section called "accumulated other comprehensive income." We will discuss this section in Chapter 23.

of legal capital, so each time a corporation issues common stock, *it records the par value (legal capital) in the Common Stock account.*

Additional Paid-In Capital

The total dollar amount the corporation receives from selling its stock is called the **market value** of the stock. Corporations normally sell common stock at a market value much higher than the par value. So, legal capital is usually only a small part of the total selling price. When a corporation sells common stock, in addition to recording the par value in a Common Stock account it also records the excess of the market value over the par value. The excess value it receives is called additional paid-in capital. **Additional paid-in capital** is the difference between the selling price and the par value in each stock transaction and is recorded in an Additional Paid-in Capital account.

Now that you have this background, we can explain how the accounting system keeps track of one kind of common stock transaction—common stock issued for cash. We will explain other kinds of common stock transactions in Chapter 24.

Common Stock Sold for Cash

To understand the issuance of common stock, assume that Unlimited Decadence Corporation sells 30,000 shares of its $3 par value common stock for $16 per share. Using the T-account approach, it records the transaction as follows:

Assets	=	Liabilities	+	Stockholders' Equity

Cash			Common Stock ($3 par)	
480,000				90,000
(+)	(−)		(−)	(+)

	Additional Paid-in Capital	
		390,000
	(−)	(+)

As a result of this transaction, Unlimited Decadence increases assets (cash) by $480,000 (30,000 × $16), the total amount of capital invested in the corporation. Because Unlimited Decadence received the $480,000 from investors, it also increases stockholders' equity by $480,000 in the following manner. To adhere to state laws, Unlimited Decadence increases its common stock account by the $90,000 (30,000 shares × $3) par value (legal capital), and increases additional paid-in capital by the $390,000 difference between the total selling price and the total par value ($480,000 − $90,000 = $390,000).

Stockholders' Equity Section of Balance Sheet

As we said earlier, the stockholders' equity section of a corporation's balance sheet has two parts: (1) contributed capital, and (2) retained earnings. Contributed capital includes common stock (the legal value) and additional paid-in capital, and shows the total capital invested in the corporation by its owners.

Exhibit 10-4 shows the stockholders' equity of Unlimited Decadence's balance sheet at December 31, 2000. As of this date, the stockholders of Unlimited Decadence have invested $8,140,000 in the corporation in exchange for 1,200,000 shares of common stock. Unlimited Decadence's common stock totals $3,600,000 ($3 par value × 1,200,000 shares), and additional paid-in capital totals $4,540,000 ($8,140,000 − $3,600,000). Because these numbers are large, Unlimited Decadence shows the amounts on its balance sheet in thousands of dollars. This is a common practice of many large corporations.

Exhibit 10-4 Unlimited Decadence Corporation

Stockholders' Equity Section of Balance Sheet
December 31, 2000
(in thousands of dollars)

Stockholders' Equity
Contributed capital
    Common stock, 1,200,000 shares issued ($3 par value)....................$ 3,600
    Additional paid-in capital... 4,540
    Contributed capital ....$ 8,140
Retained earnings 9,060
Total Stockholders' Equity $17,200

Some corporations are so large that they show their balance sheet amounts in *millions* of dollars!

The **retained earnings** reported in a corporation's stockholders' equity is the amount of its lifetime net income that has been reinvested in the corporation to date.[4] As we show in Exhibit 10-4, at December 31, 2000, the retained earnings for Unlimited Decadence is $9,060,000. The total stockholders' equity of Unlimited Decadence is $17,200,000, the sum of the $8,140,000 contributed capital and the $9,060,000 retained earnings.

Corporate Earnings

 When investors are evaluating a corporation, should they be concerned with how the corporation earned its net income? Do you think every dollar of income a corporation earns is equally important to investors? Why or why not?

The income statement of a corporation may contain several sections. Each section helps financial statement users better understand how a corporation earned its net income. Generally, a corporation will show separately (1) the earnings that resulted from its "continuing" operations, (2) the earnings that resulted from other, "nonrecurring" activities, and (3) the earnings per share of common stock. The nonrecurring earnings might include the income or loss from "discontinued operations" (such as PepsiCo, Inc.'s earnings from Pizza Hut, Taco Bell, and KFC in the year that it sold them) and any income or loss from "extraordinary" events (such as a tornado). We will discuss these nonrecurring items in Chapter 24.[5] Here, we discuss the two most common sections—income from continuing operations and earnings per share. Unlimited Decadence's income statement for the year ended December 31, 2000 (shown in Exhibit 10-5)[6] illustrates how the company reported these two sections (it did not have any nonrecurring earnings).

www.pepsico.com
www.pizzahut.com
www.tacobell.com
www.kfc.com

Income from Continuing Operations

Income from continuing operations reports a corporation's revenues and expenses that resulted from its ongoing operations. For Unlimited Decadence, this section reports the revenues and expenses from the manufacture and sale of candy bars.

This section includes **operating income,** which is determined by subtracting cost of goods sold from net sales to obtain gross profit, and then by deducting the selling expenses and the general and administrative expenses. As we show in Exhibit 10-5, the operating in-

---

[4]In its closing entries (which we discussed in Chapter 6), a corporation closes its Income Summary account to its Retained Earnings account.

[5]A corporation may also have "other comprehensive income," which we will also discuss in Chapter 24.

[6]For simplicity, we assume here that Unlimited Decadence sells only one type of candy bar. We will relax this assumption in Chapter 11.

Exhibit 10-5 Unlimited Decadence Corporation

Income Statement
For Year Ended December 31, 2000
(in thousands of dollars)

Sales (net)		$72,800
Cost of goods sold		(46,500)
Gross profit		$26,300
Operating expenses		
Selling expenses	$13,840	
General and administrative expenses	7,670	
Total operating expenses		(21,510)
Operating income		$ 4,790
Other items		
Interest revenue	$ 320	
Interest expense	(210)	
Nonoperating income		110
Pretax income from continuing operations		$ 4,900
Income tax expense		(1,960)
Net Income		$ 2,940
Earnings per share		$ 2.45

come of Unlimited Decadence for 2000 is $4,790,000. (Remember, the numbers shown are rounded to the nearest thousand dollars.)

Income from continuing operations also includes nonoperating income, in a section called **other items.** These other (nonoperating) items include revenues and expenses that frequently occur in a company but do not relate specifically to the company's primary operating activities. Interest expense, interest revenue, and gains (or losses) are common examples of other items. We will discuss gains and losses later in the book. (A company reports a $2,000 gain, for example, when it sells for $10,000 some land that it owns and that cost $8,000.) The amounts of the other items are summed to determine the other income (or loss). Under other items, Unlimited Decadence reports $320,000 of interest revenue and $210,000 of interest expense, so that its other income is $110,000.

A corporation's operating income is added to the other income to determine its pretax income from continuing operations. For Unlimited Decadence, the $4,790,000 operating income is added to the $110,000 other income to determine its $4,900,000 pretax income from continuing operations.

As we discussed earlier, corporations must pay income taxes on their earnings. **Income tax expense** is listed separately within this section. Unlimited Decadence is subject to a 40 percent income tax rate on its pretax (taxable) income, so its income tax expense is $1,960,000 ($4,900,000 × 0.40). This amount is subtracted from the pretax income from continuing operations to get the company's $2,940,000 income from continuing operations.

If Unlimited Decadence had nonrecurring earnings, it would report these items (and the related income tax expense) below income from continuing operations. Because Unlimited Decadence had no nonrecurring earnings during 2000, the income from continuing operations is called "net income."

Earnings Per Share

A corporation's net income is earned for all the corporation's stockholders. Because the common stock for most large corporations is owned by many stockholders, it is useful to report a corporation's net income on a per-share basis. **Earnings per share (EPS)** is the amount of net income earned for each share of common stock. In its simplest form, earnings per share is computed by dividing the corporation's net income for the accounting period by the average number of shares of common stock owned by all of the corporation's stockholders during the period.

All corporations must report earnings per share on their income statements, and it is the last item they show. On its income statement in Exhibit 10-5, Unlimited Decadence shows earnings per share of $2.45. We can prove that this amount is correct by dividing its net income by the number of shares of common stock[7] reported in the stockholders' equity section of its balance sheet:

$$\text{Earnings Per Share} = \frac{\text{Net Income}}{\text{Average Number of Common Shares}} = \frac{\$2,940,000}{1,200,000} = \underline{\underline{\$2.45}}$$

If a corporation has several sections on its income statement or if the number of shares that stockholders own changes during the year, the calculation of earnings per share is more complicated. We will discuss this calculation in Chapter 24.

Financial Information Used in Decision-Making

External users analyze the financial statements of a company to determine how well the company is achieving its two primary goals—remaining solvent and earning a satisfactory profit. In the case of a small company, owners and creditors can also discuss the company's financial performance with its managers. However, in a large corporation, this is usually not possible.

If investors and creditors in large corporations are given few or no opportunities to ask its managers about its operations or plans, how do they get the information they need to make business decisions? Individuals investing in large corporations must rely on publicly available information when making their investment decisions. **Publicly available information** is any information released to the public; it may come directly from the corporation or from secondary sources.

Information Reported by Corporations

4 *How does a corporation provide information to external users?*

Much of the information that investors and creditors use to evaluate a corporation comes directly from the corporation. Corporations use four methods to supply information to external users: (1) annual reports, (2) Securities and Exchange Commission (SEC) reports, (3) interim financial statements, and (4) media releases.

Annual Reports

www.potlatch.com

www.coors.com

Corporations publish their annual financial statements as part of their **annual report.** In addition to the current year's financial statements, most corporations include the financial statements of the previous two years. These are called **comparative financial statements** and are included to help external users in their analyses.

In addition to the financial statements, a corporate annual report also includes notes to the financial statements, an audit report, financial highlights or a summary, and management's discussion and analysis of the corporation's performance. In a study commissioned by Potlatch Corp., a San Francisco–based paper manufacturer, a majority of portfolio managers and securities analysts ranked annual reports as the most important documents that a company produces, including documents on computer disks and on-line services.

Notes to the financial statements inform external users of the company's accounting policies and of important financial information that is not reported in the financial statements. For example, a note may inform users of a lawsuit against the company. Adolph Coors Company's 1997 notes mentioned a lawsuit that the City of Denver has brought

---

[7]The number of shares of common stock owned by all of Unlimited Decadence's stockholders was 1,200,000 for the entire year, so the average number is also 1,200,000.

against it in regard to pollution-control issues. Although, in 1997, the lawsuit had not resulted in an additional liability for Coors, information about the lawsuit was relevant to users of its financial statements. Investors and creditors should analyze the notes to a company's financial statements before making their investment and credit decisions.

Because financial statements are so important, the Securities and Exchange Commission requires publicly-held corporations to issue audited financial statements. Banks also may require a small company to provide its audited financial statements when applying for a loan. **Auditing** involves the examination of a company's accounting records and financial statements by an independent certified public accountant (CPA). This examination enables the CPA to attest to the fairness of the accounting information in the financial statements. A corporation's annual report includes an **audit report,** such as the one we show in Exhibit 10-6 for the 1998 financial statements of Rocky Mountain Chocolate Factory, Inc.

www.rmcfusa.com

Notice that the audit report consists of three paragraphs. The first paragraph states that an audit was performed for specific years and that the company's management is responsible for preparing the financial statements. In the second paragraph, the audit report briefly describes how an audit is conducted and explains that the auditor is *reasonably* sure (it would cost too much to gather enough information to be *absolutely* sure) that the financial statements do not contain material mistakes.

What do you think makes a mistake "material"?

The third paragraph, called the "opinion paragraph," expresses the auditor's opinion about the fairness of the company's financial statements and states whether or not the audit firm believes that the statements were prepared according to GAAP.

A wide variety of users are interested in the information contained in a company's annual report.

Donald Reilly © 1973 from The New Yorker Collection. All Rights Reserved.

Exhibit 10-6   Rocky Mountain Chocolate Factory, Inc., Audit Report

Report of Independent Certified Public Accountants

Board of Directors and Stockholders
Rocky Mountain Chocolate Factory, Inc.

We have audited the accompanying consolidated balance sheets of Rocky Mountain Chocolate Factory, Inc. as of February 28, 1998 and 1997, and the related statements of operation, stockholders' equity, and cash flows for each of the three years in the period ended February 28, 1998. These financial statements are the responsibility of the Company's management. Our responsibility is to express an opinion on these financial statements based on our audits.

We conducted our audits in accordance with generally accepted auditing standards. Those standards require that we plan and perform the audit to obtain reasonable assurance about whether the financial statements are free of material misstatement. An audit includes examining, on a test basis, evidence supporting the amounts and disclosures in the financial statements. An audit also includes assessing the accounting principles used and significant estimates made by management, as well as evaluating the overall financial statement presentation. We believe our audits provide a reasonable basis for our opinion.

In our opinion, the financial statements referred to above present fairly, in all material respects, the financial position of Rocky Mountain Chocolate Factory, Inc. as of February 28, 1998 and 1997, and the results of their operations and their cash flows for each of the three years in the period ended February 28, 1998, in conformity with generally accepted accounting principles.

Grant Thornton LLP

GRANT THORNTON LLP

Dallas, Texas
April 24, 1998
(except for notes 11 and 13 as to which the dates are June 5, 1998 and May 15, 1998, respectively)

An audit report is important to external users because it provides a measure of assurance that they can rely on the information presented in the financial statements. In Exhibit 10-6, the CPA firm Grant Thornton LLP is telling investors that it believes that Rocky Mountain's financial statements are fair in that they comply with all applicable accounting standards. This type of audit report is referred to as an "unqualified" or "clean" opinion. Around 90 percent of all audit reports are unqualified. If the company's audited financial statements did not comply with GAAP, the auditor would disclose this in the audit report to warn users.

www.gt.com

Companies also include 5-, 10-, or 15-year summaries of key data from their financial statements in their annual report. These are titled **Financial Highlights** or **Financial Summaries.** Some companies merely list revenues, net income, total assets, and other key figures for recent years. Others use such items as graphs, pie charts, and ratio comparisons. As we show in Exhibit 10-7, Hewlett-Packard Company used bar graphs in its 1997 annual report to illustrate how its net revenue and net earnings have increased over time.

www.hp.com

Have you ever handed in a report and wanted the opportunity to explain what you think the report means? When a corporation releases its financial statements to the public, the corporation's managers want to provide their own analysis of its performance and financial condition. As part of the annual report, managers will include sections titled **Management's Discussion and Analysis** (MD&A) and **Letter to Shareholders.** In these sections, managers comment on how well (or poorly) the corporation performed over the past year, specifically in regard to its liquidity, capital, and results of operations. Usually these sections include a discussion about industry and market trends. Managers also discuss their plans for improvement. External users find this information useful because it explains how the corporation's current and planned operations are viewed "through the eyes of management."

Exhibit 10-7 Hewlett-Packard Company: Bar Graphs of Net Revenue and Net Earnings Included in Its 1997 Annual Report

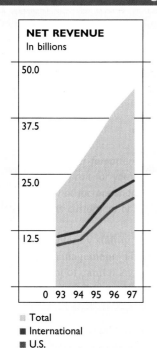

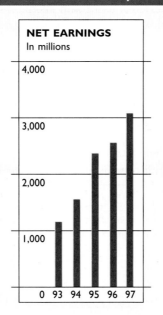

■ Total
■ International
■ U.S.

In The Walt Disney Company annual report for 1998, Mr. Michael Eisner, Chairman and CEO, used a straightforward approach to comment on the company's performance. His letter to shareholders stated: "The bad news is that 1998 was a tough year for us . . . We succumbed to the overall industry trend of paying more and more for talent in front of and behind the camera . . . In too many instances, profits did not materialize from the revenues achieved by our films." His letter then detailed Disney's strategy to improve its performance. Investors, creditors, and other interested parties certainly considered the chairman's comments as they made business decisions regarding Disney.

www.disney.com

If you were a Disney stockholder, what do you think your response would have been to Mr. Eisner's comment? Why do you think you would have reacted that way?

Securities and Exchange Commission (SEC) Reports

In addition to distributing annual reports to the public, corporations file reports with the SEC that are also available to the public. A company offering stock for public sale must file a registration statement with the SEC and must provide potential investors with a "prospectus" containing most of the same information given the SEC. The **prospectus** typically contains the corporation's financial reports and other information, such as a description of the stock to be sold, the offering price, and how the cash received from the sale will be used.

Corporations that have their stock traded on any of the national stock exchanges, such as the New York Stock Exchange, must also file annual 10-K reports with the SEC. A **10-K report** includes the corporation's annual report and other information such as officers' names, salaries, and stock ownership. Corporations file these forms electronically with the SEC. These forms are located in the SEC's Electronic Data Gathering, Analysis, and Retrieval System (commonly known as *EDGAR*). When making business decisions, investors use information in these documents and other SEC filings.

Interim Financial Statements

Companies normally use one year as their accounting period, but many companies also prepare interim financial statements. In fact, corporations registered with the SEC *must* provide external users with interim financial statements (called a *10-Q report).* **Interim financial statements** are financial statements prepared for a period of less than one year. It is most common for corporations to issue interim financial statements on a quarterly basis (every three months). These are published at the end of each quarter, and the quarterly results are also included in the corporation's annual report.

By issuing interim financial statements, corporations provide investors and creditors with new information to use to reevaluate their business decisions (such as whether or not to sell stock purchased in an earlier period) on a more frequent basis.

Media Releases

Corporations also release important financial information in a more timely manner through press conferences and interviews with the media. Research by accounting professors has shown that corporate announcements of earnings, changes in dividend policies, major contracts with the government, and other important business activities affect investors' business decisions and result in changes in a corporation's stock price.

 Suppose Unlimited Decadence announced that last quarter's earnings were double its earnings in the same quarter the previous year. How do you think this announcement would affect Unlimited Decadence's stock price? Why?

Secondary Sources of Information about Corporations

External users do not depend solely on themselves to gather and evaluate information about a corporation's financial position or performance. Data regarding corporations' performances are available through many information services. Furthermore, information about standard industries is regularly published. These industries are identified by their North American Industry Classification System (NAICS) code assigned by the U.S. government. Firms such as Dun & Bradstreet annually publish statistics about the average financial performance of corporations in each NAICS code. Increasingly, computer technology provides vast amounts of data regarding market trends, industry trends, and specific corporate information.

In addition, the financial services industry provides investment advice to investors and creditors. Financial services companies use corporations' publicly available information to evaluate the financial performance of these corporations. Stockbrokerage firms, such as A. G. Edwards and Dean Witter, closely follow market and industry trends and the performance of individual corporations in order to give advice to their clients. These firms provide services to thousands of investors by making purchases and sales of stock for them.

www.dnb.com

www.agedwards.com
www.deanwitter.com

Analysis of Financial Information

5 *How do users perform intracompany and intercompany analyses?*

How do individuals and financial services firms evaluate a corporation's operating performance and financial condition? Basically, there are two approaches. One approach is to compare the corporation's current operations and financial position with its past results or with its expected results. This approach is called **intracompany analysis.** One reason that external users perform intracompany analysis is to help determine *trends* in a corporation's financial performance. In other words, investors and creditors use trends to evaluate whether the corporation's performance is stable, improving, or declining.

 What trends in a corporation's performance do you think are most important? Why?

External users will probably want answers to the following questions about Unlimited Decadence: (1) Did Unlimited Decadence's sales increase over sales in the prior year? If so, what was the percentage growth? (2) Did Unlimited Decadence's net income change from that of the prior year? If so, what was the percentage growth or decline? (3) Is Unlimited Decadence's current ratio continuing to improve over the ratios of prior years? (4) Are Unlimited Decadence's sales growing at a higher rate than its operating expenses?

External users also use intracompany analysis to investigate whether a corporation is meeting *its* performance expectations. Investors and creditors learn about corporate performance expectations from annual reports, media releases, and financial analysts who study corporations' performances. With this data, they can answer important questions about Unlimited Decadence: (1) Did Unlimited Decadence meet the sales projections it disclosed in its prior year's annual report? (2) Did Unlimited Decadence's net income reach the level that financial analysts had predicted? (3) Did Unlimited Decadence make the capital expenditures it announced at earlier meetings? (4) What is the relationship between Unlimited Decadence's earnings and its stock price?

A second approach to analyzing a corporation's financial performance is known as intercompany analysis. **Intercompany analysis** involves comparing a company's performance with that of competing companies, industry averages, or averages in related industries. For example, investors and creditors might want to compare Unlimited Decadence's operating results and financial position with those of <u>Hershey Corporation</u> or with the averages of all companies in the confectionary industry. They may perform intercompany analyses for a single period or for several past periods.

www.hersheys.com

Companies are of many sizes, and their sizes change from year to year. Because of these size differences, intracompany and intercompany analyses are easier to conduct and to interpret if percentage analysis is used. **Percentage analysis** involves converting financial statement information from dollars to percentages. For example, suppose that Unlimited Decadence's sales increased by $2,800,000—from $70,000,000 in 1999 to $72,800,000 in 2000. At the same time, a competing company's sales also increased by $2,800,000—from $35,000,000 to $37,800,000. Since both companies' sales increased by the same dollar amount, it might be tempting to think they performed equally well. But instead of evaluating the yearly change in each company's sales only as a dollar increase of $2,800,000, think of the change as a 4% ($2,800,000 ÷ $70,000,000) increase in Unlimited Decadence's sales and an 8% ($2,800,000 ÷ $35,000,000) increase in the competitor's sales. Thinking of the change in each company's sales as a *percentage change* leads to a different conclusion. Percentage analyses are especially useful when making intercompany comparisons.

6 *What is percentage analysis, and what are its three types?*

There are three basic types of percentage analyses: ratio analysis, horizontal analysis, and vertical analysis. Recall that **ratio analysis** involves dividing an item on the financial statements by another related item (for example, net income divided by average owner's equity). We used ratio analyses in Chapters 6 through 8 to perform intracompany analysis for Sweet Temptations, and to perform intercompany analysis of JCPenney and Sears.

Horizontal analysis shows the changes in a company's operating results over time in percentages as well as in dollar amounts. Unlimited Decadence's yearly sales change that we talked about earlier is an example of horizontal analysis. **Vertical analysis** shows each item in a financial statement of a given period or date both as a percentage of another item on that statement (for example, every item on the income statement stated as a percentage of sales, or every asset stated as a percentage of total assets) and as a dollar amount. Investors and creditors use each of these types of analyses to help evaluate a corporation's performance.

Business Issues and Values

Should society expect corporations to do more than comply with laws and regulations, try to remain solvent, and earn a satisfactory profit for the owners? If so, what else should society expect? If not, what impact can this have on society?

Large corporations have the same basic goals as small companies—to remain solvent and to earn a satisfactory profit for the owners. Our society has placed limits on what companies, both large and small, can do to meet these goals. These limits may be formal laws or regulations, such as those controlling misleading advertising, product safety, and management fraud. Other limits are not laws or regulations but are norms about what society expects from the business community. For example, society expects companies to treat employees, investors, and creditors fairly, support the local economy, and "give back" some of their profits by supporting local and national charities.

There is a continuing debate over how large corporations should balance these sometimes conflicting expectations. How much severance pay should corporations offer employees who are terminated? How much profit should corporations give back to the local community?

For large corporations, these questions are difficult, in part because managers usually do not own the corporation. For example, the question of supporting charities is difficult to answer because the managers of a corporation are spending the stockholders' (not their own) resources on charities that it decides to support. How would you like someone else deciding where your donations to charity should go? On the other hand, through a corporation's identification with the charity, this support may help it increase customer loyalty and improve overall financial performance. Throughout the book we will discuss how accounting plays a role in shaping these types of corporate decisions.

Summary

At the beginning of the chapter we asked you several questions. During the chapter, we asked you to STOP and answer some other questions to build your knowledge about specific issues. Be sure you answered these additional questions. Below are the questions from the beginning of the chapter, with a brief summary of the key points relating to the answers. Use your creative and critical thinking skills to expand on these key points to develop more complete answers to the questions and to determine what other questions you have that might lead you to learn more about the issues.

1 **What are the three most common forms of business organizations and their basic characteristics?**

The three most common forms of business organizations are sole proprietorships, partnerships, and corporations. A sole proprietorship is usually small, has a limited life, and is owned by one person who has unlimited liability. A partnership is owned by two or more people (called partners) who have unlimited liability; it can be large or small, is usually governed by a partnership agreement, and has a limited life. A corporation is a legal entity incorporated in one of the states. It is usually large and usually has many owners (called stockholders) who have limited liability. A corporation may have many managers, is subject to income taxes and other government regulations, and has an unlimited life.

2 **What are the qualities that make accounting information about large corporations useful for decision-making?**

To be useful for decision-making, accounting information must be relevant, reliable, material, and valid. Relevant information has the capacity to affect a user's decision. Reliable information is capable of being verified. Information is material when the dollar amount is large enough to make a difference in a decision. Information is valid when it shows a realistic picture of what it is meant to represent.

3 **What do users need to know about the stockholders' equity section of a corporation's balance sheet and about its income statement?**

The stockholders' equity section of a corporation's balance sheet is divided into two sections: contributed capital and retained earnings. Contributed capital includes the par value (legal capital) of the common stock as well as additional paid-in capital. Retained earnings reports the total lifetime net income that has been reinvested into the corporation and not distributed to stockholders as dividends. A corporation's income statement differs from the income statement of other types of companies because the former includes income from both continuing operations and nonrecurring earnings. Since corporations are subject to income taxes, a corporation's income statement also includes income tax expense. Finally, a corporation reports earnings per share on its income statement.

4 How does a corporation provide information to external users?

A corporation provides information to external users through its annual report, Securities and Exchange Commission (SEC) reports, interim financial statements, and media releases. A corporation's annual report includes its financial statements, related notes, audit report, financial highlights, management's discussion and analysis, and other information. SEC reports include a registration statement and an annual 10-K report. A corporation usually issues interim financial statements quarterly. Media releases provide information related to important business activities.

5 How do users perform intracompany and intercompany analyses?

Users perform intracompany analysis by comparing a corporation's current operations and financial position with its past results and expected results. They perform intercompany analysis by comparing a corporation's performance with the performance of competing companies, and with industry averages or averages in related industries.

6 What is percentage analysis, and what are its three types?

Percentage analysis involves converting financial statement information from dollars to percentages. There are three types of percentage analysis: ratio analysis, horizontal analysis, and vertical analysis. Ratio analysis involves dividing a financial statement item by another related item. Horizontal analysis shows the changes in a company's operating results over time as percentages. Vertical analysis shows the items on a financial statement of a given period or date as percentages of another item on that statement.

Key Terms

additional paid-in capital *(p. 313)*
agent *(p. 304)*
annual report *(p. 316)*
articles of incorporation *(p. 307)*
auditing *(p. 317)*
audit report *(p. 317)*
capital stock *(p. 312)*
closely-held corporation *(p. 307)*
common stock *(p. 312)*
comparative financial statements *(p. 316)*
conceptual framework *(p. 310)*
contributed capital *(p. 312)*
corporation *(p. 305)*
data warehouse *(p. 309)*
distribution *(p. 309)*
double taxation *(p. 306)*
earnings per share (EPS) *(p. 315)*
enterprise resource planning (ERP) systems *(p. 309)*
finance *(p. 309)*
Financial Highlights *(p. 318)*
Financial Summaries *(p. 318)*
horizontal analysis *(p. 321)*
human resources *(p. 309)*
income from continuing operations *(p. 314)*
income tax expense *(p. 315)*

incorporation *(p. 307)*
initial public offering *(p. 307)*
intercompany analysis *(p. 321)*
intracompany analysis *(p. 320)*
interim financial statements *(p. 320)*
joint ownership *(p. 304)*
legal capital *(p. 312)*
Letter to Shareholders *(p. 318)*
limited life *(p. 303, 304)*
Management's DIscussion and Analysis *(p. 318)*
marketing *(p. 309)*
market value *(p. 313)*
material *(p. 311)*
notes to the financial statements *(p. 316)*
operating income *(p. 314)*
other items *(p. 315)*
par value *(p. 312)*
partnership *(p. 303)*
partnership agreement *(p. 304)*
percentage analysis *(p. 321)*
preferred stock *(p. 312)*
production *(p. 309)*
prospectus *(p. 319)*
publicly available information *(p. 316)*
publicly-held corporation *(p. 307)*
ratio analysis *(p. 321)*

relevant *(p. 310)*   stockholders' equity *(p. 312)*
reliable *(p. 311)*   10-K report *(p. 319)*
retained earnings *(p. 312, 314)*   unlimited liability *(p. 303, 304)*
secondary equity market *(p. 307)*   valid *(p. 311)*
sole proprietorship *(p. 303)*   vertical analysis *(p. 321)*
stockholders *(p. 305)*

S U M M A R Y
S U R F I N G

Here is an opportunity to gather information on the Internet about real-world issues related to the topics in this chapter. Go to http://www.dryden.com/account and click on the Cunningham, Nikolai, and Bazley book cover. Click on Summary Surfing, then click on this chapter number, and answer the following questions.

▶ Click on **TI** (Texas Instruments). Find the company's balance sheets. What types of stock does TI have? What is the par value per share of common stock, and how many shares were issued at the end of the most current year? What were the amounts of its retained earnings and its total stockholders' equity on December 31 of the most current year?

▶ Click on **Intel (Intel Corporation).** Find the company's income statements. What was Intel's net income for the most current year, and how does this compare with its income in the previous year? What was Intel's earnings per share for the most current year, and how does this compare with its earnings per share in the previous year? Find the Management's discussion and analysis of financial condition and results of operations. By what percent did Intel's net revenues increase from the previous year to the most current year, and what were the reasons for this growth?

Integrated Business and Accounting Situations

Answer the Following Questions in Your Own Words

Testing Your Knowledge

10-1   What is a sole proprietorship? What is meant by the terms *unlimited liability* and *limited life* as they apply to a sole proprietorship?

10-2   What is a partnership? What is meant by the terms *limited life, joint ownership, agent,* and *unlimited liability* as they apply to a partnership?

10-3   What is included in a partnership agreement?

10-4   What is a corporation? What is meant by the terms *capital stock, limited liability,* and *double taxation* as they apply to a corporation?

10-5   What is the secondary equity market? Name three organizations that are part of the secondary equity market.

10-6   Name the typical functional areas of a large corporation. How is accounting information used to manage these functions?

10-7   What is the FASB's conceptual framework, and what is the primary purpose of financial accounting information?

10-8   What is relevant accounting information, and how does it relate to materiality?

10-9 What is reliable accounting information, and how does it relate to validity?

10-10 What is the owners' equity of a corporation called, and into what two sections is it separated on a corporation's balance sheet?

10-11 What is included in contributed capital and retained earnings on a corporation's balance sheet?

10-12 What amounts are included in a corporation's common stock and additional paid-in capital accounts?

10-13 What is reported in the income from continuing operations section of a corporation's income statement?

10-14 What is the last item shown on a corporation's income statement, and how is it computed?

10-15 What is included in a corporation's annual report?

10-16 What is included in the three paragraphs of an audit report? Why is an audit report important to external users?

10-17 What is included in the management's discussion and analysis (MD&A) section of a corporation's annual report?

10-18 What is the difference between intracompany analysis and intercompany analysis?

10-19 What is the difference between horizontal analysis and vertical analysis?

Applying Your Knowledge

10-20 Companies have different forms of organization.

Required: Discuss the differences among sole proprietorships, partnerships, and corporations regarding ownership, decision-making, income taxes, the responsibility of owners for the company's debts, and the life of the company.

10-21 Suppose you were starting a new business with a friend. Your friend and you have agreed that he will invest most of the capital and that you will do most of the work. You will invest some cash and a two-year-old truck, which will be used as a delivery vehicle in the business.

Required: Briefly discuss what information you would include in the partnership agreement for the new company. Be as specific as possible.

10-22 At the end of 2000, before allocating net income, the Simon and Art partnership had total owners' equity of $100,000, consisting of Simon, capital: $60,000, and Art, capital: $40,000. During 2000 the partnership earned net income of $30,000. The partnership agreement specifies that net income is to be allocated according to three factors as follows: (a) first, each partner is to be allocated a share of net income equal to 10% of her capital amount, (b) second, Simon is to be allocated a salary of $7,000, and Art is to be allocated a salary of $10,000 as a share of net income, and (c) the remaining net income is to be allocated 60% to Simon and 40% to Art.

Required: (1) Prepare a schedule that allocates the net income to Simon and Art according to the partnership agreement. (*Hint:* The salaries paid to the partners are used only to allocate the net income; they are not included as salaries expense on the income statement.)

(2) Explain why you think factors (a) and (b) for allocating net income were included in the partnership agreement.

10-23 During 2000 the Fame and Fortune partnership had sales revenue of $200,000, cost of goods sold of $120,000, and operating expenses of $28,000. At the end of 2000, before allocating net income, the A. Fame, Capital account had a balance of $140,000, and the B. Fortune, Capital account had a balance of $70,000. In reviewing the partnership agreement, you find that annual net income is to be allocated to each partner based on three factors. (a) First, A. Fame is to be allocated a salary of $5,000, and B. Fortune is to be allocated a salary of $20,000 as a share of net income. (b) Second, each partner is to be allocated a share of net income equal to 10% of his capital account balance. (c) Third, the remaining net income is to be allocated 2/3 to A. Fame and 1/3 to B. Fortune.

Required: (1) Prepare a 2000 income statement for the Fame and Fortune partnership. At the bottom of the income statement, include a schedule that allocates the net income to each partner based on the factors in the partnership agreement. (*Hint:* The salaries paid to the partners are used only to allocate the net income; they are not included as salaries expense on the income statement.)

(2) Explain why you think factors (a) and (b) for allocating net income were included in the partnership agreement.

10-24 One way to logically divide the organization structure of a large corporation is by function.

Required: Identify the typical functional areas of a corporation, and briefly discuss what activities are performed in each area. Briefly explain how managers would use accounting information in the operations of these functional areas.

10-25 A friend of yours has recently completed a course in bookkeeping at his high school. He has been browsing through this chapter of your book and noticed the term "conceptual framework." He says: "We never had a conceptual framework in our bookkeeping class. What is this framework anyhow? Please tell me about the qualities of useful accounting information, and define each one."

Required: Prepare a written response to your friend's question.

10-26 Ryland Carpet Corporation sells 20,000 shares of its common stock for $10 per share.

Required: (1) Using T-accounts, show how Ryland Carpet Corporation would record this transaction under each of the following independent assumptions:
  (a) The stock has a par value of $2 per share.
  (b) The stock has a par value of $5 per share.
  (c) The stock has a par value of $7 per share.
(2) If you were a stockholder of Ryland Carpet Corporation, which par value would you prefer? Why?

10-27 Tiger Corporation previously had issued 10,000 shares of its $2 par value common stock for $17 per share. On December 28, 2000, it sells another 5,000 shares to investors for $20 per share.

Required: (1) Using T-accounts, (a) enter the balances in the applicable accounts for the common stock that had previously been issued, and (b) record the sale of the 5,000 shares of common stock on December 28, 2000.
(2) Prepare the contributed capital section of Tiger Corporation's December 31, 2000 balance sheet.

10-28 On December 29, 2000, Lion Corporation sells 4,000 shares of its common stock with a $5 par value to investors for $25 per share. This is the only sale of common stock during 2000. Before 2000, the corporation had issued 12,000 shares of this common stock for $21 per share. At the end of 2000, the corporation had retained earnings of $124,000.

Required: (1) Using T-accounts, (a) enter the balances in the Common Stock and Additional Paid-in Capital accounts at the beginning of 2000, and (b) record the sale of the 4,000 shares of common stock on December 29, 2000.
(2) Prepare the stockholders' equity section of Lion Corporation's December 31, 2000 balance sheet.

10-29 During all of 2000, stockholders of the Planet Pluto Corporation owned 15,000 shares of its $4 par value common stock. They had purchased this stock from the corporation for $28 per share. At the end of 2000, the Planet Pluto Corporation had an ending balance of $247,000 in its retained earnings account.

Required: Prepare the stockholders' equity section of the Planet Pluto Corporation's December 31, 2000 balance sheet.

10-30 The stockholders of Riglets Corporation owned 10,000 shares of its $5 par value common stock during all of this year. The corporation is subject to a 40% income tax rate. The corporation's balance sheet information at the end of this year and its income statement information for this year are as follows:

Common stock, $5 par value	$ (a)
Gross profit	113,000

Pretax income from continuing operations	(b)
Operating expenses	33,000
Total contributed capital	228,000
Income tax expense	(c)
Retained earnings	181,000
Net income	48,000
Additional paid-in capital	(d)
Earnings per share	(e)
Cost of goods sold	(f)
Sales (net)	240,000
Total stockholders' equity	(g)

Required: Fill in the blanks lettered (a) through (g). All the necessary information is listed. (*Hint:* It is not necessary to calculate your answers in alphabetical order.)

10-31 Braiden Corporation is subject to a 40% income tax rate. During all of this year, stockholders owned 20,000 shares of its $2 par value common stock. The corporation's income statement information for this year and its balance sheet information at the end of this year are as follows:

Sales (net)	$307,000
Net income	(a)
Total stockholders' equity	500,000
Operating expenses	(b)
Additional paid-in capital	201,000
Income tax expense	(c)
Common stock, $2 par value	(d)
Pretax income from continuing operations	(e)
Earnings per share	3.15
Total contributed capital	(f)
Gross profit	143,000
Retained earnings	(g)
Cost of goods sold	164,000

Required: Fill in the blanks lettered (a) through (g). All the necessary information is listed. (*Hint:* It is not necessary to calculate your answers in alphabetical order.)

10-32 Ringland Glass Corporation showed the following balances in its income statement accounts at the end of 2000:

Interest expense	$ 1,400
Sales (net)	420,500
Selling expenses	54,200
Interest revenue	2,200
Cost of goods sold	230,200
General expenses	31,900

The corporation pays income taxes at a rate of 40%. It had average total assets during 2000 of $500,000, and stockholders owned 30,000 shares of its common stock during all of 2000.

Required: (1) Prepare a 2000 income statement for Ringland Glass Corporation.
    (2) Compute the return on total assets of Ringland Glass Corporation for 2000. How does this compare with the industry average of 10.8%?

10-33 The stockholders of Buffalo Chips Corporation owned 40,000 shares of its common stock during all of 2000. The corporation pays income taxes at a rate of 40% and had the following balances in its income statement accounts at the end of 2000:

Administrative expenses	$ 67,400
Cost of goods sold	302,000
Interest expense	3,500
Interest revenue	1,700
Sales (net)	563,800
Selling expenses	40,600

Required: (1) Prepare a 2000 income statement for Buffalo Chips Corporation.
    (2) Compute the profit margin of Buffalo Chips Corporation for 2000. How does this compare with the industry average of 17.4%?

10-34 Stockholders of the Tomar Export Corporation owned 4,000 shares of common stock during all of this year. The corporation listed the following items in its financial statements on December 31 of this year:

Net income	$ 10,000
Current assets	15,000
Average stockholders' equity	70,000
Cost of goods sold	72,000
Total liabilities	25,000
Net sales	100,000
Current liabilities	6,000
Average inventory	9,000
Total assets	100,000

Required: Using the preceding information, compute the following ratios of the Tomar Export Corporation for this year: (1) earnings per share, (2) gross profit percentage, (3) profit margin, (4) return on owners' (stockholders') equity, (5) current ratio, (6) inventory turnover, and (7) debt ratio.

10-35 Taboue Cutlery Corporation showed the following income statement information for the years 2000 and 2001:

Taboue Cutlery Corporation
Comparative Income Statements
For Years Ended December 31

	2000	2001	Year-to-Year Increase (Decrease) Amount	Percent
Sales (net)	$60,000	$65,000	$ (a)	(b) %
Cost of goods sold	(33,600)	(c)	(d)	(e)
Gross profit	$26,400	$27,950	$ (f)	(g)
Operating expenses	(h)	(19,050)	400	(i)
Pretax operating income	$ (j)	$ 8,900	$1,150	(k)
Income tax expense	(3,100)	(3,560)	(l)	(m)
Net Income	$ 4,650	$ (n)	$ (o)	(p)
Number of common shares issued	(q)	2,700	(r)	12.6
Earnings per share	$ 1.94	$ 1.98	$ (s)	(t)

Required: (1) Determine the appropriate percentages and amounts for the blanks lettered (a) through (t). Round to the nearest tenth of a percent.

(2) Did you just do horizontal or vertical analysis? Briefly comment on what your analysis reveals.

10-36 The Clovland Corporation presents the following comparative income statements for 2000 and 2001:

Clovland Corporation
Comparative Income Statements
For Years Ended December 31

	2000	2001
Sales (net)	$90,000	$108,000
Cost of goods sold	(45,000)	(60,000)
Gross profit	$45,000	$ 48,000
Operating expenses	(20,000)	(22,000)
Pretax operating income	$25,000	$ 26,000
Income tax expense	(10,000)	(10,400)
Net Income	$15,000	$ 15,600
Number of common shares	6,800	7,000
Earnings per share	$ 2.21	$ 2.23

Required: (1) Based on the preceding information, prepare a horizontal analysis for the years 2000 and 2001. (*Hint:* To the right of the income statements, add an *Amount* column and a *Percent* column like 10-35.)

(2) Calculate the corporation's profit margin for each year. What is this ratio generally used for, and what does it indicate for the Clovland Corporation?

10-37 The Anton Electronics Corporation presents the following income statement for 2000:

Anton Electronics Corporation
Income Statement
For Year Ended December 31, 2000

Sales (net)	$135,000
Cost of goods sold	(75,000)
Gross profit	$ 60,000
Operating expenses	(33,750)
Pretax operating income	$ 26,250
Income tax expense	(10,500)
Net Income	$ 15,750
Earnings per share	$ 3.00

In addition, the average inventory for 2000 was $10,000.

Required: (1) Based on the preceding information, prepare a vertical analysis of the income statement for 2000. (*Hint:* To the right of the income statement, add a *Percent* column, and assign 100% to net sales.)

(2) Compute the corporation's inventory turnover for 2000, and briefly explain what this ratio tells you about a company.

Making Evaluations

10-38 The Toys "R" Us 1997 annual report contains the following information in the section called "Report of Management": "Management has established a system of internal controls to provide reasonable assurance that assets are maintained and accounted for in accordance with its policies and that transactions are recorded accurately on the Company's books and records. . . . The financial statements of the Company have been audited by Ernst & Young LLP, independent auditors, in accordance with generally accepted auditing standards, including a review of financial reporting matters and internal controls to the extent necessary to express an opinion on the . . . financial statements."

www.toysrus.com

Required: Suppose you were using these financial statements to make a decision about investing in Toys "R" Us. Would this information help you make your decision? If so, how would it help? If not, why do you think Toys "R" Us includes the information with its financial statements?

10-39 You have a close friend from high school who is attending college in another state. You see each other at holidays, and in between visits you correspond on a regular basis by e-mail. Here is the latest e-mail you received from your friend:

From: HT246@UA.EDU <friend>

To: Ace@AAU.EDU <you>

Subject: HELP!!!

Hey, how's it going? Sorry I don't have time to chat. I need some help. I'm taking a personal finance course. In this course, I estimate how much my annual income will be after I graduate, establish a personal monthly budget, and decide how to invest my monthly savings. As part of this, I must select a real-life corporation to invest in.

I estimated my annual income to be $75,000 (hey, you know me—I think positive), so I have a lot of savings to invest. Here's where you come in. I am having trouble getting started with the part of the assignment where I pick a real-life corporation to invest in. Luckily, dear friend, I remembered that you are taking this accounting course.

Remember how I helped you out when you were taking Poli Sci? Now it's return-the-favor time. Tell me what you know about (1) the kinds of information I need to decide whether a corporation is a good investment, (2) where I can get the information, and (3) how to analyze the information once I get it.

By the way, the assignment is due day after tomorrow, so don't send back 20 pages of techno-jargon I can't even understand. Just send what you think is most important, and tell me in words I can understand. Thanks a bunch.

Required: Using the material presented in this chapter, write an e-mail message back to your friend. Make sure you respond specifically to the three items he needs help with.

10-40 Assume that it is Friday, March 27, 1998, and that it is a great day. You receive a terrific gift from your parents—$5,000 to help support you when you start your remaining years of college. Your older sister, Rachel (who is known for her close following of the stock market), persuades you to invest the money immediately. Following her suggestion, you purchase 100 shares of common stock in Wal-Mart Corporation, whose stock is being traded on the New York Stock Exchange on that day for $50 per share.

www.wal-mart.com

Required: Using publicly available information, evaluate your investment in Wal-Mart as of March 27, 1998. Assuming you need to use this investment next year to help pay for college, evaluate whether your purchase of Wal-Mart stock is a good investment. Be sure that your evaluation includes the following:

(1) A discussion of how you performed your investigation of Wal-Mart. Make sure you document your sources (e.g., Wal-Mart's annual report, the *Wall Street Journal, Value Line Investment Survey, Standard & Poor's Stock Reports, CompuServe Inc.*).

(2) An explanation of your evaluation of your investment. Show all of the calculations you made to perform your evaluation, and what information they reveal.

(3) Your plans for the investment between now and next year when you will start using the money to pay for college.

10-41 In this chapter, we described how investors and creditors obtain information about publicly held corporations, and we began our coverage of the stockholders' equity section of a corporation's balance sheet and a corporation's income statement. Read the following item that appeared on May 16 of a recent year, on the first page of the Money section of *USA Today:*

TOY SALES: The world's largest toy retailer, hurt by weak video game sales, said [yesterday] that its first-quarter net income slipped 51%. Toys "R" Us net income fell to $18.4 million, or 7 cents a share, from $37.58 million, or 13 cents a share, a year earlier. Revenue was up slightly, at $1.49 billion, compared with $1.46 billion in the year-ago quarter. Revenue for stores open at least a year fell 10%. Toys "R" Us stock dropped 1 1/8 to $26 in heavy trading. The company has 618 toy stores in the USA, 300 international toy stores and 206 Kids "R" Us children's clothing stores.

Required: Respond to the following questions:

(1) In what month does the annual accounting period for Toys "R" Us end? How did you figure that out? Why would Toys "R" Us end its accounting period then?

(2) How many shares of stock do you think are owned by Toys "R" Us investors at the end of the first quarter of the year? How did you calculate that number?

(3) What was the market value of Toys "R" Us stock on the morning of May 15? What about on the morning of May 16? Explain why you think this change occurred.

(4) Assume you had purchased 500 shares of Toys "R" Us stock on May 15 of the previous year for $24 a share. How would you evaluate your investment's performance? As an investor, what specific information in the newspaper item would concern you the most? Why?

www.mcdonalds.com

10-42 Almost everyone has eaten at McDonald's. Big Macs and Quarter Pounders are part of many people's weekly diet. At last count, McDonald's serves over 38 million people per day. McDonald's Corporation is known not only for its fast food but also for its corporate social responsibility efforts. We have listed several social responsibility activities that McDonald's Corporation decided to undertake:

(a) McDonald's decided to sponsor Ronald McDonald Houses, where families with hospitalized children can stay near the hospital for free.

(b) McDonald's decided to become a major contributor to Jerry Lewis's fund-raising campaign to fight muscular dystrophy.

(c) McDonald's decided to employ physically and/or mentally challenged adults who find it more difficult to get jobs.

(d) Although McDonald's believed that styrofoam containers helped to maintain the quality of its food, it decided to reduce its use of styrofoam containers in response to news reports about the dangers of fluorocarbons and in response to pressures applied by nonprofit environmental groups.

In each of these cases, McDonald's senior executives probably consulted managers from some or all of the functional areas (marketing, production, human resources, finance, distribution) before making their decision.

Required: Answer the following questions. Think through your answers carefully so that you can defend the conclusions you reach.

(1) For each of the four activities listed above, list the questions you would ask to determine whether McDonald's decision to undertake this activity helps or hinders the corporation's ability to meet its basic objectives of remaining solvent and earning a satisfactory profit.

(2) For each of the four activities, analyze what functional areas will be affected and how they will be affected. Then, assuming you are the finance manager, use your analysis to write McDonald's senior executives a memo explaining the impact of activities (a) and (d) on your functional area.

(3) Now, think back through your answers to (1) and (2) with one thing in mind— information from other functional areas. More specifically, brainstorm about information that the other functional areas could provide that would improve your ability to answer questions (1) and (2). Use the knowledge you have gained about costs, profits, budgeting, and reporting to help formulate your answer.

10-43 In this chapter, we said that individuals investing in large corporations must rely on publicly available information when making their investment decisions. But some individuals may have more than just publicly available information. Consider the following situation.

Suppose you and your mom were playing golf with two of her business "cronies." While waiting to tee off at the eighth hole, one of them, the chief financial officer of her company, mentioned ("off the record") that her company had just finished the development of a new product that would "blow the socks off" the health care industry. Although she was not at liberty to discuss the product (it won't be released until early next year), she speculated that once the product was released, the company stock price would "skyrocket." She also mentioned that she intended to purchase a large number of shares of the company's stock (which is being traded on the New York Stock Exchange) later in the day, and to sell them after the product was released.

WHOA!!! This could be an opportunity for you to invest the $2,000 your wealthy Aunt Bertha gave you for your birthday. Also, your boss, coworkers, and friends might like to know about this opportunity.

Required: (1) What are the relevant facts for your decision?

(2) Are there any ethical issues involved in your decision?

(3) Who has a stake in your decision (who stands to gain and who stands to lose), and how might your decision affect these stakeholders?

(4) What do you think you should do? Why?

(5) Do you see any ethical issues in the chief financial officer's discussion and decision?

(6) Who are the stakeholders in her discussion and decision?

(7) Suppose that when you got home after the golf game, your mom asked you what you thought of the conversation at the eighth hole. How would you answer her?

(8) What do you think should happen to "level the playing field"?

10-44 Yesterday, you received the following letter for your advice column at the local paper:

Dear Dr. Decisive:

I am having a crisis with my professional life right now and could use an objective opinion. Please help! I have been working for a partnership for ten years (let's just call it "Seedman and Seedman") and have built up a strong relationship with the company's customers. I am currently earning a salary of $32,000. But last week I received from one of Seedman and Seedman's competitors a job offer (unsolicited) that included a salary of $40,000. The offer is tempting, but I like my current job. So, I met with the Seedmans to see if they could increase my salary to match the offer. Well, I wasn't prepared for their response. They offered me a share of the partnership!! But here's where it gets complicated. In order to join the partnership, I would contribute $25,000 cash but would be paid no salary until the end of the year. Then, after the net income of the partnership was determined for each year, it would be allocated as follows. First, I would be allocated a salary of $28,000, Sadie Seedman would be allocated a salary of $32,000, and Johnny Seedman would be allocated a salary of $28,000. The remaining net income (after we withdrew our salaries) would be assigned to our individual capital accounts. Sadie's share would be 50%, Johnny's 30%, and mine 20%. (If I become a partner, we could call ourselves Seedman, Seedman, and Seedling—I'd be the seedling.) If I take the other job, I plan to invest $25,000 in the stock of a high-tech company in my city.

What do you see as the advantages and disadvantages of each of my alternatives?

"Seedling"

Required: Get together with your Dr. Decisive consulting team and write a response to "Seedling."

DEVELOPING A BUSINESS PLAN FOR A MANUFACTURING COMPANY: COST-VOLUME-PROFIT PLANNING AND ANALYSIS

> "We should all be concerned about the future because we will have to spend the rest of our lives there."
>
> —Charles Kettering

1 How does the fact that a manufacturing company makes the products it sells affect its business plan?

2 How does a manufacturing company determine the cost of the goods that it manufactures?

3 Why are standard costs useful in controlling a company's operations?

4 How do manufacturing costs affect cost-volume-profit analysis?

5 What is the effect of multiple products on cost-volume-profit analysis?

6 How does a manufacturing company use cost-volume-profit analysis for its planning?

Have you ever read the ingredients in a candy bar and then wondered how these ingredients were combined to form a candy bar? It is the manufacturing process that precisely mixes these ingredients and performs the other activities necessary to form and package a tasty candy bar. To succeed, a manufacturing company must plan all aspects of its manufacturing processes.

Earlier in this book, we discussed many aspects of planning that apply to entrepreneurial service and retail companies. Now we will expand our discussion to include additional aspects of planning that apply to larger companies and specifically to manufacturing companies. Recall from our early discussion in Chapter 1 that the fact that manufacturing companies *make* the products they sell to their customers distinguishes them from service and retail companies. As you will see, although the planning processes of all types of companies are basically the same, this characteristic of a manufacturing company influences its planning processes and its business plan.

A Manufacturing Company's Business Plan

1 *How does the fact that a manufacturing company makes the products it sells affect its business plan?*

Like the entrepreneurs we discussed in Chapter 3, a manufacturing company's managers use its business plan to help them plan their company's activities, visualize the results of implementing their plans, carry out the company's plans, and later evaluate how well the company performed. A company may decide to share its business plan with potential investors and creditors. If so, they can use the company's business plan to help them learn as much as they can about the company, its plans, and how it operates so that they can make decisions about whether to invest in or lend money to the company.

A manufacturing company's business plan has much in common with the business plans of retail and service companies and contains the same components that we discussed in Chapter 3. However, since a manufacturing company makes the products that it sells, its

How does the production and sale of this candy bar fit into Hershey Food Corporation's business plan?

business plan contains an additional component useful to internal and external decision-makers—the production plan. The production plan has considerable impact on the other sections of the business plan, particularly the financial plan, which we will discuss later in this chapter.

The Production Plan

The production plan included in a manufacturing company's business plan describes how the company plans to efficiently produce its goods while maintaining a desired level of product quality. It also describes the company's plans for achieving specific levels of productivity through the use of materials, labor, equipment, and facilities. For example, Techknits, Inc. a sweater manufacturer in New York, recently purchased computerized looms. So now Techknits should describe in its production plan how it plans to complete orders for sweaters faster and more efficiently than it did previously. For example, the company plans to use these looms 24 hours a day. Whereas previously one person was needed per manual loom, one person will now be able to run four computerized looms.[1] Techknits also should explain that with this process, it will be able to turn out 60,000 sweaters a week. A company's production plan also describes the raw materials that make up the company's products, the company's production processes, and the finished products.

The Raw Materials

Raw materials are the materials, ingredients, and parts that make up a company's products. They also include materials that the company needs for production but that do not become a part of the products, such as production supplies and grease for lubricating machine parts. For example, some of the raw materials that Unlimited Decadence uses in manufacturing one of its candy bars include cocoa nibs, cocoa liqueur, sugar and other sweeteners, cocoa butter, milk products, emulsifiers, and paper (for packaging the candy bars). When Unlimited Decadence lists its raw materials in this section, it specifies any criteria that these materials must meet (such as standards or grades of cocoa). It also indicates which of them are perishable and how quickly they perish.

A company also lists its raw materials suppliers in this section. This list includes such information as the company's major suppliers and alternative suppliers, as well as a comparison of these suppliers' characteristics such as quality, delivery time and method, dependability, cost, and payment methods and schedules.

Another aspect of raw materials that a company describes in this section is the way it handles the raw materials once it receives them from its suppliers. This description includes the company's delivery inspection procedures, warehousing, and security for the raw materials. Since Unlimited Decadence's candy bar ingredients are perishable, Unlimited Decadence follows special procedures to ensure that fresh, quality raw materials go into its candy bars. In this section of its production plan, Unlimited Decadence describes how it inspects incoming raw materials for grade (percent defective) and for freedom from bugs and other contamination. Unlimited Decadence also describes unique aspects of its raw materials storage, including regulated temperature, humidity, and exposure to air.

 Picture the movement of ingredients from the warehouse of the supplier to that of Unlimited Decadence. If you were a manager at Unlimited Decadence, at what point or points in this movement would you want the ingredients to be inspected for grade, freedom from bugs, and other contamination? What is your rationale?

The Production Processes

This section typically includes a description of the employees, facilities, and equipment necessary for the manufacture of a company's products. Here, the company describes the

---

[1]John S. DeMott, "Small Factories' Big Lessons," *Nation's Business,* April 1995, 29, 30.

sequence of production steps necessary to manufacture its products and how the raw materials flow through this sequence. For example, Exhibit 11-1 lists the production steps necessary to manufacture Unlimited Decadence's Darkly Decadent candy bar. A company also describes the employees needed for each of the steps, including what their skills must be, the availability of employees with these skills, how much time they will be spending on each product, and how much this time will cost the company.

www.fairchildfurniture. com

 Fairchild of California, a sofa manufacturer near Los Angeles, employs 100 highly skilled immigrant workers to produce sofas at wages ranging from $9 to $13 per hour (depending on how many sofas each employee worked on in an hour).[2] What information about these employees do you think Fairchild should include in this section of its business plan?

A company also lists in this section all the equipment and facilities it uses or plans to use in the production process, as well as the costs associated with the use of the equipment and facilities. These associated costs include mortgage, rent, utilities, maintenance, and insurance payments. The diagram in Exhibit 11-2 illustrates the equipment that Unlimited Decadence uses to manufacture the Darkly Decadent candy bar and other candy bars. Notice that it uses an electronic control panel to regulate and automate the production process. For example, the control panel dictates how much of each ingredient is fed into the mixer from the hoppers. Since the proportion of ingredients is different for each type of candy bar, Unlimited Decadence programs different formulas into the control panel; the formulas determine the mix of ingredients for each type of candy bar. The control panel also monitors such production variables as temperature and candy density, and it adjusts the production process when these variables deviate from the acceptable range of values.

www.spanglercandy.com

 Spangler Candy Co. in Bryan, Ohio, a manufacturer of candy canes, would describe in its production processes section its partially automated factory, which doubles Spangler's output by automatically wrapping the canes in a thin plastic film, packing them in boxes of twelve (in tiny cradles to keep them from breaking), and bundling the boxes into cases. Before automation, Spangler hand-packaged the candy canes. It also would describe the costs associated with this automation, including the cost of the 215,000-square-foot warehouse where it stores the millions and millions of candy canes from February, when it begins candy cane production, until they are sold during the holiday season.[3] Can you think of any other costs that might be associated with this automated factory?

Another aspect of production that a company addresses in this section is the regulations with which it must comply and the permits and licenses that it must maintain. For

Exhibit 11-1	Production Steps Necessary to Manufacture the Darkly Decadent Candy Bar

(1) Preparing ingredients—pulverizing cocoa nibs, grinding sugar
(2) Mixing ingredients—producing chocolate paste of a rough texture and plastic consistency
(3) Refining chocolate paste—smoothing texture of paste
(4) Conching chocolate paste—dispersing sugar and milk solids in liquid fat
(5) Tempering chocolate paste—stabilizing chocolate, causing good color and texture
(6) Molding candy bars—shaping candy bars
(7) Wrapping candy bars—packaging candy bars

[2]Ibid.
[3]Ibid.

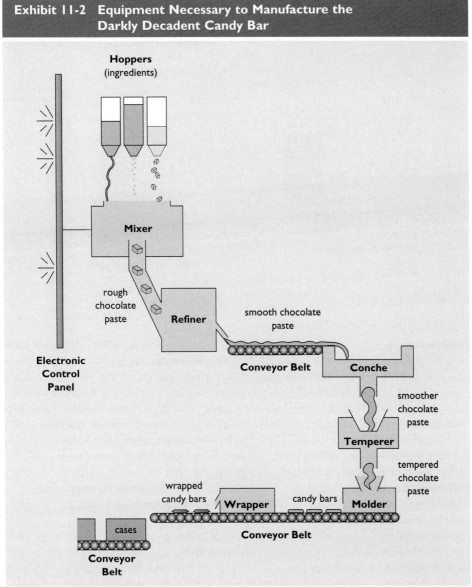

Exhibit 11-2 Equipment Necessary to Manufacture the Darkly Decadent Candy Bar

example, manufacturers in California, like those in other states, must follow national rules for clean air. In most states, regulators dictate how companies must meet these rules. However, in California, regulators allow companies to determine how they will comply with these rules. These companies include their clean air plans in this section of their business plans.[4] Recall from our discussion of regulations in Chapter 1 that these regulations, permits, and licenses also include such items as operating permits, certification and inspection licenses, state and local building codes, and recycling systems.

The Finished Products

Virtually all manufacturing companies have some form of product inspection that occurs during the production process to ensure a quality finished product. In this section of the production plan, a company describes where in the production process this quality

[4]Laura M. Litvan, "A Breath of Fresh Air," *Nation's Business,* March 1995, 53.

As a potential investor or creditor, would you have an interest in this company's clean air plan?

inspection occurs, the inspection criteria that it uses, and how it handles defective products. Since Unlimited Decadence manufactures a food product, it also discusses sanitation and pest control in this section. Regardless of the rigorous inspection procedures that a company may have, it should still have procedures in place for handling defective products that reach its customers and should describe these procedures in this section. These procedures may include warranties, guarantees, and repair and replacement policies.

A company also describes in this section how it protects, stores, and keeps track of its finished products before selling them, and how it transports them to its customers (it includes names of carriers and alternativecarriers, as well as carrier reliability, delivery schedules, shipping fees, and payment schedules). If the company's products require special shipping accommodations, such as a regulated temperature, the company describes these conditions in this section of the business plan.

By including a production plan in its business plan, a manufacturing company gives potential investors and creditors vital information about how well it can execute its production plans, meet its sales orders, stay in business, pay back its loans, and provide a return to its investors. These same production plan details give managers a plan of action and a benchmark against which to later measure the company's actual production performance.

The Financial Plan

As we mentioned earlier, the production plan influences a company's financial plan. This influence not only results from the unique production function of a manufacturing company, but is also a direct reflection of how accounting in a manufacturing company differs from that in a retail or service company. As we will discuss later in this chapter and in the next chapter, these differences add some new dimensions to both the cost-volume-profit (C-V-P) analysis and the budgeting of a manufacturing company. Before we look at these dimensions, however, we will first explore some of the ways that accounting differs between a manufacturing company and its retail and service counterparts.

Manufacturing Costs

2 *How does a manufacturing company determine the cost of the goods that it manufactures?*

A major difference between the accounting of a manufacturing company and that of a retail company is the way in which a manufacturing company accounts for inventories and cost of goods sold. As you know, a retail company has one type of inventory—goods available (ready) for sale. When it sells these goods, the retail company moves the cost of these goods from its inventory account into its cost of goods sold account. Since a manufacturing company *makes* the goods that it sells, it has *three* types of inventories: (1) the raw materials it uses either directly or indirectly in manufacturing its products, called **raw materials inventory,** (2) the products that it has started manufacturing but that are not yet complete, called **goods-in-process inventory** (also called *work-in-process inventory*), and (3) finished products that are ready to be sold, called **finished goods inventory.** Raw materials inventory and goods-in-process inventory are unique to manufacturing companies. However, a manufacturing company's finished goods inventory is the equivalent of the inventory of a retail company. Both of these inventories contain goods that are ready to be sold.

Since a manufacturing company makes the products it sells rather than purchasing them in a form ready for sale, determining the cost of the three inventories is more complex than is determining the cost of the one inventory of a retail company. For example, the cost of a retail company's inventory is usually the sum of the inventory's invoice price and shipping costs. On the other hand, the cost of a manufacturing company's finished goods inventory is the sum of all of the costs of manufacturing that inventory.

In a simple manufacturing process, three elements, or production inputs, contribute to the cost of manufacturing a product: the cost of direct materials, the cost of direct labor, and the cost of factory overhead. The sum of the costs of these three elements eventually becomes the cost of the manufactured products. Then, as each product is sold, its cost (composed of the costs of direct materials, direct labor, and factory overhead) becomes part of the total cost of goods sold. Exhibit 11-3 shows the relationships among these cost elements, the manufacturing process, the three inventories, and the cost of goods sold for Unlimited Decadence. We will discuss these elements and relationships next.

Direct Materials

Direct materials are the raw materials that physically become part of a manufactured product. In other words, direct materials are the raw materials and parts from which the product is made. Think again about that list of ingredients on the wrapper of a candy bar. These ingredients are the direct materials from which that candy bar was made. Direct materials include materials the company acquires from natural sources, such as the honey that Unlimited Decadence includes in some of its candy bars. Direct materials also include processed or manufactured products that the company purchases from other companies, such as the milk products that Unlimited Decadence purchases from Mo-o-oving Milk Products and the corn syrups that it purchases from Corn Syrups Are Us. The direct materials of many manufacturing companies also include parts or components that they purchase from other companies. For example, the microchips inside your computer were probably manufactured by a different company from the one that manufactured your computer. Since direct materials become a part of the finished product, a company includes their costs in the cost of the finished product.

 Often a company purchases its direct materials from companies in other countries. Since the General Agreement on Tariffs and Trade (GATT) was implemented, U.S. companies can purchase foreign raw materials at a lower cost. Now, for example, Tower Automotive, a major supplier of automotive frames to Detroit's automotive industry, can buy cheaper steel.[5] GATT reduces import tariffs on many products, reducing the overall cost to importers of those products. How do you think this would affect the determination of the cost of Tower Automotive's finished product?

www.towerautomotive.com

Direct Labor

Unless a factory is fully automated, factory employees help convert or assemble the direct materials into a finished product. **Direct labor** is the labor of the employees who work

---

[5]John S. DeMott, "What GATT Means to Small Business," *Nation's Business*, March 1995, 53.

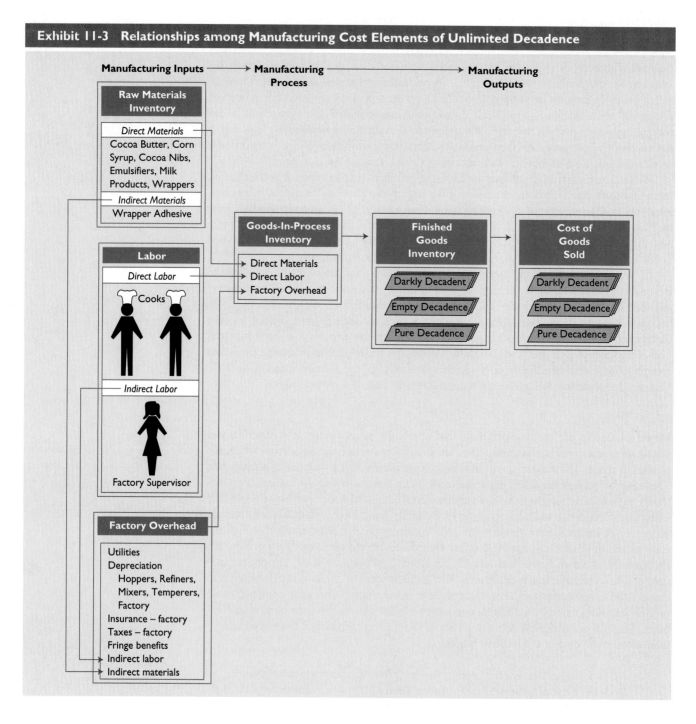

Exhibit II-3 Relationships among Manufacturing Cost Elements of Unlimited Decadence

with the direct materials to convert or assemble them into the finished product. For example, when Unlimited Decadence manufactures some of its candy bars, the labor of all the employees who operate the equipment that prepares the candy bar ingredients, mixes the ingredients, refines and tempers the chocolate paste, forms the candy bars, and packages the candy bars is direct labor. The cost of the direct labor is the wages earned by these employees. Since direct labor is the labor necessary to convert or assemble direct materials into a finished product, manufacturing companies include the cost of direct labor in the cost of the finished product. Since labor in some countries is cheaper than that in the United States, some U.S. manufacturing companies ship direct materials to those countries to be assembled. By doing this, the companies save on direct labor costs.

Do you think this candy manufacturing process has any "hidden" costs?

 Do you think the cost of shipping the direct materials to other countries and back should be included in the cost of the finished product? Why or why not?

Factory Overhead

Factory overhead includes all items, other than direct materials and direct labor, that are necessary for the manufacture of the product. Factory overhead is often called *manufacturing overhead,* or simply *overhead.* Although factory overhead items are necessary for the manufacture of products, they usually cannot be traced directly to individual products. For example, Unlimited Decadence's factory overhead includes repair and maintenance of its factory equipment. It also includes depreciation of this equipment, utilities used in the manufacturing process, insurance and property taxes on the factory and factory equipment, depreciation of the factory, and other factory costs. Unlimited Decadence's factory overhead also includes raw materials and labor that are not traceable to individual products. Because they are not traceable to products, these raw materials and labor are called **indirect materials** and **indirect labor.**

For example, although adhesive is used for each candy bar wrapper, managers think of the adhesive as an indirect material and include the cost of the adhesive in factory overhead costs. They choose this treatment because the amount and cost of adhesive per candy bar is so small that tracing it to individual candy bars, or even to cases of candy bars, is difficult. Notice in Exhibit 11-3 that before Unlimited Decadence uses indirect materials in production, it includes them with the direct materials in the raw materials inventory. Indirect labor includes the salaries of employees like custodians and maintenance workers, as well as supervisors. Managers consider the factory supervisor's salary to be indirect labor and include this salary in factory overhead costs because her job activities are too broad to be able to assign portions of her salary to individual products. Since factory overhead is necessary for the manufacture of the product, manufacturing companies include the costs of factory overhead in the cost of the finished product.

Notice that all of the overhead costs relate to what goes on in the factory. Factory overhead does not include selling costs, general and administrative costs, or other costs that we discussed earlier in the book. Although we discussed salaries, utilities, and depreciation expenses in previous chapters, these expenses did not occur in the factory and, therefore, did not relate to the manufacturing process. Since both manufacturing companies and retail companies have selling and administrative activities, the two types of companies treat these items in exactly the same way.

A manufacturing company includes manufacturing costs (direct materials, direct labor, and factory overhead) in the cost of its manufactured products, and therefore, in the cost of its inventories. Then, as the company sells its products, it transfers these costs from finished goods inventory to cost of goods sold. A retail company shows the cost of its products on hand (the invoice price and transportation costs) on its balance sheet as inventory and then as it sells these products, it transfers these costs from inventory to cost of goods sold. Exhibit 11-4 shows selling expenses and general and administrative expenses for a retail company, and how a retail company (Sweet Temptations) shows these expenses on its income statement. It also shows selling expenses, and general and administrative expenses, as well as the manufacturing costs for a manufacturing company, and how a manufacturing company (Unlimited Decadence) shows these items on its income statement. However, note that cost of goods sold includes only the cost of inventory sold, and not the total manufacturing cost for inventory produced.

Since products have three types of inputs—direct materials, direct labor, and factory overhead—why do you think candy bar labels list only the candy bars' ingredients?

Exhibit 11-4 Relationship of Costs to the Income Statements of a Retail Company and a Manufacturing Company

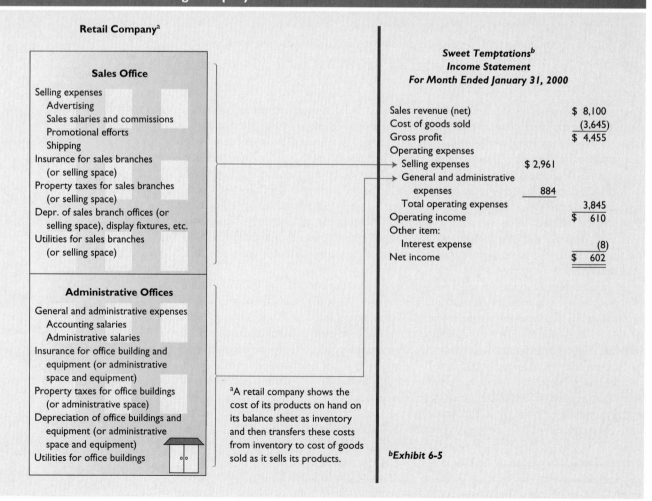

Retail Company[a]

Sales Office

Selling expenses
  Advertising
  Sales salaries and commissions
  Promotional efforts
  Shipping
Insurance for sales branches
  (or selling space)
Property taxes for sales branches
  (or selling space)
Depr. of sales branch offices (or
  selling space), display fixtures, etc.
Utilities for sales branches
  (or selling space)

Administrative Offices

General and administrative expenses
  Accounting salaries
  Administrative salaries
Insurance for office building and
  equipment (or administrative
  space and equipment)
Property taxes for office buildings
  (or administrative space)
Depreciation of office buildings and
  equipment (or administrative
  space and equipment)
Utilities for office buildings

[a]A retail company shows the cost of its products on hand on its balance sheet as inventory and then transfers these costs from inventory to cost of goods sold as it sells its products.

Sweet Temptations[b]
Income Statement
For Month Ended January 31, 2000

Sales revenue (net)		$ 8,100
Cost of goods sold		(3,645)
Gross profit		$ 4,455
Operating expenses		
Selling expenses	$ 2,961	
General and administrative expenses	884	
Total operating expenses		3,845
Operating income		$ 610
Other item:		
Interest expense		(8)
Net income		$ 602

[b]Exhibit 6-5

Standard Costs

A knowledge of how many direct materials, how many hours of direct labor, and approximately how much overhead should go into the manufacture of each product gives managers information with which to plan the materials, labor, and overhead necessary for expected levels of production. It also gives managers a benchmark against which to measure the actual usage of each of these production inputs in the manufacture of the product. Similarly, a knowledge of what the *costs* of these production inputs should be gives managers information with which to plan production costs and cash flows, and also gives them a benchmark against which to measure the actual costs of manufacturing each product. The accounting system supplies managers with standard costs and actual costs of materials, labor, and overhead to aid them in planning and controlling the operations of the company.

What Are Standard Costs?

Standard costs are the costs that *should* be incurred in performing an activity or producing a product under a given set of planned operating conditions. Management accountants, engineers, and others involved in a manufacturing activity establish the standard costs, or predetermined costs, of that activity based on a careful study of the manufacturing process. Many factors can influence these costs, so in setting standards, the group must assume that

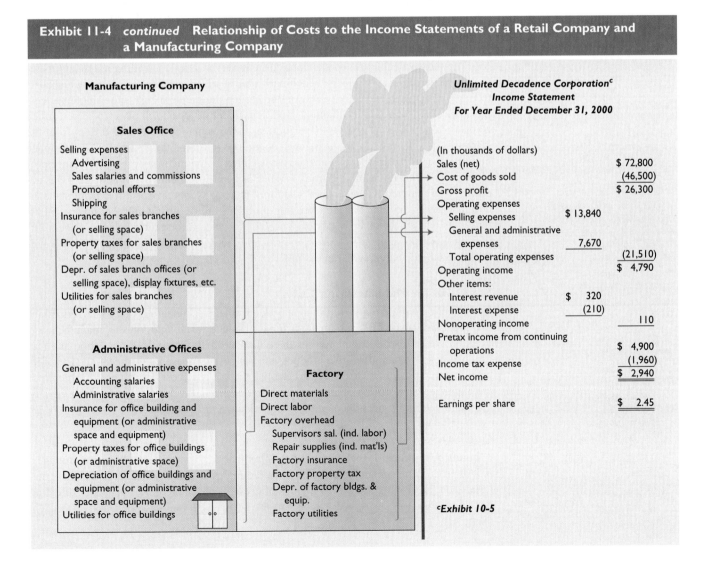

Exhibit 11-4 *continued* **Relationship of Costs to the Income Statements of a Retail Company and a Manufacturing Company**

Manufacturing Company

Sales Office

Selling expenses
  Advertising
  Sales salaries and commissions
  Promotional efforts
  Shipping
Insurance for sales branches
  (or selling space)
Property taxes for sales branches
  (or selling space)
Depr. of sales branch offices (or
  selling space), display fixtures, etc.
Utilities for sales branches
  (or selling space)

Administrative Offices

General and administrative expenses
  Accounting salaries
  Administrative salaries
Insurance for office building and
  equipment (or administrative
  space and equipment)
Property taxes for office buildings
  (or administrative space)
Depreciation of office buildings and
  equipment (or administrative
  space and equipment)
Utilities for office buildings

Factory

Direct materials
Direct labor
Factory overhead
  Supervisors sal. (ind. labor)
  Repair supplies (ind. mat'ls)
  Factory insurance
  Factory property tax
  Depr. of factory bldgs. &
    equip.
Factory utilities

***Unlimited Decadence Corporation*[c]**
Income Statement
For Year Ended December 31, 2000

(In thousands of dollars)		
Sales (net)		$ 72,800
Cost of goods sold		(46,500)
Gross profit		$ 26,300
Operating expenses		
Selling expenses	$ 13,840	
General and administrative		
expenses	7,670	
Total operating expenses		(21,510)
Operating income		$ 4,790
Other items:		
Interest revenue	$ 320	
Interest expense	(210)	
Nonoperating income		110
Pretax income from continuing		
operations		$ 4,900
Income tax expense		(1,960)
Net income		$ 2,940
Earnings per share		$ 2.45

[c]*Exhibit 10-5*

a certain set of conditions exists. For example, Unlimited Decadence bases the standard direct labor costs in its factory on the assumption that the company has direct materials of the proper specification (for example, dark chocolate versus milk chocolate) and quality entering the process as needed, equipment adjusted properly for the particular candy bar being manufactured, cooks who have the proper training and experience and who earn the normal wage rate, and so forth. The standard costs are the costs that managers expect the company to incur when these conditions exist. Together, these costs become the standard cost for each manufactured product.

 If direct materials do not meet the company's specifications or quality requirements, how might using these materials affect direct labor costs? Why would maladjusted manufacturing equipment affect direct labor costs?

Uses of Standard Costs and Variances

3 *Why are standard costs useful in controlling a company's operations?*

One reason that standards are useful in planning is that they aid in the development of budgets, as you will see in the next chapter. Later in this chapter you will see how the standard costs for direct materials, direct labor, and factory overhead become part of a manufacturing company's variable costs.

Standards also are a valuable source of information for decision-making. If they reflect current operating conditions, standard costs provide a more reliable basis for estimating costs than do actual past costs, which may reflect abnormal conditions or past inefficiencies. It is also normally less time-consuming and costly to develop cost estimates from standard costs than to perform an analysis of actual past costs each time a decision is required.

The most valuable use of standard costs, however, is in controlling company operations. Standard costs provide the benchmark against which managers compare actual costs to help them evaluate an activity. As we said earlier, the standard cost is the amount of cost that *should* be incurred if the planned conditions under which an activity is to be performed actually exist when the activity is performed. If the actual cost incurred differs from the standard cost, one or more of the planned conditions must not have existed. This difference between a standard cost and an actual cost is called a **variance.** Reporting a variance provides a *signal* that an operating problem (such as a machine being out of adjustment) is occurring and may require managers' attention. If actual costs do not differ from standard costs, managers assume that no operating problems are occurring and that no special attention is needed. In other words, *feedback* of variance information helps managers implement the *management by exception* principle that we discussed in Chapter 4. We will talk more about analyzing variances in Chapter 17.

Standards for Manufacturing Costs

You might be wondering how a company determines its standard costs. Managers establish standard costs for each manufactured product (or *output* of the manufacturing process). Remember, a company uses three inputs (direct materials, direct labor, and factory overhead) to manufacture a product, and the costs of these inputs become costs of its manufactured products. Therefore, to establish the standard cost of each product *output* of the manufacturing process, managers must first determine two standards for each *input* to the manufacturing process: a quantity standard and a price standard.

Quantity Standard

A **quantity standard** is the *amount* of an input that the company should use to produce a unit of product in its manufacturing process. Examples of quantity standards for direct materials and direct labor are the 10 pounds of cocoa beans and the 30 minutes of direct labor that Unlimited Decadence expects to use to produce one case of Darkly Decadent candy bars.

Price Standard

A **price standard** is the *cost* that the company should incur to acquire one unit of input for its manufacturing process. Examples of price standards are the expected cost per pound of the cocoa beans that Unlimited Decadence uses to produce a case of Darkly Decadent candy bars, and the expected cost per hour for the wages of the cooks who produce a case of Darkly Decadent candy bars. We will discuss quantity standards and price standards more in Chapter 17.

Cost-Volume-Profit Analysis

One of the most common forms of analysis in which managers use cost estimates based on standards is Cost-Volume-Profit (C-V-P) analysis, or break-even analysis. Recall from our discussion in Chapter 3 about C-V-P analysis in retail companies that this is a tool that managers use to evaluate how changes in sales volume, selling prices of products, variable costs per unit, and total fixed costs affect a company's profit. Managers in manufacturing companies use the same type of analysis.

4 *How do manufacturing costs affect cost-volume-profit analysis?*

Behaviors of Manufacturing Costs

As in C-V-P analysis for a retail company, the first step in C-V-P analysis for a manufacturing company is to identify the behaviors of the company's costs. Remember, a manufacturing company has three additional costs over those of a retail company: the manufacturing costs of direct materials, direct labor, and factory overhead. Like the other costs, these can ultimately be classified as variable or fixed costs.

Variable Manufacturing Costs

We just discussed how managers develop standard quantities and costs for the inputs into the production process. Since the standard quantity of direct materials and direct labor are for one unit of product, the total quantity of direct materials and direct labor that should be used in manufacturing the company's products will increase as the level of production increases. For example, assume that the standard amount of cocoa beans used to produce a case (unit) of Darkly Decadent chocolate bars is 10 pounds. If Unlimited Decadence plans to produce 25 cases of Darkly Decadent candy bars, it expects to use 250 pounds of cocoa beans (10 pounds of cocoa beans per case × 25 cases). If it plans to produce 30 cases, it expects to use 300 pounds of cocoa beans (10 pounds of cocoa beans per case × 30 cases).

Since companies develop standard costs for each unit of input, the total cost of production input increases as the quantity of direct materials and direct labor increases. If Unlimited Decadence's standard cost per pound of cocoa beans is $0.45, the cost of the cocoa beans it expects to use in producing 25 cases of Darkly Decadent candy bars is $112.50 ($0.45 per pound × 10 pounds per case × 25 cases). If it plans to produce 30 cases of the candy bar, the cost of cocoa beans it expects to use is $135 ($0.45 per pound × 10 pounds per case × 30 cases).

A **variable manufacturing cost** is constant for each unit produced but varies in total in direct proportion to the volume produced. Since the costs of direct material and direct labor are constant for each unit produced and since the total costs of direct materials and direct labor increase as total production increases, we classify these costs as variable manufacturing costs.

We also classify some (but not all) factory overhead costs as variable costs. For example, as we mentioned earlier, Unlimited Decadence classifies the adhesive used to close the candy bar wrappers as factory overhead rather than direct material because tracing this adhesive to any particular product is difficult. Since the amount of adhesive used increases as the production of cases of candy bars increases, the total cost of the adhesive increases as the production of cases of candy bars increases. We classify the adhesive's cost, then, as a variable manufacturing cost.

Fixed Manufacturing Costs

We classify all factory overhead costs that are not affected in total by changes in the volume of production within a specific period as fixed costs. At Unlimited Decadence, for example, the factory supervisor's salary is a fixed cost.

Mixed Manufacturing Costs

Mixed costs (sometimes called *semivariable costs*) are costs that behave as would the sum of a fixed cost and a variable cost. That is, mixed costs have a fixed cost component and a variable cost component.

For example, suppose that the local power company charges Unlimited Decadence a constant amount, say $0.10, for each kilowatt hour (kwh) of electricity it uses. If the amount of electricity that Unlimited Decadence uses for factory lighting remains constant each year regardless of the volume of production (say at 420,000 kwh per month), the power cost for this use is fixed at $42,000 per month (420,000 kwh × $0.10 per kwh). The amount of electricity required by the equipment used in production, however, is directly proportional to the number of cases of candy bars produced (the volume). Normally, the power cost for this use varies in proportion to the number of cases of candy bars produced. Suppose, for the sake of illustration, that we know it takes 0.5 kwh of electricity for each case of candy bars produced. The total power cost is a mixed cost because it equals the sum of a fixed component of $42,000 (from factory lighting) and a variable component (from equipment use) that increases at a rate of $0.05 per case of candy bars produced ($0.10 per kwh × 0.5 kwh per case of candy bars).

The general cost equation for the total amount of a mixed cost is as follows:

$$\text{Total mixed cost} = F + vX$$

where:

F = The fixed component
v = The rate at which the variable component increases per unit of volume
X = The volume

 This equation should look familiar to you. In Chapter 3 we used this same equation for total costs. What is the difference between total costs and a mixed cost?

The cost equation describing Unlimited Decadence's total power cost for one year is as follows:

$$\text{Total power cost} = \$42,000 + \$0.05X$$

where:

X = The number of cases of candy bars produced per year

Thus, the total power cost is $242,000 at a production volume of 4,000,000 cases of candy bars [$42,000 + $0.05(4,000,000)]. At a production volume of 4,800,000 cases of candy bars, the total power cost would be $282,000 [$42,000 + $0.05 (4,800,000)].

Exhibit 11-5 shows a graph of the mixed cost we just described. Notice that a mixed cost increases in a straight line. In other words, the mixed cost increases at a constant rate equal to the rate of its variable component ($0.05 per case of candy bars produced) as volume increases. However, unlike a variable cost, it intersects the vertical (cost) axis above the origin at an amount equal to its fixed cost component ($42,000).

Managers often separate the fixed and variable components of mixed costs and treat them independently. The fixed components of mixed costs are grouped with (and treated like) other fixed costs, and the variable components are grouped with (and treated like) variable costs. This is how we will treat them in this chapter.

Exhibit 11-5   Graph of a Mixed Cost (Total Power Cost)

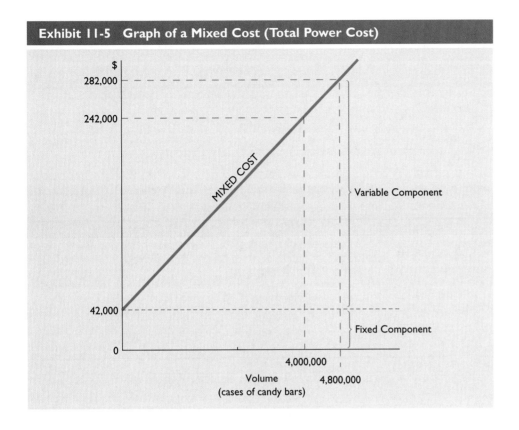

Estimating Costs

So far, we have treated variable, fixed, and mixed costs as if they are linear; if we graphed them, they would form a straight line. However, many factors other than volume can also affect costs. In reality, costs do not always behave linearly, although they *approximate* that behavior. For example, assume that Unlimited Decadence's electric bills for the factory and for candy bar production for the last six years were the following:

Year	Total Power Cost	Volume (cases)
1	$182,000	2,800,000
2	198,700	3,000,000
3	208,200	3,500,000
4	255,100	4,000,000
5	268,900	4,620,000
6	292,000	5,000,000

We can visualize the behavior of these costs by plotting them on a graph, as we show in Exhibit 11-6. This pattern of points on a graph is called a **scatter diagram.** Although the points on the scatter diagram don't form a straight line, they approximate one.

If we visualize a straight line that runs through these points and that best represents the pattern of the points, this line would intersect the vertical axis above the origin of the graph, just as would a mixed cost. Therefore, for the total power cost, we can assume a mixed behavior pattern that would be represented by the equation for a mixed cost. We then can solve the equation by estimating the fixed component and the variable component. One way to do this is by observing where the line intersects the vertical axis (the fixed cost) and how much the line increases for every unit change in volume (the variable cost). However, visually drawing the line through the scatter diagram is not very precise; if you drew a line through

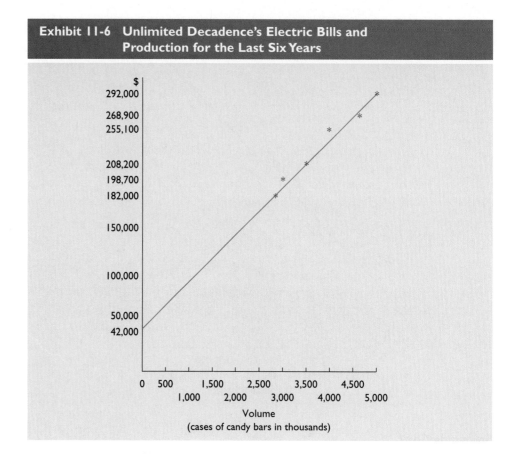

Exhibit 11-6 Unlimited Decadence's Electric Bills and Production for the Last Six Years

the points and compared your line with that of one of your classmates, you would likely see two different lines. Another method that managers often use to give a quick, shorthand estimate of fixed and variable costs is called the high-low method.

The High-Low Method

The **high-low method** assumes that any change that occurs in total costs when volume changes from the lowest volume level to the highest volume level must be due to the total variable cost change that occurs with that volume increase. (Remember, fixed costs don't change with volume.) Therefore, the variable cost per unit of volume can be estimated with the following equation:

$$v = \frac{\text{Cost change from lowest to highest volume}}{\text{Volume change from lowest to highest volume}}$$

where:

$$v = \text{The variable cost per unit of volume}$$

Going back to Unlimited Decadence's power cost and volume data for the last six years, we can figure the volume and corresponding cost changes from the lowest to the highest volume levels as follows:

	Total Power Cost	Volume (cases)
High volume	$292,000	5,000,000
Low volume	182,000	2,800,000
Change	$110,000	2,200,000

Therefore:

$$v = \frac{\$110,000}{2,200,000} = \$0.05$$

Once we determine that the variable cost estimate is $0.05 per case of candy bars, we can estimate the total variable component of the cost at either the high or the low volume level. For example, at the high volume level, the total variable cost is $250,000 (5,000,000 cases × $0.05). The total cost at that level of volume was $292,000. If we subtract the variable cost component from the total cost ($292,000 − $250,000), what we have left is the fixed cost component of $42,000. Thus, by using the high-low method, Unlimited Decadence can use the following equation to estimate the total annual power cost at any volume level:

Total Power Cost = $42,000 + $0.05X

where:

X = volume

Since fixed costs don't change with changes in volume, the fixed cost component should be the same at the low volume level. Furthermore, the variable cost per case of candy bars should be the same at both volume levels. We can test this by substituting the low volume level into the above equation:

Total Power Cost = $42,000 + $0.05(2,800,000) = $182,000

As expected, the $182,000 we computed equals the $182,000 total cost measured at the low volume level of 2,800,000 cases.

It is important to be careful when studying past cost data to establish future cost behavior patterns. In making the analysis, you should be able to answer *yes* to the following questions before using this method:

Were conditions essentially the same in all the periods the data represent?

Will the same conditions continue to exist in the future, so that the cost behavior patterns will remain the same?

Does the computed cost pattern make sense?

It is important that similar conditions existed in the time periods from which the data were obtained because abnormal conditions would distort the data and, consequently, the estimates made from the data. Suppose, for example, that during one of the years from which we obtained Unlimited Decadence's power costs, Unlimited Decadence had to add supplemental heat from electric furnaces in the factory because of an unusually cold winter. If that year happened to be the high- or low-activity year, the high-low method would produce a distorted result because of the abnormally high power cost during that year.

We also must expect that the conditions on which we are basing our estimates will continue. Otherwise, we can't count on the cost behavior patterns to stay the same. If, for example, the power company adds a surcharge or if Unlimited Decadence increases its lighting requirements, these changed conditions will also change the cost equation.

Finally, the resulting cost pattern must make sense. (Is it reasonable?) For instance, using the high-low method to estimate the relationship between sales volume and depreciation of factory equipment would give misleading results; sales volume and the depreciation of factory equipment are not directly related.

The high-low method allows decision-makers to quickly estimate the fixed and variable components of mixed costs. However, it is not the most precise method. Statistical methods such as regression analysis, which you may learn about in another class, provide more accurate results but are not as convenient. Even with these methods, however, careless interpretation can lead to misleading results. Furthermore, even the most precise estimates apply only within a certain range of volumes.

Relevant Range

Each time a management accountant prepares an analysis that involves cost estimates for a manager's decision, the requirements of the decision determine a range of volumes over which the estimates must be especially accurate. For example, if Unlimited Decadence expects to produce between 3,500,000 and 6,000,000 cases of candy bars each year and wants to decide whether or not to change its manufacturing process, cost estimates for both the existing process and the alternative process over that specific range (3,500,000 to 6,000,000 cases) would be useful in making the decision. The company would not be helped by knowing which process is less expensive to operate when producing below 3,500,000 candy bars, nor would the company care about comparing manufacturing costs for volumes above 6,000,000 candy bars. Only the range of volumes from 3,500,000 to 6,000,000 is relevant (useful) to the decision.

The **relevant range** is the range of volumes over which cost estimates are needed for a particular use and over which observed cost behaviors are expected to remain stable. The relevant range concept is extremely important because by focusing on the range of volumes for which cost estimates should be accurate, a management accountant can make cost estimates that are useful for decision-making. Decision-makers will be able to ignore cost behavior patterns outside of the relevant range. Furthermore, if the management accountant states the relevant range whenever providing cost estimates, potential users of the estimates will be alerted to the range of volumes over which the estimates are reliable.

Some costs do not fit the fixed, variable, or mixed cost behavior patterns we described. They may vary, but not in a straight line over all possible volumes. For example, Unlimited Decadence may pay less for each tub of cocoa butter that it purchases above a certain volume level than it pays for each tub that it purchases below that volume level. Other costs may be fixed over a wide range of volumes but increase abruptly to a higher amount if the upper limit of that volume range is exceeded. For example, once Unlimited Decadence's production of candy bars reaches a certain level, the capacity of its mixers will be reached. To exceed that level of production, Unlimited Decadence will have to purchase an additional mixer. When

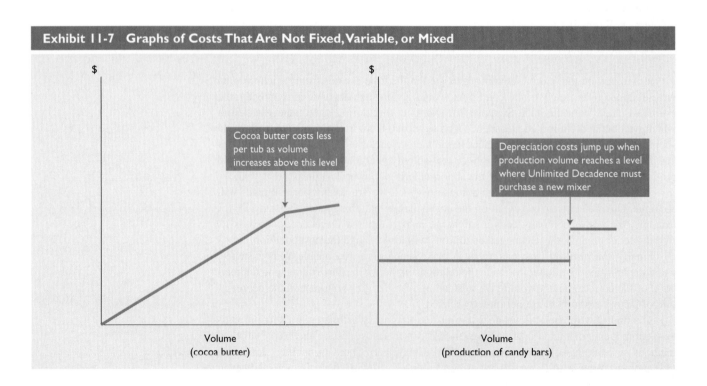

Exhibit 11-7 Graphs of Costs That Are Not Fixed, Variable, or Mixed

this occurs, Unlimited Decadence's fixed depreciation cost for mixers will jump by the amount of the new mixer's depreciation. Exhibit 11-7 presents graphs of these two cost behavior patterns.

Despite these potential cost behavior patterns, the management accountant must determine only how the costs behave within the relevant range, and in most cases, these costs fit one of the three common behavior patterns. For example, the behavior patterns shown in the graphs in Exhibit 11-7 might be estimated within the relevant range as a variable cost and a fixed cost, as we show in Exhibit 11-8.

C-V-P Computations Using the Profit Equation (Multiple Products)

Remember from our discussion in Chapter 3 that C-V-P analysis is an examination of how profit is affected by changes in the sales volume, in the selling prices of products, and in the various costs of the company. Decision-makers use C-V-P analysis to gain an understanding of the profit impact of plans that they are making. This understanding can produce more informed decisions during the planning process.

When a manufacturing company produces and sells only one product, its C-V-P computations are the same as those that Sweet Temptations used in Chapter 3, with sales volume measured in units of that product. However, most companies sell several products. When these companies (manufacturing and retail companies) perform a C-V-P analysis of their overall operations, they must consider the relative sales volumes of their different products.

This doesn't mean that the single-product analysis we described in Chapter 3 is not useful, however. Managers can use a single-product analysis to study the relationship of the cost, volume, and profit of one of a company's products as long as they can separate the costs and the sales revenues of that product from the costs and revenues caused by the production and sales of other products.

Next we will discuss C-V-P analysis in companies that sell more than one product. Our discussion assumes that you remember single-product C-V-P analysis from Chapter 3. A brief review, on your part, of the concepts and computations in Chapter 3 will help you understand the following discussion. To keep the computations simple, we will use an example involving two products, but *the procedure we are about to describe can be used with any number of products.*

5 *What is the effect of multiple products on cost-volume-profit analysis?*

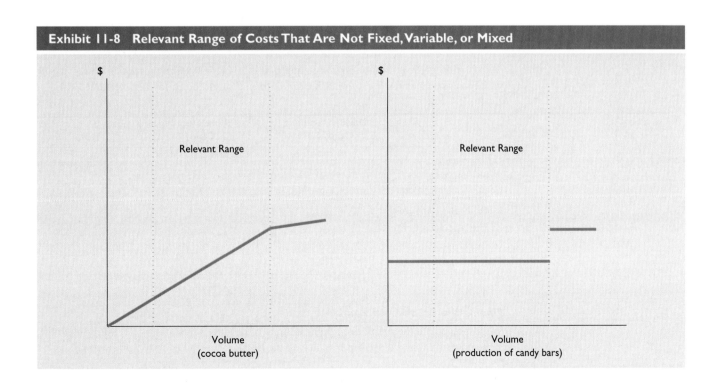

Exhibit 11-8   Relevant Range of Costs That Are Not Fixed, Variable, or Mixed

Contribution Margin for a Given Product Sales Mix

Managers can apply the single-product form of analysis to any *group* of a company's products if they know the product sales mix and the costs and sales revenues of the individual products within that group of products. The **product sales mix** is the relative proportion of units of the different products sold. In C-V-P analysis when there is more than one product, the product sales mix is considered to be one "unit." For example, if Unlimited Decadence has typically sold five cases of Darkly Decadent candy bars for every one case of Pure Decadence candy bars sold, this combination of cases of candy bars is considered to be one "unit." (Visualize a basket containing five cases of Darkly Decadent candy bars and one case of Pure Decadence candy bars.) As long as Unlimited Decadence plans to continue to sell the Darkly Decadent and Pure Decadence candy bars in that proportion, we can say that it has the same product sales mix as it had in the past.

Suppose that Unlimited Decadence estimates that its fixed costs will be $24,800,000 in the coming year and that its product sales mix will be five cases of Darkly Decadent candy bars sold for every one case of Pure Decadence candy bars. Cases of Darkly Decadent candy bars will sell for $16, require $11 of variable cost, and earn a contribution margin of $5. Cases of Pure Decadence candy bars will sell for $20 each, require $14 of variable cost, and earn a contribution margin of $6. Thus, the sales revenue, variable cost, and contribution margin per "unit" (5 cases of Darkly Decadent candy bars and 1 case of Pure Decadence candy bars) will be $100, $69, and $31, respectively. The sales revenue per "unit" is computed as follows:

$$
\begin{aligned}
\text{Selling price per "unit"} = \ & (\$16 \text{ per case of Darkly Decadent candy bars} \times \\
& 5 \text{ cases of Darkly Decadent candy bars}) + \\
& (\$20 \text{ per case of Pure Decadence candy bars} \times \\
& 1 \text{ case of Pure Decadence candy bars}) \\
= \ & \underline{\$100}
\end{aligned}
$$

The variable cost per "unit" is computed as follows:

$$
\begin{aligned}
\text{Variable cost per "unit"} = \ & (\$11 \text{ per case of Darkly Decadent candy bars} \times \\
& 5 \text{ cases of Darkly Decadent candy bars}) + \\
& (\$14 \text{ per case of Pure Decadence candy bars} \times \\
& 1 \text{ case of Pure Decadence candy bars}) \\
= \ & \underline{\$69}
\end{aligned}
$$

Therefore, the contribution margin per unit is $31 ($100 selling price per "unit" − $69 variable cost per unit). We summarize this information in the following schedule:

	Darkly Decadent Candy Bars		Pure Decadence Candy Bars		Total per "Unit"
Selling price/case	$16		$20		
Variable cost/case	(11)		(14)		
Contribution margin/case	$ 5		$ 6		
Expected sales mix (cases)	5		1		
Sales revenue	$80	+	$20	=	$100
Less: variable cost	(55)	+	(14)	=	(69)
Contribution margin	$25	+	$ 6	=	$ 31

Finding the Break-Even Point

We can calculate the break-even point in units of product sales mix by beginning with the same equation that we used in calculating the break-even point for one product:

$$\frac{\text{Unit sales volume}}{\text{(to earn zero profit)}} = \frac{\text{Total fixed cost}}{\text{Contribution margin per unit}}$$

However, keep in mind that when Unlimited Decadence uses this equation, its contribution margin per unit represents a "unit" that now consists of five cases of Darkly Decadent candy bars and one case of Pure Decadence candy bars. Since fixed costs are $24,800,000, Unlimited Decadence can find the break-even point expressed as "units" of sales volume by dividing the $24,800,000 total fixed cost by the $31 contribution margin per "unit." We can write this in equation form as follows:

$$\frac{\text{Break-even point}}{\text{(in "units")}} = \frac{\text{Total fixed cost}}{\text{Contribution margin per "unit"}}$$

$$= \frac{\$24,800,000}{\$31}$$

$$= \underline{800,000} \text{ "units"}$$

To break even, Unlimited Decadence would have to sell 800,000 "units," composed of 4,000,000 cases of Darkly Decadent candy bars (800,000 × 5 cases of Darkly Decadent candy bars) and 800,000 cases of Pure Decadence candy bars (800,000 × 1 case of Pure Decadence candy bars).

We can verify the break-even "unit" sales volume of 800,000 "units" that we just computed for Unlimited Decadence with the following profit computation:

```
Sales revenue:
    Cases of Darkly Decadent candy bars..................$64,000,000
        (4,000,000 cases @ $16 per case)
    Cases of Pure Decadence candy bars.....................16,000,000
        (800,000 cases @ $20 per case)
Total sales revenue..........................................................................  $80,000,000
Less variable costs:
    Cases of Darkly Decadent candy bars..................$44,000,000
        (4,000,000 cases @ $11 per case)
    Cases of Pure Decadence candy bars.....................11,200,000
        (800,000 cases @ $14 per case)
Total variable cost............................................................................(55,200,000)
Total contribution margin................................................................$24,800,000
Less total fixed cost.........................................................................(24,800,000)
Profit.................................................................................................$          0
```

Note in this computation that total sales revenue ($80,000,000) equals total cost ($55,200,000 variable + $24,800,000 fixed). Also note that total contribution margin equals total fixed cost ($24,800,000). In either case, profit equals $0.

Finding the Unit Sales Volume to Achieve a Target Pretax Profit

A company often states its profit goal at an amount that results in a satisfactory rate of return on owner's equity. Remember, the return on owner's equity measures how effectively managers have earned income on the amount the owners invested in the company.

In Chapter 7, in our discussion of entrepreneurial companies, we calculated the return on owner's equity as follows:

$$\text{Return on Owner's Equity} = \frac{\text{Net Income}}{\text{Average Owner's Equity}}$$

The calculation is similar for a corporation, but with two differences. One difference is that the denominator is stockholders' equity. The other difference is caused by the fact

that a corporation pays income taxes and deducts the amount of its income tax expense on its income statement to determine its net income. Since the return on stockholders' equity measures a company's efficiency in earning income on the stockholders' investment, and since income taxes are a tax *on* that income, both internal and external users are interested in the return *after* income taxes. The calculation then becomes as follows:

$$\text{Return on Stockholders' Equity} = \frac{\text{Income after Taxes}}{\text{Average Stockholders' Equity}}$$

But since internal users usually can't control the income tax expense imposed by the U.S. government, they are interested in what pretax income (profit) the company must earn to achieve its targeted after-tax income. For example, assume Unlimited Decadence estimates that its average stockholders' equity for the coming year will be $18,000,000, and assume that its managers would like it to earn a return on stockholders' equity of 18%, the industry average for confectioners. To achieve this return on stockholders' equity, Unlimited Decadence will have to earn $3,240,000 income after taxes ($18,000,000 × 18%). Suppose, then, that you want to know how many units Unlimited Decadence will have to sell to earn this desired after-tax income. To use the C-V-P equations, you must first convert the desired after-tax income to pretax income, using the following equation:[6]

$$\text{Pretax Income} = \frac{\text{After-tax Income}}{(1 - \text{Tax Rate})}$$

If we assume that Unlimited Decadence is subject to a 40 percent income tax rate, it must earn $5,400,000 [$3,240,000 ÷ (1 − 0.40)] pretax income to achieve a $3,240,000 after-tax income. The computation to determine the "unit" sales volume to achieve this target pretax income is as follows:

$$\frac{\text{"Unit" sales volume needed to}}{\text{earn a desired pretax income}} = \frac{\text{Total fixed cost} + \text{Desired pretax income}}{\text{Contribution margin per "unit"}}$$

$$\frac{\text{"Unit" sales volume needed to}}{\text{earn \$5,400,000 pretax income}} = \frac{\$24,800,000 \text{ fixed cost} + \$5,400,000 \text{ pretax income}}{\$31}$$

$$= \underline{\underline{974,194}} \text{ "units" (rounded)}$$

Therefore, at a sales mix of five cases of Darkly Decadent candy bars and one case of Pure Decadence candy bars per "unit," Unlimited Decadence will have to sell 4,870,970 cases of Darkly Decadent candy bars (974,194 × 5 cases of Darkly Decadent candy bars) and 974,194 cases of Pure Decadence candy bars (974,194 × 1 case of Pure Decadence candy bars) to earn a pretax income of $5,400,000.

---

[6]Recall that we use the following formula to compute after-tax income:

$$\text{After-tax Income} = \text{Pretax Income} - \text{Income Tax Expense}$$

Income tax expense is computed with the following formula:

$$\text{Income Tax Expense} = \text{Pretax Income} \times \text{Tax Rate}$$

We can substitute the second formula into the first formula, yielding the following revised formula for after-tax income:

$$\text{After-tax Income} = \text{Pretax Income} - (\text{Pretax Income} \times \text{Tax Rate})$$

Then, by eliminating pretax income from each of the two terms on the right side of the equation, we can restate the equation as follows:

$$\text{After-tax Income} = \text{Pretax Income} \times (1 - \text{Tax Rate})$$

Then we can find pretax income by isolating it on one side of the equation:

$$\text{Pretax Income} = \frac{\text{After-tax Income}}{(1 - \text{Tax Rate})}$$

Finding the Dollar Sales Volume to Achieve a Target Pretax Profit

When a company sells more than one product, it is often easier to represent sales volume in dollars instead of units. Earlier, we said that Unlimited Decadence would break even if it sold 800,000 "units," composed of 4,000,000 cases of Darkly Decadent candy bars and 800,000 cases of Pure Decadence candy bars. Since Darkly Decadent candy bars sell for $16 per case and Pure Decadence candy bars sell for $20 per case, Unlimited Decadence would break even when its sales revenue was $80,000,000 [(4,000,000 cases of Darkly Decadent candy bars × $16) + (800,000 cases of Pure Decadence candy bars × $20)].

A more direct way to find the dollar sales volume to achieve a desired profit is to use the company's contribution margin percentage. The *contribution margin percentage* is the ratio of the contribution margin to sales revenue or, stated another way, the contribution margin as a percentage of sales revenue. Since the contribution margin of one "unit" of Unlimited Decadence's product sales mix is $31 and the sales revenue of this "unit" is $100, its contribution margin percentage is 31% ($31 ÷ $100). We could say, then, that the contribution margin is 31% of sales revenue for this product sales mix.

Since break-even occurs when

$$\text{Contribution margin} = \text{Fixed costs,}$$

we could also say that it occurs when

$$\text{Sales revenue} \times \text{Contribution margin percentage} = \text{Fixed costs.}$$

Therefore, Unlimited Decadence could compute its break-even point (in sales dollars) as shown here:

$$\text{Break-even point (in dollars)} = \frac{\text{Total fixed cost}}{\text{Contribution margin percentage}}$$

$$= \frac{\$24,800,000}{31\%}$$

$$= \underline{\underline{\$80,000,000}}$$

Similarly, it could compute the total dollar sales volume needed to earn a desired amount of pretax income. For example, if managers want Unlimited Decadence to earn $5,400,000 pretax income, sales will have to be $97,419,355. The computation is as follows:

$$\begin{array}{l}\text{Dollar sales volume} \\ \text{needed to earn a} \\ \text{desired pretax income}\end{array} = \frac{\text{Total fixed cost} + \text{Desired pretax income}}{\text{Contribution margin percentage}}$$

$$\begin{array}{l}\text{Dollar sales volume} \\ \text{needed to earn} \\ \$5,400,000 \text{ desired} \\ \text{pretax income}\end{array} = \frac{\$24,800,000 \text{ Fixed cost} + \$5,400,000 \text{ Pretax income}}{31\%}$$

$$= \underline{\underline{\$97,419,355}}$$

 How can you verify the dollar sales volumes needed to break even and to earn a pretax profit of $5,400,000?

What If the Company Changed Its Product Sales Mix?

Remember that Unlimited Decadence's contribution margin percentage would not be 31% if its product sales mix did not remain five cases of Darkly Decadent candy bars and one case of Pure Decadence candy bars. Consider what will happen if sales of cases of Darkly Decadent candy bars change relative to sales of Pure Decadence candy bars so that Unlimited Decadence sells three cases of Darkly Decadent candy bars for every four cases of Pure Decadence candy bars. The new contribution margin percentage will be 30.47%, shown as follows:

	Darkly Decadent Candy Bars		Pure Decadence Candy Bars		Total per "Unit"
Selling price/case	$16		$20		
Variable cost/case	(11)		(14)		
Contribution margin/case	$ 5		$ 6		
Expected sales mix (cases)	3		4		
Sales revenue	$48	+	$80	=	$128
Less: variable costs	(33)	+	(56)	=	(89)
Contribution margin	$15	+	$24	=	$ 39
Contribution margin percentage ($39/$128)					30.47%
					(rounded)

With this new product sales mix, the dollar sales volume will have to be $99,113,883 [($24,800,000 fixed cost + $5,400,000 income before taxes) ÷ 30.47%] to earn a profit of $5,400,000 before income taxes. Furthermore, with the new product sales mix, total dollar sales volume will have to be $81,391,533 ($24,800,000 total fixed cost ÷ 30.47%) for Unlimited Decadence to break even.

Applications of C-V-P Analysis in a Manufacturing Environment

6 *How does a manufacturing company use cost-volume-profit analysis for its planning?*

So far, we have described fixed and variable costs as they relate to changes in sales. However, costs do not always vary with sales. They may vary with production, number of hours worked by employees, or some other measure of operating activity. Manufacturing companies incur costs to produce the products as they manufacture them. For this reason, managers of manufacturing companies usually classify the behavior of production costs based on whether or not these costs vary with the level of *production.*

As in a service or retail company, C-V-P analysis in a manufacturing company is useful in planning because it shows the potential impact of alternative plans on profit. The analysis can help managers make planning decisions and help investors and creditors evaluate the risk associated with their investment and credit decisions. In the following discussion, we illustrate how C-V-P analysis in a manufacturing company can show the potential profit impact of alternative plans.

Suppose that Unlimited Decadence is considering manufacturing the new fat-free, sugarless candy bar (to be called "Empty Decadence") that we discussed in Chapter 2. Marketing thinks it can sell 450,000 cases of these candy bars at $20 per case during the first year on the market. Purchasing has located suppliers for the sweetener and for the fat substitute. Together, all the direct materials for a case of Empty Decadence candy bars will cost $4. The production department expects to hire two new cooks to produce the Empty Decadence candy bars and has set a standard of 45 minutes of direct labor for every case of these candy bars. The human resources department expects the pay rate for these cooks to be $12 per hour. The production department estimates that variable overhead costs will increase by $0.50 per case of Empty Decadence candy bars. Marketing expects variable selling and administrative costs to increase by $1.00 because of the sale of this new product. There is currently space in the factory to manufacture the Empty Decadence candy bar, but Unlimited Decadence will have to purchase new equipment to process the sweetener and the fat substitute. The finance department has located financing for the new equipment. The production department expects depreciation and insurance on this equipment, together with the additional advertising expense, to add $1,188,000 to Unlimited Decadence's fixed costs.

Unlimited Decadence must decide whether to manufacture the Empty Decadence candy bar. Recall from Chapter 2 that there are numerous questions that Unlimited Decadence's managers should answer before they make a decision. Furthermore, there may be more than two alternatives (manufacturing or not manufacturing) to solving this issue. However, assume that Unlimited Decadence's managers are very interested in adding this new product and are gathering product information that will help them make their decision. C-V-P analysis will contribute useful information for evaluating this decision.

Managers first may want to know whether the revenue from sales of the Empty Decadence candy bar will even cover the additional costs of producing it, or whether it will "break even." We can calculate the contribution margin of each case of Empty Decadence candy bars as follows:

Sales revenue per case..		$20.00
Variable costs per case		
Direct materials	$4.00	
Direct labor ($12/hour × 3/4 hour)....................	9.00	
Additional variable overhead	0.50	
Additional variable selling and		
administrative costs...	1.00	(14.50)
Contribution margin per case...		$ 5.50

Now we can calculate the break-even point for the Empty Decadence candy bar:

$$\text{Break-even unit sales} = \frac{\text{Additional fixed costs}}{\text{Contribution margin per unit}}$$

$$= \frac{\$1,188,000}{\$5.50}$$

$$= \underline{\underline{216,000}} \text{ cases}$$

Unlimited Decadence will have to sell 216,000 cases of Empty Decadence candy bars in order for this line of candy bars to break even. Each case sold above the break-even point will cause Unlimited Decadence's profit to increase by $5.50. So, at the predicted sales level of 450,000 cases, Unlimited Decadence should earn $1,287,000 additional profit [(450,000 cases − 216,000 cases) × $5.50] on sales of the Empty Decadence candy bar.

Based on this information alone, it seems like a good idea to manufacture this new candy bar. The manager of the purchasing department, though, thinks that there is a possibility that the costs of the sweetener and the fat substitute (both direct materials) may increase in the next few months. It would be useful to know how much these costs can increase before the Empty Decadence line of candy bars will "lose money," or not be able to earn enough revenue to cover its costs. We know that costs can increase until they equal revenues, or until Empty Decadence "breaks even" at predicted sales of 450,000 cases (assuming that the marketing department's estimates are correct and that the selling price of a case of Empty Decadence candy bars doesn't change). So, we use the same formula:

$$\text{Break-even unit sales} = \frac{\text{Additional fixed costs}}{\text{Contribution margin per unit}}$$

$$450,000 = \frac{\$1,188,000}{X}$$

$$X = \$2.64$$

The contribution margin per case can decrease to $2.64 before the Empty Decadence product line will break even. If it decreases more than that, the Empty Decadence product line will lose money. In other words, the contribution margin can decrease by $2.86 (the old contribution margin of $5.50 minus the new contribution margin of $2.64). Therefore, if the only factors that change are the costs of the sweetener and the fat substitute, the direct materials can increase by $2.86 from $4.00 to $6.86 per case without the Empty Decadence product line generating a loss. We can verify this as follows:

Sales revenue per case		$20.00
Variable costs per case		
Direct materials ($4.00 + $2.86)	$6.86	
Direct labor ($12/hour × 3/4 hour)	9.00	
Additional variable overhead	0.50	
Additional variable selling and		
administrative costs	1.00	(17.36)
Contribution margin per case		$ 2.64

If Unlimited Decadence sells 450,000 cases, each will contribute $2.64, for a total contribution margin of $1,188,000, just enough to cover the additional fixed costs.

But what if marketing overestimates sales of the Empty Decadence candy bar? How much below its sales estimate can Unlimited Decadence's actual sales be before it loses money, if the cost of the sweetener and fat substitute do not change? The amount that sales (in units) can decrease without a loss, or the difference between the estimated sales volume and the break-even sales volume, is called the **margin of safety.** Managers use the margin of safety as a measure of the risk of a new plan. The higher the margin of safety is, the lower is the risk.

At the current cost estimate, break-even sales is 216,000 cases of Empty Decadence candy bars. That means that the margin of safety is 234,000 cases (450,000 cases − 216,000 cases). Sales could drop 234,000 cases below the estimate before Empty Decadence would experience a loss.

Notice that in making this calculation, we considered only the revenues and costs attributable to the Empty Decadence candy bar. Isolating these costs and revenues gives managers a clearer picture of the expected effect of adding the Empty Decadence candy bar. However, Unlimited Decadence must also consider the other effects of adding this product. For example, will the manufacture and sale of the Empty Decadence candy bar cause the sales of Unlimited Decadence's other candy bars to decrease? If so, it is possible that even though the sale of the Empty Decadence candy bar will probably generate a profit for the candy bar, *total income* for Unlimited Decadence may decrease. The decrease in the sales of other candy bars could be larger than the increase generated by the sale of the Empty Decadence candy bar. (On the other hand, maybe it would be better for Unlimited Decadence to introduce this new product before its competition does!) Wherever possible, when deciding whether to introduce a new product, managers should consider quantitative information about how the new product would affect the profits generated by the company's other products.

Summary of the C-V-P Analysis Computations for Multiple Products

Exhibit 11-9 summarizes the profit, break-even point, and sales volume computations used in our discussion of C-V-P analysis with multiple products. As in Chapter 3, we present these computations as equations that can be used to answer the basic questions that occur frequently in C-V-P analysis. Although it may be tempting to try to commit them all to memory, you should instead strive to understand how these equations relate to one another and how managers can use the answers found by applying these formulas in certain types of decision-making.

Business Issues and Values

To make smart decisions, managers must combine the results of C-V-P analysis with other factors. For example, many factors other than C-V-P analysis influence Unlimited

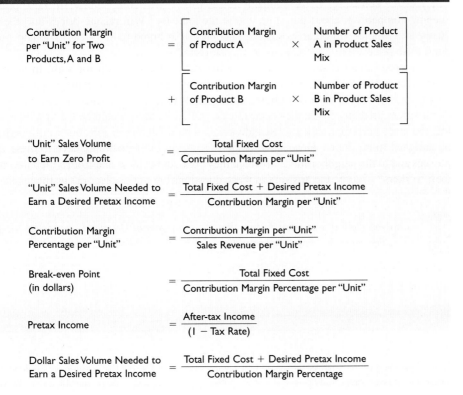

Exhibit 11-9 Summary of Cost-Volume-Profit Computations

$$\text{Contribution Margin per "Unit" for Two Products, A and B} = \left[\begin{array}{ccc}\text{Contribution Margin of Product A} & \times & \text{Number of Product A in Product Sales Mix}\end{array}\right]$$

$$+ \left[\begin{array}{ccc}\text{Contribution Margin of Product B} & \times & \text{Number of Product B in Product Sales Mix}\end{array}\right]$$

$$\text{"Unit" Sales Volume to Earn Zero Profit} = \frac{\text{Total Fixed Cost}}{\text{Contribution Margin per "Unit"}}$$

$$\text{"Unit" Sales Volume Needed to Earn a Desired Pretax Income} = \frac{\text{Total Fixed Cost} + \text{Desired Pretax Income}}{\text{Contribution Margin per "Unit"}}$$

$$\text{Contribution Margin Percentage per "Unit"} = \frac{\text{Contribution Margin per "Unit"}}{\text{Sales Revenue per "Unit"}}$$

$$\text{Break-even Point (in dollars)} = \frac{\text{Total Fixed Cost}}{\text{Contribution Margin Percentage per "Unit"}}$$

$$\text{Pretax Income} = \frac{\text{After-tax Income}}{(1 - \text{Tax Rate})}$$

$$\text{Dollar Sales Volume Needed to Earn a Desired Pretax Income} = \frac{\text{Total Fixed Cost} + \text{Desired Pretax Income}}{\text{Contribution Margin Percentage}}$$

Decadence's decision about whether to manufacture and sell the Empty Decadence candy bar; one of these factors is the hiring of the two new cooks. How much responsibility does Unlimited Decadence have when it hires new employees? Perhaps the two cooks will have to quit their secure jobs in order to work for Unlimited Decadence. Given the fact that it may be difficult for them to return to their old jobs, how sure should Unlimited Decadence be that its new product will succeed before it hires new employees? What if the two cooks are currently unemployed? Should that make a difference in Unlimited Decadence's decision?

Another factor that influences this decision is the presence or absence of health risks associated with the sweetener and fat substitute used in the Empty Decadence candy bar. Unlimited Decadence prides itself on its concern for its customers and would like to maintain its reputation of producing quality candy bars. Therefore, even if C-V-P analysis indicates that the Empty Decadence candy bar should be produced, the presence of health risks (if any) in the sweetener or fat substitute may cause managers to delay production until the company can locate safer alternatives.

Another example of other factors that companies must consider is the raising of the minimum wage. For example, in 1997, Congress raised the minimum wage from $4.25 per hour to $5.15 per hour. While this change in policy positively affected millions of minimum-wage earners, it also affected the decisions of the companies that hire these workers because an increase in the minimum wage causes companies' variable costs to increase. For instance, the owners of fast-food franchises typically hire minimum-wage workers to staff their restaurants. The fast-food industry is a "low margin" industry, which means that the average contribution margin of restaurants in this industry is low relative to that of companies in other industries. An increase in the minimum wage causes the already low contribution margins of these companies to drop lower. So companies faced with raising the wages of their minimum-wage employees have to make a difficult decision, with alternatives such as accepting lower profits, reducing staff, or raising prices. Using their critical thinking skills, managers and owners of these companies might ask the following questions when making this decision: Would accepting lower profits threaten the long-term solvency of the company? If the company raises prices, will competitors also raise prices, keeping competition about the same within the industry? Will raising prices hurt the industry as a whole? (In other words, will people eat at home more often?) If competitors don't raise prices, will the company lose customers?

A more difficult issue for these companies is the effect of reducing staff. In many of these restaurants, workers are already assigned multiple tasks. How many employees can a fast-food restaurant lay off without hurting quality, service, productivity, and morale? Furthermore, in many cases, the poorest, least-skilled workers would be the first to be laid off; the more versatile, multiskilled individuals would keep their jobs but would perhaps be assigned more duties. How much responsibility do the restaurants have to these employees and to the neighborhoods in which they conduct business and from which they hire their workers? Clearly, the answers to these questions are not as clear-cut as the results of C-V-P analysis alone.

 Can you think of any other factors that the managers of Unlimited Decadence should consider when deciding whether to produce Empty Decadence candy bars?

Summary

At the beginning of the chapter we asked you several questions. During the chapter, we asked you to STOP and answer some additional questions to build your knowledge about specific issues. Be sure you answered these additional questions. Below are the questions from the beginning of the chapter, with a brief summary of the key points relating to the answers. Use your creative and critical thinking skills to expand on these key points to develop more complete answers to the questions and to determine what other questions you have that might lead you to learn more about the issues.

1 How does the fact that a manufacturing company makes the products it sells affect its business plan?

A manufacturing company's business plan has much in common with the plans of retail and service companies. However, because a manufacturing company makes the products it sells, its business plan also includes a production plan, which affects other parts of the business plan, particularly the financial plan. The production plan describes how a company intends to manufacture and maintain the quality of the products it will sell. The plan describes the raw materials that the company will use in manufacturing its product. A description of the production process specifies how these raw materials will be converted into finished products. The production plan also describes where the company intends to store the finished products before it sells them.

2 How does a manufacturing company determine the cost of the goods that it manufactures?

Managers of a manufacturing company determine the cost of the goods that it manufactures by adding together the direct materials costs, the direct labor costs, and the factory overhead costs that it incurs in manufacturing its products. To determine the direct materials costs, managers must know how much of each raw material went into the company's products and multiply the amount of raw materials by their costs. To determine the direct labor costs, managers must know how much of each type of direct labor was necessary to manufacture the company's products and multiply the number of hours of each type of direct labor by the appropriate wages per hour. To determine the factory overhead costs, managers must add together the costs of each type of factory overhead.

3 Why are standard costs useful in controlling a company's operations?

A manufacturing company uses standard costs as a way of controlling its production. By measuring actual costs against standard costs (what the costs actually were against what the costs should have been), the managers of a company can evaluate its activities. They can determine which activities caused costs to be too high or too low and decide whether to change those activities. A company develops standards for each manufactured product by determining price and quantity standards for each input to its manufacturing process.

4 How do manufacturing costs affect cost-volume-profit analysis?

Managers of manufacturing companies treat manufacturing costs like other costs when performing cost-volume-profit analysis. Like other costs, manufacturing costs can be classified as fixed or variable costs. So, managers add the variable manufacturing costs to the other variable costs and add the fixed manufacturing costs to the other fixed costs when performing cost-volume-profit analysis.

5 What is the effect of multiple products on cost-volume-profit analysis?

C-V-P analysis is similar for a company that sells only one product and for a company that sells multiple products. With multiple products, however, managers must know the product sales mix and the costs and sales revenues of the group of products being analyzed. The C-V-P calculation for a company with multiple products results in the number of "units" of product mix that the company must sell to break even or earn a desired profit. The managers then must convert the number of "units" of product mix to the number of units of individual products. Managers may find dollar sales volume to be more useful than unit sales volume in determining the level of sales necessary to achieve a desired profit.

6 How does a manufacturing company use cost-volume-profit analysis for its planning?

C-V-P analysis helps the managers of a manufacturing company make planning decisions by showing the potential impact of alternative plans on profit. These alternative plans might include changing suppliers of direct materials, hiring production workers, buying new equipment, adding or dropping a product line, raising or lowering product costs or selling prices, or changing the planned sales volume on some of its products (and therefore also changing the planned production of those products).

Key Terms

direct labor *(p. 339)*
direct materials *(p. 339)*
factory overhead *(p. 341)*
finished goods inventory *(p. 339)*
goods-in-process inventory *(p. 339)*
high-low method *(p. 348)*
indirect labor *(p. 341)*
indirect materials *(p. 341)*
margin of safety *(p. 358)*
mixed costs *(p. 346)*

price standard *(p. 345)*
product sales mix *(p. 352)*
quantity standard *(p. 344)*
raw materials *(p. 355)*
raw materials inventory *(p. 339)*
relevant range *(p. 350)*
scatter diagram *(p. 347)*
standard costs *(p. 343)*
variable manufacturing cost *(p. 345)*
variance *(p. 344)*

Here is an opportunity to gather information on the Internet about real-world issues related to the topics in this chapter. Go to http://www.dryden.com/account and click on the Cunningham, Nikolai, and Bazley book cover. Click on Summary Surfing, then click on this chapter number, and answer the following questions.

▶ Click on **ENT** (Enterprise Corporation). Scroll down, and click on *Online Library*. Scroll down, and click on *Break-Even Analysis*. How does this article define fixed costs? How does it define variable costs? Even though it doesn't use the term, how does the article explain mixed costs? Does the article consider the labor component of production to be variable or fixed?

**SUMMARY
SURFING**

Integrated Business and Accounting Situations

Answer the Following Questions in Your Own Words

Testing Your Knowledge

11-1   Describe the purpose of the production plan.

11-2   Describe how raw materials in a manufacturing company are different from the goods that a retail company sells.

11-3   What type of information about raw materials does a manufacturing company include in its production plan?

11-4   What type of information about labor does a manufacturing company include in its production plan?

11-5   What type of information about equipment and facilities does a manufacturing company include in its production plan?

11-6   What type of information about finished products does a manufacturing company include in its business plan?

11-7   Describe the three types of inventories in a manufacturing company.

11-8   Describe the three types of production input. Give an example of each type of input for a company that builds houses.

11-9   Describe the difference between direct and indirect materials.

11-10   Describe the difference between direct and indirect labor.

11-11   How do you know if a cost should be classified as a factory overhead cost?

11-12   Define *standard* costs, and describe how managers use them.

11-13   What is a variance? How do managers use variance information?

11-14   What is the difference between a price standard and a quantity standard?

11-15   Describe a mixed cost and how it behaves.

11-16   Describe three methods that can be used to estimate the components of a mixed cost. What are the advantages and disadvantages of each?

11-17   What is a relevant range? How is C-V-P analysis affected by this concept? Why would it be useful for users of cost estimates to know the relevant range?

11-18   What is the difference between C-V-P analysis with one product and C-V-P analysis with multiple products?

11-19   Explain what is meant by a company's product sales mix. Give an example.

11-20   What happens to the results of C-V-P analysis if a company's product sales mix changes? Why does this happen?

11-21   How is a contribution margin for a product sales mix different from a contribution margin for one product?

11-22   How does a desired return on stockholders' equity help managers determine the company's target profit?

11-23   How do income taxes affect C-V-P analysis?

Applying Your Knowledge

11-24   Visit your favorite grocery store, and select a packaged product.

    Required: What raw materials went into the production of that product?

11-25   Think about how decision-makers use a business plan.

    Required: Why do you think it is important to include information about a manufacturing company's suppliers in its production plan?

11-26   Suppose you work for a company called Split Decisions and the boss has selected you to develop the production steps necessary to manufacture a banana split.

    Required: Describe the sequence of the production steps and how the raw materials flow through this sequence.

11-27 Western Brands produces western accessories. It manufactures one product, a bolo tie, from a thin 36-inch strip of leather, 1/3-inch wide, and four fancy brass rings. The leather strip is threaded through two of the rings, which act as a clasp. The remaining two rings are sewn onto the ends of the leather strip.

Western Brands purchases leather strips in 72-inch lengths that are 2 inches wide for $4.80 each and cuts them to 1/3-inch widths and then 36-inch lengths. Brass rings cost $9.60 per dozen. It takes two people 5 minutes each to produce one bolo tie. Each person earns $6 per hour.

Required: (1) What is the cost, per tie, of the direct materials?
           (2) What is the cost, per tie, of the direct labor?
           (3) What are the total direct costs for 500 ties?

11-28 The utility costs and production levels for The Cat's Pajamas for the last four months were as follows:

Month	Cost	Production Levels (pairs of pajamas)
1	$1,340	1,700
2	1,600	2,600
3	1,880	3,200
4	1,680	2,900

Required: (1) Assuming the utility cost is a mixed cost, use the high-low method with the above data to determine the variable cost per pair of pajamas and the total fixed cost per month.
           (2) If 3,150 pairs of pajamas are manufactured, what should the utility cost be?

11-29 Western Brands has estimated its factory overhead costs for the next year at two production volumes, 100,000 and 200,000. These estimates are shown below.

	Factory Overhead Costs	
	100,000 ties	200,000 ties
Depreciation on factory equipment	$ 5,000	$ 5,000
Factory rent	30,000	30,000
Factory supervisor's salary	45,000	45,000
Maintenance of factory equipment	1,950	2,200
Factory utilities	7,000	14,000
Factory supplies	3,000	6,000

Required: Estimate total factory overhead at a production level of 140,000 ties.

11-30 A company with multiple products has a break-even point of 5,000 "units."

Required: Explain the preceding sentence.

11-31 Bathtub Rings Corporation manufactures shower curtains that sell for $5.00 each and cost $3.48 to produce. It also manufactures shower-curtain rings that sell for $1.60 per box and cost $1.22 per box to produce. Fixed costs total $30,000 per year. Bathtub Rings sells five shower curtains for every box of shower-curtain rings that it sells.

Required: (1) How many of each product must Bathtub Rings sell to break even?
           (2) How many of each product must Bathtub Rings sell to earn a pretax income of $49,800?
           (3) How many of each product must Bathtub Rings sell to earn an after-tax income of $49,800 if the income tax rate is 30%?

11-32 Refer to 11-31.

Required: (1) Compute Bathtub Rings' contribution margin percentage per "unit."
           (2) Compute Bathtub Rings' break-even point in sales dollars.
           (3) What total pretax income (loss) would Bathtub Rings have if its total sales revenue amounted to $266,000?

11-33 Sí, Your Dinner! Mexican Food Company manufactures three strengths of salsa: Lightweight, Hot Stuff, and Burn Your Tongue. The selling prices and manufacturing costs of these salsas are as follows:

	Lightweight	Hot Stuff	Burn Your Tongue
Selling price per jar	$3.00	$4.00	$6.00
Manufacturing cost per jar	2.00	2.00	4.50

For every 10 jars sold, 3 are Lightweight, 3 are Hot Stuff, and 4 are Burn Your Tongue.

Required: (1) What is the contribution margin percentage per "unit"?

(2) By how much would profits change if a $1,000 advertising campaign increased the sales of Lightweight salsa by 900 jars but left sales of the other salsas unchanged?

(3) Sales are currently $10,125, and fixed costs total $2,125.
    (a) How many jars of Lightweight salsa were sold?
    (b) How many jars of Burn Your Tongue salsa were sold?
    (c) What is the current pretax income?

(4) If the sales mix changes to 2 jars of Lightweight, 4 of Hot Stuff, and 4 of Burn Your Tongue, what would be the new contribution margin percentage?

11-34 The Grandma Corporation manufactures two products—cookies and candy. Cookies have a contribution margin of $5 per box, and candy has a contribution margin of $4 per bag. Grandma's total fixed cost is currently $450,000. Grandma expects to sell two boxes of cookies for every three bags of candy sold. Boxes of cookies and bags of candy each sell for $10.

Required: (1) Compute the contribution margin percentage per "unit."

(2) At the current product mix, what total dollar sales volume is required for Grandma to earn a pretax income of $144,000?

11-35 Greco Manufacturing Corporation produces two products—olives and baklava. Olives require $3 of variable costs per bottle and sell for $5 per bottle. Baklava has variable costs of $5 per box and sells for $10. Greco's total fixed costs amount to $72,250. This year Greco sold 30,000 bottles of olives and 5,000 boxes of baklava. Greco believes that consumer tastes will shift dramatically next year. Although it expects total dollar sales volume to be the same as this year's sales volume, the product mix will change, so that one-third of the units sold will be boxes of baklava.

Required: (1) Compute Greco's pretax income for *this* year.

(2) At what dollar sales volume would Greco have broken even for *this* year?

(3) Compute Greco's expected pretax income for *next* year assuming total dollar sales volume does not change.

(4) Why does Greco expect more pretax income next year than it earned this year when the total dollar sales volume is expected to be the same? Explain.

11-36 The Boston Company (a sole proprietorship) expects to operate at a loss next year on its two products, as shown here:

	Commons	Not So Commons	Total
Production and sales (units)	100,000	20,000	120,000
Sales revenue	$200,000	$100,000	$300,000
Variable costs	(140,000)	(40,000)	(180,000)
Contribution margin	$ 60,000	$ 60,000	$120,000
Less: Fixed costs			(172,240)
Loss			($ 52,240)

Boston has two plans that it believes will improve its profit (reduce its loss) next year:

Plan A—to spend $41,000 on an advertising plan to increase the number of *Not So Commons* sold without affecting the number of *Commons* sold

Plan B—to reduce the selling price of *Not So Commons* from $5 per unit to $4 per unit; this plan should change the product mix so that one *Not So Common* is sold for every two *Commons*

Required: (1) If Boston follows neither of the two plans, so that its product mix is one *Not So Common* sold for each five *Commons* sold, what must total dollar sales volume be for the company to break even?

(2) If Boston follows Plan A, how many *Not So Commons* must it sell next year to break even? (The number of *Commons* sold will still be 100,000.)

(3) If Boston follows Plan B, what total dollar sales volume is required for it to break even?

(4) Compare your answers to (1) and (3). Explain the result obtained from this comparison.

11-37　Professional Robotics Corporation manufactures three different robots in its "domestic servants" line. Sales information for this line of product is given below:

	Butler	**Maid**	**Bartender**
Selling price per unit	$3,000	$2,500	$4,000
Variable cost per unit	750	750	1,300
Expected sales mix	1	2	4

Fixed costs are $2,500,000

Required: (1) What is Professional Robotics' break-even point, in "units" of sales mix?

(2) To break even, how many Butlers, Maids, and Bartenders must Professional Robotics sell?

(3) Suppose Professional Robotics' sales during the year were $4,800,000. Assuming a normal sales mix, how many units of each product were sold? What was Professional Robotics' pretax income?

(4) Assuming a normal sales mix and an income tax rate of 40%, how many Butlers, Maids, and Bartenders must Professional Robotics sell to earn an after-tax profit of $198,000?

Making Evaluations

11-38　Suppose you and your brother Noah, a veterinary medicine major, want to open a pet store. After long deliberations and lively discussion about the name of the corporation, you agree to name it Noah's Bark. You arrange to obtain retail space, to purchase supplies and pets, and to advertise in the newspaper. Now you are almost ready to open for business. But first you want to analyze how your plans will affect profit.

You and Noah plan to sell Labrador retrievers for $350 each, and you estimate that total fixed costs for Noah's Bark will be $6,375 ($2,000 rent, $4,000 salaries, and $375 advertising). The cost to you of purchasing the Labrador retriever puppies is $120 each. On average, you spend $60 to feed each puppy before it is sold and $30 per puppy on miscellaneous items such as dipping and grooming supplies.

Required: (1) How many dogs must Noah's Bark sell to break even?

(2) How much pretax income will Noah's Bark earn if it sells 750 dogs?

(3) How many dogs must Noah's Bark sell to earn $14,000 pretax income?

(4) What must dollar sales be to break even?

(5) What must dollar sales be to earn $14,065 pretax income?

Suppose you and your brother believe that if the selling price does not change, Noah's Bark will be able to sell 200 Labrador retrievers next year. At that unit sales volume, profit is expected to be $21,625 ([$140 contribution margin per dog × 200 dogs] − $6,375 total fixed cost). However, you are considering three alternative plans (only one of which will be followed) that you believe may allow Noah's Bark to earn even more than $21,625. These plans are as follows:

(a) Raise the selling price of the dogs to $450 per dog. With this alternative, variable costs per dog and total fixed costs do not change.

(b) Purchase only those Labrador retrievers that are descendants of American Kennel Club (AKC) ribbon winners, thus increasing the variable cost to $240 (these dogs can be purchased for $150 each). You are considering this alternative because you think the perceived improvement in the purity of the breed will increase the sales volume of dogs. With this change, neither the selling price per dog nor the total fixed cost changes.

(c) Increase total fixed costs by spending $1,000 more on advertising. With this alternative, the selling price per dog and the variable costs per dog do not change.

Required: (6) Basing your decision on C-V-P results alone, which plan should you choose? Why?

(7) What other factors might you want to consider in making this choice?

11-39 Suppose that after Noah's Bark (in 11-38) has been in business for a year, you and your brother Noah decide to sell beagles in addition to Labrador retrievers. Each beagle sells for $150, requires $60 of variable cost, and earns a contribution margin of $90. Each Labrador retriever still sells for $350, requires $210 of variable cost, and earns a contribution margin of $140. The contribution margin earned by Noah's Bark in the second year of business from beagles, from Labrador retrievers, and in total is shown here:

	Labrador Retrievers	**Beagles**	**Total**
Sales (dogs)	600	200	800
Sales revenue	$210,000	$30,000	$240,000
Less variable costs	(126,000)	(12,000)	(138,000)
Contribution margin	$ 84,000	$18,000	$102,000

Assume that fixed costs for Noah's Bark are now $76,500 per year.

Required: (1) Compute the break-even point (in sales dollars).

(2) What must sales be (in dollars) for Noah's Bark to earn $30,000 pretax income?

(3) What is the break-even point in beagles and Labs?

(4) How many beagles and Labs must Noah's Bark sell to earn a pretax income of $30,000?

(5) How many beagles and Labs must it sell to earn a net income of $30,000? The income tax rate is 40%.

Suppose you and your brother are considering three independent alternative plans (only one of which will be followed) that you believe may raise the company's income. These plans are as follows:

(a) Raise the selling price of the Labs to $450 per dog. With this alternative, variable costs per dog and total fixed costs do not change.

(b) Purchase only those Labrador retrievers that are descendants of American Kennel Club (AKC) ribbon winners, thus increasing the variable cost to $240 (these dogs can be purchased for $150 each). You are considering this alternative because you think the perceived improvement in the purity of the breed will increase the sales volume of dogs. With this change, neither the selling price per unit nor the total fixed cost changes.

(c) Increase total fixed costs by spending $1,000 more on advertising. With this alternative, the selling price per unit and the variable costs per unit do not change.

Required: (6) Based on C-V-P analysis alone, which plan should you choose? Why?

(7) What other factors might you want to consider in making this choice?

11-40 Lucas Air Service, a sole proprietorship, provides charter flights on weekdays only. Earl Lucas, the owner, is thinking of offering flying lessons on weekends. He has always protected his weekends for family time and will give up his family weekends only if he can earn at least $9,000 per year extra. Estimates of demand for lessons suggest that, weather permitting, he could teach a full six-lesson day every Saturday and Sunday for the entire year.

Earl's large plane could be used for about half of the lessons. He would borrow a smaller plane, owned by his friend Pat, for the other half. Fuel and maintenance would run about $45 per flying lesson with the large plane. With the small plane, fuel would cost $25 per lesson, and Earl would pay Pat $75 per day when he used the small plane regardless of how many lessons he gave in it.

Earl plans to use the large plane for advanced students and to charge them $75 for a lesson. He would use the small plane for beginners and charge them $65 per lesson.

Each weekend day that Earl opens for flight lessons he will incur $35 for the salary of his receptionist, utilities, and other expenses to keep his office open.

Required: (1) Prepare a schedule showing the daily profit if

(a) Earl gives from 1 to 6 advanced lessons only

(b) Earl gives from 1 to 6 beginner lessons only

(c) Earl offers both types of lessons on a given day for a total of 6 lessons (make the profit computation for only two situations: the situation where Earl gives 3 lessons of each type and the situation where Earl gives 4 advanced lessons and 2 beginner lessons).

(2) Is it more or less profitable for Earl to give 4 advanced lessons and 2 beginner lessons each day than to give 3 lessons of each kind each day?

(3) If Earl gives 3 flight lessons of each type each day, how much profit could he earn if he gives lessons for 90 days?

(4) How much profit could Earl earn if he gives 6 advanced lessons in the large plane for each of 45 days and 6 beginner lessons in the small plane for each of 45 days?

(5) How much profit could Earl earn if he gives 6 advanced lessons in the large plane for each of 60 days and 6 beginner lessons in the small plane for each of 30 days?

(6) Explain why the mix of two-thirds advanced and one-third beginner lessons seems better than the mix of half advanced and half beginner lessons in the case where only advanced or only beginner lessons are scheduled on a given day.

11-41 Golden Chocolate Inc. of Brooklyn, a manufacturer of chocolate bars, learned that a Connecticut child suffered a mild allergic reaction to the nuts in its candy bar. The wafer in the chocolate bar contains ground hazelnuts, but the candy bar's label didn't include nuts in its list of ingredients.[7] Suppose you have been hired to advise Golden Chocolates about how to respond to this situation and how to prevent related potential problems.

Required: Assume Candace Sugarbaker is the company president. Write her a memo making a recommendation or recommendations. For each recommendation, describe the effect you think it will have on Golden Chocolate's sales, fixed costs, variable costs, and break-even point. Include any other factors you think Golden's managers should consider when they make this decision.

11-42 The National Fishing Heritage Center in Grimsby, a port in northeastern England, is luring a record number of visitors (up 27 percent from last year) with some very fishy techniques: Scratch 'n' Sniff leaflets; Whiff You Were Here postcards; and "Smelloons"—balloons filled with fresh-fishy odors. Scents include "Hint of Haddock," "Compressed Cod," and "Sentiment of Seaweed."[8] The center views this effort as a major success.

Required: Working with your class team, identify the changes in fixed and variable costs caused by this tourist campaign. Besides the increase in visitors, what criteria would you use to measure the success of this effort? What questions would you ask to help you determine its success?

11-43 Chico, Maria, Elaina, and Juan are taking a year off from school to form a partnership to develop the commercial potential of a cleaning solvent they accidentally discovered in their college chemistry lab. In liquid form, their product can remove grease stains from clothing and can launder shop towels so that they appear like new. In solid form (actually a buttery consistency), it can make a mechanic's hands look like those of a baby in two minutes, and as a foam, it can lift grease and oil spots out of concrete in a jiffy.

Chico's investigation of manufacturing requirements suggests that small-scale manufacturing is quite feasible and that output could be adjusted over a wide range of volumes with little change in efficiency. Potential suppliers of raw materials have been contacted, and a long list of friends who are eager for part-time work assures the availability of direct labor.

---

[7]"Chocolate Bar Recalled as Allergy Precaution," *Columbia Daily Tribune,* April 22, 1995, 2A.

[8]"Something Fishy," *Fortune,* July 25, 1993, 14.

Maria has located a steel farm building for rent near the interstate highway in an area recently rezoned for commercial and industrial use. Initial cleanup, some insulation, additional lighting, gravel for the drive and loading area, and a small amount of additional office space are all that seem to be necessary to make the building suitable for their needs. She also has acquired a delivery van, which was used by a local florist before his retirement.

Elaina has worked out all of the details for advertising and other promotional activities that would be needed for the three forms of the product. She and Juan have determined the range of possible sales volumes for each form, assuming primary customers to be commercial laundries for the liquid, auto service centers for the solid, and service stations for the foam. Juan has determined optimal delivery routes and schedules to cover the midstate area and is now considering the possibility of adding delivery to two major metropolitan areas.

After much planning and several meetings with local financial institutions, the four have concluded that the product can be produced and marketed in only one of the three forms—liquid, solid, or foam—until successful financial performance of the venture is established. This success would require at least $30,000 of profit to be earned during the first year.

The four asked for your advice recently at a party. Rather than talk business at the party, you suggested that they send you the information they had gathered. A few days after the party, you received the following information from them:

	Liquid	Solid	Foam
Selling price	$3.00	$3.50	$11.00
Variable costs:			
Direct materials	$0.40	$0.80	$3.00
Direct labor	0.10	0.20	0.60
Variable overhead	0.15	0.30	0.90
Variable selling and administrative	0.35	0.20	0.50
Total variable costs	$1.00	$1.50	$5.00
Fixed costs:			
Factory overhead	$ 5,000	$15,000	$85,000
Selling and administrative	10,000	15,000	5,000

Sales volume information (all possible sales volumes between the estimated minimum and maximum are equally likely):

	Liquid	Solid	Foam
Maximum sales volume	20,000 bottles	40,000 tubs	25,000 cans
Minimum sales volume	12,000	15,000	5,000
Expected sales volume	16,000	27,500	15,000

Required: (1) For each of the three forms of product, what is the
   (a) maximum possible profit?
   (b) minimum possible profit?
   (c) expected profit?
   (d) sales volume needed to earn $30,000?
(2) Which form of product seems favored relative to each of the calculations you made in (1)?
(3) Which form of the product would you recommend they introduce during the first year of operations? Why?

11-44 Yesterday, you received the following letter for your advice column in the local paper:

Dear Dr. Decisive:

I read your column every day, and I think you can help me with this problem I am having with my boyfriend. This morning, as we were walking to the gym, we started having a nice, normal conversation about my aerobics class. Then, before I knew it, we had a major parting of the ways.

This all started when I mentioned that I didn't think it was fair that we had to pay a fee for each aerobics class we attended and that the $150 facilities use fee that each student pays at the beginning of the semester ought to cover it. He looked at me like I was an idiot and informed me that I was WRONG and must not have been paying attention in my accounting class. According to him, it is obvious that the aerobics fee is assessed to cover the aerobics instructor's salary. Well, it's not so obvious to me, and I need for you to tell him how wrong he is (he reads your column too). Until we get this cleared up, we can't go to the gym together. (How could I work out with such a pompous FOOL?). Just sign me . . .

"Nobody's Fool"

Required: Meet with your Dr. Decisive team and write a response to "Nobody's Fool."

CHAPTER 12

DEVELOPING A BUSINESS PLAN FOR A MANUFACTURING COMPANY: BUDGETING

"At the beginning of his undertaking, and at every successive stage, the alert business man strives to modify his arrangements so as to obtain better results with a given expenditure, or equal results with less expenditure."

—Alfred Marshall

1 *What are the similarities and differences between a large company's master budget and that of an entrepreneurial company?*

2 *What are the similarities and differences between a manufacturing company's master budget and that of a retail company?*

3 *How is a manufacturing company's operating cycle different from that of a retail company?*

4 *Is there a strategy a manufacturing company can use to complete its budget?*

5 *If a company's actual sales are different from its budgeted sales (or actual production is different from budgeted production) for the same time period, how can managers meaningfully evaluate how well the company met its cost goals?*

6 *How do budgets affect the business decisions that employees make?*

Maybe you've had an experience similar to the following: "I went into the kitchen to make birthday cupcakes for my roommate to take to his fraternity meeting, only to find that I had forgotten to buy oil the last time I went grocery shopping. So, I went to the store and purchased some oil. After I got home, I started to gather together the ingredients and discovered that my roommate had used all the eggs the last time he volunteered to cook breakfast. Back to the store! By then I had already used up the hour I had budgeted for this project, but . . . he *is* my best friend, so I persevered. (Studying for my exam could wait.) The completed project was outstanding—two dozen *yummy* cupcakes. Unfortunately, the fraternity never got to taste them. When he was ready to go to his meeting, my roommate told me there would be 36 people at the meeting!!!! Back to the store again for three dozen cupcakes (they all had to look alike). I kept the ones I made for myself."

www.saralee.com

Imagine how much larger this problem would have been if this situation had occurred at Sara Lee Corporation, a company that manufactures multiple products, including desserts, and involves numerous people in the process! Large companies invest considerable time in the planning process to prevent problems such as this from occurring, and the master budget is one tool they use for planning.

Budgeting in a More Complex Environment

1 *What are the similarities and differences between a large company's master budget and that of an entrepreneurial company?*

A large company prepares budgets for the same reasons that a smaller company does. Besides describing a company's financial plans, budgets make other contributions to its planning, operating, and evaluating processes. They:

▶ Add discipline, or order, to the planning process

▶ Help managers identify and avoid potential operating problems

▶ Quantify plans

▶ Create a "benchmark" for evaluating the company's performance

However, a large company's budgets contain elements that a smaller company's budgets do not include. We next illustrate a master budget for Unlimited Decadence Corporation, a manufacturing company, and point out the similarities and differences between it and the budget of Sweet Temptations, the entrepreneurial retail company that we discussed in Chapter 4.

The Budget Framework for Planning in a Manufacturing Company

2 *What are the similarities and differences between a manufacturing company's master budget and that of a retail company?*

As we discussed in Chapter 4, the form and the content of the individual schedules of a master budget differ from company to company for many reasons. However, even though they differ to some extent, the budget schedules of manufacturing companies and retail companies also contain many similarities because many of their activities are similar.

A master budget for a manufacturing company usually includes the following budget schedules:

1. Sales budget

2. Production budget

3. Direct materials purchases budget

4. Direct labor budget

5. Factory overhead budget

6. Selling expenses budget

7. General and administrative expenses budget

8. Capital expenditures budget

9. Cash budget

10. Projected income statement

11. Projected balance sheet

If you refer back to the budget schedules for a retail company that we discussed in Chapter 4, you will notice that a manufacturing company has more budget schedules than a retail company has. This should make sense when you remember that a manufacturing company *makes* the products that it sells rather than purchasing the products. The additional manufacturing activities must be added to the budget process. Exhibit 12-1 depicts Unlimited Decadence's master budget, composed of the eleven schedules listed above, and shows (with arrows) the important relationships among the schedules.

We will discuss the nature and purpose of these budget schedules and illustrate each of them, as we did in Chapter 4, so that you can see how Unlimited Decadence can describe its planned activities in a master budget. To simplify these illustrations, we assume in each of these budget schedules that Unlimited Decadence produces only one kind of candy—Darkly Decadent candy bars. However, companies that produce multiple products use the same procedures and logic in developing their budgets.

You should notice many similarities between the process of budgeting Unlimited Decadence's planned activities and the process that we used to describe the planned activities of Sweet Temptations. As you will see, the cyclical nature of a company's activities affects the budgeting process.

Exhibit 12-1   Interrelationships among Budget Schedules in the Master Budget

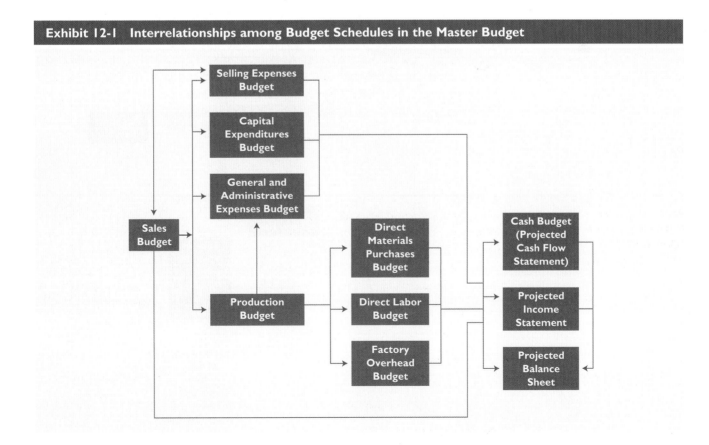

3 *How is a manufacturing company's operating cycle different from that of a retail company?*

The Operating Cycle of a Manufacturing Company

Recall from Chapter 4 that the **operating cycle** of a company is the average time it takes the company to use cash to acquire goods and services, to convert these goods and services into products or services to sell, to sell these products and services to customers, and then to collect cash from customers for the sale. We can restate this definition specifically for a manufacturing company and say that the **operating cycle for a *manufacturing* company** is the average time it takes the company to use cash to acquire direct materials to use in manufacturing goods to sell, to convert these direct materials into finished goods, to sell these goods to customers, and then to collect cash from customers for the sale. Unlimited Decadence's operating cycle is the time it takes to pay cash to purchase ingredients from its suppliers, to convert the ingredients into candy bars, to sell these candy bars to customers, and to collect cash from the customers. Exhibit 12-2 illustrates Unlimited Decadence's operating cycle. A company's master budget reflects and takes into account all the stages of its operating cycle. However, rather than beginning with expected cash payments, as the operating cycle does, a master budget begins with expected sales.

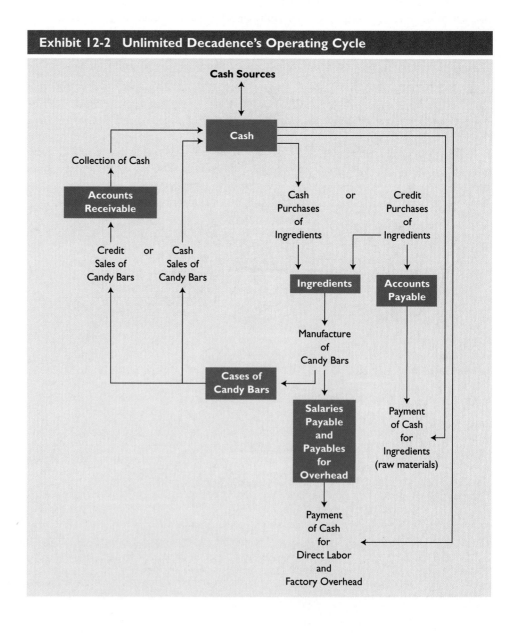

Exhibit 12-2 Unlimited Decadence's Operating Cycle

Why do you think the budget begins with expected sales rather than expected cash payments? Given what you already know about budgeting, what do you think would be the effect of beginning the budget with cash payments instead?

The Sales Budget: The Starting Point

As they do in a retail company, sales create the need for all the activities of a manufacturing company. Likewise, the sales budget directly or indirectly affects all of the other budget schedules. Remember from Chapter 4 that the **sales budget** shows the amount of inventory (in units) that the company expects to sell in each month of the budget period and the related revenues that the company expects to earn from each month's sales. Exhibit 12-3 shows Unlimited Decadence's sales budget for Darkly Decadent candy bars for the second quarter of the year 2001.[1] The sales figures are based on a market analysis conducted by Unlimited Decadence's marketing department and on the company's past sales figures. Notice that budgeted sales revenue is different from expected cash receipts in each month. This is because Unlimited Decadence gives its credit customers thirty days (n/30) to pay for their purchases,[2] so it expects to collect cash from its credit sales roughly one month after the sales occur.

4 *Is there a strategy a manufacturing company can use to complete its budget?*

 After looking at Unlimited Decadence's sales budget, do you think it has any cash customers? How do you know?

The Production Budget

After estimating sales for the quarter, managers at Unlimited Decadence must decide how many cases of Darkly Decadent candy bars to produce and when to produce them. The production budget helps managers quantify these decisions. The **production budget** is a schedule showing how many units the company should produce during each budget period both to satisfy expected sales (from the sales budget) for that period and to end each period with a desired finished goods inventory level. These production figures will form the

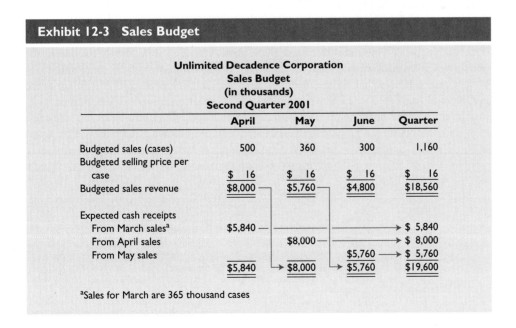

Exhibit 12-3 Sales Budget

Unlimited Decadence Corporation
Sales Budget
(in thousands)
Second Quarter 2001

	April	May	June	Quarter
Budgeted sales (cases)	500	360	300	1,160
Budgeted selling price per case	$ 16	$ 16	$ 16	$ 16
Budgeted sales revenue	$8,000	$5,760	$4,800	$18,560
Expected cash receipts				
From March sales[a]	$5,840			$ 5,840
From April sales		$8,000		$ 8,000
From May sales			$5,760	$ 5,760
	$5,840	$8,000	$5,760	$19,600

[a]Sales for March are 365 thousand cases

[1]To keep the budget schedules simple, in this chapter we assume that Unlimited Decadence sells only one type of candy bar—the Darkly Decadent candy bar. Therefore, we include only one sales budget and one production budget.

[2]We are assuming no cash discounts. If Unlimited Decadence gave its customers cash discounts, it would expect to collect cash sooner, but it also would expect to collect less cash because of the discount.

basis for estimating the expenses that the company will incur in its manufacturing activity, and that the company will show on its projected income statement for the budget period. Managers also use the desired ending finished goods inventory for the budget period in estimating the inventory costs that appear on the projected balance sheet for the budget period.

www.spanglercandy.com

In deciding what ending finished goods inventory levels to maintain, managers must balance several costs that are associated with inventories. Carrying inventories is expensive. For example, Spangler Candy Co., the Bryan, Ohio candy cane manufacturer that we discussed in Chapter 11, begins in February to produce candy canes for the Christmas holidays.[3] Since it begins its production so early in the year, it must store the candy canes in a 215,000-square-foot warehouse. Besides the cost of the warehouse, Spangler has other costs associated with its inventory. These include the costs of keeping the company's money invested in inventory of candy canes, of handling inventory, and of paying insurance and taxes. Furthermore, by storing the inventory, Spangler risks theft, damage, or obsolescence of its product.

 Why do you think there is a cost associated with keeping the company's cash tied up in inventory? What is the cost?

On the other hand, it also can be very expensive *not* to carry inventory. For example, costs can arise from having excessive production facilities just to meet peak production requirements, from working employees overtime to fill rush orders, or from losing sales because orders cannot be met. Every company must plan its inventory levels by keeping both the costs of carrying and the costs of not carrying inventory in mind, and by trying to maintain an optimal level of inventory on hand so that the combined total cost is the lowest possible amount.[4]

Sometimes, after evaluating these costs, companies set desired ending finished goods inventory levels at a constant percentage of the following period's budgeted unit sales. This policy gives the company enough units of inventory to satisfy customer demand for a constant period of time beyond the end of the period, even if the company doesn't (or can't) produce any units. It also prevents the company from accumulating too much inventory. For example, Unlimited Decadence's policy is to have an ending finished goods inventory equal to 25 percent of the next month's anticipated sales of candy bars. Therefore, if sales occur as it expects, Unlimited Decadence will always have enough units at the end of the period to satisfy customer demand for about one week without producing any new cases of candy bars. If its actual ending inventory in any month is greater than 25 percent of the next month's expected sales, it will adjust the number of cases of candy bars it plans to manufacture in the next month. In Unlimited Decadence's situation, budgeted sales and budgeted production are linked together, as shown in the following diagram:

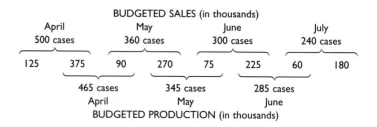

With this inventory policy, March's production would have been sufficient to cover three-fourths (75%) of March's sales and the first one-fourth (25%) of April's sales (125,000

[3]John S. DeMott, "Small Factories' Big Lessons," *Nation's Business,* April 1995, 29, 30.

[4]In Chapter 15 we will discuss how to determine the economic order quantity—the quantity that minimizes the two costs we just discussed.

cases). April's required production of 465,000 cases, then, must satisfy the last three-fourths of April's sales (375,000 cases) plus the first one-fourth of May's sales (90,000 cases) and so forth.

 What do you think should happen to next month's actual production if Unlimited Decadence sells more cases of candy bars this month than it budgeted? Why?

Other companies, particularly those experiencing seasonal demand, might be better off having a policy of allowing finished goods inventories to gradually increase during low sales periods so that they can meet increased demand during high sales periods without having to undergo large changes in production levels.

 Think about a company's factory, equipment, employees, and inventories. How do you think large changes in production levels would affect each of these factors? How would such changes affect the company's costs?

Exhibit 12-4 presents Unlimited Decadence's production budget for Darkly Decadent candy bars. Notice that we expressed this budget entirely in units (thousands of cases of candy bars). Also notice that Unlimited Decadence must have inventory available for each time period (month or quarter) equal to the sum of the budgeted sales of cases of candy bars for that time period and the desired ending inventory (in other words, enough to sell during the period and to still have the desired amount of inventory remaining after the sales). The total required cases must come from the period's beginning inventory and from any goods that Unlimited Decadence produces during the time period. Thus, for each period, the necessary production for that period is computed by subtracting the number of cases that Unlimited Decadence already has on hand at the beginning of the period (the beginning inventory) from the total number of cases required.

 By looking at this production budget, can you tell what Unlimited Decadence anticipates its July sales will be?

Notice too the relationship between the monthly and the quarterly numbers. Just as occurs with a retail company, in a manufacturing company, the budgeted unit sales for the quarter equal the sum of the budgeted unit sales for all three months of the quarter. Unlimited Decadence's total sales for the second quarter of the year 2001 (1,160,000 cases) is the sum of its monthly sales for the quarter (500,000 + 360,000 + 300,000 cases).

Exhibit 12-4 Production Budget

Unlimited Decadence Corporation
Production Budget
(in thousands of cases)
Second Quarter 2001

	April	May	June	Quarter
Budgeted sales (cases)	500	360	300	1,160
Add: Desired ending inventory of finished cases[a]	90	75	60	60
Total cases required	590	435	360	1,220
Less: Beginning inventory of finished cases	(125)	(90)	(75)	(125)
Budgeted production (cases)	465	345	285	1,095

[a]One-fourth of next month's sales

Similarly, the budgeted production for the quarter (1,095,000 cases) is the sum of the three monthly production requirements (465,000 + 345,000 + 285,000 cases). The desired ending and beginning inventories for the quarter, however, are simply equal to the desired ending inventory for the last month of the quarter (60,000 cases for June) and the beginning inventory for the first month of the quarter (125,000 cases for April), respectively. Unlimited Decadence's total requirement of cases of candy bars for the quarter is the quarter's budgeted unit sales (1,160,000 cases) plus its desired ending inventory (60,000 cases). Finally, note that each month's ending inventory is the following month's beginning inventory (April's desired ending inventory of 90,000 cases is the same as May's beginning inventory).

Look at Unlimited Decadence's production budget again. If Unlimited Decadence had a policy of keeping ending finished goods inventory at a constant level, how do you think that would change each month's production from what Unlimited Decadence currently budgeted?

Direct Materials Purchases Budget

To manufacture goods, a company must have direct materials on hand. Therefore, its managers must decide when to purchase direct materials, how many to purchase, and when to pay for these purchases. The direct materials purchases budget helps managers quantify these decisions. The **direct materials purchases budget** is a schedule that shows the number of direct material units that must be purchased in each budget period to meet production and ending direct materials inventory requirements. It also shows the costs related to those purchases and when the company expects to pay for them.

As you have probably observed, manufacturing companies often use many different direct materials in their products. They purchase these direct materials at widely differing prices. Unlimited Decadence, for example, uses sugar, milk products, cocoa beans, nuts, and emulsifiers in its products. Sugar, cocoa beans, and nuts are priced by the pound, emulsifiers by the carton, and milk products by the barrel. Because of differences like these, manufacturing companies often prepare a separate schedule for each direct material. However, despite these differences, the structures of the direct materials purchases schedules for all the direct materials are similar. Therefore, to avoid unnecessary repetition, we now illustrate Unlimited Decadence's direct materials purchases budget for only one of its direct materials—sugar.

Direct Materials Purchases Requirement

The direct materials purchases budget initially shows the direct materials, in units (pounds, barrels, or cartons), that a company needs to have on hand during each budget period. This amount is the sum of the direct materials the company expects to use in production in each budget period and the desired ending inventory of direct materials. Suppose, for example, that Unlimited Decadence purchases sugar by the pound. The total sugar that Unlimited Decadence needs to have on hand in each month is the number of pounds of sugar it requires for the budgeted production of cases of chocolates that month plus the number of pounds of sugar it desires to have in its ending inventory. Exhibit 12-5 shows Unlimited Decadence's purchases budget for sugar. Notice that in April, Unlimited Decadence needs 1,860,000 pounds of sugar for the production of 465,000 cases of candy. Its desired ending inventory is 92,000 pounds of sugar, so the total sugar that it needs to have on hand in April is the sum of both, or 1,952,000 pounds of sugar. If it needs more than the amount of the month's beginning inventory of sugar (in April, 124,000 pounds), Unlimited Decadence must purchase enough sugar to make up the difference. We computed the number of pounds of sugar that Unlimited Decadence must purchase in April (1,828,000 pounds) by subtracting the number of pounds of sugar in the beginning inventory of sugar (124,000 pounds in April) from the total inventory of sugar required in that month (1,952,000 pounds).

Unlimited Decadence determines the amount of sugar it needs for production in each budget period by multiplying its budgeted production by the standard number of

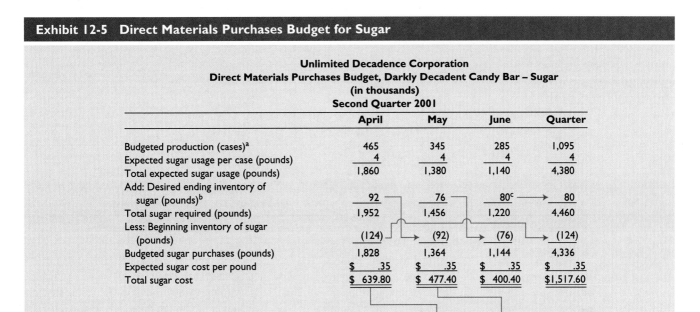

Exhibit 12-5   Direct Materials Purchases Budget for Sugar

Unlimited Decadence Corporation
Direct Materials Purchases Budget, Darkly Decadent Candy Bar – Sugar
(in thousands)
Second Quarter 2001

	April	May	June	Quarter
Budgeted production (cases)[a]	465	345	285	1,095
Expected sugar usage per case (pounds)	4	4	4	4
Total expected sugar usage (pounds)	1,860	1,380	1,140	4,380
Add: Desired ending inventory of sugar (pounds)[b]	92	76	80[c]	80
Total sugar required (pounds)	1,952	1,456	1,220	4,460
Less: Beginning inventory of sugar (pounds)	(124)	(92)	(76)	(124)
Budgeted sugar purchases (pounds)	1,828	1,364	1,144	4,336
Expected sugar cost per pound	$ .35	$ .35	$ .35	$ .35
Total sugar cost	$ 639.80	$ 477.40	$ 400.40	$1,517.60
Cash payments for purchases[c]	$ 565.95	$ 639.80	$ 477.40	$1,683.15

[a]from production budget (Exhibit 12-4)
[b]1/15 of next month's expected sugar usage
[c]Payments are made one month after credit purchases.

pounds of sugar (4 pounds) needed to produce each case of candy. It bases the standard number of pounds of sugar needed per case on its engineering studies and production data from previous periods. The desired ending inventories of sugar used in this budget result from managers' decisions based on the same kinds of cost considerations (cost of carrying versus cost of not carrying inventories) that determine the desired finished goods inventory levels appearing in the production budget.

 What other similarities do you see between the direct materials purchases budget and the production budget?

Direct Materials Purchase Cost

Managers use anticipated direct materials purchase prices (which the company may obtain from its suppliers) to convert unit purchase requirements into direct materials purchase costs. Unlimited Decadence anticipates that it will pay $0.35 per pound of sugar. Multiplying the April budgeted sugar purchases of 1,828,000 pounds by $0.35 gives the direct materials purchases cost of $639,800. Managers then use the direct materials purchases cost to budget cash payments for direct materials purchases. The company's payment arrangement with its direct materials suppliers usually determines the timing of these payments. If Unlimited Decadence pays cash for sugar, for example, its cash payment each month for purchases of sugar equals the total sugar cost for that month. On the other hand, if Unlimited Decadence always pays for sugar on the thirtieth day after its purchases (with terms of n/30, as we assume in Exhibit 12-5),[5] the cash payment for sugar purchases each month approximately equals the total budgeted sugar cost for the previous month. For example, in May, the cash payment of $639,800 equals the total sugar cost for April.

---

[5]We assume that Unlimited Decadence's supplier offers no cash discounts. If there were cash discounts, Unlimited Decadence would make cash payments earlier, but these payments would be smaller because of the discounts.

Look at the direct materials purchases budget again. Where did the beginning inventory and the ending inventory numbers for the quarter come from?

Direct materials purchase costs can also affect the selling prices of finished products as well as future sales and direct materials purchases budgets. For example, when Coca-Cola and Anheuser-Busch companies found out they would have to pay more for aluminum cans, they raised their selling prices in the first quarter of a recent year.[6] If the companies had known about this cost change when they were budgeting for the quarter, they would have shown the new costs in their direct materials purchases budgets and their new selling prices in their sales budgets.

 How do you think these companies' budgets would have been affected if their markets had been highly competitive? Why? What decisions would they have had to make?

Direct Labor Budget

Most manufacturing companies use direct labor to convert direct materials into finished goods, although some companies have completely automated factories. Managers must decide how many hours of direct labor are necessary to meet the production schedule in each budget period. The direct labor budget helps managers quantify this decision. The **direct labor budget** is a schedule that shows the hours and the cost of the direct labor required to meet the budgeted production. It also shows the cash payments the company expects to make for direct labor during each budget period.

To help you understand the concept of a direct labor budget, we illustrate a simple direct labor budget for Unlimited Decadence in Exhibit 12-6. The total hours of direct labor time required to meet each month's budgeted production of Darkly Decadent candy bars are computed by multiplying the month's budgeted production by the standard number of hours of direct labor needed to produce each unit of product. For example, to determine the amount of direct labor necessary for April's budgeted production (232,500 hours of

Exhibit 12-6   Direct Labor Budget

Unlimited Decadence Corporation
Direct Labor Budget
(in thousands)
Second Quarter 2001

	April	May	June	Quarter
Budgeted production (cases)[a]	465	345	285	1,095
Direct labor time per case (hours per case)	0.50	0.50	0.50	0.50
Total direct labor hours required	232.50	172.50	142.50	547.50
Labor rate per hour	$ 12.00	$ 12.00	$ 12.00	$ 12.00
Budgeted labor cost	$2,790.00	$2,070.00	$1,710.00	$6,570.00
Add: Beginning wages payable balance[b]	1,200.00	1,395.00	1,035.00	1,200.00
Less: Ending wages payable balance[b]	(1,395.00)	(1,035.00)	(855.00)	(855.00)
Cash payments for direct labor	$2,595.00	$2,430.00	$1,890.00	$6,915.00

[a]From production budget (Exhibit 12-4)
[b]Wages are paid two weeks after they are earned.

[6]Erle Norton, "High Raw-Material Costs Lift Price Tags," *Wall Street Journal,* April 27, 1995, A2.

labor), Unlimited Decadence's managers would multiply 465,000 cases (April's budgeted production) by 0.50 hours (the standard number of hours to produce a case of candy bars). Managers use these total direct labor hour requirements to help them anticipate the number of workers needed at various times of the year. Then they can make hiring and training plans and avoid costly overtime or production delays.

 When Techknits, Inc., the New York sweater manufacturer we mentioned in Chapter 11, computerized its looms, one person in the factory could run four looms instead of only one.[7] How do you think this change affected Techknits' direct labor budget?

In Unlimited Decadence's direct labor budget, we assume that each case of Darkly Decadent candy bars requires one-half hour of direct labor time, and that the company pays all factory employees $12 per hour. These assumptions greatly simplify the illustration because manufacturing companies usually hire employees to perform a variety of skilled and unskilled direct labor operations at many different wage rates. Notice that we based the computation of total direct labor hours required on budgeted production (from the production budget in Exhibit 12-4) and that the total from the quarter is simply the sum of the amounts for the three months. Budgeted direct labor cost is computed by multiplying the total direct labor hour requirements by the wage rate per hour. For instance, Unlimited Decadence requires 232,500 total direct labor hours in April. Multiplying this by the labor rate of $12 per hour gives the budgeted direct labor cost for April ($2,790,000). The direct labor cost for a budget period may differ from the budgeted cash *payments* for direct labor for that same period. This happens whenever the period in which employees are paid differs from the budget period in which they worked. For example, Unlimited Decadence pays wages two weeks after its employees earn them. May's budgeted cash payment for direct labor consists of the last half of April's direct labor cost ($1,395,000) and the first half of May's direct labor cost ($1,035,000).

 In what month would Unlimited Decadence budget the cash payment for the other half of May's direct labor cost?

Notice that the total cash payments for the quarter equal the sum of the cash payments for the three months in the quarter. Also notice that the beginning wages payable balance for the quarter is the same as the beginning wages payable balance for the *first month* of the quarter. The ending wages payable balance for the quarter is the same as the ending wages payable balance for the *last month* of the quarter.

 Look again at Unlimited Decadence's direct labor budget. Can you tell from the budget how much Unlimited Decadence budgeted for March's labor cost?

Factory Overhead Budget

All manufacturing companies incur overhead costs when they convert direct materials into finished goods. The **factory overhead budget** is a schedule showing estimates of all factory overhead costs and their related cash payments for each budget period. Managers base these factory overhead cost estimates on the production budget and on studies of the behavior of the various overhead costs, as we discussed in Chapter 11.

Exhibit 12-7 shows the factory overhead budget for Unlimited Decadence. Notice that we have separated fixed and variable overhead costs on this budget schedule. As you would expect, total variable costs fluctuate. Close examination reveals, in fact, that the budgeted variable cost totals for each month vary directly in proportion to changes in budgeted production levels. We show the variable cost per case of candy bars in parentheses in the variable costs section of the budget. (For instance, utilities costs are $0.05 per case.)

---

[7]John S. DeMott, "Small Factories' Big Lessons," *Nation's Business,* April 1995, 29, 30.

Exhibit 12-7 Factory Overhead Budget

Unlimited Decadence Corporation
Factory Overhead Budget
(in thousands)
Second Quarter 2001

	April	May	June	Quarter
Budgeted production (cases)ª	465	345	285	1,095
Variable overhead costs (rate):				
Indirect labor ($.12 per case)	$ 55.80	$ 41.40	$ 34.20	$ 131.40
Indirect materials ($.08 per case)	37.20	27.60	22.80	87.60
Utilities ($.05 per case)	23.25	17.25	14.25	54.75
Other variable costs ($.07 per case)	32.55	24.15	19.95	76.65
Total variable costs ($.32 per case)	$148.80	$110.40	$ 91.20	$ 350.40
Fixed overhead costs:				
Supervisory salaries	$114.00	$114.00	$114.00	$ 342.00
Depreciation of plant and equipment	150.00	150.00	150.00	450.00
Other fixed costs	240.00	240.00	240.00	720.00
Total fixed costs	$504.00	$504.00	$504.00	$1,512.00
Total factory overhead costs	$652.80	$614.40	$595.20	$1,862.40
Less: Depreciation of plant and equipment	(150.00)	(150.00)	(150.00)	(450.00)
Cash payments for factory overhead costs	$502.80	$464.40	$445.20	$1,412.40

ªFrom production budget (Exhibit 12-4)

However, fixed costs are the same in each month's budget. The fixed costs total $504,000 each month and consist of supervisory salaries, depreciation of plant and equipment, and other fixed costs.

Unlimited Decadence pays factory overhead costs (except for depreciation) in the period in which they are incurred. Recall from Chapter 5 that depreciation is an allocation of the cost (or, the difference between the original cost and the residual value) of plant and equipment to the periods of their use. There are cash flows associated with owning plant and equipment, but they are the payments associated with plant and equipment purchases (in the years that the company makes payments) and the cash receipts associated with selling or disposing of plant and equipment (in the years of disposal).[8] These cash flows do not correspond in amount in any period to the depreciation of the plant and equipment. Note that we have simply subtracted the depreciation expense ($150), which involves no corresponding cash flow, from the total factory overhead costs to determine the total monthly cash payments for factory overhead.

Selling Expenses Budget

The selling expenses budget of a manufacturing company is developed in the same way as that of a retail company. A large company typically has more complicated budgets than does a small company, however. The selling expenses budget of a large company often shows sales-determined expenses separately from sales-determining expenses. **Sales-determined expenses** result from selling activities that are necessary to support the volume of budgeted sales. Managers estimate these expenses *after* they have developed the sales budget. For example, shipping expenses are sales-determined expenses. The estimated shipping expenses increase as projected sales increase. **Sales-determining expenses** result from selling activities that affect the sales volume. Managers must deliberately decide to implement the activities that generate sales-determining expenses. Sales-determining expenses *influence* the

---

[8]A company includes these cash payments and receipts in its capital expenditures budget, which we will discuss in Chapter 20.

Where would Hershey's include the cost of this advertisement in its master budget?

preparation of the sales budget. For example, Unlimited Decadence's advertising has an impact on the number of cases of candy bars that Unlimited Decadence sells. Therefore, advertising expenses are sales-determining expenses.

 Suppose Unlimited Decadence purchased network time for a commercial to be aired during the Super Bowl. What budget periods' sales do you think this advertising expense will influence? Why?

Managers of a large company often spend a large amount of time and effort studying the factors that affect the sales volumes of its various products. Then they try to plan strategies

Exhibit 12-8 Selling Expenses Budget

	April	May	June	Quarter
Unlimited Decadence Corporation Selling Expenses Budget (in thousands) Second Quarter 2001				
Budgeted sales (cases)[a]	500	360	300	1,160
Sales-determining expenses:				
Advertising	$250	$200	$150	$ 600
Sales salaries	225	225	225	675
Other promotional efforts	100	—	—	100
Sales-determined expenses:				
Shipping (variable at $.30 per case sold)	150	108	90	348
Total selling expenses	$725	$533	$465	$1,723
Cash payments for selling expenses[b]	$725	$533	$465	$1,723

[a]From the sales budget (Exhibit 12-3)
[b]Cash payments will occur in the month of the expense.

to take advantage of those factors. In planning these strategies, they also consider general business and industry conditions, actions of competitors, and company policy.

Exhibit 12-8 shows Unlimited Decadence's selling expenses budget for the second quarter of the year 2001. Note that Unlimited Decadence has sales-determined shipping expenses of $0.30 per case *sold*. Notice also the similarity between this budget and that of Sweet Temptations (Exhibit 4-8).

General and Administrative Expenses Budget

Like the selling expenses budget, the general and administrative expenses budget of a manufacturing company is developed in the same way as that of a retail company. However, a large company like Unlimited Decadence often groups and describes expenses by administrative activity or function. For example, expenses related to accounting, research and development, and legal activities might be shown separately. Such groupings are useful because they give managers an opportunity to review the commitment of resources to each function during the planning process. The groupings also provide a standard of comparison against which managers can evaluate the actual costs incurred in each activity or function. Exhibit 12-9 shows Unlimited Decadence's general and administrative expenses budget for the second quarter of the year 2001.

 How is this budget similar to that of Sweet Temptations (Exhibit 4-9)?

Note that there are two "noncash" expenses (insurance and depreciation) that we did not include in the total cash payments for the second quarter of the year 2001. The reason we didn't include them is because Unlimited Decadence made (or will make) these cash payments in different time periods. It is common for a company to pay for some items before their costs are incurred. For example, a company may prepay insurance on its buildings and equipment. The $40,000 monthly insurance expense on Unlimited Decadence's general and administrative expenses budget reflects the expected "using up" of the insurance policy that it paid for earlier. Also, as we mentioned earlier, it is uncommon for the cash payments associated with plant and equipment purchases to coincide with the depreciation of the plant and equipment.

Exhibit 12-9 General and Administrative Expenses Budget

Unlimited Decadence Corporation
General and Administrative Expenses Budget
(in thousands)
Second Quarter 2001

	April	May	June	Quarter
Accounting and clerical expenses	$201	$201	$ 201	$ 603
Administrative salaries	134	134	134	402
General expenses:				
Insurance[a]	40	40	40	120
Property taxes[b]	99	99	99	297
Depreciation of office buildings				
and equipment	83	83	83	249
Total expenses	$557	$557	$ 557	$1,671
Schedule of cash payments:				
Accounting and clerical expenses	$201	$201	$ 201	$ 603
Administrative salaries	134	134	134	402
Property taxes[b]			1,188	1,188
Total cash payments	$335	$335	$1,523	$2,193

[a]The $40,000-per-month insurance expense is equal to the monthly reduction in the prepaid insurance account.
[b]Property taxes accrue each month and are paid in full in June each year.

Capital Expenditures Budget

Adding to plant and equipment, replacing old machinery, remodeling or relocating office facilities, or developing a new product may involve large expenditures of cash. Such expenditures often result from a company's commitments to major programs or projects that may require several years to produce benefits for the company. For example, Ford Motor Co.'s annual capital spending averages about $8.3 billion, most of which is for new product development. Its new cars take five or six years to design.[9]

Because of the cost and time requirements of major programs or projects, managers should not make capital expenditure commitments without a thorough and objective evaluation of the effect of the capital expenditures on the company's operations. Managers should also carefully plan the projects to be undertaken so that they will not interfere with the company's current operations. Such planning is aided by the capital expenditures budget. The **capital expenditures budget** is a set of schedules that shows the effects that each new project to be undertaken is expected to have on other master budget schedules. In this budget, managers use information gathered during project evaluations to show (1) the expected timing of project-related cash receipts and payments that affect the cash budget, (2) the costs of project-related assets to be acquired that affect the projected balance sheet, and (3) the project-related increases and decreases in factory overhead costs, selling expenses, general and administrative expenses, and perhaps sales that affect the budgets for those items as well as the projected income statement.

An adequate illustration of a capital expenditures budget would unnecessarily complicate our discussion of the other budgets. However, the evaluation of proposals to invest company resources in long-term projects is important. Since Unlimited Decadence is planning no capital expenditures during the second quarter of the year 2001, we will postpone our discussion of the capital expenditures budget until Chapter 20.

www2.ford.com

---

[9]James B. Treece, "Ford: Alex Trotman's Daring Global Strategy," *Business Week,* April 3, 1995, 96.

Cash Budget (Projected Cash Flow Statement)

Remember from our Chapter 4 discussion that the cash budget helps managers anticipate the approach of cash shortages or excesses in time to avoid them. If managers expect temporary cash shortages to occur, they can provide potential lenders (such as banks) with the company's cash budget to show how the company will use borrowed cash and when the managers anticipate that the company will have enough cash to repay the loan. As soon as they know when to expect temporary cash excesses, managers can begin to identify temporary investments for this excess cash.

The cash budget may have three major sections: the operating activities section, the investing activities section, and the financing activities section.[10] The **operating activities section** summarizes the cash receipts and payments that managers expect to result from the company's planned operating activities. This section shows the net cash receipts (excess of operating receipts over operating payments) or the net cash payments (excess of payments over receipts) for each budget period. When the expected net cash receipts from operating activities is added to (or the net payments are deducted from) the period's beginning cash balance, the result is the expected ending cash balance from operating activities. For example, on Unlimited Decadence's cash budget (Exhibit 12-10), the May net cash receipts of $2,254,220 are added to May's beginning cash balance of $1,949,200 to get the anticipated ending cash balance from operating activities for May of $4,203,420. Notice that April's net cash *payment* of $72,250 is *subtracted* from April's beginning cash balance to get the expected ending cash balance from operating activities for April.

The **investing activities section** summarizes the cash transactions that managers expect to result from the company's investing activities. Normally, companies include here cash payments for the purchase of property, plant, and equipment as well as for the purchase of government securities and the stocks or bonds of other companies. They also include here cash receipts from the planned disposal of old property, plant, and equipment or from the expected sale of investments in stocks and bonds of other companies.

 Why do you think these cash receipts are included in the investing activities section?

The net cash payments (receipts) from planned investment activities are subtracted from (added to) the anticipated ending cash balance from operating activities to arrive at the anticipated ending cash balance from operating and investing activities. If the anticipated ending cash balance from operating and investing activities is too low in any budget period, the company can arrange to borrow cash (a financing activity) or sell investments in time to avoid the cash shortage. If the balance is too high in any period, the company may plan to use the excess cash to repay loans taken in previous periods (another financing activity) or may invest its excess cash.

The **financing activities section** shows the cash receipts and payments associated with planned financing activities, such as those we mentioned in the previous paragraph. This section includes cash receipts from borrowing money or from selling the company's own stock. It also includes cash payments to pay back loans or to repurchase the company's own stock.

 Why do you think these cash payments are included in the financing section?

Adding the expected net financing receipts to (or deducting the net financing payments from) the anticipated cash balance from operating and investing activities gives the budgeted ending cash balance for the period. This ending cash balance is used as the cash balance for the projected balance sheet at the end of the period.

---

[10]Remember, a cash budget used for internal reporting (and sometimes used for external reporting) is similar to the cash flow statement for external reporting that we discussed in Chapter 8.

Exhibit 12-10 Cash Budget

Unlimited Decadence Corporation
Cash Budget
(in thousands)
Second Quarter 2001

	April	May	June	Quarter
Cash flows from operating activities:				
Cash receipts from:				
Sales[a]	$5,840.00	$8,000.00	$5,760.00	$19,600.00
Cash payments for:				
Sugar purchases[b]	$ 565.95	$ 639.80	$ 477.40	$ 1,683.15
Other direct materials purchases[c]	1,188.50	1,343.58	1,002.54	3,534.62
Direct labor[d]	2,595.00	2,430.00	1,890.00	6,915.00
Factory overhead[e]	502.80	464.40	445.20	1,412.40
Selling expenses[f]	725.00	533.00	465.00	1,723.00
General and administrative expenses[g]	335.00	335.00	1,523.00	2,193.00
Income taxes[h]	—	—	473.48	473.48
Total cash payments	$5,912.25	$5,745.78	$6,276.62	$17,934.65
Net cash receipts (payments) from operating activities	($ 72.25)	$2,254.22	($ 516.62)	$ 1,665.35
Add: Beginning cash balance	1,021.45[i]	1,949.20	3,183.42	1,021.45
Ending cash balance from operating activities	$ 949.20	$4,203.42	$2,666.80	$ 2,686.80
Cash flows from financing activities:				
Add: Borrowing	$1,000.00	—	—	$ 1,000.00
Less: Repayment	—	($1,000.00)	—	(1,000.00)
Interest[j]	—	(20.00)	—	(20.00)
Net cash flows from financing activities	$1,000.00	($1,020.00)	—	($ 20.00)
Ending cash balance	$1,949.20	$3,183.42	$2,666.80	$ 2,666.80

[a]From the sales budget (Exhibit 12-3)
[b]From the direct materials purchases budget (Exhibit 12-5)
[c]From the other direct materials purchases budgets (not shown in this chapter)
[d]From the direct labor budget (Exhibit 12-6)
[e]From the factory overhead budget (Exhibit 12-7)
[f]From the selling expenses budget (Exhibit 12-8)
[g]From the general and administrative expenses budget (Exhibit 12-9)
[h]From the income statement (Exhibit 12-11)
[i]From last quarter's balance sheet (Exhibit 12-12)
[j]Although interest from borrowing is in the cash flows from financing activities section of the cash budget, it is shown in the cash flows from operating activities section of the cash flow statement.

 What similarities and differences do you notice between a cash budget and the cash flow statement we discussed in Chapter 8?

Exhibit 12-10 shows Unlimited Decadence's cash budget for the second quarter of the year 2001. Notice that except for the cash payment for income taxes, the operating activities section of the cash budget merely summarizes the receipts and payments computed in the company's previous budgets. The payment of income taxes must be based on the company's projected income statement. Notice in Exhibit 12-11 on page 390, that we compute income tax expense to be $473,480. This is the same number we use for income tax *payments* in the cash budget for June because we are assuming that Unlimited Decadence pays income taxes at the end of each quarter for the income earned during the quarter.

We previously assumed that Unlimited Decadence budgeted no capital expenditures. To simplify our discussion, we further assume that the company has budgeted no other investing transactions. As a result, Unlimited Decadence's cash budget in Exhibit 12-10 does not include an investing activities section.

Notice that Unlimited Decadence's cash budget shows a net cash payment of $72,250 from operating activities in April. This reduces the beginning cash balance of $1,021,450 to $949,200. Unlimited Decadence's management has adopted the policy of not allowing its cash balance to drop below $1 million at the end of any month, however. Hence, to have enough cash on hand, the company must acquire more cash. There are two major sources of additional cash: debt capital and equity capital.

Debt Capital

Debt capital is money that a company borrows from creditors. This borrowed money, called the *principal,* must be paid back to the creditors. Furthermore, the company also must pay a specified amount of interest on the principal. This interest may take several forms:

1. A specific amount that the company pays at set intervals throughout the life of the loan

2. An amount computed on the unpaid balance and paid at the same time that the company makes partial payments on the loan

3. A set amount that the company pays all at once on the same date that it pays back the entire loan

Frequently a company signs a note payable for this debt, as we will discuss in Chapter 14.

Equity Capital

Equity capital is money that a corporation brings in through the sale of the corporation's own stock (or, as we discussed in Chapter 4, through the contribution of cash to the company by the owner or owners, in the case of sole proprietorships and partnerships). A corporation can sell its own stock to current stockholders and/or others outside the corporation, who then become additional stockholders of the company. The corporation can use the money from the sale of this stock for many purposes. There is no obligation to pay it back. However, although corporations do not necessarily return the investments of owners, most pay dividends to stockholders as a return *on* their investments. Unlike debt capital, which requires a particular amount of interest to be paid at specific times, equity capital does not require the payment of dividends. We will discuss stocks and dividends more thoroughly in Chapter 24.

In deciding whether to obtain financing through debt capital or equity capital, managers must consider several factors:

1. Whether they want the company to be obligated to a fixed cash payment (interest and principal)

2. How the interest rate on borrowed money compares with the company's anticipated dividend payments

3. Whether the current stockholders want to bring more stockholders into the company and, perhaps, share control of the company with them (meaning that the current stockholders would have relatively less "say" in the operations of the company and a smaller share of its income)

Once managers choose a type of financing, the cash budget provides information useful for planning either the payment of a dividend or the repayment of debt and the payment of its related interest. Because Unlimited Decadence's stockholders do not want to purchase more shares of Unlimited Decadence's stock or to share control of the company with new owners, Unlimited Decadence plans debt financing to cover this quarter's cash shortfalls. Unlimited Decadence has an arrangement with 2nd State Bank called a "line of

"We need two hundred million bucks by Friday—any ideas?"

©Marty Lowe. Wall Street Journal—Permission by Cartoon Features Syndicate.

credit," which allows it to borrow up to $5 million, as needed, in even million-dollar increments. In other words, the amount of money borrowed by Unlimited Decadence at any time must be evenly divisible by $1 million. At no time can the total amount borrowed by Unlimited Decadence from 2nd State Bank exceed $5 million. Unlimited Decadence computes the loan's interest at the end of each month as 1% of the loan balance at the beginning of the month. Each time Unlimited Decadence borrows money, it takes out a loan (a note payable) at the beginning of the month in which it requires the money (in this case, the beginning of April). It pays back loans plus accumulated interest on the loans at the end of the first month in which it has enough cash, in excess of $1 million, to pay back the amount of the loan plus interest.

To meet its minimum cash balance policy, Unlimited Decadence must borrow $1 million at the beginning of April, raising April's ending cash balance (and May's beginning cash balance) to $1,949,200. When this beginning balance is added to the $2,254,220 net cash receipts from May's operating activities, the projected ending cash balance from operating activities for May becomes $4,203,420.

Repayment of Debt and Interest

During periods of excess cash, management will choose to pay back loans plus the interest that has accumulated on these loans. In the case of Unlimited Decadence, since May's ending cash balance from operating activities of $4,203,420 is $3,203,420 greater than its required ending cash balance of $1 million, Unlimited Decadence plans to repay its entire loan plus interest ($1,020,000) at the end of May. The $20,000 interest is two months' interest computed on the $1 million total loan balance carried through April and May. June's $2,666,800 ending cash balance will appear on Unlimited Decadence's projected balance sheet for June 30, 2001. We will discuss short-term debt and long-term debt more thoroughly in Chapters 14 and 22 respectively.

Projected Income Statement

After generating all the previous budget schedules, managers develop a projected income statement to determine the company's profitability if it follows all its plans and if all the anticipated conditions occur. Exhibit 12-11 shows Unlimited Decadence's projected income statement for the second quarter of the year 2001. This statement is similar to Unlimited Decadence's *annual* income statement, which we discussed in Chapter 10, but with a few differences. Since Exhibit 12-11 shows a projected income statement, Unlimited Decadence computes its cost of goods sold directly on the statement. Because Unlimited Decadence is a manufacturing company, it computes its cost of finished goods available for sale ($14,684,700) by summing the beginning finished goods inventory ($1,500,000) from the end of the first quarter (March 31, 2001) balance sheet and the cost of goods manufactured this quarter ($4,752,300 direct materials used, $6,570,000 direct labor, and $1,862,400 factory overhead from the budget schedules). It then subtracts the ending finished goods inventory ($722,400) to determine its cost of goods sold ($13,962,300).

Since Unlimited Decadence is a corporation, it estimates its income tax expense by multiplying the expected income before income taxes ($1,183,700) by the anticipated 40% income tax rate. The amount of the income tax expense for the second quarter ($473,480) also appears in the cash budget for the second quarter (Exhibit 12-10). This is because we assume that Unlimited Decadence pays income taxes quarterly in the last month of the

---

Exhibit 12-11   Projected Income Statement

Unlimited Decadence Corporation
Projected Income Statement
(in thousands)
Second Quarter 2001

Sales revenue			$18,560.00[a]
Cost of goods sold			
Beginning finished goods inventory			
(125 cases at $12/case)		$ 1,500.00[b]	
Add: Cost of goods manufactured (1,095 cases):			
Direct materials used ($4.34 × 1,095)	$4,752.30[c]		
Direct labor	6,570.00[d]		
Factory overhead	1,862. 40[e]		
Total cost of goods manufactured		13,184.70	
Cost of finished goods available for sale		$14,684.70	
Less: Ending finished goods inventory		(722.40)[f]	
Cost of goods sold			(13,962.30)
Gross profit			$ 4,597.70
Operating expenses			
Selling expenses		$ 1,723.00[g]	
General and administrative expenses		1,671.00[h]	
Total operating expenses			(3,394.00)
Operating income			$ 1,203.70
Other items			
Interest expense			(20.00)[i]
Income before taxes			$ 1,183.70
Income tax expense			(473.48)[j]
Net Income			$ 710.22

[a]From the sales budget (Exhibit 12-3)
[b]From last quarter's ending balance sheet
[c]From the direct materials budgets (Exhibit 12-5 and other direct materials schedules not shown in this chapter)
[d]From the direct labor budget (Exhibit 12-6)
[e]From the factory overhead budget (Exhibit 12-7)
[f][60 cases (from Exhibit 12-4) × $12.04]. Finished goods manufactured during the quarter are expected to cost $12.04 (rounded) per case.
[g]From the selling expenses budget (Exhibit 12-8)
[h]From the general and administrative expenses budget (Exhibit 12-9)
[i]Interest expense is $20 (1% × $1,000 × 2 months).
[j]Income tax expense has been estimated based on a 40% income tax rate.

quarter in which income is earned. Unlimited Decadence's projected net income for the second quarter of 2001 is $710,220.

 Look at the cash budget again (Exhibit 12-10). Do you think the cash budget or the income statement should be developed first? Why?

Projected Balance Sheet

Finally, before implementing their plan of action, managers develop a projected balance sheet to show the resources that the company expects to have available to use and what it expects to owe creditors at the end of the quarter if it follows its plans and if anticipated conditions occur. Exhibit 12-12 shows Unlimited Decadence's *actual* balance sheet at the end of the first quarter of the year 2001 and its *projected* balance sheet for the end of the second quarter of 2001. The amounts on the projected balance sheet for Unlimited Decadence come from previous budget schedules and the previous quarter's actual balance sheet. After the second quarter of the year 2001, Unlimited Decadence expects to have $20,006,460 of total resources available to use and to owe creditors and employees a total of $2,096,240. The projected balance sheet completes the financial description of Unlimited Decadence's second-quarter plans.

Exhibit 12-12 Actual and Projected Balance Sheets

Unlimited Decadence Corporation
Balance Sheet
(in thousands)
March 31, 2001

Assets

Current assets		
Cash	$1,021.45	
Accounts receivable	5,840.00	
Raw materials inventory	134.54	
Finished goods inventory	1,500.00	
Prepaid insurance	840.00	
Total current assets		$ 9,335.99
Property, plant, and equipment		
Plant and equipment (net)	$6,408.00	
Office buildings and equipment (net)	5,301.46	
Total property, plant, and equipment		11,709.46
Total Assets		$21,045.45

Liabilities

Current liabilities		
Accounts payable	$1,754.45	
Wages payable	1,200.00	
Property taxes payable	891.00	
Total Liabilities		$ 3,845.45

Stockholders' Equity

Common stock, $3 par	$3,600.00	
Additional paid-in capital	4,540.00	
Contributed capital		$ 8,140.00
Retained earnings		9,060.00
Total Stockholders' Equity		$17,200.00
Total Liabilities and Stockholders' Equity		$21,045.45

continued

Exhibit 12-12   Actual and Projected Balance Sheets—*continued*

Unlimited Decadence Corporation
Projected Balance Sheet
(in thousands)
June 30, 2001

Assets

Current assets
Cash	$2,666.80[a]	
Accounts receivable	4,800.00[b]	
Raw materials inventory	86.80[c]	
Finished goods inventory	722.40[d]	
Prepaid insurance	720.00[e]	
Total current assets		$ 8,996.00

Property, plant, and equipment
Plant and equipment (net)	$5,958.00[f]	
Office buildings and equipment (net)	5,052.46[g]	
Total property, plant, and equipment		11,010.46
Total Assets		$20,006.46

Liabilities

Current liabilities
Accounts payable	$1,241.24[h]	
Wages payable	855.00[i]	
Total Liabilities		$ 2,096.24

Stockholders' Equity

Common stock, $3 par	$3,600.00	
Additional paid-in capital	4,540.00	
Contributed capital		$ 8,140.00
Retained earnings		9,770.22[j]
Total Stockholders' Equity		$17,910.22
Total Liabilities and Stockholders' Equity		$20,006.46

[a]From the cash budget (Exhibit 12-10)
[b]From the sales budget (Exhibit 12-3)
[c]From the raw materials purchases budget for sugar (Exhibit 12-5) and other direct materials budgets not shown in this chapter
[d]From the projected income statement (Exhibit 12-11)
[e]$840 from beginning balance sheet minus $120 from the general and administrative expenses budget (Exhibit 12-9)
[f]$6,408 book value from beginning balance sheet minus $450 depreciation from factory overhead budget (Exhibit 12-7)
[g]$5,301.46 book value from the beginning balance sheet minus $249 depreciation from the general and administrative expenses budget (Exhibit 12-9)
[h]$400.40 from the direct materials purchases budget (Exhibit 12-5) and $840.84 other direct materials (budget not shown)
[i]From the direct labor budget (Exhibit 12-6)
[j]$9,060 beginning retained earnings plus $710.22 net income minus $0 dividends

Technology and Budgeting

As you probably have observed, the budgeting process involves plenty of "number crunching." During our discussion of this process you also should have observed how the numbers within and among budgets are interrelated. It is common for managers to review their budgets, notice a problem, and go "back to the drawing board" to refine the budget. But changing any aspect of the budget causes other numbers to change also (sort of a "domino effect"). Luckily, technological developments have made this process easier and much less time-consuming, and also have minimized errors. Many companies use spreadsheet programs, such as Excel, Lotus, or Quattro Pro, to simplify their budgeting processes. These programs take into account the interrelationships among the budget numbers. When managers change a number in a budget, spreadsheet programs automatically change the other numbers that are affected by the initial change.

Responsibility Centers

A company uses the budgets we just discussed to provide a financial description of its plans. In addition, the information contained in these budgets can also be used to evaluate managers' performances. That is, after the budget period is over, the company can compare its *actual* revenues, costs, and profit with its *expected* revenues, costs, and profit from its various budgets to see how closely the company followed its plans.

A large company usually separates its operations into distinct responsibility centers for performance evaluation. A **responsibility center** is an identifiable portion or segment of a company's operations, the activities of which are the responsibility of a particular manager. Depending on the decision-making authority of that manager, a responsibility center may be evaluated as a cost center, a profit center, or an investment center.

A **cost center** is a responsibility center in which the manager who is responsible for its activities can control only the level of costs it incurs. The cost center manager has no influence over the amount of revenue ultimately received by the company or the level of investment in property, plant, and equipment used in operations. Because of this, a company evaluates a cost center manager by comparing the cost center's budgeted costs with its actual costs. For example, the foreman of a small machine shop in a large manufacturing company might be evaluated as a cost center manager. This approach is used because the foreman has no authority to influence the amount of revenue earned by (or investment made in) the machine shop, although the foreman's decisions affect the daily costs of the machine shop.

A **profit center** is a responsibility center in which the manager has decision-making authority over both costs and revenues. A company evaluates the manager of a profit center by comparing the center's budgeted profit with its actual profit. Decisions affecting revenues, such as which orders to accept and which prices to charge, affect profit. Decisions affecting costs also affect profit. Therefore profit is a convenient summary measure that a company can use to evaluate the performance of a manager who can control both costs and revenues by the decisions he or she makes.

An **investment center** is a responsibility center in which the manager has decision-making authority over costs, revenues, and the level of investment in property, plant, and equipment the center uses in its operations. A company sometimes can evaluate the manager of an investment center by judging the manager's decisions affecting the center's investment in plant and equipment separately from the manager's decisions affecting costs and revenues. More often, however, the manager's performance is evaluated using some comprehensive measure affected by all of the manager's decisions. A company commonly uses the ratio of profit earned by the center to the average investment in the center (which is sometimes called *return on average investment*) to evaluate the manager of an investment center.

Whichever type of responsibility center a company uses for a particular department or division, it must be certain that the manager has the *authority* to make decisions about the costs, revenues, or investments for which the manager is responsible. This concept is referred to as "having authority commensurate with responsibility." In the next section, we will discuss the use of flexible budgets and budget information in the evaluation of a cost center manager.

Flexible Budgets

One of the benefits of budgeting is that it provides a benchmark against which managers of a company can measure the results of actual activities to see how well the company met its goals. For a cost center, this comparison is typically quantified in a cost report. A cost report usually lists the budgeted costs, the actual costs incurred, and the differences between them. Such reports are most meaningful when the budgeted costs are developed to show the amounts expected to occur at the actual activity level attained. For example, it would be meaningful to compare the actual manufacturing costs incurred in producing

5 *If a company's actual sales are different from its budgeted sales (or actual production is different from budgeted production) for the same time period, how can managers meaningfully evaluate how well the company met its cost goals?*

500,000 cases of candy bars during a period with the costs expected at a production level of 500,000 cases of candy bars. It would be less useful to compare them with the expenses expected at the production level of 465,000 cases of candy bars budgeted before the period began. A **flexible budget** is a cost or expense budget that shows expected costs or expenses at various activity levels.

For example, Exhibit 12-13 shows a flexible budget for Unlimited Decadence's manufacturing costs. Note in this exhibit how the variable manufacturing costs (direct materials, direct labor, and variable factory overhead) vary in proportion to production volume at the variable cost rates we previously assumed.

Recall that in the direct materials purchases budget (Exhibit 12-5) we assumed that each case of Darkly Decadent candy bars requires 4 pounds of sugar costing $0.35 per pound. Thus each case requires $1.40 of sugar. We also assumed that each case requires $2.94 of other direct materials, for a total direct material cost of $4.34 per case. Similarly, each case (Exhibit 12-6) requires $6 of direct labor cost (1/2 hour at $12 per hour). The factory overhead budget in Exhibit 12-7 shows the variable factory overhead cost rates per case of Darkly Decadent candy bars manufactured. Note that the fixed factory overhead costs do not vary with production volume, however. We illustrate the use of cost reports next using data from Unlimited Decadence's flexible manufacturing cost budget (Exhibit 12-13).

Suppose that the president of Unlimited Decadence wants to evaluate the performance of the manager of the company's manufacturing operations (a cost center) for the month of April 2001, which we now assume has just passed. The basis of the performance evaluation will be a comparison of actual and budgeted manufacturing costs for April. In this comparison, the president wants to include the cost of direct materials, direct labor, and factory overhead. The company actually produced 500,000 cases of candy instead of the 465,000 cases it had budgeted earlier. Assuming the actual costs shown in Exhibit 12-14, the president prepares the *erroneous* manufacturing cost report that we present in that exhibit.

As you might expect from looking at this cost report, the president was not pleased. Many of the actual costs exceeded the April budget, and the total actual costs appear to be greater than the total expected costs by $298,800! However, the president would be mistaken in believing that the manager of the company's manufacturing operations has not kept the manufacturing costs under control.

Exhibit 12-13 Flexible Manufacturing Cost Budget

Unlimited Decadence Corporation
Flexible Cost Budget
(in thousands)

	Production Volume (Cases)			
	200	**300**	**400**	**500**
Direct materials ($4.34/case)	$ 868.00	$1,302.00	$1,736.00	$2,170.00
Direct labor ($6/case)	1,200.00	1,800.00	2,400.00	3,000.00
Factory overhead				
Variable:				
Indirect labor ($.12/case)	24.00	36.00	48.00	60.00
Indirect materials ($.08/case)	16.00	24.00	32.00	40.00
Utilities ($.05/case)	10.00	15.00	20.00	25.00
Other ($.07/case)	14.00	21.00	28.00	35.00
Fixed:				
Supervisory salaries	114.00	114.00	114.00	114.00
Depreciation	150.00	150.00	150.00	150.00
Other	240.00	240.00	240.00	240.00
Total manufacturing costs	$2,636.00	$3,702.00	$4,768.00	$5,834.00

Exhibit 12-14 Erroneous Manufacturing Cost Report

Unlimited Decadence Corporation
Manufacturing Cost Report
(in thousands)

	Original April Budget	Actual Costs	Favorable (Unfavorable) Difference
Production (cases)	465 cases	500 cases	
Direct materials ($4.34/case)	$2,018.10	$2,071.90	$ (53.80)
Direct labor ($6/case)	2,790.00	3,100.00	(310.00)
Factory overhead			
Variable:			
Indirect labor ($.12/case)	55.80	42.00	13.80
Indirect materials ($.08/case)	37.20	18.00	19.20
Utilities ($.05/case)	23.25	14.00	9.25
Other ($.07/case)	32.55	12.00	20.55
Fixed:			
Supervisory salaries	114.00	114.00	—
Depreciation	150.00	150.00	—
Other	240.00	237.80	2.20
Total manufacturing costs	$5,460.90	$5,759.70	$(298.80)

The problem with the president's report is that it compares actual costs incurred in April, costs spent in producing 500,000 cases of candy bars, with April's original planning budget, which was based on the budgeted production of only 465,000 cases of candy bars. If he thinks about it for a minute, the president shouldn't be surprised at the higher actual costs. It makes sense that costs would be higher when the company produces more cases of candy bars. Since the original production budget (Exhibit 12-4) called for the production of 465,000 cases of candy bars in April, the direct materials cost, direct labor cost, and factory overhead costs were estimated for that production level. The result is the misleading comparison in Exhibit 12-14.

We can correct the cost report, and make a meaningful cost comparison, by adjusting April's budget to show the costs expected to be incurred in producing 500,000 cases of candy bars. The flexible budget for manufacturing costs that we show in Exhibit 12-13 provides the budgeted cost information for the production level of *500,000* cases of candy bars. We used this budgeted information in the corrected manufacturing cost report in Exhibit 12-15. When April's actual costs are subtracted from the correct budgeted costs, the president has a useful cost comparison for evaluating the manager's performance regarding April's manufacturing activity.

Notice that the restatement of Unlimited Decadence's manufacturing cost budget required the adjustment of only the variable manufacturing costs. The fixed costs are expected to be the same at either production level. Note also how the cost comparison presents a very different picture of performance. The revised manufacturing cost report shows total actual costs to be *lower* than total expected costs by $74,300, a *favorable* difference.

The idea of basing cost comparisons on flexible budgets adjusted to show expected costs at the actual activity level attained is an important one for evaluating costs. Using the flexible budget in this way makes the differences computed between budgeted and actual costs calculated in cost reports more meaningful. These differences can suggest possible areas of the company's operations that may need attention, such as an inexperienced worker who uses direct materials inefficiently or a machine that needs replacement. We will discuss the evaluation of differences between expected (standard) costs and actual costs in Chapter 17.

Exhibit 12-15 Corrected Manufacturing Cost Report			

Unlimited Decadence Corporation
Manufacturing Cost Report
(in thousands)

	Original April Budget	Actual Costs	Favorable (Unfavorable) Difference
Production (cases)	500 cases	500 cases	
Direct materials ($4.34/case)	$2,170.00	$2,071.90	$98.10
Direct labor ($6/case)	3,000.00	3,100.00	(100.00)
Factory overhead			
Variable:			
Indirect labor ($.12/case)	60.00	42.00	18.00
Indirect materials ($.08/case)	40.00	18.00	22.00
Utilities ($.05/case)	25.00	14.00	11.00
Other ($.07/case)	35.00	12.00	23.00
Fixed:			
Supervisory salaries	114.00	114.00	—
Depreciation	150.00	150.00	—
Other	240.00	237.80	2.20
Total manufacturing costs	$5,834.00	$5,759.70	$74.30

 Look at the revised manufacturing cost report again (Exhibit 12-15). How might you explain the fact that actual direct labor costs were higher than the costs budgeted for the 500,000 cases produced?

Business Issues and Values

6 *How do budgets affect the business decisions that employees make?*

The master budget provides information that helps managers see the financial consequences of their planning decisions (if everything goes according to plan) before they implement those decisions. However, for everything to go according to plan, managers also must consider how their planning decisions influence the behavior of the people who will implement those plans.

Budgets can motivate employees to work toward the company's goals and can help them feel a sense of achievement when they achieve those goals. When the production supervisor at Unlimited Decadence completes production of Darkly Decadent candy bars on schedule and within budgeted costs, both she and her boss will be pleased.

On the other hand, budgets also can motivate employees to participate in activities that may be contrary to the company's goals, although these employees typically do not intend for these activities to undermine the company's goals. For example, a problem can occur when a manager's performance evaluation (or compensation) is based on how well he or she keeps costs within the budget. The message the manager gets from the budget is that actual costs should not be more than budgeted (no matter what!). When this is the case, some managers will postpone necessary expenditures so their departments will "look better" when the actual performance of the department is compared with the budget. This practice of postponing necessary expenditures can hurt the company in the long run. For example, Hasty Transfer Company, with whom Unlimited Decadence contracts to ship candy to Sweet Temptations and other retail stores around the country, must periodically have its delivery trucks serviced. Failure to perform routine maintenance on these trucks could cause expensive repair problems in the future and could delay future shipments. If its customers use a different carrier in the meantime, Hasty may permanently lose their business. As you can see, a manager who skips maintenance on the trucks during the current budget period in order to stay within the budget may cause Hasty Transfer Company much bigger problems in the future.

Another, more colorful, example of behavior being motivated by the *perceived* message involves Custer's defeat at Little Bighorn, a defeat partially caused by his inaccurate assessment of the Indians' numbers.[11] U.S. Indian agents' profits were tied to the number of Indians on the reservations: the more Indians on the reservations, the greater were the agents' profits. Any agent who reported a decrease in the Indian population took a bite out of his own paycheck. Therefore, as you might expect, the agents were reluctant to report decreases in the numbers (even though thousands of Indians had fled the reservations). Custer assumed, from the reports of the agents, that the Indians were still residing on the reservations rather than joining forces with Sitting Bull, Crazy Horse, and Gall. Consequently, he grossly underestimated the strength of his enemies and, well, the rest is history.

 How do you think the Indian agents' compensation might have been restructured to cause a better outcome?

When companies "roll over" their budgets from year to year (that is, last year's budgets become the starting point for this year's budgeting process), upper-level managers may be tempted to reduce this year's budget of a department that spent less money last year than it budgeted. Besides discouraging employees by reducing the resources they have to work with, the threat of a reduced budget usually causes employees to go on a last-minute "shopping spree," increasing end-of-budget-period expenditures in an effort to "hang on to" future resources (sometimes referred to as "use it or lose it").

 How do you think this type of last-minute spending might sabotage the company's goals?

Unfortunately, sometimes managers' efforts backfire when they try to motivate employees through budgets. For example, sometimes managers set budget goals at a level that makes these goals too difficult to accomplish. When employees recognize that they cannot attain the goals that managers have set for them, they sometimes quit trying to attain those goals. Also, sometimes efforts to be fair backfire. Departmental budgets may contain costs for activities that result in benefits for the department but over which the department manager has no control. For example, suppose Unlimited Decadence's marketing budget contains the same amount of air-conditioning costs that each other department's budget contains, even though the company has a central air-conditioning system that is used mostly to keep the kitchen-hot factory relatively cool. If Unlimited Decadence's president measures managers' performances against their budgets, a high electric bill for the company could reflect negatively on the marketing manager's performance, even though he had no control over the high air-conditioning costs. This situation could lower the manager's morale.

 Which would you prefer: your parents impose a budget on you for a week's vacation, or you participate with them in setting your vacation budget? Why?

---

[11]Evan S. Connell, *Son of the Morning Star* (San Francisco: North Point Press, 1984).

To help keep morale high, and to get better budget information, many companies use a participative budgeting process. **Participative budgeting** is budgeting in which department and division managers or teams participate with upper-level managers in the planning decisions that determine the goals and resource commitments for the activities of their departments, divisions, or teams. Upper-level company managers typically approach this process by providing mid- or lower-level managers or teams with a statement of company goals and with information about the availability of resources. A statement of company goals indicates to the budget participants the direction in which upper-level managers want the company to move. Department and division managers or teams use this information to set department, division, or team goals and to determine what resources would help them move toward the achievement of these goals. With participative budgeting, all departments, divisions, and teams, through their own goals and resources, do their part to help the company achieve the goals of upper-level managers. This situation—where department, division, or team goals support the company goals—is called **goal congruence.**

After determining goals, managers or team coordinators supply upper-level managers with information about the resource requirements necessary for each of their areas to meet these goals. Upper-level managers then review the goals and resource requirements for all areas of the company. Next, they either allocate the resources to the departments, divisions, or teams or ask them to refine and resubmit goals and resource requirements. Usually there is some "back and forth" between the areas and upper-level managers. This occurs because goals need to be refined and because often the total budget requests exceed the company's available resources.

Participative budgeting helps managers at all levels make planning decisions through this exchange of information. It helps managers arrive at decisions that complement each other and that aid the company in reaching the stated goals, and it ensures that different departments, divisions, teams, and levels of managers are aware of each other's plans and decisions.

In most large companies, budgeting is the responsibility of a budget committee, which is usually composed of representative managers of the functional areas of the company as well as other individuals affected by the budget. Having a budget committee can improve the effectiveness of the participative budgeting process by bringing these diverse individuals together to exchange information, to settle differences, to allocate resources based on the information they bring to the meeting, and to make other decisions. Having a budget committee can also improve the efficiency of the budgeting process by eliminating the time required by the "back and forth" process we just described.

Managers' participation on a budget committee takes on even more significance when a company operates in more than one country. Since countries' political, economic, and legal environments vary, communication and coordination among managers in different countries becomes more complicated. Think about how much communication and coordination must occur among the parts, assembly, and sales departments of a company. How can the parts department know how many parts to purchase or manufacture without knowing how many units will be assembled? And how can the assembly department know how many units to assemble without knowing projected sales? Now, picture Ford Motor Co., with auto-parts plants in China, an assembly plant in Poland, and a sales office in Vietnam. In addition to handling language differences, the managers of these offices and factories must be prepared to change their plans and budgets when conditions change in these countries. For example, political unrest in Poland could cause delays in shipments of parts into the country or of automobiles out of the country.

www2.ford.com

Which of Ford's budgets do you think would be affected by delays in shipments? How do you think the budgets would be affected?

As you can see, a budget can "look great on paper" but not have the effects managers intended. The improper use of budgets can cause a company to lose the potential benefits of budgeting. Therefore, great care must be used in the budgeting process. A company can use participative budgeting and budget committees to improve goal congruence, coordination, and communication within the company. The planning and decision-making that occur in the budget process require more than just consideration of the numbers. Managers must take into account how they will use the budgets and also how the budgets will affect the company's employees.

Summary

At the beginning of the chapter we asked you several questions. During the chapter, we asked you to STOP and answer some other questions to build your knowledge about specific issues. Be sure you answered these additional questions. Below are the questions from the beginning of the chapter, with a brief summary of the key points relating to the answers. Use your creative and critical thinking skills to expand on these key points to develop more complete answers to the questions and to determine what other questions you have that might lead you to learn more about the issues.

1 What are the similarities and differences between a large company's master budget and that of an entrepreneurial company?

A large company and an entrepreneurial (small) company budget for the same reasons. Both use sales budgets, purchases budgets, selling expenses budgets, general and administrative expenses budgets, cash budgets, projected income statements, and projected balance sheets. Generally, both large and small companies use similar structures for these budgets. However, a large company's selling expenses budget often shows sales-determined expenses separately from sales-determining expenses. Also, a large company's general and administrative expenses budget often shows expenses grouped by administrative activity or function. A large company often plans large programs or projects and quantifies them in a capital expenditures budget.

2 What are the similarities and differences between a manufacturing company's master budget and that of a retail company?

A manufacturing company has all of the budgets that a retail company has. However, a manufacturing company's purchases budget addresses the purchase of direct materials rather than the purchase of goods for resale. A manufacturing company develops additional budgets because of the fact that it makes the products it sells. These additional budgets include the production budget, direct labor budget, and factory overhead budget.

3 How is a manufacturing company's operating cycle different from that of a retail company?

A retail company's operating cycle is the average time it takes the company to use cash to acquire goods for resale, to sell them to customers, and then to collect cash from the customers for the sale. A manufacturing company's operating cycle is the average time it takes the company to use cash to acquire direct materials to use in manufacturing goods for sale, to convert these direct materials into finished goods, to sell these goods to customers, and then to collect cash from the customers for the sale. Although the operating cycles of these two types of companies are similar (the time involved from using cash to purchase finished products or direct materials through collecting cash from the customers for the sale of products), the difference between the two is the manufacturing company's conversion of the purchased materials into finished goods.

4 Is there a strategy a manufacturing company can use to complete its budget?

Yes, the strategy a manufacturing company can use to complete its budget is similar to that used by a retail company. The budgeting process for a manufacturing company begins with the sales budget because product sales affect all other company activities. By gathering various types of information, such as past sales data, knowledge about customer needs, industry trends, economic forecasts, and new technological developments, managers of a manufacturing company estimate the amount of inventory to be sold in each budget period. The managers plan cash collections from sales by examining the company's credit-granting policies.

After budgeting sales, managers of the manufacturing company determine the number of each of the company's products that it must manufacture in order to meet the planned sales and keep on hand a desired inventory of finished goods. Once the managers have forecasted production, they plan the amount and timing of direct materials purchases. To budget these purchases, the managers examine the costs associated with direct materials purchases and storage as well as the costs associated with not carrying enough inventory. They also consider forecasted production and the company's policy on direct materials inventory levels. After budgeting direct materials purchases, the managers plan the cash payments for these purchases by reviewing the payment agreements between the company and its suppliers.

Managers also estimate the amount of direct labor time and cost necessary to achieve the budgeted production level. They then plan the cash payments for the wages and salaries of the factory workers, basing these estimates on the agreed-upon wages for the workers and on the company's payroll schedule. The managers also use budgeted production to estimate the company's factory overhead costs. These costs may be based on agreements with indirect materials suppliers, agreed-upon wages and salaries, and past overhead costs. The managers then budget the company's selling and general and administrative expenses.

To budget all costs (expenses), the managers first must determine the behaviors of the costs (expenses). They budget fixed expenses by evaluating previous fixed expenses and then adjusting them (if necessary) according to the plans for the coming time period. They budget variable expenses by first observing what activity causes these expenses to vary, and then computing the total expenses by multiplying the cost per unit of activity by the activity level. The managers budget the cash payments for these expenses by reviewing the company's policy on the payment of expenses.

The managers then develop the cash budget, the projected income statement, and the projected balance sheet. The information for developing the cash budget comes from the other previously prepared budgets, as does the information for creating the projected income statement. The information for developing the balance sheet comes from previously developed schedules, the projected income statement, and the previous balance sheet.

5 **If a company's actual sales are different from its budgeted sales (or actual production is different from budgeted production) for the same time period, how can managers meaningfully evaluate how well the company met its cost goals?**

Managers use flexible budgets and cost reports to evaluate how well the company met its goals (as presented in the budget). Flexible budgets show expected costs at various activity levels, so if the actual activity level is different from the expected activity level, managers know what costs should have been at the actual activity level. Then, any differences between the costs budgeted and the actual costs for the actual activity level can suggest possible areas of the company's operations that may need attention.

6 **How do budgets affect the business decisions that employees make?**

Because a company uses budgets as one way to communicate to employees the company's goals and the activities needed to achieve them, managers must be sure that the budgets convey the proper messages. Employees behave in ways that they perceive will benefit them and that will, at the same time, achieve the goals of the company as communicated in the budget. But if the budget, or budget system, conveys the wrong message, employees are likely to act on the message they receive, which may not be in the best interest of the company. To maximize goal congruence through better communication, a company can use participative budgeting and a budget committee.

Key Terms

capital expenditures budget *(p. 385)*
cost center *(p. 393)*
debt capital *(p. 388)*
direct labor budget *(p. 380)*
direct materials purchases budget
  (p. 378)
equity capital *(p. 388)*
factory overhead budget *(p. 381)*
financing activities section *(p. 386)*
flexible budget *(p. 394)*
goal congruence *(p. 398)*
investing activities section *(p. 386)*

investment center *(p. 393)*
operating activities section *(p. 386)*
operating cycle *(p. 374)*
operating cycle for a *manufacturing*
  company *(p. 374)*
participative budget *(p. 398)*
production budget *(p. 375)*
profit center *(p. 393)*
responsibility center *(p. 393)*
sales budget *(p. 375)*
sales-determined expenses *(p. 382)*
sales-determining expenses *(p. 382)*

Here is an opportunity to gather information on the Internet about real-world issues related to the topics in this chapter. Go to http://www.dryden.com/account and click on the Cunningham, Nikolai, and Bazley book cover. Click on Summary Surfing, then click on this chapter number, and answer the following questions.

▶ Click on **CBS** (Canada/British Columbia Business Service Center). Under *Marketing Basics,* click on *Sales Forecasting.* In the chapter, we mentioned that the sales figures for a sales budget are based on a market analysis. Although the discussion on this Web site is geared toward small businesses, it also applies to large companies. What are the sources of information that might be useful in preparing a sales forecast? What are the factors that can affect a sales forecast? What are the steps for developing a sales forecast?

**S U M M A R Y
S U R F I N G**

Integrated Business and Accounting Situations

Answer the Following Questions in Your Own Words

Testing Your Knowledge

12-1 Explain the contributions that budgets make to the planning, operating, and evaluating processes.

12-2 What information does a sales budget convey?

12-3 Is a sales budget for a manufacturing company different from a sales budget for a retail company? Why or why not?

12-4 Describe why budgeted cash receipts in any given month might be different from budgeted sales revenue.

12-5 What information does a production budget convey?

12-6 What factors should managers consider when deciding what policy to establish about the size of the ending finished goods inventory in any budget period?

12-7 Without referring back to the chapter, write an equation that can be used to compute budgeted production for any budget period.

12-8 What information does a direct materials purchases budget convey?

12-9 What similarities do you see between the logic of the production budget and that of the direct materials purchases budget?

12-10 How does a company determine how many units of a particular direct material it needs for production in a budget period?

12-11 What information does a direct labor budget convey?

12-12 How does a company determine how many hours of direct labor are needed to meet each month's budgeted production?

12-13 How is a direct materials purchases budget similar to a direct labor budget? How is it different?

12-14 What information does a factory overhead budget convey?

12-15 Describe why depreciation is subtracted from total overhead costs in determining cash payments for factory overhead costs.

12-16 What are the similarities and differences between the selling expenses budget of a large company and that of a small company?

12-17 How can you distinguish a sales-determined expense from a sales-determining expense?

12-18 What are the similarities and differences between the general and administrative budget of a large company and that of a small company?

12-19 What information does a capital expenditures budget convey?

12-20 What information does a cash budget convey?

12-21 What are the similarities and differences between a cash budget and a cash flow statement?

12-22 How can managers predict when a company will need to borrow money, and how can they estimate how much money the company will need to borrow?

12-23 What are the similarities and differences between debt capital and equity capital?

12-24 What is a line of credit? Describe how it works.

12-25 What information does a projected income statement convey?

12-26 How are the cost of goods sold sections of the income statements of a retail company and a manufacturing company similar and different?

12-27 What information is conveyed in the projected balance sheet?

12-28 What is a responsibility center? Briefly describe the three types of responsibility center.

12-29 Describe a flexible budget. How might a flexible budget help managers make decisions?

12-30 Give three examples, in your own words, of how budgets can affect employee behavior.

12-31 What is participative budgeting, and what are its advantages?

12-32 What is a budget committee, and what are its advantages?

Applying Your Knowledge

12-33 The sales budget of Eau de Libre Corporation, a company that manufactures cologne ("One whiff makes you want to go to the library") for college students and sells the cologne mostly to students' parents, shows the following estimated sales:

September	70,000 bottles
October	40,000 bottles
November	50,000 bottles
December	60,000 bottles
January	55,000 bottles

Each bottle sells for $5. All of Eau de Libre's sales are on account, and it expects to collect accounts receivable 15 days after making the sales. It gives no cash discounts. (Assume all months have 30 days.)

Required: Prepare a sales budget for the last three months of the year, including estimated cash receipts.

12-34 Refer to 12-33. Eau de Libre's policy is to end each month with an inventory of finished goods on hand equal to 30% of the following month's estimated sales.

Required: Using the budgeted sales figures given in 12-33, prepare a production budget for the last three months of the year.

12-35 Using the budgeted sales figures in 12-33, respond to the following, treating each independently.

Required: (1) Prepare a production budget for the last three months of the year assuming that Eau de Libre wants to have 10,000 bottles in finished goods inventory at the end of each month.

(2) Prepare a production budget for the last three months of the year so that production is the same each month. Assume that Eau de Libre has a beginning finished goods inventory in October of 10,000 bottles and wants to have an ending finished goods inventory in December of 25,000 bottles.

12-36 The production budget of the Birmingham Steal Corporation, a manufacturer of baseball uniforms, shows budgeted production (in uniforms) for December and the first four months of next year as follows:

	Uniforms
December	10,000
January	4,000
February	9,000
March	15,000
April	5,000

Each uniform requires 5 yards of heavy cotton costing $3 per yard. Birmingham Steal buys cotton on credit, paying in the month following the purchase. Its supplier offers no cash discounts.

Required: For each of the following two independent situations, prepare a direct materials purchases budget for the direct materials needed in the first three months of next year:

(1) Birmingham Steal's policy is to have raw materials inventory at the end of each month equal to 50% of the following month's usage requirement.

(2) Birmingham Steal's policy is to keep raw materials inventory at the end of each month to a minimum, but without letting it fall below 5,000 yards. Assume that the

December 1 raw materials inventory has 5,000 yards of direct materials and that the company's only supplier is willing to sell a maximum of 60,000 yards of cotton to the company per month.

12-37   Refer to 12-36. Birmingham Steal Corporation uses 2 direct labor hours to produce one baseball uniform. The direct labor rate is $12 per hour. It pays three-fourths of each month's wages in the month earned. It pays the other one-fourth in the following month.

Required: Using the production information in 12-36, prepare a direct labor budget for the first three months of next year.

12-38   Refer to 12-36. Birmingham Steal Corporation's variable factory overhead costs include utilities ($.10 per baseball uniform), supplies ($.05 per uniform), and other variable costs ($.12 per uniform). Fixed factory overhead costs include supervisory salaries ($20,000 per month), depreciation of plant and equipment ($5,500 per month), and other fixed costs ($12,000 per month). Birmingham Steal makes cash payments for factory overhead costs (except for depreciation) in the month these costs are incurred.

Required: Using the production information in 12-36, prepare a factory overhead budget for the first three months of next year.

12-39   Brown's Feed Store ("We deliver to ewe") estimates its monthly selling expenses as follows:

Advertising	$22,000 per month
Sales salaries	$18,000 per month
Sales calls on customers	$ 35.00 per lot
Commissions paid to sales personnel	$ 50.00 per lot
Delivery	$ 20.00 per lot

Brown pays for selling expenses in the month after they are incurred. Using current plans, it estimates the following sales:

March	70 lots
April	90 lots
May	100 lots
June	110 lots

Required: Prepare a selling expenses budget for the second quarter for Brown's Feed Store.

12-40   Olson Construction Company builds houses. It has completed two houses: the first priced at $95,000, and the second at $120,000. Olson pays the realtor 8% of the selling price when the house is sold. Two additional houses are under construction. Brunhilde Olson, the owner, estimates that in May, the company will pay $20,000 to workers, $42,000 for direct materials, and $60,000 to other companies for work she has subcontracted. The bank will make a construction loan to Olson Construction of $50,000 at 18% per year on May 1 if the company needs it. Interest would be paid at the end of each month on that loan. If this loan is not made, the company will not be able to borrow cash until June 15. Brunhilde also wants to avoid having too much cash on hand. She has adopted a policy of investing "excess" cash in a 30-day certificate of deposit at the end of any month when the anticipated ending cash balance from operations exceeds $60,000, so that the ending cash balance is reduced to exactly $60,000. On April 30, Olson Construction Company has $25,000 cash on hand.

Required: (1) Prepare a cash budget for May, assuming that Olson Construction expects to sell only the $95,000 house.
(2) Prepare a cash budget for May, assuming that Olson Construction expects to sell both houses.

12-41   Knob-Hill Corporation, a manufacturer of door knobs, budgeted its manufacturing costs for August at a production level of 10,000 door knobs. But it actually produced 12,500 door knobs because August sales were higher than it anticipated. Budgeted and actual costs are shown here:

	Budgeted	Actual
Door knobs manufactured	10,000	12,500
Direct materials	$ 3,400	$ 4,330
Direct labor	5,500	6,750
Factory overhead		
Variable:		
Utilities	360	443
Supplies	120	162
Other	300	370
Fixed:		
Supervisory salaries	2,900	2,900
Depreciation	1,000	1,000
Other	600	660
Total manufacturing costs	$14,180	$16,615

Required: Prepare a manufacturing cost report comparing August's actual costs with a revised (flexible) budget based on the actual production level for August.

12-42 Canine Cuisine Company, owned by Goode Doggie, produces dog food that it sells in 10-pound bags for $7.00 per bag. Other information about the company includes the following:

(a) Sales estimates for the first four months of the year are as follows: January—50,000 bags, February—40,000 bags, March—55,000 bags, and April—50,000 bags. The ending inventory of dog food each month is 20% of the next month's sales estimate (in bags). All sales are cash sales.

(b) Canine Cuisine makes the dog food from a mixture of direct materials costing $.10 per pound. Each month's ending inventory of direct materials (in pounds) is 50% of the next month's usage requirement. Payment for direct materials is made in the month of purchase, with no cash discounts taken.

(c) Each bag of dog food requires 0.10 hours of direct labor costing $10 per hour. Canine Cuisine pays three-fourths of each month's direct labor cost in the month incurred and one-fourth in the following month. The wages payable for direct labor at the beginning of January was $15,500 for the 62,000 bags of dog food produced in December.

(d) Canine Cuisine's variable factory overhead costs are $1.40 per bag produced, and fixed factory overhead is $60,000 per month (which includes $25,000 of depreciation). Factory overhead costs (except for depreciation) are paid in the month after they are incurred.

(e) Canine Cuisine pays both variable selling expenses of $1.00 per bag sold and fixed selling expenses of $10,000 per month in the same month incurred.

(f) General and administrative expenses totaling $65,000 per month (including $20,000 depreciation) are all fixed. Canine Cuisine pays them (except for depreciation) in the month after they are incurred.

(g) Canine Cuisine's cash balance on January 1 is $45,000.

Required: Prepare a production budget, a direct materials purchases budget, a direct labor budget, and a cash budget for each of the first two months of the year.

12-43 Refer to 12-42. Assume that January's beginning finished goods inventory (10,000 bags) had a cost of $43,700, its budgeted production for January is 48,000 bags, and its budgeted ending finished goods inventory (8,000 bags) has a cost of $37,200.

Required: Prepare a projected income statement for the month of January for Canine Cuisine Company (assuming Canine is a sole proprietorship).

12-44 Refer to 12-42 and 12-43. At the beginning of January, Canine Cuisine Company's raw materials inventory was $24,000, its property, plant, and equipment (net) was $265,000, and its Goode Doggie, capital was $175,400. It had no goods-in-process inventory or long-term liabilities at the beginning or end of January.

Required: Prepare a projected classified balance sheet at the end of January for Canine Cuisine Company. List total current liabilities as one amount.

12-45 Mammoth Manufacturing Company set its production budget at 180,000 units per month during the second quarter of the year (assuming 45,000 units per week and four weeks per month). It developed all manufacturing cost budgets from this production budget. The following factory overhead budget for April applies to May and June as well.

Mammoth Manufacturing Company
Factory Overhead Budget
April

Budgeted production	180,000 units
Variable overhead costs:	
Utilities	$ 10,800ᵃ
Supplies	6,300ᵇ
Maintenance	5,400ᵇ
Materials handling	11,700ᵇ
Other variable costs	14,400ᵇ
Total variable overhead	$ 48,600
Fixed overhead costs:	
Supervisory salaries	$ 26,000ᵇ
Depreciation of plant and equipment	35,000
Insurance and property taxes on	
plant and equipment	14,000ᶜ
Other fixed costs	25,000ᵇ
Total fixed overhead	$100,000
Total factory overhead	$148,600

ᵃPaid in the following month
ᵇPaid in same month
ᶜInsurance was prepaid; taxes are paid in December.

Utility costs incurred in March were $10,800. The factory may have to close down during the last week in May because of some difficulty the company is having with the renegotiation of a labor contract. If this happens, production in May will fall to 135,000 units. This lost production will have to be made up in June for the company to avoid losing sales. Mammoth is concerned about the effects that closing the factory down the first week in May will have on its cash budget .

Required: On one schedule, prepare monthly factory overhead budgets (adjusting them where necessary for the effect of the one-week closing of the factory) for April, May, and June. Include the estimated monthly cash payments for factory overhead costs.

Making Evaluations

12-46 Exhibit 12-2 shows a diagram of a manufacturing company's operating cycle.

Required: Make a diagram of your own, and indicate on it where you think each budget fits. Briefly describe why you placed each budget where you did.

12-47 The quarter column in a budget sometimes sums the amounts in the other columns and sometimes doesn't sum them.

Required: Carefully describe how you can decide, when developing a budget, whether to add monthly data together to get a quarterly amount or whether to determine that quarterly amount some other way. Give an example of when you would use each method. In your example of using some other way to determine the quarterly amount, describe what that other way would be.

12-48 Suppose you and a team of managers of a company are trying to decide whether the company should obtain financing through debt capital or equity capital.

Required: What questions must you answer? How would the answers to these questions affect your decision?

12-49 Suppose you are the controller of the multinational Crescent Hardware and Software Company, which manufactures crescent wrenches and crescent rolls (and is based in the Crescent City—New Orleans). Your boss, Rosie Hammerschmidt, is interested in forming a budget committee for the company and has asked you to suggest its membership.

Required: Write Ms. Hammerschmidt a memo describing whom you would include on this committee and the rationale for each of your choices.

12-50 The Best Defense Corporation has just begun manufacturing burglar alarm systems called *Offense*. The sales estimate for April, the company's first month of operations, is 100 systems. Sales are expected to increase to 150 systems in May and 200 systems in June, and then to stay at 250 systems each month for the rest of the year. Best is planning to sell these systems for $320 each and to extend credit to its customers up to 60 days. Best gives no cash discounts. It expects to collect 10% of its accounts receivable in the month of sales, 30% in the month following sales, and 58% in the second month following sales. It estimates that 2% of its sales will not be collectible.

Required: (1) Prepare a sales budget for the first six months of Best's operations, including expected cash receipts from sales for each month.

(2) Do you agree with Best's credit policy? If so, what do you like about it? If not, what concerns do you have about the policy? In either case, what do you recommend to improve Best's credit policy?

(3) How do you think the 2% of uncollectible sales should affect the accounting equation? Why?

12-51 Stick With Us Company will begin operations next January to produce glue. Estimates of sales quantities and direct materials and direct labor costs are as follows:

Tubes to be Sold		Direct Materials and Direct Labor Costs per Tube	
January	15,000	Direct materials	
February	25,000	(4 lbs @ $1.50 per lb.)	$6.00
March	20,000	Direct labor	
April	10,000	(1/4 hr.@$9.00 per hr.)	2.25
			$8.25

The following information is also available:

(a) Monthly production should be scheduled so that the ending inventory of finished tubes of glue is 50% of the next month's expected sales of tubes.

(b) Direct materials inventory (in pounds) at the end of each month should be 25% of the next month's usage requirement. Direct materials will be paid for in the month following their purchase, with no cash discounts. Assume Stick has no direct materials inventory on January 1.

(c) Stick pays wages in the month the labor cost is incurred.

Required: (1) Prepare a production budget for January, February, and March.

(2) Prepare a direct materials purchases budget for January and February.

(3) Prepare a direct labor budget for January and February.

(4) Do you think it is reasonable for this company to set desired finished goods inventory levels as a constant percentage of the next month's expected sales, and desired direct materials inventory as a constant percentage of the next month's usage requirement? What do you think are the advantages and disadvantages of this policy?

12-52 In the chapter, we mentioned that Coca-Cola raised its selling prices after it had to pay more for aluminum cans. Suppose you were employed by Coca-Cola at that time and were involved in this decision.

Required: What other alternatives might you have considered besides raising prices? How would these alternatives have affected Coca-Cola's budgets?

12-53 Suppose that you are the head of production at Tiny Tyke Toy Company and that the accounting department has developed the following cost report for your department for the month of October.

Tiny Tyke Toy Company
Manufacturing Cost Report
October

	Original October Budget	Actual Costs	Favorable (Unfavorable) Difference
Production (units)	10,000 units	11,000 units	
Direct materials	$ 3,000	$ 3,200	$ (200)
Direct labor	12,500	13,600	(1,100)
Factory overhead			
Variable:			
Utilities	2,000	2,160	(160)
Supplies	500	540	(40)
Other	750	830	(80)
Fixed:			
Supervisory salaries	4,000	4,000	—
Depreciation	2,500	2,500	—
Other	5,500	5,550	(50)
Total manufacturing costs	$30,750	$32,380	$(1,630)

Your boss, who also has a copy of this report, has asked you to write her a memo explaining the "cost overruns" and describing a plan to keep costs more in line with the budget.

Required: Write a memo responding to your boss's request.

12-54 Yesterday, you received the following letter in the mail for your advice column in the local paper:

Dr. Decisive:

What is going on in this country? Doesn't anybody have any scruples anymore? Even my boyfriend is sliding. See if you agree with me.

My boyfriend's roommate, let's call him "Ethics," was just hired to be the new manager of the advertising department for a large furniture manufacturer. In his first few days at the company, "Ethics" learned, through the overactive company grapevine, that the company values a manager's ability to keep his or her department's costs within the limits of the budgeted costs. "Ethics" has always been concerned about his image and wants to "come on like gangbusters." Get this: he has decided to overestimate next year's budgeted costs for his department just to make himself look better on his end-of-year performance evaluation. My boyfriend says that this is normal behavior and that the company expects its managers to do this.

We just studied budgeting in my accounting class, and from what I learned, the decision made by "Ethics" will have effects both inside and outside the company. At a minimum, I can see it affecting a bank's loan decision, the way resources are allocated among the departments of the company, the activities of the employees in his department, and the success of the company as a whole. I'm sure that you agree with me that "jerk," I mean "Ethics," is not making a benign decision. Both my boyfriend and what's-his-name think I am overreacting. Will you please explain to them (in as much detail as you can) why I am right and that I am reacting in a mature, rational manner? Thanks (I read your column every day). Please sign me

"Watchdog"

Required: Meet with your Dr. Decisive team and write a response to "Watchdog."

CHAPTER OUTLINE

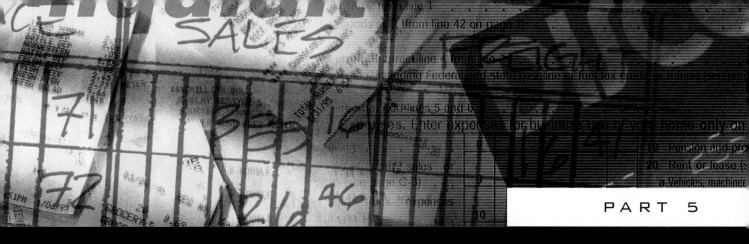

PART 5

MANAGING, REPORTING, AND EVALUATING CORPORATE LIQUIDITY

This section consists of two

chapters which discuss issues

involving a corporation's liquidity.

After reading these chapters, you

will be able to:

▶ *understand the importance of managing and reporting on a corporation's liquidity*

▶ *explain the management policies and control procedures for accounts receivable and cash receipts*

▶ *explain the management policies and control procedures for accounts payable and cash payments*

▶ *account for international sales and purchases*

▶ *report on a corporation's accrued liabilities and loss contingencies*

▶ *use intracompany and intercompany analysis to evaluate a corporation's liquidity*

REVENUES AND CASH COLLECTIONS

> *"Firms have no desire to go bankrupt, so it is no surprise that one of the crucial goals of financial management is ensuring financial viability. This goal is often measured in liquidity . . ."*
>
> —Steven A. Finkler

1 *Why is managing and reporting liquidity important?*

2 *Why might a company offer credit sales, and what management policies should exist for accounts receivable?*

3 *How does a company report credit sales and net sales?*

4 *How does a company determine the amount of its bad debts expense, and how does it report the related accounts on its financial statements?*

5 *What is an exchange rate, and how does an exchange gain (loss) arise from a credit sale made to a company in another country?*

6 *How does a company account for cash collected prior to sales?*

7 *What are the important characteristics of a note receivable, and how is interest computed?*

8 *What are the important characteristics of cash receipts management and cash payments management?*

9 *What are cash balance management and cash equivalents, and what is included under the heading of Cash and Cash Equivalents on a company's balance sheet?*

If you had an inventory of Hershey's Kisses at home or in your dorm room or apartment, how quickly do you think your inventory would "turn over"?

www.hersheys.com

www.rmcfusa.com

On Hershey Foods' (maker of "Kisses") December 31, 1997 balance sheet, the company reported that it had $415 million of cash and cash equivalents and receivables—13 percent of its total assets. If one piece of Hershey's candy sells for an average of five cents, these current asset account balances held the dollar equivalent of over 8.3 billion pieces! On February 28, 1998, Rocky Mountain Chocolate Factory's balance sheet total for the same categories was slightly less than $4 million. Given that its total assets were about $19.9 million, 20 percent of Rocky Mountain's assets were these current assets. These dollar amounts of current assets shown on Hershey Foods' and Rocky Mountain's balance sheets result from prior management decisions as well as from the accounting methods used to keep track of the various categories of balance sheet accounts.

 Hershey Food's $415 million total for the three categories of current assets is 104 times greater than Rocky Mountain Chocolate Factory's $4 million. Should you conclude that Hershey has operations that are 104 times larger than those of Rocky Mountain? Why or why not? What factors besides the amounts on the balance sheets of the two companies should you consider?

Why do these and other companies hold these current assets? Basically, large companies hold short-term assets for the same reasons as do small companies like Sweet Temptations: because the companies pay off short-term obligations as they come due, sell on credit to customers, and prepay for some items. (Companies also may hold short-term assets to sell to their customers or in anticipation of purchasing long-term assets, retiring long-term debt, or distributing cash dividends. We will discuss these issues in later chapters.) The amount that a company reports for each of these short-term assets varies within and across industries. However, one issue does not vary: effectively managing and reporting on liquidity is an important part of the accounting and finance function of every company.

In Chapters 13 and 14 we discuss liquidity. Think about these two chapters as a set. In Chapter 13, we first provide a framework for examining liquidity management and reporting issues. This framework provides a basis for discussing specific liquidity management topics. Second, we discuss management and reporting issues for accounts receivable and notes receivable as well as for a liability—unearned revenue—because they all relate to the selling of goods and services and the collection of cash from customers. We also discuss how a company accounts for credit sales to customers in other countries. We will discuss inventories and short-term investments (marketable securities) in later chapters. Finally, in Chapter 13, we evaluate management and reporting issues for a company's cash balance. In Chapter 14, we discuss management and reporting issues for accounts payable, additional types of current liabilities, prepaid items, and contingent liabilities. We also discuss how a company accounts for credit purchases from companies in other countries. We conclude the chapter with a discussion on evaluating a company's liquidity position. This evaluation section draws from information you will learn in both chapters.

As you will see, many aspects of liquidity management and reporting are similar for entrepreneurial businesses and large companies. We will concentrate on building on what you have learned in earlier chapters about these assets and liabilities. Although our focus is on large businesses that are usually organized as corporations, we will continue to use the general term *company* unless the discussion relates only to a corporation, such as when we discuss income taxes.

The Importance of Managing and Reporting on Liquidity

Recall from Chapter 7 that **liquidity** refers to how quickly a company can convert an asset into cash or can pay a liability. Cash, then, is the most liquid asset. Cash equivalents,[1] accounts receivable, and notes receivable are considered the next most liquid because they may be turned into cash in the near term. Managers and external users are interested in the liquidity of a company's assets because it affects the company's ability to pay its short-term liabilities. They assess a company's *liquidity position* by comparing the composition and amounts of its short-term assets and short-term liabilities. Also recall from Chapter 7 that managers and external users may use the quick ratio to assess liquidity. We will revisit this ratio in Chapter 14 (and discuss the current ratio in Chapter 19). **Liquidity management** refers to a company's policies and activities that control its liquidity position. In other words, it refers to how a company manages cash, receivables, and current liabilities.

Why do managers and external users need to understand liquidity? From any user's perspective, it is important to understand the types of economic resources or economic obligations that each balance sheet item represents. If an external user does not know what "cash equivalents" or "accrued expenses" are, how can he or she include them in a business decision? From a manager's perspective, it is important to understand how liquidity can be managed to improve company performance. If a manager is not aware that faster collection of receivables and slower payment of payables (without alienating the other party in each case) will increase the amount of cash that may be invested in some type of interest-earning account, how can these techniques be used to improve profits? So both external users and managers need to understand how a company's policies and activities affect its liquidity position.

In our discussion of the evaluation and management of a company's liquidity, we use an integrated approach. In other words, you need to understand what is important about each type of current asset and current liability *and* how these account balances are related to each other. We use this integrated approach for three reasons. First, managers do not make liquidity decisions for one type of cash-related activity without considering the effect on related activities. For example, managers realize that making it easier for customers to obtain credit probably makes it more difficult for the company to collect cash from credit sales. Second, external users do not evaluate a company's liquidity only by examining each current asset or liability separately. For instance, they realize that a large cash balance does not always mean that a company's liquidity position is good; for example, the company may owe a relatively large amount of short-term debt. Also, the return earned on the cash is probably low. Finally, to assess liquidity, managers and external users use financial statement ratios composed of several items.

1 *Why is managing and reporting liquidity important?*

---

[1]Cash equivalents are very short-term investments that are easily converted into cash. We will discuss them later in the chapter.

Don't let our use of an "integrated approach" worry you. To understand how to use many things, you have to understand each part and how the parts fit together. Can you drive a car safely without knowing the difference between the gas pedal and the brake pedal? We are simply applying this same logic to liquidity. Can you think of other examples in which an integrated approach to understanding is needed?

What You Need to Know to Evaluate an Account Balance

Exhibit 13-1 shows the current assets and current liabilities for Unlimited Decadence at December 31, 2000. Each asset and liability amount includes the results of all the transactions and events related to that specific account to date. To evaluate an account balance, you need to understand that company policies and activities (1) affect how these transactions and events happen (and therefore affect the account balances), and (2) occur within the larger business and economic environment.

For example, what do you need to know to evaluate an accounts receivable balance? We devote a section of this chapter to receivables, but we briefly answer this question now. The answer illustrates our approach to helping you learn about every account balance, not just accounts receivable. A year-end accounts receivable balance is calculated as follows, and the amounts appear on each of the financial statements as indicated:

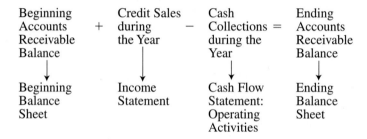

Since the ending accounts receivable balance is the net result of these three components, to evaluate a company's accounts receivable you must understand how it reports these components in each of the financial statements and how the components relate to each other. First, increases in accounts receivable result from credit sales. Thus, you need to understand how a company processes its credit sales. Equally important, you need to realize that credit policies (guidelines about which customers are given credit and about the terms of the credit) also affect accounts receivable. Second, decreases in accounts receivable result from cash collections. So, you need to understand how a company processes its cash receipts. You also need to recognize that policies about methods of cash collection and cash discounts

Exhibit 13-1	Unlimited Decadence: Balances for Current Asset and Current Liability Accounts, December 31, 2000

(in thousands)

Current assets

Cash and cash equivalents	$1,020
Marketable securities	300
Accounts receivable (net)	5,855
Short-term notes receivable	100
Inventories	1,310
Total current assets	$8,585

Current liabilities

Accounts payable	$1,450
Accrued liabilities	500
Taxes payable	2,000
Short-term notes payable	150
Total current liabilities	$4,100

affect accounts receivable. Finally, recall from Chapter 9 that companies show accounts receivable in the balance sheet at their net realizable value (Accounts Receivable [net] = Total Accounts Receivable − Estimated Amount of Uncollectible Accounts). Thus, GAAP reporting requirements and management practices affect the amount of a company's estimate of its uncollectible accounts (not included in the equation we showed earlier).

This method of analysis holds true for every account balance. Company activities and policies as well as the business and economic environment affect the transactions and events that result in a year-end account balance. To be able to evaluate the financial performance of a company, you need to understand how these factors affect each financial statement item.

Our Approach to Studying Liquidity

The highlighted areas in Exhibit 13-2 show which balance sheet items we discuss in this chapter and in Chapter 14. This should help you visualize how managers and external users approach their study of liquidity. Liquidity management can be broken down into five areas, as follows: (1) accounts receivable management, (2) cash receipts management, (3) accounts payable management, (4) cash payments management, and (5) cash balance management.

Exhibit 13-2   Analysis of a Company's Balance Sheet: Liquidity

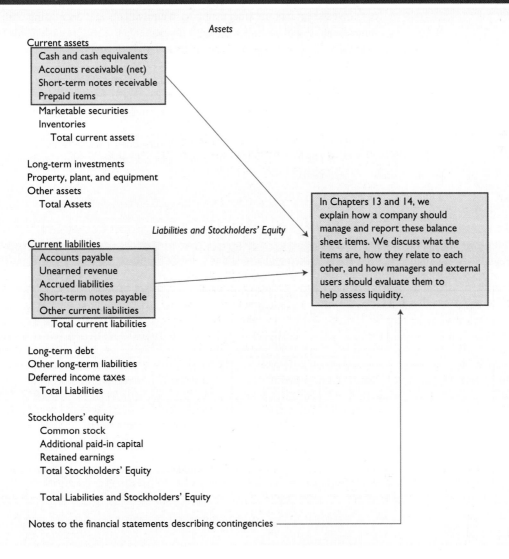

1. **Accounts receivable management** involves setting and following policies for granting credit and processing credit sales. When a company makes a credit sale, it increases accounts receivable and sales revenue.

2. **Cash receipts management** involves setting and following policies for collecting cash from credit or cash sales (or in advance of sales), processing cash collections, and depositing cash collections into the company's bank account. When a company collects (increases) cash, it also increases sales revenue or decreases accounts receivable (or increases unearned revenue, which we will discuss later in the chapter).

3. **Accounts payable management** involves setting and following policies for authorizing and making purchases and for processing credit purchases. When a company purchases an item on credit, it increases the asset acquired or the expense incurred and increases accounts payable.

4. **Cash payments management** involves setting and following policies for paying for cash or credit purchases and processing cash payments. When a company pays for purchases (decreases cash), it also decreases accounts payable or increases the asset acquired or the expense.

5. **Cash balance management** involves setting and following policies for maintaining an optimal amount of cash. A company may invest excess cash in cash equivalents or short-term marketable securities (which we will discuss in Chapter 23) to earn investment income (increasing cash equivalents and decreasing cash). When it needs additional cash, it sells these investments to meet its cash needs (increasing cash and decreasing cash equivalents or short-term marketable securities).

Exhibit 13-3 illustrates the scope of liquidity management over each of these five areas. In this exhibit, we show the financial statement items affected by liquidity management and provide *one* example of a policy and an activity for each area.

 Take some time to study Exhibit 13-3. How does it relate to our descriptions of each area? Notice what is written on the right side of the exhibit. Can you explain each of these items?

Exhibit 13-3   The Scope of Liquidity Management

Financial Statement Items	Sales		Accounts Receivable		Cash and Cash Equivalents			Accounts Payable		Assets and Expenses		Activities are recorded in the accounting system, and the account balances are reported in the financial statements.
	(−)	(+)	(+)	(−)		(+)	(−)	(−)	(+)	(+)	(−)	
Cash Management Area	Accounts receivable management		Cash receipts management		Cash balance management			Cash payments management		Accounts payable management		Company activities are managed according to company policies.
Example of Policy	Sales personnel must receive credit approval before making sale.		Cash receipts are deposited daily.		Cash balance is monitored daily to ensure proper balance.			Cash payments are made only for approved purchases.		All purchases must be approved by company employee.		Company policies influence activities.
Example of Activity	Credit sales are made to customer with approved credit.		Cash is collected from credit sale.		Excess cash is used to purchase cash equivalents.*			Cash is paid to suppliers for credit purchases.		Items are purchased on credit from supplier.		Activities are influenced by company policies.

*If the excess cash will not be needed in the near term, the company may invest in short-term marketable securities (which we will discuss in Chapter 23).

Managing Receivables

Accounts receivable are the amounts owed to a company for its credit sales. Many companies sell goods on credit as a routine part of business and expect to collect these amounts in cash within a relatively short period of time. For example, Hershey Foods had sales of $4.3 billion in 1997, and its average accounts receivable were $327 million. In the candy manufacturing industry, the number of days it takes to collect these receivables averages about 40 days. Unlimited Decadence has accounts receivable (net) of $5,855,000 at December 31, 2000.

Many companies also sell goods to customers under more formal, extended credit arrangements. In this situation, the selling company usually requires the customer to sign a promissory note. A **note** is a written legal document in which the maker of the note (in our case, the customer) makes an unconditional promise to pay another party (in our case, the selling company) a certain amount of money on an agreed future date. Because the selling company expects to receive the cash that its customer promised, the amount the customer owes is called a **note receivable.** At December 31, 2000, Unlimited Decadence has notes receivable of $100,000.

Although both accounts receivable and notes receivable are amounts owed to a company for previous credit sales, differences between the two affect how each is managed and reported. Thus, we will discuss notes receivable later in the chapter.

The Reasons for Offering Credit Sales

Why do companies grant credit? We answered this in Chapter 9 for entrepreneurial companies, and the same reasons apply equally to large companies. Briefly, these reasons are as follows: (1) It may be more convenient to sell on credit than for cash. For example, when a company is selling a product that the company has to ship, the purchaser commonly pays for the product after receiving it. (2) Offering credit may encourage a customer to buy an item that the customer might not otherwise purchase. (3) Allowing customers to pay *after* receiving the goods signals product quality and a commitment to customers.

2 *Why might a company offer credit sales, and what management policies should exist for accounts receivable?*

 Have you noticed that companies sometime sell goods on a "cash and carry" basis? What does this mean? What should companies and customers think about before using the "cash and carry" basis?

A company has two major concerns with credit sales.[2] First, credit sales require managers to be involved in receivables and cash-collection management; therefore, the company incurs additional credit management costs. Also, the company might incur additional selling costs, such as the costs of soliciting the credit customers. Second, the issue of uncollectible accounts arises. If a company cannot effectively collect cash from its credit sales, it loses some of its expected profits from credit sales. So if a company has uncollectible accounts, should it make credit sales? As long as the increase in profit (the gross profit earned from the increased sales less the cost of operating the credit activities) exceeds the cost of not collecting certain accounts, the policy of offering credit is beneficial. For example, suppose that an office supply retailer decides to sell to corporate customers and so must offer credit terms. The retailer expects its annual sales to increase by $100,000 and the following results to occur:

Gross profit on increased sales	$40,000
Less: Costs of operating the credit activities	(15,000)
Increase in profit	$25,000
Less: Uncollectible additional credit sales	(5,000)
Net increase in profit	$20,000

---

[2]In this section we are *not* discussing bank credit card (VISA, Mastercard) sales. A company treats these sales as cash sales, except that it must pay a percentage of the amount of the sale (generally between 1% and 5%) to the credit card company. So, credit cards are an example of "outsourcing" the credit evaluation and collection functions, thereby transferring the costs and risks to the credit card company.

In this example, even though the company incurred a cost from not collecting certain accounts, the decision to offer credit terms on sales to corporate customers would increase the company's profit. We will discuss accounting for the uncollectible accounts receivable later in this chapter.

 How would you, as a manager, use break-even analysis to decide whether to offer credit?

In practically every large company, the benefits from offering credit sales outweigh the associated costs. Any company that has transactions with other companies will have accounts receivable; these companies may have *only* credit sales and never make cash sales. Companies that deal only with customers who pay cash or use bank credit cards will *not* have accounts receivable.

 Can you name a company that makes all its sales on credit? that makes all its sales for cash?

Accounts Receivable Subsidiary Ledger

Recall from Chapter 6 that a company's general ledger includes all of its accounts. As a company increases in size, its general ledger also increases because of the additional accounts it needs to record specific types of accounting information. A larger company, for example, is likely to own more assets and different types of assets (e.g., buildings and equipment). In addition, it will have more customer accounts from sales on credit.

To reduce the size of the general ledger and keep up-to-date records of transactions with individual credit customers, a larger company sets up an accounts receivable subsidiary ledger. An **accounts receivable subsidiary ledger** contains the individual accounts of all the customers that purchase from the company on credit.[3] Whenever a company makes a credit sale to a customer, it records an increase in the customer's account in this subsidiary ledger. When a customer pays its account, the company records a decrease in the customer's account in this ledger. Thus, at all times the company knows the balance in each customer's account. As we will discuss later, this information is very helpful in deciding whether to extend additional credit to a customer and in determining which customers need to be reminded to pay their bills.

When a company uses an accounts receivable subsidiary ledger, it still keeps a single Accounts Receivable account in the general ledger (to maintain the equality of the accounting equation). The Accounts Receivable account is referred to as a **control account** because, in the general ledger, it takes the place of (controls) the individual customer accounts in the subsidiary ledger. The balance of the Accounts Receivable control account must always equal the total of the individual customer accounts in the accounts receivable subsidiary ledger on each balance sheet date. This means that each time a company records a transaction (e.g., credit sale, collection) in a customer's account in the subsidiary ledger, it must also record the transaction in the Accounts Receivable control account. Before the company issues its financial statements at the end of the accounting period, it prepares a schedule that lists the balance of each customer's account in the accounts receivable subsidiary ledger. It totals these balances and compares the total with the balance of the Accounts Receivable control account to prove their equality.

Accounts Receivable

In the first part of the book (particularly Chapters 5-9) we discussed credit sales and accounts receivable in an entrepreneurial environment. Some of that discussion also applies

---

[3]If a company requires customers to sign a promissory note, it may also have a subsidiary ledger for notes receivable.

to our analysis of large companies. Here are the basic management policies that apply to accounts receivable in large companies.

1. *Granting credit.* A company should have control policies to govern which customers are granted credit and how much credit it allows.

2. *Recording credit sales.* A company generally records credit sales in the accounting system when it transfers the goods to the customer.

3. *Monitoring accounts receivable balances.* A company should have control policies to monitor the accounts receivable balances of its customers. It should mail periodic (monthly) statements to its customers. It should deny additional credit to customers with overdue balances. If the total accounts receivable balance becomes relatively large, it should investigate the reasons for the growth. If cash collections have slowed, it should examine its credit policies.

4. *Reporting accounts receivable according to GAAP.* GAAP requires that every company report accounts receivable at the net realizable value on its balance sheet.

Items 1, 2, and 3 relate mainly to accounts receivable management. Item 4 refers to how a company reports accounts receivable on its balance sheet. In the following two sections we will build on these items to discuss the managing and reporting of accounts receivable in a large-company environment.

Accounts Receivable Management

Let's go back to when Sweet Temptations began operations at the end of 1999. Assume that Sweet Temptations wants to order 360 boxes of chocolates on credit from Unlimited Decadence. How does Unlimited Decadence handle this order? The following management activities should take place for receivables:

1. On December 15, 1999, Sweet Temptations asks to make purchases on credit from Unlimited Decadence. After investigating Sweet Temptations, Unlimited Decadence agrees to grant it credit. On December 18, 1999, Unlimited Decadence establishes Sweet Temptations' credit limit (the maximum dollar amount that Unlimited Decadence will allow for Sweet Temptations' accounts receivable balance) at $10,000. This credit line remains in place indefinitely until either company decides to change or cancel it.

2. On December 19, 1999, Sweet Temptations orders 360 boxes of chocolates. It contacts Unlimited Decadence to place the order. Sweet Temptations specifies the type and number of boxes it needs and uses the price of the boxes to determine the total cost of the order.

3. When taking Sweet Temptations' order, an Unlimited Decadence salesperson completes a sales order. A **sales order** is a source document (either on paper or in a computer file) that includes specific information about a sale. This means that the salesperson verifies and records the type and number of boxes of chocolates to be sold, as well as the price of the sale. Unlimited Decadence confirms that the order is for 360 boxes of chocolates at $4.50 per box, totaling $1,620. The salesperson then sends the order to the Unlimited Decadence credit department for approval.

4. Before allowing the boxes of chocolates to be shipped, Unlimited Decadence's credit department checks the status of Sweet Temptations' credit line. If its account is not overdue and the order doesn't put Sweet Temptations' credit balance above the $10,000 limit, Unlimited Decadence approves the sales order for shipment. The credit department then sends the approved sales order to the

warehouse and shipping personnel so that they can send the chocolates to Sweet Temptations.

5. Unlimited Decadence's warehouse and shipping personnel process the approved sales order. Control policies require that a shipping department employee complete a shipping document to accompany the package of chocolates and to use as evidence that the sale occurred. On December 20, 1999, Unlimited Decadence ships the boxes of chocolates.

6. Unlimited Decadence's accounting department receives copies of the approved sales order and shipping documents from the other departments involved in the sale. Using the information on the documents, the accounting department fills out a sales invoice to send to Sweet Temptations. The sales invoice provides a written record of the sale and requests that Sweet Temptations pay in accordance with the credit arrangements. Once it checks the approved sales order, shipping documents, and sales invoice for accuracy and consistency, Unlimited Decadence records the credit sale in its accounting records by increasing Accounts Receivable and Sales by the amount of the sale.

7. Unlimited Decadence mails monthly statements to all customers, periodically reviews all customers' accounts receivable balances, and investigates overdue accounts.

 How could you make these procedures simpler? What problems might be caused by simplifying the procedures?

The steps seem similar to those followed by Sweet Temptations when it makes a credit sale to a customer—and they are. In both cases, *what* took place is a credit sale. However, there are differences in *how* the credit sales take place. In other words, entrepreneurial companies and large companies do not manage credit sales and accounts receivable in exactly the same way. This is because of their different sizes and levels of complexity and their different types of customers. Unlimited Decadence's volume of credit sales and its number of credit customers require the company to adopt more extensive control policies to govern the granting of credit, the recording of credit sales, and the monitoring of accounts receivable balances.

Granting Credit

How does a company decide which customers to extend credit to and how much credit to allow? In Chapter 9 we explained that smaller companies ask potential credit customers to complete formal credit applications for evaluation and approval decisions. This process also is common for large companies. In addition, large companies use three other policies to reduce the risks associated with selling goods on credit.

First, companies often establish personnel policies that prohibit sales personnel from having the authority to approve credit sales. A salesperson who also has the ability to approve credit has an incentive to grant more credit than customers deserve, in order to increase the salesperson's dollar amount of sales. This is especially true if the company pays commissions to sales personnel.

At Unlimited Decadence, a credit department processes all credit applications. The credit manager approved Sweet Temptations' $10,000 line of credit. The credit manager reports to the Vice-President of Finance. On the other hand, the sales personnel report to the Vice-President of Sales. This organizational structure separates credit approval and sales responsibilities.

 Do you think a company's credit department and its sales department might disagree about who should be granted credit? Why or why not? How can these disagreements be resolved?

Second, before agreeing to sell goods on credit, companies sometimes require customers to submit letters of credit from their banks. A **letter of credit,** written by a customer's bank, ensures payment to the selling company when that company presents the bank with documents that show it met the conditions of the sale. In essence, the bank that issues the letter of credit guarantees that payment will be made to the seller when the transaction between the seller and the buyer is complete. If a company's sale involves a letter of credit, the risk of granting credit is reduced because the process now involves the creditworthiness of the buyer's bank.

U.S. companies commonly require letters of credit from customers when they make international sales. The letters are important because managers usually have less knowledge about business in foreign countries or about a specific foreign customer. There also may be increased risk from war, civil strife, or an inability to convert local currencies to U.S. dollars.

Third, companies that sell goods on credit to international customers sometimes purchase export insurance as a way to reduce credit risk. **Export insurance** eliminates a company's risk of not receiving payment for the goods it sold internationally; if it does not receive payment, the insurance company must pay. Regardless of the credit policies used by a company, it should approve credit before each credit sales transaction. By doing this, a company improves the collectibility of every receivable.

Recording Credit Sales in the Accounting System

According to GAAP, when collection from a sale is likely, a company records a revenue transaction in the accounting period in which it earns the revenue—usually when the selling company transfers the goods to the customer or performs the service. So, Unlimited Decadence earns revenue when it ships chocolates to its customers and when there is a high probability of collecting the receivable. Once the accounting department matches the approved sales order, shipping document, and sales invoice, it has evidence that the sale occurred, and it can record the sales transaction. Unlimited Decadence records the December 20, 1999 sale to Sweet Temptations for $1,620 (360 boxes of chocolates at $4.50 per box) as follows:

3 *How does a company report credit sales and net sales?*

Assets	=	Liabilities	+	Stockholders' Equity

Accounts Receivable (Sweet Temptations)			Sales Revenue	
1,620				1,620
(+)	(−)		(−)	(+)

Both Accounts Receivable[4] and Sales Revenue increase by $1,620 as a result of the sale.[5]

It is not always clear when credit sales have taken place and what dollar amount of sales a company should show on an income statement. For example, a company whose customers (e.g., retail stores) will resell the goods to consumers often provides the customer an opportunity to return goods that it doesn't sell. This is especially true if the product is defective or is newly developed and the retailer is not sure how many retail customers will purchase it. Similarly, some companies guarantee to have the lowest-priced products. If a customer finds a lower price on the same product elsewhere, these companies refund the difference and perhaps return an additional amount.

---

[4]Note that Unlimited Decadence uses an accounts receivable subsidiary ledger. Therefore, it records the transaction both in the Accounts Receivable control account and in the account of the individual customer, Sweet Temptations. We show this here and later in the chapter (and in Chapter 14) by listing the customer's name in parentheses in the account title.

[5]Since Unlimited Decadence uses a perpetual inventory system, it also would record an increase in Cost of Goods Sold and a decrease in Inventory for the *cost* of the inventory sold. For the sake of simplicity, we do not show the entry here or in other sales transactions later in the chapter. We discussed the perpetual inventory system in Chapter 5 and will expand on it in Chapter 19.

Would you recommend that a company not record revenue until such options have expired? For example, should the publisher of this book not record revenue until your right to return it to the bookstore has expired?

How should these types of sales policies affect a company's accounting procedures for reporting sales on the income statement and accounts receivable on the balance sheet? Recall from Chapter 6 that companies show sales revenues on the income statement at a *net* amount. **Net sales** for an accounting period equal the total sales minus the sales discounts and sales returns and allowances for that period. A **sales discount** (also called a *cash discount*) is a reduction in the invoice price because the customer pays within the discount period (we will discuss sales discounts later in the chapter). A **sales return** occurs when a customer returns goods that the company previously recorded as a sale and the customer receives a refund in exchange for the goods. A **sales allowance** occurs when a company refunds a portion of the sales price after the original sale occurred.

A company uses its accounting system to keep track of sales returns and allowances. Managers monitor the volume of returns and allowances for three basic reasons. First, a relatively high level of sales returns may indicate that sales personnel are persuading customers to make unwanted purchases. If sales personnel are not at least partly responsible for the costs associated with sales returns, they may use a lenient sales return policy, to their personal (not the company's) advantage. Perhaps you have been in a situation where the salesperson says: "Go ahead, buy it now while we have it on sale. You can always bring it back later if you change your mind." (Some companies, however, use liberal return policies as a deliberate way to generate more sales. They *encourage* sales personnel to stress the return policy when trying to make a sale because they assume that few customers will return the item.) Second, a relatively high level of sales returns may indicate problems with product quality or product demand. Therefore, many companies require sales personnel to find out why goods are being returned. Finally, a relatively high level of sales allowances may result from shipping or warehouse problems. A sales allowance often is given to customers if goods are slightly damaged or do not match the description of the goods that were ordered (e.g., if Unlimited Decadence shipped the wrong flavor of candy).

For example, assume that on April 15, 2000, Bayside Candies Company ordered 300 boxes of chocolates on credit from Unlimited Decadence for $1,350 ($4.50 per box). Further, Bayside requests that 100 of the boxes have specialized Mother's Day wrapping. On April 17, Unlimited Decadence ships the 300 boxes of chocolates and records the credit sale. When the boxes arrive at Bayside on April 19, its receiving department personnel inspect the order and find that none of the boxes have the special wrapping. On being notified of the mistake on April 20, Unlimited Decadence offers to reduce the sales price for the entire shipment by $1 per box ($300). Bayside agrees, and on April 24, 2000, Unlimited Decadence records the sales allowance[6] as follows:

Assets	**= Liabilities**	**+**	**Stockholders' Equity**

Accounts Receivable (Bayside Candies)		Sales Returns and Allowances	
Bal 1,350			
	300	300	
Bal 1,050			
(+)	(−)	(+)	(−)

 Why would both companies agree to the sales allowance rather than deciding that Bayside should return the boxes?

---

[6]We show the balance (Bal) in selected accounts in this and later chapters so that you can see the effect on account balances of recording certain transactions.

Unlimited Decadence decreases Accounts Receivable by $300 because Bayside now owes it only $1,050, not the original $1,350. It also increases Sales Returns and Allowances by $300 on the *left* side of the T-account. This is the opposite of the way that companies record increases in sales. That is, the balance of the Sales Returns and Allowance account is subtracted from the balance of the Sales Revenue account on the income statement to determine net sales. So the rule for recording increases (or decreases) in the Sales Returns and Allowances account is the *opposite* of the Sales Revenue account (where increases are recorded on the right side). An account that has the effect of reducing the balance in another account is called a **contra account.** We will discuss two other contra accounts later in the chapter.

 Can you think of other possible contra accounts?

Suppose instead that Bayside returned the 100 boxes that did not have the special wrapping. Unlimited Decadence would record the sales return of $450 ($4.50 per box) in the same way that we just showed for the sales allowance (except recording $450 rather than $300). However, since Unlimited Decadence receives the boxes back, and since it uses the perpetual inventory system, it also must record an increase in Inventory and a decrease in Cost of Goods Sold. In other words, it reverses the sale *and* the cost of the sale. If we assume that each box cost $2.50, Unlimited Decadence would record the cost of the return as follows:

Assets = Liabilities + Stockholders' Equity

Inventory			Cost of Goods Sold	
250				250
(+)	(−)		(+)	(−)

Business Issues and Values in Recording Credit Sales

How does recording credit sales affect the ability of external users to rely on the income reported on an income statement? Managers must decide how aggressively to record transactions as sales. Or, as *The Wall Street Journal* stated the question in a front-page article discussing IBM's policies for recording computer sales, "When is a sale a sale?" According to the article, in the late 1980s and early 1990s, IBM's policies became more aggressive as its sales declined. Its sales department designed more creative gimmicks to improve sales. These gimmicks included a "try and buy" plan with no initial payment and "price protection" refunds if IBM later reduced prices. A former IBM accounting manager stated that he and his accounting co-workers felt pressure to interpret sales policies more liberally.

www.ibm.com

The article reported that the CPA who led the audit of IBM's financial statements questioned IBM's accounting policies for recording computer sales. Through a private memo, he informed IBM that he believed the company was recording revenue it might never receive. The memo stated that IBM recorded revenues when goods were shipped to dealers who could return them and sometimes when goods were shipped to its own warehouses. He wrote that this latter practice was clearly inappropriate.

IBM defended its practices as being consistent with GAAP by arguing that when a shipment occurs, the earnings process is substantially complete and it is proper to record the sale. *The Wall Street Journal* reported that Amdahl Corporation and Xerox Corporation stated that they follow more conservative approaches to recording revenue. Amdahl does not record revenue for its mainframe computers until the computers are "up and running." A Xerox representative stated that although the company records revenues for small copiers at the time of shipment, it does not record revenues from sales of large copiers until "everyone says, 'Wow, it's better than sliced bread.'"

www.amdahl.com
www.xerox.com

Investors and creditors need to be aware that companies differ in how they interpret GAAP for similar sales transactions. As business deals become more complicated, defining when sales revenue is earned (and collectible) becomes more difficult.

Monitoring Accounts Receivable Balances

Although companies require customers to show that they have the *ability* to pay for credit sales, this does not mean that customers always pay. As we discussed in Chapter 9, when making credit sales, the company does not know *which* customers will not pay. (Again, if it knew at the time of sale that a particular customer would not pay, it would not make the sale.)

Large companies, like small ones, monitor customers' accounts receivable balances to help decrease the number of accounts that will be uncollectible. An accounts receivable subsidiary ledger is very useful for this purpose because it enables a company to more easily analyze each customer's account. A company mails notices to customers with overdue amounts. If a customer does not pay within a reasonable period of time, the credit manager should contact the customer to discuss the problem and try to work out a payment schedule. If that doesn't work, a company may take legal action against the customer by filing a lawsuit to force payment or may turn the account over to a collection agency.

Whether making credit sales to attract customers or to increase their convenience, a company records the costs associated with making these sales as an expense and separates them into two types: (1) the administrative expenses associated with making credit sales, and (2) the *bad debts expense* caused by customers never paying off their accounts receivable balances. The administrative expenses include the costs of processing customers' credit applications, sending out monthly statements, and contacting overdue accounts. A company records these administrative expenses when it incurs the costs. For example, assume that Unlimited Decadence incurs $1,000 in postage costs when it mails out its November 2000 monthly statements. If Unlimited Decadence uses a postage meter and had prepaid at least $1,000 of postage, it records the use of the postage in the accounting system as a $1,000 increase in Postage Expense and a $1,000 decrease in Prepaid Postage.

Bad debts expense is the expense that represents the estimated cost, for the accounting period, of the eventual noncollection of accounts receivable. A company records the expense (and a reduction in the net accounts receivable, as we will discuss later) in the accounting system through an end-of-period adjustment. Recording bad debts expense in the accounting records is not as straightforward as recording other costs. Customers do not telephone the company to announce: "We are going to keep the goods you just sold us, but

cathy® **by Cathy Guisewite**

©1997. Cathy Guisewite/Distributed by Universal Press Syndicate. Reprinted with permission.

we are never going to pay for them. Please consider us a bad debt." Rather, a company *estimates* and reports the bad debts expense in the period of the credit sale and *not* in the period when the company discovers that a customer cannot pay. This is an example of the matching principle we discussed in Chapter 9.

 Once a company has estimated the amount of accounts receivable that will be uncollectible, do you think it can just erase the total amount for accounts receivable that is in the accounting records and replace it with the net accounts receivable amount? Why, or why not? How should it make this change in the accounting records?

For example, assume that at December 31, 2000, Unlimited Decadence estimates that its bad debts expense for 2000 is $134,000 (later we will discuss how it computed this amount). It records this amount as follows:

Assets = Liabilities + Stockholders' Equity

Allowance for Bad Debts	Bad Debts Expense

	Bal 11,000		
	134,000	134,000	
	Bal 145,000		
(−)	(+)	(+)	(−)

 $134,000 probably seems like a large amount to you. How would you decide if it is a large amount for Unlimited Decadence?

Note that Unlimited Decadence did not reduce accounts receivable directly in this entry because it does not yet know which credit customers will not pay. Instead it uses an Allowance for Bad Debts account (sometimes called Allowance for Doubtful Accounts, Allowance for Uncollectible Accounts, or Provision for Credit Losses). Notice that the increase in the Allowance for Bad Debts is recorded on the *right* side of the T-account. This is the *opposite* of accounts receivable. Like Sales Returns and Allowances, Allowance for Bad Debts is a *contra* account. Subtracting its balance from the balance in the Accounts Receivable account gives the net realizable value of the accounts receivable (the amount of cash the company expects to collect) that the company reports on its balance sheet. The company includes the bad debts expense on the income statement as a part of its operating expenses.

Write-off of an Uncollectible Account

Eventually a manager will judge that certain customer accounts are uncollectible. This may occur because a customer filed for bankruptcy, left no forwarding address and cannot be found, or went out of business. At this time the company "writes off" (eliminates) the customer's account receivable, and an equal amount of the allowance for bad debts, because it knows it will not collect an amount previously included in its estimate of uncollectible accounts. It still expects to collect the same *total* amount as it did before the write-off. Therefore the write-off does *not* affect the total assets or expenses of the company. Remember that the company recorded both the expense and the reduction in the asset in the period of the credit sale by using an end-of-period adjustment.

A manager authorizing a write-off is, in essence, saying, "Now I know for whom I was creating that allowance." Therefore, the write-off does *not* affect the company's balance sheet or its income statement—the effects on those two statements were recorded when the company made the bad debt estimate. The company records the write-off by reducing the accounts receivable balance and the allowance account by the same amount. For example, assume the Chocolate Candies Cafe owes Unlimited Decadence $8,000 from a sale two years ago. Unlimited Decadence no longer believes that the amount is collectible and writes off this receivable early in 2001 as follows:

Assets			=	**Liabilities**	+	**Stockholders' Equity**

Accounts Receivable
(Chocolate Candies Cafe)   Allowance for Bad Debts

Bal 8,000			Bal 145,000
	8,000	8,000	
Bal 0			Bal 137,000
(+)	(−)	(−)	(+)

Unlimited Decadence decreases both its Allowance for Bad Debts and its Accounts Receivable by $8,000. Also, for control purposes, Unlimited Decadence will make a note of this write-off in Chocolate Candies Cafe's credit file. Note that this write-off has no effect on Unlimited Decadence's net accounts receivable:

	Before the Write-off	**After the Write-off**
Accounts receivable (assumed)	$6,000,000	$5,992,000
Less: Allowance for bad debts	(145,000)	(137,000)
Net accounts receivable	$5,855,000	$5,855,000

 Do you think managers would prefer to write off a receivable at the end of the year or wait until the next year? Explain your answer.

If the company's estimates are accurate and it writes off its uncollectible accounts before the end of the year, then the balance of its Allowance for Bad Debts account before the year-end adjustment will be zero. However, since estimates are "best guesses" and a company is unlikely to write off its accounts so quickly, a company's Allowance for Bad Debts account will frequently have a year-end balance. For example, suppose that Unlimited Decadence has a receivable from another company that declares bankruptcy. It might take more than a year for the courts to rule on how much Unlimited Decadence will receive and, therefore, how much it will write off.

In summary, a company computes the year-end balance of its Allowance for Bad Debts as follows:

Beginning Allowance Balance	+	Bad Debts Expense for the Year	−	Write-offs for the Year	=	Ending Allowance Balance

A company computes the year-end balance of its Accounts Receivable as follows:

Beginning Accounts Receivable Balance	+	Credit Sales during the Year	−	Cash Collections during the Year	−	Write-offs for the Year	=	Ending Accounts Receivable Balance

Note that this equation differs from the equation given in our discussion at the beginning of the chapter because we now include write-offs.

Technology and Receivables Management

How have computers changed your everyday life? Think about how technology affects your job or the job of a friend. How do you think technology affects large companies and their receivables management?

Do all companies manage liquidity using the same methods? No: as we discussed in Chapter 10 for enterprise resource planning (ERP) systems, an increasing number of large companies are reengineering all or parts of their accounting and finance functions, especially liquidity-management activities. **Reengineering** is the process of analyzing and redesigning an activity to make it more effective and efficient. In most cases, it involves taking advantage of new technologies.

In receivables management, reengineering has changed the way many large companies grant credit, record credit sales, and monitor receivables. For instance, General Motors Acceptance Corporation (GMAC) now approves credit applications by using a special type of computer program, called a neural network. Credit applications are entered electronically into GMAC's mainframe computer. This program, *Credit Advisor,* "thinks" like a credit analyst and decides whether or not to approve credit. GMAC reports savings in personnel costs and fewer bad debts. Countrywide Mortgage, a financing company that operates in many states, uses notebook computers and cellular-phone technology to complete customers' credit applications from remote locations (e.g., a building site). Its financial-services personnel no longer have to ask customers to fill out extensive credit applications, make a trip to its offices, or wait for weeks for credit approval. Thanks to technology, applications are processed more quickly and conveniently, allowing customers earlier access to credit.

www.gmacfs.com

www.countrywide.com

Do you think this technology means that a customer is less likely to shop around for a better deal?

Some large companies now process and record credit sales with trusted customers (called "trading partners") using Electronic Data Interchange (EDI). With EDI, the computers of the two companies are linked. When a customer wants to make a purchase, it views the seller's most recent catalogs and price lists from its own computer and submits orders directly into the seller's computerized sales-processing system. The system automatically prepares shipping documents and sales invoices, and distributes them electronically to the company's shipping department and to the customer's accounts payables management system. The computer programs have built-in controls to monitor the size and frequency of customers' orders. They print out a list of "unusual-looking" transactions daily, to be reviewed by managers to ensure that each transaction was authorized properly.

Technology also assists with monitoring a company's receivables. Computer programs electronically check the ages of customers' balances and automatically mail computerized "past due" notices to customers. The programs also change the information in the notices as the accounts become more overdue. American Express uses a computerized receivables system that tailors notices to each specific customer (and includes appropriate advertising).

Reporting Accounts Receivable

Although we explained in Chapter 9 and in the previous section that companies show accounts receivable on the balance sheet at net realizable value, we did not explain *how* they calculate the amounts of the bad debts expense and the allowance for bad debts. When a company prepares financial statements, it uses one of two methods to calculate these amounts: (1) the aging method, or (2) the percentage of sales method. The basic difference between the two is that the aging method calculates the estimate of the *balance* in the Allowance for Bad Debts account to use in determining the net realizable value for Accounts Receivable. Under this method, the bad debts expense is the amount needed to obtain the *required allowance balance.* On the other hand, the percentage of sales method calculates

4 *How does a company determine the amount of its bad debts expense, and how does it report the related accounts on its financial statements?*

the *amount of bad debts expense* to include on the income statement of the current period. It ignores any balance in the Allowance for Bad Debts. We will explain the aging method and then briefly discuss the percentage of sales method.

Aging Method of Estimating Bad Debts

A company using the **aging method** estimates the amount of bad debts based on the age of the individual amounts included in the ending balance of its Accounts Receivable (how long these amounts have been owed to the company). It does this because the older the receivable, the less likely the company is to collect it. Therefore, the aging method is generally considered to be better for estimating, at the end of the period, the net accounts receivable that will be collectible. Because of this accounts receivable focus, the aging method is called a "balance sheet approach" to estimating bad debts. Note that this method does *not* directly consider the dollar amount of credit sales that occurred during the accounting period.

> *Do you agree that the accounts receivable ending balance may include uncollected credit sales from previous periods and not include most credit sales from this period? Why or why not?*

A company uses four steps in the aging method. First, it categorizes the accounts receivable for its individual customers (from its accounts receivable subsidiary ledger) into age groups based on the length of time they have been outstanding. For example, Unlimited Decadence divides its accounts receivable into groups of balances that are (1) not yet past due, (2) 1-30 days past due, (3) 31-60 days past due, (4) 61-120 days past due, and (5) more than 120 days past due. It divides the customers' balances into groups because older accounts are more likely to be uncollectible.

Second, the company multiplies the total dollar amount for each age group by the percentage of that group's amount that it estimates to be uncollectible. It bases each group's uncollectible percentage on its past experience in collecting receivables. For example, for its December 31, 2000 balance sheet, Unlimited Decadence analyzes its past performance in collecting receivables (or uses industry estimates), develops an estimated percentage that is uncollectible for each age group, and calculates the dollar amount uncollectible for each age group as follows:

Age Group	Amount		Estimated Percentage Uncollectible		Estimated Uncollectible Amount
Not yet past due	$3,000,000	×	0.1%	=	$ 3,000
1-30 days past due	1,500,000	×	1	=	15,000
31-60 days past due	900,000	×	3	=	27,000
61-120 days past due	400,000	×	10	=	40,000
121+ days past due	200,000	×	30	=	60,000
Total	$6,000,000				$145,000

Third, the company sums the estimated uncollectible amounts to calculate the required ending balance in the Allowance for Bad Debts. As shown in the preceding schedule, the total for Unlimited Decadence on December 31, 2000 is $145,000.

Fourth, the company makes a year-end adjustment to *bring the balance in the Allowance account up to the calculated balance.* The amount of the adjustment depends on the existing balance in the Allowance account before the adjustment. We assume that before its 2000 year-end adjustment, Unlimited Decadence has a beginning balance of $11,000 in its Allowance account. For example, look at the December 31, 2000 T-accounts for Unlimited Decadence's Allowance and Bad Debts Expense accounts before the end-of-period adjustment is made:

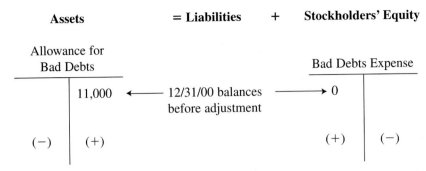

The balance in Bad Debts Expense before the adjustment is $0 because we assume that the year-end adjustment is the only time during the year that a company records bad debts. (A company could, however, record bad debts expense during the year, say quarterly.) The amount of the end-of-period adjustment is the amount needed to increase the existing balance of Allowance for Bad Debts up to the estimated amount calculated by the aging analysis. For Unlimited Decadence, the amount is calculated as follows:

$$\begin{array}{c} \text{Required end-of-period} \\ \text{adjustment} \end{array} = \begin{array}{c} \$145,000 \text{ required} \\ \text{balance} \end{array} - \begin{array}{c} \$11,000 \text{ existing} \\ \text{balance} \end{array} = \underline{\$134,000}$$

At the end of 2000, Unlimited Decadence records $134,000 as Bad Debts Expense and increases its Allowance for Bad Debts by $134,000 as follows:

	Assets	= Liabilities	+	Stockholders' Equity	

Allowance for Bad Debts

	11,000	← 12/31/00 balances before adjustment →	0		**Bad Debts Expense**
	134,000	← 12/31/00 adjustment →	134,000		
	145,000	← 12/31/00 balances after adjustment →	134,000		
(−)	(+)		(+)	(−)	

The Allowance account increases from $11,000 to the required (calculated) balance of $145,000. Unlimited Decadence subtracts this balance from the $6,000,000 ending Accounts Receivable balance to determine the net realizable value of $5,855,000, which it reports on its December 31, 2000 year-end balance sheet. It includes the bad debts expense of $134,000 on its 2000 income statement. Exhibit 13-4 summarizes the reporting of accounts receivable, using the amounts calculated above under the aging method.

In addition to using an aging analysis to determine the bad debts expense at year-end, many companies do an aging analysis on a quarterly, monthly, or more frequent basis. By watching which customers' accounts are moving to an older age group, the company can closely monitor which customers may not pay their accounts.

Percentage of Sales Method of Estimating Bad Debts

A company using the **percentage of sales method** estimates its bad debts expense by multiplying the net credit sales of the period by the percentage of these sales it estimates to be uncollectible. The company bases the percentage on its history of writing off bad debts (or on industry statistics). Because the estimate is based on the dollar amount of credit sales

Exhibit 13-4   Description of Accounts Receivable on a Balance Sheet

Unlimited Decadence
Balances for Current Asset Accounts
December 31, 2000
(in thousands)

Current assets
Cash and cash equivalents	$1,020
Accounts receivable (net)	5,855 ←
Short-term notes receivable	100
Inventories	1,610
Total current assets	$8,585

Accounts receivable (gross) is the total amount owed to a company by customers for credit sales.

Allowance for bad debts is the amount the company expects not to be paid.

Accounts receivable *(net)* is the amount the company expects to collect.

GAAP requires that a company report its accounts receivable on its balance sheet at the *net realizable value* (i.e., the amount of cash the company expects to collect from customers).

The net amount shown for Unlimited Decadence's accounts receivable represents the total amounts owed to Unlimited Decadence from customers at December 31, 2000 *less* an allowance for accounts receivable estimated to be uncollectible. The calculation is (in thousands of dollars):

Total accounts receivable owed to Unlimited Decadence	−	Allowance for bad debts	=	Accounts receivable (net)
$6,000	−	$145	=	$5,855

reported on the income statement, the percentage of sales method is called an "income statement approach" to calculating bad debts expense.

For instance, assume that Unlimited Decadence had $72 million in credit sales during 2000. Further, based on prior experience, assume it estimates that 0.2% of its credit sales will be uncollectible. If Unlimited Decadence uses the percentage of sales method, it records bad debts expense for 2000 at $144,000 ($72 million × 0.002). If we again assume that Unlimited Decadence has a beginning balance of $11,000 in its Allowance account, the balance in its Allowance for Bad Debts at the end of 2000 would be $155,000.

 Why do you think that Unlimited Decadence uses higher percentages in the aging schedule than it uses in the percentage of sales method? Since the percentage of sales and aging methods produce different amounts, is one right and the other wrong?

Notice that when a company uses the percentage of sales method, the year-end adjustment is designed so that the *calculated* amount of bad debts expense (in this case, $144,000) is the amount of the *bad debts expense* that the company reports. The year-end balance in Allowance for Bad Debts is the sum of the balance before the adjustment plus the calculated amount of bad debts expense. This method does not require any consideration of the reasonableness of the allowance balance.

What do you think managers will do if they notice that the balance of the Allowance for Bad Debts is getting larger and larger at the end of every year? Why would this happen?

Computing the Amount of Sales Made to Companies in Other Countries

As U.S. companies expand their operations, they frequently become involved in transactions with customers and suppliers in other countries. For example, a U.S. company may decide to expand its revenue opportunities by selling its products in foreign countries. Or, a U.S. company may decide that it can purchase inventory at a lower cost or acquire machinery that is more efficient from a company based in a foreign country. In each of these situations, the U.S. company must record the transaction in U.S. dollars, although the price may be stated in terms of a foreign currency. Since these types of transactions are becoming more common, even among small companies, you should have a basic understanding of these international issues. In this chapter we discuss the recording of international sales. In Chapter 14, we will discuss the recording of international purchases. But first we discuss exchange rates.

An **exchange rate** measures the value of one currency in terms of another currency. Unfortunately, some exchange rates are commonly expressed in U.S. dollars whereas others are expressed in terms of the number of foreign units that are equal to the U.S. dollar. For example, recently the British pound was quoted at a rate of $1.60. This rate means that it takes $1.60 to buy one British pound; that is, the pound is a larger unit than the U.S. dollar. In contrast, the Swiss franc was recently quoted at a rate of 1.41 francs to the U.S. dollar. This rate means that it takes 1.41 francs to buy $1; that is, the franc is a smaller unit than the dollar. To avoid confusion, in this book we always quote exchange rates in terms of the number of U.S. dollars that is equivalent to one unit of the foreign currency. Therefore, for the British pound and the Swiss franc, we use exchange rates of $1.60 for the pound and $0.71 (1 ÷ 1.41) for the franc. The general rule is that a foreign currency is converted into U.S. dollars as follows:

$$\text{Amount in U.S. Dollars} = \text{Foreign Currency Amount} \times \text{Exchange Rate}$$
$$\text{(stated in dollars)}$$

5 *What is an exchange rate, and how does an exchange gain (loss) arise from a credit sale made to a company in another country?*

When a company and its customer are in different countries that use different currencies, how do you think they arrive at an agreed-upon selling price?

We illustrate some recent exchange rates in Exhibit 13-5.

 Pick the currency of a country you have visited or would like to visit and look up its exchange rate. Is its currency larger or smaller than the U.S. dollar?

Since an exchange rate represents the price of one currency in terms of another, rates change continuously as supply and demand for currencies change. These changes are often described by terms such as strong (rising) and weak (falling). To understand these changes, consider the exchange rate for the pound in Exhibit 13-5: $1.6495. If the dollar weakens against the pound, the price (exchange rate) of the pound rises when stated in terms of the dollar. For example, a change in the rate to $1.70 would be a weakening of the dollar because it now takes more dollars to buy one pound. Saying that the dollar is weakening is the same as saying that the pound is strengthening.

 Wait a few days and look up the exchange rate you used in the previous STOP. Has the currency strengthened or weakened?

As we explained earlier, many U.S. companies conduct transactions with customers in foreign countries. Sometimes the companies agree on a price stated in U.S. dollars. For example, most sales of crude oil are stated in terms of the U.S. dollar. In these situations, there is no accounting issue; the transaction is recorded as we discussed earlier in this chapter. For example, if a U.S. oil company sells 10,000 barrels of crude oil to Mexico, the price would be quoted in dollars and not in the equivalent amount of pesos. If the price was $15 per barrel, the company would record a sale and the related cash receipt of $150,000 ($15 × 10,000).

In many situations, however, the companies agree on a price stated in terms of the foreign currency. In these cases, the U.S. company must record the transaction in U.S. dollars. Therefore, the company must convert the foreign currency amount into dollars at the exchange rate on the day of the transaction. Also, transactions between companies in different countries usually involve credit terms, if only to allow time for the processing of the orders, shipments, and payments across international borders. In addition, currency exchange rates change continuously. As a result, the exchange rate is likely to change between the date the U.S. company records a credit sale and the date it receives the payment. On the date of the cash receipt, then, the company records an exchange gain or loss to account for the difference between the selling price and the amount of the cash receipt. An **exchange gain or loss** is caused by a change in the exchange rate between the date that a company records a credit sale and the date the company collects the cash. More specifically, exchange gains and losses occur for credit sales as follows:

Exhibit 13-5 Exchange Rates

Currency (Country)	Price in U.S. Dollars
Pound (Britain)	$1.6495
Dollar (Canada)	0.6588
Euro	1.1416
Shekel (Israel)	0.2435
Yen (Japan)	0.0086
Peso (Mexico)	0.0981
Riyal (Saudi Arabia)	0.2666
Won (South Korea)	0.0009
Franc (Switzerland)	0.7081

Source: The Wall Street Journal, January 29, 1999

1. An exchange *gain* occurs when the exchange rate *increases* between the date a company records a *receivable* and the date the company *collects* the cash.

2. An exchange *loss* occurs when the exchange rate *declines* between the date a company records a *receivable* and the date the company *collects* the cash.

To understand an exchange loss that occurs when the exchange rate declines between the date a credit sale is recorded and the date the cash is collected, suppose that Unlimited Decadence sells candy to the Herrmann Company, a German company, on credit and agrees to a price of 300,000 Euros rather than a price in dollars. On the date of the sale, the exchange rate is $1.14 (1 Euro = $1.14), and therefore Unlimited Decadence records the sale of $342,000 (300,000 Euros × $1.14) as follows:

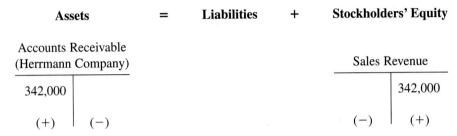

Herrmann Company has an obligation to pay 300,000 Euros regardless of the exchange rate on the date of payment. If the exchange rate is $1.12 when Herrmann pays the amount owed, Unlimited Decadence can convert those Euros into only $336,000 (300,000 Euros × $1.12). As a result, it has an exchange *loss* with $6,000 ($336,000 − $342,000), which it records at the time of the cash collection as follows:

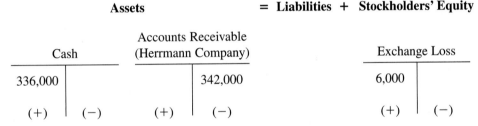

Unlimited Decadence also can compute the exchange loss by multiplying the amount of the receivable by the change in the exchange rate [300,000 Euros × ($1.14 − $1.12) = $6,000]. Remember that Herrmann Company still pays 300,000 Euros; it is Unlimited Decadence that has the exchange loss. For financial reporting purposes, Unlimited Decadence combines the amount of this exchange loss with any other exchange losses and gains, and reports the net amount in the "other items" section of its income statement.

Note that the U.S. company (Unlimited Decadence) experienced an exchange loss because it agreed to a transaction expressed in terms of a foreign currency. In such a situation, the U.S. company accepts the risks associated with changes in the exchange rate. If a U.S. company agrees to a transaction in U.S. dollars, the foreign company accepts, and the U.S. company avoids, the risks associated with changes in the exchange rate.

A potential disadvantage of selling to companies in other countries is that it may take longer to collect from them. For example, a recent Dun & Bradstreet study indicated that U.S. companies pay their bills, on average, in 30 to 60 days, whereas in Germany the average time is 30 to 90 days.

Unearned Revenue

A company usually collects cash from a customer at the time of the sale or *after* the sale, as we discussed earlier in the chapter. In some industries, however, it is common for the

6 *How does a company account for cash collected prior to sales?*

selling company to collect cash from customers *before* it delivers the goods or provides the services that the customers purchased. For example, magazine publishers require customers to pay for subscriptions before many of the issues being purchased are even written, much less delivered to the customer.

 Have you paid for goods or services in advance? What did you purchase? What are some other examples of goods or services that people pay for before they actually receive what they purchased?

When a company collects cash before it delivers the goods or services, it records a current liability often called **unearned revenue.** You may think that this is a confusing label because the term "revenue" means that the company has done what it has to do to earn revenue. However, "unearned" indicates that the earning process is not complete. Some companies use a less confusing title such as "products (or services) to be provided."

 Do you agree with the following statement? "Accounts receivable are the amounts owed to a company for credit sales already recorded, whereas unearned revenues are the amounts received by a company for sales it will record in the future." Why or why not?

A company records this liability (unearned revenue) because it accepts an obligation to provide goods or services in the future as a result of collecting cash now. Remember that a company does not record revenue until it provides the goods or services. A magazine publishing company, then, earns subscription revenue one issue at a time as it delivers magazines to customers who already paid for that issue. Every time the company delivers an issue of the magazine, it reduces that portion of the unearned revenue and increases revenue.

For example, suppose that Bookworm Publishing Corporation publishes *Enlightened Lite,* a new-age magazine that comes out monthly. The magazine publishes poetry, humorous short stories, recipes, and critiques of self-help books. Bookworm's fiscal year ends on December 31. On November 19, the company received a check for $3,600 from Aroma Health Stores for 100 annual subscriptions (12 monthly issues each, starting in December) of *Enlightened Lite.* Aroma owns 100 retail health-aid stores and wants each store manager to read the magazine. Bookworm Publishing records the cash receipt as follows:

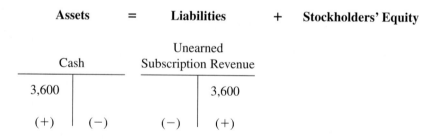

Assets	=	Liabilities	+	Stockholders' Equity

Cash		Unearned Subscription Revenue	
3,600			3,600
(+)	(−)	(−)	(+)

Bookworm increases Cash by the $3,600 it received. Because it collected the cash before it delivers any issues of the magazine to Aroma Health Stores, it increases Unearned Subscription Revenue, a current liability account, for the entire amount of the cash receipt.

 If Bookworm received payment for two-year subscriptions, do you think it would classify the entire amount as a current liability? Why or why not?

On December 1, Bookworm sends out 100 copies of its December issue of *Enlightened Lite* to Aroma Health Stores and records the event as follows:

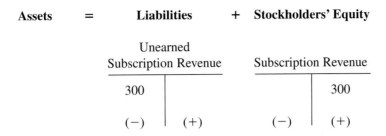

Assets   =   Liabilities   +   Stockholders' Equity

Unearned Subscription Revenue	Subscription Revenue
300	300
(−) | (+)	(−) | (+)

By sending out one issue of its magazine, Bookworm Publishing earns $300 (1/12 of the $3,600 received from Aroma). Therefore it reduces its liability to Aroma by this same amount. Every month when Bookworm mails out an issue of *Enlightened Lite* to Aroma Health Stores, it records a decrease in its liability and an increase in its revenue.

Exhibit 13-6 summarizes how Bookworm Publishing calculates the Unearned Subscription Revenue balance for Aroma Health Stores on December 31. Bookworm reports the total balance for all its customers in its Unearned Subscription Revenue account in the current liabilities section of its December 31, 2000 balance sheet.

 Why might Bookworm ship its January issue in late December?

Airline companies have significant unearned revenues because they require customers to pay before flying. For example, on its June 30, 1998 balance sheet, Delta Airlines reports an "air traffic liability" of $1,667 million, which is equal to approximately one-third of its current assets.

 Explain how this information affects your evaluation of Delta's liquidity.

In summary, a company calculates its year-end unearned revenue balance, as shown on the next page, and includes the amounts on each of the financial statements as indicated:

Exhibit 13-6   Bookworm Publishing's Year-End Subscription Revenue for One Customer: Aroma Health Stores

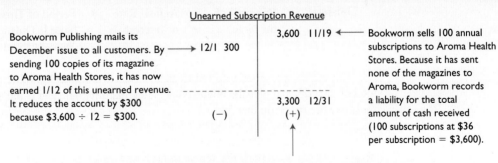

Beginning Unearned Revenue Balance	+	Cash Collected during the Year for Goods not yet Delivered or Services not yet Provided	−	Amounts Earned during the Year	=	Ending Unearned Revenue Balance
↓		↓		↓		↓
Beginning Balance Sheet: Current Liabilities		Cash Flow Statement: Operating Activities		Income Statement		Ending Balance Sheet: Current Liabilities

Notes Receivable

7 *What are the important characteristics of a note receivable, and how is interest computed?*

As we mentioned earlier, many companies also sell goods to customers in return for a promissory note. For these sales, a company manages the activities of granting credit, recording credit sales, and monitoring notes receivable balances using methods similar to those used in managing accounts receivable. For credit sales that involve promissory notes, managers and external users must still be concerned with the criteria used to judge whether a sale has actually occurred, as we discussed earlier. The same questions about transfer of goods and services to the customer and the likelihood of sales returns must be answered. So, why use a promissory note instead of an account receivable? A company may require a customer to sign a promissory note if the amount of the credit sale is relatively large, the length of time between the sale and the eventual cash collection is relatively long (and so interest is paid), or the creditworthiness of the customer is questionable. Because a promissory note is a written, legal document, many companies want the added security that is provided by a note.

 If you loaned a friend $5, would you want a note in exchange? What if you loaned $5,000?

Exhibit 13-7 provides an example of a promissory note. In our example, John Burgen Inc. makes a major purchase and agrees to pay Unlimited Decadence $10,000 plus interest (computed based on an annual interest rate of 12%) on February 1, 2001. The **principal** or **face value** of the note is the amount stated on the note—in our case, $10,000. The **maturity date** (February 1, 2001) is the specific day when the company that made and signed the note (called the **maker**) promises to pay the principal and interest amounts to the note holder (called the **payee**). Three factors determine the amount of interest owed to the payee: (1) the face value (principal) of the note, (2) the interest rate stated on the note, and (3) the length of time between the date the note is issued and the maturity date. The general rule for computing interest is as follows:

$$\text{Interest} = \begin{array}{c}\text{Principal of} \\ \text{the Note}\end{array} \times \begin{array}{c}\text{Annual Rate} \\ \text{of Interest}\end{array} \times \begin{array}{c}\text{Period of Time the} \\ \text{Note Is Outstanding in} \\ \text{Years or Fraction of a Year}\end{array}$$

This equation is often referred to as I = PRT. The **maturity value of the note** is the total of the principal plus the interest due on the maturity date and is the amount the maker must pay the payee on that date.

 Did you get all of those terms straight? Use our John Burgen Inc. example to see how well you understand this section so far. Based on our example, fill in the following blanks:

1. The maker of the note is ―――――――――――――――――――

2. The payee of the note is ―――――――――――――――――――

3. The date the note was signed is ―――――――――――――――

$ 10,000   PROMISSORY NOTE   Date August 1, 2000

_____ Six months _____ after date, for value received, I, we (and each of us)
promise to pay to _____ Unlimited Decadence Corp. _____ or order
_____ Ten Thousand _____ Dollars with interest from
_____ August 1, 2000 _____ at the rate of _12_ per cent, per _annum_ payable
_--_ annually. Principal payable and interest payable at February 1, 2001

IT IS AGREED that if this note is not paid when due or declared due hereunder, the entire principal and accrued interest thereon shall draw interest at the rate of _15_ per cent per annum, and that failure to make any payment of principal or interest when due or any default under any encumbrance or agreement securing this note shall cause the whole note to become due at once, or the interest to be counted as principal, at the option of the holder of the note. The makers and endorsers hereof severally waive presentment for payment, protest, notice of non-payment and of protest, and agree to any extension of time of payment and partial payments before, at or after maturity, and if this note or interest thereon is not paid when due, or suit is brought, agree to pay all reasonable costs of collection, including attorney's fees.

Due February 1, 2001   John Burgen, Inc
No. 125

This note is secured by: Property located at 1500 Elm Street Boulder, Colorado

4. The face value of the note is $ _____.

5. The maturity date of the note is _____.

6. The annual interest rate on the note is _____%.

7. The length of time between the date the note is issued and the maturity date is _____.

8. The amount of interest due on the maturity date is calculated to be $_____.

9. The maturity value of the note is $ _____.

How did you do?[7] Make sure you have this information correct because we will use it as we continue our notes receivable example.

Recording Receipt of a Note Receivable

Unlimited Decadence records the $10,000 sale when it receives the note from John Burgen Inc. on August 1, 2000 (the date on the note), as follows:

Assets	**=**	**Liabilities**	**+**	**Stockholders' Equity**

Notes Receivable | | | | Sales Revenue
10,000 | | | | 10,000
(+) | (−) | | | (−) | (+)

Both Notes Receivable and Sales Revenue increase by $10,000 as a result of the sale.

 Can you explain why the interest revenue may be different from the interest received in any accounting period?

[7]Here are the answers: (1) John Burgen, Inc. (2) Unlimited Decadence Corporation (3) August 1, 2000 (4) $10,000 (5) February 1, 2001 (6) 12% (7) One-half of a year (six months) (8) $10,000 × 0.12 × 1/2 = $600 (9) $10,000 + $600 = $10,600.

Recording Accrued Interest

From the day a customer signs a promissory note until the maturity date of the note, the selling company earns the interest associated with the note. It *earns* interest continuously during this time period even though it may not *collect* the interest until the maturity date. By saying that interest is earned continuously, we mean that, for example, after one day of holding a note, a company has earned one day's worth of interest. This holds true for one week, one month, and so on, regardless of when the company receives the interest.

Exhibit 13-8 shows how much interest Unlimited Decadence earns while it holds John Burgen Inc.'s $10,000 promissory note. As we show in the exhibit, we calculate one month's interest as follows:

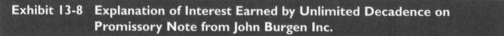

Unlimited Decadence earns $600 ($10,000 × 0.12 × 6/12) interest over the six-month life of the note. Another way to think of the total amount of interest is to multiply the interest earned per month by the number of months. Unlimited Decadence earns $100 in interest per month for six months for a total of $600.

We focus on the concept of earning interest over time because a company must report, on its financial statements for a period, the interest that it has earned during the period (even if it has not yet collected the interest). Unlimited Decadence is to receive the $10,000 face value of John Burgen Inc.'s note and the $600 in interest on February 1, 2001, but its fiscal year ends on December 31, 2000. Although Unlimited Decadence has not received any cash from John Burgen Inc., its financial statements for 2000 must include the amount of interest the company has earned through December 31, 2000.

You can see in Exhibit 13-8 that at December 31, 2000, five months have passed since Unlimited Decadence received the $10,000 note. Thus, Unlimited Decadence's accounting records should show that it earned $500 ($10,000 × 0.12 × 5/12) of interest during 2000

Exhibit 13-8 Explanation of Interest Earned by Unlimited Decadence on Promissory Note from John Burgen Inc.

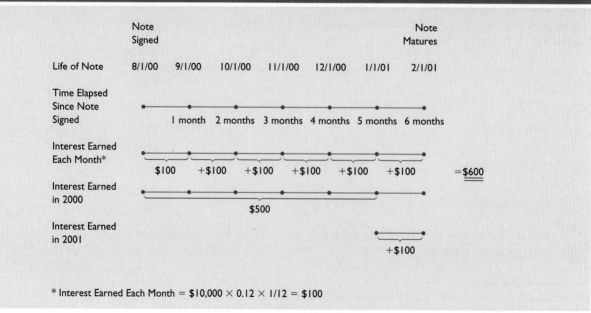

from holding John Burgen Inc.'s note. Also, the records should show that Unlimited Decadence has a legal right to collect the interest at a later date. So Unlimited Decadence makes an end-of-period adjustment to record the $500 as follows:

Assets	=	Liabilities	+	Stockholders' Equity
Interest Receivable				Interest Revenue

500				500
(+)	(−)			(−)	(+)

Both Interest Receivable and Interest Revenue increase by $500 as a result of the adjustment. Every time a company prepares financial statements, it must determine whether or not it has earned any interest that it has not yet recorded in its accounting system. If so, it makes an end-of-period adjustment to record the interest receivable that it reports as a current asset on the year-end balance sheet and the interest revenue that it reports in the "other items" section of the income statement.

Recording the Cash Receipt

Assume that on February 1, 2001, John Burgen Inc. pays Unlimited Decadence the $10,600 maturity value of the note. Unlimited Decadence records this transaction as follows:

Assets	= Liabilities + Stockholders' Equity

Cash		Notes Receivable		Interest Receivable		Interest Revenue	
		Bal 10,000		Bal 500			
10,600			10,000		500		100
		Bal 0		Bal 0			
(+)	(−)	(+)	(−)	(+)	(−)	(−)	(+)

Notice how this transaction affects Unlimited Decadence's financial statements. Cash increases by the $10,600 received from John Burgen Inc. Interest revenue increases by the $100 ($10,000 × 0.12 × 1/12) interest earned from holding the note during January, as we show in Exhibit 13-8. Unlimited Decadence reports this interest revenue on its income statement for 2001. Unlimited Decadence decreases the Notes Receivable account and the Interest Receivable account related to John Burgen Inc.'s note by $10,000 and $500, respectively, because the customer no longer owes the principal or the interest recorded in December.

Managing and Reporting Cash and Cash Equivalents

In 1998, cash and cash equivalents averaged about 15% of candy manufacturers' total assets. In Chapter 12, we discussed how a company uses a cash budget to help *plan* its management of cash. Here, we discuss how large companies manage and report cash transactions. Cash management includes three areas: (1) cash receipts management, (2) cash payments management, and (3) cash balance management.

Cash Receipts Management

8 *What are the important characteristics of cash receipts management and cash payments management?*

 Have you ever dashed to the bank to make sure your deposit gets into your bank account in time to cover checks you wrote? Do you ever keep a little extra cash in your checking account to make sure checks don't bounce? Do you think companies ever do these things too? Why or why not?

Whereas receivables management deals with making credit sales to customers and getting customers to pay, cash receipts management deals with processing customers' payments and depositing those payments into the company's bank account. Cash receipts management is important for three reasons. First, a company needs to make sure that it records its customers' payments properly. Has a company ever mishandled your payment? Maybe you sent the check to the company, the company cashed your check, and then the company sent you an overdue notice. Needless to say, the experience doesn't help to build customer loyalty. Second, cash is the most likely type of asset to be stolen. A company should have cash-receipt control policies and activities that reduce the likelihood of theft. Third, a company should process cash receipts efficiently so that the cash is available for use as soon as possible. If it handles cash receipts inefficiently, the company either loses revenue that could be earned from investing the excess cash or incurs interest costs from borrowing needed cash while waiting for the cash receipts to be processed.

In Chapter 9 we discussed controls over cash receipts in an entrepreneurial environment. Some of that discussion also applies to our large-company analysis. Here we restate relevant issues that apply to large companies.

1. *A company should separate the duties of handling cash receipts from the duties of record keeping.* A company should not have the same employees both process the cash received and also record transactions. If an employee is allowed to do both, the employee could steal cash receipts and cover up the theft by making fictitious entries in the accounting records.

2. *A company should compare incoming cash receipts with payment notices.* When a company sends out sales invoices or monthly statements, it usually includes a payment notice. A **payment notice** is the part of the invoice or statement that a customer detaches and mails back to the company with a check. A company should assign employees the responsibility of opening the mail and comparing the customers' checks with the payment notices. This ensures that customers receive credit for the amount of payment and that they have used sales discounts properly. The employees should forward the checks to the company's treasury department, total the payment notices, and forward them to the accounting department. Later, a different employee should compare the dollar total for the payment notices with the accounting records and bank deposits to verify that the other employees have processed and deposited all the receipts.

3. *A company should restrictively endorse incoming cash receipts.* Employees who are responsible for opening the company's mail should stamp the back of each check "for deposit only." This makes it more difficult for anyone to steal the checks because the endorsement makes the checks more difficult to cash.

4. *A company should make deposits daily.* A company should deposit each day's cash receipts on the day that it receives them. Then it will have access to the cash as soon as possible. This also makes it more difficult for an employee to steal (or lose) the cash receipts. Also, the employees should match the daily deposit with the dollar total of the payment notices to verify that all of the receipts were deposited in the bank.

At Unlimited Decadence, six employees open all of the mailed-in cash receipts. They do not have access to any accounting records. Here's what they do on any given day—say,

March 30, 2000. The employees open the mail and compare the payment notices with the customers' checks to make sure that the amounts match and that the customers have taken the proper sales discount. Unfortunately, some customers try to take advantage of the discount even if their payment is late. By inspecting these documents, Unlimited Decadence can monitor the use of sales discounts. The employees stamp "For Deposit Only—Unlimited Decadence" on the back of each check.

Next, working together, the employees total the payment notices and all the checks to see that the totals agree. Both totals are $300,000. One of the employees takes the checks to the treasurer, who makes the daily deposit of these receipts. Another employee takes the payment notices to the accounting department. The employees in the accounting department use the payment notices to record the cash receipts and the reduction of the accounts receivable, as follows:

Assets   **= Liabilities + Stockholders' Equity**

Cash		Accounts Receivable	
300,000			300,000
(+)	(−)	(+)	(−)

Recording Cash Receipts When Sales Discounts Are Given

Now let's discuss how sales discounts change accounting for cash receipts. In Chapter 6, we explained how a company may offer a sales (cash) discount to credit customers to encourage them to pay their accounts receivable within a relatively short period of time, usually 10 to 15 days. Recall that a sales discount is a percentage reduction of the invoice price; the selling company grants this discount in return for the customer's early payment. The sales discount arrangement is shown on the invoice in a standard format such as "2/10, n/30." This means that the selling company grants a 2% discount if the customer pays within 10 days. Otherwise the entire dollar amount of the invoice (referred to as the gross amount) is due within 30 days.

We show how a company handles sales discounts by focusing on one transaction. (In Chapter 14 we will discuss why managers usually should take advantage of the discount.) Assume that Unlimited Decadence offers discount terms of 2/10, n/30 to all its customers and that Pinecrest Candies purchases 400 boxes of chocolates on April 5, 2000 for $4.50 per box. Unlimited Decadence sends a sales invoice to Pinecrest for $1,800 (400 × $4.50). The invoice states that Unlimited Decadence will give a 2% discount to Pinecrest if it receives payment within 10 days.

On April 5, 2000, Unlimited Decadence records this sale as follows:

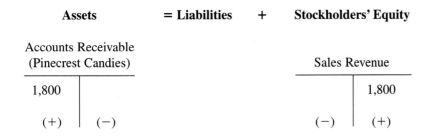

Assets   **= Liabilities**   **+**   **Stockholders' Equity**

Accounts Receivable (Pinecrest Candies)				Sales Revenue	
1,800					1,800
(+)	(−)			(−)	(+)

Now, assume that on April 12, 2000, Unlimited Decadence receives a check from Pinecrest in payment of the account receivable. Because Pinecrest pays within 10 days of the sale, it takes the 2% discount. Pinecrest's check is for $1,764, which reflects the 2% cash discount of $36 ($1,800 × 0.02). Unlimited Decadence records the April 12 cash receipt as follows:

Assets = **Liabilities + Stockholders' Equity**

Cash		Accounts Receivable (Pinecrest Candies)		Sales Discounts Taken	
1,764		Bal 1,800	1,800	36	
		Bal 0			
(+)	(−)	(+)	(−)	(+)	(−)

Note that Unlimited Decadence increases Cash by $1,764, the amount of Pinecrest's check, whereas it decreases Accounts Receivable by $1,800, the original amount of the sale. Unlimited Decadence records the $36 sales discount as an increase on the left side of Sales Discounts Taken, a contra-revenue account similar to Sales Returns and Allowances. It deducts the balances in both accounts from sales to determine net sales on its income statement.

 Why do you think that Unlimited Decadence decreases Accounts Receivable by $1,800 instead of $1,764?

Technology and Cash Receipts Management

Many large companies are reengineering their cash receipts management systems to reduce the costs of handling cash receipts and to speed up the depositing of cash receipts into their bank accounts. They often use two strategies: (1) lockbox systems, and (2) electronic cash-collection procedures.

A **lockbox system** is a cash-collection method in which customers mail their payments to the company's post office box, which is monitored by its bank. Bank employees—not company employees—compare payment notices with customers' checks, total the day's receipts, and deposit the checks. Then they send the payment notices to the company so that it can record the transactions in its accounting system. Companies that have multistate operations use several lockboxes. By using a lockbox system, a company reduces the number of employees it needs to manage cash, and it deposits its cash receipts very quickly. Wells Fargo Bank, for instance, advertises that it processes company lockbox receipts six days a week, works three shifts of employees per day, reports to the company up to four times a day, and picks up mail eight or nine times every working day.

Increasingly, companies are adopting electronic cash-collection procedures. With **electronic cash-collection procedures,** customers make payments by a direct transfer of funds from their bank accounts to the company's bank account. Electronic cash collections are commonly used by a company's EDI (Electronic Data Interchange) partners. The advantages of electronic cash-collection procedures are that there are no mailed-in receipts to open, no checks to process, and no payment notices to match. However, the company, its customers, and the banks for both parties must agree to the electronic collection procedures. Wells Fargo Bank also advertises that it performs electronic transfer services for its banking customers.

Cash Payments Management

Cash payments management deals with the cash disbursements that a company makes to pay accounts payable. (We will discuss accounts payable in Chapter 14, but we discuss cash payments management here to complement the discussion of cash receipts management and cash balance management.) Cash payments management is important for three reasons. First, a company needs to make sure that it pays suppliers the proper amount for the goods or services it received. Second, a company should control when it makes cash payments in order to take advantage of cash discounts, and it should monitor cash balances. Third, a company should manage cash payments to prevent payments for unauthorized purchases.

In Chapter 9 we discussed controls over cash payments in an entrepreneurial environment. Some of that discussion also applies to our large-company analysis. Here we restate relevant issues that apply to large companies.

1. *A company should separate cash payment duties from record-keeping duties.* A company should not have the same employees make cash payments and also record transactions. If someone is allowed to do both, the employee could make payments for personal reasons and cover them up by making fictitious entries in the accounting records.

2. *A company should pay only for approved purchases supported by proper documentation.* Before the company makes a cash payment, an employee should review the documentation provided by employees in the purchasing, receiving, and accounting departments to be sure that the information in these documents supports the payment. In addition, payments should be timed to take advantage of the selling company's sales discounts. The buying company calls these **purchases discounts,** which we will discuss in Chapter 14.

3. *A company should recheck calculations and cancel supporting documents after payment has been made.* Before writing the check, employees should recalculate the supplier's invoice. By verifying the amounts on the invoice, the company reduces the likelihood of paying an incorrect amount. After the company writes a check and mails the payment, an employee should mark "paid" on the source documents used to support the payment and send them to the accounting department. This control helps to prevent credit purchases from being paid more than once. Then the accounting department uses the documentation supporting the checks mailed that day to record the cash payments in the company's accounting system.

At Unlimited Decadence, three employees work in the cash payments area. They do not have access to Unlimited Decadence's accounting system. Every weekday morning, they receive a stack of supporting documents from the employees who work in accounts payable management. These documents are for the accounts payable that the company needs to process, pay, and mail that day.

On March 30, 2000, there are 97 sets of documents to be processed for payment. The employees check each set of documents to be certain that all 97 should be paid, and they recheck each invoice for accuracy. The computer prints all the checks, which are then signed by a manager who is authorized to sign checks and who has verified that the purchases have been approved. The employees then mail the checks to the suppliers. An employee marks the documents "Paid," calculates the total amount of the checks, and gives the documents and the cash payment total to Unlimited Decadence's accounting department. The checks total $113,000, and no cash discounts were available. On March 30, 2000, Unlimited Decadence records the following transaction:

Assets	**=**	**Liabilities**	**+**	**Stockholders' Equity**

Cash		Accounts Payable	
	113,000	113,000	
(+)	(−)	(−)	(+)

Technology and Cash Payments Management

Technology has changed the way many large companies process invoices for payment and make cash payments. An EDI system immediately authorizes the cash payment for goods accepted at a company's receiving dock when an employee completes an electronic receiving report and the supplying company submits an electronic invoice. The company's computer reads the credit terms and invoice prices, determines the day that the cash payment should be made, and releases an electronic payment to the supplier's bank account on the appropriate day.

Although not as sophisticated as EDI, many companies use computer software that automatically controls cash payments. The company enters the supplier's invoice information items (e.g., name, amount, credit terms) into the computer program when it purchases goods. The software calculates the best time for payment, given the credit terms of the purchase, and automatically prints and mails the checks on the most advantageous date. Banks provide controlled cash payment services for companies that do not have the technology available within their systems.

It is becoming more common for companies to "outsource" cash payments management. **Outsourcing** means that a company turns over the management of a function to an outside specialist. Outsourcing reduces a company's fixed personnel costs, makes new technologies such as EDI readily available, and provides additional expertise in the outsourced area. In cash payments management, outsourcing involves giving lists of approved payments to the outsourcing company for cash payment processing.

 Is the use of a lockbox system an example of outsourcing? Why or why not?

Cash Balance Management

9 What are cash balance management and cash equivalents, and what is included under the heading of Cash and Cash Equivalents on a company's balance sheet?

Whereas cash receipts management and cash payments management are concerned with the inflows and outflows of a company's operating cash, cash balance management deals with the daily amount of cash that the company keeps in its bank accounts. On any given day, a company wants to have enough cash in its bank account to cover all the payments that will clear its account on that day, but not so much cash that it forgoes earning interest by not investing any excess cash. The need to meet both of these conflicting demands on cash is what makes cash balance management important.

To accomplish both of these goals, managers need to be informed of the day's expected cash payments and deposits. Only by knowing how much cash will be coming into and going out of the bank account can they effectively manage the cash balance. This means that a company must coordinate the management of its cash receipts, of its cash payments, and of its cash balance.

If you are like most other people, you like to keep a little extra cash in your bank account just in case you miscalculate the amount in your cash balance or the date when checks are going to clear your account. You want to make sure that your checks will be honored for payment. If you make a miscalculation, this "cushion" or "safety provision" will keep your checks from being turned down for payment. In addition, you can use this extra cash if you have an unexpected expenditure. A large company usually keeps a safety provision of cash for the same reasons.

Technology and Cash Balance Management

Two features of banking allow large companies to keep very low levels of excess cash. First, changes in technology have drastically altered how companies manage cash balances. The design of new and innovative interest-earning investments has improved the investment opportunities available to cash balance managers. Large companies routinely take advantage of the money market (i.e., the market for buying and selling very short-term interest-bearing investments) by purchasing cash equivalents. **Cash equivalents** are investments that are short-term, are highly liquid, and involve very little risk. Cash balance managers of large companies manage large sums of cash so precisely that they can purchase cash equivalents for just one day. The cash equivalents are so liquid that companies

Cash Balance Management **447**

can exchange them for cash almost instantly (and earn interest on these investments) and adjust checking account balances very quickly. Communication technology provides a global marketplace for buying and selling cash equivalents.

How do you think a company computes interest for just one day?

Second, computer technology lets many banks allow large clients to monitor their checking account balances continuously. Before continuous monitoring was available, cash balance managers could only make educated guesses about when large checks would clear their bank accounts. Managers without the ability to monitor balances continuously would say: "Well, we mailed the check on Monday, it will take two days to get to the supplier and two more days before it reaches our bank. To play it safe, I'll deposit enough cash to cover the check on Wednesday afternoon." Continuous monitoring takes the guesswork out of planning for large cash withdrawals from the bank accounts. For example, Citibank supplies large customers with Citibanking, a Windows-based software program for cash balance management. Using a computer, a cash balance manager can learn which checks are going to clear the bank account later that day, can make transfers from (to) interest-earning accounts to increase (decrease) the current cash balance appropriately, and can monitor securities that the company purchased previously.

www.citibank.com

Reporting Cash Balances

In addition to checking accounts and cash equivalents, large companies may have petty cash funds, as we discussed in Chapter 9. A company includes the balance of the petty cash account, the reconciled cash balance of the checking account(s), and the cash equivalents as a current asset, Cash and Cash Equivalents, on its balance sheet. Recall that because of the liquidity of this asset, a company lists the total of Cash and Cash Equivalents as the first item of current assets. In Exhibit 13-9, we explain Unlimited Decadence's December 31, 2000 cash balance of $1,020.

Exhibit 13-9 Description of Cash and Cash Equivalents on a Balance Sheet

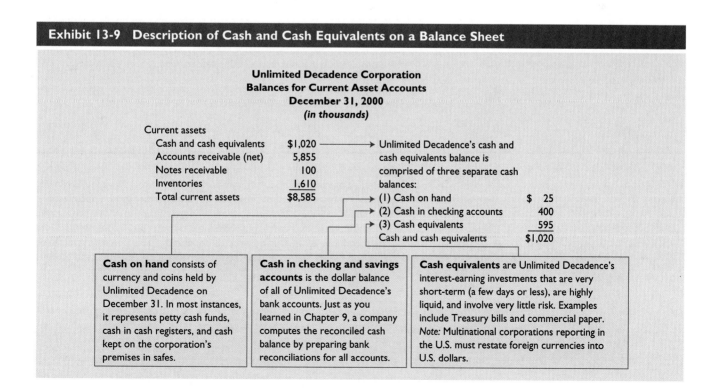

Summary

At the beginning of the chapter we asked you several questions. During the chapter, we asked you to STOP and answer some additional questions to build your knowledge about specific issues. Be sure you answered these additional questions. Below are the questions from the beginning of the chapter, with a brief summary of the key points relating to the answers. Use your creative and critical thinking skills to expand on these key points to develop more complete answers to the questions and to determine what other questions you have that might lead you to learn more about the issues.

1 Why is managing and reporting liquidity important?

Managers and external users are interested in the liquidity of a company's assets because it affects the company's ability to pay its short-term liabilities. They assess a company's liquidity position by comparing the composition and amounts of its short-term assets and its short-term liabilities. From an external user's perspective, it is important to understand the types of economic resources or economic obligations that each balance sheet item represents. From a manager's perspective, it is important to understand how liquidity can be managed to improve company performance.

2 Why might a company offer credit sales, and what management policies should exist for accounts receivable?

A company might offer credit sales because selling on credit may be more convenient than selling for cash, because offering credit may encourage customers to buy items that they might not otherwise purchase, and because allowing customers to pay after receiving the goods signals product quality and a commitment to customers. A company should have policies that cover granting credit, recognizing when a credit sale occurs, monitoring accounts receivable balances, and reporting accounts receivable according to GAAP.

3 How does a company report credit sales and net sales?

A company reports credit sales in the accounting period in which it earns the revenue—usually when it transfers the goods to the customer. A company's net sales for an accounting period equals its total sales minus the sales discounts and sales returns and allowances for that period. A sales discount is a reduction in the amount collected because the customer pays within the discount period. A sales return occurs when a customer returns goods that the company previously recorded as a sale and receives a refund in exchange for the goods. A sales allowance occurs when a company refunds a portion of the sales price after the original sale occurred.

4 How does a company determine the amount of its bad debts expense, and how does it report the related accounts on its financial statements?

A company using the aging method estimates the amount of bad debts expense based on the age of the individual accounts included in the ending balance of its Accounts Receivable. The aging method is generally considered to be better for determining the net accounts receivable that are collectible at the end of the period and is called a "balance sheet approach" for estimating bad debts. A company using the percentage of sales method estimates its bad debts expense by multiplying its net credit sales of the period by the percentage of these sales that it estimates to be uncollectible. The percentage of sales method is called an "income statement approach." Both Allowance for Bad Debts and Bad Debts Expense increase as a result of recording the estimate. A company includes Bad Debts Expense on the income statement as a part of its operating expenses. It subtracts the Allowance for Bad Debts balance from the Accounts Receivable balance, so that the net Accounts Receivable reported on its balance sheet is the net realizable value (the amount of cash it expects to collect).

5 What is an exchange rate, and how does an exchange gain (loss) arise from a credit sale made to a company in another country?

An exchange rate measures the value of one currency in terms of another currency. In this book we always quote exchange rates in terms of the number of U.S. dollars that is equivalent to one unit of the foreign currency. An exchange gain or loss is caused by a change in the exchange rate between the date a company records a credit sales transaction and the date the company collects the cash. More specifically, for credit sales, an exchange gain occurs when the exchange rate increases between the date a company records a receivable and the date the company collects the cash, and an exchange loss occurs when the exchange rate declines between the date a company records a receivable and the date the company collects the cash.

6 How does a company account for cash collected prior to sales?

When a company collects cash from customers before it delivers the goods or provides the services that they purchased, it records a current liability, often called Unearned Revenue. A company records this liability (Unearned Revenue) because it accepts an obligation to provide goods or services in the future as a result of receiving cash now. The company records revenue and reduces Unearned Revenue when it provides the goods or services.

7 What are the important characteristics of a note receivable, and how is interest computed?

The principal or face value of the note is the amount that is stated on the note. The maturity date is the date when the company that made and signed the note (called the maker) promises to pay the principal and interest amounts to the note holder (called the payee). Three factors determine the amount of interest owed to the payee: (1) the face value (principal) of the note; (2) the interest rate stated on the note; and (3) the length of time between the date the note is issued and the maturity date. The equation for computing interest is as follows:

$$\text{Interest} = \begin{array}{c}\text{Principal of} \\ \text{the Note}\end{array} \times \begin{array}{c}\text{Annual Rate} \\ \text{of Interest}\end{array} \times \begin{array}{c}\text{Period of Time the Note} \\ \text{Is Outstanding in Years} \\ \text{or Fraction of a Year}\end{array}$$

The maturity value of the note is the total of the principal plus the interest due on the maturity date.

8 What are the important characteristics of cash receipts management and cash payments management?

For cash receipts management, a company should separate the duties of handling cash receipts from record-keeping duties, compare incoming cash receipts with payment notices, restrictively endorse incoming cash receipts, and make deposits daily. For cash payments management, a company should separate cash payment duties from record-keeping duties, pay only for approved purchases with proper documentation, recheck calculations, and cancel supporting documents after payment has been made.

9 What are cash balance management and cash equivalents, and what is included under the heading of Cash and Cash Equivalents on a company's balance sheet?

Cash balance management involves having enough cash in the bank to cover all payments that will clear the company's account that day, but not so much cash that the company foregoes interest by not investing excess cash. A company invests excess cash in cash equivalents, which are investments that are short-term, are highly liquid, and involve very little risk. A company includes the balance of the petty cash account, the reconciled cash balance of the checking account(s), and the cash equivalents as a current asset, Cash and Cash Equivalents, on its balance sheet.

Key Terms

accounts payable management *(p. 418)*
accounts receivable management *(p. 418)*
accounts receivable subsidiary ledger
   (p. 420)
aging method *(p. 430)*
bad debts expense *(p. 426)*
cash balance management *(p. 418)*
cash equivalents *(p. 446)*
cash payments management *(p. 418)*
cash receipts management *(p. 418)*
control account *(p. 420)*
contra account *(p. 425)*

electronic cash-collection procedures
   (p. 444)
exchange gain or loss *(p. 434)*
exchange rate *(p. 433)*
export insurance *(p. 423)*
letter of credit *(p. 423)*
liquidity *(p. 415)*
liquidity management *(p. 415)*
lockbox system *(p. 444)*
maker *(p. 438)*
maturity date *(p. 438)*
maturity value of the note *(p. 438)*

net sales *(p. 424)*　　　　　　purchases discounts *(p. 445)*
note *(p. 419)*　　　　　　　　reengineering *(p. 438)*
note receivable *(p. 419)*　　　sales allowance *(p. 424)*
outsourcing *(p. 446)*　　　　　sales discount *(p. 424)*
payee *(p. 438)*　　　　　　　sales order *(p. 421)*
payment notice *(p. 442)*　　　sales return *(p. 424)*
percentage of sales method *(p. 431)*　unearned revenue *(p. 436)*
principal (face value) *(p. 438)*

SUMMARY SURFING

Here is an opportunity to gather information on the Internet about real-world issues related to the topics in this chapter. Go to http://www.dryden.com/account and click on the Cunningham, Nikolai, and Bazley book cover. Click on Summary Surfing, then click on this chapter number, and answer the following questions.

▶ Click on **Delta Air Lines.** Find the amount of the "air traffic liability" on its most recent balance sheet. How does this amount compare with the 1998 amount discussed in the chapter, and what does it tell you about the airline's performance?

▶ Click on **Yahoo!,** then click on *Business and Economy,* then *Finance and Investment,* then *Currency,* and then *Quotes.* Has the dollar strengthened or weakened since January 29, 1999 against each of the currencies listed both on your screen and in Exhibit 13-5?

Integrated Business and Accounting Situations

Answer the Following Questions in Your Own Words

Testing Your Knowledge

13-1　What is liquidity management, and why do users need to understand liquidity?
13-2　What does a user need to know to evaluate an account balance?
13-3　Identify the five areas of liquidity management.
13-4　Why do companies make credit sales to customers?
13-5　What is an accounts receivable subsidiary ledger, and how does it relate to the Accounts Receivable control account?
13-6　What are the basic management policies over accounts receivable for large companies?
13-7　Identify three additional controls used by large companies in granting credit.
13-8　Explain the difference between a sales discount, a sales return, and a sales allowance.
13-9　What is bad debts expense, and when is it measured and reported?
13-10　How does the reporting of bad debts affect a company's financial statements?
13-11　How does a company record the write-off of an uncollectible account, and how does the write-off affect the net accounts receivable?
13-12　Briefly explain how large companies are reengineering their liquidity management activities.
13-13　What are the two methods of calculating the bad debts expense and the allowance for bad debts?
13-14　Briefly explain how a company estimates bad debts expense using the aging method.

13-15   Briefly explain how a company estimates bad debts expense using the percentage of sales method.

13-16   Explain the meaning of (a) an exchange rate, and (b) an exchange gain and an exchange loss in regard to credit sales.

13-17   What is unearned revenue? Give an example (other than those in the chapter).

13-18   Why might a company require a customer to sign a note receivable for a credit sale?

13-19   Briefly explain how to record the receipt of a note receivable, the related accrued interest, and the payment of the note by the customer.

13-20   Identify four controls over cash receipts for large companies.

13-21   Briefly explain how a sales discount taken is recorded and reported.

13-22   Identify three controls over cash payments for large companies.

13-23   Define *cash equivalents,* and explain why a company would have them.

13-24   Identify what is included in Cash and Cash Equivalents reported on a company's balance sheet.

Applying Your Knowledge

13-25   Garcia Company has always required its customers to pay cash for purchases. It is considering making credit sales and has come to you for advice on this issue. You determine that Garcia has made sales of $800,000 each year for the past several years, on which it has earned a gross profit of 40%. Basing your calculations on industry information, you estimate that Garcia's sales will increase by 15% if it makes credit sales. However, bad debts are likely to be about 2% of credit sales, and additional variable selling expenses will be about 5% of credit sales. In addition, the cost of operating the credit department is estimated to be $30,000.

   Required: (1) Prepare a schedule to determine whether Garcia's profit will increase if it makes credit sales.
             (2) What other issues regarding profitability should Garcia consider before deciding whether to make credit sales?

13-26   Miatarus Company had gross sales for the current year of $920,000. Of these sales, 60% were credit sales with terms of 2/10, n/30. Customers took the sales (cash) discount on 90% of their credit purchases. Sales returns were $25,000, and sales allowances were $9,800.

   Required: (1) Compute the company's net sales for the current year.
             (2) Why is it important for users to know a company's gross sales and net sales?

13-27   On April 6, Softwinds Fans Corporation sold inventory costing $3,000 to Tail Company at a selling price of $5,820. On April 8, Tail returned inventory with a selling price of $760 (cost of $400) purchased on April 6 because the inventory did not match what was ordered. Softwinds uses a perpetual inventory system.

   Required: (1) Assuming that the inventory was sold for cash, prepare T-account entries for Softwinds to record the preceding transactions.
             (2) Assuming instead that the inventory was sold on credit, prepare T-account entries to record the preceding transactions.

13-28   On October 4, Shearson Woodworks sold $15,000 of merchandise on account to Lin Furniture Mart, with terms of 3/10, n/30. Shearson uses the perpetual inventory system; the cost of the inventory sold was $9,000.

   Required: (1) Assume that Lin pays for the purchase on October 12. Prepare T-account entries for Shearson to record the sale and collection.
             (2) Assume that Lin pays for the purchase on October 30. Prepare T-account entries for Shearson to record the sale and collection.

13-29   Your friend Jacob Thomon applied for a summer internship with McClellan Industries. McClellan set up its internship program for college freshmen two years ago. The program is designed to provide outstanding students who are in their early years of college with some hands-on business experience. McClellan hopes that the students' experiences will encourage them to pursue some type of business major in college.

         After submitting his application, Jacob received a letter from McClellan Industries. The letter stated that this summer's remaining internship opening is in its accounting department. It specifically mentioned that the intern will spend the summer helping reengineer the company's accounts receivable controls and policies. Jacob knows that you are taking this accounting course. He comes over to your place for some advice. He asks several questions:

(1) "What the heck is reengineering?"

(2) "What is the letter from McClellan talking about when it says 'accounts receivable controls and policies'?" "What are some of these controls and policies?"

(3) "How can accounts receivable controls and policies be reengineered?"

Required: Prepare a written response to each of Jacob's questions.

13-30 At the end of 2000, before the bad debts end-of-period adjustment, Satterly Corporation had an accounts receivable balance of $129,000 and an allowance for bad debts balance of $400. Using an aging analysis, Satterly estimated that its allowance account should have a balance of $9,000 at the end of 2000. On January 2, 2001, Satterly determined that a $1,500 account receivable was not collectible, so it wrote off the customer's account.

Required: (1) Using T-accounts, record the bad debts adjusting entry at the end of 2000.

(2) Show how the net accounts receivable would be reported on Satterly's December 31, 2000 balance sheet.

(3) Using T-accounts, record the write-off of the account receivable on January 2, 2001.

(4) Assuming no accounts receivable were collected in early January, show the net accounts receivable at the end of the day on January 2, 2001.

(5) Explain the difference between your answers to (2) and (4).

13-31 On December 31, Taylor Corporation has an accounts receivable balance of $180,000 and an Allowance for Bad Debts balance of $150. In analyzing its individual accounts receivable, Taylor determines that accounts receivable of $100,000 are not yet past due, $50,000 are between 1 and 60 days past due, $20,000 are between 61 and 120 days past due, and $10,000 are over 120 days past due. Based on past experience, Taylor estimates that it will not collect $\frac{1}{4}$ percent of accounts not yet due, 1 percent of accounts between 1 and 60 days past due, 3 percent of accounts between 61 and 120 days past due, and 10 percent of accounts over 120 days past due.

Required: (1) Prepare an aging analysis to determine the amount of Taylor Corporation's estimated uncollectible accounts at the end of the year.

(2) Using T-accounts, prepare the year-end bad debts adjustment.

(3) Show how Taylor would report its net accounts receivable on its December 31 balance sheet.

13-32 Andrews Corporation uses the aging method for its uncollectible accounts. At the end of the year, its accounts receivable were categorized as follows:

Age Group	Amount	Estimated Percentage Uncollectible
Not yet past due	$ 80,000	$\frac{1}{2}$ %
1-30 days past due	45,000	1
31-60 days past due	20,000	2
61-90 days past due	12,000	4
>90 days past due	8,000	7
	$165,000	

Before Andrews recorded the bad debts expense end-of-period adjustment, the balance in Allowance for Bad Debts was $200.

Required: (1) Calculate the amount of Andrews' estimated uncollectible accounts at the end of the year.

(2) Using T-accounts, prepare the bad debts end-of-period adjustment.

(3) Show how the net accounts receivable would be reported in Andrews' balance sheet at the end of the year.

(4) Discuss the effect on Andrews' year-end financial statements if the end-of-period adjustment had not been made in (2). Ignore income taxes.

13-33 The Redford Optical Supplies Corporation uses the percentage of sales method for estimating its bad debts expense. In 2000 the corporation sold on credit $350,000 of glasses and lenses and had sales returns and allowances for credit sales of $20,000. In past years, approximately 1 percent of net credit sales have been uncollectible. At the end of Redford's fiscal year, before the bad debts expense end-of-period adjustment is made, the accounts receivable balance was $75,000 and the allowance for bad debts balance was $300.

Required: (1) Compute the dollar amount of bad debts expense that Redford should include on its 2000 income statement.
(2) Prepare the bad debts end-of-period adjustment using T-accounts.
(3) Show how the net accounts receivable would be reported on Redford's balance sheet at the end of 2000.
(4) Discuss the effect on Redford's 2000 financial statements if the end-of-period adjustment had not been made in (2). Ignore income taxes.

13-34 Use the same facts for Redford Optical Supplies Corporation in 13-33, but assume Redford uses the aging method for calculating bad debts expense and the allowance for bad debts. In using the aging method, Redford has found that 2 percent of accounts receivable that are not yet past due at the end of any particular year are never collected and 5 percent of accounts receivable that are overdue at year-end are never collected. Of the accounts receivable balance at the end of 2000, 40% are not yet past due.

Required: (1) Compute the dollar amount of bad debts expense that Redford should include on its 2000 income statement.
(2) Show how the net accounts receivable would be reported on Redford's balance sheet at the end of 2000.

13-35 On June 20, 2000, Livingstone Company, a U.S. company, sold merchandise on credit to Schloss Company, a Swiss company, for 25,000 francs. The Livingstone Company received payment for the merchandise on July 10, 2000. The exchange rates on June 20 and July 10 were $0.70 and $0.67, respectively.

Required: (1) Prepare T-account entries for Livingstone to record the sale and collection.
(2) Prepare the July 10 T-account entry for Livingstone to record the collection if, instead, the exchange rate was $0.72 on this date.

13-36 On November 1, 2000, Lindner Corporation received $7,200 from Slater Insurance Agency in advance for six months of rent on office space.

Required: (1) Using T-accounts, record the receipt of the rent by Lindner.
(2) Using T-accounts, record Lindner's end-of-period adjustment.

13-37 Boston Publishing Company publishes a hobby magazine titled *Crocheting Today* every month. The company sells annual subscriptions for $48. On March 1, 2000, the company received payment for 1,000 subscriptions for this monthly magazine. On March 1, 2001, the company received payment for 600 annual renewals and 800 new subscriptions for this magazine. On July 2, 2001, the company received payment for another 300 subscriptions to the magazine.

Required: (1) Compute the amount of cash the company received from these subscriptions during (a) 2000 and (b) 2001.
(2) Compute the amount of revenue the company recorded from these subscriptions in (a) 2000 and (b) 2001.
(3) Explain why the cash the company received from these subscriptions during 2000 and 2001 was not recorded as revenue at the time the cash was received.
(4) Compute the amount of the liability the company owed to these subscribers at the end of (a) 2000 and (b) 2001. Explain why these amounts were current liabilities for the company.

13-38 The Nicholson Paving Corporation had the following short-term notes receivable outstanding during 2000:

Amount	Date Issued	Date Due	Interest Rate
$ 6,000	January 1, 2000	March 1, 2000	10%
8,000	May 1, 2000	November 1, 2000	12%
10,000	October 2, 2000	April 2, 2001	9%

Nicholson collects all the interest on each note on the maturity date.

Required: (1) Compute the interest revenue earned by The Nicholson Paving Corporation during 2000. For simplicity, compute interest based on the number of months that each note was outstanding.

(2) What adjusting entry (if any) does Nicholson need to make at the end of 2000?

13-39 Summertime Equipment Corporation's fiscal year ends on December 31. It has the following short-term notes receivable outstanding during 2000:

Amount	Date Issued	Life of Note	Interest Rate
$3,000	February 1	3 months	9%
5,000	September 1	6 months	10%
2,000	December 1	9 months	12%

Summertime collects all the interest on each note on the maturity date.

Required: (1) Compute the interest revenue (to the nearest month) that Summertime will report for these notes on its 2000 income statement.

(2) Compute the amount of interest receivable that Summertime will report for these notes on its 2000 ending balance sheet.

(3) Compute the interest revenue that Summertime will report for these notes on its 2001 income statement.

13-40 On April 1, 2000, O'Neill Farm Equipment Company sold a tractor to Klemme Farms for $60,000 and agreed to delay collection of the selling price until six months later (after the harvest). Klemme Farms issued a note that was dated April 1, 2000, and that had an interest rate of 10%. The tractor cost O'Neill $45,000, and it uses a perpetual inventory system. The note was paid on schedule.

Required: (1) Fill in the following blanks:

(a) The maker of the note is _____.

(b) The payee of the note is _____.

(c) The date the note was signed is _____.

(d) The face value of the note is _____.

(e) The maturity date of the note is _____.

(f) The annual interest rate on the note is _____.

(g) The length of time between the date the note is issued and the maturity date is _____.

(h) The amount of interest due on the maturity date is

_____.

(i) The maturity value of the note is _____.

(2) Using T-accounts, show how the April 1 transaction was recorded by O'Neill.

(3) Using T-accounts, show how the collection of the note receivable was recorded by O'Neill.

13-41 Farrell Corporation is preparing its ending 2000 balance sheet. In its accounting records, it has a reconciled cash balance of $47,200, petty cash of $2,700, cash equivalents of $9,300, and marketable securities of $14,000.

Required: Compute the amount that Farrell should report as Cash and Cash Equivalents on the balance sheet.

Making Evaluations

13-42 A friend of yours who owns a retail store is considering expanding her business by selling on credit to other small businesses. Knowing that you are in an accounting class, she asks for your advice.

Required: Write your friend a short report explaining the advantages and disadvantages of offering credit sales. Then write a "memo for the file" outlining how you would use your knowledge of break-even analysis to analyze the decision after you estimated the necessary information.

13-43 The Midler Boutique has significantly expanded its sales in recent years by offering a liberal credit policy. As a result, bad debt losses have also increased. The owner has prepared the following summarized income statements:

	1997	1998	1999	2000
Sales on credit	$32,000	$50,000	$70,000	$90,000
Cost of goods sold	(12,000)	(19,000)	(26,000)	(33,000)
Bad debt expense	(1,302)	(2,250)	(3,260)	(4,320)
Other expenses	(10,000)	(12,000)	(14,000)	(16,000)
Net Income	$ 8,698	$16,750	$26,740	$36,680
Accounts written off	$ 200	$ 1,000	$ 1,600	$ 2,000

The company uses the percentage of sales method to calculate its bad debts expense. The accounts written off each year relate to credit sales made in the previous year.

Required: Prepare for Ms. Midler a report that explains the trend in bad debts as compared with other items on the income statement. Does it appear that the liberal credit policy is successful? What do you think the bad debts expense for 2001 should be if credit sales were $120,000 that year?

13-44 Three years ago, Trevor and Jill Davey formed a company called The Bicycle Boutique. Sales have slowly increased each year, and the reputation of the company in the community has steadily improved. However, because of limited resources, the company has made only cash sales. With the increase in the prices for modern sophisticated bikes, the Daveys have decided that it would be desirable to offer credit card sales and to sell on credit.

Sales for the last three years have been $100,000, $140,000, and $190,000, respectively. The gross profit has consistently been 40% of sales. The Daveys believe that sales would increase by 50% next year if the "cash only" sales policy is not changed but would double under the new policy. They expect only 30% of the sales to be cash sales, with the remaining sales to be equally split between credit card sales and credit sales. The credit card receipts will be deposited immediately in a local bank. The fee on credit card sales will be 4%. It is expected that credit sales will be made evenly throughout the year, will be collected on average after two months, and that 2% will not be collectible.

To implement the new policy regarding credit sales, the company has applied for a bank loan of $150,000, to be paid back in one year. The bank will charge interest of 12% and has asked for certain financial information.

Required: (1) Prepare a schedule that shows the cash receipts expected for the next year under the old policy and under the new policy.
(2) Should the company prefer credit card sales or credit sales?
(3) Should the company implement the new policy?

13-45 Your friend has operated a business for two years and has made many sales on credit. His accountant has told him that he must estimate the amounts that will be uncollectible in the future to include in this year's financial statements. Your friend is upset because he does not want "guesses" appearing in the financial statements and because he knows that accounting information should be reliable and accurate. Since he knows that you are currently studying accounting, he buys you dinner and before picking up the check asks you for your opinion.

Required: How would you answer your friend? Explain why the accountant is suggesting that an estimate of uncollectible accounts be included in this year's financial statements and why your friend's concerns are not critical.

13-46 In the chapter, we listed the policies of **IBM, Amdahl,** and **Xerox** for recording revenue.

Required: Explain how IBM could justify recording revenue when it ships computers to a warehouse. Explain why Amdahl uses a different policy. Explain why Xerox uses two policies. Which policies do you support?

www.ibm.com
www.amdahl.com
www.xerox.com

www.circuscircus.com
www.themirage.com

13-47 According to their annual reports, <u>Circus Circus</u> and <u>Mirage Resorts,</u> operators of casinos in Las Vegas, use the following policies:

Circus Circus

Year ended January 31 (in thousands)	1998	1997	1996
Revenues	$1,419,734	$1,393,727	$1,348,983
Less: Complimentary allowances	(65,247)	(59,477)	(49,387)
	$1,354,487	$1,334,250	$1,299,596

Revenues include the retail value of rooms, food and beverage furnished gratuitously to customers. Such amounts are then deducted as complimentary allowances. The cost of such rooms, food and beverage were included as casino expenses as follows: $45.9 million, $37.9 million, and $34.5 million, for the fiscal years ended January 31, 1998, 1997, and 1996 respectively. For the three years, approximately 85%-90% of such costs were for food and beverage with the balance for rooms. Casino revenues are the net differences between the sums received as winnings and the sums paid as losses.

Mirage Resorts

The company recognizes as casino revenues the net win from gaming activities, which is the difference between gaming wins and losses. Revenues include the estimated retail value of rooms, food and beverage and other goods and services provided to customers on a complimentary basis as follows:

Year ended December 31 (in thousands)	1997	1996	1995
Rooms	$ 55,153	$ 55,125	$ 52,592
Food and Beverage	64,575	66,424	63,664
Other	7,770	7,264	6,716
	$127,498	$128,813	$122,972

After being included in gross revenues, such amounts are then deducted as promotional allowances. The estimated cost of providing these promotional allowances totaling $90.2 million in 1997, $88.3 million in 1996, and $87.2 million in 1995, have been classified primarily as casino costs and expenses.

Required: Do the two companies use the same accounting policies? Explain whether you agree with the policies. Explain which disclosure you prefer.

www.kodak.com

13-48 In its 1997 annual report, <u>Eastman Kodak Company</u> reported the following information relating to accounts receivable (amounts in millions of dollars):

	December 31	
Receivables (in millions)	1997	1996
Trade receivables	$1,930	$2,340
Miscellaneous receivables	341	398
Total (net of allowances of $112 and $90)	$2,271	$2,738

The company sells to customers in a variety of industries, markets, and geographies around the world. Adequate provisions have been recorded for uncollectible receivables. There are no significant concentrations of credit risk.

Required: (1) How can you determine if the December 31, 1997 allowance for bad debts is reasonable? (*Hint:* No calculations are required.)

(2) Sales in 1997 were $14,538 million. Assume that all sales were made on credit and that the bad debts expense for 1997 was $95 million. Compute the amount of bad debts written off in 1997 and the cash collected from sales in 1997.

13-49 In its recent annual report, <u>May Department Stores</u> disclosed the following: "During 1997, credit sales under department store credit programs were $5.8 billion, or 45.6% of 1997 revenues; this compares with 50% in 1996 and 54.5% in 1995. Sales made through third-party credit cards totaled $3.6 billion in 1997, compared with $3.0 billion in 1996 and $2.4 billion in 1995."

www.maycompany.com

Net accounts receivable consisted of (in millions):

	Jan. 31, 1998	Feb. 1, 1997
Customer accounts receivable	$2,167	$2,410
Other accounts receivable	93	119
Total accounts receivable	$2,260	$2,529
Allowance for uncollectible accounts	(96)	(104)
Accounts receivable, net	$2,164	$2,425

May's net retail sales in 1997, 1996, and 1995 were $12,352 million, $11,546 million, and $10,402 million, respectively.

Required: Evaluate (1) May Department Stores' sales performance and (2) its credit-granting performance.

13-50 Your friend works part-time at a local company. He is concerned about some of the practices he has observed and asks for your advice. "I was surprised to see the sales manager agree to open a new credit account over the phone. When I asked him about that, he said: 'We have been trying to get that account for years. I couldn't keep them waiting.' Then when I was working in the warehouse, the employees would sometimes accept returns from customers' trucks. They just wrote a note on the customer's invoice. Then I was talking to the bookkeeper about uncollectible accounts, and she said: 'Handling a bad debt is easy. I just press the delete button on my computer.' She also told me she hates the new year because that is when the company president makes her write off all the receivables. He never wants to do them at the end of the year because he says they will affect that year's performance. She also said that it upsets her to think of all the previous year's sales that are now not going to be paid for.'"

Required: Write a short report outlining the advantages and disadvantages of the activities your friend observed. For each situation, explain what policy you would recommend.

13-51 In its December 31, 1997 balance sheet, <u>UAL</u> (which owns United Airlines) reported the following amounts (in millions), respectively:

www.ual.com

	1997	1996
Current assets	$2,948	$2,682
Aircraft fuel, spare parts and supplies	355	369
Current liabilities	5,248	5,003
Advance ticket sales	1,267	1,189

Required: Using ratio analysis, explain whether or not United Airlines' liquidity position improved from December 31, 1996 to December 31, 1997. Explain which single measure of the company's liquidity you would prefer to use.

13-52 Yesterday, you received the letter shown on the following page for your advice column in the local paper:

My brother and I are having a fight over bad debts. I think he owes me $10, and he disagrees. But seriously, he is an engineer, and you know how they like all their numbers to be precise. The other day I showed him a newspaper report in which a bank president was saying that the bank had some bad real estate loans and so would have a large bad debt expense this year and for the next couple of years. My brother said that the bank president's statement was crazy and that the bank should wait until the loans were written off before recording them as an expense. I was trying to tell him that the bank should record them all as expenses now. But whoever is right, we both disagree with the bank president.

Call me "Confused Again."

Required: Meet with your Dr. Decisive team and write a response to "Confused Again."

CHAPTER 14

EXPENSES AND CASH PAYMENTS

"Ready money is Aladdin's lamp."

—George Gordon Noel Byron

1 Why does a large company make purchases on credit, and how should it manage and record accounts payable?

2 How does an exchange gain (loss) arise from a credit purchase made from a company in another country?

3 What are accrued liabilities, and what types does a company often have?

4 What types of taxes do an employee and a company incur, and how does the company record them?

5 How is accounting for a short-term note payable similar to accounting for a short-term note receivable?

6 What are prepaid items, and how does a company account for them?

7 What are loss contingencies, and how does a company report or disclose them?

8 What can external users learn from analyzing a company's liquidity?

If you had an inventory of Hershey's Hugs at home or in your dorm room or apartment, how many times a year do you think you would "turn over" your inventory?

www.herseys.com

www.rmcfusa.com

Hershey Foods' (maker of "Hugs") December 31, 1997 balance sheet listed $796 million of current liabilities—24 percent of its total assets. If one piece of Hershey's candy sells for an average of five cents, these current liability account balances held the dollar equivalent of over 15.9 billion pieces! On February 28, 1998, Rocky Mountain Chocolate Factory's balance sheet total for current liabilities was $3.5 million. Given that its total assets were about $19.9 million, Rocky Mountain's current liabilities were equal to 17.6 percent of its total assets. These dollar amounts of current liabilities shown on Hershey Foods' and Rocky Mountain's balance sheets resulted from prior management decisions as well as from the accounting methods used to keep track of the various categories.

 Hershey Foods' $796 million in current liabilities is over 227 times greater than Rocky Mountain's $3.5 million. Can you conclude that Hershey is in a much worse financial situation than Rocky Mountain? Why or why not? What factors should you consider besides the amounts on the balance sheets of the two companies?

As we discussed in Chapter 13, managers and external users assess a company's liquidity position by comparing the composition and amounts of the company's current assets *and* its current liabilities. If you have information only about a company's current assets, you cannot properly assess liquidity.

In this chapter, we continue our discussion of the balance sheet items that affect a company's liquidity position. In Chapter 13 we provided an analysis of the management and reporting of three current assets—cash, accounts receivable, and notes receivable—and a current liability, unearned revenue. All these items relate to the reporting of revenue. In this chapter we describe and analyze how a company manages and reports its current liabilities and one current asset, all of which relate to the reporting of expenses.

We organize the chapter as follows. First, we discuss the management and reporting of accounts payable. We explain how companies manage purchases on credit and accounts payable, including purchases discounts, and how they report accounts payable in the balance sheet. Second, we discuss additional types of current liabilities. These other liabilities are an important aspect of a company's liquidity. For example, although Hershey Foods reported in its December 31, 1997 balance sheet that it owed $796 million in current liabilities, 82 percent of these liabilities were *not* accounts payable. Third, we discuss prepaid items, an asset that relates to payments of expenses. Finally, we discuss how to evaluate a company's liquidity position using information from Chapter 13 and this chapter.

Managing and Recording Accounts Payable

Recall from Chapter 9 that accounts payable are the amounts owed by a company to its suppliers for previous credit purchases of inventory and supplies. A large company makes purchases on credit for many of the same reasons that a small company does: (1) purchasing on credit is often more convenient than purchasing with cash, (2) purchasing on credit delays paying for purchases and, by doing so, results in a short-term "loan" from the supplier, and (3) purchasing on credit gives the company an opportunity to assess the quality of the item before making the cash payment. At December 31, 2000, Unlimited Decadence owes $1,450,000 in accounts payable, as we showed in Exhibit 13-1.

Accounts payable management involves establishing procedures, policies, and activities that govern credit purchases. One procedure that a large company will use to help manage its accounts payable is to create an accounts payable subsidiary ledger. An **accounts payable subsidiary ledger,** which contains the individual accounts of all the suppliers that sell to the company on credit, works the same way as an accounts receivable subsidiary ledger (discussed in Chapter 13). Whenever the company purchases on credit or pays a supplier, it records the transaction in the individual supplier's account in the subsidiary ledger. In this way, the company keeps up-to-date records of its transactions with its suppliers. As we will discuss later, this is important so that the company can monitor its purchases discounts, returns, and allowances. The company also keeps an Accounts Payable **control account** in the general ledger to control the individual supplier accounts in the subsidiary ledger and to help the company monitor its existing total Accounts Payable balance. The balance of the Accounts Payable control account must always be equal to the total of the accounts payable subsidiary ledger on each balance sheet date. Thus, when a company records an accounts payable transaction in the individual subsidiary ledger account, it must also record the transaction in the control account. Before the company issues its financial statements, it prepares a schedule of the individual supplier account balances to prove the equality of the Accounts Payable control account and the subsidiary ledger.

In general, companies should establish the following policies over credit purchases:

1. *A company should separate purchasing duties from record-keeping duties and/or from control of the asset.* Separating these duties helps prevent one employee from making a purchase through the company and stealing the purchased goods for personal use. For example, say that one employee is in charge of processing the accounting records for a company's computer purchases *and* also has the authority to order its equipment. In this situation, the employee could order a notebook computer to be delivered to his or her office, process the purchase for the company to make the payment, take the computer home, and then later remove the computer from the company's accounting records.

2. *A company should restrict the ability of employees to obligate the company to pay for credit purchases.* A company should set up a purchasing department to control the purchasing process. This department should investigate potential suppliers and identify the best prices and payment terms for goods that meet the company's quality standards. Restricting purchases to employees in the purchasing department should prevent other employees from making unnecessary or costly credit purchases.

3. *A company should authorize cash payments only for goods that have been received and properly documented.* Because a company should separate the duties related to purchasing, record keeping, and control of assets, it needs some type

1 *Why does a large company make purchases on credit, and how should it manage and record accounts payable?*

of documentation to ensure that it doesn't make cash payments for goods that it didn't order or didn't receive. A company should authorize cash payments only if the purchase order and the receiving report match the supplier's invoice—that is, only if the supplier's invoice reflects what the company received from the supplier and what the company ordered. If the receiving report indicates a problem with purchased goods and the company keeps the goods anyway (e.g., the goods have minor damage), the accounts payable department should ask the supplier for a reduction in the sales price (known as a purchases allowance).

4. *A company should require the submission of accounts payable documents to the cash payments department in a timely manner to take advantage of purchases discounts.* Recall from Chapter 13 that a selling company often offers sales discounts to customers if they pay by a certain date. The company buying the goods refers to this as a purchases discount. Accounts payable department employees should analyze the potential savings from taking purchases discounts and, when beneficial, notify cash payments personnel that they should make a timely payment.

Here's an example. Suppose that on July 3, 2000, Unlimited Decadence is running low on cocoa. The employee who monitors cocoa for the company contacts the purchasing department and requests that more cocoa be purchased (in Chapter 15, we will discuss how much a company should buy). The purchasing department checks the purchases budget to see if this seems like a reasonable and expected request. If so, an employee in the purchasing department checks current prices for cocoa and completes a purchase order, which is approved by a supervisor. The **purchase order** documents the details of a purchase (e.g., item number, quantity, price) and provides a written record of the purchase approval. The purchasing department sends a copy of the approved purchase order to Unlimited Decadence's cocoa supplier, Cool Cocoa Inc. So, Unlimited Decadence has now completed its order for, say, $35,000 of cocoa.

Cool Cocoa ships the cocoa to Unlimited Decadence and mails it an invoice. When the cocoa arrives at Unlimited Decadence's receiving dock on July 24, 2000, the employees check the goods against a copy of the purchase order to see that the correct goods arrived. If the goods match the purchase order, the employees accept delivery of the goods and complete a form called a receiving report. The **receiving report** documents the type, quantity, and condition of goods received by the company.

Employees in the accounting department match the July 3, 2000 purchase order with the corresponding receiving report and the invoice from the supplier. If all the information on each document is consistent, since Unlimited Decadence uses a perpetual inventory system and an accounts payable subsidiary ledger, it records the transaction as follows:

Assets	**=**	**Liabilities**	**+**	**Stockholders' Equity**
Raw Materials Inventory		Accounts Payable (Cool Cocoa, Inc.)		
35,000			35,000	
(+) | (−)		(−) | (+)		

Purchases Discounts

A **purchases discount** (also called a *cash discount*) is a reduction in the invoice price because the purchaser pays within the discount period. In Chapter 13, we explained how a company may offer a sales (cash) discount to credit customers to encourage them to pay their accounts receivable within a relatively short period of time, usually 10 to 15 days.

Recall that a sales discount is a percentage reduction of the invoice price that the selling company grants in return for the customer's early payment. The sales discount is shown on the invoice in a standard format such as "2/10, n/30." This means that the selling company grants a 2% discount if the customer pays within 10 days. Otherwise the entire dollar amount of the invoice (referred to as the gross amount) is due within 30 days.

 Explain whether, as a manager, you would be more interested to know the amount of the purchases discounts taken or the amount of the available discounts that the company did not take.

Now we discuss how a company handles purchases discounts. Again we focus on the transaction in which Unlimited Decadence purchases cocoa at a cost of $35,000. Assume that Cool Cocoa offers discount terms of 2/10, n/30. On July 24, 2000, Unlimited Decadence receives the cocoa. It has two alternate methods to use to record the purchase—the gross method and the net method.

Recording Purchases Using the Gross Method

If Unlimited Decadence uses the gross method, it records the purchase of the cocoa on July 24, 2000, at the total invoice price of $35,000, as we illustrated earlier. The purchasing department employees forward the purchase documents to the cash payments department so that the company can make the payment within the discount period.

Assume that on July 31, 2000, Unlimited Decadence pays for the cocoa by mailing a check. Because it pays within 10 days of the purchase, it takes the 2% discount. Its check is for $34,300, the $35,000 invoice price less the $700 (2% × $35,000) discount. Unlimited Decadence records the cash payment as follows:

Assets				=	Liabilities	+	Stockholders' Equity
Cash		Raw Materials Inventory			Accounts Payable (Cool Cocoa Inc.)		
		Bal 35,000			Bal 35,000		
	34,300		700	35,000			
		Bal 34,300			Bal 0		
(+)	(−)	(+)	(−)	(−)	(+)		

Cash decreases by $34,300, the amount of the check, whereas Accounts Payable decreases by $35,000, the original amount of the purchase. Even though Unlimited Decadence paid only $34,300, it reduces Accounts Payable by $35,000 because it has satisfied its entire obligation to Cool Cocoa. Unlimited Decadence records the $700 purchases discount as a decrease in the Raw Materials Inventory account because inventory should be recorded at the acquisition cost—in this case, $34,300. It reports any balance in the Accounts Payable account at the end of the accounting period as a current liability on the year-end balance sheet.

Alternatively, if Unlimited Decadence does *not* pay within the 10-day discount period, when it does pay it simply reduces both Cash and Accounts Payable by $35,000.

 Do you think a company could treat the amount of purchases discounts it takes as an increase in income? Why or why not?

Recording Purchases Using the Net Method

If Unlimited Decadence uses the net method, it records the purchase of the cocoa at the total invoice price less the discount (that is, the net price), or $34,300, as follows:

Assets	=	Liabilities	+	Stockholders' Equity

Raw Materials Inventory		Accounts Payable (Cool Cocoa, Inc.)	
34,300			34,300
(+)	(−)	(−)	(+)

Now on July 31, 2000, when Unlimited Decadence pays for the cocoa by mailing a check, it takes the 2% discount and only pays $34,300, which it records as follows:

Assets	=	Liabilities	+	Stockholders' Equity

Cash		Accounts Payable (Cool Cocoa, Inc.)	
	34,300	34,300	Bal 34,300
			Bal 0
(+)	(−)	(−)	(+)

Alternatively, if Unlimited Decadence does not pay within the 10-day discount period, it must pay $35,000, which it records as follows:

Assets	=	Liabilities	+	Stockholders' Equity

Cash		Accounts Payable (Cool Cocoa, Inc.)		Purchases Discounts Lost	
	35,000	34,300	Bal 34,300	700	
			Bal 0		
(+)	(−)	(−)	(+)	(+)	(−)

Cash decreases by $35,000, the amount of the check, whereas Accounts Payable decreases by $34,300, the original amount at which Unlimited Decadence recorded the purchase. Unlimited Decadence records the $700 difference as Purchases Discounts Lost, which is an expense account similar to interest expense.

Management Issues

Although most companies use the gross method, the net method has advantages for the managers of a company. Managers typically take advantage of purchases discounts. Think about how much it costs not to! Consider the Unlimited Decadence example. If the company takes advantage of the discount, it pays 2% less by paying 20 days earlier (the 30 days allowed for payment minus the 10-day discount period). This is an approximate annual interest cost of 36% (2% × [360 ÷ 20])! Unlimited Decadence would save even if it had to borrow money from a bank to pay for the purchases within the discount period.

 What do you think would be the interest cost if the company didn't pay for 60 days? What other consequences might follow from this decision?

Given the high cost of *not* taking a discount, managers should be interested in knowing if any discounts have not been taken. The net method indicates this fact directly because the Purchases Discounts Lost account keeps track of any discounts *not taken.* In contrast, the gross method only keeps track of the discounts that *were taken* (by reducing the Inventory account). It does not show the discounts that were available but were *not* taken.

Purchases Returns and Allowances

Recall from Chapter 13 that a company may report a sales return or allowance that it gives a customer for, say, damaged goods. The customer (the purchaser) has a purchases return or allowance. A **purchases return** occurs when a company *returns* goods that it previously recorded as a purchase and receives a refund in exchange for the goods. A **purchases allowance** occurs when a company *keeps* the goods that it previously recorded as a purchase and later receives a refund of a portion of the purchase price.

A company uses its accounting system to keep track of purchases returns and allowances. Managers monitor the volume of returns and allowances for three basic reasons. First, a relatively high level of purchases returns may indicate that the purchasing department personnel are being persuaded to make unwanted purchases. As we discussed in Chapter 13, some companies want their sales personnel to encourage a purchase by reminding the customers how easy it is to return the item. Second, a relatively high level of purchases returns may indicate problems with the suppliers' product quality. Therefore, companies should require purchasing department personnel to find out why goods are being returned. Finally, a relatively high level of purchases allowances may result from suppliers' shipping or warehouse problems. A purchases allowance is often obtained if goods are slightly damaged or do not match the description of the goods that were ordered.

For example, assume that on September 7, 2000, Unlimited Decadence ordered 10,000 pounds of sugar on credit from Sugar Supply Company for $0.35 per pound, for a total cost of $3,500. On September 18, Unlimited Decadence receives the sugar and records the purchase (using the gross method) in its Raw Materials Inventory and Accounts Payable accounts. Its receiving department personnel inspect the order and find that the sugar is of the wrong quality. After being notified of the mistake on September 20, Sugar Supply Company offers to reduce the sales price for the entire shipment by $0.05 per pound ($500). Unlimited Decadence agrees because it can use the sugar in a different candy bar without affecting the quality, and it records the purchases allowance as follows:

Assets	=	**Liabilities**	+	**Stockholders' Equity**

Purchases Returns and Allowances		Accounts Payable (Sugar Supply Co.)	
			Bal 3,500
	500	500	
			Bal 3,000
(−)	(+)	(−)	(+)

 Why would both companies agree to the purchases allowance rather than agreeing that Unlimited Decadence will return the sugar?

Unlimited Decadence decreases Accounts Payable by $500 because it now owes only $3,000, not the original $3,500. It also increases Purchases Returns and Allowances by $500 on the *right* side of the T-account, which is a *contra* account to the Raw Materials Inventory account. So the rule for recording increases (or decreases) in the Purchases Returns and Allowances account is the *opposite* of the rule for the Raw Materials Inventory account (where increases are recorded on the left side). The company would record a purchases return in the same way. It would subtract the balance of the Purchases Returns and Allowances account from the balance of the Raw Materials Inventory account to determine the net cost of the inventory. A company could reduce the Raw Materials Inventory account directly, but recording the returns and allowances in a separate account is a way for the company to keep track, for control purposes, of the returns and allowances taken.

 Why do you think a company reports accounts receivable net, but accounts payable gross?

Purchase Transactions in a Foreign Currency

2 *How does an exchange gain (loss) arise from a credit purchase made from a company in another country?*

As we explained in Chapter 13, many U.S. companies conduct transactions with customers in foreign countries. Here we discuss transactions involving the purchase of inventory when the company and its supplier agree on a price stated in terms of the foreign currency. In these cases, the U.S. company must record the purchase in U.S. dollars. Therefore, the company must convert the foreign currency amount into dollars at the exchange rate on the day of the transaction. As we discussed in Chapter 13, transactions between companies in different countries usually involve credit terms, if only to allow time for the processing of the orders, shipments, and payments across international borders. In addition, currency exchange rates change continuously. As a result, the exchange rate is likely to have changed between the date the U.S. company records a credit purchase and the date it makes the payment for that purchase. On the date of payment, then, the company must record an exchange gain or loss to account for the difference between the purchase price and the amount of the cash payment. An **exchange gain or loss** is caused by a change in the exchange rate between the date that a company records a credit purchase and the date that the company pays the cash. More specifically, exchange gains and losses occur for credit purchases as follows:

1. An exchange *gain* occurs when the exchange rate *declines* between the date a company records a *payable* and the date the company *pays* the cash.

2. An exchange *loss* occurs when the exchange rate *increases* between the date a company records a *payable* and the date the company *pays* the cash.

To understand an exchange gain that occurs when the exchange rate declines between the date a credit purchase is recorded and the date the cash is paid, suppose that Unlimited Decadence purchases sugar from a Brazilian company and agrees to a price of 400,000 reals rather than a price in dollars. On the date of the purchase, the exchange rate is $0.51 (one real = $0.51); therefore, Unlimited Decadence records the purchase of the inventory at $204,000 (400,000 reals × $0.51) as follows:

Assets	=	Liabilities	+	Stockholders' Equity
Raw Materials Inventory		Accounts Payable (Brazilian Co.)		
204,000			204,000	
(+)	(−)	(−)	(+)	

The Brazilian company has a right to receive 400,000 reals, and Unlimited Decadence is obligated to pay sufficient dollars that will convert to 400,000 reals on the date that the payment is made. Now assume that the exchange rate on the date of payment is $0.49 (one real = $0.49). In this case, since only $0.49 now buys one real, Unlimited Decadence will have to pay fewer dollars to buy 400,000 reals. That is, the real has become less expensive. More specifically, Unlimited Decadence has to pay only $196,000 (400,000 reals × $0.49). Therefore, it has incurred an exchange *gain* of $8,000 ($204,000 − $196,000), which it records at the time of the cash payment as follows:

Assets	=	Liabilities	+	Stockholders' Equity
Cash		Accounts Payable (Brazilian Co.)		Exchange Gain
	196,000	204,000			8,000
(+)	(−)	(−)	(+)	(−)	(+)

The exchange gain occurs because Unlimited Decadence has to pay only $196,000 to settle the debt it originally recorded at $204,000. It can also compute the gain by multiplying the amount owed by the change in the exchange rate [400,000 reals × ($0.51 − $0.49) = $8,000]. Remember that the Brazilian company still receives 400,000 reals; it is Unlimited Decadence that has the exchange gain. For financial reporting purposes, Unlimited Decadence combines the amount of the exchange gain with any other exchange gains or losses and reports the net amount in the "other items" section of its income statement.

Note that the U.S. company (Unlimited Decadence) experienced the exchange gain because it agreed to a transaction expressed in terms of a foreign currency. In such situations, the U.S. company accepts the risks associated with exchange rate changes. When the transaction is expressed in U.S. dollars, the foreign company accepts, and the U.S. company avoids, the risks associated with exchange rate changes.

Technology and Accounts Payable Management

As for the other areas of liquidity management, a rethinking of accounts payable management and the emergence of new technology are changing accounts payable policies and activities for many large companies. Companies often use three innovations.

First, many large companies, as part of their ERP systems, are reengineering the purchase requisition and ordering process for small-dollar purchases. Streamlining this process can save large companies millions of dollars. Using a traditional purchasing system, processing one purchase order costs between $50 and $300 regardless of the cost of the goods being ordered. According to the president of American Express Travel Services Group, the cost of processing the paperwork often exceeds the value of the items being purchased! Realizing this, many companies are replacing their old process with a procurement card system.

www.americanexpress. com

Similar to a credit card, a **procurement card** permits employees responsible for keeping supplies in stock to purchase directly from suppliers. The card records each transaction electronically with the company's bank. The company's accounting system processes only the aggregate total of all of these purchase transactions instead of processing each individual transaction. Electronic controls prevent misuse of the card by restricting which suppliers can access the card and limiting the dollar amount of purchases charged each month.

Procurement cards eliminate the need for purchase requisitions, reduce the handling of invoices, speed up the delivery of supplies, and lower costs. For example, by adopting the use of procurement cards, Eli Lilly & Co. drastically reduced purchasing costs. Instead of processing 2,700 small purchases per month, as it did under the old system, Eli Lilly's accounting system now processes the same activities with only one combined transaction!

www.lilly.com

Second, many companies use EDI technology (as we discussed in Chapter 13) in their accounts payable management, mainly for large-dollar inventory purchases from trading partners. Under EDI, when a company purchases raw materials, its purchasing department personnel access its trading partner's current inventory price lists and then, using these prices, place the purchase order electronically. Computer controls restrict (1) who can place orders, (2) which trading partners the purchasing department personnel can use for specific types of purchases, and (3) the size and frequency of orders.

With EDI, electronic invoices received from trading partners automatically update the company's accounts payable system. The computer checks the information on the invoice (price, description of goods, quantity, etc.) against the electronic purchase order, confirms receipt of the proper goods by checking computerized inventory-receiving reports, and

www.nees.com

approves the transaction for entry into the accounting records. New England Electric Systems (NEES) Corporation adopted EDI technology for its accounts payable management system in 1994 and has reported that it now processes large-dollar invoices in one to three days rather than three weeks!

Third, some companies are outsourcing accounts payable in much the same way that they outsource cash payments. Outsourcing accounts payable may provide several benefits. First, it reduces the fixed personnel costs associated with managing accounts payable internally. Second, the company gains immediate access to new and efficient technologies, such as EDI, that it may not otherwise have. Third, by using the knowledge of accounts payable specialists, the company is likely to improve its controls over accounts payable. According to National City Corporation, companies that change to outsourcing accounts payable report immediate cost reductions of 10% to 20% as a result of these benefits.

www.national-city.com

www.oxychem.com

One disadvantage of computerized systems is that they work only as well as they are programmed. An article in the *The Wall Street Journal* reported that, for example, Occidental Chemical had reduced its accounts payable staff by one-third, to 40 employees, but that duplicate payments to suppliers and missed discounts had doubled to at least $500,000 annually.

 How would Occidental Chemical use breakeven analysis in making the decision to change its accounts payable procedures?

Additional Current Liabilities

Accounts payable is not the only current liability shown on a company's balance sheet. Remember that accounts payable represent only amounts owed to suppliers for credit purchases of supplies and inventory. Companies also engage in many other activities that lead to reporting current liabilities. For instance, when a company's employees work for a day, the company incurs an obligation to pay them. There are many specific current liabilities that a company might report on its balance sheet. We discuss three of the most common types: (1) accrued liabilities, (2) taxes, and (3) short-term notes payable.

Accrued Liabilities

3 *What are accrued liabilities, and what types does a company often have?*

On its December 31, 1997 balance sheet, Hershey Foods reported $372 million of accrued liabilities, which was almost 47% of its total of $796 million in current liabilities. For managers and external users to assess a company's liquidity, they must understand what accrued liabilities are and why companies report them.

Accrued liabilities are short-term obligations (other than accounts payable) that a company owes at the end of an accounting period and that result from the company's operating activities during the period. A company's utility bill that covers the last month in an accounting period (and that it will pay in the next accounting period) is an example of an accrued liability. In most instances, a company records its accrued liabilities by making end-of-period adjustments to its accounts. It makes these adjustments so that it records all the expenses for the accounting period and the related amounts it owes at the end of the period and correctly reports them in the period's financial statements.

 Assume that it is March 31, 2000, and Unlimited Decadence is about to prepare its financial statements for the first quarter of 2000. Its Utilities Expense account is as follows:

Utilities Expense

(+)	(−)
16,800	
14,800	

Do you think Unlimited Decadence's accounting system shows all of its utilities expense for the first quarter of 2000? Why or why not? What does Unlimited Decadence need to do, if anything, to ensure that it includes the proper amount of utilities expense in its income statement?

We discuss two specific types of accrued liabilities: (1) salaries (wages) and (2) warranties.

Accrued Salaries

Many manufacturing companies, such as candy manufacturers, pay employees weekly or biweekly (e.g., every other Friday). During an accounting period, a company records salaries as an expense on the day that it pays the employees. At the end of an accounting period, however, its employees may have worked several days since their last payday. The amount of salaries that a company owes its employees on the balance sheet date is called **accrued salaries, salaries payable,** or **wages payable.**

For example, assume that Unlimited Decadence is preparing its financial statements for the year ending December 31, 2000. Further, assume that it pays its employees $1 million of salaries each week (five-day week), with every Wednesday being payday. Exhibit 14-1 shows Unlimited Decadence's pay schedule for the week that includes December 31, 2000. Notice that December 31, 2000 is on a Sunday. This means that on December 31, 2000, Unlimited Decadence owes its employees for the work they performed on Thursday and Friday of this week (since the last payday). As we show in Exhibit 14-1, the salaries

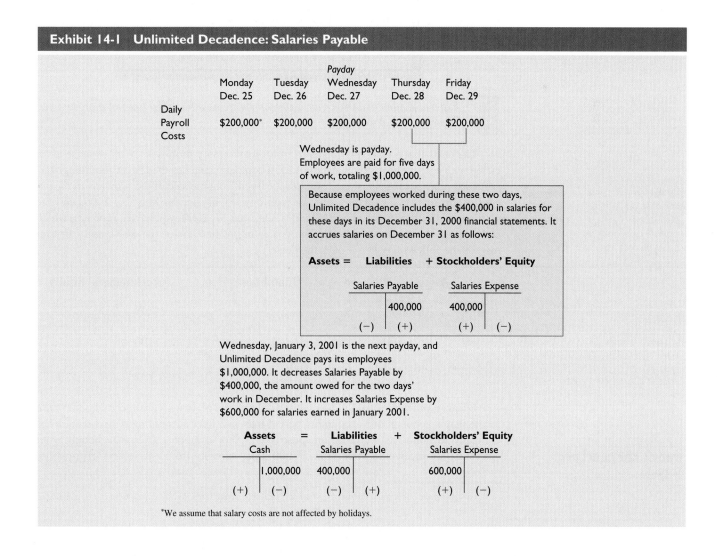

Exhibit 14-1 Unlimited Decadence: Salaries Payable

*We assume that salary costs are not affected by holidays.

for these two days total $400,000. To ensure that its financial statements correctly include these salaries, Unlimited Decadence makes the entry shown in Exhibit 14-1.

Both Salaries Expense and Salaries Payable increase by the amount of the salaries owed, $400,000. Unlimited Decadence includes the $400,000 salaries expense for the last two working days of the year in the total salaries expense that it reports as an operating expense on its income statement for 2000. It reports the $400,000 salaries payable as part of its accrued liabilities in the current liabilities section of its December 31, 2000 balance sheet.[1] As you can see in Exhibit 14-1, on the next payday (January 3, 2001), Unlimited Decadence pays $1 million but has an expense of only $600,000 for 2001 because its employees worked only three days in January (we assume that salary costs are not affected by holidays).

Warranty Liabilities

When a company offers a warranty on a product it sells, it agrees to repair or replace it for a specified period of time if it is defective. Do you check what type of warranty comes with the products you purchase? Depending on the type of product, you may see all sorts of warranties: "30 days parts and labor," "3 years bumper-to-bumper," "complete satisfaction or your money back." Here's what is written on the side of a package of M&M's Chocolate Candies:

GUARANTEE OF QUALITY AND FRESHNESS
"M&M's"® Chocolate Candies are made of the finest food ingredients. They should reach you in excellent condition. If not, we will replace them. Questions or Comments? Call **1-800-627-7852** M-F, 8:30 AM to 5 PM Eastern (Cont. US). Please save the unused product and the wrapper.

 Explain whether you think that a company increases the selling price of a product because it offers a warranty.

The costs that a company incurs to fulfill its warranty promises are an expense associated with selling the goods. Under GAAP, a company matches the cost of providing warranties as an expense against the revenues it earned from the sale of the products *in the period of the sale.* For example, suppose you buy a Chrysler on May 20, 2000, and the warranty is for three years or 36,000 miles. On June 17, 2000, you have a problem, which the dealer fixes at a cost of $100. The dealer bills Chrysler for the $100, and Chrysler records the following when it pays the dealer:

Assets	=	Liabilities	+	Stockholders' Equity
Cash				Warranty Expense

	100			100	
(+)	(−)			(+)	(−)

Because warranties tend to last for several months or years, customers who purchase a company's goods in one accounting period may in a later accounting period require the company to honor its warranty on those goods. For example, when you bought your Chrysler, you received a three-year, 36,000-mile warranty from Chrysler Corporation.

www2.chryslercorp. com

---

[1]In this discussion and our previous discussions on salaries, we ignore payroll taxes. We will discuss them in a later section on taxes.

So when Chrysler prepares its financial statements for the period ending December 31, 2000, it calculates and records the estimated cost of meeting the remaining warranties on current-period sales. Suppose that on December 31, 2000, Chrysler estimates that the warranty on the car it sold you in 2000 will cost another $900 before expiring. It records this warranty cost as follows:

Assets	**=**	**Liabilities**	**+**	**Stockholders' Equity**

Accrued Warranty Liability		Warranty Expense	
	900	100	
		900	
		Bal 1,000	
(−)	(+)	(+)	(−)

By recording this estimate, Chrysler increases its Warranty Expense by $900, to $1,000, for your car. As a result of this accrual, its Warranty Expense account for 2000 now includes all of the warranty costs associated with the sale made in 2000. Chrysler records and reports the total warranty expense for *all* its sales for the year as an operating expense on its 2000 income statement. Also, as a result of this accrual, its Accrued Warranty Liability increases by $900, the estimated cost of the remaining warranties. Chrysler records and reports the total accrued warranty liability for *all* its sales in the liability section of its December 31, 2000 balance sheet. During the next three years, whenever you claim the warranty associated with the 2000 sale, Chrysler will reduce the accrued warranty liability and will reduce cash or inventory.

 Since your warranty has a life of three years, explain whether Chrysler should report all of the warranty liability as a current liability or part of the warranty liability as a current liability and part as a noncurrent liability.

Warranty costs can substantially affect a company's profitability. For example, a recent article in *The Wall Street Journal* reported that Chrysler's warranty costs in 1995 were $959 per vehicle, for a total of $2.38 billion. Ford said that its costs were "a couple of hundred dollars less." Although the warranty expense reduces net income, providing a warranty to customers should increase sales. However, increasing or excessive warranty costs usually signal problems with the quality of the goods that a company manufactures and sells. Managers and external users monitor a company's warranty costs to determine if a company has quality-control problems.

 Explain whether you would or would not purchase an extended warranty on your new television.

Taxes

A **tax** is an amount of money that a government requires a taxable entity (e.g., an individual or a company) to pay. For example, in the United States, if you earn a certain minimum amount of personal income, the federal government requires you to pay income taxes. Companies incur many different kinds of taxes, including federal and state payroll taxes ("social security" and "unemployment" taxes), federal and state income taxes, state and local sales taxes (if they sell to retail customers), and state and local property taxes.

4 *What types of taxes do an employee and a company incur, and how does the company record them?*

At December 31 of any year, do you have a personal income tax liability or asset? Why?

Managers and external users should understand that taxes are a significant cost of doing business. For instance, in 1997 Hershey Foods earned $554 million in income before income taxes. In that same year, it reported income tax expense of $218 million. Keep in mind that the $218 million does not include the amounts for other types of taxes that Hershey incurred during 1997.

Taxes that a company owes but has not paid at the balance sheet date are referred to as **accrued taxes,** or **taxes payable.** We explain three types of taxes: payroll, income, and sales taxes.

Payroll Taxes

If you talk about payroll taxes with a company's managers or its employees, you may hear two different perspectives. You may hear an employee say: "There is a big difference between the amount of income I earn (the **gross pay**) and the amount of my take-home pay (the **net pay**). Taxes take a big chunk out of my paycheck." The amount of an employee's net pay is usually quite a bit smaller than the gross pay because the employer is required by law to withhold certain taxes from the employee's earnings and send those taxes to the government.

On the other hand, you may hear a manager say: "The wages we pay our employees are only part of our total payroll costs. The cost of payroll taxes adds tremendously to our labor costs." This manager is referring to the fact that, in the United States, federal and state governments require employers to pay certain taxes on their employees' earnings.

A company's accounting system must keep track of the payroll taxes incurred by both the employees and the company. In the next three sections, we describe three types of payroll taxes and show how Unlimited Decadence calculates the net pay of one employee for a single pay period.

Federal and State Income Taxes on Employees

Calculating federal and state income taxes for individual taxpayers in the United States is complex, and paying personal income taxes is the employee's, not the employer's, responsibility. However, employers, such as Unlimited Decadence, are required to withhold federal and state income taxes from their employees' pay and periodically to send the money withheld to the appropriate tax authorities. Governments set up this "pay-as-you-go" withholding of income taxes to increase the likelihood of collecting the taxes that are due.

A company, with the aid of its employees and government forms, calculates the dollar amount of taxes to withhold from each employee's paycheck for each pay period throughout the year. This amount varies considerably among employees depending on a variety of tax-related factors, including how much income they earn, their tax status (married or single), and the number of dependents they claim. If an individual employee's

pay varies between pay periods, the company calculates this withholding amount each time it pays the employee. Every pay period, the company deducts the appropriate amount of tax from each employee's gross pay.

For example, assume that Charlie Hill earns $15 per hour working for Unlimited Decadence as a machine operator. Further assume that he works 40 hours per week. Mr. Hill's gross pay for the pay-week (remember that Unlimited Decadence's payday is Wednesday) ending February 23, 2000, is $600 ($15 × 40 hours). However, Mr. Hill does not receive a paycheck for this gross amount. Unlimited Decadence uses federal and state income tax tables to determine how much federal and state income tax to withhold from Mr. Hill's pay. In this example, we assume that Mr. Hill's federal and state income tax withholdings total $95.

Federal Social Security and Medicare Taxes

Unlimited Decadence also must withhold federal social security and Medicare taxes from Mr. Hill's gross pay. Under the Federal Insurance Contributions Act (FICA), the U.S. government collects social security taxes from employees *and* employers. The amounts generated from FICA taxes provide the cash used to pay current benefits to qualified participants in the government's social security and Medicare system. In other words, the government does *not* save the dollars you pay into the system while you are in the workforce to support your financial needs during your retirement years. These dollars go to support those who are currently retired and eligible for benefits.

 When you retire in, say, 2050, who do you think will pay your social security benefits?

For both the employer and the employee, FICA taxes are composed of two parts: (1) social security taxes, and (2) Medicare taxes. Congress periodically increases the FICA rates. At the time we wrote this book, the social security tax rate was 6.20% of wages and salaries up to $72,600—neither you nor the company you worked for would pay social security tax on any wages or salaries you earned in excess of $72,600 per year. The Medicare tax rate was 1.45%, with no upper limit on the amount of salary taxed.

 Do you think Mr. Hill will have social security and Medicare taxes deducted from his gross pay every week during 2000? Why or why not?

Using the rates in effect when we wrote this book, Unlimited Decadence calculates social security and Medicare payroll tax deductions for Mr. Hill as follows:

Mr. Hill's Social Security Taxes
Withheld from His Weekly Pay
= Gross Pay × 6.20%
= $600 × 0.062
= $37.20

Mr. Hill's Medicare Taxes
Withheld from His Weekly Pay
= Gross Pay × 1.45%
= $600 × 0.0145
= $8.70

Mr. Hill's Total FICA Taxes
Withheld from His Weekly Pay
= Social Security Taxes + Medicare Taxes
= $37.20 + $8.70
= $45.90

Based on these calculations, Unlimited Decadence withholds $45.90 in FICA taxes from Mr. Hill's gross pay. Assuming Mr. Hill has no other employee deductions,[2] his net pay for the week is $459.10 ($600 − $95 − $45.90).

---

[2]Employees often pay for programs such as medical insurance, union dues, and charitable contributions (e.g., the United Way) through payroll deductions. The employer must keep track of the appropriate deductions from each employee's pay and send the correct amounts to the various agencies.

Remember that *both* the employee *and* the employer pay FICA taxes. Thus, after withholding $45.90 from Mr. Hill's pay, Unlimited Decadence must pay $91.80 ($45.90 for the employee portion of the tax withheld from the employee's paycheck plus $45.90 for the employer portion of the tax) of FICA taxes to the government.

Federal and State Unemployment Taxes

Under the Federal Unemployment Tax Act (FUTA), federal and state governments collect unemployment taxes from companies to support unemployment insurance payments to workers who lose their jobs. These FUTA taxes are paid only by employers (*not* employees). At the present time, FUTA taxes are assessed at a maximum rate of 6.2% on the first $7,000 paid to each employee in each year. Of the 6.2%, 5.4% is paid to the state if it levies an approved unemployment tax. However, most states allow a company with a good employment record to receive a good "merit rating" and receive a reduction in the tax rate.

To determine whether Unlimited Decadence is required to pay FUTA taxes on Mr. Hill's February 23, 2000 gross pay, it must calculate the amount of wages earned this year by Mr. Hill. The week ending February 23, 2000 is the eighth week of the year. Including his February 23 paycheck, Mr. Hill has received $4,800 so far this year ($600 per week × 8 weeks). Because Mr. Hill has not yet received $7,000 during 2000, Unlimited Decadence is required to pay FUTA taxes on Mr. Hill's gross pay. Using the 6.2% rate, Unlimited Decadence must pay $37.20 ($600 × 6.2%) in FUTA taxes to the U.S. government because of Mr. Hill's work during the week ending February 23, 2000. However, it pays no FUTA taxes on any income it pays an employee above $7,000 during the year.

Recording Payroll and Payroll Taxes

Computerized payroll systems are designed to calculate an employee's gross pay and net pay. The payroll software is constantly updated for changes in pay rates, payroll taxes, or other employee deductions to ensure that a company accounts for its payroll properly. Even though computers make the payroll calculations, it is important that managers, investors, and creditors understand how payroll taxes affect a company's expenses. For example, if you don't understand payroll tax laws, it is easy to underestimate the total cost associated with hiring new employees.

Exhibit 14-2 Payroll and Employee Payroll Taxes: Unlimited Decadence

Employee payroll taxes that affect Mr. Hill's net pay for the week ending February 23, 2000, are as follows:

$600.00	Gross pay (40 hours × $15)
(95.00)	Federal and state income tax withheld
(45.90)	FICA taxes withheld (social security taxes of $37.20 and medicare taxes of $8.70)
$459.10	

On February 23, 2000, Unlimited Decadence records Mr. Hill's salary as follows:

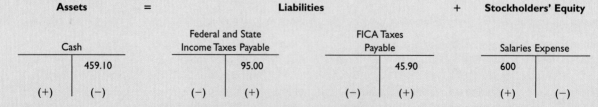

Salaries Expense increases by the $600 gross amount of Mr. Hill's pay—Unlimited Decadence's cost of his salary for the week. Two liability accounts increase by $95 and $45.90 because Unlimited Decadence collects these taxes for the government and owes these amounts. Cash decreases by the $459.10 amount of Mr. Hill's net pay. If Unlimited Decadence owes payroll tax liabilities at year-end, it reports them in the current liability section of its balance sheet.

Exhibit 14-2 shows the impact of the payroll tax items on Charlie Hill's net pay. Mr. Hill's gross pay of $600 is reduced by $95 in federal and state income tax withholding and $45.90 in social security and Medicare taxes, resulting in net pay of $459.10. We also show how Unlimited Decadence records Mr. Hill's weekly pay in its accounting system. Note that it bases the amount of salary expense on Mr. Hill's gross pay. The gross pay is part of the cost to Unlimited Decadence for his employment. The amount of taxes withheld from Mr. Hill's pay are liabilities of Unlimited Decadence until it pays them to the governmental agencies. If it owes these taxes at the balance sheet date, Unlimited Decadence reports the amounts as current liabilities on its ending balance sheet. Then when Unlimited Decadence pays the government for these taxes, it reduces the related liabilities.

Exhibit 14-3 shows how Unlimited Decadence records the employer-related payroll taxes it incurred as a result of employing Mr. Hill for the week. Recall that Unlimited Decadence incurred $45.90 in FICA taxes and $37.20 in FUTA taxes because of Mr. Hill's employment. As a result of Mr. Hill's employment for the week ending February 23, 2000, Unlimited Decadence records an increase of $83.10 ($45.90 + $37.20) in its Payroll Taxes Expense and an increase in each tax liability. If Unlimited Decadence owes these taxes at the balance sheet date, it reports these amounts as current liabilities on its ending balance sheet. When Unlimited Decadence pays the government for these taxes, it reduces the related liabilities.

Remember that we based our example on only one employee, Mr. Hill. Unlimited Decadence's total expense for employees' salaries for the week ending February 23, 2000, and for every week, is the sum of these expenses for all employees. Also, if Unlimited Decadence accrues salaries (or wages) at the end of an accounting period as we showed earlier, it accrues payroll taxes at the same time.

Income Taxes

In Chapter 10 we explained that one major difference between a corporation and a partnership or sole proprietorship is that a corporation is subject to federal and state income taxes. Therefore, a corporation must include the effects of its own income taxes on its financial statements. It includes income tax expense on its income statement because income taxes are a cost of doing business. Similarly, if it owes federal and/or state income

Exhibit 14-3 Employer Payroll Taxes: Unlimited Decadence

Employer payroll taxes for Unlimited Decadence caused by Mr. Hill's employment for the week ending February 23, 2000, are as follows:

$45.90   Employer's FICA taxes owed on Mr. Hill's gross pay (social security taxes of $37.20 and medicare taxes of $8.70)
  37.20   FUTA taxes owed on Mr. Hill's gross pay
$83.10

On February 23, 2000, Unlimited Decadence records the payroll taxes associated with Mr. Hill's salary as follows:

Assets =	Liabilities		+ Stockholders' Equity
	FUTA Taxes Payable	FICA Taxes Payable	Payroll Tax Expense
	37.20	45.90	83.10
(−)	(+)	(−)	(+)	(−) (+)	(−)

Two liability accounts increase by $37.20 and $45.90. Payroll Tax Expense increases by the $83.10 cost of employing Mr. Hill. If Unlimited Decadence owes payroll tax liabilities at year-end, it reports them in the current liability section of its balance sheet.

taxes at the end of an accounting period, it reports these amounts as current liabilities on its ending balance sheet.

As we explained in Chapter 10, a corporation computes the income tax expense related to its "income before income taxes" each time it prepares an income statement; it computes this expense by multiplying its pretax income by the applicable tax rate. Since a corporation usually pays its income taxes after the end of the accounting period, it must accrue an expense and a liability through an end-of-period adjustment.[3]

For example, assume that Unlimited Decadence's income before income taxes for 2000 is $4.9 million (as we showed in Exhibit 10-5) and that it is subject to an income tax rate of 40%. Its income tax expense for 2000 is $1.96 million ($4.9 million $\times$ 0.40), and it records this amount as follows:

Assets	=	Liabilities	+	Stockholders' Equity	
		Income Taxes Payable		Income Tax Expense	
		1,960,000	1,960,000		
(−)		(+)	(+)		(−)

Both Income Tax Expense and Income Taxes Payable increase by $1.96 million, the amount of the taxes. Unlimited Decadence reports the Income Tax Expense amount on its 2000 income statement and reports the Income Taxes Payable amount with its other taxes payable in the current liabilities section of its December 31, 2000 balance sheet.

Sales Taxes

So far in this book, whenever we discussed sales, for simplicity we ignored sales taxes. However, most states and local communities in the United States require customers to pay a sales tax on many types of products purchased. A company is required to collect state and local sales taxes from its retail customers at the time they purchase its products. (States usually require sales tax to be paid only on sales to the final retail purchaser and not on sales

Some corporations claim that computing their income taxes is complicated? Do you agree?

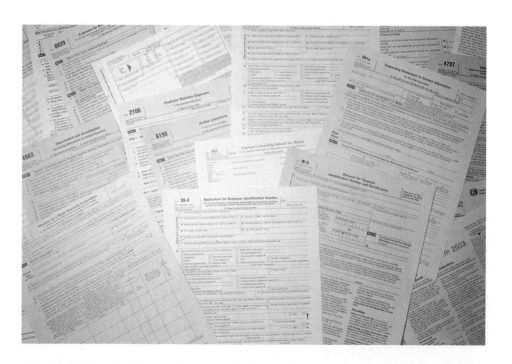

---

[3]Like individuals, corporations are required to make tax payments throughout the year. For simplicity, we ignore this issue.

from a manufacturing company to a retail company.) Almost every time you purchase a product, you hear the salesperson say, "And with sales tax, your total comes to . . ."

At the time of sale, a company is acting as a collection agency for the state and/or local government. Therefore the sales tax it collects and then pays is neither a revenue nor an expense. The collection of the tax from the customer, however, does create a liability for the company because it receives cash that it owes to the state. It eliminates the liability when it pays the state. For example, if Unlimited Decadence makes a $10,000 credit sale that is subject to a 5% sales tax, it records the transaction as follows:

Assets		=	**Liabilities**		+	**Stockholders' Equity**	
Accounts Receivable			**Sales Taxes Payable**			**Sales Revenue**	
10,500				500			10,000
(+)	(−)		(−)	(+)		(−)	(+)

Accounts Receivable increases by $10,500, which is the amount of the sale ($10,000) plus the amount of the 5% tax ($10,000 × 5% = $500). Sales Revenue increases by $10,000, the amount of the sale. Because Unlimited Decadence must pay the amount of the sales tax to the state and local government at a later date, Sales Taxes Payable increases by $500. When Unlimited Decadence pays the sales tax to the state, it reduces the Sales Taxes Payable. If it has not paid these taxes by the balance sheet date, Unlimited Decadence reports them as a current liability on its ending balance sheet.

Other Taxes

Companies in the United States are also subject to many other types of taxes. At the state level, companies are required to pay franchise taxes. A franchise tax is simply a tax that the state levies on all companies for "doing business" in the state. For example, California collects around $22 billion annually in company franchise taxes. It bases the amount of the franchise tax on the company's income in the preceding year.

Almost all companies are required to pay property taxes. These are often called *ad valorem* taxes. Municipalities, school districts, counties, states, and other governmental entities that have taxing authority may levy property taxes on a company's land, buildings, or equipment. For example, the state of Iowa levies taxes on the value of a company's equipment. Local governments generally tax a company on the value of its land and buildings.

A company records the costs of its franchise taxes, property taxes, and other types of taxes as expenses in the accounting period in which it incurs them. If it has not paid these taxes by the end of an accounting period, it reports them in the current liability section of its ending balance sheet.

Short-Term Notes Payable

As we discussed in Chapter 13, some companies also sell goods to customers in return for a promissory note. When a company is the maker of the promissory note, it records a short-term note payable. A company may purchase goods using a promissory note for one of several reasons: (1) because the dollar amount of the purchase is relatively large compared with most of the selling company's credit sales, (2) because the purchasing company does not want to pay for the goods within the normal time frame offered by the selling company's credit department, or (3) because the purchasing company's credit worthiness is questionable.

Accounting for short-term notes payable is a "mirror image" of accounting for short-term notes receivable. Whereas a company earns interest revenue during the time it holds a note receivable, a company incurs interest expense during the time it owes a note

5 *How is accounting for a short-term note payable similar to accounting for a short-term note receivable?*

payable. The amount of interest expense that a company incurs depends on the face value of the note, the note's interest rate, and the note's life. At the end of the accounting period, the company computes any accrued interest in the same way that we discussed for notes receivable. For notes payable, however, a company records the amount of interest as Interest Expense and Interest Payable. In addition to reporting the face value of short-term notes payable as a current liability on its balance sheet, a company includes the amount of interest payable in its total for accrued liabilities. The company reports the related interest expense in the "other items" section of its income statement.

 Do you think that a balance sheet would be more useful if the assets and liabilities related to revenues were separated from the assets and liabilities related to expenses? Why or why not?

Prepaid Items

6 *What are prepaid items, and how does a company account for them?*

A company often pays for goods or services *after* it has acquired or used them, as we discussed earlier in the chapter. In some industries, however, it is common for the buying company to pay cash *before* the selling company delivers the goods or provides the services that the buying company purchased. For example, landlords require tenants to pay rent before being allowed to use the property, and insurance companies require policyholders to pay premiums before their policy is in effect.

 Why do you think that in some industries, purchasers are required to pay in advance, whereas in others they pay in arrears?

When a company pays for goods or services before using them, it doesn't record the expense at this time. Instead it records a current asset often called a **prepaid item.** Sometimes companies call this asset a *prepaid expense,* but many people think it is confusing to have the term "expense" in the name of an asset. Also, don't forget that many other assets are eventually going to be recorded as expenses and could also be labeled prepaid expenses.

 Would you call a building a prepaid expense? Why, or why not?

A purchasing company records a prepaid item as an asset because it has paid for a good or service that it will use in the future. It records an expense for the portion of the asset it uses, and it reduces the prepaid item as an end-of-period adjustment. The company includes the expense as an operating expense on its income statement and the remaining amount of the prepaid item as a current asset on its ending balance sheet. For example, a company paying $12,000 on October 1 for a one-year insurance policy records an asset, called prepaid insurance. At the end of the year, it records insurance expense for the amount used up, $3,000 [($12,000 ÷ 12) × 3 months], and reduces the prepaid insurance by the same amount. On the ending balance sheet, it reports the prepaid insurance at $9,000 ($12,000 − $3,000).

 Do you agree with the following statement? "Payables are the amounts owed because the company will record an expense in the future, whereas prepaids are the amounts that have already been recorded as an expense." Why or why not?

Loss Contingencies

7 *What are loss contingencies, and how does a company report or disclose them?*

If you are deciding whether to invest in a company, would you want to know if the company promised to pay off another company's debt if it went unpaid? Would you want to know that the company is a defendant in a major lawsuit and may have to pay a large amount in damages if it loses? We are sure that your answer to both these questions is "yes." If this company has to pay off another company's debts or loses a major lawsuit, the financial situation of the company may drastically change. Its risk would be higher, and its financial flexibility and liquidity would be lower. In an investment decision about this company, you would probably like to have two additional pieces of information about each of these situations so you can make a more informed investment decision. First, you would want to know how likely it is that the company will actually have to pay. Second, you would want some estimate of what the dollar amount of the payment may be.

Situations such as the two described above are referred to as contingencies. A **contingency** is an existing condition that will lead to a gain or loss if a future event occurs (or fails to occur). A gain is like a revenue because it increases stockholders' equity, and a loss is like an expense because it reduces stockholders' equity. For example, the company faces a monetary loss *if* it loses the lawsuit. GAAP has more detailed rules for *loss* contingencies and the related liability (or reduction of an asset) because these affect investors and creditors negatively.

 Of the topics we have discussed in Chapters 13 and 14, can you think of any that are examples of loss contingencies?

GAAP requires a company to either report or disclose certain information about loss contingencies in its financial statements depending on two conditions: (1) the likelihood that the future event will occur, and (2) the ability to estimate the dollar amount associated with the contingency. The likelihood that the future event will occur falls into three levels, according to GAAP:

1. *Probable:* the chance that the future event will occur is likely

2. *Reasonably possible:* the chance that the future event will occur is more than remote but less than probable

3. *Remote:* the chance that the future event will occur is slight

Note that these levels are not defined in terms of a percentage probability. Their application requires good judgment.

The method that a company is required to use to report or disclose loss contingencies depends on the degree of certainty and measurability associated with the future event.

1. *Report in the financial statements:* a company reports an estimated loss from a loss contingency in its financial statements as a reduction in income (either as an expense or as a loss) and a liability (or reduction of an asset) if *both* of the following conditions are met:
   (a) it is *probable* that the future event related to the loss contingency will occur, and
   (b) the amount of the loss can be *reasonably estimated.*

2. *Disclose in the notes to the financial statements:* a company discloses an estimated loss from a loss contingency in the notes to its financial statements if it is *reasonably possible* that the future event related to the loss contingency will occur.

 How do you think a company would report or disclose a loss contingency that is probable but not measurable? measurable but not probable?

If the likelihood of the future event related to a loss contingency is remote, GAAP does not require that a company report an estimated loss in its financial statements or disclose the estimated loss in the notes (unless it is a guarantee of another company's debt).

Since a contingency requires an estimate, a company will rarely consider a single amount. Instead it will evaluate alternate amounts. When a single amount is the best estimate, the company uses that amount. Otherwise the company uses the minimum amount of the range of its estimates.

Do you think that companies have contingent assets? If so, what is an example? If not, why not?

www.johnsonandjohn-
son.com

In the notes to its financial statements in a recent annual report, Johnson & Johnson Corporation discussed four loss contingencies related to pending legal proceedings. First, it disclosed that it was involved in numerous product liability cases, many of which concerned adverse reactions to drugs and medical devices. Although the damages claimed were substantial and the company was confident of the warnings that accompanied such products, it stated that predicting the ultimate outcome of the litigation was not feasible. Second, it disclosed that it had "self-insured" for product liability since January 1, 1986, because insurance was unavailable. The company had established "reserves" to cover expected costs. Third, Johnson & Johnson was a defendant in a large number of individual and class-action suits brought by retail pharmacies that alleged price discrimination and price fixing. The company believed these claims were without merit. Fourth, it commented that it was involved in a number of patent, trademark, and other lawsuits incidental to its business. Finally, the company concluded that these issues together would not have a material adverse effect on its income, cash flows, or balance sheet. Thus we see that the company did not include the effects of these suits in its financial statements because they were not probable, not measurable, or not material.

Evaluation of a Company's Liquidity Position

8 *What can external users learn from analyzing a company's liquidity?*

In these two chapters we have discussed how a company manages and reports the current assets (except inventory and marketable securities) and liabilities that affect its liquidity position. It is important for you to understand these assets and liabilities and how they relate to each other as we discuss the evaluation of a company's liquidity.

External users evaluate a company's liquidity position for two main reasons. First, they evaluate the company's liquidity to help assess its ability to meet short-term obligations. External users realize that if a company cannot pay its obligations as they come due, it risks going out of business. A company that fails to pay its short-term obligations will have difficulty purchasing on credit or borrowing money. Second, external users evaluate a company's liquidity to help assess its financial flexibility. A company in a good liquidity position can take better advantage of business opportunities such as aggressively marketing its products or investing for growth.

External users must understand two basic aspects of accounting to be able to evaluate a company's liquidity position. First, they need to know the assets and liabilities that affect liquidity. You learned about this aspect in these two chapters. Second, investors and creditors must understand how to perform financial statement analysis. In Chapter 10 we described several types of financial statement analyses. Here, we will apply what you learned in these chapters.

Recall from Chapter 10 that investors and creditors use ratio analysis, horizontal analysis, and vertical analysis to evaluate liquidity. They may perform these types of analyses only on the company being evaluated (intracompany analysis), and/or they may compare the company's liquidity position with industry averages and with the liquidity positions of similar companies (intercompany analysis). We separate our discussion of evaluating company liquidity into two sections: intracompany analysis and intercompany analysis.

Intracompany Analysis of Liquidity

www.rmcfusa.com

Assume that you are a stockholder in Rocky Mountain Chocolate Factory. On May 27, 1998, you received Rocky Mountain's 1998 annual report, and you turned to the February 28, 1998 and February 28, 1997 comparative balance sheets to determine how well the company has managed its liquidity position. We show amounts included as current assets and current liabilities on these balance sheets in Exhibit 14-4. Note that the company uses a *fiscal year* that is different from the calendar year.

 Why do you think the company has a balance sheet dated at the end of February?

How would you start your analysis? You should probably perform three steps. First, you should examine the balance of each account that affects liquidity for both years. Think about the liquidity management policies and activities that affect each balance. For instance, ask yourself: "Are the balances on February 28, 1998 similar to those on February 28, 1997?" "Did any balances change dramatically? If so, what could have caused the change?" By familiarizing yourself with the balances, you can anticipate the findings that percentage analysis or ratio analysis may produce.

For example, we can see in Exhibit 14-4 that Rocky Mountain's accounts (and notes) receivable (net) balance on February 28, 1998 ($2,174,618) is substantially larger than it was on February 28, 1997 ($1,496,682). There are several possible explanations for this increase. Some explanations are positive, whereas others indicate potential problems. If accounts receivable increased because of an overall increase in credit sales to good customers, the increase is good news. If the increase in accounts receivable is not accompanied by an increase in sales from the fiscal year ending February 28, 1997 to the fiscal year ending February 28, 1998, this increase may signal a slowdown in cash collections. You can get a better picture of the changes that occurred in these balances by using horizontal analysis to calculate the percentage change in the balances from 1997 to 1998. Accounts (and notes) receivable, for instance, increased by 45% ($2,174,618 ÷ $1,496,682 = 1.45, rounded) from 1997 to 1998. Rocky Mountain's sales increased by 5% (amounts not shown in Exhibit 14-4), so its accounts receivable increased by a much larger percentage. You can also compare the percentage increase in receivables with percentage changes in other liquidity-related accounts. But note that receivables may not all have the same liquidity. For example, a company may expect to collect accounts receivable sooner than notes receivable. Note also that Rocky Mountain's allowance for doubtful accounts (allowance for bad debts) increased in 1998, but by a much smaller percentage than the total receivables. The company may not be managing its receivables as well but may be more optimistic about collecting them, thereby sending a mixed signal about its liquidity.

Exhibit 14-4 Rocky Mountain Chocolate Factory, Inc.: Current Asset and Current Liability Amounts as a Percentage of Total Assets				
	February 28, 1998	**%**	**February 28, 1997**	**%**
CURRENT ASSETS				
Cash and cash equivalents	$1,795,381	9.0	$ 792,606	4.2
Accounts and notes receivable—trade, less allowance for doubtful accounts of $214,152 and $202,029	2,174,618	10.9	1,496,682	8.0
Inventories	2,567,966	12.9	2,082,566	11.2
Other	888,170	4.5	1,365,772	7.3
Total current assets	$7,426,135	37.4	$5,737,626	30.7
CURRENT LIABILITIES				
Current maturities of long-term debt	$1,132,900	5.7	$ 847,881	4.5
Accounts payable	1,296,769	6.5	799,671	4.3
Accrued salaries and wages	707,737	3.6	465,338	2.5
Other accrued expenses	339,481	1.7	867,961	4.6
Deferred income	0	0	93,000	0.5
Total current liabilities	$3,476,887	17.5	$3,073,851	16.5

Note: Total assets at February 28, 1998 are $19,867,892 and at February 28, 1997 are $18,666,130.

If a company's accounts receivable increased by 45%, would you expect a similar increase in its accounts payable? Why or why not?

Second, you should examine how Rocky Mountain's liquidity position has changed from February 28, 1997 to February 28, 1998, by converting the dollar balances for each current asset and current liability to percentages of the company's total assets. This is done by dividing the balance of each current asset and current liability by the amount of total assets. This vertical analysis is important because although the current-year account balances may be significantly different from the account balances of the past year, the whole company may have grown by the same proportion. Rocky Mountain's total assets at February 28, 1998 and February 28, 1997 are $19,867,892 and $18,666,130, respectively. In Exhibit 14-4, for each year we calculated each of Rocky Mountain's current asset and current liability balances as a percentage of that year's total assets. For example, the increase in Rocky Mountain's accounts payable balance from $799,671 to $1,296,769 may seem more significant when we realize that the relation to total assets has increased from 4.3% to 6.5%.

 What other insights do you gain by examining Exhibit 14-4? What questions about Rocky Mountain's liquidity position occur to you when you examine this exhibit?

Third, you should calculate liquidity ratios for February 28, 1997 and February 28, 1998. Two of the most commonly used ratios are the quick ratio and the accounts receivable turnover ratio.[4] We introduced these ratios in earlier chapters. The quick ratio is calculated as follows:

$$\text{Quick Ratio} = \frac{\substack{\text{Cash and Cash Equivalents} + \text{Short-Term Investments} \\ + \text{Accounts Receivable} + \text{Notes Receivable (short-term)}}}{\text{Current Liabilities}}$$

The quick ratio compares the company's dollar amount of those current assets that can be most easily converted into cash with the dollar amount of the company's current liabilities. The larger the ratio, the better position the company is in to meet its short-term obligations. The quick ratio of Rocky Mountain on February 28, 1998 is 1.14 and on February 28, 1997 is 0.74. Since the 1998 ratio is higher than the 1997 ratio, this trend indicates an improvement in Rocky Mountain's liquidity position.

 When computing the quick ratio, would you include unearned revenue in the denominator? Why or why not?

The accounts receivable turnover ratio is calculated as follows:

$$\text{Accounts Receivable Turnover} = \frac{\text{Net Sales}}{\text{Average Net Accounts Receivable}}$$

Dividing net sales[5] by average net accounts receivable shows how many times the average accounts receivable are *turned over,* or collected, during each accounting period. Notice that we use the *average* net accounts receivable, as opposed to the balance at the beginning or the end of the accounting period, as the denominator in this ratio. The average net accounts receivable is calculated as follows:

---

[4]We will discuss the current ratio and the inventory turnover ratio for large companies in Chapter 19.
[5]As we discussed in Chapter 7, if a company's net *credit* sales are known, you should use this amount in the calculation.

$$\text{Average Net Accounts Receivable} = \frac{\overset{\text{Beginning Net}}{\text{Accounts Receivable}} + \overset{\text{Ending Net}}{\text{Accounts Receivable}}}{2}$$

A company uses this average amount because it is usually a better measure of the dollar amount of accounts receivable that the company managed during the accounting period than is the accounts receivable balance at the beginning or the end of the year. The accounts receivable turnover ratio is a measure of the efficiency with which a company collects its receivables. As a general rule, the higher the turnover, the better it is for the company because the company has fewer resources tied up in accounts receivable, collects these resources at a faster pace, and usually has fewer uncollectible accounts. Too high a turnover rate, however, might indicate that the company is too aggressive in its collection policies and is alienating its customers. A company often divides its accounts receivable turnover into the number of days in the business year; this shows the average number of days required for the company to collect its accounts receivable. External users compare a company's average collection period with the number of days the company gives its customers to pay for credit purchases (i.e., credit terms). This comparison provides investors and creditors with an indication of how effectively the company manages its accounts receivable and cash receipts.

Using information from Rocky Mountain's annual report, we calculated the company's accounts receivable turnover ratio and its average collection period (assuming a 365-day business year) for fiscal 1998 and fiscal 1997, as you can see in Exhibit 14-5.

Exhibit 14-5 Rocky Mountain Chocolate Factory, Inc.: Accounts Receivable and Accounts Payable Ratios

Fiscal Year Ending February 28, 1998

$$\text{Accounts Receivable Turnover} = \frac{\$20,659,076}{(\$1,496,682 + \$2,174,618) \div 2} = 11.3$$

$$\text{Number of Days in Collection Period} = \frac{365 \text{ days}}{11.3} = 32 \text{ days}$$

$$\text{Accounts Payable Turnover} = \frac{\$10,960,966}{(\$799,671 + \$1,296,769) \div 2} = 10.5$$

Fiscal Year Ending February 28, 1997

$$\text{Accounts Receivable Turnover} = \frac{\$19,682,622}{(\$1,463,901 + \$1,496,682) \div 2} = 13.3$$

$$\text{Number of Days in Collection Period} = \frac{365 \text{ days}}{13.3} = 27 \text{ days}$$

$$\text{Accounts Payable Turnover} = \frac{\$11,017,119}{(\$998,520 + \$799,671) \div 2} = 12.3$$

Note: Listed below are the dollar numbers we used to calculate the accounts receivable ratios for Rocky Mountain. Make sure you understand how each ratio was calculated.

Net sales	Cost of sales
1998: $20,659,076	1998: $10,960,966
1997: $19,682,622	1997: $11,017,119

Net accounts receivable	Accounts payable
2/28/1998: $2,174,618	2/28/1998: $1,296,769
2/28/1997: $1,496,682	2/28/1997: $ 799,671
2/29/1996: $1,463,901	2/29/1996: $ 998,520

(For simplicity, we assumed that all the receivables are accounts receivable, since the notes receivable are listed as trade receivables rather than receivables from loans.) As you can see, Rocky Mountain's collection period has increased from 27 days in fiscal 1997 to 32 days in fiscal 1998. Thus, Rocky Mountain is collecting its accounts receivable less effectively.

Another ratio that some users find helpful is the accounts payable turnover ratio, which is calculated as follows:

$$\text{Accounts Payable Turnover} = \frac{\text{Cost of Goods Sold}}{\text{Average Accounts Payable}}$$

This ratio measures the number of times that accounts payable turn over during the year. Using information from Rocky Mountain's annual report, we calculated the company's accounts payable turnover ratio for fiscal 1998 and fiscal 1997, as we show in Exhibit 14-5. As you can see, Rocky Mountain's accounts payable turnover has decreased from 12.3 in fiscal 1997 to 10.5 in fiscal 1998. The accounts payable turnover ratio may also be divided into the number of days in the business year to show the average payment period in days. The higher (lower) the turnover, the shorter (longer) is the time between the purchase of inventory and the payment of cash. Thus, Rocky Mountain is paying its accounts payable slower in 1998 than 1997. A company with too low an accounts payable turnover may not be paying creditors on a timely basis and may be in financial difficulty. Alternatively, a company with too high a turnover may be paying too quickly and losing the "free" credit provided by accounts payable. A user may prefer to compute the accounts payable turnover ratio using purchases as the numerator because purchases are more closely related to accounts payable than is cost of goods sold. Since companies typically don't report purchases, the external user needs to compute the amount by adding the ending inventory to the cost of goods sold and subtracting the beginning inventory.

 Can you use the information in Exhibit 14-4 to discover other useful information?

Intercompany Analysis of Liquidity

When you complete an *intra*company analysis of a company's liquidity position, you learn how the company's position has changed since previous years. However, to gauge how well the company has managed its liquidity, you also should use *inter*company analysis to compare the company's liquidity position with the liquidity position of similar companies or with industry averages. Investors and creditors can find industry-level financial data from information services companies such as Dun & Bradstreet, Moody's, and Standard & Poor's.

www.dnb.com
www.moodys.com
www.standardpoor.com

By comparing Rocky Mountain's February 28, 1998 and February 28, 1997 quick ratios and its fiscal 1998 and 1997 accounts receivable turnover ratios, numbers of days in its collection period, and accounts payable turnover ratios, we can analyze Rocky Mountain's liquidity position. But are the ratios and amounts good or bad? Do the fiscal 1998 accounts receivable turnover ratio of 11.3 and the collection period of 32 days indicate that the company's accounts receivable are being managed effectively? In Exhibit 14-6, we list the industry averages for candy manufacturers.

By studying Exhibit 14-6, you can see that Rocky Mountain has a better-than-average quick ratio. This means Rocky Mountain has slightly more cash, short-term investments, and accounts and notes receivable compared with its total dollar amount of current liabilities. Its accounts receivable turnover (and the collection period) are worse than the industry averages. Furthermore, its accounts payable turnover is much slower than the industry average. So, Rocky Mountain's liquidity position is getting worse (as we discussed earlier in the chapter), and it is also generally worse than the industry average. Therefore, investors and creditors may have some concerns about Rocky

	Rocky Mountain 1998	Industry Averages
Exhibit 14-6 **Comparison of Industry Averages for Liquidity: Rocky Mountain Chocolate Factory and Other Candy Manufacturers**		
Quick Ratio	1.14	1.0
Accounts Receivable Turnover Ratio	11.3	14.5
Number of Days in Collection Period	32	25.0
Accounts Payable Turnover Ratio	10.5	18.1

Mountain's current overall liquidity position, and may need to monitor the company's ongoing overall liquidity position.

 If some companies in the industry make significant cash sales, how would your interpretation of their quick ratios and their accounts receivable turnover ratios be affected?

Business Issues and Values

In this chapter and Chapter 13 we explained how companies record and report several types of current assets and current liabilities using GAAP. We also explained how managers, investors, and creditors use financial statements to assess a company's liquidity position. Because investors and creditors make business decisions that are based on their assessment of a company's financial statements, a manager may be tempted to make the company appear more liquid, or more financially flexible, than it really is.

In Chapter 13, we discussed how some companies record credit sales very aggressively, stretching their interpretations of GAAP. By recording credit sales before the revenue is earned, a company may *overstate* its accounts receivable and net income for the accounting period. Alternatively, a company might understate its expected future sales returns, which would overstate sales (net) and net income. Also, because the dollar amount in accounts receivable is higher than it should be, the quick ratio may be overstated.

When it comes to reporting current liabilities, a manager may be tempted to *understate* the company's liabilities. For example, a company may intentionally underestimate warranty liabilities by using a lower estimate of warranty claims outstanding at year-end. Similarly, a company may indicate that a loss contingency is only remotely possible even though it knows that the probability is much higher.

If a company's current liabilities are understated, its quick ratio is higher than it should be. Thus, the company's liquidity position looks better, making the company seem to have more financial flexibility. By relying on these inflated ratios, external users may make wrong business decisions—make a loan to a company that is more risky than they believed it was or pay more than they should for shares of a company's common stock. If managers intentionally misstate financial statements, they have broken the law. They have committed what is called "management fraud" and can be arrested and prosecuted for their actions.

 Do you think a manager should be pessimistic about warranty costs or contingent liabilities to make sure that the company's liquidity position is not overstated? Why or why not? What should the manager do?

At the beginning of the chapter we asked you several questions. During the chapter, we asked you to STOP and answer some additional questions to build your knowledge about specific issues. Be sure you answered these additional questions. Below are the questions from the beginning of the chapter, with a brief summary of the key points relating to the answers. Use your creative and critical thinking skills to expand on these key points to develop more complete answers to the questions and to determine what other questions you have that might lead you to learn more about the issues.

1 Why does a large company make purchases on credit, and how should it manage and record accounts payable?

A large company makes purchases on credit for many of the same reasons that a small company does: (1) purchasing on credit is often more convenient than purchasing with cash, (2) purchasing on credit delays paying for purchases and, by doing so, results in a short-term "loan" from the supplier, and (3) purchasing on credit gives the company an opportunity to assess the quality of the item before making the cash payment. In general, a company should establish the following policies for credit purchases: (1) separate purchasing duties from record-keeping duties and/or control of the asset, (2) restrict the ability of employees to obligate the company to pay for credit purchases, (3) authorize cash payments only for goods that have been received and properly documented, and (4) require submission of accounts payable documents to the cash payments department in a timely manner to take advantage of purchases discounts. When the company purchases inventory and uses the gross method, it increases inventory and accounts payable for the total amount of the purchase. When it pays for the purchases and takes a discount, it decreases cash for the net amount, inventory for the amount of the discount, and accounts payable by the gross amount of the purchase. Alternatively, if the company does not pay within the discount period, it simply reduces cash and accounts payable. If a company uses the net method, it records the inventory at the total invoice price less the discount (that is, at the net price). When it pays the invoice, it reduces cash and accounts payable by the net amount. Alternatively, if it does not pay within the discount period, it decreases cash by the gross amount, decreases accounts payable by the net amount, and records the difference as purchases discounts lost, which is an expense account similar to interest expense.

2 How does an exchange gain (loss) arise from a credit purchase made from a company in another country?

An exchange gain or loss is caused by a change in the exchange rate between the date that a company records a credit purchase transaction and the date that the company pays the cash. More specifically, an exchange gain occurs when the exchange rate declines between the date a company records a payable and the date the company pays the cash, and an exchange loss occurs when the exchange rate increases between the date a company records a payable and the date the company pays the cash.

3 What are accrued liabilities, and what types does a company often have?

Accrued liabilities are short-term obligations (other than accounts payable) that a company owes at the end of an accounting period and that result from the company's operating activities during the period. Examples include a company's utility bill for the last month in an accounting period (which it will pay in the next accounting period), salaries (wages) that have been earned by employees but have not yet been paid, and warranties that apply to products sold during the period and that will be honored in future year(s).

4 What types of taxes do an employee and a company incur, and how does the company record them?

If an employee earns a certain minimum amount of personal income, the federal government requires the employee to pay income taxes, as well as social security and Medicare taxes. A company incurs federal and state payroll taxes (social security and unemployment taxes), federal and state income taxes, state and local sales taxes (if it sells to retail customers), and state and local property taxes. For the employee, the company records gross pay as an expense, deducts taxes owed by the employee, and pays the employee the net pay. It sends the employee's taxes withheld to the appropriate governments. The company also records its payroll expenses and later sends the amounts to the appropriate governments.

5 **How is accounting for a short-term note payable similar to accounting for a short-term note receivable?**

Accounting for a short-term note payable is a "mirror image" of accounting for a short-term note receivable. Whereas a company earns interest revenue during the time it holds a note receivable, a company incurs interest expense during the time it owes a note payable. The amount of interest expense that a company incurs depends on the face value of the note, its interest rate, and its life. At the end of the accounting period, the company computes any accrued interest in the same way it does for a note receivable. For notes payable, however, a company records the amount of interest as interest expense and interest payable. In addition to reporting the face value of a short-term note payable as a current liability on its balance sheet, a company includes the amount of interest payable in its total for accrued liabilities. The company reports the related interest expense in the "other items" section of its income statement.

6 **What are prepaid items, and how does a company account for them?**

Prepaid items arise when a purchasing company pays cash before the selling company delivers the goods or provides the services that were purchased. For example, landlords require tenants to pay rent before being allowed to use the property, and insurance companies require policyholders to pay premiums before their policy is in effect. A purchasing company records a prepaid item as an asset because it has paid for a good or service that it will use in the future. It records an expense for the portion of the asset it uses and reduces the prepaid item as an end-of-period adjustment. The company includes the expense as an operating expense on its income statement and the remaining amount of the prepaid item as a current asset on its ending balance sheet.

7 **What are loss contingencies, and how does a company report or disclose them?**

A contingency is an existing condition that will lead to a gain or loss if a future event occurs (or fails to occur). GAAP requires a company to either report or disclose certain information about loss contingencies in its financial statements depending on two conditions: (1) the likelihood that the future event will occur, and (2) the ability to estimate the dollar amount associated with the contingency. The likelihood that the future event will occur falls into three levels, according to GAAP: (1) probable, (2) reasonably possible, and (3) remote. The method that a company is required to use to report or disclose loss contingencies depends on the degree of certainty that is associated with the future event: (1) if it is probable that the future event related to the loss contingency will occur and the amount of the loss can be reasonably estimated, a company reports an estimated loss from a loss contingency on its financial statements as a reduction in income (either as an expense or a loss) and as a liability (or reduction of an asset); (2) if it is reasonably possible that the future event related to the loss contingency will occur, a company discloses an estimated loss from a loss contingency in the notes to its financial statements. If the likelihood of the future event related to a loss contingency is remote, GAAP does not require that a company report an estimated loss in the financial statements or disclose the loss in the notes (unless it is a guarantee of another company's debt).

8 **What can external users learn from analyzing a company's liquidity?**

External users evaluate a company's liquidity position for two main reasons. First, they evaluate the company's liquidity to help assess its ability to meet short-term obligations. External users realize that if a company cannot pay its obligations as they come due, it risks going out of business. A company that fails to pay its short-term obligations will have difficulty purchasing on credit or borrowing money. Second, external users evaluate a company's liquidity to help assess its financial flexibility. A company in a good liquidity position can take better advantage of business opportunities such as aggressively marketing its products or investing for growth. External users must understand two basic aspects of accounting to be able to evaluate a company's liquidity position. First, they need to know the assets and liabilities that affect liquidity. Second, they must understand how to perform financial statement analysis using ratio analysis, horizontal analysis, and vertical analysis. They may perform these types of analyses only on the company being evaluated (intracompany analysis), and/or they may compare the company's liquidity position with industry averages and with the liquidity positions of similar companies (intercompany analysis).

Key Terms

accounts payable subsidiary ledger *(p. 461)*	**procurement card** *(p. 467)*
accrued liabilities *(p. 468)*	**purchase order** *(p. 462)*
accrued salaries *(p. 469)*	**purchases allowance** *(p. 465)*
accrued taxes *(p. 472)*	**purchases discount** *(p. 462)*
contingency *(p. 479)*	**purchases return** *(p. 465)*
control account *(p. 461)*	**receiving report** *(p. 462)*
exchange gain or loss *(p. 466)*	**salaries payable** *(p. 469)*
gross pay *(p. 472)*	**tax** *(p. 471)*
net pay *(p. 472)*	**taxes payable** *(p. 472)*
prepaid item *(p. 478)*	**wages payable** *(p. 469)*

SUMMARY SURFING

Here is an opportunity to gather information on the Internet about real-world issues related to the topics in this chapter. Go to http://www.dryden.com/account and click on the Cunningham, Nikolai, and Bazley book cover. Click on Summary Surfing, then click on this chapter number, and answer the following questions.

▶ Click on **Yahoo!**, then *Business and Economy*, then *Finance and Investment*, then *Currency* and then *Quotes*. Has the dollar strengthened or weakened against the Brazilian real since Unlimited Decadence's purchase discussed in the chapter? If the company purchased sugar when the exchange rate was $0.51 and paid at the current exchange rate, would the company have an exchange gain or loss?

▶ Click on **FreeEDGAR**, click on *SEARCH FILINGS*, type "Hershey Foods" and click on *SEARCH*, then click on *COMPANY FILINGS*, then on HERSHEY FOODS CORP. beside the 10K filed in March of the most recent year (e.g., 3/16/98), then on EX-13: 1997 ANNUAL REPORT. Explain how the company's liquidity has changed in the last year.

Integrated Business and Accounting Situations

Answer the Following Questions in Your Own Words

Testing Your Knowledge

14-1 Why does a large company make purchases on credit?

14-2 What is an accounts payable subsidiary ledger, and how does it relate to the Accounts Payable control account?

14-3 What are the basic management policies over credit purchases for large companies?

14-4 What is the difference between a purchase order and a receiving report?

14-5 Briefly explain how a company records and reports a purchases discount taken under (a) the gross method and (b) the net method.

14-6 Explain the difference between a purchases return and a purchases allowance.

14-7 Explain the difference between an exchange gain and an exchange loss in regard to credit purchases.

14-8 Briefly explain what innovations a company might use for its accounts payable management.

14-9 What are accrued liabilities, and what effect do they have on a company's financial statements?

14-10 What are accrued salaries? How is the dollar amount of salaries payable calculated at the end of an accounting period?

14-11 What is a product warranty? What does the dollar amount of accrued warranty liability reported on a company's ending balance sheet represent?

14-12 Identify three types of payroll taxes, and explain whether employees, employers, or both are responsible for each type of tax.

14-13 Why might a company be required to issue a short-term note payable when it purchases inventory? How does the company report this note on its ending balance sheet?

14-14 What is a prepaid item, and how is it adjusted at the end of an accounting period?

14-15 What is a loss contingency, and what are the two conditions that must be considered in determining how to account for it?

14-16 When does a company report a loss contingency in its financial statements?

14-17 hen does a company disclose a loss contingency in the notes to its financial statements?

14-18 Why do external users evaluate a company's liquidity position?

14-19 Briefly discuss how you would use intracompany analysis to evaluate a company's liquidity management.

14-20 How is a company's quick ratio calculated, and what does it show?

14-21 How is a company's accounts receivable turnover ratio calculated, and what does it measure?

14-22 How is a company's accounts payable turnover ratio calculated, and what does it measure?

14-23 Briefly discuss how you would use intercompany analysis to evaluate a company's liquidity management.

Applying Your Knowledge

14-24 On May 3 Morgan Furnace Company, which uses a perpetual inventory system, purchased $8,000 of furnaces from Tam Mfg. on credit with terms 3/10, n/30.

Required: (1) Using T-accounts and the gross method, record Morgan's purchase and payment assuming (a) Morgan paid for the purchase on May 12, and instead (b) Morgan paid for the purchase on May 30.

(2) Using T-accounts and the net method, record Morgan's purchase and payment assuming (a) Morgan paid for the purchase on May 12, and instead (b) Morgan paid for the purchase on May 30.

14-25   On September 21 the purchasing department of Sherman Hardware Corporation purchased raw materials costing $7,500 on credit from Adams Supply Company. Adams offered Sherman purchases discount terms of 2/15, n/30. Sherman uses a perpetual inventory system and the gross method of recording purchases discounts.

Required: (1) Using T-accounts, show how Sherman records the credit purchase and its cash payment in its accounting system (a) if Sherman's accounting department waits 30 days from the date of the purchase before it pays Adams for this purchase, and instead (b) if Sherman's accounting department pays for the purchase within 15 days from the date of the purchase.

(2) If Sherman sells this inventory for $12,000, what is the gross profit from the sale under (a) and (b)? Explain the difference between these two amounts.

(3) What would your answers to (2) be if Sherman had been using the net method of recording purchases discounts? What is the reason for any difference between your answers to (2) and (3)?

(4) What is the approximate interest cost (percentage) assuming a 360-day year if Sherman chooses not to pay for its purchases within the purchases discount period?

14-26   On July 1, Nikko Company purchased merchandise costing $14,000 on credit from Ham Company under terms n/30. When it received the merchandise, an inspection revealed that some was of inferior quality. Instead of returning the merchandise to Ham, Nikko was granted an allowance of $1,700, and it planned to sell the merchandise at its annual "sidewalk sale." Nikko uses the gross method to record its purchases.

Required: (1) Using T-accounts, show how Nikko Company would record the purchase, allowance, and payment.

(2) What source documents would be used to record each transaction?

(3) What is the net amount of the inventory after these transactions have been recorded?

14-27   On January 15, Seagle Company, a U.S. company, acquired machinery on credit from Cleese Company, a British company, for 12,000 pounds. The Seagle Company paid for the machine on January 30. The exchange rates on January 15 and January 30 were $1.65 and $1.60, respectively.

Required: (1) Prepare T-account entries for Seagle to record the purchase and the payment.

(2) Prepare the January 30 T-account entry for Seagle to record the payment if, instead, the exchange rate was $1.72 on this date.

14-28   The Clinkscales Brass Fittings Company has 100 employees, each of whom earns $440 per week for a five-day work week (Monday through Friday). The employees are paid every Thursday at the end of the day. September 30, the end of the company's fiscal year, falls on Monday.

Required: (1) Using T-accounts, record the end-of-period adjustment for salaries on September 30.

(2) Using T-accounts, record the entry for the payment of salaries on October 3.

(3) Explain the effect on Clinkscales' financial statements for the fiscal year if it had not made the end-of-period adjustment in (1). Ignore income taxes.

14-29   On October 2, 2000, Scotch Company purchased two acres of land from Irist Company at a cost of $10,000. The Scotch Company signed (issued) a one-year, 10% note requiring it to repay the $10,000 principal plus $1,000 interest on October 1, 2001 to Irist Company. Irist Company had originally purchased the land for $10,000.

Required: (1) Using T-accounts, record the purchase of the land and the December 31 end-of-period adjustment for Scotch Company.

(2) Using T-accounts, record the sale of the land and the December 31 end-of-period adjustment for Irist Company.

14-30 The following list of accounts and account balances was taken from the accounting records of Mane Lettering Company:

Account Title	Account Balance Before Adjustment	Account Balance After Adjustment
Prepaid Insurance	$2,400	$1,800
Salaries Payable	0	7,300
Unearned Rent Revenue	9,800	5,600

Required: Using T-accounts, for each account enter the beginning balance, prepare the end-of-period adjustment that caused the change in the account balance, and enter the ending balance.

14-31 On December 31 of the current year, Rulem Company provides you with the following information:
(a) Accrued interest on a note payable amounts to $850 at year-end.
(b) Prepaid insurance that expired during the year totals $2,500 at year-end.
(c) Unearned rent revenue that was earned during the year totals $3,600 at year-end.

Required: (1) Using T-accounts, record the end-of-period adjustment of Rulem for each of the preceding items.
(2) Explain the effect on Rulem's current financial statements if each of the end-of-period adjustments had not been made. Ignore income taxes.

14-32 During 2000, Ryan Appliance Wholesalers sold electric toasters with one-year warranties. By the end of the year, the company had repaired 300 toasters at an average cost (paid in cash) of $8 each. On December 31, 2000, the company estimated that, in 2001, it would repair, at an average cost of $8 per toaster, 500 toasters sold in 2000.

Required: (1) Using T-accounts, record the repair of the toasters during 2000.
(2) Using T-accounts, record the end-of-period adjustment for 2000.
(3) Show how the warranty expense and liability would be reported on the company's 2000 financial statements.

14-33 Lisa Renet manages Seasons Catering Company. Her annual salary is $78,000, which is earned evenly over the year. Each month, Renet has $1,200 in federal and state income taxes withheld. For simplicity, assume the FICA tax rate is 8% up to a maximum salary of $70,000. Assume that FUTA taxes are 6.2% on the first $7,000 of an employee's gross pay. Renet pays $50 per month for medical insurance; the company withholds this amount from her paycheck and also contributes an equal amount.

Required: (1) For the month of February, calculate (a) Renet's net pay and (b) Seasons Catering Company's salary expense and payroll tax expense associated with Renet's employment.
(2) For the month of December, calculate (a) Renet's net pay and (b) Seasons Catering Company's salary expense and payroll tax expense associated with Renet's employment.
(3) Are the amounts you calculated in (1) the same as the amounts you calculated in (2)? Why or why not?

14-34 For the employees of McKinley Plastics Company, the gross pay and the federal income tax withheld in the first week of February 2000 were as follows:

Employee	Gross Pay	Income Tax Withheld
Carver, James	$600	$ 84
Webb, Steve	700	108
Bailey, Doreen	800	154

For simplicity, assume FICA taxes are withheld at an 8% rate. FUTA taxes are 6.2%. Each employee has a $5 union fee deducted from each paycheck.

Required: (1) Compute the net amount paid to each employee.
(2) Compute the total salaries expense and payroll tax expense incurred by McKinley for the first week of February.
(3) Using T-accounts, record (a) the salaries expense and (b) the payroll tax expense of McKinley for the first week of February, assuming the FICA taxes, FUTA taxes, and union dues will be remitted by McKinley in March.

14-35   During 2000, Caran Cutlery Company made cash sales of $90,000, on which a 6% sales tax was imposed. The sales tax was collected from the customer at the time of each sale. By the end of the year, 75% of the sales tax collected had been remitted to the state.

Required: (1) Using T-accounts, show how Caran Cutlery should record the preceding events for 2000.
(2) Show how Caran Cutlery would report the sales tax liability at the end of 2000.

14-36   On December 31, 2000, Adams Advertising Company was preparing its 2000 financial statements and estimated that its property taxes for the period from July 1, 2000 to June 30, 2001 would be $50,000. On February 10, 2001, Adams received and paid its property tax bill for $50,000.

Required: (1) Using T-accounts, show how Adams should record the preceding events on (a) December 31, 2000, and (b) February 10, 2001.
(2) What would be the effect on the 2000 financial statements if Adams had not recorded its property taxes on December 31, 2000? Ignore income taxes.

14-37   On August 1, 2000, Taft Trailer Company purchased inventory for $60,000 and issued a 10%, six-month note due February 1, 2001 to the seller. The company uses a perpetual inventory system and pays all interest on the maturity date.

Required: (1) Using T-accounts, record (a) the purchase of the inventory, (b) the accrual of interest at year-end, and (c) the repayment of the note.
(2) Show how Taft Trailer Company would report the liabilities at the end of 2000.

14-38   On October 30, 2000, Sheller Manufacturing Company (whose fiscal period is a calendar year) paid six months' rent in advance on its factory, at $10,000 a month.

Required: (1) Using T-accounts, record the payment of the rent and any other entry you think is appropriate in 2000.
(2) Show how the rent accounts would be reported on Sheller's 2000 financial statements.
(3) If Sheller had recorded the entire $60,000 as rent expense on October 31, 2000, what adjustment at the end of 2000 would you recommend to correct its accounting records? Why?

14-39   Wanchez Company is a defendant in a lawsuit resulting from injuries sustained by a customer. During 2000, the customer filed suit against the company for $700,000; the company's lawyers feel that the customer is at least partially at fault. The suit is expected to be "settled" in 2001.

Required: For each of the following alternatives, show how the company would report or disclose the preceding information in its 2000 annual report.
(1) The company's lawyers think that the lawsuit will probably be settled for between $50,000 and $100,000, with $80,000 being the most likely amount.
(2) The company's lawyers think that it is reasonably possible the customer will win the lawsuit. If so, the amount of the settlement will likely be somewhere between $50,000 and $100,000.

14-40   At the beginning of 2000, Fresco Manufacturing Company had accounts receivable (net) of $36,000. During 2000, Fresco made net sales of $420,000 under terms of 1/10, n/30, while operating on a 300-day business year. At the end of 2000, the company had current liabilities of $60,000, as well as the following current assets:

Cash and cash equivalents	$12,000
Accounts receivable (net)	40,000
Notes receivable	12,000
Inventories	83,000
Marketable securities	6,000
Prepaid items	4,000

Required: (1) Compute Fresco's quick ratio at the end of 2000. How does this compare with the industry average of 1.05?

(2) Compute Fresco's accounts receivable turnover ratio and the number of days in its collection period. What do you think of its collection efforts?

Making Evaluations

14-41 If you have (or used to have) a job, think about the controls you have seen regarding purchases and cash payments.

Required: Explain the controls you observed. Are there any areas in which you would recommend improvements?

14-42 Your friend works at a local company part-time helping with the accounts payable. He has observed that the company uses the gross method of accounting for purchases discounts and wonders what the differences are between this method and the net method.

Required: Write a short report explaining the difference between the gross and the net methods, and include your recommendation about which method the company should use.

14-43 Use your paycheck stub from a job where you work (or have worked).

Required: Determine the amount of your gross pay and net pay. Analyze how your pay affects the company's financial statements. Can you identify the payroll costs the company incurred by employing you?

14-44 The Zanzibar Company has a significant increase in business around Christmas. In past years it has hired 10 extra employees for December, with each employee working 200 hours. As a result of using seasonal employees, the company pays the full 5.4% of the 6.2% FUTA tax to the state on these salaries as well as on the salaries of its 20 year-round employees. The company is confident that if it did not have this seasonal employment problem, it could achieve a merit rating and could pay only 4.6% to the state for the FUTA tax. The company estimates that hiring each employee costs $50 in interviewing and processing costs. As an alternative for 2000, Zanzibar Company is considering using employees provided by Temphelp, a company that specializes in providing temporary employees. Zanzibar would have to pay Temphelp $6 per hour per employee, but Temphelp would pay all social security and federal and state unemployment taxes.

Required: Using the rates provided in this chapter, what is the company wage rate at which it would make no difference to Zanzibar Company if it hired its own employees or used Temphelp?

14-45 In 1990, Adolph Coors reported in its income statement a "special charge" of $30 million. On the following pages are some related disclosures from its 1990 and 1995 annual reports.

www.coors.com

Required: Why did the income statement for 1990 include $30 million whereas Note 7 refers to $18.6 million? Why did the company record the amount in 1990? What does the term "jointly and severally liable" (in Management's Discussion) mean? Why did the company record $30 million instead of $4.5 billion? Why did the company record the effects of the insurance settlement only in 1994?

CONSOLIDATED STATEMENT OF INCOME

Adolph Coors Company and Subsidiaries

	For the years ended		
	December 30, 1990	December 31, 1989	December 25, 1988
	(In thousands, except per share data)		
Sales	$2,050,110	$1,934,337	$1,680,968
Less—federal and state beer excise taxes	186,756	170,467	159,271
Net sales	1,863,354	1,763,870	1,521,697
Costs and expenses:			
Cost of goods sold	1,273,840	1,232,028	1,021,084
Marketing, general and administrative	462,911	433,435	408,348
Research and project development	22,219	22,991	22,723
Special charge (Note 7)	30,000	—	—
Asset write-downs (Note 7)	—	41,670	—
Total operating expenses	1,788,970	1,730,124	1,452,155
Operating income	74,384	33,746	69,542
Other (income) expense:			
Interest income	(4,183)	(6,119)	(8,894)
Interest expense	371	1,699	2,642
Miscellaneous—net	13,996	12,534	(1,181)
Total other (income) expense	10,184	8,114	(7,433)
Income before income taxes	64,200	25,632	76,975
Income taxes (Note 4)	25,300	12,500	30,100
Net income	$ 38,900	$ 13,132	$ 46,875
Net income per share of common stock	$1.05	$0.36	$1.28

See notes to consolidated financial statements.

NOTE 7:

Special Charge and Asset Write-Downs

Included in 1990 is a special pre-tax charge of $30,000,000 for potential costs related to remediation of the Lowry Landfill Superfund site. The Company has received notice from the U.S. Environmental Protection Agency that it is a "potentially responsible party" under the Comprehensive Environmental Response Compensation and Liability Act (as amended by the Superfund Amendment and Reauthorization Act) and may be required to share in the cost of study and any clean-up of the Lowry Landfill Superfund site. The impact of this charge on 1990 net earnings was $18,600,000, or $0.50 per share. The ultimate remediation methods and appropriate allocation of costs for Lowry are not yet final. The Company, in cooperation with certain other users of the landfill, is vigorously studying the site in an effort to understand the scope of the problem and recommend appropriate remedies.

██ CONSOLIDATED STATEMENT OF INCOME

Adolph Coors Company and Subsidiaries

	For the years ended		
	December 31, 1995	December 25, 1994	December 26, 1993
	(In thousands, except per share data)		
Sales	**$2,060,595**	$2,040,330	$1,946,592
Less – federal and state excise taxes	**385,216**	377,659	364,781
Net sales	**1,675,379**	1,662,671	1,581,811
Costs and expenses:			
Cost of goods sold	**1,091,763**	1,062,789	1,036,864
Marketing, general and administrative	**503,503**	492,403	454,130
Research and project development	**15,385**	13,265	13,008
Special (credits) charges (Note 9)	**(15,200)**	(13,949)	122,540
Total operating expenses	**1,595,451**	1,554,508	1,626,542
Operating income (loss)	**79,928**	108,163	(44,731)
Other income (expense):			
Interest income	**1,345**	1,546	2,580
Interest expense	**(11,863)**	(11,461)	(15,780)
Miscellaneous — net	**3,868**	5,972	1,101
Total other income (expense)	**(6,650)**	(3,943)	(12,099)
Income (loss) before income taxes	**73,278**	104,220	(56,830)
Income tax expense (benefit) (Note 5)	**30,100**	46,100	(14,900)
Net income (loss)	**$ 43,178**	$ 58,120	($ 41,930)
Net income (loss) per share of common stock	**$1.13**	$1.52	($1.10)
Weighted average number of outstanding shares of common stock	**38,170**	38,283	37,989

See notes to consolidated financial statements.

NOTE 9:

Fourth quarter results for 1994 include a net special credit of $13.9 million and resulted in income of $0.22 per share after tax. Two non-recurring items contributed to the net credit. First, the Company reached a settlement with a number of its insurance carriers which enabled it to recover a portion of the costs associated with the Lowry Landfill Superfund site (see Note 12). Offsetting this was an impairment reserve for the write-down of certain distributor assets.

MANAGEMENT'S DISCUSSION AND ANALYSIS OF FINANCIAL CONDITION AND RESULTS OF OPERATIONS

Adolph Coors Company and Subsidiaries

Environmental

The Company has received notice from the U.S. Environmental Protection Agency (EPA) that it is a "potentially responsible party" (PRP) under the Comprehensive Environmental Response Compensation and Liability Act for the Lowry Landfill Superfund site (the site). Under the laws governing Superfund sites, PRPs may be jointly and severally liable for the entire amount of the clean-up at these sites. Lowry is a legally permitted landfill owned by the City and County of Denver that accepted waste materials from a variety of sources from the 1960s until 1980.

In mid-1988, the EPA released a "Preliminary Identification of Remedial Alternatives" (PIRA) for the site which included a wide range of cost estimates and time frames for clean-up. According to the EPA's PIRA, the estimated total costs of the overall site remedies deemed plausible ranged from $151.3 million to $4.5 billion.

In December 1990, the EPA issued a revised list of volumes contributed. This list indicates the Company contributed approximately 20% of the volume at the site. During the fourth quarter of 1990, the Company recorded a special pre-tax charge of $30.0 million related to potential remediation costs for the site. Net income was reduced by $18.6 million, or $0.50 per share, as a result of this charge. The Company's actual total cost of remediation will depend upon a number of factors, such as the selected method of remediation, timing of work, number of financially solvent PRPs ultimately responsible for payment, the allocation of the liability, effect of inflation and development of remediation technology. Until the ultimate remediation methods and appropriate allocation of costs for the site have been determined, the Company cannot accurately predict the total cost of remediation for the site. The Company does not anticipate significant cash outlays for remediation within the near term. The Company, in cooperation with certain other users of the landfill, is vigorously studying the site in an effort to understand the scope of the problem and recommend appropriate remedies.

While it is impossible to predict the eventual aggregate cost to the Company for environmental and related matters, management believes that the payments for these matters will be made over a period of years in amounts which, except as set forth above with respect to the Lowry Landfill Superfund site, would not be material in any one year to the Company's consolidated results of operations or financial position.

14-46   The Slamming Sam Golf Club Company decided to expand its manufacturing operations as a result of receiving a new order for golf clubs from a distributor. On July 1, 2000, the company acquired a new machine for manufacturing the clubs, from a supplier at a cost of $500,000. The supplier offers to accept either immediate payment or a nine-month note with interest of 10%. The company expects to produce 5,000 clubs during the remaining six months of the year and incur materials costs of $30 for each club evenly over the period. Since Slamming Sam will not sell the clubs to the public until the spring of 2001, the materials supplier offers terms of immediate payment less a 5% discount if paid within ten days, or full payment within two months, or delayed payment until 2000 with interest charged at 12% after two months until full payment is received.

Required: Compute the amount of the liabilities that the company will have on December 31, 2000 under each of the alternative situations. (Assume a 360-day year.)

14-47   According to Fortune magazine, the following amounts were used to compute the "net profits" of the movie *Indecent Proposal:*

Gross receipts	$162,235,826
Less: Distribution fees	56,338,707
Gross after distribution fees	$105,897,119
Less: Accounts receivable (net of distribution fees)	5,163,725
Balance	$100,733,394
Less: Distribution expenses	55,062,679
Balance	$ 45,670,715
Less: Interest on negative cost	8,002,432
Negative cost	73,418,212
Net profits	$(35,749,929)

Many of the second-tier stars, writers, and producers receive bonuses based on net profits.

Required: Explain what you think each of the items represents. Explain whether the calculation of the net profits seems reasonable to you.

14-48 In its 1997 annual report, <u>Newmont Mining</u> disclosed that it "is involved in several matters concerning environmental obligations associated with former mining activities. Based on the Corporation's best estimate of its liability for these matters, $52.2 million and $49.8 million were accrued for such obligations at December 31, 1997 and 1996, respectively. Depending on the ultimate resolution of these matters, the Corporation believes that it is reasonably possible that the liability for these matters could be as much as 70% greater or 15% lower than the amount accrued at December 31, 1997."

www.newmont.com

Required: Why did the company accrue these amounts? Why did the amount increase during 1997? How will the company report the effects of an increase or a decrease in its estimate?

14-49 <u>Adolph Coors</u> reports the following in its income statement (in thousands):

www.coors.com

Year Ended	Dec. 28, 1997	Dec. 29, 1996	Dec. 31, 1995
Sales–domestic and international	$2,208,231	$2,121,367	$2,075,917
Less–beer excise taxes	386,080	379,311	385,216
Net sales	$1,822,151	$1,742,056	$1,690,701

Required: (1) Why do you think that Coors uses a different date for each year-end?
   (2) In the chapter, we explained that sales taxes are not included as part of revenue. Explain why you think that Coors uses its form of disclosure for beer excise taxes.

14-50 In a recent annual report, <u>Quaker Oats</u> disclosed the following:

www.QuakerOats.com

On December 18, 1990, Judge Prentice H. Marshall of the United States District Court for the Northern District of Illinois entered judgment against the Company in favor of Sands, Taylor & Wood Co., holding that the use of the words "thirst aid" in advertising Gatorade thirst quencher infringed the Plaintiff's rights in the trademark THIRST-AID. On July 9, 1991, Judge Marshall entered a judgment of $42.6 million, composed of $31.4 million in principal, prejudgment interest of $10.6 million, and fees, expenses and costs of $0.6 million. The order enjoined use of the phrase "THIRST-AID" in connection with the advertising or sale of Gatorade thirst quencher in the United States. The Company appealed the judgment. On September 2, 1992, the Court of Appeals for the Seventh Circuit affirmed the finding of infringement, but found that the monetary award was an inequitable "windfall" to the Plaintiff, and it therefore remanded the case to the District Court. On June 7, 1993, Judge Marshall issued a judgment on remand of $26.5 million, composed of $20.7 million in principal, prejudgment interest of $5.4 million, and fees, expenses and costs of $0.4 million. The Company appealed this judgment. On September 13, 1994, the Court of Appeals affirmed the lower court's award of a reasonable royalty and prejudgment interest, but again remanded the case to allow the District Court to explain the enhancement of the royalty award. On April 11, 1995, Judge Marshall affirmed his prior ruling and the Company filed another appeal. Management, with advice from outside legal counsel, has determined that the Court of Appeals' opinion appears to indicate a range of exposure between $18 million and $30 million.

Required: Explain when you think that Quaker Oats should have recorded the effects of the litigation in the financial statements. How much do you think it should have recorded?

www.generalmills.com

14-51 The annual report for General Mills is included in Appendix C.

Required: (1) Compute the quick ratio on May 31, 1998, and May 25, 1997, as well as the accounts receivable turnover ratio, and the accounts payable turnover ratio for fiscal years 1998 and 1997. The accounts receivable and accounts payable at May 26, 1996 were $337.8 and $590.7, respectively. Write a short report evaluating the performance of General Mills.

(2) In Management's Discussion and Analysis, the company discloses that sales volume grew 8% in 1998 compared with 1997. Compute the average amount by which the company's sales prices changed from 1997 to 1998. How is your answer affected because 1998 was a 53-week fiscal year?

(3) The company does not disclose when it records revenue. Explain when you think it should record revenue. Explain why you think the company did not disclose its policy.

(4) Compute the company's interest expense for the fiscal year 1998 on its current notes payable. Ignore amounts reclassified to long-term debt.

14-52 Yesterday, you received the following letter for your advice column in the local paper:

Dear Dr. Decisive:

Following a trip with my girlfriend and my family, I recently [see Chapter 5] wrote to ask you whether frequent flyer miles are an asset or an expense for a company that has accumulated them. Soon thereafter, we started arguing about whether the airline has a liability for frequent flyer miles "earned" by its customers. I say no. For example, I earned 12,000 miles on my trip to Hawaii, but I have to have 25,000 miles to get a free ticket. And I doubt I will travel much in the next few years because my parents won't take me on another trip. My girlfriend says there is a liability because many business executives fly all the time and get lots of miles that they use. But I respond that they often don't have time to use the miles. Then my smart-aleck little brother, who thinks he knows everything, agreed with my girlfriend but asked how the airline would know how much to record as the value of the liability. Help me before my girlfriend dumps me for my little brother.

Please sign me: "Wrestling Fan (Part 2)."

Required: Meet with your Dr. Decisive team and write a response to "Wrestling Fan (Part 2)."

CHAPTER OUTLINE

PART 6

MANAGING, REPORTING, AND EVALUATING OPERATIONS IN A CORPORATE ENVIRONMENT

This section consists of five chapters

which discuss issues involving a

corporation's operating activities.

After reading these chapters, you

will be able to:

▶ *understand the relevant costs and revenues in short-term planning decisions*

▶ *know how to use job order costing and process costing in managing a corporation's manufacturing activities*

▶ *calculate and use standard costs for direct materials, direct labor, and factory overhead to control a corporation's operations*

▶ *apply activity-based costing in a corporation's operations*

▶ *understand how a corporation uses the FIFO, LIFO, or average cost method to report its inventory*

▶ *use a corporation's inventory and cost of goods sold disclosures for evaluating its operations*

CHAPTER 15

SHORT-TERM PLANNING DECISIONS

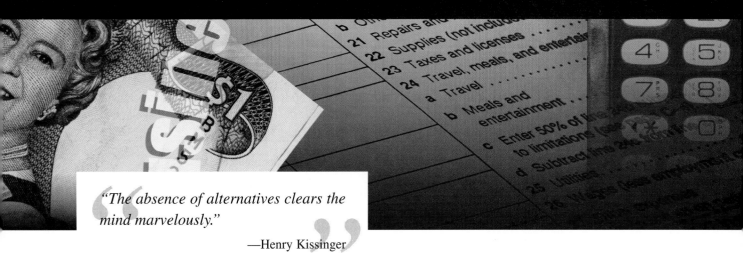

"The absence of alternatives clears the mind marvelously."

—Henry Kissinger

1 *How do relevant costs and revenues contribute to sound decision-making?*

2 *What types of costs and revenues are relevant to decision-making?*

3 *How can a company determine how much inventory to order?*

4 *How does a company determine when to drop a product?*

5 *What is a make-or-buy decision, and what issues does a company consider in this decision?*

6 *How does a company determine whether to sell a product or to process it further?*

7 *What is a product-mix decision, and what issues does a company consider in this decision?*

8 *What other factors should a company consider when making inventory decisions?*

Think about the decisions you have made so far today: what to wear, what to have for breakfast, whether to wash the breakfast dishes right away or wait until later, whether to stop for gas on the way to school or on the way back, what route to take to school, how fast to drive, whether to change lanes, where to park, what route to walk to class . . . whew! Now think about the decisions you made in the last year. They included decisions similar to the ones we have just listed, but they may also have included major decisions, such as where to go to school, what to major in, what career to choose, or even whether to get married. Some of these decisions are easy to make, and others require processing a mind-boggling amount of information and possible outcomes. (What if you consider and weigh all the pertinent factors and still end up in a career that you dislike or married to the wrong person?) Whether decisions affect just today or have long-term effects, organizing and analyzing this information and these possibilities helps the decision-making process.

A company also faces a wide array of decisions, from very simple to extremely complicated. To help a company make sense of the information and possibilities related to business decisions, managers use accounting information as one input in their decision-making processes. In this chapter we discuss the use of accounting information for short-term decisions involving inventory planning.

Both merchandising and manufacturing companies make short-term inventory-planning decisions. However, because of the production function, a manufacturing company faces a larger number and variety of these decisions than does a merchandising company. Some common inventory-planning decisions involve determining answers to the following questions:

1. How many units of inventory should the company make or buy?

2. Should the company drop an unprofitable product?

3. Should the company make or buy a component that becomes a part of a product?

4. Should the company sell a product "as is" or process it further into a different product?

5. Which products should the company advertise?

6. What is the most profitable "product mix" for the company when one of its resources is scarce?

In this chapter, we will emphasize the inventory decisions made by manufacturing companies. But before we look at each of these decisions, we will briefly review decision-making, discuss the relevant costs and revenues for decision-making, and present the general characteristics or types of information that help managers make better, or more informed, decisions.

Decision-making

1 *How do relevant costs and revenues contribute to sound decision-making?*

Recall from our Chapter 2 discussion of critical thinking that there are several steps in decision-making: (1) recognizing the need for a decision (defining the problem), (2) identifying alternative solutions, (3) evaluating the alternative solutions, and (4) making the decision (choosing the best alternative). Although accounting information may be useful in any of these steps, it is particularly helpful in evaluating alternatives (step 3). When a company evaluates each decision alternative, the key question is, "What difference does it make?" One important area where decision alternatives make a difference is in a company's profit. It is important that a company analyze the changes in its costs and revenues caused by each decision alternative so that it understands the profit impact of each alternative. This information can then be weighed against any other considerations that are important to the decision, such as how the alternative affects employees, the community, or the environment.

Relevant Costs and Revenues

The profit impact of a decision is often one of the most important issues in evaluating decisions like the ones we listed above. To understand the profit impact of a decision, managers must carefully analyze the costs and revenues that the decision affects—or the *relevant* costs and revenues. **Relevant costs** and **relevant revenues** are *future* costs and revenues that will change as a result of a decision.

It is important to know that a cost or a revenue that is relevant for one decision may not be relevant for another. For example, the temperature outside is relevant for a decision about what to wear today, but is irrelevant for a decision about what classes to take next semester. Likewise, the cost of sugar Unlimited Decadence uses in producing its Darkly Decadent candy bar is relevant for deciding whether to continue producing the candy bar, but is irrelevant for deciding whether to replace equipment.

An important part of preparing an analysis for a decision is to identify the costs and/or revenues that are relevant to that decision. All relevant costs and revenues should be included in this analysis because incomplete profit information could result in an incorrect decision. Costs and revenues that are *not* relevant to a decision should be omitted from the analysis because they are not helpful in making the decision. Also, if treated improperly, they might result in an incorrect decision.

Determining Relevant Costs and Revenues for a Decision

For a particular decision, a manager must ask two questions to identify the relevant costs and/or revenues: (1) what activities are necessary for the company to carry out the decision? and (2) by how much will the costs and/or revenues be affected if the company undertakes the activities?

As you will see, many inventory decisions involve only costs. Hence, we focus the remaining discussion on identifying relevant costs for an activity. However, the same procedures are used for identifying relevant revenues for an activity.

What Activities are Necessary for the Company to Carry Out the Decision?

The key to identifying potentially relevant costs is to have a good understanding of the company's activities that are necessary to carry out the decision. Why? Because these activities are the *cause* of all relevant costs. Thus only costs that the company incurs as a *result* of performing these activities can be relevant. Therefore, two large groups of costs can immediately be eliminated from consideration.

First, *no cost incurred prior to making the decision is relevant.* Since the decision must be made before the activities can be carried out, all costs that the company incurs as a result of the activities must be *future* costs. Thus only future costs are relevant. Past costs (sometimes called *sunk* costs) therefore can be eliminated from consideration. Consider the following situation: suppose you are driving to a party at a friend's new house and you make a wrong turn. Now you have a decision to make about what route to take from your present location to your friend's house. (The decision involves an action you will take from *now* into the future.) The fact that you made a wrong turn in the past has nothing to do with the decision alternative (what route to take) that you must choose now. For this decision, the costs of the driving that you have done so far (the mileage) and of the wrong turn (your lost time) are sunk costs. (Whatever decision you make now, you will not regain either the mileage or your lost time.) Similarly, the cost of a machine that a company purchased last year is not relevant to a decision about how the company should use the machine in production this year. (The company already purchased the machine and has incurred this cost whether or not it uses the machine in production this year.)

 Suppose it is November and you are trying to decide whether to go to the beach or to a ski resort for Spring Break. Do you think the cost of the swimming suit you bought last year is relevant to that decision? Why or why not? Do you think the cost of a beach hotel or a ski resort condominium is relevant to that same decision? Why or why not?

2 *What types of costs and revenues are relevant to decision-making?*

Second, *future costs that a company will incur for activities that are not necessary to carry out the decision are not relevant.* These costs relate to other activities that would be undertaken regardless of the outcome of this decision. For example, the cost of sugar to be used in the next year's production of candy bars, although a future cost, is not relevant to Unlimited Decadence's decision to replace an old machine with a new one. This is because the company will use the sugar in the production of candy bars whether it uses the old machine or a new one.

 Assuming you have already decided to go somewhere for Spring Break, do you think your March apartment rent or your spring-semester dorm payment is relevant to the decision about whether to go to the beach or to a ski resort? Why or why not?

Remember, the key question in evaluating a decision is, "What difference does it make?" Past costs, as well as future costs associated with activities that are not related to the decision, remain the same no matter what the decision is. For these costs, the answer to the above question is, "It makes no difference." Hence these costs are irrelevant and should not be considered in the analysis.

By How Much Will the Costs and/or Revenues be Affected if the Company Undertakes the Activities?

The costs that remain for further analysis are the costs required by the decision. Even some of these costs may not be relevant, however. *A specific cost is relevant only if the total amount that the company will incur is affected by the decision.* This fact cannot always be determined until the amounts of the potential relevant costs are estimated, however. Thus the cost-estimation step has two purposes: to provide estimates of relevant costs and to further eliminate irrelevant costs.

For example, suppose Unlimited Decadence is considering two processes to produce the Pure Decadence candy bar. For this decision, it analyzes two potentially relevant costs: direct materials and direct labor. Process 1 requires 2 ounces of one artificial sweetener and 1 hour to produce one case of candy bars. Process 2 requires 4 ounces of a different artificial sweetener and 1.5 hours to produce one case of candy bars. The first artificial

Hm-m-m . . . the beach or the mountains? The mountains or the beach? Beach? Mountains? Mountains? Beach? Is there any way to do both?

sweetener costs $0.60 per ounce, and the second one costs $0.30 per ounce. Direct labor cost is $10 per hour. Are either of these costs relevant to Unlimited Decadence?

The direct materials cost is *not* relevant because the cost of the sweetener to produce a case of candy bars will be $1.20 regardless of which process Unlimited Decadence uses (4 ounces × $0.30 or 2 ounces × $0.60). The direct labor cost, on the other hand, *is* relevant because with Process 1, the labor will cost $10 (1 hour × $10), but the labor will cost $15 (1.5 hours × $10) if Unlimited Decadence uses Process 2. Note that only by estimating these costs do we discover the irrelevance of direct materials cost.

Exhibit 15-1 shows the three-step process by which a manager identifies and separates relevant costs from irrelevant costs. Notice in the first step that we removed all past costs. In the second step, we removed any future costs that are not necessary to carry out the decision. In the third step, we eliminated those costs that would not differ from one decision alternative to another. Then, the only costs left are future costs that a company would incur in different amounts to carry out the decision alternatives. These costs are the relevant costs to include in the decision analysis.

 Which of the following costs are relevant or irrelevant to your decision about whether to go to the beach or to the ski resort? Why?

1. *gas for the trip from your college to the beach and from your college to the ski resort*

2. *the cost of paying your kid brother to feed your fish and pick up your mail*

3. *the cost of ski rentals*

4. *the cost of the ski lessons that you took the last time you went skiing*

5. *the cost of your March car payment*

Other Cost (and Revenue) Concepts for Short-Term Decisions

Three additional cost (and revenue) concepts are important for short-term decisions about inventory because they suggest the reason why certain costs (or revenues) might be relevant for a given decision.

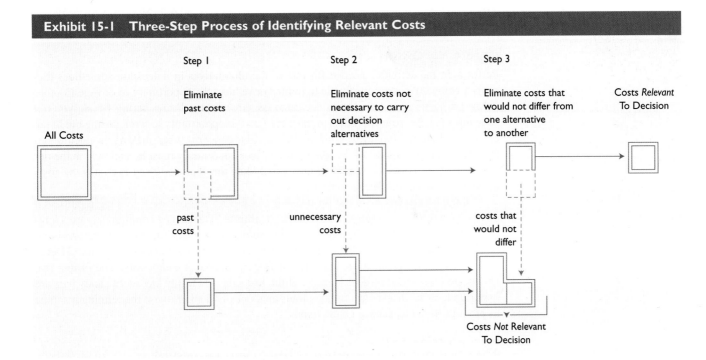

Exhibit 15-1   Three-Step Process of Identifying Relevant Costs

Incremental Costs

In some decisions, one of the alternatives may require activities that a company does not need if it chooses another alternative. In many other decisions, one of the alternatives may require activities at a higher volume than required by another alternative. When either situation occurs, the additional activity usually causes additional costs to be incurred. Cost increases of this type are called incremental costs. **Incremental costs** are cost increases resulting from a higher volume of activity or from the performance of an additional activity. They are *always* relevant when the higher volume of activity, or the additional activity, is not necessary for all the alternatives. For example, suppose Unlimited Decadence must decide whether or not to accept a customer's special order for its Darkly Decadent candy bars. The customer wants special packaging with the customer's name displayed prominently on the boxes it has ordered. The incremental costs of the special packaging are relevant because Unlimited Decadence would have to incur these costs only if it accepts the order. The incremental revenues also are relevant because Unlimited Decadence would receive them only if it accepts the order.

Avoidable Costs

In many other short-term inventory decisions, one of the alternatives involves either discontinuing an activity or decreasing its volume. When a company decreases the volume of an activity or when it discontinues the activity, certain costs necessary to support that activity may be reduced or may no longer have to be incurred. **Avoidable costs** are the costs that a company must incur to perform an activity at a given level, but that it can avoid if the company reduces or discontinues the activity. For example, in late 1993 Ford Motor Company decided to eliminate separate operations for cars sold in the United States, Europe, Asia, and South America, to consolidate operations, and to reduce duplication of effort.[1] As a result, it planned to cut the number of its suppliers of everything from office supplies to machine tools from 50,000 to 5,000 suppliers by 1997. Ford estimated that this action would reduce its costs (avoidable costs), including ordering and shipping costs, by $1 billion!

Suppose a company currently makes a part that it uses in one of its products. If it decides to buy that part instead of making it, the cost of the raw materials used in producing that part is an avoidable cost. If the company stops making the part, do you think the depreciation cost of the factory is an avoidable cost? Why or why not?

Opportunity Costs

Performing the activities needed for one of the alternatives in a decision sometimes disrupts a company's other profitable activities or reduces its opportunity to engage in other future profitable activities. If you decide to go snow skiing during Spring Break, you not only must pay for your trip but also must give up the opportunity to work during the break and earn additional money. A company has similar concerns when making production decisions. The profit impact of this disruption or lost opportunity must be included in the decision analysis. This is commonly done by including the *opportunity costs* among the costs to be incurred for that alternative.

Opportunity costs are the profits that a company forgoes by following a particular course of action. For example, suppose that Unlimited Decadence continuously uses a refining machine to produce Darkly Decadent candy bars. A decision to use the refining machine for a short time to produce Pure Decadence candy bars would cause Unlimited Decadence to decrease production and sales of Darkly Decadent candy bars. The profits that Unlimited Decadence forgoes because of the lost sales of Darkly Decadent candy bars are opportunity costs that it must include in its analysis of whether to use the refining machine to produce Pure Decadence candy bars.

---

[1]James B. Treece, "Ford: Alex Trotman's Daring Global Strategy," *Business Week,* April 3, 1995, 97.

DILBERT® reprinted by permission of United Features Syndicate, Inc.

Illustration of Determining Relevant Costs and Revenues (Special Order)

In this section we show how Unlimited Decadence used the three-step process we described earlier to determine the relevant costs and revenues for a simple inventory decision. Suppose Unlimited Decadence's sales manager returned from a trip to Wyoming, where a movie theater chain offered him $250,000 for 20,000 cases of Darkly Decadent candy bars. Although tempted to jump at the opportunity to increase sales, Unlimited Decadence's sales manager decided to analyze the decision alternatives first. A quick check with the production supervisor assured the sales manager that the plant had the excess capacity to produce an additional 20,000 cases of Darkly Decadent candy bars without giving up production of other candy bars. Therefore, Unlimited Decadence would not incur an opportunity cost by choosing to accept the offer. Because this offer was below the company's normal $16 per case selling price, the sales manager made an analysis of the relevant costs and revenues before deciding whether or not to accept the offer.

The sales manager asked the company's accountant to provide him with some cost information from the company's records. We show this information in Exhibit 15-2. The sales manager recognized that this data could be misleading because the accountant based the amounts on records of Unlimited Decadence's *past* operations, whereas the decision involved *future* operations. Therefore, before looking at the data, he thought through the decision in the following way:

Exhibit 15-2 Cost Data for the Wyoming Sale

Manufacturing costs per unit:
Direct materials	$ 4.34
Direct labor	6.00
Factory overhead:	
Variable	.32
Fixed	1.26
Total manufacturing costs	$11.92

Selling costs:
Advertising	$50,000
Trip to Wyoming	$ 550

Steps 1 and 2

There were only two alternatives to the decision. The company could refuse to accept the offer or could accept it. If Unlimited Decadence refused the offer, it would not engage in cost-incurring activities related to accepting the offer, and it would earn no additional revenue. In other words, Unlimited Decadence would incur no incremental costs or revenues if it did not accept the offer. If it accepted the offer, however, Unlimited Decadence would have to manufacture the 20,000 cases of candy bars and ship them to Wyoming in order to earn the sales revenue. These activities would generate incremental costs and revenues.

 Do you agree with the sales manager's conclusion that there were only two alternatives? Can you think of any others?

After looking at the data in Exhibit 15-2, the sales manager penciled in some comments on the projected cost sheet as a result of his thinking in Step 1. Exhibit 15-3 shows the revised data.

By thinking through the activities needed to carry out the decision to accept the offer, the sales manager recognized that two of the listed costs were not relevant. As we show in Exhibit 15-3, he eliminated the cost of the sales manager's trip to Wyoming because it was a past cost (Step 1). He also eliminated advertising because this cost is related to activities that are not necessary to carry out the decision (Step 2). The offer had already been made, so no advertising would be needed. Finally, he recognized that costs related to shipping (incremental costs) would be incurred if the offer was accepted.

Step 3

Next, after deciding what costs he thought might be relevant, he estimated these costs. After obtaining a bid of $6,000 from Hasty Transfer Company to ship the candy bars to Wyoming, he gathered additional information about the manufacturing costs for the candy bars. He found that the past direct materials, direct labor, and factory overhead costs per unit were still good estimates of those costs for the coming year. The total fixed factory overhead would not increase if Unlimited Decadence were to accept the offer and produce 20,000 additional cases of Darkly Decadent candy bars.

With this information, the sales manager eliminated the fixed factory overhead from the analysis (Step 3) because although it would be a future cost incurred to support manufacturing activity, the amount would not be affected by the decision. Having finally identified and estimated all of the relevant costs, the sales manager included the relevant revenue and then made a decision.

The analysis in Exhibit 15-4 clearly shows all the incremental costs and revenues from accepting the order. It shows that accepting the order would result in an increase in company revenues of $250,000 but an increase in company costs of only $219,200. Therefore Unlimited Decadence's profit (before income taxes) would increase by $30,800. Since rejecting the offer would produce no additional profit, the sales man-

---

Exhibit 15-3 Cost Data for the Wyoming Sale (Revised)

Manufacturing costs per unit:	
Direct materials	$ 4.34
Direct labor	6.00
Factory overhead:	
Variable	.32
Fixed	1.26
Total manufacturing costs	$11.92
Selling costs:	
~~Advertising~~ .... ~~$50,000~~ *omit; activity not required*	
~~Trip to Wyoming~~ .... ~~$ 550~~ *omit; past cost*	
Shipping costs .... ?	

Exhibit 15-4 Relevant Costs and Revenues for the Wyoming Sale

	Accept Offer (20,000 cases)	Reject Offer
Relevant revenues	$250,000	$0
Relevant costs:		
Manufacturing costs:		
Direct materials ($4.34 per case)............. $ 86,800		0
Direct labor ($6 per case) 120,000		0
Variable factory overhead ($0.32 per case)... 6,400		0
Total manufacturing costs $213,200		$0
Shipping costs.. 6,000		0
Total relevant costs......................................	(219,200)	(0)
Increase in profit	$ 30,800	$0

ager should have accepted the offer if he based his decision only on the accounting information.

How do you think Unlimited Decadence's regular customers would react to Unlimited Decadence selling Darkly Decadent candy bars to the theater chain in Wyoming at less than its normal selling price? Would there be any opportunity costs for Unlimited Decadence?

Now that we have described and illustrated the steps involved in identifying relevant costs and revenues for decision-making, we will discuss several common short-term inventory decisions for a variety of companies. The kinds of decisions we discuss below can sometimes be very complex and can, in some situations, be more properly evaluated as long-term decisions (which we will discuss in Chapter 20). We have made the illustrations relatively simple to emphasize the treatment of relevant costs and revenues in the decisions. For simplicity, we ignore income taxes.

Deciding How Many Units of Inventory to Buy

3 *How can a company determine how much inventory to order?*

Most companies carry inventory ranging from a few items to hundreds of products. As we discussed in Chapter 12, carrying inventory requires an investment of money in the inventory. A company should have enough inventory on hand to avoid lost sales or to have flexibility in scheduling production. On the other hand, it should not hold too much inventory because the excess money invested is an opportunity cost—the company could invest the money elsewhere to earn a profit. Recall that in Chapter 13 we had a similar discussion about how much cash a company should hold in its checking account.

In managing the level of its inventory, a company must determine the optimal amount to order for each item of inventory. One technique used for this decision is called the economic order quantity (EOQ) method.[2] The EOQ method assumes that there is a total inventory cost, consisting of the sum of the total carrying costs and the total ordering costs for the inventory. **Carrying costs** are the costs per unit of keeping an inventory item on hand. Carrying costs include the costs for such items as storage and handling, insurance, property taxes, deterioration, and obsolescence. Carrying costs also include the cost of capital tied up in the inventory.[3] Total carrying costs increase as the units in inventory

---

[2]Another technique many companies use is related to a just-in-time operating environment. In this environment, companies maintain minimum inventory levels. We will discuss just-in-time operating environments further in Chapter 18.

[3]The cost of capital is the opportunity cost or profit forgone from having money invested in inventory instead of using that money elsewhere. We will briefly discuss the cost of capital in Chapter 20, but it is beyond the scope of this chapter.

increase. **Ordering costs** are the costs of placing and receiving each inventory order. Ordering costs include the costs for activities such as preparing the purchase order, making long-distance phone calls, shipping and handling the inventory order, and receiving the order. (We discussed many of these activities in Chapter 14 in the context of accounts payable management.) Note that ordering costs are separate from the price of the inventory item. That is, the purchase price of the inventory item is *not* included in the ordering costs. Since ordering costs occur with each order, total ordering costs increase as the number of *orders* increase, rather than as the number of units in inventory increase. For example, Unlimited Decadence pays $2.50 ordering costs for each order of sugar. If it orders 600 pounds of sugar, its ordering costs are $2.50. However, if it places two orders for 300 pounds of sugar for each order, its ordering costs are $5.00 even though the increase in inventory is the same.

The basic idea behind the EOQ method is that total carrying costs increase as a company keeps larger inventories on hand, while total ordering costs decrease because fewer orders are needed. (If inventories held become larger, there is certainly no need to order *more* inventory.) On the other hand, total ordering costs increase as the number of orders increase, but since the company is placing orders more often, it doesn't have to keep as much inventory on hand, so total carrying costs decrease. So, there is a tradeoff between the size of a company's inventory and the number of orders it places. The EOQ method determines the optimal quantity of inventory that a company should order to minimize its *total* inventory costs.

Consider the following situation. Suppose on a Saturday afternoon you and a group of your friends are crowded around the television to watch football and you decide to order pizza before the game starts. In trying to decide how much to order, you note that a small pizza costs $8, a medium pizza costs $12, and a large pizza costs $15. Furthermore, the delivery charge is $1. You could order 6 large pizzas now and maybe 6 small pizzas later, or 12 medium pizzas now and maybe throw some away. Or you might order some other combination of pizzas. How would you figure out the combination of pizzas to order that would minimize your costs? Wouldn't it be useful to have a formula to use?

A company minimizes its total inventory costs by "balancing" the total carrying costs with the total ordering costs. The EOQ method uses the following equation to determine the optimal amount of inventory to order each time a company places an order:

For a Merchandising Company	For a Manufacturing Company
$$EOQ = \sqrt{\frac{2SO}{C}}$$	$$EOQ = \sqrt{\frac{2UO}{C}}$$

where: S = total annual sales
        O = order cost per order
        C = carrying cost per unit
	where: U = total annual raw materials used
	        O = order cost per order
	        C = carrying cost per unit

To keep the calculations simple, the EOQ method makes several assumptions (such as that sales, or raw materials used in production, can be estimated perfectly). Companies use some other approaches in more complex situations to manage inventory levels. However, these approaches are beyond the level of this book. The following illustration shows how to use the EOQ method to determine how many units of inventory to buy.

Suppose Unlimited Decadence expects to sell 5 million cases of Darkly Decadent candy bars next year. These candy bars will require 20 million pounds of sugar to manufacture. The company has estimated that its relevant carrying costs are $1.00 per pound and that its relevant ordering costs for sugar are $62.50 per order. Its managers want to decide the optimal order quantity of sugar. Based on the preceding information, they make the following calculation:

$$EOQ = \sqrt{\frac{2 \times 20,000,000 \times \$62.50}{\$1.00}}$$

$$EOQ = \sqrt{2,500,000,000}$$

$$EOQ = \underline{\underline{50,000 \text{ pounds}}}$$

Thus, based on the EOQ method, Unlimited Decadence should buy 50,000 pounds of sugar for its inventory each time it places an order.

 How do you think using the EOQ method would affect Unlimited Decadence's raw materials purchases budget? How do you think using the EOQ method would affect the company's controls over raw materials purchases? Try to be as specific as you can.

Deciding Whether to Drop a Product

Over its life, a company that sells more than one product will change the specific products it sells. For example, music stores used to sell mostly albums and tapes. Now, they sell mostly tapes and compact disks. A company will add to its inventory new products that it hopes will be profitable and will drop old products that are no longer profitable. Ordinarily, products do not become unprofitable overnight. More often there is a gradual decline in profitability. As a company begins to notice a product's decline in profitability, it normally does whatever it can to slow that decline, including reducing prices, increasing advertising, searching for new markets, and/or modifying the product. We do not consider the decisions related to these efforts because they can be very complex. But we *are* concerned about developing management accounting information that will highlight the profitability (or the decline in profitability) of individual products, so that the company will continue to produce and sell a product when it is profitable and will drop it when it is unprofitable. Proper analysis of the cost and revenue information can also help a company avoid either carrying a product too long or dropping it too soon.

The key to deciding whether a company should drop a product is to determine the costs that it would not incur (i.e., the avoidable costs) and the revenues that it would not earn if it discontinued production and sale of the product. Avoidable costs are *always* relevant to a decision to drop a product. These costs are the only future costs that the company would *not* incur if it dropped the product. All other costs would be the same in either case.

Once a company determines the avoidable costs, its decision to drop the product, based on accounting information alone, is straightforward. *A company should drop a product only if the total avoidable costs are more than the revenue it would lose if it dropped the product.* Another way of saying this is that a company should drop a product if the relevant "cost savings" from dropping the product are greater than the relevant "lost revenues." Under this condition, the total company profit will be higher if it drops the product than if it continues to produce and sell the product. In the following discussion we illustrate how Unlimited Decadence would analyze the relevant costs and revenues for a decision about dropping the Divinely Decadent candy bar.

Suppose the managers at Unlimited Decadence wonder whether the Divinely Decadent candy bar is really a profitable product. The accounting department has assembled preliminary estimates for next year's operations to analyze the expected profitability of the candy bar. We show these estimates in Exhibit 15-5. Unfortunately, this information suggests that Unlimited Decadence would produce and sell the Divinely Decadent candy bar at a $10,900 loss.

Notice that the profit computation we show in Exhibit 15-5 separates the variable and fixed costs, and lists the fixed costs so that they can be analyzed individually. The first

4 *How does a company determine when to drop a product?*

Exhibit 15-5 **Expected Profit Computation**

UNLIMITED DECADENCE CORPORATION
Expected Profit of Divinely Decadent Candy Bars and Other Candy Bars

	Divinely Decadent Candy Bars	Other Candy Bars	Total
Sales revenue	$ 21,647,500	$ 57,984,500	$ 79,632,000
Less variable costs	(15,462,500)	(32,912,500)	(48,375,000)
Contribution margin	$ 6,185,000	$ 25,072,000	$ 31,257,000
Less fixed costs:			
Advertising	$ 1,920,000	$ 2,880,000	$ 4,800,000
Depreciation: Buildings	825,000	1,675,000	2,500,000
Depreciation: Equipment	69,400	990,600	1,060,000
Insurance	128,000	352,000	480,000
Property taxes	302,000	1,062,000	1,364,000
Salaries	351,500	7,048,500	7,400,000
General and administrative	2,600,000	5,100,000	7,700,000
Total fixed costs	$(6,195,900)	$(19,108,100)	$(25,304,000)
Profit (loss)	$(10,900)	$ 5,963,900	$ 5,953,000

question the Unlimited Decadence managers should ask is, "Which costs can be avoided if Unlimited Decadence drops the Divinely Decadent candy bar?" The following information is important about the costs listed in the exhibit.

1. The variable costs for each product are accurate. Therefore, Unlimited Decadence expects the variable costs assigned to the Divinely Decadent candy bars ($15,462,500) to be very close to the actual variable costs incurred. Thus, these variable costs are avoidable costs.

2. The advertising expense of $1,920,000 for the Divinely Decadent candy bars consists of $1,400,000 specifically related to advertising these candy bars and $520,000 allocated to the Divinely Decadent candy bars from general advertising for all company products. Therefore, only the $1,400,000 cost specifically related to the Divinely Decadent candy bars is avoidable. (Unlimited Decadence will continue general advertising for all company products whether or not it drops the Divinely Decadent candy bar.)

3. The depreciation of $825,000 on the portion of the factory buildings that Unlimited Decadence uses to manufacture the Divinely Decadent candy bars is a sunk cost because it is based on the *past* purchase cost of the buildings. It is not relevant to this decision. However, if Unlimited Decadence stops production of the Divinely Decadent candy bar, it will be able to use the space it currently uses for this production to spread out its production facilities for other candy bars. This would improve the efficiency of the production of other candy bars. Unlimited Decadence estimates that this improved efficiency would increase the profit it earns on the other candy bars by $910,000. If Unlimited Decadence continues to produce the Divinely Decadent candy bars, it will lose this profit increase. Thus, Unlimited Decadence will incur an opportunity cost of $910,000 related to space usage if it continues the production of the Divinely Decadent candy bar.

4. The depreciation of $69,400 on the factory equipment used to produce the Divinely Decadent candy bar is also a sunk cost because it is based on the past purchase cost of the equipment. It is not relevant to this decision. Because of the age

of the equipment, Unlimited Decadence cannot sell it. Furthermore, it cannot use the equipment in the production of other candy bars. Therefore, Unlimited Decadence will give the equipment to a local scrap dealer if it discontinues the production of the Divinely Decadent candy bar.

 What if Unlimited Decadence could sell this equipment? Do you think the selling price would be relevant to this decision? If so, how would it affect Unlimited Decadence's profit under each alternative? If not, why not?

5. A discussion with Unlimited Decadence's insurance agent suggests that the company's insurance expense for insurance coverage on equipment and inventories would decrease by $128,000 if Unlimited Decadence discontinues production of the Divinely Decadent candy bar.

6. Unlimited Decadence will be able to avoid the property taxes of $302,000 because of the reduction in the inventory of Divinely Decadent candy bars if it discontinues production of the candy bar.

7. The salaries of $351,500 related to Divinely Decadent candy bar production are for four shift managers and a production superintendent. Unlimited Decadence will lay off all four shift managers if it discontinues production of the Divinely Decadent candy bar. Therefore, their total salaries of $279,000 are avoidable. Instead of laying off the production superintendent, Unlimited Decadence would make her the new manager of the production planning and scheduling department. Her salary ($72,500) is not avoidable. If Unlimited Decadence continues to produce and sell the Divinely Decadent candy bar, the company will have to hire a new manager for production planning and scheduling from outside the company. The personnel department estimates that to hire such a person would cost the company $46,000. This $46,000, therefore, is avoidable if Unlimited Decadence discontinues production of the Divinely Decadent candy bar. Thus, the total avoidable salaries costs are $325,000 ($279,000 + $46,000).

8. Unlimited Decadence does not expect the $2,600,000 of general and administrative expenses allocated to Divinely Decadent candy bar production to be affected by the decision to drop the product. They are not avoidable.

As a result of this analysis, we can show the profit effects of a decision to stop the production and sale of the Divinely Decadent candy bar by comparing the costs that Unlimited Decadence would avoid with the revenues that it would lose. We show this comparison in Exhibit 15-6.

Exhibit 15-6 shows the "cost savings," or relevant costs, of $18,527,500 that Unlimited Decadence would avoid if it dropped the Divinely Decadent candy bar. It also shows the "lost revenues," or relevant revenues, of $21,647,500 that Unlimited Decadence would not earn if it dropped the Divinely Decadent candy bar. Costs that Unlimited Decadence cannot avoid and revenues that it would not lose are not relevant to this decision. Hence, we do not show them in the exhibit. Note that the revenues lost exceed the avoidable costs by $3,120,000. Thus profit would *decrease* by $3,120,000 if Unlimited Decadence discontinued production and sale of the Divinely Decadent candy bar. Based on this information alone, Unlimited Decadence's decision, therefore, would be to continue the production and sales of the Divinely Decadent candy bar.

As we show in Exhibit 15-7, we could rearrange the relevant costs and revenues into an income statement format to compute the $6,185,000 contribution margin ($21,647,500 sales revenues lost − $15,462,500 variable costs avoided) that Unlimited Decadence would lose if it discontinued the product, and we then can deduct from this amount the $3,065,000 of avoidable fixed costs. The contribution margin that Unlimited Decadence would lose exceeds the avoidable fixed costs by $3,120,000 ($6,185,000 − $3,065,000), confirming that

Exhibit 15-6 Analysis for the Decision to Drop a Product

UNLIMITED DECADENCE CORPORATION
*Relevant Costs and Revenues for the Decision
to Drop Divinely Decadent Candy Bars*

		Stop Production
Avoidable costs:		
Variable costs		$ 15,462,500
Fixed costs		
Advertising	$1,400,000	
Opportunity cost for space usage	910,000	
Insurance	128,000	
Property taxes	302,000	
Salaries	325,000	
Total fixed costs		3,065,000
Total avoidable costs (cost savings)		$ 18,527,500
Sales revenue lost		(21,647,500)
Profit lost		$ (3,120,000)

Exhibit 15-7 Alternate Analysis for Decision to Drop a Product

		Stop Production
Sales revenue lost		$(21,647,500)
Less: Variable costs avoided		15,462,500
Contribution margin lost		$ (6,185,000)
Less: Avoidable fixed costs (cost savings)		
Advertising	$1,400,000	
Opportunity cost for space usage	910,000	
Insurance	128,000	
Property taxes	302,000	
Salaries	325,000	3,065,000
Profit lost		$ (3,120,000)

profit would decrease by $3,120,000 if Unlimited Decadence were to discontinue the production and sale of the Divinely Decadent candy bar.

Deciding Whether to Make or Buy a Part or Product

5 *What is a make-or-buy decision, and what issues does a company consider in this decision?*

Many products require a manufacturing process to convert basic direct materials into completed products of inventory. These products seldom are produced entirely by one company. For example, think about the many companies involved in the manufacture of automobiles. There are companies that manufacture steel, glass, paint, rubber, plastic, and so on. Other companies use these materials to produce parts such as lights, radios, air conditioners, fuel pumps, and tires. Any company that buys parts (or components) from other companies may question whether it would be less costly to produce a part than to purchase it from an outside supplier. That is, the company faces a *make-or-buy decision*.

Many factors affect the make-or-buy decision. If a company has to buy the equipment required to manufacture a particular part and has to develop the know-how to produce that part, it may be much more costly to make the part than to buy it from the present supplier, but not always. Consider <u>Aquapore Moisture Systems, Inc.,</u> based in Phoenix, Arizona. It saved costs by deciding to make a "part," when possible, rather than purchasing it.[4] Aquapore manufactures garden hoses from worn-out tires (the "part"), which it has traditionally purchased from scrap dealers. As a result of a search by its environmental team for opportunities to reduce and recycle waste, the company found more than 30,000 pounds of rubber chunks left over from the hose-manufacturing process. After comparing the relevant costs and revenues, Aquapore decided to purchase a $20,000 machine to grind the rubber chunks into small pieces that it could use to make more hoses. Now, the company has virtually no waste from hose production and, in 1995, saved about $9,000 a month as a result of lower disposal costs and a reduction in the number of worn-out tires the company had to buy.

<u>www.aquapore.com</u>

How do you think the public's knowledge of Aquapore's production methods affects the general perception of the company's environmental consciousness? Do you think this public perception has the potential to affect the company's profits? If so, how and why? If not, why not?

A company can sometimes obtain a short-term cost advantage by making a part. This might occur when the company already has the equipment required for making the part and when it is not fully using that equipment for other production. In this situation, the company might be able to produce the part with little or no incremental costs. This cost advantage may not be long-lasting, however. (What if the company finds that it needs to use the equipment soon for other production?) A decision to make a currently purchased part to obtain a short-term cost advantage may be unwise if the company is likely to reverse the decision in the near future. Valuable business relationships with suppliers might be damaged by a decision to make a part instead of buying it.

Another reason for making a part that a company is currently purchasing involves the issues of quality and supplier reliability. Both of these factors can affect the company's overall costs as well. Poor-quality parts can cause increases in production costs for a company. A company may have to rework products that do not meet minimum quality standards, or may have to replace parts that break during the manufacturing process or after customers purchase the products. Reworking products and replacing parts add to the cost of manufacturing the product. For example, even though Unlimited Decadence doesn't use parts in its products, poor-quality ingredients can have the same effect for it as poor-quality parts have for other manufacturers. Substandard cocoa beans might make it more difficult to refine the chocolate. To overcome this problem, Unlimited Decadence might decide to lengthen the refining process, but this action would also raise the cost of manufacturing the candy bars. Poor-quality parts can also cause customer dissatisfaction with a company's product. This dissatisfaction may lead to a loss of sales (resulting in opportunity costs).

Do you think that Aquapore has an unlimited supply of parts for its garden hoses? Why or why not?

Recently, in an effort to appease customers, <u>Mazda Corporation</u> recalled certain Mazda models to replace faulty seat belts. What specific additional costs do you think Mazda incurred as a result of this measure? What potential liabilities did it try to minimize?

<u>www.mazdausa.com</u>

If the supplier of parts is unreliable, production delays may result that also can cause increases in production costs and lost sales. For example, if late parts cause production delays, the company later may ask its employees to work overtime in order to meet expected product sales. Without the overtime production, the company might temporarily or permanently lose sales if its customers purchase from its competitors. When negotiations with a supplier fail to correct quality and reliability problems, a company may consider producing its own parts.

---

[4]Laura M. Litvan, "Gold from Garbage," *Nation's Business,* July 1995, 53.

The decision to make or buy a part involves an analysis of the relevant costs for each alternative. In the following illustration, we show how to consider various activities and their related costs in a make-or-buy decision.

Process Control Company manufactures the electronic control panel that Unlimited Decadence uses to control some of its production processes. Process Control currently purchases 1,000 computer chips per month from an outside supplier at a cost of $5.40 per chip for use in manufacturing the panel. Due to the discontinuation of another product, Process Control has some unused and unsalable machinery that could make as many as 2,000 chips in one production run. Process Control believes its employees have the production skills to make the chips and, in fact, that it can make a better-quality chip than is available from its current supplier. Because of the lower quality of the purchased chip, the company estimates that it currently incurs excess manufacturing costs of $0.60 for each purchased chip used in production. Process Control can avoid this cost by making the higher-quality chip. Exhibit 15-8 shows the relevant cost comparison for the make-or-buy decision.

Notice in Exhibit 15-8 that Process Control's cost study shows no incremental fixed costs related to making or buying the chip. All relevant costs in this situation are variable costs. The comparison shows that making 1,000 chips per month rather than buying them would save Process Control $2,200 ($6,000 − $3,800) per month. A comparison of the per-unit variable costs shows that the company would save $2.20 ($6.00 − $3.80) for each chip made. In this case, based on this information alone, the company would decide to make as many chips as it needs, up to the maximum that the available machinery can produce.

The decision is not so straightforward, however, if there are some relevant fixed costs involved. Suppose that Process Control does not have the machinery it needs to make the chip, but can lease the machinery for a fixed cost of $2,640 per month. All the other costs remain the same. In this case, the cost of making 1,000 chips is $6,440 ($3,800 + $2,640) per month, and the cost of purchasing 1,000 chips is $6,000 per month. Here, Process Control would prefer to buy the chip (again, considering this information alone). When fixed costs are involved, Process Control should consider the total cost of each *alternative* rather than comparing the total (fixed + variable) costs per *chip*. If it needs more or less than 1,000 chips, Process Control may be misled by comparing total costs per chip because fixed costs per chip change when the volume changes, as we discussed in Chapter 11.

If the number of chips that Process Control needs is likely to change, a different form of analysis is more helpful. The cost of buying the chip is $6.00 per chip purchased. The total cost of making the chip now includes a fixed cost of $2,640 per month and a variable cost of $3.80 per chip made. Exhibit 15-9 shows a graph of the expected costs of both making and buying the chip as the volume needed per month varies.

Exhibit 15-8   Analysis for the Make-or-Buy Decision

PROCESS CONTROL COMPANY
Relevant Costs for the Make-or-Buy Decision

	Make Chip	Buy Chip
Expected monthly requirements (chips)	1,000	1,000
Relevant costs:		
Direct materials	$2,200	
Direct labor	1,050	
Variable overhead	550	
Chip purchase cost		$5,400
Excess manufacturing costs incurred in production of electronic control panels as a result of lower-quality purchased chips	—	600ª
Total relevant costs	$3,800	$6,000
Relevant costs per unit	$ 3.80	$ 6.00

ª$0.60 × 1,000

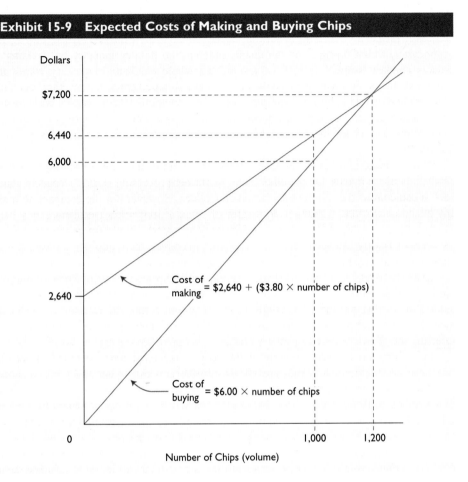

Exhibit 15-9 Expected Costs of Making and Buying Chips

Note from the graph in Exhibit 15-9 that Process Control's expected total cost of making the chip is higher than the total cost of buying the chip at a volume of 1,000 units. The graph also shows that at a volume below 1,200 units, the total cost of making the chip is always higher, and at a volume above 1,200 units, the total cost of buying the chip is always higher. This form of analysis is useful because it not only helps in making the correct current decision, but also shows the volume level at which the decision would change. Based on accounting information alone, the correct decision is to continue buying the chip because the purchase cost at the expected volume of 1,000 chips is less than the cost of making the chips.

 Can you think of any alternatives other than continuing to purchase parts from the current supplier or making them? Remembering back to Chapter 10, what organizational function do you think is responsible for this type of decision? How can accounting information help?

Deciding Whether to Sell a Product or Process It Further

Many companies face the decision of whether to sell a product "as is" or to use it as a direct material in the manufacture of another product. For instance, a meatpacker can sell animal fat or make soap out of it, a textile mill can sell yarn or weave cloth out of it, and an oil refinery can sell the kerosene produced in refining oil or process it further to increase

6 *How does a company determine whether to sell a product or to process it further?*

www.tyson.com

www.mcdonalds.com

gasoline output. (You will make a similar decision when you graduate. Will you take the product of your education—your mind—and sell it to the job market as is, or will you process it further by working toward an advanced degree?) Consider Tyson Foods, Incorporated, which became the dominant leader in the poultry industry by deciding to process chicken further.[5] Instead of just selling whole chickens to grocery stores and restaurant chains, Tyson anticipated the need to have prepared chicken items that need only to be cooked or reheated. For example, Tyson Foods supplied McDonald's with its first Chicken McNuggets! These innovations resulted in Tyson Foods possessing a 25 percent share of the poultry market. The corporation is pursuing a similar strategy with pork and fish products.

Now suppose that Unlimited Decadence can sell all of the cases of Darkly Decadent candy bars that it makes. On the other hand, by further processing Darkly Decadent candy bars, it can convert them into fancy boxed chocolates. However, for the company to make any boxed chocolates, it must give up sales of some of its Darkly Decadent candy bars. The problem is to determine whether Unlimited Decadence should forgo selling some of the cases of Darkly Decadent candy bars in order to convert them into fancy boxed chocolates. The company faces a *sell-or-process-further decision*.

In a sell-or-process-further decision, a company compares the "profit" from selling the product "as is" with the "profit" from using the product as a direct material in the manufacture of another product. This analysis involves subtracting the relevant costs (incremental costs and opportunity costs) from the relevant revenues under each alternative and selecting the alternative (sell or process further) that provides the higher "profit."

For Unlimited Decadence, none of the costs it incurs to produce Darkly Decadent candy bars to the point where they are ready for further processing into fancy boxed chocolates are relevant to the decision. These costs must be incurred whether Unlimited Decadence sells Darkly Decadent candy bars "as is," or whether it processes them further and sells them as boxed chocolates. The only costs that are relevant are the incremental costs of selling cases of Darkly Decadent candy bars (costs that Unlimited Decadence incurs if it sells the candy bars, but not if it processes them further) and the incremental costs of further processing and selling fancy boxed chocolates (costs that Unlimited Decadence incurs if it further processes the candy bars into boxed chocolates, but not if it sells the candy bars).

Both the revenue from the sale of Darkly Decadent candy bars (if not processed further) and the revenue from the fancy boxed chocolates (if processed further) are relevant as long as they are different from each other. Next, we illustrate how to consider the relevant costs and revenues in a sell-or-process-further decision.

Unlimited Decadence believes that it might increase its profits by giving up the sale of some of its Darkly Decadent candy bars sales to produce and sell higher-priced fancy boxed chocolates. To analyze this alternative, Unlimited Decadence estimates its relevant revenue and cost information. We show this information in Exhibit 15-10.

First, Unlimited Decadence estimates its revenues. It determines that it would have to give up sales of 31,250 cases of Darkly Decadent candy bars at $16 per case, totaling $500,000, if it processes the candy bars further into fancy boxed chocolates. If it processes the candy bars further, the marketing department estimates that it can sell 200,000 boxes of fancy chocolates at $5 per box, totaling $1,000,000. These are the relevant revenues for this decision that we show in Exhibit 15-10.

Although Unlimited Decadence would not have to expand the factory for the additional processing, it would have to lease new packaging equipment at a fixed cost of $14,000 per year. In addition, Unlimited Decadence would reassign molding equipment it is currently using full-time in the production of other candy bars to this added processing. This reassignment would reduce the production capability slightly for other candy bars.

---

[5]Thomas Heath, (*Washington Post*), "Tyson Foods Finds Unwelcome Spotlight Blazing upon It," *Des Moines Register*, July 30, 1995, Sec. J, 1, 2.

Exhibit 15-10 Analysis for the Sell-or-Process-Further Decision

UNLIMITED DECADENCE CORPORATION

Relevant Costs and Revenues for the Sell-or-Process-Further Decision

	Sell (as candy bars)		Process Further (as boxed chocolates)	
Revenue		$500,000[a]		$1,000,000[b]
Relevant costs:				
Fixed leasing costs	—		$14,000	
Variable opportunity cost of using fully utilized molding equipment ($0.05 × 200,000)	—		10,000	
Variable labor and overhead costs ($0.40 × 200,000)	—		80,000	
Variable selling costs	$ 9,375[c]		19,400[d]	
Total incremental costs		(9,375)		(123,400)
Difference ("profit")		$490,625		$ 876,600

[a]31,250 cases × $16
[b]200,000 boxes × $5
[c]31,250 × $0.30
[d]200,000 × $0.097

The lost sales for the other candy bars would result in variable opportunity costs of $0.05 per box of fancy chocolates packaged, or a total of $10,000. Furthermore, variable costs of converting the candy bars into boxed chocolates include direct labor and variable overhead costs of $0.40 per box of chocolates, or a total of $80,000. Unlimited Decadence expects delivery costs and the cost of fancy display cartons to cause variable selling costs to be $0.097 for each *box* of chocolates (totaling $19,400) as compared to $0.30 for each *case* of candy bars (totaling $9,375). We show the estimates of these relevant costs for this decision in Exhibit 15–10.

Exhibit 15-10 shows that the difference between the relevant revenue and relevant costs is $385,975 ($876,600 − $490,625) higher under the "process further" alternative than it is under the "sell" alternative. This means that processing candy bars further to make and sell 200,000 boxes of fancy chocolates results in a profit increase of $385,975. This occurs because the increase in revenue of $500,000 ($1,000,000 − $500,000) is $385,975 more than the $114,025 ($123,400 − $9,375) increase in costs. Thus, considering this accounting information alone, Unlimited Decadence's decision should be to further process enough candy bars to satisfy the demand for boxes of fancy chocolates.

Notice that we didn't show the manufacturing costs required to produce the candy bars. Unlimited Decadence must incur these costs in the same amount regardless of which alternative it chooses; therefore, these costs are not relevant to the decision.

Decisions Involving Product Mix

Companies that produce and sell several items of inventory face a common problem. They have to decide how many units of each product to produce and sell. This is called a *product-mix decision*. For example, over several years in the early 1990s, General Motors Corporation's Cadillac Division changed its product mix by dropping to zero the number of Fleetwood Broughams, Allantes, and Cimarrons it produced, and by importing the Catera from Germany for sale in the United States.[6] (As part of the promotion for the

7 *What is a product-mix decision, and what issues does a company consider in this decision?*

www.gm.com

6Jerry Flint, "A German Cadillac," *Forbes*, July 31, 1995, 60.

new Catera, the Cadillac Division changed the name of the car from the German Opel Omega.)

A product-mix decision involves two issues. First, a company can influence the sales volume of each of its products (or a combination of its products) in many ways, such as by sales activities (advertising), promotional campaigns, and the number of sales personnel used for each product. Second, many companies operate with limited productive capacity (for example, with a limited number of machines or a limited amount of time that these machines can be operated) and, as a result, cannot produce as much of every product as they can sell. Thus, the decision about how much to produce and sell of each product can be very complex.

 How do you think the Cadillac Division was able to analyze its product mix when some of its product costs were in U.S. dollars and some were in euros?

In this section, we illustrate only two very simplified situations, but they should be helpful to you in providing an understanding of how a company uses management accounting information in its product-mix decisions.

Deciding How to Spend Advertising Dollars

The first situation we discuss involves deciding which product a company should advertise. For simplicity, we make the following assumptions:

1. The company currently spends a budgeted amount on advertising for each of several products.

2. The company has added a fixed amount of money to its coming year's advertising budget. The question is, "On which *one* of the several products should the company spend the additional advertising money?"

3. Studies by the marketing department provide reliable estimates of the additional sales volume (units) that would result from spending the additional advertising money on each of the products.

4. The company has enough factory equipment to produce the additional units of any of the products that would be sold as a result of the additional advertising.

In this situation, the company's profit increases if the contribution margin resulting from increased sales is more than the increase in advertising cost. The problem is to choose which product should be advertised so that the largest possible profit increase is obtained. *When the increase in fixed costs* (the additional advertising money is a fixed amount) *does not change between alternatives, the company earns the highest profit from the alternative that produces the largest increase in contribution margin above the increase in fixed costs.* This is the key to the decision. Management accounting information shows the contribution margin per unit for each of the products, while the marketing department information shows the additional sales volume that the advertising would produce. The computation required to evaluate the alternatives simply involves comparing the additional contribution margin for each alternative with the additional advertising cost.

To illustrate, we assume that Unlimited Decadence produces three products—Darkly Decadent candy bars, Pure Decadence candy bars, and Divinely Decadent candy bars—and that it has increased its advertising budget by $200,000. The company plans to spend the entire $200,000 on advertising for one of the candy bars. Exhibit 15-11 shows the contribution margin per unit and the estimated sales volume increases that the advertising would produce for each product. It also shows the calculations that Unlimited Decadence would make to evaluate each alternative.

As you can see in Exhibit 15-11, Unlimited Decadence can increase its profit by spending the additional $200,000 to advertise either Darkly Decadent candy bars or Pure Decadence candy bars. Spending the additional $200,000 to advertise Divinely Decadent

Exhibit 15-11	Analysis for the Product-Mix Decision

UNLIMITED DECADENCE CORPORATION
Analysis of Product-Mix Decision

	Divinely Decadent	Darkly Decadent	Pure Decadence
Selling price per case	$28	$16	$20
Variable costs per case	(20)	(11)	(14)
Contribution margin per case	$ 8	$ 5	$ 6
Sales volume increase resulting from additional advertising (cases)	× 20,000	× 76,000	× 60,000
Additional contribution margin	$160,000	$380,000	$360,000
Additional advertising cost	(200,000)	(200,000)	(200,000)
Increase (decrease) in profit	$(40,000)	$180,000	$160,000

candy bars would *decrease* Unlimited Decadence's total profit by $40,000. Unlimited Decadence can obtain the largest profit increase by advertising the Darkly Decadent candy bar. The profit increase would be $180,000. Although the contribution margin *per unit* for Darkly Decadent candy bars is the lowest of the three products, the increase in its sales volume is highest. It is high enough, in fact, to cause an increase in the total contribution margin for Darkly Decadent candy bars that is more than the increase in the total contribution margin of either of the other two products and more than the increase in fixed costs. Thus Unlimited Decadence should spend the additional advertising money on Darkly Decadent candy bars.

Deciding How Many Units to Produce

The second situation we discuss involves deciding how many units a company should produce of each of several products. For simplicity, in our discussion of the product-mix decision, we make the following assumptions:

1. The company's production is limited by a single scarce resource.

2. The combined customer demand for the company's products exceeds its limited production capacity.

Remember from our discussion in Chapter 11 that by changing its product mix, a company may also change its total contribution margin.

 How would a change in a company's product mix result in a change in its total contribution margin?

What do we mean by a single scarce resource? Here is an example. As you have been told many times, there are only 24 hours in a day. When we run out of the 24 hours, nothing we do will help us accomplish more in that day. The 24 hours compose our scarce resource and our limit. Similarly, when a company has a limited scarce resource (available machine time, for example), it can manufacture products only until it exhausts the resource. *Therefore, the company earns the highest profit by using up the scarce resource to manufacture the product mix that produces the highest total contribution margin.* In other words, the product-mix decision involves making the most profitable use of this resource. Therefore, the manager must know both the contribution margin per product and how much of the scarce resource the company uses for each of the products. Given this information, the product that makes the most profitable use of a resource is the one that produces the highest contribution margin *per unit of the scarce resource.* The correct decision, using this information alone, is for the company to first produce the product that makes the most profitable use of the scarce resource, until its demand is satisfied, and then to produce the product that makes the next most profitable use of the resource, and so on until the scarce resource is fully used.

Again, assume Unlimited Decadence produces three products: Divinely Decadent, Darkly Decadent, and Pure Decadence candy bars. Each kind of candy bar uses emulsifiers that are in short supply because of a strike at the supplier's factory. Unlimited Decadence has only 625 pounds (10,000 ounces) of emulsifiers in its inventory and will receive no more for three weeks. So, in this case, emulsifiers are the single scarce resource that will drive our analysis. During this time, Unlimited Decadence expects to be able to sell 12,000 cases (units) of Divinely Decadent candy bars, 5,000 cases of Darkly Decadent candy bars, and 15,000 cases of Pure Decadence candy bars. Unlimited Decadence must decide how many cases of each product to produce and sell during the next three weeks. Exhibit 15-12 shows the contribution margin per case for each product, the direct materials needed for each product, and the contribution margin earned per ounce of emulsifiers.

Notice in Exhibit 15-12 that Divinely Decadent candy bars have the *highest* contribution margin per *unit* (case). If Unlimited Decadence stopped the analysis here, it would choose to produce only Divinely Decadent candy bars and not make the most profitable decision. It would run out of emulsifiers, leaving the demand for the other candy bars unmet. Remember that the focus of this decision is on the scarce resource (emulsifiers), and Divinely Decadent candy bars also require the most emulsifiers per case. As a result, they have the *lowest* contribution margin per *ounce* of the scarce emulsifiers of all three candy bars. Darkly Decadent candy bars make the most profitable use of emulsifiers by having the *highest contribution margin per ounce*. Pure Decadence candy bars have the second highest contribution margin per ounce. Therefore, the company should produce as many cases of Darkly Decadent candy bars as it can until the demand for Darkly Decadent candy bars is satisfied, then produce Pure Decadence candy bars until their demand is satisfied. Finally, the company should produce Divinely Decadent candy bars if any emulsifiers are still available.

In this situation, Unlimited Decadence should use 3,125 ounces (5,000 cases × 0.625) of emulsifiers to produce 5,000 cases of Darkly Decadent candy bars and use the remaining 6,875 ounces (10,000 − 3,125) of emulsifiers to produce 5,500 cases (6,875 ÷ 1.25) of Pure Decadence candy bars. Since demand for Pure Decadence candy bars would not be completely satisfied, Unlimited Decadence would produce no cases of Divinely Decadent candy bars. With this product mix, the total contribution margin would be higher than for any other product mix. For example, if Unlimited Decadence used the 10,000 ounces of emulsifiers to produce 3,125 cases (10,000 ÷ 3.2) of Divinely Decadent candy bars, the total contribution margin would be $25,000 (10,000 ounces × $2.50 per ounce). If it used the emulsifiers to produce 8,000 cases (10,000 ÷ 1.25) of Pure Decadence candy bars, the total contribution margin would be $48,000 (10,000 ounces × $4.80 per ounce). If it used 3,125 ounces of emulsifiers to produce 5,000 cases of Darkly Decadent candy bars and the remaining 6,875 ounces to produce 5,500 cases of Pure Decadence candy bars, however,

Exhibit 15-12   Computation of Contribution Margin per Unit of a Scarce Resource

UNLIMITED DECADENCE CORPORATION
Computation of Contribution Margin per Ounce of Emulsifiers

	Divinely Decadent	Darkly Decadent	Pure Decadence
Estimated sales (cases)	12,000	5,000	15,000
Contribution margin per case	$8	$5	$6
Direct materials (emulsifiers) usage per case (ounces)	÷ 3.2	÷ 0.625	÷ 1.25
Contribution margin per ounce of emulsifiers	$2.50	$8	$4.80

the total contribution margin would be \$58,000 [(3,125 ounces $\times$ \$8 per ounce) + (6,875 ounces $\times$ \$4.80 per ounce)]. No other possible mix can earn a higher contribution margin during the three weeks that emulsifiers are in short supply.

 Don't take our word for it. Try to find a mix of candy bars that can produce a higher contribution margin.

In more complicated situations, a company faces many product interdependencies and several scarce resources. For these cases, the company often uses linear programming or some other mathematical programming techniques to determine the optimal product mix. You can study these techniques, which are extensions of what we discussed here, in more advanced courses.

Business Issues and Values

You probably noticed in our discussions of various inventory decisions that we always said what the best decision would be, *using only the accounting information.* Management accounting information provides useful information to *help* managers make decisions, but it shouldn't be used in a "vacuum." Other issues affect decisions as well, and a company's managers might make decisions that have undesirable consequences if they don't consider all these issues.

For example, after a company's managers determine the optimum quantity of inventory to order, other issues that they might want to consider when making this decision include the following:

8 *What other factors should a company consider when making inventory decisions?*

1. Can the supplier even provide this quantity at one time? If not, should the company consider adding another supplier?

2. If the product is perishable, can the company use up the entire order before it deteriorates?

In making a decision to drop an unprofitable product, a company's managers should consider other related issues. For example, in some cases, dropping an unprofitable product might affect sales of another related product. (If movie theaters stopped making and selling popcorn, the sale of soft drinks would surely decrease!) Furthermore, the company should consider the effect on its employees of dropping a product. What if dropping an unprofitable product necessitates "laying off" employees?

 When __Black & Decker__ stopped producing Molly fasteners (a type of wall anchor) several years ago, it closed its Temple, Pennsylvania, plant.[7] When it laid off plant employees, it decided to give them severance pay to help them during the time they were trying to find new jobs. How do you think a company would include employee severance pay in its analysis of a decision to drop a product? What effect do you think this cost would have on the decision?

www.blackanddecker.com

Even if a product turns out to be profitable, the company might consider dropping it for some other reason. For example, if new research indicates that a product is hazardous, the company would be disregarding the well-being of its customers (and perhaps the community in which it manufactures the product) by continuing to produce it.

Management accounting provides an excellent means of determining relevant revenues and costs for particular decisions. By combining this information with other relevant issues, managers can make informed, intelligent decisions.

---

[7]Keith Herman, "An Accounting Checklist for Plant Closings," *Management Accounting,* July 1994, 30.

Summary

At the beginning of the chapter we asked you several questions. During the chapter, we asked you to STOP and answer some additional questions to build your knowledge about specific issues. Be sure you answered these additional questions. Below are the questions from the beginning of the chapter, with a brief summary of the key points relating to the answers. Use your creative and critical thinking skills to expand on these key points to develop more complete answers to the questions and to determine what other questions you have that might lead you to learn more about the issues.

1 How do relevant costs and revenues contribute to sound decision-making?

Both merchandising and manufacturing companies make short-term inventory-planning decisions. Regardless of the type of inventory-planning decision these companies make, one factor that they consider is the profit impact of the decision. They can determine the profit impact of the decision by analyzing relevant costs and revenues.

2 What types of costs and revenues are relevant to decision-making?

Relevant costs and revenues are future costs and revenues that will change as a result of a decision. If they do not change from one decision alternative to another, costs and revenues are not considered relevant to the decision. They will not sway the decision one way or another. By considering only relevant costs and revenues, managers eliminate the possibility of misusing irrelevant information and thereby making incorrect decisions. To identify relevant costs and revenues, managers first identify the company's activities necessary to carry out the decision and then estimate the costs and/or revenues that are affected by these activities. These costs and revenues can include incremental costs and revenues, avoidable costs, and opportunity costs.

3 How can a company determine how much inventory to order?

A company can determine how much inventory to order by using the economic order quantity (EOQ) method. The EOQ method assumes that there is a total inventory cost consisting of the sum of the total carrying costs and the total ordering costs for the inventory. This method determines the optimal quantity of inventory to order that minimizes the total inventory cost—that is, by "balancing" the total carrying costs with the total ordering costs. For a merchandising company, the EOQ is the square root of [(2 × total annual sales × order cost per order) ÷ carrying cost per unit]. For a manufacturing company, the EOQ is the square root of [(2 × total annual raw materials used × order cost per order) ÷ carrying cost per unit].

4 How does a company determine when to drop a product?

A company determines when to drop a product by estimating the costs that it would not have to incur (i.e., the avoidable costs) and the revenues that it would not earn if production and sale of the product were discontinued. The company should drop the product only if its total avoidable costs are more than the revenue it would lose from dropping the product.

5 What is a make-or-buy decision, and what issues does a company consider in this decision?

In a make-or-buy decision, a company decides whether producing a part would be less costly than purchasing it from an outside supplier. In making this decision, the company compares the relevant incremental costs of producing the part with the relevant costs of purchasing the part. In addition to cost factors, the company should consider the quality of the produced part versus the quality of the purchased part, the reliability of the supplier, and the company's desired long-term business relationship with the supplier.

6 How does a company determine whether to sell a product or to process it further?

A company determines whether to sell a product or to process it further by comparing the "profit" from selling the product "as is" with the "profit" from using the product as a direct material in the manufacture of another product. This analysis involves subtracting the relevant costs from the relevant revenues under each alternative, and selecting the alternative (sell or process further) that provides the higher "profit."

7 **What is a product-mix decision, and what issues does a company consider in this decision?**

In a product-mix decision, a company decides how many units of each product to produce and sell. In making this decision, a company considers two issues. First, the company considers the impact of activities such as increased advertising on the sales volume of each of its products. Second, the company considers the impact of a limited productive capacity (scarce resource) on the production of each of its products. For the first issue, when the increase in fixed costs (i.e., additional advertising money) does not change among alternatives, the company earns the highest profit from the alternative that produces the largest increase in contribution margin above the increase in fixed costs. For the second issue, the company earns the highest profit by using up the scarce resource to manufacture the product mix that produces the highest contribution margin per unit of scarce resource.

8 **What other factors should a company consider when making inventory decisions?**

Management accounting information identifying the effect on profit of each decision alternative is just a starting point for analyzing a decision. Managers also should consider other potential effects of each decision alternative, such as effects on other company products, on employees, and on customers.

Key Terms

avoidable costs *(p. 508)*
carrying costs *(p. 511)*
incremental costs *(p. 508)*
opportunity costs *(p. 508)*

ordering costs *(p. 512)*
relevant costs *(p. 505)*
relevant revenues *(p. 505)*

Here is an opportunity to gather information on the Internet about real-world issues related to the topics in this chapter. Go to http://www.dryden.com/account and click on the Cunningham, Nikolai, and Bazley book cover. Click on Summary Surfing, then click on this chapter number, and answer the following questions.

▶ Click on **AICPA.** Click on CEFM. Scroll down, then click on *Publications*. Scroll down and click on *Selecting the Optimum Product Line for an Enterprise.* How can an unprofitable product make a significant contribution to the overall profitability of a company?

S U M M A R Y
S U R F I N G

Answer the Following Questions in Your Own Words

Testing Your Knowledge

15-1   What are relevant costs and relevant revenues?

15-2   Explain why past costs are irrelevant.

15-3   Since past costs are irrelevant in decision-making, why do you think keeping past cost records can be helpful in the decision-making process?

15-4   Why should irrelevant costs and revenues be omitted from a decision analysis?

15-5   What is the difference between incremental costs and avoidable costs?

15-6   Under what circumstances is an avoidable manufacturing cost relevant in the make-or-buy decision?

15-7   Under what circumstances is an incremental manufacturing cost relevant in a make-or-buy decision?

15-8   In a decision to make a previously purchased component, think of two incremental costs that might not be avoidable if the decision is reversed a year later. Why would this happen?

15-9   Explain, by using an example, how a fixed cost can be an incremental cost.

15-10 Why might it be valuable to distinguish between relevant fixed costs and relevant variable costs for a short-term decision?

15-11 When are variable costs not relevant in a short-term decision?

15-12 Define an opportunity cost, and give an example of such a cost.

15-13 Describe how carrying costs and ordering costs interact with each other. Given this interaction, what does the EOQ method accomplish?

Applying Your Knowledge

15-14 Carlos Garcia, who is paid $8 per hour, is the only person who is trained to operate a machine that is critical in the production of bicycle seats. Each bicycle seat has a contribution margin of $6 and requires 1/4 hour of processing time on the machine. Sales of bicycle seats are limited only by scarce time on this machine.

Required: What is the opportunity cost to the company if Carlos becomes sick and leaves work an hour early one day?

15-15 Gorilla Grills has just discontinued its lowest line of high-quality barbecue grills. In its inventory, Gorilla has 40,000 grills that cost $60 per grill to manufacture. At the current selling price of $90, it may take as long as eight years for Gorilla to sell the grills. A foreign buyer has just offered the company $2 million for all the units.

Required: Is the $60-per-unit manufacturing cost relevant in deciding whether or not to accept the offer? List the costs and revenues that you think would be relevant.

15-16 Water Works ended its busy season with an inventory of 15,000 plastic rafts that cost $180,000 to manufacture. The company has two choices. One is that it can store the rafts for six months and sell them for $8 each during the following year. Storage would cost $8,500, and Water Works knows that at least 30% of the rafts would deteriorate during storage. The deteriorated rafts would have no value. The only other alternative is to have a clearance sale now and sell the rafts for $6.20 each. Water Works believes that all of the rafts can be sold if it spends $15,000 to advertise the sale.

Required: Based on this information, prepare an analysis showing the relevant costs and revenues of each alternative, and decide which alternative Water Works should choose.

15-17 Tiger Company sells large, stuffed tigers. It expects to sell 3,200 units of this inventory item next year. The company has estimated that its relevant carrying costs are $1.20 per unit and that its relevant order costs are $30 per order.

Required: What is Tiger Company's optimal order quantity? Based on this quantity, how often should Tiger Company place orders?

15-18 On a chilly Saturday morning, Roy Parker bought 30 dozen doughnuts for $72, took 10 gallons of hot coffee, and went to a farm auction. He sold all the coffee and all but 6 dozen of the doughnuts before heading for home late in the afternoon. Knowing that he could not eat 6 dozen donuts himself and that they would be worthless by the next day, he began to consider how he might sell the remaining doughnuts. Only one possibility occurred to him. If he drove across town and left the doughnuts in the lunchroom at the plant where he worked, he was sure that workers on the late shift would be happy to buy the doughnuts. He figured the 20-mile round trip to the plant would cost him about $0.25 per mile. It would take him about an hour to make the trip, and he decided that it would be worthwhile to drive to the plant if he were compensated $10 for his time. Roy believes that workers will "forget" to pay for 1 dozen of the doughnuts.

Required: Prepare an analysis to determine how much Roy would have to charge per doughnut on the doughnuts he sells at the plant to reach his profit goal.

15-19 Happy Apparati Company produces small electrical appliances. The manufacturing costs per unit to produce a small toaster are shown here:

Direct materials	$ 6.50
Direct labor	3.75
Variable overhead	4.25
Fixed overhead	6.00
Total manufacturing cost per unit	$20.50

Variable selling costs to obtain and fill orders normally average $1.50 per unit when Happy sells the toasters to local customers. Recently, however, Happy paid $40,000 to advertise its various products in an international trade magazine. The company has just received an order from a large mail-order merchandising company in Brazil for 700 toasters at a total offering price of $12,000. The merchandising company is willing to pay all shipping charges except the initial packaging, which costs $0.75 per toaster.

Required: Compute the total incremental cost that Happy Apparati would expect to incur if it accepted and filled this order. Should Happy produce and sell the 700 toasters to the Brazilian company?

15-20 Houston Hobby produces several products that are sold by hobby shops across the country. Production of one product, a small model rocket, uses all available machine hours on machine 12A. The rocket, which provides a contribution margin of $1.90 per unit, requires 0.05 machine hours per unit to produce. Houston Hobby would like to use machine 12A in the production of other products. This production would take about 250 hours.

Required: Compute the opportunity cost of using 250 machine hours on machine 12A for other production.

15-21 Armand Leggitt Company manufactures table legs and chair arms. It owns a lathe that it is not currently using. The lathe, which Armand Leggitt purchased nine years ago for $40,000, has a current book value of $4,000. Armand Leggitt can get $4,800 for the lathe if it sells it now. Armand Leggitt has just received an order for 50,000 table legs; it cannot accept the order unless it keeps the lathe for use in producing the order. If Armand Leggitt keeps the lathe for this purpose, the lathe will have no residual value after the company completes the order. The direct materials, direct labor, and variable overhead costs that Armand Leggitt would incur to produce the order total $50,900. The customer has offered $55,000 for the table legs.

Required: Prepare a schedule to help Armand Leggitt Company determine whether it should accept the order for the table legs.

15-22 The Porter Wagon Company produces sleds, scooters, and wagons. Scooters are not as popular as they used to be, and the company is considering dropping this product. Porter currently sells 5,000 scooters per year for $25 each. Variable manufacturing and selling costs total $17 per scooter. Fixed costs of $45,000 can be avoided if scooters are not produced.

Required: Prepare an analysis to answer each of the following independent questions.

(1) Given this information, by how much would Porter's profit increase if production of scooters is discontinued?

(2) If Porter can increase the sales volume of scooters to 6,000 units per year by spending an additional $10,000 per year on advertising, should Porter continue scooter production?

(3) If Porter can increase the sales volume of scooters to 7,000 per year by reducing its selling price to $20 per scooter, should Porter continue scooter production?

15-23 Buzz Telephone Company manufactures telephones and answering machines. Buzz currently buys a connector for its phones for $1.80 per unit. Buzz's president asked for cost estimates for making this product and received the following report:

Costs per Unit of Making Connectors

Direct materials	$0.75
Direct labor	0.30
Variable overhead	0.35
Fixed overhead	0.80
Total manufacturing cost per unit	$2.20

If Buzz makes the connector, production would take place in its machine shop. No additional plant and equipment would be necessary; however, the company would have to hire someone to inspect the connectors before they could be used in producing the company's other products. The inspector's salary would be $15,000 per year.

Required: (1) Compute the incremental costs of making and of buying the connector in quantities of 25,000 units per year. Should the company make the connector or buy it?

(2) Compute the incremental costs of making and of buying the component in quantities of 50,000 units per year. Should the company make the component or buy it?

(3) How many units of the component would have to be produced so that the total costs of making them would be equal to the total costs of buying them?

15-24 Mane Street sells 3,000 economy-size bottles of shampoo for $10 per bottle. The cost to manufacture the shampoo is $5.00 per bottle. Further variable processing costs of $4 per bottle for the shampoo would convert it into a shampoo/conditioner, which Mane Street could sell for $18 per bottle. Variable selling costs are $1 per bottle for the shampoo, but for the shampoo/conditioner they would be $2.50 per unit.

Required: Based on this information and assuming that Mane Street can sell 3,000 bottles of shampoo/conditioner, prepare an analysis to answer each of the following questions.

(1) Should Mane Street process the shampoo further into a shampoo/conditioner?

(2) If the selling price per unit of the shampoo/conditioner dropped to $15 per bottle, should Mane Street process the shampoo further into a shampoo/conditioner?

15-25 Uncommon Scents, which makes and sells perfume and body lotion, has $10,000 to spend on advertising. The company has estimated that using the $10,000 to advertise perfume would increase sales of perfume by 5,000 bottles. Uncommon Scents is uncertain how many additional tubes of body lotion it could sell by spending the $10,000, however. The perfume has a contribution margin of $8.50 per bottle, and the body lotion has a contribution margin of $2.50 per tube.

Required: Given this information, prepare an analysis to answer each of the following independent questions.

(1) If spending the $10,000 on body lotion would increase its sales by 15,000 tubes, which product should Uncommon Scents advertise?

(2) If spending the $10,000 on body lotion would increase its sales by 20,000 tubes, which product should Uncommon Scents advertise?

(3) By how many tubes would sales of body lotion have to increase to justify spending the $10,000 on body lotion instead of perfume?

15-26 Light the Night Manufacturing Company can sell a maximum of 4,000 desk lamps and 10,000 floor lamps. Desk lamps have a contribution margin of $6 per lamp and require 1 machine hour to produce. Floor lamps have a contribution margin of $15 per lamp and require 3 machine hours to produce. Light the Night currently has 6,400 machine hours available each month.

Required: Given this information, prepare an analysis to answer each of the following questions.

(1) How many desk lamps and floor lamps should Light the Night produce each month to earn the maximum monthly total contribution margin?

(2) What is the maximum amount Light the Night should pay per month to lease one additional machine, which can be used 360 hours per month?

Making Evaluations

15-27 The percentage of Americans who drink coffee was the same in 1995 (50%) as it was in 1985. But the type of coffee that Americans purchased shifted during that time. Growing at a rate of 7-10% per year, by 1995 the number of coffee drinkers who purchased coffee beans rather than ground coffee reached 20%. However, rather than change their product mix to reflect the market, Maxwell House, Folgers, and Nestle cut prices. Maxwell House cut its price per can of ground coffee by $0.30 in 1995.

www.kraft.com
www.pg.com
www.nestle.com

Required: What factors and issues do you think Maxwell House weighed in making this decision?

15-28 Show Time Company currently manufactures the hands it uses in the assembly of grandfather clocks. Cost estimates to make each set of hands are as follows:

Direct materials	$ 8.00 per set
Direct labor	4.00 per set
Variable overhead	2.00 per set
Fixed overhead	$13,000 per year

Required: (1) Prepare an analysis to answer each of the following independent questions.

(a) Assume that all variable costs are avoidable and that the company needs 4,000 sets of hands annually. How much of the fixed overhead must be avoidable in order for the company to prefer to buy the sets from an outside supplier at $17 per set instead of continuing to make them?

(b) Assume that all variable costs are avoidable, that the company needs 4,000 sets of hands annually, and that only $6,000 of fixed costs are avoidable. Below what purchase price per set of hands would the company prefer to buy the components from an outside supplier instead of continuing to make them?

(c) Assume that all variable costs are avoidable, that $3,000 of fixed overhead is avoidable, and that the purchase price of a set of hands is $20. Below what number of sets needed would the company prefer to buy the sets of hands from an outside supplier instead of continuing to make them?

(2) Suppose fixed overhead costs include the following:

Rent	$ 5,000
Depreciation, equipment	3,600
Property taxes	300
Foreman's salary	3,000
Routine maintenance	600
Utilities	500
	$13,000

List the fixed costs that you think Show Time could avoid (at least partially) if it purchased sets of hands. What are your reasons for including each of these costs on the list?

15-29 Music, Music, Music Company has just completed a study suggesting that sales of two of its products, sheet music and compact disks, could be increased by spending more on advertising. The following table shows how many additional units of the two products could be sold if advertising for each is increased:

Amount Spent on Advertising Sheet Music	Additional Sales of Sheet Music
$1,000	400 units
2,000	800
3,000	1,100
4,000	1,200

Amount Spent on Advertising Compact Disks	Additional Sales of Compact Disks
$1,000	400 disks
2,000	800
3,000	1,200
4,000	1,600

Sheet music has a contribution margin of $7.00 per unit, and compact disks have a contribution margin of $6.00 per unit. The company has a total of $4,000 to spend on additional advertising. The head of marketing, Harry Hill, has asked your boss for a recommendation about how much to spend on advertising for each product in order to increase profit by the greatest amount, and your boss has passed the question on to you.

Required: (1) Compute the increase in the company's profit if the $4,000 is spent on advertising sheet music alone.

(2) Compute the increase in the company's profit if the $4,000 is spent on advertising compact disks alone.

(3) Compute the increase in the company's profit if only $3,000 is spent on advertising sheet music alone. How do you explain the difference between this increase in profit and the increase in profit you computed in (1)?

(4) Write a memo to Mr. Hill (sending a copy to your boss) recommending how much additional advertising to spend on each product (up to $4,000 total) in order to increase profit by the greatest amount. Be sure to include the reasoning behind your recommendation.

15-30 Woodchuck Manufacturing produces quality tools for woodworking. Woodchuck has been forced to increase prices by about 40% over the last few years, mostly because of the increased costs of purchased components and other direct materials used in the manufacture of its products. Although Woodchuck will always have a market for its products among craftsmen who appreciate quality, the company is losing much of its business to companies manufacturing low-quality tools. Some of Woodchuck's departments are operating at about half of their usual capacity.

Chuck Woods, the company's founder and president (and your dad's next-door neighbor), would not allow his name to be associated with poor-quality tools. He feels that some price reductions are necessary, however, to keep sales from falling. He is concerned more about providing jobs for his employees than about earning a large profit. If sales fall much further, he will not be able to do either, however. Not a single employee has been laid off, nor has anyone received less than a full paycheck, even though many skilled machinists have pushed brooms and done odd jobs these last few months.

Recently, one of Chuck's foremen suggested that the company attempt to manufacture some of the components currently being purchased. Chuck and his foreman talked at great length, finally choosing to study the possibility of manufacturing a ³/₄-inch chuck that is used on hand drills, drill presses, and lathes. Everyone was quite excited when it was determined that the kind of equipment needed to manufacture the chuck was owned by the company and was not currently in use. Production would be no problem for the skilled machinists employed by Woodchuck.

It took about a week for Chuck's accountant to find all the information necessary to prepare the report that follows:

Dec. 15

Dear Chuck:

I'm sorry to report that after careful study of the costs of manufacturing ³/₄-inch chucks, I've concluded that we can't afford to make them. We currently use about 1,000 chucks of this size per month and are now buying them for $6.50 each. The costs to manufacture 1,000 chucks per month would be:

Direct materials	$1,850
Direct labor	1,900
Variable overhead	1,175
Fixed overhead	3,800
Total	$8,725

I'm sorry to bring you this bad news just before the holidays, Chuck. We buy hundreds of other components. Perhaps one of them would be cheaper to make than to buy. I'll be glad to make the cost estimates.

Lief Schmidt

Chuck knows you are studying accounting and has asked your opinion.

Required: Prepare a brief analysis of this situation and write Chuck a letter explaining your recommendation about whether his company should make or buy this component, and whether it also would be worthwhile to consider making rather than buying other components. What other issues should Chuck consider in making his decision?

15-31 Sunnydays Nursery School has been in operation for about five years. The school has never had any trouble filling its limit: 36 children for the morning session, 36 different children for the afternoon session, and 18 children who stay all day and are served a hot lunch. Currently, monthly tuition is $60 for half-day children and $120 for all-day children. The school has a long waiting list of children whose parents want to enroll them for half-days.

All-day children have never been accepted at the school unless their parents qualify for aid under the state's day-care program. Under this program the state pays half of the monthly tuition up to a maximum of $100. New regulations that take effect on January 1 would require accreditation before state funds can be paid under this program. This would require that at least one teacher be certified by the state for teaching at the preschool level. Currently, none of the school's three teachers can qualify for certification.

The director of the school feels that the loss of state funds would pose a serious threat to the school. She believes that a certified teacher could be hired, although this would cost the school $900 per month.

Monthly tuition could be raised to $75 for half-day children and $150 for all-day children. The director is uncertain how this would affect enrollment, however. Alternatively, the school could give up the all-day children who currently receive aid. Several other day-care centers in town (some charging as little as $100 per month) have room to take all of the all-day children.

Monthly operating costs for the school are as follows:

Rent	$ 300
Utilities	160
Salaries	2,400
Insurance	100
Toys and supplies	360
Lunches	378
Total Monthly Cost	$3,698

Toys and supplies are variable at rates of $5 per half-day child per month and $10 per all-day child per month.

Required: (1) What problem does the director have to solve?

(2) Suppose the director has placed you on an advisory committee to make a recommendation about a solution to the problem. With your committee, make a list of possible alternatives that she could consider.

(3) Assume that the director has reviewed all possible choices and has reduced the decision to two possible alternatives: (a) to close the all-day program, not to raise tuition, and not to hire the new teacher; and (b) to keep the all-day program open, to raise tuition, and to hire the new teacher. List the costs and revenues that you think will be relevant in the analysis of these two alternatives and give a reason for including each on the list.

(4) With your committee, make a list of other information you would like to have before advising the director on which of the two alternatives she should choose.

15-32 Midwest Watchamacallits sells Thingamajigs ("Jigs") and Thingamaboppers ("Boppers"). In late April the company found itself with only 500 hours of machine time available for the coming month because of the untimely malfunction of an accelerator attached to one of its two operating rod-catch assemblers, which are used in the production of its two products. Although May is not normally a month of high demand, losing one of its two assemblers creates definite problems. Data on the two products are shown here:

	Jigs	Boppers
Selling price per unit	$60	$85
Variable costs per unit	(30)	(40)
Contribution margin per unit	$30	$45
Assembler machine hours per unit	0.25	0.50
Expected May demand (units)	1,600	600

Midwest is already committed to pay $1,000 for advertising one (but not both) of the products to increase its demand beyond the estimates shown earlier. The company still has time to select the product to be advertised, however. The marketing department believes that demand for either product could be increased by 100 units with advertising.

Required: Explain how the machine problem would alter the company's advertising decision.

15-33 Pringle Paper Products is considering converting some of its fine writing paper into fancy stationery. The company currently is able to sell all of the fine writing paper it can produce, but it believes that its profit might be improved by giving up some of its fine writing paper sales to produce higher-priced stationery. Although the plant would not have to be expanded for this new processing, new printing equipment would have to be leased for a cost of $14,000 per year. In addition, packaging equipment currently in full-time use in other production would be reassigned to this new processing, thus slightly reducing production capability for another product. The lost sales for this other product would result in opportunity costs of $.025 per box of stationery packaged. Costs of converting the fine writing paper into fancy stationery include direct labor and overhead costs totaling $0.40 per box of stationery. Increased delivery costs and the cost of fancy display cartons are expected to cause variable selling costs to be higher for fancy stationery than for writing paper. The company believes that customer demand will be 40,000 boxes of stationery per year for an indefinite number of years. Pringle estimates that if it does not convert some of its writing paper into fancy stationery, it will earn $50,000 revenue and incur $2,000 in variable selling costs on that writing paper. It also estimates that if it does convert this writing paper into stationery, it will earn $140,000 revenue and incur $5,000 in variable selling costs for the stationery.

Required: (1) Prepare an analysis showing the relevant costs and revenues of each alternative, and decide which alternative should be chosen based on this analysis.

(2) Do you think your decision might change if you knew the manufacturing costs required to produce the fine writing paper? Why or why not?

(3) What if customer demand turns out to be less than 40,000 boxes of stationery per year? At a minimum, how many boxes of stationery must Pringle sell to justify your decision in (1)?

15-34 Yesterday, you received the following letter for your advice column in the local paper:

Dear Dr. Decisive:

I am a very organized person and prefer to think through things before I do them. My boyfriend, on the other hand, is a real slob and claims that he is just being "spontaneous" when he acts first and thinks later. This is becoming a real problem for us, and I am beginning to wonder what we see in each other. Here's a typical example of how different we are.

Yesterday, I was telling him about my plans for Spring Break and all the decisions my roommate and I are going to have to make. See, my roommate and I are planning to meet some old high school friends at Gulf Shores, Alabama during Spring Break. Classes will be over for Spring Break on a Friday and will not start again until a week from the following Monday.

But I'm not even sure I should go. I'm on a very limited budget. If I don't go, I'll stay on campus, live in the sorority house, and work. I'll have to eat my meals out, though, because my sorority house won't serve meals during the break.

Despite my boyfriend's ridicule of my thoroughness, I have made the following list of choices that my roommate and I have to make:

Transportation:	Car (rent)	Length of stay:	Ten days
	Bus		Five days
	Train	Go or not:	Go
	Motorhome		Stay at school and work
	Plane		
Lodging:	Tent		
	Motorhome		
	Motel		
	Condominium		

Anyway, I need your help. I know there's an organized way of making sense of all of these choices and deciding what to do. My boyfriend says I should just go (that's what he would do). Now that he's made the decision (in his mind), he doesn't want to talk about it any more.

Help!!! How can I make a decision? Is there a process? Maybe when my boyfriend sees your response, he will see the value of being organized.

Call me . . .
"Organized, but Undecided."

P.S. Why do you think my boyfriend is so eager for me to go out of town?

Required: Meet with your Dr. Decisive team and write a response to "Organized, but Undecided."

CHAPTER 16

INVENTORY AND OPERATIONS

"*Economic efficiency consists of making things that are worth more than they cost.*"

—John Maurice Clark

1 How does the way a manufacturing company determines the cost of its inventories and cost of goods sold differ from the way a merchandising company determines them?

2 How does a cost accounting system help a manufacturing company assign costs to its products?

3 Since overhead is not a physical part of the product, how does a company include the cost of overhead in the cost of its products?

4 Why is there more than one type of cost accounting system?

5 What is a job order cost accounting system, and how does a company use this system?

6 What is a process cost accounting system, and how does a company use this system?

www.herseys.com

Did you know that <u>Hershey Foods Corporation</u> manufactures more than just candy bars? Hershey Foods Corporation does manufacture candy bars, including the following brands: Hershey's, Reese's, Y&S, Kit Kat, Peter Paul, and Sweet Escapes, to name a few. But it also manufactures Chuckles, Good & Plenty, Jolly Rancher gummis, Luden's throat drops, Twizzlers, baking chocolate, hot cocoa mix, coconut flakes, ice cream topping, butterscotch syrup, ice cream bars, and chocolate pudding.[1]

It costs Hershey Food Corporation a different amount to produce each of these products because the mix of direct materials, the amount and type of direct labor, and the use of factory overhead differ from product to product. To set selling prices high enough to make a desired profit, Hershey must know the cost of each product it manufactures. Moreover, when it makes a sale, Hershey must know the cost of the product it is selling so that it can reduce its Finished Goods Inventory account and increase its Cost of Goods Sold account by that amount. How do you think Hershey determines the cost of each inventory item that it sells? Furthermore, how do you think it determines the costs of its goods-in-process and finished goods inventories?

The process of determining and accumulating the costs of products and activities within a company is called **cost accounting**. Although cost accounting is primarily concerned with determining the cost of producing a product, it may also involve calculating the cost of operating a particular department or the cost of a manufacturing process or marketing technique. In this chapter, we introduce two of the most common types of cost accounting systems that companies use to assign manufacturing costs to products: the job order costing system and the process costing system. In Chapter 17, we will discuss how a company uses standards in its cost accounting system to plan and control its operations. Then, in Chapter 18, we will discuss recent manufacturing developments, the changing information needs of managers in modern manufacturing environments, and a relatively new modification of cost accounting systems, called activity-based costing.

Although our discussion focuses on manufacturing companies, other companies use cost accounting systems as well. Service companies such as airlines, banks, hospitals, and social service agencies also have developed cost accounting systems by modifying many of the ideas and procedures we describe.

Common Elements of Cost Accounting Systems

1 *How does the way a manufacturing company determines the cost of its inventories and cost of goods sold differ from the way a merchandising company determines them?*

As we discussed in Chapter 11, there are three production inputs to the manufacture of a product: direct materials, direct labor, and factory overhead. Exhibit 16-1 (a copy of Exhibit 11-3) illustrates the relationships among these manufacturing inputs, the manufacturing process, the three inventories, and cost of goods sold for Unlimited Decadence. Take a minute to review these relationships before you read on.

In the cost accounting systems we are about to discuss, the *costs* of the three inputs systematically become the cost of the goods-in-process inventory, the cost of the finished goods inventory, and the cost of goods sold. The company, in essence, "attaches" these three manufacturing costs to the products as it manufactures them, moving the costs with the products as they move from being goods-in-process to finished goods to goods sold. So by the time Hershey finishes manufacturing a batch of Reese's Pieces, it has accumulated the costs of manufacturing them and has assigned these costs to finished goods inventory. When it sells the candy, the manufacturing costs associated with the Reese's Pieces (or "attached to them") become the resulting cost of goods sold. The manufacturing costs associated with the unsold Reese's Pieces remain the costs of the ending inventories.

2 *How does a cost accounting system help a manufacturing company assign costs to its products?*

[1]Hershey Foods Corporation, *1998 Annual Report.*

Exhibit 16-1   Relationships among Manufacturing Cost Elements of Unlimited Decadence

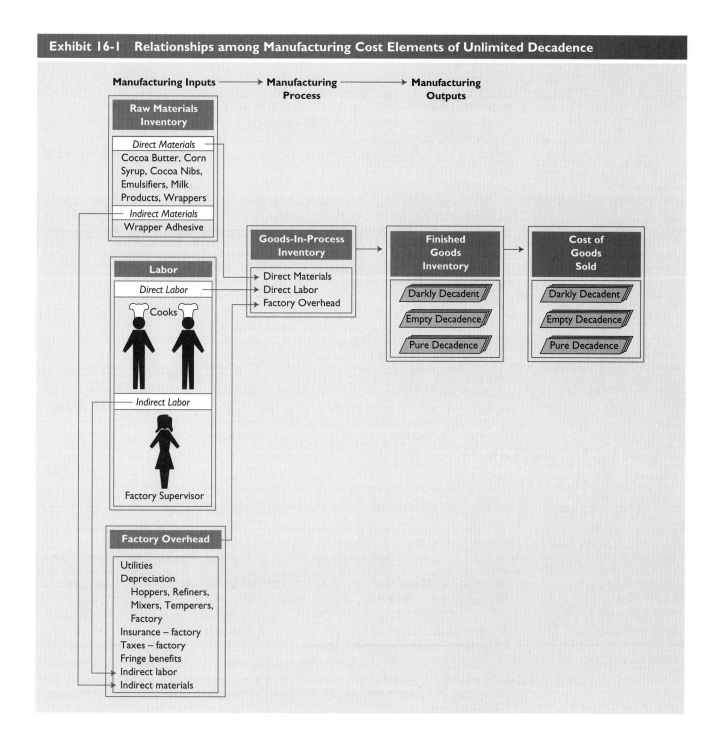

Raw Materials Costs

Remember from Chapter 11 that raw materials include both direct materials and indirect materials. Since direct materials physically become part of the product and are one of the three production inputs, companies include the cost of direct materials as one of the three manufacturing costs that make up the cost of the finished product. However, it is difficult to associate the cost of indirect materials with specific products, so companies normally include indirect materials costs as part of *factory overhead.*

God makes the snake

3 *Since overhead is not a physical part of the product, how does a company include the cost of overhead in the cost of its products?*

4 *Why is there more than one type of cost accounting system?*

Labor Costs

Recall that direct labor is the labor of the employees who work with the direct materials to convert or assemble them into the finished products. Companies include the cost of direct labor (usually based on the hourly rate they pay these employees) in the cost of the product as one of the three manufacturing costs. However, they usually include *additional* payroll costs (payroll taxes, pensions, and other fringe benefits associated with these employees) as part of *factory overhead*. Also, since it is difficult to associate the cost of indirect labor with specific products, companies usually include the wages earned by these employees and the additional payroll costs of indirect labor as part of *factory overhead*.

Factory Overhead Costs

Although factory overhead items are necessary to manufacture a product, they cannot be traced *directly* to each unit produced. However, factory overhead is one of the three production inputs. So, companies include the *total* cost of factory overhead items (including indirect materials and indirect labor) in the cost of the products as one of the three manufacturing costs. As you will see, they then use an allocation process to assign these overhead costs to *individual* products. For example, it would be difficult for Hershey to trace the cost of factory air conditioning to a case of Mounds candy bars. But it *could* allocate a portion of the monthly air-conditioning cost to the Mounds candy bars manufactured that month based on the proportion of the factory's cubic feet that it devotes to manufacturing Mounds candy bars. In that case, if the company uses one-fourth of the factory space to manufacture the Mounds candy bars, it would allocate one-fourth of the air-conditioning cost to these candy bars. Then it could assign this cost to individual cases of Mounds by dividing the allocated cost by the number of cases of Mounds manufactured during the month. Although factory overhead includes a large number and a wide variety of different manufacturing costs, companies normally treat these costs together as a single cost.

The Structure of Cost Accounting Systems

Manufacturing companies incur costs as they acquire the goods and services they use as inputs to the manufacturing process, and it is relatively easy for them to determine the total cost of each *input*. The task of the cost accounting system is to classify the costs incurred according to *activities* performed and then to assign the costs to the product *output* of those activities. As you will see, cost accounting systems classify these costs as products flow through the manufacturing process.

The Perpetual Inventory System

Most cost accounting systems use a perpetual inventory system to record the costs of the raw materials, goods-in-process, and finished goods inventories. As we described and illustrated in Chapter 6, in a perpetual inventory system the company keeps a continuous record of the balance in an inventory account. For a merchandising company, this involves increasing the Inventory account for the cost of all merchandise purchases and decreasing this account for the cost of merchandise sold.

A manufacturing company uses the perpetual system for all three inventory accounts. It increases the Raw Materials Inventory account for the cost of the raw materials it purchases and decreases the account for the cost of the raw materials it uses in production. It increases the Goods-in-Process Inventory account for the cost of direct materials, direct labor, and factory overhead it uses in production and decreases this account for the cost of the products it completes. It increases the Finished Goods Inventory account for the cost of the products it completes and decreases the account for the cost of the products it sells.

Does this make sense? Take a minute and diagram with T-accounts, arrows, and descriptions the perpetual inventory system of a manufacturing company. Label the arrows with a description of the costs they represent. Here's a start:

| Raw Materials Inventory | Goods-in-Process Inventory | Finished Goods Inventory | ? |

How Costs Flow through the Accounts

Under the perpetual inventory system, manufacturing costs almost seem as if they flow through the accounts, paralleling the flow of products through the manufacturing process. These costs enter the system as the company incurs them, flowing into the goods-in-process inventory as the company uses direct materials, direct labor, and factory overhead to manufacture products. Once they are in the Goods-in-Process Inventory account, the company assigns, or *applies*, the costs to specific products as manufacturing operations take place.

Exhibit 16-2 is an expansion of Exhibit 16-1 and illustrates how the costs of the inputs "attach" to the candy bars that Unlimited Decadence manufactures. Notice that the "flow" of costs from the cost of the inputs through the cost of goods sold parallels the physical flow of the candy bars through the manufacturing process. Each arrow from the right side of one account to the left side of another account represents an entry transferring costs from one account to the next by decreasing one account and increasing the next. Note also that manufacturing costs become an expense (cost of goods sold) only when Unlimited Decadence sells finished goods inventory.

Companies most commonly use one of two kinds of cost accounting systems to assign manufacturing costs to manufactured products: *job order costing* or *process costing* (either of which may be enhanced by *standard costing* and *activity-based costing*). These cost accounting systems are a practical way for a manufacturing company to get timely information for the following five activities:

1. Planning the company's manufacturing operations

2. Deciding what products to manufacture, what operations to use in their production, how many units of each to produce, and perhaps even what selling prices to charge

3. Evaluating the performance of manufacturing operations, departments, and individual employees

4. Maintaining control over manufacturing costs and discovering ways to reduce costs and improve efficiency

5. Preparing financial statements

 How do you think knowing the cost of manufacturing its products helps a company in each of the above five activities?

We will discuss job order costing and process costing systems next, standard costing in Chapter 17, and activity-based costing in Chapter 18. Because job order costing is easiest to understand, we will discuss it first.

Exhibit 16-2   Physical Flow of Candy Bars and Flow of Costs for Unlimited Decadence

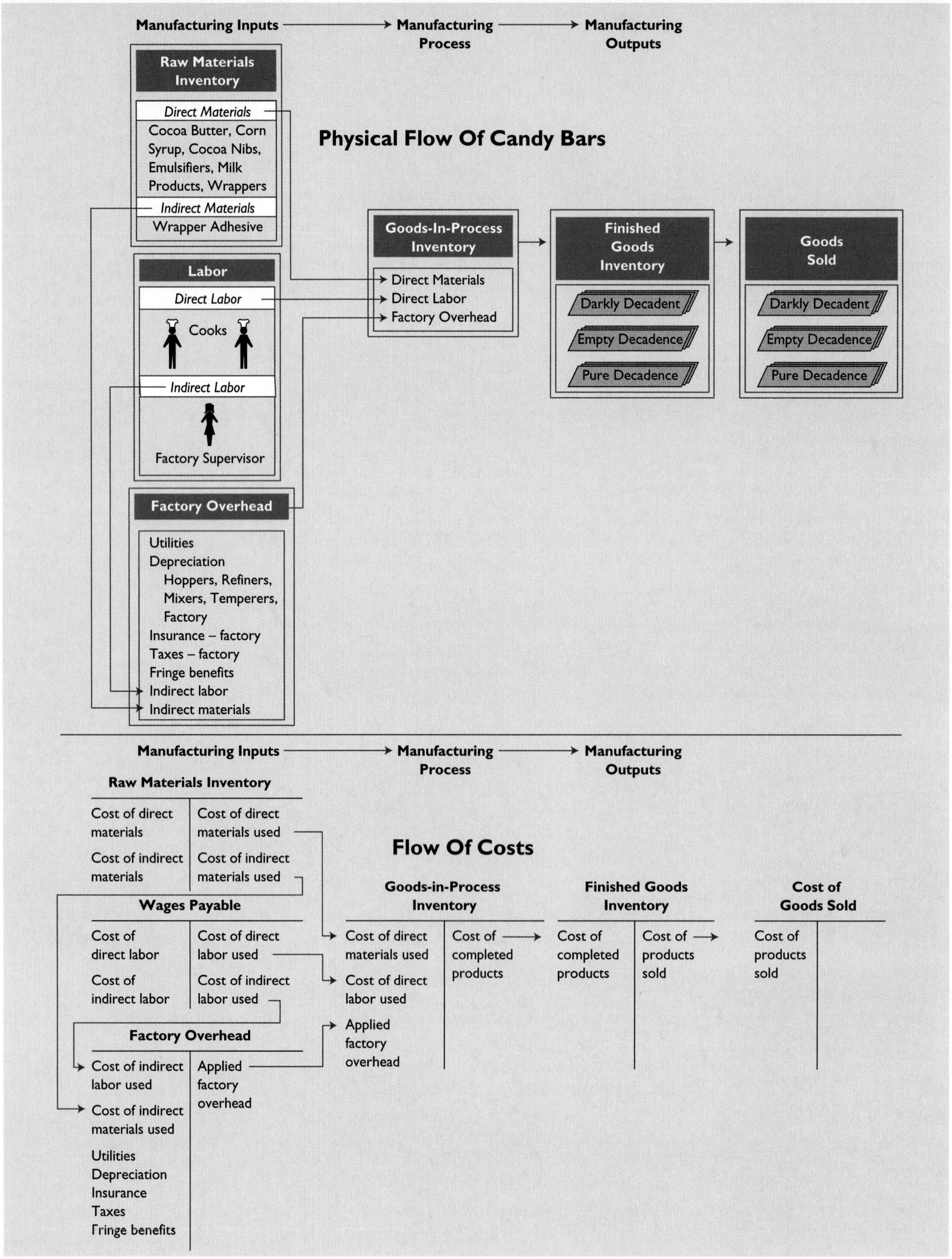

Manufacturing Inputs ⟶ Manufacturing Process ⟶ Manufacturing Outputs

Physical Flow Of Candy Bars

Raw Materials Inventory

Direct Materials
Cocoa Butter, Corn Syrup, Cocoa Nibs, Emulsifiers, Milk Products, Wrappers

Indirect Materials
Wrapper Adhesive

Labor

Direct Labor
Cooks

Indirect Labor
Factory Supervisor

Factory Overhead
Utilities
Depreciation
   Hoppers, Refiners,
   Mixers, Temperers,
   Factory
Insurance – factory
Taxes – factory
Fringe benefits
Indirect labor
Indirect materials

Goods-In-Process Inventory
→ Direct Materials
→ Direct Labor
→ Factory Overhead

Finished Goods Inventory
Darkly Decadent
Empty Decadence
Pure Decadence

Goods Sold
Darkly Decadent
Empty Decadence
Pure Decadence

Manufacturing Inputs ⟶ Manufacturing Process ⟶ Manufacturing Outputs

Flow Of Costs

Raw Materials Inventory

| Cost of direct materials | Cost of direct materials used |
| Cost of indirect materials | Cost of indirect materials used |

Wages Payable

| Cost of direct labor | Cost of direct labor used |
| Cost of indirect labor | Cost of indirect labor used |

Factory Overhead

Cost of indirect labor used	Applied factory overhead
Cost of indirect materials used	
Utilities	
Depreciation	
Insurance	
Taxes	
Fringe benefits	

Goods-in-Process Inventory

Cost of direct materials used	Cost of completed products
Cost of direct labor used	
Applied factory overhead	

Finished Goods Inventory

| Cost of completed products | Cost of products sold |

Cost of Goods Sold

| Cost of products sold | |

Job Order Costing

Some manufacturing companies produce products in a wide variety of sizes and colors, or with other unique features that might be requested by specific customers. For example, in furniture manufacturing, companies might produce sofas in several styles with many up-holstery options. Tables, chairs, dressers, and cabinets may vary in type of style, wood, and finish. Sally Industries in Jacksonville, Florida, builds robots—complete with custom designs and scripted, complex body movements—for theme parks such as Universal Studios. Since they are customized, the robot characters, such as E.T. (the extraterrestrial) on a bicycle, have an enormous number of unique variables such as blinking eyes, rotating wrists, and girth. Similarly, Unlimited Decadence might fill special orders, such as an order for distinctively labeled boxed chocolates.

When a company manufactures one unit of a unique product or manufactures a unique group of products, it treats that unit or group as a **job order**, or "job." (Each of Sally Industries' robots, or sometimes each *group* of robots, is a job order.) A job order may require more than one manufacturing activity.

One characteristic of a job order is that determining when the job starts and ends is easy. A company often starts a job as a result of a "sales order" from a specific customer for a small number of particular items. The job ends when the order is complete. A "job" could be:

1. a set of mahogany chairs in a furniture factory;

2. the first printing of a textbook in a publishing company;

3. a dozen plows in the plant of a farm-implement manufacturer;

4. a car or truck being serviced at a garage;

5. a set of custom-designed memo pads in a print shop;

6. a construction project;

7. a custom set of kitchen cabinets;

8. an audit by a public accounting firm;

5 *What is a job order cost accounting system, and how does a company use this system?*

www.sallycorp.com
www.universalstudios.
com

Examples of customized robots manufactured by Sally Industries.

9. a robot for a theme park; or

10. an order of specially sized and packaged candy.

 Do you think colleges and universities think of individual courses, like this one, as job orders? Do you think they regard individual students as job orders? Why or why not?

In job order manufacturing, production departments such as machine shops or assembly and finishing departments may perform manufacturing operations on hundreds of different jobs in a month's time. Also, the individual jobs may require manufacturing operations in several production departments. For example, the robots that Sally Industries manufactures go through seven functional areas: mechanical, pneumatic, art, scenic, electronics, programming/audio, and shop administration.[2]

In this kind of manufacturing environment, a company's cost accounting system must determine how much of each department's manufacturing costs to apply to each job on which that department worked. For example, if Sally Industries' art department worked on both E.T. and the Seven Dwarfs, the cost accounting system would determine how much of the art department's costs to apply to E.T. and how much to apply to the Seven Dwarfs. The system would do this for each of the functional areas. The cost accounting system best suited for this situation is known as job order cost accounting or job order costing. A **job order cost accounting system** keeps track of the costs applied to each job order.

The Job Order Cost Sheet

When a company uses job order costing, the individual job is the key to product or service costing. The company accumulates direct materials, direct labor, and factory overhead costs for each individual job on a *job order cost sheet* or in a computerized job order cost file as it manufacturers the job. Throughout our discussion of job order costing, we will illustrate a job order cost sheet. Keep in mind, however, that electronic job order costing systems accumulate costs for jobs in the same way, except that electronic systems use computers. Exhibit 16-3 shows an example of a job order cost sheet for a special order from Sweet Temptations for 250 cases of smaller-sized specially packaged Darkly Decadent candy bars. Unlimited Decadence completed the order on March 12 and will sell this order to Sweet Temptations for $16 per case.[3]

Note how a job order cost sheet has separate columns for the direct materials, direct labor, and factory overhead costs applied to a job, and a place to summarize these costs after the job is finished. To determine its total goods-in-process inventory, the company adds together the total accumulated costs of each incomplete job (from the job order cost sheets for each job). When it completes a job, the company takes the total costs applied to the job (summarized on that job's job order cost sheet) out of the Goods-in-Process Inventory account and adds them to the Finished Goods Inventory account. When it sells products from finished goods inventory, the company takes the costs out of the Finished Goods Inventory account and adds them to the Cost of Goods Sold account. The job order cost sheet for the special order is the source document that Unlimited Decadence uses when it records each of these events in its accounting system. We will discuss each of these issues in the following sections, using selected information from the job order cost sheet in Exhibit 16-3.

How a Company Applies Raw Materials Costs to Jobs

When a company purchases raw materials, it places them in the raw materials storeroom and records their cost in the Raw Materials Inventory account. For example, Unlimited Decadence would record a credit purchase of sugar costing $639,800 as follows:

---

[2]Thomas L. Barton and Frederick M. Cole, "Accounting for Magic," *Management Accounting*, January 1991, 28.

[3]Because this is a special order, Unlimited Decadence keeps track of the costs of the order (and any other special orders) separately using job order costing. In other production situations, it may use process costing, which we will discuss later in the chapter.

Exhibit 16-3 Job Order Cost Sheet: Unlimited Decadence

Job Order Cost Sheet

Product Description *Darkly Decadent Candy Bars*	**Job Order Number** *101*
Notes *Rush Order!!!*	**Units Required** *250 Cases*
Special Sizing and Packaging	**Date Started** *March 10*
	Date Completed *March 12*

	Direct Materials		Direct Labor		Factory Overhead Applied
Date	Request Number	Cost	Labor Ticket Number	Cost	
3-10	541	$ 350	380	$ 84	
			381	96	
			382	96	
			383	84	
			384	90	
			387	96	
			388	72	
			389	96	
3-11	549	735	400	96	
			401	90	
			405	96	
			407	84	
			408	96	
			409	78	
			411	96	
			412	96	
3-12			413	54	
		$ 1,085		$ 1,500	125 hours @ $3.16 = $395

Summary of Costs

Direct Material	$1,085
Direct Labor	1,500
Factory Overhead	395
Total Job Cost	$2,980
Units	250
Cost per Case	$11.92

Assets	**=**	**Liabilities**	**+**	**Stockholders' Equity**

Raw Materials Inventory		Accounts Payable	
639,800			639,800
(+)	(−)	(−)	(+)

The company supports the Raw Materials Inventory account with records that show thereceipts, issues, and current balance for each type of individual raw material item, such as sugar, cocoa beans, and emulsifiers.

The storekeeper, who is responsible for all raw materials kept in the storeroom at the company, must receive a written authorization form, known as a *raw materials requisition* (or *request*), before issuing raw materials for use in the factory.[4] Unlimited Decadence uses these forms (like the one in Exhibit 16-4) to trace to specific jobs the quantity and cost of *direct* materials it uses in the manufacturing process and to apply these costs directly to those jobs.

 Can you think of another reason the storekeeper needs an authorization before releasing raw materials into the factory?

Note that the raw materials requisition we show is for sugar to be used on job order number 101 and gives the information needed (requisition number 541, cost $350, and job order number 101) for the March 10 entry for direct materials on the job order cost sheet we show in Exhibit 16-3.

Unlimited Decadence also can use the information on raw materials requisition forms to assign to the Factory Overhead account the total cost of *indirect* materials used. Exhibit 16-5 shows a summary of Unlimited Decadence's raw materials requisitions for March 10. Notice that two requisitions (numbers 545 and 547) were for indirect materials. Unlimited Decadence will apply these costs to jobs along with other indirect manufacturing costs, as we will discuss later. This form also provides Unlimited Decadence with the information it needs to decrease the Raw Materials Inventory account by the total cost of all raw materials issued and to decrease the individual raw materials records for the cost of each type of raw material (e.g., sugar, cocoa, emulsifiers) issued.

 Why do you think companies keep records for each type of raw material that they use?

Thus, raw materials requisitions have several purposes. They:

Exhibit 16-4   Raw Materials Requisition: Unlimited Decadence

	Raw Materials Requisition			# _541_
Item No.	Description	Quantity	Cost per Unit	Cost
885	Sugar	1,000 lbs.	$0.35	$350

Requested for Job Order # _101_
or general factory use _____
by _J. Jones_   Date _3/10_

Issued by _T. Hall_
Date _March 10_
Received by _J. Jones_   Date _3/10_

Exhibit 16-5 Raw Materials Requisition Summary: Unlimited Decadence

Raw Materials Requisition Summary				
Direct Materials				
Job Order Number	Requisition Number	Department	Amount	Job Order Total
101	541	4	$ 350	$ 350
102	543	3	4,600	
102	544	4	2,100	6,700
103	542	2	4,150	
103	546	3	300	4,450
104	540	2	3,000	3,000
			Total Direct	$14,500
Indirect Materials				
	545	4	$40	
	547	3	49	
			Total Indirect	$ 89
Summary for Date 3-10			Total Raw Materials	$14,589
Notes:				

1. Instruct the storekeeper to issue materials to particular factory departments

2. Transfer responsibility for materials used from the storekeeper to production personnel

3. Associate the cost of direct materials used with particular jobs, and the cost of indirect materials used with factory overhead

4. Inform the company of the amount by which the Raw Materials Inventory account should be reduced and the Goods-in-Process Inventory and Factory Overhead accounts increased

For example, the total March 10 raw materials requisitions of $14,589 included $14,500 for direct materials and $89 for indirect materials. Unlimited Decadence records the issuance of these materials in its accounting system (assuming that it has a beginning balance in its Raw Materials Inventory of $30,200) as follows:

Assets   **= Liabilities + Stockholders' Equity**

Raw Materials Inventory		Goods-in-Process Inventory		Factory Overhead	
	14,589	14,500		89	
(+)	(−)	(+)	(−)	(+)	(−)

 Notice that we listed factory overhead on the asset side of the equation along with the two inventory accounts. Why do you think we consider factory overhead an asset?

The $14,589 reduction in the raw materials inventory is supported by a total of $14,589 of reductions in the individual raw materials records. The $14,500 increase in goods-in-process inventory is supported by recording appropriate amounts totaling $14,500 on

individual job order cost sheets. Recording the $350 cost of sugar from requisition number 541 on the job cost sheet for job order number 101 in Exhibit 16-3 is one example of an entry on an individual job order cost sheet that supports the increase in goods-in-process inventory.

 What do you think happens to the physical direct materials and the accounting for them when the production department doesn't use all of the direct materials issued to it for a particular job? What do you recommend should be done?

How a Company Applies Factory Labor Costs to Jobs

In a job order cost accounting system, a company also applies factory labor costs both directly and indirectly to jobs. Recall that direct labor is the labor of employees who work with the raw materials to convert or assemble them into the finished product. The wages earned by machine operators, for example, are direct labor costs of manufacturing candy. The company can trace these direct labor costs to specific jobs on the basis of labor tickets (or computer files) that are kept by the employees and that show the amount of time the employees spent on each specific job. Exhibit 16-6 shows labor ticket #413, from one of Unlimited Decadence's wrapping machine operators on March 12. Note that the $54 cost on this labor ticket is the same $54 that is recorded on the job order cost sheet in Exhibit 16-3 for job order number 101.

A company uses these labor tickets to apply direct labor costs to jobs in the same way that it uses raw materials requisitions to apply direct materials costs to jobs. The time spent on a specific job multiplied by the employees' hourly wage rates gives the direct labor cost to be applied to that particular job for the manufacturing operation performed.

The direct application of labor costs to specific jobs, however, is only for time spent working on those jobs. The same employees may spend time cleaning and oiling machinery, waiting for work, or making equipment adjustments. The company applies the wages for this time *indirectly* to jobs by adding them to factory overhead along with other indirect labor costs. The company also normally applies overtime premiums, the employer's share of payroll taxes, and the cost of fringe benefits, such as vacation pay, to indirect labor.

 Why do you think a company indirectly *applies the cost of time spent on such activities as cleaning and oiling machinery, waiting for work, or making equipment adjustments even though the company considers the same employees to be direct labor?*

Recall that indirect labor is the labor of the employees who are needed for the operation of the production process but who do not convert or assemble the direct materials into the finished product. Since the costs of this work can't be traced directly to jobs, a com-

Exhibit 16-6	Labor Ticket: Unlimited Decadence

Labor Ticket   # _413_

Date _March 12_   Employee Number _2-3-195_

Operation _Wrap & Package Candy_   Department Number _4_

Started _1:00 p.m._   Job Order Number _101_

Completed _5:30 p.m._   Verified by _cfm_

Time	Rate	Amount
4½ hours	$12.00	$54.00

pany applies wages paid for supervision, maintenance, materials handling, storekeeping, inspecting, and so on *indirectly* to jobs by adding them to factory overhead first and then "spreading them over" the jobs. A company records direct and indirect labor costs in a manner similar to that used to record direct and indirect materials costs. For example, suppose Unlimited Decadence's payroll records show that wages of factory personnel for a day total $18,658. If a summary of labor tickets shows that $18,001 is for direct labor on specific jobs and $657 is for indirect labor, Unlimited Decadence records these costs in the T-accounts as follows:

Assets				=	Liabilities	+ Stockholders' Equity

Goods-in-Process Inventory		Factory Overhead			Wages Payable	
14,500		89				
18,001		657				18,658
(+)	(−)	(+)	(−)	(−)	(+)	

Unlimited Decadence uses the labor tickets to determine the amounts (totaling $18,001) that it records (applies) on the individual job order cost sheets and to support the $18,001 increase in the goods-in-process inventory. Notice that the T-accounts also include the amounts of direct materials ($14,500) and indirect materials ($89) that Unlimited Decadence previously recorded in them.

How a Company Applies Factory Overhead Costs to Jobs: Predetermined Overhead Rate

As you just saw, the amount of direct materials cost a company applies to a particular job is the specific cost of the direct materials the company used to manufacture the job. The company traces this amount to the job with information from raw materials requisitions. Similarly, the amount of direct labor cost the company applies to a job is the specific wages earned by the factory employees for the hours they worked on that job. The company traces this direct labor cost to each job through information recorded on labor tickets. Note that a company incurs direct materials costs and direct labor costs because of specific manufacturing activities performed on specific jobs, and that the company easily traces them to particular jobs.

Factory overhead costs are quite different, however. A company incurs almost all factory overhead costs for the general benefit of all manufacturing activity and not specifically because of individual jobs. For example, although all jobs benefit from the use of the building, no individual job can be considered the cause for incurring depreciation on the building. But, because all jobs benefit from the building, the company should apply some of the building's depreciation cost to each job. The same is true for all factory overhead costs. However, individual factory overhead costs cannot be applied *directly* to a job in the way that the company applies direct labor and direct materials costs. Instead, the company adds together all factory overhead costs (including indirect materials and indirect labor) and applies them *indirectly* to jobs by assigning amounts to jobs in proportion to the amount of manufacturing activity devoted to each job. But what is the measure of manufacturing activity? For this purpose, a company might use direct labor hours, machine hours, or direct labor cost to measure the manufacturing activity devoted to each job. If the company uses machine hours, for example, a job requiring 10 hours of machine time would have twice as much factory overhead applied to it as a job requiring 5 hours of machine time. Sally Industries assigns overhead costs to jobs using direct labor hours as its measure of manufacturing activity. This is because producing and *customizing* robots is highly labor-intensive, so the more hours employees log in on a job, the higher are the labor *and* the overhead costs for that job.

Do you think using direct labor hours as the measure of manufacturing activity might cause the proportion of factory overhead allocated to each job to be different from that allocated when the measure is machine hours? Why or why not?

This procedure does not apply to each job the exact amount of factory overhead resulting from the manufacture of that job. However, it does apply factory overhead cost roughly in proportion to the factory overhead benefits the individual jobs received, which is a desirable and reasonable result.

 Suppose a company applied factory overhead costs to jobs by using a procedure that caused it to apply a larger proportion of factory overhead cost to a job than the proportion of factory overhead benefits that the job received. How would this affect the factory overhead costs that the company applied to other jobs during the same time period? How might this procedure affect managers' decisions about pricing, advertising, or dropping products?

For various reasons, a company may not know the exact amount of overhead cost it incurred for manufacturing until the end of the year. For example, the company normally receives a property tax bill or computes depreciation on factory equipment once a year. However, the company usually completes jobs in less than a year. To use a perpetual inventory system with a goods-in-process inventory, a company must be able to include overhead costs in its inventories as it manufactures and completes products. To apply factory overhead costs to individual jobs when manufacturing operations take place or when the company completes jobs, the company estimates the amount of its overhead cost for the year and sets an estimated overhead *rate* (cost per direct labor hour, machine hour, or direct labor dollar, for example) at the beginning of the year. Such a rate is called a predetermined overhead rate. A company figures its **predetermined overhead rate** at the beginning of a year by dividing the year's budgeted factory overhead cost by the budgeted total volume of manufacturing activity (however it is measured) for the year. For example, suppose that Unlimited Decadence wants to apply factory overhead costs to jobs based on the number of direct labor hours (DLH) worked on each job. If it expects to incur $7,584,000 of factory overhead costs during the year and expects factory employees to work 2,400,000 DLH during that same time period, the predetermined overhead rate is set as follows:

$$\text{Predetermined Overhead Rate} = \frac{\text{Expected factory overhead cost for the year}}{\text{Expected direct labor hours for the year}}$$

$$= \frac{\$7,584,000}{2,400,000 \text{ DLH}}$$

$$= \underline{\$3.16/\text{DLH}}$$

Having determined this rate at the beginning of the year, the company uses it to apply factory overhead costs to jobs throughout the whole year. A job requiring 25 hours of direct labor will have $79 (25 DLH × $3.16/DLH) applied to it whether Unlimited Decadence produces it in January or December. Another job requiring 125 direct labor hours will have five times as much factory overhead cost applied (125 DLH × $3.16/DLH = $395) as the job requiring 25 hours of direct labor effort.

Unlimited Decadence records the application of factory overhead of $395 to a job requiring 125 direct labor hours during the month (assuming a predetermined overhead rate of $3.16 per DLH) in its accounting system as follows:

Assets   **=   Liabilities   +   Stockholders' Equity**

Goods-in-Process Inventory		Factory Overhead	
14,500		89	
18,001		657	
395			395
(+)	(−)	(+)	(−)

Unlimited Decadence also applies the factory overhead cost to the specific job, as you can see in the factory overhead column of the job order cost sheet in Exhibit 16-3.

As Unlimited Decadence incurs *actual* factory overhead costs, it accumulates them on the left side of the Factory Overhead account. For instance, if Unlimited Decadence pays $4,000 for factory utilities, it records this actual cost as follows:

Assets   **=   Liabilities   +   Stockholders' Equity**

Cash		Factory Overhead	
	4,000	89	
		657	
		4,000	
(+)	(−)	(+)	(−)

Notice that the actual factory overhead costs increase the Factory Overhead account and that the *applied* factory overhead costs decrease the account by the amount transferred out of Factory Overhead and into the Goods-in-Process Inventory account.

 If the Factory Overhead account has a positive or negative balance, what do managers know?

How a Company Records the Completion of Jobs

When a company completes a job, it removes the completed products from the factory and takes them to the finished goods storeroom or ships them to customers immediately. At the same time, the company computes the cost per unit by dividing the total cost applied on the job order cost sheet by the number of units in the job. Then, the company transfers the job's cost (calculated on the job order cost sheet) from the Goods-in-Process Inventory account into the Finished Goods Inventory account. For example, Unlimited Decadence records the completion of job order #101 ($2,980 = 250 cases × $11.92 per case) as follows:

Assets   **=   Liabilities   +   Stockholders' Equity**

Goods-in-Process Inventory		Finished Goods Inventory	
14,500	2,980	2,980	
18,001			
395			
(+)	(−)	(+)	(−)

Unlimited Decadence then removes the job order cost sheet of the completed job from the goods-in-process supporting records.

How a Company Records the Sale of Finished Goods

When a company uses a perpetual inventory system for the finished goods inventory, it must make two entries to record a sale. First, it records the revenue from the sale. So, when Unlimited Decadence sells the 250 cases from completed job order #101 to Sweet Temptations on credit at a price of $4,000 (250 × $16 selling price per case), it records the revenue from this sale as follows:

	Assets		=	Liabilities	+	Stockholders' Equity	
	Accounts Receivable					Sales	
4,000							4,000
(+)		(−)				(−)	(+)

Second, the company transfers the cost of the cases that it sells from the Finished Goods Inventory account to the Cost of Goods Sold account by decreasing the Finished Goods Inventory account and increasing the Cost of Goods Sold account. For example, Unlimited Decadence transfers from its Finished Goods Inventory account[5] to the Cost of Goods Sold account the $2,980 cost of the 250 cases (250 × $11.92) delivered to Sweet Temptations as follows:

	Assets		=	Liabilities	+	Stockholders' Equity	
Finished Goods Inventory						Cost of Goods Sold	
Bal 2,980		2,980				2,980	
(+)		(−)				(+)	(−)

What Happens to Overapplied and Underapplied Overhead?

As we mentioned earlier, by using a predetermined overhead rate to apply factory overhead, a company does not have to wait to assign overhead costs to jobs until the end of the year when it knows the total *actual* factory overhead cost incurred. The actual factory overhead costs, however, may not equal the expected factory overhead costs for the year. For instance, for various reasons, when a company uses direct labor hours as a measure of manufacturing activity, the number of direct labor hours that factory employees actually work may differ from the expected number of hours. When differences occur, a balance remains in the Factory Overhead account at the end of the year.

 If the company uses machine hours as a measure of manufacturing activity instead of direct labor hours, how might you explain a difference between actual and applied factory overhead costs?

If the company incurs more factory overhead costs than it applies during the year, at the end of the year the total of the left side (the *actual* overhead cost) of the Factory Overhead account exceeds the total of the right side (the applied overhead cost), indicating that the company has "underapplied" factory overhead by the amount of the difference. If the company applies more factory overhead than it incurs, the total of the right side (the applied overhead cost) exceeds the left side (the actual overhead cost) of the Factory Overhead

---

[5]For simplicity, we only show a $2,980 balance on the left side of the Finished Goods Inventory account for the total costs of job order #101. In reality, the Finished Goods Inventory account would have a balance for the costs of *all* the completed jobs that have not yet been sold.

account at the end of the year, indicating that the company has "overapplied" factory overhead. When a company overapplies or underapplies factory overhead, the recorded cost of the year's jobs is too much or too little. As a result, when the jobs are completed and sold, the cost of goods sold recorded in the accounting system will be larger or smaller than the actual cost of goods sold. Fortunately, a company can often estimate its factory overhead costs and activity levels quite accurately. As a result of this accuracy, the amount by which it over- or underapplies factory overhead is seldom very large. In this case, when the amount is small, the company transfers the balance of the Factory Overhead account at year-end to the Cost of Goods Sold account. (However, if the amount is large, the company also transfers a portion of it to the Goods-In-Process Inventory and Finished Goods Inventory accounts because their balances are also larger or smaller than the actual costs of the goods-in-process and finished goods inventories.)

For example, suppose that Unlimited Decadence's factory employees actually worked 2,500,000 direct labor hours and that it actually incurred $7,640,000 of factory overhead costs. Throughout the year Unlimited Decadence incurred and recorded factory overhead costs of $7,640,000 on the left side of its Factory Overhead account. The company, however, applied factory overhead at a predetermined overhead rate of $3.16 ($7,584,000 ÷ 2,400,000 DLH) on each direct labor hour worked. As a result, the total amount that Unlimited Decadence applied by the end of the year (and recorded on the right side of the Factory Overhead account) is $7,900,000 (2,500,000 DLH × $3.16/DLH).[6] Thus, Unlimited Decadence *overapplied* its factory overhead by $260,000 ($7,900,000 applied − $7,640,000 incurred). Assume that during the year, Unlimited Decadence sold candy bars costing $50,000,000 (direct materials cost, direct labor cost, and *applied* factory overhead cost) and recorded cost of goods sold of that amount. At the end of the year, Unlimited Decadence will transfer the $260,000 balance of factory overhead to cost of goods sold, reducing cost of goods sold, as follows:

Assets		=	**Liabilities**	+	**Stockholders' Equity**	
Factory Overhead					Cost of Goods Sold	
7,640,000	7,900,000				50,000,000	
260,000						260,000
Bal　　0					Bal 49,740,000	
(+)	(−)				(+)	(−)

Note that the entry to Factory Overhead reduces its balance to zero at the end of the year, indicating that the amount of factory overhead Unlimited Decadence has applied is now equal to its actual overhead costs. Since the Factory Overhead account now has a zero balance, Unlimited Decadence can use this account next year to accumulate the factory overhead costs it incurs and applies during that year.

Note also that the entry to cost of goods sold reduces its balance from $50,000,000 to $49,740,000. This makes sense because by overapplying factory overhead by $260,000, Unlimited Decadence added more than the actual total of factory overhead to the Goods-in-Process Inventory account. This excess flows to finished goods inventory as Unlimited Decadence completes jobs and to cost of goods sold as it sells them. Thus, when Unlimited Decadence overapplies factory overhead, it also overstates the Cost of Goods Sold account balance. The reduction of that account by $260,000 offsets this overstatement. Similarly, if Unlimited Decadence underapplied factory overhead (the Factory Overhead account would have a balance in its right side at year-end), it would understate the Cost

---

[6]In Chapter 17 we will explain what a company does with the costs associated with the difference between the 2,400,000 expected direct labor hours and the 2,500,000 actual direct labor hours.

of Goods Sold account balance. To correct for this understatement, Unlimited Decadence would increase the Cost of Goods Sold account (and reduce the Factory Overhead account).

 As a manager, would you prefer that factory overhead be overapplied or underapplied? Why?

You just saw that job order costing systematically moves the costs of manufacturing products through the inventory accounts and into cost of goods sold as the jobs *physically* move through the inventories and then are sold. We next discuss and illustrate the process costing system. As you will see, although this system assigns costs to manufactured products, as does the job order costing system, it accomplishes the task differently.

Process Costing

6 *What is a process cost accounting system, and how does a company use this system?*

www.fritolay.com

The job order cost accounting system we discussed in the previous section is well suited for a company that produces unique products in small quantities for customer orders. In some industries, however, companies produce large volumes of identical units of products. In many cases the nature of the products or the high demand for each requires the company to organize the manufacturing operations of each product *separately* to obtain smooth, continuous, and efficient production. For example, Frito-Lay produces Lay's Potato Chips in a long, continuous process and Fritos in a separate long, continuous process. Hence, it organizes production so that it works on only one type of product in each process.

Many times production of a product requires only one manufacturing process, but at other times it requires several processes. In these cases the product normally flows from one operation or process to another continuously as the company completes each stage of its production. The company performs manufacturing operations on large quantities of identical units of that product continuously over long periods of time. Examples of such manufacturing can be found in the production of potato chips, paper, flour, some chemicals, cars, and many other products.

The cost accounting system best suited to apply manufacturing costs to a product manufactured in this way is the process cost accounting system. A **process cost accounting system** keeps track of the costs applied to a product as it moves through one or more manufacturing processes. That is, a process cost accounting system uses a manufacturing *process* (like molding, trimming, baking, and painting) rather than an individual job as the point of cost accumulation. So, with this system, a company uses raw materials requisitions and labor tickets to trace to specific *processes* the quantity and cost of direct materials and direct labor it uses in production and to apply these costs directly to the processes. As manufacturing takes place, a company adds the direct materials, direct labor, and factory overhead costs of each process to a Goods-in-Process Inventory account set up for that particular process (so molding, trimming, baking, and painting would each have its own Goods-in-Process Inventory account). As products move from process to process, the company transfers the products' costs from the Goods-in-Process Inventory account for the first process to that for the next process, or enters manufacturing costs directly into computer-based systems to accumulate the costs for each manufacturing process. The company uses a *process cost sheet* to assign the manufacturing costs for a particular process to individual products. In the following discussion, we focus on the process cost sheet, but keep in mind that computerized process costing systems accumulate costs similarly. The process cost sheet supports the amounts listed in the Goods-in-Process Inventory account for that process. Since a company using the process cost accounting system manufactures only one type of product (such as Fritos) continuously through a process, it applies the accumulated manufacturing costs of that process to the units of that product (bags of Fritos)—usually at the end of each month.

Process Costing When There Is Only One Process

Sometimes a company manufactures a product completely in a single process. For example, consider Lady MacBeth Company, from whom Unlimited Decadence purchases cleaning supplies. Lady MacBeth manufactures a cleaning solvent by mixing several chemicals in a single mixing process that takes 36 hours. The company applies all of the manufacturing costs it incurs in that mixing process during a month to the gallons of cleaning solvent it manufactures during the month.

As Lady MacBeth incurs these costs, it records them in the same way that we described for job order costing except that the costs are added to the Goods-in-Process Inventory account for the *process* (rather than for the job), as well as to the process cost sheet (rather than to individual job order cost sheets).

When There Is No Beginning or Ending Goods-in-Process Inventory

The simplest process costing situation is when a process has no inventory of unfinished products at either the beginning or the end of a month. In this case, during the month the company starts and completes all of the products it manufactures in that month. It assigns the *average* cost per unit of direct materials, direct labor, and factory overhead to each product it completes. However, in process costing, companies often combine the direct labor cost and the factory overhead cost on the process cost sheet and assign them to units as a single cost element called *conversion cost* (sometimes called *processing cost*) in order to simplify computations. Since this is a common practice, we will use it throughout the remainder of the chapter. **Conversion costs** are the direct labor and factory overhead costs necessary to convert raw materials into a finished product. Thus our discussion of single-process manufacturing involves assigning two cost elements to products: direct materials cost and conversion cost.

 When a company combines direct labor and factory overhead costs, it is applying factory overhead costs the same way it is applying direct labor costs—by direct labor hour. Can you explain why?

For example, suppose that during April, Lady MacBeth Company produced 1,500 gallons of cleaning solvent in a single mixing process. It had no unfinished gallons of solvent at the beginning or end of April. During the month, the company recorded a total of $7,500 [(a) $3,000 of direct materials, (b) $2,000 of direct labor, and (c) $2,500 of applied factory overhead] in the Goods-in-Process Inventory account as follows:

Assets			=	Liabilities	+	Stockholders' Equity

Goods-in-Process Inventory		Raw Materials Inventory		Factory Overhead		Wages Payable	
(a) 3,000		(a) 3,000					(b) 2,000
(b) 2,000							
(c) 2,500				(c) 2,500			
(+)	(−)	(+)	(−)	(+)	(−)	(−)	(+)

On the process cost sheet, Lady MacBeth treated these costs as two types of manufacturing costs, $3,000 of direct materials and $4,500 ($2,000 + $2,500) of conversion cost, and assigned them to the 1,500 gallons of cleaning solvent, as we show in Exhibit 16-7.

Lady MacBeth recorded the transfer of the $7,500 cost of completed gallons of solvent to finished goods inventory from the goods-in-process inventory at the end of the month as follows:

Exhibit 16-7 Process Cost Sheet for One Process (No Beginning or Ending Inventories)

LADY MACBETH COMPANY
Process Cost Sheet

	Total Costs Accumulated in Goods-in-Process Inventory		Bottles		Average Costs per Bottle
Direct Materials	$3,000	÷	1,500	=	$2
Conversion	4,500	÷	1,500	=	3
Total	$7,500				

Costs Assigned

To bottles completed and transferred to finished goods inventory			
Direct materials	1,500 bottles @ $2	=	$3,000
Conversion	1,500 bottles @ $3	=	4,500
Total Costs Assigned			$7,500

Assets   =   Liabilities   +   Stockholders' Equity

Goods-in-Process Inventory		Finished Goods Inventory	
Bal 7,500	7,500	7,500	
Bal 0		Bal 7,500	
(+)	(−)	(+)	(−)

From this total, Lady MacBeth assigned each completed bottle of solvent the same amount of cost ($2.00 per gallon average direct materials cost plus $3.00 per gallon average conversion cost).

It is important to note the steps used in these computations, because with some modification the same steps can be used to handle much more complex situations. The three steps are as follows:

1. Compute the total for each type of manufacturing cost ($3,000 direct materials costs and $4,500 conversion costs)

2. Compute the average direct materials cost per product ($2 per gallon) and the average conversion cost per product ($3 per gallon)

3. Assign the total cost to the products by multiplying the number of products times the average costs per product [(1,500 gallons × $2 direct materials costs) + (1,500 gallons × $3 conversion costs) = $7,500 total cost]

But what happens if a process contains unfinished products at the end of a month? We next discuss how a company modifies these steps in such a case.

When There Is Ending Goods-in-Process Inventory

Because manufacturing a product takes time, and because production is continuous, at the end of a month we often find that a particular process has products that are only partially completed. That is, the process has an ending inventory of goods-in-process. When this occurs, the company must modify the cost-assignment procedure so that it assigns costs both to products it completes and transfers out of the process, and to unfinished products left in the process.[7] This modification involves counting the unfinished products as well as those completed and transferred, computing the average costs per unit for all products counted, and assigning costs to all products.

Usually, it is easy to count physical products, regardless of whether they are completed or unfinished. Ford Motor Company can count finished cars as they roll off the production line, and it also can count how many cars are still on the production line in different stages of completion. Regarding product costs, the reason for counting the products is to compute an average cost per unit for direct materials and conversion to use in assigning costs to the products involved. However, it doesn't make sense to assign the same amount of cost to unfinished products as to completed products. (Surely, the unfinished products did not cost as much to make, so far, as did the finished products.) So, to assign reasonable costs to products, a company counts its unfinished products and completed products differently.

www2.ford.com

> Suppose at the end of the month, Ford Motor Company's painting department has 100 cars that are half-painted. Do you think the cost of painting these cars so far is as much as the cost of painting other cars that are complete? If so, explain why. If not, what manufacturing costs are left to add to the half-painted cars?

A company that uses the process cost accounting system counts each *completed* product as a whole unit. It counts each *unfinished* product as a part of a whole unit—that part being the estimated percent that the product is complete. For example, Lady Macbeth would count a bottle of solvent that is 80% complete as 80% of a whole bottle. Normally,

What types of costs must still be incurred to complete these products?

[7]To simplify this introductory discussion, we are ignoring the possibility that a third group of units—lost or spoiled units—might also result from the month's operations. Accounting for the costs of spoilage or lost units is complex, and we do not discuss it in this book.

though, the company does not examine unfinished products individually. Instead, it estimates the average percentage of completion for all unfinished products as a group. It then "counts" the unfinished products by multiplying the total number of unfinished physical products by their average percentage of completion. When physical products in a process are counted this way they are called **equivalent units**. The number of equivalent units in a group of unfinished physical products is the total number of physical products multiplied by their average percentage of completion. A group of 500 completed products that are 100% complete counts as 500 (500 × 100%) equivalent units, whereas a group of 500 unfinished products that are 40% complete counts as 200 (500 × 40%) equivalent units. Thus, Lady MacBeth would count 10 gallons of solvent that are 40% complete (or 40% mixed) as 4 whole gallons (10 × 40%), 300 gallons that are 80% complete as 240 whole gallons (300 × 80%), and so on.

The reason such equivalent unit computations are useful is that they allow a company to assign costs to products in proportion to their percentage of completion. This is desirable because, for example, it is usually fair to assume that the cost incurred to bring 500 products to 40% completion is the same as the cost incurred to complete 200 whole products. Using equivalent units to compute per-unit costs allows a company to assign costs to completed and unfinished products in proportion to the amount of resources each group used.

A company usually does not incur direct materials costs and conversion costs at the same rate, however. The company often adds all direct materials to a process at the beginning of the process, and conversion normally takes place uniformly as the factory employees convert or assemble the direct materials into products. An example of this is Milliken & Co., a leading textile manufacturer in Spartanburg, South Carolina, which adds bolts of fabric completely to a process before dying, bleaching, or other treating occurs. Other examples are in the manufacture of chemicals and in food-processing operations, where all ingredients must be added before mixing, blending, or packaging operations can take place. In these cases, all physical units in the process are 100% complete with regard to direct materials even though their conversion may be only 10% complete. Therefore, these types of companies count equivalent units separately for direct materials and for conversion because *unfinished* products may be at different stages of completion for each respective cost.

In this chapter we always make equivalent unit computations separately for direct materials and for conversion. To simplify these computations, we assume that direct materials are *always* added at the beginning of conversion so that both completed and unfinished products are always 100% complete with regard to direct materials. We also assume that conversion takes place uniformly. Thus, whereas *completed* products are 100% complete with regard to conversion, *unfinished* products are always less than 100% converted.

Let's return to Lady MacBeth Company. Suppose that during July, Lady MacBeth incurred a total of $12,400 in the mixing process and added these costs to the Goods-in-Process Inventory account. Lady MacBeth always adds direct materials at the beginning of processing, whereas conversion (mixing) takes place uniformly. Information for the mixing process during July is as follows:

www.milliken-kex.com/
html/global.htm

Total Costs Accumulated in Goods-in-Process Inventory (all added during July)		Production Information (physical products)	
Direct materials	$ 7,000	Completed & transferred	1,000
Conversion	5,400	Ending inventory (50% processed)	400
Total	$12,400	Total	1,400

Since 400 unfinished gallons of solvent remain in mixing at the end of July, we must assign the direct materials and conversion costs incurred in July to those gallons as well as to the gallons that Lady MacBeth completed and transferred out of mixing to finished goods inventory. To compute the costs per bottle, we must count the equivalent units for

Exhibit 16-8   Process Cost Sheet (Ending Inventory)

LADY MACBETH COMPANY
Process Cost Sheet (July)

Equivalent Units

	Physical Units	Equivalent Units for Direct Materials	Equivalent Units for Conversion
Completed and transferred	1,000	1,000	1,000
Ending inventory (50% processed)	400	400	200[a]
Total	1,400	1,400	1,200

[a]400 × 50%

Average Costs per Equivalent Unit

	Total Costs Accumulated in Goods-in-Process Inventory		Equivalent Units		Average Costs per Equivalent Unit
Direct materials	$ 7,000	÷	1,400	=	$5.00
Conversion	5,400	÷	1,200	=	4.50
Total	$12,400				

Costs Assigned

To units completed and transferred to finished goods inventory:

Direct materials	1,000 equivalent units @ $5.00 =	$5,000	
Conversion	1,000 equivalent units @ $4.50 =	4,500	$ 9,500

To ending (July 31) goods-in-process inventory (unfinished units):

Direct materials	400 equivalent units @ $5.00 =	$2,000	
Conversion	200 equivalent units @ $4.50 =	900	2,900
Total costs assigned			$12,400

both direct materials and conversion. We show this count in the upper part of the process cost sheet in Exhibit 16-8.

Notice that in the computation of equivalent units for completed gallons of solvent, we count each of the 1,000 *completed* gallons as a full equivalent unit for both direct materials and conversion. We count the ending inventory of 400 *unfinished* gallons, however, as only 200 equivalent units for conversion because the processing of the 400 gallons is only 50% complete. In other words, these gallons have been mixing for 18 of the 36 hours. For direct materials, however, we count each unfinished bottle as a full equivalent unit. This is because Lady MacBeth added all direct materials at the beginning of processing. Thus, although the unfinished gallons are only 50% processed, they are 100% complete with regard to direct materials. We can use the 1,400 equivalent units for direct materials to compute the average direct materials cost per equivalent unit. Similarly, we can use the 1,200 equivalent units for conversion to compute the average conversion cost per equivalent unit. We show these computations in the middle part of the process cost sheet in Exhibit 16-8. To determine the $5.00 average cost per equivalent unit for direct materials, we divide the $7,000 of direct materials costs by the 1,400 equivalent units for direct materials. To determine the $4.50 average cost per equivalent unit for conversion, we divide the $5,400 of conversion costs by the 1,200 equivalent units for conversion.

We now can assign direct materials costs and conversion costs separately to completed and unfinished gallons of solvent based on the average costs per equivalent unit. We can do this for each group (both completed and unfinished gallons of solvent) by multiplying the average costs per equivalent unit by the number of equivalent units in the group. We show these computations in the lower part of the process cost sheet in Exhibit 16-8.

We determine the $9,500 total cost of the units completed and transferred to finished goods inventory in three steps. First, we multiply the 1,000 equivalent units for direct materials by the $5.00 average direct materials cost to determine the $5,000 total direct materials costs for the units transferred. Second, we multiply the 1,000 equivalent units for conversion by the $4.50 average conversion cost to determine the $4,500 total conversion costs for the units transferred. Finally, we combine these two costs to determine the $9,500 total cost of the units transferred.

Next, we determine the $2,900 total cost of the unfinished units in the ending goods-in-process inventory in three steps. First, we multiply the 400 equivalent units for direct materials by the $5.00 average direct materials cost to determine the $2,000 total direct materials costs for the unfinished units. Second, we multiply the 200 equivalent units for conversion by the $4.50 average conversion cost to determine the $900 total conversion costs for the unfinished units. Finally, we combine these two costs to determine the $2,900 total costs of the units transferred.

Notice in this computation that the total costs assigned ($12,400) equals the total costs that accumulated in the Goods-in-Process Inventory account. Based on this cost assignment, we transfer the $9,500 cost of the completed units to the Finished Goods Inventory account from the Goods-in-Process Inventory account as follows:

| **Assets** | | | | **= Liabilities + Stockholders' Equity** |

Goods-in-Process Inventory		Finished Goods Inventory		
Bal 12,400	9,500	9,500		
Bal 2,900		Bal 9,500		
(+)	(−)	(+)	(−)	

After the preceding entry to transfer the $9,500 cost of completed units to the Finished Goods Inventory account, the ending balance of the Goods-in-Process Inventory account for mixing is $2,900. This is the amount of cost we assigned on the process cost sheet to the unfinished gallons of solvent. This will become the cost of the August beginning goods-in-process inventory for the mixing process.

 How does this method compare with the method that we used for a process without a beginning and ending inventory? Are the steps the same? What are the similarities and differences?

When There Are Both Beginning and Ending Balances in Goods-in-Process Inventory

When a company has partially completed products in a process at the beginning of a month, the Goods-in-Process Inventory account for that process has a beginning balance equal to the cost assigned to those units at the end of the previous month. Additional costs incurred during the current month increase this balance. Thus, at the end of the month, the total cost accumulated in the Goods-in-Process Inventory account consists of (1) the beginning inventory balance and (2) additional costs added during the current month.

A company with a beginning balance in its goods-in-process inventory uses one of several methods to determine the amount of the total cost to assign to completed and unfinished products at the end of the month. We illustrate the average cost method because it is both simple and widely used.[8] The **average cost method** assigns the total costs of direct materials and conversion separately to products at the *average* costs per equivalent unit by simply adding the amount of each type of cost in the beginning inventory to the amount of that cost type incurred during the month. The remaining steps are the same as those we discussed earlier.

So let's see what happens to the cost of Lady MacBeth's cleaning solvent in August. Remember that Lady MacBeth ended July with 400 unfinished gallons of cleaning solvent in its goods-in-process inventory, and that it assigned $2,000 direct materials costs and $900 conversion costs to these gallons. During August, Lady MacBeth started 1,200 additional gallons of cleaning solvent. It completed and transferred 1,300 gallons during August and ended August with 300 gallons (60 percent processed) still in process. Lady MacBeth incurred $11,908 of additional costs ($6,000 direct materials and $5,908 conversion) in the mixing process. We add these costs to the Goods-in-Process Inventory account, bringing the balance to $14,808 ($2,900 + $11,908) for the mixing process during August as we show below:

Cost Information		Production Information (physical units)	
Costs in beginning inventory (Aug. 1)		Beginning inventory	400
Direct materials	$ 2,000	Added in August	1,200
Conversion	900	Total	1,600
Costs added during August		Completed & transferred	1,300
Direct materials	6,000	Ending inventory (60% processed)	300
Conversion	5,908	Total	1,600
Total	$14,808		

Lady MacBeth must assign the total of $14,808 ($2,000 + $6,000 for direct materials and $900 + $5,908 for conversion) to gallons of solvent for August. We show all of the computations needed to assign the $14,808 total costs to Lady MacBeth's Goods-in-Process Inventory account and Finished Goods Inventory account at the end of August on the process cost sheet in Exhibit 16-9.

 How does this method compare with the method that we used in the example for a process without a beginning and ending inventory? Are the three steps the same? Be sure to note the similarities and differences.

Note in these computations on the process cost sheet in Exhibit 16-9 that we did not use the number or stage of completion of the *beginning* goods-in-process inventory units. The average cost method does not use this information.

Process Costing When There Are Multiple Processes

As we mentioned earlier, manufacturing some products involves more than one process. For example, look at Exhibit 16-10, which illustrates the six conversion processes necessary for Unlimited Decadence to manufacture its Darkly Decadent candy bars. In cases like this, the products transferred out of a process may not be ready for sale but instead may require further conversion in another process. Handling this situation requires very little modification of the steps we illustrated for assigning process costs in single-process manufacturing.

[8]Besides the average cost method, a manufacturing company also may use the last-in, first-out (LIFO) or the first-in, first-out (FIFO) methods to apply costs to its inventory. LIFO and FIFO are more complicated, so we don't discuss them here. However, the general idea is the same as the LIFO and FIFO methods that a retail company uses to cost its inventory, as we will discuss in Chapter 19.

Exhibit 16-9 Process Cost Sheet (Beginning and Ending Inventory)

LADY MACBETH COMPANY
Process Cost Sheet (August)

Equivalent Units

	Physical Units	Equivalent Units for Direct Materials	Equivalent Units for Conversion
Completed and transferred	1,300	1,300	1,300
Ending inventory (60% processed)	300	300	180[a]
Total	1,600	1,600	1,480

[a] $300 \times 60\%$

Average Costs per Equivalent Unit

	Cost in Beginning Goods-in-Process Inventory	Costs Added during August	Total Costs Accumulated in Goods-in-Process Inventory		Equivalent Units		Average Costs per Equivalent Unit
Direct materials	$2,000	$ 6,000	$ 8,000	÷	1,600	=	$5.00
Conversion	900	5,908	6,808	÷	1,480	=	4.60
Total	$2,900	$11,908	$14,808				

Costs Assigned

To units completed and transferred to finished goods inventory
    Direct materials   1,300 equivalent units @ $5.00 = $6,500
    Conversion   1,300 equivalent units @ $4.60 = 5,980 $12,480

To ending (Aug 31) goods-in-process inventory
    Direct materials   300 equivalent units @ $5.00 = $1,500
    Conversion   180 equivalent units @ $4.60 =   828   2,328
        Total costs assigned $14,808

Exhibit 16-11 shows three diagrams of simple arrangements for multiple-process manufacturing. Companies use these and many more complex arrangements in manufacturing a variety of products. The arrows in these diagrams show the flow of products from one process to the next until the products have been converted into finished goods inventory. In these multiple-process situations, manufacturing *costs* flow from one Goods-in-Process Inventory account to the next in a manner corresponding to the flow of products through the processes. As a company completes the conversion of its products, the company removes the costs assigned to them from the last process and transfers them to the Finished Goods Inventory account.

Consider the case of Unlimited Decadence's Gluttonous Gooey Gob candy bars, "chewy peanut clusters surrounded by pure milk chocolate, caramel, and marshmallows." Gluttonous Gooey Gobs require conversion in two processes—mixing and molding. Unlimited Decadence assigns costs to mixing the same way it would if Gluttonous Gooey Gobs required only one process—mixing. However, the entry it uses to record the transfer of the costs of the completed Gluttonous Gooey Gobs *out* of the mixing Goods-in-Process Inventory account differs from that made in the single-process case. In the single-process case, the company transfers completed products to finished goods inventory. In this case, however, Unlimited Decadence transfers the completed Gluttonous Gooey Gobs from

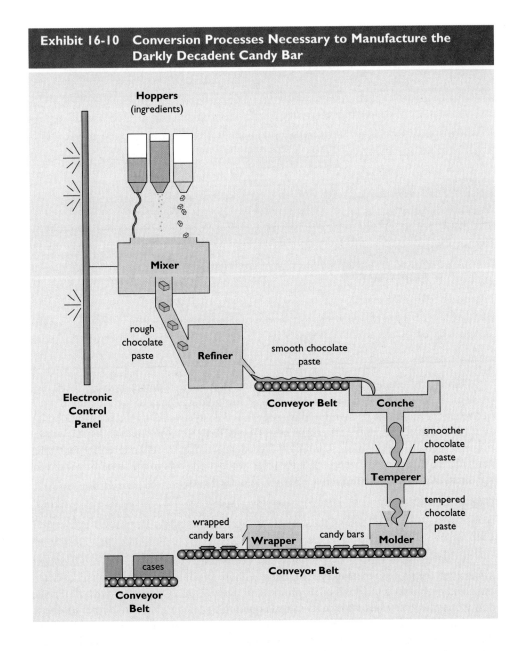

Exhibit 16-10   Conversion Processes Necessary to Manufacture the Darkly Decadent Candy Bar

mixing into molding, where they become goods-in-process inventory for molding. There-fore, Unlimited Decadence transfers the costs assigned to the completely mixed Glutto-nous Gooey Gobs from the Mixing Goods-in-Process Inventory account to the Molding Goods-in-Process Inventory account. For example, if Unlimited Decadence has assigned $1,200 of cost to the Gluttonous Gooey Gobs processed in mixing, when it transfers them from mixing to molding it records the transfer as follows:

Assets		=	Liabilities	+	Stockholders' Equity

Goods-in-Process Inventory: Mixing		Goods-in-Process Inventory: Molding	
Bal 1,200	1,200	1,200	
(+)	(−)	(+)	(−)

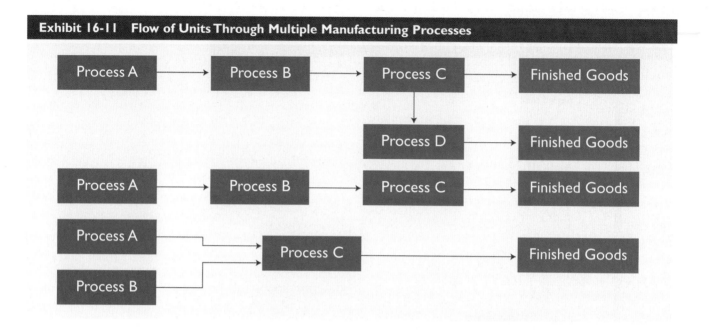

Exhibit 16-11 Flow of Units Through Multiple Manufacturing Processes

Unlimited Decadence treats these costs as an additional, separate type of cost, called *prior production cost*, on the process cost sheet for molding. That is, the molding Goods-in-Process account has its own molding conversion costs *as well as* the prior production cost (direct materials and conversion costs) transferred in from the mixing Goods-in-Process account. In addition, Unlimited Decadence makes a separate equivalent units computation on the process cost sheet for prior production costs in the same way it did for the direct materials and conversion costs we discussed earlier.

 In computing equivalent units for prior production costs, what percentage do you think you should use to indicate the percentage of completion?

We have just discussed two popular cost accounting systems: the job order costing system and the process costing system. Each of these systems allows a company to determine and accumulate the costs of its products or activities. In Chapter 17 we will discuss how a company uses standards in its cost accounting system to plan and control its operations. In Chapter 18 we will discuss some recent developments in modern manufacturing philosophies and processes. You will see how these developments have prompted activity-based costing, a modification of the job order and the process costing systems. We will discuss the activity-based costing system and some of its advantages and disadvantages.

Summary

At the beginning of the chapter we asked you several questions. During the chapter, we asked you to STOP and answer some additional questions to build your knowledge about specific issues. Be sure you answered these additional questions. Below are the questions from the beginning of the chapter, with a brief summary of the key points relating to the answers. Use your creative and critical thinking skills to expand on these key points to develop more complete answers to the questions and to determine what other questions you have that might lead you to learn more about the issues.

1 How does the way a manufacturing company determines the cost of its inventories and cost of goods sold differ from the way a merchandising company determines them?

Whereas a merchandising company assigns costs to its inventory and cost of goods sold based on what it paid for the goods, a manufacturing company assigns these costs based on the costs of manufacturing its inventories. These costs include the costs of direct materials, direct labor, and factory overhead, and they flow through the inventory accounts (raw materials, goods-in-process, and finished goods) as the products flow through the production process to the finished goods warehouse.

2 How does a cost accounting system help a manufacturing company assign costs to its products?

A cost accounting system assigns the costs of manufacturing products (direct materials costs, direct labor costs, and factory overhead costs) to the goods-in-process inventory, by job or by process, as the company manufactures the products. Then, as the jobs or processes are completed, it assigns these costs to individual products.

3 Since overhead is not a physical part of the product, how does a company include the cost of overhead in the cost of its products?

A company usually assigns overhead to products in proportion to the amount of a manufacturing activity, such as direct labor hours, devoted to the manufacture of the products. At the beginning of the year, the company estimates its total annual overhead costs and the level of manufacturing activity. Then, it computes an overhead rate by dividing the estimated costs by the estimated level of activity. As the product is manufactured, the company multiplies the actual level of manufacturing activity (direct labor hours) by the overhead rate. It adds the resulting amount to the Goods-in-Process Inventory account before determining individual product costs.

4 Why is there more than one type of cost accounting system?

Each cost accounting system is a practical way for a manufacturing company to get timely information about its manufacturing operations, and each is specifically suited for a particular type of manufacturing environment. Job order cost accounting is used by a company that manufactures unique products in small quantities for customer orders. Process costing is better suited for a company that manufactures products, where one manufacturing process, or several processes, continuously produces large volumes of identical units.

5 What is a job order cost accounting system, and how does a company use this system?

In a job order cost accounting system, a company keeps track of its costs to manufacture inventory for each job order. It accumulates the costs of direct materials, direct labor, and factory overhead for each individual job on a job order cost sheet. As a company uses direct materials and direct labor, it adds their costs to the Goods-in-Process Inventory account. As it uses indirect materials and indirect labor, and as it incurs other manufacturing costs, the company adds these costs to the Factory Overhead account. The company then increases the Goods-in-Process Inventory account for the factory overhead by applying overhead based on a predetermined overhead rate. When the job is completed, the company transfers the total costs from the Goods-in-Process Inventory account to the Finished Goods Inventory account. When the units of inventory in the job are sold, the company transfers the costs from the Finished Goods Inventory account to the Cost of Goods Sold account. The company adjusts cost of goods sold for any difference between the actual factory overhead incurred and the factory overhead applied.

6 What is a process cost accounting system, and how does a company use this system?

In a process cost accounting system, a company keeps track of its costs to manufacture inventory for each manufacturing process. As manufacturing takes place, the company accumulates the costs of direct materials and conversion (direct labor and factory overhead) for each manufacturing process on a process cost sheet. As a company incurs direct materials and conversion costs in a manufacturing process, it increases the Goods-in-Process Inventory account by the costs of that process. The company then assigns an average cost for direct materials and conversion to each of the units of inventory that flow through that process during the period. To determine the units manufactured for the period, the company counts each completed unit as a whole unit and counts each partially completed unit as an equivalent unit. As units move to the next process, the company transfers the average cost for the prior process out of the Goods-in-Process Inventory account for that process to the Goods-in-Process Inventory account for the next process. After the units of inventory are complete, the total average costs are transferred from the last Goods-in-Process Inventory account to the Finished Goods Inventory account. When units of inventory are sold, the company transfers the average cost per unit sold from the Finished Goods Inventory account to the Cost of Goods Sold account.

Key Terms

average cost method *(p. 561)*	**job order** *(p. 543)*
conversion costs *(p. 555)*	**job order cost accounting system** *(p. 544)*
cost accounting *(p. 538)*	**predetermined overhead rate** *(p. 550)*
equivalent units *(p. 558)*	**process cost accounting system** *(p. 554)*

SUMMARY SURFING

Here is an opportunity to gather information on the Internet about real-world issues related to the topics in this chapter. Go to http://www.dryden.com/account and click on the Cunningham, Nikolai, and Bazley book cover. Click on Summary Surfing, then click on this chapter number, and answer the following questions.

▶ Click on **Bobs Candies.** Then click on *How Canes Are Made.* Identify as many types of direct materials costs, direct labor costs, and factory overhead costs as you can from what you see. Explain why you classified these costs the way you did.

Integrated Business and Accounting Situations

Answer the Following Questions in Your Own Words

Testing Your Knowledge

16-1   Describe the manufacturing environment for which job order costing is best suited.

16-2   Describe a perpetual inventory system and how it works in a job order costing system.

16-3   How do job order cost sheets support the Goods-in-Process Inventory account in a job order system?

16-4   Explain what it means to apply costs.

16-5   What is the purpose of a raw materials requisition (or request)?

16-6   How do you know whether a raw material is a direct material or an indirect material?

16-7   What are the purposes of labor tickets?

16-8   How do you know whether a labor cost is for direct labor or indirect labor? Give two examples of indirect labor.

16-9   Why does a company bother to distinguish direct materials from indirect materials and direct labor from indirect labor?

16-10   Why are factory overhead costs not applied directly to job orders, when the other two manufacturing input costs are applied directly?

16-11   Why does a company predetermine its overhead rate?

16-12   Under what conditions is factory overhead overapplied and underapplied? In either of these cases, why does a company adjust the balance in its Cost of Goods Sold account?

16-13   Describe the manufacturing environment for which process costing is best suited.

16-14   In a process costing system, what are conversion costs and why are they called conversion costs?

16-15   How do process cost sheets support the Goods-in-Process Inventory account in a process costing system?

16-16   In a process costing system, what are prior production costs? How are these costs treated on the process cost sheet?

16-17   Describe, as precisely as you can, how a company computes equivalent units for a group of units in goods-in-process inventory.

16-18   Why does a company compute equivalent units separately for materials and for conversion costs?

Applying Your Knowledge

16-19   During May, Bigg Production Company made a $21,700 credit purchase of raw materials. A summary of raw materials requisitions shows the following raw materials issued into production:

Direct materials for	
Job order 101	$ 7,560
Job order 102	3,030
Job order 104	2,750
Job order 105	1,890
Total direct materials	$15,230
Total indirect materials	340
Total raw materials issued	$15,570

Required: (1)   Use T-accounts to show the effect of the purchase of raw materials on Bigg's accounts.

(2)   Use T-accounts to show the effect of the issue of raw materials on Bigg's accounts.

16-20 A summary of labor tickets shows the following labor costs for Bigg Production Company during May:

Direct labor for		
Job order 101	(310 hours)	$3,100
Job order 102	(280 hours)	2,800
Job order 104	(200 hours)	2,000
Job order 105	(80 hours)	800
Total direct labor	(870 hours)	$ 8,700
Total indirect labor		1,305
Total direct and indirect labor		$10,005

Required: Use T-accounts to show the effect of direct and indirect labor costs on Bigg's accounts.

16-21 Bigg Production Company could set its predetermined overhead rate based on the year's expected factory overhead cost and either the year's expected direct labor hours or direct labor cost (dollars). Bigg expects this year's factory overhead costs to be $126,000. It also expects that its employees will work 12,000 direct labor hours this year and that this labor will cost $120,000.

Required: (1) What is Bigg's predetermined overhead rate per direct labor hour?
(2) What is Bigg's predetermined overhead rate per direct labor dollar?
(3) Refer to 16-20. How much total overhead would Bigg apply to the job orders in May if it used the predetermined overhead rate per direct labor hour? Use T-accounts to show how applying the overhead would affect Bigg's accounts.
(4) Refer again to 16-20. How much total overhead would Bigg apply to the job orders in May if it used the predetermined overhead rate per direct labor dollar?

16-22 Heavy Metal Products computed its predetermined overhead rate to be $13.50 per machine hour (with expected overhead costs of $124,200 and with 9,200 expected machine hours for the year).

Required: (1) If actual factory overhead costs were $130,000 and total actual machine hours were 9,500 for the year, by how much did Heavy Metal over- or underapply overhead? Use T-accounts to record the actual and applied factory overhead, and to transfer the over- or underapplied overhead to the Cost of Goods Sold account.
(2) What if, instead, actual factory overhead costs were $118,100 and total actual machine hours were 8,900 for the year? Use T-accounts to record the actual and applied factory overhead and to transfer the over- or underapplied overhead to the Cost of Goods Sold account.

16-23 Protez Company produces crankers based on customers' special orders. During October, it started and completed one job order (#89), which contained 80 crankers. The following cost information is available for October.
(1) *Materials Requisitions:* $8,768 direct materials
(2) *Labor Time Cards:* 860 hours of direct labor at $12 per hour
(3) *Factory Overhead:* Factory overhead costs are applied to job orders at a predetermined overhead rate of $6.20 per direct labor hour.

Below is job order cost sheet #89.

Job Order Cost Sheet #89	
Direct Materials	$_____
Direct Labor	_____
Factory Overhead	_____
Total Job Cost	$_____
Units	_____
Cost per Unit	$_____

Required: Complete job order cost sheet #89 for Protez Company.

16-24 Multiple Times Corporation, manufacturer of watches, clocks, and stopwatches, had the following costs and units on its job cost sheets for its job orders for July:

Job order 16	$12,350	(300 stopwatches)
Job order 17	35,800	(1,100 alarm clocks)
Job order 18	6,170	(40 cuckoo clocks)
Job order 19	15,850	(250 sports watches)
Job order 20	27,000	(1,000 standard watches)

Multiple Times completed job orders 16, 17, 18, and 20 during the last week of July. It sold job orders 17 and 18 entirely and 300 watches out of job order 20. Revenues from these credit sales totaled $96,425.

Required: (1) Record the balance in Multiple Times' Goods-in-Process Inventory T-account during the last week of July (the balance before recording the completion of the job orders). Now use T-accounts to record the effect on Multiple Times' accounts of the completion of the job orders during the last week of July.

(2) Use T-accounts to record the effect on Multiple Times' accounts of its sales during the last week of July. Determine the ending balance in the Finished Goods Inventory T-account.

16-25 Woods Custom Furniture Manufacturing worked on a single job order during the entire month of August. It started the job at the beginning of the month and completed and sold the job at the end of the month. The following related events occurred during the month:

(1) Woods made a credit purchase of $18,000 of raw materials.

(2) Woods issued $15,200 of direct materials and $450 of indirect materials into production.

(3) Woods' employees worked 995 direct labor hours at $10.00 per hour. Indirect labor cost Woods $1,700.

(4) The factory returned $110 of direct materials to the storeroom.

(5) Woods' factory overhead, other than indirect labor and materials, amounted to $23,650 as follows:

Depreciation on factory and equipment	$13,500
Insurance (previously paid in advance)	2,200
Property taxes (to be paid in December)	1,600
Other factory overhead (all cash payments)	6,350
Total	$23,650

(6) Woods applied factory overhead at a predetermined overhead rate of $30 per direct labor hour.

(7) Woods completed the job order and transferred it to finished goods inventory.

(8) Woods sold the job order for $105,000 on credit.

Required: Using T-accounts, show the effect of each of these events on Woods' accounts.

16-26 PETROIL Refining Company produces one of its products in refining process B.

Required: Compute the number of equivalent units for conversion cost in each of the following groups:

(1) 1,400 completed tanks

(2) 550 tanks (1/2 processed)

(3) 600 tanks (1/3 processed)

(4) 300 tanks (20% processed) and 440 tanks (25% processed)

(5) 200 completed tanks and 100 tanks (75% processed)

16-27 Refer to 16-26.

Required: Compute the number of equivalent units for direct materials cost for each of the five groups, assuming that PETROIL adds direct materials at the beginning of refining process B.

16-28 Suppose that PETROIL Refining Company has no beginning inventory in refining process B in May. During May, it accumulated the following costs in its Goods-in-Process Inventory account:

Direct materials	$3,300
Conversion	4,125
Total	$7,425

PETROIL completed and transferred 500 tanks to the finished goods inventory during May. At the end of May, 250 unfinished tanks were still in process. They were 100% complete for direct materials but only 50% complete for conversion.

Required: (1) Prepare the schedules that PETROIL would include on its process cost sheet to assign the total direct materials and conversion costs to the completed tanks and to the ending inventory of unfinished tanks.

(2) Using T-accounts, record the transfer of the costs of completed tanks from the goods-in-process inventory to the finished goods inventory.

16-29 Apollo Chemical Company produces procoline in its mixing process. There is no inventory in the mixing process at the beginning of February. Apollo adds direct materials at the beginning of processing. During February, it completed 1,400 bottles of procoline and transferred them from the mixing process to the finished goods inventory. At the end of February, 300 bottles (80% processed) remained in the mixing process. Apollo incurred the following costs in the mixing process during February:

Direct materials	$3,910
Direct labor	1,674
Factory overhead	2,590
Total	$8,174

Required: (1) Prepare the schedules that Apollo would include on its process cost sheet to assign the direct materials and conversion costs incurred in the mixing process to the completed and unfinished bottles of procoline.

(2) Using T-accounts, record the transfer of the costs of completed bottles of procoline from the goods-in-process inventory to the finished goods inventory.

16-30 Greyson Grinding Company produces an abrasive powder in a grinding process. This process had an inventory at the beginning of February, to which Greyson had assigned the following costs:

Direct materials	$6,700
Conversion	760
Total beginning goods-in-process inventory balance	$7,460

Greyson added the following additional costs to the Goods-in-Process Inventory account during February:

Direct materials	$18,500
Direct labor	14,410
Factory overhead	26,830
Total	$59,740

Greyson added direct materials at the beginning of processing. It completed and transferred 16,000 bags of powder to the finished goods inventory during February. At the end of February, 2,000 bags of powder were unfinished (40% processed).

Required: (1) Prepare the schedules that Greyson would include on its process cost sheet to assign the total costs accumulated in the Goods-in-Process Inventory account at the end of February to the completed and the unfinished bags of powder.

(2) Using T-accounts, record the transfer of the costs of completed bags of powder from the Goods-in-Process Inventory account to the Finished Goods Inventory account.

16-31   ERIC Industries manufactures dribbits in a single process. It adds direct materials at the beginning of processing. ERIC's cost and production information for the months of July and August is as follows:

Cost Information

	July	August
Costs in beginning inventory		
Direct materials	$ 41,500	$?ᵃ
Conversion	10,430	?ᵃ
Costs added during month		
Direct materials	77,300	87,500
Conversion	24,850	32,880
Total	$154,080	$?ᵃ

ᵃTo be computed

Production Information (physical units)

	July	August
Beginning inventory	500	300
Added during the month	600	800
Total	1,100	1,100
Completed and transferred	800	900
Ending inventory		
July (60% processed)	300	
August (30% processed)		200
Total	1,100	1,100

Required: (1) Prepare the schedules that ERIC would include on its process cost sheet to assign the total costs accumulated in the goods-in-process inventory at the end of July to the completed and unfinished units.

(2) Repeat (1) for August.

16-32   The Genuine Products Company manufactures "antique tables" in two processes. First, Genuine Products adds direct materials at the beginning of an assembly process in which the tables are assembled with precut and finished tops and legs. It then transfers the completed tables into an "aging" process in which they are nicked, scratched, and water-spotted by two skilled craftsmen. It adds no new direct materials to the aging process. At the end of the aging process, Genuine Products transfers the tables to the finished goods inventory. Genuine Products has the following cost and production information for the two processes during the month of March:

Cost Information

	Assembly	Aging
Beginning inventory costs:		
Prior production	—	$2,200
Direct materials	$ 950	—
Conversion	240	77
Costs added during March:		
Prior production	—	?ᵃ
Direct materials	11,300	—
Conversion	7,800	3,895
Total	$20,290	?ᵃ

ᵃTo be computed

Production Information (physical units)

	Assembly	Aging
Beginning inventory	40	20
Added	310	320
Total	350	340
Completed and transferred	320	325
Ending inventory		
(50% processed)	30	
(40% processed)		15
Total	350	340

Required: (1) Prepare the schedules that Geunine Products would included on its process cost sheet to assign the total costs accumulated in each of the two Goods-in-Process Inventory accounts at the end of March to the completed and unfinished tables.

(2) Using T-accounts, record the transfer of the costs of completed tables out of the two Goods-in-Process Inventory accounts at the end of March.

Making Evaluations

16-33 The Machine Shop uses lathes, drill presses, and other metal-working equipment to do machining to customer order. It grinds valves; cuts, drills, and bends sheet metal; and welds. A large portion of The Machine Shop's business is fabrication of machine parts for machine repair work by other companies in the vicinity. The company also often repairs brush hogs and other equipment for local farmers.

Required: What kind of cost accounting system would you recommend that The Machine Shop use? What features of the system that you recommended would be useful to the company, and why would each of these features be useful?

16-34 Chemicals-R-Us operates a large plant in the Midwest. It manufactures several common acids that are in high demand. In fact, several of its acid departments operate 24 hours per day, 7 days a week. Equipment in most of Chemicals' departments is specialized. For example, mixing vats and piping are lined for sulfuric acid production. This is not necessary for several other chemicals produced by the company. Chemicals-R-Us keeps a huge storage warehouse near the factory to hold finished chemicals because demand fluctuates greatly and in some months exceeds the company's production capability.

Required: What kind of cost accounting system would you recommend that Chemicals-R-Us use? What characteristics of the company caused you to make your recommendation? What features of the system that you recommended would be useful to the company?

16-35 LUBCO Inc. has opened a new plant to expand production of a compound that is experiencing increased industrial use. You are the production manager of the new plant, which is supposed to be capable of twice the rate of output of the old plant and of a slightly lower processing cost per gallon. Just when you thought things were going great, you received the following memo from Pete Duncan, the vice-president of production for the company:

Dear_____:

What the_____is going on over there? I put you in charge of the new plant because I thought you could handle it best. But look at the mess your factory is in. The production performance for Compound A62 is erratic. Look at the numbers:

Old Plant

	Cost Incurred	Gallons of Completed Output	Cost per Gallon
Jan.	$240,000	20,000	$12.00
Feb.	$240,000	20,000	$12.00
March	$240,000	20,000	$12.00
April	$240,000	20,000	$12.00
May	$240,000	20,000	$12.00
June	$240,000	20,000	$12.00

New Plant

	Cost Incurred	Gallons of Completed Output	Cost per Gallon
Jan.	$441,000	35,000	$12.60
Feb.	$487,500	39,000	$12.50
March	$483,750	43,000	$11.25
April	$501,200	40,000	$12.53
May	$500,400	45,000	$11.12
June	$569,600	40,000	$14.24

You've had a production cost per gallon lower than that of the old plant in only two of the six months that the new plant has been operating. And this most recent month is the worst of all. Your per-unit cost is almost 20% higher. If you've got problems, let me know. And if you can't get things turned around soon, I'll come over and run that plant myself.

Pete

Because the vice-president was particularly concerned about cost performance in June, the most recent month, you have gathered the following information for June from your records and those offered by the cost accountant of the old plant.

	Old Plant	New Plant
June production (gallons):	Physical Units	Physical Units
Beginning Inventory	0	0
Started	20,000	48,000
Total	20,000	48,000
Completed	20,000	40,000
Ending Inventory	0	8,000 (75% complete)
Total	20,000	48,000
June costs:		
Direct materials	$200,000	$480,000
Conversion	40,000	89,700
Total	$240,000	$569,700

Required: Write a memo to Pete Duncan describing your assessment of the performance of your new plant relative to that of the old plant.

16-36 Aboveboard Inboard and Outboard Motors is a boat dealership. The company sells new and used boats, and provides repair service as well. Suppose you are the manager of used boat sales. One of your primary sources for used boats is the company's new boat operation, which takes trade-ins. You inspect and make offers on boats traded in. Your cost for each boat includes your offer price plus the parts and labor you purchase from the company's service operation to recondition the boat, an assignment of "overhead," and a sales commission.

You have the following information with which to establish prices for five boats taken in on trade during the second week of August:

Offer Price

Boat A	$ 500
Boat B	1,200
Boat C	900
Boat D	2,100
Boat E	2,300

Parts Requisition Summary:

	Requisition	Part	Amount	Total
Boat A	16710	42-21003	$ 21.95	
		42-21004	6.50	
		30-12500	65.35	
		30-12901	4.35	
		30-12911	9.15	$107.30
	16725	5-4100	30.50	30.50
Boat B	16760	42-21103	23.95	
		42-21104	6.50	
		80-65000	13.50	43.95
Boat C	16801	50-81400	43.50	43.50
Boat D	16900	20-92500	1.50	
		80-65300	14.95	16.45
Boat E	16911	30-13100	80.15	
		30-13600	4.90	
		30-13610	9.05	94.10
	16914	95-20200	180.00	180.00

Labor Summary

Mechanic	Boat	Allowed Time	Operation
Repair Shop			
Wu, Lin	A	2 hr	Depth gauge
		1	Starter motor
		1	Tune
		2	Anchor engine
	C	1	Replace light assembly
	D	1	Replace battery connection
Guptil, Ann	B	1	Replace interior light assembly
		1	Change rotor assembly
	E	2	Speed gauge
		3	Overhaul engine
Body Shop			
Austin, Les	B	4	Sand, waterproof bow and stern
	D	1	Touch up, buff

Aboveboard's repair shop charges $30 per hour for labor. Its body shop charges $35 per hour.

You assign "overhead"—which includes your salary, rent, utilities, advertising, insurance, property taxes, and supplies—equally at a predetermined rate to the boats you sell. You estimated this year's total of these indirect costs to be $72,800 and total sales for the year to be 520 used boats.

You pay sales personnel strictly on a commission basis at a rate of 10% of sales revenue from the boats they sell. The dealership wants to earn an average of $50 per used boat sold.

Required: Determine the prices to be charged for the five used boats taken in on trade during the second week of August and discuss the similarities and differences between your pricing computations and the procedures of a job order cost accounting system for a manufacturing company.

16-37   Your boss, Festus B. Thorneapple, stopped by your office today. Among other things, he said:

> I know that we apply overhead to jobs in proportion to their relative number of direct labor hours and that we currently allocate overhead at a rate of $60 per direct labor hour. But that bothers me a little. Here's why. I know, for example, that we expect to use 10 direct labor hours and 500 KWH of electricity on the Smith job. And we expect to use 100 direct labor hours and 100 KWH of electricity on the job for Calloway Corp. According to my calculations, that means that we will allocate $600 in overhead costs to the Smith job (10 direct labor hours × $60 per direct labor hour) and $6,000 to the Calloway job (100 direct labor hours × $60 per direct labor hour). The thing that bothers me is that we use much more electricity for the Smith job than for the Calloway job. Since our utility costs are overhead costs, it seems like we should be allocating more overhead costs to the Smith job. I looked at the numbers, and if we applied overhead based on KWH, we would apply overhead at a rate of $11 per KWH, which would change the costs of both jobs.
>
> Anyway, to make a long story short, this made me start wondering whether we are making faulty decisions based on the way we are allocating overhead costs. To start with, how might applying overhead costs based on KWH affect our decisions about what selling prices to charge? Our current policy is to set the selling price at 1.6 times the cost of a job. We have projected that the Smith job will cost $1,800 ($600 factory overhead + $1,000 direct materials + $200 direct labor) and the Calloway job will cost $11,000 ($6,000 factory overhead + $3,000 direct materials + $2,000 direct labor). So, we're planning to sell the Smith job for $2,880 (1.6 × $1,800) and the Calloway job for $17,600 (1.6 × $11,000). If we were to change our method of applying overhead costs from using direct labor hours to using KWH, how would that affect our decisions about the selling prices to charge for these jobs? When you get a chance, will you please think about this and write me a memo addressing this question?

Required: Write your boss a memo responding to his question.

16-38 Yesterday, you received the following letter for your advice column in the local paper:

Dear Dr. Decisive:

My roommate and I belong to a service club on campus. Next month, the club is going to hold a bake sale and plans to give the profits to the homeless shelter downtown. We would like to make the largest profit possible, but the members can't agree on how to do that. Even my roommate and I don't agree. She says (and most of the club members agree with her) that the bake sale will make the most profit if each person decides what he or she wants to bake for the sale, gets reimbursed for the cost of the ingredients from the club, and then the club sells everything. She says that's what her high school basketball team did to finance their trips, and they had plenty of money. (I think their parents contributed most of the money for the trips, but that's a different issue.) I am trying to convince the members of the club that what I learned in my accounting class is relevant here: knowing the cost of baking the goods that the club will sell will help the club (1) plan what to bake, (2) decide how many of each type of baked good it wants to sell, (3) decide how much to charge for each item, and (4) make the largest profit.

I know that most of the club members read your column because we try to guess what your answers are going to be before we read your answers. I also think that they pay attention to what you say. So, will you please explain why I am right? My roommate will buy my dinner if you agree with me.

"Correct on Campus"

Required: Meet with your Dr. Decisive Team and write a response to "Correct on Campus."

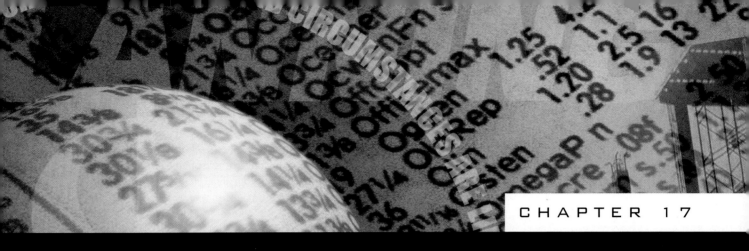

INVENTORY AND CONTROL

"Idealism increases in direct proportion to one's distance from the problem."
—John Galsworthy

1 *What is a price standard and a quantity standard, and how does a company compute a standard cost?*

2 *What is included in a company's direct materials price and quantity standards?*

3 *When a company compares its actual direct materials costs to its direct materials standards, how does it determine what caused the difference between the two?*

4 *What is included in a company's direct labor price and quantity standards?*

5 *When a company compares its actual direct labor costs to its direct labor standards, how does it determine what caused the difference between the two?*

6 *What does a company include in its factory overhead price and quantity standards, and what volume does it use to set its predetermined rates?*

7 *When a company compares its actual factory overhead costs to its factory overhead standards, how does it determine what caused the difference between the two?*

8 *How does a company use its manufacturing cost variances to control its operations?*

What measures do you use to describe your personal level of fitness? Do you use weight? body fat composition? cholesterol levels? triglyceride levels? strength? resting heart rate? blood pressure? Whatever measures you use, you probably compare them against standards, such as the ideal weight for a 21-year-old woman or man, or the average resting heart rate of serious runners, or the range of reasonable blood pressures. If your fitness level is "substandard," perhaps you alter your diet, change your exercise program, or visit with your doctor to get ideas for moving your fitness level closer to the standard—or to control your weight, body fat composition, cholesterol level, and so forth.

A company also tries to measure and control its "fitness." In earlier chapters, we discussed how a company uses ratios, industry averages, and comparisons with competitors' ratios to evaluate its performance. A company also uses its cost accounting system to measure its "fitness." When a company's costs deviate from its standards, the company uses this information to locate problems and fix them or, in other words, to *control* its operations.

In Chapter 16 we discussed cost accounting systems primarily in regard to *product costing.* We described two types of cost accounting systems: job order and process cost accounting systems. Most manufacturing companies use these systems, or some combination of these systems, to assign direct materials, direct labor, and factory overhead costs to the products they make. But they also use the information from these same cost accounting systems to help managers *plan* and *control* company operations.

In this chapter we will emphasize the use of cost accounting systems in controlling a company's operations. Our discussion focuses on the development of *standard costs* and how managers use them to evaluate the manufacturing activities of a company, or the company's manufacturing "fitness."

More about Standard Costs

1 *What is a price standard and a quantity standard, and how does a company compute a standard cost?*

Remember from our discussion in Chapter 11 that **standard costs** are the costs that a company *should* incur in performing an activity or producing a product under a given set of planned operating conditions. As you saw in Chapter 12, standard costs are useful in planning because they aid in the development of budgets. Managers can use standard costs to help them develop, for any level of planned production, raw materials budgets, direct labor budgets, and factory overhead budgets. Managers can also use standard costs of selling activities (such as costs of finished goods warehouse operations, shipping, and delivery) and standard costs of some general and administrative expenses to help them prepare the selling expenses budget and the general and administrative expenses budget.

However, the most valuable use of standard costs is in controlling a company's operations. As you saw in Chapter 12, managers can use flexible budgeting in their control activities. A "flexible budget" for manufacturing costs shows the standard cost for direct materials, for direct labor, and for factory overhead at various levels of production. Managers can use this flexible budget information as a benchmark against which to measure the actual costs of production. If an actual production cost is different from the standard cost budgeted for the actual level of production (in other words, if there is a *variance),* one or more of the planned conditions must not have existed. When the actual cost is greater than the standard cost, the variance is *unfavorable.* When the actual cost is less than the standard cost, the variance is *favorable.* By analyzing this unfavorable or favorable variance, managers can determine which of the planned conditions did not exist and decide what changes, if any, to make in the company's operations.

 Can you think of a situation where it really might not be favorable for the company if the actual cost of some activity is less than the standard cost of that activity?

Recording Standard Costs in the Accounts

When a manufacturing company uses a **standard cost system,** it normally assigns standard costs rather than actual costs to each of its inventory accounts (Raw Materials

Inventory, Goods-in-Process Inventory, and Finished Goods Inventory). This simplifies cost recording by *eliminating* the following tasks:

1. Keeping detailed records of actual costs to support the raw materials inventory; the supporting raw materials inventory records can be kept in *physical quantities* only

2. Recording *actual* costs on job order cost sheets in job order costing

3. Calculating *actual* costs per unit in process costing

By assigning standard costs to inventory accounts, managers avoid assigning different costs to identical units in inventory just because problems (such as inefficient production by a new employee, a machine breakdown, or the use of faulty materials) result in production costs that are higher for some units than for others. Thus, a company that uses a standard cost system does not record in inventory the costs that result from inefficiency in manufacturing operations. Rather, it measures these costs as variances and treats them separately from the costs of inventories. In this chapter, as we discuss the calculations of variances for direct materials, direct labor, and factory overhead, we will show you how standard costs affect the inventory accounts.

Manufacturing Cost Standards

To understand variance computations and to know what they mean, you need to understand how a company establishes a standard cost for each product it manufactures. Unlimited Decadence, for example, has a standard cost for each case of candy bars it produces. But as you know, a company calculates the cost of its manufactured products by adding together the costs of its *inputs*—direct materials, direct labor, and factory overhead. (The *cost* of Unlimited Decadence's candy bars is made up of the costs of the ingredients, labor, and overhead that went into manufacturing the candy bars.) These input costs are based on the quantity of inputs for each product and their costs. Therefore, a company establishes the *standard* cost of a unit of product output (e.g., a case of candy bars) by determining two standards for each *input* to the manufacturing process. The two standards for each of these inputs are a price standard and a quantity standard.

A **price standard** is the *cost* that a company should incur to acquire one unit of *input* for a manufacturing process. Examples of price standards include the cost per pound for direct materials and the cost per hour for direct labor. Unlimited Decadence's direct materials purchases budget, which we discussed and illustrated in Chapter 12, shows that the standard price for a pound of sugar is $0.35. Its direct labor budget shows that the standard cost for labor is $12 per hour.

A **quantity standard** is the *number* of units of an *input* that a company should use to produce one unit of product *output*. For example, Unlimited Decadence uses 4 pounds of sugar and 0.5 hours of direct labor (product input) for each case of Darkly Decadent candy bars it produces (product output). These amounts—4 pounds per case and 0.5 hours per case—are the quantity standards for direct materials and direct labor.

A company determines the **standard cost of an input** *for one unit of product output* by multiplying the quantity standard of the input by its price standard. So at Unlimited Decadence, the standard cost of sugar for one case of Darkly Decadent candy bars is $1.40 (4 pounds × $0.35). The standard cost of labor for a case of Darkly Decadent candy bars is $6 (0.5 hours × $12).

A manufacturing company spends a lot of time and effort designing its products and its manufacturing operations for efficient production. It tries to determine the least costly way of manufacturing each product, while maintaining high product quality, by considering (1) the prices of various types, sizes, and qualities of direct materials, and (2) the expected direct labor and factory overhead costs that would result from using different combinations of direct labor and machine operations. This planning process results in a set of specific conditions for the production of the company's products. The company determines price and quantity standards for direct materials, direct labor, and factory overhead from these planned conditions.

Exhibit 17-1 shows the standard manufacturing cost for one case of Darkly Decadent candy bars. The planned conditions for the production of these candy bars provide the basis for all of the illustrations and exhibits in this chapter.

Notice in Exhibit 17-1 how we computed the standard costs per case of candy bars by multiplying the quantity standard for each input by its price standard. For example, we determined the $1.40 standard sugar cost of a case of Darkly Decadent candy bars by multiplying the quantity standard (4 pounds per case of Darkly Decadent candy bars) by the price standard ($0.35 per pound of sugar). To simplify the illustration, we show how Unlimited Decadence computed the standard cost of one direct material—sugar. We show a summary figure, $2.94, for the total standard cost of all the other direct materials, although in reality, Unlimited Decadence would have computed the standard cost of each of the direct materials. Also notice that we set the standard factory overhead rates (price standards for factory overhead) separately for variable and fixed overhead ($0.64 per hour variable and $2.52 per hour fixed). We established the quantity standards for fixed and variable factory overhead by determining the number of direct labor hours (DLH) required per case of candy bars under planned operating conditions (0.5 direct labor hours per case). In Chapter 16, under the job order cost accounting system, we applied *total* factory overhead to the cost of a case of candy bars at a rate of $3.16 per direct labor hour.

Standard Costs and Variances for Direct Materials

2 *What is included in a company's direct materials price and quantity standards?*

You just learned that a company sets standard costs for each of the direct materials it uses to manufacture its products. But how does it determine the standard costs for direct materials and compute the variances between standard and actual direct materials costs? And how do the standard costs and variances affect its cost accounting system?

Direct Materials Price and Quantity Standards

Before a company uses standard costs for its direct materials, it first sets its direct materials price and quantity standards.

Direct Materials Price Standard

As we discussed earlier, a **direct materials price standard** shows the *cost* that a company should incur to acquire one unit of a direct material for production. The cost includes two factors: (1) the invoice price (less any expected discounts) to be paid to normal suppliers when the company purchases materials in expected quantities, and (2) any transportation costs the company expects to pay.

**Exhibit 17-1   Standard Manufacturing Cost:
Case of Darkly Decadent Candy Bars**

UNLIMITED DECADENCE
Darkly Decadent Candy Bars

Inputs	Standard Quantity and Price	Standard Cost per Output Unit
Direct materials (sugar)	4 pounds @ $0.35	$ 1.40
Other direct materials	(assumed)	2.94
Direct labor	0.5 DLH @ $12.00	6.00
Factory overhead		
Variable	0.5 DLH @ $0.64	0.32
Fixed	0.5 DLH @ $2.52	1.26
Total standard cost per case		$11.92

Direct Materials Quantity Standard

A **direct materials quantity standard** shows the *amount* of a direct material that a company should use to produce one unit of product. This amount includes three factors: (1) the amount of materials that should end up in each "good" unit[1] of product; (2) an allowance for materials normally lost through various manufacturing operations ("waste"); and (3) an allowance for normal amounts of spoiled production ("spoilage"—products that are not "up to snuff" and, therefore, unacceptable for sale). In this way the direct materials quantity standard shows the average (normal) amount of a material that the company should use per unit of product when it performs manufacturing operations under planned conditions.

 Why do you think both direct materials that are normally lost through various manufacturing operations and normal amounts of spoiled production are included in the direct materials quantity standard?

Setting Standards for Direct Materials

Exhibit 17-2 shows the computations of the direct materials price and quantity standards for the sugar used by Unlimited Decadence to produce Darkly Decadent candy bars, the product whose standard cost we showed in Exhibit 17-1.

Notice the conditions that are important in setting the price standard. Price standards are influenced by the type, size, and quality of the required direct materials, but they also are influenced by several other conditions. Planned purchase quantities affect the invoice price. The supplier's terms (n/30) also affect the purchase cost. Finally, both shipping by normal freight carriers and unloading and inspecting in the usual manner determine the transportation cost per pound of material. Together these conditions determine the standard price per pound to make the required sugar available for production.

Many conditions also influenced the determination of the direct materials quantity standard in Exhibit 17-2. For example, the size of the 50-pound bags of sugar (in relation

Exhibit 17-2 Direct Materials Price and Quantity Standards

UNLIMITED DECADENCE
Direct Materials Price and Quantity Standards for Sugar
Case of Darkly Decadent Candy Bars

Price standard (dollars per pound)[a]	
Invoice price	$0.24
Transportation charges	0.11
Standard price per pound	$0.35
Quantity standard (pounds per case)[b]	
Material content per completed unit	3.90 pounds
Allowance for waste in pouring, mixing, refining, molding	0.10 pounds
Standard quantity per case	4.00 pounds

[a]Materials are purchased in 50-pound bags in multiples of 20. At that quantity the normal supplier charges 0.24 per pound. If purchased in smaller quantities, the price would be 0.25 per pound. The normal supplier offers terms of n/30. Materials are to be shipped by rail from the supplier to St. Louis, where they are to be picked up by a local trucking company and brought to the plant, unloaded, inspected, and stacked in the storeroom at a total cost of $110 for each 20 bags (1,000 pounds) purchased.
[b]The manufacturing process involves pouring the 50-pound bags of sugar into bins, followed by mixing the sugar with other ingredients, refining the chocolate mix, and molding it into candy bars. During these processes, an average of 1.25 pounds of sugar is lost from each bag (when the sugar is poured into the bins and when chocolate paste is left in the mixing, refining, and molding equipment). Materials lost through pouring, mixing, refining, and molding are hauled away at no charge by a shelter for the homeless.

---

[1]In our later discussion, one unit always refers to one "good" unit.

to the size of the desired product) affects the pouring, mixing, refining, and molding operations and determines the resulting sugar content of the product and the allowance for waste. In determining that no allowance for normal spoilage is necessary for this product, Unlimited Decadence also considers the quality of the sugar as well as the proper adjustment of the equipment, the skill level of the laborers, and the condition of the storage areas for the direct materials and candy bars. Careful study of these conditions enables the engineering and production department personnel to determine the standard quantity of direct materials to be budgeted and used per unit of product.

Direct Materials Price and Quantity Variances

3 *When a company compares its actual direct materials costs to its direct materials standards, how does it determine what caused the difference between the two?*

A company that uses standard costs for its direct materials compares these standard costs with actual costs by computing a direct materials price variance and a direct materials quantity variance.

Direct Materials Price Variance

How would you determine the standard cost of one batch of brownies?

When a company purchases direct materials under conditions other than those planned, the cost per direct material unit may differ from the price standard. If this occurs, it causes a direct materials price variance. A **direct materials price variance** is the difference between the standard cost that a company *should have incurred* to acquire the direct materials and the actual cost it *did* incur to acquire the direct materials. The company computes this variance by multiplying the actual number of direct material units *purchased* by the difference between the standard price and the actual price per direct material unit. Companies normally compute direct materials price variances at the time they purchase materials. Unlimited Decadence makes the computation for its sugar[2] as we show next, assuming it purchased (on credit) 1,500,000 pounds of sugar for the production of Darkly Decadent candy bars at an actual cost of $540,000 ($0.36 per pound):

Direct Materials Price Variance:

Standard purchase cost	1,500,000 lbs. @ $ 0.35	= $ 525,000
− Actual purchase cost	1,500,000 lbs. @ $ 0.36	= (540,000)
Direct materials price variance	1,500,000 lbs. @ $(0.01)	= $ (15,000) unfavorable

In the computation of the direct materials price variance, the standard purchase cost (what the company *should* have paid) is found by multiplying the total actual quantity purchased by the direct materials price standard ($0.35 from Exhibit 17-2). As a result, Unlimited Decadence computes the $15,000 unfavorable direct materials price variance as the difference between the standard and the actual purchase costs ($525,000 − $540,000). Or it can compute the variance by multiplying the actual number of units purchased times the difference between the standard price and the actual price per unit [1,500,000 pounds × ($0.35 − $0.36)]. The direct materials price variance for sugar is *unfavorable* because the actual purchase price per unit is higher than the standard price. In other words, the company paid more than it should have paid for the sugar. If the actual purchase price per unit is less than the standard price, the direct materials price variance is *favorable*. We set up all the variance calculations in this chapter so that *a negative number means an unfavorable variance and a positive number means a favorable variance.*

 Do you think a company should always try to pay less than the standard price for its direct materials if it can? Why or why not?

---

[2]Unlimited Decadence also computes direct materials price and quantity variances for its other direct materials. We do not show those computations here.

Direct Materials Quantity Variance

When operating conditions that actually occur during production differ from those planned, the actual quantity of direct materials the company uses to produce a given number of products may differ from the standard direct materials quantity budgeted for that number of products. The **standard direct materials quantity budgeted** is the amount of direct materials that *should be used* for the company's actual production level. It is computed by multiplying the actual number of units produced by the direct materials quantity standard per unit. For example, if Unlimited Decadence produces 360,000 cases of Darkly Decadent candy bars, it should use 1,440,000 pounds (360,000 cases produced × 4 pounds per case from Exhibit 17-2) of direct materials (sugar).

The **direct materials quantity variance** is the difference between the standard cost of the quantity of direct materials that a company *should have used* for the actual number of units produced and the standard cost of the quantity of direct materials that it *did* use to produce those units. In other words, a direct materials quantity variance indicates that the company used more or less direct materials for the actual number of units produced than the standard direct materials quantity budgeted for that number of units. We illustrate this computation next, assuming Unlimited Decadence produced 360,000 cases of Darkly Decadent candy bars during the month and used 1,480,000 pounds of direct materials (sugar) in that production:

Direct Materials Quantity Variance:

Standard quantity budgeted at standard price	1,440,000ᵃ lbs. @ $0.35 =	$ 504,000
− Actual quantity used at standard price	1,480,000 lbs. @ $0.35 =	(518,000)
Direct materials quantity variance	(40,000) lbs. @ $0.35 =	$ (14,000) unfavorable

ᵃ360,000 cases of candy bars × 4 pounds per case = 1,440,000 pounds.

The key to computing the direct materials quantity variance is a correct computation of the standard direct materials quantity budgeted. Remember that the standard direct materials quantity budgeted is computed by multiplying the *actual* number of units produced by the direct materials quantity standard for one unit (360,000 cases of Darkly Decadent candy bars × 4 pounds per case = 1,440,000 pounds). Notice in the computation of the direct materials quantity variance that both the standard direct materials quantity budgeted and the actual direct materials used are multiplied by the $0.35 price standard for the direct materials (sugar). Thus, Unlimited Decadence can compute the direct materials quantity variance by finding the difference between the standard direct materials quantity *budgeted* for the actual number of cases produced and the actual direct materials *used,* and multiplying that difference by the direct materials price standard [e.g., (1,440,000 − 1,480,000) × $0.35]. Notice also that the $14,000 direct materials quantity variance for sugar is *unfavorable* because the actual quantity of direct materials used is more than the standard quantity budgeted for the production of 360,000 cases of Darkly Decadent candy bars. If the actual quantity of direct materials used is less than the standard quantity budgeted for a given output, the direct materials quantity variance is *favorable*.

 If a case of Darkly Decadent candy bars requires 4 pounds of sugar, what do you think would cause Unlimited Decadence to use more sugar in the production of these candy bars?

Recording Direct Materials Variances

To assign standard costs to inventories, a company must separate variances from actual costs and record the variances separately in variance accounts. A company records its direct materials price variances at the time it purchases direct materials. Unlimited Decadence records the credit purchase of 1,500,000 pounds of sugar for the production of

Darkly Decadent candy bars as follows (this entry relates to the direct materials price variance computation we showed earlier):

Assets	=	Liabilities	+	Stockholders' Equity

Raw Materials Inventory			Accounts Payable		Unfavorable Direct Materials Price Variance	
525,000				540,000	15,000	
(+)	(−)		(−)	(+)	(+)	(−)

Note that Unlimited Decadence recorded the $540,000 actual purchase cost of the 1,500,000 pounds of sugar (1,500,000 lbs. @ $0.36) as Accounts Payable. (It *does owe* its supplier the actual purchase price of the sugar!) However, it added the $525,000 standard cost of these direct materials (1,500,000 lbs. @ $0.35) to Raw Materials Inventory. Thus *it keeps the Raw Materials Inventory account at standard cost*. The $15,000 unfavorable direct materials price variance (1,500,000 lbs. @ $0.01) is recorded in the left side of a separate account entitled Unfavorable Direct Materials Price Variance. Note that all "variance" accounts are "temporary" stockholders' equity accounts. As we briefly discuss later, a company normally closes its variance accounts to its Cost of Goods Sold account (an expense account) at the end of the accounting period. Thus, the rules for recording unfavorable and favorable variances relate to the rules for recording expenses. An unfavorable variance (i.e., more cost than planned) increases cost of goods sold (expense), so *an increase in an **unfavorable** variance is recorded on the **left** side of the variance account*. A favorable variance (less cost than planned) decreases cost of goods sold, so it is like *contra-expense* (we discussed contra accounts in Chapter 13). So *an increase in a **favorable** variance is recorded on the **right** side of the variance account.*

 Why do you think variance accounts affect stockholders' equity? If a company did not use a standard costing system, do you think its total stockholders' equity would be the same as or different from what it would be if the company were using a standard costing system? Why?

A company records its direct materials quantity variances as it *uses* direct materials. Unlimited Decadence records the use of 1,480,000 pounds of sugar to produce 360,000 cases of Darkly Decadent candy bars as follows (this entry relates to the direct materials quantity variance computation we showed earlier):

Assets		=	Liabilities	+	Stockholders' Equity

Raw Materials Inventory		Goods-in-Process Inventory				Unfavorable Direct Materials Quantity Variance	
Bal 525,000	518,000	504,000				14,000	
(+)	(−)	(+)	(−)			(+)	(−)

Note that Unlimited Decadence reduced the Raw Materials Inventory account by the $518,000 standard cost of the *actual* sugar used (1,480,000 lbs. @ $0.35). This 1,480,000 pounds is the quantity of sugar that it actually moved out of the raw materials warehouse and into production. However, it added the $504,000 standard cost of the *standard direct materials quantity budgeted* (1,440,000 lbs. @ $0.35) to the Goods-in-Process Inventory account.[3] Thus *it also keeps the Goods-in-Process Inventory account at standard cost.* Note that the $14,000 unfavorable direct materials quantity variance is recorded in the left side of the Unfavorable Direct Materials Quantity Variance account. Later in this chapter, after we discuss direct labor and factory overhead variances, we will discuss how managers use the direct materials price and quantity variance.

A Diagram of Direct Materials Variance Computations

An illustration of the variance computations may be helpful in understanding the preceding computations and the amounts appearing in the entries we just described. With prices on the vertical dimension and quantities on the horizontal dimension, actual cost totals, standard cost totals, and variances appear as areas of the rectangles in Exhibit 17-3.

The area of the entire rectangle (actual quantity purchased × actual price) is the $540,000 total actual cost of direct materials purchased (1,500,000 lbs. @ $0.36). The long, thin horizontal rectangle (1) labeled as the direct materials price variance ($15,000 unfavorable) has an area equal to the actual quantity purchased times the difference between the standard price paid and the actual price [1,500,000 lbs. × ($0.35 − $0.36)]. When the $15,000 unfavorable direct materials price variance is subtracted from the $540,000 total actual purchase cost, the $525,000 remainder represents the standard cost of the actual quantity purchased (1,500,000 lbs. @ $0.35). Note in Exhibit 17-3 that the rectangle (2, 3, and 4) representing this $525,000 remainder is divided into three smaller rectangles. From left to right, the three rectangles represent (2) the $504,000 standard cost of the standard quantity of sugar Unlimited Decadence should have used in manufacturing 360,000 cases (1,440,000 lbs. @ $0.35), (3) the $14,000 unfavorable direct materials quan-

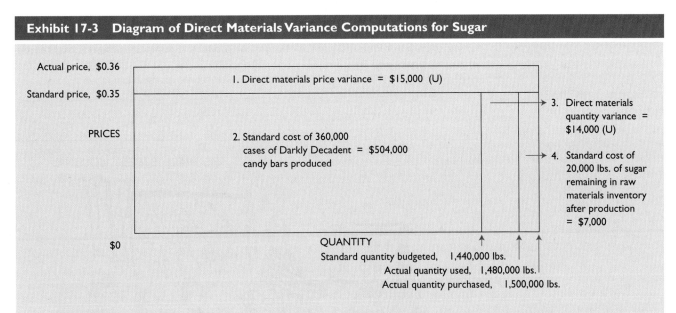

Exhibit 17-3   Diagram of Direct Materials Variance Computations for Sugar

1. The direct materials price variance is $0.01 for each pound of sugar purchased. For 1,500,000 pounds purchased, the total unfavorable direct materials price variance is $15,000.
2. The standard cost of sugar for producing cases of Darkly Decadent candy bars is $0.35 per pound. For 360,000 cases, the standard number of pounds budgeted is 1,440,000 for a standard cost of $504,000.
3. But Unlimited Decadence used 40,000 additional pounds of sugar. The standard cost of those extra pounds, at $0.35 per pound, is $14,000 — the unfavorable direct materials quantity variance.
4. The standard cost of 20,000 pounds of sugar remaining in raw materials inventory from the purchase, at $0.35 per pound, is $7,000.

---

[3]Unlimited Decadence also adds $1,058,400 of standard cost [360,000 cases × 3 $2.94 (from Exhibit 17-1)] for other direct materials to the Goods-in-Process Inventory account. We do not show that entry here.

tity variance [(1,440,000 − 1,480,000 lbs.) × $0.35], and (4) the $7,000 standard cost of the 20,000 pounds of unused direct materials (sugar) remaining from this purchase in the raw materials inventory for future use [(1,500,000 − 1,480,000 lbs.) × $0.35].

Standard Costs and Variances for Direct Labor

4 *What is included in a company's direct labor price and quantity standards?*

A company also determines standard costs and computes variances for the direct labor it uses to manufacture its products. This section shows how a company determines standard costs for direct labor, how it computes variances between standard and actual direct labor costs, and how it records the standard direct labor costs and variances in its cost accounting system.

Direct Labor Price and Quantity Standards

Before a company uses standard costs for its direct labor, it first sets its direct labor price and quantity standards.

Direct Labor Price Standard

A **direct labor price standard** shows the current wage rate that a company should incur per hour for a specific type of direct labor employed in production. Examples of different types of direct labor include machinists, welders, painters, assembly workers, and cooks. For Unlimited Decadence, direct labor includes employees who work as mixers, refiners, molders, and wrappers. Direct labor price standards also may be set to include an allowance for payroll taxes and fringe benefits. Although a company that does not use a standard cost system normally treats these additional payroll costs as factory overhead costs, it is common for a company that *does use* a standard cost system to include such items in its direct labor price standards. In setting the price standard for each manufacturing operation required to make one unit of product, a company assumes that the operation is performed by a properly trained operator earning the usual wage rate for that operation.

THE WALL STREET JOURNAL

"We've found the key to productivity. Its Fred, down in the shop. He makes the stuff."

From The Wall Street Journal. Reprinted by permission of Cartoon Features Syndicate.

Direct Labor Quantity Standard

A **direct labor quantity standard** shows the amount of direct labor time that a company should use to produce one unit of product. A company sets direct labor quantity standards in a two-step process. First, it carefully studies the time required to perform the direct labor operations needed to produce a product. Then, it allows for normal amounts of labor time used for personnel rest breaks, machine adjustments and idle time, and production of normal amounts of spoiled units. A direct labor quantity standard shows the direct labor time the company expects to use per unit when it performs manufacturing operations under planned conditions.

Setting Standards for Direct Labor

Exhibit 17-4 shows the computations of the price and quantity standards for the direct labor used in producing Darkly Decadent candy bars. For simplicity we assume that the same labor rate is earned by all workers in each direct labor operation.

In Exhibit 17-4 the direct labor price standard of $12 per hour includes the basic wage rate of $9.60 in both departments plus payroll tax and fringe benefit allowances that total $2.40. Unlimited Decadence set the quantity standard for direct labor by adding the standard hours per unit of product for the various required labor operations and the normal amounts of rest breaks and machine adjustments. Mixing (0.15 hours) and refining operations (0.25 hours) prepare the direct materials so that they are ready for the molding and wrapping operations (0.1 hours). After the molding and wrapping operations are completed, the cases of Darkly Decadent candy bars are finished. At that time each case should have had a total of 0.5 direct labor hours devoted to it.

Direct Labor Price and Efficiency Variances

A company that uses standard costs for its direct labor compares those standard costs with actual direct labor costs by computing a direct labor price variance and a direct labor efficiency variance.

Direct Labor Price Variance

The **direct labor price variance** is the difference between the cost that a company *should have incurred* for the actual labor hours worked [at the standard direct labor price (rate)

Exhibit 17-4 Direct Labor Price and Quantity Standards

UNLIMITED DECADENCE
*Direct Labor Price and Quantity Standards for
a Case of Darkly Decadent Candy Bars*

Price standard (dollars per direct labor hour)[a]

Basic wage rate	$ 9.60
Payroll taxes (Social Security and unemployment compensation)..	1.44
Fringe benefits (vacation pay, insurance, etc.)...	0.96
Standard price (rate) per direct labor hour..	$12.00

Quantity standard (direct labor hours per case)

Mixing operations..	0.15 hours
Refining operations	0.25
Molding and wrapping operations	0.10
Standard direct labor quantity per case..	0.50 hours

We assume in this exhibit that payroll taxes total 15% of the basic wage rate. We assume fringe benefits to be 10% of the basic wage rate. We use these rates for simplicity.

per hour] and the actual direct labor cost it *did* incur for the number of actual labor hours worked. It is also known as the direct labor *rate* variance. The direct labor price (rate) variance shows how much of the difference between the standard and actual direct labor costs can be explained by the difference between the standard and actual labor rates. A company computes the direct labor price variance by multiplying the actual direct labor hours worked by the difference between the direct labor price standard and the actual direct labor price per hour. We illustrate this computation next, assuming 182,000 direct labor hours were worked (to produce 360,000 cases of Darkly Decadent candy bars) at a total direct labor cost of $2,165,800 ($11.90 per hour):

Direct Labor Price Variance:

Actual hours at standard price	182,000 hours @ $12.00 =	$ 2,184,000
− Actual direct labor cost	182,000 hours @ $11.90 =	(2,165,800)
Direct labor price variance	182,000 hours @ $ 0.10 =	$ 18,200 favorable

Note that we computed the direct labor cost that Unlimited Decadence should have incurred for the actual hours worked by multiplying the actual hours times the direct labor price standard ($12.00 from Exhibit 17-4). As a result, we can compute the $18,200 favorable direct labor price variance as the difference between the standard direct labor cost and the actual direct labor cost ($2,184,000 − $2,165,800) or by multiplying the actual number of hours worked by the difference between the standard price and the actual price (rate) per hour [182,000 hours × ($12.00 − $11.90)]. This direct labor price variance is *favorable* because the actual direct labor rate per hour is less than the direct labor price standard. If the actual rate per hour exceeds the standard rate, the direct labor price variance is *unfavorable*.

 Can you think of a situation where a favorable direct labor price variance may actually be unfavorable for a company? Why would this be the case?

Direct Labor Efficiency Variance

When actual operating conditions during production differ from the planned conditions, the total actual direct labor hours that a company's employees work may differ from the standard direct labor hours budgeted for the number of products manufactured. Here, the **standard direct labor hours budgeted** is the number of direct labor hours that *should be used* for the company's actual production level. A company computes the standard direct labor hours budgeted by multiplying the actual number of units produced by the standard direct labor hours per unit (the direct labor quantity standard). For example, when Unlimited Decadence produces 360,000 cases of Darkly Decadent candy bars, it should use 180,000 direct labor hours (360,000 cases produced × 0.5 standard direct labor hours per case from Exhibit 17-4).

The **direct labor efficiency variance** is the difference between the standard cost of the direct labor hours that a company *should have used* for the actual number of units produced and the standard cost of the direct labor hours that it *did* use to produce those units.[4] In other words, a direct labor efficiency variance indicates that the *actual* direct labor hours that the company's employees worked on the actual number of units produced were more or less than the standard direct labor hours *budgeted* for that number of units. We illustrate the computation next, assuming Unlimited Decadence produced 360,000 cases of Darkly Decadent candy bars during the month and its employees worked 182,000 actual direct labor hours:

5 *When a company compares its actual direct labor costs to its direct labor standards, how does it determine what caused the difference between the two?*

---

[4]The direct labor efficiency variance is sometimes called the direct labor quantity variance because its computation is similar to the direct materials quantity variance. However, employees may react negatively to being thought of as a quantity rather than as efficient contributors to the company's activities. Hence, we refer to the variance as the direct labor efficiency variance.

Direct Labor Efficiency Variance:

Standard hours budgeted at standard price	180,000 hours[a] @ $12.00 =	$ 2,160,000
−Actual hours at standard price	182,000 hours @ $12.00 =	(2,184,000)
Direct labor efficiency variance	(2,000) hours @ $12.00 =	$ (24,000) unfavorable

[a]360,000 cases of candy bars × 0.5 hours per unit = 180,000 hours.

   The key to computing the direct labor efficiency variance is a correct computation of the standard direct labor hours budgeted. Remember that a company computes the standard direct labor hours budgeted by multiplying the *actual* number of units produced by the direct labor quantity standard for one unit (360,000 cases × 0.5 hours per case = 180,000 standard direct labor hours budgeted). This means that employees of Unlimited Decadence should have worked 180,000 direct labor hours when they produced 360,000 cases of Darkly Decadent candy bars. Notice in the efficiency variance computation that both the standard direct labor hours budgeted and the actual direct labor hours are multiplied by the $12.00 price standard. Thus the $24,000 unfavorable direct labor efficiency variance can be computed by finding the difference between the standard direct labor hours budgeted (for the actual number of cases produced) and the actual direct labor hours worked, and multiplying that difference by the direct labor price standard [e.g., (180,000 − 182,000) × $12]. Notice also that the $24,000 direct labor efficiency variance is *unfavorable* because the employees actually worked more hours than the standard direct labor hours budgeted for the production of 360,000 cases of Darkly Decadent candy bars. If the actual direct labor hours worked are less than the standard direct labor hours budgeted for a given output, the direct labor efficiency variance is *favorable*.

 Can you think of a situation where a favorable direct labor efficiency variance may actually be unfavorable for the company? Why would this be the case?

Recording Direct Labor Variances

A company records both the direct labor price variance and the direct labor efficiency variance at the time production takes place. In a standard cost system, a company adds the standard cost of direct labor to the Goods-in-Process Inventory account. Unlimited Decadence records the use of 182,000 direct labor hours for the production of 360,000 cases of Darkly Decadent candy bars as follows (this entry relates to the computations of both the direct labor price variance and the direct labor efficiency variance we showed earlier):

Assets		=	Liabilities		+	Stockholders' Equity			
						Favorable Direct Labor Price Variance		Unfavorable Direct Labor Efficiency Variance	
Goods-in-Process Inventory			Wages Payable						
504,000									
1,058,400[5]									
2,160,000				2,165,800			18,200	24,000	
(+)	(−)		(−)	(+)		(−)	(+)	(+)	(−)

   Note that Unlimited Decadence recorded the actual direct labor cost incurred (182,000 hours @ $11.90 = $2,165,800) as Wages Payable. However, it added the $2,160,000 standard cost for 360,000 cases of Darkly Decadent candy bars (180,000 standard direct labor hours budgeted @ $12 per hour) to the Goods-in-Process Inventory account to keep that account at standard cost. (Notice it includes the standard costs for direct materials we recorded earlier.)

[5]Standard costs for direct materials other than sugar (360,000 cases × $2.94; from Exhibit 17-1).

Also note that it recorded the $18,200 favorable direct labor price variance and the $24,000 unfavorable direct labor efficiency variance in separate variance accounts.

Standard Costs and Variances for Factory Overhead

6 *What does a company include in its factory overhead price and quantity standards, and what volume does it use to set its predetermined rates?*

Factory overhead includes all manufacturing costs other than direct materials and direct labor costs. As we discussed in Chapter 16, it includes the costs of items such as depreciation, insurance, and property taxes on factory plant and equipment, utilities, maintenance, indirect labor, indirect materials, supervision, and factory supplies. Because of the large number and variety of these costs, a company typically combines them and applies them to units of product as a single cost element, *factory overhead* (or simply *overhead*), through the use of predetermined overhead rates. As we discussed in Chapter 16, the company commonly determines these rates prior to production. It then *applies* factory overhead to Goods-in-Process Inventory in an amount equal to the predetermined rate multiplied by the number of direct labor hours (or machine hours or other measure of activity) worked in production.

Factory Overhead Price and Quantity Standards

Before a company uses standard costs for its factory overhead, it first sets its factory overhead price and quantity standards.

Factory Overhead Price Standards

The **price standards for factory overhead** are the standard predetermined overhead rates. A company often establishes separate rates for variable and fixed factory overhead. The variable factory overhead rate is the sum of all the variable overhead costs per unit of product. The company computes its fixed factory overhead rate by determining the budgeted amount of annual fixed factory overhead and dividing that amount by the estimated annual volume of manufacturing activity (measured in standard direct labor hours, machine hours, or other measure of activity).[6]

Factory Overhead Quantity Standard

The **quantity standard for factory overhead** is the volume of production activity (direct labor hours, machine hours, or other measure of activity) that *should be used* to produce one unit of product. If a company uses direct labor hours to apply factory overhead, the quantity standard for overhead is the same as the quantity standard for direct labor. If it uses machine hours or some other measure of activity for overhead application, it must determine a separate quantity standard showing the budgeted machine hours (or other activity) required to produce one unit of product. Although a company may use several measures of activity for budgeting and applying factory overhead, the most commonly used measure is standard direct labor hours. Unlimited Decadence uses standard direct labor hours for budgeting and applying factory overhead.

Setting Standards for Factory Overhead

Exhibit 17-5 shows the computation of standard factory overhead rates at three volumes (expressed in standard direct labor hours) using overhead costs from the flexible overhead budget in that exhibit.

Notice in Exhibit 17-5 that the fixed factory overhead budget is $504,000 per month (or $6,048,000 per year) at each of the three volumes shown. This is because Unlimited Decadence does not expect fixed overhead costs to be affected by changes in the volume (all of these volumes are within the relevant range of activity). As a result, however, *the fixed factory overhead rate per standard direct labor hour depends on the volume of stan-*

---

[6]In Chapter 18 we will discuss activity-based costing, which uses additional measures of activity to apply factory overhead.

Exhibit 17-5   Flexible Overhead Budget and Rate Computation

UNLIMITED DECADENCE
Flexible Factory Overhead Budget for Darkly Decadent Candy Bar

Volume *(cases per month)*	360,000	400,000	440,000
Volume *(standard direct labor hours)*	180,000	200,000[a]	220,000

Factory overhead costs:

Variable:			
Indirect labor ($0.12/case)	$ 43,200	$ 48,000	$ 52,800
Indirect materials ($0.08/case)	28,800	32,000	35,200
Utilities ($0.05/case)	18,000	20,000	22,000
Other variable overhead ($0.07/case)	25,200	28,000	30,800
Total variable overhead ($0.32/case)	$115,200	$128,000	$140,800
Fixed:			
Supervisory salaries	$114,000	$114,000	$114,000
Depreciation of plant and equipment	150,000	150,000	150,000
Other fixed overhead	240,000	240,000	240,000
Total fixed overhead	$504,000	$504,000	$504,000
Total factory overhead	$619,200	$632,000	$644,800

Standard Overhead Rate Computations at Each Volume

	180,000 Standard Direct Labor Hours	200,000 Standard Direct Labor Hours	220,000 Standard Direct Labor Hours
Variable	$\frac{\$115,200}{180,000\ \text{DLH}} = \$0.64/\text{DLH}$	$\frac{\$128,000}{200,000\ \text{DLH}} = \$0.64/\text{DLH}$	$\frac{\$140,800}{220,000\ \text{DLH}} = \$0.64/\text{DLH}$
Fixed	$\frac{\$504,000}{180,000\ \text{DLH}} = \$2.80/\text{DLH}$	$\frac{\$504,000}{200,000\ \text{DLH}} = \$2.52/\text{DLH}$	$\frac{\$504,000}{220,000\ \text{DLH}} = \$2.29/\text{DLH}$
Total	$\frac{\$619,200}{180,000\ \text{DLH}} = \$3.44/\text{DLH}$	$\frac{\$632,000}{200,000\ \text{DLH}} = \$3.16/\text{DLH}$	$\frac{\$644,800}{220,000\ \text{DLH}} = \$2.93/\text{DLH}$

[a]Recall that the quantity standard for direct labor is 0.5 hours per case. Thus the standard direct labor hours budgeted for a unit volume of 400,000 units is 200,000 hours (400,000 units × 0.5 hours per case).

dard direct labor hours used to compute the rate. Note that the fixed factory overhead rate is a different amount at each of the three volumes. Hence, the total factory overhead rate is different at each volume as well. Thus, if a company expects monthly production volumes to fluctuate and computes the monthly fixed overhead rate based on each month's volume, the fixed overhead (and total overhead) rates will also fluctuate.

It is usually not desirable to allow fixed factory overhead rates to change because of fluctuating production volume.

Why do you think it is not desirable to allow fixed factory overhead rates to change because of changes in production volume?

To avoid this problem, a company usually computes its standard fixed overhead rate using a volume that reflects the normal activity or practical capacity of its manufacturing operations. **Normal activity** is the average of the company's expected annual production volumes, usually computed for three to five years into the future. It is closely related to the average sales volume expected over that future period.

Why do you think expected annual production volumes and expected average sales volumes are closely related?

Practical capacity is the volume of activity at which the company's manufacturing facilities are capable of operating per year under *practical* conditions, allowing for usual levels of efficiency. It is closely related to the physical size of the manufacturing facilities, which typically does not change much from year to year. Computing the fixed factory overhead rate using the overhead budget at either normal activity or practical capacity provides stability to the fixed factory overhead rate (and therefore to the total overhead rate), which would not exist if a company used the expected monthly or annual production volume.

Variable factory overhead rates are not influenced by the volume chosen for the rate computation. The reason is that the total budgeted variable factory overhead cost varies directly in proportion to volume. Thus a company uses the standard variable overhead rate to budget variable overhead cost regardless of the volume at which it is computed. Observe in Exhibit 17-5 that the standard variable overhead rate for producing Darkly Decadent candy bars is $0.64 per standard direct labor hour at each of the three volumes.

Throughout our discussion of factory overhead variances we assume that normal activity for Unlimited Decadence is 4,800,000 cases of Darkly Decadent candy bars (2,400,000 standard direct labor hours) per year and that the company used that volume to set its standard predetermined fixed overhead rates. Unlimited Decadence's predetermined overhead rates are as follows:

Variable overhead rate = $0.64 per standard direct labor hour
Fixed overhead rate   = 2.52 per standard direct labor hour
                        ($6,048,000 ÷ 2,400,000 DLH)
Total overhead rate   = $3.16 per standard direct labor hour

Applying Factory Overhead Costs in a Standard Cost System

7 *When a company compares its actual factory overhead costs to its factory overhead standards, how does it determine what caused the difference between the two?*

Overhead application is slightly different when a company uses a standard cost system instead of an actual cost system (as we discussed in Chapter 16). When a company does not have a standard cost system but applies factory overhead using a predetermined overhead rate per direct labor hour, it computes the amount applied by multiplying the *actual direct labor hours worked* by the predetermined overhead rate. When a company uses a standard cost system, however, it computes the amount of factory overhead applied by multiplying the *standard direct labor hours budgeted* for the actual number of units produced by the standard predetermined overhead rate. (The number of standard direct labor hours budgeted for factory overhead costs is the *same* as the number of standard direct labor hours budgeted for direct labor costs.) For example, suppose that employees of a company with a predetermined overhead rate of $3 per direct labor hour actually work 105 hours to produce 50 units that should have taken 2 standard direct labor hours per unit to produce. If the company is *not* using a standard cost system, it will apply $315 (105 actual hours × $3 per hour) of factory overhead to those units. If it *is* using a standard cost system, however, it will apply only $300 [100 (50 units × 2 hours) standard direct labor hours *budgeted* × $3 per hour] to those units.

Factory Overhead Variances

Factory overhead variances arise when the actual amount of factory overhead cost incurred during a period differs from the amount of factory overhead cost applied.

Total Overhead Variance

The **total overhead variance** is the difference between total factory overhead cost *applied* and total factory overhead cost *incurred* in a standard cost system. The computation of the $56,600 unfavorable total overhead variance experienced by Unlimited Decadence during a month when Unlimited Decadence produced 360,000 cases of Darkly Decadent candy bars and incurred actual overhead costs of $625,400 is as follows:

Total Overhead Variance:

Total overhead cost applied	
(180,000 standard direct labor hours budgeted @ $3.16)	$568,800
−Total overhead cost incurred	(625,400)
Total overhead variance	$ (56,600) unfavorable

Note in this computation that Unlimited Decadence multiplies the *standard direct labor hours budgeted* to produce 360,000 cases of Darkly Decadent candy bars (360,000 cases × 0.5 standard direct labor hours per case = 180,000 hours) by the total predetermined overhead rate ($3.16 per hour) to compute the $568,800 total overhead cost applied. It subtracts the $625,400 total overhead cost incurred to compute the $56,600 unfavorable total overhead variance. When the total overhead cost incurred is more than the total overhead cost applied, as in the preceding computation, the total overhead variance is *unfavorable*. When the amount incurred is less than the amount applied, the total overhead variance is *favorable*.

To improve managers' understanding of the reasons why the total overhead variance occurred, companies usually divide the total overhead variance into at least two separate overhead variances. Next, we will discuss two of these overhead variances that together make up the total overhead variance: the overhead budget variance and the fixed overhead volume variance.

Overhead Budget Variance

The **overhead budget variance** is the difference between the total overhead *budgeted* and the total overhead *incurred*. The total overhead budgeted is the amount of factory overhead cost that a company *should* incur to produce a given number of units under planned operating conditions. A company computes the total overhead budgeted by multiplying the standard direct labor hours budgeted for the actual number of units produced by the variable overhead rate, and then adding the result to the budgeted fixed overhead. When the company incurs an actual total factory overhead cost that exceeds the total overhead budgeted, the overhead budget variance is *unfavorable*. Incurring less cost than budgeted results in a *favorable* budget variance.

 Does this make sense? What is the difference between the overhead budget variance and the total overhead variance?

Next, we show the computation of the $6,200 unfavorable overhead budget variance for the month when Unlimited Decadence produced 360,000 cases of Darkly Decadent candy bars. Unlimited Decadence computes the total overhead budgeted by first multiplying the 180,000 standard direct labor hours budgeted by the $0.64 variable overhead rate to determine the $115,200 budgeted variable overhead cost. It adds this amount to the $504,000 budgeted fixed overhead cost to determine the $619,200 total overhead budgeted. It subtracts the $625,400 total overhead cost incurred (that we used in the total overhead variance computation) to determine the $6,200 unfavorable overhead budget variance.

Overhead Budget Variance:

Total overhead budgeted (based on 180,000		
standard direct labor hours budgeted):		
Variable (180,000 hours @ $0.64)	$115,200	
Fixed	504,000	$619,200
−Total overhead cost incurred		(625,400)
Overhead budget variance		$ (6,200) unfavorable

The overhead budget variance arises when the actual costs of the individual overhead items differ from those budgeted. To provide useful control information, a company normally reports the overhead budget variance *item by item* so that its managers can judge which items need attention. We show such a breakdown of the overhead budget variance in Exhibit 17-6. For this illustration, we assumed the actual amounts incurred, whereas we took the budgeted amounts from Exhibit 17-5.

In Exhibit 17-6 five of the seven overhead items in the overhead budget variance report show unfavorable variances. Indirect labor and indirect materials, in particular, show very large unfavorable variances relative to their budgeted amounts. Together they make up over 80% [($2,600 + $2,400) ÷ $6,200] of the total unfavorable overhead budget variance. By directing the attention of Unlimited Decadence's managers to these two items, the overhead budget variance report enables them to use the management-by-exception principle.

 How do you think knowing the indirect labor and indirect materials variances would enable managers to use the management-by-exception principle?

Fixed Overhead Volume Variance

The **fixed overhead volume variance** is the difference between the amount of *applied* fixed overhead and the amount of *budgeted* fixed overhead. A company computes this variance by subtracting the total budgeted fixed overhead cost from the amount of applied fixed overhead cost (standard direct labor hours budgeted for the actual number of units produced multiplied by the standard fixed overhead rate per hour). It is *unfavorable* when the budgeted fixed overhead is more than the applied fixed overhead and *favorable* when the budgeted fixed overhead is less than the applied fixed overhead.

 Does this make sense to you? Why do you think the fixed overhead volume variance is unfavorable when the budgeted fixed overhead is more than the applied fixed overhead?

The fixed overhead volume variance arises solely because of the difference between the way fixed overhead is applied and the way it is budgeted. A company *applies* fixed overhead by multiplying the predetermined fixed overhead rate by the standard direct labor hours budgeted for the actual number of units produced. (So when the volume of production changes, the total amount of fixed overhead applied changes.) However, a company *budgets* total fixed overhead at the total amount it expects to incur regardless of its production volume.

Unlimited Decadence expected to incur total fixed overhead costs of $504,000 per month (see Exhibit 17-5), or $6,048,000 per year. Recall that the company used a normal activity of 200,000 standard direct labor hours per month (2,400,000 per year) to compute its standard fixed overhead rate of $2.52 per standard direct labor hour. It applied fixed

Exhibit 17-6 Overhead Budget Variance Report

UNLIMITED DECADENCE
Overhead Budget Variance Report

	Budgeted Overhead at 180,000 Standard Direct Labor Hours Budgeted	Actual Overhead Costs Incurred	Overhead Budget Variance
Indirect labor	$ 43,200	$ 45,800	$ (2,600) unfavorable
Indirect materials	28,800	31,200	(2,400) unfavorable
Utilities	18,000	18,400	(400) unfavorable
Other variable overhead	25,200	25,050	150 favorable
Supervisory salaries	114,000	114,500	(500) unfavorable
Depreciation of plant and equipment	150,000	150,000	0
Other fixed overhead	240,000	240,450	(450) unfavorable
Total	$619,200	$625,400	$ (6,200) unfavorable

overhead at this rate. During the month when Unlimited Decadence produced 360,000 cases, the number of standard direct labor hours budgeted for that output was 180,000 direct labor hours (360,000 × 0.5). At this volume, Unlimited Decadence *applied* $453,600 (180,000 standard direct labor hours budgeted × $2.52 per standard direct labor hour) of fixed overhead to that output. The amount of fixed overhead *budgeted*, however, was $504,000. The fixed overhead volume variance is computed as follows:

Fixed Overhead Volume Variance:

Fixed overhead applied (180,000 standard direct labor hours budgeted at $2.52 per hour)	$453,600
−Fixed overhead budgeted	(504,000)
Fixed overhead volume variance	$(50,400) unfavorable

Exhibit 17-7 shows both the amount of fixed overhead that Unlimited Decadence would apply at various levels of standard direct labor hours and the amount of fixed overhead budgeted. It also shows the $50,400 unfavorable fixed overhead volume variance we computed earlier.

Notice in Exhibit 17-7 that for all volumes *below* the normal activity of 200,000 standard direct labor hours, the amount of fixed overhead applied is less than the amount budgeted. This results in an *unfavorable* fixed overhead volume variance. Remember that fixed costs do not change as a result of changes in volume. A company underapplies fixed overhead when the actual volume of production output is less than normal activity and requires fewer standard direct labor hours than does normal activity. The company has achieved

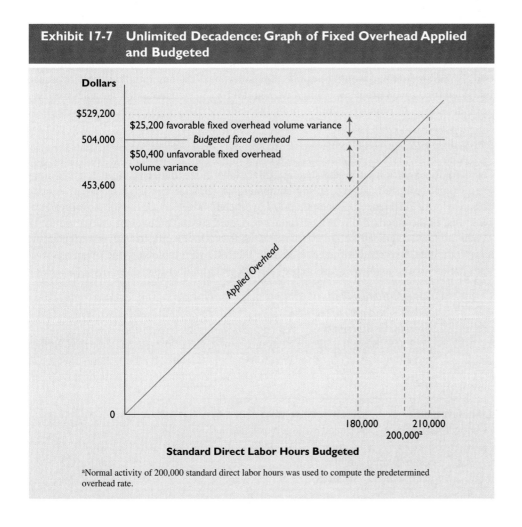

Exhibit 17-7   Unlimited Decadence: Graph of Fixed Overhead Applied and Budgeted

[a]Normal activity of 200,000 standard direct labor hours was used to compute the predetermined overhead rate.

less than a normal product output with the same fixed costs, and the fixed overhead applied is less than that budgeted—an *unfavorable* condition. For all volumes *above* normal activity, the company has achieved more than a normal product output with the same fixed costs. The amount of fixed overhead applied is more than the amount budgeted, and this results in a *favorable* fixed overhead volume variance. A company overapplies fixed overhead when the actual volume of production is greater than normal activity and requires more standard direct labor hours than does normal activity. In this case, the amount of fixed overhead applied is more than that budgeted—a *favorable* condition. For example, if Unlimited Decadence had produced 420,000 cases, 210,000 standard direct labor hours (420,000 cases × 0.5 hours per case) would have been budgeted for that volume of production. Applied fixed overhead would be $529,200 (210,000 standard direct labor hours budgeted × $2.52 per hour). But the fixed overhead cost should not have changed because Unlimited Decadence produced more cases than it expected to produce. The fixed overhead cost (the amount budgeted) would still be $504,000. In this case the fixed overhead volume variance would be $25,200 favorable ($529,200 applied − $504,000 budgeted). We also show this variance in Exhibit 17-7.

The only time that a company will *not* have a fixed overhead volume variance (that is, its volume variance will be zero) is when the number of standard direct labor hours used to apply fixed overhead to actual product output (the standard direct labor hours budgeted) is exactly equal to the production volume (the normal activity) the company used to compute its fixed overhead rate. Note in Exhibit 17-7 that when the standard direct labor hours budgeted are 200,000, the normal activity level that Unlimited Decadence used to compute its predetermined overhead rates, the amount of fixed overhead applied equals the amount budgeted ($504,000) and the fixed overhead volume variance is zero.

It is important to understand that *there can never be a "variable" overhead volume variance*. The reason is that variable overhead is applied in the same way it is budgeted: at a constant rate per standard direct labor hour. For a month when Unlimited Decadence produces 360,000 cases of Darkly Decadent candy bars (for which 180,000 standard direct labor hours are budgeted), its variable overhead budget is $115,200 (see Exhibit 17-5). This is the same amount that would be applied in that month. The amount of variable overhead budgeted for a given production volume (in units) equals the amount of variable overhead applied to the units produced. For Unlimited Decadence, the variable overhead rate is $0.64 per standard direct labor hour. The amount of variable overhead budgeted and applied is $115,200 (180,000 standard direct labor hours budgeted × $0.64 per hour).

A company applies variable overhead by multiplying the variable overhead rate per standard direct labor hour by the standard direct labor hours budgeted for the actual number of units produced. Therefore, the company can compute the fixed overhead volume variance as the difference between the *total* overhead budgeted and the total overhead applied (using the standard direct labor hours budgeted for the number of units produced). When the fixed overhead volume variance is added to the overhead budget variance, the sum is the total overhead variance. Notice in the following table how the overhead variances relate to one another as differences between the total overhead *incurred, budgeted,* and *applied.*

	Actual Overhead Incurred	*Overhead Budgeted at 180,000 Standard Direct Labor Hours Budgeted*	*Overhead Applied at 180,000 Standard Direct Labor Hours Budgeted*
Variable overhead	$120,450	$115,200 (180,000 hours @ $0.64)	$115,200 (180,000 hours @ $0.64)
Fixed overhead	504,950	504,000	453,600 (180,000 hours @ $2.52)
Total overhead	$625,400	$619,200	$568,800 (180,000 hours @ $3.16)

$6,200 unfavorable overhead budget variance

$50,400 unfavorable fixed overhead volume variance

$56,600 unfavorable total overhead variance

The fixed overhead volume variance shows that the volume of units produced in a period was more or less than the volume used to set the predetermined standard overhead rate. This difference in production volume could have resulted from a sales volume that was higher or lower than expected (so the company would have had to adjust its volume of production). An unfavorable fixed overhead volume variance could be a symptom of an inefficiency or problem in the manufacturing process.

To complete our discussion of overhead variance computations, in Exhibit 17-8 we show graphically how the fixed factory overhead volume variance and the overhead budget variance together make up the total overhead variance. In this exhibit we show both the total overhead budgeted and the total overhead applied at various levels of standard direct labor hours budgeted. We also show the actual overhead incurred. We show the overhead budget variance, the fixed overhead volume variance, and the total overhead variance for the month when Unlimited Decadence produced 360,000 cases of Darkly Decadent candy bars (when 180,000 standard direct labor hours were budgeted).

Note in Exhibit 17-8 how we add the $6,200 unfavorable overhead budget variance and the $50,400 unfavorable fixed overhead volume variance to show the $56,600 unfavorable total overhead variance. Note also that the $50,400 unfavorable fixed overhead volume variance appears as the difference between the total overhead *budgeted* and the total overhead *applied* using the 180,000 standard direct labor hours budgeted. The $56,600 unfavorable total overhead variance appears as the difference between the actual overhead incurred and the total overhead applied at 180,000 standard direct labor hours.

Exhibit 17-8   Unlimited Decadence: Graph of Factory Overhead Variance

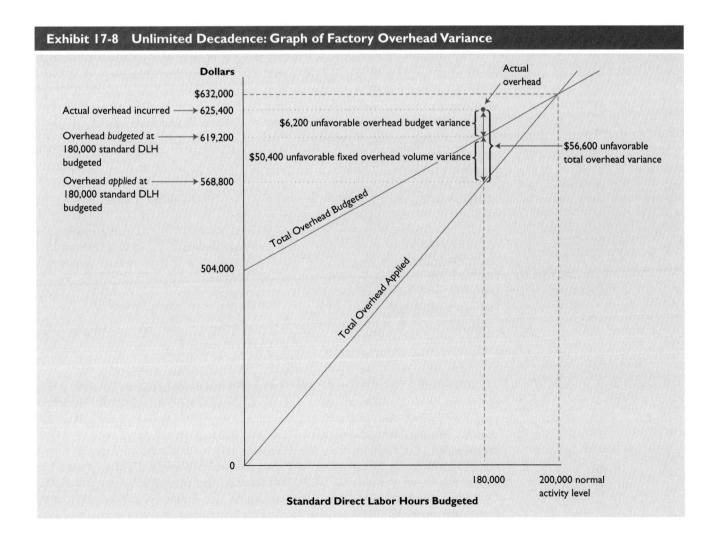

Recording Factory Overhead Variances

As we discussed in Chapter 16, a company records the factory overhead costs it actually *incurred* as increases in the Factory Overhead account. The company records the factory overhead costs it *applied* (at standard) as decreases in the Factory Overhead account (and increases in the Goods-in-Process Inventory account). To understand the application of standard factory overhead costs, recall that Unlimited Decadence applied $568,800 of standard factory overhead (from Exhibit 17-8). It records the application as follows:

Assets		= Liabilities	+ Stockholders' Equity

Factory Overhead		Goods-in-Process Inventory	
625,400		504,000	
		1,058,400	
		2,160,000	
	568,800	568,800	
(+)	(−)	(+)	(−)

Note that the $568,800 standard amount of factory overhead applied to the Goods-in-Process Inventory account (180,000 standard direct labor hours budgeted × $3.16 total overhead rate) is removed from the Factory Overhead account. Thus, a company records *standard* factory overhead costs in the Goods-in-Process Inventory account just like it records the standard costs for direct materials and direct labor (which we show in the Goods-in-Process account above for the amounts we recorded earlier).

The balance in the Factory Overhead account at the end of a period equals the total overhead variance for the period. Companies usually remove this balance from the account at the end of each month so that the overhead budget variance and the fixed overhead volume variance (which together make up the total overhead variance) are recorded in separate overhead variance accounts. The balance of Unlimited Decadence's factory overhead account is $56,600 after it records $625,400 of actual factory overhead costs incurred (from Exhibit 17–6) and after it applies $568,800 of standard overhead costs. Unlimited Decadence transfers this balance to the separate overhead variance accounts as follows:

Assets		= Liabilities	+	Stockholders' Equity			

Factory Overhead				Unfavorable Overhead Budget Variance		Unfavorable Fixed Overhead Volume Variance	
625,400	568,800						
	56,600			6,200		50,400	
Bal 0							
(+)	(−)			(+)	(−)	(+)	(−)

By recording direct materials, direct labor, and factory overhead as we illustrated in this chapter, Unlimited Decadence records the $4,291,200 standard manufacturing cost of producing 360,000 cases of Darkly Decadent candy bars in its Goods-in-Process Inventory account. This standard cost consists of $1,562,400 standard direct materials cost ($504,000 for sugar and $1,058,400 for other direct materials), $2,160,000 standard direct labor cost, and $568,800 standard factory overhead cost. Although we do not illustrate it here, Unlimited Decadence transfers the $4,291,200 standard cost of completed cases of Darkly Decadent candy bars ($11.92 per case from Exhibit 17-1 for the 360,000 cases) from the Goods-in-Process Inventory account to the Finished Goods Inventory account when it completes the units. As it sells the candy bars, it removes this standard cost from the

Finished Goods Inventory account and adds it to the Cost of Goods Sold account. So, in addition to the three inventory accounts, the Cost of Goods Sold account is also recorded at standard cost.

At the end of an accounting period for which a company prepares financial statements, its variance accounts for direct materials, direct labor, and factory overhead will have balances. If the company's standards reflect current planned conditions, these balances will be small. Companies normally transfer these variance account balances at the end of the period to the Cost of Goods Sold account. Transferring these variance balances to Cost of Goods Sold causes the expense to reflect actual costs rather than standard costs, so that the company reports its actual net income on its income statement. If the total (net) amount of these variances is not small, a more complicated procedure is required. This procedure is beyond the scope of this book.

Using Manufacturing Cost Variances to Control Operations

The standard costs are the costs that a company expects to incur when its manufacturing operations are running as smoothly as its managers have planned. When problems occur in these operations, however, variances arise. If a machine is out of adjustment, it can cause more direct materials usage and result in an unfavorable direct materials quantity variance. The purchase of a less-expensive grade of material than needed for the production of a product causes a favorable direct materials price variance, but it also could cause more direct materials usage and result in an unfavorable direct materials quantity variance. Similarly, assigning a new unskilled employee with a lower wage rate to a job requiring a more-skilled, higher-paid worker causes a favorable direct labor price variance, but it also could lead to unfavorable direct materials quantity and direct labor efficiency variances. *Standard cost variances result from problems that change the actual manufacturing conditions from the planned conditions.* Variances can be thought of as the "symptoms" of those problems.

By looking at these "symptoms," managers attempt to use cost variance information to determine what problems are affecting the efficient performance of their company's manufacturing activities in somewhat the same way a doctor uses symptoms to diagnose a medical ailment. The doctor knows that the symptoms observed in a patient may be the result of a temporary physical condition that will go away without medical help. But the doctor also knows that if the symptoms are not the result of a temporary condition, the specific medical problem must be identified before he or she can prescribe effective treatment. Finally, the doctor knows that the symptoms may indicate an illness that cannot be cured.

Similarly, variances from standard costs can result from temporary operating problems that will run their course and come to an end without managers' attention. For example, a small batch of low-quality direct materials that goes into a manufacturing process may cause more waste or extra processing time, but these problems will disappear when the faulty material is used up.

 What circumstances might cause managers to decide to scrap the low-quality direct materials and not try to use them up in production?

Variances can also be caused by uncontrollable changes in operating conditions, such as labor rate changes resulting from a new union contract or changes in direct materials prices. However, variances may result from operating problems that, if identified, can be corrected so that future operations will be more efficient.

To make variance computations more helpful to managers in identifying specific problems, management accountants follow three general rules:

1. They try to measure variances as quickly as they can after the variances occur.

2. They try to measure variances in as much detail as is helpful in pinpointing specific problems.

8 *How does a company use its manufacturing cost variances to control its operations?*

3. They try to report variances to managers who are in a position to identify and correct the problems that are likely to have caused the variances.

Measuring Variances Quickly

Variances should be measured as quickly as possible after they occur so that managers can recognize problems early and correct them before they cause too much damage. Although the variance computations we showed for Unlimited Decadence were based on a period of a month, many companies compute variances weekly or even daily to help identify problems more quickly. Two practices followed by many companies in computing direct materials variances provide an excellent example of how management accountants attempt to follow this general rule.

Direct materials price variances can be computed either as materials are purchased or as they are used. Most companies compute direct materials price variances at the time of purchase (as we did in our computation) because these variances are caused by problems arising at the time of purchase. To wait until materials are used (perhaps months after purchase) would delay recognition and correction of those problems.

Direct materials quantity variances also can be computed quickly after they occur. Many companies allow the storekeeper to issue only the standard amount of direct materials required for a given amount of products when the materials requisition is presented. If this amount of materials is not enough to complete production, an additional materials requisition must be presented before more direct materials are issued. This practice ensures that there is a document indicating that an unfavorable direct materials quantity variance is occurring. The supervisors of production operations can then be alerted.

Measuring Variances in Detail

The reason for measuring variances in detail is that these detailed variance computations provide better clues to help managers identify specific problems. We have already discussed some examples of the kinds of detailed computations that are helpful. Rather than computing a single total manufacturing cost variance, for example, we discussed computations of separate variances for each input to the manufacturing process (direct materials, direct labor, and factory overhead). In addition, we described price and quantity variance computations for direct materials and direct labor and showed the overhead budget variance reported on an item-by-item basis.

Recall our illustration of the direct labor efficiency variance. The production of Darkly Decadent candy bars required direct labor hours to be worked in mixing, refining, and molding and wrapping operations (see Exhibit 17-4). Using the direct labor quantity standard (0.5 DLH per case) computed in Exhibit 17-4, we determined that 180,000 standard direct labor hours were budgeted to produce 360,000 cases (360,000 × 0.5). We subtracted the 182,000 actual direct labor hours worked from these standard direct labor hours budgeted and multiplied the excess hours (2,000) by the $12 direct labor price standard to compute the overall $24,000 unfavorable direct labor efficiency variance. However, it is more helpful for identifying the problem(s) causing that variance if a company measures the excess labor hours worked in each individual operation or each production department. Then the company can compute the direct labor efficiency variances for the individual operations or departments and correct any problems causing these variances.

For example, recall that the production process includes mixing, refining, and molding and wrapping. Suppose that of the total 182,000 actual direct labor hours, 55,250 actual direct labor hours were worked in mixing, 89,650 actual direct labor hours were worked in refining, and 37,100 actual direct labor hours were worked in molding and wrapping. Exhibit 17-4 shows that the direct labor quantity standard is 0.15 hours in mixing, 0.25 hours in refining, and 0.10 hours in molding and wrapping. Thus the standard direct labor hours budgeted for 360,000 cases is 54,000 hours (360,000 × 0.15) in mixing, 90,000 hours (360,000 × 0.25) in refining, and 36,000 hours (360,000 × 0.10) in molding and wrapping operations. Unlimited Decadence can compute the direct labor efficiency variance for each operation, as we show here:

Direct Labor Efficiency Variances:

Mixing [(54,000 − 55,250) × $12]	$(15,000) unfavorable
Refining [(90,000 − 89,650) × $12]	4,200 favorable
Molding and wrapping [(36,000 − 37,100) × $12]	(13,200) unfavorable
Total unfavorable variance	$(24,000)

Note in this computation that the direct labor efficiency variances for mixing ($15,000) and for molding and wrapping ($13,200) are unfavorable because the actual direct labor hours are more than the standard direct labor hours budgeted. In refining, however, the $4,200 direct labor efficiency variance is favorable. The value of this more detailed direct labor efficiency variance computation is that it helps focus managers' attention on individual operations or departments. In this way, operations that are inefficient can be found. Operations that are especially efficient also can be recognized. Investigations of the causes of both unfavorable and favorable variances can often help improve the efficiency of future operations.

Reporting Variances

To be useful, manufacturing cost variance information must be communicated to managers who can correct problems in the manufacturing operations by the actions they take or the decisions they make. By measuring variances in enough detail to separate variances incurred in different operations or departments, or during different work shifts in the same department, a company can provide various managers with reports showing the variances that result from the operations for which they are responsible. These reports can help the managers identify and correct their departments' operating problems.

Reporting favorable variances to managers is just as important as reporting unfavorable variances. Favorable variances normally indicate that performance of manufacturing activities was better than planned and may indicate opportunities for continued good performance. The company can reward employees who have done a particularly good job and can share with other employees new or innovative production methods that may have caused the favorable variances. *Favorable* variances, however, are not always good. They sometimes can result from potentially serious problems. For example, the $4,200 favorable direct labor efficiency variance computed for the refining operations could be an indication of employees' hasty and sloppy processing, which might lead to customer dissatisfaction and lost sales. Thus, both unfavorable and favorable variances may be indications of potential trouble. So, it is important that managers understand what caused the unfavorable and favorable variances.

Of course, not all manufacturing cost variances deserve managers' attention. Some variances result from minor problems that are not long-lasting and not serious enough for managers to incur the cost of investigating the problems. Other variances may quickly be recognized as resulting from permanent and uncontrollable changes in operating conditions, suggesting the need for revision of the price or quantity standards. For example, a direct labor price variance may be caused by increased wage rates resulting from a new union contract. A company should note this change in conditions and revise the direct labor price standard.

By considering the absolute or relative size of variances, managers direct their attention to the operations that are most likely to benefit from attention. That is, the detailed variance analysis can enable managers to use the principle of *management by exception.* Variance computations are especially helpful when they are computed quickly after they occur and are reported to the managers who can take corrective action.

The Flexibility of Variances

Although variance analysis is a technique developed and used by manufacturing companies, it is flexible enough to be used by other types of organizations. Take Old Rosebud,

What are some of the variable costs per day to board this horse?

for example.[7] Old Rosebud is a 400-acre farm in the Kentucky Bluegrass that specializes in boarding thoroughbred horses. In evaluating its operations, Old Rosebud uses four variances: a sales volume variance [(budgeted boarding days − actual boarding days) × the budgeted daily contribution margin per mare]; a sales price variance [(budgeted boarding rate − actual boarding rate) × actual boarding days]; a variable cost variance [(budgeted variable costs per mare per day − actual variable costs per mare per day) × actual boarding days]; and a fixed cost variance (budgeted fixed costs − actual fixed costs). To get the most meaningful information from its variance analysis, Old Rosebud computes a variable cost variance for each variable cost individually.

During one year, variance analysis helped Old Rosebud's managers discover that sales volume had decreased significantly because of an economic downturn that caused a decline in breeding activities, which in turn decreased the demand for thoroughbred horse boarding (which showed up in the unfavorable sales volume variance). But surprisingly, the biggest problem for the company concerned *price*. The unfavorable sales price variance was almost twice as large as the sales volume variance! In an effort to attract boarders from its competitors, Old Rosebud had lowered boarding prices. What Old Rosebud discovered through its analysis was that at the volume of boarding days that it had achieved in that year, *if it had not lowered its boarding rates* it would have earned six times more income than it actually achieved!

 How are Old Rosebud's variances similar to and different from those that we discussed earlier in the chapter?

Business Issues and Values

Earlier we mentioned that variances help managers locate problems as soon as possible so that they can begin to correct them. Many companies use variances to locate the manager who has responsibility in the area in which the problem is occurring. But though this is

---

[7]Hans Sprohge and John Talbott, "Applications in Accounting: New Applications for Variance Analysis," *Journal of Accountancy*, April 1989, 137–141.

useful for assigning responsibility for *fixing* a problem, companies must use special care in assigning responsibility for the *cause* of the problem. For example, suppose a company has an unfavorable direct materials quantity variance. There are several possible causes of this type of unfavorable variance:

1. Maybe a machine was out of alignment, causing it to produce bad parts. If so, the production department probably had to produce that part again with different direct materials (using at least twice the standard amount of materials). Perhaps this is the production manager's responsibility. Maybe the machine should have been aligned more often. Or maybe it was one unique incident that a proper alignment schedule could not have prevented.

2. Maybe new, inexperienced employees were being trained during the time period in which the variances occurred. The learning mistakes of these "trainees" may have caused the variance. In this case, perhaps the variance was uncontrollable, but the variance would still point to the production manager.

3. Maybe a messy factory floor was interfering with clean operations and causing the factory workers to make mistakes. Again, the production manager has responsibility for the factory floor.

So, at first glance, it looks as though the production manager has responsibility for fixing the problem and *may have* responsibility for causing the problem. But what if the cause of the problem is that the purchasing department decided to purchase direct materials from a new supplier, and these materials were of a lower quality than those purchased from the original supplier? It is possible that the new direct materials didn't hold up as well in the production process, causing more materials to have been used in order to get "good" products. If so, then the responsibility for causing and fixing the problem belongs to the purchasing manager. Incorrectly identifying the responsibility for a problem can delay the correction of the problem. Furthermore, holding managers responsible for correcting problems over which they have no control may lead to severe morale problems.

Variances point to problems and to *possible* causes of problems. To solve the problems, managers must know the causes, and to do that, they must use their creative thinking skills to identify alternate possible causes. This process will help ensure that the problem is addressed quickly and directly.

Summary of Variance Computations

Exhibit 17-9 shows, in equation form, the computations of the variances we have discussed. Note the similarity between the direct materials variance computations and the direct labor variance computations.

Exhibit 17-9   Summary of Variance Computations

Direct materials price variance $=$ Actual direct materials units purchased $\times$ (Standard price per unit of direct materials $-$ Actual price per unit of direct materials)

Direct materials quantity variance $=$ (Standard direct materials quantity budgeted for actual units produced $-$ Actual direct materials used) $\times$ Direct materials price standard

Direct labor price variance $=$ Actual direct labor hours worked $\times$ (Standard direct labor price per hour $-$ Actual direct labor price per hour)

continued

Exhibit 17-9 Summary of Variance Computations *continued*

Direct labor efficiency variance = (Standard direct labor hours budgeted for actual units produced − Actual direct labor hours worked) × Direct labor price standard

Total overhead variance = (Standard direct labor hours budgeted for actual units produced × Standard total overhead rate per direct labor hour) − Actual total overhead cost incurred

Overhead budget variance = [Total budgeted fixed overhead + (Standard direct labor hours budgeted for actual units produced × Standard variable overhead rate per direct labor hour)] − Actual total overhead cost incurred

Fixed overhead volume variance = (Standard direct labor hours budgeted for actual units produced × Standard fixed overhead rate per direct labor hour) − Total budgeted fixed overhead

Summary

At the beginning of the chapter we asked you several questions. During the chapter, we asked you to STOP and answer some other questions to build your knowledge about specific issues. Be sure you answered these additional questions. Below are the questions from the beginning of the chapter, with a brief summary of the key points relating to the answers. Use your creative and critical thinking skills to expand on these key points to develop more complete answers to the questions and to determine what other questions you have that might lead you to learn more about the issues.

1 What is a price standard and a quantity standard, and how does a company compute a standard cost?

A price standard is the *cost* that a company should incur to acquire one unit of *input* for a manufacturing process. A quantity standard is the *number of units* of an input that a company should use to produce one unit of product in a manufacturing process. A company determines the standard cost of an input for one unit of product output by multiplying the quantity standard of the input by its price standard.

2 What is included in a company's direct materials price and quantity standards?

A direct materials price standard includes two factors: (1) the invoice price (less any expected discounts) to be paid to normal suppliers when the company purchases materials in expected quantities; and (2) any transportation costs the company expects to pay. A direct materials quantity standard includes three factors: (1) the actual amount of materials that should end up in each "good" unit of product; (2) allowances for materials normally lost through various manufacturing operations; and (3) allowances for normal amounts of spoiled production (products that are not "up to snuff" and, therefore, are unacceptable for sale). The direct materials quantity standards show the average (normal) quantity of materials that the company should use per unit of product when it performs manufacturing operations under the planned conditions.

3 When a company compares its actual direct materials costs to its direct materials standards, how does it determine what caused the difference between the two?

A company uses direct materials variances to help it determine the causes of differences between actual and standard direct materials costs. A direct materials price variance is the difference between the cost that the company should have incurred (at the standard price) to acquire the direct materials and the actual cost it *did* incur to acquire direct materials. A company computes this variance by multiplying the actual number of direct material units *purchased* by the difference between the standard price and the actual price per direct material unit. Companies normally compute direct materials price variances at the time they purchase materials. The direct materials quantity variance is the difference between the standard cost of the quantity of direct materials that a company *should have used* for the actual number of units produced and the standard cost of the direct materials that it *did* use to produce those units.

4 What is included in a company's direct labor price and quantity standards?

A direct labor price standard shows the current hourly wage rate that a company should incur for a specific type of direct labor employed in production. Direct labor price standards also may be set to include an allowance for payroll taxes and fringe benefits. A direct labor quantity standard shows the amount of direct labor time that a company should use to produce one unit of product. A company sets direct labor quantity standards in a two-step process. First, it carefully studies the time required to perform the direct labor operations needed to produce a product. Then, it allows for normal amounts of labor time used for personnel rest breaks, machine adjustments and idle time, and production of normal amounts of spoiled units.

5 When a company compares its actual direct labor costs to its direct labor standards, how does it determine what caused the difference between the two?

A company uses direct labor variances to help it determine the causes of differences between actual and standard direct labor costs. A direct labor price variance is the difference between the cost that a company should have incurred for the actual labor hours worked [at the standard direct labor price (rate) per hour] and the actual direct labor cost it did incur for the number of actual labor hours worked. A company computes this direct labor price variance by multiplying the actual direct labor hours worked by the difference between the direct labor price standard and the actual direct labor price per hour. The direct labor efficiency variance is the difference between the standard cost of the direct labor hours that a company *should have used* for the actual number of units produced and the standard cost of the direct labor hours that it *did* use to produce those units. In other words, the *actual* direct labor hours that the company's employees worked on the actual number of units produced were more or less than the standard direct labor hours *budgeted* for that number of units.

6 What does a company include in its factory overhead price and quantity standards, and what volume does it use to set its predetermined rates?

The price standards for factory overhead are the standard predetermined overhead rates. A company often establishes separate rates for variable and fixed factory overhead. The variable factory overhead rate is the sum of all the variable overhead costs per unit of product. The company computes its fixed factory overhead rate by determining the amount of budgeted annual fixed factory overhead and dividing that amount by the estimated annual volume of production activity (measured in standard direct labor hours, machine hours, or other measure of activity). The quantity standard for factory overhead is the volume of production activity (direct labor hours, machine hours, or other measure of activity) that should be used to produce one unit of product. If a company uses direct labor hours to apply factory overhead, the quantity standard for overhead is the same as the quantity standard for direct labor. If it uses machine hours or some other measure of activity for overhead application, it must determine a separate quantity standard showing the budgeted machine hours (or activity) required under planned operating conditions to produce one unit of product. A company usually computes its standard fixed overhead rate using a volume that reflects the normal activity or practical capacity of its manufacturing operations. Normal activity is the average of the company's expected annual production volumes, usually computed for three to five years into the future. It is closely related to the average sales volume expected over that future period. Practical capacity is the volume of activity at which the company's manufacturing facilities are capable of operating per year under practical conditions, allowing for usual levels of efficiency. It is closely related to the physical size of the manufacturing facilities, which typically does not change much from year to year.

7 When a company compares its actual factory overhead costs against its factory overhead standards, how does it determine what caused the difference between the two?

A company uses factory overhead variances to help it determine the causes of differences between actual and standard factory overhead costs. The total overhead variance is the difference between total factory overhead cost *applied* and total factory overhead cost *incurred* in a standard cost system. The overhead budget variance is the difference between the total overhead *budgeted* and the total overhead *incurred*. The total overhead budgeted is the amount of factory overhead cost that a company *should* incur to produce a given number of units under planned operating conditions. A company computes the total overhead budgeted by multiplying the standard direct labor hours budgeted for the actual number of units produced by the variable overhead rate, and then adding the result to the budgeted fixed overhead. The fixed overhead volume variance is the difference between the amount of *applied* fixed overhead and the amount of *budgeted* fixed overhead. A company computes this variance by subtracting the total budgeted fixed overhead cost from the amount of applied fixed overhead cost (the standard direct labor hours budgeted for the actual number of units produced times the standard fixed overhead rate per hour).

8 **How does a company use its manufacturing cost variances to control its operations?**

Managers attempt to use cost variance information to determine what problems are affecting the efficient performance of their company's manufacturing activities. To make variance computations more helpful to managers in identifying specific problems, management accountants try to measure variances as quickly as they can after the variances occur, to measure variances in as much detail as is helpful in pinpointing specific problems, and to report variances to managers who are in a position to identify and correct the problems that are likely to have caused the variances.

Key Terms

direct labor efficiency variance *(p. 588)*
direct labor price standard *(p. 586)*
direct labor price variance *(p. 587)*
direct labor quantity standard *(p. 587)*
direct materials price standard *(p. 580)*
direct materials price variance *(p. 582)*
direct materials quantity standard
(*p. 581*)
direct materials quantity variance
(*p. 583*)
fixed overhead volume variance *(p. 594)*
normal activity *(p. 591)*
overhead budget variance *(p. 593)*
practical capacity *(p. 592)*
price standard *(p. 579)*

price standard for factory overhead
(*p. 590*)
quantity standard *(p. 579)*
quantity standard for factory overhead
(*p. 590*)
standard costs *(p. 578)*
standard cost system *(p. 578)*
standard cost of an input for one unit of
product output *(p. 579)*
standard direct labor hours budgeted
(*p. 588*)
standard direct materials quantity
budgeted *(p. 583)*
total overhead variance *(p. 592)*

SUMMARY SURFING

Here is an opportunity to gather information on the Internet about real-world issues related to the topics in this chapter. Go to http://www.dryden.com/account and click on the Cunningham, Nikolai, and Bazley book cover. Click on Summary Surfing, then click on this chapter number, and answer the following questions.

▶ Click on **Hershey Foods Corporation.** Then click on *Hershey's Cookbook.* Now click on *Greatest Chocolate Recipes . . . and More!* M-m-m-m!! YUM! Click on *SEARCH* and then on *HOT COCOA.* What are the direct materials and direct labor quantity standards for Hot Cocoa? How would you determine the direct materials and direct labor price standards?

Integrated Business and Accounting Situations

Answer the Following Questions in Your Own Words

Testing Your Knowledge

17-1 What is a standard cost system?

17-2 What is the difference between a price standard and a quantity standard?

17-3 How does a company compute the standard cost of an input per unit of output in its manufacturing operations?

17-4 What costs are included in a direct materials price standard?

17-5 What amounts are included in a direct materials quantity standard?

17-6 Distinguish between a direct materials price variance and a direct materials quantity variance.

17-7 Why is a direct materials price variance usually computed at the time of purchase?

17-8 How does a company record the purchase of direct materials (on credit) in a standard cost system?

17-9 How does a company record the use of direct materials in a standard cost system?

17-10 What does a direct labor price standard include?

17-11 What amount does a direct labor quantity standard include?

17-12 Distinguish between a direct labor price variance and a direct labor efficiency variance.

17-13 How does a company record wages for direct labor in a standard cost system?

17-14 What are the price standards for factory overhead?

17-15 What is the quantity standard for factory overhead?

17-16 Distinguish between an overhead budget variance and a fixed overhead volume variance.

17-17 Explain how a company records its factory overhead incurred and factory overhead applied.

17-18 What is the balance in a company's factory overhead account at the end of the period, and how does the company remove this balance?

17-19 What rules do management accountants follow to make variance computations more helpful?

17-20 Why is it useful for managers to have a "breakdown" of the standard cost variances for individual operations or departments?

17-21 Should managers investigate all variances to identify the problems causing them? Briefly discuss.

Applying Your Knowledge

17-22 The Morgan Company plans to purchase material X in 5-gallon drums (1,000 at a time) at an invoice price of $21 per drum and to take a 2% cash discount by paying for the material within 10 days. Freight and receiving costs for a shipment of 1,000 drums should total $920. During April, a rush order for one of Morgan's products caused an emergency cash purchase of 1,000 gallons of material X from an alternate supplier. The alternate supplier delivered the material the next day, charging Morgan $4,500 with no cash discount. Freight and receiving costs totaled $180.

Required: (1) Compute the direct materials price standard (per gallon) for material X.
(2) Compute the direct materials price variance related to the emergency purchase.

17-23 The Melton Company has set the standard direct materials cost for one of its products at $12 per unit (4 pounds per unit @ $3 per pound). During March, Melton purchased 4,100 pounds of this direct material on credit at a total cost of $12,050 and used 3,800 pounds to produce 930 units of product.

Required: (1) Compute Melton's direct materials price and quantity variances for March.

(2) Using T-accounts, prepare the entries for Melton to record (a) the purchase of this direct material and (b) the use of this direct material.

17-24 Playtime Products makes large dollhouses. The standard cost of the carpet used for their construction is $8.40 per dollhouse (6 square feet @ $1.40 per square foot). During September, Playtime paid $25,140 to purchase carpet, half of which was used to produce dollhouses during that month. Direct materials variances related to the purchase and use of this carpet during September were as follows:

Direct materials price variance   = $(2,040) unfavorable
Direct materials quantity variance = $210 favorable

Required: Compute the following related amounts: (1) the number of square feet of carpet material purchased in September, and (2) the number of dollhouses produced in September.

17-25 Foster Furniture uses a standard cost system. One model of sofa has a standard direct labor cost of $111 (10 hours per sofa @ $11.10 per hour). During the first week of October, Foster manufactured 15 of these sofas. Because of illness, one of the regular employees was replaced during that week by a new, untrained employee. Employees worked a total of 157 direct labor hours at an average labor cost of $10.80 per hour on the sofas. The direct labor price variance and the direct labor efficiency variance for the production of the sofas resulted from substituting the untrained employee for the regular skilled worker.

Required: (1) Compute the direct labor price variance and the direct labor efficiency variance.

(2) How much extra direct labor cost was incurred in the production of the sofas because of the substitution of the untrained employee?

17-26 The Morristown Manufacturing Company incurred $60,500 of direct labor cost in its machine shop during the month of June. This cost was the result of 5,910 direct labor hours worked to produce 2,000 units of product. The direct labor quantity standard is 3 direct labor hours per unit, and the direct labor price standard is $10 per direct labor hour.

Required: (1) Compute the direct labor price variance.

(2) Compute the standard direct labor hours budgeted.

(3) Compute the direct labor efficiency variance.

(4) Using T-accounts, prepare the entry to record the wages incurred for direct labor.

17-27 The SpitShine Company produced 5,400 gallons of brass polish in January. The direct labor quantity standard for this polish is 0.2 hours per gallon, and the direct labor price standard is $12 per hour. During January, the following direct labor variances were recorded:

Direct labor price variance   = $(660) unfavorable
Direct labor efficiency variance = $(240) unfavorable

Required: Compute the following related amounts: (1) the actual direct labor hours worked during January, and (2) the average actual wage rate paid per direct labor hour in January.

17-28 The Roberts Company produces product X, which is in high demand. Mr. Roberts, the owner, believes that three or four times as many units could be sold as his five employees are capable of making. Direct materials and direct labor quantity standards and price standards are as follows:

Direct materials quantity standard.......................... 1.3 pounds per unit
Direct labor quantity standard................................ 6 hours per unit
Direct materials price standard .... $10 per pound
Direct labor price standard .... $12 per hour

Factory overhead is budgeted and applied on the basis of standard direct labor hours. Practical capacity is 9,000 standard direct labor hours. The factory overhead budget at practical capacity shows $45,000 of variable overhead and $18,000 of fixed overhead.

Required: (1) Compute the standard variable and fixed overhead rates per direct labor hour based on the budget at practical capacity.

(2) Compute the standard direct materials, direct labor, variable overhead, and fixed overhead costs per unit of product X.

17-29 Refer to 17-28. At the beginning of this year the Roberts Company leased a new machine—for $4,500 per year—that would allow production of a unit of product X out of 1 pound of direct materials in 4 direct labor hours. Mr. Roberts was so happy with the efficiency of this new machine that he raised the labor rate he paid his employees to $13 per hour. This change did not affect the total variable overhead budgeted at practical capacity.

Required: (1) Revise the quantity and price standards for direct materials, direct labor, and factory overhead so that they reflect the expected changes resulting from the new machine.

(2) Compute the revised total standard cost per unit of product X.

17-30 Hugland Company budgets its factory overhead on the basis of a normal activity of 100,000 standard direct labor hours (DLH) per year. It estimates that its variable factory overhead is $4 per DLH and its fixed factory overhead is $600,000 per year. Hugland applies its factory overhead using a predetermined rate based on the preceding information. Hugland has a direct labor quantity standard of 2 hours per unit of product. During the current year, Hugland produced 48,000 units of product and incurred actual factory overhead costs of $990,000.

Required: Compute Hugland's (1) predetermined overhead rate, (2) total overhead variance, (3) overhead budget variance, and (4) fixed overhead volume variance.

17-31 The total annual factory overhead budget of the Reynolds Company is given by the following cost equation:

Total overhead cost budgeted = $78,000 + $3.50X
where
X = standard direct labor hours

The Reynolds Company has a practical capacity of 20,000 standard direct labor hours, but it expects to operate at a normal activity level of 15,000 standard direct labor hours. The direct labor quantity standard is 5 hours per unit of product. Last year the company produced 2,400 units and incurred $124,900 of overhead costs.

Required: (1) Using the factory overhead budget at *practical* capacity, (a) compute the variable and fixed overhead rates per direct labor hour; (b) compute the overhead budget variance; and (c) compute the fixed overhead volume variance.

(2) Using the factory overhead budget at *normal* activity, repeat all the computations required in (1).

(3) Discuss the similarities and differences between your computations in (1) and (2).

17-32 The Brimestone Company produces several products. The company's factory overhead rates were determined in 2000 at its normal activity of 90,000 units (180,000 standard direct labor hours budgeted) per year, as shown here:

	Factory Overhead Budget at 90,000 Units (180,000 standard direct labor hours budgeted)	**Standard Factory Overhead Rates per Hour**
Variable	$180,000	$1
Fixed	540,000	3
Total	$720,000	$4

During 2000, 82,500 units were produced and actual factory overhead totaled $702,500 (all of which was paid in cash except depreciation of $300,000 on factory and equipment).

Required: (1) Compute (a) the total overhead variance, (b) the overhead budget variance, and (c) the fixed overhead volume variance.
(2) Using T-accounts, prepare entries to record (a) factory overhead incurred and (b) factory overhead applied.
(3) Using T-accounts, prepare the entry to record the overhead budget variance and the fixed overhead volume variance.

17-33 The Sanford Corporation produces a single product and uses a standard cost system. Fixed and variable overhead costs are applied to this product on a standard machine hour basis. Sanford uses its normal activity of 100,000 standard machine hours to set its standard overhead rates. Summary data from Sanford's flexible budget are as follows:

Standard Machine Hours per Year	Total Overhead Costs Budgeted per Year
80,000	$124,000
90,000	132,000
100,000	140,000
110,000	148,000

The standard machine hour requirement for Sanford's product is 2 machine hours per unit. Last year 45,000 units were produced, and actual overhead costs were $132,800.

Required: (1) Compute the fixed and variable overhead rates per standard machine hour. (*Hint:* Total overhead cost is a *mixed* cost that can be separated into fixed and variable components.)
(2) Compute the amount of fixed overhead cost *budgeted* at 80,000, 90,000, 100,000, and 110,000 standard machine hours, respectively.
(3) Compute the amount of fixed overhead cost *applied* at 80,000, 90,000, 100,000, and 110,000 standard machine hours, respectively.
(4) Compute last year's fixed overhead volume variance.
(5) Draw two lines, one representing the amount of fixed overhead *budgeted* and the other representing the amount of fixed overhead *applied*, on a graph using the vertical axis to measure dollars and the horizontal axis to measure standard machine hours. On this graph, show the fixed overhead volume variance computed in (4).
(6) Compute last year's overhead budget variance.

17-34 The Glover Company produces Product A, for which the following standards have been set:

Direct materials (3 pounds @ $2.50 per pound)	$ 7.50
Direct labor (1 hour @ $12.20 per hour)	12.20
Total factory overhead (1 direct labor hour @ $7 per hour)	7.00
Standard manufacturing cost per unit of A	$26.70

The fixed factory overhead rate was determined from the fixed factory overhead budget of $76,000 at a normal activity of 20,000 standard direct labor hours (20,000 units of Product A) per month.

Actual data recorded during April:

Units of Product A produced:	13,000
Direct materials purchased:	100,000 pounds @ $2.47 per pound
Direct materials used:	39,620 pounds
Direct labor cost:	13,025 hours @ $12.48 per hour
Total factory overhead cost:	$125,000

Required: (1) Compute the following:
(a) Fixed factory overhead rate per standard direct labor hour
(b) Variable factory overhead rate per standard direct labor hour

        (c) Direct materials price and quantity variances

        (d) Direct labor price and efficiency variances

        (e) Overhead budget variance

        (f) Fixed overhead volume variance

    (2) Using dollars on the vertical axis and standard direct labor hours budgeted on the horizontal axis, graph the amount of total factory overhead budgeted and total factory overhead applied as standard direct labor hours vary. Clearly show the fixed factory overhead volume variance and the overhead budget variance for April on this graph.

17-35 The Pierless Paint Company produces an exterior house paint known as Pierpont 163. Two direct materials are combined in the manufacture of this paint: pier and pont. Pierpont 163 is sold in 1-gallon cans, the standard costs of which are shown here:

Standard cost per gallon: Pierpont 163

Material pier:...	0.8 gallons @ $4.00 per gallon	$3.20
Material pont:..	0.4 pounds @ $0.60 per pound	.24
Direct labor:...	0.01 hours @ $10.00 per hour	.10
Variable overhead:......................................	0.01 direct labor hours @ $8.00 per hour[a]	.08
Fixed overhead:	0.01 direct labor hours @ $22.00 per hour[a]	.22
Total standard cost per gallon		$3.84

[a]Overhead rates were computed at normal activity of 2,000 standard direct labor hours per month.

Inventory records last month show:

Item	Beginning Inventory	Purchases	Ending Inventory
Material pier	80,000 gallons	126,000 gallons @ $3.80 per gallon	30,000 gallons
Material pont	35,000 pounds	135,000 pounds @ $0.62 per pound	90,000 pounds

Additional production information from last month:

Gallons of Pierpont 163 produced:.. 212,000 gallons

Actual direct labor cost (2,180 direct labor hours @ $9.70 per hour):..... $21,146

Actual overhead costs:.. $63,575

Required: Compute the following variances:

    (1) Direct materials price and quantity variances for (a) material pier and (b) material pont

    (2) Direct labor price and efficiency variances

    (3) Overhead budget variance

    (4) Fixed overhead volume variance

17-36 The Hammond Manufacturing Company produces Yagis. Standard costs per Yagi are as follows:

	Standard Cost per Yagi
Direct materials:	
Aluminum tubing (144 feet @ $0.40 per foot)...	$ 57.60
Hardware (1 package @ $5.00 per package)	5.00
Direct labor (3 direct labor hours @ $9.60 per hour)......................................	28.80
Factory overhead:	
Variable (3 direct labor hours @ $2.00 per hour)...................................	6.00
Fixed (3 direct labor hours @ $4.00 per hour)	12.00
Standard manufacturing cost per Yagi	$109.40

Factory overhead is budgeted and applied on the basis of standard direct labor hours. The overhead rates were set at a practical capacity of 5,600 standard direct labor hours per year.

Actual production and cost data from last year:

Yagis produced:	1,350
Aluminum tubing purchased (on credit):	280,000 feet @ $0.41 per foot = $114,800
Aluminum tubing used:	196,400 feet
Hardware purchased (on credit):	1,360 packages @ $4.95 per package = $6,732
Packages of hardware used:	1,360 packages
Direct labor cost:	4,120 direct labor hours @ $9.70 per hour = $39,964
Total factory overhead cost:	$32,050 (assume all was paid in cash except for depreciation of $4,500 on equipment)

Required: (1) Calculate the direct materials price and quantity variances for each direct material.

(2) Calculate the direct labor price and efficiency variances.

(3) Calculate the overhead budget variance.

(4) Calculate the fixed overhead volume variance.

(5) Using T-accounts, prepare the entries to record (a) the purchase and use of the raw materials, (b) the wages incurred for direct labor, (c) the factory overhead incurred and applied, and (d) the overhead budget variance and the fixed overhead volume variance.

Making Evaluations

17-37 The Oldtown Clock Company makes walnut veneer clocks that look like antiques. A new clock to be manufactured requires a veneer strip 6 inches wide and 18 inches long. Oldtown's supplier of walnut veneer will sell veneer in 6-inch-wide strips that are 8 feet long for $12.50 per strip. The supplier is also willing to sell Oldtown 6-inch-wide strips in 6-foot lengths at a price of $9.60 per strip.

The veneer strips must be carefully cut by hand into 18-inch lengths in Oldtown's cutting department. Each 6-inch cut across the strip should take 3 minutes. Direct labor rates in the cutting department are $8.00 per hour. No other manufacturing costs are affected by the company's choice of buying 6- or 8-foot strips. The odd-sized pieces of veneer that are left after cutting have no value.

Required: (1) Assuming the veneer strips are purchased in 6-foot lengths, compute the expected direct materials cost of the veneer and the expected direct labor cost that would be incurred per clock in the cutting department.

(2) Assuming the veneer strips are purchased in 8-foot lengths, compute the expected direct materials cost of the veneer and the expected direct labor cost that would be incurred per clock in the cutting department.

(3) Considering your answers to (1) and (2), should Oldtown purchase the veneer strips in 6- or 8-foot lengths?

(4) Assuming the veneer strips are purchased in 6-foot lengths, determine (for the veneer strips and for veneer cutting operations) the following: (a) the direct materials quantity standard (in feet per clock); (b) the direct materials price standard per foot; and (c) the direct labor quantity standard (in hours per clock).

17-38 The Ranger Company produces Ringos. The president of the company has recently been puzzled by apparent problems causing direct labor price variances that she cannot identify. You are asked to help the president understand the source of the direct labor price variances. The president informs you that 7 direct labor hours should be worked to produce each Ringo and that the standard direct labor cost totals $84 per Ringo. During April, 700 Ringos were produced, 4,900 direct labor hours were worked, and direct labor cost incurred was $59,374.

Required: (1) Given the preceding information, compute the direct labor price and efficiency variances.

(2) Suppose on further investigation you discover that 990 of the 4,900 direct labor hours were worked in Ranger's Department A and the rest in Department B. Furthermore you discover that production of each Ringo should require the following:

Department A : 2 direct labor hours @ $11.00 per hour = $22.00
Department B: 5 direct labor hours @ $12.40 per hour =   62.00
Total direct labor cost per Ringo $84.00

You also discover that during April, $10,890 of the direct labor cost was incurred in Department A and $48,484 in Department B. Given this additional information, compute the direct labor price and efficiency variances for Department A and Department B separately.

(3) Comment on the results obtained in (1) and (2).

17-39 The Cozyhome Company makes doghouses. These houses are built in two departments. Department A cuts ¾-inch plywood into two shapes (1 and 2) and paints the pieces with quick-drying paint. Doghouses are assembled in Department B using three pieces of shape 1 and two pieces of shape 2. Direct labor quantity standards for the operations of these two departments are shown here:

Department A : Cutting and painting
    Shape 1 .... 0.21 hours per piece
    Shape 2 .... 0.25 hours per piece
Department B: Assembly
    Assembly .... 1 direct labor hour per doghouse

On August 18, actual production was as follows:

Department A:
    Pieces of shape 1: .... 80 cut and painted
    Pieces of shape 2: .... 40 cut and painted
Department B:
    Doghouses: .... 20 assembled

Three laborers worked 8 hours each in Department A and three laborers worked 8 hours each in Department B. All workers earn $10.00 per hour. At the beginning of the day, six pieces of shape 1 but no pieces of shape 2 were ready for assembly.

Required: (1) Compute the standard direct labor cost of one doghouse.
        (2) Compute the standard direct labor hours budgeted in Departments A and B for the work done in the Cozyhome shop on August 18.
        (3) Compute the direct labor efficiency variances occurring in each of the departments.
        (4) Write a brief report on the direct labor performance of the two departments and include a suggestion on how, in the future, managers might avoid the problem that occurred on August 18.

17-40 "... and Roy, you know as well as anyone else that while our sales volume is down, we've got to cut costs. Your department's unit costs are up 2% this June. We just can't have any more of this or I'll have to find someone who can keep the costs down." Roy Lilley, a production department manager for the JJS Company, left the meeting room very upset. He had just been severely criticized by the production supervisor because of inefficiency in his department. The basis for that criticism was the following report:

DEPARTMENT 40-00 (ROY LILLEY)
COST REPORT: MAY AND JUNE

	May	June
Production (units)	20,000	16,000
Direct labor hours	4,000	3,100
Costs:		
Direct materials	$10,000	$ 8,400
Direct labor	30,000	22,000

(continued)

(continued)	**May**	**June**
Factory overhead	40,000	34,875
Total	$80,000	$65,275
Cost per unit	$ 4.00	$ 4.08

Roy felt that something was wrong. It seemed to him that his department had worked harder than any of the others to keep costs down. This same episode occurred last summer too, and Roy had almost quit his job because of it.

The cost accounting system used by the JJS Company applies all costs incurred each month to the units produced. Actual total overhead costs, for example, are computed at the end of the month and assigned to the month's production at an actual rate per direct labor hour. In May, total overhead costs had been $100,000 while 10,000 actual direct labor hours were worked in the factory. In June, overhead costs were $90,000 while direct labor hours had dropped to 8,000.

Required: Discuss how useful the cost report is in judging the performance of Roy Lilley's department during June. Also discuss how a standard cost system could be used to prepare another performance report for Department 40-00, one that would be more useful to Roy Lilley and to the production supervisor.

17-41 Missouri Briar Company is a manufacturer of corncob pipes. The company has grown rapidly over the past 10 years. Originally a small supplier of cheaply made pipes for novelty and souvenir shops, the company now supplies large quantities of high-quality pipes to pipe shops throughout the country. Several grades of pipes are sold. The best pipes—Grade A—smoke more sweetly than the finest imported briar pipes. Demand continues to grow. Profit seems to have leveled off over the past two years, however. Pipe production does not seem to be as efficient as it used to be.

Producing a pipe involves several distinctly different operations that require special labor skills. Production starts with "rough cobbing," in which seasoned cobs are cut and drilled. Next comes a critical "sorting" operation, in which the cut and drilled cobs are sorted by quality and shape and sent to different departments set up to produce different grades of pipes.

In these departments, "plugging," "stemming," and "finishing" operations are performed. More skill is required, and a great deal more time is taken in the production of Grade A pipes than in the production of Grade B or Grade C pipes. "Final grading" is the last operation performed. It is an inspection process aimed at maintaining quality. Grade A pipes that do not pass inspection are downgraded and sold as Grade B or C pipes. Grade B pipes that do not pass inspection are downgraded and sold as Grade C pipes. Grade C pipes that do not pass inspection are sold as novelties.

During the last two years Alex Hrechko, the president of Missouri Briar Company, has noticed that the average direct materials and direct labor cost per pipe have increased considerably, although he is not sure why. Alex is worried that things are out of control.

Some data from the last three years are presented in the following table:

	1998 Average Direct Costs Per Pipe			1999 Average Direct Costs Per Pipe			2000 Average Direct Costs Per Pipe		
	Pipes Produced	Materials	Labor	Pipes Produced	Materials	Labor	Pipes Produced	Materials	Labor
Grade A	20,000	$ .90	$1.20	20,000	$ .95	$1.30	21,250	$1.00	$1.45
Grade B	30,000	.86	1.10	31,000	.89	1.23	33,750	.94	1.40
Grade C	40,000	.85	1.00	46,000	.88	1.14	53,750	.93	1.35
Novelty	10,000	.84	.95	13,000	.87	1.10	16,250	.91	1.30
Total	100,000			110,000			125,000		

Required: Discuss in what ways the data given in the table are deficient for evaluating the performance of the company's manufacturing operations. Also discuss how a standard cost system could improve the president's ability to control the manufacturing operations of his company.

17-42 Carmen A., the supervisor of purchasing operations, is responsible for buying needed materials at the most favorable delivered prices for the Long Manufacturing Company. She is evaluated on the basis of net materials price variances each month. Harlan D., the production supervisor, is responsible for producing the company's products in the desired quantities, attaining appropriate quality standards, and meeting the production schedules that have been adopted. He is evaluated on the basis of net direct materials quantity variances for all materials used each month as well as direct labor efficiency and overhead budget variances.

   During January, Carmen obtained a 30% quantity discount off a slightly lower than standard price for a one year's supply of dingers from a new supplier. Normally, dingers are purchased in much smaller quantities. Dingers are critical to the quality of several of the company's products and to the efficiency of direct materials and direct labor usage in several manufacturing processes. The dingers purchased by Carmen in January are of inferior quality.

   Required: Discuss the effects that the January purchase of inferior dingers will have on the performance evaluation of both Carmen A. and Harlan D. and the likely effects on company profit. Suggest a way to change the performance evaluation system so that it might be more fair to the individuals involved and might improve company profitability as well.

17-43 Bill C., the supervisor of purchasing operations, is responsible for buying needed materials for the Short Manufacturing Company at the most favorable delivered prices. He is evaluated on the basis of net materials price variances each month. Peggie C., the production supervisor, is responsible for producing the company's products in the desired quantities, attaining appropriate quality standards, and meeting the production schedules that have been adopted. She is evaluated on the basis of net direct materials quantity variances for all materials used each month as well as direct labor efficiency and overhead budget variances.

   During February the company's sales manager, Toni C., landed two huge orders for one of the company's products. These two orders were obtained because Toni promised the customers almost immediate delivery; she would not have obtained the orders otherwise. Toni C. is evaluated on the basis of total sales dollars from orders she obtains. In fact, she receives a fixed percentage sales commission based on her sales dollars.

   To obtain enough direct materials for the production required, Bill C. placed rush orders with the company's regular supplier and with several other suppliers at above standard prices. He also made special and costly shipping arrangements in order to have direct materials available in time for production.

   Peggie C. used several old machines that had been previously taken out of production because they were inefficient, and she employed several inexperienced machine operators in order to complete production in time to meet the deadlines she was given.

   Required: Discuss how Toni C.'s promises of "almost immediate delivery" will affect her own performance evaluation and those of Bill C. and Peggie C. Also discuss the likely effects that her promises will have on company profit. Suggest ways to change the performance evaluation system so that it might be more fair to the individuals involved and might improve company profitability as well.

17-44 Yesterday, you received the following letter for your advice column in the local paper:

Dear Dr. Decisive:

My roommate and I bought a new desk for our room and thought we could just load it up in his truck, carry it up to our room, and use it. WRONG! As it turned out, there was *some assembly required.* In the middle of our "assembly," we discovered that we were two screws short of what we needed. Well, as if this wasn't bad enough, my roommate, the accounting major, started thinking about standards. He told me that this desk didn't have the standard amount of direct materials included with it. Then he started mumbling about variances and how there were favorable and unfavorable variances (the direct materials variance was favorable for the company that sold us the desk but was unfavorable for us, or something like that). Anyway, one thing led to another, and the next thing I knew we were arguing about whether a favorable variance is always favorable for the company. I think the answer is yes. Otherwise, why would a variance be called favorable? My roommate says I'm wrong, and besides, I'm on his *unfavorable* side right now because it was my idea to buy the desk. I think if you say I'm right, he will see both the favorable and the unfavorable side of me. Please help settle our dispute.

"Two-Sided"

Meet with your Dr. Decisive team and write a response to "Two-Sided."

CHAPTER 18

MODERN DEVELOPMENTS IN MANAGING OPERATIONS

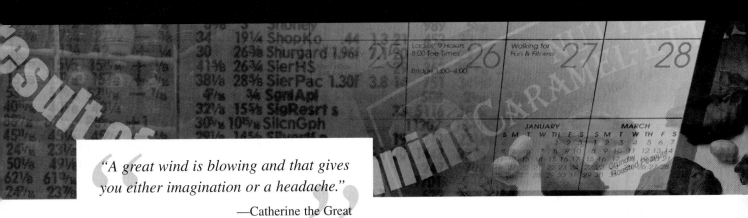

"A great wind is blowing and that gives you either imagination or a headache."

—Catherine the Great

1 *How has the global economy caused companies to become more competitive?*

2 *As part of its efforts to become more competitive, how can a company measure quality and the costs of quality?*

3 *How does just-in-time production help a company reduce its costs, operate more efficiently, and control quality?*

4 *How have improved technology and factory layouts helped companies become more competitive?*

5 *When a company uses activity-based costing, what three stages does it follow to allocate factory overhead costs to products?*

6 *How does activity-based costing improve managers' decisions?*

Suppose that you have always had an interest in running competitively. When you were little and raced the other kids, you consistently won. Suppose also that, as you grew up, you competed in school track-and-field events and won state track meets and that you recently won a national track-and-field competition that makes you eligible to run in the Olympics. How will you evaluate your chances of winning in the Olympics? And how will you prepare to win? Remember, the people you will be competing against also have won school track-and-field events and other track meets, and have proven themselves to be the best in their own countries. Furthermore, some of them have practiced in environments that are different from (and maybe better than) yours; they are perhaps aware of more successful running techniques than you use, and they may wear more technologically advanced running shoes than you do. With this in mind, as you look for ways to improve your performance, you might practice in an environment similar to that of the Olympic venue, hire an additional coach known for his or her innovative techniques, search for ways to run more efficiently (to eliminate the wasted motion that adds to your time), and learn more about the best available running shoes.

Today, companies face a similar situation. Many no longer compete only in their own countries; world competition has become commonplace. Even companies that are well-established in their own countries cannot afford to be complacent about their success because companies in other countries (as well as in their own country) are eager to win the competition for customers by using improved technology, by selling high-quality products at lower prices, and by meeting shorter delivery schedules. Consequently, to make themselves more competitive, many companies have adopted a Japanese philosophy called *kaizen*, or continuous improvement. These companies consistently strive for higher-quality products and services, more efficient operations, and lower costs.

www.alexanderdoll. com

Here's what can happen when a company focuses on improvement. <u>Alexander Doll Company,</u> a New York City manufacturer of collectible dolls, in an effort to improve its operations, set up a team of employees to evaluate its production line.[1] At the time, production was spread out over three floors, which caused extra handling that not only damaged the dolls but also wasted time. Furthermore, the factory scheduled production so that the dolls moved from process to process in batches. This batch processing caused a collection, or "log jam," of dolls before each process as batches of dolls waited their turn while the process finished a previous batch. By combining all the operations at one location (on one floor) and by processing the dolls continuously, rather than in batches, Alexander Doll Company achieved dramatic improvements.

For instance, the distance each doll traveled through the production process went down from 630 to 40 feet, and the time to complete a doll dropped from 90 days to 90 *minutes*! The production area decreased from 2,010 to 980 square feet, and the average productivity per person per day increased from 8 to 25 dolls. Even with this substantial betterment, the company plans to continue to make improvements. Managers of companies like Alexander Doll Company have found that better information obtained from their companies' accounting systems supports their ability to continuously improve their companies in these areas.

Do you suppose Alexander Doll Company uses a job order or a process cost accounting system? Why?

1 *How has the global economy caused companies to become more competitive?*

Effects of Modern Developments on Competition

As we discussed in Chapter 2, many factors affect the current business environment, but global competition, alone, has forced companies to reassess everything from operations to customer service. This additional competition has accelerated the rate of technological advances, allowing companies to produce and sell a wider assortment of products and services. Because of the increasing rate of technological change, many products and services appeal to customers for shorter periods of time before more-advanced products and services capture their attention. Advances in communication and transportation have provided customers with worldwide product information and greater access to these products.

[1]Roberta Maynard, "A Company Is Turned Around through Japanese Principles," *Nation's Business,* February 1996, 9.

Global competition not only has *contributed* to the rate of change in the business environment but is a *part* of that change. Now, instead of just trying to maintain their share of customers or to gain customers by successfully competing against companies in their own countries, companies also must defend or increase their share of customers by competing with companies from other countries.

A company uses numerous strategies to make itself more competitive, including the following:

1. Selling a better (higher-quality) product than that offered by any of its competitors

2. Responding to customer needs and wants, and providing superior customer service

3. Reducing the amount of time between receiving a customer's order and delivering the product

4. Selling a product equal in quality to that of its competitors but at a lower price

Along with the philosophy of continuous improvement, several other management philosophies and production techniques have emerged that help a company implement these strategies and compete more effectively. As you will see in this chapter, a company's accounting system can be reconfigured to support these philosophies and techniques. Next, we will discuss these management philosophies and techniques and the related information needs of managers.

The Issue of Quality

Because providing a better-quality product or service gives companies a "leg up" on their competition, managers are giving the issue of quality increasing attention and using it as a selling point for their companies' products. For example, Leisure Life Limited, a manufacturer of small boats, includes the following paragraph in its sales brochures:

> Every Leisure Life Limited boat must pass a rigorous test of nearly 100 quality checks during assembly and before shipping. . . . Our boats have earned the reputation of being the highest quality in the industry, and for good reason. Compare the quality of design, construction, and attention to detail of any Leisure Life Limited boat against any other small boat and you will agree that our reputation is well deserved.

As more companies export their products to other countries as a means of expanding their set of customers, they may choose to adopt **ISO 9000,** a set of quality standards set up by the International Organization for Standardization, a consortium of European countries. They may adopt these standards not only because they agree with them, but also because many large potential customers in Europe *require* that their suppliers adhere to these standards. Both Leisure Life's statement of quality and ISO 9000 are consistent with a management philosophy called "total quality management," which we will discuss next.

Total Quality Management

Total Quality Management (TQM) is a management philosophy or approach that focuses on a company's customers. These customers can be consumers—what we normally picture as the customers of the company. But the "customers" may also exist *inside* the company. Departments or divisions may serve all or some of the employees of other departments or divisions of the company. For example, if a company has an employee cafeteria, the employees of the company who eat lunch in the cafeteria are the cafeteria's customers.

Under the TQM philosophy, all employees of the company work as a team with their external and internal customers, as well as with their suppliers, to foster continuous

2 *As part of its efforts to become more competitive, how can a company measure quality and the costs of quality?*

www.leisurelife.com

improvement in the company to meet or exceed the expectations of the customers. The ideal is 100 percent quality rather than, say, 95 percent quality. (Think about it. If you take 120 credit hours during your undergraduate program, that's about 1,800 actual hours spent in the classroom. Do you want 5%, or 90 of those hours, filled with misinformation? How would you know which 90 of the 1,800 hours contained misinformation? Perhaps worse yet, when you are ill do you want 5% of your doctor's education to be filled with misinformation?)

 How do you think including its suppliers on the team helps a company meet or exceed its customers' expectations?

The atmosphere of continuous improvement must be supported by an information system that provides continuous feedback to help all employees perform better. When this feedback is available, employees can measure information about the activities of the company against benchmarks and can take corrective action when necessary. As you will see next, one important component of TQM and the measurement of quality is the integrated accounting system. This integrated accounting system may be part of a company's *enterprise resource planning system* (ERP). As we discussed in Chapter 10, under an ERP system, a company stores information in an electronic "data warehouse." Managers can "data mine" the information in this data warehouse to extract useful information for TQM, as we discuss in the following sections.

How Can the Integrated Accounting System Measure Quality?

Have you ever purchased a product that didn't measure up to your expectations of quality? What did you do about it? If the company from whom you purchased the product is "lucky," *it* will notice the problem before you do, recall the product, and fix or replace it. Or if *you* notice the problem first, you will return it for warranty work or replacement. In those cases, the company can "make it right" and perhaps maintain your goodwill. But if, instead, the company is "unlucky," and you decide to harbor a grudge and never purchase a product from that company again, the company stands to lose more than the cost of the warranty work or replacement—it stands to lose all of your future business (and perhaps the future business of all the people you tell about your experience with that product). The costs of flaws in products that reach the customers are called **external failure costs.** These costs occur *after* the product leaves the company. Since managers are focused on continuous improvement, including the reduction of external failure costs, they are usually interested in monitoring both the cost of external failures and the number of those failures.

www.mattel.com

For example, in 1997 Mattel's new Cabbage Patch Kids Snacktime doll caused quite a stir. Children were getting their hair and fingers caught in the doll's mouth. As a result, Mattel decided to recall the doll, pay a $40 refund to doll owners, and pull the remaining dolls from store shelves. In total, Mattel's dollar measure of its external failure cost was $8 million. As we discussed in previous chapters, some companies use a Warranty Expense account and a Sales Returns and Allowances account to help them keep track of some of their external failure costs. An integrated accounting system most useful to managers measures the *number* of warranty repairs, product replacements, and product recalls as well as all their costs (costs of raw materials, labor, overhead, and shipping), and you can be sure Mattel's internal records contain this information as well.

 How do you think the integrated accounting system could measure the cost of losing future business or the cost of customer ill will?

Because of the risk of losing or alienating their customers, companies prefer to catch product defects *before* their products leave the company, or to prevent defects altogether. The costs of catching product defects inside the company are called **appraisal costs.** The salaries of product inspectors and equipment testers, and the costs of materials used in the inspecting and testing processes, are examples of appraisal costs that the accounting system captures and communicates. The integrated accounting system also captures and

**"We jacked up our prices to insure that you receive the
same quality and service in the future."**

Bernard Schoenbaum © 1995 from The New Yorker Collection. All Rights Reserved.

Do you think price is always
related to quality?

communicates the number of inspections and tests conducted, at what point (or points) in
the production process they are conducted, and how many defects the inspectors and
testers find.

The costs of reworking defective products after the inspectors and testers find the defects (the wages of factory employees who rework the defective products, the cost of replacement parts and materials, and overhead costs) and the amount of time that the factory
is "down" while employees trace and fix the cause of the defects are called **internal failure costs.** The integrated accounting system provides information about these costs as well
as the number of defective products reworked. For instance, earlier in the book we used
the Purchases Returns and Allowances account to help keep track of some of these internal failures.

 *What do you think are the similarities between internal and external failure costs?
How do these costs differ from each other?*

Companies can minimize external failure costs, appraisal costs, and internal failure
costs by preventing defects from occurring in the first place. The costs of preventing flaws
and defects are called **prevention costs.** These costs include employee-training costs (for
example, salaries of trainers, salaries of employees during their training time, and costs of
training facilities). A case in point is Taco Inc., a Cranston, Rhode Island, manufacturer of
heating and cooling equipment.[2] As part of its employee-training program, one of Taco's
managers teaches a class on the ISO 9000 international quality standards. Taco Inc.'s prevention costs include the manager's salary while teaching the class, the salaries of the employees while taking the class, and the costs of the Taco Learning Center (consisting of two
classrooms, a computer lab room, a library, and a conference room). Prevention costs also
include equipment-maintenance costs (wages of maintenance employees and costs of indirect materials).

www.taco-hvac.com

[2]Michael Barrier, "Closing the Skills Gap," *Nation's Business*, March 1996, 27.

Why do you think equipment-maintenance costs are considered to be prevention costs?

The integrated accounting system provides information about training and equipment-maintenance costs, as well as other information that managers might want to know about prevention costs. This information includes, for instance, the number of employees trained, the number of training seminars, the number of machines maintained, and the number of maintenance orders over a specified time period.

 If you were the president of a company, which of the four costs of quality could you most easily justify? Why?

But what if a company wants to take quality a step further and not just reduce defects, but manufacture a higher-quality product than it has previously manufactured? Many times, a higher-quality product costs more to manufacture than does one of lower quality. To keep its profit the same, a company trying to increase the quality of its product would have to raise selling prices (or sell more units) to make up the difference in cost, or would have to lower other costs. Otherwise, it would end up with less profit.

In the past, managers tried to balance the value of the increased quality against the related increase in costs—the increase in quality might not be worth the additional costs of a higher-quality product if the company's customers seemed satisfied with the current level of product quality. Now, however, managers realize that a competitor of the company may succeed at providing a better product without raising prices or incurring higher costs, or may manage to sell an equal-quality product at a lower price. Furthermore, the competitor may shorten the time it needs to deliver high-quality products to customers.

As companies have learned, one way a competitor can manufacture higher-quality products without raising prices or incurring higher costs is by reducing other costs enough to cover the increased costs of manufacturing a higher-quality product. The competitor can sell an equal-quality product at a lower price by reducing the costs of manufacturing the product without reducing quality.

A company can reduce its product costs, as well as the amount of time between the customer order and the delivery of the product, by eliminating or reducing inefficiencies in its production process and by using improved technology. One way a company can reduce inefficiencies is by identifying those activities that are not adding value to its products or services and then minimizing or eliminating those activities. By "adding value," we mean making products or services more valuable to customers. For example, consider the following categories of manufacturing activities: production, inspection, transfer, idle time, and storage. Of these categories, only production activities add value to the products.

Although inspection activities are necessary to ensure that products meet a specified level of quality, they do not give the customer a higher level of quality; instead, they help the company maintain the expected level of quality. Transfer activities simply move products from one part of the factory to another. Idle time is factory time not used for production and includes setup time, "log jam" or queue time that occurs when products are waiting behind other products for processing, maintenance time, and repair time. Storage activities involve warehousing products between the time of their manufacture and the time of their sale or delivery. It is only the conversion of raw materials and parts into finished products that adds value to products. Many companies have found that changing from traditional production strategies to just-in-time production strategies has helped them reduce these inefficiencies.

3 *How does just-in-time production help a company reduce its costs, operate more efficiently, and control quality?*

Just-In-Time (JIT) Strategies for Manufacturing Companies

Many companies use **just-in-time strategies** to reduce costs by reducing or eliminating inventories, streamlining the factory and increasing operational efficiencies, and controlling quality. The approach to production these companies use differs from that of traditional manufacturing companies.

Traditional manufacturing companies (in this case, those other than JIT-oriented companies) base their production and inventory orders on forecasts of demand for their products. Think back to our Chapter 12 discussion of a manufacturing company's budgets. Remember that we based Unlimited Decadence's production budget on predicted sales. That is, Unlimited Decadence planned to produce in any given month enough candy bars so that the combination of its production and its beginning inventory for the month would cover that month's predicted sales as well as one-half of the following month's predicted sales. Based on its sales budget, Unlimited Decadence planned to build up inventories of finished goods in anticipation of future sales, and also to have extra inventory on hand in case it underestimated sales. Its production budget influenced production scheduling as well as planned orders of raw materials, as shown in its raw materials purchases budget. Based on the production budget (which was based on forecasted sales), Unlimited Decadence planned to build up its raw materials inventory in anticipation of future production. So, in traditional manufacturing, the sales forecast "pushes" the products through the production process. Hence, we could call the production process in a traditional factory **push-through production.**

The practice of building up inventories can cause companies to operate inefficiently. For example, inventory ties up resources such as cash (which a company doesn't get back until it sells the inventory and collects the related receivables), floor space, and labor, keeping the company from using these resources for other purposes. By minimizing inventories, companies also minimize this kind of inefficiency and the costs associated with it.

 What costs do you think are associated with tying up cash, floor space, and labor?

Unlike traditional companies, companies that use JIT strategies minimize their inventories. Suppliers deliver materials and parts to these companies just in time for production of the orders placed by the company's customers, so there is no buildup (or there is minimal buildup) of raw materials inventories. Goods-in-process inventory moves through production just in time for the next process, so incomplete products don't build up after one process while waiting to enter the next process (which they may do in a conventional factory). When these companies complete orders, they deliver the orders directly to their customers rather than to the storeroom or warehouse, avoiding a buildup of finished goods inventories. In these companies, production is based on customers' orders rather than on a forecast of what customers *might* order. So, customers' orders "pull" the products through the production process, from the customers' orders backward through the production process to the purchase of raw materials. Because of this characteristic, production in a JIT factory is called **pull-through production.** Exhibit 18-1 illustrates push-through and pull-through production. In the exhibit, you can see that pull-through production even *looks* more efficient than push-through production.

Notice in the JIT portion of Exhibit 18-1 that there is no finished goods inventory. This is usually the case because a company that uses a JIT system ordinarily ships its finished products to its customers immediately after manufacturing the products. In this situation, the company may choose to record its product costs (for direct materials, direct labor, and factory overhead) *directly* in its Cost of Goods Sold account. Under this system, if the company does have a finished goods inventory on hand at the end of its accounting period, the company "backs out" the costs of the products still on hand from its Cost of Goods Sold account, and records these costs in a Finished Goods Inventory account. This method and variations of this method are sometimes referred to as **back-flush costing.**

 Notice that we said that a company using JIT strategies minimizes its inventories. Why do you think the company doesn't just eliminate its inventories altogether?

Exhibit 18-1 Push-Through and Pull-Through Production

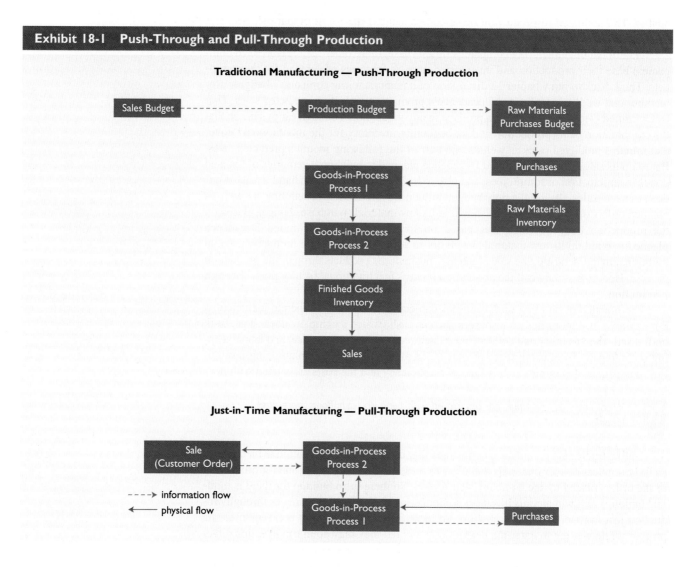

Along with inventory buildups, another source of inefficiency in the production process is numerous setup times. A company that manufactures a variety of products may use some of the same machines for different products. For example, Unlimited Decadence could use the hoppers, mixer, refiner, conche, temperer, molder, and wrapper in different combinations to manufacture most of its candy bars. Many times, when a company uses a machine for manufacturing more than one product, workers on the production line must set the machine up differently for each product. For the Unlimited Decadence factory to mold a candy bar in a unique shape, the molder would have to be set up to produce candy bars in that shape. So each time production switched from a candy bar with one shape to one with a different shape, the machine setup would take time away from production and would occupy labor so that it could not be used productively somewhere else. The more setups a company has, the longer will be the total production time. In trying to eliminate inefficiencies and costs, a company that has a JIT factory also tries to minimize setup times. As you will see later in this chapter, manufacturing technology has improved setup times for a company that takes advantage of this technology.

A company using JIT production also reduces inefficiencies and costs in its factory by minimizing **product defect rates,** the percentage of defective products manufactured. Besides bringing production to a grinding halt while employees locate and fix the problem that caused the defects, product defects also slow delivery times because of the production delays. (Remember, the company maintains zero or minimal finished goods inventories, so it can't deliver "spare" products when the factory shuts down.) Furthermore, defects can raise the costs of inspecting the products if, as a result of these defects, the company decides to make more regular inspections. Defects also can raise the costs of production because of the additional costs of correcting the defects.

One way a company minimizes its product defect rates is by choosing, and closely working with, a supplier that emphasizes quality. This way the company can be assured that it makes its products with high-quality raw materials and parts. In addition, the company can minimize its product defect rates by training its factory employees to detect product defects and by emphasizing regular equipment-maintenance and ongoing defect prevention. Many companies also take advantage of advances in technology and improve their factory layouts to minimize their defect rates.

 If a company has a philosophy of continuous improvement and is able to reduce inefficiencies in its factory, how do you think that will affect the company's standard costs? Why?

The Effect of Improved Technology and Factory Layout

As we mentioned earlier, technology has had a significant effect on world competition. Improvements in factory layouts have enhanced this effect. This combination of improvements in technology and factory layouts not only allows a company to manufacture higher-quality products and minimize its defect rates, but also allows the company to manufacture a wider variety of products at a lower cost than otherwise would be possible. We will discuss flexible manufacturing systems and manufacturing cells next. Both enhance JIT systems, but both also work well in more-traditional factories.

4 *How have improved technology and factory layouts helped companies become more competitive?*

Flexible Manufacturing Systems

Many companies have found that by investing in flexible manufacturing systems, they can make their factories operate more efficiently. **Flexible manufacturing systems** are computerized networks of automated equipment that use computer software to control such tasks as machine setups, direct materials and parts selection, and product assembly. Exhibit 18-2 illustrates Unlimited Decadence's flexible manufacturing system, which is run by an electronic control panel. The control panel selects the ingredient mix for each type of candy bar that Unlimited Decadence produces with this system, designates the amount of time each machine spends on each type of candy bar, monitors the temperature and candy density, and directs the packaging of each type of candy bar. Furthermore, it causes adjustments to be made to the production process when any of these variables deviate from an acceptable range of values.

A company that manufactures a wide variety of products stands to benefit the most from flexible manufacturing systems; since the equipment is automated, setup costs are almost zero. Computers drive each setup, and many times the setup involves merely using different software rather than requiring a physical change in the machinery. So each setup takes less time, causes lower labor costs, and results in fewer mistakes than when employees must make physical changes in the machinery for each setup.

In many flexible manufacturing systems, computer software also drives the selection and delivery of parts and materials needed for current production. Some companies have computer-driven robots that select parts and materials and that either deliver them to the production area or put the parts on a computerized belt that will deliver the parts to the production area. As part of their ERP systems, some companies using JIT production have computer systems "networked" to their suppliers' computers. With this arrangement, the computer that is running production can order parts and other raw materials electronically from suppliers so that they will arrive at the factory just in time for production. After the parts and materials arrive in the production area, computer-driven machinery assembles them into products.

Exhibit 18-2   Unlimited Decadence's Flexible Manufacturing System

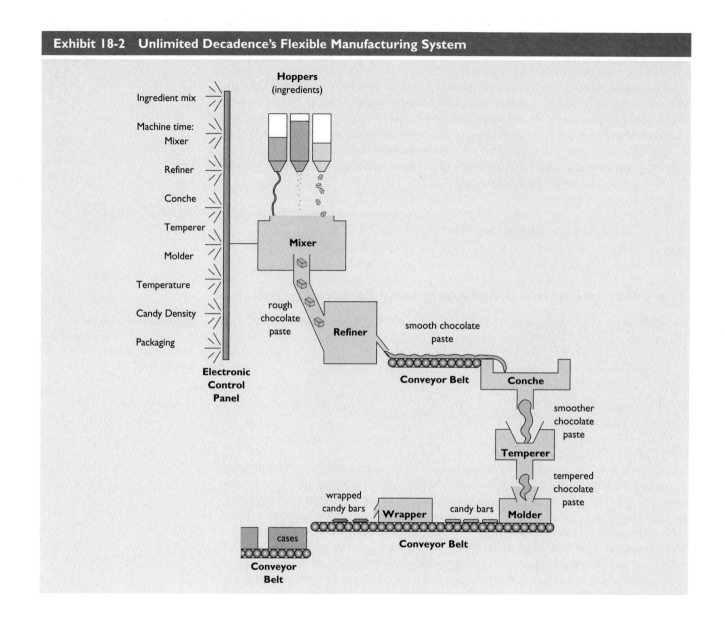

 How do you think switching from a traditional factory to a flexible manufacturing system would affect the costs of materials, labor, and overhead relative to each other? Why?

www.fujielectronic.co.
jp/eng/index-e.html

A decade ago, Fuji Electric, a Japanese manufacturer of electronic machinery, began changing from a traditional manufacturing system to a flexible manufacturing system.[3] Now Fuji's factory is automated and uses information in bar codes on its products, read by automated scanners, to direct machine setups, materials and parts selection, and product assembly. Currently it takes 24 hours, on average, from the time a customer places an order until Fuji delivers that order. It used to take three days. Additionally, Fuji now uses one-third as many factory workers, keeps about one-third less inventory on hand, and produces three times the variety of products it did when it used a traditional system!

Fuji's experience demonstrates that, besides reducing labor costs by using automated equipment instead of labor, flexible manufacturing systems make factories more efficient

[3]Thomas A. Stewart, "Brace for Japan's Hot New Strategy," *Fortune*, September 21, 1992, 62ff.

by reducing setup times and overall production times. Producing each type of product doesn't require a separate production line; the same machines can be used to manufacture a greater assortment of products. Keep in mind, however, that although converting to a flexible manufacturing system reduces some costs, it may increase other costs, including equipment costs and any interest the company must pay on money borrowed to acquire the equipment. Managers must consider these cost tradeoffs when deciding whether to convert to a flexible system. We will discuss equipment purchase decisions (capital budgeting decisions) in Chapter 20.

Manufacturing Cells

Many companies have found that by reconfiguring the layouts of their factories, they can improve manufacturing efficiency. In a traditional factory, products move through the factory from process to process until they are completed. Typically, a company groups together, in an area of the factory called a department or process, those machines that perform similar tasks. For instance, a candy factory might have a pulverizing department, a mixing department, a refining department, a conching department, a tempering department, a molding department, and a packaging department. Specialized employees, assigned to a process or department, perform a specific task on each product that moves through that department or process. Other employees maintain the factory equipment and may even specialize in maintaining particular types of equipment. Products may travel a considerable distance across the factory to get from process to process.

When a company reconfigures its factory to use manufacturing cells, it moves its machines from processes or departments to *cells*. Each cell is responsible for manufacturing a specific product, or "family" of products, and is made up of the machines needed to manufacture that product or family. The company assigns workers to each cell and trains them to operate and maintain *all* the machines in the cell (a much more interesting job than just doing one particular task day after day). These employees also are responsible for making decisions about production in their cells (like whether to shut down production in the cell when a product flaw or defect is discovered)—decisions that production supervisors in a traditional factory typically make. Products move from machine to machine (process to process) within the cell until they are finished. Exhibit 18-3 shows how Unlimited Decadence might organize its factory under a traditional layout and one with manufacturing cells.

 How do you think Exhibit 18-3 would be different if the factory using manufacturing cells was a JIT factory?

Manufacturing cells are more efficient than the traditional factory layout because products don't have to travel as far to get from process to process. Labor costs may be reduced because employees are able to perform a greater variety of tasks. (There is less need for specialized employees who are limited to doing a few tasks, who do only those tasks when needed, and who may have idle time when their specialty is not needed.) Furthermore, employee morale may be better in a factory that uses manufacturing cells. Also, because of the employees' greater involvement in total production (including making decisions that traditionally would have been a manager's decision), employees take more pride in their work, tend to take "ownership" in their work, and are more inclined to do quality work.

Activity-Based Costing

In today's competitive world market, a company needs accurate and timely cost information to compete effectively. As we have been discussing, one way a company competes is by minimizing costs and inefficiencies in its operations. To do this, the company's managers must know which of its activities create value for its customers and which do not. Then they can manage costs by becoming more efficient in performing value-adding activities and by working to eliminate, or minimize, non-value-adding activities. Managing costs requires a

Is this a traditional factory layout or a manufacturing cell layout?

Exhibit 18-3   Unlimited Decadence: Traditional Factory vs. Manufacturing Cells

Traditional Factory

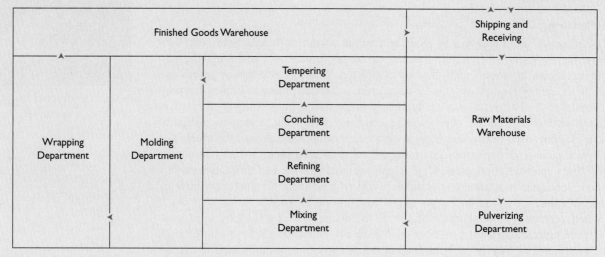

Factory with Manufacturing Cells

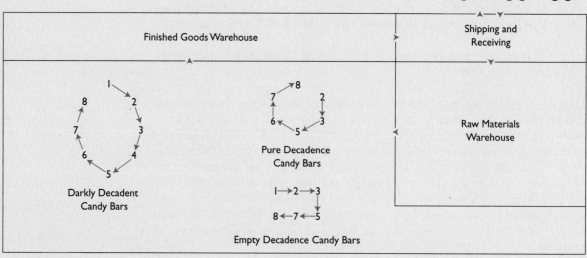

1 Pulverizing	4 Refining	7 Molding
2 Mixing	5 Conching	8 Wrapping
3 Refining	6 Tempering	

good understanding of which activities, or factors related to these activities, cause the company to incur costs.

For planning, operating, and evaluating decisions, the managers of a company need good estimates of product and service costs based on realistic assumptions. But as factories have become more automated, there are fewer direct labor costs and what appear to be more fixed factory overhead costs. Both job order costing and process costing, using direct labor hours or machine hours to allocate factory overhead costs, assume that all overhead costs result from one type of activity (such as direct labor or machine usage). But if you think about it, some overhead costs may have nothing to do with direct labor or machine usage. For example, air-conditioning costs may be more directly related to the number of cubic feet in the factory than they are related to either direct labor or machine usage. Numerous factors can cause a company to incur overhead costs, such as purchase orders, machine setups, inspections, and floor space occupied. So, more-traditional methods of determining product and service costs may no longer provide relevant information. Activity-based costing, however, enhances the results of job order costing and process costing by providing companies with more precise cost information that results from taking into account these numerous factors in the allocation of factory overhead.

A manufacturing company uses activity-based costing in conjunction with job order costing and process costing. Under both job order costing and process costing, a company allocates its factory overhead costs to individual units of product. Conventional job order costing and process costing both follow a multiple-stage overhead-allocation process that allocates overhead costs to jobs or processes, and then allocates the costs of jobs or processes to units of the product. A company using **activity-based costing** also follows a multiple-stage process to allocate factory overhead to units of product under either a job order cost accounting system or a process cost accounting system. However, as we will discuss in the next section, the first stage is different from that used in conventional costing. Furthermore, the stages are based on the assumption that many of the factory overhead costs (both fixed and variable overhead costs) that a company incurs are the result of activities not related to direct labor hours. (In fact, some of these costs may stay the same as direct labor hours increase or decrease, and so may *appear to be* fixed costs. Other costs may appear to vary with direct labor hours, perhaps because the company separated mixed costs into fixed and variable components by using direct labor hours as its measure of volume.) As you will see, this more realistic assumption provides a more precise measurement of the true cost of a manufactured product than does the assumption that all overhead costs *are* directly related to direct labor hours. Knowing the true cost of each of a company's products helps its managers make better decisions.

Three-Stage Allocation Process

In the first stage of activity-based costing, instead of allocating factory overhead costs to departments, a company allocates factory overhead costs to activity pools. Each **activity pool** is a grouping of related activities. For example, the company would accumulate the factory overhead costs related to purchasing raw materials in a pool for purchasing activities. The activities of purchasing raw materials include several sub-activities that involve locating suppliers, processing purchase orders, receiving shipments of inventory, transporting the newly-received inventory to the raw materials warehouse, and processing accounts payable related to the purchases. These activities cause the company to incur certain overhead costs, such as the salaries of the purchasing agents, dock receivers, materials handlers, and accounts payable clerks, the cost of supplies used in these activities, and depreciation of the forklifts that transport the materials. Similarly, the company would accumulate the costs of activities related to setting up equipment in a pool for machine setups; it would accumulate the costs of activities related to conducting inspections in a pool for quality inspections; and it would accumulate the costs of activities related to shipping merchandise to customers in a pool for order shipments. The activities on which the company bases these pools are often called **cost drivers** because they each drive, or cause the company to incur, certain overhead costs. The overhead costs the company allocates to each

5 *When a company uses activity-based costing, what three stages does it follow to allocate factory overhead costs to products?*

Exhibit 18-4 Examples of Cost Drivers

Number of direct labor hours	Number of machine hours
Number of purchase orders	Number of deliveries
Number of material movements	Number of inspections
Number of products reworked	Number of hours of training time
Number of employees	Number of part types
Number of square feet of floor space	Number of machine setups

activity pool are the costs incurred by the company as a result of engaging in the activities represented by the pool. Exhibit 18-4 lists some examples of cost drivers. As each cost driver (e.g., number of purchase orders, number of direct labor hours) increases, the company can expect its related costs in the cost pool to increase. So the costs in the cost pool are variable costs and vary in proportion to the increases or decreases in the cost driver.

In the second stage of activity-based costing, the company assigns the factory overhead costs accumulated in each activity pool to jobs (or processes) based on the relative number of activities (*driver units*) needed to complete the jobs (or processes). For example, if a company has only two processes, one needing three setups and the other needing seven setups, the company will allocate the total costs accumulated in the machine setup pool to the two processes in a three-to-seven ratio. So if the machine setup pool contains costs totaling $10,000, the company will allocate $3,000 (3/10 × $10,000) to the first process and $7,000 (7/10 × $10,000) to the second process.

In the third stage, the company assigns the total factory overhead costs allocated to each job (or process) equally to the individual units of product in the job (or process). So if each process in the above example had 500 units, the company would assign each unit in the first process a setup cost of $6 ($3,000 ÷ 500 units) and each unit in the second process a setup cost of $14 ($7,000 ÷ 500 units). Exhibit 18-5 illustrates the three-stage allocation process that Unlimited Decadence uses in activity-based costing.

Activity-Based Costing Computations

As we showed in Chapter 17, Unlimited Decadence uses direct labor hours as a means of allocating factory overhead costs to products. But direct labor hours don't drive all its overhead costs and probably don't reflect the amount of each activity used by different products. For instance, Unlimited Decadence uses 10 ingredients in its Darkly Decadent candy bars. In ordering these ingredients, it has to process 10 purchase orders (one for each ingredient). It has to process these purchase orders regardless of whether or not its factory is totally automated (whether or not it has *any* direct labor hours). The salaries of the employees who process these orders are considered to be indirect labor costs, which are part of factory overhead. So in this case, overhead costs should increase for each purchase order processed. If Unlimited Decadence's factory were totally automated, it could not allocate these factory overhead costs to its products based on direct labor hours because there would be no direct labor hours! But even if a company does have direct labor in its factory, if it uses direct labor hours to allocate all factory overhead costs to products, it may distort the individual costs (such as the costs of processing purchase orders) included in the total cost of each of its products. Here's how this can happen.

Suppose that Unlimited Decadence plans to produce and sell two products (the Darkly Decadent candy bar and the Pure Decadence candy bar) during the coming year. The production and sales volume of the Pure Decadence candy bar will be relatively low compared with that of the Darkly Decadent candy bar. Assume that the normal activity of Unlimited Decadence is a production volume of 5,000,000 cases of Darkly Decadent candy bars and 1,000,000 cases of Pure Decadence candy bars. Each case of Darkly Decadent candy bars takes 0.5 direct labor hours (DLH) to produce. Each case of Pure Decadence candy bars

Exhibit 18-5 Three-Stage Allocation Process Used by Unlimited Decadence for Activity-Based Costing

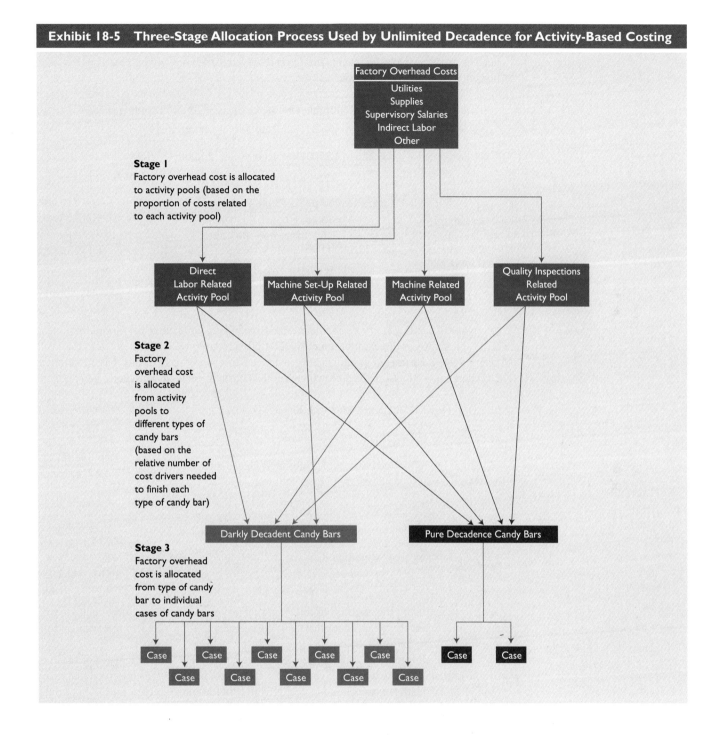

takes 0.75 direct labor hours. At normal activity, employees of Unlimited Decadence have to work 3,250,000 direct labor hours (DLH), computed as follows:

Darkly Decadent candy bars:	5,000,000 cases × 0.5 DLH	=	2,500,000 DLH
Pure Decadence candy bars:	1,000,000 cases × 0.75 DLH	=	750,000 DLH
Total direct labor hours			3,250,000 DLH

Assume Unlimited Decadence estimates that its variable factory overhead will be $0.64 per direct labor hour and its total fixed factory overhead costs will be $8,320,000 at its normal activity level.[4] If it uses direct labor hours as a basis for applying factory overhead costs to the two products, its *predetermined overhead rate* will be $3.20 per direct labor hour, computed as follows:

$$\begin{array}{ll} \text{Predetermined} \\ \text{Overhead Rate} \end{array} = \frac{\text{Total Variable Overhead Costs} + \text{Total Fixed Overhead Costs}}{\text{Total Direct Labor Hours}}$$

$$= \frac{\$0.64 \ (3{,}250{,}000 \ \text{DLH}) + \$8{,}320{,}000}{3{,}250{,}000 \ \text{DLH}}$$

$$= \frac{\$2{,}080{,}000 + \$8{,}320{,}000}{3{,}250{,}000 \ \text{DLH}}$$

$$= \frac{\$10{,}400{,}000}{3{,}250{,}000 \ \text{DLH}}$$

$$= \underline{\$3.20/\text{DLH}}$$

Note that this $3.20 rate includes $0.64 per direct labor hour of variable overhead costs and $2.56 per direct labor hour ($8,320,000/3,250,000 DLH) of fixed overhead costs. Using this $3.20 rate to assign factory overhead to each case of candy bars, Unlimited Decadence would assign the following overhead costs to each case of candy bars:

Darkly Decadent candy bars ($3.20×0.5 DLH): $1.60/case

Pure Decadence candy bars ($3.20×0.75 DLH): $2.40/case

So at its normal activity level, Unlimited Decadence would apply the total overhead costs to the two types of candy bars as follows:

Darkly Decadent candy bars...	($1.60 × 5,000,000 cases):	$ 8,000,000
Pure Decadence candy bars...	($2.40 × 1,000,000 cases):	2,400,000
Total factory overhead applied:		$10,400,000

However, using this method of allocating factory overhead costs to products doesn't take into account the effect that other activities—such as setups, machine hours, and inspections—have on overhead costs.

Suppose Unlimited Decadence decides to use activity-based costing to assign factory overhead costs to the two types of candy bars. It does so because it has observed that many of the factory overhead costs it incurs result from activities unrelated to direct labor hours. It has also observed that the proportion of these activities needed to produce the various candy bars is different than the proportion of direct labor hours needed to produce these candy bars. For example, the production of Pure Decadence candy bars is done in smaller batches than the Darkly Decadent candy bars. Therefore, production of Pure Decadence candy bars requires more machine setups than production of Darkly Decadent candy bars. Furthermore, since Pure Decadence candy bars are of higher quality, their production requires a longer use of the mixer, refiner, conche, and temperer machines. In addition, to ensure the higher quality, more inspections are made during the production process. As we

---

[4]The total factory overhead costs and the direct labor hours given here are different from those in Chapters 12 and 17 because there, for simplicity, we assumed that Unlimited Decadence was producing only one type of candy bar.

discuss later, activity-based costing is more expensive to use, but Unlimited Decadence's managers think that it will provide more-accurate overhead cost allocations to the two candy bars. Using activity-based costing, the managers will reexamine all of its overhead costs to see how it can better associate changes in these costs with various cost drivers. It may find that some overhead costs still vary with direct labor hours, that some costs vary with other cost drivers, and that some costs are still fixed.

For example, suppose that Unlimited Decadence identifies the following activity pools and their related cost drivers in total and for each type of candy bar (remember, Unlimited Decadence is producing five times as many cases of Darkly Decadent as Pure Decadence candy bars):

| Activity Pool/Cost Driver | Expected Number of Activities (Driver Units) | | |
	Darkly Decadent	Pure Decadence	Total Driver Units
Direct labor related activities/ *direct labor hours* (DLH)	2,500,000 DLH	750,000 DLH	3,250,000 DLH
Machine setup related activities/ *machine setups* (MS)	232,000 MS	568,000 MS	800,000 MS
Machine related activities/ *machine hours* (MH)	3,000,000 MH	1,000,000 MH	4,000,000 MH
Quality inspections related activities/ *inspections* (IN)	600,000 IN	400,000 IN	1,000,000 IN
General factory	(not associated with an identifiable cost driver)		

And suppose, also, that Unlimited Decadence has been able to trace $3,900,000 of its factory overhead costs (its previous $2,080,000 variable overhead costs and $1,820,000 of its previous fixed overhead costs) to these cost pools. It also has been able to determine the cost per activity (driver unit), as we show in the schedule at the bottom of this page.

Unlimited Decadence would allocate the $3,900,000 variable (traceable) overhead costs in the activity pools and the remaining $6,500,000 fixed overhead costs ($8,320,000 previous fixed overhead costs − $1,820,000) to the two types of candy bars, as we show in the schedule at the top of the next page.

Note that Unlimited Decadence calculated the variable overhead cost per case for each type of candy bar ($0.48 for the Darkly Decadent candy bar and $1.50 for the Pure Decadence candy bar) by dividing the total variable (traceable) overhead costs by the normal production of that candy bar. It determined the fixed overhead cost per case in the same manner as it had earlier. First, it calculated a $2 fixed overhead rate per direct labor hour by dividing the total remaining fixed overhead costs ($6,500,000) by the total direct labor hours (3,250,000). It then applied the overhead to each case of candy bars based on the number of direct labor hours needed to produce a case of each candy bar. Unlimited Decadence then

Activity Pool	(a) Traceable Costs	(b) Total Driver Units	(a) ÷ (b) Rate per Driver Unit
Direct labor related	$ 650,000	3,250,000	$0.20/DLH
Machine setup related	800,000	800,000	$1.00/MS
Machine related	1,320,000	4,000,000	$0.33/MH
Quality inspections related	1,130,000	1,000,000	$1.13/IN
Total variable (traceable) costs	$3,900,000		

	Darkly Decadent		Pure Decadence		Total Amount
	Driver Units	Amount	Driver Units	Amount	
Variable overhead:					
Direct labor related (at $0.20/DLH)	2,500,000 DLH	$ 500,000	750,000 DLH	$ 150,000	$ 650,000
Machine setup related (at $1.00/MS)	232,000 MS	232,000	568,000 MS	568,000	800,000
Machine related (at $0.33/MH)	3,000,000 MH	990,000	1,000,000 MH	330,000	1,320,000
Quality inspections related (at $1.13/IN)	600,000 IN	678,000	400,000 IN	452,000	1,130,000
Total variable overhead costs		$2,400,000		$1,500,000	$3,900,000
Variable overhead cost per case		$0.48[a]		$1.50[b]	
Fixed overhead cost per case		1.00[c]		1.50[d]	
Total overhead cost per case		$1.48		$3.00	

[a]$2,400,000 total variable overhead costs ÷ 5,000,000 cases of Darkly Decadent candy bars
[b]$1,500,000 total variable overhead costs ÷ 1,000,000 cases of Pure Decadence candy bars
[c]$6,500,000 fixed overhead costs ÷ 3,250,000 DLH = $2; $2 × 0.5 DLH
[d]$6,500,000 fixed overhead costs ÷ 3,250,000 DLH = $2; $2 × 0.75 DLH

added the $0.48 variable overhead cost per case and the $1.00 fixed overhead cost per case to determine the $1.48 total overhead cost per case for the Darkly Decadent candy bars. Thus, $1.48 is the *predetermined overhead rate* for each case of Darkly Decadent candy bars. It added the $1.50 variable overhead cost per case and the $1.50 fixed overhead cost per case to determine the $3.00 total overhead cost per case for the Pure Decadence candy bar. Thus, $3.00 is the *predetermined overhead rate* for each case of Pure Decadence candy bars.

So, using activity-based costing, Unlimited Decadence would apply $1.48 of factory overhead costs to each case of Darkly Decadent candy bars and $3.00 to each case of Pure Decadence candy bars, as follows:

Darkly Decadent candy bars ($1.48 × 5,000,000 cases) = $ 7,400,000
Pure Decadence candy bars ($3.00 × 1,000,000 cases) = 3,000,000
Total factory overhead applied = $10,400,000

Recall that, using only direct labor hours to allocate overhead costs, Unlimited Decadence allocated $1.60 of factory overhead costs (totaling $8,000,000) to each case of Darkly Decadent candy bars and $2.40 of factory overhead costs (totaling $2,400,000) to each case of Pure Decadence candy bars. Using activity-based costing has caused Unlimited Decadence to "rethink" the overhead costs of each of its products. As it expected, Unlimited Decadence has determined that some of its variable overhead costs continue to vary with direct labor hours, but that other variable overhead costs vary with the cost drivers of machine setups, machine hours, and quality inspections. It also has discovered that some of the overhead costs that it had assumed were fixed are instead variable costs.

For decision-making purposes, the managers of a company may express, for each activity pool, the total number of driver units required for each product on an "average per unit" basis. Thus, for instance, since the normal activity of Unlimited Decadence for Pure Decadence candy bars is 1,000,000 cases, these candy bars require the following average driver units per case for each activity pool:

Activity Pool	Average Number of Driver Units per Case
Direct labor related	0.75 DLH/case (750,000 total driver units ÷ 1,000,000 cases)
Machine setup related	0.568 MS/case (568,000 ÷ 1,000,000)
Machine related	1.00 MH/case (1,000,000 ÷ 1,000,000)
Quality inspections related	0.40 IN/case (400,000 ÷ 1,000,000)

If a company uses this approach, the managers determine its variable cost per unit of product by multiplying the average number of driver units per unit of product by the rate per driver unit for each activity pool. Unlimited Decadence would compute its $1.50 variable cost per case of Pure Decadence candy bars as follows:

Average Number of Driver Units per Case	Rate per Driver Unit	Variable Cost per Case
0.75 DLH	$0.20/DLH	$0.15
0.568 MS	1.00/MS	0.568
1.00 MH	0.33/MH	0.33
0.40 IN	1.13/IN	0.452
Variable cost per case		$1.50

This approach enables the managers to more easily see, for each activity pool, how a change in the average number of driver units per unit of product would affect the variable cost of that unit. For instance, if Unlimited Decadence increased its machine hours from 1 to 2 to produce a case of Pure Decadence candy bars, the variable cost per case for machine hours would increase from $0.33 (1 MH × $0.33) to $0.66 (2 MH × $0.33), and the total variable cost per case would increase to $1.83 ($1.50 + an additional $0.33).

 Does this make sense to you? Try this approach with the Darkly Decadent candy bars. Did you get $0.48 variable overhead cost per case?

For cost management purposes, the managers of a company may also periodically measure the average consumption (use) of cost driver units per unit of product. This measurement helps them assess the progress the company is making in its attempt to continuously improve the efficiency of manufacturing activities. For example, managing product quality by preventing product defects might reduce the need for frequent inspections, which might reduce costs. For Unlimited Decadence, reducing the number of inspections per case of Pure Decadence candy bars from 0.40 IN/case to 0.10 IN/case would reduce variable costs per case by $0.339 [(0.40 − 0.10) × $1.13] even though the cost per inspection would remain at $1.13.

Activity-Based Costing for Service Companies

In our discussion of activity-based costing so far, we focused on the assignment of factory overhead to the units manufactured in a manufacturing company. Service companies also have "overhead" and also may use activity-based costing to assign this overhead to the services that they provide. A service company that uses activity-based costing goes through the same three-stage allocation process that we discussed for a manufacturing company. Namely, a service company allocates its overhead costs to activity pools based on cost drivers, assigns the overhead costs accumulated in each pool to jobs based on the relative number of activities needed to complete the jobs, and assigns the total overhead costs in each job to the individual units in the job. However, a service company defines "overhead costs," "jobs," and "units" differently than does a manufacturing company. A service company might be, for instance, an auto repair shop, a bank, a hospital, or a CPA firm. Here, we briefly discuss the similarities and differences between the assignment of overhead for service companies and manufacturing companies, using these four service companies as examples.

In the first stage, a service company assigns its overhead costs to activity pools. But, what are its "overhead costs"? Some kinds of overhead costs are incurred by both service companies and manufacturing companies; for example, utilities, insurance, and depreciation. However, there are distinct differences in the cost elements of a service company as compared to a manufacturing company. Since a service company does not manufacture a product, it does not have direct materials and direct labor as we defined them for a manufacturing company. It may have materials directly related to providing the service, however. These might include auto repair parts, deposit slips, prescription drugs, or audit working papers. It will also have the labor that worked directly on the service provided to the customer. So, the wages and salaries paid to an auto mechanic, a teller, a nurse, or an auditor may be considered direct labor. As you can see, what one service company thinks is its "direct materials" and "direct labor" may be much different from that of another service company. As a result, since the remaining costs of operating a service company are its "overhead," these types of costs are also likely to differ from that of one service company to another. For instance, as significant overhead costs, an auto repair shop would have machine lubricant costs while a bank would have security costs. A hospital would have food costs, while a CPA firm would have secretarial costs. Hence, the overhead costs that service companies allocate to their activity pools are likely to be more heterogeneous than those of manufacturing companies.

A service company has some cost drivers that are similar to those of a manufacturing company. For instance, a service company might use the number of direct labor hours, employees, square feet of floor space, or hours of training time as its cost drivers. However, it might also use other cost drivers such as numbers of repair parts orders, checking accounts, patient days, or number of audit hours. Each service company must identify the cost drivers appropriate for its type of overhead activity.

In the second stage, a service company assigns the overhead costs in each activity pool to the jobs based on the relative number of activities used to complete each job. (Generally, service companies think of their operations as relating to discrete jobs rather than processes.) Here, jobs don't involve the manufacture of a product, but rather the completion of a service. For instance, for an auto repair shop, a job might be the replacement of an engine while for a bank, a job might involve granting a car loan to a customer. For a hospital, a job might involve surgery and hospital care for a patient while for a CPA firm, a job might be an audit "engagement." Whichever way a service company defines its jobs, it assigns its overhead costs in each activity pool to each job using that activity pool in proportion to the relative use of the activities by each job.

For example, suppose a hospital creates an activity pool for its general care activity, including costs such as maintenance, housekeeping, dietary, and laundry. Using patient days as the cost driver (because the costs in this pool tend to increase with the level of hospital occupancy), the hospital can calculate a predetermined overhead rate per patient day. Then, by multiplying that predetermined rate by the number of days individual patients stay in the hospital, the hospital can calculate and assign its general care costs to those patients in proportion to their length of stay.

The third stage of the overhead allocation process, where a service company assigns the total overhead costs for each job to the units in the job, generally is very simple. In most cases the job involves one customer, so the customer is the "unit." Therefore, the total overhead costs are assigned to the customer of the engine repair, the car loan, the surgery and hospital care, or the audit engagement. Although service companies may have more heterogeneous overhead costs than manufacturing companies, the objective is still the same in activity-based costing. The goal is to assign overhead costs to jobs in a fair and equitable manner.

Activity-Based Costing and Managers' Decisions

The more precise information provided by activity-based costing can help managers make better decisions. For instance, when managers add the total factory overhead cost per unit to the per-unit costs of direct materials and direct labor to determine the unit cost for a product, they have a better idea of the true product cost. This is because they were able to trace costs to the activities that affect these costs. With this more precise product cost information, managers can make better decisions about setting normal selling prices. Activity-based costing information also may be helpful for making better decisions about what price to charge a customer for a special order, whether to drop a product, whether to make or buy a part, whether to sell a product or process it further, and what to set as the product mix, as well as for making better decisions involving cost-volume-profit analysis.

6 *How does activity-based costing improve managers' decisions?*

In these decisions, however, managers must be careful in how they analyze costs. For instance, in some decisions, the *total* overhead cost per unit (variable overhead cost per unit + fixed overhead cost per unit) is not applicable because the fixed cost *per unit* depends on the production level. Under activity-based costing, Unlimited Decadence was able to identify—with several activity pools—some of what it had previously assumed were fixed overhead costs, so that these costs were recognized to be variable costs. This change reduced its total fixed overhead costs. The remaining fixed overhead costs, however, *still are fixed in total*. Therefore, the $1.00 fixed overhead cost per case of Darkly Decadent candy bars and the $1.50 fixed overhead cost per case of Pure Decadence candy bars apply only at Unlimited Decadence's normal activity level of 5,000,000 cases of Darkly Decadent candy bars and 1,000,000 cases of Pure Decadence candy bars. Furthermore, even if a company's production volume doesn't change, these per-unit costs may not be relevant for certain decisions. The point is that the managers of a company using activity-based costing make decisions in the same way that managers of other companies make decisions—by considering the *relevant* costs (both fixed and variable) and revenues that will change as a result of the decision, as we discussed in Chapter 15.

Let's consider the impact of activity-based costing on managers' decisions involving cost-volume-profit (C-V-P) analysis. In Chapter 11, in our discussion of C-V-P analysis, we said that in the coming year, Unlimited Decadence planned to produce and sell Darkly Decadent candy bars for $16 per case and Pure Decadence candy bars for $20 per case. The variable costs per case were $11 and $14, respectively. These variable costs included costs for direct materials, direct labor, and variable factory overhead (allocated based on direct labor hours), along with other nonmanufacturing variable costs. With contribution margins of $5 per case for Darkly Decadent candy bars and $6 per case for Pure Decadence candy bars, and with total fixed costs (both manufacturing and nonmanufacturing) of $24,800,000, we determined that when the sales mix was 5 cases of Darkly Decadent candy bars to 1 case of Pure Decadence candy bars, Unlimited Decadence would have to sell 4,000,000 cases of Darkly Decadent candy bars and 800,000 cases of Pure Decadence candy bars to break even, as we show in the schedule at the top of the next page.

The more precise overhead cost allocation of activity-based costing shifts $1,820,000 of the $24,800,000 total fixed cost to variable costs, decreasing the total fixed costs to $22,980,000. Thus, the variable costs for Darkly Decadent candy bars increase by $0.16 [$0.48 new variable overhead cost per unit − ($0.64 old variable overhead cost per DLH×0.5 DLH per unit)], from $11 to $11.16 per case, and the contribution margin decreases to $4.84 per case ($16 selling price − $11.16). The variable costs for Pure Decadence candy bars increase by $1.02 [$1.50 − ($0.64 × 0.75 DLH)], from $14 to $15.02 per case, and the contribution margin decreases to $4.98 per case ($20 selling price − $15.02).

If Unlimited Decadence recomputed the break-even point (assuming the same sales mix) using the variable costs and fixed costs determined by activity-based costing, its break-even sales volume would change, as follows:

Sales revenue:
    Cases of Darkly Decadent candy bars.. $64,000,000
        (4,000,000 cases @ $16 per case)
    Cases of Pure Decadence candy bars... 16,000,000
        (800,000 cases @ $20 per case)
Total sales revenue.. $80,000,000
Less: Variable costs:
    Cases of Darkly Decadent candy bars.. $44,000,000
        (4,000,000 cases @ $11 per case)
    Cases of Pure Decadence candy bars... 11,200,000
        (800,000 cases @ $14 per case)
Total variable cost.. (55,200,000)
Total contribution margin... $24,800,000
Less: Total fixed cost .... (24,800,000)
    Profit.. $ 0.00

$$\begin{array}{c} \text{Break-even point} \\ \text{(in "units")} \end{array} = \frac{\text{Total fixed costs}}{\text{Contribution margin per "unit"}}$$

$$= \frac{\$22,980,000}{(\$4.84 \times 5 \text{ cases}) + (\$4.98 \times 1 \text{ case})}$$

$$= \frac{\$22,980,000}{\$29.18}$$

$$= \underline{787,526} \text{ "units" (rounded up)}$$

Since there are five cases of Darkly Decadent candy bars and one case of Pure Decadence candy bars in every "unit" of sales mix, Unlimited Decadence would have to sell 3,937,630 cases of Darkly Decadent candy bars (787,526 × 5 cases) and 787,526 cases of Pure Decadence candy bars (787,526 × 1 case) to break even. In other words, with the current sales mix, sales price, and recomputed variable costs, contribution margins, and total fixed costs, Unlimited Decadence would have to sell less of each kind of candy bar in order to break even, as we show in the schedule below.

Sales revenue:
    Cases of Darkly Decadent candy bars.................................... $63,002,080
        (3,937,630 cases @ $16 per case)
    Cases of Pure Decadence candy bars...................................... 15,750,520
        (787,526 cases @ $20 per case)
Total sales revenue... $78,752,600
Less: Variable costs:
    Cases of Darkly Decadent candy bars.................................... $43,943,960[a]
        (3,937,630 cases @ $11.16 per case)
    Cases of Pure Decadence candy bars...................................... 11,828,640
        (787,526 cases @ $15.02 per case)
Total variable cost.. (55,772,600)
Total contribution margin $22,980,000
Less: Total fixed cost.. (22,980,000)
    Profit.. $ 0.00

[a]Rounded to balance, since we previously rounded the number of "units"

For Unlimited Decadence to achieve a desired pretax income of $5,400,000, using direct labor hours to allocate overhead costs, we determined in Chapter 11 that it would have to sell 4,870,970 cases of Darkly Decadent candy bars and 974,194 cases of Pure Decadence candy bars. However, using activity-based costing, Unlimited Decadence would have to sell 4,862,920 (972,584 × 5) cases of Darkly Decadent candy bars and 972,584 cases of Pure Decadence candy bars to earn $5,400,000 of pretax income, as follows:

$$\frac{\text{``Unit'' sales to earn \$5,400,000}}{\text{pretax income}} = \frac{\text{Total fixed costs + Desired pretax income}}{\text{Contribution margin per ``unit''}}$$

$$= \frac{\$22,980,000 + \$5,400,000}{\$29.18}$$

$$= \underline{972,584} \text{ ``units'' (rounded up)}$$

So, with the current sales mix, Unlimited Decadence would have to sell less of each kind of candy bar to earn its desired profit.

 Suppose Unlimited Decadence determined that it would have to sell more of each kind of candy bar to earn its desired profit. Do you think that should affect its decision about whether to use activity-based costing? Why or why not?

What if Unlimited Decadence decided to change its sales mix? Activity-based costing shows that the contribution margin is lower for both Darkly Decadent candy bars and Pure Decadence candy bars. However, the contribution margin for Pure Decadence candy bars is *significantly* lower (from $6 to $4.98) than Unlimited Decadence had planned when it had based its overhead allocation on direct labor hours. Therefore, Unlimited Decadence should carefully consider these decreased contribution margins when deciding whether to change its sales mix.

 How many cases of each type of candy bar do you think Unlimited Decadence would have to sell to earn a pretax income of $5,400,000 if its sales mix changed to 3 cases of Darkly Decadent candy bars for every 4 cases of Pure Decadence candy bars? Do you think Unlimited Decadence should try to achieve this sales mix? What other questions might you ask before you make this decision?

As we mentioned earlier, other management decisions of a company can be affected by the use of activity-based costing. For example, a switch to activity-based costing caused the automotive division of Slade Manufacturing to raise selling prices on some of its products.[5] This decision resulted in $1.2 million in additional revenues. Clearly, managers must know product costs in order to make these decisions. Keep in mind, however, that managers need to know more than product costs to make these decisions. As we discussed in Chapter 2, decision-makers should gather *all* the relevant facts before identifying and evaluating alternative solutions to problems and then making decisions. Consider the following decision about whether or not to try to meet a customer's expectations.

Business Issues and Values: Can Satisfying Customers Be a Bad Decision?

In our previous discussion about TQM, we said that companies with this philosophy fostered continuous improvement to meet or exceed their customers' expectations. However, there is a major difference between fostering continuous improvement to meet or exceed the expectations of the customers and meeting *unreasonable* demands of customers. After trimming down production to make its operations more efficient, a company must evaluate whether the revenues it will earn from satisfying its customers is greater than the costs

[5]Robin Cooper, Robert S. Kaplan, Lawrence S. Maisel, Eileen Morrissey, and Ronald M. Oehm, "From ABC to ABM," *Management Accounting*, November 1992, 55.

of meeting all its customers expectations, and then must decide whether to continue to try to meet these expectations. Remember, the overall goal of a company is to earn a profit, so decisions must be made with that in mind. Activity-based costing can help the managers of a company isolate which customers cannot be satisfied profitably.

But profit should not be the sole criterion for making a decision about a customer. For example, a company may want to retain a customer even though it may not be profitable to do so. If the customer is new, the company may think that satisfying this customer may lead to a long-term *profitable* relationship. Other unprofitable customers may provide other benefits to the company, such as leading-edge insights into technology or industry trends, or the ability to give the company credibility that helps it attract other customers. So with this additional information, the company should be able to evaluate the advantages and disadvantages of trying to keep this type of customer happy and should then make a decision.

Of course, the managers of a company can make good decisions only if they have good information to support those decisions. Consequently, each company should choose a cost accounting system that supports its information needs.

Choosing Which Cost Accounting System to Use

A company should choose the cost accounting system (job order costing, process costing, or one of these systems enhanced by activity-based costing) that best meets its particular needs. However, a cost accounting system can be expensive to set up and operate. For example, under activity-based costing, identifying cost drivers and allocating overhead costs to products based on these cost drivers can be both time-consuming and expensive. Thus, a company also must consider whether the benefits gained from the information that the accounting system communicates exceed the costs of getting that information. Many companies have chosen not to use activity-based costing because of the expense of obtaining the information they would need in operating that system. As you saw earlier, both the ability of a particular cost accounting system to provide needed information and the cost of operating that system depend largely on the way a company organizes its manufacturing operations and the nature and variety of the products it produces.

Modern manufacturing systems with features such as computer control of manufacturing operations, robotics, quickly adjustable multipurpose machinery, tight quality control, and minimum (if not zero) inventory levels present a challenge to management accountants because one cost accounting system alone may not suit a company's needs. Therefore, companies with such modern manufacturing operations may create hybrid costing systems by adapting many of the product costing techniques we described in this and previous chapters. Such systems might be described as partly job order costing systems, partly process costing systems, and partly activity-based costing systems. These companies also may develop new techniques. The important requirement is that a company's cost accounting system meet the information needs of its managers and employees.

Summary

At the beginning of the chapter we asked you several questions. During the chapter, we asked you to STOP and answer some other questions to build your knowledge about specific issues. Be sure you answered these additional questions. Below are the questions from the beginning of the chapter, with a brief summary of the key points relating to the answers. Use your creative and critical thinking skills to expand on these key points to develop more complete answers to the questions and to determine what other questions you have that might lead you to learn more about the issues.

1 How has the global economy caused companies to become more competitive?

Instead of just competing against companies in their own countries, companies must also compete against companies from other countries. The additional competition of the global economy has accelerated the rate of technological advances, allowing companies to produce and sell a wider assortment of products and services. Many of these products and services appeal to customers for shorter periods of time because more-advanced products and services soon capture their attention. Advances in communication and transportation have provided customers with worldwide product information and greater access to these products.

2 As part of its efforts to become more competitive, how can a company measure quality and the costs of quality?

A company can measure external failure costs by counting the number and measuring the costs of warranty repairs, product replacements, and product recalls. It can measure appraisal costs by counting the number of inspections and tests conducted, noting where in the production process they are conducted, and counting how many defects the inspectors and testers find. It also can measure the salaries of product inspectors and equipment testers, and the costs of materials used in the inspecting and testing processes. A company can measure internal failure costs by assessing the number of defective products reworked, the costs of reworking defective products, and the amount of time that the factory is "down" while employees trace and fix the cause of the product defects. It can measure prevention costs by tallying employee-training costs and equipment-maintenance costs, and by counting the numbers of employees trained, training seminars given, machines maintained, and maintenance orders taken.

3 How does just-in-time production help a company reduce its costs, operate more efficiently, and control quality?

A company using just-in-time production reduces its costs and operates more efficiently by minimizing inventory levels and, therefore, tying up less cash, floor space, and labor. It also minimizes the number of setup times. It controls quality by minimizing product defect rates. It accomplishes this by choosing, and closely working with, a supplier that emphasizes quality, by training its factory employees to detect product defects, by emphasizing regular equipment maintenance and ongoing defect prevention, and by taking advantage of advances in technology and improving factory layouts.

4 How have improved technology and factory layouts helped companies become more competitive?

Improvements in technology and factory layouts allow companies to manufacture higher-quality products and minimize their defect rates, and also to manufacture a wider variety of products at a lower cost than otherwise would be possible. Flexible manufacturing systems minimize setup and production times. Manufacturing cells minimize the time that products spend moving from process to process, and also minimize labor costs. These improvements allow companies to sell higher-quality products at lower prices.

5 When a company uses activity-based costing, what three stages does it follow to allocate factory overhead costs to products?

In the first stage, a company allocates its factory overhead costs to activity pools, or groupings of costs of related activities. In the second stage, it assigns the factory overhead costs accumulated in each activity pool to jobs or processes based on the relative number of activities (driver units) needed to complete the jobs or processes. In the third stage, the company assigns the total factory overhead costs allocated to each job or process equally to the individual units of product resulting from that job or process.

6 How does activity-based costing improve managers' decisions?

Activity-based costing helps managers better understand not only the behavior of a company's factory overhead costs, but also what company activities drive that behavior. So in making a decision, a manager can more precisely predict the cost effects of any particular decision alternative. Without activity-based costing, some costs may appear to be fixed and therefore managers may assume that these costs will not change from one decision alternative to another. Or, managers may assume that a variable cost varies with direct labor hours when, in reality, it does not. But when a company uses activity-based costing, managers see that some "fixed" costs, in fact, may vary with specific company activities and some variable costs may vary with some measure of volume other than direct labor hours. They also see that these costs may be different from one decision alternative to another. This insight helps managers make better decisions because they can better see the effects that different decision alternatives have on costs, and because they can better determine which costs are relevant for those decisions.

Key Terms

activity-based costing *(p.629)*

activity pool *(p. 629)*

appraisal costs *(p. 620)*

back-flush costing *(p. 623)*

cost drivers *(p. 629)*

external failure costs *(p. 620)*

flexible manufacturing systems *(p. 625)*

internal failure costs *(p. 621)*

ISO 9000 *(p. 619)*

just-in-time strategies *(p. 622)*

prevention costs *(p. 621)*

product defect rates *(p. 624)*

pull-through production *(p. 623)*

push-through production *(p. 623)*

total quality management (TQM) *(p. 619)*

SUMMARY SURFING

Here is an opportunity to gather information on the Internet about real-world issues related to the topics in this chapter. Go to http://www.dryden.com/account and click on the Cunningham, Nikolai, and Bazley book cover. Click on Summary Surfing, then click on this chapter number, and answer the following questions.

▶ Click on **AICPA.** Scroll down and click on *Center for Excellence in Financial Management*, then click on *Business Issues*. Click on Business Management. Then, under "Competitive Advantage," click on Implementing Just-in-Time Production Systems. How does the American Production and Inventory Control Society define JIT? Where else can a company use JIT besides in manufacturing?

▶ Click on **AICPA.** Scroll down and click on *Center for Excellence in Financial Management*, then click on *Business Issues*. Click on Business Management. Then, under "Activity-Based Management," click on Implementing Activity-Based Costing (ABC). Besides allowing a company to develop more accurate and relevant product, process, service, and activity costs, how else does ABC help a company improve operations? How do banks use ABC?

Integrated Business and Accounting Situations

Answer the Following Questions in Your Own Words

Testing Your Knowledge

18-1 List two strategies a company might use to make itself more competitive.
18-2 Briefly explain TQM.
18-3 What are external failure costs? Give two examples. What accounts might be used to keep track of these costs?
18-4 What is the relationship between appraisal costs and internal failure costs?
18-5 What are prevention costs, and what costs do they help minimize?
18-6 Explain the difference between push-through production and pull-through production.
18-7 Briefly explain how JIT production and inventory work.
18-8 Briefly explain how a flexible manufacturing system works.
18-9 Briefly explain how a company uses manufacturing cells.
18-10 Briefly explain the three stages of activity-based costing.
18-11 Briefly explain what is meant by a "cost driver" in activity-based costing.

Applying Your Knowledge

18-12 Curl-Up-and-Dry Corporation manufactures hair dryers, curling irons, and hot rollers. As part of its "new" image, Curl-Up is placing special emphasis on quality products. To initiate the company's quality-improvement program, Buzz Whitehair has gathered together the following list of items from the integrated accounting system related to quality and asked you to help him organize it so that he can determine what quality improvements to make. The following items relate to last month's activities:
(a) Scheduled maintenance performed on eight casing machines
(b) $31,545 paid to product inspectors
(c) 56 warranty repairs done
(d) $45,650 paid to employees in training
(e) Factory down 10 hours for unscheduled repairs after inspectors found product defects
(f) Raw materials costing $11,575 were used to repair recalled products
(g) Found 210 product defects
(h) Spent $500 on materials used in testing hair dryers
(i) Spent $310 shipping replacements for broken hair appliances still under warranty
(j) Held 12 training seminars around the country

Required: For each item in the list, indicate whether it is (a) an external failure cost or measure, (b) an appraisal cost or measure, (c) an internal failure cost or measure, or (d) a prevention cost or measure.

18-13 Thun Company produces two products, Tweeters and Woofers, and uses activity-based costing. The company's normal activity level is 100,000 units of Tweeters and 80,000 units of Woofers. It has developed the following "activity" information for these products.

Cost Drivers	Expected Number of Activities (Driver Units)		
	Tweeters	Woofers	Total
Purchase orders (PO)	60,000	30,000	90,000
Direct labor hours (DLH)	40,000	8,000	48,000

It has $76,800 of fixed factory overhead costs that are not associated with an identifiable cost driver. It traces its $188,400 total variable overhead costs to the following activity pools related to the previous cost drivers:

Activity Pool	Traceable Costs
Purchase related	$126,000
Direct labor related	62,400

Thun assigns its fixed factory overhead costs to units based on 48,000 direct labor hours. It takes 0.4 direct labor hours to produce a unit of Tweeters and 0.1 direct labor hours to produce a unit of Woofers.

Required: Determine Thun's total overhead cost per unit of each product.

18-14 Brandt Company uses activity-based costing. The company produces Flims and Flams (microscopic parts used in rocket engines), and its normal activity level is 40,000 cases of Flims and 100,000 cases of Flams. Brandt has $511,200 total factory overhead cost at this expected production volume. It traces its $341,200 total variable factory overhead costs to two activity pools as follows: direct labor related, $197,200; inspection related, $144,000. In regard to these activity pools, Brandt expects to use 68,000 direct labor hours (DLH), of which 8,000 are for Flims and 60,000 are for Flams. It expects the factory to conduct 80,000 inspections (IN), of which 20,000 are for Flims and 60,000 are for Flams.

Brandt has $170,000 of fixed factory overhead costs that are not traceable to an identifiable cost driver. It assigns these costs to cases based on 68,000 direct labor hours. It takes 0.2 direct labor hours to produce a case of Flims and 0.6 direct labor hours to produce a case of Flams.

Required: (1) Determine Brandt's total overhead cost per case of Flims and per case of Flams.

(2) Assuming Brandt produces 40,000 cases of Flims and 100,000 cases of Flams during the coming year, apply its factory overhead to each case of the products.

18-15 Demolition Derby produces two products, Igniters and Blasters, and its normal activity is 300,000 cartons of Igniters and 100,000 cartons of Blasters. It uses activity-based costing, and has developed the following "activity" information for these products.

Cost Drivers	Expected Number of Activities(Driver Units)		
	Igniters	**Blasters**	**Total**
Direct labor hours (DLH)	60,000	40,000	100,000
Square feet of floor space (SF)	600,000	200,000	800,000
Material moves (MM)	350,000	50,000	400,000

Demolition Derby has $300,000 of fixed factory overhead costs that are not associated with an identifiable cost driver. It traces its $1,100,000 total variable factory overhead costs to its activity pools related to the previous cost drivers as follows: direct labor related, $500,000; floor space related, $200,000; and material moves related, $400,000. Demolition Derby assigns its fixed factory overhead costs to cartons based on 100,000 direct labor hours. It takes 0.2 direct labor hours to produce a carton of Igniters and 0.4 direct labor hours to produce a carton of Blasters.

Required: (1) Determine Demolition Derby's total overhead cost per carton of each product.

(2) For each activity pool, determine the average driver units per carton of Blasters. Verify the total variable overhead cost per carton of Blasters, which you computed in (1).

18-16 Toga Toga Company produces two products, Greek Letters and Roman Numerals, and uses activity-based costing. The normal activity for Toga Toga Company is 400,000 sets of Greek Letters and 200,000 sets of Roman Numerals. It has developed the following partially completed schedules of "activity" information for these products:

Activity Pool	Traceable Cost	Total Driver Units	Rate per Driver Unit
Direct labor related	$ (a)	300,000 DLH	$2.00/DLH
Machine set-up related	300,000	600,000 MS	(b)
Purchase related	560,000	(c) PO	$1.40/PO
Total variable O/H costs	$ (d)		

Variable Overhead	Greek Letters Driver Units	Greek Letters Amount	Roman Numerals Driver Units	Roman Numerals Amount	Total Amount
$2.00/DLH	(e)	$480,000	(f)	$ (g)	$ (h)
$0.50/MS	500,000 MS	(i)	100,000 MS	50,000	300,000
$1.40/PO	300,000 PO	420,000	100,000 PO	140,000	560,000
Total variable O/H costs		$ (j)		$310,000	$ (k)
Variable overhead cost per set		$ (l)		$ (m)	
Fixed overhead cost per set		(n)		(o)	
Total overhead cost per set		$ (p)		$ (q)	

Toga Toga Company has $450,000 of fixed factory overhead costs that are not associated with an identifiable cost driver. It assigns its fixed factory overhead costs to sets based on 300,000 direct labor hours. It takes 0.6 direct labor hours to produce a set of Greek Letters and 0.3 direct labor hours to produce a set of Roman Numerals.

Required: Determine the missing amounts (a) through (q) in Toga Toga's schedules.

18-17 Color Me Pink Company produces two products, Crayons and Markers. Its normal activity is 600,000 boxes of Crayons and 200,000 boxes of Markers. Color Me Pink uses activity-based costing and has developed the following "activity" information for these products.

Cost Drivers	Expected Number of Activities (Driver Units) Crayons	Markers	Total
Machine hours (MH)	160,000	40,000	200,000
Direct labor hours (DLH)	300,000	160,000	460,000
Color changes (CC)	1,200,000	400,000	1,600,000

Color Me Pink traces its $2,585,000 total variable factory overhead costs to thefollowing activity pools:

Activity Pool	Traceable Costs
Machine hours related	$ 800,000
Direct labor related	345,000
Color change related	1,440,000

Color Me Pink has $920,000 of fixed factory overhead costs that are not traceable to an identifiable cost driver and assigns these costs to boxes based on 460,000 direct labor hours. It takes 0.5 direct labor hours to produce a box of Crayons and 0.8 direct labor hours to produce a box of Markers.

Required: (1) Determine Color Me Pink's total overhead cost per box of Crayons and per unit of Markers.
(2) For each activity pool, determine the average driver units per box of Markers. Verify the total variable overhead cost per box of Markers, which you computed in (1).

18-18 Blapp Company manufactures both Prangs and Floppers. It uses activity-based costing to assign its manufacturing costs, and has developed the following "normal activity" information related to its activity pools:

Product	Production (Units)
Prangs	500,000
Floppers	500,000

Driver Units (Expected Number of Activities)

	Cost Drivers			
Product	**Purchase Orders (PO)**	**Square Feet of Floor Space (FS)**	**Direct Labor Hours (DLH)**	**Reworks (R)**
Prangs	300,000	200,000	200,000	100,000
Floppers	150,000	200,000	300,000	150,000
Total driver units	450,000	400,000	500,000	250,000

Blapp has $2,925,000 of total factory overhead costs at its expected production volume. It traces its $2,325,000 total variable overhead costs to the activity pools related to the previous cost drivers as follows: purchase related, $450,000; floor space related, $1,200,000; direct labor related, $400,000; and rework related, $275,000. Blapp has $600,000 of fixed factory overhead costs that are not associated with an identifiable cost driver. It assigns these costs to units based on 500,000 direct labor hours. It takes 0.4 direct labor hours to produce a unit of Prangs and 0.6 direct labor hours to produce a unit of Floppers.

Required: (1) Determine Blapp's total overhead cost per unit of Prangs and per unit of Floppers.

(2) Assuming Blapp produces 500,000 Prangs and 500,000 Floppers during the coming year, apply its factory overhead to each unit of the products.

18-19 Rough Razor Company produces two types of razors, Cutters and Slicers, and uses activity-based costing. Rough Razor has a normal activity of 450,000 cases of Cutters and 600,000 cases of Slicers. It has developed the following "activity" information for these products.

	Expected Number of Activities (Driver Units)		
Cost Drivers	**Cutters**	**Slicers**	**Total**
Purchase orders (PO)	60,000	20,000	80,000
Machine setups (MS)	50,000	100,000	150,000
Inspections (IN)	20,000	80,000	100,000
Direct labor hours (DLH)	90,000	180,000	270,000

Rough Razor traces its $898,000 total variable overhead costs to the following activity pools related to the previous cost drivers:

Activity Pool	*Traceable Costs*
Purchase related	$336,000
Machine setup related	315,000
Inspection related	85,000
Direct labor related	162,000

Rough Razor has $405,000 of fixed factory overhead costs that are not associated with an identifiable cost driver. It assigns these costs to cases based on 270,000 direct labor hours. It takes 0.2 direct labor hours to produce a case of Cutters and 0.3 direct labor hours to produce a case of Slicers.

Required: Determine Rough Razor's total overhead cost per case of Cutters and per case of Slicers.

Making Evaluations

18-20 Refer to 18-12. Suppose that after helping Buzz organize his list, you get the following voice-mail message from Buzz: "Thanks for your help in organizing my list of quality items. You used four categories of costs and other measures of quality to organize the list, and I'm hoping you can help me figure out how to use these categories to help the company get the most 'bang' for its 'buck.' Curl-Up-and-Dry's annual budget meeting is coming up next month, and I want to be sure to balance the resources allocated to each of these categories to ensure the maximum quality improvement for the company. But it seems like the four categories you used are interrelated. When I go to the meeting, I want to recommend that we focus on, and allocate more money to, one of the four costs of quality. I also want to be able to justify my recommendation. Which category do you think we should focus on, and how will the focus on that one category affect the costs and other measures of quality in the other categories?"

Required: Write Buzz a memo outlining your recommendation and how you think the focus you recommend will affect the other costs and measures of quality.

18-21 Night Light Inc. manufactures a popular type of dorm room lamp. College students claim that this lamp, alone, has saved thousands of friendships because it allows one person to study with books and papers completely illuminated while other students sleep in blissful darkness. However, Night Light recently has suffered a public relations nightmare. Lately, it has experienced an unprecedented high number of warranty repairs and product recalls. And worse, because of the popularity of the lamp, the newspapers have been illuminating the public about this development. It seems no one has been left in the dark. After a lengthy investigation into the cause of the problem, a lightbulb went off in the production manager's head. It seems that a faulty part from a supplier had caused most of the warranty and recall problems. Dwight, the production manager (and also your cousin), has come to you for some consulting services.

Required: Write Dwight a memo recommending alternative courses of action that his company might take to get the product and the company's reputation turned around.

18-22 Jones Company has just asked Smith Company to sell it 100 Sprackets for $80 per unit. Smith normally sells Sprackets for $84 each. Smith produces and sells several products, and prices each product at 200% of the product's cost. Smith Company's cost of producing Sprackets under its traditional costing system is based on the following information:

Direct materials .... (4 parts @ $2.50 per part)
Direct labor... (2 DLH @ $12 per hour)
Total factory overhead .... ($4 per DLH)

Smith's controller says: "There is no way we can accept this order; it would not be profitable. We need to sell our products for at least 200% of our cost in order to cover our selling and administrative expenses, and earn a reasonable profit. We would earn only about 190% of our cost on this order." Smith's factory accountant says: "Yes, we should accept Jones' order. If we accept the order, we will make more than 200%."

Smith's factory accountants and engineers have been working on installing activity-based costing in its factory. Below are its variable factory overhead rates for the activity pools used in producing Sprackets.

Rate per Driver Unit	Average Driver Units per Spracket
Direct labor related (at $0.25/DLH)..............................	2 DLH
Machine setup related (at $0.40/setup)........................	4 setups
Quality inspections related (at $0.50/inspection)	3 inspections

Because Smith has identified more factory overhead costs as being variable under activity-based costing, each product has different variable costs per unit and its fixed overhead rate has been reduced from $2.10 per DLH to $0.80 per DLH.

Required: (1) Compute the cost per Spracket that Smith's controller must be using to justify his comment.

(2) Compute the cost per Spracket that Smith's factory accountant must be using to justify her comment.

(3) Discuss who is "right" and what accounts for the difference in the costs and selling prices per Spracket.

18-23 Fritz Company manufactures and sells various products. The president of Fritz comes to you (the chief factory accountant) with a concern. She says: "I am concerned about how well our Plappers are selling. Our Plappers are just as good as the next company's, but we are losing sales, and I've determined this is because our $130 selling price per unit is too high. But based on our cost accounting system, we have to sell our products at a gross profit of at least 40% of our selling price in order to cover our selling and administrative expenses. Based on the following costs from our system, we can't afford to reduce our selling price, so perhaps we should drop this product from our product line. Check this out for me."

Direct materials (2 parts at $5 per part)	$10
Direct labor (4 DLH at $14 per hour)	56
Total factory overhead ($3 per DLH)	12
Total cost per Plapper	$78

You have been working with engineers to design and implement activity-based costing in the company's factory. You have found that some factory overhead costs that you previously assumed were fixed are instead variable costs. Based on your findings, you have developed several activity pools and have found that each product has variable costs per unit different from what you previously assumed. The rate per driver unit and the average driver units per Plapper for each activity pool in regard to Fritz Company's variable factory overhead are as follows:

Rate per Driver Unit	Average Driver Units per Plapper
Direct labor related (at $0.50/DLH)	4 DLH
Material movement related (at $0.20/movement)	5 movements
Machine hours related (at $0.60/machine hour)	2 machine hours
Inspection related (at $0.40/inspection)	6 inspections

Under activity-based costing, Fritz Company's fixed factory overhead rate is reduced from $1 per direct labor hour (under the old costing system) to $0.60 per direct labor hour.

Required: (1) Based on Fritz Company's traditional costing approach, prove that it is earning a 40% gross profit rate on its sales of Plappers.

(2) Based on the new activity-based costing approach, determine what selling price Fritz Company could charge for Plappers to obtain its target gross profit. Write the president a short memo explaining your findings and making a recommendation.

18-24 Paller Metal Products uses activity-based costing and currently manufactures Component X for use in one of its products. Ople Company has approached the president of Paller with an offer to sell Component X to Paller at a price of $14 per unit for all the units that Paller needs in production. The units would be sold on credit (terms 2/10, n/30) to Paller and would be shipped from Ople's factory FOB shipping point, with the shipping costs being $0.75 per unit. The president sends you (the factory accountant) an e-mail that says:

I want to know whether or not to accept this offer. I have started to analyze our costs and have developed, based on our cost records, the following schedule for Component X (CompX). I don't know much about activity-based costing, so I didn't fill in the cost for the variable factory overhead.

CompX

Direct materials	$7
Direct labor (0.4 DLH × $15)	6
Variable factory overhead	?
Fixed factory overhead (0.4 DLH × $5)	2
Total Cost per Unit	$?

Analyze our costs to produce CompX, complete the schedule (showing supporting calculations), and make a recommendation to me as soon as possible.

Under its activity-based costing system, Paller allocates its variable factory overhead to activity pools. CompX goes through three of these activity pools. Paller's cost records indicate that the average driver units for CompX in each activity pool and the rate per driver unit are as follows:

Activity Pool/Cost Driver	Average Driver Units per CompX	Rate per Driver Unit
Direct labor related/Direct labor hours (DLH)	1.00 DLH	$0.50/DLH
Setup related/Number of setups (SU)	0.80 SU	$0.35/SU
Inspection related/Number of inspections (IN)	0.35 IN	$0.60/IN

You determine that Paller's total fixed factory overhead costs will not change if it discontinues manufacturing CompX.

Required: Prepare a memo to the president in response to his e-mail.

18-25 Yardguard Company manufactures and sells a variety of "home improvement" products. One product, a lawn mower, is in such high demand that the company has operated both of the departments it uses to produce mowers at the departments' maximum capacity for several years. The company expects to be able to sell all of the mowers it can produce for many years at $180 per mower. The major reason for the popularity of the Yardguard mower is its quiet and reliable engine. Engines are manufactured in Department A. Mower housing, engine mounting, and testing of the mowers take place in Department B. Yardguard uses activity-based costing to assign variable factory overhead to its products. Cost information relating to mower manufacturing in the two departments is as follows:

	Department A	Department B
Expected production	25,000 engines	25,000 mowers
Variable manufacturing costs per unit:		
Direct materials	$17	$21[a]
Direct labor	10	13
Variable factory overhead	?[b]	16
Fixed factory overhead	$24 per engine	$ 8 per mower
Selling and administrative costs		
Variable: $20 per mower sold		
Fixed: $300,000		

[a]Excluding engines
[b]Mowers go through three activity pools (purchase related, materials movement related, and inspection related) for the assignment of variable factory overhead in Department A. The rate per driver unit is $5 per purchase order, $3 per materials movement, and $2 per inspection. The average driver units per engine are 0.4 purchase orders, 1.0 materials movement, and 0.5 inspections.

Yardguard recently has been offered $75 per engine for 5,000 engines for the coming year and must decide whether or not to accept the offer. If the company accepts this offer, it will produce and sell only 20,000 mowers. In this case, the company's total fixed factory overhead costs for each department will not change. The controller of Yardguard has asked you, a management accountant for the company, to prepare an analysis of this offer.

Required: (1) Write the controller a memo that recommends whether or not to accept the offer for 5,000 engines. Include in the memo (a) a schedule of the pretax profit Yardguard would earn by *not* accepting the offer, and (b) a schedule of the pretax profit Yardguard would earn by accepting the offer.

(2) What minimum price per engine would make the offer acceptable?

18-26   Altus Company produces and sells two products, Hinkels and Quirts. During the coming year, its normal activity level of production is 400,000 cases of Hinkels and 100,000 cases of Quirts. Each case of Hinkels requires 0.6 DLH, and each case of Quirts requires 0.8 DLH. Altus has been budgeting and applying its factory overhead on the basis of 320,000 standard direct labor hours (DLH). Based on this activity level, Altus has computed its estimated total variable factory costs to be $1,280,000 and its total fixed factory overhead costs to be $1,520,000. Its standard costs for direct labor and direct materials for a case of each product are as follows:

	Hinkels	**Quirts**
Direct labor	$6	$ 8
Direct materials	5	10

At this activity level, Altus has no nonfactory variable costs, and it estimates its nonfactory fixed costs to be $2,000,000. Altus expects to sell each case of Hinkels for $21 and each case of Quirts for $30, and desires to earn a pretax income of $300,000.

Required: (1) Compute Altus Company's (a) variable factory overhead cost per direct labor hour and (b) fixed factory overhead cost per direct labor hour.

(2) Compute Altus Company's total cost per case of (a) Hinkels and (b) Quirts.

(3) Compute Altus Company's break-even point in "units" and in cases of Hinkels and Quirts.

(4) Compute the volume (in "units" and in cases of Hinkels and Quirts) that Altus Company must produce and sell to achieve its desired pretax income.

Now suppose that Altus Company uses activity-based costing to budget and apply its factory overhead at its normal activity level (400,000 cases of Hinkels and 100,000 cases of Quirts). Based on an analysis by its management accountants and engineers, Altus has identified several activity pools and their related cost drivers. It also has recognized that $1,000,000 of factory overhead costs that it previously considered to be fixed costs are variable costs. Thus, it traced its $2,280,000 total variable factory overhead costs to these cost pools and computed a rate per driver for each activity pool as follows:

Activity Pool/Cost Driver	Traceable Costs	Total Driver Units	Rate per Driver Unit
Purchase related/Purchase orders (PO)	$ 440,000	200,000	$2.20/PO
Material move related/Material moves (MM)	615,000	150,000	4.10/MM
Machine related/Machine hours (MH)	265,000	100,000	2.65/MH
Direct labor related/Direct labor hours (DLH)	960,000	320,000	3.00/DL
Total variable (traceable) costs	$2,280,000		

Altus has determined that at its normal activity level, Hinkels and Quirts will use the following number of driver units in each activity pool:

	Number of Driver Units	
Cost Driver	Hinkels	Quirts
PO	150,000	50,000
MM	110,000	40,000
MH	60,000	40,000
DLH	240,000	80,000

Altus has $520,000 fixed factory overheads that are not associated with an identifiable cost driver. It assigns these costs to cases based on 320,000 direct labor hours.

Required: (5) Using activity-based costing, determine Altus Company's total factory overhead cost per case of (a) Hinkels and (b) Quirts.

(6) Using activity-based costing, compute Altus Company's total cost per case of (a) Hinkels and (b) Quirts.

(7) Using activity-based costing, compute Altus Company's break-even point in "units" and in cases of Hinkels and Quirts.

(8) Using activity-based costing, compute the volume (in "units" and in cases of Hinkels and Quirts) that Altus Company must produce and sell to achieve its desired pretax income.

(9) Explain why Altus Company's total cost per case in (6) differs from that in (2).

(10) Explain why Altus Company's volumes needed to reach its break-even point and earn its desired pretax income in (7) and (8) are lower than the volumes needed to reach its break-even point and earn its desired pretax income in (3) and (4).

18-27 Jim Q is the president of Kluger Company, a medium-sized manufacturing company that sells a variety of products. The company has been in business for many years and has had a history of increasing production, sales, and profits. Jim's compensation arrangement states that he receives a salary plus a bonus based on the company's performance. The bonus is 10 percent of the amount by which the company's actual profit exceeds its target profit for the year. In computing its "profit," the company disregards income taxes and Jim's bonus. The company uses C-V-P analysis to determine the production and sales units needed to achieve its yearly target profit. The "units" that the company produces and sells are based on a constant product mix of all its products. The company also uses traditional flexible budgeting based on normal activity to determine its variable and fixed costs. During the past year, the company had a target profit of $1.2 million, based on estimated total fixed costs of $6 million, an estimated $0.60 contribution margin per unit, and a planned production (and sales) volume of 12 million units. During that year, its actual production (and sales) volume also was 12 million units. For the coming year, the company has used the same estimates, except that it has set its target profit at $1.8 million based on planned production (and sales) of 13 million units.

You are a management accountant who just started working for Kluger. You are knowledgeable about activity-based costing and have done some fairly extensive studies about the company's factory overhead. You have determined that many of the factory overhead costs that the company has always considered to be fixed do, in fact, vary with different cost drivers. You have set up several activity pools based on these cost drivers and, as a result of applying activity-based costing, have found a very high correlation between Kluger's estimated and actual variable factory overhead costs, as well as its estimated and actual fixed overhead costs, over the past several years. Based on these findings, you are confident that the company's contribution margin is $0.50 per unit and that its total fixed costs are $4 million.

One day, you meet Jim Q in the lunchroom and he says, "Do you have any ideas about how we can better manage our factory costs?" You respond that you would like to implement activity-based costing in the factory. He says: "I've studied activity-based costing, and I don't think it would help the company. Setting up all these activity pools is too much work, costs too much, and doesn't give us any better information than we had before. Let's just stay with the traditional flexible budgeting that we use now." You are surprised by Jim's response and go back to your office to think about what he said.

Required: (1) Draw a graph of Kluger's total estimated fixed costs and contribution margin for last year under traditional flexible budgeting (TFB). Label the lines on your graph.

(2) On the same graph that you drew in (1), draw Kluger's total estimated fixed costs and total contribution margin under activity-based costing (ABC). Label the new lines on your graph.

(3) Using the graph, briefly explain why Jim Q may prefer traditional flexible budgeting.

(4) How could Jim's compensation arrangement be changed so that he might be more receptive to implementing activity-based costing? Give an illustration for this past year and for the coming year.

18-28 Yesterday, you received the following letter for your advice column in the local paper:

Dear Dr. Decisive:

My sister and my best friend are dating, which has its good points and its bad points. One of the bad points is that sometimes I get caught in the middle of their disagreements. For example, last night, a newspaper article about a local manufacturing company started the most recent debate. According to the article, the company is losing competitive ground. The company has a traditional factory and, until recently, has been a leader in its industry. Since it is a mainstay of our community, its predicament has been the talk of the town.

Anyway, my sister and my best friend were trying to "solve" this company's problem, and started talking about TQM, JIT, flexible manufacturing systems, and manufacturing cells. My sister, who has always been fascinated by machinery and processes, said that a company that uses total quality management, flexible manufacturing systems, and manufacturing cells is using just-in-time manufacturing. In fact, she thinks they are all one and the same. My friend (who has never been in a factory in his life) says that a company can have total quality management, flexible manufacturing systems, and manufacturing cells and not be using just-in-time manufacturing.

Well, to get to the point, my problem is that I sided with my sister, and my best friend is acting like my *EX*-best friend. I think he'll come around, though, when he sees that you agree with my sister and me. Please hurry!!! My sister will always be my sister, but your answer may be just in time to save my friendship.

"Stuck in the Middle"

Required: Meet with your Dr. Decisive team and write a response to "Stuck in the Middle."

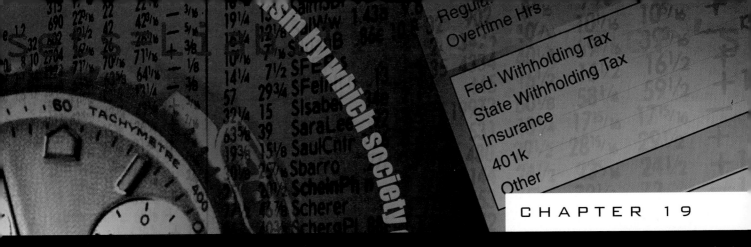

CHAPTER 19

REPORTING INVENTORY

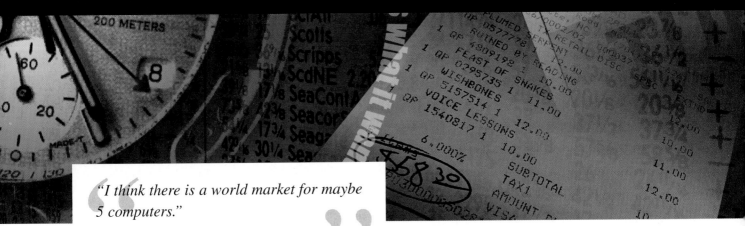

"I think there is a world market for maybe 5 computers."

—Thomas Watson, chairman of IBM, 1943

1 *How does a company determine the costs and amounts of inventory that it includes in the inventory reported on its balance sheet?*

2 *What alternative cost flow assumptions may a company use for determining its cost of goods sold and ending inventory?*

3 *How do alternative cost flow assumptions affect a company's financial statements?*

4 *How do a company's inventory and cost of goods sold disclosures help a user evaluate the company?*

5 *How does a company apply the lower-of-cost-or-market method to report the inventory on its balance sheet?*

6 *What methods may a company use to estimate its cost of goods sold and inventory?*

7 *How and why does a company report its operating cash flows under the indirect method on its cash flow statement?*

On Hershey Foods' (maker of Reese's Peanut Butter Cups) December 31, 1997 balance sheet, the company shows that it owns $506 million of inventory—15.3 percent of its total assets. On February 28, 1998, Rocky Mountain Chocolate Factory's balance sheet total for inventory was $2.6 million. Given that its total assets were about $19.9 million, 13.1 percent of Rocky Mountain's assets were inventory. These dollar amounts shown on Hershey Foods' and Rocky Mountain's balance sheets result from prior budgeting, purchasing, and inventory management decisions, as well as the accounting methods used to keep track of inventory.

Hershey Foods' $506 million in inventory is over 195 times greater than Rocky Mountain's $2.6 million. Can we conclude that Hershey manufactures about 195 times the amount of candy produced by Rocky Mountain? Why or why not? What factors besides the amounts on the balance sheets of the two companies should we consider?

A company uses the term **inventory** to describe its assets that are (1) ready for sale, (2) being produced for sale, or (3) ready for use in a production process. So when you walk into a Wal-Mart store, everything you see on the shelves, as well as the goods in the warehouse, is inventory. If you visited a Ford factory, the completed cars waiting for shipment, the partially completed cars on the production line, and the parts waiting to be added to the cars are inventory. So you can see that inventory is an important asset for both retail and manufacturing companies.

Retail companies often refer to their inventory as *merchandise inventory*. They purchase this inventory for resale from wholesalers or directly from manufacturers. As we discussed in earlier chapters, manufacturers have several types of inventory because they make their products. Their inventories include *raw materials inventory, goods-in-process inventory*, and *finished goods inventory*. Remember, merchandise inventory for a retailer and finished goods inventory for a manufacturer are essentially equivalent because they both are products ready to be sold to customers. For simplicity, in this chapter our inventory calculations use the merchandise inventory of a retailer, but in our evaluation discussion, we include both retail and manufacturing companies. As we discussed briefly in Chapter 7, a company reports inventory as a component of current assets on its balance sheet at the cost it incurred to buy or manufacture the inventory.

Does the fact that a company reports inventory at its historical cost affect the usefulness of this balance sheet information? How?

In previous chapters we discussed several issues regarding inventories. In Chapter 6, we discussed the differences between the perpetual and the periodic inventory systems. Recall that a company uses the **perpetual inventory system** to keep a continuous record of the cost of inventory on hand and the cost of inventory sold. It uses a **periodic inventory system** when it does *not* need to keep a continuous record of the inventory on hand and sold. Instead, it determines the inventory on hand by a physical count at the end of the accounting period.

In Chapter 9, we briefly discussed simple controls for the ordering, accepting, and storing of inventory. We also explained the specific identification method of accounting for inventory. Under the **specific identification method**, a company assigns a specific cost (what it paid for that specific unit) to each unit of inventory it sells and to each unit that it holds in its ending inventory.

In Chapters 15 through 18, we explained how a company's managers use accounting information to help them make decisions regarding inventory planning, inventory operations, and inventory control. The inventory planning issues we discussed for a manufacturing company included using relevant revenues and costs for making decisions such as whether to make or buy a product or part of a product, and whether to sell a product as is or process it further. The inventory operations issues involved using job order and process costing for manufactured inventory, as well as activity-based costing and just-in-time

Do you think this company is using the perpetual inventory system or the periodic inventory system? Why?

inventory systems. The inventory control issues dealt with standard costs and the use of variance analysis to control manufacturing operations. In this chapter, we explain how a company reports its inventory and cost of goods sold on the financial statements it includes in its annual report. We discuss how a company records the acquisition of inventory, computes cost of goods sold, records cost of goods sold, and related issues. We also describe how a company's inventory and cost of goods sold disclosures help external users assess the company's liquidity, profitability, and operating capability.

 If you prepared a personal balance sheet, what would you include as inventory? Why?

Reporting Inventory on the Balance Sheet

Let's assume that you decide to start a T-shirt business on campus and that you form a corporation with your parents and yourself as shareholders. You have an agreement with a wholesale company that will supply shirts with your designs printed on them. Now suppose you purchase 500 shirts with a special design on them to sell at the homecoming football game. You pay $6 per shirt but intend to sell them for $15 each. When you have the boxes of shirts, what value should you assign to them? Should it be $6 per shirt because that is what you paid for them? Or since you designed a creative homecoming message on the shirts, should the value be higher, say $10 a shirt? Or since you are very confident that you can sell all the shirts, is the $15 selling price the best value? Or because you have agreed to pay a commission of $1 per shirt to the students who sell them, is $14 a shirt perhaps best?

 Can you think of another value that might be appropriate? If you decide to use the cost, what costs in addition to the $6 cost of the shirt might you include in the cost of inventory?

The alternatives we considered in assigning a value to the inventory of shirts illustrate why managers and external users, in order to make informed business decisions, need to understand how a company accounts for and reports on its inventory. In our T-shirt example we did not apply any accounting rules to help decide what value to use. A company using GAAP, however, is required to base its inventory reporting on two accounting concepts we introduced earlier in the book—the *historical cost concept* and the *matching principle*. Let's review these concepts.

Recall that the historical cost concept states that a company records its transactions on the basis of the dollars exchanged (in other words, the cost) in the transaction. Once the company records a transaction, it usually retains the *cost* involved in the transaction in its accounting records. So your company would report the T-shirts at $6 per shirt under GAAP.

Some accounting and business experts express concerns about the usefulness of historical costs for inventory. They say, "Since the manufacturing activities of a company like Ford add value to the product, we should record that added value and report the inventory at an amount higher than the cost." In other words, they question the *relevance* of presenting this historical cost amount. Supporters of the historical cost concept argue that until the company has a transaction with a buyer at an agreed price, there is insufficient evidence to support any other value than the cost. They say, "Companies earn a profit by selling, not by manufacturing items or putting them on the shelves." So they argue that cost *is* the relevant value.

 To whom might the $15 selling price be relevant?

Supporters of historical cost also argue that the *reliability* of historical costs and GAAP's emphasis on *conservatism* (which we discuss later in the chapter) outweigh any potential increase in relevance that would be gained from using any other measure of value, such as the selling price.

In essence, GAAP supporters say: "If we report inventory at the selling price (or any amount above the cost), then we also have to record the profit before we sell the item—after all the balance sheet has to balance. But profit doesn't occur until we sell the inventory at a specified price. Everyone thinks they can sell their inventory at a desired price, but it doesn't always happen!"

 Which accounts do you think would be affected, and how would they be affected, if a company records its inventory at more than it paid for its inventory?

Until someone actually buys the T-shirt for $15, we are not sure how reliable that dollar amount is. Assume, for example, that you recorded the inventory in your records at $15 per shirt and that your parents, as investors, made a business decision based on your $15 estimate. Now suppose that on the day of the homecoming game, it rained and game attendance was low, so you decided to sell shirts for only $10 at halftime. Then your income would be $5 less per shirt. So, the company's investors would have been hurt by the estimate you recorded. With historical cost accounting, at least external users "know what they are getting." For example, if we polled ten accountants, all ten would conclude that the historical cost was $6 per shirt, and all ten would later report the same income and asset amounts. If a company recorded inventory at its selling price rather than at its historical cost, those same ten accountants would probably differ in their estimates of the selling price of the shirts, and would therefore report different income and asset amounts.

 Whose side do you take on this discussion—the supporters or the critics of the historical cost concept? Explain your position.

The matching principle states that to determine its net income for an accounting period, a company computes the total expenses involved in earning the revenues of the period and deducts them from the revenues earned in that period. Therefore, a company reports the inventory expense, usually known as **cost of goods sold**, in the period in which it sells the item and reports the revenue from the sale. For example, Unlimited Decadence reports the cost of the chocolates it sells to Sweet Temptations in the same period in which it reports the revenue from the sales.

So, the historical cost concept and the matching principle provide the basis for how a company accounts for inventory and reports it in the company's financial statements. In this chapter we will address five important issues: (1) computing the historical cost and the amount of inventory, (2) using alternative inventory cost flow assumptions, (3) using a company's inventory and cost of goods sold disclosures for evaluation, (4) using the lower-of-cost-or-market rule, and (5) estimating the cost of inventory and the cost of goods sold. In addition, since inventory is the last current asset of the operating cycle that we will discuss, we will revisit the cash flows from operating activities section of the cash flow statement.

Computing the Historical Cost and the Amount of Inventory

How does a company determine the costs and amounts of inventory that it includes in the inventory reported on its balance sheet?

The cost of each unit of inventory includes all the costs incurred to bring the item to its existing condition and location. Thus the cost of inventory includes the purchase price (less any purchases discounts), sales tax, applicable transportation costs, insurance, customs duties, and similar costs. When a cost, such as the cost of ordering the inventory, is difficult to associate with a particular inventory item, many companies record it as a general and administrative expense. A company determines the cost of each unit of inventory by reviewing the source documents (e.g., invoices) it uses to record the purchase of the inventory.

When a company takes a physical inventory, it counts the units of inventory in its stores and warehouses (and factories). The company also may own additional units of inventory that are in transit. **In transit** means that a freight company is in the process of delivering the

What do you think is the inventory in this picture?

inventory from the selling company to the buying company. The company (the buyer or the seller) that has economic control over the items in transit includes them in its inventory. Typically, economic control transfers at the same time legal ownership transfers.

A company may buy or sell inventory under terms of FOB (free on board) shipping point or FOB destination. **FOB shipping point** means that the selling company transfers ownership to the buyer at the place of sale (shipping point)—that is, *before* the inventory is in transit. The selling company excludes these items in transit from its inventory; the buying company includes them in its inventory. The buying company is responsible for any transportation costs incurred to deliver the items, and includes those costs as a cost of its inventory (rather than immediately recording them as an expense). **FOB destination** means that the selling company transfers ownership to the buyer at the place of delivery (after transit is completed). The selling company includes these items in transit in its inventory until delivery takes place; the buyer excludes them. In this case, the selling company is responsible for any transportation costs incurred to deliver the items and includes those costs in its selling expenses.

 Why do you think the selling company includes transportation costs on the income statement, whereas the buying company includes transportation costs on the balance sheet?

Using Alternative Inventory Cost Flow Assumptions

Once a company has determined the number of units in its ending inventory and the cost of the units it purchased during the period, it must determine how to allocate the total cost of these units (the cost of goods available for sale) between the ending inventory (balance sheet) and the cost of goods sold (income statement). The following diagram shows this relationship:

2 *What alternative cost flow assumptions may a company use for determining its cost of goods sold and ending inventory?*

| Cost of Beginning Inventory + Cost of Purchases (or Goods Manufactured) | = | Cost of Goods Available for Sale | = | Cost of Ending Inventory ⟶ Balance Sheet + Cost of Goods Sold ⟶ Income Statement |

If the cost of each unit of inventory is the same during the period, the company simply allocates these costs to ending inventory and cost of goods sold according to how many units it has left and how many it has sold. It is more difficult to determine which costs a company includes in the ending inventory and which costs it includes in the cost of goods sold when the costs it incurred to acquire the units changed during the period. Such changes are common in the current economic environment. GAAP allows a company to choose one of four alternative cost flow assumptions to allocate its cost of goods available for sale between ending inventory and cost of goods sold:

1. Specific identification

2. First-in, first-out (FIFO)

3. Average cost

4. Last-in, first-out (LIFO)

A company must disclose in its annual report the method it uses, and it must use that method consistently every year. Since we discussed the specific identification method in Chapter 6, in this chapter we will focus on the FIFO, average cost, and LIFO methods. We will discuss each of the methods for Granola Goodies Company, using the information in Exhibit 19-1. For simplicity, we use a month rather than the more common quarterly or annual accounting period used by actual companies.

The company has a beginning inventory (1,000 units) of $5,000 and makes two purchases (500 and 900 units) during January for a total cost of $8,150 ($2,750 + $5,400). During the month it sold 1,300 (400, 700, and 200) units. Therefore it must divide its cost of goods available for sale (for its 2,400 units available) of $13,150 ($5,000 + $8,150) between the 1,300 units it sold (the cost of goods sold) and its ending inventory of 1,100 units. For illustration purposes, we first assume that Granola Goodies Company uses the *perpetual inventory system.* (Later we will discuss how each of the cost flow assumptions is applied under the periodic inventory system.) Under the perpetual system, the company records the cost of goods sold each time it sells a unit, and updates its inventory account each time the physical inventory changes (each time it makes a purchase or a sale). Note that we assume the company makes only three sales during the month.

When the costs to acquire the inventory have changed during the period, each of the inventory cost flow assumptions produces different amounts for the cost of goods sold and the ending inventory balance. It is important to understand that these *cost* flow assumptions may *not* be related to the actual *physical* flow of the goods in inventory. Typically a company will use a FIFO physical flow of its inventory to reduce the risk of obsolescence, but may still use any of the cost flow assumptions to allocate its cost of goods available for sale between ending inventory and cost of goods sold.

Exhibit 19-1	**Granola Goodies Company: Inventory Information**	
Beginning inventory, January 1	1,000 units @ $5.00 per unit	$ 5,000
January 7 sale	(400) units	
January 12 purchase	500 units @ $5.50 per unit	2,750
January 20 sale	(700) units	
January 24 purchase	900 units @ $6.00 per unit	5,400
January 26 sale	(200) units	
Cost of goods available for sale		$13,150
Ending inventory, January 31	1,100 units	

Notes: 1. The units are sold for $13 per unit.
2. Granola Goodies Company uses the perpetual inventory system.
3. 2,400 (1,000 + 500 + 900) units are available for sale during January.

First-In, First-Out (Perpetual)

When a company uses the **first-in, first-out (FIFO)** cost flow assumption, it includes the *earliest (first)* costs it incurred in the cost of goods sold as it sells its products, leaving the *latest* costs in ending inventory. (In other words, the company *assumes* that it sells the inventory in the same order as it purchased it—*even if it may not actually sell the inventory in the same order.*) Under the FIFO cost flow assumption, Granola Goodies Company computes the cost of goods sold to be $6,650 and the ending inventory to be $6,500, as we show in Exhibit 19-2. The exhibit has two parts: the upper part shows a diagram of the "flow" of costs; the lower part shows schedules computing the cost of goods sold and the ending inventory.

The company sold 1,300 units. Using the FIFO cost flow assumption, the company moves the first costs it incurred into cost of goods sold first. The most recent costs it incurred remain in inventory. Therefore, the 400 units sold on January 7 have a cost of $5 per unit from the beginning inventory. After the sale, the cost of 600 units from the beginning inventory remain in inventory. On January 12, the company purchased 500 units at $5.50 per unit. For the January 20 sale of 700 units, 600 units have a cost of $5 per unit

---

Exhibit 19-2 Granola Goodies Company: First-In, First-Out Cost Flow Assumption (Perpetual Inventory System)

Diagram

		Inventory			Cost of Goods Sold	
	Units in Inventory	Cost per Unit	Total Cost of Units in Inventory	Units Sold	Cost per Unit	Total Cost of Units Sold
1/1 Beg. Inv.	1,000	@$5.00	= $5,000			
1/7 Sale	−400		(2,000)	400	@$5.00	= $2,000
	600	@$5.00	= $3,000			
1/12 Purchase	500	@$5.50	= 2,750			
	1,100		$5,750			
1/20 Sale	−600		(3,000)	600	@$5.00	= $3,000
	−100		(550)	100	@$5.50	= $ 550
	400	@$5.50	$2,200			
1/24 Purchase	900	@$6.00	= 5,400			
	1,300		$7,600			
1/26 Sale	−200	@$5.50	(1,100)	200	@$5.50	= $1,100
	1,100 {200	@$5.50	$6,500	1,300		$6,650
	900	@$6.00				

Schedules

Cost of Goods Sold (1,300 units):

January 7	400 units @ $5.00 per unit (from beginning inventory)	$2,000
January 20	700 units: 600 units @ $5.00 per unit (from beginning inventory)	3,000
	100 units @ $5.50 per unit (from January 12 purchase)	550
January 26	200 units @ $5.50 per unit (from January 12 purchase)	1,100
	1,300	$6,650

Ending Inventory (1,100 units):

Ending Inventory = Beginning Inventory + Purchases − Cost of Goods Sold
  $6,500   = $5,000   + $8,150   − $6,650

or

Ending Inventory = 200 units @ $5.50 per unit (from January 12 purchase) $1,100
        + 900 units @ $6.00 per unit (from January 24 purchase)   5,400
                                  $6,500

from the beginning inventory and 100 units have a cost of $5.50 from the January 12 purchase. After this sale, the cost of 400 units from the January 12 purchase remains in the Inventory account. On January 24, the company purchased 900 units at $6 per unit. For the January 26 sale, the 200 units have a cost of $5.50 from the January 12 purchase. This leaves the cost of the other 200 units from the January 12 purchase in the Inventory account. The cost of the ending inventory includes the cost of these 200 units remaining from the January 12 purchase ($1,100), as well as the cost of the 900 units the company purchased on January 24 ($5,400). So the total cost of the 1,100 units in ending inventory is $6,500.

Average Cost (Perpetual)

When a company uses the average cost flow assumption under the perpetual inventory system, it must compute an average cost per unit after each purchase and then assign this new average cost to items sold until the next purchase (when it computes another new average cost). This method is called the **moving average** cost flow assumption; because this method involves tedious calculations, we will not discuss it further. However, we will show the computations for the average cost method under the periodic inventory system later.

Last-In, First-Out (Perpetual)

When a company uses the **last-in, first-out (LIFO)** cost flow assumption, it includes the *latest (last)* costs it incurred before a sale in its cost of goods sold and the earliest costs (part or all of which are costs it incurred in previous periods) in ending inventory. (In other words, it *assumes* that the order in which it sells the inventory items is the reverse of the order in which it purchased them. Remember, however, that these *cost* assumptions are not necessarily the same as the actual *physical* flows of the inventory.) Under the LIFO cost flow assumption, Granola Goodies Company computes the cost of goods sold to be $6,950 and the ending inventory to be $6,200, as we show in Exhibit 19-3. Again, this exhibit has two parts: the upper part shows a diagram of the "flow" of costs; the lower part shows schedules computing the cost of goods sold and the ending inventory.

The company sold 1,300 units. Using the LIFO cost flow assumption, the company moves the most recent costs it incurred to purchase inventory into cost of goods sold first. The earliest costs it incurred remain in the Inventory account. The 400 units sold on January 7 have a cost of $5 per unit from the beginning inventory. On January 12, the company purchased 500 units at $5.50 per unit. For the January 20 sale of 700 units, the first 500 of these units have a cost of $5.50 per unit from the January 12 purchase, and the remaining 200 units have a cost of $5 from the beginning inventory. (Remember that we are *assuming* that the most recent units purchased are sold first, even though that may not be the case.) On January 24, the company purchased 900 units at $6 per unit. For the January 26 sale, the 200 units sold have a cost of $6 per unit from the January 24 purchase. The cost of the ending inventory, then, includes the cost of the remaining 700 units from the January 24 purchase and the cost of 400 units from January's beginning inventory. So, the total cost of the 1,100 units in ending inventory ($6,200) includes the cost of 400 units remaining from the beginning inventory ($2,000) plus the cost of 700 units remaining from the purchase on January 24 ($4,200).

First-In, First-Out (Periodic)

In the previous illustrations of inventory cost flow assumptions, we assumed the use of the *perpetual* inventory system. In that system, a company computes the cost of goods sold and the inventory balance as each sale is made. When a company uses the *periodic* inventory system, it first computes the cost of the inventory balance at the end of the period (by taking a physical inventory at the end of the period). It then computes the cost of goods sold at the end of the period by subtracting the cost of the ending inventory from the total cost of goods available for sale for the period.

Exhibit 19-3 Granola Goodies Company: Last-In, First-Out Cost Flow Assumption (Perpetual Inventory System)

Diagram

	Inventory			Cost of Goods Sold		
	Units in Inventory	Cost per Unit	Total Cost of Units in Inventory	Units Sold	Cost per Unit	Total Cost of Units Sold
1/1 Beg. Inv.	1,000	@$5.00	= $5,000			
1/7 Sale	−400		(2,000)	400	@$5.00	= $2,000
	600	@$5.00	= $3,000			
1/12 Purchase	500	@$5.50	= 2,750			
	1,100		$5,750			
1/20 Sale	−500		(2,750)	500	@$5.50	= $2,750
	−200		(1,000)	200	@$5.00	= $1,000
	400	@$5.00	$2,000			
1/24 Purchase	900	@$6.00	= 5,400			
	1,300		$7,400			
1/26 Sale	−200		(1,200)	200	@$6.00	= $1,200
	1,100 { 400	@$5.00	$6,200	1,300		$6,950
	700	@$6.00				

Schedules

Cost of Goods Sold (1,300 units):

January 7	400 units @ $5.00 per unit (from beginning inventory)	$2,000
January 20	700 units: 500 units @ $5.50 (from January 12 purchase)	2,750
	200 units @ $5.00 (from beginning inventory)	1,000
January 26	200 units @ $6.00 per unit (from January 24 purchase)	1,200
	1,300	$6,950

Ending Inventory (1,100 units):

Ending Inventory = Beginning Inventory + Purchases − Cost of Goods Sold
  $6,200 = $5,000 + $8,150 − $6,950

or

Ending Inventory = 700 units @ $6.00 per unit (from January 24 purchase) $4,200
        + 400 units @ $5.00 per unit (from beginning inventory) 2,000
                              $6,200

Using the FIFO cost flow assumption, the company includes the earliest (first) costs it incurred in cost of goods sold. The most recent (last) costs it incurred remain in ending inventory. On January 31, Granola Goodies Company has an ending inventory of 1,100 units. As we show in Exhibit 19-4, the company computes the cost of the 1,100 units in the ending inventory to be $6,500, consisting of the most recent costs incurred, which are the cost of the 900 units from the January 24 purchase ($5,400) and the cost of 200 units from the January 12 purchase ($1,100). It computes the $6,650 cost of goods sold by subtracting the $6,500 ending inventory from the $13,150 ($5,000 + $8,150) cost of goods available for sale. The cost of goods sold (for the 1,300 units sold) includes the earliest costs— the cost of the 1,000 units in beginning inventory ($5,000) plus the cost of 300 units from the January 12 purchase ($1,650). Note that, when the company uses FIFO, the cost of goods sold and the cost of the ending inventory are the same amounts under both the perpetual and periodic inventory systems, as we show in Exhibits 19-2 and 19-4. This will always be true when a company uses FIFO because it always includes in the ending inventory the latest costs that it incurred to acquire inventory.

Exhibit 19-4   Granola Goodies Company: First-In, First-Out Cost Flow Assumption (Periodic Inventory System)

Inventory Information

Beginning inventory, January 1	1,000 units @ $5.00 per unit	$ 5,000
January 12 purchase	500 units @ $5.50 per unit	2,750
January 24 purchase	900 units @ $6.00 per unit	5,400
Cost of goods available for sale in January	2,400 units	$13,150
Sales during January	(1,300) units	
Ending inventory, January 31	1,100 units	

Calculations

Ending Inventory (1,100 units):

900 units @ $6.00 per unit (from January 24 purchase)	$5,400
200 units @ $5.50 per unit (from January 12 purchase)	1,100
1,100	$6,500

Cost of Goods Sold (1,300 units):

Cost of Goods Sold = Beginning Inventory + Purchases − Ending Inventory
$6,650   = $5,000   + $8,150 − $6,500

or

Cost of Goods Sold = 1,000 units @ $5.00 per unit (from beginning inventory)	$5,000
+300 units @ $5.50 per unit (from January 12 purchase)	1,650
	$6,650

Average Cost (Periodic)

When a company uses the **average cost** flow assumption, it allocates the average cost per unit for the period to both the ending inventory and the cost of goods sold. That is, it combines the costs of all the units available for sale, computes the average cost, and assigns the resulting average cost to the units in both the ending inventory and the cost of goods sold. As we show in Exhibit 19-5, Granola Goodies Company computes its average cost per unit of $5.48 (rounded) by dividing the total cost of goods available for sale ($13,150) by the number of units available for sale during the period (2,400, which includes the 1,000 units in the beginning inventory plus the 1,400 units purchased).

The company computes the ending inventory balance to be $6,028 for the 1,100 units remaining on hand at the average cost of $5.48 per unit and computes the cost of goods sold as $7,122, which includes the 1,300 units sold at the average cost of $5.48 per unit (adjusted for a $2 rounding error).

Last-In, First-Out (Periodic)

Using the LIFO cost flow assumption, the company includes the most recent (last) costs it incurred in cost of goods sold. The earliest (first) costs it incurred remain in ending inventory. Granola Goodies Company has an ending inventory of 1,100 units. As we show in Exhibit 19-6, under LIFO, the company computes the cost of the 1,100 units in ending inventory to be $5,550, consisting of the earliest costs incurred, which are the cost of the entire beginning inventory ($5,000) and the cost of 100 units from the January 12 purchase ($550). It computes the $7,600 cost of goods sold by subtracting the $5,550 ending inventory from the $13,150 cost of goods available for sale. The $7,600 cost of goods sold (for the 1,300 units sold) includes the latest costs—the cost of the units from the January 24 purchase ($5,400) and the cost of 400 units from the January 12 purchase ($2,200).

Note that the cost of goods sold and the ending inventory under the LIFO perpetual method ($6,950 and $6,200, as we show in Exhibit 19-3) differ from those under the LIFO

Exhibit 19-5 Granola Goodies Company: Average Cost Flow Assumption (Periodic Inventory System)

Average Cost per Unit = Cost of Goods Available for Sale ÷ Number of Units Available for Sale
= $13,150 ÷ 2,400
= $5.48 per Unit (rounded)

Ending Inventory (1,100 units):

Ending Inventory = Number of Units × Average Cost per Unit
= 1,100 × $5.48
= $6,028

Cost of Goods Sold (1,300 units):

Cost of Goods Sold = Beginning Inventory + Purchases − Ending Inventory
$7,122 = $5,000 + $8,150 − $6,028

or

Cost of Goods Sold = Number of Units Sold × Average Cost per Unit
= 1,300 × $5.48 = $7,122 (adjusted for $2 rounding error)

Exhibit 19-6 Granola Goodies Company: Last-In, First-Out Cost Flow Assumption (Periodic Inventory System)

Ending Inventory (1,100 units):

1,000 units @ $5.00 per unit (from beginning inventory) $5,000
100 units @ $5.50 per unit (from January 12 purchase)... 550
1,100 .... $5,550

Cost of Goods Sold (1,300 units):

Cost of Goods Sold = Beginning Inventory + Purchases − Ending Inventory
$7,600 = $5,000 + $8,150 − $5,550

or

Cost of Goods Sold = 900 units @ $6.00 per unit (from January 24 purchase)................................ $5,400
+400 units @ $5.50 per unit (from January 12 purchase)................................ 2,200
$7,600

periodic method ($7,600 and $5,550, as we show in Exhibit 19-6). The differences result from the assumptions each makes about the timing of the sales. Under the perpetual system, the company computes the cost of goods sold when each sale is made and therefore includes the cost(s) of the *most recent purchase(s) at that time*. Under the periodic system, the company treats the whole accounting period (a month in this example) as a single unit, and assumes that all the sales are made after all the purchases. Under this assumption, it computes the cost of goods sold after recording the cost of all the units purchased during the period. Therefore, the cost of goods sold always includes the costs of the *latest purchases of the period*. For example, Granola Goodies' first sale occurs on January 7, and under the *perpetual* system the company assumes that the cost of goods sold for those units is taken from the beginning inventory of $5.00 per unit since that is the only inventory on hand at the time of the sale. Under the *periodic* system, however, since the number of units purchased exceeds the number of units sold for the month, the company includes none of the cost of the beginning inventory in the cost of goods sold. Instead, it takes the cost of the 1,300 units sold from the cost of the most recent purchases (January 24 and January 12) of the period.

 Do you think a large retail company could apply the average or the LIFO cost flow assumption under the perpetual inventory method? Why or why not?

Additional Periodic Illustration

Exhibit 19-7 continues the Granola Goodies Company *periodic* inventory system example through February so that we can give you another illustration of the differences between FIFO and LIFO. It is important to note that the beginning inventory for February is the ending inventory for January and that, therefore, the amounts for the two cost flow assumptions differ. The calculations otherwise follow the same procedures as for January.

Effects of the Three Alternatives

3 *How do alternative cost flow assumptions affect a company's financial statements?*

As you just saw, the FIFO, average, and LIFO cost flow assumptions affect a company's financial statements differently. We will discuss the advantages and disadvantages of these assumptions in this section.

Effects on the Financial Statements

The choice made by managers to adopt the FIFO, the average, or the LIFO cost flow assumption affects both the income statement and the balance sheet. If costs are *rising*, cost of goods sold is lower under FIFO because the first costs moved into cost of goods sold are the earliest (lower) costs. Since cost of goods sold is lower, gross profit (sales − cost of goods sold) is higher and net income is higher. Under LIFO, the most recent (higher) costs are moved into cost of goods sold first, making it higher than the cost of goods sold under FIFO. Therefore, the gross profit and net income under LIFO are lower than under FIFO. If costs are *falling,* the relationships between FIFO and LIFO are reversed. In both cases the average cost amounts are between those of FIFO and LIFO. Using the Granola Goodies Company example, the following comparative ending inventory and gross profit figures result from selling 1,300 units for $16,900 in *January* (assuming a selling price of $13 per unit and the use of the periodic system):

	FIFO		**Average Cost**		**LIFO**	
Sales		$16,900		$16,900		$16,900
Cost of goods available for sale	$13,150		$13,150		$13,150	
Ending inventory	(6,500)		(6,028)		(5,550)	
Cost of goods sold		(6,650)		(7,122)		(7,600)
Gross profit		$10,250		$ 9,778		$ 9,300

Since Granola Goodies is experiencing rising costs, you can see that under FIFO, its ending inventory is highest, its cost of goods sold is lowest, and therefore its gross profit is highest. In contrast, LIFO results in the lowest ending inventory, the highest cost of goods sold, and therefore the lowest gross profit. It is often said that FIFO takes a balance sheet approach by reporting the inventory at the cost of its most recent purchases, a cost that is close to its replacement cost. The **replacement cost** is the cost (including any transportation costs ordinarily incurred) that a company would have to pay at the balance sheet date to purchase (replace) an item of inventory (based on purchasing inventory in normal quantities from the usual suppliers). Although FIFO reports ending inventory at close to replacement cost, it understates cost of goods sold when costs are rising because cost of goods sold is *not* close to the amount the company paid for its most recent purchases. In contrast, since LIFO includes the most recent costs in cost of goods sold first, it takes an

> ### Exhibit 19-7   Granola Goodies Company: Ending Inventory and Cost of Goods Sold for February (Periodic Inventory System)

Additional Information

Beginning Inventory, February 1	1,100 units	
February 7 purchase	400 units @ $6.20 per unit	$2,480
February 19 purchase	800 units @ $6.40 per unit	$5,120
Units available for sale	2,300 units	
Ending inventory, February 28	(1,300) units	
Sales during February	1,000 units	

First-In, First-Out

Beginning Inventory = 200 units @ $5.50 per unit + 900 units @ $6.00 per unit (from Exhibit 19-4)
= $6,500

Ending Inventory	= 800 units @ $6.40 per unit	$5,120
	+400 units @ $6.20 per unit	2,480
	+100 units @ $6.00 per unit	600
	=1,300 units	$8,200

Cost of Goods Sold = Beginning Inventory + Purchases − Ending Inventory
= $6,500 + $7,600 (i.e., $2,480 + $5,120) − $8,200
= $5,900

or

Cost of Goods Sold = 200 units @ $5.50 per unit (from beginning inventory)	$1,100
800 units @ $6.00 per unit (from beginning inventory)	4,480
	$5,900

Last-In, First-Out

Beginning Inventory = 1,000 units @ $5.00 per unit + 100 units @ $5.50 per unit (from Exhibit 19-6)
= $5,550

Ending Inventory	= 1,000 units @ $5.00 per unit	$5,000
	+100 units @ $5.50 per unit	550
	+200 units @ $6.20 per unit	1,240
	= 1,300 units	$6,790

Cost of Goods Sold = Beginning Inventory + Purchases − Ending Inventory
= $5,550 + $7,600 − $6,790
= $6,360

or

Cost of Goods Sold = 800 units @ $6.40 per unit (from February 19 purchase)	$5,120
200 units @ $6.20 per unit (from January 12 purchase)	1,240
	$6,360

income statement approach by matching the most recent costs against revenues. However LIFO understates ending inventory because the cost of the ending inventory is *not* close to the amount the company paid for its most recent purchases.

Note that we made a simplifying assumption in the Granola Goodies Company example for January and that this assumption has made the differences less than they might otherwise be. We assumed that the beginning inventory consisted of 1,000 units at $5 under all three methods. Recall, however, that the beginning inventory of the period is the ending inventory of the previous period. Therefore the use of each method in the previous period (assuming costs changed) means that the beginning inventory would differ under each of the alternatives, just as the ending inventory for January differs under each method. You can see this relationship in the calculations for February (Exhibit 19-7), in which the beginning inventory is different in all three situations. This factor can become very significant when a company uses the LIFO cost flow assumption. If the number of units in a company's inventory increases during each period, it carries over the costs in the beginning inventory for each period. Therefore, a company using LIFO builds up *layers* of costs in its inventory.

To understand this, look back at Exhibit 19-7. The February ending LIFO inventory for Granola Goodies of $6,790 includes three layers of cost: $5, $5.50, and $6.20 per unit. As years pass, however, these costs will become very outdated. For example, many companies adopted LIFO in the late 1930s and others during the period of high inflation in the middle of the 1970s. The inventories they report in today's balance sheets include elements of costs from many years ago that usually bear little or no relationship to the costs of the current period or to the costs that will be incurred to replace the inventory. Therefore, users say that the LIFO inventory cost in the balance sheet is *not relevant*.

 Do you think the LIFO cost of goods sold is relevant? Why or why not?

Income Measurement

At this point, you may be having some difficulty understanding LIFO. It may seem to be a counter-intuitive method, and we have just said that the LIFO inventory cost in the balance sheet is not relevant. So the next issue is very important. Many users of financial statements argue that LIFO results in a better measure of income when costs are rising. To understand this point, consider Granola Goodies Company in *January*. If the company uses the FIFO method (perpetual inventory system), it will be selling units for $13 and, for 1,100 of the units, recording cost of goods sold of $5 per unit and a gross profit of $8 per unit during January. The company has to replace the inventory during the month by paying $5.50 or $6 per unit, however, so the company must use $.50 or $1 more of the gross profit to buy the replacement units of this inventory. Therefore, only $7.50 or $7 represents the real gross profit of Granola Goodies Company (the amount of the gross profit that is left to cover the company's operating costs after it replaces the inventory it sold). A **holding gain** (or **inventory profit**) is the artificial profit that results when a company records cost of goods sold at an historical cost that is lower than the replacement cost of the units sold. In this example, the holding gain is $.50 or $1 per unit sold. Since the holding gain cannot be distributed to the owners as dividends without reducing the ability of the company to replace the units of inventory sold, many users argue that the holding gain should be excluded from the calculation of income.

 Why do you think inventory profit is called a "holding gain"?

Impact of Tax Rules

Why would the managers of a company select LIFO for financial reporting when it results in lower reported income? *If the company is a corporation, LIFO is allowed for income tax purposes only if LIFO is also used for the financial statements.* (Any of the other methods may be used for calculating corporate taxable income, regardless of which method is used for financial reporting.) And why would managers of a company select LIFO for income tax purposes? If we assume rising costs, the use of LIFO results in lower taxable income (because of higher cost of goods sold) and consequently in the payment of less income taxes. For instance, according to their recent annual reports, three major U.S. companies—General Motors, Ford, and General Electric—have together saved around $1.9 billion in taxes by using LIFO instead of FIFO. This tax saving is a very strong, practical argument in favor of LIFO because companies using LIFO avoid cash payments for income taxes and therefore have more cash available than they otherwise would for such things as paying employees, investing in property and equipment, reducing liabilities, or paying dividends.

www.gm.com
www2.ford.com
www.ge.com

 Do you think you pay less when you purchase a car because the manufacturer uses LIFO?

Managers' Selection of an Inventory Cost Flow Assumption

If the managers of a company expect that the costs of acquiring inventory will increase in the future, then we should expect them to select LIFO because of the lower income taxes that the company will have to pay. Of course, the income the company reports in its financial statements also will be lower. Reporting a lower income, however, does not mean that the company's stock price goes down. There is much evidence that investors understand how LIFO affects net income and that the stock price of a company is *not* lower because the company reports a lower income under LIFO. Instead, the stock price should be higher because the company pays less taxes. Alternatively, if the managers expect that the costs of acquiring inventory will *decrease* in the future, then we should expect them to select FIFO or average cost because the company would again pay lower income taxes.

Although the managers are able to select one of the four (including specific identification) cost flow assumptions to account for a company's inventory, once they make the selection, they are required by GAAP to consistently apply that method from period to period. If the managers make a change, they must disclose the effects of the change (the difference between what net income would have been under the old method, and what it is under the new method) in the company's annual report. Managers also may select more than one method by using a different cost flow assumption for different types of inventory. For example, if a retail company is selling clothing that has rising costs and computers that have falling costs, the company may select LIFO for the clothing and FIFO for the computers.

 If costs are decreasing, explain how the three methods would affect a company's inventory, cost of goods sold, and gross profit.

Disclosure in the Financial Statements

A company reports its inventory in the current assets section of its balance sheet, usually immediately after receivables. It discloses its inventory cost flow assumption (FIFO, average, or LIFO) and its method of valuing the inventory (we will discuss these methods later in the chapter) usually in a note to the financial statements. It deducts cost of goods sold from net sales on the income statement to determine gross profit.

Using Inventory and Cost of Goods Sold Disclosures for Evaluation

Up to this point in the chapter we have focused on reporting inventory and cost of goods sold. Understanding these issues provides the foundation needed to learn how external users study a company's inventory and cost of goods sold disclosures to help them evaluate its *liquidity, profitability,* and *operating capability* (efficiency)—measures of how well a company uses its assets to generate revenue and cash flows.

Investors and creditors evaluate inventory and cost of goods sold, like other parts of the financial statements, by performing *intra*company and *inter*company analysis, through the use of horizontal analysis, vertical analysis, and ratio analysis. We will discuss intracompany analysis first, followed by intercompany analysis. We will use Intel Corporation's 1997 annual report to provide the information we need to explain intracompany analysis. Intel primarily manufactures and sells computer chips and is classified as part of the electronics components industry. We selected Intel because inventory is very important to electronics manufacturers. (We will also discuss Intel's property, plant, and equipment in Chapter 21.)

4 *How do a company's inventory and cost of goods sold disclosures help a user evaluate the company?*

www.intel.com

 Would you expect Intel to use the FIFO, average, or LIFO cost flow assumption? Why?

Intracompany Analysis of Inventory: Intel Corporation

Exhibit 19-8 presents information taken from Intel's 1997 annual report—its balance sheets, income statements, cash flow statements, and notes. Since we discussed liquidity,

Exhibit 19-8	Inventory Disclosures: Intel

Consolidated Balance Sheets (in part)

December 27, 1997 and December 28, 1996

(In millions—except per share amounts)	1997	1996
Assets		
Current assets:		
Cash and cash equivalents	**$ 4,102**	$ 4,165
Short-term investments	**5,630**	3,742
Trading assets	**195**	87
Accounts receivable, net of allowance for doubtful accounts of $65 ($68 in 1996)	**3,438**	3,723
Inventories	**1,697** ←	1,293
Deferred tax assets	**676**	570
Other current assets	**129**	104
Total current assets	**15,867**	13,684

Consolidated Statements of Income (in part)

Three years ended December 27, 1997

(In millions—except per share amounts)	1997	1996	1995
Net revenues	**$25,070**	$20,847	$16,202
Cost of sales	**9,945**	9,164	7,811

Consolidated Statements of Cash Flows (in part)

Three years ended December 27, 1997

(In millions)	1997	1996	1995
Cash flows provided by (used for) operating activities:			
Net income	**6,945**	5,157	3,566
Adjustments to reconcile net income to net cash provided by (used for) operating activities:			
Changes in assets and liabilities:			
Accounts receivable	**(285)**	(607)	(1,138)
Inventories	**(404)**	711	(835)

Notes (in part)

Inventories. Inventories are stated at the lower of cost or market. Cost is computed on a currently adjusted standard basis (which approximates actual cost on a current average or first-in, first-out basis). Inventories at fiscal year-ends were as follows:

(In millions)	1997	1996
Raw materials	**$ 255**	$ 280
Work in process	**928**	672
Finished goods	**514**	341
Total	**$1,697**	$1,293

including the current and quick ratios, in Chapter 7, we do not repeat that discussion here. However, recall that liquidity is a measure of how quickly an asset can be turned into cash and that the *current ratio* (current assets divided by current liabilities) and the *quick ratio* (quick assets divided by current liabilities) are used to evaluate a company's liquidity.

 Compute the quick and current ratios for Intel on December 27, 1997, and December 28, 1996, if the current liabilities are $6,020 million and $4,863 million for these dates respectively. How has the company's liquidity changed?

More information can be gained by analyzing the information disclosed on Intel's financial statements. The operating activities section of the cash flow statement confirms that Intel's inventory increased by $404 million in 1997. (As we will discuss later in this chapter, the increase is subtracted from net income in the cash flow statement because Intel purchased more inventory than it sold.) The income statement shows that during 1997, the company had cost of goods sold of $9,945 million. Using just the information from these two financial statements, we can figure out the total cost incurred (in millions) by Intel to acquire (manufacture or purchase) inventory in 1997 as follows:

$$\text{Beginning} + \text{Cost of Inventory} - \text{Ending} = \text{Cost of Goods}$$
$$\text{Inventory} \qquad \text{Acquired} \qquad \text{Inventory} \qquad \text{Sold}$$

or
$$\$1,293 + \text{Cost of Inventory} - \$1,697 = \$9,945$$
$$\text{Acquired}$$

Therefore, Cost of Inventory Acquired $= \$9,945 + \$1,697 - \$1,293$
$$= \$10,349$$

Comparing the cost of inventory acquired in a given year with that of previous years will enable you to understand how a company's manufacturing (or purchasing) activities have increased (or decreased).

 What was the cost of inventory acquired in 1996 if the beginning inventory was $2,004 million?

Now we discuss two questions about inventory and cost of goods sold.

Question #1: Does Intel Sell Its Inventory Profitably?
We discussed profitability, including the gross profit percentage, in Chapter 6. A variation of the gross profit percentage is the cost of goods sold (cost of sales) as a percentage of net sales (net revenues), which we compute for Intel as follows (in millions):

	1997	1996	1995
Cost of goods sold Net sales	$\frac{\$\,9,945}{\$25,070} = 39.7\%$	$\frac{\$\,9,164}{\$20,847} = 44.0\%$	$\frac{\$\,7,811}{\$16,202} = 48.2\%$

Thus we see that Intel's costs compared with selling prices have decreased in each of the last two years. Therefore, its gross profit percentage has increased in those years.

Another comparison we can make is to see if the company's increase in inventory affected its sales. In 1997 Intel increased its inventory by $404 million and increased its sales by $4,223 ($25,070 − $20,847), a multiple of 10.5 ($4,223 ÷ $404); a good result! This suggests that the increased inventory helped sales! By comparison, in 1996 Intel decreased its inventory by $711 million and increased its sales by $4,645 ($20,847 − $16,202).

 Why do you think that Intel increased its inventory while it increased its sales in 1997, but decreased its inventory while it increased its sales in 1996, whereas its cost of goods sold divided by its sales decreased?

Question #2: Does Intel Use Its Inventory Efficiently?

For a company using LIFO, the lower ending inventory cost (assuming rising costs) affects the computation and evaluation of current assets, working capital, and any financial ratios that include inventory, thereby reducing comparability between it and other companies. We discussed the inventory turnover ratio (cost of goods sold divided by average inventory) in Chapter 7 as a means of evaluating operating capability (efficiency). We do not repeat that discussion here but instead look at this ratio and related issues that arise when we compare two (or more) companies.

 Compute the inventory turnover ratio, and the inventory turnover in days, for Intel in 1997. How do these compare with the amounts for 1996 if the inventory at the beginning of 1996 was $2,004 million?

Intercompany Analysis within an Industry

One limitation of intracompany analysis is that it fails to provide an external comparison of the company's performance. Do we know how well Intel is performing relative to other companies in the electronics components industry? *Intercompany analysis* provides this relative analysis. We discussed intercompany comparisons of liquidity in Chapter 14. Here, we focus our discussion on those special issues, related to evaluating operating capability (efficiency), that are raised by the use of alternative cost flow assumptions. In Chapter 21 we will discuss the comparison of Intel to industry norms using property, plant, and equipment.

Listed below are three alternatives that may exist when comparing companies that have significant amounts of inventory. For this discussion, we will assume a comparison of just two companies and will treat the FIFO and average cost methods as interchangeable, since they are not likely to result in materially different amounts.

 Why do you think that the FIFO and the average cost methods are not likely to result in materially different amounts? Do you think that the LIFO and the average cost methods are likely to differ materially? Why or why not?

Alternative #1: Both Companies Use the FIFO or the Average Cost Flow Assumption

When you are comparing two companies that use the FIFO or average cost flow assumption, you have the simplest situation. The ending inventory amounts of the companies are comparable because they are the latest costs of the period. Although the cost of goods sold amounts are based on the earliest costs of the period, including the costs of the beginning inventories, these amounts should be comparable (unless the companies have very different inventory turnovers and significant changes in their costs).

 Why do you think that different inventory turnovers and significant changes in costs would affect the comparability of the cost of goods sold for two companies?

Alternative #2: Both Companies Use the LIFO Cost Flow Assumption

When you are comparing two companies that use the LIFO cost flow assumption, you might think that you have another simple situation. But be careful! Since cost of goods sold is computed from the latest costs of the period, the two cost of goods sold amounts are comparable (again assuming similar inventory turnovers). However, the ending inventory amounts of the two companies are *not* comparable because they are the earliest costs. As we discussed previously in the chapter, the inventory under LIFO is made up of "layers" of costs from periods since the company adopted LIFO. Therefore, a company that adopted LIFO in 1975 would have a very different inventory cost from that of a company that adopted LIFO in 1990, even if their physical inventories are exactly the same. Also, two companies that adopted LIFO in the same year would not have comparable ending inventory costs because each company would have added layers of different amounts in each period.

To overcome these limitations of comparing the LIFO balance sheet amounts, companies must disclose the costs of their ending inventories under an alternative, more comparable, cost flow assumption, such as FIFO, average, current, or replacement cost. Fortunately, you don't have to worry about the distinction between these titles—for our purposes, they all mean the same because the amounts are unlikely to be significantly different. Therefore, you can think of them all as being the same as the FIFO inventory value. We will refer to them as **non-LIFO** amounts. Also, rather than disclose the amounts directly, companies often disclose the *difference* between the LIFO and the non-LIFO ending inventory amounts. Sometimes they call this difference the **LIFO reserve**.

 How might this discussion affect your computation of the inventory turnover ratio?

Since the inventory turnover ratio uses the (average) inventory for the year, the ratio computations are not relevant (or comparable) when they are based on LIFO inventory values. Therefore, it is preferable to base the ratio on the non-LIFO cost of the inventory disclosed rather than the LIFO amount reported on the balance sheet.

Exhibit 19-9 shows the inventory amounts and related disclosures for Wal-Mart. If we use the nonrelevant "LIFO cost" amounts on the balance sheets, we would compute the inventory turnover ratio for 1997 (the fiscal year ending January 31, 1998) as follows:

www.wal-mart.com

$$\text{Inventory Turnover} = \frac{\text{Cost of Goods Sold}}{\text{Average Inventory}}$$

$$= \frac{\$93,438}{(\$15,897 + \$16,497) \div 2}$$

$$= \underline{\underline{5.77}}$$

 Why do you think that Wal-Mart uses a January 31 year-end instead of the more commonly used December 31?

Using the preferable non-LIFO (replacement cost) amounts shown on the balance sheet, we compute the inventory turnover ratio as follows:

$$\text{Inventory Turnover} = \frac{\text{Cost of Goods Sold}}{\text{Average Inventory}}$$

$$= \frac{\$93,438}{(\$16,193 + \$16,845) \div 2}$$

$$= \underline{\underline{5.66}}$$

Dividing these two ratios into 365 days gives the inventory turnover as 63.3 days and 64.5 days, respectively. While a 1.2 day difference may not seem significant for Wal-Mart, the difference may be more significant for other companies you analyze and for intercompany comparisons.

 Do you think that General Motors and Ford would have the same inventory turnover ratio amounts if they were equally efficient? Why or why not?

www.gm.com
www2.ford.com

Exhibit 19-9   Inventory Disclosures: Wal-Mart

CONSOLIDATED BALANCE SHEETS (in part)

(Amounts in millions)

January 31,	1998	1997
Assets		
Current Assets:		
Cash and cash equivalents	$ 1,447	$ 883
Receivables	976	845
Inventories		
At replacement cost	16,845	16,193
Less LIFO reserve	348	296
Inventories at LIFO cost	16,497	15,897
Prepaid expenses and other	432	368
Total Current Assets	19,352	17,993

CONSOLIDATED STATEMENTS OF INCOME (in part)

(Amounts in millions except per share data)

Fiscal years ended January 31,	1998	1997	1996
Revenues:			
Net sales	$117,958	$104,859	$93,627
Other income—net	1,341	1,319	1,146
	119,299	106,178	94,773
Costs and Expenses:			
Cost of sales	93,438	83,510	74,505
Operating, selling and general and administrative expenses	19,358	16,946	15,021

NOTES TO CONSOLIDATED FINANCIAL STATEMENTS (in part)

Inventories
The Company uses the retail last-in, first-out (LIFO) method for domestic Wal-Mart discount stores and Supercenters and cost LIFO for SAM's Clubs. International inventories are on other cost methods. Inventories are not in excess of market value.

Alternative #3: One Company Uses FIFO/Average While the Other Uses LIFO

The most complex situation arises when the two companies you are comparing use different cost flow assumptions. This should not happen too often because, as we discussed earlier, managers should choose a cost flow assumption based on the expected cost changes in that industry. Since users normally make comparisons within an industry, companies within that industry will generally select the same cost flow assumption.

In this situation, we again use the disclosures made by the company. But this time we use the company's disclosures to convert the LIFO beginning and ending inventory amounts, as well as the cost of goods sold amount, to non-LIFO amounts. We illustrate this conversion in Exhibit 19-10 using Wal-Mart's disclosures given in Exhibit 19-9. First, we take the LIFO information from Wal-Mart's balance sheet and income statement and compute the cost of inventory acquired during the year ($94,038) following the procedures we

Exhibit 19-10 Computation of Non-LIFO Amounts for Wal-Mart

	Beginning Inventory	+	(in millions) Cost of Inventory Acquired	−	Ending Inventory	=	Cost of Goods Sold
LIFO	$15,897 (1)	+	$94,038 (3)	−	$16,497 (1)	=	$93,438 (2)
LIFO Reserve	296 (4)			−	348 (4)	=	(52) (3)
Non-LIFO	$16,193 (4)	+	$94,038 (5)	−	$16,845 (4)	=	$93,386 (3)

(1) Balance sheet information
(2) Income statement information
(3) Calculated amount
(4) Balance sheet information from Wal-Mart; often presented in the notes instead
(5) Amount is the same under either method

discussed earlier. This cost is the same under any inventory cost flow assumption. Then we add the $296 and $348 LIFO Reserve amounts to the LIFO beginning inventory and ending inventory, respectively, and subtract the $52 difference in the Reserve from the LIFO cost of goods sold. This results in the $16,193 non-LIFO beginning inventory, the $16,845 non-LIFO ending inventory, and the $93,386 non-LIFO cost of goods sold. We now have the non-LIFO amounts of ending inventory and cost of goods sold, which are necessary for us to compare two companies using different inventory cost flow assumptions. Note that we can convert only a LIFO company to non-LIFO and not the other way around, because non-LIFO companies are not required to make disclosures of LIFO amounts.

You must be careful when you use this approach. If the LIFO reserve *increases* during the year, then the non-LIFO cost of goods sold is *lower* than the LIFO amount. Alternatively, if the LIFO reserve *decreases* during the year, then the non-LIFO cost of goods sold is *higher* than the LIFO amount. For Wal-Mart, the LIFO reserve increased during 1997 and therefore its non-LIFO cost of goods sold is *lower* than the LIFO amount.

 In Exhibit 19-10, did the difference between the cost of goods sold amounts move in the direction (increase or decrease) that you would expect? Why or why not?

So you see that for any ratio that uses inventory or cost of goods sold to measure liquidity, profitability, or operating efficiency, you need to understand which cost flow assumption the company is using. You also need to consider whether to use the financial statement amounts or to modify them by using the additional information disclosed.

Business Issues and Values

Earlier we said that there should not be many situations in which two companies in the same industry use different cost flow assumptions, because managers should choose a cost flow assumption based on the expected cost changes in that industry. However, look at the following recent disclosures for Nike and Reebok:

www.nike.com
www.reebok.com

Nike

"Inventories are stated at the lower of cost or market. Cost is determined using the last-in, first-out (LIFO) method for substantially all U.S inventories. Non-U.S. inventories are valued on a first-in, first-out (FIFO) basis."

Reebok

"Inventory, substantially all finished goods, is recorded at the lower of cost (first-in, first-out method) or market.

Do you consider these two companies to be in the same industry? Have the two companies made different choices for their primary cost flow assumptions? Why do you think the managers made the choices that they did?

U.S. companies usually don't use LIFO for their international operations (and non-U.S. companies usually don't use LIFO) because they cannot use it for income tax reporting in those other countries. Therefore, when a U.S. company with international operations, such as Nike, experiences rising costs, it will overstate income because it includes holding gains in income. Similarly, a non-U.S. company with rising inventory costs will overstate its income if it doesn't use LIFO.

When a company using LIFO reduces the physical quantity of inventory from the beginning of the year to the end of the year, it has a **LIFO liquidation.** Then the company includes lower costs from previous periods in its cost of goods sold and reports a **LIFO liquidation profit**—the extra profit that results from reporting a lower cost of goods sold than it would have if it had not had a LIFO liquidation. Companies are required to disclose this LIFO liquidation profit. For example, General Electric reported LIFO liquidation profits of $59 million, $58 million, and $88 million in 1997, 1996, and 1995, respectively. Whereas a reduction in inventory quantities may be caused by managers making sound decisions, such as developing more-efficient inventory management, it also can be caused by managers deliberately reducing inventory quantities (a company reducing its beginning inventory by selling more inventory than it purchased) to "increase" profit.

www.ge.com

 Explain whether you think it is desirable for a company's income to be influenced by managers' choices, rather than just from economic transactions and events.

Using the Lower-of-Cost-or-Market Method

5 *How does a company apply the lower-of-cost-or-market method to report the inventory on its balance sheet?*

The GAAP requirement that companies report their inventories at historical cost (under any one of the four alternative cost flow assumptions) is modified in one situation. When the market value of a company's inventory falls below its cost, the company is required to reduce, or "write down," the inventory to that market value. This is called the **lower-of-cost-or-market (LCM) method.** The company reports the inventory at the lower market value on its balance sheet and includes the corresponding "loss" on its income statement (typically by increasing cost of goods sold).

The use of the term *market value* here may lead to confusion. You should understand that *market value* refers to the cost to the company of replacing the item of inventory and *not* to the selling price the company charges its customers. As we discussed earlier, the replacement cost is the cost (including any transportation costs ordinarily incurred) that a company would have to pay at the balance sheet date to purchase (replace) an item of inventory (based on purchasing inventory in normal quantities from the usual suppliers). A decline in the replacement cost of the inventory is the result of declining costs for the supplier of the inventory.

For example, suppose that Cane Candy Company has 100 boxes of candy for which it paid $50 per box. If the replacement cost declines to $40 per box, the company includes the inventory on its balance sheet at $40 per box because the $50 cost is an overstatement of the resource—inventory—that the company will use to generate future revenues. The company has lost $10 per unit by owning the inventory while its cost declined. If the company had delayed the purchase, it could have acquired the inventory for only $40 per unit.

The lower-of-cost-or-market method is an example of applying the conservatism principle. The **conservatism principle** holds that a company should apply GAAP in such a way that there is little chance that it will overstate assets or income. Therefore, companies record a loss (or an increase in an expense) when there is evidence of a loss, whereas they must wait to record a gain (or an increase in a revenue) until an actual transaction occurs. This principle does *not* mean that a company should understate its assets or income; rather, it states that when there is a doubt about the likely effect of an accounting method, the company should report the more conservative amount. The rationale for the conservatism principle is that the users of financial statements are least likely to be misled if a company uses the least favorable valuation; conservatism also tends to offset the optimistic view of the company's managers. Many users disagree with the conservatism principle, however, because they believe that accounting should strive to obtain the best valuation, with a bias neither toward nor against conservatism. Furthermore, since the long-term income of the company is the same whether conservatism is applied or not, reducing its income or asset values in the current period will result in higher income in the future than the company would otherwise report. Therefore, conservatism may be unfair to present stockholders and biased in favor of prospective stockholders because of the lower valuation. Nevertheless, the conservatism principle has affected several accounting practices, including the lower-of-cost-or-market method.

 How do you think conservatism could be unfair to present shareholders?

Another argument in favor of the lower-of-cost-or-market method is based on the assumption that the relationship between cost and selling price remains fairly constant. That is, it is common for companies to set their selling prices at a certain percentage (called the *markup*) above the cost of the inventory. For example, if a company normally sells for $100 units that cost $50, the markup is 100% of cost. If the replacement cost of the inventory drops to $40, the company would write down its inventory to this $40 cost and record a $10 loss. We might expect the company to reduce the selling price to $80, thus maintaining its 100% markup on this cost. Use of the lower-of-cost-or-market method thus separates the loss on holding the inventory ($10) from the gross profit that results from selling the inventory ($80 − $40). Also note that the company records the loss associated with the decline in value in the period of the decline, not in the period in which the inventory is ultimately sold.

 Whose side do you take on this discussion—the supporters or the critics of the conservatism principle? Explain your position.

Companies often apply the lower-of-cost-or-market method separately to *each item* in inventory, as we show in the following example for Jordan Company (which uses FIFO):

Item	Quantity	Unit Cost	Unit Market	Total Cost	Total Market	Lower-of-Cost or-Market
A	100	$20	$18	$ 2,000	$ 1,800	$ 1,800
B	200	30	31	6,000	6,200	6,000
C	200	25	20	5,000	4,000	4,000
D	100	40	43	4,000	4,300	4,000
				$17,000	$16,300	$15,800

The value of the inventory under the lower-of-cost-or-market method applied to individual items is $15,800. (If the company applied the method to the total inventory, its inventory value would be $16,300.) In this case, the company reduces the inventory and records a loss of $1,200 ($17,000 cost − $15,800 market value) as follows:

676 CHAPTER 19 *Reporting Inventory*

| **Assets** | = | **Liabilities** | + | **Stockholders' Equity** |

Inventory			Cost of Goods Sold

Bal 17,000	1,200		1,200
Bal 15,800			
(+)	(−)		
			(+)	(−)

Note that the $1,200 entry on the right side of the Inventory account reduces the balance to $15,800 ($17,000 − $1,200). In this example, we assume that the company includes the $1,200 loss as part of cost of goods sold (it could also report it as a Loss in the "other items" section of its income statement). Jordan Company includes the $15,800 inventory in the current asset section of its balance sheet as follows:

Inventory, at lower-of-cost-or-market value (FIFO cost, $17,000) $15,800

 Would you prefer that a company report the loss separately from cost of goods sold? Why or why not?

Note that the company discloses both the cost and the market value of its inventory, as well as the method used to compute the cost of its inventory. When we discussed the conservatism principle earlier, we pointed out that the reduction in a company's income in the current period is offset in later periods by income that is higher than it would otherwise report. In the Jordan Company example, if we assume that the replacement cost of the inventory is *not* less than the cost at the end of the *second* year, its income in the second year will be $1,200 higher than the income otherwise would have been because the beginning inventory is $1,200 lower, resulting in a lower cost of goods sold.

 How does a lower beginning inventory result in a lower cost of goods sold?

www.apple.com

To understand the importance of the lower-of-cost-or-market method, consider the following disclosure made in 1997 by Apple Computer: "Gross margin increased from 10% to 19% of sales during 1997, primarily as a result of a $616 million charge in the second quarter of that related principally for the write-down of certain inventory."

 Would you expect the replacement cost of the inventory to be less than the actual cost of the inventory for a company that uses FIFO? one that uses average cost? one that uses LIFO? Explain why.

Estimating the Cost of Inventory and the Cost of Goods Sold

6 *What methods may a company use to estimate its cost of goods sold and inventory?*

Sometimes a company needs to estimate the cost of its inventory. If a company is using the periodic inventory system, managers may estimate the cost of the inventory during the year so that they can prepare the internal (e.g., monthly) financial statements without incurring the cost of taking a physical inventory. Also, if a company has a loss of inventory in a fire or theft, or if the inventory accounting records are destroyed, it may need to estimate its loss. Companies often use one of two methods to estimate the cost of inventory. Companies use the gross profit method in the special situations just described, whereas retailing companies such as supermarkets and department stores routinely use the retail inventory method for preparing financial statements.

What kind of evidence do you think an insurance company would want to see supporting this company's inventory fire loss claim?

Gross Profit Method

A company uses the **gross profit method** to estimate the cost of its inventory by first determining the historic gross profit percentage (gross profit ÷ net sales) based on the income statements of previous periods. It then multiplies its net sales of the current period by the historic gross profit rate to determine its estimated current gross profit. Next, it subtracts the estimated current gross profit from the net sales to determine the estimated cost of goods sold. Finally, it subtracts the estimated cost of goods sold from the cost of goods available for sale to determine its estimate of the ending inventory.

For example, suppose that the beginning inventory of Watson Company for the current period is $12,000, net purchases are $48,000, and net sales are $70,000. If the historic gross profit rate based on the company's income statements of previous periods is 40%, we can estimate the ending inventory of the current period in four steps as follows:

Step 1: Estimate the current gross profit

$$\text{Gross Profit} = \text{Net Sales} \times \text{Historic Gross Profit Percentage}$$
$$= \$70,000 \times 40\%$$
$$= \$28,000$$

Step 2: Estimate the cost of goods sold

$$\text{Cost of Goods Sold} = \text{Net Sales} - \text{Gross Profit}$$
$$= \$70,000 - \$28,000$$
$$= \$42,000$$

Step 3: Determine the actual cost of goods available for sale

$$\text{Cost of Goods Available for Sale} = \text{Beginning Inventory} + \text{Net Purchases}$$
$$= \$12,000 + \$48,000$$
$$= \$60,000$$

Step 4: Estimate the ending inventory

$$\text{Ending Inventory} = \text{Cost of Goods Available for Sale} - \text{Cost of Goods Sold}$$
$$= \$60,000 - \$42,000$$
$$= \underline{\$18,000}$$

We illustrate these relationships in income statement format as follows (Steps 1–4 are listed in parentheses):

Net sales			$70,000	(100%)
Cost of goods sold:				
Beginning inventory	$12,000			
Net purchases	48,000			
Cost of goods available for sale (actual)	(3)	$60,000		
Less: Ending inventory (estimated)	(4)	(18,000)		
Cost of goods sold (estimated)			(2) (42,000)	(60%)
Gross Profit (estimated)			(1) $28,000	(40%)

The accuracy of the gross profit method depends on the reasonableness of the historic gross profit percentage. Since the percentage is based on the gross profit and net sales relationships of past periods, it is an accurate estimate of the gross profit rate of the current period only if the gross profit relationships have not changed. If a company knows that conditions have changed, it should adjust the gross profit percentage so that the estimated cost of the ending inventory will be more accurate.

If a company uses the gross profit method to estimate a casualty loss (e.g., loss from fire), it calculates the amount of the loss by subtracting the cost of any salvaged inventory from the cost of the inventory it estimates that it had on hand before the casualty.

Retail Inventory Method

Retail companies generally find it easier and less expensive to base their inventory accounting system on the retail value of their inventory. They mark their merchandise and put it on display at the retail price. During the physical inventory, it is easier to count the inventory at retail prices than to identify the cost of each item. The *cost* of the inventory must be included in the financial statements, however.

A company uses the **retail inventory method** to estimate the cost of its inventory by multiplying the retail value of the ending inventory by the cost-to-retail ratio of the current period (this method approximates the average cost flow assumption). To apply this method, the company completes the following steps:

1. Compute the total goods available for sale (beginning inventory plus net purchases) at *both* cost and retail value (selling price). The company must keep detailed records of the beginning inventory and the net purchases at both cost and retail prices to compute these amounts.

2. Compute a cost-to-retail ratio by dividing the cost of the goods available for sale by the retail value of the goods available for sale.

3. Compute the ending inventory at retail by subtracting the net sales for the period from the retail value of the goods available for sale.

4. Compute the ending inventory at cost by multiplying the ending inventory at retail by the cost-to-retail ratio.

We illustrate these steps for the retail inventory method in the following example, using the same cost and sales information from the gross profit method and assuming the retail amounts (Steps 1 through 4 are listed in parentheses):

	Cost	Retail	
Beginning inventory	$12,000	$ 20,000	
Purchases (net)	48,000	80,000	
Goods available for sale	$60,000	$100,000	(1)
Cost-to-retail ratio $\dfrac{\$60,000}{\$100,000} = 0.60$			(2)
Less: Sales (net)		(70,000)	
Ending inventory at retail		$ 30,000	(3)
Ending inventory at cost (0.60 × $30,000)	$18,000		(4)

Watson Company had goods with a retail value of $100,000 available for sale during the period and made net sales of $70,000. Therefore the retail value of the ending inventory is $30,000. Since the company's costs are 60% of the retail value, the cost of the ending inventory is $18,000. Watson Company reports this cost on its ending balance sheet.

Note that the retail inventory method is an estimating procedure and is useful for quarterly financial statements. It does not eliminate the need for taking a periodic physical inventory, however, especially at the end of the fiscal year. For example, if Watson Company takes a physical inventory and finds that the retail value of the inventory is $29,000, the cost of the inventory it reports on the balance sheet is $17,400 (0.60 × $29,000) because this amount is more accurate than the $18,000 we computed earlier. The company adds the difference of $600 to its cost of goods sold on its income statement for the period.

 Why would a company's accounting system report a quantity of inventory that differs from the physical count?

Summary of Estimating Methods

The gross profit method and the retail inventory method are similar because they both estimate the cost of inventory by using a profit percentage. However, the retail inventory method is more sensitive to price changes because it uses a current period estimate of the profit percentage, whereas the gross profit method uses an estimate based on past periods. We can summarize the two methods as follows:

Gross Profit Method	Retail Inventory Method
Cost of goods available for sale Less: Cost of goods sold (sales × gross profit rate)	Retail value of goods available for sale Less: Sales (net)
	Ending inventory at retail × Cost-to-retail ratio
Ending inventory at cost	Ending inventory at cost

Cash Flows from Operating Activities

In Chapter 8 we introduced the cash flow statement of a company. This statement has three sections: (1) cash flows from operating activities, (2) cash flows from investing activities, and (3) cash flows from financing activities. We discussed only the basic issues about the cash flow statement in Chapter 8. Here, we discuss additional issues about the cash flows from operating activities section. We will discuss other issues concerning the cash flows from investing and financing activities in later chapters.

The cash flows from operating activities section reports on the company's cash flows from all transactions and other events that involve acquiring, selling, and delivering goods for sale, as well as providing services. These transactions involve changes in cash, accounts receivable, accounts payable, inventory, and other current assets and current liabilities. They also involve revenues and expenses. To further explain the cash flows from operating activities, we will review how revenues, expenses, current assets, and current liabilities are related in a company's operating cycle.

Operating Cycle

Recall that a company's **operating cycle** is the average time required to pay for inventory, sell the inventory, and collect on the sales. To begin its operating cycle, the company acquires inventory by paying cash or increasing accounts payable. When the company makes cash or credit sales during the current accounting period, it increases cash or accounts receivable and revenues. It also increases cost of goods sold and reduces inventory. When the company collects its accounts receivable, it increases cash and decreases accounts receivable. When the company pays its accounts payable, it decreases accounts payable and cash. These collections of accounts receivable and payments of accounts payable may occur in an accounting period after the company has recorded the sales revenue and cost of goods sold.

Companies also have differences in the timing of other expenses and the related cash payments. For example, a company may report an expense (e.g., rent, insurance) in the current period even though it paid for the item in a previous period. Therefore, the expense is accompanied by a reduction in an asset (e.g., prepaid rent, prepaid insurance). Also, a company may report an expense (e.g., salaries, interest) in the current period even though it will pay for it in a future period. Therefore, the expense is accompanied by an increase in a liability (e.g., salaries payable, interest payable).

Each part of the company's operating cycle may affect both net income and the net cash flow from operating activities. Each may be affected differently, however, because of differences in when the company records revenues and expenses and when it receives or pays cash. You (as a user of accounting information) need to understand the changes in each of the company's current assets and current liabilities to determine their impact on operating cash inflows and outflows.

Also, changes in some noncurrent assets (property and equipment) affect the company's net income but do not result in an operating cash inflow or outflow. For instance, when a company records depreciation for equipment, it increases depreciation expense and decreases the equipment's book value. Although depreciation expense decreases net income (and a noncurrent asset), there is no operating cash outflow. Similarly, a gain or loss on the sale of property and equipment is included in the company's net income, but does not result in a cash flow from *operating* activities—the cash flow from the sale is a cash flow from an *investing* activity. You also must analyze each of the changes in these noncurrent asset accounts to determine the effect on the company's cash flows from operating activities.

Methods of Reporting Cash Flows from Operating Activities

As we introduced in Chapter 8, there are two methods of computing a company's cash flows from operating activities reported on its cash flow statement—the direct method and the indirect method. In Chapter 8 we discussed and illustrated the direct method because it is easier to understand and more closely follows how a company analyzes its operating cash flows in its cash budget. In this chapter we explain the indirect method because it is the method that most companies (over 90 percent) use in their cash flow statements and, therefore, is the one that users are most likely to encounter, and need to interpret. To help you understand the indirect method, we use an example to compare the direct method and the indirect method.

Direct Method

As we discussed in Chapter 8, under the **direct method,** a company subtracts its operating cash outflows from its operating cash inflows to determine the net cash provided by (or used in) operating activities. For a corporation, the operating cash inflows include: (1) collections from customers, (2) collections of interest and dividends, and (3) other operating receipts. The operating cash outflows include: (1) payments to suppliers, (2) payments to employees, (3) payments of interest, (4) payments of income taxes, and (5) other operating payments. A company computes its operating cash inflows and operating cash outflows based on an analysis like the one we used in Exhibit 8-9. To understand this method, suppose that Frank Corporation, a retail company, shows the following income statement information for the current year:

Sales revenue	$360,000
Cost of goods sold	(150,000)
Salaries expense	(70,000)
Rent expense	(14,000)
Depreciation expense	(40,000)
Gain on sale of land	12,000
Interest expense	(8,000)
Income tax expense	(36,000)
Net Income	$ 54,000

Its beginning and ending balance sheets show the following changes in current assets and current liabilities:

Accounts receivable decreased by $35,000
Inventory increased by $20,000
Prepaid rent increased by $2,000
Accounts payable increased by $13,000
Salaries payable increased by $4,000
Interest payable decreased by $1,000
Income taxes payable increased by $3,000

Furthermore, during the year the Frank Corporation sold land that cost $25,000 for $37,000 cash, resulting in the $12,000 gain reported on its income statement.

Under the direct method, Frank Corporation reports its cash flows from operating activities on the cash flow statement as follows:

Cash Flows from Operating Activities:		
Cash Inflows:		
Collections from customers	$ 395,000	
Cash inflows from operating activities		$395,000
Cash Outflows:		
Payments to suppliers	$(157,000)	
Payments to employees	(66,000)	
Payments for rent	(16,000)	
Payment of interest	(9,000)	
Payment of income taxes	(33,000)	
Cash outflows for operating activities		(281,000)
Net cash provided by operating activities		$114,000

Next we provide a schedule that shows how Frank Corporation calculated each of the preceding amounts, followed by an explanation of each calculation.

Income Statement	Amount		Balance Sheet Change			Cash Flow
Sales revenue	$360,000	+	Decrease in accounts receivable	$35,000	=	$395,000
Cost of goods sold	(150,000)	+	Increase in inventory	(20,000)		
		−	Increase in accounts payable	13,000	=	(157,000)
Salaries expense	(70,000)	−	Increase in salaries payable	4,000	=	(66,000)
Rent expense	(14,000)	+	Increase in prepaid items	(2,000)	=	(16,000)
Interest expense	(8,000)	+	Decrease in interest payable	(1,000)	=	(9,000)
Income tax expense	(36,000)	−	Increase in income taxes payable	3,000	=	(33,000)
Depreciation expense	(40,000)		Not included			
Gain	12,000		Not included			
Income flow	$ 54,000		Operating cash flow			$114,000

Because accounts receivable *decreased* between the beginning and the end of the year, we know that the company's cash collections were *more* than its sales. Therefore, we compute the $395,000 cash received from customers by adding the decrease in accounts receivable ($35,000) to the sales revenue ($360,000). This is the only cash receipt, so that the cash inflows from operating activities were $395,000.

Because inventory *increased* between the beginning and the end of the year, we know that the company purchased *more* inventory than it sold. Therefore, we compute the purchases of $170,000 by adding the increase in inventory ($20,000) to the cost of goods sold ($150,000). Because accounts payable *increased* between the beginning and the end of the year, we know that the company paid for *less* inventory than it purchased. Therefore, we compute the $157,000 cash paid to suppliers by subtracting the increase in accounts payable ($13,000) from the purchases ($170,000). Because salaries payable *increased* between the beginning and the end of the year, we know that the company paid its employees *less* than they earned (and less than the company recorded as an expense). Therefore, we compute the $66,000 cash paid to employees by subtracting the increase in salaries payable ($4,000) from the salaries expense ($70,000).

Because prepaid rent *increased* between the beginning and the end of the year, we know that the company paid more to its landlord than it recorded as an expense. Therefore, we compute the $16,000 cash paid for rent by adding the increase in prepaid rent ($2,000) to the rent expense ($14,000). Because interest payable *decreased* between the beginning and the end of the year, we know that the company paid its lenders *more* than it recorded as an expense. Therefore, we compute the $9,000 cash paid to its lenders by adding the decrease in interest payable ($1,000) to the interest expense ($8,000). Because income taxes payable *increased* between the beginning and the end of the year, we know that the company paid the government *less* than its income tax expense.[1] Therefore, we compute the $33,000 cash paid for income taxes by subtracting the increase in income taxes payable ($3,000) from the income tax expense ($36,000). These cash outflows for operating activities total $281,000, so that the net cash provided by operating activities was $114,000. Note that the depreciation expense and the gain on the sale of the land are not included because they did not involve cash flows from operating activities. Note also that we didn't introduce any new concepts in this analysis. We just used summary amounts from the balance sheets and income statement (as we briefly introduced in Chapter 8) rather than having internal information about transactions.

The direct method has the advantages of being easy to understand and similar to the upper part of the cash budgets that we discussed in Chapters 4 and 12. External users have

---

[1] A company also may have a change in its deferred income tax liability; it treats this change like a change in its income tax payable to determine its cash paid for income taxes. We will discuss deferred income taxes more fully in Chapter 22.

criticized the method, however, because it does not "tie" the net income that a company reports on its income statement to the net cash provided by operating activities that the company reports on its cash flow statement. Also, the direct method does not show how the changes in the parts (i.e., current assets and current liabilities) of a company's operating cycle affected its operating cash flows.

Indirect Method

When a company uses the indirect method to report the net cash provided by operating activities on its cash flow statement, the two criticisms of the direct method are resolved. Under the **indirect method,** a company adjusts its net income to the net cash provided by operating activities. To do this, it lists net income first and then makes adjustments (additions or subtractions) to the net income (1) to include any changes in the current assets (other than cash) and current liabilities involved in the company's operating cycle that affected cash flows differently than they affected net income, and (2) to eliminate amounts that were included in its net income but that did not involve an operating cash flow. In other words, under the indirect method, a company's income flows are converted from an *accrual* basis to a *cash* basis.

> **7** *How and why does a company report its operating cash flows under the indirect method on its cash flow statement?*

 Would you expect that, for a typical company, its net cash flow from operating activities would be greater or less than its net income? Explain your answer.

We use Frank Corporation's income statement and balance sheet information, shown earlier, to illustrate the indirect method. Frank Corporation reports its net cash flow from operating activities under the indirect method on its the cash flow statement as follows:

Cash Flows from Operating Activities

Net income..	$ 54,000
Adjustments for differences between net income and cash flows from operating activities:	
Add: Decrease in accounts receivable	35,000
Increase in accounts payable..	13,000
Increase in salaries payable	4,000
Increase in income taxes payable	3,000
Depreciation expense	40,000
Less: Increase in inventory	(20,000)
Increase in prepaid rent...	(2,000)
Decrease in interest payable..	(1,000)
Gain on sale of land...	(12,000)
Net cash provided by operating activities...	$114,000

First, note that the net cash provided by operating activities ($114,000) is the same under both the direct and the indirect methods. Now, why did we make each adjustment to convert net income to the net cash provided by operating activities? We will discuss these adjustments as they relate to sales revenue, cost of goods sold, expenses, and noncash items. First, as we discussed earlier, since accounts receivable decreased by $35,000, we know that the company's cash collections were more than its sales revenue, so it must have collected some accounts receivable related to sales from the previous period. Since the current sales of $360,000 are lower than the amount of cash that Frank collected, its net income of $54,000 is lower than it would have been if Frank had counted the amount of cash it collected this period from sales of the previous period. Therefore, we add the $35,000 decrease in accounts receivable to net income as one step in computing the net cash provided by operating activities. Also note that adding the decrease in accounts receivable to sales revenue (the direct method) has the same effect as adding the decrease to net income (the indirect method).

Next, because inventory increased by $20,000, we know that the company purchased more inventory than it sold. So the cost of goods sold is not the same as the amount of inventory that Frank purchased. Since the cost of goods sold is subtracted from sales in computing income, we subtract the increase in inventory from the net income to show the additional outflow from purchasing more inventory. However, because accounts payable increased by $13,000, we know that the company paid for less inventory than it purchased. Therefore, we add the increase in accounts payable to net income to compute the net cash inflow. Remember that a *lower* cash *outflow* means that the *net* cash *inflow* is *higher*. Also note that (1) adding the increase in inventory to cost of goods sold (the direct method) has the same effect as subtracting the increase from net income (the indirect method), and (2) subtracting the increase in accounts payable from purchases (the direct method) has the same effect as adding the increase to net income (the indirect method).

 Does this make sense? Why does adding the increase in inventory to cost of goods sold have the same effect as subtracting the increase from net income?

Because prepaid rent increased by $2,000, we know that the company paid its landlord more than it recorded as an expense, so we subtract the increase in prepaid rent from net income to compute the net cash inflow. Because salaries payable increased by $4,000, we know that the company paid its employees less than it recorded as an expense, so we add the increase in salaries payable to net income to compute the net cash inflow. Because income taxes payable increased by $3,000, we know that the company paid the government less than it recorded as an expense, so we add the increase in income taxes payable to net income to compute the net cash inflow. Also note that (1) adding the increase in prepaid rent to rent expense (the direct method) has the same effect as subtracting the increase from net income (the indirect method), (2) subtracting the increase in salaries payable from salaries expense (the direct method) has the same effect as adding the increase to net income (the indirect method), and (3) subtracting the increase in income taxes payable from income tax expense (the direct method) has the same effect as adding the increase to net income (the indirect method).

Because interest payable decreased by $1,000, we know that the company paid its lenders more than it recorded as an expense, so we subtract the decrease in interest payable from net income to compute the net cash inflow. Also note that adding the decrease in interest payable to interest expense (the direct method) has the same effect as subtracting the decrease from net income (the indirect method).

 Explain why subtracting the increase in salaries payable from salaries expense is the same as adding the increase to net income.

Next, we add the $40,000 depreciation expense to the net income because it was subtracted to determine net income but there was no cash outflow. Finally, we subtract the $12,000 gain on the sale of the land from net income because it was added to determine net income but there was no inflow of cash from operating activities. The cash received from the sale is classified as an *investing* activity. We will discuss these issues more in Chapter 21.

 How would the company report on its cash flow statement an increase in accounts receivable during the year? a decrease in inventory? a loss on a sale of a machine? Explain each of your answers.

In the previous example, we included only a few adjustments to convert the net income to the net cash provided by operating activities. Some companies, however, have more; we show the common adjustments under the indirect method in Exhibit 19-11.

 If a company uses the indirect method in its cash flow statement, would you be able to compute its operating cash flows under the direct method?

Exhibit 19-11   Adjustments to Convert Net Income to Net Cash Provided by Operating Activities

Net Income

Plus

> Depreciation expense
> Decrease in accounts receivable
> Decrease in inventory
> Decreases in other current assets related to operating activities
> Increase in accounts payable
> Increase in salaries payable
> Increase in income taxes payable
> Increases in other current liabilities related to operating activities
> Losses on sales of assets

Minus

> Increase in accounts receivable
> Increase in inventory
> Increases in other current assets related to operating activities
> Decrease in accounts payable
> Decrease in salaries payable
> Decrease in income taxes payable
> Decreases in other current liabilities related to operating activities
> Gains on sales of assets

Equals

Net Cash Provided by Operating Activities

Steps to Complete under the Indirect Method

Based on the previous example, we can identify six steps that a company completes under the indirect method to compute the net cash provided by operating activities that it reports on its cash flow statement:

1. Compute the increase or decrease during the year in each current asset and current liability account

2. List the company's net income first in the cash flows from operating activities section

3. *Add* the *decrease* in each current *asset* and the *increase* in each current *liability* to the net income

4. *Subtract* the *increase* in each current *asset* and the *decrease* in each current *liability* from the net income

5. *Add* the depreciation *expense* and any *losses* on the sale of property and equipment assets to the net income; *subtract* any *gains* on the sale of property and equipment assets from net income

6. Compute the net cash provided by (or used in) operating activities

To illustrate, we assume that Symes Syrup Company earned net income of $36,000 for 2000. It included depreciation expense of $17,000 in the operating expenses deducted from sales revenue to determine this net income. Step 1 involves determining the changes in the current assets and current liabilities. A review of the 2000 ending and beginning balance sheets for Symes Syrup Company shows the following current assets and current liabilities:

Accounts	Balances 12/31/2000	12/31/1999	Changes (Step 1)
Accounts receivable	$14,000	$10,000	$4,000
Inventory	20,000	28,500	(8,500)
Accounts payable	11,500	21,000	(9,500)
Salaries payable	6,000	4,000	2,000

Based on this information, the cash flows from operating activities section of Symes Syrup Company's 2000 cash flow statement is as follows (Steps 2-6 are listed in parentheses before the items):

Cash Flows from Operating Activities
(2) Net income	$36,000
Adjustments for differences between net income and cash flows from operating activities:	
(3) Add: Decrease in inventory	8,500
Increase in salaries payable	2,000
(5) Depreciation expense	17,000
(4) Less: Increase in accounts receivable	(4,000)
Decrease in accounts payable	(9,500)
(6) Net cash provided by operating activities	$50,000

Symes Syrup Company would include this section with the cash flows from investing activities and the cash flows from financing activities sections (not discussed here) to complete its cash flow statement for 2000.

 If a company uses the direct method in its cash flow statement, would you be able to compute its operating cash flows under the indirect method?

Using Information about Cash Flows from Operating Activities

While net income is a good indicator of the performance of a company, the net cash provided by operating activities also provides useful information—the company needs to generate sufficient cash to pay its bills, and typically generate that cash from operating activities.

 What type of company would you expect not to generate sufficient cash from its operating activities to pay its normal recurring bills?

Also, a user may be interested in looking at the difference between net income and the net cash provided by operating activities because this difference may provide additional useful information. For example, if the net cash provided by operating activities is less than net income because of a significant increase in accounts receivable, this may indicate that the company is having difficulty collecting its bills or has changed the type of customer to which it makes sales and to which it has extended its credit terms. As another example, if the net cash provided by operating activities is greater than net income because of a significant increase in accounts payable, this may indicate that the company is having difficulty paying its bills, or is delaying payment so much that it may damage its relationships with its suppliers.

Since a company may use either the direct or the indirect method to report its net cash provided by operating activities, a user may have difficulty comparing two companies that use different methods. Fortunately, when a company uses the direct method, it must also disclose the results of the indirect method in the notes to its financial statements. When a company uses the indirect method, it must disclose its payments for interest and for income taxes. However, the company has no obligation to report the other operating cash inflows or outflows.

Many users find the direct method easier to understand. So when a company uses the indirect method, a user may want to compute the cash flows under the direct method, using the logic that we discussed earlier in the chapter. However, the company may not disclose sufficient information to perform the analysis in as much detail as we used. For example, a company may not disclose salaries payable separately in the balance sheet, or it may include in accounts payable more than just amounts owed to suppliers. Also, a manufacturing company includes factory employees' salaries in its cost of inventory and therefore in its cost of goods sold. Thus the user will not be able to compute separate amounts for payments to suppliers and for payments to employees. Instead, the user will have to combine these amounts with the other operating payments.

 What other items might make it impossible to compute separate amounts for payments to suppliers and payments to employees?

S u m m a r y

At the beginning of the chapter we asked you several questions. During the chapter, we asked you to STOP and answer some additional questions to build your knowledge about specific issues. Be sure you answered these additional questions. Below are the questions from the beginning of the chapter, with a brief summary of the key points relating to the answers. Use your creative and critical thinking skills to expand on these key points to develop more complete answers to the questions and to determine what other questions you have that might lead you to learn more about the issues.

1 How does a company determine the costs and amounts of inventory that it includes in the inventory amount reported on its balance sheet?

The cost of each unit of inventory includes all the costs incurred to bring the item to its existing condition and location. Thus the cost of inventory includes the purchase price (less any purchases discounts), sales tax, applicable transportation costs, insurance, customs duties, and similar costs. When a cost, such as the cost of ordering the inventory, is difficult to associate with a particular inventory item, many companies record it as a general and administrative expense. When a company takes a physical inventory, it counts the units of inventory in its stores and warehouses (and factories). The company also counts any additional units of inventory that it owns that are in transit. A company may buy or sell inventory under terms of FOB (free on board) shipping point or FOB destination. FOB shipping point means that the selling company transfers ownership to the buyer at the place of sale (shipping point)—that is, before the inventory is in transit. The selling company excludes these items in transit from its inventory while the buying company includes them in its inventory. The buying company is responsible for any transportation costs incurred to deliver the items and includes these costs as a cost of its inventory (rather than immediately recording them as an expense). FOB destination means that the selling company transfers ownership to the buyer at the place of delivery—that is, after transit is completed. The selling company includes these items in transit in its inventory until delivery takes place, and the buyer excludes them. In this case, the selling company is responsible for any transportation costs incurred to deliver the items and includes these costs in its selling expenses.

2 **What alternative cost flow assumptions may a company use for determining its cost of goods sold and ending inventory?**

A company may use the FIFO, the average, or the LIFO cost flow assumption. When a company uses the first-in, first-out (FIFO) cost flow assumption, it includes the earliest (first) costs it incurred in the cost of goods sold and the latest costs in the ending inventory. That is, the first costs it incurred are the first costs it includes as costs of the units sold. When a company uses the average cost flow assumption, it allocates an average cost per unit to both the ending inventory and the cost of goods sold. When a company uses the last-in, first-out (LIFO) cost flow assumption, it includes the latest (last) costs incurred in its cost of goods sold and the earliest costs (part or all of which are costs it incurred in previous periods) in the ending inventory.

3 **How do alternative cost flow assumptions affect a company's financial statements?**

The choice made by managers to adopt the FIFO, the average, or the LIFO cost flow assumption has an impact on both the income statement and the balance sheet. If costs are rising, gross profit (sales − cost of goods sold), income, and ending inventory are higher under FIFO and lower under LIFO. Ending inventory is higher under FIFO and lower under LIFO because under LIFO the oldest costs remain in this inventory. The average cost amounts are between those of FIFO and LIFO. If costs are falling, the relationships are reversed. Many users of financial statements argue that LIFO results in a better measure of income when costs are rising and that holding gains should be excluded from income. If the company is a corporation in the United States, LIFO is allowed for income tax purposes only if it is also used for the financial statements. If costs are rising, the use of LIFO results in lower taxable income and, consequently, in the payment of less income taxes; therefore the company has more cash available than it otherwise would for such things as paying employees, investing in property and equipment, reducing liabilities, or paying dividends. If the managers of a company expect that the costs of acquiring inventory will increase in the future, then they should select LIFO because of the lower income taxes that the company will have to pay. Alternatively, if the managers expect that the costs of acquiring inventory will decrease in the future, then they should select FIFO or average cost because the company would pay lower income taxes.

4 **How do a company's inventory and cost of goods sold disclosures help a user evaluate the company?**

As with other parts of financial statements, a user evaluates inventory and cost of goods sold by performing intracompany and intercompany analysis, through the use of horizontal analysis, vertical analysis, and ratio analysis. For any ratio that uses inventory or cost of goods sold to measure liquidity, profitability, or operating efficiency, a user needs to understand which cost flow assumption the company is using. For a company using LIFO, the lower ending inventory cost (assuming rising costs) affects the computation and evaluation of current assets, working capital, and any financial ratios that include inventory, thereby reducing comparability between it and other companies. The use of alternative cost flow assumptions raises special issues related to evaluating liquidity, profitability, and operating capability (efficiency). Three alternatives may exist when comparing companies that have significant amounts of inventory: (1) both companies use the FIFO or the average cost flow assumption, (2) both companies use the LIFO cost flow assumption, and (3) one company uses the FIFO or the average cost flow assumption while the other uses the LIFO cost flow assumption. The user needs to consider whether to use the financial statement amounts or to modify them by using the additional information disclosed.

5 **How does a company apply the lower-of-cost-or-market method to report the inventory on its balance sheet?**

When the market value of a company's inventory falls below its cost, the company reduces, or "writes down," the inventory to that market value. The company reports the inventory at the lower market value on its balance sheet and includes the corresponding loss on its income statement (typically by increasing cost of goods sold). The market value is the cost of replacing the inventory item.

6 **What methods may a company use to estimate its cost of goods sold and inventory?**

A company uses the gross profit method if it is using the periodic inventory system and managers want to estimate the cost of the inventory during the year so that they can prepare the internal (e.g., monthly) financial statements without incurring the cost of taking a physical inventory. Also, if a company has a loss of inventory in a fire or theft, or if the accounting records are destroyed, it may need to estimate its loss. A company uses the gross profit method to estimate the cost of its inventory by first determining the historic gross profit percentage (gross profit ÷ net sales) based on the income statements of previous periods. It then multiplies its net sales of the current period by the historic gross profit percentage to determine its estimated current gross profit. Next, it subtracts the estimated current gross profit from the net sales to determine the estimated cost of goods sold. Finally, it subtracts the estimated cost of goods sold from the cost of goods available for sale to determine its estimate of the ending inventory.

Retailing companies such as supermarkets and department stores routinely use the retail inventory method for preparing financial statements. They complete the following steps: (1) compute the total goods available for sale (beginning inventory plus net purchases) at *both* cost and retail value (selling price), (2) compute a cost-to-retail ratio by dividing the cost of the goods available for sale by the retail value of the goods available for sale, (3) compute the ending inventory at retail by subtracting the net sales for the period from the retail value of the goods available for sale, and (4) compute the ending inventory at cost by multiplying the ending inventory at retail by the cost-to-retail ratio.

7 **How and why does a company report its operating cash flows under the indirect method on its cash flow statement?**

Under the indirect method, a company adjusts its net income to the net cash provided by operating activities. To do this, the company (1) computes the increase or decrease during the year in each current asset and current liability account, (2) lists its net income first in the cash flows from operating activities section, (3) adds the decrease in each current asset and the increase in each current liability to the net income, (4) subtracts the increase in each current asset and the decrease in each current liability from the net income, (5) adds the depreciation expense and any losses on the sale of property and equipment assets to the net income and subtracts any gains on the sale of property and equipment assets from net income. A company uses the indirect method because this method "ties" the net income that it reports on its income statement to the net cash provided by operating activities that it reports on its cash flow statement. Also, the indirect method shows how the changes in the parts (i.e., current assets and current liabilities) of a company's operating cycle affected its operating cash flows.

Key Terms

average cost *(p. 662)*
conservatism principle *(p. 674)*
cost of goods sold *(p. 656)*
direct method *(p. 681)*
first-in, first-out (FIFO) *(p. 659)*
FOB shipping point *(p. 657)*
FOB destination *(p. 657)*
gross profit method *(p. 677)*
holding gain or inventory profit *(p. 666)*
indirect method *(p. 683)*
inventory *(p. 654)*
in transit *(p. 656)*
last-in, first-out *(p. 660)*

LIFO liquidation *(p. 674)*
LIFO liquidation profit *(p. 674)*
LIFO reserve *(p. 671)*
lower-of-cost-or-market (LCM) method *(p. 674)*
moving average *(p. 660)*
non-LIFO *(p. 671)*
operating cycle *(p. 680)*
periodic inventory system *(p. 654)*
perpetual inventory system *(p. 654)*
replacement cost *(p. 664)*
retail inventory method *(p. 678)*
specific identification method *(p. 654)*

**SUMMARY
SURFING**

Here is an opportunity to gather information on the Internet about real-world issues related to the topics in this chapter. Go to http://www.dryden.com/account and click on the Cunningham, Nikolai, and Bazley book cover. Click on Summary Surfing, then click on this chapter number, and answer the following questions.

▶ Click on **Procter & Gamble.** Find the most recent *Annual Report*, then find *Consolidated Balance Sheet* and *Summary of Significant Accounting Policies* (in the *Notes to the Consolidated Financial Statements*) and answer these questions. How much does Procter & Gamble report as inventories for the current year? What accounting method or methods does the company use for its inventories? Now click on **Colgate-Palmolive.** Find the notes labeled *Summary of Significant Accounting Policies* and *Supplemental Balance Sheet Information* in the most current *Annual Report* and answer these questions. How much does Colgate-Palmolive report as inventories for the current year? What accounting method or methods does the company use for its inventories? Evaluate the comparability of the information disclosed by the two companies.

▶ Click on **JCPenney.** Find the most recent *Annual Report,* then find the *Consolidated Balance Sheets* and *Notes to Consolidated Financial Statements* and answer these questions. By how much would JCPenney's inventory be different in the most recent year if it used non-LIFO? By how much would JCPenney's cost of goods sold be different in the most recent year if it used non-LIFO?

Integrated Business and Accounting Situations

Answer the Following Questions in Your Own Words

Testing Your Knowledge

19-1   What three types of assets may a company include in its inventory?

19-2   What is the difference between merchandise inventory and finished goods inventory?

19-3   What is the difference between the perpetual and the periodic inventory methods?

19-4   Company X purchases inventory under terms FOB destination from Company Y, and the goods are still in transit. Which company includes the goods in its inventory? Why? How would your answers change if the purchase had been made under terms FOB shipping point?

19-5   Explain which costs are included in cost of goods sold and ending inventory under the (a) FIFO, (b) average cost, and (c) LIFO cost flow assumptions.

19-6   Explain the impact of FIFO and LIFO on a company's income statement and balance sheet if costs are rising.

19-7   Where does a company report its ending inventory and its inventory cost flow assumption in its financial statements?

19-8   Explain the difference between intracompany and intercompany analysis.

19-9   Explain what is meant by a "LIFO liquidation profit."

19-10   Explain what is meant by the lower-of-cost-or-market (LCM) method.

19-11   Under the LCM method, what does "market value" mean?

19-12 How does a company use the gross profit method to estimate its ending inventory?

19-13 How does a company use the retail inventory method to estimate its ending inventory?

19-14 Explain what is meant by a company's "operating cycle" and how the cycle affects cash flows related to accounts receivable and accounts payable.

19-15 How does a company determine its net cash provided by operating activities under the direct method?

19-16 How does a company determine its net cash provided by operating activities under the indirect method?

19-17 Identify the steps a company completes under the indirect method to compute its net cash provided by operating activities.

Applying Your Knowledge

19-18 The Schulte Tape Company has a beginning inventory for May of $2,500 (250 tapes at $10 each) and makes the following purchases and sales of tapes during May:

May	5	Purchases	150 tapes @ $11 = $1,650
	12	Sales	160 tapes
	22	Purchases	150 tapes @ $12 = 1,800
	25	Sales	80 tapes

Required: Compute the cost of goods sold and the ending inventory if the company uses the following:
(1) The perpetual inventory system and the FIFO cost flow assumption
(2) The perpetual inventory system and the LIFO cost flow assumption
(3) The periodic inventory system and the FIFO cost flow assumption
(4) The periodic inventory system and the LIFO cost flow assumption

19-19 The Gomez Folding Chair Company has 400 chairs (at $15 each) in its beginning inventory for July. It makes the following purchases and sales of chairs during July:

Date	Purchases	Sales
July 6	200 chairs @ $16 each	
14		220 chairs @ $30 each
21	140 chairs @ $17 each	
29		100 chairs @ $31 each

Required: Compute the cost of goods sold and the ending inventory if the company uses the following:
(1) The perpetual inventory system and the FIFO cost flow assumption
(2) The perpetual inventory system and the LIFO cost flow assumption
(3) The periodic inventory system and the FIFO cost flow assumption
(4) The periodic inventory system and the LIFO cost flow assumption

19-20 The Russell Video Company had 200 videos in its April 1 inventory. It uses the perpetual inventory system and made the following purchases and sales of videos during April and May.

April	9	Purchases	20 videos for $15 each
	17	Sales	30 videos
	24	Purchases	50 videos for $16 each
	26	Sales	20 videos
May	8	Sales	30 videos
	15	Purchases	60 videos for $17 each
	22	Sales	50 videos

The FIFO and the LIFO costs of the videos in the April 1 inventory were $12 and $8, respectively.

Required: (1) Compute the cost of goods sold and the ending inventory for each month if the company uses the following:
(a) The FIFO cost flow assumption
(b) The LIFO cost flow assumption

(2) Which cost flow assumption provides the more realistic balance sheet amount for ending inventory? Why? Which provides the more realistic measure of income? Why?

19-21 The Caldwell Company had 50 electric motors in its November 1 inventory. The company uses the perpetual inventory system and made the following purchases and sales of electric motors during November and December.

Nov. 12	Sales..	40 electric motors
20	Purchases..	100 electric motors for $65 each
29	Sales..	80 electric motors
Dec. 4	Purchases..	100 electric motors for $75 each
10	Purchases..	50 electric motors for $80 each
16	Sales..	140 electric motors

The FIFO and the LIFO costs of the electric motors in the November 1 inventory were $64 and $50, respectively.

Required: (1) Compute the cost of goods sold and the ending inventory for each month if the company uses the following:
  (a) The FIFO cost flow assumption
  (b) The LIFO cost flow assumption
(2) Which cost flow assumption provides the more realistic balance sheet amount for ending inventory? Why? Which provides the more realistic measure of income? Why?

19-22 The Ginther Power Tool Company had 100 air compressors in its January 1 inventory. It uses the periodic inventory system and made the following purchases of air compressors during January and February.

January 10	50 air compressors for $100 each
20	40 air compressors for $102 each
February 5	20 air compressors for $104 each
18	60 air compressors for $108 each

Sales during January and February were 80 air compressors and 100 air compressors, respectively. The FIFO, the average, and the LIFO costs of the air compressors in the January 1 inventory were $97, $95, and $62, respectively.

Required: (1) Compute the ending inventory and the cost of goods sold for each month if the company uses the following:
  (a) The FIFO cost flow assumption
  (b) The average cost flow assumption
  (c) The LIFO cost flow assumption
(2) Which cost flow assumption provides the most realistic balance sheet amount for ending inventory? Why? Which provides the most realistic measure of income? Why?

19-23 The Johnson Watch Company had 300 watches in its July 1 inventory. The company uses the periodic inventory system and made the following purchases of watches during July and August.

July 8	40 watches for $20 each
27	100 watches for $21 each
Aug. 18	50 watches for $22 each
24	60 watches for $23 each

Sales during July and August were 200 watches and 150 watches, respectively. The FIFO, the average, and the LIFO costs of the watches in the July 1 inventory were $19, $18, and $13, respectively.

Required: (1) Compute the ending inventory and the cost of goods sold for each month if the company uses the following:
  (a) The FIFO cost flow assumption
  (b) The average cost flow assumption
  (c) The LIFO cost flow assumption

(2) Which cost flow assumption provides the most realistic balance sheet amount for ending inventory? Why? Which provides the most realistic measure of income? Why?

19-24 The Brabham Kite Company had the following FIFO costs and replacement costs of kites for its ending inventory.

Item #	Number of Units	Unit Cost	Unit Replacement Cost
804	100	$10	$11
603	150	12	10
331	320	8	5
928	70	20	22

Required: (1) Compute the value of the ending inventory under the lower-of-cost-or-market method applied to individual items.

(2) How are the company's financial statements affected by the application of the lower-of-cost-or-market method?

(3) Show how the ending inventory would be reported on the company's balance sheet.

19-25 The Seaman Company's ending inventory of vacuum cleaner parts included the following items:

Item #	Number of Units	Unit Cost (FIFO)	Unit Replacement Cost
A12B	50	$100	$90
L15C	150	76	82
P27X	200	60	55
W08S	400	10	9

Required: (1) Compute the value of the ending inventory under the lower-of-cost-or-market method.

(2) Using T-accounts, prepare the entry to record the reduction of the inventory to its market value.

(3) Show how the ending inventory would be reported on the company's balance sheet.

(4) If, at the end of the next year, none of the items in inventory has a market value below cost, how will the income statement for that year be affected by the application of the lower-of-cost-or-market method in this year?

19-26 On March 31, Ireland Peat Company needs to estimate its ending inventory for preparation of its first quarter's financial statements. The following information is available:

Inventory, January 1 .... $30,000
Purchases (net) 40,000
Sales (net)... 85,000

A study of past income statements indicates that a gross profit percentage of 25% of net sales is appropriate.

Required: Compute the cost of goods sold and the ending inventory.

19-27 On September 1, a fire destroyed all but $3,000 of Redster Company's inventory. The following information is available from the company's accounting records:

Inventory, January 1 .... $ 24,000
Purchases (net), January 1 through August 31 67,000
Sales (net), January 1 through August 31 100,000

Based on recent history, Redster's gross profit has averaged 30% of net sales.

Required: Compute the estimated loss of inventory from the fire.

19-28 Lotus Tire Company estimates its ending inventory for its quarterly financial statements by using the gross profit method. The following information is available from its accounting records:

	First Quarter	Second Quarter
Inventory, Jan. 1	$30,000	
Purchases	38,000	$50,000
Purchases returns	3,000	5,000
Sales	70,000	80,000
Sales returns	3,000	2,000

The company uses a gross profit percentage of 30% of net sales.

Required: (1) Compute the cost of goods sold and the ending inventory for each quarter.

(2) How would your answer for the second quarter change if the company's gross profit percentage dropped to 28% for that quarter?

19-29 Scheckter Department Store uses the retail inventory method. At the end of the first quarter, the following information is available:

	Cost	Retail
Inventory, Jan. 1	$15,000	$18,000
Purchases	47,000	86,000
Purchases returns	3,000	4,000
Sales		90,000
Sales returns		5,000

Required: (1) Compute the cost of goods sold and the gross profit for the first quarter.

(2) If the company took a physical inventory at the end of the first quarter and the retail value was $14,000, what is the cost of the ending inventory?

(3) What may have caused the difference in the answers for (1) and (2)?

19-30 Burris Department Store uses the retail inventory method. At the end of the first quarter, the following information is available:

	Cost	Retail
Inventory, Jan. 1	$ 5,000	$ 9,000
Purchases	35,000	68,000
Purchases returns	2,000	3,000
Sales		65,000
Sales returns		2,000

Required: (1) Compute the cost of goods sold and the gross profit for the first quarter.

(2) If the company took a physical inventory at the end of the first quarter and the retail value was $10,000, what is the cost of the ending inventory?

(3) What may have caused the difference in the answers for (1) and (2)?

19-31 The following information is taken from the accounting records of Tilder Company for the current year:

Net income, $47,000
Increase in inventory, $4,600
Decrease in accounts receivable, $8,500
Depreciation expense, $10,000
Decrease in salaries payable, $1,000
Gain on sale of land, $3,000
Increase in accounts payable, $6,200

Required: Prepare the cash flows from operating activities section of Tilder's cash flow statement for the current year.

19-32 In the current year, Faldo Company earned net income of $61,000. Included in the computation of net income was $12,500 of depreciation expense and a loss of $4,000 on the sale of land. During the year, the company had the following changes in its current assets and current liabilities:

Increases	Decreases
Accounts receivable, $5,700	Inventory, $7,400
Salaries payable, $3,000	Accounts payable, $9,600

Required: (1) Prepare the cash flows from operating activities section of Faldo's cash flow statement for the current year.

(2) What does your answer to (1) reveal compared with Faldo's net income?

19-33   During the current year, Woods Company earned net income of $56,000. Depreciation expense of $11,000 was included in the computation of net income. Woods' accounting records show the following beginning and ending balances in its current assets and current liabilities for the year:

Account	Ending Balance	Beginning Balance
Accounts receivable	$56,700	$37,200
Inventory	34,400	43,100
Prepaid rent	2,000	0
Accounts payable	25,600	33,000
Salaries payable	1,300	0

Required: (1) Prepare the cash flows from operating activities section of Woods' cash flow statement for the current year.

(2) What does your answer to (1) reveal compared with the company's net income?

Making Evaluations

19-34   Birkin Company uses the FIFO inventory cost flow assumption. It includes the following amounts in the company's financial statements:

Inventory, January 1	$100,000
Purchases	300,000
Cost of goods sold	250,000
Inventory, December 31	150,000

The company sells only one product, and purchases and sales are made evenly throughout the year. The replacement cost of the inventory at January 1 and December 31 is $125,000 and $187,500, respectively. The cost of the company's purchases was 25% higher at the end of the year than at the beginning.

Required: The owner of Birkin Company asks you to analyze the preceding information and tell her the following:

(1) How much would the cost of goods sold be if it was computed on the basis of the average replacement cost for the period?

(2) What is the amount of the holding gain (inventory profit) included in the income computed on a FIFO basis?

(3) Did the number of units in inventory increase or decrease during the year?

19-35   Nike disclosed the following in its 1998 annual report (in millions):   **www.nike.com**

Inventory valuation: Inventories are stated at the lower of cost or market. Cost is determined using the last-in, first-out (LIFO) method for substantially all U.S. inventories. Non-U.S. inventories are valued on a first-in, first-out (FIFO) basis.

	May 31	
	1998	1997
Finished goods	$1,303.8	$1,248.4
Work-in-process	34.7	50.2
Raw materials	58.1	40.0
	$1,396.6	$1,338.6

The excess of replacement cost over LIFO cost was $21.9 million and $20.7 million at May 31, 1998 and May 31, 1997, respectively.

The company also disclosed that its costs of sales were $6,065.5 and $5,503.0 in 1998 and 1997 respectively.

www.reebok.com

Reebok disclosed the following in its 1997 annual report:

Inventory valuation: Inventory, substantially all finished goods, is recorded at the lower of cost (first-in, first-out method) or market.

Required: (1) Why do you think that Nike and Reebok use different cost flow assumptions?
(2) Why do you think that Nike uses a different method for its international inventories than it uses in the United States?
(3) Explain why a user might want to convert Nike's inventory and cost of goods sold to non-LIFO amounts.
(4) Compute the amounts of Nike's beginning and ending inventories for 1998 and its 1998 cost of goods sold under a non-LIFO method.
(5) Compute Nike's inventory turnover ratio for 1998 using (a) the LIFO amounts and (b) the non-LIFO amounts.
(6) What is the cumulative effect at May 31, 1998 on Nike's cost of goods sold from using LIFO?

www.coca-cola.com

19-36 Coca-Cola disclosed the following in its 1997 annual report:

Inventories: Inventories consist primarily of raw materials and supplies and are valued at the lower of cost or market. In general, cost is determined on the basis of average cost or first-in, first-out methods.

www.pepsico.com

PepsiCo disclosed the following in its 1997 annual report (in millions):

Inventories: Inventories are valued at the lower of cost (computed on the average, first-in, first-out or last-in, first-out method) or net realizable value.

Year-end	1997	1996
Raw materials and supplies	$400	$484
Finished goods	332	369
	$732	$853

The cost of 43% of 1997 inventories and 39% of 1996 inventories was computed using the last-in, first-out method.

Required: (1) Why do you think that Coca-Cola and PepsiCo use different cost flow assumptions? Why do you think that PepsiCo uses all three cost flow assumptions? Is there anything you find surprising about PepsiCo's disclosures?
(2) Explain why a user might want to convert PepsiCo's inventory and cost of goods sold to non-LIFO amounts.

www.kelloggs.com

19-37 Kellogg Company disclosed the following in its 1997 annual report:

Inventories: Inventories are valued at the lower of cost (principally average) or market.

www.**QuakerOats**.com

Quaker Oats disclosed the following in its 1997 annual report (in millions):

Inventories: Inventories are valued at the lower of cost or market, using various cost methods, and include the cost of raw materials, labor and overhead. The percentages of year end inventories valued using each of the methods is as follows:

December 31	1997	1996
Last-in, first-out (LIFO)	65%	53%
Average quarterly cost	30%	39%
First-in, first-out (FIFO)	5%	8%

If the LIFO method of valuing these inventories was not used, total inventories would have been $8.6 million and $15.3 million higher than reported as of December 31, 1997 and 1996, respectively.

	1997	1996
Cost of goods sold	$2,564.9	$2,807.5
Inventories	256.1	274.9

Required: (1) Why do you think that Kellogg and Quaker Oats use different cost flow assumptions? Why do you think that Quaker Oats uses all three cost flow assumptions?

(2) Explain why a user might want to convert Quaker Oats' inventory and cost of goods sold to non-LIFO amounts.

(3) Compute the amounts of Quaker Oats' beginning and ending inventories for 1997 and its 1997 cost of goods sold under a non-LIFO method.

(4) Compute Quaker Oats' inventory turnover ratio for 1997 using (a) the LIFO amounts and (b) the non-LIFO amounts.

(5) What is the cumulative effect on Quaker Oats' cost of goods sold of using LIFO?

19-38 JCPenney disclosed the following in its "Management's Discussion and Analysis" section of its 1997 annual report:

www.**jcpenney**.com

FIFO operating earnings increased to $1,371 million in 1997, up 15.9 per cent compared with $1,183 million in 1996. The increase was principally the result of improvements to gross margin and managing of selling, general, and administrative (SG&A) expenses. FIFO gross margin increased by 70 basis points in 1997 compared with 1996, despite a very promotional first half of the year. The Company recorded a LIFO credit of $20 million in both 1997 and 1996. SG&A expenses were well managed across all areas of the Company, particularly advertising, and were flat as a percentage of sales as compared with 1996.

FIFO operating earnings were $1,183 million in 1996 compared with $1,199 million in 1995. Sales in JCPenney stores were soft in the first half of 1996 compared with 1995 and accelerated in the second half as inventory levels rose and the Company implemented aggressive marketing programs to drive traffic in the stores. FIFO gross margin declined by 70 basis points in 1996 compared with 1995, primarily as a result of aggressive marketing programs designed to boost sales volumes and reduce inventory levels. In 1995, the Company recorded a $7 million LIFO credit. SG&A expenses were well managed in 1996, improving by 40 basis points as a percent of sales.

Required: Assume you are a financial analyst. Write a report on JCPenney's performance for those of your clients who you know are not financially sophisticated. (A LIFO credit is the same as a change in the LIFO reserve for the year.)

19-39 May Department Stores Co. disclosed the following in its 1997 annual report:

www.**maycompany**.com

Earnings before interest and taxes (EBIT) for the past three years were as follows:

(dollars in millions)	1997	1996	1995	Increase 1997	Increase 1996
Operating earnings	$1,578	$1,509	$1,410	4.6%	7.0%
Percent of revenues	12.5%	12.6%	12.9%		

EBIT presented above includes a LIFO (last-in, first-out) credit of $5 million, $20 million, and $53 million in 1997, 1996, and 1995, respectively.

EBIT, excluding LIFO, is presented below on a supplementary basis for comparative purposes:

(dollars in millions)	1997	1996	1995	Increase 1997	Increase 1996
Operating earnings	$1,573	$1,489	$1,357	5.7%	9.6%
Percent of revenues	12.4%	12.4%	12.4%		

Cost of Sales

Cost of sales includes cost of merchandise sold and buying and occupancy costs. Cost of sales was $8.73 billion in 1997, compared with $8.23 billion in 1996, a 6.2% increase. The overall increase resulted from a 7.0% increase in sales. As a percent of revenues, cost of sales increased 0.3% from 68.5% in 1996 to 68.8% in 1997. Approximately 0.2% of this increase relates to the finance charge component of revenues decreasing 5.7% with no corresponding decrease in cost of sales. The remaining increase was caused by the decrease in the LIFO credit.

Cost of sales was $8.23 billion in 1996, compared with $7.46 billion in 1995, a 10.2% increase. The overall increase resulted from a 9.9% increase in sales (52 weeks in 1996 versus 53 weeks in 1995). As a percent of revenues, cost of sales increased 0.4% from 68.1% in 1995 to 68.5% in 1996. This increase was caused primarily by the decrease in the LIFO credit.

The impact of LIFO on cost of sales, as a percent of revenues, is shown below:

	1997	1996	1995
Cost of sales	68.8%	68.5%	68.1%
LIFO credit	(0.1)	(0.2)	(0.5)
Cost of sales before LIFO	68.9%	68.7%	68.6%

Required: Assume you are a financial analyst. Write a report that explains May's inventory disclosure for those of your clients who you know are not financially sophisticated. (A LIFO credit is the same as a change in the LIFO reserve for the year.)

19-40 When Janet Guthrie arrived at her dress shop on the morning of June 15, 2000, she found that thieves had broken in overnight and stolen much of her merchandise. The agent of Alright Insurance Company agreed to visit in the afternoon and promised he would write a check for the amount of the loss if she could verify it. Janet took a physical inventory of the merchandise not stolen and determined that its cost was $2,000. Janet needs to make an estimate of the loss so that she can collect the insurance money and buy new merchandise. She asks for your help, and you agree to look at her accounting records. She tells you that the store has been in business since January 1, 1999, and that she does not use the retail method of accounting for inventory. You obtain the following information:

Inventory, January 1, 1999	$ 7,000
Purchases, 1999	49,000
Purchases, 2000	33,000
Sales (net), 1999	80,000
Sales (net), 2000	50,000
Purchases returns, 1999	4,000
Purchases returns, 2000	2,500
Inventory, January 1, 2000	16,000
Physical inventory after theft	2,000

Required: How much would you recommend that Janet settle for with the insurance company? What is the major assumption underlying your answer?

19-41 Intel disclosed the following selected amounts (in millions) in its 1997 annual report: **www.intel.com**

Net revenues	$25,070
Cost of sales	9,945
Research and development	2,347
Marketing, general and administrative	2,891
Interest expense	27
Interest income	799
Income tax expense	3,714
Decrease in accounts receivable	$ 285
Increase in inventories	404
Decrease in other assets (net)	97
Increase in accounts payable	438
Increase in accrued compensation and benefits	140
Increase in income taxes payable	179
Depreciation	2,192
Net loss on retirements of property, plant, and equipment	130
Increase in deferred income tax liability	6

Required: (1) Explain the advantages of (a) the indirect method and (b) the direct method of reporting the cash flows from operating activities. Explain which method you prefer.

(2) Calculate Intel's net cash provided by operating activities for 1997 under the direct method, computing a single amount for all the operating payments other than those for interest and for income taxes.

(3) Calculate Intel's net cash provided by operating activities for 1997 under the indirect method.

(4) Calculate Intel's operating cash flow margin (discussed in Chapter 8) for 1997. In 1996, Intel's operating cash flow margin was 41.9% ($8,743 ÷ $20,847). Explain how the company's performance has changed.

19-42 Rocky Mountain Chocolate Factory disclosed the following selected amounts in its **www.rmcfusa.com**
1998 annual report:

Sales	$20,659,076
Franchise and royalty fees	3,104,906
Cost of sales	10,960,966
Franchise costs	1,106,172
Sales and marketing	1,290,516
General and administrative	1,763,757
Retail operating expenses	6,043,810
Interest expense	664,852
Interest income	114,732
Income tax expense	788,640
Increase in accounts and notes receivable (trade)	$158,353
Increase in inventories	485,400
Decrease in other assets	74,872
Increase in accounts payable	497,098
Increase in refundable income taxes	250,159
Decrease in accrued liabilities and deferred income	379,081
Increase in deferred income tax liability	767,666
Depreciation and amortization	1,335,715
Net losses on sales and disposals	943,609

Required: (1) Explain the advantages of (a) the indirect method and (b) the direct method of reporting the cash flows from operating activities. Explain which method you prefer.

(2) Calculate Rocky Mountain's net cash provided by operating activities for 1998 under the direct method, computing a single amount for all the operating payments other than those for interest and for income taxes.

(3) Calculate Rocky Mountain's net cash provided by operating activities for 1998 under the indirect method.

www.generalmills.com **19-43** The annual report for General Mills is included in Appendix C.

Required: (1) Calculate the cash flows from operating activities for 1998 under the direct method. Ignore unusual items and earnings (losses) from joint ventures, and compute a single amount for all the operating payments other than those for interest and for income taxes. Since you are ignoring certain items, don't be surprised if your answer is not the same as the cash flows from operating activities reported by General Mills.

(2) Using General Mills' reported amounts, evaluate for 1997 and 1998 the company's cash flows from operating activities using the three cash flow ratios we discussed in Chapter 8. The company reported total assets and total stockholders' equity at the end of 1996 of $3,294.7 million and $307.7 million, respectively.

19-44 Yesterday, you received the following letter for your advice column in the local paper:

Dear Dr. Decisive:

I think I must be losing my mind! I have just been looking over some annual reports with my girlfriend. I was trying to impress her with my knowledge. But then I started to explain to her about inventory, cost of goods sold, and such measures of performance as gross profit and inventory turnover. I got lost trying to explain why some companies use one method, other similar companies use a different method, and others use *three* different methods. Is all this just to help keep accountants in jobs? My girlfriend made sense when she said, "When I go in a clothing store, I just pick the one that is on top of the pile, but when I buy food I always look for the package with the latest expiration date. Is there an accountant watching me through the security camera to check which I buy?"

Call me "Inventory-ily Impaired."

Required: Meet with your Dr. Decisive team and write a response to "Inventory-ily Impaired."

CHAPTER OUTLINE

MANAGING, REPORTING, AND EVALUATING NONCURRENT ASSETS IN A CORPORATE ENVIRONMENT

This section consists of two chapters

which discuss issues involving a

corporation's noncurrent assets.

After reading these chapters, you

will be able to:

▶ *Understand the time value of money and the present value of future cash flows*

▶ *Compute the net present value of a capital expenditure proposal*

▶ *Know how to make a capital investment decision*

▶ *Explain how a corporation values and reports property, plant and equipment, and intangible assets on its financial statements*

▶ *Understand how different depreciation methods affect a corporation's financial statements*

▶ *Use a corporation's noncurrent asset information in intracompany and intercompany analyses*

CAPITAL EXPENDITURE DECISIONS

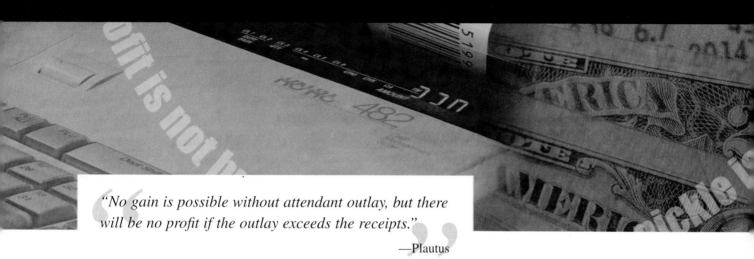

"No gain is possible without attendant outlay, but there will be no profit if the outlay exceeds the receipts."

—Plautus

1 What is a capital expenditure, and what are the four steps in a capital expenditure decision?

2 What does a company include in the initial cost of a capital expenditure proposal?

3 What are the relevant costs of a capital expenditure proposal, and how do operating income, depreciation, and ending cash flows affect these costs?

4 How does a company determine the rate of return it requires on a capital expenditure proposal?

5 How does a company use the net present value method to evaluate a capital expenditure proposal?

6 What is the difference between the payback method and the average rate of return on investment method for evaluating a capital expenditure proposal?

7 How does a company decide which capital expenditure proposal to accept when it has proposals that accomplish the same thing, or when it cannot obtain sufficient cash to make all of its desired investments?

Have you ever purchased, or considered purchasing, a car? If so, you probably considered how the car looked, how much power it had, how comfortable it was, how it performed on the road, and how it compared with other cars. More importantly, you most certainly weighed, not only the price of the car, but also how much the payments would be and when you would make them (including payments for upkeep and repairs). Furthermore, you probably considered how well the car would retain its value and what its potential value would be when you are ready to sell it. A company makes a similar decision when it invests in property and equipment and in certain long-term projects.

In this chapter we will discuss a company's long-term decision-making involving capital expenditures. Like the decision to purchase a car, a capital expenditure decision involves considering related cash receipts and payments that occur at different times, perhaps over several years. Therefore, in this type of decision-making, a manager must understand such issues as how to estimate cash receipts and payments, what cash receipts and payments are relevant to the decision to make a capital expenditure, and what steps must be completed in the process of making the decision. Many of these issues are the same as those we discussed in Chapter 15 on short-term decision-making. As you will see, however, a key difference between the two types of decisions is that for long-term decision-making, the manager needs to consider the time value of money and therefore must have an understanding of present value computations.

Capital Expenditure Decisions

❚ *What is a capital expenditure, and what are the four steps in a capital expenditure decision?*

A **capital expenditure** decision is a long-term decision in which a company determines whether or not to make an investment (cash payment) at the time of the decision in order to obtain future net cash receipts totaling more than the investment. The future net cash receipts related to the investment provide a "return" on the investment. This "return" is what makes a company want to make a capital expenditure (investment).

Most companies have a large number and a wide variety of investment (capital expenditure) opportunities each year. They can expand factory or office size, replace old equipment, purchase additional new equipment, introduce new products, increase inventories, start an employee-training program, or engage in a special advertising campaign, to name a few. These opportunities or "projects" come to the attention of a company's managers in the form of *proposals* to invest cash. Because these proposals involve estimating future cash receipts and payments over several years, capital expenditure decisions are sometimes referred to as *capital budgeting* decisions.

 Other than the purchase of a car, can you think of any personal capital expenditure decisions you have made or will make? What cash receipts and payments are related to those decisions?

Making a Capital Expenditure Decision

As a general rule, *a capital expenditure proposal is acceptable to a company when its return on investment is greater than the cost to the company of providing the cash to make the investment.* Therefore, to determine whether a capital expenditure proposal is acceptable, a company must complete four steps. First, the company must determine the initial cash payment needed to make the investment. Second, the company must estimate the future cash receipts and payments (cash flows) expected from the investment, and the time period over which it expects these future cash receipts and payments to occur. Third, the company must determine its cost of providing the cash to make the investment. Finally, the company must determine whether the estimated future cash flows will provide it a return that is sufficient (after adjusting for the time value of money) to cover the cost of providing the cash to make the investment. If the cash flows of a proposal will produce a return on investment that is higher than the cost of providing the cash to make the investment, the difference contributes to the long-term "profitability" of the company. This makes the proposal acceptable for the company. If the return on investment will be less than the cost, the proposal is undesirable and should be rejected. We will discuss each of the preceding steps in the following sections.

Determining the Initial Cash Payment

Whenever a company makes a capital expenditure decision, one of the first questions it asks is, "What is this going to cost?" The question may be broken down into two parts: (1) the initial cost and (2) the cost(s) incurred in later years. We will discuss any costs incurred in later years in the estimated future cash receipts and payments section of this chapter. The **initial cost** is the expected cash payment to be made to put the proposal into operation. In other words, it is the capital that the company must expend (the *capital expenditure*) to make the investment.

For instance, a company may be deciding whether or not it should invest in a new machine that it will use for six years. A vendor has quoted a price of $10,000 for the machine. The company expects to pay transportation costs of $800 to get the machine to its factory, and costs of $400 for installing the machine. The initial cost of this capital expenditure proposal is $11,200, computed as follows:

Cost of machine	$10,000
Transportation costs	800
Installation costs	400
Initial cost	$11,200

This $11,200 is the cash payment that the company must make to put the machine into operation (the initial cash payment). In some cases, a capital expenditure proposal may require the investment of additional *working capital*. For instance, a new piece of equipment may require an investment in additional raw materials inventory. In this case, for capital expenditure decision-making, the additional cost of the investment in raw materials inventory should be included in the initial cost of the equipment. However, with just-in-time inventory systems, additional investments in inventory may not be necessary.

 Why do you think additional investments in inventory may not be necessary with a just-in-time inventory system?

You may think that determining the initial costs of a proposed capital expenditure is easier than estimating expected future cash flows because initial costs are incurred at the present time and therefore are more "definite" and "accurate." In many situations this is true, but not always. In some cases initial costs involve the use of estimates that are not very precise and that include large numbers. For instance, take the example of a company that is considering a capital expenditure to build a new 100,000-square-foot factory. What is the initial cost of the factory? The initial cost includes the cost of construction, the cost of all the equipment that goes into the factory, training costs for the employees, and many other costs. A contractor may give a "rough estimate" of the cost of construction but is not likely to spend much time on the estimate if the company is only considering building the factory. The U.S. government does print estimated "per-foot" costs of construction, but they are just that—estimates. And these estimates vary from city to city and by type of construction. So determining the initial cost of this type of capital expenditure can rely heavily on estimates. Nonetheless, a good estimate is better than a guess!

Estimating Future Cash Flows

The expected future net cash receipts help to provide the return on an investment. As we show in the following diagram, these net future cash receipts may come in three forms: (1) future cash receipts only, (2) future cash receipts that are more than future cash payments, or (3) savings of future cash payments.

2 *What does a company include in the initial cost of a capital expenditure proposal?*

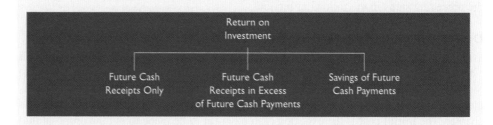

The return from some investments comes from future cash receipts only. An example of this is when a company buys stocks or bonds of another company to receive dividends or interest. The dividends or interest received plus the eventual selling price of the securities (all cash receipts) provide a return when they are more than the amount initially invested in the securities.

In other cases, both future cash receipts and payments affect the return from the investment. For example, suppose Unlimited Decadence invests in additional equipment to be able to produce and sell more cases of Darkly Decadent candy bars. If the cash receipts from increased sales are more than the cash payments for increased production and selling costs, the increase in the net cash receipts (the difference between the future cash receipts and cash payments) provides a return on the investment when it is more than the amount that Unlimited Decadence initially invested in the additional equipment.

Finally, some investments do not involve increasing future cash receipts, but instead involve *reducing future cash payments*. The effect on a company's cash, however, is the same. The benefit received by the decrease in future cash payments also can provide a return on the investment. For example, suppose that a local newspaper invests $3,000 today in an employee-training program that is expected to save $1,000 in payments for labor costs each year for five years. This investment has the same expected return for the newspaper as would investing $3,000 to increase cash receipts from sales of advertising space in the paper by $1,000 each year for five years.

Determining Relevant Cash Flows

3 *What are the relevant costs of a capital expenditure proposal, and how do operating income, depreciation, and ending cash flows affect these costs?*

Whether you are dealing with future cash receipts only, net future cash receipts, or savings in future cash payments, it is important to identify the relevant cash flows and to estimate the number of years over which these cash flows will occur. **Relevant cash flows** are future cash flows that differ, either in *amount* or in *timing*, as a result of accepting a capital expenditure proposal. That is, relevant cash flows are (1) the *additional* future cash flows (either future receipts or payments) over and above a company's existing cash flows, or (2) the *savings* in future cash payments. Relevant cash flows may be either *variable* or *fixed* cash flows. Again, the key is whether there is a change to the company's cash flows as a result of accepting the proposal. The reason that cash flows differing in amount or in timing are relevant is that they affect the company's long-term profitability.

Capital expenditure decisions involve whether or not to engage in a long-term investment: to buy a machine or not to buy it, to expand the size of the factory or not to expand it, to introduce a new product or not to introduce it, and so on. We refer to alternatives such as *not* buying the machine, *not* expanding the size of the factory, or *not* introducing the new product as the *"do-nothing"* alternative. Choosing the do-nothing alternative does not change a company's cash flows. On the other hand, choosing to accept a capital expenditure proposal—whether it is to buy a new machine, expand the size of the factory, or introduce a new product—*does* cause changes in the company's cash flows. In evaluating a capital expenditure proposal, *it is useful to think of the do-nothing alternative as having zero cash flows and the capital expenditure proposal as having cash flows equal to the **changes** it causes.* This approach helps you focus on the relevant cash flows from the proposal.

Deciding what cash flows are relevant for a capital expenditure decision is similar to deciding what costs are relevant for a short-term decision. Cash receipts and payments that occurred *prior* to the capital expenditure decision are irrelevant because they cannot be affected by the decision. They are *sunk costs*. Cash flows that result from activities *not* required for any of the decision alternatives also cannot be relevant (even if they are future cash flows) because selecting any of the alternatives will not affect them. To be relevant to a particular capital expenditure decision, cash flows must

1. occur in the future,

2. result from activities that are required by the proposal, and

3. cause a change in the company's existing cash flows.

Operating Income and Annual Cash Flows

When a company estimates its relevant future cash flows from a capital expenditure proposal, it uses the "best" available information for its predictions. Frequently, the best available information is its expected future additional operating revenues and/or expenses. Most revenues and expenses of a company result in related cash receipts and payments of the same amounts at approximately the same points in time. For example, a company usually collects cash from credit sales very soon after the sales occur. Similarly, a company normally pays wages to employees soon after the employees earn them. As a result, cash receipts from accounts receivable and cash payments for wages payable in a year are likely to be about the same as the sales revenue and wages expense for the year. Of course, sometimes large differences occur. For example, sometimes a company prepays expenses for several years. In this case the company considers the amount of the cash payment and the year in which it makes the payment rather than the annual expense.

Treatment of Depreciation

Depreciation is another expense for which the related cash flows occur in different years and in different amounts than the expense. For example, if Unlimited Decadence plans to purchase a machine for $1,000 cash and use the machine until it sells it at the end of 10 years for the estimated residual value of $100, the yearly "straight-line" depreciation expense for each of the 10 years will be $90 [($1,000 − $100) ÷ 10]. Since it plans to pay cash for the machine on the date of purchase, Unlimited Decadence would make no cash payments for the machine in any of those years, however.

The planned purchase and the resale of this machine involve only two relevant cash flows. The first is the cash payment of $1,000 to purchase the machine. The second is the $100 cash receipt at the end of year 10. A capital expenditure analysis should focus on the amounts and timing of these cash flows and *not* on the $90 yearly depreciation expense. It is important to understand that we are not ignoring this major cost; we are simply treating it in a different way.[1]

 Even though depreciation is not a cash flow, it affects a corporation's income tax payments. How do you think depreciation expense would affect a corporation's income tax payments over the life of the related asset?

Ending Cash Flows

A capital expenditure proposal may have some relevant cash flows occurring at the end of the project's life. For instance, in the example we just presented for depreciation, there was a cash receipt (the residual value) at the end of the machine's life. Another example relates to the earlier discussion of the possibility of investing in additional working capital (e.g.,

---

[1]The depreciation that a company includes on its tax return provides yearly cash savings in income taxes. However, for simplicity, we do not consider these cash flows in this chapter.

inventory) at the beginning of a project. If this occurs, the company will "recover" the working capital at the end of the project (when the company sells the final items of inventory), and will treat this "recovery" as a cash receipt. Not all proposals have cash receipts at the end of the project's life. In fact, in some cases there will be an additional cash payment. For instance, it is sometimes necessary to pay someone to haul off fully depreciated and used-up factory equipment.

When a company decides to accept a capital expenditure proposal, it stores the information it used to analyze the proposal in its integrated accounting system. Later, then, it may use the information in its accounting process. For instance, suppose that based on a capital expenditure analysis, a company decides to purchase a new machine. As the company uses this machine, it retrieves the information about the machine's estimated life and estimated residual value from its integrated accounting system for use in its depreciation expense calculations, as you will see in Chapter 21.

Determining the Required Return on Investment

4 *How does a company determine the rate of return it requires on a capital expenditure proposal?*

For any capital expenditure proposal, the question arises as to the company's required return on the investment. The required return is equal to the cost of providing cash for the investment, and is expressed as a percentage rate. For instance, a 15% rate means that the cost is 15 cents per year for every dollar invested. A company's financial position improves as a result of accepting a capital expenditure proposal only when the proposal provides a return on investment that is higher than the cost of providing the cash for the investment (in this case, greater than 15%).

The rate that measures the cost to a company of providing cash for investments is called the company's "cost of capital." A company's **cost of capital** is the weighted-average cost (rate of return) it must pay to all sources of capital. Remember, a company receives its capital from short-term borrowing (e.g., issuing notes payable), long-term borrowing (e.g., issuing bonds payable), and stockholders (e.g., selling stock). Each of these creditor and stockholder groups demands a "return on their investment" in the form of interest, dividends, or increased market value. The key to determining a company's cost of capital is to combine these returns into an "average" return.

There are several ways a company may compute its average cost of capital. One simple way is to determine the return demanded by each group and then weight this rate by the proportion of the company's total capital that the group has provided. For instance, suppose a company's total capital consists of 40% liabilities and 60% stockholders' equity. The liabilities pay an interest rate of 8%, and stockholders expect a return of 12%. In this example, the company's weighted average cost of capital is 10.4%, computed as follows:

	Proportion of equity		Required return		
Debt	40%	×	8%	=	3.2%
Stockholders' equity	60%	×	12%	=	7.2%
Cost of capital					10.4%

A company's cost of capital is the *cutoff rate* used to distinguish between acceptable and unacceptable capital expenditure proposals. In other words, the return on the proposed capital expenditure must be equal to or greater than the company's cost of capital to be acceptable. In this example, the return must be equal to or greater than 10.4%. In this book we are not concerned with computing a company's cost of capital. We stress that a proper cutoff rate must be set and used consistently in evaluating whether capital expenditure proposals will benefit a company. Throughout the rest of this chapter and in the homework, we will refer to this cutoff rate as the company's **required rate of return.**

Determining Acceptable Capital Expenditure Proposals

*The return on an investment comes from the receipt of future **net** cash receipts that total more than the investment.* For example, if a $100 investment provides a net cash receipt of $121 two years later, the investment earns a return. The receipt of $121 can be thought of as the sum of (1) a return *of* the investment ($100), plus (2) a return *on* the investment ($21). Regarding a capital expenditure proposal, the question is whether the expected return *on* the investment is high enough to make the investment acceptable. An *acceptable* rate of return on a capital expenditure proposal is one that is *equal to* or *higher than* the company's required rate of return. An *unacceptable* rate of return is *lower* than the required rate of return, in which case the proposal should be rejected.

A company may use several methods to analyze whether the rate of return on a capital expenditure proposal is acceptable. We will discuss three: (1) the net present value method, (2) the payback method, and (3) the average rate of return on investment method. Before we discuss these methods, however, you need to understand the concept of the time value of money and the computation of "present value."

The Time Value of Money and Present Value

Since capital expenditure decisions involve cash payments and cash receipts occurring at different times, often over several years, a manager must consider the time value of money in these decisions. *No analysis that ignores the time value of money can provide a sound basis for making capital expenditure decisions.*

To understand the time value of money, consider whether you would rather receive $1 today or $1 next year. Your answer should be that you would rather receive $1 today because a dollar held today is worth more than a dollar received a year from now. If you received $1 today and put it in an interest-bearing account, you would have more than $1 a year from now. If you waited until next year to receive $1, you would have only $1 a year from now. The difference between the two amounts is *interest*, which reflects the *time value of money*.

To illustrate the time value of money, suppose that you have $100 on January 1, 1999, and can invest it at 10%. This money will grow over the next three years as shown in the following table:

Year	Amount at Beginning of the Year	Interest at 10%	Amount at End of the Year
1999	$100	$10.00	$110.00
2000	110	11.00	121.00
2001	121	12.10	133.10

Therefore you would rather have $100 today than $100 in one year because the $100 today grows to $110 in one year. Alternatively, the table shows that the following amounts, given the 10% interest rate and their respective dates, have *equivalent* values:

▶ $100 at the beginning of 1999

▶ $110 at the end of 1999 (beginning of 2000)

▶ $121 at the end of 2000 (beginning of 2001)

▶ $133.10 at the end of 2001 (beginning of 2002)

 Why do you think these four amounts are equivalent?

Einstein discovers that time is actually money.

Since these amounts have equivalent values, if you were asked which amount you wanted to receive, you would be indifferent about the four alternatives, given the 10% rate.

It is important to know that the dollar amounts have a time and an interest rate attached to them. Whenever you are considering the time value of money, you must always know the date at which the dollar amount is measured and the appropriate interest rate. A dollar received or paid in 1999 does not have the same value as a dollar received or paid in 2000.

Definition of Present Value

There is an important term that is widely used whenever the time value of money is being considered. The **present value** is the value today of a certain amount of dollars paid or received in the future. Either the payor or the receiver of money can use the present value concept.[2] In the preceding example, $100 is the present value at the beginning of 1999 of $133.10 to be paid or received at the end of 2000 when the interest rate is 10%.

The concept underlying present value is compound interest. **Compound interest** is interest that accrues on both the principal and the past (unpaid) interest. Thus during 1999, interest of 10% accrues on the principal of $100, making a total of $110 at the end of 1999. In 2000, interest of 10% accrues on the $110 (the principal *and* the 1999 interest). The interest amounts to $11 for 2000. Similarly, in 2001, interest of $12.10 is accrued on $121 ($100 + $10 + $11) so that the total amount is $133.10 at the end of 2001.

The computation of a present value is necessary in many situations. In this chapter, we will use present value computations in evaluating capital expenditure proposals. In later

---

[2]Another concept sometimes used is future value. The **future value** is the value at a future date of a certain amount of dollars paid or received today. Since present value is more commonly used, for simplicity we do not discuss future value in this book.

chapters, we will use present value computations in accounting for items such as investments in bonds, bonds payable, leases, and mortgages. As you will see, formulas and tables simplify present value computations.

Present Value Formulas and Tables

Formulas or tables may be used instead of preparing year-by-year calculations of present values. But first you must understand that there are two types of future cash flows, a single amount and an annuity.

Present Value of a Single Future Amount

A single future **amount** is a one-time future cash flow. For example, if Unlimited Decadence plans to use a mixing machine for three years and then sell it, the cash it will receive from the sale is a single future amount. The general relationship between the present value and a future amount is shown in the following equation:

$$PV = \frac{FA}{(1 + i)^n}$$

where:

$$PV = \text{Present value}$$
$$FA = \text{Future amount}$$
$$i = \text{Interest rate}$$
$$n = \text{Number of periods}$$

Using the same example of 10% and three years, if the future amount of $133.10 is known, the present value is calculated as follows:

$$PV = \frac{FA}{(1 + i)^n}$$

$$= \frac{\$133.10}{(1 + 0.10)^3}$$

$$= \frac{\$133.10}{1.331}$$

$$= \underline{\underline{\$100}}$$

A table can simplify the calculation process even more. Table 20-1 at the end of this chapter is entitled Present Value of $1 Due in n Periods, but you can use it to figure the present value of any single future amount. With information from the table, you can compute a present value by using the following simple formula:

$$PV = FA \times \text{Present Value of \$1 Factor}$$

A **factor** is a decimal amount in the table. If you look up the factor for 10% and three periods in Table 20-1,[3] you will find that it is 0.7513. This represents the present value of *$1* received or paid at the end of three years. The present value of *$133.10* received or paid at the end of three years, using a 10% interest rate, is 133.10 times the present value of $1. Another way of saying this is that the present value of $133.10 is $133.10 times the 0.7513 factor, as follows:

---

[3]The factors in Table 20-1 were computed using the equation for the present value of $1 factor shown at the beginning of Table 20-1.

$$PV = FA \times \text{Present Value of \$1 Factor for 3 Periods at 10\%}$$
$$= \$133.10 \times 0.7513$$
$$= \underline{\underline{\$100}}$$

 What do you think the present value of $10 received or paid at the end of three years is, using a 10% interest rate?

The process of converting a future amount to a present value is known as *discounting*, and the rate used is often called the **discount rate.** Thus, we can say that the $133.10 future amount is discounted to the $100 present value by multiplying it by the 0.7513 present value of $1 factor for three periods at the 10% discount rate.

Present Value of an Annuity

In many situations we are not concerned with the present value of a single future amount but with the present value of an annuity. An **annuity** is a series of *equal* periodic future cash flows. These cash flows may be either received or paid. For example, if on January 1 Unlimited Decadence purchased a new mixing machine that will require $200 of maintenance at the end of each of the next three years, the three $200 payments are an annuity. In this book we will assume that the first cash flow in an annuity occurs at the *end* of the first year. Thus, if an annual annuity begins on January 1, 2000, the first cash flow occurs on December 31, 2000.

We could compute the present value on January 1, 2000 of a three-year $200 annuity at 10% by treating it as three separate single future amounts and using Table 20-1, but there is an easier way. Instead of using Table 20-1, we will use Table 20-2 at the end of the chapter.

 How would you compute the present value for the preceding example using Table 20-1?

Table 20-2 is entitled Present Value of an Annuity of $1 per Period, but you can use it to compute the present value of an annuity of any amount. The present value is computed using the following simple formula:

$$PV \text{ of an Annuity} = \begin{array}{c} \text{Periodic Amount of} \\ \text{an Annuity} \end{array} \times \begin{array}{c} \text{Present Value of} \\ \text{an Annuity Factor} \end{array}$$

If you look up the factor for 10% and three periods in Table 20-2,[4] you will find that it is 2.4869. This is the present value of *$1* received or paid at the end of each of the next three years using a 10% discount rate. Therefore, you can compute the present value of an annuity of $200 received or paid at the end of each year for the next three years using a 10% discount rate as follows:

$$PV \text{ of Annuity} = \text{Annuity} \times \text{Present Value of Annuity Factor for 3 Periods at 10\%}$$
$$= \$200 \times 2.4869$$
$$= \underline{\underline{\$497.38}}$$

Another way of saying this is that the annuity of $200 received or paid at the end of each year for the next 3 years is discounted to a present value of $497.38.

Many calculators have the capacity to compute the present value of a single future amount and the present value of an annuity. The calculation process follows exactly the same concepts that we discussed earlier. These calculators use equations to determine each factor whenever a calculation is made. If you use a calculator to make your present value

---

[4]The factors in Table 20-2 were computed using the equation for the present value of an annuity factor, shown at the beginning of Table 20-2. The factor in Table 20-2 for a given year and interest rate also may be computed by summing the factors in Table 20-1 for each year prior to and including the given year for that interest rate.

computations, you may find an occasional "rounding" error between your answer and what is shown in this book. That is because the calculator does not round its factors, whereas the factors in Tables 20-1 and 20-2 are rounded to four decimal places.

Present Value Examples

In making capital expenditure decisions, you may need to compute both the present value of a single future amount and the present value of an annuity. To help you better understand these computations, we provide the following examples.

Example 1

Compute the present value of a $100 cash receipt at the end of 5 years if the interest rate is 12%.

$$\text{Present Value} = \text{Future Amount} \times \text{Present Value of \$1 Factor}$$
$$= \$100 \times 0.5674$$
$$= \underline{\underline{\$56.74}} \text{ (receipt)}$$

Example 2

Compute the present value of cash receipts of $300 at the ends of years 1, 2, and 3 if the interest rate is 14%.

$$\text{Present Value} = \text{Annuity} \times \text{Present Value of Annuity Factor}$$
$$= \$300 \times 2.3216$$
$$= \underline{\underline{\$696.48}} \text{ (receipt)}$$

Example 3

Compute the present value of a $200 cash receipt at the ends of years 1 and 2, and a $300 cash receipt at the end of year 3, if the interest rate is 10%.

$$\text{Present Value} = (\$200 \times 1.7355) + (\$300 \times 0.7513)$$
$$= \underline{\underline{\$572.49}} \text{ (receipt)}$$

Example 4

Compute the present value of a $500 cash receipt at the end of 10 years together with a $300 cash payment at the end of 2 years, if the interest rate is 8%.

$$\text{Present Value} = (\$500 \times 0.4632) - (\$300 \times 0.8573)$$
$$= \underline{\underline{(\$25.59)}} \text{ (net payment)}$$

Example 5

Compute the present value of a $500 cash receipt at the end of each year for 5 years, together with a $200 cash payment at the end of each year for 5 years, if the interest rate is 12%.

$$\text{Present Value} = (\$500 - \$200) \times 3.6048$$
$$= \underline{\underline{\$1,081.44}} \text{ (net receipt)}$$

If you used a calculator to solve the examples, your answers might be a few cents different from those shown because of rounding errors. Also, in Examples 3, 4, and 5 there are other ways to compute the present value of the cash receipts and payments, but all result in the same present value that we computed in each example.

 What is another way of computing the present value for Example 3?

www.exxon.com

A dramatic example of the time value of money involves the 1989 spill of crude oil in Alaska's Prince William Sound by the oil tanker *Exxon Valdez*. Exxon Corporation, the owner of the tanker that spilled 11 million gallons of oil into the sound, agreed to pay $1 billion for damages to the sound and in government fines—the largest amount that had been assessed for an environmental violation at that time. But Exxon was allowed to pay the fine over a 10-year period. Furthermore, these payments were tax deductible in the years that Exxon paid them. Compare the full $1 billion that Exxon Corporation could have been asked to pay at the time of the fine with what it did pay—the $486 million present value of the net payments (payments minus related tax deductions). By extending its payments over 10 years (and because the payments were tax deductible), Exxon reduced its actual costs to less than half of the assessed damages and fine!

Now that you understand the time value of money and what we mean by present value, we can now discuss how a company makes capital expenditure decisions. As we mentioned earlier, a company has the choice of using one or more of several approaches to evaluating capital expenditure proposals. We will begin our discussion with the net present value method.

Net Present Value Method

5 *How does a company use the net present value method to evaluate a capital expenditure proposal?*

The net present value method is one approach to evaluating whether or not to undertake a capital expenditure proposal. It considers the time value of money and involves a three-step process:

1. Determine the initial cash payment (investment) required to implement the capital expenditure proposal

2. Determine the present value of the expected future net cash receipts from the capital expenditure proposal

3. Determine the net present value by subtracting the amount of Step 1 from the amount of Step 2

Step 1 involves determining the expected cash payment (investment) needed to put the proposal into operation. This investment is already stated at its present value, since it takes place at the present time, just before putting the project into operation.[5] Step 2 involves first estimating the expected future cash receipts and payments (and the length of time over which the company expects these cash receipts and payments to occur), as we discussed earlier. It then involves discounting the expected future *net* cash receipts

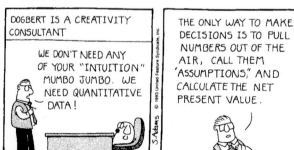

DILBERT® reprinted by permission of United Features Syndicate, Inc.

---

[5]Another way of looking at this is to consider that the initial investment takes place in time period *zero*, which always has a present value factor of 1.0, regardless of the discount rate. Some books will multiply the initial cash payment by 1.0 to determine the present value. Since we consider this approach to be extra work to get the same result, we do not use it in this book.

(future cash receipts minus future cash payments) for each year to their present value using the company's required rate of return (its cost of capital).

Step 3 involves computing the net present value. The **net present value** of a capital expenditure proposal is the present value of the expected future net cash receipts and payments minus the initial cash payment (investment). When the net present value is zero or positive, the capital expenditure proposal is acceptable because the project will earn at least the company's required rate of return. When the net present value is negative, the capital expenditure proposal is not acceptable because it will earn less than the company's required rate of return.[6] We can summarize these decision rules as follows:

When the net present value is:	The decision rule is:
Zero	Acceptable; rate of return on the proposal is equal to the required rate of return
Positive	Acceptable; rate of return on the proposal is greater than the required rate of return
Negative	Not acceptable; rate of return on the proposal is less than the required rate of return

We will illustrate the net present value method with two examples.

Capital Expenditure Proposal: Build New Factory

In the first example, Unlimited Decadence is considering building a new factory. The new factory will be 100,000 square feet. Construction costs are estimated to be $70 per square foot, or a total of $7,000,000 (100,000 × $70). Equipment, installation, and training costs are expected to be $1,920,000. The company estimates that the new factory will be used for 12 years, after which it (and the equipment) will be sold for $1,000,000 (the residual value). Therefore, it computes its expected depreciation on the factory and equipment to be $660,000 per year. The factory is expected to increase the company's operating revenues by $8,000,000 per year and to increase its operating expenses (including depreciation) by $6,660,000 per year. Unlimited Decadence's required rate of return is 14 percent. Should Unlimited Decadence build this factory?

To analyze this capital expenditure proposal, Unlimited Decadence first determines the initial cost of the investment. In this case, the initial cost is $8,920,000 ($7,000,000 + $1,920,000). The company then determines the amounts and timing of its additional future cash flows. In this example, Unlimited Decadence estimates it will have $8,000,000 additional cash *receipts* from operations in years 1 through 12. The company estimates it will have $6,000,000 additional cash *payments* for operations in years 1 through 12. (Note that although Unlimited Decadence estimated that operating expenses would be $6,660,000 per year, it *excludes* the $660,000 depreciation from the analysis because the depreciation does not involve a yearly cash payment.) Therefore, its expected future *net* operating cash receipts are $2,000,000 per year for years 1 through 12. Unlimited Decadence also estimates that it will have a $1,000,000 cash receipt from the residual value at the end of year 12.

Since the company's required rate of return is 14 percent, it uses this percentage as the discount rate to compute the present value of the future cash flows. We show the computation of the net present value of building this factory in Exhibit 20-1. Unlimited Decadence computed the present value of its expected future cash flows first. Note that Unlimited Decadence listed each type of cash flow along with the year(s) during which it expects the cash

---

[6]Some companies use a "time-adjusted rate of return" method. This method determines (by trial and error) the rate that, when used to discount the cash flows from the proposal, gives a net present value of *zero*. Then a company knows exactly what rate of return a proposal will earn. We use the net present value method because it is an easier approach and shows acceptable proposals with rates of return that are equal to or greater than the required rate of return.

Exhibit 20-1   Capital Expenditure Proposal: Build New Factory

Present Value of Expected Future Net Cash Receipts

Type	Years	Future Amount	×	14% Discount Factor	=	Present Value
Net operating cash receipts	1-12	$2,000,000[a]		5.6603[b]		$11,320,600
Residual value	12	1,000,000		0.2076[c]		207,600
Present value of expected future net cash receipts						$11,528,200

Investment (Initial Cash Payments)

Type	Amount
Factory (100,000 sq. ft. × $70/sq. ft.)..	$7,000,000
Equipment, installation, training...	1,920,000
Initial investment...	(8,920,000)
Net present value...	$ 2,608,200

Decision: Project is acceptable.

[a]$8,000,000 operating receipts − $6,000,000 operating payments
[b]From Table 20-2 (annuity), n = 12, i = 14%
[c]From Table 20-1 (single amount), n = 12, i = 14%

flow to occur and the future amount of the cash flow. It then multiplied each future amount by the appropriate present value factor for the 14% required rate of return.

The net operating cash receipts are an annuity because they occur in the same amounts each year. The present value factor of an annuity for 12 years at 14% comes from Table 20-2 at the end of this chapter; it is 5.6603. The present value of the net operating cash receipts is $11,320,600. Since the $1,000,000 residual value is a single cash receipt at the end of year 12, the 0.2076 present value factor comes from Table 20-1 at the end of the chapter. The present value of the residual value, then, is $207,600.

The sum of the two present values of the future cash flows is the $11,528,200 present value of the expected future net cash receipts. This amount minus the $8,920,000 initial investment results in the $2,608,200 *positive* net present value. The capital expenditure proposal to build the new factory is acceptable because it has a positive net present value. This means that the rate of return on the proposal is greater than the 14% rate of return that Unlimited Decadence requires on its capital expenditures.

Capital Expenditure Proposal: Purchase Wrapper Machine

Now assume that Unlimited Decadence is considering replacing its existing "wrapper" machine with a new improved one. In addition to wrapping the candy bars, the new wrapper machine also would count and box the candy bars. Currently, this counting and boxing has to be done by an employee. The new machine costs $30,000 to buy, and installation costs are expected to be $500. The old machine could be sold for $400.

Unlimited Decadence expects to use the new machine for four years, after which it can sell the machine for $1,000 (the residual value). The new machine will not increase production. However, because the machine does the counting and boxing, Unlimited Decadence estimates that the new machine will save $10,000 per year in employee labor costs. Unlimited Decadence's required rate of return is 14%. Should it purchase the new wrapper machine?

The initial cost of the investment is $30,100, which is the $30,000 cost of the new machine plus the $500 installation cost less the $400 received from the residual value of the old machine. The future cash flows consist of expected "savings" in cash payments of $10,000 each year for four years (remember, these are treated like cash receipts) and a $1,000 cash receipt from the residual value at the end of year 4.

Exhibit 20-2 Capital Expenditure Proposal: Purchase Wrapper Machine

Present Value of Expected Future Net Cash Receipts

Type	Years	Future Amount	×	14% Discount Factor	=	Present Value
Savings in wages	1-4	$10,000		2.9137[a]		$29,137
Residual value	4	1,000		0.5921[b]		592
Present value of expected future net cash receipts						$29,729

Investment (Initial Cash Payments)

Type	Amount	
Cost of machine...	$30,000	
Installation and testing..	500	
Less: Residual value of old machine..	(400)	
Present value of initial investment...		(30,100)
Net present value...		$ (371)

Decision: Project is *not* acceptable.

[a]From Table 20-2 (annuity), n = 4, i = 14%
[b]From Table 20-1 (single amount), n = 4, i = 14%

Unlimited Decadence used its 14% required rate of return as the discount rate to compute the present value of its expected future cash flows. We show the computations of the net present value of purchasing the wrapper machine in Exhibit 20-2.

The present value of the future net cash receipts totals $29,729. It consists of two present values: the $29,137 present value of the $10,000 annuity from the savings in labor costs for each of years 1 through 4 and the $592 present value of the new machine's $1,000 residual value received at the end of year 4.

Unlimited Decadence subtracted the $30,100 initial investment from the $29,729 to determine the *negative* net present value of $371. The capital expenditure proposal to purchase a new wrapper machine is *not* acceptable because it has a negative net present value. This means that the rate of return on the project is less than the 14% rate of return that Unlimited Decadence requires on its capital expenditures.

Alternative Methods for Evaluating Capital Expenditure Proposals

In addition to the net present value method, there are several other methods a company might use to evaluate a capital expenditure proposal. We will discuss two: (1) the payback method and (2) the average rate of return on investment method.

6 *What is the difference between the payback method and the average rate of return on investment method for evaluating a capital expenditure proposal?*

Payback Method

The payback method evaluates a capital expenditure proposal based on the payback period. The **payback period** is the length of time required for a return *of* the initial investment. That is, it is the length of time needed for the future net cash receipts to "pay back" the initial cash payment for the capital expenditure.

To illustrate, we will use the previous example in which Unlimited Decadence was considering whether to purchase a wrapper machine. The initial investment was $30,100, and the expected future net cash receipts were $10,000 in years 1 through 4 and $1,000 at the end of year 4. The following schedule shows how Unlimited Decadence computed the payback period:

	Amount to Pay Back at Beginning of Year	Net Annual Cash Receipts Expected	Total Amount Paid Back at Year-End	Amount Left to Pay Back at Year-End
Year 1	$30,100	$10,000	$10,000	$20,100
Year 2	20,100	10,000	20,000	10,100
Year 3	10,100	10,000	30,000	100
Year 4	100	11,000	30,100	—

The schedule shows that $30,000 of the investment would be paid back by the end of Year 3. Since only $100 of the investment would remain unpaid at the beginning of year 4, and $11,000 of net cash receipts are expected in Year 4, the $100 would be paid back in 0.009 years ($100 ÷ $11,000), or after a little more than 3 days (0.009 × 365 days) of Year 4. Thus the payback period is 3.009 years.

Sometimes a company will use the payback period computation to determine whether a capital expenditure proposal is acceptable. It does this by setting a maximum payback period for acceptable proposals. A capital expenditure proposal with a payback period longer than the maximum period would not be acceptable. In addition, a company also might use the payback period to judge whether one capital expenditure proposal is better than another. The company would judge the proposal with the shorter payback period to be better.

Unfortunately, the payback period is *not* a good measure for either purpose. There is no objective way to determine an appropriate payback period. Hence, setting a maximum payback period is arbitrary. A project may have a short payback period for a return *of* the investment and be considered an acceptable proposal. However, the project may provide no return *on* the investment. Therefore, such a project would not contribute to the overall profitability of the company and thus the company should not consider it acceptable.

 Think of a numerical example to illustrate a project that has a short payback period but no return on the investment.

Another project may have a payback period longer than the maximum payback period and be judged to be unacceptable under this method. However, the project may provide a large return *on* the investment later in the project's life and thus may be considered acceptable under another method. *The problem with the payback method is that the payback period focuses on the return **of** the investment and completely ignores the return **on** the investment.* The payback period computation, by itself, cannot provide a sound basis for making capital expenditure decisions.

Average Rate of Return on Investment Method

Another approach that a company sometimes will use in making capital expenditure decisions is the average rate of return on investment method. The **average rate of return on investment** is the average return *on* the investment per year, per dollar invested. It is usually expressed as a percentage per year. The company compares this percentage per year for a proposal against its minimum required rate of return to determine whether the proposal is acceptable.

A company computes the average rate of return on investment by dividing the total net cash receipts from an investment (the return on investment) by the number of years over which the cash will be received times the dollars invested. Since this is a "mouthful," we show the computation in equation form below. In this equation, the total net cash receipts is the numerator and is equal to the total cash receipts minus the total cash payments (including the initial investment).

$$\text{Average Rate of Return on Investment} = \frac{\text{Total Cash Receipts} - \text{Total Cash Payments}}{\text{Years} \times \text{Investment}}$$

To understand this method, consider Unlimited Decadence's proposal for purchasing a wrapper machine, which we discussed earlier. The average rate of return for this proposal is 9.1%, computed as follows:

$$\begin{array}{l} \text{Average Rate} \\ \text{of Return on} \\ \text{Investment} \end{array} = \frac{(\$10,000 + \$10,000 + \$10,000 + \$10,000 + \$1,000) - \$30,100}{4 \times \$30,100}$$

$$= \frac{\$10,900}{\$120,400}$$

$$= \underline{\underline{9.1\%}}$$

Since 9.1% is less than Unlimited Decadence's minimum required rate of return of 14%, the method shows that the proposal is unacceptable.

In contrast to the payback period computation, the average rate of return *does* consider the return *on* investment. The average rate of return on investment method, however, does not provide a good basis for making capital investment decisions. The reason is that *the average rate of return on investment method does not consider the time value of money.* For a proposal that has cash flows occurring late in the life of the project, the "averaging" process may lead a company to erroneously accept a capital expenditure proposal that will not contribute to its profitability.

 Given what you have learned about present value analysis, how do you think the averaging process might lead a company to accept a proposal that has cash flows occurring late in the life of the project, so that the project would not contribute to its profitability?

Although companies sometimes use the payback method and the average rate of return on investment method to evaluate capital expenditure proposals, these methods do not consider the return on investment, do not account for the time value of money, or both. Therefore, they should not be used *by themselves* for capital expenditure decisions. Some companies use these methods in conjunction with the net present value method to help screen potentially acceptable proposals and to provide supporting analyses.

 What additional information do you think a combination of the three methods could provide that a company would not get using the net present value method alone?

Selecting Alternative Proposals for Investment

Capital expenditure decisions would be much easier if a company could invest in all proposals that it identified as being acceptable. This is not always possible, however. Consider the following two situations in which a company must select between two or more proposals that it has identified as being acceptable.

7 *How does a company decide which capital expenditure proposal to accept when it has proposals that accomplish the same thing, or when it cannot obtain sufficient cash to make all of its desired investments?*

Mutually Exclusive Capital Expenditure Proposals

Capital expenditure proposals often arise because of alternative ways a company has to perform an activity, do a job, or provide a service. Sometimes there are several alternatives. In this situation, the capital investment alternatives are called "mutually exclusive." **Mutually exclusive capital expenditure proposals** are proposals that accomplish the same thing, so that when one proposal is selected, the others are not. For example, a company might be considering air conditioning its offices. Although several makes and models of air conditioners may be available, each with a different set of cash flows, one is enough to do the job.

A company evaluating mutually exclusive capital expenditure proposals completes a two-step process. In the first step, the company analyzes each proposal to determine whether or not it is acceptable. The company does this analysis using the net present value method we discussed earlier. If more than one proposal is acceptable (i.e, has a positive net present value), a second step is necessary. In the second step, the company selects one of the acceptable alternatives by *choosing the proposal with the highest positive net present value*. When the company selects a proposal in this way, the analysis in the first step provides the information needed for the second step.

For example, suppose that Unlimited Decadence is considering replacing a "mixer" machine with a new, improved one. There are three different mixer machines on the market, only one of which can be selected. All have the same life and cost about the same, but each would provide different savings in electricity, labor costs, and so on. As the first step in analyzing these mutually exclusive proposals, Unlimited Decadence prepared a net present value analysis for each proposal. Below are the resulting net present values for each machine:

Machine	Net Present Value
A	$6,300
B	(2,200)
C	4,700

In this situation, Unlimited Decadence would eliminate Machine B after the first step because it has a negative net present value. In the second step, it would select Machine A because Machine A has a higher positive net present value than Machine C.[7]

Occasionally, a company considers several mutually exclusive capital expenditure proposals with the requirement that it *must* select one proposal. That is, the alternative of not investing at all is not an available choice. This might happen, for instance, when a company must obtain equipment or facilities to comply with a law. When one of the capital expenditure proposals must be accepted, *the best proposal is the one with the highest (most positive) net present value, **even if that net present value is negative***.

Suppose, for example, that a recently established safety ordinance requires that Unlimited Decadence add additional lights to its factory parking lot. The additional lights require a cash payment, although they will provide no cash receipts. Normally, Unlimited Decadence would not make such a capital expenditure because it would result in a negative net present value. Because of the new law, however, *not* investing in additional lights is an unacceptable alternative. If several proposals for additional lighting would comply with the safety ordinance, Unlimited Decadence would choose the proposal with the least negative net present value.

Capital Rationing

The previous analyses identified acceptable capital expenditure proposals. If a company has enough cash available, all acceptable capital expenditures could be made (including one selected from each set of mutually exclusive proposals). Sometimes, however, a company finds itself with a larger number of acceptable capital expenditure proposals than it can finance. When this occurs, the company must make its capital expenditure decisions in a situation known as capital rationing. **Capital rationing** occurs when a company cannot obtain sufficient cash to make all of the investments that it would like to make. A difficult decision arises when this happens. The company must choose which of the acceptable proposals to invest in, which to delay until sufficient funds become available, and which to forget altogether, if necessary.

[7]Choosing the better alternative may be more complicated when the mutually exclusive capital expenditure proposals require a different amount of investment or when the numbers of years over which they affect the company's cash flows differ. We do not discuss procedures to handle such situations in this book.

Many approaches to handling this problem have been suggested. A detailed study of these approaches is beyond the scope of this book. However, we will discuss the general idea for one approach. This approach involves looking at the acceptable capital expenditure proposals to find all the possible combinations that do not require a larger total investment of cash than is available. Under this approach, *a company chooses the combination of capital expenditure proposals that provides the highest total net present value for the total investment available.*

For example, suppose that Unlimited Decadence has $200,000 cash available for capital expenditures during the current budget period and has the following three proposals that are acceptable because of their positive net present values:

Proposal	Initial Investment Required	Net Present Value
A	$200,000	$120,000
B	110,000	80,000
C	90,000	50,000

Unlimited Decadence could accept capital expenditure proposal A, which would use the entire $200,000 cash available for investment. Or it could undertake both proposals B and C with the $200,000 cash available. In this case, Unlimited Decadence should select proposals B and C because together they provide a higher total net present value of $130,000 ($80,000 + $50,000) than proposal A's $120,000 net present value.

Business Issues and Values

Although the methods we discussed seem to be relatively easy to implement through tables and formulas, not all capital expenditure proposals are easy to quantify. For example, consider the decision about whether to invest in an employee-fitness program.[8] Corporations such as Johnson & Johnson, Tenneco, PepsiCo, IBM, and Kimberly-Clark have invested in wellness programs with facilities alone costing between $1.8 million and $11 million. On top of the costs of the facilities, these corporations added the costs of the salaries and benefits for fitness center employees, health screenings, and incentives for employees. Mattel Corporation estimates that it spends from $75 to $100 per employee on its fitness program. But how do these corporations measure the benefits of their programs, and how far into the future do they have to go before they start seeing these benefits? Companies have been able to measure such factors as the percentage decline in employee smoking and the decline in insurance claims of employees who quit smoking, the average number of insurance claims for exercisers versus nonexercisers, rates of absenteeism for smokers versus nonsmokers and exercisers versus nonexercisers, and reductions in insurance costs. However, many of these factors can't be measured for years after the initial investment, and some other factors can't be quantified at all. For example, the increase in employee morale from company fitness programs is harder to measure but no less important.

In making capital expenditure decisions, companies need to consider *all* the relevant factors, including the difficult-to-measure ones. Otherwise, in cases like this, a company might put an arbitrary limit on the time horizon of the project (and therefore not see the long-term benefits of the project) or might not consider the nonquantifiable benefits of the project. Thus, the company might decide against a capital expenditure that is actually in its best interests.

www.johnsonand
johnson.com
www.tenneco.com
www.pepsico.com
www.ibm.com
www.Kimberly-
Clark.com
www.mattel.com

If you were deciding whether or not to purchase an exercise bike, what costs and benefits would you consider?

[8]Otto H. Chang and Cynthia Boyle, "Fitness Programs: Hefty Expense or Wise Investment?" *Management Accounting*, January 1989, 45-46.

Summary

At the beginning of the chapter we asked you several questions. During the chapter, we asked you to STOP and answer several additional questions to build your knowledge about specific issues. Be sure you answered these additional questions. Below are the questions from the beginning of the chapter, along with a brief summary of the key points relating to the answers. Use your creative and critical thinking skills to expand on these key points to develop more complete answers to the questions and to determine what other questions you have that might lead you to learn more about the issues.

1 **What is a capital expenditure, and what are the four steps in a capital expenditure decision?**

A capital expenditure is a long-term investment (cash payment) made by a company in order for it to obtain future net cash receipts totaling more than the investment. In making a capital expenditure decision, a company completes four steps. First, the company must determine the initial cash payment needed to make the investment. Second, the company must estimate the future cash receipts and payments (cash flows) expected from the investment and the time period over which it expects these future cash receipts and payments to occur. Third, the company must determine its cost of providing the cash to make the investment. Finally, the company must determine whether the estimated future cash flows will provide a return that is sufficient (after adjusting for the time value of money) to cover the cost of providing the cash to make the investment.

2 **What does a company include in the initial cost of a capital expenditure proposal?**

The initial cost of a capital expenditure proposal is the expected cash payment necessary to put the proposal into operation. In other words, it is the capital that the company must expend to make the investment. It includes such items as the cost of an asset, transportation costs, and installation costs.

3 **What are the relevant costs of a capital expenditure proposal, and how do operating income, depreciation, and ending cash flows affect these costs?**

The relevant costs of a capital expenditure proposal are future cash flows that differ, either in amount or in timing, as a result of accepting a capital expenditure proposal. That is, relevant costs are (1) the additional future cash flows (either receipts or payments) to a company's existing cash flows, or (2) the savings in future cash payments. Frequently, the best available information to use in predicting these relevant costs is the expected future additional operating revenues and/or expenses. Most revenues and expenses of a company (the company's operating income) result in related cash receipts and payments of the same amounts at approximately the same points in time. But depreciation is an expense for which the related cash flows occur in different years and in different amounts than the expense, so a company does not consider depreciation expense when it predicts relevant cash flows. A company considers ending cash flows related to the capital expenditure to be relevant costs.

4 **How does a company determine the rate of return it requires on a capital expenditure proposal?**

The rate of return that a company requires on a capital expenditure proposal is the cost to the company of providing the cash for the investment. It is the weighted-average cost the company must pay to all its sources of capital. This rate of return is called the company's cost of capital.

5 **How does a company use the net present value method to evaluate a capital expenditure proposal?**

A company evaluates a capital expenditure proposal using the net present value method by considering the time value of money in a three-step process. Step 1 involves determining the expected cash payment needed to put the proposal into operation (the investment). This investment is already stated at its present value, since it takes place at the present time, just prior to putting the project into operation. Step 2 involves first estimating the expected future cash receipts and payments (and the length of time over which the company expects these cash receipts and payments to occur). It then involves discounting the expected future *net* cash receipts (future cash receipts minus future cash payments) for each year to their present values using the company's required rate of return (its cost of capital). Step 3 involves computing the net present value, by subtracting the initial cash payment (from Step 1) from the present value of the expected future net cash 7receipts and payments (from Step 2). When the net present value is positive, the capital expenditure proposal is acceptable. When the net present value is negative, the capital expenditure proposal is not acceptable because it will earn less than the company's required rate of return.

6 **What is the difference between the payback method and the average rate of return on investment method for evaluating a capital expenditure proposal?**

A company using the payback method evaluates a capital expenditure proposal based on the length of time required for a return of the initial investment. A company using the average rate of return on investment method compares a company's average return on the investment per year, per dollar invested, against the company's minimum required rate of return to determine whether the proposal is acceptable.

7 **How does a company decide which capital expenditure proposal to accept when it has several proposals that accomplish the same thing, or when it cannot obtain sufficient cash to make all of its desired investments?**

A company evaluating several proposals that accomplish the same thing (called mutually exclusive proposals) completes a two-step process. In the first step, the company analyzes each proposal to determine whether or not it is acceptable. The company does this analysis using the net present value method. If more than one proposal is acceptable (i.e,. has a positive net present value), a second step is necessary. In the second step, the company selects one of the acceptable alternatives by choosing the proposal with the highest positive net present value. One approach to deciding which capital expenditure proposal to accept when a company cannot obtain sufficient cash to make all of its desired investments (called capital rationing) involves looking at the acceptable capital expenditure proposals to find all possible combinations of proposals that do not require a larger total investment of cash than is available. A company chooses the combination of capital expenditure proposals that provides the highest total net present value for the total investment available.

Key Terms

amount *(p. 713)*
annuity *(p. 714)*
average rate of return on investment
  (p. 720)
capital expenditure *(p. 706)*
capital rationing *(p. 722)*
compound interest *(p. 712)*
cost of capital *(p. 710)*
discount rate *(p. 714)*
factor *(p. 713)*

future value *(p. 712)*
initial cost *(p. 707)*
mutually exclusive capital expenditure
  proposals *(p. 721)*
net present value *(p. 717)*
payback period *(p. 719)*
present value *(p. 712)*
relevant cash flows *(p. 708)*
required rate of return *(p. 710)*

Here is an opportunity to gather information on the Internet about real-world issues related to the topics in this chapter. Go to http://www.dryden.com/account and click on the Cunningham, Nikolai, and Bazley book cover. Click on Summary Surfing, then click on this chapter number, and answer the following questions.

▶ Click on **Gold's Gym Enterprises, Inc.** Then click on *ABOUT GOLD'S GYM*. According to the "Gold's Gym Story," what kinds of capital expenditure decisions have its managers made?

▶ Click on **Gold's Gym Enterprises, Inc.** Then click on *ABOUT GOLD'S GYM* and then on *The Mecca of Bodybuilding*. What future cash receipts and cash payments do you think its managers considered in deciding whether Gold's Gym should invest in The Mecca?

SUMMARY
SURFING

Table 20-1

Present Value of $1 Due in n Periods

$$Factor = \frac{1}{(1+i)^n}$$

(n) Period	1%	2%	3%	4%	5%	6%	7%	8%	9%	10%	12%	14%	15%	16%	18%	20%	24%
1	.9901	.9804	.9709	.9615	.9524	.9434	.9346	.9259	.9174	.9091	.8929	.8772	.8696	.8621	.8475	.8333	.8065
2	.9803	.9612	.9426	.9246	.9070	.8900	.8734	.8573	.8417	.8264	.7972	.7695	.7561	.7432	.7182	.6944	.6504
3	.9706	.9423	.9151	.8890	.8638	.8396	.8163	.7938	.7722	.7513	.7118	.6750	.6575	.6407	.6086	.5787	.5245
4	.9610	.9238	.8885	.8548	.8227	.7921	.7629	.7350	.7084	.6830	.6355	.5921	.5718	.5523	.5158	.4823	.4230
5	.9515	.9057	.8626	.8219	.7835	.7473	.7130	.6806	.6499	.6209	.5674	.5194	.4972	.4761	.4371	.4019	.3411
6	.9420	.8880	.8375	.7903	.7462	.7050	.6663	.6302	.5963	.5645	.5066	.4556	.4323	.4104	.3704	.3349	.2751
7	.9327	.8706	.8131	.7599	.7107	.6651	.6227	.5835	.5470	.5132	.4523	.3996	.3759	.3538	.3139	.2791	.2218
8	.9235	.8535	.7894	.7307	.6768	.6274	.5820	.5403	.5019	.4665	.4039	.3506	.3269	.3050	.2660	.2326	.1789
9	.9143	.8368	.7664	.7026	.6446	.5919	.5439	.5002	.4604	.4241	.3606	.3075	.2843	.2630	.2255	.1938	.1443
10	.9053	.8203	.7441	.6756	.6139	.5584	.5083	.4632	.4224	.3855	.3220	.2697	.2472	.2267	.1911	.1615	.1164
11	.8963	.8043	.7224	.6496	.5847	.5268	.4751	.4289	.3875	.3505	.2875	.2366	.2149	.1954	.1619	.1346	.0938
12	.8874	.7885	.7014	.6246	.5568	.4970	.4440	.3971	.3555	.3186	.2567	.2076	.1869	.1685	.1372	.1122	.0757
13	.8787	.7730	.6810	.6006	.5303	.4688	.4150	.3677	.3262	.2897	.2292	.1821	.1625	.1452	.1163	.0935	.0610
14	.8700	.7579	.6611	.5775	.5051	.4423	.3878	.3405	.2992	.2633	.2046	.1597	.1413	.1252	.0985	.0779	.0492
15	.8613	.7430	.6419	.5553	.4810	.4173	.3624	.3152	.2745	.2394	.1827	.1401	.1229	.1079	.0835	.0649	.0397
16	.8528	.7284	.6232	.5339	.4581	.3936	.3387	.2919	.2519	.2176	.1631	.1229	.1069	.0930	.0708	.0541	.0320
17	.8444	.7142	.6050	.5134	.4363	.3714	.3166	.2703	.2311	.1978	.1456	.1078	.0929	.0802	.0600	.0451	.0258
18	.8360	.7002	.5874	.4936	.4155	.3503	.2959	.2502	.2120	.1799	.1300	.0946	.0808	.0691	.0508	.0376	.0208
19	.8277	.6864	.5703	.4746	.3957	.3305	.2765	.2317	.1945	.1635	.1161	.0829	.0703	.0596	.0431	.0313	.0168
20	.8195	.6730	.5537	.4564	.3769	.3118	.2584	.2145	.1784	.1486	.1037	.0728	.0611	.0514	.0365	.0261	.0135
21	.8114	.6598	.5375	.4388	.3589	.2942	.2415	.1987	.1637	.1351	.0926	.0638	.0531	.0443	.0309	.0217	.0109
22	.8034	.6468	.5219	.4220	.3418	.2775	.2257	.1839	.1502	.1228	.0826	.0560	.0462	.0382	.0262	.0181	.0088
23	.7954	.6342	.5067	.4057	.3256	.2618	.2109	.1703	.1378	.1117	.0738	.0491	.0402	.0329	.0222	.0151	.0071
24	.7876	.6217	.4919	.3901	.3101	.2470	.1971	.1577	.1264	.1015	.0659	.0431	.0349	.0284	.0188	.0126	.0057
25	.7798	.6095	.4776	.3751	.2953	.2330	.1842	.1460	.1160	.0923	.0588	.0378	.0304	.0245	.0160	.0105	.0046
26	.7720	.5976	.4637	.3607	.2812	.2198	.1722	.1352	.1064	.0839	.0525	.0331	.0264	.0211	.0135	.0087	.0037
27	.7644	.5859	.4502	.3468	.2678	.2074	.1609	.1252	.0976	.0763	.0469	.0291	.0230	.0182	.0115	.0073	.0030
28	.7568	.5744	.4371	.3335	.2551	.1956	.1504	.1159	.0895	.0693	.0419	.0255	.0200	.0157	.0097	.0061	.0024
29	.7493	.5631	.4243	.3207	.2429	.1846	.1406	.1073	.0822	.0630	.0374	.0224	.0174	.0135	.0082	.0051	.0020
30	.7419	.5521	.4120	.3083	.2314	.1741	.1314	.0994	.0754	.0573	.0334	.0196	.0151	.0116	.0070	.0042	.0016

Table 20-2

Present Value of an Annuity of $1 per Period

$$Factor = \frac{1 - \frac{1}{(1 + i)^n}}{i}$$

(n) Number of Periods	1%	2%	3%	4%	5%	6%	7%	8%	9%	10%	12%	14%	15%	16%	18%	20%	24%
1	0.9901	0.9804	0.9709	0.9615	0.9524	0.9434	0.9346	0.9259	0.9174	0.9091	0.8929	0.8772	0.8696	0.8621	0.8475	0.8333	0.8065
2	1.9704	1.9416	1.9135	1.8861	1.8594	1.8334	1.8080	1.7833	1.7591	1.7355	1.6901	1.6467	1.6257	1.6052	1.5656	1.5278	1.4568
3	2.9410	2.8839	2.8286	2.7751	2.7232	2.6730	2.6243	2.5771	2.5313	2.4869	2.4018	2.3216	2.2832	2.2459	2.1743	2.1065	1.9813
4	3.9020	3.8077	3.7171	3.6299	3.5460	3.4651	3.3872	3.3121	3.2397	3.1699	3.0373	2.9137	2.8550	2.7982	2.6901	2.5887	2.4043
5	4.8534	4.7135	4.5797	4.4518	4.3295	4.2124	4.1002	3.9927	3.8897	3.7908	3.6048	3.4331	3.3522	3.2743	3.1272	2.9906	2.7454
6	5.7955	5.6014	5.4172	5.2421	5.0757	4.9173	4.7665	4.6229	4.4859	4.3553	4.1114	3.8887	3.7845	3.6847	3.4976	3.3255	3.0205
7	6.7282	6.4720	6.2303	6.0021	5.7864	5.5824	5.3893	5.2064	5.0330	4.8684	4.5638	4.2883	4.1604	4.0386	3.8115	3.6046	3.2423
8	7.6517	7.3255	7.0197	6.7327	6.4632	6.2098	5.9713	5.7466	5.5348	5.3349	4.9676	4.6389	4.4873	4.3436	4.0776	3.8372	3.4212
9	8.5660	8.1622	7.7861	7.4353	7.1078	6.8017	6.5152	6.2469	5.9952	5.7590	5.3282	4.9464	4.7716	4.6065	4.3030	4.0310	3.5655
10	9.4713	8.9826	8.5302	8.1109	7.7217	7.3601	7.0236	6.7101	6.4177	6.1446	5.6502	5.2161	5.0188	4.8332	4.4941	4.1925	3.6819
11	10.3676	9.7868	9.2526	8.7605	8.3064	7.8869	7.4987	7.1390	6.8052	6.4951	5.9377	5.4527	5.2337	5.0286	4.6560	4.3271	3.7757
12	11.2551	10.5753	9.9540	9.3851	8.8633	8.3838	7.9427	7.5361	7.1607	6.8137	6.1944	5.6603	5.4206	5.1971	4.7932	4.4392	3.8514
13	12.1337	11.3484	10.6350	9.9856	9.3936	8.8527	8.3577	7.9038	7.4869	7.1034	6.4235	5.8424	5.5831	5.3423	4.9095	4.5327	3.9124
14	13.0037	12.1062	11.2961	10.5631	9.8986	9.2950	8.7455	8.2442	7.7862	7.3667	6.6282	6.0021	5.7245	5.4675	5.0081	4.6106	3.9616
15	13.8651	12.8493	11.9379	11.1184	10.3797	9.7122	9.1079	8.5595	8.0607	7.6061	6.8109	6.1422	5.8474	5.5755	5.0916	4.6755	4.0013
16	14.7179	13.5777	12.5611	11.6523	10.8378	10.1059	9.4466	8.8514	8.3126	7.8237	6.9740	6.2651	5.9542	5.6685	5.1624	4.7296	4.0333
17	15.5623	14.2919	13.1661	12.1657	11.2741	10.4773	9.7632	9.1216	8.5436	8.0216	7.1196	6.3729	6.0472	5.7487	5.2223	4.7746	4.0591
18	16.3983	14.9920	13.7535	12.6593	11.6896	10.8276	10.0591	9.3719	8.7556	8.2014	7.2497	6.4674	6.1280	5.8178	5.2732	4.8122	4.0799
19	17.2260	15.6785	14.3238	13.1339	12.0853	11.1581	10.3356	9.6036	8.9501	8.3649	7.3658	6.5504	6.1982	5.8775	5.3162	4.8435	4.0967
20	18.0456	16.3514	14.8775	13.5903	12.4622	11.4699	10.5940	9.8181	9.1285	8.5136	7.4694	6.6231	6.2593	5.9288	5.3527	4.8696	4.1103
21	18.8570	17.0112	15.4150	14.0292	12.8212	11.7641	10.8355	10.0168	9.2922	8.6487	7.5620	6.6870	6.3125	5.9731	5.3837	4.8913	4.1212
22	19.6604	17.6580	15.9369	14.4511	13.1630	12.0416	11.0612	10.2007	9.4424	8.7715	7.6446	6.7429	6.3587	6.0113	5.4099	4.9094	4.1300
23	20.4558	18.2922	16.4436	14.8568	13.4886	12.3034	11.2722	10.3711	9.5802	8.8832	7.7184	6.7921	6.3988	6.0442	5.4321	4.9245	4.1371
24	21.2434	18.9139	16.9355	15.2470	13.7986	12.5504	11.4693	10.5288	9.7066	8.9847	7.7843	6.8351	6.4338	6.0726	5.4509	4.9371	4.1428
25	22.0232	19.5235	17.4131	15.6221	14.0939	12.7834	11.6536	10.6748	9.8226	9.0770	7.8431	6.8729	6.4641	6.0971	5.4669	4.9476	4.1474
26	22.7952	20.1210	17.8768	15.9828	14.3752	13.0032	11.8258	10.8100	9.9290	9.1609	7.8957	6.9061	6.4906	6.1182	5.4804	4.9563	4.1511
27	23.5596	20.7069	18.3270	16.3296	14.6430	13.2105	11.9867	10.9352	10.0266	9.2372	7.9426	6.9352	6.5135	6.1364	5.4919	4.9636	4.1542
28	24.3164	21.2813	18.7641	16.6631	14.8981	13.4062	12.1371	11.0511	10.1161	9.3066	7.9844	6.9607	6.5335	6.1520	5.5016	4.9697	4.1566
29	25.0658	21.8444	19.1885	16.9837	15.1411	13.5907	12.2777	11.1584	10.1983	9.3696	8.0218	6.9830	6.5509	6.1656	5.5098	4.9747	4.1585
30	25.8077	22.3965	19.6004	17.2920	15.3725	13.7648	12.4090	11.2578	10.2737	9.4269	8.0552	7.0027	6.5660	6.1772	5.5168	4.9789	4.1601

Integrated Business and Accounting Situations

Answer the Following Questions in Your Own Words

Testing Your Knowledge

20-1 What is a capital expenditure decision? Give three examples of capital expenditure opportunities.

20-2 When is a capital expenditure proposal acceptable to a company?

20-3 What four steps must a company complete to determine whether or not a capital expenditure proposal is acceptable?

20-4 What is the initial cost of a capital expenditure proposal? Give three examples of items included in the initial cost of purchasing a machine.

20-5 Identify three forms of expected net future cash receipts.

20-6 What are relevant cash flows? How are cash inflows and outflows that occurred prior to a capital expenditure decision included in relevant cash flows?

20-7 Briefly discuss how depreciation expense on a machine is treated in a capital expenditure analysis.

20-8 What is a company's cost of capital? How does it relate to the required rate of return on a capital expenditure?

20-9 What is an acceptable rate of return on a capital expenditure proposal?

20-10 What is meant by "the time value of money"?

20-11 What is the relationship between "present value" and "compound interest"?

20-12 Explain how to compute the present value of a future amount.

20-13 Explain how to compute the present value of an annuity.

20-14 Define the net present value of a capital expenditure proposal. Identify what amount of net present value indicates an acceptable (unacceptable) proposal.

20-15 Define the payback period. Why is the payback period a poor measure for determining whether a capital expenditure proposal is acceptable?

20-16 Briefly explain why the average rate of return on investment method is better than the payback method in judging whether a capital expenditure proposal is acceptable. Does your answer mean that the average rate of return on investment method is a good method for making capital investment decisions?

20-17 What are mutually exclusive capital expenditure proposals? Give an example.

20-18 Define capital rationing. Identify an investment approach that a company could use in a capital rationing situation.

Applying Your Knowledge

20-19 The following are four sets of cash flows:
  (a) A single $200 cash inflow at the end of year 5.
  (b) A series of $100 cash inflows at the end of years 1, 2, 3, 4, and 5.
  (c) A cash inflow of $300 at the end of year 3 and a cash inflow of $400 at the end of year 5.
  (d) A series of cash outflows of $60 at the end of years 1 through 10.

  Required: Determine the present value of each of the sets of cash flows using a discount rate of 12%.

20-20 The following are four sets of cash flows:
  (a) A single $300 cash inflow at the end of year 5.
  (b) A series of $200 cash inflows at the end of years 1, 2, 3, 4, and 5.
  (c) A cash inflow of $400 at the end of year 3 and a cash inflow of $500 at the end of year 5.
  (d) A series of cash outflows of $80 at the end of years 1 through 10.

  Required: Determine the present value of each of the sets of cash flows using a discount rate of 10%.

20-21 The following are two *independent* questions.

    (a) The Delta Company sells a new type of pecan shelling machine that it claims will save a constant amount of labor costs at a particular company each year for 10 years. Delta suggests that this savings would have a present value (at 16%) of $14,499.60 to the company. What is the amount of the annual labor cost savings being claimed?

    (b) The Sigma Company sells a small mechanical apparatus with a complicated solid-state control unit that attaches to an automobile's carburetor. Sigma claims the apparatus will save the average car owner $100 per year in gasoline bills that should be worth over $800 (present value) to the owner using a discount rate of 10%. If the apparatus can save $100 per year, how many years would it have to be used for the present value of the savings to exceed $800?

    Required: Prepare an analysis to answer each of the questions.

20-22 Tom Hammond is considering investing $5,000 in a tract of farmland a group of his friends is planning to buy. His share of the expected selling price of the land after five years would be $8,500.

    Required: (1) Compute the net present value of the land investment, assuming a 12% required rate of return.

             (2) Should Tom make the investment? Why or why not?

20-23 The McKenzie Company is considering buying a machine that would increase the company's cash receipts by $2,200 per year for five years. Operation of the machine would increase the company's cash payments by $100 in each of the first two years, $200 in the third and fourth years, and $300 in the fifth year. The machine costs $6,000 and would have a residual value of $500 at the end of the fifth year.

    Required: (1) Assuming a 16% required rate of return, compute the net present value of the machine investment being considered by McKenzie Company.

             (2) Should McKenzie Company make the investment? Why or why not?

20-24 Carmichael Radio Company, a distributor of radio towers and antennas, is considering buying the entire inventory of West Tower Company, which manufactures extremely large, heavy-duty towers, and which is going out of business. These towers would cost $250,000 delivered to Carmichael's warehouse. Carmichael plans to sell these towers to special customers. Carmichael's required rate of return is 20%.

    Required: Compute the net present value of Carmichael's investment for *each* of the following assumed patterns of cash inflows that could result from the sale of these towers.

           (1) Cash inflows of $100,000 each year for 6 years.

           (2) Cash inflows of $60,000 each year for 8 years.

           (3) Cash inflows of $200,000 during the first year, $100,000 in each of the second and third years, and $50,000 in each of the fourth and fifth years.

20-25 Bowler Company is considering purchasing a packaging machine for $20,000 that will have a residual value of $100 after 10 years. It would be depreciated using the straight-line method. The machine would reduce labor costs in the shipping department by $8,000 per year. Experience with such machines suggests that finished goods that could be sold for $3,500 would be ruined each year by the packaging machine. Ownership of the machine also would increase property taxes and insurance (paid annually) by $200 per year. Bowler's required rate of return is 20%.

    Required: (1) Prepare an analysis to determine whether the purchase of this machine is an acceptable capital expenditure for Bowler.

             (2) What is the highest price Bowler should be willing to pay for the packaging machine?

20-26 Keeler Company is considering purchasing an overhead conveyor system for $200,000 that will have a residual value of $3,000 after eight years. This conveyor system would be depreciated on a straight-line basis. The conveyor system would reduce labor costs in the shipping department by $60,000 per year. Experience with such systems indicates that $7,000 would be spent each year on maintenance to keep it operating properly. Ownership of the new conveyor system also would increase property taxes and insurance by $2,000 per year. Keeler's required rate of return is 16%.

Required: (1) Prepare an analysis to determine whether the purchase of this overhead conveyor system is an acceptable capital expenditure for Keeler.

(2) What is the highest price Keeler should be willing to pay for the overhead conveyor system?

20-27 A company is considering the following three capital expenditure proposals:

(a) Proposal A—An investment of $10,000 promising cash receipts of $3,700 per year for 5 years.

(b) Proposal B—An investment of $10,000 promising a single cash receipt of $20,000 after 5 years.

(c) Proposal C—An investment of $10,000 promising a cash receipt of $2,000 each year for 4 years and $12,000 in the fifth year.

Required: (1) Prepare an analysis to determine the acceptability of each of the capital expenditure proposals, assuming a 16% minimum required rate of return.

(2) If only one of the three proposals can be selected for investment, which one should it be? Write a brief justification for your selection.

20-28 A company is considering the following three capital expenditure proposals:

(a) Proposal A—An investment of $12,000 promising cash receipts of $2,600 per year for 20 years.

(b) Proposal B—An investment of $12,000 promising a single cash receipt of $390,000 after 20 years.

(c) Proposal C—An investment of $12,000 promising a cash receipt of $2,300 each year for 19 years and $45,000 in the 20th year.

Required: (1) Prepare an analysis to determine the acceptability of each of the capital expenditure proposals, assuming a 20% minimum required rate of return.

(2) If only one of the three proposals can be selected for investment, which one should it be? Write a brief justification for your selection.

20-29 A company is considering the following investment proposals:

(a) $12,000 invested in a savings account that pays $240 (in cash) quarterly.

(b) $12,000 invested in a delivery van, which would reduce delivery expenses so that cash payments are decreased by $1,200 per year for 10 years.

(c) $12,000 invested in land, for which real estate taxes of $100 would be paid each year. The company expects to be able to sell the land after 8 years for $25,000.

Required: Compute the payback period for each of the proposals.

20-30 Refer to 20-23.

Required: Compute the payback period of McKenzie Company for this machine.

20-31 Refer to 20-23.

Required: Compute the average rate of return on investment for the machine being considered by McKenzie Company.

20-32 Refer to 20-22.

Required: Compute the average rate of return on Tom Hammond's land investment.

20-33 Merimac Company can accept either capital expenditure proposal A or B (but not both), or it can reject both proposals. Proposal A requires an investment of $700 and promises increased net cash inflows of $220 for each of the next five years. Proposal B requires an investment of $700 and promises increased net cash inflows of $250 per year for the next four years and $100 in the fifth year. The company's required rate of return is 20%.

Required: (1) Prepare an analysis to determine which (if either) of the proposals should be selected for investment.

(2) How would your answer to (1) be altered if one of the two proposals must be selected?

20-34 The Mosely Company has identified the following capital expenditure proposals as acceptable. Only $50,000 is available for investment, however.

Investment Proposal	Required Investment	Net Present Value
A	$10,000	$ 4,000
B	20,000	12,000
C	10,000	5,000
D	30,000	16,000
E	10,000	7,000
F	20,000	13,000

Required: Determine the combination of proposals to be selected.

Making Evaluations

20-35 The Greenville Manufacturing Company is considering replacing an old machine that cost the company $80,000 five years ago. This machine could be used for 10 more years, at which time it would have no residual value. If it were sold now, net receipts from its disposal would be $25,000. The old machine requires five operators to run it, each earning $22,000 per year.

The new machine, which costs $145,000, has an estimated life of 10 years and a residual value of $6,000 at the end of that time. The new machine requires only three operators, each earning $30,000 per year. Actual direct materials costs would be slightly less with the new machine because materials waste (currently $4,000 per year) could be cut in half.

Maintenance on the old machine, which currently runs approximately $3,000 per year, would be decreased by 40% with the new machine. At present, power costs are $20,000 per year. The new machine would require 5% less power. Greenville estimates that the revenues associated with the product produced by the old machine, $150,000 per year, would not be changed by purchasing the new machine. Greenville's required rate of return is 20%.

Required: (1) Prepare a schedule of the relevant cash flows for this capital expenditure proposal to replace the old machine. Indicate any cash flows that are not relevant, and explain why they are not relevant.

(2) Compute the net present value of the proposal. Is this proposal acceptable?

(3) What maximum amount should Greenville be willing to pay for the new machine?

20-36 Several years ago, Dane Company signed a contract to supply 5,000 units of a special product each year to one of its customers at a price of $20 per unit. This contract, which runs for five more years, is noncancelable.

Dane is currently producing the product with an old machine that can be kept running for five more years if $12,000 of maintenance cost per year is incurred. Other operating costs to produce this product with the old machine (excluding maintenance) total $60,000 per year. The old machine has no residual value now and will have none after the contract is fulfilled.

East Company has recently offered to sell Dane 5,000 units of this product per year over the next five years for $14 per unit. Dane had almost decided to accept this offer from East as the best-possible way to satisfy its contract when a new machine capable of producing the 5,000 units each year for $56,000 total cash operating costs per year became available. This new machine would cost $55,000 and would have a residual value of $10,000 after five years. Dane's required rate of return is 16%.

Required: (1) Is purchasing 5,000 units of the product per year from East Company preferable to producing them on the old machine? Explain.

(2) By computing the net present value of this proposal, determine the acceptability of the capital expenditure proposal to buy the new machine.

(3) If East Company withdraws its offer to supply the units, would your answer to (2) change? Explain, supporting your explanation with computations if necessary.

20-37 Porter Paper Company has just been ordered by the court to install a pollution-control device on the exhaust system of one of its production processes. The company's required rate of return is 20%. Two devices are available on the market.

Device A costs $20,000 and is expected to last 12 years, after which it would have a zero residual value. It costs $600 per year to operate and maintain.

Device B costs $12,000 and would last only six years, after which it would have a residual value of $1,000. If device B is purchased, Porter would have to replace it in six years. The second unit would have an expected cost at that time of $18,000. The second unit would also be expected to have a residual value of $1,000 at the end of its six-year life. Both the first and second unit of device B cost $700 per year to operate and maintain.

Required: (1) By computing the net present value of the investment for each of the devices, determine which pollution-control device Porter should purchase.

(2) How much *per year* would the court have to fine Porter for ignoring the order to ensure that it would be less expensive (in terms of present value of costs) for the company to comply with the court order by purchasing one of the devices?

(3) Suppose the court fine is less than the cost of complying with the court order. What else should Porter Paper consider as it decides what to do?

20-38 Wayne Industries is considering introducing a new product. Wayne believes it can sell 32,000 units of this product per year for 10 years at a price of $9 per unit. Wayne estimates that the cost of producing the product would be $3 per unit. Additional production costs of $75,000 would be required during the first year, however, while the production department became familiar with the techniques required to produce the new product. Cash payments for advertising this product are expected to be $50,000 per year. Variable selling costs are expected to be about $2 per unit sold.

Wayne Industries has already spent $300,000 on research and development of this product. If the new product is introduced, an additional $220,000 would have to be invested immediately to obtain the additional plant and equipment necessary for production. This additional plant and equipment would have a residual value of $100,000 after 10 years. Wayne's required rate of return is 20%.

Required: (1) Prepare a schedule of the relevant annual net cash flows for this capital expenditure proposal to introduce this new product.

(2) Compute the net present value of the proposal.

(3) Discuss whether Wayne should accept this proposal.

20-39 Midus Muffin Shops, a chain of fast-foods shops serving breakfast 24 hours a day, is considering opening a shop in Danville. The shop could be opened in one of two ways, either by building the shop between a west-side shopping center and Danville's small college campus or by buying a vacant building on the edge of the downtown business district. The investment required in either case is $100,000. An extensive analysis of the potential of these two locations, however, suggests that the expected cash inflows and outflows from their operations would be very different.

The downtown location would have a much greater volume of customers than the west-side location for at least five years. Furthermore, this volume would be concentrated between 6 a.m. and 11:30 p.m., allowing considerable savings in wages during the early-morning hours. The volume of the west-side location would be smaller and more uniform throughout the day and night.

The costs of upkeep for the new west-side building should be considerably less than for the older building downtown, however. Furthermore, an interstate highway currently under construction 100 miles to the north is expected eventually to come through Danville within three blocks of the west-side location after five or more years, increasing the potential volume of customers to that shop by a considerable amount.

Required: Assume that you are a consultant to Midus and have been assigned to make a recommendation to the company about what to do in Danville. Write the president of Midus a memo describing the approach that should be used to make this decision, listing the important factors that you expect to influence the decision, and requesting specific information that you will need to evaluate the decision alternatives.

20-40 Mary T. lives with her mother and is an administrative secretary for a large architectural company in a small midwestern city. She earns $19,000 per year. She dreams of being an architect, however. New architects in her company start at $29,000 per year. Mary has been accepted at several universities. Because she is bright and ambitious, she believes she can graduate in four years (including summer school) unless she works part-time, in which case she would need five years to graduate. She has been looking at college catalogues for several months, calculating the total costs for tuition, fees, room and board, books and supplies, and so on. She has tabulated these costs and ruled out all but one school because of the high out-of-state tuition. She has estimated the following costs per year of attending the state university:

Tuition and fees	$2,800
Room and board	3,500
Books and supplies	500
Automobile	600
Clothes	400
Miscellaneous	200
Annual Cost	$8,000

Although it seems like a lot of money, Mary believes her total cost over four years ($32,000) would be paid back before she finishes her second year working as an architect. Before she resigns from her job, she comes to you for your opinion.

Required: Write Mary a letter describing how she should evaluate this decision. Make some tentative calculations using any of the preceding information that you feel is relevant and assuming any additional information that is necessary to demonstrate how she should consider the monetary aspects of her decision. Disregard income taxes.

20-41   Yesterday, Sandy received a note from her father, who is now 45 years old, asking for advice in starting his plans for retirement. The pertinent parts of that note are as follows:

> . . . and you know how much your mom and I like to travel. I was thinking that my pension from the company plus social security wouldn't be enough to allow us much travel during those years while we're still young enough to be active. Assuming our health continues, we'd like to supplement our retirement income 'til we're about 75. I thought you might be able to clear my thinking a bit since you're taking those business classes at the university.

> It isn't investment advice that I'm asking for. You know that I'll just put anything I save in certificates of deposit at the Community Saving and Loan. I think I should be able to average about 6% interest per year there. The main things I'm having trouble thinking about are whether I should start saving now or wait 'til you finish school, and whether to retire at 55, 60, or 65.

> Incidentally, your Grandpa just told me that he put $25,000 in U.S. savings bonds in my name when he sold the drugstore. I was 20 years old then. They've probably earned only about 4% per year, so I doubt whether they will help much. What do you think?

> Someone at work told me that if I had a certain amount of money saved when I retired, I could withdraw about 9% of that amount every year for 20 years before the money ran out. Could that be possible? By my reckoning that would be 180% of what I started with. If it's true, maybe I could retire at 55 after all. I'd like your explanation, though, before I rely on that idea.

Required: Assuming that you are Sandy, write a note to your dad to answer his questions in order to help him begin his retirement planning. (Ignore income tax considerations.)

20-42   Miss Priss Cosmetics currently reimburses its forty saleswomen for the use of their personal automobiles for the business. Terri K., company sales manager, has been trying without success to persuade the company to buy a number of cars to be used by her sales staff in the future, however. Terri's assistant has estimated the costs of operating company-owned automobiles an expected 30,000 miles per year on the basis of accounting records for automobiles used by company executives. The cost estimates in comparison with average mileage reimbursements are as follows:

Comparisons of Annual Costs of Company Automobiles with Annual Mileage Reimbursements

Company-Owned Car

Gas and oil	$1,800
Tires	300
Maintenance	400
Insurance and property taxes	500
Licenses, parking, tolls, etc.	200
Washing and waxing	100
Depreciation ($16,500 − $1,500) ÷ 3 years	5,000
Total Annual Operating Costs	$8,300

Mileage Reimbursement

30,000 @ $0.30	$9,000

The company is currently paying $0.30 per mile on an average of 30,000 miles driven by each saleswoman, and the sales manager believes that considerable savings are possible if the company buys cars to be used by sales personnel. She was recently questioned by John Q., the company's financial vice-president, about high costs in her department at a recent managers' meeting. Straining to keep her temper, she responded that if the company weren't so tight, it could save $28,000 per year by buying automobiles for the sales staff instead of paying that high mileage rate. She had the annual cost comparison to stick in his face if he challenged her on her statement.

At previous meetings, Terri had emphasized that a fleet of clean new cars with the company name on them would improve the company image and increase brand-name recognition, both factors leading to increased future sales. She emphasized that this would be especially true given that many of the sales routes would be lengthened next year to an average of 36,000 miles per year and would include areas where the company's products had not previously been sold. Terri had repeatedly been told that it would be too expensive for the company to buy cars for the sales staff to use, which is why she had instructed her assistant to prepare the cost comparison shown above.

Required: (1) Assume that Miss Priss Cosmetics has a cost of capital of 10% and that you are the company's financial vice-president. Write the sales manager a brief memo explaining why it would not be desirable for the company to buy cars for her staff in spite of the annual costs estimated by her assistant. Ignore the lengthening of sales routes and the possibility that sales might be increased.

(2) Now assume that you are the sales manager. Write the financial vice-president a memo describing how the analysis in (1) would be affected by (a) longer sales routes and (b) possible sales increases due to an improved company image and name recognition.

20-43 Yesterday, you received the letter shown on the following page for your advice column in the local paper:

Dear Dr. Decisive:

Last weekend, my roommate (let's just call him "Crunch") and I were visiting my father. Crunch and my father have a lot in common—Crunch is a varsity football player (left tackle), and Dad is a diehard football fan. Anyway, Crunch and I were looking through one of Dad's billions of football scrapbooks and came across an article describing the contracts of two NFL quarterbacks. Well, a good weekend got better because we were soon in the middle of one of our famous friendly debates. We couldn't (and still can't) agree on which quarterback got the better deal. According to the article, each quarterback received a six-year contract. "Lightning Z" would earn a total of $45 million, or an average of $7.5 million per year, and "Zinger B" would earn a total of $40.5 million, or an average of $6.75 million per year. So, the article said that, based on annual average salaries, "Lightning Z" was the higher-paid player. I agree with the article—it's an obvious conclusion—but Crunch disagrees with me.

According to the contracts, here's how each was supposed to be paid:

Year	Lightning Z	Zinger B
1998	$ 3 million	$13 million
1999	$10 million	$ 8.325 million
2000	$ 8.275 million	$ 7.675 million
2001	$ 6.55 million	$ 6.75 million
2002	$ 7.825 million	$ 3 million
2003	$ 9.35 million	$ 1.75 million
Total	$45 million	$40.5 million

Before contract negotiations, Lightning Z was about to enter the last year of a previous contract in which he was supposed to earn $4.5 million in 1998. To negotiate a better contract in later years, and to help his team, he "gave up" $1.5 million in salary in 1998. (This gave his team enough room below the salary cap to hire a top draft pick in 1998.) Zinger B negotiated a $10 million signing bonus (which he received at the beginning of 1998) as part of his $13 million 1998 salary.

You can see that even after giving up $1.5 million in 1998, Lightning Z is clearly getting the better deal. Crunch says Zinger B has the better deal because he is getting more money "up front."

Please help me convince Crunch that even though he knows his football (and is quite good at playing football), I'm right about this. A lot is riding on this. Whoever loses (and your answer is the deciding factor) must buy the winner two tickets to the next Chiefs game. I'm still trying to decide whom to take with me (maybe Crunch, maybe not).

"Undecided"

Required: Meet with your Dr. Decisive team and write a response to "Undecided."

CHAPTER 21

REPORTING PROPERTY, PLANT AND EQUIPMENT, AND INTANGIBLES

"Something rare and remarkable is going on, as companies buy equipment at fierce rates. The benefits could be enormous."
—Joseph Spiers, *Fortune*, April 3, 1995

1 *What types of assets does a company include in its property, plant, and equipment, and how does the company compute its historical costs?*

2 *Why does a company depreciate its property, plant, and equipment, and what are the causes of depreciation?*

3 *How does a company calculate its depreciation expense, and why does it compute depreciation expense differently for financial reporting than for income taxes?*

4 *How does a company evaluate the impairment of its property, plant, and equipment?*

5 *How does a company record and report the disposal of property, plant, and equipment?*

6 *How do external users evaluate information about a company's property, plant, and equipment?*

7 *What are intangible assets and natural resource assets, and what does a company report about them?*

www.hersheys.com

www.rmcfusa.com

In Hershey Foods' (maker of Caramello Candy Bars) December 31, 1997 balance sheet, the company shows that it owns $1,648 million (net) in property, plant, and equipment—50% of its total assets. On Rocky Mountain Chocolate Factory's February 28, 1998 balance sheet, its property, plant, and equipment was $9.7 million (net). Given that its total assets were about $19.9 million, 49% of Rocky Mountain's assets are included in property, plant, and equipment. These dollar amounts shown on Hershey Foods' and Rocky Mountain's balance sheets result from prior capital budgeting decisions and the accounting methods the companies used to keep track of property, plant, and equipment.

Hershey Foods' $1.6 billion in property, plant, and equipment is almost 165 times greater than Rocky Mountain Chocolate's $9.7 million. Can we conclude that Hershey manufactures about 165 times the amount of candy produced by Rocky Mountain? Why or why not? What factors besides the amounts on the balance sheets of the two companies should be considered?

A company uses the term **property, plant, and equipment** to describe all of the physical (tangible), long-term assets it uses in its operations. So when you walk into a Wal-Mart store, the land, building, and equipment (including its cash registers as well as shelves) are property, plant, and equipment. If you visited a Ford factory, the land, building, and manufacturing machinery are property, plant, and equipment. If you visited either company's head office, the land, building, and equipment (including computers and office furniture) are property, plant, and equipment. As we discussed briefly in Chapter 7, a company reports these assets in a separate section of the balance sheet, often called *property, plant, and equipment, long-term* assets, or *fixed* assets. It reports land at its original cost because of the assumption that the land does not get used up, but it reports the other property, plant, and equipment assets at their cost, less their accumulated depreciation.

What long-term assets can you identify in this picture?

In Chapter 19, we explained how companies report on inventory and how external users use a company's disclosures of inventory and cost of goods sold for evaluation. In this chapter, we explain how companies report on their property, plant, and equipment and depreciation expense in the financial statements included in their annual reports. Because many companies also have intangible assets and/or natural resource assets, we discuss the accounting issues related to these assets.

Issues Involved in Reporting Property, Plant, and Equipment

Make a list of a few long-term assets you own. Your list may include your watch or jewelry, a computer, a car, etc. Next, use your best judgment to write down a dollar value for each asset. How did you decide which value to use? Did you have any problems deciding what value to assign? Write down why you chose the values you selected for each of your assets.

Exhibit 21-1 shows the list for Jennifer Book, a business student. In addition to writing her list, Jennifer explained why she had some difficulty deciding the dollar values to assign to her assets. Perhaps your difficulties were similar to hers. Let's examine the problems she encountered assigning values.

As we show in Exhibit 21-1, Jennifer lists her computer, clothes, car, and wedding ring as some of her long-term assets. We see that Jennifer has doubts about the appropriate dollar values to list for her assets. For example, even though she purchased the computer in 1998 for $2,000, she knows that she could not sell it for that amount today. She has used the computer a lot, and technology has improved substantially since her purchase. She concludes that $800 is the best value to list. For her clothes, she decides to list them at $0 because she knows that she won't sell them—eventually she will give them to a charity. However, for her car, which she bought two years ago for $18,000 and plans to keep for another four years, she lists the value at $12,000—two-thirds of its original cost. "I am not going to sell the car for another 4 years, so the 'blue book' value doesn't seem relevant to me," she says. The $600 Jennifer lists for her wedding ring represents the amount she and her husband paid for the ring at the time of the purchase—the ring's dollar value at the time she acquired the asset. Although Jennifer decided to write down $600, she expresses

What types of assets does a company include in its property, plant, and equipment, and how does the company compute their historical costs?

Exhibit 21-1 Jennifer Book's List of Four Assets She Owns and Some Issues with Assigning Dollar Values to Them

Asset	Value	Issues in Deciding Dollar Value
Computer	$800	I paid about $2,000 for the computer when I bought it in 1998. But I'm sure I couldn't sell it for that amount today. The way computers get outdated so fast, I figure it is worth less than half of what I paid for it.
Clothes	$0	Even though I paid about $2,500 for them, I will give them away when they wear out or are out of style. Therefore, I don't see that I should give them any value.
Car	$12,000	I bought the car two years ago for $18,000, but I am not going to sell it for another 4 years, so the "blue book" value doesn't seem relevant to me. Since I have owned the car for one-third of the time I plan to own it, I assigned a value of $12,000.
Wedding ring	$600	This is the amount my husband and I paid for the ring in 1997. I think it is worth much more than $600 now, but I am not sure how much more. I saw a ring like mine in a jewelry store for $1,100, but you know stores charge a huge markup. Of course, I really only paid for half of it.

some concerns about it. She thinks the ring is worth more than $600 today (although she has no intention of selling it) because she saw a similar ring selling for $1,100. On the other hand, she points out that she purchased the ring jointly with her husband and so has only $300 invested in the ring.

 Do you agree with Jennifer's decisions? Was she consistent in her approach to valuing the assets? Why or why not? Did you have valuation problems similar to Jennifer's? Do you think that a long-term asset you own is worth more than its original cost, but do not know its value? Or, on the other hand, do you have a long-term asset that you think is no longer worth what you paid for it, but you do not know what amount to write down?

The difficulties that Jennifer had in assigning dollar values for long-term assets illustrate why financial statement users, in order to make informed business decisions, need to understand how companies account for and report on property, plant, and equipment. Notice that Jennifer did not use any accounting rules to help her decide. A company, however, is required to use GAAP, which for property, plant, and equipment is based on two accounting concepts we introduced earlier in the book—the *historical cost concept* and the *matching principle*. Let's review these concepts.

Recall that the historical cost concept states that a company records its transactions on the basis of the dollars it exchanged (in other words, the cost) in the transaction. Once a company records a transaction, it usually retains the *cost* involved in the transaction in its accounting records. For instance, in 1985, Unlimited Decadence paid $35,000 for 10 acres of land on which to build its headquarters. At the end of 2000, real estate professionals estimate that the land has a market value greater than $85,000. Under the historical cost concept, Unlimited Decadence continues to show the land on its 2000 ending balance sheet at $35,000.

 Which accounts would be affected, and how would they be affected, if a company records its property, plant, and equipment at more than the company paid for them?

Many accounting and business experts express concerns about the usefulness of the historical cost concept. They ask, "How does including the $35,000 cost of the land in Unlimited Decadence's 2000 ending balance sheet help investors and creditors make business decisions?" In other words, they question the *relevance* of presenting this historical cost amount. Supporters of the historical cost concept argue that if the company has no intention of selling the asset, then the market value is *not* relevant. Since Unlimited Decadence has no intention of selling its headquarters building and the land underneath it, the $85,000 is not relevant.

 To whom might the market value be relevant?

Supporters of historical cost also argue that the *reliability* of historical costs and GAAP's emphasis on *conservatism* outweigh any potential increase in relevance that might be gained from using the market value. In essence, GAAP supporters say: "We know that Unlimited Decadence paid $35,000 for its land. Until someone actually buys the land from Unlimited Decadence for $85,000, we are not sure how reliable that dollar amount is. If an investor made a business decision based on the $85,000 estimate and the land was later sold for only $50,000, that investor might have been hurt by our estimate. With historical cost accounting, at least external users know what information they are getting." Also we know that all accountants would conclude that the historical cost was $35,000, whereas they probably would differ in their estimates of the market value.

 Whose side do you take on this discussion—the supporters or the critics of the historical cost concept? Explain your position.

The matching principle states that to determine its net income for an accounting period, a company computes the total expenses involved in earning the revenues of the period and deducts them from the revenues earned in that period. Because property, plant, and equipment provide benefits every period that they are used and because they have a finite life, a company includes a portion of their cost as an expense in its measurement of net income for each accounting period that the company benefits from their use. For example, Unlimited Decadence owns machines that wrap its candy bars after they are produced. Each accounting period in which it uses a candy-wrapping machine, it matches a portion of the cost of the machine against the revenues it recorded during the period. Recall from Chapter 5 that the part of the cost of property, plant, and equipment that a company allocates as an expense to each accounting period in which the company uses the asset is called **depreciation expense**. The recording of depreciation expense is an end-of-period adjustment. Also recall from Chapter 7 that **accumulated depreciation** is the total depreciation recorded on an asset to date, and that the **book value** of an asset, or **net asset value**, is the cost of the asset less its accumulated depreciation.

So, the historical cost concept and the matching principle provide the basis for how a company accounts for property, plant, and equipment and reports on them in its financial statements. In the next sections we will address seven important issues: (1) computing the historical cost of property, plant, and equipment, (2) the reasons for depreciating property, plant, and equipment, (3) calculating depreciation expense for both financial reporting and income taxes, (4) recording the impairment of property, plant, and equipment, (5) disposing of property, plant, and equipment, (6) reporting property, plant, and equipment and depreciation expense in a company's annual report, and (7) using information about a company's property, plant, and equipment and depreciation expense to evaluate its operations.

Computing the Cost of Property, Plant, and Equipment

The total cost of an asset classified as property, plant, and equipment includes all the costs a company incurs to acquire the asset *and* to get it ready for use. These costs may include the invoice price (less any cash discounts), sales taxes, transportation charges, and installation costs.

 Do you think that this principle is the same as the one that we discussed in Chapter 19 for recording inventory? Why or why not?

For instance, suppose that Unlimited Decadence purchases a vertical agitator machine with a contract price of $40,000 on terms of 2/10, n/30. The company incurs sales tax of 5%, transportation costs of $2,300, and installation costs of $1,200. The company deducts the cash discount of $800 (2% × $40,000) and pays the net invoice price of $39,200 ($40,000 − $800). Given this information, we can calculate the cost[1] of the machine as follows:

Contract price	$40,000
Sales tax	2,000
Transportation costs	2,300
Installation costs	1,200
Less: Cash discounts available	(800)
Acquisition cost	$44,700

---

[1]The discount should be deducted from the cost of the machine whether or not it is taken. If it is not taken, the amount of the discount not taken is treated as interest expense.

Note that although these costs may be incurred at various times, Unlimited Decadence includes in the cost of the machine all the costs to acquire the asset and get it ready for its intended use because they are necessary for the machine to be able to produce the benefits for which it was purchased. Since Unlimited Decadence will benefit from using the machine over its intended life, it allocates the cost of the machine as an expense over its life, and *not* in the period in which it acquired the machine. Therefore, Unlimited Decadence records the machine as an item of property, plant, and equipment at $44,700.

Assume you are starting a typing service in your home. You purchase new computer equipment and supplies to start the company. Listed below are the types of costs you incurred while setting up the computer equipment. Would you categorize each cost as (a) a cost that is part of the acquisition cost of the computer equipment, (b) a cost that is an expense of the current period for the company, or (c) neither (a) nor (b)? Why?

1. Purchase price of the computer

2. Purchase price of the printer

3. Purchase price of the computer and printer cables

4. Purchase price of three boxes of paper

5. Charges for delivery and setup of the computer equipment

6. Purchase price of the pizza eaten while setting up the computer equipment

7. Charges for delivery of the pizza

8. Costs of installing special electrical outlets for the computer equipment

9. Cost of replacing the lamp that was broken during the delivery

Reasons for Depreciating Property, Plant, and Equipment

2 *Why does a company depreciate its property, plant, and equipment, and what are the causes of depreciation?*

The assets a company includes in its property, plant, and equipment provide it with benefits for more than one year. As we stated earlier in the chapter, the *matching* principle requires that a company match the expenses involved in obtaining the revenues of the period against the revenues it recorded in that accounting period. Unlimited Decadence expects its vertical agitator machine to last three years. Each year, this machine mixes ingredients for the candy that Unlimited Decadence sells. Therefore, each year, Unlimited Decadence matches part of the machine's historical cost against the revenue produced by the sale of the candy that this machine helped manufacture that year.

Causes of Depreciation

Think more about the long-term assets you may personally own. Assume you own a car and a computer. What factors cause these particular assets to depreciate? The number of miles you drive your car each year and how hard you drive it are the most likely factors that determine how many years it will last. On the other hand, a computer's life is more likely to be limited by technological innovations (e.g., you want a faster, more powerful computer to run new software).

A company's property, plant, and equipment depreciate for two primary reasons: (1) physical causes and (2) functional causes, as we illustrate in Exhibit 21-2. **Physical causes** include wear and tear due to *use,* deterioration and decay caused by the passage of *time,* and damage and destruction. For example, Unlimited Decadence's vertical agitator machine may have parts that break or wear out. **Functional causes** limit the life of the asset, even though the physical life is not exhausted. An asset is made obsolete because new technology is introduced or because the asset is no longer suitable for the company's operations even though it still may be physically sound. So, depreciation on a car tends to be from physical causes (but may be from functional causes if you want to

Exhibit 21-2   Depreciation Issues

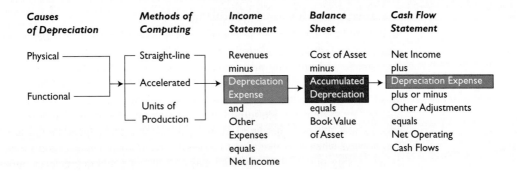

Causes of Depreciation	Methods of Computing	Income Statement	Balance Sheet	Cash Flow Statement
Physical	Straight-line	Revenues minus	Cost of Asset minus	Net Income plus
Functional	Accelerated	Depreciation Expense	Accumulated Depreciation	Depreciation Expense plus or minus
	Units of Production	and Other Expenses equals Net Income	equals Book Value of Asset	Other Adjustments equals Net Operating Cash Flows

purchase a new car to be "cool"), whereas depreciation on a computer tends to be from functional causes.

 Think about the assets you own. What would be the primary cause for each type of asset to depreciate?

Service Life and Residual Value

There are three factors involved in the calculation of the depreciation amount: (1) the **cost** of the asset; (2) the **estimated service life** of the asset, which is the life over which a company expects the asset to be useful; and (3) the **estimated residual value** of the asset, which is the cash the company estimates it will receive from the sale or disposal of the asset at the end of its estimated service life. The service life often is referred to as the *economic life,* and the residual value as the *salvage value.*

Managers must estimate the service life and the residual value when the company acquires the asset. They do this by analyzing how the physical and functional causes of depreciation will affect the asset. The managers' estimate of the service life also directly affects the estimate of the residual value. In some cases, managers will plan to keep the asset until its physical life is exhausted. In this case, the estimated residual value will be close to zero. Alternatively, managers may plan to dispose of the asset well before its physical life is exhausted. In this situation, the estimated residual value may be relatively large. For example, airlines often sell planes long before the end of their physical lives. Although managers sometimes find it difficult to estimate the service life and the residual value of an asset, they must make realistic estimates using the best information available. Because of the difficulty of estimating the residual value, many companies use an arbitrary amount, such as 10 percent of the cost. The company's estimates of an asset's useful life and residual value affect the amount of depreciation it records for the asset. The estimates of the service life and residual value should be consistent with the estimates used in the capital expenditure decisions that we discussed in Chapter 20.

 Think of an asset you own. Identify the residual values and service lives that you could select. Would other people with the same asset use the same amounts?

Depreciation Is an Allocation of Cost, Not a Valuation

A company does not record depreciation in an attempt to estimate the value of an asset. By that, we mean that depreciating an asset is not an attempt to estimate the market value of an asset *during* its life. Depreciation involves matching the acquisition (historical) cost of the asset, as an expense, against the revenue it helps to earn. Therefore, it is only at the time of acquisition and at the end of the life of an asset (if the original estimate of the residual value is accurate) that the book value (the cost of the asset less the accumulated depreciation) is equal to its market value. During the life of the asset, the book value is the *cost* of the remaining benefits that the company expects to obtain from the asset, and *not* the value of those benefits.

Systematic and Rational Allocation of Costs

Since precisely measuring the benefits that a particular asset provides is usually impossible, the underlying principle is that a company matches the depreciation expense in a "systematic and rational" manner against its revenue. **Systematic** means that the calculation follows a formula and is not determined in an arbitrary manner. As you will see, the straight-line method and the alternative methods, which we will discuss later in the chapter, are systematic. **Rational** means that the amount of the depreciation relates to the benefits that the asset produces in any period. Thus, managers should use the *straight-line method* when it is likely that the asset will produce equal benefits each period over its life. Using this method, the company records an equal depreciation amount each period and matches this expense against the benefits (revenues) each period. An *accelerated depreciation method* records the highest amount of depreciation in the first year of the asset's life and lesser amounts in each subsequent year. Therefore, managers should use an accelerated method when the asset produces benefits that are highest early in the life of the asset and when the benefits decline in each succeeding period. Managers may select different depreciation methods for different types of assets because the patterns of benefits generated by each type of asset vary.

 Can you think of an asset for which accelerated depreciation is appropriate? Explain why.

Calculating Depreciation Expense

3 *How does a company calculate its depreciation expense, and why does it compute depreciation expense differently for financial reporting than for income taxes?*

Earlier, we discussed why GAAP requires that a company record property, plant, and equipment in its accounting records at historical cost (GAAP's requirements for relevant and reliable information) and why a company depreciates property, plant, and equipment (GAAP's requirement that costs be matched as expenses against revenues they helped to earn). In the next sections, we will focus on how a company determines the specific amounts that it records as depreciation. This understanding will help you analyze the reporting of property, plant, and equipment in financial statements. To illustrate depreciation expense, first we will briefly discuss the straight-line method of depreciation. Then we will explain an accelerated depreciation method that some companies use.

Straight-Line Depreciation

A company using the **straight-line method** computes depreciation expense by allocating the cost of an asset, less its estimated residual value, equally to each period of the asset's estimated service life. This is the simplest and most commonly used way that companies calculate depreciation. The straight-line method is appropriate when the company expects to use the asset approximately equally in each period. If the benefits are equal in each period, the total *remaining* benefits decline equally each period. This pattern of depreciation occurs, for example, when physical deterioration and decay occur at a steady rate over the life of the asset. Then a company records an equal amount of depreciation expense each period by using the straight-line method. The amount of the straight-line depreciation is computed as follows:

$$\text{Depreciation per Year} = \frac{(\text{Cost} - \text{Estimated Residual Value})}{\text{Estimated Service Life}}$$

The cost less the residual value is known as the **depreciable cost.** It is the estimated total portion of the acquisition cost that the company will allocate to depreciation expense over its service life. Sometimes a company may express depreciation in terms of a rate per year. For straight-line depreciation, a company computes this rate by dividing 100% by the estimated life.

For example, suppose that Unlimited Decadence buys a blending machine (that it uses to mix ingredients) for $25,000 on January 1, 2000, and estimates that it will sell the machine for $2,500 (the residual value) after using it for 5 years (the service life). Unlimited Decadence computes the straight-line depreciation expense as follows:

$$\text{Depreciation per Year} = \frac{(\$25,000 - \$2,500)}{5 \text{ years}}$$

$$= \$4,500$$

The $22,500 depreciable cost of the blending machine is the acquisition cost of $25,000 less the $2,500 residual value. This $22,500 is allocated equally to each year of the asset's 5-year life, or at the rate of $4,500 per year. The straight-line rate is 20% (100% ÷ 5). So Unlimited Decadence could also compute the straight-line depreciation expense by multiplying the depreciable cost by the straight-line rate ($22,500 × 20% = $4,500).

Companies generally record depreciation in their accounting records as an end-of-period adjustment. If a company prepares financial statements only on an annual basis, the end-of-period depreciation adjustment records depreciation expense for the entire year. If a company prepares financial statements every quarter, it records depreciation expense each quarter only for that quarterly period. Accumulated depreciation shows the total depreciation that the company has recorded as of the end of the period (including the depreciation recorded for the same asset in previous periods).

Unlimited Decadence records the annual depreciation expense we just calculated for its blending machine in its accounting records at December 31, 2000 as follows:

Assets	**=**	**Liabilities**	**+**	**Stockholders' Equity**

Accumulated Depreciation: Blending Machine				Depreciation Expense: Blending Machine
	4,500			4,500
(−)	(+)			(+) (−)

In Chapter 7, when we first explained accumulated depreciation, we recorded the amount directly on the right side of the asset account. Here we record it in a separate account so that it is easier for managers to know both the cost and the accumulated depreciation of an asset, and to prepare the company's annual report which requires the disclosure of both amounts. Accumulated Depreciation is a *contra*-account—the company records increases on the right side of the account and subtracts the balance from the related asset account to compute the book value of the asset. For example, on its December 31, 2000 balance sheet, Unlimited Decadence would report the $20,500 book value of its blending machine as follows:

Property, Plant, and Equipment
Machinery $25,000
Less: Accumulated depreciation .... (4,500)
$20,500

A company should keep separate asset, depreciation expense, and accumulated depreciation accounts for each type of asset. Separate asset and accumulated depreciation accounts allow users to easily check the historical cost and accumulated depreciation for each type of asset, and are needed for the disclosures we will discuss later. We show a summary of the annual straight-line depreciation expense, the accumulated depreciation, and the book value over the life of Unlimited Decadence's blending machine in the top part of Exhibit 21-3.

In the lower part of Exhibit 21-3, we also use our blending machine example to help explain the relationships among the historical cost of an asset, accumulated depreciation, and book value. First, keep in mind that the blending machine's historical cost, $25,000, does not change during its service life. This follows GAAP's reliance on the historical cost concept. Second, note that when Unlimited Decadence places the blending machine into service at the start of 2000, accumulated depreciation equals $0. At the end of each year, Unlimited Decadence records annual depreciation expense of $4,500 and increases the blending machine's accumulated depreciation by this $4,500. By the end of the fifth year of the blending machine's service life (year 2004), accumulated depreciation totals $22,500 ($4,500 annual depreciation expense × 5 years), and the book value is $2,500, the estimated residual value. Note also how the book value of the blending machine changes over its service life. At the start of 2000, the $25,000 historical cost of the blending machine and its book value are equal. Then the blending machine's book value

Exhibit 21-3   Straight-Line Depreciation: Unlimited Decadence's Blending Machine

Straight-Line Depreciation Schedule:
Blending Machine

Year	Depreciation Expense	Accumulated Depreciation	Book Value at the End of the Year
2000	$4,500	$ 4,500	$20,500
2001	4,500	9,000	16,000
2002	4,500	13,500	11,500
2003	4,500	18,000	7,000
2004	4,500	22,500	2,500

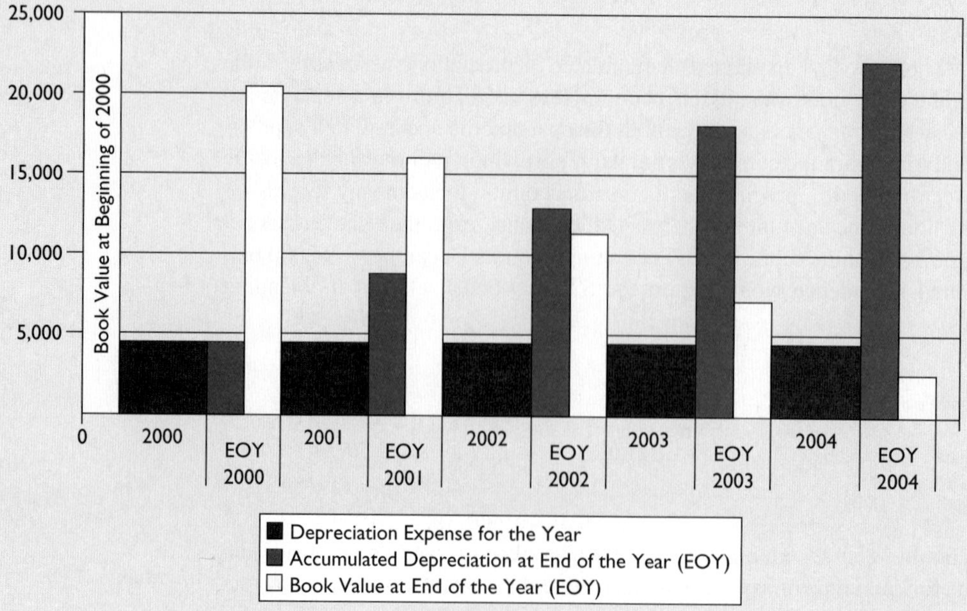

■ Depreciation Expense for the Year
■ Accumulated Depreciation at End of the Year (EOY)
☐ Book Value at End of the Year (EOY)

declines by $4,500 each year as a result of the recording of depreciation expense and accumulated depreciation. At the end of 2004, Unlimited Decadence's blending machine has been fully depreciated so that its book value ($2,500) equals its estimated residual value.

 If a company purchases a used asset, do you think it starts with a balance in Accumulated Depreciation? Why or why not?

Partial Period Depreciation

In the previous example, Unlimited Decadence purchased the blending machine on January 1, 2000, so we computed a full year of depreciation. But companies do not always purchase property, plant, and equipment on the first day of the year! So how does a company compute depreciation expense when it buys an asset during the year?

A common approach is to compute depreciation expense to the nearest whole month. Thus, if Unlimited Decadence purchased the blending machine on April 3, 2000, it would compute the depreciation expense for 2000 based on 9 months to be $3,375 ($4,500 × 9/12). Then in 2001 through 2004, its depreciation expense would be $4,500 per year. Finally, it would use the machine through the first three months of 2005. So the depreciation expense for 2005 for this machine would be $1,125 ($4,500 × 3/12), and the book value would be $2,500 on April 1, 2005.

Accelerated Depreciation Methods

In 1997, over 90 percent of U.S. companies used straight-line depreciation for at least *some* of their assets. So, not all companies use the straight-line method. GAAP allows a company's managers to choose among several additional methods, including (1) the double-declining-balance method, (2) the sum-of-the-years'-digits method, and (3) the units-of-production method. Double declining balance and sum of the years' digits are two **accelerated depreciation methods**, which record the highest depreciation in the first year of an asset's service life and lower depreciation in subsequent years. We will discuss the units-of-production method later in the chapter.

Double-Declining-Balance Method

A company using the **double-declining-balance method** computes depreciation expense by multiplying the book value of an asset at the beginning of the period by twice the straight-line rate. The double-declining depreciation rate is computed by dividing 200% by the asset's estimated life. Note that the double-declining-balance method uses twice the *rate* that is used for the straight-line method (*not* twice the amount). In addition, the residual value is *not* considered in the calculation of the depreciation expense under the double-declining-balance method. A company using this method bases its depreciation calculation on the asset's book value rather than its depreciable cost. However, the asset is not depreciated below the estimated residual value. In other words, its book value must not drop below its residual value. Using the double-declining-balance method, a company computes the depreciation expense as follows:

$$\text{Depreciation per Year} = \frac{200\%}{\text{Estimated Service Life}} \times \text{Book Value at the Beginning of the Year}$$

Here's how Unlimited Decadence would compute depreciation expense for its blending machine if it used the double-declining-balance method. Recall that Unlimited Decadence purchased the blending machine at the beginning of 2000 for $25,000, and that the machine had an estimated residual value of $2,500 and an estimated service life of 5 years. Since the asset has a life of 5 years, the double-declining-balance depreciation rate is 40% (200% ÷ 5) per year. Unlimited Decadence would calculate the depreciation expense each year as follows:

		Double-Declining-Balance Depreciation Schedule: **Blending Machine**			
Year	**Book Value at** **the Beginning** **of the Year**	**Depreciation** **Calculation**	**Depreciation** **Expense**	**Accumulated** **Depreciation**	**Book Value** **at the End** **of the Year**
2000	$25,000	40% × $25,000	$10,000	$10,000	$15,000
2001	15,000	40% × 15,000	6,000	16,000	9,000
2002	9,000	40% × 9,000	3,600	19,600	5,400
2003	5,400	40% × 5,400	2,160	21,760	3,240
2004	3,240		740[a]	22,500	2,500

[a]40% × $3,240 = $1,296, but depreciation expense is limited to $740 so that the asset's book value equals its $2,500 estimated residual value.

Note that Unlimited Decadence bases the calculation of the depreciation in the first year on the total acquisition cost of $25,000 and *not* on the acquisition cost less the estimated residual value. In the year 2004, it must make a modification to the usual calculations because a company should *not* depreciate the asset below its estimated residual value. Therefore, in 2004, Unlimited Decadence records depreciation expense of only $740 (instead of 40% × $3,240, or $1,296). This is exactly the amount of depreciation expense needed to reduce the book value to $2,500 at the end of the year so that the book value is equal to the estimated residual value.

 During the first year of the blending machine's useful life, would the straight-line method or the double-declining-balance method cause Unlimited Decadence to report the higher net income? the higher total assets? the higher stockholders' equity? Would this be true during the last year of the blending machine's useful life? Why or why not?

Sum-of-the-Years'-Digits Method

GAAP allows a company's managers to select another accelerated depreciation method called the sum-of-the-years'-digits method. The **sum-of-the-years'-digits method** computes depreciation expense by multiplying the depreciable cost (cost − residual value) of an asset by a fraction that declines each year.[2] The declining fraction that is used depends on the length of the asset's useful life. Because few companies use the sum-of-the-years'-digits method and because its effects on a company's financial statements are similar to those of the double-declining-balance method, we do not go through the detailed calculations of this method.

Comparison of Depreciation Methods

Now that we have discussed the straight-line and accelerated methods of depreciation allowed by GAAP, let's compare the effects of each type of method on a company's financial statements. In Exhibit 21-4 we graph the amount of depreciation expense incurred each year of the blending machine's useful life under the straight-line and the double-declining-balance methods. This exhibit shows that the amount of depreciation expense that Unlimited Decadence records each year for its blending machine depends on which depreciation method the company selects.

In Exhibit 21-5 we show how the blending machine's book value changes during the five years of its useful life for each of the two depreciation methods. Notice that at the start

[2]The numerator of the fraction changes each year and is the years' digits, used in reverse order. So for an asset with a 5-year life, the numerator is 5 in the first year, 4 in the second year, and so on. The denominator is the sum of the years' digits [i.e. (1 + 2 + 3 + 4 + 5)], or [n(n + 1) ÷ 2]. So for a 5-year asset, the denominator is 15 [i.e., (5 × 6) ÷ 2]. Therefore, the fractions (or rates) for a 5-year asset are $\frac{5}{15}$, $\frac{4}{15}$, $\frac{3}{15}$, $\frac{2}{15}$, and $\frac{1}{15}$.

Exhibit 21-4   Depreciation Expense for Blending Machine under Different Methods

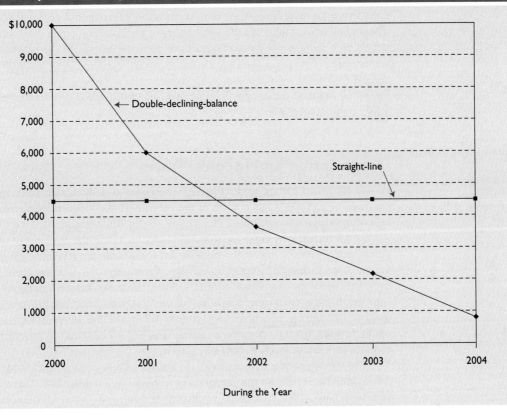

Exhibit 21-5   Book Value of Blending Machine under Different Depreciation Methods

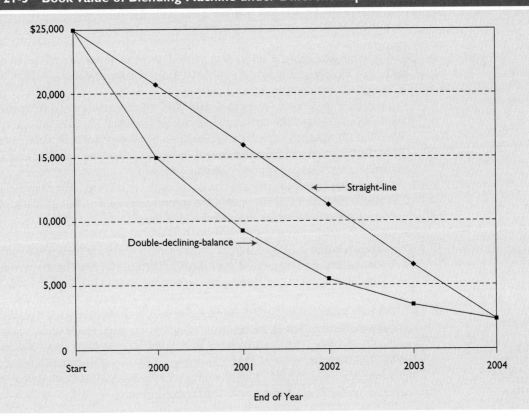

of the machine's useful life, its book value is the same under each method ($25,000). The $25,000 is the machine's acquisition cost. The decline in book value each year results from the recording of annual depreciation expense and accumulated depreciation. The ending book values are the same for both methods and equal the asset's actual residual value if the company's managers have correctly estimated the residual value and the service life.

 If you were a manager for Unlimited Decadence, which depreciation method would you choose? Why?

Depreciation and Income Taxes

As we explained earlier, under GAAP, a corporation deducts depreciation expense from revenues as part of its calculation of net income. It also deducts depreciation expense in reporting *taxable* income on its income tax return. But because the depreciation rules under GAAP differ from those for computing income taxes, the amounts of depreciation expense in any year for financial reporting and for income tax reporting are different. These amounts are different because financial reporting and the Internal Revenue Code have different objectives. An objective of GAAP is to prepare income statements that fairly present the income-producing activities of the company and that are useful to decision-makers. In contrast, two objectives, among others, of the Internal Revenue Code are to obtain revenue for the operation of the federal government and to provide investment incentives for certain kinds of business activity.

The managers of a corporation have a responsibility to the stockholders to minimize the income taxes paid by the corporation without violating the law. Therefore, it is desirable for a corporation to record, for income tax purposes, as much depreciation as possible early in the life of an asset. Higher depreciation in the early years of an asset's life reduces the corporation's taxable income in those years, thereby reducing the income taxes paid in those years. To accomplish this, companies use an accelerated depreciation method acceptable under the Internal Revenue Code—the **Modified Accelerated Cost Recovery System (MACRS)**—for income tax purposes.

 If the total depreciation for both methods is the same over the life of the asset, why do managers consider the use of MACRS to be advantageous?

There are three major ways in which MACRS depreciation is different from GAAP depreciation: (1) MACRS defines the *tax life* of the asset, (2) MACRS uses *no residual value,* and (3) MACRS specifies a depreciation percentage for each year. In contrast, for GAAP depreciation, managers estimate the *service life* and the *residual value* of the asset and select a method based on the matching principle.

Companies frequently disclose the use of different methods. For example, in a note to Wal-Mart's 1997 financial statements, the corporation explains that its financial statement and tax depreciation methods are different, as follows:

> **Depreciation . . .** Depreciation . . . for financial statement purposes is provided on the straight-line method over the estimated useful lives of the various assets. For income tax purposes, accelerated methods [MACRS] are used. . .

Exhibit 21-6 shows MACRS depreciation (except for buildings) as a percentage of the cost of an asset for each of the tax lives. Buildings are depreciated under the straight-line method over either 27.5 years (residential buildings) or 39 years (non- residential buildings). Three longtime users of MACRS—General Motors, Ford, and General Electric— have together saved around $20 billion in taxes by using MACRS rather than straight-line depreciation for taxes, thereby lowering taxable income.

www.gm.com
www2.ford.com
www.ge.com

Exhibit 21-6 Percentage of an Asset's Cost Used to Compute MACRS Depreciation

Year of Life	Tax Life of Asset in Years[a]					
	3	5	7	10	15	20
1	33.33%	20.00%	14.29%	10.00%	5.00%	3.750%
2	44.45	32.00	24.49	18.00	9.50	7.219
3	14.81	19.20	17.49	14.40	8.55	6.677
4	7.41	11.52	12.49	11.52	7.70	6.177
5		11.52	8.93	9.22	6.93	5.713
6		5.76	8.92	7.37	6.23	5.285
7			8.93	6.55	5.90	4.888
8			4.46	6.55	5.90	4.522
9				6.56	5.91	4.462
10				6.55	5.90	4.461
11				3.28	5.91	4.462
12					5.90	4.461
13					5.91	4.462
14					5.90	4.461
15					5.91	4.462
16					2.95	4.461
17						4.462
18						4.461
19						4.462
20						4.461
21						2.231

[a]The percentages are based on the half-year convention—depreciation for half a year is recorded in the year of acquisition and in the final year of depreciation for tax purposes. The percentages are also based on a change to the straight-line method in the period in which the straight-line depreciation exceeds the amount calculated under the accelerated method.

 Do you think you pay less when you purchase a car because the car manufacturer uses MACRS for its income taxes?

Subsequent Expenditures

After purchasing an asset, a company often makes additional expenditures on the asset during its economic life. The company classifies these costs as either capital expenditures or operating expenditures. A **capital expenditure** is a cost that increases the benefits the company will obtain from an asset. An **operating expenditure** is a cost that only maintains the benefits that the company originally expected from the asset.

 If you own a car, which of your costs would you classify as capital expenditures? operating expenditures?

A *capital* expenditure increases the benefits to be obtained from an asset either by significantly increasing the usefulness of the asset or by extending its life. Examples of capital expenditures (often called *renewals* and *betterments*) include additions, improvements, and unusual repairs such as adding a new wing to a building, installing additional insulation, or repairing a boiler in such an extensive way that its life is extended. A company records a capital expenditure as an addition to the cost of the asset. The company includes the additional cost in the calculation of the depreciation expense it records over the remaining life of the asset.

The major item of *operating* expenditures is routine repair and maintenance costs. For example, if a company buys a delivery truck that it expects to use for 150,000 miles, it knows that it will have to perform repairs and maintenance during that time. Thus, each routine repair merely maintains the ability of the truck to last for 150,000 miles and does not extend the asset's life or increase its usefulness. A company records an operating expenditure (sometimes called a *revenue expenditure*) as an expense when incurred.

It is important for a company to record an additional cost correctly as a capital or operating expenditure. Managers must use good judgment. An error in classification may have a significant effect on the company's financial statements. For example, suppose a company incorrectly records the cost of adding a new wing to a building as a repairs expense. As a result, the company overstates the repairs expense on its income statement and understates net income in the period of the expenditure. Also, it understates the asset—Building—on its balance sheet and therefore understates depreciation expense (thereby overstating net income) for the rest of the life of the asset.

Or suppose a company incorrectly records routine repairs to machinery as an increase in the machinery account. Then, it understates the repairs expense on its income statement and overstates net income. It overstates the asset—Machinery—on its balance sheet and therefore overstates depreciation expense (thereby understating net income) for the rest of the life of the asset. You can see that the correct classification of subsequent expenditures is important to the measurement of net income.

 Explain which of the two errors may be more likely to occur.

Impairment of Property, Plant, and Equipment

4 *How does a company evaluate the impairment of its property, plant, and equipment?*

Recall that an asset of a company is an economic resource that will provide future benefits to the company, and that the company reports its property, plant, and equipment at book value (historical cost − accumulated depreciation). The future economic benefits that the property, plant, and equipment will provide are the expected net cash flows that the company will receive from using the assets in its operations. But what if the market value of these assets is less than their book value? In this case, these assets may not provide sufficient future net cash flows to "recover" the book value. Then it may be argued that the book value is *not* a good measure of the cost of the expected future benefits. So an asset is **impaired** when the expected future cash flows are less than the book value of the asset.

Under GAAP, a company must review its property, plant, and equipment assets (and certain identifiable intangible assets discussed later in the chapter) to see if they are impaired. Impairment exists whenever events or changes in circumstances indicate that the book value of the assets may not be recoverable through the net cash flows that the company will receive from those assets. Examples of events or changes in circumstances that indicate that assets may be impaired include a significant decrease in the market value of the assets, a significant change in the way the assets are used, a significant change in the business or regulatory environment, a current period operating loss, or a negative cash flow from operating activities. In making this review, a company may look at each individual asset or at groups of related assets (e.g., a production line or a factory).

 Why does each of the examples indicate that the company may not be able to generate net cash inflows that equal or exceed the book value of the asset?

If the book value of an asset is not recoverable through the future cash flows expected from that asset, then a company must reduce the book value of that asset and record an impairment loss. For each property, plant, and equipment asset, a company computes the impairment loss as the difference between the asset's book value and its lower market value. The market value is the amount at which the asset could be bought or sold in a current transaction between willing parties. However, market prices frequently will not be available for a used asset. Therefore, a company may use the present value of the estimated future cash flows generated by the asset as a measure of its market value. The discount rate that a company uses to determine the present value is the rate of return that the company would require for a similar investment with similar risks. For example, this could be the rate the company used to evaluate capital budgeting projects, as we discussed in Chapter 20. When the company records the impairment loss, it reduces the asset's book value to the lower market value. It reports the impairment loss on the income statement as part of income from continuing operations, and reports the new (reduced) book value on the ending balance sheet. The reduced book value (i.e., market value) becomes the new "cost" of the asset, and the company uses this new cost to compute the depreciation over the remaining life of the asset. Once a company has written an asset down, if the market value subsequently increases, the company may not write it back up.

 Is the impairment of property, plant, and equipment similar to the lower-of-cost-or-market method for inventory? Why or why not?

To understand an impairment loss, suppose that Unlimited Decadence determines that a building and some machinery are impaired and that their market value of $2 million is $500,000 less than the book value of $2.5 million. Unlimited Decadence reduces the book value of its property, plant, and equipment assets on its balance sheet from $2.5 million to $2 million. It also reports a loss of $500,000 in income from continuing operations on its income statement. Unlimited Decadence will depreciate the new "cost" of $2 million over the remaining useful life of the assets.

External User Perspective: Evaluation of GAAP for Asset Impairment

GAAP for an asset impairment is intended to enhance the usefulness of a company's financial statements by requiring the company to report the loss when it is incurred and to show the lower market value of its productive assets. The information is more relevant because the company reports the loss in current income, and because the asset amount shows the lower market value of the company's investment, thereby helping users assess the *re-*

Suppose you are a passenger on this plane and are reading American Airlines' 1995 annual report. What do you think the company means when it refers to its airplanes as "impaired"? Should you get off the plane immediately?

turn on investment, operating capability, and *risk* of the company. The information also improves comparability across companies.

These principles do allow significant flexibility for a company's managers, however. For example, they do not require that a company review its assets for impairment on a regular basis, because that would be very costly. Also, estimating future cash flows is subjective. For example, the company could use current or expected cost and volume information. Furthermore, the discount rate used to calculate the present value of those cash flows is a management choice. Also note that the reduction in the asset's book value will "guarantee" future profits because of the reduced depreciation expense in future periods.

www.pepsico.com
www.AA.com

To illustrate asset impairment, in 1995 PepsiCo and American Airlines reported impairment losses of $520 million and $193 million, respectively. It is interesting to note that PepsiCo evaluated each individual restaurant, whereas American Airlines evaluated types of aircraft—in this case, the impairment related to DC-10 aircraft. PepsiCo also reported that its depreciation expense in 1995 was reduced by $21 million as a result of the impairment. In 1996 and 1997 PepsiCo again reported impairment losses of $373 million and $200 million respectively—equivalent to a lot of cans of soft drinks and bags of potato chips! In 1997, General Motors reported an impairment loss of over $1 billion!

 Do you think that the reporting of impairment losses creates both relevant and reliable information? Why, or why not?

Disposing of Property, Plant, and Equipment

5 *How does a company record and report the disposal of property, plant, and equipment?*

Although property, plant, and equipment lasts longer than one year, it doesn't last forever. At some point, Unlimited Decadence's blending machine will stop blending and its vertical agitator will stop shaking. After a few years, even if the machines are still functioning, newer models may make the current ones obsolete. Even though Unlimited Decadence might be able to continue using the machine, it may find it difficult to compete with companies that upgrade their machines.

When a company disposes of a depreciable asset, one of three things happens: (1) the asset is sold for an amount equal to its book value at the date of disposal; (2) the asset is sold for an amount greater or less than its book value on that date, in which case the company records a gain or loss; or (3) the asset is traded for another asset.

Regardless of the reason for the disposal, a company records and reports depreciation expense for the current period up to the date of disposal. For example, if Unlimited Decadence starts its fiscal year on January 1 and sells its blending machine on July 30, 2003, it reports depreciation expense on the machine for seven months in its 2003 income statement. The blending machine had not been fully depreciated at the start of 2003, and it was used to help Unlimited Decadence earn income during the first seven months of the year.

Then, when a company disposes of the property, plant, and equipment, it removes the balances in both the specific asset account and the related accumulated depreciation account from its accounting records. Disposals range from the very simple, where there is no cash involved and the book value is zero, to more complex transactions in which the company receives cash and reports a gain or loss on the disposal because the actual selling price of the asset is not equal to its book value. A company reports any gain or loss in the "other items" section of its income statement, as we discussed in Chapter 10. (This is similar to the procedure a company uses to record the impairment of an asset.)

To illustrate a disposal involving the sale of an asset, we assume that Unlimited Decadence sells office equipment for $1,500. The equipment had originally cost $10,000 and has a current book value of $1,000 (accumulated depreciation is $9,000). Therefore, Unlimited Decadence reports a gain of $500 (the cash received of $1,500 − the book value of $1,000). Based on this information, Unlimited Decadence records the sale as follows:

Assets						= Liabilities +	Stockholders' Equity	
Cash		Office Equipment		Accumulated Depreciation: Office Equipment			Gain on Sale of Equipment	
1,500			10,000	9,000				500
(+)	(−)	(+)	(−)	(−)	(+)		(−)	(+)

 If Unlimited Decadence sold the equipment for $800 instead, how would you record the sale?

When a company trades in an old asset for a new asset, it pays cash for the difference between the market value of the new asset and the market value of the old asset traded in. The company records the new asset at its market value, reduces its cash for the amount paid, and removes the cost and accumulated depreciation of the old asset from its accounting records. The company also records a gain or loss for the difference between the market value of the old asset and its book value.[3] The company reports the gain or loss in the "other items" section of its income statement.

For instance, assume Unlimited Decadence purchases a new machine that has a market value of $7,000—by paying $5,000 cash and trading in an old machine with a market value of $2,000. The old machine has a book value of $3,000 ($11,000 cost − $8,000 accumulated depreciation). In this case, Unlimited Decadence records the new equipment at $7,000, reduces cash by $5,000, eliminates the cost of $11,000 and the $8,000 accumulated depreciation on the old machine, and records a $1,000 loss ($2,000 market value − $3,000 book value of the old equipment).

Reporting Property, Plant, and Equipment and Depreciation Expense

We have used the title Property, Plant, and Equipment in this chapter because it is the title most companies use in their balance sheets. You may come across titles such as Plant and Machinery, Land and Buildings, Fixed Assets, or for a retail company, Property and Equipment. For example, Intel Corporation uses the term "Property, Plant and Equipment" and Deere & Company uses "Property and Equipment," even though both are manufacturing companies.

The types and extent of property, plant, and equipment information reported in companies' annual reports vary from one company to another. However, GAAP requires all companies to disclose the following items in their financial statements or in the notes accompanying these statements:

1. Depreciation expense for the period

2. Balances of major classes of depreciable assets by nature (such as buildings or equipment) or function (such as candy manufacturing or transportation) on the balance sheet date

3. Accumulated depreciation, either by major classes of assets or in total, on the balance sheet date

www.intel.com
www.deere.com

---

[3]Accounting for exchanges of assets can be very complex. GAAP distinguishes between "dissimilar" and "similar" asset exchanges. For certain asset exchanges, GAAP limits the amount of gain or loss that a company records. These rules apply to exchanges between "dealers" and "nondealers." Our example is between a dealer and a nondealer, so that a company trading in an asset records a gain or loss as we discuss. For more information, see D. Marcinko and E. Petri, "A Clarification of Certain Issues Arising Out of Nonmonetary Exchanges," *Journal of Accounting Education,* 9 (2), fall, 1991, pp. 365-372. We do not discuss the more complicated exchanges in this book.

4. A general description of the method or methods used in computing depreciation with respect to the major classes of depreciable assets, and how these methods differ from those used for income taxes

We show PepsiCo's property, plant, and equipment disclosures on December 27, 1997 in Exhibit 21-7.

 Examine PepsiCo's disclosures. Find where it makes each required disclosure. What other important information did PepsiCo disclose? Why do you think PepsiCo made these disclosures? What do the disclosures tell you about PepsiCo's management decisions concerning property, plant, and equipment? What additional disclosures do you think might be useful?

Exhibit 21-7   Disclosures of Property, Plant, and Equipment: PepsiCo

Consolidated Balance Sheet (in part)

(in millions except per share amount)
PepsiCo, Inc. and Subsidiaries
December 27, 1997 and December 28, 1996

	1997	1996
Property, Plant and Equipment, net	$6,261	$6,086

Notes to Consolidated Financial Statements (in part)

Property, Plant and Equipment. Property, plant and equipment (PP&E) are stated at cost, except for PP&E that have been impaired, for which the carrying amount is reduced to estimated net realizable value. Depreciation is calculated on a straight-line basis over the estimated useful lives of the assets.

	1997	1996
Land	$ 365	$ 361
Buildings and improvements	2,623	2,543
Machinery and Equipment	7,513	7,253
Construction in progress	793	751
	11,294	10,908
Accumulated depreciation	(5,033)	(4,822)
	$ 6,261	$ 6,086

INDUSTRY SEGMENTS

	1997	1996	1995
Depreciation Expense			
Beverages	$444	$440	$445
Snack Foods	394	346	304
Corporate	7	7	7
	$845	$793	$756

Although we have used the term "depreciation expense" throughout the chapter, a manufacturing company includes some of that "expense" as part of the cost of the inventory that it manufactures, as we discussed in Chapter 16. Many companies also use a "functional" classification for their expenses. In this case, the company allocates the depreciation expense among its functional classifications, such as cost of goods sold, selling, and general and administrative expenses.

Property, Plant, and Equipment and the Cash Flow Statement

A company reports purchases and sales of property, plant, and equipment as investing cash flows on its cash flow statement. A company adds back depreciation expense to net income if it computes the net cash provided by operating activities under the indirect method, because depreciation is a noncash expense that was subtracted from revenue in calculating net income. A company subtracts (adds) gains (losses) on disposals of property, plant, and equipment from (to) net income if it computes the net cash provided by operating activities under the indirect method, because it included gains and losses on disposals of property, plant, and equipment in calculating income but the gains and losses did not affect cash flows from operating activities. The company shows the cash it received from the disposal of the asset as an *investing* cash inflow on the cash flow statement.

Using Information about Property, Plant, and Equipment and Depreciation Expense

Up to this point in the chapter we have focused on reporting property, plant, and equipment. These issues provide the foundation you need for understanding how external users use a company's property, plant, and equipment disclosures to help them evaluate its operating capability and operating efficiency. A company's **operating capability** is its ability to maintain its level of physical output. For instance, external users evaluate Unlimited Decadence's disclosures to help them determine if it can maintain or increase the number of chocolates it produces and sells. **Operating efficiency** refers to how well a company uses its assets to generate revenue.

As with other parts of financial statements, external users use property, plant, and equipment for evaluation by performing intracompany and intercompany analysis—through the use of horizontal analysis, vertical analysis, and ratio analysis. We will discuss intracompany analysis first, followed by intercompany analysis. We use Intel Corporation's 1997 annual report to provide the information we need to explain intracompany analysis. We selected Intel because property, plant, and equipment are very important to "electronic computer" manufacturers and because Intel provides a substantial amount of information in its annual report.

6 *How do external users evaluate information about a company's property, plant, and equipment?*

Intracompany Analysis of Property, Plant, and Equipment: Intel Corporation

Exhibit 21-8 presents property, plant, and equipment information taken from Intel's 1997 Annual Report—its balance sheet, income statement, and cash flow statement. Intel's financial statements provide more information than just the net changes in its property, plant, and equipment. You can get more detailed information by analyzing the property, plant, and equipment information on the balance sheet *and* on the cash flow statement. The operating activities section of its cash flow statement reveals that Intel recorded $2,192 million in (straight-line) depreciation expense during 1997. It also shows that the company incurred a net loss of $130 million on retirements (disposals) of property, plant, and equipment. (Remember that depreciation is not a cash flow but is added to net income on the cash flow statement because it is a noncash expense used in computing net income. Similarly, the net loss is also added.) Finally, the investing activities section of Intel's cash flow

Exhibit 21-8   Selected Financial Information: Intel

Financial Statement Information Taken from Intel's 1997 Annual Report Relating to Property, Plant, and Equipment

Balance Sheet Information

December 27, 1997 and December 28, 1996

(In millions—except per share amounts)	1997	1996
Property, plant and equipment:		
Land and buildings	$ 5,113	$ 4,372
Machinery and equipment	10,577	8,729
Construction in progress	2,437	1,161
	18,127	14,262
Less accumulated depreciation	7,461	5,775
Property, plant and equipment, net	10,666	8,487
Total assets	$28,880	$23,735

Income Statement Information

Three years ended December 27, 1997

(In millions—except per share amounts)	1997	1996	1995
Net revenues	$25,070	$20,847	$16,202
Cost of sales	9,945	9,164	7,811
Research and development	2,347	1,808	1,296
Marketing, general and administrative	2,891	2,322	1,843
Operating costs and expenses	15,183	13,294	10,950
Operating income	9,887	7,553	5,252

Cash Flow Statement Information

Three years ended December 27, 1997

(In millions)	1997	1996	1995
Cash and cash equivalents, beginning of year	$ 4,165	$ 1,463	$ 1,180
Cash flows provided by (used for) operating activities:			
Net income	6,945	5,157	3,566
Adjustments to reconcile net income to net cash provided by (used for) operating activities (in part):			
Depreciation	2,192	1,888	1,371
Net loss on retirements of property, plant, and equipment	130	120	75
Cash flows provided by (used for) investing activities:			
Additions to property, plant, and equipment	(4,501)	(3,024)	(3,550)

statement shows that during 1997 the company added $4,501 million of new property, plant, and equipment. Using the information from these two financial statements, we can determine the total dollar changes that occurred for Intel's property, plant, and equipment accounts during 1997. We show these calculations in Exhibit 21-9.

 Analyze Exhibit 21-9. Can you explain each item included in Intel's Property, Plant, and Equipment and Accumulated Depreciation T-accounts?

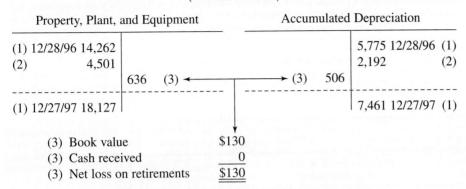

Exhibit 21-9   Analysis of Intel's Property, Plant, and Equipment

(in millions of dollars)

Property, Plant, and Equipment		Accumulated Depreciation
(1) 12/28/96 14,262		5,775 12/28/96 (1)
(2) 4,501		2,192 (2)
	636 (3) ◄──────► (3) 506	
(1) 12/27/97 18,127		7,461 12/27/97 (1)

(3) Book value $130
(3) Cash received   0
(3) Net loss on retirements $130

(1) The beginning and ending balances for Property, Plant, and Equipment and Accumulated Depreciation are taken from Intel's balance sheets.

(2) The increases in Property, Plant, and Equipment (due to $4,501 additions) and Accumulated Depreciation (due to $2,192 depreciation expense) and the $130 net loss on retirements are taken from Intel's cash flow statement.

(3) From the information provided in (1) and (2), we calculated the $636 decrease in Property, Plant, and Equipment and the $506 decrease in Accumulated Depreciation. Because Intel did not disclose any cash inflow from selling the Property, Plant, and Equipment, we know that the loss ($130) is equal to the difference between the asset's book value ($636 cost − $506 accumulated depreciation) and the cash received ($0).

Listed below are three specific questions that relate to Intel Corporation's operating capability and efficiency. You can ask these same three questions (as well as others) when using information about any company's property, plant, and equipment for intracompany analysis. Under each question, we explain how financial analysis helps external users answer these questions.

Question #1: Does Intel Own Enough Property, Plant, and Equipment to Maintain Production or Increase the Amount of Electronic Components Above What It Produced Last Year?

To answer this question, we first examine Intel's comparative balance sheets to see how its property, plant, and equipment changed from the end of the previous year (1996) to the end of the current year (1997). From the balance sheet information provided in Exhibit 21-8 we see that the company's ending 1996 net property, plant, and equipment balance was $8,487 million and its 1997 net balance was $10,666 million (a big company!). So, Intel's dollar amount of property, plant, and equipment (net) increased by $2,179 million ($10,666 million − $8,487 million). That is a 26% ($2,179 million ÷ $8,487 million) increase from the end of 1996 to the end of 1997. At the end of 1997, Intel has invested 37% ($10,666 ÷ $28,880) of its total assets in property, plant, and equipment (net), as compared with 36% ($8,487 ÷ $23,735) at the end of 1996. Intel's increase ($2,179) in property, plant, and equipment (net) during 1997 and the increase in property, plant, and equipment as a proportion of total assets provide evidence that Intel can increase its production (operating capability) during the coming year.

We present additional information from Intel's annual report in Exhibit 21-10. This exhibit also provides information useful in answering questions #1 and #2. The top bar graph in Exhibit 21-10 shows Intel's capital additions over the past 10 years. We will discuss the bottom bar graph later.

Study these two bar graphs. What information, in addition to that provided in Intel's financial statements, do the bar graphs provide? How useful is this additional information?

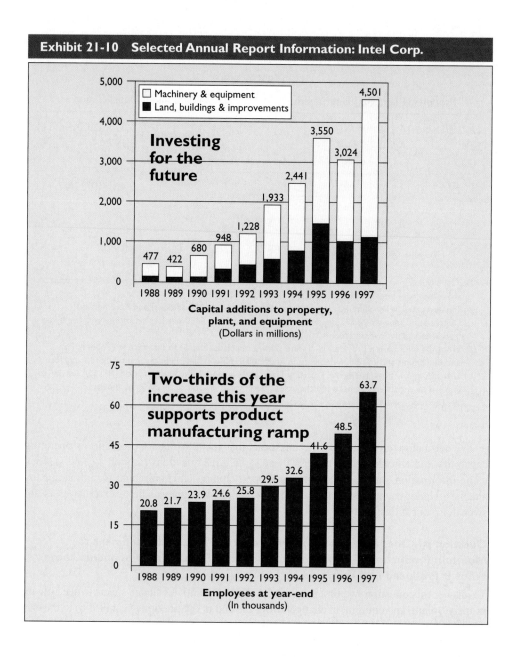

Exhibit 21-10   Selected Annual Report Information: Intel Corp.

Question #2: Does Intel's 1997 Increased Investment in Property, Plant, and Equipment Produce Significant Increases in Net Revenue?

We learned from our analysis in Exhibit 21-9 that Intel increased its investment in property, plant, and equipment during 1997 by $3,865 ($4,501 purchased − $636 sold). Another analysis will help determine if this increased investment in property, plant, and equipment was converted into increased revenue for Intel. According to Intel's income statement, net revenues for 1996 were $20,847 million. In 1997, net revenues totaled $25,070 million, a $4,223 million increase over 1996. Thus, net revenues increased from 1996 to 1997 by 20% ($4,223 ÷ $20,847). This provides evidence that the demand for Intel's products at least partially justifies the company's 1997 increased investment in property, plant, and equipment. The 1997 increase in net revenues is 1.09 times the increase in the property, plant, and equipment ($4,223 million ÷ $3,865 million). Of course, the increase in revenues in 1997 would also result from increased investments in property, plant, and equipment purchased in previous years and used in operations during 1997.

Describe a situation in which a company's financial statements indicate that the company may have a problem maintaining operating capability. Specifically, what trends in property, plant, and equipment and sales revenue would signal this problem?

Question #3: Does Intel Use Its Property and Equipment Efficiently?

A common way that external users evaluate how efficiently a company is using its property, plant, and equipment is to relate property, plant, and equipment to revenues. They do this by calculating a net revenues to net property, plant, and equipment ratio as follows:

$$\frac{\text{Net Revenues}}{\text{Net Property, Plant, and Equipment}}$$

The higher the ratio, the larger the dollar amount of net revenue produced by each dollar invested in net property, plant, and equipment. In 1996, Intel's ratio was 2.46 ($20,847 million ÷ $8,487 million). On average, every dollar Intel had invested in net property, plant, and equipment generated $2.46 in net revenue during 1996. For 1997, the ratio was 2.35 ($25,070 million ÷ $10,666 million). Based on the calculations of this ratio, Intel's operating efficiency appears to have decreased slightly in 1997 compared to 1996. (Note that for simplicity we used the ending rather than average amount of net property, plant, and equipment.)

Intel provides an additional measure of operating activity that is not a required disclosure under GAAP—the number of employees at year-end. We show this in the bottom chart in Exhibit 21-10. We can now compute Intel's gross fixed assets per employee and revenue per employee as additional indicators of the company's efficiency. In 1996, Intel's gross fixed assets per employee was $294,062 ($14,262 million ÷ 48,500), and its revenue per employee was $429,835 ($20,847 million ÷ 48,500). In 1997, Intel's gross fixed assets per employee was $284,568 ($18,127 million ÷ 63,700), and its revenue per employee was $393,564 ($25,070 million ÷ 63,700). Both measures indicate that Intel's efficiency declined slightly in 1997. The large amounts are also indicative of Intel's capital-intensive, high-technology focus.

 Can you think of industries where you would expect the revenue-per-employee ratio and the gross-fixed-assets-per-employee ratio to be much lower than Intel's? Which ones? Why? Can you think of one where the ratios would be higher? Which ones? Why?

Intercompany Analysis within an Industry

In the prior sections, you learned a lot about Intel's property, plant, and equipment. This information indicated that Intel is increasing its operating capability, but that its operating efficiency has decreased slightly. As we have stated in earlier chapters, one limitation of intracompany analysis is that it fails to provide an external comparison of the company's performance. Our analysis of Intel gives us "mixed signals" as to its performance each year, but we do not know how well it is performing relative to other companies in the "electronic computers manufacturing" industry. *Inter*company analysis provides this relative analysis.

When an external user evaluates a company's operating capability and efficiency, the user needs a basis on which to judge the company's performance. Industry information provides a good initial measure of performance expectations. The investor or creditor is asking, "Is this company performing better or worse than the average company in the same line of business?" For example, Exhibit 21-11 shows the average 1997 net sales to net property, plant, and equipment ratios for four industries. The 1997 average ratios for the two manufacturing industries shown—candy products and the electronic computers manufacturing industry—are 10.2-to-1 and 18.0-to-1, respectively. However, the retail grocery stores industry and the advertising agencies industry have much higher 1997 net sales to net property, plant, and equipment ratios of 19.9-to-1 and 31.9-to-1. Thus, a company with

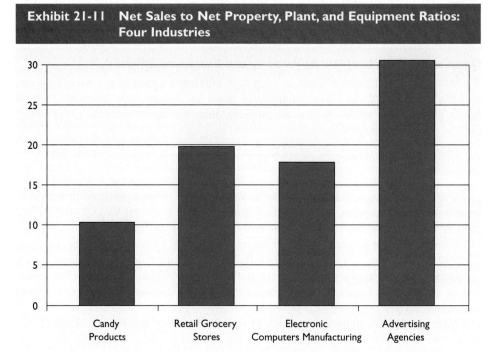

Exhibit 21-11   Net Sales to Net Property, Plant, and Equipment Ratios: Four Industries

a 10-to-1 ratio may be acceptable in the candy products industry but would be viewed poorly in the retail grocery stores industry.

 Why do you think the two manufacturing industries have such different ratios from those of the retail grocery stores and advertising agencies industries?

In the previous section we calculated Intel Corporation's 1997 net sales to net property, plant, and equipment ratio to be 2.35. Now we can incorporate electronic computers manufacturing industry information into our evaluation. In addition to seeing that Intel's ratio worsened from 1996 to 1997, from 2.46 (or 2.46 to 1) to 2.35, we now see that Intel's ratio is also well below the industry average of 18.0.

What does this tell us about Intel's operating capability and efficiency? One interpretation is that Intel is not operating as efficiently as many other companies in this industry. However, because this ratio relies on historical cost amounts for property, plant, and equipment, users of this ratio need to interpret a below-industry average ratio carefully. For example, Intel's relatively low ratio may be because Intel uses modern, more costly property, plant, and equipment that has not been depreciated much. Recall that the net property, plant, and equipment of Intel is about 37% of its total assets at the end of 1997. The industry average is only 20%. Also remember that Intel's property, plant, and equipment balance increased 26% from the end of 1996 to the end of 1997. These facts might suggest that Intel's relatively low ratio is due to the company's significant investment in new property, plant, and equipment. Also, the ratio may be affected by the age of the assets as we discuss later.

 Can you think of another reason why Intel's ratio may be lower than the industry average?

Intercompany Comparisons with Major Competitors

Our comparison of Intel's operating capability and performance with the average level of performance for the industry raised questions about Intel's performance. Although industry data is a good place to start making intercompany comparisons, the evaluation should not stop there. Industry averages show a composite performance measure of many different companies. A clearer picture of Intel's relative operating capability and efficiency may be obtained by comparing Intel with its major competitors.

Exhibit 21-12 shows the 1997 net sales to net property, plant, and equipment ratio for the electronic computers manufacturing industry, for Intel, and for two of its largest competitors—AMD Corporation and National Semiconductor Corporation. By singling out Intel's major competitors, we see that the largest companies in this industry all have net sales to net property, plant, and equipment ratios well below the 18.0 industry average. Therefore the industry average may not be representative of the operations of these particular companies. For example, these large companies may rely more on high-tech equipment and less on skilled labor to produce their products.

www.amd.com
www.nsc.com

 Do you think that General Motors, Ford, and DaimlerChrysler would have the same ratios if they were equally efficient? Why or why not?

www.gm.com
www2.ford.com
www3.daimlerchrys.
com

We do not repeat this extensive discussion of intercompany analysis in other chapters. However, you should think about how you would perform this analysis for inventories in Chapter 19 and for other topics in the remaining chapters of this book.

Estimating the Average Age and the Average Life of Property, Plant, and Equipment

Two additional issues related to analyzing a company's property, plant, and equipment involve estimating the average age and the average life of these assets. The average age is important because the older a company's property, plant, and equipment, the less likely it is that the company will be able to maintain its *operating capability* in the future. Also, the average age may affect a user's evaluation of a company's *profitability* over time, or in comparison to another company.

Exhibit 21-12 Intercompany Comparisons: Net Sales to Net Property, Plant, and Equipment Ratios for Selected Companies in the Electronic Computers Manufacturing Industry

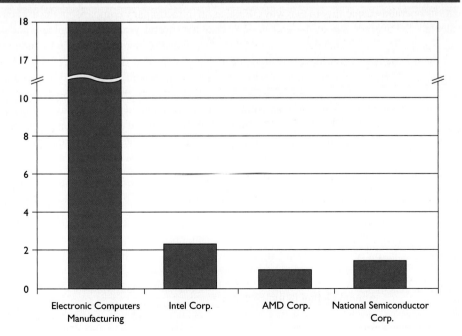

The average life of a company's property, plant, and equipment is important because it affects the company's *profitability* through its depreciation expense. The longer the life, the lower is the depreciation expense and the higher the net income. Similarly, the shorter the life, the higher is the depreciation expense and the lower the net income.

Unfortunately, companies do not provide useful disclosures of the average age and the average life of their property, plant, and equipment. (They are required to disclose the lives for each category of property, plant, and equipment, but these disclosures are usually too vague to be useful.) So, if a user wants to analyze a company's property, plant, and equipment to help evaluate the company's operating capability and profitability, the user must estimate the average age and average life of these assets. In the following sections, we explain how to make these estimates assuming that a company uses the straight-line depreciation method. This is a reasonable assumption because most companies use this method.

Average Age

To compute the average age of a company's property, plant, and equipment, you need to think about the balance in accumulated depreciation. This balance represents the lifetime depreciation that the company has recorded on the property, plant, and equipment that it currently owns. Also remember that under the straight-line depreciation method a company's accumulated depreciation increases by approximately the same amount each year. Therefore the average age of a company's property, plant, and equipment may be computed as follows:

$$\text{Average Age} = \text{Accumulated Depreciation} \div \text{Annual Depreciation Expense}$$

Companies are required to disclose both the accumulated depreciation and the annual depreciation expense. However, since a company is only required to disclose a single amount of accumulated depreciation, a user can only calculate a single average age for all of the company's property, plant, and equipment. Also a company typically buys and sells assets every year, so this calculation will only result in an approximate measure of the average age. Using Intel's disclosures shown in Exhibit 21-8, we can estimate the average age of its property, plant, and equipment at the end of 1997 to be 3.4 years ($7,461 accumulated depreciation at the end of 1997 ÷ $2,192 depreciation expense for 1997). As we would expect for a technologically advanced company, its property, plant, and equipment is not very old.

A user may use the average age of a company's property, plant, and equipment to evaluate its operating capability in two ways. First, as an intracompany comparison, the user can calculate the average age at the end of each year for several years to determine whether the average age has changed over time. If the average age is increasing, this may indicate that the company's operating capability is decreasing because it is using older assets in its operations. If the average age is decreasing, this may indicate that the company's operating capability is increasing because it is using newer assets in its operations. Second, as an intercompany comparison, the user can compare the average age of the company's property, plant, and equipment to that of its competitors. If the average age of a company's property, plant, and equipment is higher than its competitors, this may indicate that the company has less operating capability. And if the average age of its property, plant, and equipment is lower than its competitors, the company may have more operating capability.

Average Life

To compute the estimated average life that a company's managers have decided to use to calculate depreciation expense for its property, plant, and equipment, you use the formula for the calculation of depreciation (assuming use of the straight-line method):

$$\text{Annual Depreciation Expense} = \frac{\text{Cost} - \text{Residual Value}}{\text{Estimated Life}}$$

Therefore,

$$\text{Estimated Life} = \frac{\text{Cost} - \text{Residual Value}}{\text{Annual Depreciation Expense}}$$

Companies are required to disclose both the cost of their property, plant, and equipment and the annual depreciation expense. So a user must estimate the residual value in order to compute the estimated life. As we mentioned earlier in the chapter, many companies use an arbitrary residual value such as zero or 10%, and either would be a reasonable assumption to make for most companies. However, either assumption would not be as reasonable for a company that has major investments in non-manufacturing real-estate assets (such as office buildings), or for a company in an industry where assets are often sold well before the end of their useful lives (such as a major airline). It is also appropriate to subtract the cost of any land and construction in process (partially completed buildings) from the cost of the property, plant, and equipment, since neither is depreciated. As with the estimated average age of a company's property, plant, and equipment, the user must understand that this calculation provides an approximation of the estimated life used by the company to calculate its depreciation expense. Using Intel's disclosures shown in Exhibit 21-8, we estimate that its managers decided that the average useful life of its property, plant, and equipment (assuming a zero residual value) is 7.2 years [($18,127 cost − $2,437 construction in progress = $15,690 adjusted cost) ÷ $2,192 depreciation expense for 1997]. As we would expect for a technologically-based company, its property, plant, and equipment does not have a very long useful life.

A user may use this estimate of the average life of a company's property, plant, and equipment to evaluate its operating capability by assessing whether the average life seems reasonable for the company, or whether the average life used by the company is significantly different from that used by its competitors. Furthermore, the user can assess how the average life used affected the company's profitability. If the user thinks the average life used by the company is too long (or too short), the user can re-compute the company's annual depreciation expense to determine how the change in depreciation expense affects the company's income. For example, suppose a user thought that the average life Intel's managers used was too short and wanted to know what effect an increase of 20% in the average life of Intel's property, plant, and equipment would have on its 1997 operating income. Since we computed the average life to be 7.2 years, a 20% increase would result in a revised average life of 8.64 years. Dividing the $15,690 adjusted cost (that we computed earlier) by this 8.64 average life results in a revised depreciation expense of $1,816, which is $376 less than the $2,192 actual 1997 depreciation expense. So with a 20% longer life assigned to its property, plant, and equipment, Intel's 1997 operating income would have been 3.8% higher ($376 ÷ $9,887 operating income, from Exhibit 21-8).

By changing the average life of a company's property, plant, and equipment to one that is more reasonable, or to one that is closer to the average life used by a competitor, a user can also re-compute the company's return on assets. The numerator will change because of the revised depreciation expense as we just computed, and the denominator will change by the revised accumulated depreciation. Then the user may have a better comparison of the profitability of the two companies.

 Compute the estimated average age and average life of General Mills' property, plant, and equipment using the information in Appendix C.

Disclosures in SEC Filings

A company must disclose more information about property, plant, and equipment in its annual 10-K filing with the Securities and Exchange Commission than GAAP requires. SEC requirements indicate that investors and creditors may want more than the historical cost amounts provided in the financial statements in order to make their business decisions. A company's managers also may discuss activities related to property, plant, and equipment in the letter to shareholders or the management's discussion and analysis section of the company's 10-K report. The 10-K report also often contains other types of statistical data that can be used to help external users assess a company's outlook for the future.

In Exhibit 21-13, we show *selected* information from the 10-K report that Rocky Mountain Chocolate Factory, Inc., submitted to the SEC for the year ended February 28, 1998. This report included financial statements, management's discussion and analysis, and other information.

 Study Exhibit 21-13. What does this information tell you about Rocky Mountain's activities related to property, plant, and equipment? How would you use the information?

Business Issues and Values

The *actual* net cost of a company's property, plant, and equipment asset is the difference between the purchase price of the asset and the actual residual value. This net cost is not known with certainty until the company disposes of the asset. Meanwhile, the managers of the company have to make important decisions regarding the allocation of the *estimated* net cost as an expense to each accounting period. For depreciation expense, they have to estimate the pattern of benefits (to decide which method to use), the life of the asset, and the residual value. In addition, to determine any impairment loss, they have to compute the market value, probably by discounting the future cash flows the asset is estimated to generate.

Each of these decisions allows for considerable flexibility, and if the managers' estimates are in error, a company *could* report a depreciation amount each year that is quite different from the "correct" amount. So the flexibility may sometimes cause reporting problems for the company and interpretation problems for users. For example, if managers underestimate the annual depreciation expense early in the life of the asset, the company will report income amounts that are too high in those years. To offset this early underestimate of depreciation expense, the managers will, in later years, have to increase the annual depreciation expense, or the company will report a loss on the sale of the asset. (With lower accumulated depreciation, the book value of the asset will be higher than expected at the end of its service life.) In either case, the company will report an income amount that is too low in those years. Since these potential effects extend over the lives of the assets, it may be many years before external users (and the managers) are aware of the misstated income. Therefore, ratios involving income and property, plant, and equipment assets will be misleading during those years, perhaps causing users to make misguided decisions. Furthermore, unethical managers might deliberately *understate* the annual depreciation expense (by overstating the estimated life and/or the residual value) in order to *overstate* annual income and any related ratios. Such a manipulation of income is, of course, a violation of accounting principles and could result in legal sanctions against the managers.

Intangible Assets

7 *What are intangible assets and natural resource assets, and what does a company report about them?*

Up to this point in the chapter, we focused on managing, reporting, and evaluating a company's property, plant, and equipment. All types of property, plant, and equipment (land, buildings, machines, etc.) have at least two things in common—they have useful lives longer than one year, and they are *tangible*. Tangible means "having a physical substance" (i.e., they can be seen or touched). Many companies also have another category of long-term assets called *in*tangible assets. **Intangible assets** are a company's long-term assets that do *not* have physical substance. These assets have value to a company because they provide it with specific *legal rights* or *economic benefits*. For example, some companies own intangible assets such as patents, copyrights, trademarks and tradenames, franchises, and computer software. Unlimited Decadence Corporation (if it were a real corporation) would own the tradenames (i.e., the exclusive legal right to use a name or symbol) for the words "Unlimited Decadence," "Empty Decadence," and "Pure Decadence." No other company could use these labels without its approval.

Exhibit 21-13 Selected Financial Information: Rocky Mountain Chocolate Factory

BALANCE SHEET (in part)	February 28 1998	February 28 1997
Property and Equipment—At Cost		
Land	$ 513,618	$ 122,558
Building	3,665,581	3,644,357
Machinery and equipment	6,023,347	5,449,261
Furniture and fixtures	2,072,208	2,267,437
Leasehold improvements	1,389,608	1,410,948
Transportation equipment	293,357	246,499
	$13,957,719	$13,141,060
Less accumulated depreciation and amortization	4,285,276	3,400,719
	$ 9,672,443	$ 9,740,341

	For the Year Ended		
CASH FLOW STATEMENT (in part)	February 28, 1998	February 28, 1997	February 29, 1996
Cash Flows from Investing Activities			
Purchase of property and equipment	$(1,984,940)	$(2,251,598)	$(4,853,283)
Net cash used in investing activities	$(2,209,718)	$(2,269,848)	$(4,918,818)

NOTES TO FINANCIAL STATEMENTS (in part)

Property and Equipment: Property and equipment are recorded at cost. Depreciation and amortization are computed using the straight-line method based upon the estimated useful life of the asset. Leasehold improvements are amortized on the straight-line method over the lives of the respective leases or the service lives of the improvements, whichever is shorter.

Store Concept

The Company seeks to establish a fun and inviting atmosphere in its Rocky Mountain Chocolate Factory store locations.

Unlike most other confectionery stores, each Rocky Mountain Chocolate Factory store prepares certain products, including fudge and caramel apples, in the store. Customers can observe store personnel making fudge from start to finish, including the mixing of ingredients in old-fashioned copper kettles and the cooling of the fudge on large marble tables, and are often invited to sample the store's products. The Company believes that an average of approximately 40% of the revenues of Company-owned and franchised stores are generated by sales of products prepared on the premises. The Company believes the in-store preparation and aroma of its products enhance the ambiance at Rocky Mountain Chocolate Factory stores, are fun and entertaining for its customers and convey an image of freshness and home-made quality.

Rocky Mountain Chocolate Factory stores have a distinctive country Victorian decor, which further enhances their friendly and enjoyable atmosphere. Each store includes finely-crafted wood cabinetry, copper and brass accents, etched mirrors and large marble tables on which fudge and other products are made. To ensure that all stores conform to the Rocky Mountain Chocolate Factory image, the Company's design staff provides working drawings and specifications and approves the construction plans for each new franchised or Company-owned store. The Company also controls the signage and building materials that may be used in the stores.

The average store size is approximately 1,000 square feet, approximately 650 square feet of which is selling space. Most stores are open seven days a week. Typical hours are 10 a.m. to 9 p.m., Monday through Saturday, and 12 noon to 6 p.m. on Sundays. Store hours in tourist areas may vary depending upon the tourist season.

continued

Exhibit 21-13   Selected Financial Information: Rocky Mountain Chocolate Factory, cont'd

Manufacturing Operations

General.   The Company manufactures its chocolate candies at its factory in Durango, Colorado. All products are produced consistent with the Company's philosophy of using only the finest, highest quality ingredients with no artificial preservatives to achieve its marketing motto of "the peak of perfection in handmade chocolates." It has always been the belief of management that the Company should control the manufacturing of its own chocolate products. By controlling manufacturing, the Company can better maintain its high product quality standards, offer unique, proprietary products, manage costs, control production and shipment schedules and potentially pursue new or under-utilized distribution channels.

Manufacturing Processes.   The manufacturing process primarily involves cooking or preparing candy centers, including nuts, caramel, peanut butter, creams and jellies, and then coating them with chocolate or other toppings. All of these processes are conducted in carefully controlled temperature ranges, and the Company employs strict quality control procedures at every stage of the manufacturing process. The Company uses a combination of manual and automated processes at its factory. Although the Company believes that it is currently preferable to perform certain manufacturing processes, such as dipping of some large pieces, by hand, automation increases the speed and efficiency of the manufacturing process. The Company has from time to time automated processes formerly performed by hand where it has become cost-effective for the Company to do so without compromising product quality or appearance.

The Company seeks to ensure the freshness of products sold in Rocky Mountain Chocolate Factory stores with frequent shipments and production schedules that are closely coordinated with projected and actual orders. Most Rocky Mountain Chocolate Factory stores do not have significant space for the storage of inventory, and the Company encourages franchisees and store managers to order only the quantities that they can reasonably expect to sell within approximately two to four weeks. For these reasons, the Company generally does not have a significant backlog of orders.

Ingredients.   The principal ingredients used by the Company are chocolate, nuts, sugar, corn syrup, peanut butter, cream and butter. The factory receives shipments of ingredients daily. To ensure the consistency of its products, the Company buys ingredients from a limited number of reliable suppliers. In order to assure a continuous supply of chocolate and certain nuts, the Company frequently enters into purchase contracts for these products having durations of 6 to 18 months. Because prices for these products may fluctuate, the Company may benefit if prices rise during the terms of these contracts, but it may be required to pay above-market prices if prices fall. The Company has one or more alternative sources for all essential ingredients and therefore believes that the loss of any supplier would not have a material adverse effect on the Company and its results of operations. The Company currently also purchases small amounts of finished candy from third parties on a private label basis for sale in Rocky Mountain Chocolate Factory stores.

Properties

The Company's manufacturing operations and corporate headquarters are located at its 53,000 square foot manufacturing facility which it owns in Durango, Colorado. During fiscal 1998, the Company's factory produced approximately 2.0 million pounds of chocolates, up from 1.7 million pounds in fiscal 1997. The factory has the capacity to produce approximately 3.5 million pounds per year. In January 1988, the Company acquired a two-acre parcel adjacent to its factory to ensure the availability of adequate space to expand the factory as volume demands.

As of April 30, 1998, all 37 Company-owned stores were occupied pursuant to non-cancelable leases of five to ten years having varying expiration dates, most of which contain optional 5-year renewal rights. The Company does not deem any individual store lease to be significant in relation to its overall operations.

The Company acts as primary lessee of some franchised store premises, which it then subleases to franchisees, but the majority of existing locations are leased by the franchisee directly. Current Company policy is not to act as primary lessee on any further franchised locations. At April 30, 1998, the Company was the primary lessee at 50 of its 185 franchised stores. The subleases for such stores are on the same terms as the Company's leases of the premises. For information as to the amount of the Company's rental obligations under leases on both Company-owned and franchised stores, see Note 6 of Notes to financial statements.

In Exhibit 12-12, why do you think that Unlimited Decadence doesn't show any intangible assets on its balance sheet?

Intangible assets are similar to a company's tangible assets of property, plant, and equipment in several respects: they have an expected life of more than one year; they derive their value from their ability to help provide revenue for the company; and the company records their cost as an expense in the periods in which it receives their benefits. However, intangible assets generally have five characteristics that make them different from tangible assets:

1. They do not have a physical substance but usually result from legal rights.

2. There is generally a higher degree of uncertainty regarding their future benefits.

3. Their value is subject to wider fluctuations because it may depend on competitive conditions.

4. They may have value only to a particular company.

5. They may have expected lives that are very difficult to determine.

As with property, plant, and equipment, a company initially records an intangible asset at its acquisition cost, and then allocates this cost as an expense over the asset's useful life. However, this expense is called **amortization expense** rather than depreciation expense, even though the matching concept underlies both expenses.[4] Before we explain each type of intangible asset mentioned earlier, we will discuss accounting for research and development costs because this accounting may affect the dollar amounts that a company includes in its financial statements as intangible assets. We will discuss amortization expense in a later section.

Research and Development Costs

Many companies engage in research and development (R&D) to improve their products or services. Expenditures on R&D by technologically oriented companies may be a major part of their total costs each period. In 1997, Intel Corporation incurred $2,347 million in R&D costs, which was over 15% of its operating expenses.

Research is aimed at the discovery of new knowledge intended for use in developing a new or improved product or process. **Development** is the translation of research into a plan or design for a new or improved product or process. The costs included in R&D are those for items such as materials, depreciation on assets used in R&D projects, the salaries of R&D employees, and a reasonable allocation of general and administrative costs. Each year many companies spend large amounts of money on R&D because they expect to receive total future benefits that exceed the total costs incurred. However, not all R&D projects are successful. Some projects of a company will be unsuccessful (the costs will exceed the benefits), and others will be successful (the benefits will exceed the costs). But overall, the company's managers must expect the total benefits to exceed the total costs. If a company expects benefits to exist for many periods in the future, it could be argued that the company should record the cost of acquiring these benefits as an asset. However, most projects do not provide benefits that exceed costs. For example, one recent study reported that only 1 out of every 20 to 25 ideas becomes a successful product and that only 1 of every 10 to 15 new products becomes a hit. Therefore, because of the uncertainty of the success of each R&D project, GAAP requires a company to *record all R&D costs as an expense when it incurs them.* This uncertainty is why Intel includes its total R&D costs of $2,347 million in its 1997 income statement as an operating expense.

---

[4]A company also is required to evaluate its intangible assets for any impairment loss, as we discussed earlier in the chapter.

Usually, increases in a company's expenses are viewed negatively because they reduce net income. Do you think this is true for R&D costs? Why or why not?

Patents

A **patent** is an exclusive right granted by the U.S. government (or the government of another country) giving the owner of an invention the control of its manufacture or sale for 20 years from the date of the patent application.[5] The owner of a patent cannot renew it, but may extend its effective life by obtaining a new patent on modifications and improvements to the original invention. Alternatively, competition may make its *useful* life much less than 20 years. As a general rule, a company records the costs of obtaining a patent in an intangible asset account entitled Patents. Recall, however, that a company records as an expense all the R&D costs associated with the internal development of an invention. Therefore, the costs that a company records as an asset for a patent primarily are the costs of processing the patent application and any legal costs incurred, which may be relatively small. For example, IBM had 1,724 patents in 1997 yet reported no patent asset on its balance sheet because they were internally developed. Alternatively, if a company purchases a patent from another company, it records the entire acquisition cost as an asset.

www.ibm.com

 If a company develops its own invention, it does not show the costs of development as an asset on its balance sheet. However, if a company purchases a patent from another company, it shows the entire purchase price as an intangible asset. Do you think GAAP is treating this issue fairly? Why would GAAP require patents to be accounted for in these ways?

Copyrights

A **copyright** is an exclusive right granted by the U.S. government (or the government of another country) to publish or sell literary or artistic products for the life of the

THE WALL STREET JOURNAL

"I believe in truth in advertising, *too*, Hargreave. . . but I *don't* think we should call our new video game 'gimme your quarter!'"

From *The Wall Street Journal.* Reprinted by permission of Cartoon Features Syndicate.

---

[5]Before 1994, the legal life of a patent was 17 years from the date of grant.

author plus an additional 70 years. Copyrights cover such items as books, music, and films.

 Are you allowed to make copies of this book and sell them to your friends? Why or why not?

As with patents, a company records the costs of *obtaining* the copyright in an intangible asset account, called Copyrights. The costs of *producing* the copyrighted item are accounted for separately. For example, a film company accounts for the costs of producing a film separately from the copyright on the film. Therefore, the film company records another asset for these costs, entitled, for example, Film Production.

Trademarks and Tradenames

A **trademark** or **tradename** is an exclusive right granted by the U.S. government (or the government of another country) to use a name or symbol for product identification. Pepsi and Quaker Oats, for example, are tradenames. Rocky Mountain Chocolate Factory disclosed in its 10-K report:

www.QuakerOats.com

> The trade name "Rocky Mountain Chocolate Factory," the phrases "The Peak of Perfection in Handmade Chocolates" and "America's Chocolatier," as well as all other trademarks, service marks, symbols, slogans, emblems, logos and designs used in the Rocky Mountain Chocolate Factory system, are proprietary rights of the Company. All of the foregoing are believed to be of material importance to the Company's business. The registration for the trademark Rocky Mountain Chocolate Factory has been granted in the United States and Canada. Applications have also been filed to register the Rocky Mountain Chocolate Factory trademark in certain foreign countries. The Company has not attempted to obtain patent protection for the proprietary recipes developed by the Company's master candy-maker and is relying upon its ability to maintain the confidentiality of those recipes.

The right to a trademark or tradename lasts for 20 years and is renewable indefinitely as long as the company uses the trademark or tradename continuously. Again, a company records only the costs directly associated with obtaining the trademark or tradename, in an intangible asset account. The company records the costs of promoting the name and producing the product separately, as marketing expense and inventory, respectively.

For many companies, trademarks and tradenames are one of their most valuable assets. Yet, as we mentioned, GAAP allows companies that have internally developed valuable trademarks to show only the direct costs of obtaining their trademarks (e.g., filing fees). For instance, since Unlimited Decadence internally developed its tradenames, it does not report an intangible asset on its balance sheet. As with patents, if a company purchases an established trademark from another company, it reports the trademark as an intangible asset at the purchase price.

Franchises

A **franchise** is an agreement entered into by two parties. For a fee, one party (the franchisor) gives the other party (the franchisee) rights to perform certain functions or sell certain products or services over the legal life of the franchise, all of which is specified in the franchise agreement. In addition, the franchisor may agree to provide certain services to the franchisee. For example, many McDonald's restaurants are locally owned and operated under a franchise agreement with the McDonald's Corporation. As with other intangibles, a franchisee records the cost it incurred to acquire the franchise as an intangible asset.

www.mcdonalds.com

 What kinds of services do you think that McDonald's provides to its franchisees?

Computer Software Costs

A company that designs software for sale (rather than for its own information systems) incurs three types of costs associated with the software. First, **software production costs** are the costs of designing, coding, testing, and preparing documentation and training materials. The company includes these costs in R&D expense until it establishes the technological feasibility of the product. The company establishes *technological feasibility* either on the date of the completion of a detailed program design or, in its absence, on the completion of a working model of the product. After this date, the company records all additional software production costs as an intangible asset until the product is available for sale to customers. After the product is ready for sale, the company records any software production costs incurred as an expense. We can summarize the accounting for software production costs as follows:

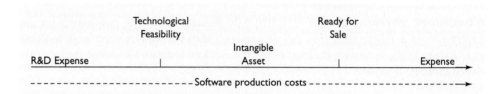

We will discuss the rules for the amortization of intangibles later. However, there is a special rule for computer software costs. The amortization expense is the greater of the following amounts: (1) the cost of the intangible asset multiplied by the ratio of *current* gross revenues from the software to the estimated *total* amount of gross revenues from the software, or (2) the straight-line method. The company amortizes the intangible asset for the software production costs over the expected life of the product, which will typically be a relatively short period, such as five years, because of technological change.

Generally, as a result, companies assign most computer software production costs to an expense because, for many companies, technological feasibility occurs after they complete the detailed logic of the program and begin coding. For many companies, software may be a significant, or perhaps the only, revenue-producing "asset" of a company. As the U.S. economy moves toward intangible outputs and creative processes, one may argue that accounting should accommodate this transition by allowing companies to record the results of creative processes as assets when future cash inflows are probable.

The second category of computer software costs is the **unit cost** of producing the software, such as costs of the disks and the duplication of the software, packaging, documentation, and training materials. The company reports these unit costs as inventory and then as cost of goods sold when it reports the related revenue. The third category of computer software costs is the **maintenance and customer-support costs** that the company incurs after it releases the software. It records these costs as an expense when it incurs them.

A different set of rules apply to the costs of software that a company develops for internal use, such as an airline's computer reservation system or a company's management information system. A company records the costs that it incurs in the preliminary stage of development as an expense. The company starts to record software costs as an asset when managers authorize and commit to funding a computer software project and (a) it is probable that the project will be completed and (b) the software will be used to perform the function intended. The company then amortizes the asset using the straight-line method over the estimated useful life of the software, unless another method provides better matching. The company adds the costs for upgrades and enhancements of the software to the asset, whereas it records the costs incurred for maintaining the software as an expense. It also records the training costs for using the software as an expense. The company must also record any impairment, as we discussed earlier.

Goodwill

Goodwill is another intangible asset that may appear on a company's balance sheet. Goodwill is often called "excess of cost over net assets of acquired companies." A company may record goodwill when it purchases another company or a significant portion of another company. When a company purchases another company, it records each of the identifiable *net* assets (assets minus liabilities) at its market value. **Goodwill** is the difference between the total price a company paid to buy another company and the market value of the identifiable net assets it acquired.

Why would a purchasing company be willing to pay the owners of the purchased company more than the market value of its identifiable net assets? The reason is that companies do not record some "assets" under GAAP. For example, Unlimited Decadence has established a reputation for high-quality products, innovative marketing, and dedicated employees. These characteristics make Unlimited Decadence more valuable than the sum of its recorded net assets. If another company decides to buy Unlimited Decadence, it is also buying Unlimited Decadence's reputation. Therefore, the company should be willing to pay more than just the market value of the net assets that Unlimited Decadence includes on its balance sheet. A company records any purchased goodwill separately as an intangible asset at its purchase price.

Amortization of Intangibles

Recall that a company records R&D costs, as well as such costs as marketing and employee-training costs, as expenses when it incurs them. On the other hand, since a company records as assets the costs of the intangible assets we discussed earlier, it must allocate these costs as expenses over the periods in which it expects the assets to produce benefits. **Amortization expense** is the portion of the acquisition cost of an intangible asset that a company allocates as an expense to each accounting period over the asset's service life. Therefore, it is exactly the same concept as depreciation expense, with only a change in the title. Note that a company amortizes the cost of an intangible asset over its expected *service* life and not necessarily over its legal life. For example, although a patent has a maximum legal life of 20 years, its expected service life may be less than 20 years. A company allocates the cost of the patent as an expense over the lesser of the two periods—its actual service life or its legal life of 20 years. As you have seen, some intangibles have very long lives and, in the case of trademarks and tradenames, potentially indefinite lives. Because of the difficulty of determining benefits so far into the future, however, GAAP imposes a maximum economic (service) life of 40 years. The **general rule for amortization of intangible assets** is that the expected life of the intangible asset is the lesser of the service life or the legal life, up to a maximum of 40 years. In computing the amount of the amortization expense, a company uses the *straight-line* method unless it has convincing evidence that an alternative method provides a better matching of expenses against revenues. We summarize these issues in Exhibit 21-14.

The recording of amortization expense is slightly different from the recording of depreciation expense because GAAP does not require a company to report separately the accumulated amortization on its intangible assets. Therefore, many companies reduce the intangible asset directly for the annual amortization amount. For example, a company records the $2,000 annual amortization on its patents as follows:

Exhibit 21-14 Expensing the Cost of Intangibles

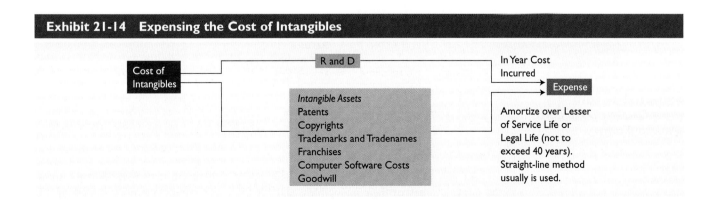

Assets	=	Liabilities	+	Stockholders' Equity

Patents			Amortization Expense	
	2,000		2,000	
(+)	(−)		(+)	(−)

Companies must also evaluate their intangibles for impairment, as we discussed earlier in the chapter for property, plant, and equipment. For example, in 1994 Eli Lilly purchased PCS Health Systems for $4.1 billion and reported an impairment loss on its goodwill of $2.4 billion in 1997.

Reporting a Company's Intangible Assets

Companies usually list their intangible assets on the balance sheet in a separate section called Intangibles, which is often presented below Property, Plant, and Equipment. Intangible assets are reported at cost less the accumulated amortization. Companies usually show the book value as a single net amount because, as we discussed earlier, GAAP does not require the reporting of both the cost and the accumulated amortization of intangibles. However, GAAP does require that companies disclose the method and the period of amortization. Exhibit 21-15 shows how PepsiCo reports its intangible assets on its balance sheet and the related disclosures in the notes.

Using Information about Intangible Assets for Evaluation

GAAP for intangibles reflects a concern that a company report relevant and reliable amounts for its assets. External users should understand that the market value of a company's intangible asset is often much greater than the book value that the company reports on its balance sheet. Further, as we explained earlier, external users must be aware that many companies possess a tremendous amount of "goodwill" that they do not show on their balance sheets because they did not purchase it. Thus, we can make the distinction between the costs of *internally developed* goodwill, which a company records as an expense as incurred, and the costs of *purchased* goodwill, which a company records as an asset.

Intracompany and intercompany analyses of intangibles should take this into consideration. Therefore, external users should not rely solely on the annual reports of a company and its competitors. They should use additional sources of information when evaluating intangibles. One CPA went so far as to say, "GAAP is of little use to financial analysts studying brand names because the only time these assets are shown at their true market value is when a company is acquired." However, some countries, such as Great Britain, allow companies to report internally developed intangibles on their balance sheets.

In the following table, we use *Financial World's* estimates of the dollar values of several tradenames and compare them with the balance sheet amounts shown for Intangibles (net) for the companies that own the tradenames:

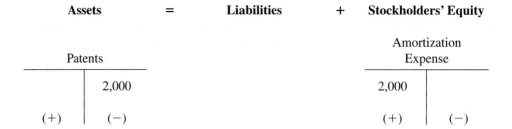

Company	Tradename	Balance Sheet Amount for Intangibles	Estimated Value
Mattel	Barbie	$149 million	$2.2 billion (14.8 times the balance sheet amount)
Quaker Oats	Quaker Oats	$493 million	$697 million (1.4 times the balance sheet amount)
Levi Strauss	Levi's	$341 million	$5.0 billion (14.7 times the balance sheet amount)

www.mattel.com
www.QuakerOats.com
www.levi.com

As you can see, the companies' historical cost financial statements did not show the market values of their intangibles, and for these companies, the book values of the

Consolidated Balance Sheet (in part)

(in millions except per share amount)
PepsiCo, Inc. and Subsidiaries
December 27, 1997 and December 28, 1996

	1997	1996
ASSETS		
Intangible Assets, net	**$5,855**	$6,036

Notes to Consolidated Financial Statements (in part)

Intangible Assets. Intangible assets are amortized on a straight-line basis over appropriate periods, generally ranging from 20 to 40 years.

	1997	1996
Reacquired franchise rights	**$2,780**	$2,917
Trademarks	**625**	650
Other identifiable intangibles	**152**	122
Goodwill	**2,298**	2,347
	$5,855	$6,036

Identifiable intangible assets primarily arose from the allocation of purchase prices of businesses acquired. Amounts assigned to such identifiable intangibles are based on independent appraisals or internal estimates. Goodwill represents the residual purchase price after allocation to all identifiable net assets.

The above amounts are net of accumulated amortization of $1.7 billion and $1.5 billion at year-end 1997 and 1996, respectively.

intangibles are less than their market values. However, stock market studies of companies that own visible brand names have found that the stock prices for these companies do reflect the market value of the brand names. Using these higher values in ratios, such as return on assets, will reduce the apparent profitability of the company.

 Do you consider the cost of your education to be an asset or an expense? Why?

Business Issues and Values: Accounting for Intangibles

Earlier we explained that companies could amortize goodwill over as much as 40 years. Now consider that the goodwill consists of "assets" such as quality products and reputation, skilled and motivated employees, or a positive image among consumers. An important question to ask is, how long will the benefits from those items last? Will it be 40 years or longer? Or will it be much less than 40 years? For example, when IBM purchased LOTUS (the company—not the software!) for $3.52 billion, it classified $1.7 billion as goodwill. IBM is amortizing the goodwill over five years.

A user may want to estimate the average life that a company uses for the amortization of its intangible assets. (The user would typically not be as interested in the average age of the intangibles because they are not replaced in the same way as property, plant, and

www.ibm.com

equipment, and they usually are not a material amount.) The user can then evaluate how a different average life might affect the company's amortization expense (and net income). For example, the user may be interested in the average life a company uses to amortize its goodwill. If the company is using a 40-year life, for instance, and the user believes that a ten-year life is more appropriate, the user would multiply the amortization expense by 4 (40 ÷ 10) and assess its impact on the company's reported income. To illustrate how to compute the average life, we show Pfizer's disclosures in Exhibit 21-16. We also show our computation of the estimated actual "average" life that Pfizer used for the amortization of its goodwill. Do you agree that the company's disclosures are appropriate, or do you think that they could be considered misleading? Note that we are *not* suggesting that they are wrong!

www.pfizer.com

Exhibit 21-16 Analysis of the Disclosure of Goodwill: Pfizer Inc.

All amounts in millions

BALANCE SHEETS (in part)

December 31,	1997	1996
Assets		
Goodwill, less accumulated amortization 1997: $152; 1966: $115	$1,294	$1,424

NOTES TO CONSOLIDATED FINANCIAL STATEMENTS (in part)
Goodwill

Goodwill represents the difference between the purchase price of acquired businesses and the fair value of their net assets when accounted for by the purchase method of accounting. We amortize goodwill evenly over periods not exceeding 40 years.

CALCULATIONS		
December 31,	1997	1996
Goodwill (net)	$1,294	$1,424
+Accumulated amortization	152	115
Cost of goodwill	$1,446	$1,539

Amortization expense for 1997 = Change in accumulated amortization
$$= \$152 - \$115$$
$$= \$37$$

Alternative 1
Assume goodwill disposed of on January 1, 1997

Life of goodwill = Cost of goodwill that was amortized in 1997 ÷ Amortization expense
$$= \$1,539 \div \$37$$
$$= 41.6 \text{ years}$$

Alternative 2
Assume goodwill disposed of on December 31, 1997

Life of goodwill = Cost of goodwill that was amortized in 1997 ÷ Amortization expense
$$= \$1,446 \div \$37$$
$$= 39.1 \text{ years}$$

CONCLUSION

The company used an average life of 40 years, as compared with the disclosure that states the company uses a life "not exceeding 40 years."

As you have seen, accounting rules require that a company record many costs as expenses even though they can be expected to generate benefits in future periods. For example, the costs of marketing, hiring and training employees, and research and development are all recorded as expenses, even though managers incur these costs with the expectation of obtaining future benefits. These costs are often referred to as "internally developed intangibles." Managers sometimes are tempted to record such costs as assets rather than as expenses in order to increase the company's income for the current year (by reducing the expenses). For example, suppose that one of an executive's responsibilities is to oversee the development of a new computer system. Should the company add part of the executive's salary to the cost of the computer software, rather than recording it as an expense?

Can you think of a company whose total market value exceeds the market value of its net assets because of each of the above "intangible" items? What factors do you think could affect the lives of the "assets" that compose goodwill?

Remember, GAAP applies to financial reporting in the United States. Under International Accounting Standards, intangibles must be amortized over a maximum of 20 years. Also, in some countries, including Great Britain, goodwill may be "written off" immediately by reducing stockholders' equity. These differences make it more difficult to compare U.S. companies with non-U.S. companies.

Natural Resource Assets

In addition to property, plant, and equipment and intangible assets, some companies have natural resource assets (sometimes called *wasting assets*). A **natural resource asset** is an asset that is used up as it is extracted, mined, dug up, or chopped down. Examples of natural resource assets are oil, coal, gravel, and timber. A company usually reports its natural resource assets in a separate section of the balance sheet. They may appear above or below property, plant, and equipment, depending on the relative importance of the two categories of assets to the particular company. A company accounts for these assets in the same manner as it accounts for its other categories of physical, long-term assets. That is, it records the cost as an asset and then allocates that cost as an expense over the expected service life of the asset. **Depletion expense** is the portion of the cost (less the estimated residual value) of a natural resource asset that a company allocates as an expense to each accounting period over the asset's service life. Thus, we see that companies use three different titles—**depreciation** for property, plant, and equipment, **amortization** for intangible assets, and **depletion** for natural resource assets—for the single concept of the allocation of the cost of an asset as an expense against the benefits (revenues) the asset produces. Companies often compute depletion expense using the units-of-production (or activity) method.

Units-of-Production Method

A company uses the **units-of-production method** to compute depletion expense based on the amount of a natural resource asset that is used up (activity level). That is, the company allocates the depletable cost (cost minus estimated residual value) as an expense each year based on the actual production and sale of the natural resource for that year. This method is appropriate because it results in an equal depletion expense for every unit sold. For example, suppose that Deep Pit Mine Company purchased a copper mine for $10 million and estimates that the mine will produce 10,000 tons of copper. (We will ignore the residual value in this example.) Deep Pit computes the depletion *rate* on the basis of the total estimated number of tons (lifetime activity level), as follows:

$$\text{Depletion Rate} = \frac{\text{Cost} - \text{Estimated Residual Value}}{\text{Total Estimated Lifetime Activity Level}}$$

$$= \frac{\$10 \text{ million} - \$0}{10,000 \text{ tons}}$$

$$= \underline{\$1,000 \text{ per ton}}$$

Then it computes the depletion expense for the year by multiplying the depletion rate times the number of tons mined and sold during the year. For example, assume that Deep Pit mined and sold 500 tons of copper in 2000. Under the units-of-production method, the company calculates its annual depletion expense as follows:

$$\text{Depletion Expense} = \text{Rate per Ton} \times \text{Actual Number of Tons Mined and Sold}$$

$$= \$1,000 \times 500$$

$$= \underline{\$500,000}$$

The company records the $500,000 as an increase in the depletion expense and as a decrease directly in the asset (Copper Mine) account to reduce its book value. The company reports the book value of the natural resource asset on its balance sheet. Because estimating the expected production of a natural resource asset is difficult, a company may revise its expected production after several years as a result of new geological information. As a result, it then calculates a new depletion rate by dividing the remaining book value (less any estimated residual value) by the remaining estimated production.

Although in this example we illustrate depletion of a mine using the units-of-production method, the managers of a company may apply the method to other assets. For instance, Unlimited Decadence could have based the depreciation of its blending machine (which we discussed earlier in the chapter) on the number of pounds of ingredients processed by the machine each accounting period or on the number of hours it operates. When compared with the straight-line method, the activity method produces a constant depreciation rate per *unit* (pound of ingredients sold, for Unlimited Decadence), but the total depreciation expense will vary per *year* as the activity level (number of pounds sold) varies.

Summary

At the beginning of the chapter we asked you several questions. During the chapter, we asked you to STOP and answer some additional questions to build your knowledge about specific issues. Be sure you answered these additional questions. Below are the questions from the beginning of the chapter, with a brief summary of the key points relating to the answers. Use your creative and critical thinking skills to expand on these key points to develop more complete answers to the questions and to determine what other questions you have that might lead you to learn more about the issues.

1 **What types of assets does a company include in its property, plant, and equipment, and how does the company compute its historical costs?**

A company includes all of the physical (tangible), long-term assets it uses in its operations in property, plant, and equipment, including land, building, machinery, and equipment. The total cost of an asset classified as property, plant, and equipment includes all the costs a company incurs to acquire the asset and to get it ready for use. These costs may include the invoice price (less any cash discounts), sales taxes, transportation charges, and installation costs.

2 **Why does a company depreciate its property, plant, and equipment, and what are the causes of depreciation?**

The assets a company includes in its property, plant, and equipment provide it with benefits for more than one year. A company depreciates property, plant, and equipment because the matching principle requires that the company match the expenses involved in obtaining the revenues of the period against the revenues it recorded in that accounting period. A company's property, plant, and equipment depreciate for two primary reasons: (1) physical causes and (2) functional causes. Physical causes include wear and tear due to use, deterioration and decay caused by the passage of time, and damage and destruction. Functional causes limit the life of the asset, even though the physical life is not exhausted. An asset is made obsolete because new technology is introduced or because the asset is no longer suitable for the company's operations even though it still may be physically sound.

3 How does a company calculate its depreciation expense, and why does it compute depreciation expense differently for financial reporting than for income taxes?

A company may use the straight-line method to compute depreciation expense by allocating the cost of an asset, less its estimated residual value, equally to each period of the asset's estimated service life. The straight-line method is appropriate when the company expects to use the asset approximately equally each period. A company also may use the following: (1) the double-declining-balance method, (2) the sum-of-the-years'-digits method, and (3) the units-of-production method. The double-declining-balance method and the sum-of-the-years'-digits method are two accelerated depreciation methods. A company using the double-declining-balance method computes depreciation expense by multiplying the book value of an asset at the beginning of the period by twice the straight-line rate. A company using the units-of-production method allocates the cost of an asset, less its estimated residual value, equally to each unit produced by that asset.

In any year, the depreciation expense a company records for financial reporting differs from the amount it records for income tax reporting because the rules are different: financial reporting and the Internal Revenue Code have different objectives. An objective of GAAP is to prepare income statements that fairly present the income-producing activities of the company and that are useful to decision-makers. In contrast, two objectives, among others, of the Internal Revenue Code are to obtain revenue for the operation of the federal government and to provide certain kinds of investment incentives for business activity. Companies use the Modified Accelerated Cost Recovery System (MACRS) of depreciating assets for income tax purposes. MACRS depreciation is different from GAAP depreciation because (1) MACRS defines the tax *life,* (2) MACRS uses *no residual value,* and (3) MACRS specifies a depreciation percentage for each year. In contrast, for GAAP depreciation, managers estimate the service life and the residual value of the asset, and select a method based on the matching principle.

4 How does a company evaluate the impairment of its property, plant, and equipment?

A company must review its property, plant, and equipment assets (and certain identifiable intangible assets) for impairment whenever events or changes in circumstances indicate that the book value of the assets may not be recoverable through the net cash flows that the company will receive from those assets. Examples of such events or changes in circumstances include a significant decrease in the market value of the assets, a significant change in the way the assets are used, a significant change in the business or regulatory environment, a current period operating loss, or a negative cash flow from operating activities. If the book value of an asset is not recoverable through the future cash flows expected from that asset, then a company records an impairment loss. The impairment loss is computed as the difference between the asset's book value and its lower market value. The market value may be computed by discounting the expected future cash flows to their present value using the company's applicable discount rate.

5 How does a company record and report the disposal of property, plant, and equipment?

When a company disposes of property, plant, and equipment, regardless of the reason for the disposal, it records depreciation expense for the current period up to the date of disposal. Then, the company removes the balances in the asset account and in the related accumulated depreciation account from its accounting records. Disposals range from the very simple, in which there is no cash involved and the book value is zero, to more complex transactions in which the company receives cash and reports a gain or loss on the disposal because the actual selling price is not equal to the book value.

6 **How do external users evaluate information about a company's property, plant, and equipment?**

External users use information about a company's property, plant, and equipment and depreciation expense to help evaluate its operating capability and operating efficiency. A company's operating capability is its ability to maintain its level of physical output. Operating efficiency refers to how well a company uses its assets to generate revenue. External users make their evaluations by performing intracompany and intercompany analysis—through the use of horizontal analysis, vertical analysis, and ratio analysis.

7 **What are intangible assets and natural resource assets, and what does a company report about them?**

Intangible assets are long-term assets that do not have a physical substance. These assets have value to a company because they provide specific legal rights or economic benefits. Intangible assets include patents, copyrights, trademarks and tradenames, franchises, computer software costs, and goodwill. A company reports its intangible assets on its balance sheet at their cost less accumulated amortization. It reports the amortization expense for these intangible assets on its income statement. Amortization expense is the portion of the acquisition cost of an intangible asset that a company allocates as an expense to each accounting period over the asset's service life. The general rule for the amortization of intangible assets is that the expected life of the intangible asset is the lesser of the service life or the legal life, up to a maximum of 40 years. In computing the amount of its amortization expense, a company uses the straight-line method unless it has convincing evidence that an alternative method provides a better matching of expenses against revenues.

A natural resource asset is an asset that is used up as it is extracted, mined, dug up, or chopped down. Examples of natural resource assets are oil, coal, gravel, and timber. A company reports the book value of its natural resource assets on its balance sheet and reports depletion expense for these assets on its income statement. Depletion expense is the portion of the cost (less the estimated residual value) of a natural resource asset that a company allocates as an expense to each accounting period over the asset's service life. A company often computes depletion expense using the units-of-production (or activity) method. Under the units-of-production method, the company computes a depletion rate and then multiplies the rate by the number of units mined and sold during the year to determine the depletion expense.

Key Terms

accelerated depreciation methods
  (p. 747)
accumulated depreciation (p. 741)
amortization (p. 777)
amortization expense (p. 769, 773)
book value (p. 741)
capital expenditure (p. 751)
copyright (p. 770)
cost (p. 743)
depreciable cost (p. 744)
depreciation (p. 750)
depreciation expense (p. 741)
depletion (p. 777)
depletion expense (p. 777)
development (p. 769)
double-declining-balance method
  (p. 747)
estimated residual value (p. 743)
estimated service life (p. 743)
franchise (p. 771)
functional causes (p. 742)
general rule for amortization of
  intangible assets (p. 773)
goodwill (p. 773)

impaired (p. 752)
intangible assets (p. 766)
maintenance and customer-support
  costs (p. 772)
Modified Accelerated Cost Recovery
  System (MACRS) (p. 750)
natural resource asset (p. 777)
net asset value (p. 741)
operating capability (p. 757)
operating efficiency (p. 757)
operating expenditure (p. 751)
patent (p. 770)
physical causes (p. 742)
property, plant, and equipment (p. 738)
rational (p. 744)
research (p. 769)
software production costs (p. 772)
straight-line method (p. 744)
sum-of-the-years'-digits method
  (p. 748)
systematic (p. 744)
trademark or tradename (p. 771)
unit cost (p. 772)
units-of-production method (p. 777)

Here is an opportunity to gather information on the Internet about real-world issues related to the topics in this chapter. Go to http://www.dryden.com/account and click on the Cunningham, Nikolai, and Bazley book cover. Click on Summary Surfing, then click on this chapter number, and answer the following questions.

▶ Click on **Intrawest**. Find the company's most recent financial statements and related notes. Do you agree with the lives and method used by Intrawest for its properties assets? By how much would the lives have to be different for you to believe there would be a material impact on its financial statements?

▶ Click on **Procter & Gamble**. Find the company's most recent financial statements and related notes. How much property, plant, and equipment does Procter & Gamble report for the current year? What depreciation method or methods does the company use? How much was the company's research and development cost? Now click on **Colgate-Palmolive**. Find the company's financial statements and related notes. How much property, plant, and equipment does Colgate-Palmolive report for the current year? What depreciation method or methods does the company use? How much was the company's research and development cost? Evaluate the comparability of the information disclosed by the two

SUMMARY SURFING

Integrated Business and Accounting Situations

Answer the Following Questions in Your Own Words

Testing Your Knowledge

21-1 What does a company include in its property, plant, and equipment?

21-2 At what amount does a company report each of its property, plant, and equipment assets?

21-3 Explain the difference between depreciation expense and accumulated depreciation. What is the book value of an asset?

21-4 What costs does a company include in the total cost of a machine it acquires?

21-5 Why does a company depreciate a building?

21-6 Explain what is meant by the (a) physical causes and (b) functional causes of depreciation.

21-7 Identify the three factors involved in the calculation of depreciation.

21-8 What do we mean when we say that depreciation expense is matched against revenue in a "systematic and rational" manner?

21-9 Explain how a company computes straight-line depreciation expense.

21-10 Explain how a company computes double-declining-balance depreciation expense.

21-11 Identify the three ways in which MACRS depreciation for income taxes is different from GAAP depreciation.

21-12 What is a capital expenditure, and how is it accounted for? What is an operating expenditure, and how it is accounted for?

21-13 When is an asset impaired, and how does a company compute the amount of an impairment loss on an asset?

21-14 How does a company account for the disposal of a machine that it has been using in its operations?

21-15 Explain how a company accounts for the trade-in of a used asset for a new asset.

21-16 What items of information does GAAP require that a company disclose about its property, plant, and equipment? How does a company report its property, plant, and equipment transactions on its cash flow statement?

21-17 What are intangible assets? Give three examples.

21-18 What are research and development, and how does a company record its research and development costs?

21-19 Explain the difference between a patent, a copyright, and a trademark or tradename.

21-20 What are the three types of computer software costs for a company that designs software for sale, and how does the company account for them?

21-21 What is goodwill, and what is it frequently called on a company's balance sheet?

21-22 What is amortization expense, and how is it generally computed?

21-23 What is depletion expense, and how is it computed under the units-of-production method?

Applying Your Knowledge

21-24 The Young Outdoor Clothing company owned the following assets at the end of its accounting period:
(a) Land on which it had built a warehouse
(b) Land on which it is planning to build a new store two years from now
(c) A retail store
(d) Shelving used for the display of products
(e) Old cash registers that were replaced by point-of-sale systems and will be sold next year
(f) Goods held for sale in a warehouse

Required: Which of the assets are the company's property, plant, and equipment? Explain your reasoning.

21-25 Hawkins Publishing Company acquired a new copying machine. The machine had a contract price of $6,000 and was purchased on terms of 2/10, n/30. The bill was paid within 10 days. The sales tax rate is 6% on the contract price. Delivery costs paid by the company were $200. Modifications to the room in which the copier was installed were $150, of which $20 was the result of damage caused by an accident. After a month of use, a service representative repaired damage caused by an employee unfamiliar with the machine, at a cost of $50.

Required: What is the cost of the copying machine? Justify any item(s) you did not include.

21-26 Jackson Company purchased a milling machine on January 1, 2000 for $60,000. The machine had an expected life of 10 years and a residual value of $2,000.

Required: (1) Compute the depreciation for 2000 and 2001 under each of the following methods: (a) straight line and (b) double declining balance.
(2) Show how the company would report the book value of the machine on its December 31, 2001 balance sheet under each method.

21-27 On January 1, 2000, Desmond Photo Developing Company purchased a machine for printing pictures. The cost of the machine was $80,000, and the estimated life and residual value are five years and $10,000 respectively.

Required: (1) Compute the depreciation expense for 2000 and 2001 under each of the following methods: (a) straight line and (b) double declining balance.
(2) Show how Desmond would report the book value of the machine on its December 31, 2001 balance sheet under each method.

21-28 The Mingus Ice Cream Company purchased a delivery truck on January 1, 2000 for $40,000. The company expected the truck to be driven for 100,000 miles and then sold for $6,000 at the end of 2003. The truck was driven 20,000 miles in 2000.

Required: Compute the depreciation for 2000 under each of the following methods: (1) straight line and (2) units of production (miles driven).

21-29   The Tatum Tax Service Company purchased a computer system on January 1, 2000 for $50,000. The company expected the computer system to be used for four years and have a residual value of $6,000.

Required: Prepare a depreciation schedule for the life of the asset under each of the following methods: (1) straight line and (2) double declining balance.

21-30   The Prentiss Poster Company purchased a printing machine for $18,000 on April 2, 2000. The company estimated the life and residual value of the machine as four years and $2,000, respectively. The company uses the straight-line depreciation method, and its fiscal year ends December 31. The company sells the machine on March 31, 2004.

Required: Compute the depreciation expense, accumulated depreciation, and book value for each fiscal year over the life of the machine.

21-31   The Paul Cleaning Company purchased an industrial cleaning machine on January 1, 2000 for $60,000. The machine had an expected life of five years, a residual value of zero, and a life of three years under the Modified Accelerated Cost Recovery System for income taxes.

Required: For each year of the machine's service life, compute the depreciation expense reported (a) on the company's financial statements (using the straight-line method) and (b) on the company's income tax returns.

21-32   The following events occurred for a company during the year:
(a) Installed a solar energy collector in a warehouse
(b) Installed a hydraulic lift door in a delivery truck
(c) Put a new roof on a warehouse
(d) Painted a new advertising logo on the fleet of company trucks
(e) Redecorated offices
(f) Repaired a company car involved in an accident; the car was not covered by insurance

Required: Classify the preceding items as capital expenditures or operating expenditures. Explain your reasoning.

21-33   The Brooks Legal Services Company paid for the following items with cash during 2000:
(a) Installation of energy-efficient windows in offices, $8,500
(b) Overhaul of machine to extend its original life by three years, $1,000
(c) Replacement of dead trees on landscaping around office building, $700
(d) Repainting of all offices, $1,000
(e) Installation of facilities for handicapped employees in office building, $4,900
(f) Replacement of tires on company trucks, $5,300

Required: Using T-accounts, prepare entries to record the preceding transactions. Explain your reason for how you recorded each item.

21-34   On December 31, 2000, Franklin Company has an asset that is impaired. The machine cost $100,000 on January 1, 1997, and has accumulated depreciation of $40,000 at the end of 2000. The company estimates that the machine will produce net cash inflows of $13,000 each year for the next four years, and the company uses a discount rate of 12%.

Required: (1) Compute the impairment loss on the machine.
(2) Using T-accounts, prepare the entry to record the impairment loss.

21-35   Brown Hydraulic Engineering Company owns a machine that originally cost $25,000. The accumulated depreciation account now has a balance of $18,000.

Required: Using T-accounts, prepare entries to record the disposal of the machine if it is sold for cash in the amount of: (1) $7,000, (2) $1,000, or (3) $12,000.

21-36   The Snowdon Mining Company purchased a machine for $80,000 on January 1, 1997. The company depreciates the asset using the straight-line method over five years to a zero residual value. On December 31, 2000, the company sells the machine.

Required: Using T-accounts, prepare entries to record the disposal of the machine if it is sold for cash in the amount of: (1) $16,000, (2) $11,000, and (3) $17,000. Assume the company has recorded depreciation expense for 2000.

21-37 Scafell Die Cutting Company owns a machine that originally cost $70,000 and currently has accumulated depreciation of $52,000. The company trades in the machine to a dealer on a new model, which has a selling price (market value of) $90,000. The old machine has a market value of $15,000, so Scafell pays $75,000 in the exchange.

Required: (1) What is the amount at which Scafell records the new machine?
(2) What is the gain or loss that Scafell records on the trade-in of the old machine?
(3) How would your answer to (2) change if Scafell pays only $70,000 in the exchange?

21-38 The Everest Sweater Company reports the following items in its financial statements for 2000 and 2001.

	2000	2001
Sales	$67,000	$73,000
Sales returns	2,000	3,000
Property, plant, and equipment	26,000	32,000
Accumulated depreciation	7,000	10,000

Required: Compute the net revenues to net property, plant, and equipment ratio for 2000 and 2001. Evaluate your results.

21-39 The Larsone Company uses the straight-line method with no residual value to depreciate its property, plant, and equipment. On its 2000 income statement, Larsone reported depreciation expense of $15,000 and net income of $20,000. On its December 31, 2000 balance sheet, Larsone reported the following amounts:

Property, plant, and equipment	$150,000
Less: Accumulated depreciation	(30,000)
Property, plant, and equipment (net)	$120,000

Required: (1) Compute the average age of Larsone's property, plant, and equipment.
(2) Compute the average life of Larsone's property, plant, and equipment.
(3) If a user decides the average life of Larsone's assets should be 2 years shorter, compute Larsone's revised depreciation expense for 2000.
(4) Compute Larsone's return on assets for 2000 (a) using its reported amounts, and (b) using the 2-year shorter life. Use the ending amount of property, plant, and equipment (net) as the total assets and ignore income taxes.

21-40 The Noyce Company was involved in the following transactions:
(a) Purchased a patent from another company
(b) Developed a design for a new type of machine for use in its production process
(c) Purchased a franchise for exclusive regional sale of a product
(d) Obtained a trademark on a new product
(e) Developed an advertising campaign for a new product
(f) Purchased another company for more than the market value of its identifiable net assets

Required: (1) Explain whether the company should record an intangible asset for each of the preceding items. If not, how would it record each item?
(2) For each item recorded as an intangible asset, indicate the maximum life over which the company may amortize it.

21-41 The Nevis Company owns the following intangible assets:
(a) A new patent purchased for $34,000
(b) A copyright purchased for $16,000
(c) A trademark purchased for $35,000
(d) A franchise purchased for $55,000
The company amortizes the assets using the straight-line method over the maximum allowable life.

Required: Using T-accounts, record the amortization expense in the first year of each asset's life.

21-42 The Skiddaw Company purchased land for $11 million in 2000. The company expects to be able to mine 1 million tons of molybdenum from this land over the next 20 years, at which time the residual value will be zero. During 2000, the company mined and sold 30,000 tons; during 2001, it mined and sold 40,000 tons.

Required: Compute the depletion expense for 2000 and 2001.

21-43 The Bonnington Company purchased a coal mine for $1.4 million in 2000. The company expected to be able to mine 500,000 tons of coal from this mine over the next 10 years, after which it expected to sell the land for $200,000. During 2000, the company mined and sold 20,000 tons of coal. Early in 2001, the company revised its estimate of the total remaining tons to be mined to 580,000 tons. During 2001, the company mined and sold 40,000 tons.

Required: Using T-accounts, record the depletion expense for 2000 and 2001.

Making Evaluations

21-44 Coltrane Corporation is a newly formed company and has purchased a building, office equipment, a machine to be used in production, and three company cars. The company is considering which depreciation method to select for each asset for financial reporting. The president wants to report the highest possible net income and pay the lowest possible income taxes. He also argues that the building is unlikely to go down in value in the next five years, so there is no need to depreciate it for that time. He wants to "save the depreciation" until later in the life of the building, when the value will go down. The chief accountant agrees that it is possible to minimize the payment of income taxes, but argues that it is incorrect to select a depreciation method in order to maximize net income or to relate to the value of the asset. She also points out that the value of the cars decreases significantly as soon as they are driven away from the dealer.

Required: (1) Evaluate the correctness of each argument.
(2) Which depreciation method do you think the chief accountant will likely suggest for each asset? Explain your reasoning.

21-45 Ten years ago, Davis Corporation purchased some equipment for $200,000. The company is depreciating the equipment on a straight-line basis and is now about to replace it. The income tax rate has been 40%. The president is shocked to find out that the company does not have enough cash available to replace the equipment because the purchase price has doubled. The president lends the company enough money to buy the new equipment but says, "Now we will record twice as much depreciation as before so that we don't have this problem again."

Required: (1) Considering only the preceding facts, by how much do you think the cash balance of the company will have changed over the life of the equipment?
(2) Can the company implement the president's proposed depreciation policy? Do you agree that it would be more desirable?

21-46 Charlotte Parker is considering purchasing either Gordon Company or Rollins Company. Both companies started business five years ago, and at that time, each company purchased property, plant, and equipment for $110,000 and decided to depreciate the assets over 10 years with no residual value. Gordon Company uses straight-line depreciation, and Rollins Company uses double-declining-balance depreciation. The two companies have very similar products and reputations, and their total assets (other than property, plant, and equipment) and total liabilities on their balance sheets are very similar.

Required: (1) Compute the book value of the property, plant, and equipment for each company at the end of five years.
(2) Which company represents the more desirable purchase? Explain your reasoning. Ignore income taxes.
(3) Would your answer to (2) change if income taxes are considered and both companies are corporations?

www.pfizer.com

21-47 <u>Pfizer</u> reported that its depreciable property and equipment at December 31, 1997 had a cost of $6,458 million (rounded) and accumulated depreciation of $2,321 million (rounded). The company uses the straight-line depreciation method. Assume the assets have no residual value and that the average life of the assets is 20 years.

Required: (1) What is the average age of the assets on December 31, 1997? Round your answer to the nearest whole year.

(2) If the company used the double-declining-balance method instead, what would be the amount of accumulated depreciation on December 31, 1997? Round each of your calculations to the nearest million, and the depreciation percentage to the nearest whole number.

(3) How much depreciation expense would be recorded in 1998 under the straight-line and double-declining-balance methods, respectively?

(4) Explain whether you agree with Pfizer's use of the straight-line method.

www.wal-mart.com

21-48 <u>Wal-Mart</u> disclosed the following in its annual report for its fiscal year ending January 31, 1998 (in millions):

	January 31,	
	1998	1997
Property, Plant, and Equipment, at cost		
Land	$ 4,691	$ 3,689
Buildings and improvements	14,646	12,724
Fixtures and equipment	7,636	6,390
Transportation equipment	403	379
	$27,376	$23,182
Less: Accumulated depreciation	5,907	4,849
Net property, plant, and equipment	$21,469	$18,333

	1998	1997
Cash flows from operating activities		
Net income	$ 3,526	$ 3,056
Adjustments to reconcile net income to net cash provided by operating activities:		
Depreciation and amortization	1,634	1,463
Cash flows from investing activities		
Payments for property, plant, and equipment	$ (2,636)	$ (2,643)

Wal-Mart uses the straight-line depreciation method. Assume that the assets have no residual value, that the amortization is not material, and that all acquisitions of property, plant, and equipment were cash transactions.

Required: (1) Compute the estimated average age of the depreciable property, plant, and equipment at the end of the 1998 fiscal year. Round your answer to the nearest whole year.

(2) Compute the estimated average life of the depreciable property, plant, and equipment at the end of the 1998 fiscal year. Round your answer to the nearest whole year.

(3) In evaluating Wal-Mart's property, plant, and equipment, why would you want to estimate the average age and the average life of these assets? What else might you want to know?

www.kodak.com

21-49 <u>Eastman Kodak</u> disclosed the following in its 1997 annual report (in millions):

	December 31,	
	1997	1996
Properties		
Land	$ 185	$ 193
Buildings and building equipment	2,693	2,788
Machinery and equipment	9,062	8,996
Construction in progress	884	608
	$12,824	$12,585

Accumulated depreciation	(7,315)	(7,163)
Property and equipment, net	$ 5,509	$ 5,422
⋮		
Total assets	$13,145	$14,438

	1997	1996
Revenues		
Sales	$14,538	$15,968
Cash flows from operating activities		
Income	$ 5	$ 1,011
Adjustments to reconcile net income to net cash provided by operating activities:		
Depreciation and amortization	828	903
Cash flows from investing activities		
Additions to properties	$ (1,485)	$ (1,341)
Proceeds from sales of properties	109	124

Eastman Kodak uses the straight-line depreciation method. Assume that the assets have no residual value, that the amortization is not material, and that all acquisitions of property, plant, and equipment were cash transactions.

Required: (1) Compute the estimated average age and average life of the property, plant, and equipment at the end of 1997. Round your answers to the nearest whole year.

(2) Compute the gain or loss on the sale of the property, plant, and equipment in 1997.

(3) If the company consistently had (a) gains or (b) losses on the sales of property, plant, and equipment, explain what you would conclude.

(4) Compute the dollar increase in the company's net property, plant, and equipment for 1997. What is this increase as a percentage?

(5) At the end of 1997, what percent of the company's total assets was invested in net property, plant, and equipment? How does this compare to 1996?

(6) What do you conclude about the company's operating capability for 1998?

(7) Compute the company's net revenues-to-net property, plant, and equipment ratio for 1997 and for 1996. What do these results indicate about the company's operating efficiency?

21-50 Eastman Chemical Company disclosed the following in its 1997 annual report (in millions):

www.eastman.com

	Dec. 31, 1997
Properties at Cost	
Balance at beginning of year	$7,530
Additions	749
Deductions	(175)
Balance at end of year	$8,104
Accumulated Depreciation	
Balance at beginning of year	$4,010
Provision for depreciation	327
Deductions	(114)
Balance at end of year	$4,223

Cash Flow Statement	1997
Proceeds from sales of assets	$ 20

Required: (1) Using T-accounts, re-create the transactions that affected Properties and Accumulated Depreciation during 1997. Assume that all acquisitions and sales of property, plant, and equipment were cash transactions.

(2) If Eastman Chemical Company used a longer estimated life, explain whether its gain or loss on the sale of property, plant, and equipment would be larger or smaller.

www.generalmills.com   **21-51**   General Mills' 1998 fiscal year annual report is included in Appendix C. Use this annual report to answer the following questions.

Required: (1) Why does the company use the straight-line depreciation method?
(2) Do you agree with the way the company lists Land, Buildings and Equipment in its balance sheet?
(3) Compute the estimated age and average life of the property, plant, and equipment at the end of the 1998 fiscal year. Round your answers to the nearest whole year. Assume that the assets have no residual value and the amortization is not material.
(4) Compute the estimated gain or loss on the sale of the property, plant, and equipment during the 1998 fiscal year.
(5) Compute the sales-to-net land, buildings, and equipment ratio for the 1998 and 1997 fiscal years. What do these results indicate about the company's operating efficiency?
(6) If GAAP allowed General Mills to record prepaid advertising as an expense instead of an asset, would the effects on the 1998 ending total assets and earnings before taxes and earnings (losses) from joint ventures be material? Assume that the prepaid advertising relates to the production costs of advertising that will take place in the next year.

www.pepsico.com   **21-52**   PepsiCo's disclosures of intangibles were shown in the chapter. For (2) and (3) below, assume any disposals of intangibles occurred at the end of 1997.

Required: (1) Why does the company use the straight-line amortization method?
(2) Compute the average age of the intangibles at December 27, 1997.
(3) Compute the average estimated life of the intangibles at December 27, 1997.
(4) Do you agree with the life used by PepsiCo?
(5) Explain whether PepsiCo purchased or sold intangibles in 1997.

www.colgate.com   **21-53**   Colgate-Palmolive disclosed the following amounts (in millions) in its 1997 annual report:

	1997	1996	1995
Income before income taxes	$ 1,102.3	$ 954.6	$ 363.5
Maintenance and repairs	113.6	107.1	108.2
Capital expenditures	478.5	459.0	431.8
Media advertising	637.0	565.9	561.3
Research and development	169.4	162.7	156.7
Total assets (Dec. 31)	7,538.7	7,901.5	7,642.3

Required: If GAAP allowed the company to record maintenance and repairs, media advertising, and research and development costs as assets and amortize them over three years, would the effects on the 1997 income before income taxes and ending total assets be material? Assume that the costs were incurred at the beginning of each year.

21-54 Yesterday, you received the following letter for your advice column in the local paper:

Dear Dr. Decisive:

Recently a group of us went to see a movie. And guess what we started to talk about when we got back to the dorm?! All the people whose names are listed at the end of the movie. Including the accountant. Can you get me that job? But seriously, one thing led to another, and we started to discuss how the movie company accounts for the costs of a movie. We thought we had that figured out, and we were all about to get some sleep when one of my friends asked how the company would depreciate the movie. That kept us up much too late. Then one of my friends showed me the annual report of COMSAT Corporation. And you won't believe what we found. "Costs of series satellites that are lost at launch or that fail in orbit are carried, net of any insurance proceeds, in the property accounts. The remaining net amounts are depreciated over the estimated service life of a satellite of the same series." Now tell me that accountants aren't weird! Please help us with these issues.

Call me "Sleepless in the Dorm."

www.comsat.com

Required: Meet with your Dr. Decisive team and write a response to "Sleepless in the Dorm."

CHAPTER OUTLINE

MANAGING, REPORTING, AND EVALUATING LONG-TERM FINANCING AND INVESTING ACTIVITIES IN A CORPORATE ENVIRONMENT

This section consists of three

chapters which discuss issues

involving a corporation's long-term

financing and investing activities.

After reading these chapters, you

will be able to:

▶ *Identify the factors that affect interest rates*

▶ *Know how a corporation accounts for its bond issues and capital leases*

▶ *Explain how different methods of accounting for investments in stocks and bonds affect a corporation's financial statements*

▶ *Describe a corporation's capital structure*

▶ *Understand a corporation's income statement and earnings per share*

▶ *Use a corporation's long-term debt, investment, and earnings information for evaluating its financial position and performance*

LONG-TERM DEBT AND OTHER FINANCING ISSUES

"If you think nobody cares if you're alive, try missing a couple of car payments."

—Earl Wilson, newspaper columnist

1 *How does a corporation compute the periodic payment, the interest expense, and the repayment of the principal on a loan?*

2 *What is a bond, what are its characteristics, and why does a corporation issue bonds?*

3 *What are the factors that affect long-term interest rates?*

4 *Why does a corporation issue bonds at less than or more than their face value?*

5 *How does the interest expense each period compare with the interest paid in that period when a corporation issues bonds at a discount or a premium?*

6 *What are zero-coupon bonds, and how does a corporation account for the interest on them?*

7 *How do long-term debt and interest expense disclosures help external users evaluate a corporation?*

8 *What is a lease? What is a capital lease, and what impact does it have on a lessee's financial statements?*

9 *Why do deferred income taxes arise, and how does a corporation report them in its financial statements?*

10 *What is a defined-benefit pension plan, and how does a corporation account for it?*

www.hersheys.com

www.rmcfusa.com

In Hershey Foods' (maker of Peter Paul Mounds) December 31, 1997 balance sheet, the company shows that it owes a total of $1,029 million of long-term debt—31 percent of its total liabilities and stockholders' equity. Rocky Mountain Chocolate Factory's long-term debt was $6 million on its February 28, 1998 balance sheet. Given that its total liabilities and stockholders' equity was about $19.9 million, 30 percent of Rocky Mountain's capital is provided by long-term debt. These dollar amounts shown on Hersheys' and Rocky Mountain's balance sheets result from decisions by managers and from the accounting methods the companies used to keep track of long-term debt.

 Hershey Foods' $1,029 million of long-term debt is over 171 times greater than Rocky Mountain's $6 million. Can we conclude that Hershey is much riskier than Rocky Mountain? Why or why not? What factors besides the amounts on the balance sheets of the two companies should you consider?

To be able to evaluate a company's liquidity and financial flexibility, as well as its ability to finance operations over the long run, both external and internal users must be familiar with how it issues and reports any long-term debt. Users also must be knowledgeable about how "market forces" affect the ability of a company to issue long-term debt. Typically, when a company borrows from a bank, the debt is called a note payable, whereas when it borrows from individual investors, the debt is called bonds payable. The primary difference between the two is that bonds can be sold on a "capital market," such as the New York Exchange, in the same way as stocks. Also, notes payable are usually issued at their face value, whereas bonds may be issued at their face value, at a premium, or at a discount, as we will discuss later in the chapter.

In Chapter 21, we explained how a company reports on its property, plant, and equipment. In this chapter, we will discuss one of the primary ways that a company finances its acquisition of those assets—the issuance of long-term debt.

 If you prepared a personal balance sheet, what would you include as long-term debt?

If a bank asked you to list your long-term liabilities and their amounts on your loan application, what information about your long-term liabilities would you want to have with you?

Valuing Long-Term Debt

Make a list of a few of your long-term liabilities. Your list may include your car loan, a student loan, a mortgage, etc. Next, use your best judgment to write in a value for each liability. How did you decide which amount to use? Did you have any problems deciding what values to assign? Write down why you chose the amounts you selected for each of your liabilities.

In Exhibit 22-1, we show the list for Jennifer Book, the business student we introduced in Chapter 21. In addition to writing her list, Jennifer explained why she had some difficulty deciding on the values to assign to her liabilities. Perhaps your difficulties were similar to hers. Let's examine the problems she encountered in assigning the amounts.

As we show in Exhibit 22-1, Jennifer lists a family obligation, a "loan" from her grandparents, a car loan, and her student loan as her long-term liabilities. We see that Jennifer has doubts about the appropriate amount to list for her liabilities. For example, she lists her family obligation at the cost of the food but is unsure whether to include the costs of her time. Her grandparents gave her a check for $5,000 on her 18th birthday to help her with college, but she is unsure whether it is a loan or a gift. So she assumes there is a 20% chance of repaying her grandparents and assigns a value of $1,000.

 Do you think that a gift to Jennifer is the equivalent of an investment in her—that is, stockholders' equity? Why or why not?

When Jennifer bought her car two years ago, she borrowed $14,000 but recently has received a bank statement showing that she has paid $2,000 of principal. She is uncertain how to handle the principal of the loan that will be outstanding when she plans to sell the car. Finally, for her student loan she schedules the cash flows so that she can compute their present value, but she is uncertain whether to use the rate on the loan of 6% or the market rate of 10%. Also she is unsure whether to include the amounts she will borrow for her senior year.

Exhibit 22-1	Jennifer Book's List of Four Liabilities Owed and Some Issues with Assigning Dollar Values to Them	

Liability	Value	Issues in Deciding Dollar Value
Family	$100	We have a family tradition of alternating cooking Christmas dinner. Next year it's my turn, and I think the food will cost me $100. But it will take me a lot of time. Perhaps I should also include the cost of my time for shopping and cooking.
Grandparents	$1,000	My grandparents gave me a check for $5,000 on my 18th birthday to help me with college. They wrote "loan to help with college," but I am pretty sure they don't expect me to repay them when I get a job after graduation. I will assume there is a 20% chance of repaying them, so I will assign a value of $1,000.
Car loan	$12,000	When I bought the car two years ago for $18,000, I took out a loan for $14,000, but I just got a bank statement showing that I have paid $2,000 of principal so far. But I will still have some of the loan outstanding when I plan to sell the car in four years. What should I do about that?
Student loan	$12,000	Since I don't have to start repaying this loan until after I graduate, I decided to compute the present value. The loan is at a subsidized rate of 6%, but I know that market rates are about 10%. So I laid out a schedule of all the cash payments I will have to make and discounted them at 10%. I also know I will borrow more in my senior year, but I left those out. I don't see how I can have a liability until I have the cash.

Do you agree with Jennifer's decisions? Was she consistent in her approach to valuing the liabilities? Why or why not? Did you have valuation problems similar to Jennifer's? Do you have a long-term liability that you think is worth less (or more) than its face value, but you don't know how much?

The difficulties Jennifer had in assigning dollar values for long-term liabilities illustrate why financial statement users need to understand how companies account for and report on long-term debt in order to make informed business decisions. In our example, Jennifer Book had difficulty deciding the value to assign to her liabilities. Notice that she did not use any accounting rules to help her decide. A company, however, is required to use GAAP, which for long-term debt is based on three accounting concepts we introduced earlier in the book—the *historical cost concept,* the *concept of a transaction,* and the *matching principle.* Let's review these concepts.

Recall that the historical cost concept states that a company records its transactions on the basis of the dollars exchanged (in other words, the cost) in the transaction. Once a company records a transaction, it usually retains the *cost* involved in the transaction in its accounting records. For instance, assume in July 2000, Unlimited Decadence Corporation borrowed $100,000 for five years at 11% to finance the purchase of some machinery. It is required to make a payment on the loan only once a year. At the end of 2000, interest rates on that type of loan have increased to 12%. Under the historical cost concept, Unlimited Decadence continues to show the debt on its balance sheet at $100,000.

Do you think that the present value of the payments on the loan discounted at 11% are greater or less than those same payments discounted at 12%? Explain your answer.

Many accounting and business experts are concerned about the usefulness of the historical cost concept. They ask, "How does including the $100,000 amount of the loan on Unlimited Decadence's 2000 ending balance sheet help investors and creditors evaluate its liquidity?" In other words, they question the *relevance* of reporting this historical cost amount. They believe that it would be more useful to report the current market value of the loan because if the company paid the loan off early, it would pay the market value of the loan. Supporters of the historical cost concept argue that the $100,000 *is* relevant for evaluating the company's long-term liquidity, and if the company has no intention of paying off the liability this year, then the current market value is *not* relevant.

To whom might the market value be relevant?

Supporters of historical cost also argue that the *reliability* of historical costs outweighs any potential increase in relevance that might be gained from using a measure of current value. In essence, GAAP supporters say: "We know that Unlimited Decadence borrowed $100,000 at 11%. We are not sure how reliable a measure the current interest rate is. With historical cost accounting, at least financial statement users know what they are getting." Also we know that all accountants would conclude that the amount borrowed was $100,000, whereas they would probably differ in their estimates of the value based on a current market interest rate.

Whose side do you take on this discussion—the supporters or the critics of the historical cost concept? Explain your position.

The concept of a transaction means that a company must have engaged in a transaction in order to record a liability (or an asset). Thus, budgeted cash outflows for an amount that a company will borrow in the future do not create a liability until the amount is borrowed.

If a company hires a new CEO and agrees to pay her $1 million per year for five years, do you think the company has a liability? Why or why not?

The matching principle states that to determine its net income for an accounting period, a company computes the total expenses involved in earning the revenues of the period and deducts them from the revenues earned in that period. Because long-term debt provides benefits every period that it is outstanding, a company includes the cost of the borrowing as an expense in determining its net income for each accounting period. For example, Unlimited Decadence borrowed $100,000 at 11%. In each accounting period during which the company has use of the money, it matches the cost of borrowing against the revenues recorded during the period. **Interest expense** is the cost to a company of borrowing money for a period, and a company records it as an end-of-period adjustment.

So, the historical cost concept, the transaction concept, and the matching principle provide the basis for how a company accounts for its long-term debt and reports this debt in its financial statements. Next we will address four important issues: (1) loan payments and interest, (2) the nature of bonds, (3) why a company issues bonds, and (4) bonds issued at face value. However, companies do not always issue bonds at their face value, because the market rate of interest may differ from the interest rate stated on the bonds. Therefore, we will also discuss the factors affecting interest rates and how the market rate of interest affects bond selling prices. In later sections, we will discuss other long-term debt issues, including leases, mortgages, deferred income taxes, and retirement benefits. In the appendix to this chapter, we discuss the accounting for bonds that are sold at a discount or premium and that pay interest semiannually.

 Do you think the fact that a company reports its long-term debt at historical cost affects the usefulness of this balance sheet information? If so, how?

Loan Payments and Interest

Individuals and businesses have many types of loans. For example, individuals may take out a loan to pay for college, to buy a car, or to purchase a house; a company may take out a loan to buy a specific item of property or to finance its general operations. All these loans have similar characteristics and involve many of the same issues. Since it is important for you to understand these issues, we start by explaining those related to a simple loan. Let's assume that when you graduate, you decide to buy a car and take out a loan of $20,000 to pay for it. The loan is for four years and has an interest rate of 10%. The typical loan requires equal monthly payments (an annuity), but for simplicity, we will assume that this loan requires an equal single payment at the end of each year (this is still an annuity). Don't be concerned about this simplification: it does not affect the issues we discuss—it simply means we can discuss 4 payments instead of 48! So the first issue is the amount of the annual payment. Car dealers and banks determine these payments according to the present value principles we discussed in Chapter 20. Note that since you are borrowing $20,000 today, this is the present value amount. The periodic payment is the amount of an annuity that has a present value equal to the amount borrowed. Since the present value of an annuity is computed as follows:

Present Value of Annuity = Periodic Payment × Present Value of Annuity Factor

and since the amount borrowed is the present value amount, the periodic payment is computed as follows:

Periodic Payment = Amount Borrowed ÷ Present Value of Annuity Factor Based on the Interest Rate and the Life of the Loan

Each periodic payment on the loan consists of two components: (1) interest expense and (2) a portion of the principal balance. The interest expense is based on the interest rate

How does a corporation compute the periodic payment, the interest expense, and the repayment of the principal on a loan?

and the balance (called the **book value**) in the liability account at the beginning of the period. The interest expense and the repayment of principle are computed as follows:

$$\text{Interest Expense} = \text{Periodic Interest Rate} \times \text{Book Value of Loan at the Beginning of the Period}$$

$$\text{Repayment of Principal} = \text{Periodic Payment} - \text{Interest Expense}$$

The four annual payments are an annuity, so we need to look at Table 20-2 (at the end of Chapter 20) to find the appropriate factor to use. The factor for 10% and 4 years is 3.1699. Therefore the annual payment is computed as follows:

$$\text{Annual Payment} = \text{Amount Borrowed} \div \text{Present Value of Annuity Factor}$$

$$= \$20,000 \div 3.1699$$

$$= \$6,309.35 \text{ (rounded)}$$

The interest expense for the first year is calculated as follows:

$$\text{Interest Expense} = \text{Periodic Interest Rate} \times \text{Book Value of Loan at the Beginning of the Year}$$

$$= 10\% \times \$20,000$$

$$= \$2,000$$

The remaining portion of the payment is $4,309.35 ($6,309.35 − $2,000.00) and is the repayment of the principal. So at the beginning of the second year, the balance (principal) of the loan, or the *book value* of the loan, is $15,690.65 ($20,000 − $4,309.35). The interest for year 2 is 10% × $15,690.65, or $1,569.07 (rounded). The remaining portion of the payment is $4,740.28 ($6,309.35 − $1,569.07) and is the repayment of the principal. So at the beginning of the third year, the book value of the loan is $10,950.37 ($15,690.65 − $4,740.28). By now we hope you follow the process, but here are the calculations for the final two years:

$$\text{Interest, year 3} = 10\% \times \$10,950.37 = \$1,095.04 \text{ (rounded)}$$

$$\text{Repayment of principal, year 3} = \$6,309.35 - \$1,095.04 = \$5,214.31$$

$$\text{Book value of loan, beginning of year 4} = \$10,950.37 - \$5,214.31 = \$5,736.06$$

$$\text{Interest, year 4} = 10\% \times \$5,736.06 = \$573.61 \text{ (rounded)}$$

$$\text{Repayment of principal, year 4} = \$6,309.35 - \$573.61 = \$5,735.74$$

So you see that the balance of your loan is now eliminated because your final payment includes a repayment of principal of $5,735.74, which is equal to the book value of the loan at the beginning of Year 4 of $5,736.06 (allowing for a $0.32 rounding error).

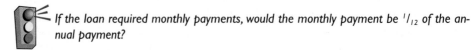 *If the loan required monthly payments, would the monthly payment be $^1/_{12}$ of the annual payment?*

In this example, we have not discussed how to record the loan or the asset (the car). We will discuss those issues later in the chapter, but if you prepared personal financial statements, you would record the car as an asset and the loan as a liability. Then, at the end of each year, you would record both the interest expense on the loan (as we just calculated) and the depreciation on the car (as we discussed in Chapter 21). You would report the depreciation expense and interest expense in your income statement. We now turn our discussion to situations in which companies borrow money under formal agreements, often called bonds.

 How would you respond if a friend asked you why you paid a total of $25,237.40 (4 × $6,309.35) for a $20,000 car (assuming you borrowed 100% of the cost of the car)?

Bond Characteristics

Virtually every company borrows money. In Chapter 14 we discussed notes payable, which a company issues when it borrows money for a short time. When a company borrows a large amount of money from investors for a long time, it usually issues bonds. A **bond** is a type of note in which a company agrees to pay the holder of the bond its face value at the maturity date and to pay interest on the face value periodically at a specified rate. Thus the company that issues the bond, the *borrower,* receives money when it sells the bond to the holder (purchaser) of the bond, the *lender.* We will now explain some terms related to bonds. The **face value** (also called the *par value*) is the amount of money that the issuer promises to pay on the maturity date. The face value is the same concept as the principal of a note. The **maturity date** is the date on which the issuer of the bond agrees to pay the face value to the holder. The issuer also agrees to pay interest each period. The **contract rate** (also called the *stated* or *nominal* rate) is the rate at which the issuer of the bond pays interest on the face value each period until the maturity date. All this information is printed on a bond certificate or related documents, provided to the owner of the bond. A **bond certificate** is a serially numbered legal document that specifies the face value, the annual interest rate, and the maturity date.[1] A company usually issues bonds so that each bond has a face value of $1,000. It may sell the entire bond issue to one purchaser or to numerous individual purchasers. Thus a $100,000 bond issue will consist of 100 bonds, each with a $1,000 face value. In addition, the bond issue usually specifies that interest is paid twice each year (semiannually), although it may state the contract rate in annual terms on the bond certificate. The interest rate per semiannual period, therefore, is 1/2 of the stated annual rate. For example, a $1,000, 10% bond pays interest of $50 ($1,000 × 10% × 1/2) twice each year (every six months), for a total of $100 per year.

2 What is a bond, what are its characteristics, and why does a corporation issue bonds?

User Analysis Perspective: Reasons for Issuing Bonds

A company (corporation) can obtain large amounts of money (capital) for a long time in two ways. The first way is to sell common stock, which we briefly discussed in Chapter 10 and will discuss more completely in Chapter 24. Selling common stock provides a corporation with permanent capital, since it has no obligation to repay the stockholders. In addition, it has no legal obligation to pay dividends, although many corporations choose to do so. Because the stockholders are the owners of a corporation, selling more stock spreads ownership rights, voting rights, and the corporation's earnings over more shares. The second way a corporation can obtain long-term capital is to borrow the money by, for example, issuing bonds, which obligate the corporation to repay the amount borrowed and also to pay interest each period. The payment of interest is a legal obligation, and if the corporation issuing the bonds (the borrower) fails to pay the interest on the face value, the holder of the bonds (the lender) can take legal action to enforce payment, which may cause the borrower to declare bankruptcy. The bondholders are creditors of the corporation; they are not the owners and therefore have no voting rights.

[1]The bond certificate may contain other provisions as well. For instance, bonds may be registered, convertible, zero-coupon, serial, and callable, to name a few. We will briefly discuss zero-coupon and callable bonds later in the chapter.

The main reason why the managers of a corporation may decide that it should issue bonds instead of common stock is that the earnings available to the common stockholders can be increased through leverage. **Leverage** is the use of borrowing by a corporation to increase the return to common stockholders. It also is called *trading on equity*. If a corporation can borrow money by issuing bonds and can use the money to invest in a project that provides greater income than the interest that it must pay on the bonds, the corporation and its stockholders will be better off (they will earn a higher income). One measure of the return to common stockholders is earnings per share, which we discussed in Chapter 10. When a corporation successfully uses leverage, it increases its earnings per share.

For example, assume that a corporation currently has 10,000 shares of common stock held by stockholders, income before income taxes of $100,000, and an income tax rate of 40%. The managers have decided to expand its operations by building a factory, at a cost of $300,000. They expect the factory to provide additional pretax income of $50,000 per year. The corporation is considering selling 6,000 additional shares of common stock for $50 per share or issuing bonds with a face value of $300,000 and a 10% interest rate. We show the effects of these two alternatives in Exhibit 22-2.

First, let's look at financing the expansion by issuing bonds for $300,000. In this case (the middle column of Exhibit 22-2), the corporation has interest expense of $30,000 ($300,000 × 10%), which it records as an expense on the income statement. After subtracting the income tax expense, its net income increases by $12,000 (from $60,000 to $72,000) when it uses bond financing. Since it does not increase the number of common shares with bond financing, it also reports an *increase* in its earnings per share from $6.00 to $7.20 ($72,000 ÷ 10,000).

Now suppose the corporation decides to finance the expansion by issuing common stock. In this case (the right column of Exhibit 22-2), the corporation has no additional interest expense, so it reports an increase in its income before income taxes of $50,000 and an increase in net income of $30,000 (from $60,000 to $90,000). Although its net income increases by more than it does under the bond financing alternative, the corporation also increases the number of common shares by 6,000, to 16,000. Therefore, it reports a *decrease* in its earnings per share from $6.00 to $5.63 ($90,000 ÷ 16,000). In this situation, although financing by issuing bonds does not increase net income by as much as selling common stock, bond financing has a more favorable impact on the earnings per share of current stockholders and is of greater benefit to them.

The reason for this advantageous result is that the new factory is expected to earn a pretax return (additional earnings ÷ investment) of nearly 17% ($50,000 ÷ $300,000), whereas the pretax interest cost on the bonds is only 10%. Stockholders benefit from leverage when a corporation borrows money at 10% to earn a return of 17%.

Exhibit 22-2　Use of Leverage through Bond Financing

	Before Expansion	Bond Financing	Stock Financing
Earnings before interest and income taxes	$100,000	$150,000	$150,000
Interest expense	—	(30,000)	—
Income before income taxes	$100,000	$120,000	$150,000
Income tax expense	(40,000)	(48,000)	(60,000)
Net Income	$ 60,000	$ 72,000	$ 90,000
Number of shares of common stock	10,000	10,000	16,000
Earnings per share	$6.00	$7.20	$5.63

How much would the corporation report as net income and earnings per share under the bond and stock financing alternatives if the expansion was not as successful and the new factory provides additional pretax income of only $15,000?

Although stockholders may benefit when a corporation borrows money, there is a limit to the amount of money it can borrow. As the amount of money the corporation borrows increases, its risk of default increases, so that the interest rate it will have to pay also increases. At some point the interest rate will exceed the rate that the corporation can earn from an investment (so earnings per share will decrease), lenders will refuse to lend it more money, or the managers will decide that the risk of borrowing has become too high. Thus all companies have a limit on the amount of money they can borrow.

 Explain whether you are using leverage if you borrow money to pay for your college education.

Bonds Issued at Face Value

If a company issues bonds for the amount of their face value, the recording and reporting are straightforward because the cash received from the sale equals the face value. For example, assume that on January 1, 2000, Unlimited Decadence issues 10%, 10-year bonds with a face value of $200,000 for $200,000 cash. When it issues these bonds, Unlimited Decadence records the face value in a liability account called Bonds Payable, as follows:

Assets	=	**Liabilities**	+	**Stockholders' Equity**

Cash		Bonds Payable	
200,000			200,000
(+)	(−)	(−)	(+)

Besides increasing cash, Unlimited Decadence reports the $200,000 bonds payable as a long-term liability on its balance sheet. It reports the cash received as a cash inflow from a financing activity on its cash flow statement.

Interest Expense and Payment

As we discussed earlier, bonds issued by companies usually pay interest semiannually. Unlimited Decadence pays interest each June 30 and December 31. Therefore, it computes the semiannual interest expense on these dates as follows:

$$\text{Semiannual Interest Expense} = \text{Face Value of Bonds} \times \left(\text{Annual Contract Rate} \div \text{Number of Interest Payments per Year} \right)$$

Since the interest payment is based on the face value of the bonds and the company issued the bonds for the amount of the face value, the interest expense and interest payment are equal. The company computes them as follows:

Semiannual Interest Expense and Interest Payment = $200,000 × (10% ÷ 2)

= $10,000

Note that since the interest expense and interest payment are equal, the company does not reduce the principal amount, as we discussed earlier for the $20,000 car loan. Unlimited Decadence records each semiannual interest expense and payment as follows:

Assets	=	Liabilities	+	Stockholders' Equity

Cash				Interest Expense
	10,000			10,000	
(+)	(−)			(+)	(−)

Also, note that since the company increases interest expense, it decreases its stockholders' equity. Unlimited Decadence reports the $10,000 interest expense in the "other items" section on its income statement. It includes the cash paid as a cash outflow from operating activities on its cash flow statement.

Accrual of Interest

Companies may issue bonds at any time during the year, but they still pay interest every six months from the date of issuance. For instance, if a company issues bonds on May 1, then it pays interest every October 31 and April 30. In this situation, the company issuing the bonds must be sure it reports the correct amount of interest expense on its annual income statement and the bond interest owed at the end of the year on its ending balance sheet. So the company *accrues* the interest it owes from the date of the last interest payment to the end of the year.

 What do you think is the primary difference between the payments on a car loan and the payments on a bond?

To illustrate, assume that Layth Company issued 12%, 10-year bonds with a face value of $300,000 for $300,000 cash on September 1, 2000. It pays interest on these bonds every February 28 and August 31. At the end of 2000, the company has not yet paid any interest, but it *owes* interest for four months (from September 1 through December 31). Therefore, the company must report four months of interest expense on its 2000 income statement and four months of interest owed on its ending 2000 balance sheet. The company computes its interest expense and interest owed to date as follows:

$$\text{Interest Expense for} = \text{Semiannual Interest} \times \text{Fraction of Period}$$
$$\text{Fraction of Period} \quad \text{Expense} \qquad \text{since Interest Last Paid}$$

$$= [\$300,000 \times (12\% \div 2)] \times 4/6$$

$$= \$12,000$$

Note that we determine the interest expense for the four months by computing the semiannual interest amount and then multiplying this amount by the fraction of the semiannual period since the bonds were issued (since the company has not yet paid interest). In this case the company's bonds were outstanding for four months of the six-month interest period. Therefore, it records the interest expense and interest owed on December 31, 2000, as follows:

Assets	=	Liabilities	+	Stockholders' Equity

		Interest Payable		Interest Expense
			12,000		12,000	
		(−)	(+)		(+)	(−)

Layth Company reports the interest expense in the "other items" section on its 2000 income statement and the interest payable as a current liability on its 2000 balance sheet. When the company makes its first $18,000 semiannual interest payment on February 28, 2001, it will record interest expense of $6,000 for the two months of the interest period in 2001 and will eliminate the $12,000 interest payable recorded at the end of 2000. This pattern of accruing interest will continue every year for the life of the bonds.

 Using T-accounts, record the February 28 entry for the $18,000 interest payment.

Factors Affecting Bond Interest Rates

In the examples of a car loan and bonds issued at face value, we assumed an interest rate. Several factors affect interest rates, including the policies of the Federal Reserve Board (which affect the supply and demand for money in the national economy), federal regulations, and the budget surplus or deficit of the federal government. Long-term interest rates for corporations, however, include three *primary* factors:

3 *What are the factors that affect long-term interest rates?*

▶ The risk-free rate

▶ The expected inflation rate

▶ The risk premium

The **risk-free rate** is the rate that a borrower would pay, and a lender would receive, when there is no risk of default by the borrower and when no inflation is expected. Borrowing by the U.S. government is considered to be risk free because the government will not default. Since the United States is not inflation free, most U.S. government borrowing reflects the effect of the risk-free rate plus the expected inflation rate. The interest rate includes the **expected inflation rate** so that the borrower pays additional interest to compensate for the expected inflation over the life of the borrowing. Inflation causes the value of the dollar that eventually is repaid to be worth less than the dollar that was originally lent, so the added interest compensates for this decline. Most borrowings of the federal government illustrate the risk-free rate plus the expected inflation because they are considered to be risk-free, but occur in an inflationary environment. However, in recent years the U.S. government has issued "inflation indexed" bonds whose principal amounts are adjusted to reflect inflation. Therefore, the interest rate on these borrowings is the risk-free rate. The **risk premium** is the additional interest that a borrower, such as a company, pays when there is a possibility that it will default. The higher the risk of default, the higher is the risk premium. So a company that has a higher risk of default will have to pay a higher rate of interest to its lenders.

To illustrate the nature of these three components, at the time of writing this book the following rates (called *yields,* which we explain later) existed on selected borrowings:

Borrower	Maturity Date	Yield
U.S. Government (inflation indexed)	2008	3.8%
U.S. Government	2008	4.6
Duke Energy	2008	6.3
Duke Energy	2023	6.8
Phillips Petroleum	2023	7.5

Thus the risk-free rate until 2008 to 3.8%. The risk-free rate plus the inflation expectation until 2008 is 4.6% per year. Thus, the market is expecting inflation of 0.8% per year until 2008. Since Duke Energy does have some risk of default, the risk premium associated with the borrowing that will mature in 2008 is 1.7%. The risk premium for the 2023 borrowing of Duke Energy is 0.5% because there is a longer time period in which Duke

www.phillips66.com

Energy could have financial problems and a longer period of potential inflation. The risk premium for <u>Phillips Petroleum</u> is 0.7%, which indicates that its likelihood of default is higher than Duke Energy's. We do not expect you to compute an interest rate for a particular situation. However, an understanding of the components of long-term interest rates is helpful in understanding both general business issues and accounting for bonds that are issued at less than or more than their face value (which we will discuss in the next section and in the appendix to this chapter), as well as accounting for investments in bonds (which we will discuss in Chapter 23).

 Look in a newspaper to find the current yields of each of the bonds listed above. Have expectations of inflation changed? Have any of the risk premiums changed?

Bonds Issued at Less Than or More Than Face Value

4 *Why does a corporation issue bonds at less than or more than their face value?*

A company must follow certain steps when it issues bonds, such as receiving approval from the regulatory authorities (for example, the Securities and Exchange Commission). It also must publish the terms of the bond issue, such as the contract rate, maturity date, and interest payment dates, and must print the bond certificates. When a company decides to issue bonds, it usually deals with a securities broker(s) or investment banker(s). The broker and the company agree on a price for the bonds, and the company sells the bonds to the broker. The broker then sells the bonds to its customers and plans to make a profit on this service. The company issuing (selling) the bonds deals with a broker to avoid the problem of having to find the purchasers and having to be involved in cash transactions with each purchaser.

 Do you think this is similar to the relationship among a manufacturer, a wholesaler, and a retailer?

The broker and the company base the selling price on the terms of the bond issue and the components of the long-term interest rate, as we discussed earlier. They determine the rate that they believe best reflects current market conditions. This market rate of interest is called the yield. The **yield** is the market rate at which the bonds are issued.[2] Although the yield is stated as a percentage, it is usually referred to as a yield instead of a yield rate. The yield is often called the *effective rate*. The yield on a bond issue may be different from the contract rate set by the company and printed on the bond certificates. The managers of the company set the contract rate, whereas the marketplace determines the yield. The difference between the contract rate and the yield may result from a difference of opinion between the broker and the company about the yield at which the bonds will be sold. It also may result from a change in economic conditions between the date the terms of the bond were set and the date the bonds are issued. Sometimes companies issue bonds for which the yield is equal to the contract rate, in which case it sells the bonds at face value, as we illustrated earlier. However, often these rates are not equal. When this is the case, a company sells the bonds at less than or more than their face value.

Bond Selling Prices

Once the broker and the company have set the terms of a bond issue and determined the yield, they calculate the selling price of the bonds. We explain the calculation in the appendix to this chapter. However, we can state some general rules now. If the yield is *more* than the contract rate, the company will receive (and the purchasers of the bonds will pay) a selling price that is *less* than the face value of the bonds; that is, the company will sell the bonds at a *discount*. Since the contract rate is less than the market rate of interest for

---

[2]After a company issues bonds, the yield on these bonds will fluctuate in the bond market as changes occur in the risk premium and the expected inflation rate. It is the yield at the time of issuance, however, that a company uses in accounting for its bonds payable.

similar bonds, the company's bonds are worth less in comparison and, therefore, sell for less. Alternatively, if the yield is *less* than the contract rate, the company will receive (and the purchasers of the bonds will pay) a selling price that is *more* than the face value of the bonds; that is, the company will sell the bonds at a *premium*.

 Why do you think purchasers are willing to pay a premium for bonds that have a contract rate greater than their yield?

The issuance price of bonds sold at a discount or a premium is usually quoted as a percentage of the face value. For example, a company issuing bonds that have a face value of $200,000 and that are quoted at 97 (i.e., 97% of the face value) sells these bonds at a discount for $194,000 ($200,000 × 0.97). Bonds that have a face value of $100,000 and that are quoted at 102 are sold at a premium for $102,000 ($100,000 × 1.02). When a company sells bonds (whether at a premium or a discount), it records the selling price in the Bonds Payable account. For example, the company selling bonds with a face value of $200,000 for $194,000 would record the sale as follows:

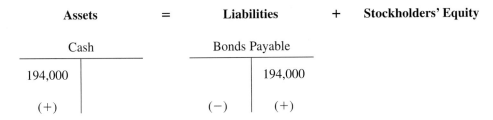

The $194,000 is the *book value* of the bonds.

Users need to understand why bonds sell at a price different from the face value when the yield is different from the contract rate. Remember that the selling price is the amount received by the company (and paid by the purchasers) at the time it issues the bonds, and that the face value is the amount that the company will pay (and the purchasers will receive) on the maturity date. The difference between the selling price and the face value means that the company incurs a cost (and the purchasers earn a return) on the bonds' selling price equal to the yield required by the market on the date of issue. For instance, a company sells bonds at a discount because the yield is higher than the contract rate. Remember that when a company sells a bond at a discount, it borrows less than the face value of the bond but still must pay back the entire face value of the bond on its maturity date. The difference (the discount) between the lower selling price and the face value, combined with the contract interest paid by the company each interest period, results in a cost to the company (and return to the purchasers) equal to the higher yield. Alternatively, a company sells bonds at a premium because the yield is lower than the contract rate. When a company sells a bond at a premium, it borrows more than the face value of the bond but only pays back the face value of the bond on its maturity date. The difference (the premium) between the higher selling price and the face value, offset by the contract interest paid by the company each interest period, results in a cost to the company (and return to the purchasers) equal to the lower yield. We know this paragraph may be difficult to understand, but we will be explaining the issues more as we go through the chapter and in the appendix to this chapter.

 If the yield on two bonds is the same, would you prefer to buy a bond that sells at a discount or one that sells at a premium? Explain your answer.

Bond Interest Expense

Interest expense is the cost of borrowing money. When a company sells bonds at a discount, the amount of money it receives (borrows) is less than the face value of the bonds. But the total amount of cash the company pays (the interest and principal) is the same amount it would pay if it sold the bonds at their face value. The excess of the total amount

5 *How does the interest expense each period compare with the interest paid in that period when a corporation issues bonds at a discount or a premium?*

"When interest rates go up, bond prices go down. When interest rates go down, bond prices go up. But please don't ask me why."

© 1998 Sidney Harris

paid over the amount borrowed is the total (lifetime) interest. When a company sells bonds at a discount, that difference is higher than it would be if the company sold the bonds for their face value. Not only the *amount* of interest but also the *rate* of interest is higher in this situation.

Because a company issuing bonds at a discount or premium incurs a cost (yield) either higher (for bonds sold at a discount) or lower (for bonds sold at a premium) than the contract rate, the interest *expense* it records each semiannual period is either higher or lower than the interest *paid* in that period (remember, the borrower pays the contract rate). A company computes the interest expense on bonds payable each period as follows:

$$\text{Interest Expense for Period} = \text{Book Value of Bonds Payable} \times \text{Yield at Beginning of Period}$$

When a company sells bonds at a *discount,* its interest expense each period is *higher* than the interest it pays in that period. When a company sells bonds at a *premium,* its interest expense each period is *lower* than the interest it pays in that period. The difference between the interest expense and the interest paid is the amount of the discount or premium that the company *amortizes* each period. As you will see, by the maturity date, the company will have amortized all the discount or premium so that the book value of the bonds payable equals the face value (the amount the borrower pays the lender).

We show the relationships between the yield and the contract rate, as well as the related impact on the selling price and the interest expense, in Exhibit 22-3. Because

Exhibit 22-3	Relationships between Bond Selling Prices and Interest Expense	

Yield Compared to Contract Rate	Bonds Sell at	Annual Interest Expense Compared to Annual Interest Payment
Yield > Contract Rate	Discount	Interest Expense > Interest Paid
Yield = Contract Rate	Face Value	Interest Expense = Interest Paid
Yield < Contract Rate	Premium	Interest Expense < Interest Paid

the accounting procedures for the amortization of a discount or premium on bonds that pay interest each period are complex, we do not show them here. We will illustrate the calculations and the accounting procedures for these bonds in the appendix to this chapter. We do, however, illustrate the amortization of the discount on zero-coupon bonds in the next section.

Zero-Coupon Bonds

In the previous sections, we discussed bonds on which a company pays interest *each period*. In recent years, many companies have issued a slightly different type of bond called a zero-coupon bond. **Zero-coupon bonds** are bonds that pay no interest each period. That is, the only cash flows associated with the bonds are the amount borrowed (which is less than the face value of the bonds) and the payment of the face value on the maturity date. The face value includes the amount borrowed plus the interest. Even though the bonds *pay* no interest each period, the company still reports an interest *expense* each period because it has incurred interest on the amount borrowed. The selling price of zero-coupon bonds is the present value of the face value (using the *annual* yield),[3] and therefore is always less than the face value. Recall from Chapter 20 that the present value is the value today of a certain amount of dollars paid or received in the future. (You should go back to Chapter 20 if you need to review the concept of, and calculations for, present value.) The *discount* is the difference between the selling price and the face value. The company computes the annual interest expense by multiplying the annual yield by the book value of the bonds at the beginning of the year. This way of computing interest expense is called the **effective interest method**. Since the company pays no cash for interest each year, it records the annual interest expense as an increase in the book value of the bonds payable each year, so that the book value on the maturity date is equal to the face value (the amount the borrower pays the lender). Similarly, although the purchasers *receive* no interest, they earn interest *revenue* each year.

For example, suppose that, on January 1, 2000, Unlimited Decadence issues 10-year, zero-coupon bonds with a face value of $1 million. The bonds are sold to yield 10%. The selling price of the bonds is calculated by discounting the face value (a single future amount) using the 10% yield and the 10-year life of the bonds, as follows:

Selling Price of the Bond Issue = Present Value of the Face Value

= Face Value × Present Value of $1 Factor for
10 Periods at 10%

= $1,000,000 × 0.3855 (from Table 20-1 at the
end of Chapter 20)

= $385,500

Notice that the $385,500 selling price of the zero-coupon bonds is much less than the $1 million face value. This is why many people refer to them as *deep discount* bonds. Unlimited Decadence records the sale of the bonds as follows:

Assets	=	Liabilities	+	Stockholders' Equity

Cash			Bonds Payable	
385,500				385,500
(+)	(−)		(−)	(+)

[3]A zero-coupon bond may also be valued using a semiannual yield. We use the annual yield for simplicity.

6 What are zero-coupon bonds, and how does a corporation account for the interest on them?

The company computes the $38,550 interest expense for 2000 by multiplying the book value of the bonds payable at the beginning of the period by the annual yield, as follows:

$$\text{Interest Expense for Period} = \text{Book Value of Bonds Payable} \times \text{Annual Yield at Beginning of Period}$$

$$= \$385,500 \times 10\%$$

$$= \$38,550$$

Since Unlimited Decadence does not *pay* any interest, on December 31, 2000, it records the amount of the interest as an increase in the book value of the liability. This is called *amortizing* a portion of the discount, and the company records the interest expense and amortization as follows:

Assets	=	**Liabilities**	+	**Stockholders' Equity**

	Bonds Payable		Interest Expense
	Bal 385,500		
	38,550	38,550	
	Bal 424,050		
(−)	(+)	(+)	(−)

Unlimited Decadence reports the new $424,050 book value of the bonds as a long-term liability on its December 31, 2000 balance sheet as follows:

Long-term debt
   10% bonds payable (face value $1,000,000), due 12/31/09 $424,050

Unlimited Decadence also reports the $38,550 interest expense in the "other items" section of its 2000 income statement. It computes its interest expense for 2001 as follows:

$$\text{Interest Expense for Period} = \text{Book Value of Bonds Payable} \times \text{Annual Yield at Beginning of Period}$$

$$= (\$385,500 + \$38,550) \times 10\%$$

$$= \$424,050 \times 10\%$$

$$= \$42,405$$

Each year for 10 years, Unlimited Decadence increases the book value of the bonds by the amount of that year's amortization so that at the end of their 10-year life, their book value will be $1 million (the face value of the bonds). Unlimited Decadence will then pay $1 million to the bondholders to retire the liability.

Retirement of Bonds

As we mentioned earlier, whether a company issues bonds at a premium or at a discount, on the maturity date the book value of the bonds payable is equal to the face value because of the amortization process over the life of the bonds. Therefore, when the company pays the face value on the maturity date, it retires the bonds and eliminates the bond liability.

Sometimes a company retires bonds prior to their maturity date. This may occur if the bonds are traded on a "capital market" and the company purchases them from the investors at their market price on the day of the purchase. Also the bond certificate may include a provision that allows the issuer to purchase them. These bonds are called **callable bonds**. When bonds are callable, the company that issued the bonds has the right to recall (retire) the bonds before the maturity date at a *call price* that was specified when the bonds were issued, rather than at their market price. The call price is higher than the *original* selling price.

 Would you buy bonds from a company if the call price was less than the face value? Why or why not?

When a company retires bonds, the price paid may be more, less, or the same as the current book value of the bonds. When the cash paid to retire bonds is less than the book value of the bonds, the company records an *extraordinary gain* on the retirement. Or, if the cash paid to retire bonds is more than the book value of the bonds, the company records an *extraordinary loss* on the retirement. A company reports extraordinary gains and losses on its income statement, as we briefly discussed in Chapter 10 and will discuss more in Chapter 24.

To understand the early retirement of bonds, suppose that a company pays $205,000 to retire bonds with a current book value of $198,000. In this situation, the company incurs a $7,000 ($205,000 − $198,000) extraordinary loss to retire the bonds, and it records the retirement as follows:

Assets	=	Liabilities	+	Stockholders' Equity
Cash		Bonds Payable		Extraordinary Loss

			Bal 198,000		
205,000	198,000			7,000	
			Bal 0		
(+) (−)		(−) (+)		(+) (−)	

The $198,000 reduction of the Bonds Payable account eliminates the liability because the current book value was $198,000. The Extraordinary Loss account is like an expense account, so an increase in the loss account causes a decrease in stockholders' equity. As you will see in Chapter 24, the company reports the $7,000 loss in a section of its income statement called "extraordinary items."

Similarities between Loans and Bonds Payable

Now that we have discussed loans (such as a car loan) and bonds, it is helpful to understand the similarities between the two. In both cases, the following statements apply:

1. The initial amount recorded by the company is the present value of the future cash flows.

2. The interest expense for the period is the book value of the liability at the beginning of the period multiplied by the interest rate (yield).

3. The book value of the liability at any time is the present value of the remaining cash flows.

So you see that the principles followed are the same. The differences are in the form of the agreement rather than its substance. Of course, loans and bonds can have different characteristics than the ones we discussed.

Reporting Long-Term Debt and Interest

We have used the title Long-Term Debt in this chapter because that is the title many companies use in their balance sheet. You may come across titles such as Long-Term Liabilities or Noncurrent Liabilities. The types and extent of long-term debt disclosures reported in an annual report vary from one company to another. However, GAAP requires all companies to disclose information about the terms of the debt, the interest expense, and the interest paid in their financial statements or the notes accompanying those statements. We show excerpts from PepsiCo's annual report for 1997 in Exhibit 22-4.

www.pepsico.com

Examine PepsiCo's disclosures. Do you understand these disclosures? What do they tell you about PepsiCo's managers' decisions concerning long-term debt? What additional disclosures do you think might be useful?

Using Long-Term Debt and Interest Expense Disclosures for Evaluation

7 *How do long-term debt and interest expense disclosures help external users evaluate a corporation?*

So far in the chapter, we have focused on the issues involved in reporting long-term debt. Knowledge of these issues provides you with the foundation necessary to understand how external users evaluate a company's long-term debt and interest expense disclosures to assess its long-term financial flexibility, risk, and liquidity. **Financial flexibility** refers to a company's ability to adapt to change. Financial flexibility enables a company to increase (or reduce) its operating activities in response to changing economic conditions. For example, this concept relates to a company's ability to raise additional capital resources to adapt to a changing environment. **Risk** is a measure of the uncertainty of a company's future performance. **Long-term liquidity** relates to the amount of cash a company will generate over the long run to pay off its liabilities as they become due.

Exhibit 22-4   PepsiCo's Disclosures Related to Debt

Consolidated Balance Sheet (in part)

(in millions except per share amount)
PepsiCo, Inc. and Subsidiaries
December 27, 1997 and December 28, 1996

LIABILITIES AND SHAREHOLDERS' EQUITY	1997	1996
Current Liabilities		
Accounts payable and other current liabilities	$ 3,617	$ 3,378
Income taxes payable	640	413
Total Current Liabilities	4,257	3,791
Long-term Debt	4,946	8,174
Other Liabilities	2,265	1,997
Deferred Income Taxes	1,697	1,575
Shareholders' Equity		
Capital stock, par value 1 2/3¢ per share: authorized 3,600 shares, issued 1,726 shares	29	29
Capital in excess of par value	1,314	1,201
Retained earnings	11,567	9,184
Currency translation adjustment	(988)	(768)
	11,922	9,646
Less: Treasury stock, at cost: 224 shares and 181 shares in 1997 and 1996, respectively	(4,986)	(3,023)
Total Shareholders' Equity	6,936	6,623
Total Liabilities and Shareholders' Equity	$20,101	$22,160

As with other parts of financial statements, external users evaluate long-term debt by performing intracompany and intercompany analysis—through the use of percentage analysis (trend analysis and ratio analysis). We will discuss only intracompany analysis in this chapter, using the disclosures from PepsiCo's 1997 annual report given in Exhibit 22-4. You can also perform intercompany analysis following the procedures we discussed in Chapter 21.

Exhibit 22-4   PepsiCo's Disclosures Related to Debt, cont'd

Consolidated Statement of Income

(in millions except per share amounts)
PepsiCo, Inc. and Subsidiaries
Fiscal years ended December 27, 1997, December 28, 1996 and December 30, 1995

	1997	1996	1995
Net Sales	$20,917	$20,337	$19,067
Costs and Expenses, net			
Cost of sales	8,525	8,452	8,054
Selling, general and administrative expenses	9,241	9,063	8,133
Amortization of intangible assets	199	206	208
Unusual items	290	576	66
Operating Profit	2,662	2,040	2,606
Interest expense	(478)	(565)	(629)
Interest income	125	91	114
Income from Continuing Operations Before Income Taxes	2,309	1,566	2,091
Provision for Income Taxes	818	624	669
Income from Continuing Operations	1,491	942	1,422
Income from Discontinued Operations, net of tax	651	207	184
Net Income	$ 2,142	$ 1,149	$ 1,606
Income Per Share – Basic			
Continuing operations	$ 0.98	$ 0.60	$ 0.90
Discontinued operations	0.42	0.13	0.12
	$ 1.40	$ 0.73	$ 1.02
Average shares outstanding	1,528	1,564	1,576
Income Per Share – Assuming Dilution			
Continuing operations	$ 0.95	$ 0.59	$ 0.88
Discontinued operations	0.41	0.13	0.12
Net Income	$ 1.36	$ 0.72	$ 1.00
Average shares outstanding	1,570	1,606	1,608

See accompanying Notes to Consolidated Financial Statements.

Consolidated Statement of Cash Flows (in part)

Supplemental Cash Flow Information			
Interest paid	$ 462	$ 538	$ 621
Income taxes paid	696	611	741

continued

Exhibit 22-4	PepsiCo's Disclosures Related to Debt, cont'd

Notes to Consolidated Financial Statements (in part)

Note 10 – Long-term Debt

	1997	1996
Long-term debt		
Commercial paper (5.4%)	$ –	$1,176
Notes due 1998-2011 (6.5% and 6.4%)	2,643	3,111
Various foreign currency debt, due 1998-2001 (5.2% and 5.5%)	809	1,448
Zero coupon notes, $1.0 billion due 1998-2012 (10.5% and 7.9%)	480	930
Euro notes due 1998-1999 (5.8% and 5.5%)	500	700
Other, due 1998-2020 (7.5% and 7.1%)	514	809
	$4,946	$8,174

The interest rates in the above table include the effects of associated interest rate and currency swaps at year-end 1997 and 1996. See Note 11 for a discussion of PepsiCo's use of interest rate and currency swaps, its management of the inherent credit risk and fair value information related to debt and interest rate and currency swaps.

PepsiCo enters into currency swaps to hedge its currency exposure on certain non-U.S. dollar denominated debt. At year-end 1997, the aggregate carrying amount of the debt was $629 million and the payables under related currency swaps were $104 million, resulting in a net effective U.S. dollar liability of $733 million with a weighted average interest rate of 5.8%, including the effects of related interest rate swaps. At year-end 1996, the carrying amount of this debt aggregates $1.8 billion and the receivables and payables under related currency swaps aggregate $54 million and $59 million, respectively, resulting in a net effective U.S. dollar liability of $1.8 billion with a weighted average interest rate of 5.6%, including the effects of related interest rate swaps.

At year-end 1997 and 1996, PepsiCo's unused revolving credit facilities covering potential borrowings aggregate $2.75 billion and $3.5 billion, respectively. The 1997 facilities expire in 2002. These credit facilities exist largely to support the issuances of short-term borrowings and are available for general corporate purposes.

At year-end 1997 and 1996, $2.1 billion and $3.5 billion, respectively, of short-term borrowings were classified as long-term debt, reflecting PepsiCo's intent and ability, through the existence of the unused credit facilities, to refinance these borrowings.

The annual maturities of long-term debt through 2002 are: 1998-$2.1 billion, 1999-$939 million, 2000-$746 million, 2001-$353 million and 2002-$330 million.

Intracompany Analysis of Long-Term Debt: PepsiCo

Listed below are three specific questions that relate to PepsiCo's long-term financial flexibility, risk, and liquidity. You can ask these same three questions (as well as others) when evaluating any company's long-term debt and interest expense using intracompany analysis. Under each question, we explain how financial analysis helps external users answer these questions.

Question #1: Is PepsiCo's Long-Term Financial Flexibility Reasonable?

To answer this question, we first examine PepsiCo's comparative balance sheets to see how much of its total assets (which is equal to total liabilities plus shareholders' equity) is financed by long-term debt. In Chapter 7 we discussed the debt ratio (total liabilities ÷ total assets) as a measure of a company's financial flexibility.

 What is the debt ratio in 1997 and 1996 for PepsiCo, and how has the company's financial flexibility changed?

A variation of the debt ratio is the debt-to-equity ratio, which is computed by dividing total liabilities by total shareholders' equity. Yet another variation results from dividing *long-term* debt by shareholders' equity. This ratio is a better measure of a company's long-term financial flexibility because its numerator includes only long-term debt.

The lower the ratio is, the more likely a company can finance needed capital by issuing long-term debt, thereby increasing its leverage (as we discussed earlier in the chapter). We compute this ratio for PepsiCo as follows:

	1997	1996
Long-term debt	$\dfrac{\$4,946}{\$6,936} = 0.71$	$\dfrac{\$8,174}{\$6,623} = 1.23$
Shareholders' equity		

This analysis shows that PepsiCo has substantially reduced its reliance on long-term debt from 1997 to 1996 in financing its activities and that, therefore, its financial flexibility has increased.

Question #2: Can PepsiCo Pay Its Interest Obligations Each Period?

External users often use the times interest earned ratio (also called the interest coverage ratio) to evaluate a company's ability to meet its interest obligations through its annual earnings. It is a measure of the financial risk of creditors' (especially long-term creditors') investments in the company's long-term debt. A user typically uses income before income taxes plus interest expense as the numerator of the times interest earned ratio. As you can see from Exhibit 22-4, PepsiCo's income statement includes a section called "income from discontinued operations." We will discuss this section in Chapter 24. But for now, be aware that when a company's income statement includes both income from continuing operations and income from discontinued operations, the user typically adds interest expense to pretax income from continuing operations in the numerator. Excluding income from discontinued operations is appropriate because it generally does not affect the long-run interest-paying ability of a company. As a general rule, the higher the times interest earned ratio, the better able the company is to meet its interest obligations. We compute the ratio for PepsiCo as follows:

Times Interest Earned = (Income from Continuing Operations before Income Taxes + Interest Expense) ÷ Interest Expense

1997   ($2,309 + $478) ÷ $478 = 5.83

1996:   ($1,566 + $565) ÷ $565 = 3.77

So you see that PepsiCo's interest coverage has improved significantly in 1997 as compared to 1996; therefore, this aspect of its financial risk has decreased.

Continued interest *payments* (which are legal commitments) are endangered by low earnings over an extended period of time. Because both earnings and interest *expense* are based on accrual accounting, the times interest earned ratio is slightly inaccurate, since it should include only cash outflows for interest and cash inflows from earnings. Such refinements are usually not made to this ratio, however.

Question #3: Does PepsiCo Have Sufficient Long-Term Liquidity?

One way to evaluate a company's long-term liquidity is to examine its cash flow obligations compared to its operating cash flows. From the discussion in Note 10 of Exhibit 22-4, notice that PepsiCo has total maturities of long-term debt over the next *five* years of $4.468 billion ($2.1 billion + $939 million + $746 million + $353 million + $330 million). Its cash flows from operating activities for the past *three* years total $9.253 billion (we do not show these yearly amounts in Exhibit 22-4). Although we are comparing *past* cash flows to *future* obligations, these amounts suggest that PepsiCo would be able to pay off its long-term debts as they become due even if it did not borrow any additional amounts. Furthermore, in Note 10 PepsiCo discloses that it has $2.75 billion of unused revolving credit at the end of 1997. This analysis suggests that PepsiCo has sufficient long-term liquidity.

 What information would you need to help you decide whether PepsiCo could afford to buy Coca-Cola Company *(ignore antitrust considerations)?*

www.coca-cola.com

Leases

8 *What is a lease? What is a capital lease, and what impact does it have on a lessee's financial statements?*

Many companies choose to lease an asset rather than buy it. A **lease** is an agreement giving the right to use property, plant, or equipment without transferring legal ownership of the item. For instance, when Unlimited Decadence leases a computer from IBM, it acquires the right to use the computer for the period of the lease, but it does not acquire legal ownership. IBM remains the legal owner of the computer. The **lessee** is the company that acquires the right to use the item. The **lessor** is the company that gives up the use of the item. For instance, Unlimited Decadence is the lessee and IBM is the lessor in this example. In a lease, the lessee agrees to make periodic lease payments to the lessor for the right to use the leased item.

There are several reasons a company might lease instead of buy. First, a lease may not require a down payment to acquire the use of an asset, so a lessee with a cash shortage may be able to save its cash. Second, a lease may allow a lessee to avoid the risk of obsolescence, since the leased item may be returned to the lessor at the end of the lease. Third, if the lessee is a corporation, it may obtain a tax benefit because it can take a tax deduction on its income tax return for the total lease payment.

Before we discuss how a company accounts for leases, you should understand the similarities between leasing an asset and purchasing an asset on credit. For example, if a company purchases a building for use in its operations by issuing a 30-year mortgage, it records an asset (the building) and a long-term liability (the mortgage payable). Although the company owns the building, the mortgage company has a legally secured interest in the building to protect its financial interests.

Now suppose another company leases a building for 30 years for use in its operations. It does not acquire legal ownership of the building but agrees to make lease payments for 30 years. In both the mortgage and the lease situations, the company purchasing the building and the company leasing the building will each use the building in its operations, and each is committed to making payments for 30 years. External users of financial statements usually are not concerned with the legal differences between a purchase and a lease. In the lease situation, it is *not* appropriate for the lessee to leave the asset and the liability off its balance sheet just because it does not "legally" own the building. Instead, the lessee should report that it has an asset because it has the use of the building for 30 years, and it should report a liability because it has a 30-year commitment to make lease payments. In other words, a lessee's financial statements are more helpful to external users if the statements report on the economic substance of the transaction. That is, the purchaser of the building and the lessee of the building both have engaged in similar economic transactions. Therefore, the lessee should record both an asset and a long-term liability, in the same way as does the purchaser. This is an example of the accounting principle that states that **economic substance is more important than legal form**—the lessee records an asset that it does not legally own. However, some leases (such as when you rent an apartment) are short term, and the economic substance is *not* like a purchase.

There are two types of leases for financial reporting purposes, a capital lease and an operating lease. A lease is a **capital lease** if it transfers the risks and benefits of ownership from the lessor to the lessee. A lessee records an asset and a liability for a capital lease.[4]

---

[4]A lease transfers the risks and benefits of ownership if the lease agreement meets any one of the following criteria: (1) the lease transfers ownership to the lessee at the end of the lease, (2) the lease includes a bargain-purchase option, (3) the lease is for 75 percent or more of the economic life of the property, or (4) the present value of the lease payments is 90 percent or more of the market value of the property. The specific calculations are beyond the scope of this book.

On the other hand, a lease is an **operating lease** if it does *not* transfer the risks and benefits of ownership (such as the lease on an apartment). If a lease is an operating lease, the accounting is simple. The *lessee* records each lease payment as rent expense, which it reports as an operating expense on its income statement. The *lessor* records each lease payment as rent revenue, which it reports on its income statement. Note that the *lessor* includes the asset on its balance sheet under a title such as Property Leased to Others, records depreciation expense on the asset, and reports the depreciation expense as an operating expense on its income statement.

Capital Lease

If a lease is a capital lease, the lessee records an operating asset and a long-term liability. It records both the asset and the liability at the present value of the lease payments agreed to in the lease. Determining the interest rate to use in the present value calculation is complex, so we will always assume a rate. For example, suppose that Unlimited Decadence signs a capital lease for a computer with HiTech Company having the following terms:[5]

Lease date	January 1, 2000
Annual lease payments at end of year	$4,000
Life of lease	5 years
Interest rate	10%
Date of first payment	December 31, 2000

Unlimited Decadence computes the amount at which to record the asset and the liability as follows:

Present Value of Lease Payments = Periodic Lease Payment × Present Value of Annuity Factor for 5 Periods at 10%

= $4,000 × 3.7908 (from Table 20-2)

= $15,163 (rounded)

Unlimited Decadence (the lessee) records an asset and a liability on January 1, 2000, as follows:

Assets	=	**Liabilities**	+	**Stockholders' Equity**

Leased Property		Capital Lease Obligation	
15,163			15,163
(+)	(−)	(−)	(+)

Since Unlimited Decadence records an asset, it must depreciate the cost over the life of the lease. Assuming straight-line depreciation (and no residual value), the depreciation is $3,033 ($15,163 ÷ 5, rounded) for each year of the lease. On December 31, 2000, Unlimited Decadence records the depreciation as follows:

[5]Most leases require payments at the beginning of the lease, and often more frequently than once a year. These issues make the accounting procedures much more complex but do not change the basic issues we discuss in this chapter.

Assets		**=**	**Liabilities**	**+**	**Stockholders' Equity**

Leased Property				Depreciation Expense	
Bal 15,163	3,033			3,033	
Bal 12,130					
(+)	(−)			(+)	(−)

Unlimited Decadence reports the $12,130 ($15,163 cost − $3,033 accumulated depreciation) book value of the leased property[6] in the property, plant, and equipment section of its December 31, 2000 balance sheet. It reports the $3,033 depreciation expense on its 2000 income statement. Each year the company reports the same amount of depreciation expense and reduces the book value of the leased asset by $3,033.

Each $4,000 lease payment includes both interest and principal. Every year when Unlimited Decadence records the payment, it must separate the payment into the interest expense portion and the portion that reduces the lease obligation. It computes the yearly interest expense by multiplying the book value of the lease obligation at the beginning of the year by the interest rate. It reduces the lease obligation by the difference between the cash payment and the interest expense.

At the end of 2000, Unlimited Decadence computes its interest expense and reduction of lease obligation as follows:

$$\text{Interest Expense} = \text{Book Value of Lease Obligation} \times \text{Interest Rate}$$
$$\text{at Beginning of Year}$$

$$= \$15,163 \times 10\%$$

$$= \$1,516 \text{ (rounded)}$$

$$\text{Reduction of Lease Obligation} = \text{Cash Payment} - \text{Interest Expense}$$

$$= \$4,000 - \$1,516$$

$$= \$2,484$$

Unlimited Decadence records the lease payment on December 31, 2000, as follows:

Assets		**=**	**Liabilities**		**+**	**Stockholders' Equity**	

Cash			Capital Lease Obligation			Interest Expense	
	4,000		2,484	Bal 15,163		1,516	
				Bal 12,679			
(+)	(−)		(−)	(+)		(+)	(−)

The book value of the capital lease obligation now is $12,679 ($15,163 − $2,484). Unlimited Decadence reports the amount to be paid next year ($4,000) as a current liability and the remaining portion ($8,679) as a long-term liability on its December 31, 2000 balance sheet. The company reports the $1,516 interest expense on its 2000 income statement.

---

[6]Some companies record the accumulated depreciation in a separate contra account called Accumulated Depreciation on Leased Property. The contra-account balance then is subtracted from the Leased Property cost to determine the book value. Our method is less complex and conveys similar information.

It includes the interest paid in the cash flows from operating activities section, and reports the reduction of the capital lease obligation in the cash flows from financing activities section of its cash flow statement.

Each year, the company computes and records the interest expense and the reduction of the lease obligation in the same manner. For 2001, the interest expense is $1,268 ($12,679 × 10%, rounded), and the reduction of the lease obligation is $2,732 ($4,000 − $1,268). Using this method, the company will reduce the lease obligation to zero by the end of the lease life.

 Explain why the book value of the asset and the liability are not equal during each year (after the initial recording of the asset and the liability).

Impacts of Capital Lease Accounting

By recording a lease as a capital lease because the risks and benefits of ownership are transferred, a company's financial statements provide external users with better information to assess the profitability, financial flexibility, and operating capability of the company.

Recording an asset and a liability for a capital lease has a negative effect on the company's income in the first years of the lease because the interest expense and the depreciation expense are higher than the rent expense that it would record under an operating lease. (Later in the lease, the total expenses under the capital lease are lower than the rent expense because the interest expense is lower each year.) With a capital lease, the company records an asset, so the return on assets [(net income + interest expense) ÷ average total assets] is reduced. Since the income is reduced and the assets are increased, this financial reporting allows for more valid comparisons with companies that purchase their assets.

In regard to a company's financial flexibility, recording an asset and a liability for a capital lease also has a negative effect on the company's debt ratio (total liabilities ÷ total assets). The effect is negative because the numerator and the denominator increase by the same amount, thereby increasing the proportion of debt to assets. Again, this financial reporting allows for more valid comparisons with companies that purchase their assets.

 Suppose a company has assets of $200 and liabilities of $100. It enters into a capital lease with a value of $30. Compute the debt ratio before and after recording the capital lease.

In regard to a company's operating capability, recording an asset and a liability for a capital lease provides more information about the ability of the company to maintain a given level of operations. This financial reporting gives a better picture of the total property, plant, and equipment that the company uses in its operations and again helps with intercompany comparability.

Lessor Accounting for a Capital Lease

Although this is a chapter on long-term debt, we will briefly discuss the lessor's accounting for the asset involved in a capital lease. The lessor in a capital lease reports the "sale" of the asset on credit and a receivable, like a "mirror image" of the lessee's "purchase" and liability. Since the lessee records the payments to be *made* as a liability, to be consistent the lessor records the payments to be *received* as an asset. Since the lessee records the payments it makes on the lease as interest expense and a reduction in its liability, the lessor records the payments received as interest revenue and a reduction in its receivable. The difference between a sale using a lease and a typical credit sale is that the lessor offers credit for the term of the lease rather than for, say, 30 days.

Business Issues and Values

Many lessees have numerous leases that fail the criteria that would make them capital leases. Therefore, these are classified as operating leases. Two industries in which this is common are airlines and retailers. For its operating leases, a company must disclose the cash flows that it is obligated to make on those leases. It must disclose the amount it will pay each year for the next five years and the total amount it must pay for all years thereafter. An external user should examine this disclosure to see if the cash flows are significant. If so, the user can compute an approximate present value of the cash flows to determine the effect on the liabilities (and assets) of the company. To illustrate, Delta Airlines disclosed the following in its 1998 annual report:

www.delta-air.com

> At June 30, 1998, the Company's minimum rental commitments under capital leases (primarily aircraft) and noncancelable operating leases with initial or remaining terms of more than one year were as follows (in millions):

Years Ending June 30	Capital Leases	Operating Leases
1999	$100	$ 950
2000	67	950
2001	57	940
2002	57	960
2003	48	960
After 2003	71	10,360
Total minimum lease payments	$400	$15,120
Less: Amounts representing interest	88	
Present value of future minimum capital lease payments	312	
Less: Current obligations under capital leases	63	
Long-term capital lease obligations	$249	

Some aspects of this disclosure may surprise you. Delta's operating leases (which it does not report on its balance sheet) involve much higher cash flows than its capital leases. Its operating leases also appear to have longer lives than the capital leases. Note also that Delta reports the present value of the capital leases but not of the operating leases. To compute the present value of the operating leases, an external user has to discount the annual operating lease cash flow for each of the five years (and for the years after 2003) to its present value, and sum the present values to determine the total present value (as we did with capital budgeting in Chapter 20). To do so, the user has to assume the number of years after 2003 over which the remaining operating lease payments of $10.360 billion are to be made and also has to assume an interest rate. In its 1998 balance sheet, Delta disclosed that it had long-term debt of $1.533 billion and total noncurrent liabilities of $5.079 billion. Therefore, no matter what life and interest rate the external user selects, the present value of the operating leases represents a significant obligation for Delta and, if considered to be debt, would significantly affect the user's perception of the company's risk and financial flexibility.

Some companies also deliberately structure leases so that they fail the criteria for being a capital lease (thus the companies avoid recording their long-term lease liabilities). Such companies do this in the belief that external users will be "fooled" by the low amount of debt they report on their balance sheets and will therefore believe the companies have less risk. However, since each company must report the future cash flows for operating leases, external users can perform the present value analysis we just discussed and avoid being misled.

Mortgages Payable

Earlier we compared the purchase of a building (by signing a mortgage payable) with the lease of a building. Since accounting for a mortgage payable is similar to accounting for a lease obligation (and for a loan, as we discussed earlier in the chapter), we will briefly discuss mortgages here. A **mortgage payable** is a long-term liability for which the lender has a specific claim against an asset of the borrower. For example, most homeowners purchase their homes by issuing a mortgage. That is, they borrow the money from a lender, and the lender is assigned a secured claim on the home. A company also may acquire an asset through a mortgage. When a company acquires an asset in this way, it records the cost of the asset and the mortgage payable. The typical mortgage requires equal monthly payments (an annuity), and these payments are determined by a present value of an annuity calculation. Each mortgage payment consists of interest and of a reduction of the mortgage obligation. The company computes and records the interest expense and the liability reduction in the same way as we discussed for lease payments, except on a monthly basis.

Deferred Income Taxes

In earlier chapters, for simplicity we assumed that the amount of a corporation's income tax expense for a period is the same as its income tax obligation for that period. The income tax *expense* is the amount that the corporation reports on its income statement, whereas the income tax *obligation* is the amount that the corporation must pay the government(s) for that year. In our discussion for some topics, we explained that the rules for computing taxable income are different from the rules for determining pretax accounting income. One of the major differences is depreciation. In Chapter 21 we explained that most corporations use the straight-line method for financial reporting but use the Modified Accelerated Cost Recovery System (MACRS), a type of accelerated depreciation, for income tax reporting. When a corporation uses these methods, its pretax accounting income is different from its taxable income in any given year. Although the two amounts of depreciation in any year are different, the *total* depreciation expense over the life of the asset is the same (assuming a zero residual value). Therefore, the yearly difference in the depreciation amounts computed by these two methods is known as a temporary difference.

A **temporary difference** occurs when a corporation records an expense (or a revenue) for financial reporting in a period different from that used for income tax reporting, but the total lifetime expense (or revenue) is the same for both. In the case of depreciation expense, in the early years of an asset's life the MACRS depreciation expense that a corporation reports on its income tax return is usually *greater* than the depreciation expense that the corporation reports on its income statement. This causes taxable income to be *less* than its pretax accounting income, as we discussed in Chapter 21. However, in future years the temporary difference reverses, and the corporation's MACRS depreciation expense is *less* than the income statement depreciation expense. This causes its taxable income to be *greater* than its pretax accounting income. These *taxable differences* in future years will cause the corporation to owe additional taxes because of the higher taxable income. **Deferred Tax Liability** is the account a corporation uses to report on its balance sheet the amount of its future additional income taxes resulting from taxable temporary differences.

To determine its deferred tax liability at the end of a given year, a corporation multiplies the income tax rate times its expected future taxable temporary differences.[7] It then makes an adjustment to its beginning deferred tax liability. (These computations are beyond the scope of this book.) The corporation's income tax expense is the sum of its current income tax obligation (based on its taxable income for the year) and its deferred taxes for the year. For example, if for 2000 Barbre Corporation's income tax obligation is $9,000 and the increase in its deferred tax liability is $480, the corporation's income tax expense is $9,480, and it records these amounts as follows:

9 *Why do deferred income taxes arise, and how does a corporation report them in its financial statements?*

---

[7]If the tax rate has been changed (e.g., by the U.S. Congress) for future years, a corporation uses that new rate to compute the amount of its deferred tax liability.

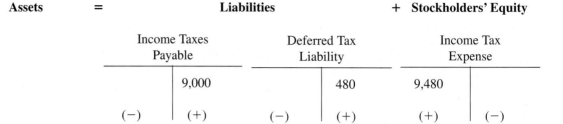

Assets	=	Liabilities		+	Stockholders' Equity

Income Taxes Payable		Deferred Tax Liability		Income Tax Expense	
	9,000		480	9,480	
(−)	(+)	(−)	(+)	(+)	(−)

Barbre Corporation reports the $9,480 income tax expense on its 2000 income statement, the $9,000 income taxes payable as a current liability (assuming that it did not make any interim tax payments for 2000), and the $480 deferred tax liability as a long-term liability on its December 31, 2000 balance sheet.[8]

A corporation also may have a deferred tax asset. **Deferred Tax Asset** is the account a corporation uses to report on its balance sheet the amount by which its future income taxes will be reduced by deductible temporary differences. For example, as we discussed in Chapter 14, using GAAP, a company records warranty expense in the period of the sale. However, the corporation deducts the warranty costs on its income tax return when it pays them. Therefore, the amount of the warranty expense in the period of the sale is usually *greater* than the warranties paid. However, in future years the temporary difference reverses and the corporation's warranty payments are *greater* than the income statement warranty expense, causing its taxable income to be *less* than its pretax accounting income. These *deductible differences* in future years will cause the corporation to owe fewer taxes because of its lower taxable income.

External User Perspective: Analysis of Deferred Tax Reporting

Deferred income tax reporting is controversial. Typically, over time a corporation increases its depreciable assets either because it is growing larger or because it replaces its assets at a higher cost. When these assets increase, the MACRS depreciation expense that the corporation reports on its income tax return each year is consistently higher than the depreciation expense it reports on its income statement. Therefore, the corporation's taxable income each year is *always* less than its pretax accounting income, so that the deferred tax liability accumulates and will not be paid. Another way of saying this is that the corporation's deferred income tax liability will decrease only if its income tax obligation is greater than its income tax expense; this will occur only when its investment in depreciable assets decreases over time. For this reason, many external users of financial statements argue that deferred income taxes are not a "real" liability and that the deferred tax procedures should *not* be used. Instead, they suggest that the income tax expense a corporation reports on its income statement should be equal to its income tax obligation for the period. So these external users ignore a corporation's deferred income taxes in their evaluation of its profitability, financial flexibility, and liquidity.

Note also that, although a corporation reports deferred taxes as a liability (or asset) on its ending balance sheet, they are very different from any other liability (asset)—there is no other entity that claims that the corporation owes it money. Specifically, the federal government does not have a claim because the corporation has filed its tax return and has paid (or will pay) any amounts it owes for the current year.

 Use Exhibit 22-4 to find the difference in PepsiCo's debt ratio in 1997 if you exclude deferred income taxes from its liabilities.

---

[8]Many other temporary differences cause deferred taxes. A corporation also may have *permanent* differences between its taxable income and its pretax accounting income; these do *not* cause deferred taxes. As a result, accounting for income taxes is very complex, and we discuss only the basic issues here.

Retirement Benefits

A person who retires usually has three sources of retirement income: savings, social security, and a pension. Many companies, especially larger ones, have pension plans for their employees. A **pension plan** is an agreement by a company to provide income to its employees after they retire. A **defined-contribution plan** specifies the amount that the company must contribute to the plan each year while its employees work. A **defined-benefit plan** specifies the amount that the company must pay to its employees each year during their retirement. For example, a retired employee might receive an annual pension income under a defined-benefit plan based on the following formula:

$$\text{Annual Pension Income} = \text{Average of Last 5 Years' Pay} \times \underset{\text{of Service}}{\text{Number of Years}} \times 0.02$$

Therefore, an employee who worked for 40 years for a company and had an average salary of $100,000 for the last 5 years of service receives $80,000 per year ($100,000 × 40 × 0.02) during retirement until death.

For a defined-benefit plan, to pay each employee's future pension benefits, a company must pay ("fund") an annual amount to a "funding agency" during each year that the employee works. The funding agency (e.g., insurance company) is responsible for safeguarding and investing the assets of the pension plan and for making payments to the retired employees. An *actuary*, who is trained to calculate risks and premiums, determines the amount that the company contributes. The computations involve present value analyses and are based on assumptions about future pay rates, life expectancies, and expected rates of return.

The agreement to pay future retirement benefits causes the company to incur a pension expense each year that the employee works. However, in some cases, a company pays

10 *What is a defined-benefit pension plan, and how does a corporation account for it?*

How does a defined-benefit pension plan add to the enjoyment of this couple?

CHAPTER 22 *Long-Term Debt and Other Financing Issues*

less to the funding agency in a given year than it records as pension expense. This is because GAAP defines the amount of the expense whereas federal law specifies the amount the company must pay. When this occurs, the company records a pension obligation. For instance, if Crabtree Company computes its yearly pension expense to be $8,900 but pays only $8,000 to its funding agency, it records a $900 liability as follows:

Assets		=	Liabilities		+	Stockholders' Equity	
Cash			Pension Obligation			Pension Expense	
	8,000			900		8,900	
(+)	(−)		(−)	(+)		(+)	(−)

Crabtree Company reports the $8,900 pension expense as an operating expense on its income statement and reports the $900 pension obligation as a long-term liability on its ending balance sheet. Alternatively, the company could pay more than the pension expense, in which case it will decrease any previous pension obligation (or, if none, record a pension asset).

The computation of pension expense is very complex and beyond the scope of this book. However, it is important for external users to know that the obligation of the company to its employees for the work they have done to date, called the **projected benefit obligation** (computed using present value techniques), is *not* reported as a liability on the company's balance sheet. Also the **assets of the pension plan** that will be used to pay the retirement benefits are *not* reported as assets on the company's balance sheet (because they are under the control of the "funding agency"). The company discloses both amounts in the notes to its financial statements, however. External users should look at the difference between these two amounts because it may affect their evaluation of the company's liquidity, risk, and financial flexibility. For example, if the projected benefit obligation exceeds the pension plan assets, the company will have to increase its payments to the plan in future years, thereby increasing its risk and reducing its financial flexibility.

Companies that provide a pension plan for their employees may also provide other retirement benefits, often referred to as OPEBs (other postemployment benefits). Healthcare benefits are the most common form of OPEB, but some companies also provide such items as dental and life insurance benefits. A company that provides OPEBs to its employees also computes and records an OPEB expense. Usually the company does not "fund" these other retirement benefits, so that its OPEB obligation exceeds the OPEB assets (zero in this case).

How Long-Term Debt Transactions Affect the Cash Flow Statement

A company generally reports long-term debt transactions involving cash in the financing activities section of its cash flow statement. It reports the cash received from the issuance of notes payable or bonds payable—whether issued at face value, at a premium, or at a discount—as a cash inflow from financing activities. It reports the cash paid to retire notes payable and bonds payable as cash outflows for financing activities. It includes the cash paid for interest, however, in the operating activities section. Even though the interest paid is related to a financing activity, GAAP requires it to be included as an operating cash flow because the interest expense is included in the company's income statement. A lease payment includes both interest and principal. Thus, a company includes the interest portion of a lease payment as a cash outflow for operating activities and the principal portion (the reduction of the lease obligation) as a cash outflow for financing activities. A company includes income tax payments and pension payments as cash outflows for operating activities.

If a company's interest payments are less than its interest expense (because of accrued interest), explain whether the difference is added to or subtracted from net income in computing the net cash flow from operating activities.

Summary

At the beginning of the chapter we asked you several questions. During the chapter, we asked you to STOP and answer some additional questions to build your knowledge about specific issues. Be sure you answered these additional questions. Below are the questions from the beginning of the chapter, with a brief summary of the key points relating to the answers. Use your creative and critical thinking skills to expand on these key points to develop more complete answers to the questions and to determine what other questions you have that might lead you to learn more about the issues.

1 How does a corporation compute the periodic payment, the interest expense, and the repayment of the principal on a loan?

The periodic payment is the amount of an annuity that has a present value equal to the amount borrowed; it is computed as follows:

Periodic Payment = Amount Borrowed ÷ Present Value of Annuity Factor Based on the Interest Rate and the Life of the Loan

The interest expense is computed as follows:

Interest Expense = Periodic Interest Rate × Book Value of Loan at the Beginning of the Period

The repayment of principal is computed as follows:

Repayment of Principal = Periodic Payment − Interest Expense

2 What is a bond, what are its characteristics, and why does a corporation issue bonds?

A bond is a type of note in which a company agrees to pay the holder the face value at the maturity date and to pay interest periodically at a specified rate on the face value. The face value (also called the *par value*) is the amount of money that the issuer promises to pay on the maturity date. The maturity date is the date on which the issuer of the bond agrees to pay the face value to the holder. The contract rate is the rate at which the issuer of the bond pays interest each period until the maturity date. A bond certificate is a legal document that shows the face value, the annual interest rate, and the maturity date. The main reason managers of a company (corporation) may decide to issue bonds instead of common stock is that the earnings available to the common stockholders can be increased through leverage. Leverage is the use of borrowing by a company to increase the return to common stockholders. If a corporation can borrow money by issuing bonds and use the money to invest in a project that provides greater income than the interest that must be paid on the bonds, the corporation and its stockholders will be better off (they will earn a higher return).

3 What are the factors that affect long-term interest rates?

Several factors affect long-term interest rates, including the policies of the Federal Reserve Board (whose policies affect the supply and demand for money in the national economy), federal regulations, and the budget surplus or deficit of the federal government. Long-term interest rates for corporations, however, include three *primary* factors. First, interest rates include the risk-free rate, which is the rate that a borrower would pay, and a lender would receive, when there is no risk of default by the borrower and when no inflation is expected. Most borrowing by the U.S. government is considered to be risk free because the government will not default. Second, interest rates include the expected inflation rate, so the borrower pays additional interest to compensate for the expected inflation over the life of the borrowing. Third, interest rates include the risk premium, which is the additional interest that the borrower pays when there is a possibility that it may default.

4 **Why does a corporation issue bonds at less than or more than their face value?**

When a company decides to issue bonds, it usually deals with a securities broker (or an investment banker). The broker and the company agree on a price for the bonds, and the broker pays the company for them. The broker and the company base this selling price on the terms of the bond issue and the components of the long-term interest rate. They determine the rate that they believe best reflects current market conditions. This market rate of interest is called the *yield* and is the rate at which the bonds are issued. The yield on a bond issue may be different from the contract rate set by the company. The managers of the company set the contract rate, whereas the marketplace determines the yield. If the yield is more than the contract rate, the company will receive a selling price (and the purchasers of the bonds will pay) less than the face value of the bonds; that is, the company will sell the bonds at a discount. Alternatively, if the yield is less than the contract rate, the company will receive a selling price (and the purchasers of the bonds will pay) more than the face value of the bonds; that is, the company will sell the bonds at a premium.

5 **How does the interest expense each period compare with the interest paid in that period when a corporation issues bonds at a discount or a premium?**

Because a company issuing bonds incurs a cost (yield) either higher (for bonds sold at a discount) or lower (for bonds sold at a premium) than the contract rate, the interest expense recorded in each semiannual period is different from the interest paid. When a company sells bonds at a discount, its interest expense each period is higher than the interest it pays that period. When a company sells bonds at a premium, its interest expense each period is lower than the interest it pays that period. The difference between the interest expense and the interest paid is the amount of the discount or premium that the company amortizes each period.

6 **What are zero-coupon bonds, and how does a corporation account for the interest on them?**

Zero-coupon bonds are bonds that pay no interest each period. That is, the only cash flows associated with the bonds are the amount borrowed (which is less than the face value of the bonds) and the payment of the face value on the maturity date. Zero-coupon bonds always sell at a discount. The discount is the difference between the selling price and the face value. A company computes the annual interest expense by multiplying the annual yield by the book value of the bonds at the beginning of the year. Since the company pays no cash for interest each year, it records the annual interest expense as an increase in the book value of the bonds payable each year, so that the book value on the maturity date is equal to the face value (the amount the borrower pays the lender).

7 **How do long-term debt and interest expense disclosures help external users evaluate a corporation?**

External users evaluate a company's long-term debt and interest expense disclosures to help them evaluate its long-term financial flexibility, risk, and liquidity. A company's financial flexibility refers to its ability to raise additional capital. Financial flexibility enables a company to increase (or reduce) its operating activities in response to changing economic conditions. A company's risk is a measure of the uncertainty of its future performance. A company's long-term liquidity relates to the amount of cash it will generate over the long run to pay off its liabilities as they become due. As with other parts of financial statements, external users evaluate long-term debt by performing intracompany and intercompany analysis—through the use of percentage analysis (trend analysis and ratio analysis).

8 **What is a lease? What is a capital lease, and what impact does it have on a lessee's financial statements?**

A lease is an agreement giving a company the right to use property, plant, or equipment without transferring legal ownership of the item. The *lessee* is the company that acquires the right to use the item. The *lessor* is the company that gives up the use of the item. A capital lease is a lease in which the risks and benefits of ownership are transferred from the lessor to the lessee. If a lease is a capital lease, the lessee reports an operating asset and a long-term liability on its balance sheet at the present value of the lease payments agreed to in the lease. The company computes the amount at which to record the asset and the liability as follows:

Present Value of = Periodic Lease Payment × Present Value of Annuity Factor Based on
Lease Payments   the Interest Rate and the Life of the Lease

The lessee must depreciate the cost of the asset over the life of the lease. It also must separate the lease payment into the interest expense portion and the portion that reduces the lease obligation, as follows:

Interest Expense = Book Value of Lease Obligation at Beginning of Year × Interest Rate

Reduction of Lease Obligation = Cash Payment − Interest Expense

The lessee reports the depreciation expense and the interest expense related to the lease on its income statement.

9 **Why do deferred income taxes arise, and how does a corporation report them in its financial statements?**

Deferred taxes arise because a temporary difference occurs when a corporation records an expense (or a revenue) for financial reporting in a period different from that used for income tax reporting, but the total lifetime expense (or revenue) is the same for both. A common type of temporary difference involves depreciation expense. In the early years of an asset's life, the MACRS depreciation expense that a corporation reports on its income tax return is usually greater than the depreciation expense that the corporation reports on its income statement. However, in future years the temporary difference reverses and the corporation's MACRS depreciation expense is less than the income statement depreciation expense, causing its taxable income to be greater than its pretax accounting income. These taxable differences in future years will cause the corporation to owe additional taxes because of the higher taxable income. Deferred Tax Liability is the account that a corporation uses to report on its balance sheet the amount of its future additional income taxes resulting from taxable temporary differences. To determine its deferred tax liability at the end of a given year, a corporation multiplies the income tax rate times its expected future taxable temporary differences. It then makes an adjustment to its beginning deferred tax liability. A corporation also may have deductible temporary differences (e.g., warranty costs). Deferred Tax Asset is the account that a corporation uses to report on its balance sheet the amount by which its future income taxes will be reduced by deductible temporary differences. The corporation's income tax expense reported on its income statement is the sum of its current income tax obligation (based on its taxable income for the year) and its deferred taxes for the year.

10 **What is a defined-benefit pension plan, and how does a corporation account for it?**

A defined-benefit pension plan is an agreement that specifies the amount a company must pay to its employees each year during their retirement. For this plan, the company pays an annual amount to a funding agency, which is responsible for safeguarding the assets and paying the retirement benefits. The company records the difference between its annual pension expense and the amount it pays to the funding agency as an increase (decrease) in its long-term pension obligation, which the company reports as a long-term liability on its balance sheet. The company discloses the projected benefit obligation and the pension plan assets in the notes to its financial statements.

Key Terms

assets of the pension plan *(p. 822)*
bond *(p. 799)*
bond certificate *(p. 799)*
book value *(p. 798)*
callable bonds *(p. 809)*
capital lease *(p. 814)*
contract rate *(p. 799)*
deferred tax asset *(p. 820)*
deferred tax liability *(p. 819)*
defined-benefit plan *(p. 821)*
defined-contribution plan *(p. 821)*

economic substance is more important than legal form *(p. 814)*
effective interest method *(p. 807)*
expected inflation rate *(p. 803)*
face value *(p. 799)*
financial flexibility *(p. 810)*
interest expense *(p. 797)*
lease *(p. 814)*
lessee *(p. 814)*
lessor *(p. 814)*
leverage *(p. 800)*

Appendix: Accounting for Bonds That Are Sold at a Discount or Premium and That Pay Interest Semiannually

In the chapter we discussed why companies issue bonds at a discount or at a premium—the yield on the bonds is different from the contract rate. We also illustrated the accounting for a zero-coupon bond, for which a company incurs interest expense each year but does not pay any interest until the maturity date. In this appendix, we discuss how a company accounts for bonds payable that it sells at a discount or a premium and that pay interest semiannually.

Calculating the Selling Price of Bonds

We can calculate the selling price of a bond issue that pays interest each semiannual period using a present value computation when we know the maturity date, face value, contract rate, and yield. The **selling price** is the present value of the cash flows that the company agrees to pay under the terms of the bond issue. A bond issue has two cash flows: (1) the face value paid on the maturity date and (2) the semiannual interest paid on each interest payment date. In "present value language," the face value is a *single future amount,* and the semiannual interest payments are an *annuity.* The selling price is computed as follows:

Selling Price of Bond Issue = Present Value of Face Value + Present Value of Interest Payments

The present value of the face value is computed as follows:

Present Value of Face Value = Face Value × Present Value of $1 Factor

Remember that we list the present value of $1 factors in Table 20-1 at the end of Chapter 20. Also, you need to understand that the company pays interest payments semiannually and computes the amount of the interest paid by multiplying the face value by half the contract rate. It computes the present value of the interest payments as follows:

Present Value of Interest Payments = Periodic Interest Payment × Present Value of Annuity Factor

We list the present value of annuity factors in Table 20-2 at the end of Chapter 20. The present value factors in each of the preceding equations are based on the *yield* and the life of the bonds. Recall from our earlier discussion that the yield on the bonds is the market rate of interest when the bonds are *issued.* The yield is the cost to the company of the money it borrows, and also is the return that will be earned on the purchase price by the purchasers of the bonds. Although bond yields are stated in terms of annual rates, the actual yield for each interest period is *half* the annual yield because bonds pay interest semiannually. Since the yield is stated in terms of a semiannual rate, the life of the bonds also must be stated in semiannual periods. These items are computed as follows:

Semiannual Yield = Annual Yield ÷ 2

Number of Semiannual Periods = Life of Bonds in Years × 2

Thus, the company discounts the cash payments that it agrees to make for the bonds at the semiannual yield for the number of semiannual periods in the life of the bonds.

Bonds Issued at a Discount

When a company sells bonds at a discount, the yield earned by investors is more than the contract rate. We illustrate the accounting for bonds issued at a discount by assuming that Unlimited Decadence issues bonds with the following terms:

Date of sale	January 1, 2000
Face value	$100,000
Contract rate	10%
Interest payment dates	June 30 and December 31
Maturity date	December 31, 2003

We use a short life of 4 years to simplify the calculations. However, companies typically issue bonds with much longer lives. For example, IBM recently issued $850 million of bonds with a 100-year life!

www.ibm.com

The selling price of Unlimited Decadence's 10% bonds is the present value of the future cash payments that it has agreed to make. These payments are the $100,000 face value on the maturity date and a $5,000 [$100,000 × (10% ÷ 2)] interest payment every 6 months. The $100,000 is a single future amount, and the $5,000 semiannual interest payments are an annuity.

If Unlimited Decadence sells the bonds to yield 12%, it discounts the cash payments at 6% (12% ÷ 2) per semiannual period for 8 (4 years × 2) semiannual periods. The selling price of this bond issue is $93,789, computed as follows:

Present Value of Face Value = Face Value × Present Value of $1 Factor for 8 Periods at 6%

= $100,000 × 0.6274 (from Table 20-1)

= $62,740

Present Value of Interest Payments = Periodic Interest Payment × Present Value of Annuity Factor for 8 Periods at 6%

= $5,000 × 6.2098 (from Table 20-2)

= $31,049

Selling Price of Bond Issue = Present Value of Face Value + Present Value of Interest Payments

= $62,740 + $31,049

= $93,789

In this case, Unlimited Decadence sells the bonds at a discount of $6,211, the difference between the $100,000 face value and the $93,789 selling price, because the yield is *higher* than the contract rate. The company has a cost of 12% (6% semiannually) on its borrowing, and the purchasers obtain a 12% return (6% semiannually) on their investment. Unlimited Decadence records the sale of these bonds at a discount on January 1, 2000, as follows:

Assets	=	**Liabilities**	+	**Stockholders' Equity**
Cash		Bonds Payable		
93,789		93,789		
(+) (−)		(−) (+)		

The $93,789 is the *book value* of the bonds payable on the date of their sale.[9]

Unlimited Decadence makes its first interest payment of $5,000 on June 30, 2000. This amount is *not* the interest expense for the period. For bonds sold at a discount (or premium), the company computes the **interest expense** by multiplying the book value of the bonds payable at the beginning of the period times half the annual yield. This way of computing interest expense is called the **effective interest method.** As we discussed earlier, when a company sells bonds at a discount, the interest expense is greater than the interest paid. Remember that Unlimited Decadence will pay $100,000 at the end of 4 years, not $93,789. Unlimited Decadence computes the interest expense for the first period (January 1 through June 30, 2000) to be $5,627.34, as follows:

$$\text{Interest Expense for Period} = \text{Book Value at Beginning of Period} \times (\text{Yield} \div 2)$$

$$= \$93,789 \times (12\% \div 2)$$

$$= \$5,627.34$$

Since the company has interest *expense* of $5,627.34 but *pays* interest of only $5,000, it increases its bond liability by $627.34. The process of increasing the bonds payable for the difference between the interest expense and the interest paid is called *amortizing* a portion of the $6,211 discount.[10] On June 30, 2000, Unlimited Decadence records the interest expense as follows:

Assets		=	Liabilities	+	Stockholders' Equity	
Cash			Bonds Payable		Interest Expense	
	5,000.00		Bal 93,789.00 627.34		5,627.34	
			Bal 94,416.34			
(+)	(−)		(−) (+)		(+)	(−)

Note that the discount amortization has *increased* the Bonds Payable book value to $94,416.34 ($93,789 + $627.34).

On December 31, 2000, Unlimited Decadence records its interest expense for the second semiannual period in the same way as we showed above. In this case, however, it computes the interest expense of $5,664.98 by multiplying the $94,416.34 book value of the bonds payable at the beginning of the second period by the 6% semiannual yield. Since it pays the interest of $5,000, it amortizes $664.98 ($5,664.98 − $5,000) of the discount as an increase in the bonds payable. Thus, the book value of the bonds payable is $95,081.32 ($94,416.34 + $664.98) at the end of 2000, and Unlimited Decadence reports this amount (rounded) as a long-term liability on its December 31, 2000 balance sheet as follows:

> *Long-term debt*
> 10% bonds payable (face value $100,000), due 12/31/03 $95,081

Note that the company reports the face value in parentheses or in the notes to the financial statements. The company reports $11,292 ($5,627.34 + $5,664.98, rounded) interest expense for the whole year in the "other items" section on its 2000 income statement. In Exhibit 22-5, we show the

---

[9]Some companies would instead record the Bonds Payable account at the face value ($100,000) and would then create a contra account called Discount on Bonds Payable for $6,211. These companies would subtract the contra-account balance from the Bonds Payable face value to determine the $93,789 book value of the bonds. Our method is less complex and conveys similar information.

[10]Some companies amortize the discount (or premium) using the *straight-line* method. Under this method, they allocate an equal portion of the discount (or premium) to interest expense each period and increase the bonds payable by that same amount each period. Because the interest expense under this method does not reflect the actual yield, we do not discuss it further.

Exhibit 22-5   Bond Calculations: Issued at a Discount

Date	Cash Paid[a]	Interest Expense[b]	Amortization of Discount[c]	Book Value of Bonds[d]
1/1/00				$ 93,789.00
6/30/00	$5,000.00	$5,627.34	$627.34	94,416.34
12/31/00	5,000.00	5,664.98	664.98	95,081.32
6/30/01	5,000.00	5,704.88	704.88	95,786.20
12/31/01	5,000.00	5,747.17	747.17	96,533.37
6/30/02	5,000.00	5,792.00	792.00	97,325.37
12/31/02	5,000.00	5,839.52	839.52	98,164.89
6/30/03	5,000.00	5,889.89	889.89	99,054.78
12/31/03	5,000.00	5,945.22[e]	945.22	100,000.00

[a]Face Value × (Annual Contract Rate ÷ Number of Interest Payments Each Year), or $100,000 × (10% ÷ 2)
[b](Annual Yield ÷ Number of Interest Payments Each Year) × Book Value of the Bonds at the Beginning of the Period (from previous line); at 6/30/00, (12% ÷ 2) × $93,789.00 = $5,627.34
[c]Interest Expense − Cash Paid; at 6/30/00, $5,627.34 − $5,000.00 = $627.34
[d]Book Value of Bonds (from previous line) + Amortization of Discount; at 6/30/00, $93,789.00 + $627.34 = $94,416.34
[e]Adjusted for rounding error of $1.93

calculations for the entire life of the bonds. Note that after the company has recorded its interest for the 8 semiannual periods, on the December 31, 2003 maturity date the book value is equal to the $100,000 face value. This is because Unlimited Decadence has amortized all of the discount. So the liability is equal to the amount that Unlimited Decadence must pay on that date.

Bonds Issued at a Premium

When a company sells bonds at a premium, the yield earned by investors is less than the contract rate. We illustrate the accounting for bonds issued at a premium by assuming the same information for the Unlimited Decadence bond issue in the previous example except that the yield now is 8%. Therefore, the company computes the $106,733.50 selling price by discounting the future cash flows using a 4% semiannual yield for 8 semiannual periods as follows:

Present Value of Face Value = Face Value × Present Value of $1 Factor for 8 Periods at 4%

= $100,000 × 0.7307 (from Table 20-1)

= $73,070

Present Value of Interest = Periodic Interest Payment × Present Value of Annuity Factor
Payments   for 8 Periods at 4%

= $5,000 × 6.7327 (from Table 20-2)

= $33,663.50

Selling Price of Bond Issue = Present Value of Face Value + Present Value of Interest Payments

= $73,070 + $33,663.50

= $106,733.50

In this case Unlimited Decadence sells the bonds at a premium of $6,733.50, the difference between the $106,733.50 selling price and the $100,000 face value, because the yield is *lower* than the contract rate. The company has a cost of 8% (4% semiannually) on its borrowing, and the purchasers obtain an 8% return (4% semiannually) on their investment. Unlimited Decadence records the sale of these bonds at a premium on January 1, 2000, as follows:

Assets	=	Liabilities	+	Stockholders' Equity

Cash	Bonds Payable
106,733.50	106,733.50
(+)　　(−)	(−)　　(+)

The $106,733.50 is the book value of the bonds payable.[11]

Unlimited Decadence makes its first $5,000 interest payment on June 30, 2000. It computes the interest expense by multiplying the book value of the bonds payable at the beginning of the period by half the annual yield. As we discussed earlier, when a company sells bonds at a premium, the interest expense is less than the interest paid. For Unlimited Decadence, the interest expense for the first period is $4,269.34 ($106,733.50 × 0.04, rounded). Since the company has interest *expense* of $4,269.34 but *pays* interest of $5,000, it amortizes the $730.66 difference (premium reduction) as a decrease in bonds payable. On June 30, 2000, Unlimited Decadence records the interest as follows:

Assets	=	Liabilities	+	Stockholders' Equity

Cash	Bonds Payable	Interest Expense
	Bal 106,733.50	
5,000.00	730.66	4,269.34
	Bal 106,002.84	
(+)　　(−)	(−)　　(+)	(+)　　(−)

Note that the premium amortization has decreased the Bonds Payable book value to $106,002.84 ($106,733.50 − $730.66).

On December 31, 2000, Unlimited Decadence records its interest for the second semiannual period in the same way as we showed above. In this case, however, it computes the interest expense to be $4,240.11 by multiplying the $106,002.84 book value of the bonds at the beginning of the

---

Exhibit 22-6　Bond Calculations: Issued at a Premium

Date	Cash Paid[a]	Interest Expense[b]	Amortization of Premium[c]	Book Value of Bonds[d]
1/1/00				$106,733.50
6/30/00	$5,000.00	$4,269.34	$730.66	106,002.84
12/31/00	5,000.00	4,240.11	759.89	105,242.95
6/30/01	5,000.00	4,209.72	790.28	104,452.67
12/31/01	5,000.00	4,178.11	821.89	103,630.78
6/30/02	5,000.00	4,145.23	854.77	102,776.01
12/31/02	5,000.00	4,111.04	888.96	101,887.05
6/30/03	5,000.00	4,075.48	924.52	100,962.53
12/31/03	5,000.00	4,037.47[e]	962.53	100,000.00

[a]Face Value × (Annual Contract Rate ÷ Number of Interest Payments Each Year), or $100,000 × (10% ÷ 2)
[b](Annual Yield ÷ Number of Interest Payments Each Year) × Book Value of the Bonds at the Beginning of the Period (from previous line); at 6/30/00, (8% ÷ 2) × $106,733.50 = $4,269.34
[c]Cash Paid − Interest Expense; at 6/30/00, $5,000.00 − $4,269.34 = $730.66
[d]Book Value of Bonds (from previous line) − Amortization of Premium; at 6/30/00, $106,733.50 − $730.66 = $106,002.84
[e]Adjusted for rounding error of $1.03

---

[11]Some companies would instead record the Bonds Payable account at the face value ($100,000) and would then create a Premium on Bonds Payable account for $6,733.50. The company adds the premium to the Bonds Payable face value to determine the $106,733.50 book value of the bonds. Our method is less complex and conveys similar information.

second period by the 4% semiannual yield. Since it pays interest of $5,000, it amortizes $759.89 ($5,000 − $4,240.11) of the premium as a decrease in the bonds payable. Thus, the book value of the bonds payable is $105,242.95 ($106,002.84 − $759.89) at the end of 2000, and Unlimited Decadence reports this amount (rounded) as a long-term liability on its December 31, 2000 balance sheet. The company reports $8,509 ($4,269.34 + $4,240.11, rounded) interest expense for the whole year on its 2000 income statement. In Exhibit 22-6, we show the calculations for the entire life of the bonds. Note that after the company has recorded its interest for the 8 semiannual periods, on the December 31, 2003 maturity date the book value is equal to the $100,000 face value. This is because Unlimited Decadence has amortized all the premium. So the liability is equal to the amount that Unlimited Decadence must pay on that date.

 What is the difference between the payments on a bond issued at face value and the payments on a bond issued at a premium or discount?

Integrated Business and Accounting Situations

Answer the Following Questions in Your Own Words

Testing Your Knowledge

22-1 What three concepts or principles affect how a company accounts for and reports on long-term debt in its financial statements?

22-2 Define the terms *bond, face value, maturity date, contract rate,* and *bond certificate.*

22-3 Explain what is meant by "leverage" (or trading on equity).

22-4 Explain how a company computes interest expense when it issues bonds at face value.

22-5 How does a company determine the amount of interest expense to accrue at the end of an accounting period when it issues bonds at face value?

22-6 Identify the three components that determine the yield on a bond issue.

22-7 Under what condition will a company sell a bond at a discount? at a premium?

22-8 When a company sells bonds at a discount, is its interest expense higher or lower than the interest paid? Why? How would your answer change if the company sold the bond issue at a premium?

22-9 For bonds sold at a discount or a premium, how does a company compute its interest expense?

22-10 What is meant by the phrase "amortizing a portion of the discount (or premium)" in regard to interest expense?

22-11 What are callable bonds, and how does a company record their retirement?

22-12 What is a lease? What is the difference between a lessee and a lessor?

22-13 When does a lessee company record an asset and a liability for a lease?

22-14 What is the difference between a capital lease and an operating lease?

22-15 How does a lessee company record a capital lease?

22-16 How does a lessee company compute the interest expense for a capital lease? How does this affect the lease obligation?

22-17 How does a lessor company account for a capital lease?

22-18 For income taxes, what is a temporary difference, a deferred tax liability, and a deferred tax asset?

22-19 For retirement benefits, what is a pension plan? a defined-benefit plan? Where does a company report the projected benefit obligation and the assets of its pension plan?

22-20 How does a company report its long-term debt transactions on its cash flow statement?

22-21 (Appendix). How does a company compute the selling price of a bond issue?

Applying Your Knowledge

22-22 On January 1, 2000, Allen Fritz borrowed $15,000 from a bank to buy a car. The loan has an interest rate of 8% and requires equal annual payments at the end of each year for the next three years.

Required: Determine the equal annual amounts that Fritz must pay at the end of each year for the next three years to repay the loan.

22-23 On January 1, 2000, Latriece Johnson borrowed $10,000 from her uncle to help finance her college education. She and her uncle sign a "contract" that charges her 6% interest and requires her to repay the loan in equal annual payments at the end of each year for the next four years.

Required: (1) Determine the equal annual amounts that Johnson must pay at the end of each year for the next four years to repay the loan.

(2) Prepare a schedule for each of the four years to show how much of each annual payment is for interest and how much is for principal. Use the following column headings: Year, Beginning Balance, Interest, Principal, Ending Balance.

22-24 The Underhill Ski Corporation has been operating at a very stable level, consistently earning $200,000 income before income taxes. The company is evaluating the possibility of expanding its operations to include snowboards. It has calculated that building a new plant would cost $1.2 million, and it estimates that pretax income would increase by $150,000 as a result of the expansion. The company currently has 100,000 shares of common stock held by stockholders. Its income tax rate is 40%. The company is considering whether to finance the expansion by selling bonds with a face value of $1.2 million and a 10% interest rate or by selling 60,000 additional shares of common stock for $20 per share to obtain the $1.2 million.

Required: (1) Compute the company's earnings per share under each method of financing.

(2) Which method of financing would you recommend? Explain your reasoning.

22-25 On January 1, 2000, Miles Shredding Machine Company issued 10%, 20-year bonds with a face value of $300,000 for $300,000. The bonds pay interest semiannually on June 30 and December 31.

Required: (1) How much interest expense does Miles record in 2000?

(2) What is the book value of the bonds on December 31, 2000? Show how the company reports this on its December 31, 2000 balance sheet.

22-26 The Martinez Company issued 12-year, zero-coupon bonds with a face value of $500,000 on January 1, 2000. The bonds were sold to yield 8%.

Required: (1) Compute the selling price of the bonds.

(2) Compute the interest expense for 2000 and 2001.

(3) What is the book value of the bonds on December 31, 2001?

22-27 The Weimer Company issued 7-year, zero-coupon bonds with a face value of $300,000 on January 1, 2000. The bonds were sold to yield 12%.

Required: (1) Compute the selling price of the bonds.

(2) Using T-accounts, record the interest expense for 2000 and 2001.

(3) What is the book value of the bonds on December 31, 2001?

22-28 The Porter Luggage Company has 9% bonds outstanding with a face value of $80,000. The bonds pay interest on June 30 and December 31. On July 1, 2000, when the bonds have a book value of $81,000, Porter calls them for $83,000.

Required: (1) Using T-accounts, record the retirement of the bonds.

(2) Show how Porter would report the resulting gain or loss on its 2000 income statement.

22-29 The Duran Furniture Company shows the following items in its 2000 and 2001 financial statements:

	2000	2001
Income before income taxes	$98,000	$104,000
Interest expense	10,000	16,000
Long-term debt, end of year	125,000	200,000
Stockholders' equity, end of year	150,000	200,000

Required: (1) Compute the (a) long-term debt to stockholders' equity ratio and (b) times interest earned ratio, for 2000 and 2001.

(2) Briefly discuss your ratio results in regard to the company's financial risk.

22-30 On January 1, 2000, Thompson Cement Company leased a machine from Hexad Equipment Company. The lease was a capital lease, and Thompson recorded the asset and the liability at $84,000 based on a 10% interest rate and a 5-year life. Thompson makes a lease payment of $22,159 at the end of each year. The company uses the straight-line depreciation method for the leased asset, and expects the asset to have no residual value.

Required: What are (1) the interest expense and (2) the depreciation expense for Thompson Cement Company for 2000?

22-31 Use the information in 22-30 but assume that Thompson classified the lease as an operating lease.

Required: (1) How much expense related to the lease will Thompson Cement Company record in 2000?

(2) Which company will report the machine on its balance sheet at the end of 2000? Why?

22-32 On January 1, 2000, Eton Horse Breeding Company leased a Mercedes from Elite Cars for the president's use. The lease specified that $30,000 was to be paid at the end of each year for five years. Eton classified the lease as a capital lease with an interest rate of 10%. It uses the straight-line method of depreciation with a zero residual value.

Required: (1) Show how Eton would report the depreciation expense and the interest expense for the lease on its 2000 income statement.

(2) Show how Eton would report the leased asset and the lease liability on its December 31, 2000 balance sheet.

(3) Briefly discuss how this lease affects Eton's risk, financial flexibility, and liquidity.

22-33 Holliday Company purchased a hotel for $360,000 and made a 20% down payment. It financed the remainder with a 20-year mortgage at 12%, with monthly payments. The present value of an annuity of 1% for 240 periods is 90.8194.

Required: (1) Compute the amount of the monthly mortgage payment.

(2) Using T-accounts, prepare entries to record the (a) purchase of the building, (b) first monthly payment, and (c) second monthly payment.

22-34 At the end of 2000, Lucero Child Care Corporation reported taxable income for the year of $27,000 on its income tax return. It is subject to a 40% income tax rate, and its 2000 income taxes will be paid in early 2000. For 2000, the company computed a $700 increase in its long-term deferred tax liability.

Required: (1) Using T-accounts, prepare the entry to record the company's income taxes for 2000.

(2) If the company had a beginning long-term deferred tax liability of $4,800, show how it would report its income tax obligations on its December 31, 2000 balance sheet.

22-35 Mullen Rafting Company operates a pension plan for the benefit of its employees. The company computed its pension expense for 2000 to be $60,000, but paid $58,000 to its funding agency at the end of the year.

Required: (1) Using T-accounts, prepare the entry to record the company's pension expense for 2000.

(2) Assuming the company had a pension liability of $14,000 at the beginning of 2000, show how it would report its pension liability on its December 31, 2000 balance sheet.

(3) Where would you find the amounts of the company's projected benefit obligation and the assets of its pension plan? What is your evaluation if its projected benefit obligation is greater than the pension plan assets?

22-36 (Appendix). Mark Paint Company issues 10-year, 10% bonds with a face value of $200,000 on January 1, 2000. The bonds pay interest semiannually.

Required: Compute the issuance price of the bonds if (1) the company sells the bonds to yield 12%, and (2) the company sells the bonds to yield 8%.

22-37 (Appendix). On January 1, 2000, Loveland Tractor Company issues 10-year, 9% bonds with a face value of $100,000. The bonds pay interest semiannually and are issued to yield 10%.

Required: (1) What is the selling price of the bonds? What is the amount of the discount?

(2) How much interest expense does the company record in 2000?

(3) Show how the company reports the book value of the bonds on its December 31, 2000 balance sheet.

22-38 (Appendix). Use the same information as in 22-37 except that Loveland Tractor Company issues the bonds to yield 6%.

Required: (1) What is the selling price of the bonds? What is the amount of the premium?
(2) How much interest expense does the company record in 2000?
(3) Show how the company reports the book value of the bonds on its December 31, 2000 balance sheet.

22-39 (Appendix). The James Wood Stove Company issued 2-year, 10% bonds with a face value of $100,000 for $96,535.50 on January 1, 2000. The bonds pay interest semiannually on June 30 and December 31, and were issued to yield 12%.

Required: (1) Using T-accounts, prepare all the entries related to the bonds over the 2-year life.
(2) Summarize how the company would report the cash flows on this bond issue in its cash flow statements over the 2-year life.

22-40 (Appendix). The Linjo Insecticide Company issued 2-year, 8% bonds with a face value of $400,000 for $414,873.60 on January 1, 2000. The bonds pay interest semiannually on June 30 and December 31 and were issued to yield 6%.

Required: (1) Using T-accounts, prepare all the entries related to the bonds over the 2-year life.
(2) Summarize how the company would report the cash flows on the bond issue in its cash flow statements over the 2-year life.

Making Evaluations

22-41 At a board of directors meeting of Temple Battery Company to discuss the issuance of bonds with a face value of $100,000, the following comments were made:

▶ "At current market rates, I think the bonds will sell to yield 10%. Therefore, we should have a contract rate of 11% so that the bonds will sell at a premium. Like anyone else, investors view premiums as favorable, and we should do anything we can to get favorable reactions."

▶ "I agree that the yield will be 10%, but I think we should have a contract rate of 8% so that the bonds will sell at a discount. We all know people like to get a good deal, and if they can buy the bonds for less than face value, I'm sure the bonds will sell very easily."

▶ "If the yield is 10%, we should have a contract rate of 10%. Since we need exactly $100,000 to finance our expansion, that is the best alternative."

Required: Critically evaluate each of the above comments.

22-42 The Byrne Bus Company is planning to acquire some machinery. It is considering three methods of acquiring the machinery, which has a 6-year life and no residual value:

(a) Buy the machinery for $50,000, pay $10,000 down, and borrow the balance from a bank at 10% for 6 years. The company will pay interest on December 31 of each year.
(b) Lease the machinery under a 6-year lease, which it would classify as a capital lease. The lease would require a payment of $15,000 at the end of each year. The leased asset would revert back to the lessor at the end of the lease.
(c) Lease the machinery under a 1-year lease, which it would classify as an operating lease. The company could renew the lease each year for 5 more years. The lease payment, which is due when the lease is signed, is $15,000.

Required: (1) Prepare an analysis (using assumptions that you think are appropriate) of the cash flows the company would pay over the 6 years under each alternative.
(2) Explain how each of the alternatives would affect the company's financial statements.
(3) Which alternative would you recommend?

www.wal-mart.com

22-43 Wal-Mart reported the following amounts in its 1998 financial statements (in millions):

Jan. 31	1998	1997
Cash and cash equivalents	$ 1,447	$ 883
Total assets	45,384	39,604
Total shareholders' equity	18,503	17,143

	1998	1997	1996
Interest expense	$ 555	$ 629	$ 692
Income before income taxes	5,719	4,877	4,359
Net income	3,526	3,056	2,740
Net cash provided by operating activities	7,123	5,930	2,383
Net cash used in investing activities	(4,421)	(2,068)	(3,332)
Net cash (used in) provided by financing activities	(2,138)	(3,062)	987

Annual maturities of long-term debt during the next five years are as follows:

Fiscal years ending January 31	Annual Maturity
1999	$1,039
2000	815
2001	2,018
2002	52
2003	559
Thereafter	3,747

During 1998, Wal-Mart issued and repaid long-term debt of $547 and $554, respectively.

Required: (1) Compute Wal-Mart's long-term debt to shareholders' equity ratio at the end of the 1998 and 1997 fiscal years. How has its financial flexibility changed?

(2) Compute Wal-Mart's times interest earned ratio in the fiscal years 1998 and 1997. Explain whether you are concerned about its ability to pay its interest obligations each period.

(3) Explain whether you are concerned about Wal-Mart's ability to pay its long-term debt obligations. Explain whether you would like any additional information to help you answer this question.

www.exxon.com

22-44 Exxon reported the following (partial) information related to its debt in the notes to its 1997 financial statements (in millions):

Dec. 31	1997	1996
Guaranteed zero-coupon notes due 2004, face value ($1,146) net of unamortized discount	$538	$482
Guaranteed debt securities due 1999-2011	143	150

Required: (1) What was the interest expense on the zero coupon notes (bonds) in 1997? What is the annual yield on these notes? Assume that Exxon did not issue or retire any notes during 1997.

(2) What will be the interest expense on the zero-coupon notes (bonds) in 1998? Explain how the interest will affect Exxon's financial statements.

(3) Explain whether Exxon issued the guaranteed debt securities at a discount or a premium. Assume that it did not issue or retire any of the bonds in 1997.

www.sears.com

22-45 Sears Roebuck reported the following (partial) information in the notes to its 1997 financial statements:

Lease and Service Agreements
Minimum lease obligations excluding taxes, insurance, and other expenses payable directly by the company for leases in effect as of Jan. 3, 1998 were:

	Operating Leases (millions of dollars)
1998	$ 340
1999	311
2000	268
2001	235
2002	210
After 2002	1,102
Future minimum obligations	$2,466

Required: (1) What would be the effects on the relevant balance sheet items at January 3, 1998, and on the relevant income statement items for the 1997 fiscal year if the operating leases were recorded as capital leases instead? Assume the company makes each year's lease payments at the end of the year. Use a 10% interest rate and straight-line depreciation over a 9-year life with no residual value. Assume the "After 2002" payments have a present value of $500 million. Round to two decimal places.

(2) How do these calculations affect the January 3, 1998 balance sheet and the ratios used to evaluate the company?

(3) The company reported "long-term debt and capital lease obligations" of $13,071 at January 3, 1998. Do the operating leases have a material effect on your understanding of the company's obligations?

22-46 The following excerpts are from United Airlines' 1997 financial statements (in millions):

www.ual.com

Total assets at December 31, 1997	$15,803
Total stockholders' equity at December 31, 1997	2,337

Lease Obligations

Future minimum lease payments as of December 31, 1997 under operating leases having initial or remaining noncancellable lease terms in excess of one year are as follows:

Payable during	Operating Leases
1998	$ 1,419
1999	1,395
2000	1,402
2001	1,380
2002	1,357
After 2002	19,562
Total minimum lease payments	$26,515

Required: (1) What would be the effects on the relevant balance sheet items at December 31, 1997, and on the relevant income statement items for 1998 if the operating leases were recorded as capital leases instead? Assume the company makes each year's lease payments at the end of the year. Use a 10% interest rate and straight-line depreciation over a 20-year life with no residual value. Assume the "After 2000" payments have a present value of $6 million. Round to two decimal places.

(2) Are the effects of your calculations material to the December 31, 1997 balance sheet?

22-47 PepsiCo disclosed the following (partial) information in the income taxes note to its 1997 financial statements (in millions):

www.pepsico.com

The details of the provision for income taxes on income are:

Current: Federal	$598
Foreign	110
State	59

Deferred: Federal	$ 23
Foreign	15
State	13

Deferred tax liability
Property, plant, and equipment ... $500
Deferred tax asset
Various current liabilities ... $459
Income taxes paid: ... $696

Required: (1) What is the amount of PepsiCo's income tax expense for 1997?
(2) What is the amount of PepsiCo's current income tax obligation to federal, foreign, and state governments for 1997? Why is this obligation different from the income tax expense? Why is it different from the income tax paid?
(3) Explain why PepsiCo has a deferred tax liability from property, plant, and equipment.
(4) Explain why PepsiCo has a deferred tax asset from various accrued liabilities.

www.bethsteel.com

22-48 At December 31, 1997, Bethlehem Steel reported total assets of $4,802.6 million and total stockholders' equity of $1,215 million. In its notes, it disclosed that its pension plan had a projected benefit obligation of $5,495 million and plan assets of $4,930. The company also disclosed that the discount rate used to compute the projected benefit obligation was 7.75%, up from 7.25% in the previous year.

Required: (1) Compute Bethlehem Steel's debt ratio with and without considering the pension plan. How does consideration of the pension plan affect your assessment of Bethlehem Steel's risk and financial flexibility?
(2) Explain whether the increase in the discount rate increased or decreased the projected benefit obligation.

www.generalmills.com

22-49 Use the 1998 fiscal year annual report of General Mills (in Appendix C) to answer the following questions.

Required: (1) How much was General Mills' interest expense for 1998?
(2) How much interest did General Mills pay in 1998?
(3) What will be the interest expense on the 11.7% zero-coupon notes (bonds) in 1999? for the last six months in 2004? (Use an annual yield.)
(4) Has General Mills issued any long-term debt at a discount or a premium?
(5) Does General Mills have significant operating leases that would affect your understanding of the company's financial position?
(6) What is the amount of General Mills' income tax expense for 1998?
(7) What is the amount of General Mills' current income tax obligation to federal, state and local, and foreign governments for 1998? Why is this obligation different from the income tax expense? Why is it different from the income tax paid?
(8) Explain why General Mills has a deferred tax liability from depreciation.
(9) Explain why General Mills has a deferred tax asset from accrued liabilities.
(10) Are General Mills' pension plan assets greater or less than its projected benefit obligation at May 31, 1998?

22-50   Yesterday, you received the following letter for your advice column in the local paper:

Dear Dr. Decisive:

I recently took a trip and flew on Frontier Airlines. When I got back I decided to look at the company's annual report. Was I surprised! The airline has no planes listed on its balance sheet. But I definitely flew on one. How can this be? And how can I evaluate the company's performance if it reports ticket sales on the income statement but has no assets on its balance sheet? Then I took another look at the balance sheet and I saw that the company had a liability for "accrued maintenance expense." Does that mean the company is saving money by not doing maintenance? That would be scary!

Call me "Flying without a Plane."

Required: Meet with your Dr. Decisive team and write a response to "Flying without a Plane."

CHAPTER 23

INVESTMENTS IN STOCKS AND BONDS OF OTHER COMPANIES

"Competition is a lot like codliver oil. First it makes you sick. Then it makes you better."

—AMD Inc. advertisement

1 *How does a company classify its investments on its financial statements?*

2 *How does a company record and report its investments that are available for sale?*

3 *How does a company record and report its investments in companies over which it has significant influence?*

4 *When and why does a company prepare consolidated financial statements?*

5 *How does a company record and report its investments in bonds that it expects to hold until maturity?*

To evaluate a company's liquidity and financial flexibility, both external and internal users must be familiar with how the company records and reports its investments. A company may make various types of investments for various reasons. For example, when a company has excess cash, it has several choices. If it wants to invest for a short time with very little risk, it may invest in cash equivalents, as we discussed in Chapter 13. If the company wants to invest for a longer time and accept more risk, it may invest in securities (either stocks or bonds). A company makes this investment because it expects to receive dividends or interest, and to participate in an increase in the market value of the securities.

In addition, a company may purchase long-term investments in stocks of other corporations, either because it expects them to be more profitable than investing in property, plant, and equipment, or for strategic reasons. For example, a company can obtain some influence, or even control, over the operations of its suppliers or customers by purchasing stock of these companies, voting at the stockholders' meetings, and having member(s) on the board of directors. A company also may invest in the stocks of corporations that have an operating cycle different from its own. In doing this, the company hopes that the income earned from owning the stock will help to offset any cyclical declines in the income from its own business, and will therefore smooth its earnings trend. A company may make a long-term investment in the bonds of other companies either to develop a financial relationship with another company or to obtain a relatively safe source of continued interest revenue.

Classifications of Investments

1 *How does a company classify its investments on its financial statements?*

Recall from Chapters 10 and 22 that a corporation may issue (sell) stocks and bonds to investors. Recall that **common stock** is the ownership unit of a corporation and that common stockholders are the owners of a corporation.[1] These owners have the right to vote on corporate policies and the right to share in the corporation's net income by receiving dividends. **Bonds** are a type of note in which a company agrees to pay the holder the face value on the maturity date and to pay interest on the face value periodically at a specified rate. Bondholders are creditors of a company. Although bondholders cannot vote, they do "share" in the company's income by receiving interest.

A company (called the *investor*) may choose to invest in the common stock of another company (called the *investee*). How the investor company accounts for its investments in stock depends on its "influence" over the investee. *Influence* is defined by the percentage ownership the investor company has in the investee; percentage ownership relates to the number of votes the investor company has. If an investor company has **no** influence over the investee (less than 20% ownership), it has an investment in "available-for-sale stock."[2] The investor company typically makes this investment to receive dividends and participate in an increase in the market value of the stock. The company reports this investment on its balance sheet using the *market value method*. If the investor company has **significant influence** over the investee (between 20% and 50% ownership), it has an equity investment. It has a larger ownership (equity) interest in the investee and that larger interest provides it with significant influence. The investor company reports this investment using the *equity method*. If the investor company has **control** over the investee (more than 50% ownership), the investee is no longer a separate *economic* entity from the investor company, so the investor company prepares *consolidated* financial statements.

---

[1]Investors also may purchase *preferred stock*. For simplicity, in this chapter we focus on investments in common stock, although the principles we discuss for investments in common stock that are available for sale also apply to preferred stock.

[2]Some companies, such as banks, also make investments in "trading securities." *Trading securities* are securities that a company holds for a very short time (often only a few days) to earn profits from short-term differences in the selling prices of the securities. We do not discuss trading securities in this book.

Do you think a company could own less than 20% and have significant influence? more than 20% and not have significant influence? less than 50% and have control? more than 50% and not have control? Why or why not?

A company also may choose to invest in another company's bonds. How the investor company reports its investments in bonds depends on how long it expects to hold the bonds. If the company expects to sell the bonds before their maturity date, it calls them "available-for-sale bonds" and reports this investment using the *market value method.* If the company expects to hold the bonds for their entire life, it calls them "held-to-maturity bonds" and reports this investment using the *amortized cost method.* We summarize the method a company uses to report each type of investment in Exhibit 23-1, and we will explain these methods in later sections of this chapter.

Market Prices of Stocks and Bonds

A company (just like an individual) usually makes an investment in stocks or bonds of publicly traded companies through a stockbroker. A **stockbroker** is a person or company that buys and sells (*trades*) stocks and bonds for other people or companies. As we discussed in Chapter 10, the stocks and bonds of large corporations are traded on organized securities exchanges, such as the New York Stock Exchange, the Tokyo Stock Exchange, or the Stockholm Stock Exchange. The stocks and bonds of other corporations are traded in the over-the-counter market, such as NASDAQ, in which brokers deal directly with each other rather than through a stock exchange.

The market prices of these stocks and bonds are quoted daily and are reported in many newspapers. For example, the stock of IBM was recently listed as follows:

www.ibm.com

52 weeks		Symbol	Dividend	Yield %	Price Earnings	Volume 100s	High	Low	Close	Net Change
High	Low									
$170^9/_{16}$	$95^5/_8$	IBM	.88	.5	26	36,873	170	$163^3/_4$	165	$-4^7/_{16}$

This information indicates that the stock has sold at a high of $170^9/_{16}$ per share and a low of $95^5/_8$ per share in the last 52 weeks. The symbol used on the stock exchange is IBM. The annual dividend is $0.88 per share, which is a yield (the dividend as a percentage of the market price) of 0.5% on the closing market price. The closing market price is

---

Exhibit 23-1   Accounting for Investments

Type of Investment	Method
Investments in Common Stock	
Amount of Influence	
No influence (less than 20% ownership)	Market value method
Significant influence (20% to 50% ownership)	Equity method
Control (more than 50% ownership)	Consolidation method
Investments in Bonds	
Available-for-sale	Market value method
Held-to-maturity	Amortized cost method

26 times the earnings per share for the last four quarters. On the date of this quotation, 3,687,300 shares were traded, the high price for the day was $170 per share, the low price was $163¾ per share, and the closing price was $165 per share, which was a decrease in price of $4⁷⁄₁₆ over the closing price of the previous day.

 Look up the listing of IBM's stock. Which items have changed? By how much have they changed?

Bonds of IBM were also listed recently, as follows:

Bonds	Current Yield	Volume	Close	Net Change
8⅜ 19	6.8	22	123³/₈	− 1⅛

This information indicates that the bonds have a contract rate of 8⅜% and mature in the year 2019. The bonds currently yield 6.8% (the annual interest as a percentage of the market price), and on the date of this quotation 22 bonds were traded. The closing price was 123³/₈% per bond, which was a decrease of 1⅛ from the closing price of the previous day. This bond price is quoted as a percentage of the face value of the bond and not as a dollar amount. Since bonds have a face value of $1,000, this quote means a price of $1,233.75 (123³/₈% × $1,000).

 Look up the listing of IBM's bonds. Which items have changed? By how much have they changed?

These quoted market prices show the prices an investor had to pay to purchase or sell the securities on the date the prices were quoted. In addition, the investor has to pay a fee to the stockbroker to make a purchase or a sale. Thus, when a company purchases securities, it records the purchase in an Investment account (asset) at the cost of acquisition, which is the quoted market price on the date of the purchase plus any commissions paid to stockbrokers, and any transfer or sales taxes that are imposed. For simplicity, in this chapter we ignore stockbroker's commissions and sales taxes. We use the term *market value* in this book, but the term *fair value* is often used also.

 Is this principle different from the way other assets are initially recorded? Explain why or why not.

Market Value Method

2 *How does a company record and report its investments that are available for sale?*

As we mentioned earlier, there are several methods a company may use to account for an investment in stocks and bonds. For stocks, the choice of method depends on the amount of *influence* the investor has over the investee. For bonds, the choice depends on the *intent* of the investor.

A company uses the market value method for investments in **available-for-sale securities**. These securities may be common stock or bonds. In the case of common stock available for sale, the investor does *not* have significant influence because it owns less than 20% of the investee. In the case of bonds available for sale, the investor does *not* expect to hold the bonds until their maturity date. Available-for-sale securities sometimes are called *marketable securities*.

Brown   Courtesy The Christian Science Monitor

"Laddie Boy up $^{7}/_{8}$ . . . .Alpo up $^{1}/_{2}$
. . .Purina Dog Chow down $^{1}/_{4}$. . ."

Three general issues arise in accounting for investments in available-for-sale securities. First, when should a company record the revenue from the investment? Second, what dollar amount should it report for the asset (Investment) on its balance sheet at the end of the year? Third, how should it compute the gain or loss when it sells the securities? The answer to the first question varies between stocks and bonds. An investor company records dividend revenue on stock paid by the investee when it receives the dividends.[3] The investor records interest revenue on bonds in the period the interest is earned. In other words, interest accrues (is earned) continuously over time, whereas dividends are discretionary periodic payments. As we discussed earlier, the answer to the second question is that an investor reports investments in available-for-sale securities (both stocks and bonds) at their *market value* at year-end. The answer to the third question is that an investor computes the gain or loss on the sale of securities by comparing the cash received from the sale with the *cost* of the securities that it sold.

For example, suppose that on January 1, 2000, Unlimited Decadence purchased 200 shares of Fox Company common stock for $4,000 and 8 bonds of Crow Company for $8,000 because it had excess cash to invest. The bonds have a face value of $8,000, have a contract rate of 10%, and pay interest semiannually on June 30 and December 31. Unlimited Decadence records the investment on January 1, 2000 at a cost of $12,000, as follows:

	Assets		**=**	**Liabilities**	**+**	**Stockholders' Equity**

Cash		Investment in Available-for-Sale Securities	
	12,000	12,000	
(+)	(−)	(+)	(−)

"Each one of us is responsible for managing our own portfolios in this life's uncertain market."

From *The Wall Street Journal.* Reprinted by permission of Cartoon Features Syndicate.

Unlimited Decadence has exchanged one asset, Cash, for another asset, Investments in Available-for-Sale Securities. A company's **investments portfolio** includes all of its investments in the securities of other companies. Thus, Unlimited Decadence's $12,000 portfolio of investments in available-for-sale securities on January 1, 2000 consists of 200 shares of common stock costing $4,000 and 10 bonds costing $8,000.

Recording Dividends and Interest

A company records dividend revenue when it receives the cash dividend. Thus, if Unlimited Decadence receives $200 of dividends on the Fox Company common stock during 2000, it records the receipt as follows:

Assets	=	Liabilities	+	Stockholders' Equity
Cash				Dividend Revenue

200					200
(+)	(−)			(−)	(+)

Unlimited Decadence reports dividend revenue in the "other items" section on its 2000 income statement, and the cash received in the operating activities section of its cash flow statement.

A company records interest revenue as the interest is earned during the year. Thus, Unlimited Decadence records $400 [$8,000 face value × (10% contract rate ÷ 2)] of interest revenue semiannually on June 30 and on December 31, 2000, as follows:

Assets	=	Liabilities	+	Stockholders' Equity
Cash				Interest Revenue

400					400
(+)	(−)			(−)	(+)

Unlimited Decadence reports the $400 interest revenue in the "other items" section on its 2000 income statement and the cash received in the operating activities section of its cash flow statement.

Reporting Ending Market Value

At the end of the year, a company reports its portfolio of investments in available-for-sale securities on its ending balance sheet at the market value of the portfolio. If the market value of the portfolio is greater than the cost, the company increases its Investments account and also increases an Unrealized *Increase* in Market Value of Investments account for the difference between the market value and the cost. If the market value of the portfolio is *less* than the cost, the company decreases its Investments account and increases an Unrealized *Decrease* in Market Value of Investments account for the difference between the cost and the market value.[4] Both the Unrealized Increase and the Unrealized Decrease accounts are stockholders' equity accounts that represent the "gain" or "loss" from the change in market value. It is important to note that the company does not include the change in value in its income statement—we will discuss how the company reports it later in the chapter. The "gain" or "loss" is called "unrealized" because the company has not sold the securities and has not collected cash relating to the change in market value.

To understand this concept, suppose that at the end of 2000, the Fox Company stock has a market value of $4,600 and the Crow Company bonds have a market value of $7,900. Unlimited Decadence prepares a schedule of the change in market value of its investments as we show in Exhibit 23-2.

Why do you think the market value of the bonds decreased?

Based on the schedule, Unlimited Decadence records the following on December 31, 2000:

Assets	=	Liabilities	+	Stockholders' Equity
Investments in Available-for-Sale Securities				Unrealized Increase in Market Value of Investments
Bal 12,000				
500				500
Bal 12,500				
(+) (−)				(−) (+)

Exhibit 23-2 Schedule to Compute Market Value of Investments in Available-for-Sale Securities

Security	1/1/00 Cost	12/31/00 Market Value	Increase (Decrease)
Fox stock	$ 4,000	$ 4,600	$600
Crow bonds	8,000	7,900	(100)
Totals	$12,000	$12,500	$500

[4]The Unrealized Decrease account is a contra stockholders' equity account. Therefore, it is increased by an entry on the left side and decreased by an entry on the right side.

As we show, the balance of the Investments account now is $12,500, and Unlimited Decadence reports this market value as an asset on its December 31, 2000 balance sheet. If the company intends to sell the investments during 2001, it reports the Investments account as a current asset. Otherwise, it reports the Investments account as a long-term asset. Note that this classification is based on the intent of the managers. A company must report the *balance* of the Unrealized Increase (or Decrease) account on its ending balance sheet, directly after retained earnings, in a component of its stockholders' equity section called "accumulated other comprehensive income (loss)."[5] So, Unlimited Decadence reports the $500 balance in the Unrealized Increase account as accumulated other comprehensive income in the stockholders' equity section of its ending 2000 balance sheet, as follows:

Stockholders' Equity (in part)	
Accumulated other comprehensive income	
Unrealized increase in market value of investments	$500

If Unlimited Decadence holds the investments at the end of the second year, it prepares a schedule similar to the one illustrated. It then increases or decreases the Investments account and the Unrealized Increase (or Decrease) account, and reports the new *balance* in the Unrealized Increase (or Decrease) account as accumulated other comprehensive income in the stockholders' equity section of its balance sheet.

Sale of Investments

When a company sells an investment, it must record the cash received, reduce the Investments account, adjust the Unrealized Increase (or Decrease) account, and record any gain or loss on the sale. The company computes the gain or loss by comparing the cash received from the sale of the securities with the *cost* of the securities sold. For example, suppose that on October 1, 2001, Unlimited Decadence sold the 200 shares of Fox Company common stock for $4,800. It computes the $800 gain on the sale by comparing the cash received with the *cost* of the investment, as follows:

Cash received	$4,800
Cost	(4,000)
Gain on sale	$ 800

Since Unlimited Decadence reported the investment in the common stock available-for-sale securities at $4,600 (see Exhibit 23-2) at the end of 2000, it eliminates this amount from the Investments account. Also, it must reduce the Unrealized Increase account by the $600 portion related to the investment in the common stock. This $600 is now part of the $800 "real" gain from the sale of the common stock. Unlimited Decadence reports this $800 gain on its income statement for 2001. If it doesn't remove the $600 unrealized increase from stockholders' equity, it will be double-counting—it would include the amount both in retained earnings (as part of net income) and as a component of stockholders' equity (the accumulated other comprehensive income). Unlimited Decadence records this transaction on October 1, 2001, as follows:

---

[5]A company must also report the *change* in the Unrealized Increase (Decrease) account as "other comprehensive income (or loss)" in its financial statements, as we discuss in Chapter 24. Under GAAP, a company would report its unrealized increase (decrease) after deducting income taxes. In this discussion, for simplicity we ignore income taxes. Since the company does not pay income taxes until it sells the securities, the company also would report a deferred tax liability (asset). We discussed deferred taxes in Chapter 22.

Assets			= Liabilities +		Stockholders' Equity		

Cash		Investments in Available-for-Sale Securities		Unrealized Increase in Market Value of Investments		Gain on Sale of Investments	
		Bal 12,500			Bal 500		
4,800			4,600	600			800
		Bal 7,900		Bal 100			
(+)	(−)	(+)	(−)	(−)	(+)	(−)	(+)

Unlimited Decadence reports the Gain on Sale of Investments in the "other items" section of its 2001 income statement. Note that after the sale, the Investments account has a balance of $7,900, which is the market value of the Crow Company bonds at the end of 2000. The Unrealized Increase account has a balance of $100 on the left side of the account, and so the company renames it "Unrealized Decrease in Market Value of Investments" and the rules for increasing or decreasing a contra-account then apply to this account.

 Explain why the Unrealized account now has a balance on the left side.

At the end of 2001, Unlimited Decadence would prepare a schedule similar to Exhibit 23-2 to determine the change in the market value of the Crow Company bonds since December 31, 2000. It then would increase or decrease the Investments and Unrealized Decrease accounts accordingly.

How Market Value Method Investment Transactions Affect the Cash Flow Statement

A company reports the cash it paid for investments in available-for-sale securities as a cash outflow for an investing activity on its cash flow statement. It reports the cash it received from the sale of these investments as a cash inflow from an investing activity. It includes the dividends (and interest) it received as cash inflows from operating activities. If the company uses the indirect method for reporting its cash flows from operating activities, it subtracts the gain on the sale of an investment from the net income (or adds the loss to net income). It does not report adjustments of the Investments account for changes in the market value on its cash flow statement.

 Why do you think a company does not report these adjustments of the Investments account in its cash flow statement?

External User Perspective: Evaluation of the Market Value Method

From an external user's perspective, there are several advantages when a company uses the market value method to report its investments in available-for-sale securities. First, the current market price is a good indicator of the cash that the company will receive if it sells the securities. This information helps both external and internal users evaluate the *liquidity* of the company. Second, the company may receive the market value of the securities easily through a sale, which is an indication of the company's *financial flexibility*. Third, changes in market value are an indicator of the success of the *investment strategy* of the company's managers. Finally, the market value is easily determined and is *reliable*.

Note that under GAAP, this is the only asset for which a company uses market (fair) value when it is *higher* than cost. For inventory, a company uses the lower-of-cost-or-market method. For property, plant, and equipment as well as intangibles, a company may record an impairment. But in both of these situations, a company records only decreases in value, whereas for available-for-sale securities it records both increases and decreases. The reason for the different rule is primarily because the market value of securities can be obtained reliably—securities have a readily available market, whereas such a market does not exist for other types of assets.

When the FASB was developing the rules for investments in available-for-sale securities that we have discussed, some people argued that a company should also be able to report its liabilities at market (fair) value. However, the FASB did not allow this because the Board members believed that the market values of *most* liabilities were not *reliable* because the liabilities do not trade on established markets. So, companies would have to estimate the market values of those liabilities. But, not allowing "revaluation" of liabilities to their market value created inequities for some companies. Consider, for example, a bank that holds debt securities as assets and also has debt of its own. Now assume that interest rates rise. As interest rates increase, the present value of the future cash flows decreases. Therefore, the market value of the debt securities held as assets decreases, resulting in a "loss." However, the market value of the bank's liabilities also decreases, resulting in a "gain." Therefore, allowing the bank to report its liabilities at market value would allow it to "offset" the effects of the changes in interest rates.

Another issue that arises because changes in market value are not included in income is *gains trading*. This occurs when the managers of a company select a security to sell from its investment portfolio because the sale will result in a gain. Thus, these managers are selecting the security based on the effect the sale will have on the company's income statement (and thus "managing" earnings), and not necessarily on whether the security *should* be sold.

 Suppose a company owns Security A, which cost $5,000, and Security B, which cost $20,000. Each security now has a market value of $10,000. As a manager, explain which security you would sell and why would you choose that security to sell.

Disclosures of Available-for-Sale Securities

www.pfizer.com

To illustrate how a company reports its investments in available-for-sale securities, we show the disclosures of Pfizer in Exhibit 23-3. Note that the company owns both available-for-sale securities, which it reports at market value, and held-to-maturity securities, which it reports at amortized cost.

Equity Method

3 *How does a company record and report its investments in companies over which it has significant influence?*

As we discussed earlier, a company whose investment in the common stock of another company enables it to have significant influence (but not control) over the operations of the other company uses the *equity method* to account for its investment. Significant influence occurs when the investor owns between 20% and 50% of the investee's common stock.

 Explain whether you think a company has significant influence at 21% ownership but not at 19%.

At this level of ownership, there are several reasons why the equity method is appropriate:

1. The market value of the common stock of the investee is not a good indicator of the total value of the investment. The price of a share of stock on the stock

Exhibit 23-3   Pfizer Inc.: Disclosure of Available-for-Sale Securities

Notes to Consolidated Financial Statements (in part):

Investments in Debt and Equity Securities

Information about our investments follows:

(millions of dollars)	1997	1996	1995
Amortized cost and fair value of			
held-to-maturity debt securities:*			
Corporate debt	$ 626	$ 602	$ 682
Certificates of deposit	655	657	350
Municipals	56	29	222
Other	104	81	186
Total held-to-maturity debt securities	1,441	1,369	1,440
Cost and fair value of available-for-sale			
debt securities	686	636	—
Cost of available-for-sale equity			
securities	81	81	68
Gross unrealized gains	106	73	50
Gross unrealized losses	(4)	(8)	(8)
Fair value of available-for-sale equity			
securities	183	146	110
Total investments	$2,310	$2,151	$1,550

*Gross unrealized gains and losses are immaterial.

These investments are in the following captions in the Balance Sheet:

(millions of dollars)	1997	1996	1995
Cash and cash equivalents	$ 636	$ 640	$ 153
Short-term investments	712	487	1,109
Long-term loans and investments	962	1,024	288
Total investments	$2,310	$2,151	$1,550

The contractual maturities of the held-to-maturity and available-for-sale debt securities as of December 31, 1997 were as follows:

(millions of dollars)	Within 1	Years Over 1 to 5	Over 5 to 10	Over 10	Total
Held-to-maturity debt securities:					
Corporate debt	$ 567	$ 54	$ 4	$ 1	$ 626
Certificates of deposit	646	9	—	—	655
Municipals	56	—	—	—	56
Other	79	—	15	10	104
Available-for-sale debt securities:					
Certificates of deposit	—	256	189	—	445
Corporate debt	—	91	150	—	241
Total debt securities	$1,348	$410	$358	$11	$2,127
Available-for-sale					
equity securities					183
Total investments					$2,310

market on any given day is the result of supply and demand on that day. If an investor company sold over 20% of the shares of an investee company, this large number of shares would sell at a market price different from the market price of a small number of shares.

2. The dividends received are not a good indicator of the increase in the investor company's wealth. For example, suppose an investee company earns $60,000 and pays dividends of $6,000. If an investor company owns 25% of the shares, it would receive dividends of $1,500, but this amount does not represent its share of the income accumulated by the investee company. Since the investee has earned $60,000 and the investor "owns" 25% of the income, the investor's wealth has increased by $15,000 on this investment.

3. The investor may be able to influence the dividend policy and thereby affect the cash payments it receives.

For these reasons, reporting of income on the accrual basis (equity method) by the investor is preferable to reporting of income on the basis of the cash received.

The equity method approach for reporting the value of the investment and for reporting income differs from the approach used in the market value method. Under the equity method, the investor company accounts for the investment and income as follows:

$$\text{Investment} = \text{Cost} + \text{Income Earned} - \text{Dividends Received}$$

where:

$$\text{Income Earned} = \text{Investee's Net Income} \times \text{Investor's Ownership \%}$$

and:

$$\text{Dividends Received} = \text{Total Dividends Paid by Investee} \times \text{Investor's Ownership \%}$$

The investor company records as income its share of the investee company's net income (it *accrues* the income as it earns it). When the investor company records this income, it also *increases* the book value of the Investment (asset) account by the same amount. It does *not* record the receipt of dividends as income. Instead, it records the receipt as a *decrease* in the book value of the Investment account. This accounting by the investor company is a "mirror image" of the accounting by the investee company. When the *investee* company earns income, it increases its stockholders' equity, and when it pays dividends, it decreases its stockholders' equity. For the *investor* company, the book value of the Investment account increases as its share of the investee company's stockholders' equity increases (as income is earned), and decreases as its share of the investee company's stockholders' equity decreases (as dividends are received). Consequently, if the investor company were to record dividends received as income, it would double-count income because it has already recorded as income its share of the investee company's income, out of which the dividends are received.

Comprehensive Example

To understand the equity method, suppose that the managers of Unlimited Decadence wanted to obtain significant influence over a supplier, Sanchez Sugar Company.

 What reasons do you think a company might have for wanting to influence the operations of one of its suppliers?

So on January 1, 2000, Unlimited Decadence purchased 30% of Sanchez Sugar Company's common stock for $60,000. At this time Sanchez reported total assets of $300,000, total liabilities of $100,000, and total stockholders' equity of $200,000 on its beginning 2000 balance sheet. Unlimited Decadence records this investment on January 1, 2000, as follows:

	Assets		**=**	**Liabilities**	**+ Stockholders' Equity**

Cash		Investment in Sanchez Sugar Company	
	60,000	60,000	
(+)	(−)	(+)	(−)

Note that this $60,000 investment represents 30% of the $200,000 stockholders' equity of Sanchez. For simplicity, we assume that Unlimited Decadence is able to purchase its investment on the stock market for an amount that is equal to its share of the book value (assets minus liabilities) of Sanchez Sugar Company. As we discussed in Chapter 21, it is more likely that Unlimited Decadence would have to pay more than the book value.

At the end of 2000, Sanchez reports net income of $40,000 and pays dividends of $10,000. Since Unlimited Decadence owns 30% of Sanchez's stock, the income it has earned from its investment is $12,000, computed as follows:

Income Earned = Sanchez's Net Income × Unlimited Decadence's Ownership %

$$= \$40,000 \times 30\%$$

$$= \underline{\underline{\$12,000}}$$

Unlimited Decadence records its share of Sanchez's 2000 net income as follows:

Assets	**=**	**Liabilities**	**+**	**Stockholders' Equity**

Investment in Sanchez Sugar Company		Income from Investment in Sanchez Sugar Company	
Bal 60,000			
12,000			12,000
Bal 72,000			
(+)	(−)	(−)	(+)

Unlimited Decadence reports the $12,000 income from the investment in Sanchez Sugar Company (sometimes referred to as "equity income") in the "other items" section on its 2000 income statement. The dividends of Sanchez that Unlimited Decadence receives are computed as follows:

Dividends Received = Total Dividends × Unlimited Decadence's
Paid by Sanchez   Ownership %

$$= \$10,000 \times 30\%$$

$$= \underline{\underline{\$3,000}}$$

Unlimited Decadence records the receipt of its share of Sanchez's 2000 dividends as follows:

| Assets | = | Liabilities | + | Stockholders' Equity |

Cash		Investment in Sanchez Sugar Company	
3,000		Bal 72,000	3,000
		Bal 69,000	
(+)	(−)	(+)	(−)

As we show, the balance in the Investment account is now $69,000. Unlimited Decadence can verify the $69,000 book value of its Investment in the Sanchez account at the end of 2000 as follows:

Cost of investment...	$60,000
+ Share of Sanchez's net income ($40,000 × 30%)..	12,000
− Dividends received from Sanchez ($10,000 × 30%)	(3,000)
Book Value of Investment at Year-end...	$69,000

Unlimited Decadence reports this $69,000 as a long-term investment on its December 31, 2000 balance sheet. It includes the dividends received as a cash flow from operating activities in its cash flow statement.

To better understand the rationale of the equity method, consider the stockholders' equity of Sanchez (the investee) after it records the preceding events. The investment by Unlimited Decadence has no effect on Sanchez's stockholders' equity because Unlimited Decadence purchased 30% of the *existing* common stock.

 Why do you think that Unlimited Decadence's purchase of existing stock did not affect Sanchez's stockholders' equity?

On the other hand, the earning of income and the payment of dividends by Sanchez do affect its stockholders' equity. By looking at the changes in the accounting equation, we can examine the effects of these events. The income and dividends have the following impact on Sanchez's stockholders' equity in its balance sheet:

	Stockholders' Equity
Earning income	+$40,000
Payment of dividends.	− 10,000
Net Effect	+$30,000

The net effect is a $30,000 increase in the stockholders' equity of Sanchez. Since Unlimited Decadence owns 30% of Sanchez, it owns 30%, or $9,000, of the increase in Sanchez's stockholders' equity. Note that Unlimited Decadence's equity investment increased by $9,000 ($12,000 − $3,000) in 2000. Also note that Unlimited Decadence reported $12,000 equity income from its investment in Sanchez, which is 30% of Sanchez's net income. So the equity method reflects a proportional financial relationship between the amounts reported by the investor and by the investee.[6]

How Equity Method Investment Transactions Affect the Cash Flow Statement

A company reports the cash it paid for equity investments as a cash outflow for an investing activity on its cash flow statement. It reports the cash it received from the sale of these investments as a cash inflow from an investing activity. If the company uses the indirect method for reporting its cash flow from operating activities, it subtracts the gain on the sale of an investment from the net income (or adds the loss to net income). It does this because the gain (loss) is included in its net income but does not affect its *operating* cash flows. If the company uses the indirect method for reporting its cash flows from operating activities, it subtracts the increase in the book value of the equity investment from its net income because that is the amount by which the income reported exceeds the dividends (cash) received. The company includes dividends received as a cash inflow from operating activities.

 Does this make sense to you? Can you explain why a company subtracts the increase in the book value of the investment from net income in its indirect-method cash flow statement?

External User Perspective: Evaluation of the Equity Method

Some external users of financial statements criticize the equity method because the investor company reports income that is greater than the cash it received as dividends. They argue that the cash received from dividends is a more useful measure of the investor company's income. This criticism is not consistent with the accrual concept used in accounting. In accrual accounting, a company reports income in the year in which it is earned and not necessarily when it receives cash. The equity method is another example of reporting income on an accrual basis. It is the best way to report on an investor's income from an investee when the investor has enough of an ownership percentage in the investee to significantly influence the investee's operations and dividend policy.

Business Issues and Values

The managers of an investor company may choose to purchase more than 20% of an investee's stock so that the company can use the equity method. For example, buying 19% of a company's common stock would result in the use of the market value method, and the investor company would record dividends received as income. If the managers instead bought 21%, the investor company would use the equity method and would record 21% of the investee's income as its income. If the investee's net income was larger than the dividends it paid, then the investor company's income would be increased by use of the equity method instead of the market value method. Alternatively, the managers of the investor company could argue that they have significant influence with less than 20% ownership and then use the equity method.

 Under what circumstances might the managers of a company prefer not to buy more than 20% of an investee's common stock?

---

[6]The total stockholders' equity of Sanchez now is $230,000 ($200,000 beginning + $30,000 increase). The value of a 30% share is $69,000 (30% × $230,000). Note that this amount is the balance (book value) in Unlimited Decadence's Investment in Sanchez Sugar Company account. These amounts are equal because Unlimited Decadence purchased its investment for a price equal to 30% of Sanchez's stockholders' equity (book value) at that time. Usually a company will pay more than its share of the book value, but this situation raises complex issues that are beyond the scope of this book.

Consolidated Financial Statements

4 *When and why does a company prepare consolidated financial statements?*

When an investor company owns more than 50% of the common stock of another company, the investor has **control** over the investee.[7] In this situation, the investor company is called the **parent company**. On the other hand, the investee company that has more than 50% of its common stock owned by the investor (parent) company is called the **subsidiary company**. The parent and subsidiary companies remain separate legal entities and keep separate accounting records during the year. The reasons for this separation include income tax, legal liability, and international issues that are beyond the scope of the book. Users of financial statements, however, are interested in financial statements that report the combined activities of the parent and the subsidiaries over which it has control. Therefore, at the end of the year the parent company reports the net income, cash flows, and ending balance sheets of both companies in its financial statements as if the separate legal entities were one economic entity. That is, it publishes a single set of "consolidated" financial statements. **Consolidated financial statements** are the combined financial statements of the parent company and all other companies over which it has control.

 Explain whether, and why, you think a company has control at 51% ownership but not at 49%.

www.hersheys.com

For example, Hershey Foods' consolidated financial statements show the combined results of at least four separate companies, including a subsidiary in Canada. An investor who owns common stock in Hershey Foods does not want four different sets of financial statements that report separately on the activities of each of the companies. So instead Hershey publishes one set of consolidated financial statements. *The separate legal entities are treated as a single economic entity for financial reporting purposes.* So consolidated financial statements are another example of the principle of economic substance taking precedence over legal form.

The consolidated financial statements include the sum of the information in the accounting records of the separate companies. Thus, the parent company adds the assets of the separate companies together, as well as their liabilities, to prepare the consolidated balance sheet. It adds their revenues together, as well as their expenses, to prepare the consolidated income statement. It adds their operating cash flows together, as well as their investing and financing cash flows, to prepare the consolidated cash flow statement. However, the parent and subsidiary companies often buy from and sell to one another, as well as have other "intercompany" transactions. Since the companies are separate legal and accounting entities, they record these transactions in their own accounting systems. To avoid double-counting, the parent company "eliminates" (excludes) from the consolidated financial statements those items that are recorded in both accounting systems. For example, if the parent company makes a loan to the subsidiary company, the parent's note receivable and the subsidiary's note payable (as well as any related interest revenue and interest expense) would be eliminated. So the parent company prepares consolidated financial statements at the end of the year by combining the yearly information in each company's accounting records *after* the eliminations. Also recall from Chapter 21 that a parent company reports (and amortizes) goodwill when it has control over a subsidiary company and prepares consolidated financial statements.

When a parent buys a subsidiary, it records its cost in an Investment account. During the year, the parent company accounts for its investment in the subsidiary using the equity method we discussed earlier. At the end of the year, to prepare its consolidated financial statements, the parent company makes the various eliminations (including the elimination of the Investment account). Because these eliminations are complex and

---

[7]The FASB is discussing the substitution of the concept of economic control for the concept of legal control currently used. This proposal would result in the preparation of consolidated financial statements at less than 50% ownership.

because consolidated financial statements look similar to those that are not consolidated, we do not discuss the accounting procedures for preparing consolidated financial statements. Appendix C includes the consolidated financial statements of General Mills Corporation.

When a company controls another company but purchases less than 100% of the common stock, the holders of the remaining shares are known as the *minority interest*. So if a parent company purchases 70% of a subsidiary's shares, the owners of the remaining 30% are the minority interest. In this case, the parent company includes 100% of the subsidiary company's revenues and expenses, and assets and liabilities, in its consolidated financial statements. The minority interest is reported in two ways. First, the minority interest percentage multiplied by the subsidiary's net income is subtracted in computing the net income on the consolidated income statement. Second, the minority interest percentage multiplied by the subsidiary's stockholders' equity is included separately in the stockholders' equity section of the consolidated balance sheet.

Why do you think the minority interest is subtracted on the consolidated income statement?

Business Issues and Values

As we discussed above, the parent company includes the assets and liabilities of the subsidiary in its consolidated balance sheet. Note that under the equity method, the investor company includes an Investment account but does not specifically report the investee's liabilities. (The equity method is sometimes referred to as *one-line consolidation* because the Investment account contains the amount of the investor company's current investment in the *net assets* [assets − liabilities] of the investee company.) Therefore, if the managers of a parent company believe they can exercise control with less than 50% ownership, they may purchase that lower amount to avoid consolidation and avoid adding the liabilities on the parent company's balance sheet. External users must read the notes to the financial statements to learn about the investee's liabilities (and other information).

Segment Reports

Although external users believe that consolidated financial statements are important in evaluating the overall performance of a company, they also like to know information about its operating segments. These users think that evaluations of the income and assets of the separate segments are useful in evaluating each segment's performance, including the segments' *return on investment* and *operating capability*. Because users need this information, the notes to a company's consolidated financial statements include information about its different segments. That is, to provide more useful information, GAAP requires a company to "break down" its consolidated financial statements into **segment reports**. We show a diagram of this relationship in Exhibit 23-4.

An operating segment is a component (e.g., department, division, or subsidiary) of a [company that earns revenues and] incurs expenses, (2) whose performance is reviewed [by the chief operating] executive, and (3) for which financial information is [available. The segment information a] company reports includes the following for each segment:

[1.] certain revenues (i.e., sales) and expenses

3. *General information* (e.g., types of products, information for geographic areas)

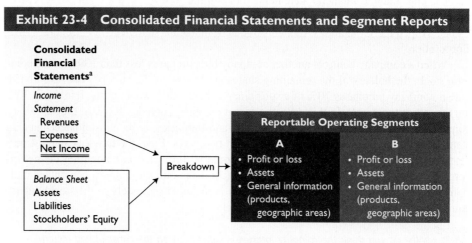

Exhibit 23-4 Consolidated Financial Statements and Segment Reports

aThere are no cash flow reporting requirements for segments.

For example, the three major U.S. car manufacturers (before Chrysler became Daimler-Chrysler) reported their segments and geographic areas as we show below.

	General Motors	**Ford**	**Chrysler**
Segments	North American Operations International Operations General Motors Acceptance Corporation Delphi Hughes	Automotive Financial Services	Automotive Operations Financial Services
Geographic Areas	United States Canada and Mexico Europe Latin America All Other	United States Europe All Other	United States Canada Other

What other geographic areas do you think a large corporation might have?

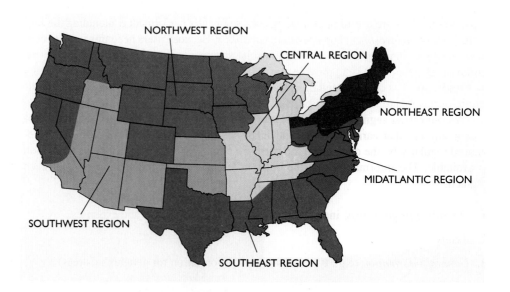

Explain whether you think the segment and geographic information is useful for comparing <u>General Motors</u>, <u>Ford</u>, and <u>Chrysler</u>.

www.gm.com
www2.ford.com
www.daimlerchrysler.com

Uses of Segment Information

External users can use the segment information of a company to evaluate how well each segment is doing over time or in comparison with other companies. For instance, by comparing the sales of a segment over time, users can find out which parts of the company are growing fastest. Also, by dividing a segment's operating profit by its net sales, users can compute the *profit margin* of each segment. Or, by dividing a segment's operating profit by its average total assets, they can compute the *rate of return* of the segment. They can compare these ratios with the segment's ratios in prior years or with the ratios of other companies' segments. When comparing the results with those of the segments of other companies, however, users must be sure that each company has identified its operating segments in the same way. Because each company defines its own segments, users are more likely to use segment reports for intracompany analysis than for intercompany analysis.

We do not show the procedures for preparing segment reports because they are complex. However, we show the segment reports accompanying <u>PepsiCo's</u> consolidated financial statements in Exhibit 23-5. We recommend that you look at this exhibit now.

www.pepsico.com

Exhibit 23-5   PepsiCo: Segment and Geographic Disclosures

Note 17 – Business Segments (in part)

INDUSTRY SEGMENTS	1997	1996	1995
NET SALES			
Beverages	$10,541	$10,587	$10,467
Snack Foods	10,376	9,750	8,600
	$20,917	$20,337	$19,067
OPERATING PROFIT [a]			
Beverages	$ 1,114	$ 890	$ 1,309
Snack Foods	1,695	1,608	1,432
Combined Segments	2,809	2,498	2,741
Equity Income/(Loss)	84	(274)	38
Unallocated Expenses, net	(231)	(184)	(173)
	$ 2,662	$ 2,040	$ 2,606
Amortization of Intangible Assets			
Beverages	$ 155	$ 165	$ 167
Snack Foods	44	41	41
	$ 199	$ 206	$ 208
Depreciation Expense			
Beverages	$ 444	$ 440	$ 445
Snack Foods	394	346	304
Corporate	7	7	7
	$ 845	$ 793	$ 756

	1997	1996	1995
Identifiable Assets*			
Beverages	$ 9,752	$ 9,816	$10,032
Snack Foods	6,998	6,279	5,451
Investments in Unconsolidated Affiliates	1,201	1,147	1,253
Corporate	2,150	468	1,464
Net Assets of Discontinued Operations	–	4,450	4,744
	$20,101	$22,160	$22,944
Capital Spending			
Beverages	$ 618	$ 648	$ 563
Snack Foods	873	973	768
Corporate	15	9	34
	$ 1,506	$ 1,630	$ 1,365
United States	$ 996	$ 1,109	$ 928
International	510	521	437
	$ 1,506	$ 1,630	$ 1,365
Acquisitions and Investments in Unconsolidated Affiliates			
Beverages	$ 43	$ 75	$ 318
Snack Foods	76	–	82
	$ 119	$ 75	$ 400
United States	$ 3	$ 15	$ 37
International	116	60	363
	$ 119	$ 75	$ 400

*Identifiable assets reported by PepsiCo at the end of 1994 were $9,566 for Beverages and $5,044 for Snack Foods.

Exhibit 23-5   PepsiCo: Segment and Geographic Disclosures—continued

GEOGRAPHIC AREAS[b]

	Net Sales			Segment Operating Profit (Loss)[c]			Identifiable Assets		
	1997	1996	1995	1997	1996	1995	1997	1996	1995
Europe	$ 2,327	$ 2,513	$ 2,451	$ (133)	$ (88)	$ (7)	$ 1,130	$ 1,224	$ 1,382
Canada	941	946	889	105	116	94	1,013	1,045	1,054
Mexico	1,541	1,314	1,204	214	105	135	685	583	550
United Kingdom	859	810	751	106	159	139	1,582	1,542	1,408
Other	1,371	1,346	1,371	(50)	(342)	103	1,670	1,698	1,672
Total International	7,039	6,929	6,666	242	(50)	464	6,080	6,092	6,066
United States	13,878	13,408	12,401	2,567	2,548	2,277	10,670	10,003	9,417
Combined Segments	**$20,917**	**$20,337**	**$19,067**	**$ 2,809**	**$ 2,498**	**$ 2,741**	**16,750**	16,095	15,483
Investments in Unconsolidated Affiliates							1,201	1,147	1,253
Corporate							2,150	468	1,464
Net Assets of Discontinued Operations							–	4,450	4,744
							$20,101	**$22,160**	**$22,944**

[a] See Unusual Items Affecting Comparability on page 32.
[b] The results of centralized concentrate manufacturing operations in Puerto Rico and Ireland have been allocated based upon sales to the respective geographic areas.
[c] The unusual items reduce combined segment operating profit by $290 (United States – $74, Europe – $96, Mexico – $(17), United Kingdom – $53, Other – $84) in 1997, $576 (Europe – $69, Mexico – $4, Other – $503) in 1996 and $66 (Europe – $62, Other – $4) in 1995 (see Unusual Items Affecting Comparability on page 32).

Which of PepsiCo's segments has the highest net sales? the highest operating profit? the highest return on assets? the highest capital spending? Which of PepsiCo's geographic areas outside the United States has the highest net sales? the highest operating profit? the highest return on assets?

www.generalmills.com

In Appendix C, note that General Mills does not provide segment disclosures because it operates in only one business segment. General Mills describes its business as the "manufacture and marketing of consumer food products." It describes its businesses as ready-to-eat cereals, desserts, flour and baking mixes, dinner and side dishes, snack products and beverages, yogurt products, food service and international foods operations. However, it does provide geographic disclosures in Note 19.

Do you agree with General Mills' decision not to provide segment disclosures?

Investments in Held-to-Maturity Bonds: Amortized Cost Method

5 *How does a company record and report its investments in bonds that it expects to hold until maturity?*

An investor company may invest in bonds that it expects to hold to maturity. It makes this investment to establish a financial relationship with the investee company or to obtain a relatively consistent source of continuing interest revenue. For instance, a bank often purchases bonds in order to earn interest for a defined period of time.

When a company purchases bonds as an investment and has both the *intent* and the *ability* to hold the bonds until maturity, it records the purchase price (the cost) in an Investment in Held-to-Maturity Bonds account. It may purchase the bonds for the same as, more than, or less than their face value. As we discussed in Chapter 22, if the yield is the same as the contract rate, it purchases the bonds at face value. If the yield is *more* than the contract rate, it purchases the bonds at a *discount* (less than face value). If the yield is *less* than the contract rate, it purchases the bonds at a *premium* (more than face value).

 Think back to our discussion of the sale of bonds in Chapter 22. Explain why a company purchases bonds at a discount when their yield is more than the contract rate.

If a company purchases held-to-maturity bonds at a discount or a premium, it uses the *amortized cost method* (which is another name for the effective interest method, which we discussed and illustrated in Chapter 22) to record its interest revenue each period. The company determines its interest revenue as follows:

Interest Revenue for Period = Book Value of Investment at Beginning of Period × Yield

The book value of the investment at the beginning of the period is the balance in the investment account at that time.

How the company accounts for the amortization of the discount or premium depends on whether the bonds are zero-coupon bonds (which pay the accumulated interest on the maturity date) or are bonds that pay interest semiannually. We will discuss zero-coupon bonds in the next section. We will discuss the accounting for an investment in bonds that are purchased at a discount or a premium and that pay interest semiannually in the appendix at the end of the chapter.

Zero-Coupon Bonds

Recall from Chapter 22 that **zero-coupon bonds** pay no interest each period. That is, they accrue interest each period, but *pay* interest on the maturity date. Therefore, zero-coupon bonds are always purchased at a discount. A company with an investment in zero-coupon bonds records the amount of interest it earns each period as interest revenue and as an increase in its Investment account (this is called amortizing the discount). In other words, this accounting is a "mirror image" of the accounting for zero-coupon bonds we discussed in Chapter 22.

For example, assume that on January 1, 2000, Beany Biscuit Company purchased for $385,500 (at a 10% yield) all of Unlimited Decadence's 10-year, $1,000,000 face value zero-coupon bonds that we discussed in Chapter 22. Beany computed the purchase price (present value) by discounting the $1,000,000 face value using the 10% yield and the 10-year life [$385,500 = $1,000,000 × 0.3855 (from Table 20-1 at the end of Chapter 20)]. Beany expects to hold the bonds until maturity and records the purchase as follows:

	Assets		=	Liabilities	+	Stockholders' Equity

	Cash	Investment in Held-to-Maturity Bonds	
	385,500	385,500	
(+)	(−)	(+)	(−)

Since the yield is 10% annually, at the end of 2000 Beany computes the interest revenue to be $38,550 ($385,500 beginning book value × 10% yield) and records it on December 31, 2000, as follows:

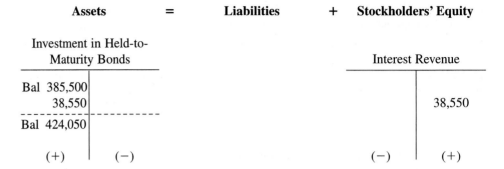

Assets	**=**	**Liabilities**	**+**	**Stockholders' Equity**

Investment in Held-to-Maturity Bonds

Bal 385,500
    38,550

Bal 424,050

(+)   (−)

Interest Revenue

                38,550

(−)   (+)

Beany reports the $424,050 balance in the Investment in Held-to-Maturity Bonds account as a long-term asset on its balance sheet and reports the $38,550 interest revenue in the "other items" section of its income statement.

At the end of 2001, Beany computes its interest revenue as $42,405 ($424,050 beginning book value × 10% yield) and records the amount in the same way as in 2000. Each year it increases the Investment account so that, at the end of the 10-year life of the bonds, the book value will be $1 million. Beany will then collect $1 million from Unlimited Decadence to retire the investment.

Exhibit 23-6   A Summary of Investments in Stocks and Bonds of Other Companies

Partial Balance Sheet for a Hypothetical Company
December 31, 2000

Assets

Cash and cash equivalents	$ 5,000
Investments in available-for-sale securities	27,000
Accounts receivable (net)	63,000
Inventories	84,000
Equity investments	76,000
Investments in held-to-maturity bonds	22,000
Property, plant, and equipment (net)	145,000
Goodwill	62,000
Total Assets	$484,000

Cash equivalents are investments that are short-term, highly liquid, and involve very little risk (we discussed cash equivalents in Chapter 13).

Investments in available-for-sale securities are investments in stocks of other companies when the investor has no significant influence (or bonds which the investor does not intend to hold until their maturity date). The investor reports these securities on the balance sheet at market value.

Equity investments are investments in stocks of other companies when the investor has significant influence. The investor reports them on the balance sheet at cost plus the investor's share of the investee's income minus the dividends received from the investee.

Investments in held-to-maturity bonds are investments in bonds for which the investor has the intent and ability to hold them to maturity. The investor company reports them on the balance sheet at amortized cost.

Goodwill arises when a parent company has control over a subsidiary company and prepares consolidated financial statements. The parent measures goodwill as the difference between the purchase price of the subsidiary and the market value of the net assets acquired. (We also discussed goodwill in Chapter 21).

Effects of Investments in Held-to-Maturity Bonds on the Cash Flow Statement

A company reports the cash it paid for investments in bonds it expects to hold until maturity as a cash outflow for investing activities on its cash flow statement. It reports the cash it received at the maturity of these investments in two places: it reports the amount it received equal to its original investment as a cash inflow from an investing activity; it reports the amount of interest it received as a cash inflow from operating activities. If the company uses the indirect method to compute the cash flows from operating activities, it subtracts the increase in the book value of the investment (from the amortization of the discount) from net income. It adds the decrease in the book value of the investment (from the amortization of the premium) to net income. It does this because the increase or decrease represents the amount by which the income it reported differs from the cash it received as interest.

External User Perspective: Evaluation of Amortized Cost Method

Earlier in the chapter, we explained why the market value method is preferable for valuing available-for-sale securities. So why does a company use the amortized cost method for a held-to-maturity bond? The reason is because the bond will not be sold. As we discussed in Chapter 21, it may be argued that the market value of an asset that will not be sold is *not* relevant because the company will not receive any cash until the bond matures. However, some people argue that the market value of a bond held as an investment is relevant because its value reflects changes in the marketplace since it was purchased.

To help you review the four methods we have discussed in this chapter, we show a hypothetical balance sheet and related descriptions in Exhibit 23-6.

Summary

At the beginning of the chapter we asked you several questions. During the chapter, we asked you to STOP and answer some additional questions to build your knowledge about specific issues. Be sure you answered these additional questions. Below are the questions from the beginning of the chapter, with a brief summary of the key points relating to the answers. Use your creative and critical thinking skills to expand on these key points to develop more complete answers to the questions and to determine what other questions you have that might lead you to learn more about the issues.

1 How does a company classify its investments?

An investor company may choose to invest in an investee company's common stock. How the investor company accounts for its investments in stock depends on its "influence" over the investee. Influence is defined by the percentage ownership the investor company has in the investee. If an investor company has no influence over the investee (less than 20% ownership), it has an investment in "available-for-sale stock," and the company reports this investment on its balance sheet using the market value method. If it has significant influence over the investee (between 20% and 50% ownership) over the investee, it has an equity investment, and it reports this investment using the equity method. If it has control over the investee (more than 50% ownership), it prepares consolidated financial statements. An investor company also may choose to invest in an investee company's bonds. How the investor company reports its investments in bonds depends on how long it expects to hold the bonds. If the company expects to sell the bonds before the maturity date, it calls them "available-for-sale bonds" and reports this investment using the market value method. If the company expects to hold the bonds for their entire life, it calls them "held-to-maturity bonds" and reports this investment using the amortized cost method.

2 How does a company record and report its investments that are available for sale?

A company uses the market value method for investments in available-for-sale securities. These securities may be common stock or bonds. Available-for-sale securities are sometimes called *marketable securities.* The company records dividends paid by the investee as revenue when it receives the dividends. The company records interest on bonds as revenue for each period they are owned. In other words, interest accrues continuously over time, whereas dividends are discretionary periodic payments. The company reports dividend revenue and interest revenue on its income statement and reports its investments in available-for-sale securities (both stocks and bonds) on its balance sheet at their market value at year-end. It reports the unrealized increase or decrease in the market value of its investments in available-for-sale securities in the accumulated other comprehensive income (loss) component of the stockholders' equity section on its ending balance sheet. The company computes the gain or loss on the sale of an investment in available-for-sale securities by comparing the cash it received from the sale with the cost of the securities that it sold.

3 How does a company record and report its investments in companies over which it has significant influence?

A company whose investment in the common stock of another company enables it to have significant influence over the operations of the other company uses the equity method to account for its investment. Significant influence occurs when the investor owns between 20% and 50% of the investee's common stock. Under the equity method, the investor company accounts for the investment and income as follows:

$$\text{Investment} = \text{Cost} + \text{Income Earned} - \text{Dividends Received}$$

where:

$$\text{Income Earned} = \text{Investee's Net Income} \times \text{Investor's Ownership \%}$$

and:

$$\text{Dividends Received} = \text{Total Dividends Paid by Investee} \times \text{Investor's Ownership \%}$$

The company reports the book value of the investment as a long-term asset on its balance sheet. It reports the income earned in the "other items" section on its income statement.

4 When and why does a company prepare consolidated financial statements?

When an investor company owns more than 50% of the common stock of another company, the investor has control over the investee. The investor company that owns more than 50% of the common stock of the investee is the parent company. The investee company that has more than 50% of its common stock owned by the investor (parent) company is the subsidiary company. The parent and the subsidiary companies remain separate legal entities and keep separate accounting records during the year. Users of financial statements are interested in financial statements that report the combined activities of the parent and the subsidiaries over which it has control, however. Therefore, at the end of the year the parent company reports the net income, cash flows, and ending balance sheets of both companies in its financial statements as if the separate legal entities were one economic entity. That is, the parent company publishes a single set of "consolidated" financial statements. Consolidated financial statements are the combined financial statements of the parent company and all other companies over which it has control.

5 How does a company record and report its investments in bonds that it expects to hold until maturity?

When a company purchases bonds as an investment and has both the intent and the ability to hold the bonds until maturity, it records the purchase price (the cost) in an Investment in Held-to-Maturity Bonds account. It may purchase the bonds for the same as, less than, or more than their face value. If the yield is the same as the contract rate, it purchases the bonds at face value. If the yield is more than the contract rate, it purchases the bonds at a discount (less than face value). If the yield is less than the contract rate, it purchases the bonds at a premium (more than face value). When a company invests in zero-coupon bonds, it always purchases them at a discount. It determines its interest revenue for the period by multiplying the book value of the investment at the beginning of the period by the yield. It also records an increase in its Investment account of the same amount. The company reports the book value of the investment as a long-term asset on its balance sheet. It reports the interest revenue in the "other items" section of its income statement.

Key Terms

Appendix: Accounting for an Investment in Held-to-Maturity Bonds That Pay Interest Semiannually

In the chapter, we discussed how a company calculates and records interest revenue on an investment in zero-coupon bonds that it intends to hold to maturity. In this appendix, we illustrate how a company calculates and records interest revenue on an investment in bonds that pay interest semiannually and that it expects to hold to maturity.

Bonds Purchased at a Discount

To illustrate the accounting for an investment in bonds purchased at a discount, we assume that Baker Company, a supplier of candy ingredients, purchases bonds of Unlimited Decadence with the following terms:

Date of sale:	January 1, 2000
Face value:	$100,000
Contract rate:	10%
Interest payment dates:	June 30 and December 31
Maturity date	December 31, 2003

Baker Company purchases the bonds at a yield of 12%. Therefore, it pays $93,789, which is a discount of $6,211 ($100,000 face value − $93,789 purchase price). (This is the same bond issue that we discussed in the appendix to Chapter 22, so please refer to that appendix if you want to see the present value calculations for determining the purchase/selling price.) Baker Company records the purchase on January 1, 2000, as follows:

Assets		=	**Liabilities**	+	**Stockholders' Equity**

Cash		Investment in Held-to-Maturity Bonds	
	93,789	93,789	
(+)	(−)	(+)	(−)

The $93,789 is the book value of the investment at the time of purchase.

On June 30, 2000, Baker receives its first $5,000 [$100,000 face value × (10% contract rate ÷ 2)] semiannual interest receipt. It computes the interest revenue using the *amortized cost* method. For bonds purchased at a discount, the interest revenue is *more* than the interest received because the yield is *more* than the contract rate. Baker's interest revenue for the first semiannual inerest period is $5,627.34 [$93,789 book value × (12% yield ÷ 2)]. It records the $627.34 difference between the interest revenue and the interest receipt as an *increase* in the Investment in Held-to-Maturity Bonds account. This is called *amortizing* a portion of the $6,211 discount. Baker Company records the interest revenue as follows:

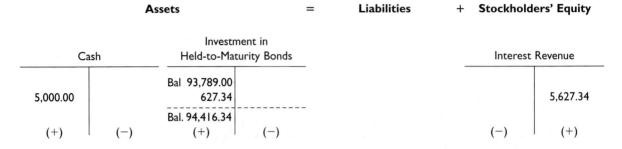

| Assets | = | Liabilities | + | Stockholders' Equity |

Note that the amortization of the discount increases the book value of the Investment account to $94,416.34 ($93,789 + $627.34).

On December 31, 2000, Baker records its interest revenue for the second semiannual interest period in the same way. In this case, however, the interest revenue is $5,664.98 ($94,416.34 × 6%). Since it receives interest of $5,000, it amortizes $664.98 as an increase in the investment. Thus, the book value of the investment increases to $95,081.32 ($94,416.34 + $664.98) at the end of 2000. Baker Company reports this amount as a long-term investment on its December 31, 2000 balance sheet as follows:

> *Long-term investments*
>   Investment in held-to-maturity bonds ($100,000 face value) $95,081

Baker Company reports the $11,292 ($5,627.34 + $5,664.98, rounded) interest revenue in the "other items" section on its 2000 income statement. After the company has recorded all of its interest for the 8 semiannual periods, on the December 31, 2003 maturity date the book value of the investment will equal the $100,000 face value because Baker will have amortized all the discount.

Bonds Purchased at a Premium

A company accounts for bonds purchased at a premium in the same way that it accounts for bonds purchased at a discount. It records the purchase price in the Investment in Held-to-Maturity Bonds account, and since it purchased the bonds at a premium, this amount is greater than the face value. It computes the interest revenue using the amortized cost method. For bonds purchased at a premium, the interest revenue is *less* than the interest received because the yield is *less* than the contract rate. A company records the difference between the interest revenue and the interest received as a *decrease* in the Investment account, because it is amortizing part of the premium.

If the yield is 8% when Baker Company purchases the Unlimited Decadence bonds, it records the purchase price of $106,733.50 in the Investment in Held-to-Maturity Bonds account. (Again, you should review the appendix to Chapter 22 for the present value calculations.) Since you should now be familiar with recording interest, we do not show the changes in the accounts and the accounting equation. On June 30, 2000, Baker records Interest Revenue of $4,269.34 [$106,733.50 × (8% ÷ 2)], an increase in Cash of $5,000, and a decrease in the Investment account of $730.66 ($5,000 − $4,269.34). On December 31, 2000, Baker records Interest Revenue of $4,240.11 [($106,733.50 − $730.66) × 4%], an increase in Cash of $5,000, and a decrease in the Investment account of $759.89. On the December 31, 2003 maturity date, the book value of the investment will equal the $100,000 face value because Baker will have amortized all the premium.

Here is an opportunity to gather information on the Internet about real-world issues related to the topics in this chapter. Go to http://www.dryden.com/account and click on the Cunningham, Nikolai, and Bazley book cover. Click on *Summary Surfing,* then click on this chapter number, and answer the following questions.

▶ Click on **IBM** and find the most recent *Annual Report.* Select *Notes to Financial Statements,* and find the section *Marketable Securities and Other Investments,* and answer these questions. What was the carrying value of IBM's current marketable securities and of its marketable securities-noncurrent at December 31 of the most recent year? Now go back and select *Statement of Financial Position* and answer this question. What was the net unrealized gain (or loss) on marketable securities at December 31 of the most recent year?

▶ Click on **Exxon.** Find the most recent *Annual Report,* then click on the note labeled *Equity Company Information* and answer these questions. What was Exxon's share of the net income of companies in which it had an investment accounted for by the equity method in the most recent year? its share of the total assets at the end of the most recent year? its share of the net assets at the end of the most recent year?

Integrated Business and Accounting Situations

Answer the Following Questions in Your Own Words

Testing Your Knowledge

23-1 What method does a company use to account for its investment in common stock when it has (a) less than 20% ownership, (b) between 20% and 50% ownership, and (c) more than 50% ownership?

23-2 What method does a company use to account for its investment in bonds that it expects to be (a) available for sale, and (b) held to maturity?

23-3 Under the market value method, how does a company report its investment in available-for-sale securities on its year-end balance sheet?

23-4 When a company using the market value method sells an investment, how does it compute the gain (loss)?

23-5 Under the equity method, how does a company account for its investment and income?

23-6 Under the equity method, how does a company compute the income that it has earned on its investment?

23-7 Under the equity method, how (and why) does a company account for the dividends that it receives on its investment?

23-8 Under the consolidation method, what are (a) the parent company, (b) the subsidiary company, and (c) consolidated financial statements?

23-9 What is an operating segment of a company, and what information does a company report about each of its operating segments?

23-10 What is the relationship between the yield and the contract rate when a company purchases bonds at a discount? at a premium?

23-11 How does a company compute the interest revenue on its investment in held-to-maturity zero-coupon bonds?

23-12 How does a company report its investment in held-to-maturity zero-coupon bonds on its year-end balance sheet?

23-13 How does a company report its investment transactions on its cash flow statement?

23-14 (Appendix). Under the amortized cost method, how does a company that purchases bonds at a discount record the discount amortization when it receives interest?

Applying Your Knowledge

www.att.com

23-15 The following information for AT&T's stock and bonds was recently listed as follows:

STOCK

| 52 weeks | | | | Yield | Price | Volume | | | | Net |
High	Low	Symbol	Div	%	Earnings	100s	High	Low	Close	Change
71⅛	48⅜	T	1.32	1.9	20	92780	72¼	70⅝	71	—

BONDS

Bonds	Current Yield	Volume	Close	Net Change
8⅛ 24	7.5	21	108⅜	−1¼

Required: Explain the meaning of each item listed.

23-16 On January 2, 2000, Castle Brush Company purchased 400 shares of Bass Company for $9,200 and 10 bonds of Trout Company for $10,000. The bonds have a $10,000 face value and an 8% contract rate, and pay interest on June 30 and December 31. Castle classifies these investments as available-for-sale securities. During 2000, it received the semiannual interest payments on the Trout Company bonds, and on December 12 it received a cash dividend of $1.50 per share on the Bass stock. At the end of 2000, the Bass stock had a market value of $9,900, and the Trout bonds had a market value of $9,800.

Required: (1) Using T-accounts, record all of the preceding investment transactions and events for Castle.

(2) Show how Castle would report the investment information on its December 31, 2000 balance sheet, assuming it expects to sell the investments in 2001.

23-17 At the beginning of January 2000, Belford Buckle Company held 500 shares of Wirl common stock in its investment portfolio of available-for-sale securities. These shares had cost $9,000 and had a market value of $9,500 on January 1, 2000. During 2000, Belford had several other transactions relating to its investments in available-for-sale securities, as follows. On January 8, Belford purchased 400 shares of Nirt common stock for $6,000, and on July 1, Belford purchased 10%, $10,000 bonds of Fess Company for $10,000. The bonds pay interest on June 30 and December 31. On August 6, Belford sold the 500 shares of Wirl common stock for $9,900. On December 15, Belford received cash dividends of $1 per share on the Nirt common stock, and on December 31 it received the interest on the Fess bonds. At the end of December, the Nirt shares had a market value of $5,700, and the Fess bonds had a market value of $10,200.

Required: (1) Using T-accounts, record the preceding 2000 investment transactions and events for Belford (keep track of the balance in the Investments account).

(2) Show how Belford would report the results of the investment transactions and events on its 2000 income statement and on its December 31, 2000 balance sheet (assuming it expects to sell the investments in 2001).

23-18 At the beginning of 2000, Morton Tile Corporation's investment in available-for-sale securities consisted of 600 shares of Teal Company common stock that had a cost of

$18,000 and a market value of $18,900. During 2000, the company engaged in the following transactions relating to this portfolio:

March 3:	Sold 400 shares of Teal stock for $31 per share
June 7:	Purchased 500 shares of Loom stock for $10,500 and 700 shares of Prat stock for $5,600
November 20:	Sold the remaining 200 shares of Teal stock for $29 per share
December 15:	Received dividends of $1 per share on the Loom stock and $0.50 per share on the Prat stock

On December 31, 2000, the Loom stock had a market value of $10,000, and the Prat stock had a market value of $6,700.

Required: (1) Using T-accounts, record the preceding 2000 investment transactions and events for Morton (keep track of the balance in the Investments account).

(2) Show how Morton would report the results of the investment transactions and events on its 2000 income statement and on its December 31, 2000 balance sheet (assume it expects to sell the investments in 2001).

23-19 On January 1, 2000, Jackson Pen Company purchased 10,000 shares of Rizzo Company for $50,000. This represented 40% of Rizzo's common stock selling on the stock market. On that date, the book value of Rizzo's stockholders' equity was $125,000. At the end of 2000, Rizzo reported net income of $35,000 and paid total dividends of $16,000.

Required: (1) How much does Jackson Pen Company report as income for 2000 in regard to its investment in Rizzo?

(2) What does Jackson Pen Company report as the book value of its investment in Rizzo on its December 31, 2000 balance sheet?

(3) Using T-accounts, prepare Jackson Pen Company's entries to record its investment, income, and dividends in regard to Rizzo (keep track of the balance in the Investment account).

23-20 On January 1, 2000, Foley Aircraft Company purchased on the stock market 25% of Pet Helicopter Inc.'s 80,000 shares of common stock, paying $5.25 per share. On that date, the book value of Pet's stockholders' equity was $420,000. On December 31, 2000, Foley reported a balance in its investment account for Pet of $120,000. Pet did not pay dividends in 2000.

Required: (1) How much did Foley pay for its investment in Pet?

(2) How much did Foley report as its 2000 income in regard to its investment in Pet?

(3) What was the total net income of Pet during 2000?

23-21 Carter Company purchased, on the stock market, 48,000 of the 120,000 shares of Chavous Company on January 1, 2000 for $240,000. The condensed balance sheet of Chavous on that date is as follows:

Assets	$1,000,000	Liabilities	$ 400,000
		Stockholders' equity	600,000
			$1,000,000

At the end of 2000, Chavous reported net income of $150,000 and paid dividends of $40,000.

Required: (1) Using T-accounts, record the preceding events in 2000 for Carter Company (keep track of the balance in the Investment account).

(2) Show how Carter Company would report the results of the preceding events on its 2000 income statement and on its December 31, 2000 balance sheet.

(3) Assuming that Chavous' liabilities remained unchanged, prepare a condensed balance sheet for Chavous on December 31, 2000.

(4) Explain the relationship between the change in the stockholders' equity of Chavous and the change in the balance of Carter's Investment account since the purchase of the investment.

23-22 On January 1, 2000, Hoffman Company purchased 12-year, zero-coupon bonds issued by Martinez Company. The bonds have a face value of $500,000 and were purchased to yield 8%. Hoffman expects to hold these bonds until maturity, so it uses the amortized cost method to account for its investment.

Required: (1) Compute the purchase price of the bonds.
(2) Compute the interest revenue for 2000 and 2001.
(3) What is the book value of the bonds on December 31, 2001?

23-23 On January 1, 2000, Courtwright Company purchased 7-year, zero-coupon bonds issued by Weimer Company. The bonds have a face value of $300,000 and were purchased to yield 12%. Courtwright expects to hold these bonds until maturity, so it uses the amortized cost method to account for its investment.

Required: (1) Compute the amount that Courtwright pays for the bonds.
(2) Using T-accounts, record the interest revenue for 2000 and 2001.
(3) How much will Courtwright report as its investment on December 31, 2001?

23-24 During 2000, Bashor Company entered into the following investment transactions:
(a) Purchased available-for-sale securities for $57,000
(b) Purchased held-to-maturity bonds for $102,000
(c) Sold available-for-sale securities for $33,000 at a gain of $3,000
(d) Received interest of $4,600 on available-for-sale securities
(e) Received dividends of $5,000 on investments accounted for under the equity method
(f) Reported $8,000 increase in investment in available-for-sale securities because of increase in year-end market value
(g) Received dividends of $3,500 on available-for-sale securities
(h) Received interest of $9,000 on investments in held-to-maturity bonds

Required: Show how Bashor would report the preceding transactions on its 2000 cash flow statement (assuming it uses the direct method of reporting cash flows from operating activities).

23-25 (Appendix). On January 1, 2000, Robinson Steel Company purchased 12%, 10-year bonds with a face value of $100,000 for $112,463. At this price the bonds yield 10%. Interest on the bonds is paid on June 30 and December 31. The company expects to hold these bonds until maturity, so it uses the amortized cost method to account for its investment.

Required: (1) Compute the interest revenue that Robinson records in 2000 (round to the nearest dollar).
(2) What would Robinson report as the balance in its Investment in Bonds account on its December 31, 2000 balance sheet?

23-26 (Appendix). On January 1, 2000, Norel Company purchased 10%, 10-year bonds with a face value of $200,000 for $177,059. Based on this purchase price, the bonds yield 12%. Interest on the bonds is paid on June 30 and December 31. Norel expects to hold these bonds until maturity, so it uses the amortized cost method to account for its investment.

Required: (1) Compute the interest revenue that Norel records in 2000 (round to the nearest dollar).
(2) What would Norel report as the balance in its Investment in Held-to-Maturity Bonds account on its December 31, 2000 balance sheet?

23-27 (Appendix). On January 1, 2000, Nairne Gas Company purchased investments in the bonds of two companies:

	Simon Co.	**Fraser Co.**
Purchase price	$52,346	$37,282
Face value	$50,000	$40,000
Contract rate	9%	7%
Yield	8%	8%

Both bond issues pay interest on June 30 and December 31. The company expects to hold the bonds until maturity.

Required: (1) Using T-accounts, prepare the entries for Nairne to record all the events for the investments during 2000 (round all calculations to the nearest dollar, use a single Investments account, and keep track of the balance in the Investments account).

(2) Show how Nairne would report its interest revenue on the bonds on its 2000 income statement.

(3) Show how Nairne would report its investments in the bonds on its December 31, 2000 balance sheet.

23-28 (Appendix). On January 1, 2000, Winfrey Silicone Company purchased investments in the bonds of two companies:

	Bates Co.	**Clever Co.**
Purchase price	$86,524	$74,361
Face value	$90,000	$70,000
Contract rate	9%	11%
Yield	10%	10%

Both bond issues pay interest on June 30 and December 31. The company expects to hold the bonds until maturity.

Required: (1) Using T-accounts, prepare the entries for Winfrey to record all the events for the investments during 2000 (round all calculations to the nearest dollar, use a single Investments account, and keep track of the balance in the Investments account).

(2) Show how Winfrey would report its interest revenue on the bonds on its 2000 income statement.

(3) Show how Winfrey would report its investments in the bonds on its December 31, 2000 balance sheet.

Making Evaluations

23-29 The board of directors of Oxford Company is discussing the method that the company should use for the valuation of the company's available-for-sale securities. Some of the comments are as follows:

▶ "We should use cost, because until we sell the securities we don't know if we have made any money."

▶ "If we use cost, we are effectively misleading the users of the financial statements, and as a member of the Board of Directors, I don't feel I'm fulfilling my responsibilities."

▶ "Market value may also be misleading. If the price is up in one period and down in the next, we will report a loss in the second period although we may have a profit overall."

Required: Describe what the speaker of each of these comments means, and prepare a counterargument for each of them.

23-30 In its 1997 financial statements, Intel disclosed the following amounts (in millions): **www.intel.com**

	December 27, 1997		**December 28, 1996**	
	Cost	**Estimated Fair Value**	**Cost**	**Estimated Fair Value**
Available-for-sale securities:	$11,355	$11,445	$8,840	$9,027

Realized gains on available-for-sale securities in 1997 were $106 million.

Cash Flow from Investing Activities (1997)

Purchases of available-for-sale investments	$(9,224)
Maturities of available-for-sale investments	?
Sales of available-for-sale investments	153

Required: (1) Using T-accounts, re-create the transactions and events that affected Intel's available-for-sale securities during 1997. Assume that the securities sold in 1997 had a fair value of $98 at December 28, 1996.

(2) What can you assume about the intent of Intel's managers regarding their investments in available-for-sale securities?

www.coca-cola.com

23-31 In its 1997 annual report, Coca-Cola disclosed the following (partial) information:

On December 31, 1997 and 1996, available for sale and held to maturity securities consisted of the following (in millions):

Securities	Cost	Gross Unrealized Gains	Gross Unrealized Losses	Estimated Fair Value
Dec. 31, 1997				
Available for Sale	$ 448	$ 93	$ (5)	$ 536
Held to Maturity	1,591	—	—	1,591
Dec. 31, 1996				
Available for Sale	$ 546	$259	$(8)	$ 797
Held to Maturity	1,608	—	(9)	1,599

Cash Flow from Investing Activities

Purchases of investments	$(459)
Proceeds from disposals of investments	?

Required: (1) Using T accounts, re-create the transactions and events that affected Coca-Cola's (a) available-for-sale securities and (b) held-to-maturity securities during 1997. The company reported that it had no realized gains or losses from sales of securities. Assume that held-to-maturity securities with a cost of $17 matured in 1997 and the company did not purchase any held-to-maturity securities in 1997.

(2) What can you assume about the decisions of Coca-Cola's managers regarding its held-to-maturity securities?

(3) Explain how Coca-Cola would report any gain on the sale (disposals) of investments in the operating activities section of its cash flow statement (a) under the direct method and (b) under the indirect method.

23-32 Minnow Company had the following summarized balance sheet at January 2, 2000, and income statement for 2000:

Current assets	$ 250,000	Current liabilities	$ 25,000
Noncurrent assets	900,000	Noncurrent liabilities	125,000
		Stockholders' equity	1,000,000
	$1,150,000		$1,150,000

Revenue	$350,000
Expenses	(150,000)
	$200,000
Income tax expense	(80,000)
Net Income	$ 120,000

On January 2, 2000, Shark Company purchased 20% of the shares of Minnow Company on the stock market for $10 per share. Minnow Company has 100,000 shares of common stock outstanding and paid dividends of $50,000 in 2000. On December 31, 2000, the Minnow Company shares were listed on the stock market at $15 per share.

Required: (1) If Shark Company classifies the investment as an available-for-sale security, show the effects on its financial statements for 2000.

(2) If Shark Company uses the equity method, show the effects on its financial statements for 2000.

(3) How would your answers to (1) and (2) change if the market price of the shares at year-end was $8 per share?

(4) How would your answers to (1) and (2) change if Minnow Company had a net loss of $120,000 in 2000?

23-33 In its 1997 annual report, Coca-Cola disclosed that it owns 44% of Coca-Cola Enterprises, which it accounts for under the equity method. It disclosed the following (partial) summary information for Coca-Cola Enterprises at December 31, 1997 (in millions):

www.coca-cola.com

Current assets	$1,813
Noncurrent assets	15,674
Current liabilities	3,032
Noncurrent liabilities	12,673

Coca-Cola's balance sheet included the following amounts:

Current assets	$ 5,969
Investment in Coca-Cola Enterprises	184
Total assets	16,940
Current liabilities	7,379
Stockholders' equity	7,311

Required: (1) Compute the current ratio for (a) Coca-Cola and (b) Coca-Cola Enterprises.

(2) Compute the total liabilities to total assets ratio for (a) Coca-Cola and (b) Coca-Cola Enterprises.

(3) Compare the liquidity and financial flexibility of Coca-Cola and Coca-Cola Enterprises.

(4) Explain why you think Coca-Cola may have purchased only 44% of Coca-Cola Enterprises.

(5) If Coca-Cola used the consolidation method to account for its investment in Coca-Cola Enterprises, what would be the effects on its balance sheet? Compute the total liabilities to total assets ratio after the consolidation.

23-34 Sheri Clark has extensive experience working in shops that sell greeting cards and small gifts. She decided that she wanted to purchase her own store, and she found two that had the appropriate characteristics. The balance sheets of the two stores at December 31, 2000, were as follows:

	Store A	Store B
Cash	$ 10,000	$ 20,000
Accounts receivable	40,000	70,000
Inventory	30,000	100,000
Furniture	62,500	125,000
Less: Accumulated depreciation	(40,000)	(25,000)
Intangible assets	10,000	0
	$112,500	$290,000
Accounts payable	$ 25,000	$ 50,000
Bank loan	40,000	80,000
Owner's equity	47,500	160,000
	$112,500	$290,000

Both owners are willing to sell their companies for 125% of the value of the net assets (assets minus liabilities) as reported on their balance sheets. An investigation of the two balance sheets reveals the following:

Accounts receivable: Store B has appropriately provided for bad debts, whereas Store A has not. It appears that $5,000 of Store A's accounts receivable may not be collectible.

Inventory: Store A uses the LIFO cost flow assumption, whereas Store B uses FIFO. The replacement cost of Store A's inventory is $20,000 higher than its balance sheet amount.

Furniture: Store A uses the MACRS depreciation method to prepare its financial statements, whereas Store B uses the straight-line method. Each store purchased its furniture two years ago.

Intangible assets: Store A's intangible asset is the cost of the promotional campaign that was undertaken when the store opened.

Required: Prepare for Sheri Clark a memo that recommends which of the two stores she should buy.

23-35 In the chapter, we discussed three methods of valuing investments in stocks: (a) the market value method, (b) the equity method, and (c) consolidation. Each method results in different amounts appearing in various sections of a company's financial statements.

Required: (1) In what situation does a company use each of the three methods?
(2) Explain how a company reports the results of the three methods on its financial statements.
(3) Explain the justification for requiring the use of each of the three different methods from the perspective of the users of the financial statements.

www.dupont.com

23-36 Du Pont disclosed the following in its 1997 financial statements with respect to the equity method used for Investments in Affiliated Companies (amounts in millions):

	December 31 1997
Equity in Earnings of Affiliates, 1977	$ 682
Investment in Affiliates, 12/31/97	3,477
Investment in Affiliates, 12/31/96	2,278
Investments in Affiliates, 1997	2,283

Required: (1) Using T-accounts, re-create the transactions and events that affected the Investments in Affiliated Companies in 1997. (*Hint:* You need to compute the dividends received.)
(2) Explain why Du Pont recorded the transactions in this way.

www.QuakerOats.com
www.snapple.com

23-37 On December 6, 1994, Quaker Oats purchased Snapple for $1.7 billion (it sold the company in 1997). In its consolidation process, Quaker Oats included the following intangible assets along with the related amortization periods.

Goodwill	$1,300.7	40 years
Trademark *Snapple*	440.0	40
Trademark *Made from the Best Stuff on Earth*	6.0	7
Proprietary formulas	75.0	15
Distribution rights	30.0	30
Distribution network	7.0	10

Required: (1) Explain whether you agree with the lives used by Quaker Oats.
(2) Assume that a manager is considering the allocation of the amount Quaker Oats paid (the cost) to purchase (invest in) Snapple. Among the assets purchased were inventory, land, buildings, machinery, and goodwill. Explain how the manager might prefer to allocate the costs.

23-38 On January 1, 2000, Ant Company had 100,000 shares of common stock outstanding and the following summarized balance sheet:

Current assets	$ 200,000	Current liabilities	$ 100,000
Noncurrent assets	1,000,000	Noncurrent liabilities	700,000
		Stockholders' equity	400,000
	$1,200,000		$1,200,000

The market value of all Ant's assets and liabilities is equal to their book values. On January 2, 2000, Elephant Company purchased 50% of the shares of Ant Company for $10 cash per share on the stock market. Elephant Company had the following summarized balance sheet at January 1, 2000:

Current assets	$ 700,000	Current liabilities	$ 90,000
Noncurrent assets	900,000	Noncurrent liabilities	160,000
		Stockholders' equity	1,350,000
	$1,600,000		$1,600,000

Required: (1) If Elephant Company uses the equity method, prepare its balance sheet on January 2, 2000.

(2) If Elephant Company prepares consolidated financial statements instead, prepare its consolidated balance sheet on January 2, 2000. Assume the goodwill is $300,000 and the minority interest is $200,000.

(3) Compute the debt ratio for each balance sheet. Explain which debt ratio you think better measures the company's risk.

23-39 In the chapter, we showed the disclosures of PepsiCo's operating segments.

www.pepsico.com

Required: Write PepsiCo's shareholders a memo that evaluates the performance of PepsiCo's segments. Include appropriate ratio analyses.

23-40 Refer to General Mills' annual report in Appendix C.

www.generalmills.com

Required: (1) Using T-accounts, re-create the transactions and events that affected General Mills' available-for-sale (marketable) securities during 1998. Ignore the marketable securitites included in "Other Current Assets." (*Hint:* Some of the relevant information is included in Note 5, and you have to compute the unrealized increase in the market value of the securities at the beginning of the year.) Assume that the cost of the securities sold is equal to their market value at May 25, 1997.

(2) Does General Mills have investments that it accounts for under the equity method?

(3) If General Mills included the increase in the market value of its marketable securities in its income statement, would the effect on earnings before taxes and earnings (losses) from joint ventures be material?

23-41 Yesterday, you received the following letter for your advice column in the local paper:

Dear Dr. Decisive:

I am becoming addicted to reading annual reports. I had no idea they could contain so much information—and that sometimes they could be so difficult to understand. I understand that accountants (in the interest of their employment opportunities?) use four methods to report on investments. Please explain to me why each of the methods is used but, more important, why there are four different methods.

Call me "Investment Curious."

Required: Meet with your Dr. Decisive team and write a response to "Investment Curious."

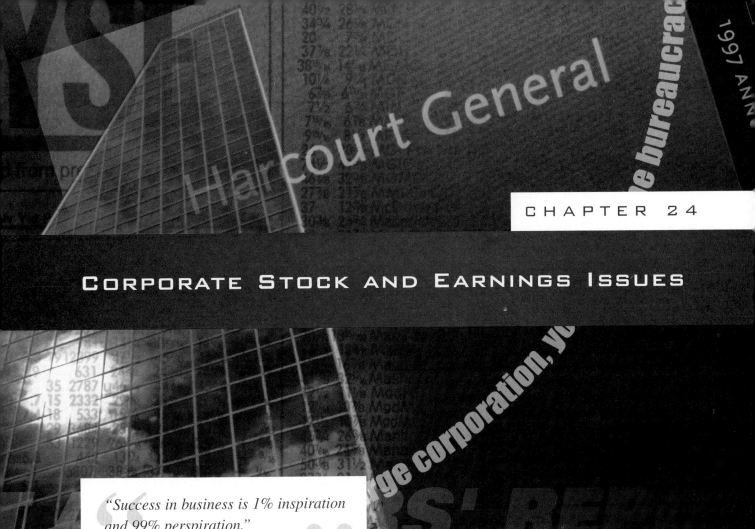

CHAPTER 24

CORPORATE STOCK AND EARNINGS ISSUES

"Success in business is 1% inspiration and 99% perspiration."

—Thomas Edison

1 What are the rights of a corporation's stockholders?

2 What is important for an external user to know about a corporation's capital stock transactions?

3 What are the characteristics of a corporation's treasury stock, and how does it record and report this stock?

4 What are compensatory stock options, and how does a corporation report them?

5 How does a corporation report its results from discontinued operations and extraordinary items?

6 How does a corporation compute and report its earnings per share?

7 What kinds of dividends can a corporation distribute, and what are their characteristics?

8 How and why does a corporation report the changes in its stockholders' equity?

We began our discussion of corporations in Chapter 10. There we noted that corporations are separate legal entities, and that states have enacted laws to govern how a corporation records and reports its stockholders' equity items on its balance sheet. We also briefly discussed the differences between a corporation's income statement and that of a sole proprietorship or a partnership.

To evaluate a corporation's *risk, financial flexibility,* and *return on capital,* both external and internal users must be familiar with how the corporation issues and reports on its capital stock, and with how and why it reports its nonrecurring income and related cash flows. In this chapter, we will expand on the discussion of corporations from Chapter 10 by explaining different kinds of capital stock transactions, two types of nonrecurring earnings, the computation of earnings per share, the alternative forms of dividends, the impact of these items on the cash flow statement, and related issues.

Corporate Capital Structure

A sole proprietorship has a single owner, and a partnership usually has only a few owners. In both types of company, each owner has a separate Owner's Capital account for reporting the owner's equity on the company's balance sheet. The ending balance of each Owner's Capital account includes the investments by the owner plus the owner's share of the company's net income earned to date less the owner's withdrawals. A corporation usually has many owners and frequent changes in ownership, making it almost impossible to keep separate capital accounts for each owner as is done for a sole proprietorship or a partnership. Furthermore, state laws require special accounting procedures for the owners' equity of a corporation; these laws were established to protect the absentee owners of a corporation as well as its creditors.

As we discussed in Chapter 10, **stockholders' equity** is the term used for the owners' equity of a corporation. The stockholders' equity on a corporation's balance sheet includes at least two parts: contributed capital and retained earnings. Each is governed by the laws of the state in which the company is incorporated. We show the basic format (with assumed numbers of shares and dollar amounts) of the stockholders' equity section of a corporation's balance sheet as follows:

Stockholders' Equity

Contributed capital	
Capital stock, $5 par, 20,000 shares authorized,	
10,000 shares issued and outstanding...	$ 50,000
Additional paid-in capital...	70,000
Total contributed capital...	$120,000
Retained earnings..	90,000
Total Stockholders' Equity...	$210,000

A corporation includes the total amount of investments made by its stockholders in **Contributed Capital**. We discuss each of the accounts and the related transactions in the following sections. A corporation reports the balance in its **Retained Earnings** account as the second part of its stockholders' equity. The amount the corporation reports as its retained earnings is the total lifetime corporate income that it has reinvested and that it has *not* distributed to stockholders as dividends. Later in this chapter we will also discuss the accounting issues relating to retained earnings. Since the laws of each state govern some of the stockholders' equity issues that a corporation faces, we will explain only the general issues in this chapter. A particular state's laws might require another procedure or disclosure.

Capital Stock and Legal Capital

Capital stock is the ownership unit in a corporation. **Stockholders** (or **shareholders**) are the owners of a corporation, and their evidence of corporate ownership is a stock certificate. A **stock certificate** is a serially numbered legal document that indicates the number of shares of capital stock owned by a stockholder. It also may include additional information such as the legal capital and the method of transferring the capital stock to another owner.

Stockholders' Rights

Shares of stock are transferable between individuals, and the owners of a corporation may be a diverse set of stockholders who are not involved in its management. Because of this separation of ownership and management, each stockholder may have the following rights:

I *What are the rights of a corporation's stockholders?*

1. The right to attend stockholders' meetings and to vote in setting and approving major policies and actions of the corporation. Included are policies and actions concerning such items as mergers with other companies, acquisitions of other companies, sales of major portions of the corporation, and the issuance of additional stock and bonds.

2. The right to vote in the election of the board of directors. A **board of directors** is a group of individuals that has the responsibility and authority to supervise the corporation's ordinary business activities, make future plans, and take whatever action is necessary in managing the corporation. Voting to elect the board of directors (and the *chair of the board*) also takes place at the stockholders' meetings.

3. The right to share in net income by receiving dividends from the corporation. The board of directors decides on the payment of dividends, however.

4. The right to purchase additional capital stock if it is issued—a right known as the *preemptive right*. The **preemptive right** is the right to maintain a proportionate (pro rata) share of additional capital stock if it is issued. This right often is very significant for small, privately held corporations for which control is very important, but it is less important for corporations with large numbers of shareholders who each own a relatively small number of shares. Stockholders may give up their preemptive right, for example, to allow the corporation to acquire another company by issuing a large number of additional shares of stock to obtain sufficient capital to do so.

5. The right to share in the distribution of the assets of the corporation if it is liquidated (terminated). If a corporation is terminated, creditors have first priority in the collection of their claims; stockholders receive any remaining assets.

Legal Capital

A corporation may issue capital stock in several ways: for cash, in noncash exchanges, to employees through stock options, and in other transactions. The dollar amount that a corporation reports in the Capital Stock account for each capital stock transaction depends on the laws of the state in which the corporation is incorporated. Because stockholders have a *limited liability* to protect creditors, state laws usually set a legal capital for all corporations. **Legal capital** is the amount of stockholders' equity of a corporation that it cannot distribute to stockholders. A corporation may not pay dividends or reacquire capital stock if these activities will reduce the legal capital. The definition of legal capital varies from state to state. In most states, however, the legal capital is the total par value or stated value of the issued capital stock.

 How do you think legal capital protects a corporation's creditors?

Par Value Stock

A common way a corporation establishes its legal capital is by assigning a par value to each share of capital stock. The **par value** of capital stock is a monetary amount that the corporation designates as the legal capital per share in its articles of incorporation. The par value per share is printed on each stock certificate. The total legal capital of a corporation is determined by multiplying the par value per share by the number of shares issued. Generally, states require that a corporation separately account for its legal capital. Consequently, as you will see shortly, for each issuance of capital stock, a corporation records the total dollar amount of the par value in a capital stock account.

The par value of a share of capital stock is usually very low, such as $10, $2, or even less per share. For example, the par value of General Motors' stock is $1⅔ per share. Since a corporation usually issues capital stock at a price much higher than the par value, the legal capital is usually only a small part of the total amount received. The total amount the corporation receives is the *market* value, the price at which the stock is issued. It is important for users to understand that the par value of capital stock has *no* direct relationship to its market value at any time.

No-Par Stock

Many states also allow the issuance of no-par capital stock. **No-par capital stock** does not have a par value. Some states require that the entire amount received by the corporation when it issues no-par stock be designated as legal capital, and the corporation records this amount in the capital stock account. Many states, however, allow the corporation's board of directors to set a stated value per share of no-par stock. The **stated value** of no-par stock is the legal capital per share of stock. The stated value per share, when multiplied by the number of shares issued, is the total amount of legal capital, and is the amount the corporation records in its capital stock account.

 Look at General Mills' *Consolidated Balance Sheet in Appendix C. Does General Mills have par, no-par, or stated value common stock?*

Additional Paid-In Capital

A corporation may issue capital stock in several kinds of transactions. In addition to following state laws for recording the par or stated value in a capital stock account, a corporation also records the excess value received, known as the additional paid-in capital. **Additional paid-in capital** is the difference between the market value (selling price) and the par (or stated) value in each stock transaction, and the corporation records it in its Additional Paid-in Capital account. Corporations may call this account *Additional Paid-in Capital on Capital Stock, Additional Paid-in Capital in Excess of Par (or Stated) Value, Premium on Capital Stock,* or *Contributed Capital in Excess of Par (or Stated) Value.* For simplicity, in this chapter we call it *Additional Paid-in Capital.* Additional paid-in capital sometimes arises from transactions not involving the original issuance of capital stock. We will discuss these transactions later in the chapter.

The concept of legal capital has a significant impact on corporate reporting, particularly as it applies to stockholders' equity. As we just described, a corporation uses a capital stock account to report its legal capital, and an additional paid-in capital account to report the remainder of the total amount of capital contributed by stockholders. However, most external users are interested in the total contributed capital.

Classes of Capital Stock

Corporations may issue two (or more) classes of capital stock—common stock and preferred stock. If a corporation issues only one class of capital stock, it refers to this stock as common stock. **Common stock** is capital stock that shares in all the stockholders' rights. However, some corporations issue more than one type of common stock, such as Class A and Class B common stock. Usually one type of common stock has much greater voting rights than the other in order to preserve control by the original shareholders. For example, both Ford and Coors have two types of common stock, thus preserving the voting rights of members of the Ford and Coors families. A corporation also may issue **preferred stock,** which is capital stock for which stockholders receive certain additional rights in exchange for giving up some of the usual stockholders' rights. The additional rights may involve the right to receive a dividend before any dividend is paid to common stockholders, and the right to convert the preferred stock to common stock at a later date. Preferred stockholders may give up the right to vote in exchange for these additional rights. Alternatively, the preferred stock may be callable or redeemable. We will briefly discuss the conversion of preferred stock to common stock and the recall or redemption of preferred stock later in this chapter.

Does General Mills have preferred stock (see Appendix C)?

A corporation often issues preferred stock with a par value. When a corporation issues both common stock and preferred stock, it uses a Common Stock account and a Preferred Stock account to report the legal capital of each kind of stock. It also uses an Additional Paid-in Capital on Common Stock account and an Additional Paid-in Capital on Preferred Stock account to report the differences between the market values (selling prices) it received and the par (or stated) values of each kind of stock. We also use these titles in this book. When a corporation issues both classes of stock, it expands the contributed capital component of its stockholders' equity to include the additional items (using assumed numbers of shares and dollar amounts), as follows:

Stockholders' Equity

Contributed capital
Preferred stock, $100 par, 2,000 shares authorized,
   600 shares issued and outstanding .... $ 60,000
Additional paid-in capital on preferred stock 72,000
Common stock, $10 par, 30,000 shares authorized,
   9,000 shares issued and outstanding 90,000
Additional paid-in capital on common stock 43,000
   Total contributed capital $265,000
Retained earnings 173,000
   Total Stockholders' Equity $438,000

Now that you have this background, we will discuss recording and reporting the various types of capital stock transactions. Since most capital stock is common stock, our examples are in terms of common stock. The entries in the T-accounts and the balance

www2.ford.com
www.coors.com

Is this what a corporation means by "preferred stock"?

PREFERRED STOCK

Reprinted by permission of TIAA-CREF.

sheet reporting are the same for preferred stock, however, except for the changes in the account titles from common stock to preferred stock.

Capital Stock Transactions

2 *What is important for an external user to know about a corporation's capital stock transactions?*

www.lucent.com

A corporation's articles of incorporation authorize the issuance of capital stock. This authorization lists the classes of stock that the corporation may issue, their par or stated values, the number of authorized shares of each class, and in the case of preferred stock, any preference provisions. After a corporation has issued all of its authorized stock, it must obtain stockholder approval and reapply to the state if it wants to issue more shares. Hence, a corporation usually obtains authorization to issue more stock than it initially plans to sell.

Users need to understand the difference between authorized capital stock and issued capital stock. **Authorized capital stock** is the number of shares of capital stock (both common and preferred) that the corporation *may* legally issue. For example, on December 23, 1998 Lucent Technologies announced that it would double the number of its authorized shares to 6 billion to give it "more flexibility for stock splits or acquisitions." On the other hand, **issued capital stock** is the number of shares of capital stock that a corporation *has* legally issued to its stockholders as of the balance sheet date. On December 23, 1998 Lucent had only issued 1.3 billion shares. As we showed earlier, a corporation reports the numbers of shares authorized and issued for each class of stock in the stockholders' equity section of its balance sheet.

 How many common shares had General Mills issued at May 31, 1998 (see Appendix C)?

A corporation may issue common stock for cash, in noncash exchanges, and in other transactions. We will discuss each of these alternatives next.

 Would you be more interested to know the number of shares a corporation is authorized to issue or the number of shares it has issued? Explain why.

Issuance for Cash

Depending on the state in which it is incorporated, a corporation may issue common stock as stock with a par value, as no-par stock with a stated value, or as true no-par stock. For simplicity, in this book we assume common stock has a par value. In most cases a corporation issues common stock for cash, at a price above the par value. For example, assume that a corporation issues 300 shares of its $10 par value common stock for $16 per share. The corporation records this transaction as follows:

Assets	=	Liabilities	+		Stockholders' Equity		
Cash				**Common Stock**		**Additional Paid-in Capital**	
4,800					3,000		1,800
(+)	(−)			(−)	(+)	(−)	(+)

If the corporation had only this one stock transaction, it would report total contributed capital of $4,800 in stockholders' equity on its year-end balance sheet. A corporation may incur miscellaneous costs for the issuance of common stock, including legal fees, accounting fees, stock certificate costs, and other costs. When the corporation pays these costs, it reduces the Additional Paid-in Capital account, because the costs are considered to be a reduction in the amount received rather than an expense.[1]

---

[1] At the time of the original formation of a corporation, however, it reports these costs as an expense.

Why do you think these additional costs may not be recorded as an expense?

Noncash Issuance of Stock

Sometimes a corporation issues common stock for assets other than cash or for services performed. When this occurs, the corporation must use a correct value to record the transaction. Finding a correct value is particularly challenging when intangible assets such as patents or copyrights are involved, because it is difficult to value these assets. The general rule is to record the transaction at the market value of the stock issued or of the assets received, whichever is more *reliable*. For instance, at the time of the transaction, the stock may be selling on the stock market at a specified price. In this case the stock would have a known value (the stock market price), and therefore the corporation would use this value to record the transaction.

For example, suppose that Unlimited Decadence issues 1,000 shares of $3 par value common stock in exchange for a patent. The stock is currently selling for $18 per share on the stock market. Unlimited Decadence would use a value of $18,000 ($18 × 1,000) to record the transaction as follows:

Assets	=	Liabilities	+	Stockholders' Equity			
Patents				**Common Stock**		**Additional Paid-in Capital**	
18,000					3,000		15,000
(+)	(−)			(−)	(+)	(−)	(+)

Alternatively, a corporation's stock may not trade on a stock market. In this case the market value of the asset received may be more reliable, and the corporation should use it to record the transaction. The corporation may base this value on a review of recent transactions involving similar assets or on an appraisal by an independent appraiser.

Users need to understand the impact on the financial statements of an error in recording the noncash issuance of common stock. Suppose, for instance, that a corporation issued stock for equipment and that it recorded the transaction at too high a value. In this case the corporation would overstate both its assets and its stockholders' equity. In addition, since equipment is a depreciable asset, the initial error would cause an overstatement each year in the depreciation expense, resulting in an understatement of net income. With net income understated and assets and stockholders' equity overstated, the company's return on assets and return on stockholders' equity would be understated. The corporation's financial statements, and many of its ratios, would be correct only at the end of the asset's useful life. If the corporation initially recorded the equipment at too low a value, opposite errors would result. The managers of a corporation must use good judgment in recording noncash issuances of common stock to avoid errors in the corporation's financial statements of current and later periods.

Do you think that managers might prefer to overstate or understate the value of a noncash stock transaction? Explain why.

Transfer of Stock between Stockholders

The preceding discussions involving the sale of stock for cash and in noncash exchanges dealt only with the issuance of stock by the corporation to its stockholders. Later, stockholders may trade (i.e., purchase and sell) the corporation's stock. In this case the corporation is not directly involved in the transaction, and no stockholders' equity accounts are affected. Therefore, the corporation makes no entry in its accounts, and the value of these trades does *not* affect its financial statements. However, it must keep records of the names and addresses of the stockholders for mailing reports and dividends.

 In General Mills' annual report in Appendix C, its stock price on May 31, 1998 was $54½. What is the total value of the company's issued shares? By how much does that amount exceed the amount reported in the balance sheet? Why?

Convertible, Callable, and Redeemable Preferred Stock

Earlier we mentioned that a corporation may issue two classes of stock, common and preferred. One of the preferences that preferred stockholders might receive is the right to exchange (convert) the preferred stock for common stock at a later date. **Convertible preferred stock** is preferred stock that is exchangeable into common stock at the option of the individual stockholders. Usually the corporation establishes, at the time it issues the preferred stock, the number of common shares into which it will convert each preferred share. Another feature of preferred stock usually involves the right to a set dividend. For instance, at the end of 1997, Bethlehem Steel had issued 5.123 million shares of cumulative (which we discuss later in the chapter) convertible preferred stock at $48 per share. Each share had a right to a $3.50 annual dividend and was convertible into 2.39 shares of common stock.

www.bethsteel.com

Both the conversion preference and the dividend feature are advantages to the preferred stockholder. Since the stockholder can convert each share of preferred stock into a specified number of shares of common stock, the market price of the convertible preferred stock tends to rise in proportion to any rise in the market price of the common stock. When the market price of the common stock falls, however, the right to a set dividend on the preferred stock tends to stabilize the market value of the preferred stock.

 What would you expect the stock market price of Bethlehem Steel's preferred stock to be if its common stock currently sells for $10 per share? if its common stock currently sells for $30 per share?

Preferred stock also may be callable. A corporation may recall (or retire) **callable preferred stock** at its option. It states the call price on the stock certificate, and this price is usually several dollars above the issuance price. Stockholders owning nonconvertible preferred stock must give up their shares when the shares are called by the corporation. Stockholders owning convertible preferred stock usually have the choice of conversion or recall. The primary reason a corporation issues callable preferred stock relates to dividends. Retirement of the preferred stock enables the corporation to save its preferred stock dividend payments, thereby increasing its cash available for common stock dividends or for other purposes.

When a corporation issues convertible or callable preferred stock, it records the issuance in the same manner as the issuance of common stock. After issuance, the corporation discloses the conversion, call, or redemption feature in a note to its financial statements. When the stockholder converts preferred stock to common stock, the corporation eliminates the par value of the converted preferred stock and the additional paid-in capital on the preferred stock (the total contributed capital for the converted preferred stock). Then it assigns this amount to common stock in two steps. First, it determines the par value of the common stock issued and adds that amount to the common stock account. Then it adds the remaining contributed capital from the converted preferred stock to the additional paid-in capital on the common stock. Thus, the conversion of preferred stock to common stock affects the components of contributed capital but not the total contributed capital.

For example, assume that at incorporation, Anglar Corporation issues 40 shares of $100 par value convertible preferred stock for $110 per share and 1,000 shares of $5 par

How do you think a corporation decides when it is time to call in shares of its preferred stock?

value common stock for $20 per share. Each share of preferred stock is convertible into 6 shares of common stock. Later, stockholders convert all the shares of preferred stock into common stock. The impact on contributed capital before and after the conversion of all the preferred stock is shown in the following stockholders' equity sections of Anglar's balance sheet:

Before Conversion		**After Conversion**	
Contributed capital			
Preferred stock, $100 par	$ 4,000		
Additional paid-in capital on preferred stock	400	Contributed capital	
Common stock, $5 par	5,000	Common stock, $5 par	$ 6,200[a]
Additional paid-in capital on common stock	15,000	Additional paid-in capital	18,200[b]
Total contributed capital	$24,400	Total contributed capital	$24,400
Retained earnings (assumed)	35,000	Retained earnings (assumed)	35,000
Total Stockholders' Equity	$59,400	Total Stockholders' Equity	$59,400

[a]$5,000 + (40 × 6 × $5)
[b]$15,000 + [$4,400 − (40 × 6 × $5)]

Note that the conversion did not change the corporation's $24,400 total contributed capital because the $4,400 of contributed capital for the preferred stock was replaced by the same amount for the common stock. Also note that the corporation ignores the market value of the stock on the date of the conversion.

 Why do you think that GAAP requires the corporation to ignore the market value of the stock on the date of the conversion?

Preferred stock also may be **redeemable**. Redeemable preferred stock is subject to mandatory retirement at a specified maturity date and price, or at the option of the owner.[2] The primary difference between callable preferred stock and mandatory redeemable preferred stock is that callable preferred stock *may* be retired whereas redeemable preferred stock *must* be retired at the specified date or at the stockholder's request. When a corporation issues redeemable preferred stock, it records the issuance in the same manner as the issuance of callable preferred stock. After issuance, the corporation discloses the redeemable preferred stock in a separate section of the balance sheet, usually between liabilities and stockholders' equity, often referred to as the "mezzanine" section of the balance sheet. Alternatively, the corporation may include the redeemable preferred stock in the stockholders' equity section but must include the phrase "redeemable preferred stock" in the title of the section, such as "Total Stockholders' Equity and Redeemable Preferred Stock." The purpose of these disclosure formats is to alert the user to the future cash outflow—a characteristic usually associated with liabilities.

When a corporation recalls or redeems preferred stock, it eliminates the par value of the retired preferred stock and the related additional paid-in capital and reduces cash for the call or redemption price. Since the cash it pays to retire the stock is usually more than the original issuance price, it also reduces retained earnings. The excess cash payment above the original issuance price is a return to the stockholders. For example, suppose in the above example that Anglar Corporation's 40 shares of preferred stock were redeemable at $125 per share, or a total of $5,000. The impact on contributed capital and retained earnings before and after the redemption of all the preferred stock is shown as follows:

---

[2]Some redeemable preferred stock may be retired at the option of the company.

Before Redemption		After Redemption	
Redeemable preferred stock, $100 par	$ 4,000		
Additional paid-in capital on redeemable			
preferred stock	400		
Contributed capital		Contributed capital	
Common stock, $5 par	5,000	Common stock, $5 par	$ 5,000
Additional paid-in capital on common stock	15,000	Additional paid-in capital	15,000
Total contributed capital	$24,400	Total contributed capital	$20,000
Retained earnings (assumed)	35,000	Retained earnings	34,400ª
Total Stockholders' Equity	$59,400	Total Stockholders' Equity	$54,400

ª{$35,000 − [(40 × $125) − $4,400]}

Note that the $5,000 redemption (or recall) of preferred stock eliminates the $4,000 par value of the redeemable preferred stock and the related $400 additional paid-in capital and reduces retained earnings by $600 on the corporation's balance sheet. The corporation's income statement is not affected.

 Why do you think that GAAP does not allow the corporation to record a $600 loss?

Treasury Stock

3 *What are the characteristics of a corporation's treasury stock, and how does it record and report this stock?*

www.dow.com

In most states a corporation may reacquire its own previously issued capital stock, after which it holds the stock in its treasury. **Treasury stock** is a corporation's own capital stock that (1) stockholders fully paid for and the corporation issued, (2) the corporation later reacquired, and (3) the corporation currently holds. For instance, at the end of 1997, Dow Chemical held nearly 102 million shares of its own capital stock as treasury stock, for which it paid $5,935 million.

What was the cost of General Mills' treasury stock at May 31, 1998 (see Appendix C)?

A corporation may acquire treasury stock for various reasons: (1) to have shares available to issue for employee-purchase plans, (2) to have shares available to issue in the conversion of convertible preferred stock, (3) to invest excess cash (intending to later sell the shares for a higher price), (4) to have shares available to issue in the acquisition of other companies, (5) to reduce the number of shares outstanding and to increase earnings per share, in order to help maintain the market price of its stock, (6) to have shares available to use in the issuance of a stock dividend, and (7) to concentrate ownership of the shares to assist in the defense against hostile takeovers. Treasury stock transactions may be subject to legal and stock exchange regulations.

External users need to understand several features about treasury stock. Treasury stock clearly is *not* an asset of the corporation—a corporation cannot own itself. A corporation cannot report a gain or a loss from reacquiring its own stock; this restricts a corporation from influencing its net income by buying and selling its own stock. Consequently, a corporation reports treasury stock as a reduction of its stockholders' equity, as we will discuss next. Treasury stock generally does not have the stockholders' rights we discussed earlier; it has no voting or preemptive rights, cannot participate in dividends, and has no rights at liquidation.

When a corporation originally issues capital stock, it increases its stockholders' equity and the number of shares outstanding. When it acquires treasury stock, it does just the opposite. The corporation reduces its stockholders' equity (and the number of shares outstanding). You should understand the difference between issued capital stock and outstanding capital stock. Recall that issued capital stock is the number of shares that a corporation has issued to stockholders. **Outstanding capital stock** is the number of shares that the corporation has issued to stockholders and that the stockholders still hold as of a specific date. Thus, the difference between *issued* capital stock and *outstanding* capital stock is the number of shares being held by a corporation as *treasury* stock. A corporation may reissue treasury stock for the reasons we mentioned earlier, in which case it increases stockholders' equity and the number of shares outstanding.

 Would you be more interested to know the number of shares a corporation has issued or the number of shares it has outstanding? Explain why.

Acquisition of Treasury Stock

When a corporation reacquires its capital stock, it records the *cost* it pays as an increase in a Treasury Stock account and a decrease in Cash. The corporation ignores the par value of the stock in recording the reacquisition since it already accounted for the par value when it first issued the stock. During the time between reacquisition and reissuance, the corporation treats the Treasury Stock account as a contra stockholders' equity account. (Since it is a contra account to stockholders' equity, it is increased on the left side.) If the corporation issues a balance sheet during this period, it deducts the cost of the treasury stock from the total of contributed capital and retained earnings.

 By how much is General Mills' stockholders' equity reduced by treasury stock (see Appendix C)?

For example, suppose that Duong Corporation previously issued 5,000 shares of $10 par value common stock for $12 per share. The corporation decides to reacquire 400 shares of this common stock, and it purchases these shares on the stock market at a cost of $14 per share. The corporation records the reacquisition of the stock at $5,600 ($14 × 400) as follows:

Assets	=	**Liabilities**	+	**Stockholders' Equity**
Cash				Treasury Stock
5,600				5,600
(+) | (−)				(+) | (−)

Note that the corporation recorded the treasury stock at its *cost* per share and that it ignored the stock's original par value. If the corporation prepared a balance sheet before reissuing these shares, it would report the stockholders' equity as follows:

Stockholders' Equity

Contributed capital	
Common stock, $10 par, 40,000 shares authorized, 5,000 shares issued,	
4,600 shares outstanding	$50,000
Additional paid-in capital	10,000
Total contributed capital	$60,000
Retained earnings (assumed)	35,000
Total contributed capital and retained earnings	$95,000
Less: Treasury stock (400 shares at $14 per share)	(5,600)
Total Stockholders' Equity	$89,400

In the example, Duong Corporation subtracts the $5,600 cost of the treasury stock from the $95,000 total of contributed capital and retained earnings to determine its

$89,400 total stockholders' equity. Note that it also reports the numbers of shares authorized, issued, and outstanding.

Reissuance of Treasury Stock

A corporation may reissue treasury stock at a price above, below, or equal to its cost (the amount it paid when it reacquired the shares). It records the reissuance by reducing the Treasury Stock account for the *cost* of the shares reissued, and it treats the difference between the cash it receives and this cost as an adjustment of Additional Paid-in Capital. If it receives more cash than the cost of the reissued treasury stock, it records the excess as an increase in Additional Paid-in Capital. If it receives less cash than the cost, it reduces Additional Paid-in Capital by the amount of the difference. Since a corporation may reacquire treasury stock at different dates and costs, it keeps records so that it will know the cost information when it reissues the stock.

Explain why you think a corporation increases Additional Paid-in Capital for the excess of the cash it receives over the cost of the reissued treasury stock. Is this consistent with what you know about the components of the stockholders' equity section? Why or why not?

To understand the reissuance, assume that Duong Corporation reissues 300 shares of the treasury stock from our earlier example at $15 per share. It records this reissuance as follows:

| Assets | = Liabilities + | Stockholders' Equity |

Cash		Treasury Stock		Additional Paid-in Capital
		Bal 5,600		Bal 10,000
4,500			4,200	300
		Bal 1,400		Bal 10,300
(+)	(−)	(+)	(−)	(−)	(+)

Note that the corporation reduces the Treasury Stock account by the $4,200 cost of the reissued shares and increases Additional Paid-in Capital by $300, the difference between the $4,500 proceeds and this cost. After this transaction, the corporation reports the stockholders' equity as follows:

Stockholders' Equity

Contributed capital	
Common stock, $10 par, 40,000 shares authorized, 5,000 shares issued,	
4,900 shares outstanding	$50,000
Additional paid-in capital	10,300
Total contributed capital	$60,300
Retained earnings (assumed)	35,000
Total contributed capital and retained earnings	$95,300
Less: Treasury stock (100 shares at $14 per share)	(1,400)
Total Stockholders' Equity	$93,900

Note that stockholders' equity of Duong Corporation has increased by $4,500 (from $89,400 before it reissued the treasury stock, to $93,900), that the number of shares outstanding has increased by 300 (from 4,600 to 4,900), and that the number of shares of treasury stock has decreased to 100 shares.

When a company reissues treasury stock, why doesn't it record a gain or a loss?

Stock Options

Another way in which corporations issue stock is through stock options. Many stock options are issued to employees as part of their compensation. A corporation's **compensatory stock options** are intended to provide additional compensation to its employees (often a select group of employees, such as its top managers). Under a compensatory stock option plan, employees, in exchange for their services, receive the option to buy shares of their corporation's common stock at a fixed price for a certain period of time.[3] For example, suppose Unlimited Decadence grants an option to an employee as follows:

4 What are compensatory stock options, and how does a corporation report them?

Date of grant:	January 1, 2000
Number of options:	10,000
Option price per share:	$20
Options first exercisable:	January 1, 2004
Options expire:	January 1, 2010
Price per share of common stock on 1/1/2000:	$20

In this case the employee must work for Unlimited Decadence for four years (called the *service period* or *vesting period*), until January 1, 2004, before he or she has the right to exercise the options and purchase the common stock. Then the employee has another six years, until January 1, 2010, in which to exercise the options. It is very important to note that during those six years, the employee can purchase 10,000 shares of common stock for $20 each. This amount is referred to as the *option price, exercise price,* or *strike price.* This option price is the amount the employee pays to buy shares, *no matter what the current stock market price is.* For example, if the stock has a market price of $100 per share in 2006 and the employee exercises the options, he or she would pay $200,000 (10,000 × $20) and receive shares worth $1 million (10,000 × $100). So you can see how a compensatory stock option is considered to be part of an employee's compensation!

In addition to providing compensation, compensatory stock options are designed to encourage employees to make decisions that cause the market price of the corporation's stock to increase, thereby providing a benefit to all its stockholders. These options are particularly popular in high-technology and bio-technology corporations, as well as in new corporations (called *start-up* corporations). For instance, a start-up corporation probably does not have sufficient cash available to pay high salaries to attract the best employees; therefore, it offers compensatory stock options in addition to a lower cash salary.

We will explain only the most commonly used GAAP for recording and disclosing compensatory stock options because the issues are very complex. The corporation that issues the stock option we described above does *not* report an expense for these options on its income statement, either at the time of issuance, during the service period, or at the date of exercise. So even though the employee is $800,000 better off in our example, the option has no affect on the corporation's net income. This partly explains why compensatory stock options are an increasingly popular form of compensation. They can result in significant benefits for employees but no expense, or cash outflow, for the corporation. Also, if the corporation pays its employees a *lower* cash salary when it also provides a stock option plan, its income is *higher* because of the lower salary expense!

---

[3]Options may be granted to nonemployees, they may be noncompensatory, and they may have variable terms. These topics are beyond the scope of this book.

When the employee exercises the option, the corporation increases its cash and stock-holders' equity for the amount paid by the employee—$200,000 in our example. Note that Unlimited Decadence records that it has sold stock for $200,000 even though it could have sold the stock for $1 million. Thus it has an opportunity cost of $800,000.

 Do you agree that a corporation that issues a stock option should not record an expense? Why or why not?

Because the GAAP for recording compensatory stock options is so controversial, a corporation must disclose in the notes to its financial statements the amount that its net income would be if it included the "expense" of the stock options it grants. This amount is often referred to as the "pro forma" net income. To compute its pro forma net income the corporation must first determine its "cost" of the stock options. The computation of this cost is very complex and is based on an "option pricing" model. The cost then is allocated to the "service period"—four years in the Unlimited Decadence example. This amount is the "expense" that the corporation subtracts in the computation of its pro forma net income and discloses in its notes. Therefore, an external user can use the pro forma net income instead of the reported net income in order to understand the performance of a corporation that has issued stock options.

www.microsoft.com

As an example of the effects of this disclosure, Microsoft reported that its 1997 net income was $3.5 billion. However, the disclosures in the notes reported that this income would have been $401 million *less* if it had included the expense of its compensatory stock options in its income statement!

A corporation's annual report discloses relatively little information about its executives' compensation, which often includes compensatory stock options. An external user can find more information in the corporation's "Proxy Statement," which is filed with the Securities and Exchange Commission and is sent to shareholders before the corporation's annual meeting. In particular, the Proxy Statement includes detailed information about the five employees who have the highest compensation.

External User Analysis: Liabilities vs. Stockholders' Equity

In the early chapters of this book, we explained that a corporation's liabilities are amounts it owes to creditors (creditors' equity) and that its stockholders' equity is the owners' residual interest, measured by subtracting the corporation's liabilities from its assets. In the later chapters of this book, we have seen several issues that complicate the distinction between the two categories. In this chapter, we have discussed redeemable (and callable) preferred stock, which will result in a cash outflow when the stock is redeemed. We also discussed deferred income tax liabilities (and assets), which might not be considered liabilities (and assets) if they will continue to increase in the future. We also discussed operating leases, which will require future cash payments but which are not included as liabilities on the corporation's balance sheet and are instead disclosed in the notes to its financial statements. So, an external user must be careful when looking at the equity part of a corporation's balance sheet; the user should consider the related notes and should carefully examine how much debt the corporation owes and how much stockholders' equity it reports.

Corporate Earnings

The stockholders' equity section of a corporation's balance sheet includes contributed capital and retained earnings. Contributed capital reports the total amount of investments made by stockholders into the corporation. Retained earnings is the amount of the corporation's lifetime income not distributed as dividends to stockholders. As we discussed in Chapter 10, how a corporation reports its net income differs from how a sole proprietorship or a partnership reports its income because of the effect of income taxes, discontinued operations, extraordinary items, and the disclosure of earnings per share. A corporation may distribute dividends to both preferred and common stockholders, after "declaring" them at an earlier date. A corporation may pay cash dividends or distribute stock dividends. We will discuss each of these topics in the following sections.

Corporate Income Statement

The net income (loss) that a corporation reports on its income statement for a period is the amount of income that it transfers to retained earnings at the end of its accounting period. But, a corporation's income statement provides much more information than just net income (loss). This statement may have several major sections, as follows:

1. Income from continuing operations
   (a) Operating income
   (b) Nonoperating income (other items)
   (c) Income tax expense related to continuing operations

2. Results of discontinued operations
   (a) Income (loss) from operations of a discontinued segment (net of income taxes)
   (b) Gain (loss) on disposal of discontinued segment (net of income taxes)

3. Extraordinary gains or losses (net of income taxes)

4. Net income (the sum of items 1, 2, and 3)

5. Earnings per share

Not all corporate income statements contain these sections. We show Unlimited Decadence Corporation's income statement, which includes each section, in Exhibit 24-1 using assumed amounts.[4] Also included in Exhibit 24-1 is the note to the financial statements describing the computation of earnings per share.

Income from Continuing Operations

We discussed the income from continuing operations section of a corporate income statement in Chapter 10. This section includes a corporation's *operating income*, which it determines by subtracting cost of goods sold from net sales to obtain gross profit, and then subtracting the selling expenses and general and administrative expenses. It also includes the nonoperating income (or expense), which is the sum of the *"other items."* These other items include recurring items, such as interest expense and revenue, which are not part of the corporation's primary operations, as well as ordinary (as opposed to extraordinary) gains and losses, such as those related to the sale of equipment; losses from the impairment of property, plant, and equipment (or intangibles); and "restructuring" losses.

A corporation reports the total of the operating income and the nonoperating income as "income before income taxes" *if* it does not report results of discontinued operations or extraordinary items (which we discuss later). If it does include either of these items, it reports the total of the operating income and nonoperating income as "pretax income from continuing operations." In Exhibit 24-1, Unlimited Decadence's operating income is $7,000, its nonoperating income is $1,000, and its pretax income from continuing operations totals $8,000. (Note that all amounts in Unlimited Decadence's income statement are in thousands.)

A corporation has income tax expense, which is based on its pretax accounting income. It *pays* income taxes based on its "taxable income." The difference between the

---

[4]In this chapter, we assume that Unlimited Decadence has a vending machine segment, VendoBar, that it sells in 2000.

Exhibit 24-1 Income Statement for Unlimited Decadence Corporation

Unlimited Decadence Corporation
Income Statement
For Year Ended December 31, 2001

(in thousands)

Sales (net)		$80,000
Cost of goods sold		(51,000)
Gross profit		$29,000
Operating expenses		
Selling expenses	$14,000	
General and administrative expenses	8,000	
Total operating expenses		(22,000)
Operating income		$ 7,000
Other Items		
Gain on sale of equipment	$ 500	
Interest revenue	700	
Interest expense	(200)	
Nonoperating income		1,000
Pretax income from continuing operations		$ 8,000
Income tax expense of continuing operations		(3,200)
Income from continuing operations		$ 4,800
Results of discontinued operations		
Loss from operations of discontinued		
VendoBar Segment (net of $200 income tax credit)	$ (300)	
Gain on sale of discontinued VendoBar Segment		
(net of $600 income tax expense)	900	600
Income before extraordinary loss		$ 5,400
Extraordinary loss from tornado (net of $800		
income tax credit)		(1,200)
Net income		$ 4,200
Basic earnings per share (see Note A)		
Income from continuing operations		$ 3.16
Results of discontinued operations		0.46
Extraordinary loss from tornado		(0.92)
Basic earnings per share		$ 2.70

Labels on the left (brackets): Income from Continuing Operations; Results of Discontinued Operations; Extraordinary Loss; Net Income; Earnings per Share

Notes to the Financial Statements (in part)

Note A: Preferred dividends of $690 were deducted from net income and income from continuing operations in computing earnings per share. The weighted average number of common shares outstanding is 1,300 shares.

income tax expense and the income tax obligation causes deferred taxes, as we discussed in Chapter 22. A corporation's pretax accounting income is the sum of its pretax income from continuing operations, results of discontinued operations, and extraordinary items.[5] To determine its *total* income taxes, the corporation multiplies its taxable income by the income tax rate. Because actual income tax computations are complex, for simplicity we assume an income tax rate of 40% for all discussion and end-of-chapter homework materials. Because GAAP requires the corporation to report on its income statement the income tax expense (or income tax credit, in the case of a loss) related to each of these sections, the corporation makes a separate income tax computation for each section.

For example, in 2001, Unlimited Decadence has a pretax income from continuing operations of $8,000, a pretax loss from operations of its discontinued VendoBar segment of $500, a pretax gain on the sale of its discontinued VendoBar Segment of $1,500, and a

---

[5]It is not necessary to understand the meaning of both *results of discontinued operations* and *extraordinary items* for computing income taxes. It may be helpful, however, to read the later sections of this chapter, which deal with these items, in conjunction with the remainder of this section.

pretax extraordinary loss of $2,000. It computes its total income taxes and the income taxes related to each item, as we show in the following tax schedule.[6] Note that the two items of loss reduced the income taxes in the amounts of $200 and $800, respectively. These amounts are called *income tax credits*.

	Pretax Amount		Income Tax Rate		Income Taxes
Pretax income from continuing operations	$8,000	×	0.40	=	$3,200
Pretax loss from operations of discontinued segment	(500)	×	0.40	=	(200)
Gain (pretax) on sale of discontinued segment	1,500	×	0.40	=	600
Extraordinary loss (pretax)	(2,000)	×	0.40	=	(800)
Taxable Income and Income Taxes	$7,000	×	0.40	=	$2,800

As we show in Exhibit 24-1, Unlimited Decadence lists the $3,200 income tax expense for continuing operations as a separate item on the income statement and deducts this amount from the $8,000 pretax income from continuing operations to determine its $4,800 income from continuing operations.

Any items that a corporation includes in the results from discontinued operations section or as extraordinary gains and losses are reported "net of income taxes." That is, for each of these items, the corporation deducts the income tax expense (or income tax credit, in the case of a loss) *directly* from each item, and reports only the *after-tax* amount in its net income. It shows the income tax expense or credit in parentheses on the income statement, however. In Exhibit 24-1, Unlimited Decadence reports the loss from operations of its discontinued VendoBar Segment at the after-tax amount of $300 ($500 less the income tax credit of $200 from the tax schedule), the gain on sale of its discontinued VendoBar Segment at $900 ($1,500 − $600), and the extraordinary loss at $1,200 ($2,000 − $800).

Results of Discontinued Operations

Many corporations, sometimes called *conglomerates*, have several major divisions (segments) that sell different products or services. A corporation occasionally sells one of these segments—called a *sale of a discontinued segment*. The corporation usually sells the segment because it is not making enough profit (or is operating at a loss), or because the corporation is restructuring its activities. A **segment** is a separate major line of business whose assets, results of operations, and activities can clearly be separated from the rest of the corporation. Examples of transactions involving the sale of a segment include the sale by a communications company of all its radio stations or the sale by a food distributor of its wholesale supermarket division.

5 *How does a corporation report its results from discontinued operations and extraordinary items?*

 When PepsiCo *sold its* Pizza Hut *restaurants, do you think the sale was reported as the sale of a discontinued segment? Why or why not?*

www.pepsico.com

The sale of a discontinued segment is an important event for a corporation because of the effects on its future earnings potential and on the evaluation of its past earnings. For this reason, a corporation reports certain information about the sale separately on its income statement in a section called *results of discontinued operations*. By reporting this information separately, a corporation helps external users to evaluate the continuing part of the corporation, and thereby to assess the future potential of the corporation. That is, the current (and past) performance of the discontinued segment normally is not helpful in predicting how the remaining segments will perform in the future. The corporation includes two items in the discontinued operations section:

---

[6]For simplicity, in this discussion and end-of-chapter homework questions, we ignore deferred income taxes. Therefore, we assume Unlimited Decadence has no deferred tax liability.

1. *The income (or loss) from the operations of the discontinued segment for the year.* When a corporation operates the discontinued segment for part (or all) of the year before the sale of the segment, it must compute the pretax income (loss) from these operations.

2. *The gain (or loss) from the sale of the discontinued segment.* When the corporation sells the assets of the discontinued segment, it records a gain or loss (the difference between the selling price and the book value of the assets). It computes this gain or loss in the same way that it computes the gain or loss from the sale of an individual asset, as we discussed in Chapter 21.

The corporation deducts the related income taxes from both these pretax income (loss) amounts, and reports the after-tax income (loss) amounts related to the discontinued segment on its income statement. It adds together the after-tax operating income (loss) and the after-tax gain (loss) on the sale of the discontinued segment in the results of discontinued operations section of the income statement. As we discussed earlier, in Exhibit 24-1 Unlimited Decadence reported two amounts related to its discontinued VendoBar Segment—a $300 loss (after an income tax credit of $200) from the segment's operations, and a $900 gain (after income taxes of $600) from the sale of the segment.

Although we do not illustrate it here, Unlimited Decadence also adjusts its comparative income statements of the previous years to report separately the amounts of income earned by the segment in those years. It also separately classifies the assets and liabilities of the segment on its comparative balance sheets of previous years. Separating out these amounts allows external users to evaluate the corporation's segment(s) that will continue to exist separately from the segment the corporation has sold.

www.harsco.com

For instance, Harsco Corporation reported income from continuing operations of $100 million for 1997 and reported that it discontinued the operations of its defense business. Related to this discontinued operation, the corporation reported income of $28 million and a gain on the disposal of $150 million (both amounts net of tax). Harsco's net income was $278 million for 1997.

Which income amount would you use to evaluate Harsco's performance?

Extraordinary Gains and Losses

Sometimes an event or transaction causes an extraordinary gain or loss for a corporation. An **extraordinary item** is an event or transaction that is (1) *unusual in nature* and (2) *infrequent in occurrence*. Examples of events that are likely to be extraordinary items are an earthquake, a tornado, a flood, an expropriation of assets by a foreign country, and a prohibition under a newly enacted law. These may be thought of as acts of God or acts of politicians! For instance, in its income statement for 1996, The Coastal Corporation reported

www.coastalcorp.com

an extraordinary loss of $85.6 million (net of income taxes) as a result of discontinuing certain regulatory accounting principles relating to natural gas. Extraordinary items are so abnormal in regard to a corporation's current and potential earnings that GAAP requires the corporation to report the related gains or losses separately on its income statement.

 Do you think that earthquake damage would be an extraordinary item in California? in Florida? Why or why not?

A corporation reports extraordinary gains or losses, net of income taxes, in a separate section of its income statement, directly below the results of discontinued operations section (or if there is no such section, after income from continuing operations). In Exhibit 24-1, Unlimited Decadence reports a $1,200 extraordinary loss from a tornado (after deducting an $800 income tax credit).

Most gains and losses are *not* considered to be extraordinary. For example, the writedown of inventories and the sale of property, plant, and equipment result in ordinary gains and losses. A corporation reports these gains and losses in the nonoperating income section as "other items" and includes them in its pretax income from continuing operations.

Like discontinued operations, a corporation reports extraordinary items separately so that external users can focus on income from continuing operations as they evaluate the corporation's performance. Although an extraordinary loss has caused a loss for the shareholders, it is not likely to occur again and so should be treated differently by external users in their analysis.

External User Perspective: Profitability Ratio Analysis

In Chapters 6 and 7, we introduced three ratios that external users use to evaluate a company's profitability: (1) profit margin, (2) return on owners' (stockholders') equity, and (3) return on total assets. In this chapter, we discussed the various sections of a company's income statement, including income from continuing operations, results of discontinued operations, and extraordinary items. As we discussed, the latter two items are "nonrecurring" and are reported below income from continuing operations. When a user evaluates a company with these ratios, the user may make adjustments in these ratios to maintain comparability across time for that company, and across companies in the industry. Let's see how to do this by using the information for Unlimited Decadence in Exhibit 24-1 for the year 2001.

The profit margin is computed by dividing net income by net sales. So, Unlimited Decadence's profit margin is 5.3% ($4,200,000 ÷ $80,000,000). However, a user who is evaluating a corporation's profitability by computing its profit margin may omit any results of discontinued operations or extraordinary items from the numerator. Then Unlimited Decadence's profit margin is 6.0% ($4,800,000 ÷ $80,000,000).

The return on stockholders' equity is computed by dividing net income by average stockholders' equity. We will assume that Unlimited Decadence's average stockholders' equity is $18,000,000 (not shown in Exhibit 24-1). So, Unlimited Decadence's return on equity is 23.3% ($4,200,000 ÷ $18,000,000). However, a user evaluating a corporation's performance by computing its return on equity may omit any results of discontinued operations or extraordinary items from the numerator. In this case, Unlimited Decadence's return on stockholders' equity is 26.7% ($4,800,000 ÷ $18,000,000).

The return on total assets is computed by dividing net income plus interest expense by average total assets. We will assume that Unlimited Decadence's average total assets are $28,000,000 *including* the $4,000,000 average net assets of the discontinued segment (not shown in Exhibit 24-1). So, Unlimited Decadence's return on total assets is 15.7% [($4,200,000 net income + $200,000 interest expense) ÷ $28,000,000]. However, a user evaluating a corporation's profitability by computing its return on total assets may omit the results of the discontinued operations and extraordinary items from the net income in the numerator, as well as the net assets of the discontinued segment from the average total assets in the denominator. In this case, Unlimited Decadence's return on assets is 20.8% [($4,800,000 + $200,000) ÷ $24,000,000].

These modified calculations of the profit margin, return on stockholders' equity, and return on total assets should be better measures of Unlimited Decadence's performance and better indicators of its future performance. Also, since a company reclassifies its previous years' income statements and balance sheets to separately report the results of discontinued operations, the user can recalculate the ratios for previous years to see the trends in the performance of the company's continuing operations. Of course, users should not totally ignore the results of discontinued operations, which may indicate that the company is changing directions or that the company's managers have made poor decisions in the past in managing the segment.

The user must also be careful to examine whether the operating income section of the income statement includes "non operating" income, such as losses on the impairment of property, plant, and equipment (or intangibles), or restructuring losses. Determining the amounts of these losses may require careful reading of the notes to the financial statements. For example, in 1997 General Motors recorded charges (reductions) against income of $6.4 billion based on its "competitiveness studies." These charges had the effect of "reducing net sales and revenues by $548 million and increasing cost of sales, depreciation and amortization, and other deductions by $1.7 billion, $4.1 billion, and $72 million, respectively.

www.gm.com

Earnings per Share

6 *How does a corporation compute and report its earnings per share?*

The owners (stockholders) of a corporation hold shares of stock as evidence of ownership. Because owners can readily transfer these shares, the stock of many corporations sells on organized stock markets like the New York Stock Exchange and in the "Over The Counter" market. Stockholders invest (or sell their investments) in a corporation for many reasons, including the likelihood of receiving future dividends or participating in any future increase (or decrease) in the stock market price. The corporation's current and estimated future earnings influence both these factors.

To predict a corporation's future earnings, dividends, and stock market price, investors prepare many kinds of analyses. One of the items of financial information that they use in these analyses is the corporation's *earnings per share*. Earnings per share is probably the most frequently cited information in a financial analysis of a corporation. Each corporation reports its earnings per share (abbreviated as EPS) on its income statement, directly below the net income. For instance, PepsiCo reported earnings per share of $1.40 on its income statement for 1997, based on net income of $2,142 million and 1,528 million average common shares.

wwww.pepsico.com

Earnings per share computations can be very complicated; here we explain the computation of "basic earnings per share," and we will discuss "diluted" earnings per share later. **Basic earnings per share** is a corporation's net income per share available to its common stockholders. In its simplest form, a corporation computes its basic earnings per share by dividing its net income by the number of common shares outstanding during the entire year. A corporation, however, may report several components of net income and may have preferred stock outstanding that has first priority to dividends (as we discussed earlier in the chapter). It also may have shares of common stock outstanding for only part of a year because it issued common stock during the year. Therefore, a corporation computes this basic earnings per share amount as follows:

$$\text{Basic Earnings per Share} = \frac{\text{Net Income} - \text{Preferred Dividends}}{\text{Weighted Average Number of Common Shares Outstanding}}$$

Net Income and Preferred Dividends

Common stockholders are the *residual* owners of the corporation. Therefore, the earnings per share amount applies *only* to common shares, and the numerator includes only the earnings available to common stockholders. If a corporation has no preferred shares outstanding, it uses net income as the numerator. If a corporation has outstanding preferred stock, however, it deducts the preferred dividends for the current period from the net income to determine the earnings available to common stockholders. To understand the computation of the numerator, assume that Unlimited Decadence (from Exhibit 24-1) had preferred stock outstanding during 2001 and that the dividends on this preferred stock amounted to $690,000. The numerator of Unlimited Decadence's 2001 earnings per share is $3,510,000, computed by subtracting the $690,000 preferred dividends from the $4,200,000 net income. We will summarize these computations later.

Weighted Average Common Shares

Since a corporation earns its net income over the entire year, it should relate the earnings to the weighted average number of common shares outstanding during the year. If a corporation has not issued any common shares during the year, it uses the common shares outstanding for the entire year as the denominator. When the corporation has issued common shares during the year, it multiplies these shares by the fraction of the year (in months) that they are outstanding. It adds the result to the beginning number of shares to determine the weighted average number of common shares outstanding during the year. It uses this number as the denominator in the earnings per share calculation.

Assume Unlimited Decadence had 1,200,000 common shares outstanding during all of 2001. On August 1, 2001, it issued an additional 240,000 common shares, so that it had a total of 1,440,000 common shares outstanding at the end of the year. Its weighted average number of common shares outstanding during 2001 is 1,300,000, determined by adding 1,200,000 + 100,000 weighted average shares (240,000 × 5/12), computed as follows:

Months Shares Are Outstanding	Shares Outstanding	×	Fraction of Year Outstanding	=	Weighted Average
January-December	1,200,000		12/12		1,200,000
August-December	240,000		5/12		100,000
Total Weighted Average Common Shares					1,300,000

 If a corporation purchases treasury stock, does its weighted average number of common shares increase or decrease? Does its basic earnings per share increase or decrease?

Computation, Reporting, and Disclosure

A corporation reports its basic earnings per share on the income statement directly below net income. In addition, it reports the earnings per share related to the major components of net income. It computes the earnings per share for the income from continuing operations by subtracting the preferred dividends from the income from continuing operations and dividing the result by the weighted average common shares. It computes the earnings per share amounts for the results of discontinued operations and extraordinary items by dividing the respective amounts (disregarding the preferred dividends) by the weighted average common shares. It discloses the amount of the preferred dividends deducted from the numerator and the weighted average number of common shares used in the denominator in the notes to its financial statements.

The basic earnings per share of Unlimited Decadence for 2001 are $2.70, as we calculate in the following schedule. We also show the earnings per share for each component of the income statement. The earnings per share amounts, of course, total $2.70, and Unlimited Decadence reports them on its income statement, as we show in Exhibit 24-1. The note to Unlimited Decadence's financial statements discloses the preferred dividends and weighted average shares.

Item	Computations	EPS
Basic earnings per share	$$\frac{\$4,200,000 - \$690,000}{1,300,000}$$	= $2.70
Components:		
Income from continuing operations	$$\frac{\$4,800,000 - \$690,000}{1,300,000}$$	= $3.16
Results of discontinued operations	$$\frac{\$600,000}{1,300,000}$$	= 0.46
Extraordinary loss from tornado	$$\frac{\$(1,200,000)}{1,300,000}$$	= (0.92)
Basic earnings per share		$2.70

Diluted Earnings per Share

A corporation has a **complex capital structure** when it has issued stock options and convertible securities (bonds or preferred stock). These securities are known as **potential common shares** because they can be used by the holder to acquire common stock. Since conversion of these securities into common stock would affect the earnings available to each common stockholder, the corporation must report its diluted earnings per share in addition to basic earnings per share. **Diluted earnings per share** includes the effects of all potential common shares that would reduce earnings per share. For example, Microsoft's diluted earnings per share in 1997 was $2.63 per share, as compared with its basic earnings per share of $2.87 per share, a decrease of 8%.

We will not illustrate the computation of diluted earnings per share because it is very complex. We will, however, explain why diluted earnings per share is lower than basic earnings per share. Two types of potential common shares affect the computation of diluted earnings per share—stock options and convertible securities.

Stock options reduce earnings per share because the computation of diluted earnings per share *assumes* that the employees exercised the options at the beginning of the year to acquire comon stock.[6] These additional shares would increase the denominator of the earnings per share computation. This larger denominator would result in a lower earnings per share.

Convertible securities reduce earnings per share because the computation *assumes* that each security was converted into common stock at the beginning of the year. This assumed conversion causes two changes in the earnings per share computation—an increase in both the numerator and the denominator. The denominator increases by the number of shares that would be issued due to the assumed conversion. If convertible bonds are assumed to be converted into common stock, the numerator increases because net income would be larger, since the interest expense on the bonds would not be paid. If preferred stock is assumed to be converted into common stock, the preferred dividends would not be paid and the earnings available to common stockholders would increase.

External User Analysis: Price/Earnings Ratio

Many users consider a corporation's earnings per share to be the single most useful indicator of its performance. They look at the amount of earnings per share, the change in earnings per share from the previous period, and the trend in earnings per share as important indicators of the success, or failure, of the corporation. Since one of the important results of a corporation's performance is the market price of its common stock, another important and widely used measure is the **price/earnings ratio,** which is computed as follows:

$$\text{Price/Earnings Ratio} = \text{Market Price per Share} \div \text{Earnings per Share}$$

The price/earnings ratio indicates how much investors are willing to pay per dollar of *current* earnings. So a higher price/earnings ratio often is thought to mean that the corporation has better prospects for *future* growth. For example, at the time of the writing of this book, the following amounts were reported for selected corporations:

---

[6]The computation assumes that the employees paid the option price (which is *lower* than the market price) to the corporation in cash, and that the corporation issued the shares of stock to the employees. Then, the computation assumes that the corporation used the cash to purchase treasury stock at the average market price which is *higher* than the option price. Given these assumptions, the corporation would have been able to purchase fewer shares than the number that it issued due to the exercise of the options. To compute diluted earnings per share, the corporation subtracts the assumed shares reacquired as treasury stock from the assumed shares issued for the stock options and adds the difference to the denominator of the basic earnings per share computation. These assumptions are made so that all corporations compute diluted earnings per share in a consistent manner.

Company	Market Price per Share	Earnings per Share[a]	Price/Earnings Ratio
PepsiCo	$ 38½	$1.33	29
Coca-Cola	64¾	1.51	43
Intel	116⅞	3.25	36
Microsoft	134⅜	2.04	66

[a]Amounts computed and rounded to the nearest cent

The differences in the price/earnings ratios indicate, for example, that investors believe that Coca-Cola will experience higher growth in earnings per share than PepsiCo. Therefore, they are willing to pay a higher price per dollar of current earnings for Coca-Cola's stock than for PepsiCo's stock. Similarly, investors expect Microsoft to grow faster than Intel. The price/earnings ratios also show that the expectation of growth for Coca-Cola is between those for the two computer companies. The price/earnings ratio also can be used to predict future stock prices. For example, if an investor expects that PepsiCo will earn $2 per share in the next year and that the price/earnings ratio will not change, the stock price should be $58 ($2 × 29).

www.cocacola.com
www.pepsico.com
www.microsoft.com
www.intel.com

 Look up in a newspaper the market price per share and the price/earnings ratio for each of the four companies listed above. Compute the earnings per share. Which amounts have changed?

Business Issues and Values

The requirement that a corporation must disclose the "expense" of its stock options in the notes to its financial statements was very controversial, even causing bills to be introduced in Congress. Some people wanted the corporation to include the expense directly in its income statement. Those who supported this approach argued that stock options are part of the employees' compensation and therefore should be an expense. Those who were against the expense being reported argued that there is no expense because the corporation has *no cash outflow*. The controversy particularly surrounds executive compensation—many executives like the idea of being compensated in a way that does not affect a corporation's net income! These arguments do not mean that stock options are bad—they are designed to encourage employees to make decisions that cause the market price of a corporation's stock to increase and provide a benefit to all its stockholders.

Earlier we gave the example of Microsoft. (By the way, Bill Gates does *not* participate in the stock options.) Microsoft reported a net income in 1997 of $3.5 billion, or $2.63 per share. Including the effect of its stock options would reduce its net income to $3.1 billion, or $2.32 per share. So, a stock price of, say, $70 would be 30 times the adjusted earnings per share amount but only about 27 times the reported amount.

 Look up Microsoft's price/earnings ratio in a newspaper. How is the market evaluating Microsoft?

Another issue to understand is where the stock comes from when employees exercise options. A corporation could distribute either treasury stock or authorized but unissued common stock. Microsoft chooses to use treasury stock. In 1997, it paid about $3.1 billion to purchase treasury stock to issue to employees who exercised stock options! The $3.1 billion is a cash expenditure that does not affect income—it reduces cash and stockholders' equity.

When a corporation uses authorized but unissued common stock, of course it does not pay any cash. However, the issuance of additional shares reduces the ownership interests of current shareholders and also reduces earnings per share. Therefore, *if* the price/earnings ratio remains the same, the corporation's stock price would also decrease.

 Does this make sense? Explain how the corporation's stock price would decrease if the price/earnings ratio remains the same.

Cash Dividends

7 *What kinds of dividends can a corporation distribute, and what are their characteristics?*

Corporations often distribute cash dividends. (We will discuss another "type" of dividend later in the chapter.) A corporation's net income increases its net assets, and it records the net income in retained earnings, but the distribution of cash dividends has the opposite effect. The corporation records the distribution as a decrease in its *assets*, and it also records this decrease in retained earnings. Thus the phrase "retained earnings paid out in dividends," which some corporations use in discussing dividends, is somewhat misleading. A corporation pays cash dividends out of *cash,* and it decreases retained earnings because the payment is a return of capital to the stockholders.

A corporation must meet legal requirements and have enough cash available to pay dividends. The board of directors is responsible for setting a corporation's dividend policy. The board determines the amount and timing of the dividends, considering legal requirements, compliance with contractual agreements, and the financial well-being of the corporation. Legal requirements vary from state to state, but most states require a corporation to have a positive balance in retained earnings before it may declare dividends. In evaluating the financial well-being of the corporation, the board of directors should consider several factors including the impact of the payment of a dividend on cash, current assets, and working capital; the corporation's ability to finance expansion projects with the remaining assets; and the effect of the dividend on the stock market price per share. The payment of dividends should be in the financial long- and short-term best interests of the corporation and its stockholders.

 Explain whether you think that a corporation that reports a loss for the year would pay dividends.

A sole proprietorship or a partnership can arrange for owner withdrawals very quickly. When the owner wants to withdraw cash, the company writes a check to the owner from its checking account, the company records the withdrawal, and the owner cashes the check for personal use. In contrast, a corporation cannot distribute dividends so quickly. The corporation may have many stockholders and therefore may require extensive record keeping. As a result, the dividend process is usually spread out over a period of several weeks.

Three dates are significant for a cash dividend (or any type of dividend): (1) the date of declaration, (2) the date of record, and (3) the date of payment. For instance on August 18, 1998, Whirlpool Corporation declared a 34¢ per-share quarterly dividend, payable on September 11, 1998, to shareholders of record on August 31, 1998.

www.whirlpool.com

On the **date of declaration**, the board of directors declares that a dividend will be paid to stockholders of record on a specified future date, typically about four to six weeks later. On the declaration date, the corporation becomes legally liable to pay the future dividend. At this time, the corporation determines the total amount of the dividend liability to common stockholders, as well as any dividend liability to preferred stockholders (we will discuss this later). The corporation normally declares dividends on a *per-share basis.* That is, it sets a dollar amount per common share outstanding at the time of declaration. It determines the total amount of the dividend liability by multiplying the dividends per share by the number of common shares outstanding on the date of declaration. The corporation records the liability by reducing Retained Earnings and increasing a current liability (Dividends Payable).

It takes the corporation some time to process the dividend checks, and investors need to determine whether they want to buy or sell the stock based on the dividends. Thus, the corporation needs to specify a *cut-off* date—the date of record. On the **date of record**, only investors listed as stockholders of the corporation (the stockholders of record) can participate in the dividend. The date of record usually occurs several weeks after the declaration date and several weeks before the payment date, as specified in the dividend provisions. After the date of record, the corporation begins processing the dividend checks to the stockholders of record. On the **date of payment**, the corporation mails the dividend checks. The corporation records the payment by reducing cash and eliminating the current liability.

 Explain why you might buy or sell stock between the date of declaration and the date of record.

For example, assume that on November 15, 2000, Unlimited Decadence declared a 60¢ per-share dividend on its 1,200,000 outstanding common shares. These dividends were payable on December 29, 2000, to stockholders of record as of December 15, 2000. On November 15, Unlimited Decadence recorded the declaration of the $720,000 dividends (1,200,000 × $0.60) as follows:

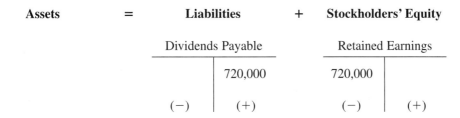

Assets	=	**Liabilities**	+	**Stockholders' Equity**
		Dividends Payable		Retained Earnings
		720,000		720,000
	(−)	(+)	(−)	(+)

On December 29, 2000, Unlimited Decadence recorded the payment of the dividends as follows:

Assets	=	**Liabilities**	+	**Stockholders' Equity**
Cash		Dividends Payable		
720,000		720,000		
(+)	(−)	(−)	(+)	

If a corporation's accounting period ended between the date of declaration and the date of payment, it would report the Dividends Payable account as a current liability on its balance sheet.

Cash Dividends on Preferred Stock

As we discussed earlier in the chapter, some investors consider certain stockholder rights to be more important than others. To appeal to these investors, a corporation may issue preferred stock. The rights of preferred stockholders are included on the stock certificate. The two important rights for dividends are (1) a preference as to dividends, and (2) accumulation of dividends. Preferred stock may be issued with one or both of these rights.

Preference as to Dividends

Holders of preferred stock have a preference as to dividends. A **dividend preference** is a right of preferred stockholders to receive a dividend before a corporation pays a dividend to common stockholders. A corporation usually issues preferred stock with a par value and expresses the dividends as a percentage of this value. For instance, assume that a corporation has outstanding 1,000 shares of 10%, $50 par value preferred stock. The corporation must pay $5 per share ($50 par × 10%), which totals $5,000 ($5 × 1,000 shares), as dividends to preferred stockholders before it can pay *any* dividends to common stockholders.

This preference to dividends does *not* guarantee that the corporation will pay a preferred dividend in any given year, since the board of directors can decide not to pay any dividends. To protect preferred stockholders further, the corporation may include on the preferred stock certificate a provision that requires the accumulation of dividends.

 Would you purchase preferred stock without a cumulative provision? Explain why or why not.

Cumulative Preferred Stock

Stockholders are not legally entitled to receive dividends unless the corporation's board of directors has declared these dividends. If the board of directors does not declare dividends in a given year, the corporation will never be required to pay that dividend to a holder of *non*cumulative preferred stock. For this reason, corporations rarely issue noncumulative preferred stock because investors consider this feature to be a distinct disadvantage.

Most preferred stock is cumulative. The corporation must pay the holders of **cumulative preferred stock** all dividends of the current period and the accumulated *unpaid* dividends of past periods before it can pay any dividends to common stockholders. Any dividends not declared on cumulative preferred stock in a given period become **dividends in arrears**. Dividends in arrears accumulate from period to period. The dividends in arrears are *not* a liability to the corporation because no liability exists until the dividend declaration. Any dividends in arrears, however, are very important to external users, and the corporation discloses them in a note to the financial statements.

To understand dividends in arrears, assume that a corporation has 2,000 shares of 8%, $100 par value cumulative preferred stock outstanding. Each share of stock is entitled to an $8 annual dividend (8% × $100 par value). Suppose the corporation does not declare dividends in 1998 and 1999. Preferred stockholders are entitled to dividends in arrears of $16,000 (2,000 × $8) at the end of 1998 and $32,000 (2,000 × $8 × 2 years) at the end of 1999. At the end of 2000, the corporation would have to pay dividends of $48,000 (for three years) to preferred stockholders before it could pay any dividends to common stockholders.

Stock Dividends

www.civitasbank.com

Occasionally a corporation may declare and distribute a *stock* dividend. A **stock dividend** is a proportional (pro rata) distribution of additional shares of a corporation's own stock to its stockholders. For instance, on August 18, 1998, Civitas Bank declared a 5% stock dividend, "payable" on September 18, 1998 to shareowners of record on August 28, 1998.

 As an investor, would you generally prefer to receive a cash dividend or a stock dividend? Explain why.

Note that a stock dividend is very different from a cash dividend. A stock dividend differs from a cash dividend in that the corporation does *not* distribute assets. After a stock dividend, each stockholder holds the same percentage of ownership in the corporation as the stockholder held prior to the distribution. For instance, assume that a corporation has 10,000 common shares outstanding, that one stockholder owns 2,000 shares, and that the corporation issues a 10% stock dividend. After the stock dividend, the corporation has 11,000 shares outstanding (10,000 × 1.10), and the stockholder now owns 2,200 (2,000 × 1.10) shares. The stockholder owns 20% of the outstanding common stock *both prior to and after* the stock dividend. What occurs, from an accounting standpoint, is a rearrangement of stockholders' equity. Total stockholders' equity of the corporation does not change, but its retained earnings decreases by the dollar amount of the dividend and its contributed capital increases by the same amount because of the additional number of shares issued. As you will see shortly, the corporation calculates the dollar amount of the stock dividend differently depending on whether the dividend is "small" or "large."

Is this rancher participating in a stock dividend?

Some stockholders view stock dividends unfavorably because, when they receive a stock dividend: (1) the stockholders receive no corporate assets; (2) theoretically, the total market value of their investment does not increase because the increased number of shares is offset by a decrease in the stock market price per share due to a larger number of shares participating in the same corporate earnings; and (3) the corporation's ability to pay future cash dividends may be limited because it decreases retained earnings by the amount of the stock dividend and most states set legal dividend restrictions based on a positive balance in retained earnings.

Some stockholders, however, welcome stock dividends because (1) they see stock dividends as evidence of corporate growth and sound financial policy; (2) other investors also may look favorably on the stock dividends and purchase the stock, causing the stock market price *not* to decrease proportionally; (3) the corporation may continue to pay the same cash dividend per share, in which case stockholders will receive higher total dividends; and (4) the market price may decrease to a lower trading range (the range of prices that investors are willing to pay for stock), making the stock more attractive to additional investors.

 Explain why you think making the stock attractive to additional investors would seem positive to current stockholders.

Small Stock Dividends

For reporting purposes, GAAP distinguishes between small and large stock dividends. A **small stock dividend** is 20% or less of the previously outstanding common shares.[7] A corporation may issue a small stock dividend in order to continue a pattern of dividend *distributions* to stockholders when no cash is available for a cash dividend. For a small stock dividend, GAAP assumes that the size of the dividend does not significantly affect the stock market price of the outstanding shares. Thus, the market price at which the corporation's stock is selling is considered to be the "value" of the stock issued in the stock

---

[7]GAAP states that a small stock dividend is less than 20% or 25%. For simplicity, we use 20%.

dividend, and the corporation records the stock dividend at this price. It reduces retained earnings and increases contributed capital by an amount equal to the current market value on the date of declaration for the additional shares of the stock dividend.

To understand the reporting of a small stock dividend, assume that Crabtree Corporation declares and issues a 10% stock dividend. Before the stock dividend, Crabtree has 10,000 shares of $10 a common stock outstanding. The common stock is selling for $19 per share, so the 1,000 share (10,000 shares × 10%) stock dividend has a current market value of $19,000. The corporation records the small stock dividend by reducing Retained Earnings by $19,000, increasing Common Stock for the $10,000 par value, and increasing Additional Paid-in Capital for $9,000 ($19,000 − $10,000). Crabtree Corporation's stockholders' equity before and after the issuance of the small stock dividend is as follows:

	Stockholders' Equity		
	Before Stock Dividend	**Change**	**After Stock Dividend**
Contributed capital			
Common stock, $10 par, 40,000 shares authorized, 10,000 and 11,000 shares issued and outstanding	$100,000	+ $10,000 =	$110,000
Additional paid-in capital	70,000	+ 9,000 =	79,000
Total contributed capital	$170,000		$189,000
Retained earnings	140,000	− 19,000 =	121,000
Total Stockholders' Equity	$310,000		$310,000

Note that the total stockholders' equity prior to and after the stock dividend is $310,000. The components have changed, with retained earnings decreasing by $19,000 and contributed capital increasing by the same amount, and with the issued shares increasing from 10,000 to 11,000.

Large Stock Dividends and Stock Splits

Sometimes the market price of a corporation's common stock increases to the point where it is not as attractive to certain investors. Many corporations believe a wide distribution of ownership increases the demand for their stock, improves their public image, and increases their product sales to their stockholders. To reduce the market price so that it falls within the trading range of most investors, a corporation may authorize a large stock dividend or a stock split.

A **large stock dividend** is greater than 20% of the previously outstanding common shares. The size of a large stock dividend is likely to cause a substantial decrease in the stock market price of the outstanding shares. Thus, the market price at which the corporation's stock is selling cannot be considered to be the "value" of the stock issued in the dividend. Therefore, a corporation does *not* record a large stock dividend at the current market price, but uses the *par* (or *stated*) value of the stock instead. For a large stock dividend, a corporation reduces retained earnings and increases contributed capital by the total par value for the additional shares of the stock dividend. Therefore, although the amount of one component decreases and the amount of the other component increases, there is no change in total stockholders' equity. To illustrate a large stock dividend, we will use the same facts for Crabtree Corporation except that now we will assume that it declares and issues a 100% stock dividend. The corporation issues an additional 10,000 (10,000 × 100%) shares and records the stock dividend at the par value of $100,000 (10,000 × $10). After the dividend, the corporation has issued a total of 20,000 shares of common stock.

Stockholders' Equity

	Before Stock Dividend	Change			After Stock Dividend
Contributed capital					
Common stock, $10 par, 40,000 shares authorized, 10,000 and 20,000 shares issued and outstanding	$100,000	+ $100,000	=		$200,000
Additional paid-in capital	70,000				70,000
Total contributed capital	$170,000				$270,000
Retained earnings	140,000	− 100,000	=		40,000
Total Stockholders' Equity	$310,000				$310,000

A stockholder who previously owned 40 shares of common stock will own 80 shares after the large stock dividend. The additional number of shares participating in the same amount of corporate earnings should cause a proportional decrease in the market price per share. Like a small stock dividend, a large stock dividend has no effect on total stockholders' equity.

A stock split is similar to a large stock dividend. A **stock split** is a decrease in the par value per share of a corporation's common stock and a proportional increase in the number of shares authorized and issued. For example, on November 13, 1997, The Clorox Company authorized a four-for-three stock split in the form of a 33% stock dividend, payable December 15, 1997 to shareholders of record on December 1, 1997." Since a stock split affects the number of authorized shares and the legal capital, each stock split must be approved by the stockholders and the state in which the corporation is incorporated.

To illustrate a stock split, we will use the same facts for Crabtree Corporation except that now we will assume that it declares a 2-for-1 stock split with a reduction to a $5 par value. After the split, the corporation has issued a total of 20,000 shares of $5 par value common stock (still a total par value of $100,000).

www.clorox.com

Stockholders' Equity

Contributed capital	
Common stock, $5 par, 80,000 shares authorized, 20,000 shares issued and outstanding	$100,000
Additional paid-in capital	70,000
Total contributed capital	$170,000
Retained earnings	140,000
Total Stockholders' Equity	$310,000

Note that no component of stockholders' equity is changed by the stock split—but the number of shares authorized and issued has doubled and the par value is half its original amount. A stockholder who previously owned 40 shares of $10 par value common stock will own 80 shares of $5 par value common stock after the stock split. The additional number of shares participating in the same amount of corporate earnings will cause a proportional decrease in the market price per share.

As an investor, explain whether you would prefer a company to issue a large stock dividend or a stock split.

Comprehensive Income

A corporation that has "unrealized gains and losses" must report its annual *comprehensive income*. Comprehensive income is a measure of a corporation's performance that includes the corporation's: (1) net income (or loss) and (2) "other" comprehensive income (or loss). A corporation's other comprehensive income (or loss) includes items such as the "unrealized increase or decrease in the value of available-for-sale securities" (which we discussed in Chapter 23) and the "gain or loss from converting the financial statements of a foreign subsidiary into U.S. dollars." These items are reported net of income taxes. GAAP requires each corporation to report its comprehensive income so that external users have more complete information to evaluate the corporation's profitability, financial flexibility, and operating capability. A corporation reporting comprehensive income has the option of including a schedule adding net income and the other items of comprehensive income either on the bottom of its income statement, in a separate statement, or in its statement of changes in stockholders' equity (which we will discuss in the next section of this chapter).

To illustrate the computation of other comprehensive income, recall from Chapter 23 that Unlimited Decadence's investments in available-for-sale securities increased from $12,000 to $12,500 in 2000. Under the market value method, Unlimited Decadence would report the $500 *increase* in its Unrealized Increase in Market Value of Investments account as its other comprehensive income for 2000. Unlimited Decadence would then add this $500 unrealized increase in the market value of its investments in available-for-sale securities to its net income for 2000 and report the total combined amount as its comprehensive income for 2000. A corporation reports the *accumulated* other comprehensive income as a separate component in the stockholders' equity section of its balance sheet. We illustrated this disclosure in Chapter 23 for the $500 *balance* of Unlimited Decadence's Unrealized Increase in Market Value of Investments account at the end of 2000.

Statement of Changes in Stockholders' Equity

8 *How and why does a corporation report the changes in its stockholders' equity?*

As you can see from the discussion in this chapter, in a single accounting period a corporation may have many transactions affecting its contributed capital. In addition, a corporation increases retained earnings by the net income and decreases it by the dividends of the accounting period. External users are interested in the changes in a corporation's stockholders' equity because these changes may have an impact on the corporation's *risk* and *financial flexibility*. To disclose its stockholders' equity activities, each corporation reports the changes in the different classes of capital stock (including the number of shares issued), in each additional paid-in capital account, in treasury stock, and in retained earnings for the accounting period.[8] Most corporations report this information on a statement of changes in stockholders' equity. A **statement of changes in stockholders' equity** is a supporting schedule to the stockholders' equity section of the balance sheet.[9]

We show the statement of changes in stockholders' equity (and the reported ending stockholders' equity) of Barth Corporation in Exhibit 24-2, using assumed amounts. In the top part of Exhibit 24-2 we list the stockholders' equity account titles across the top of the schedule, and we list the beginning balances in the respective columns. Then we briefly explain each of the transactions that affected the components of stockholders' equity in the explanation column. We include the shares issued and dollar amounts under the appropriate column. For instance, the second line indicates that the corporation allocated the $18,000 cash received from issuing 1,000 shares of common stock as follows: $10,000 to the Common Stock account and $8,000 to Additional Paid-in Capital. Note that we list the

---

[8]As we discussed in the previous section, a corporation may also report its comprehensive income in this statement.

[9]When a corporation has not issued or reacquired any capital stock during the accounting period, it may choose to prepare a statement of retained earnings. **A statement of retained earnings** is a schedule that starts with the beginning balance in retained earnings, adds the amount of net income, and subtracts the amount of dividends to determine the ending balance of retained earnings. This schedule is similar to the schedule of changes in owner's equity for a sole proprietorship (see Exhibit 6-7) as well as the retained earnings column of Exhibit 24-2, and we do not illustrate it here.

Exhibit 24-2 **Reporting Changes in Stockholders' Equity and Ending Stockholders' Equity**

BARTH CORPORATION
Statement of Changes in Stockholders' Equity
Schedule A
For Year Ended December 31, 2000

Explanation	Common Stock Shares Issued	Common Stock $10 Par Value	Additional Paid-in Capital	Retained Earnings	Treasury Stock
Balances, 1/1/2000	6,000	$60,000	$26,000	$67,000	$(4,500)
Issued for cash	1,000	10,000	8,000		
Reissued treasury stock					
(100 shares at $17, cost $15)			200		1,500
Net income				49,000	
Dividends (cash)				(20,000)	
Balances, 12/31/2000	7,000 (1)	$70,000 (2)	$34,200 (3)	$96,000 (4)	$(3,000) (5)

BARTH CORPORATION
Stockholders' Equity
December 31, 2000
(see Schedule A)

Contributed Capital		
Common stock, $10 par, 30,000 shares authorized,		
7,000 shares issued (1), 6,800 shares outstanding	$70,000 (2)	
Additional paid-in capital	34,200 (3)	
Total contributed capital		$104,200
Retained earnings		96,000 (4)
Total contributed capital and retained earnings		$200,200
Less: Treasury stock (200 shares at a cost of $15 per share)		(3,000) (5)
Total Stockholders' Equity		$197,200

amounts in the treasury stock column in parentheses because treasury stock is a negative component of stockholders' equity. We then total the columns, and include the column headings and totals in the stockholders' equity section of the balance sheet, as we show in the bottom part of Exhibit 24-2. Note that the items and amounts listed in stockholders' equity (which we have numbered 1 through 5 for clarity) correspond to the columns and totals in the statement of changes in stockholders' equity.

How Capital Stock Transactions Affect the Cash Flow Statement

A corporation generally reports capital stock transactions involving cash in the financing activities section of its cash flow statement. It reports the cash collected from the sale of stock (including sales to employees for stock options) and from the reissuance of treasury stock as cash inflows from financing activities. It reports the cash paid to acquire treasury stock and paid for cash dividends as cash outflows for financing activities.

 Why do you think a dividend that a corporation paid is a cash flow from a financing activity whereas a dividend that it received is a cash flow from an operating activity?

A corporation reports the cash flows from its income from continuing operations in the operating activities section of its cash flow statement, using either the direct or the indirect method, as we discussed in Chapters 8 and 19. On the other hand, the corporation reports any cash it received from the disposal of a discontinued segment as a cash inflow from investing activities because it involves the sale of property, plant, and equipment (as well as other assets). A corporation also reports any cash it received (or paid) from an extraordinary item (other than the early retirement of debt that we discussed in Chapter 22) as a cash inflow (outflow) from investing activities.

Although not affecting cash, the noncash issuance of stock (e.g., issuance of stock for land) increases both a corporation's assets (an investing activity) and its stockholders' equity (a financing activity). Similarly, the conversion of preferred stock to common stock both increases and decreases a corporation's stockholders' equity (both are financing activities). A corporation discloses these types of transactions in a note accompanying its financial statements. The corporation does not disclose the issuance of a stock dividend or a stock split in this way because neither is considered by GAAP to be a financing activity.

Summary

At the beginning of the chapter we asked you several questions. During the chapter, we asked you to STOP and answer some additional questions to build your knowledge about specific issues. Be sure you answered these additional questions. Below are the questions from the beginning of the chapter, with a brief summary of the key points relating to the answers. Use your creative and critical thinking skills to expand on these key points to develop more complete answers to the questions and to determine what other questions you have that might lead you to learn more about the issues.

1 **What are the rights of a corporation's stockholders?**

A corporation's stockholders may have the following rights: (1) the right to attend stockholders' meetings and to vote in setting and approving major policies and actions of the corporation; (2) the right to vote in the election of the board of directors; (3) the right to share in net income by receiving dividends from the corporation; (4) the right to purchase additional capital stock if it is issued—a right known as the *preemptive right;* and (5) the right to share in the distribution of the assets of the corporation if it is liquidated (terminated).

2 **What is important for an external user to know about a corporation's capital stock transactions?**

It is important for an external user to understand the difference between authorized capital stock and issued capital stock. Authorized capital stock is the number of shares of capital stock (both common and preferred) that the corporation may legally issue. On the other hand, issued capital stock is the number of shares of capital stock that a corporation has legally issued to its stockholders as of the balance sheet date. A corporation may issue common stock for cash, in noncash exchanges, and in other transactions. A corporation may issue common stock with a par value, as no-par stock with a stated value, or as true no-par stock. In most cases a corporation issues common stock for cash, at a price above the par value. When a corporation issues common stock for assets other than cash, or for services performed, it must use a correct value to record the transaction. The general rule is to record the transaction at the market value of the stock issued or the assets received, whichever is more reliable.

3 **What are the characteristics of a corporation's treasury stock, and how does it record and report this stock?**

Treasury stock is a corporation's own capital stock that (1) stockholders fully paid for and the corporation issued, (2) the corporation later reacquired, and (3) the corporation currently holds. External users need to understand several features about treasury stock. Treasury stock is not an asset of the corporation. A corporation cannot report a gain or a loss from reacquiring its own stock; this restricts a corporation from influencing its net income. Consequently, a corporation reports treasury stock as a reduction of stockholders' equity. Treasury stock generally does not have voting or preemptive rights, cannot participate in dividends, and has no rights at liquidation. When a corporation reacquires its capital stock, it records the cost as an increase in a Treasury Stock account (which reduces stockholders' equity) and a decrease in Cash. On its balance sheet, the corporation deducts the cost of the treasury stock from the total of contributed capital and retained earnings. A corporation may reissue treasury stock at a price above, below, or equal to its cost. The corporation records the reissuance by reducing the Treasury Stock account for the cost of the shares reissued, and treats the difference between the cash received and this cost as an adjustment of Additional Paid-in Capital. If it receives more (less) cash than the cost of the reissued treasury stock, it records the excess as an increase (decrease) in Additional Paid-in Capital.

4 What are compensatory stock options, and how does a corporation report them?

A corporation's compensatory stock options are intended to provide additional compensation to its employees (often a select group of employees, such as the top managers). Under a compensatory stock-option plan, employees, in exchange for their services, receive the option to buy shares of the corporation's common stock at a fixed price for a certain period of time. In addition to providing compensation, stock options are designed to encourage employees to make decisions that will increase the price of the stock and thereby provide a benefit to all stockholders. The corporation that issues compensatory stock options does not report an expense for these options on its income statement. If the corporation pays its employees a lower cash salary when it also provides a stock-option plan, its income is higher because of the lower salary expense. When the employee exercises the option, the corporation increases cash and stockholders' equity for the amount paid by the employee. Because the GAAP for stock options is so controversial, a corporation must disclose in the notes to its financial statements the amount that its net income would be if it included the "expense" of the compensatory stock options it grants. Therefore, an external user can use this pro forma net income instead of the reported net income in order to understand the performance of a corporation that has issued compensatory stock options.

5 How does a corporation report its results from discontinued operations and extraordinary items?

Many corporations have several major divisions (segments) that sell different products or services. A corporation occasionally sells one of these segments—a sale of a discontinued segment. The corporation reports certain information about the sale separately on its income statement in a section called results of discontinued operations. The results of discontinued operations section includes two items: (1) the income (or loss) from the operations of the discontinued segment for the year, and (2) the gain (or loss) from the sale of the discontinued segment. The corporation deducts the related income taxes from both these pretax income (loss) amounts, and reports the after-tax income (loss) amounts related to the discontinued segment in the results of discontinued operations section. The corporation also reclassifies its comparative income statements of previous periods to report separately the amounts of income generated by the segment in those periods. It also separately classifies the assets and liabilities of the segment on its comparative balance sheets of previous years.

An extraordinary item is an event or transaction that is (1) unusual in nature and (2) infrequent in occurrence. These extraordinary items are so abnormal in regard to a corporation's current and potential earnings that GAAP requires the corporation to report the related gains or losses separately on its income statement. A corporation reports extraordinary gains or losses, net of income taxes, in a separate section of its income statement, directly below the results of discontinued operations section.

6 How does a corporation compute and report its earnings per share?

Earnings per share is a corporation's net income per share available to its common stockholders. A corporation computes its basic earnings per share amount as follows:

$$\text{Basic Earnings per Share} = \frac{\text{Net Income} - \text{Preferred Dividends}}{\text{Weighted Average Number of Common Shares Outstanding}}$$

If a corporation has not issued any common shares during the year, it uses the common shares outstanding for the entire year as the denominator. When the corporation has issued common shares during the year, it uses the weighted average number of common shares outstanding during the year as the denominator. It reports basic earnings per share on the income statement directly below net income. In addition, it reports the earnings per share related to the major components of net income. It discloses the amount of the preferred dividends deducted from the numerator and the weighted average number of common shares used in computing earnings per share in a note to its financial statements.

A corporation has a complex capital structure when it has issued stock options and convertible securities (bonds or preferred stock). These securities are known as potential common shares because they can be used by the holder to acquire common stock. Since conversion of these securities into common stock would affect the earnings available to each common stockholder, the corporation must report its diluted earnings per share amount that includes the effects of all potential common shares that would reduce earnings per share. Two types of potential common shares affect the computation of diluted earnings per share—stock options and convertible securities.

7 **What kinds of dividends can a corporation distribute, and what are their characteristics?**

A corporation may distribute cash dividends, but must meet legal requirements and have enough cash available in order to pay dividends. Three dates are significant for a cash dividend (or any type of dividend): (1) the date of declaration, (2) the date of record, and (3) the date of payment. On the date of declaration, the board of directors formally declares that a dividend will be paid to stockholders of record on a specified future date, typically four to six weeks later. On the declaration date, the corporation becomes legally liable to pay the future dividend. The corporation records the liability by reducing Retained Earnings and increasing a current liability (Dividends Payable). Only investors listed as stockholders of the corporation (the stockholders of record) on the date of record can participate in the dividend. On the date of payment, the corporation mails the dividend checks and records the payment by reducing cash and eliminating the current liability.

Holders of preferred stock have a preference as to dividends. A dividend preference is a right of preferred stockholders to receive a dividend before a corporation may pay a dividend to common stockholders. This preference to dividends does not guarantee that the corporation will pay a preferred dividend in any given year, since the board of directors can decide not to pay any dividends. To protect preferred stockholders further, the corporation may include on the preferred stock certificate a provision that requires the accumulation of dividends. The corporation must pay the holders of cumulative preferred stock all dividends of the current and past periods before it can pay any dividends to common stockholders. Any dividends not declared on cumulative preferred stock in a given period become dividends in arrears. The dividends in arrears are not a liability to the corporation because no liability exists until the dividend declaration.

A stock dividend is a proportional (pro rata) distribution of additional shares of a corporation's own stock to its stockholders. For reporting purposes, GAAP distinguishes between a small and a large stock dividend. A small stock dividend is 20% or less of the previously outstanding common shares. A corporation records a small stock dividend at the current market value of the stock on the date of declaration. A large stock dividend is greater than 20% of the previously outstanding common shares. A corporation records a large stock dividend at the par (or stated) value of the stock. A stock split is similar to a large stock dividend. A stock split is a decrease in the par value per share of a corporation's common stock and a proportional increase in the number of shares authorized and issued.

8 **How and why does a corporation report the changes in its stockholders' equity?**

A corporation reports the effects of changes in its stockholders' equity in a statement of changes in stockholders' equity, which is a supporting schedule to the stockholders' equity section of the balance sheet. External users are interested in the changes in a corporation's stockholders' equity because these changes may have an impact on the corporation's risk and financial flexibility. To disclose its stockholders' equity activities, the corporation reports the changes in its different classes of capital stock (including the number of shares issued), in each additional paid-in capital account, in treasury stock, and in retained earnings (net income and dividends) for the accounting period in its statement of changes in stockholders' equity

Key Terms

additional paid-in capital *(p. 880)*	**capital stock** *(p. 879)*
authorized capital stock *(p. 882)*	**common stock** *(p. 880)*
basic earnings per share *(p. 896)*	**compensatory stock options** *(p. 889)*
board of directors *(p. 879)*	**complex capital structure** *(p. 898)*
callable preferred stock *(p. 884)*	**convertible preferred stock** *(p. 884)*

cumulative preferred stock *(p. 902)*
date of declaration *(p. 900)*
date of payment *(p. 900)*
date of record *(p. 900)*
diluted earnings per share *(p. 898)*
dividend preference *(p. 901)*
dividends in arrears *(p. 902)*
extraordinary item *(p. 894)*
issue capital stock *(p. 882)*
large stock dividend *(p. 904)*
legal capital *(p. 879)*
no-par capital stock *(p. 880)*
outstanding capital stock *(p. 886)*
par value *(p. 880)*
potential common shares *(p. 898)*
preemptive right *(p. 879)*

preferred stock *(p. 881)*
price/earnings ratio *(p. 898)*
redeemable *(p. 885)*
segment *(p. 893)*
small stock dividend *(p. 903)*
stated value *(p. 880)*
statement of changes in stockholders' equity *(p.906)*
statement of retained earnings *(p. 906)*
stock certificate *(p. 879)*
stock dividend *(p. 902)*
stockholders' equity *(p. 878)*
stockholders or shareholders *(p. 879)*
stock split *(p. 905)*
treasury stock *(p. 886)*

Here is an opportunity to gather information on the Internet about real-world issues related to the topics in this chapter. Go to http://www.dryden.com/account and click on the Cunningham, Nikolai, and Bazley book cover. Click on Summary Surfing, then click on this chapter number, and answer the following questions.

▶ Click on **Intel.** Find the most recent *Annual Report,* then find the *Consolidated Statements of Income* and answer this question. How much was Intel's basic and diluted earnings per share for the most recent year reported?

▶ Click on **Exxon.** Find the most recent *Annual Report.* How many stock options did Exxon grant during the most recent year? How many stock options (shares) were outstanding at the end of the year? What is the average exercise price of the stock options? How many stock options are exercisable at the end of the year?

**S U M M A R Y
S U R F I N G**

Integrated Business and Accounting Situations

Answer the Following Questions in Your Own Words

Testing Your Knowledge

24-1   What are the two parts of stockholders' equity, and what is included in each part?

24-2   List the basic rights of a stockholder. Which right do you consider to be the most important?

24-3   What is legal capital? How does a corporation determine the total legal capital when its capital stock has a par value?

24-4   What is the difference between common stock and preferred stock?

24-5   What is the meaning of the following terms: (a) authorized capital stock, (b) issued capital stock, (c) outstanding capital stock, and (d) treasury stock? What is the difference between issued capital stock and outstanding capital stock?

24-6 If a corporation issues common stock for an asset other than cash, what amount does it use to record the transaction?

24-7 What is convertible preferred stock? How does the conversion of preferred stock to common stock affect a corporation's contributed capital?

24-8 What are callable preferred stock and redeemable preferred stock?

24-9 What is treasury stock? Why might a corporation acquire treasury stock?

24-10 How does a corporation report treasury stock on its balance sheet? What is the effect of the acquisition of treasury stock on the corporation's basic earnings per share?

24-11 What are the major sections (and items in each section) of a corporation's income statement?

24-12 How does a corporation report total income tax expense on its income statement?

24-13 What is a segment of a corporation? What information for the sale of a discontinued segment does a corporation report on its income statement, and where does it report it?

24-14 What is an extraordinary item? Where and how does a corporation report gains or losses from extraordinary items on its income statement?

24-15 How is basic earnings per share computed? Where and how does a corporation report this amount on its income statement?

24-16 What are the three dates of importance regarding dividends?

24-17 Define the following terms regarding preferred stock: (a) dividend preference, (b) cumulative, and (c) dividends in arrears.

24-18 What is a stock dividend? Distinguish between a small and a large stock dividend, and explain what amounts a corporation uses to record the declaration of each dividend.

24-19 How are a stock split and a large stock dividend alike? How are they different?

24-20 What is a statement of changes in stockholders' equity? What changes in specific accounts does a corporation report on this statement?

24-21 How does a corporation report the impact of its capital stock transactions on its cash flow statement?

Applying Your Knowledge

24-22 On January 8, 2000, Ryland Carpet Corporation is incorporated and is authorized to issue 20,000 shares of $5 par value common stock. On January 9, 2000, it issues 1,000 shares at $12 per share, and on July 3, 2000, it issues another 800 shares at $15 per share.

Required: (1) Using T-accounts, record the two issuances of common stock for Ryland.
(2) Prepare the contributed capital section of Ryland's December 31, 2000 balance sheet.

24-23 On January 3, 2000, Mark Razor Corporation is incorporated and is authorized to issue 2,000 shares of $100 par value preferred stock and 25,000 shares of $3 par value common stock. During 2000, Mark issues 800 shares of preferred stock for $112 per share and 9,000 shares of common stock for $17 per share.

Required: (1) Using T-accounts, record the two issuances of capital stock for Mark.
(2) Prepare the contributed capital section of Mark's December 31, 2000 balance sheet.

24-24 Antley Company issued 200 shares of $10 par value common stock in exchange for five acres of land.

Required: Using T-accounts, record the acquisition of the land for each of the following independent situations: (a) the common stock is currently selling on the stock market for $80 per share, and (b) the land is appraised at $15,000, but the common stock is not actively traded in the stock market.

24-25 Thompson Corporation is authorized to issue 60,000 shares of $5 par value common stock and 3,000 shares of $100 par value preferred stock. During the current period it engages in the following transactions:
(a) Sells 10,000 shares of common stock for $13 per share
(b) Sells 1,000 shares of preferred stock for $123 per share
(c) Acquires a building by paying $10,000 cash and issuing 5,000 shares of common stock and 500 shares of preferred stock. The common stock is currently selling for $15 per share; the preferred stock is selling for $125 per share. No reliable appraisal value is available for the building.

Required: (1) Using T-accounts, record the preceding transactions for Thompson.

(2) How would your answer to (c) change if the building was appraised at $149,000? Why?

24-26 The community of Happy Rock donated land to Jipem Window Corporation for the site of a new factory. The land was reliably appraised at $18,000.

Required: Explain how Jipem should record, if at all, the receipt of the land.

24-27 At incorporation, Gasser Furnace Corporation issued 75 shares of $100 par value preferred stock for $108 per share and 2,000 shares of $10 par value common stock for $36 per share. Each share of preferred stock was convertible into three shares of the common stock. One year later, the preferred stockholders elected to exercise the conversion option on 50 shares of preferred stock.

Required: (1) Prepare the contributed capital section of Gasser's balance sheet at the time of incorporation.

(2) Prepare the contributed capital section of Gasser's balance sheet immediately after the conversion.

(3) Explain the change in total contributed capital.

24-28 On January 1, Amitroy Company had 20,000 shares of $5 par value common stock outstanding. The shares were originally issued at a price of $12 per share. During the year, the following stock transactions occurred:

March 4: The company reacquired 2,000 shares of its common stock at a cost of $12 per share.

April 5: The company sold 1,000 shares of the treasury stock for $14 per share.

July 9: The company sold the remaining 1,000 shares of the treasury stock for $11 per share.

Required: (1) Using T-accounts (including dates), record all the preceding transactions in one set of accounts for Amitroy.

(2) What is the final net effect on the accounts after these transactions are recorded? Why?

24-29 On January 1, 2000, Rollo Awning Corporation had 8,000 shares of $10 par value common stock outstanding. These shares were originally issued at $25 per share. During 2000, Rollo entered into the following transactions:

(a) Reacquired 2,500 shares of its common stock for $26 per share

(b) Sold 1,250 shares of the treasury stock for $28 per share

(c) Sold 750 shares of the treasury stock for $23 per share

Required: (1) Using T-accounts, record all the preceding stock transactions in one set of accounts for Rollo.

(2) Prepare the stockholders' equity section of Rollo's balance sheet at December 31, 2000 (assume that 30,000 shares are authorized and that retained earnings is $40,000).

24-30 The following is a list of selected accounts and ending account balances taken from the accounting records of Dean Company on December 31, 2000:

Account Title	Amount
Additional paid-in capital on preferred stock	$11,000
Common stock	80,000
Preferred stock	50,000
Treasury stock	6,000
Retained earnings	90,000
Additional paid-in capital on common stock	33,000

Additional information:

(a) Preferred stock has a $100 par value; 1,000 shares are authorized.

(b) Common stock has a $10 par value; 10,000 shares are authorized, 8,000 shares have been issued, and 7,500 shares are outstanding.

(c) During 2000, Dean reacquired 1,500 shares of common stock at $12 per share; 1,000 shares were reissued at $13 per share.

Required: (1) Prepare the stockholders' equity section of the December 31, 2000 balance sheet for Dean Company.

(2) At what average price were the outstanding shares of preferred stock issued?

(3) At what average price were the 8,000 shares of common stock issued?

24-31   The following information is available for Teresa Textile Corporation for the year ended December 31, 2000: (1) pretax income from continuing operations, $29,000; (2) loss from operations of discontinued Segment B (pretax), $6,500; (3) extraordinary gain (pretax), $4,200; and (4) loss on sale of discontinued Segment B (pretax), $5,000. The corporation is subject to a 40% income tax rate. It had no preferred stock outstanding, and 6,000 shares of common stock were outstanding during all of 2000.

Required: Prepare the lower portion of Teresa Textile Corporation's 2000 income statement, starting with pretax income from continuing operations.

24-32   At the beginning of 2000, Deavels Corporation had 1,000 shares of 9%, $100 par value preferred stock and 16,500 shares of common stock outstanding. On June 1, Deavels issued 3,000 additional shares of common stock. On December 31, 2000, Deavels reported net income of $37,105, paid dividends for 2000 on the preferred stock, and paid a $1 per-share dividend on each share of common stock outstanding.

Required: Compute the basic earnings per share of Deavels Corporation for 2000.

24-33   The records of Stringer Cable Corporation show the following *pretax* items on December 31, 2000:

Cost of goods sold	$42,000
Extraordinary loss from tornado	1,500
General and administrative expenses	8,000
Interest revenue	700
Sales	78,000
Interest expense	200
Gain on sale of discontinued Segment R	1,000
Selling expenses	13,000
Loss from operations of discontinued Segment R	3,000

Additional information:
(a) There were 2,000 shares of common stock outstanding on January 1, 2000. On July 1, 2000, the corporation issued 4,000 additional shares of common stock.
(b) The corporation paid dividends for the current year on 200 shares of 8%, $100 par value preferred stock outstanding. No dividends were paid to common stockholders.
(c) The corporation is subject to a 40% income tax rate.

Required: Prepare the income statement of Stringer Cable Corporation for 2000

24-34   The records of the Lundgren Chemicals Corporation show the following *pretax* items on December 31, 2000:

Cost of goods sold	$65,000
Extraordinary loss from flood	2,250
General and administrative expenses	12,000
Interest revenue	700
Interest expense	300
Loss on sale of discontinued Segment Q	250
Income from operations of discontinued Segment Q	800
Selling expenses	23,000
Sales	119,400

Additional information:
(a) There were 3,000 shares of common stock outstanding on January 1, 2000. On July 1, 2000, the corporation issued 6,000 common shares.
(b) The corporation paid dividends for the current year on 500 shares of 7%, $100 par preferred stock outstanding. Dividends of $6,000 were paid on common stock.
(c) The corporation is subject to a 40% income tax rate.

Required: Prepare the income statement of Lundgren Chemicals Corporation for 2000.

24-35   On October 1, Sewel Corporation declares a cash dividend on its 1,600 outstanding shares of 9%, $100 par value preferred stock. These dividends are payable on December 2, to stockholders of record as of November 15. On November 1, the company declares a $1.05 per-share cash dividend on its 9,000 outstanding shares of common stock. These dividends are payable on December 16, to stockholders of record as of November 30.

Required: Using T-accounts, prepare entries for Sewel Corporation to record the declaration and payment of each dividend.

24-36   The stockholders' equity section of the January 1, 2000 balance sheet for Turner Tennis Corporation follows:

Contributed capital
    Common stock, $10 par, 60,000 shares authorized,
        30,000 shares issued and outstanding $300,000
    Additional paid-in capital 100,000
Total contributed capital $400,000
Retained earnings 325,000
Total Stockholders' Equity $725,000

Early in 2000, the corporation declared and issued a 15% stock dividend. On the date of declaration, the common stock was selling for $16 per share.

Required: (1) Prepare the stockholders' equity section of Turner's balance sheet after the issuance of the stock dividend.
        (2) Explain the change(s) in the stockholders' equity section.

24-37   The stockholders' equity accounts of Quiser Corporation on January 1, 2000 were as follows:

Preferred stock, 8%, $100 par (5,000 shares authorized) $100,000
Additional paid-in capital on preferred stock 12,000
Common stock, $10 par (80,000 shares authorized) 200,000
Additional paid-in capital on common stock 37,000
Retained earnings 172,000
                                                                                                                                  $521,000

During 2000, the company entered into the following capital stock transactions:

Date	Transaction
May 15	Declared a 15% stock dividend on the common stock outstanding. The stock is to be distributed on June 28. The common stock is currently selling for $18 per share.
June 28	Issued the stock dividend declared on May 15.
Nov. 1	Declared the annual cash dividend on the outstanding preferred stock and a $1.20 annual cash dividend on the outstanding common stock. These dividends are to be paid on December 15.
Dec. 15	Paid the cash dividends declared on November 1.

Required: (1) Using T-accounts, prepare entries to record the preceding transactions for Quiser.
        (2) Prepare the stockholders' equity section of the December 31, 2000 balance sheet for Quiser (assume that 2000 net income was $101,000).
        (3) Compute Quiser's return on stockholders' equity for 2000.

24-38   The Fife Office Equipment Corporation is authorized to issue 1,000 shares of 8%, $100 par value preferred stock and 20,000 shares of $10 par value common stock. The December 31, 1999 stockholders' equity accounts showed the following balances:

Common stock, $10 par .... $ 80,000
Additional paid-in capital on common stock 61,000
Retained earnings 78,000
                                                                                                                                  $219,000

During 2000, the corporation engaged in the following capital stock transactions:

Date	Transaction
Jan. 3	Issued 250 shares of preferred stock at $104 per share
Mar. 1	Issued 3,000 shares of common stock for land. The common stock is selling at $22 per share.
Sept. 30	Reacquired 500 shares of common stock at $23 per share.
Nov. 1	Declared the 8% dividend on the outstanding preferred stock and a $1 per-share dividend on the outstanding common stock, to be paid on December 16.
Dec. 16	Paid the dividends on the preferred stock and common stock.

In addition, during 2000 the company earned net income of $46,000.

Required: (1) Prepare Fife's statement of changes in stockholders' equity for the year ended December 31, 2000.
(2) Prepare the stockholders' equity section of Fife's December 31, 2000 balance sheet.
(3) Compute Fife's return on stockholders' equity for 2000.

24-39 During 2000, Herley Transport Corporation entered into the following long-term debt and capital stock transactions:
(a) Issued 5,000 shares of common stock for $18 per share
(b) Issued 1,000 shares of preferred stock for $110 per share
(c) Reacquired 1,000 shares of common stock for $19 per share
(d) Issued long-term bonds for $100,000
(e) Paid interest of $10,000 on long-term bonds
(f) Paid dividends of $16,000 on preferred stock
(g) Paid dividends of $34,000 on common stock

Required: Show how Herley would report the preceding transactions on its 2000 cash flow statement (assuming it uses the direct method for reporting cash flows from operating activities).

Making Evaluations

24-40 At the beginning of the current year, Blong Chocolate Corporation issued common stock in exchange for equipment. The president of the company has asked your advice. He states: "I don't know how the company should record this transaction. However, even if the company recorded the transaction at too high or too low a price, it should not make any difference. This transaction does not affect net income for the current accounting period because it does not involve a revenue or expense account. Furthermore, since it occurs during the current accounting period, the future financial statements of the company will not be affected."

Required: Prepare a written evaluation of the president's comments. Include a suggestion for recording the transaction.

24-41 At the beginning of 2000, Zing Corporation reacquired 500 shares of its own common stock for $20 per share. During 2000 it reissued 200 of these treasury shares for $25 per share. As of December 31, 2000, the company had not yet reissued the remaining treasury stock.

The president of Zing Corporation has suggested that the 300 shares of treasury stock be shown as an asset on the corporation's December 31, 2000 balance sheet and that the $1,000 "gain" be shown on the income statement. He also feels the treasury stock should be considered as outstanding shares and should not be distinguished from common stock issued.

Required: (1) Explain what treasury stock is.
(2) Explain why a corporation might acquire treasury stock.
(3) What is outstanding common stock? What is the difference between issued common stock and outstanding common stock?
(4) Identify how the president of Zing Corporation arrived at the $1,000 gain. Explain whether you agree that treasury stock should be shown as an asset and that the gain be shown on the income statement.

www.bestbuy.com

24-42 In its 1997 annual report, Best Buy disclosed the following:

> The securities are convertible into shares of the Company's common stock at the rate of 2.222 shares per security (equivalent to a conversion price of $22.50 per share). The preferred securities are subject to mandatory redemption in November 2024 at the liquidation preference price. The company has the option to defer distributions on the securities for up to 60 months. A deferral of distributions may result in the conversion of the preferred securities into Series A Preferred Stock of the Company. The

company has the right to cause the conversion rights to expire any time after three years from the date of issuance in the event the Company's Common Stock price exceeds $27 per share for 20 out of 30 consecutive trading days.

Required: Write an owner of the securities a short memo explaining the alternatives that may arise.

24-43 Intel disclosed the following (partial) information about its compensatory stock options in its 1997 annual report (in millions except stock price per share):

	Number of Shares	Weighted Average Exercise Price
Options granted in 1997	31.5	$72.46
Options exercised in 1997	23.6	6.11
Options exercisable at Dec. 28, 1996	57.3	5.72
Options exercisable at Dec. 27, 1997	57.6	7.33

www.intel.com

The range of exercise prices for options outstanding at December 27, 1997 was $2.52 to $97.94 per share. Intel's 1997 income was $6,945 million, and its basic earnings per share was $4.25. Assume that Intel's stock price on December 27, 1997 was $75 per share.

Required: (1) Explain the effects of the options on Intel's 1997 financial statements.
(2) What is the opportunity cost to Intel of the options exercisable at December 27, 1997?
(3) If all the exercisable options at the end of 1996 were exercised, what would be the effect on Intel's 1997 earnings per share? Assume that the exercise occurs at the beginning of 1997.
(4) Intel disclosed that its basic earnings per share would have been $4.12 if it had included an expense for stock options in its 1997 income statement. Explain which earnings per share amount you would use to evaluate Intel.

24-44 Callaway Golf (maker of Big Bertha golf clubs) disclosed the following (partial information) in its 1997 annual report:

www.callawaygolf.com

The Company has a Promotion, Marketing and Endorsement Stock Incentive Plan. Under this plan, up to 3,560,000 shares of Common Stock may be granted in the form of options or other stock awards to golf professionals and other parties at prices which may be less than the market value of the stock at the grant date.

Required: (1) If you were a golf professional, explain whether you would like to be included in the Promotion, Marketing and Endorsement Stock Incentive Plan instead of receiving cash payments for promotional fees.
(2) If you were a shareholder of Callaway Golf, explain whether you would support the Promotion, Marketing and Endorsement Stock Incentive Plan.

24-45 According to *Fortune* (July 24, 1995), Anthony O'Reilly, CEO of Heinz and the company's second-largest shareholder, became eligible to exercise four million stock options—already in the money for $60 million—in addition to the 750,000 he was given in the previous year. Heinz's returns have trailed its peer group.

www.heinz.com

Required: (1) What do you think "already in the money" means in regard to the relationship between the option price of the four million options and the market price of the common stock?
(2) What was the expense on Heinz's income statement of the previous year for the 750,000 options O'Reilly was given?
(3) Do you believe that the CEO deserved his stock options?

24-46 Kmart disclosed the following income statements and notes to the financial statements in its 1996 annual report:

Kmart Corporation
Consolidated Statements of Operations
(dollars in millions, except per share data)

	Fiscal Year Ended		
	January 31, 1996	January 25, 1995	January 26, 1994
Sales	$34,389	$32,514	$33,295
Licensee fees and other income	265	286	294
	34,654	32,800	33,589
Cost of merchandise sold, including buying and occupancy costs	26,996	24,868	24,950
Selling, general and administrative expenses	7,554	7,376	7,477
Store restructuring and other charges	—	—	1,130
Asset impairment charges	532	—	—
Gain on pension curtailment	(124)	—	—
Interest expense:			
Debt, net	220	258	302
Capital lease obligations and other	226	235	192
	35,404	32,737	34,051
Income (loss) from continuing retail operations before income taxes and equity income	(750)	63	(462)
Equity in net income of unconsolidated companies	38	52	52
Income tax provision (credit)	(222)	11	(150)
Net income (loss) from continuing retail operations before extraordinary items and the effect of accounting changes	(490)	104	(260)
Discontinued operations including the effect of accounting changes, net of income taxes of $59 and $(91), respectively	—	75	(169)
Gain (loss) on disposal of discontinued operations, net of income taxes of $88, $282, and $(248), respectively	(30)	117	(521)
Extraordinary items, net of income taxes of $(27) and $(6), respectively	(51)	—	(10)
Effect of accounting changes, net of income taxes of $(36)	—	—	(14)
Net income (loss)	$ (571)	$ 296	$ (974)
Earnings (loss) per common share:			
Continuing retail operations	$ (1.08)	$ .21	$ (.59)
Discontinued operations	—	.16	(.37)
Gain (loss) on disposal of discontinued operations	(.06)	.26	(1.14)
Extraordinary items	(.11)	—	(.02)
Effect of accounting changes	—	—	(.03)
Net income (loss)	$ (1.25)	$ .63	$ (2.15)
Weighted average shares (millions)	459.9	456.6	456.7

See accompanying Notes to Consolidated Financial Statements.
The Consolidated Statements of Operations for prior periods have been restated for discontinued operations.

Notes to Consolidated Financial Statements (in part):
3) Discontinued Operations and Dispositions
Discontinued operations include Borders Group, Inc. ("Borders Group"), OfficeMax, Inc. ("Office-Max"), The Sports Authority, Inc. ("The Sports Authority"), Coles Myer, Ltd. ("Coles Myer"), PACE Membership Warehouse, Inc. ("PACE") and Furr's/Bishop ("Furr's") cafeteria chains.

1995 Activity
Discontinued operations for 1995 include the Borders Group, whose initial public offering ("IPO") was completed in June 1995. In this IPO, Kmart sold 87% of its equity interest for net proceeds of approximately $493. Additionally, in July 1995, the Borders Group agreed to purchase all of Kmart's remaining 13% interest which resulted in net proceeds of approximately $73. As a result of these transactions, the Company recorded an after tax loss of $185.

Also in July 1995, OfficeMax completed the public offering of Kmart's remaining equity interest in OfficeMax. Kmart received net proceeds of approximately $360 and recorded an after tax gain of $107.

In October 1995, The Sports Authority completed the public offering of Kmart's remaining equity interest in The Sports Authority. Kmart received approximately $151 in net proceeds and recorded an after tax gain of $48.

As the Company no longer owns any interest in the aforementioned entities, they are accounted for as discontinued operations in the accompanying financial statements.

In November 1995, Kmart disposed of the assets of its automotive service centers at a book value of approximately $84 receiving approximately $50 in cash and the balance in a five-year interest-bearing note. Under the terms of the agreement, the centers will continue to operate at Kmart locations in exchange for various rents and fees for services provided by Kmart. The Company also disposed of certain Senior Notes of Thrifty PayLess Holdings, Inc. ("TPH") acquired in 1993 in connection with the sale of PayLess Drug Stores Northwest, Inc. ("Payless") for approximately $102.

1994 Activity

Discontinued operations for 1994 include OfficeMax, whose IPO was completed in November 1994. This IPO reduced Kmart's interest in OfficeMax from over 90% to approximately 25% and resulted in net proceeds of approximately $642. Also, in November 1994, the IPO of The Sports Authority was completed reducing Kmart's interest from 100% to approximately 30% and resulted in net proceeds of approximately $254. These transactions resulted in an after tax gain of $101.

Additionally, in November 1994, Kmart completed the sale of its 21.5% equity interest in Coles Myer, an Australian retailer which operates department and general merchandise stores including certain stores using the "Kmart" name. Net cash proceeds of $928 were realized from the sale resulting in an after tax gain of $48. As part of the transaction, Kmart extended a long-term license agreement that allows Coles Myer to use the "Kmart" name in Australia and New Zealand.

In January 1995, Kmart charged $32 to loss on disposal of discontinued operations for sublease exposure related to lease guarantees on properties sublet to Furr's, which was sold by Kmart in 1986.

Due to the 1995 completion of the divestitures of the Borders Group, OfficeMax and The Sports Authority, results of these operations for 1994 and 1993 have been restated and accounted for as discontinued operations. The results of Coles Myer and the charge for Furr's have also been included as discontinued operations. Kmart's interest in the results of these operations was an after tax gain of $75 during 1994.

1993 Activity

In January 1994, PACE sold the assets and lease obligations of 93 of its warehouses and virtually all of the inventory and membership files in the 34 warehouses not included in the transaction to Sam's Club, a division of Wal-Mart, for approximately $774 in cash. Operations of the 34 remaining PACE sites not included in the transaction were discontinued, and PACE was subsequently divested in August 1995. Included in this loss was the write-off of unamortized goodwill of $395, a provision for the expected remaining lease obligations in the warehouses not sold, other PACE liabilities and a provision for additional costs anticipated during the wind-down of PACE operations.

The loss on disposal of discontinued operations in 1993 of $521 includes the losses on disposal of PACE assets and the divestiture of PayLess. The operations of these businesses were reclassified to discontinued operations to reflect their respective plans for disposition. The sale of PayLess was completed in April 1994 to TPH and its subsidiary Thrifty PayLess, Inc. for approximately $595 in cash, $100 in Senior Notes of TPH and approximately 46% of the common equity of TPH.

Kmart had originally intended to complete the divestiture of its TPH equity interest within a one year time frame and had, accordingly, classified the results of operations as a component of discontinued operations. During the latter part of 1994, Kmart pursued the disposition of its interest in TPH, but did not locate an acceptable buyer during this time frame. Therefore, management reclassified the results of operations for PayLess in 1993 and prior from discontinued operations to continuing retail operations.

4) Store Restructuring and Other Charges

On January 5, 1994 the Kmart Board of Directors approved a restructuring plan involving domestic and Canadian Kmart stores, Builders Square and the Walden division of the Borders Group. As a result, in the fourth quarter of 1993, Kmart recorded a pretax charge (Store Restructuring and Other Charges) of $1,348, $862 after tax. The portion of the charge associated with the Borders Group, $218 pretax and $139 after tax, has subsequently been restated as discontinued operations. The remaining restructuring provision included anticipated costs of $1,130 associated with Kmart stores which were to be closed and relocated, enlarged or refurbished in the U.S. and Canada and the closing and relocation of certain Builders Square stores. These costs included lease obligations for store closings as well as fixed asset writedowns, primarily furniture and fixtures, and inventory dispositions and related operating losses for all affected stores. The restructuring provision also included $20 to increase the reserve for lease obligations for stores closed as part of Kmart's 1989 restructuring plan. Other charges included the estimated costs of $76 for re-engineering programs (principally

continued

severance) and other non-recurring charges and an accural of $12 for a non-routine legal judgment resulting from the insolvency of an insurer.

The following table sets forth the 1993 restructuring plan and related activity through January 31, 1996:

		Activity to Date			
	Provision Recorded	Cash Costs Incurred	Noncash Costs and Asset Writedowns	Changes In Estimate	Reserve at January 31, 1996
1993 Restructuring Plan:					
Lease obligation costs	$ 577	$166	$ (75)ᵃ	$ (57)	$429
Asset writedowns	181	—	201	49	29
Inventory disposition costs and related operating losses	264	35	159	13	83
Re-engineering and other non-recurring charges	76	54	25	12	9
Non-routine legal accrual	12	7	—	(5)	—
	$1,110	$262	$310	$ 12	$550

ᵃRepresents $35 and $40 for interest expense accreted during 1995 and 1994 on discounted lease obligations.

Cash costs incurred for the 1993 restructuring plan of $262, include $177, $80 and $5 for 1995, 1994 and 1993, respectively. Noncash charges of $310 include $159, $146 and $5 for the same periods, respectively.

Changes in estimate are representative of management's assessment in the fourth quarter of 1995 and 1994, that based on actual experiences to date, certain charges will be higher than originally planned while others will be less than planned.

Builders Square and Kmart Canada have substantially completed their restructuring plans during 1995. Actual results were in line with the original reserve of $226 and $39 for Builders Square and Canada, respectively.

The 1989 restructuring plan, with the $20 addition in 1993, included $526 for stores which were closed and relocated, enlarged or refurbished, and through January 31, 1996, $509 was charged against this reserve. Cash costs relating to the 1989 restructuring plan were $54, $53 and $82 for 1995, 1994 and 1993, respectively. There were no noncash charges for 1995 compared to $29 and $137 for 1994 and 1993, respectively.

The restructuring obligation is included primarily in "Other long-term liabilities" in the Consolidated Balance Sheets.

5) Asset Impairment Charges

Kmart adopted Financial Accounting Standard No. 121 "Accounting for the Impairment of Long-Lived Assets and for Long-Lived Assets to Be Disposed Of" ("FAS 121") in the fourth quarter of 1995. This statement requires companies to record impairments of long-lived assets, certain identifiable intangibles, and associated goodwill on an exception basis, when there is evidence that events or changes in circumstances have made recovery of an asset's carrying value unlikely. In conducting its review, management considered, among other things, its current and expected operating cash flows together with a judgment as to the fair value the Company could receive upon sale of its investment. Based on this review, Kmart recorded a $532 pretax charge, $390 after tax, relating to Builders Square and certain international operations.

6) Extraordinary Items

The Company entered into agreements whereby holders of approximately $550 of certain real estate related debt agreed to eliminate put features which would have required Kmart to purchase the debt from the holders if Kmart's long-term debt rating was lowered to non-investment grade or the lowest level of investment grade rating in certain cases. As a result, Kmart recorded an extraordinary noncash charge of $51, net of income taxes, primarily relating to make-whole premiums payable under such agreements.

In August 1993, Kmart called for early redemtpion of all $200 of its 8⅛% debentures due January 1, 1997. The debentures were redeemed at 100% of the principal amount plus interest accured to the date of redemption. In April 1993, Kmart called for early redemption of all $200 of its 10½% Sinking Fund Debentures due December 1, 2017. The resulting redemption premium of $10, net of applicable income taxes, was reported as an extraordinary item.

Required: Identify the income amounts you would use in your evaluation of Kmart's performance for the three-year period. Explain why you chose these amounts.

24-47 Small Corporation shows the following items of stockholders' equity:

Common stock, $10 par (40,000 shares authorized, 10,000 shares issued and outstanding)	$100,000
Additional paid-in capital on common stock	80,000
Retained earnings	160,000
	$340,000

The company's common stock currently is selling for $30 per share on the stock market. The board of directors is considering the following *alternative* actions in regard to "dividends":
(a) Payment of a $3 per share cash dividend
(b) Distribution of a 15% stock dividend
(c) Distribution of a 40% stock dividend
(d) Distribution of a 2-for-1 stock split, reducing the par value to $5 per share

The board has always paid a cash dividend and is not very familiar with stock dividends and stock splits. It is also unsure of the effect that each of these alternatives would have on stockholders' equity and has asked for your advice.

Required: (1) Explain what is meant by a stock dividend and a stock split, including an explanation of which, if either, is really a "dividend."
(2) Explain what is likely to happen to the market price per share of common stock as a result of a stock dividend or a stock split.
(3) For each alternative, determine the amount of each item of stockholders' equity for Small Corporation immediately after the cash payment or the issuance of the common stock. Show your calculations for each amount that changed.
(4) Assume that the company's total assets before any of these transactions was $700,000. Compute the ratio of stockholders' equity to total assets for each situation. Explain the differences between the ratios.

24-48 At the end of its first year of operations, Lynn Company had a fire that destroyed many of its accounting records. It was able to save information on the following accounts and ending account balances related to stock transactions and dividends:

Amount	Balance
Cash (from stock and dividends paid)	$77,400
Equipment	77,000
8% preferred stock, $100 par	70,000
Additional paid-in capital on preferred stock	7,000
Common stock, $5 par value	35,000
Additional paid-in capital on common stock	55,000
Retained earnings	7,400

In addition, the company's managers were able to recall that during the first year, the following events occurred:

(1) The company acquired equipment with an appraised value of $77,000 by issuing 700 shares of preferred stock.
(2) Net income was $20,000.
(3) The company distributed the annual dividends on the preferred stock outstanding and on the common stock outstanding.
(4) The company sold 7,000 shares of common stock.

Required: On the basis of the preceding information, using T-accounts where applicable, show how all the transactions affected Lynn Company's financial statements.

24-49 The bookkeeper for Cortez Company prepared the following statements for the year ended December 31, 2000:

December 31, 2000
Expense and Profits Statement

Sales (net)		$220,000
Less: Selling expenses		(27,200)
Net sales		$192,800
Add: Interest revenue		1,300
Add: Gain on sale of equipment		4,900
Gross sales revenues		$199,000
Less: Costs of operations		
Cost of goods sold	$139,100	
Dividend costs ($0.50 per share for 8,300 common shares outstanding the entire year)	4,150	
Extraordinary loss due to earthquake (net of $2,400 income tax credit)	3,600	(146,850)
Taxable revenues		$ 52,150
Less: income tax on continuing income		(14,800)
Net income		$ 37,350
Miscellaneous deductions:		
Loss from operations of discontinued Segment L (net of $1,200 income tax credit)	$ 1,800	
Administrative expenses	21,800	(23,600)
Net Revenues		$ 13,750

Retained Revenues Statement
For Year Ended December 31, 2000

Beginning retained earnings	$ 65,000
Add: Gain of sale of segment L (net of $1,800 income tax expense)	2,700
Recalculated retained earnings	$ 67,700
Add: Net revenues	13,750
	$ 81,450
Less: Interest expense	(1,100)
Ending retained earnings	$ 80,350

You determine that the preceding account balances are correct but, in certain instances, have been incorrectly titled or classified.

Required: (1) Review both statements and indicate where each incorrectly classified item should be classified. Also indicate any other errors you find.

(2) Prepare a corrected 2000 income statement and retained earnings statement for Cortez Company.

24-50 Baker Company reports a retained earnings balance of $54,600 at the beginning of 2000. The following information is available for 2000:

(a) The company declared and paid a 62-cent cash dividend per share on the 5,000 shares of common stock that were outstanding the entire year.

(b) The company incurred a pretax $10,000 loss as a result of an earthquake, which is unusual and infrequent for the area.

(c) The company sold division P in May. From January through May, division P had incurred a pretax loss from operations of $6,000. A pretax gain of $5,500 was earned on the sale of division P.

(d) The company reported sales (net) of $99,600, cost of goods sold of $57,900, and operating expenses of $18,200.

The company is unclear how to report the various preceding items in its financial statements as well as how to compute its profit margin. It has asked for your advice.

Required: (1) Assuming that all "pretax" items are subject to a 40% income tax rate, prepare Baker Company's income statement for 2000.

(2) Prepare Baker Company's retained earnings statement for 2000.

(3) Compute the company's profit margin. Discuss your computations.

24-51   Refer to General Mills' annual report in Appendix C.   **www.generalmills.com**

Required: (1) What was General Mills' total stockholders' equity at May 31, 1998?

        (2) How many shares of common stock are authorized? How many were issued at May 31, 1998? How many were outstanding at May 31, 1998?

        (3) What is the par value per share of the common stock?

        (4) What was the cost of the treasury stock at May 31, 1998?

        (5) What were the basic and diluted earnings per share for the year ended May 31, 1998?

        (6) What were the cash dividends declared for the year ended May 31, 1998?

        (7) What were the dividends per share for each of the last 5 years?

        (8) If all General Mills' stock options at the end of 1997 that were (a) exercisable were exercised, what would be the effect on basic earnings per share in 1998 and (b) outstanding were exercised, what would be the effect on basic earnings per share for 1998? Assume that the exercise occurs at the beginning of 1998 and therefore ignore the actual exercise of stock options that occurred in 1998.

24-52   Yesterday, you received the following letter for your advice column in the local paper:

Dear Dr. Decisive:

My mother and father both work full-time to help my sisters and me go to school. I realize they get paychecks every month, but I have just found out they get "paid" even more. My mother recently went back to work, and she is employed by a high-tech company where all employees get paid stock options. She gets 500 options every year. My father just got promoted to vice-president, and he was paid 10,000 options. Is my family rich? And what do these options cost the company?

Call me "Options for All."

Required: Meet with your Dr. Decisive team and write a response to "Options for All."

THE PROFESSION OF ACCOUNTANCY

"The best augury of a man's success in his profession is that he thinks it is the finest in the world."

—George Eliot

1 *What are the general fields that make up the profession of accountancy?*

2 *What do industry (or management) accountants do?*

3 *What broad categories of service do public accountants perform?*

4 *In what types of jobs may an accountant work as a governmental accountant?*

5 *What are some examples of organizations of professional accountants?*

1 *What are the general fields that make up the profession of accounting?*

Perhaps you are wondering what the profession of accountancy is all about. Accountancy has emerged as a profession, alongside other professions such as medicine, law, and architecture. The study and the practice of accountancy require a broad understanding of concepts in such areas as business, economics, sociology, psychology, and public administration, as well as an in-depth knowledge of specialized accounting areas.

The four general fields of accountancy include (1) public accounting, (2) industry accounting, (3) governmental accounting, and (4) education, each of which has several accounting specialty areas. Close to 48 percent of accountants work in industry accounting, and 45 percent work in public accounting. Of the remaining 8 percent, 5 percent work in governmental accounting and 3 percent in education.[1] We summarize industry, public, and governmental accounting in Exhibit A-1 and discuss them briefly here.

Industry Accounting

2 *What do industry (or management) accountants do?*

A company employs an industry (or management) accountant to perform its internal (management) accounting activities and to prepare its financial reports. A high-level manager, such as the company's **controller,** usually coordinates these activities. This manager frequently reports directly to a top manager of the organization, such as the chief financial officer—an indication of how important the accounting functions are to the company's operations.

Another indication of the importance of management accounting is the Certificate in Management Accounting (CMA). The CMA is granted to those who meet specific educational and professional standards and who pass a uniform CMA examination, administered twice yearly by the Institute of Management Accountants. Although the CMA is not required as a license to practice, accountants holding the CMA are recognized as professional experts in the area of management accounting.

www. rutgers.edu/ Accounting/raw/ima. htm

Management accounting activities encompass several areas: budgeting, cost accounting, and financial reporting, which we discussed briefly in Chapter 1, as well as designing and operating accounting systems, internal auditing, and tax accounting. We discuss the last three of these areas next.

Exhibit A-1 The Profession of Accountancy

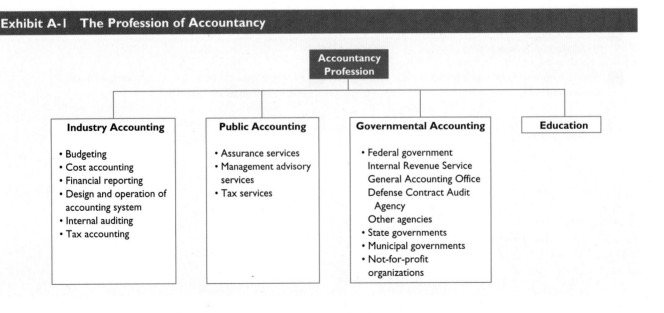

[1]AICPA Web Site, 1999.

Design and Operation of an Integrated Accounting System

One duty of the management accountant is to design and operate a company's integrated accounting system, which may be a part of its bigger enterprise resource planning (ERP) system (which we discussed in Chapter 10). This function is sometimes referred to as **general accounting** because of the wide variety of activities involved. These activities include, among others, determining the portion of the accounting system that will be computer or manually operated, integrating the accounting activities for different departments, and designing accounting procedures, forms, and reports.

Internal Auditing

One part of the design of an accounting system is establishing good internal control. **Internal control** involves the procedures needed to safeguard a company's economic resources and to promote the efficient and effective operation of its accounting system. Internal auditing is a part of a company's internal control procedures and has as its purpose the review of the company's operations to ensure that all company employees are following these procedures. Internal auditing is becoming increasingly important because, as you will see shortly, the procedures for a company's *external* audit depend, to a great degree, on the quality of its internal control. As evidence of professionalism in internal auditing, an accountant may earn a Certificate of Internal Auditing (CIA), awarded by the Institute of Internal Auditors, Inc. Although not a license to practice, this certificate states that the holder has met specified educational and practical experience requirements and has passed the uniform CIA examination.

www. theiia.org

Tax Accounting

Although companies often assign their tax work to the tax services department of a public accounting firm, many of them maintain their own tax departments as well. Accountants with expertise in the tax laws that apply to the company make up the staff of these departments. These accountants handle income tax planning and the preparation of the company's state, federal, and foreign income tax returns. They also work on real estate taxes, personal property taxes (such as taxes on inventories), and other taxes.

Public Accounting

A public accountant is an independent professional who provides accounting services to clients for a fee. Many accountants practice public accounting as individual practitioners or work in local or regional public accounting firms. Others work in large public accounting firms that have offices in most major U.S. and international cities. These firms provide accounting services to large corporations, some of which span the United States as well as the world in their activities.

3 *What broad categories of service do public accountants perform?*

Most public accountants are **certified public accountants** (CPAs). A CPA has met the requirements of, and holds a license to practice accounting issued by, the state in which he or she works. States use licensing to help ensure that public accountants provide high-quality, professional services. Although the licensing requirements vary from state to state, all CPAs must pass the Uniform CPA Examination. The "CPA exam" is a national examination given by the American Institute of Certified Public Accountants (AICPA) twice a year across the United States. In addition to passing the exam, a CPA must have met a state's minimum educational and practical experience requirements to be licensed in that state.

www. aicpa.com

But what do public accountants *do?* We discuss several services that public accountants provide to their client next. These services include assurance services, management advisory services, and tax services.

Assurance Services

As a result of the information age, the volume of all types of information has grown, and much of that information is readily available to companies, governments, organizations,

MOMMA

CHAPTER ONE: Wanda awoke to find herself in the secret lair of the handsomest man in the world. He was tall and dark, and had the romantic air of a charming international rogue. Boldly, he swept her into his powerful arms. "My name is Jean-Pierre," he said, with a devilish smile. "I am a Certified Public Accountant."

and individuals. Since decision-makers increasingly rely on such information, they need assurance that the information is valid for the purposes for which they intend to use it. In this regard, "an assurance involves expression of a written or oral conclusion on the reliability and/or relevance of information and/or information systems."[2] Auditing evolved from a need for a specific type of assurance service.

Auditing

Accounting information is one type of information for which decision-makers need assurance. One way a company communicates accounting information is by issuing financial statements. Managers of the company issuing the statements are responsible for preparing these statements. But because of the potential bias of these managers, external users of the financial statements need objective assurance that the statements *fairly* represent the results of the activities of the company. Therefore, both the New York Stock Exchange and the American Stock Exchange, as well as the Securities and Exchange Commission, require that the set of financial statements that certain companies (those offering equity securities for public sale) issue every year be audited. This audited set of financial statements is called an **annual report**. Similarly, a bank may require a company to provide audited financial statements when the company applies for a loan. For the same reason, other types of economic entities, such as universities and charitable organizations, also issue audited financial statements. But what does it mean to be audited?

Auditing involves the examination, by an *independent* CPA, of a company's accounting records and financial statements. Based on the evidence gathered in the auditing process, including evidence about the quality of the company's internal control, the CPA expresses a professional, unbiased opinion about (or attests to) the fairness of the accounting information in the company's financial statements. Auditing plays an important role in society because many external users rely on CPAs' opinions when making decisions about whether to engage in activities with companies, universities, charitable organizations, and other economic entities.

Other Assurance Services

Recently, because of their customers' needs for assurance about other types of information, public accounting firms have begun to expand their assurance services. In the interest of helping public accounting firms serve their customers, the AICPA, through one of its

www.nyse.com
www.amex.com
www.sec.gov

---

[2]AICPA-sponsored meeting of representatives of small and medium-sized firms, regulators, and scholars.
[3]AICPA Special Committee on Assurance Services.

committees,[3] identified some specific opportunities for these firms to provide assurance services. Exhibit A-2 summarizes some of these opportunities.

Management Advisory Services

During an audit by a public accounting firm, the CPA makes a careful study of the company's accounting records, which are part of its integrated information system. Thus the public accounting firm has a good knowledge of the strengths and weaknesses of the operating activities and the information system of the company. In addition to auditing departments, many public accounting firms have separate management advisory services departments to conduct special studies to advise client companies about improving their internal operations and to aid client managers in their various activities. These departments, in part, help to provide some of the assurance services we discussed earlier.

Management advisory services in public accounting firms include the design or improvement of a company's financial accounting system for identifying, measuring, recording, retaining, and reporting accounting information. These services also may include assistance in areas such as developing cost-control systems, planning manufacturing facilities, and installing computer operations. To provide these services, public accounting firms also must have employees who have a strong understanding of the industries in which their clients operate. Therefore, in addition to hiring accountants, public accounting firms hire people with other specialties—people such as lawyers, industrial engineers, and systems analysts.

Tax Services

The federal government, governments of other countries, and most state governments require companies and individuals to file income tax returns and to pay taxes. Because of the high tax rates, complex tax regulations, and special tax incentives today, most companies (and individuals) can benefit from carefully planning their activities to minimize or postpone their tax payments. This is called **tax planning.** Many public accounting firms have separate tax services departments that employ tax professionals who are experts in the various federal, foreign government, and state tax regulations. These tax professionals assist companies and individuals in tax planning. In addition to tax planning, the tax services departments of public accounting firms frequently prepare client company or individual income tax returns that reflect the results of these tax-planning activities.

Governmental and Quasi-Governmental Accounting

Certain governmental and quasi-governmental agencies also employ accountants. The Internal Revenue Service, for example, is responsible for the collection of federal income taxes. State revenue agencies also perform similar functions. Administrators of other

4 *In what types of jobs may an accountant work as a governmental accountant?*

Exhibit A-2   Opportunities for Providing Assurance Services

▶ Assessing whether an entity has identified all its risks and is effectively managing them
▶ Evaluating whether an entity's performance measurement system contains relevant and reliable measures of its progress toward its goals and objectives
▶ Assessing whether an entity's integrated information system (or its ERP system) provides reliable information fordecision-making
▶ Assessing whether systems used in electronic commerce provide appropriate data integrity, security, privacy, and reliability
▶ Assessing the effectiveness of health care services provided by HMOs, hospitals, doctors, and other providers
▶ Assessing whether various caregivers are meeting specified goals regarding care for the elderly

federal, state, and local government agencies are responsible for the control of both tax revenues and tax expenditures. These agencies hire accountants to provide accounting information for use in the administration of these activities.

Administrators of federal, state, municipal, and other not-for-profit organizations such as colleges and universities, hospitals, and mental health agencies are responsible for the organizations' efficient and effective operations. The accounting information needed by these organizations is similar to that needed by companies. But because they are not-for-profit organizations financed in part by public funds, these organizations are required to use somewhat different accounting procedures (sometimes called *fund accounting*). These organizations hire accountants to design and operate their accounting systems.

Several other governmental organizations also employ accountants. As we mentioned in Chapter 1, the Securities and Exchange Commission (SEC) is responsible for overseeing the reported financial statements of certain companies and has the legal authority to establish accounting regulations for them. The SEC employs accountants to identify appropriate accounting procedures and to verify that companies are following existing regulations. The General Accounting Office (GAO) is responsible for cooperating with various agencies of the federal government in the development and operation of their accounting systems to improve the management of these agencies. It also oversees the administration of government contracts and the spending of federal funds. The Defense Contract Audit Agency (DCAA) audits all federally funded defense contracts. Its work resembles the audit services of public accounting firms. Other federal and state agencies, such as the Federal Bureau of Investigation, the Environmental Protection Agency, and the Federal Communications Commission, also employ accountants to prepare and use accounting information.

As evidence of professionalism in governmental accounting, an accountant may become a Certified Government Financial Manager (CGFM). A CGFM must have met specified educational and practical experience requirements and must have passed a uniform CGFM exam.

www.sec.gov

www.gao.gov

www.dtic.mil/dcaa

www.fbi.gov
www.epa.gov
www.fcc.gov

Professional Organizations

5 *What are some examples of organizations of professional accountants?*

In Chapter 1, we mentioned several organizations that influence generally accepted accounting principles (GAAP). In addition, a number of *professional* organizations also influence accounting standards and facilitate communication among members of the profession.

As we discussed in Chapter 1, the AICPA is the national professional organization of CPAs. In addition to influencing accounting principles, the AICPA influences auditing standards. The Auditing Standards Board of the AICPA develops auditing standards that govern the way CPAs perform audits. The AICPA also prepares and grades the CPA examination and dispenses the results to the individual states, which then issue licenses to those who have passed the examination and who meet the other qualifications of the state. The AICPA publishes the *Journal of Accountancy*.

www.rutgers.edu/ Accounting/raw/ feisr1/cfri.htm
www.rutgers.edu/ Accounting/raw/ima. htm

www.aaa-edu.org

The Financial Executives Institute (FEI) is an organization of financial executives of major corporations, such as the chief financial officer, financial vice-presidents, and controllers. The FEI publishes *Financial Executive.*

The Institute of Management Accountants (IMA) is an organization of management accountants and others interested in management accounting. Besides influencing the practice of management accounting, the IMA prepares and grades the CMA examination. The IMA publishes *Management Accounting.*

The American Accounting Association (AAA) is the national professional organization of academic and practicing accountants interested in both the academic and the research aspects of accounting. Through their research, AAA members, many of whom are accounting practitioners, influence the setting of accounting standards. The AAA publishes *The Accounting Review, Issues in Accounting Education,* and *Accounting Horizons.*

Summary

At the beginning of the appendix we asked you several questions. Below are the questions from the beginning of the appendix, with a brief summary of the key points relating to the answers. Use your creative and critical thinking skills to expand on these key points to develop more complete answers to the questions and to determine what other questions you have that might lead you to learn more about the issues.

1 What are the general fields that make up the profession of accountancy?

The four general fields of accountancy include (1) industry accounting, (2) public accounting, (3) governmental accounting, and (4) education.

2 What do industry (management) accountants do?

A company employs an industry (or management) accountant to perform its internal (management) accounting activities and to prepare its financial reports. Management accounting activities encompass several areas: budgeting, cost accounting, preparation of financial reports, design and operation of accounting systems, internal auditing, and tax accounting.

3 What broad categories of services do public accountants perform?

The broad categories of services that public accountants perform include assurance services, management advisory services, and tax services. An assurance is a conclusion expressed on the reliability and/or relevance of information and/or information systems. Auditing evolved from a need for assurance services. Auditing involves the examination, by an independent CPA, of a company's accounting records and financial statements. Based upon the evidence gathered in the auditing process, the CPA expresses a professional, unbiased opinion about (or attests to) the fairness of the accounting information in the financial statements. Management advisory services include the design or improvement of the financial accounting system for identifying, measuring, recording, retaining, and reporting accounting information. These services also may include assistance in areas such as developing cost control systems, planning manufacturing facilities, and installing computer operations. Tax services involve assisting companies and individuals in tax planning. In addition to tax planning, the tax services also include preparing company or individual income tax returns that reflect the results of these tax planning activities.

4 In what types of jobs may an accountant work as a governmental accountant?

The Internal Revenue Service is responsible for administering the collection of federal income taxes. State revenue agencies also perform similar functions. Administrators of other federal, state, and local government agencies are responsible for the control of both tax revenues and tax expenditures. These agencies hire accountants to provide accounting information for use in the administration of these activities. Administrators of federal, state, municipal, and other not-for-profit organizations such as colleges and universities, hospitals, and mental health agencies are responsible for their efficient and effective operations. Accountants hired by these organizations design and operate the accounting systems of these organizations. Several other governmental organizations also employ accountants. The Securities and Exchange Commission, the General Accounting Office, the Defense Contract Audit Agency, and other federal and state agencies, such as the Federal Bureau of Investigation, the Interstate Commerce Commission, the Environmental Protection Agency, and the Federal Communications Commission, also employ accountants to prepare and use accounting information.

5 What are some examples of organizations of professional accountants?

The American Institute of Certified Public Accountants is the national professional organization of CPAs. The Financial Executives Institute is an organization of financial executives of major corporations, such as the chief financial officer, financial vice-presidents, and controllers. The Institute of Management Accountants is an organization of management accountants and others interested in management accounting. The American Accounting Association is the national professional organization of academic and practicing accountants interested in both the academic and research aspects of accounting.

Key Terms

annual report *(p. 928)*

auditing *(p. 928)*

certified public accountants *(p. 927)*

controller *(p. 926)*

general accounting *(p.927)*

internal control *(p. 927)*

tax planning *(p. 929)*

QUESTIONS

QA-1 What does a company's controller do?

QA-2 What do you know about an accountant who holds a Certificate in Management Accounting (CMA)?

QA-3 What is internal control?

QA-4 What is the purpose of internal auditing?

QA-5 What do you know about an accountant who holds a Certificate of Internal Auditing (CIA)?

QA-6 What are the responsibilities of the accountants who work in a company's tax department?

QA-7 What do you know about an accountant who is a certified public accountant (CPA)?

QA-8 What is an assurance?

QA-9 What is auditing?

QA-10 What do management advisory services include?

QA-11 What tax services does a public accounting firm's tax department perform?

QA-12 What different types of jobs might a governmental accountant hold?

QA-13 What do you know about an accountant who is a Certified Government Financial Manager (CGFM)?

QA-14 What are four professional organizations of accountants and who are their members?

RECORDING, STORING, AND REPORTING ACCOUNTING INFORMATION

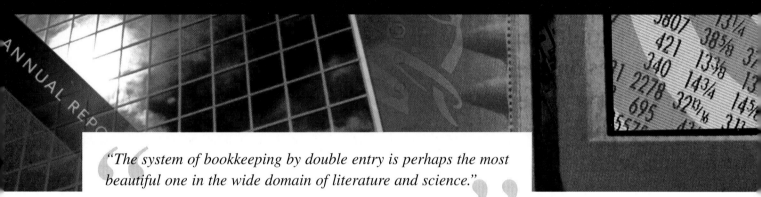

"The system of bookkeeping by double entry is perhaps the most beautiful one in the wide domain of literature and science."

—E. T. Freedley, 1852

1 *What is a debit entry, and what is a credit entry?*

2 *What are the rules for recording increases and decreases in asset and liability accounts?*

3 *What are the rules for recording increases and decreases in owner's equity accounts?*

4 *What are the major steps in a company's accounting cycle?*

5 *What is the difference between journalizing and posting?*

6 *What are adjusting entries, and what are the three types of adjusting entries?*

7 *What are closing entries, and how do they relate to the Income Summary account?*

8 *How are accounting procedures modified for corporations?*

In Chapter 5, we explained transactions and source documents, as well as the entity, monetary unit, and historical cost concepts as they apply to a company's accounting process. We explained that the accounting process accumulates information and reports the results of the company's activities. We introduced an accounting system in terms of the accounting equation: Assets = Liabilities + Owner's Equity. And we explained the dual effect of recording transactions. We discussed several accounting principles and concepts related to net income, including the concept of an accounting period, the earning process, the matching principle, and accrual accounting. We also used a column approach to illustrate how to record and retain the information from a company's transactions so that the information could be reported in the company's balance sheet.

In Chapter 6, we noted that the column approach is unmanageable when a company has many transactions for which it needs to keep detailed records. We discussed the concept of a T-account and explained how a company uses separate T-accounts to record the changes in each of its asset, liability, and owner's equity items. We then expanded the discussion to include the recording of transactions in revenue and expense T-accounts so that the information could be reported on the company's income statement. From then on throughout the book, we used T-accounts in conjunction with the accounting equation to explain the impact of transactions on a company's accounting system.

The T-account and accounting equation approach worked well to explain the accounting process without getting "bogged down" in specific accounting procedures. This approach enabled you to focus more on understanding how to use the information generated by this process. However, many of you will become accounting majors and will need to have a basic understanding of the specific accounting procedures a company uses in operating its accounting system. Others of you also may be interested in understanding these procedures. The purpose of this appendix is to explain debit and credit rules, the accounting cycle, and how companies record transactions in journals, post and retain transaction information, record adjusting and closing entries, and prepare financial statements. To help explain some of these procedures, we will review what we discussed in earlier chapters. For simplicity, our discussion will focus on a sole proprietorship, but we will explain the differences for corporations later in the chapter.

Accounts

Recall that an accounting system is a means by which a company identifies, measures, records, and retains accounting information about its activities so that it can report this information in its financial statements. In an accounting system, a company uses **accounts** to record and retain the monetary information from its transactions. It uses separate accounts for each asset, liability, and owner's equity item, as well as for each revenue and expense item. The number of accounts as well as the types and names of the accounts for each company depend on the particular company's operations, and on whether it is a sole proprietorship, partnership, or corporation. A **general ledger** is the entire set of accounts that a company uses. For this reason, accounts sometimes are referred to as *general ledger accounts*.

An account can take several physical forms. It might be a location on a computer disk or tape, or, in the case of a manual system, on a sheet of paper. The general ledger might be a computer file (on disk or tape), or a loose-leaf binder containing all the accounts of a manual system. Regardless of the physical form, a company uses each account for recording and accumulating accounting information about a financial statement item.

Debits and Credits

1 *What is a debit entry, and what is a credit entry?*

In a manual system, accounts may have several different forms. For convenience, in this appendix we will continue to use the T-account form, as we show below. Recall that the title is written across the top of each T-account, and that each T-account has a left side and a right side. The left side is called the **debit** side, and the right side is called the **credit** side. The left (debit) and the right (credit) sides of each account are used for recording and accumulating the monetary information from transactions. A **debit entry** is a monetary amount recorded (debited) on the left side of an account. A **credit entry** is a monetary amount recorded (credited) on the right side of an account.

Title of Account

Left (debit) side	Right (credit) side

Recording Rules

Each account accumulates information about how much it has increased or decreased as a result of various transactions. As we explained in Chapter 6, whether a company records increases or decreases on the left or the right side of an account depends on the type of account (on where the account "fits" within the accounting equation). Expanding the discussion from Chapter 6, we now introduce the *debit and credit rules*. For assets, liabilities, and owner's equity accounts,[1] these rules relate to the side of the accounting equation on which the account is located. For withdrawal, revenue, and expense accounts, these rules relate to whether the transactions increase or decrease owner's equity. That is, when an owner withdraws money from a company, the effect of the withdrawal is that the owner's equity in the company decreases. When the company earns revenue, the ultimate effect of the revenue increase is to increase the owner's equity. When the company incurs expenses, the ultimate effect of the expense increase is to decrease the owner's equity.

The debit and credit rules are as follows:

1. **Asset accounts (accounts on the left side of the accounting equation) are increased by debit entries (amounts recorded on the left side of a T-account) and decreased by credit entries.**

2. **Liability accounts (accounts on the right side of the equation) are increased by credit entries (amounts recorded on the right side of a T-account) and decreased by debit entries.**

3. *Permanent* **owner's equity, or capital, accounts (accounts on the right side of the equation) are increased by credit entries and decreased by debit entries.** *Temporary* **owner's equity accounts have the following rules:**

   (a) **Withdrawal accounts are increased by debit entries and decreased by credit entries.**

   (b) **Revenue accounts are increased by credit entries and decreased by debit entries.**

   (c) **Expense accounts are increased by debit entries and decreased by credit entries.**

Exhibit B-1 illustrates the debit and credit rules as they relate to the accounting equation.

A company uses the double entry rule for recording its accounting information. The **double entry rule** states that in the recording of a transaction, the total amount of the debit entries must equal the total amount of the credit entries for the transaction. The use of both the double entry rule and the debit and credit rules in recording transactions ensures that the accounting equation remains in balance.

At any given time, an account may have a number of debit and credit entries in it. The **balance of an account** is the difference between the total increases and the total decreases

2 *What are the rules for recording increases and decreases in asset and liability accounts?*

3 *What are the rules for recording increases and decreases in owner's equity accounts?*

---

[1]Owner's equity accounts may be *permanent* or *temporary*. Permanent owner's equity accounts are those that a company reports on its balance sheet. Temporary owner's equity accounts are used only to compute a company's net income or withdrawals for the accounting period.

Exhibit B-1 Accounting Equation and Debit/Credit Rules

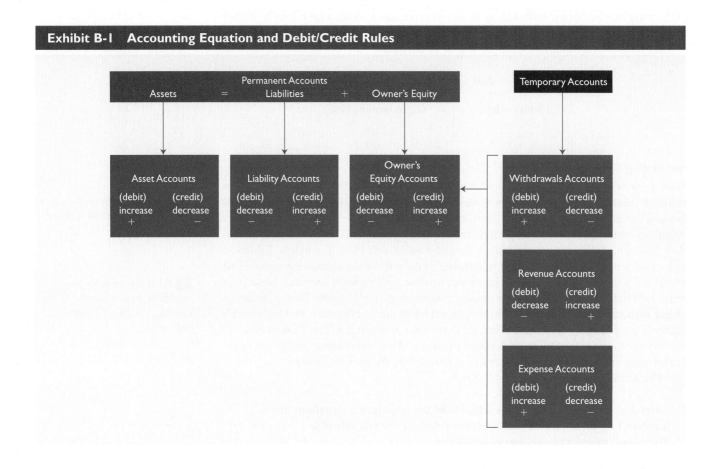

recorded in the account. Typically, total increases exceed total decreases. Therefore, each asset account normally has a debit balance because the total increases (debits) exceed the total decreases (credits) in the account. Similarly, each liability and permanent owner's equity account normally has a credit balance because the total increases (credits) exceed the total decreases (debits) in each account. For the temporary owner's equity items, revenue accounts normally have credit balances, whereas expense and withdrawal accounts normally have debit balances. The following list summarizes the normal balances in the various accounts.

Accounts	Normal Balance
Assets	Debit
Liabilities	Credit
Owner's capital	Credit
Owner's withdrawals	Debit
Revenues	Credit
Expenses	Debit

Accounting Cycle

4 *What are the major steps in a company's accounting cycle?*

Now that you are familiar with the rules for recording and accumulating information in the various accounts, we will discuss the steps that a company completes during each accounting period to record, retain, and report the monetary information from its transactions. These steps are called the **accounting cycle**. The major steps include: (1) recording (journalizing) the transactions in the general journal, (2) posting the journal entries to the accounts in the general ledger, (3) recording (and posting) adjusting entries, (4) preparing the financial statements, and (5) recording (and posting) closing entries. We will discuss and illustrate each of these steps, along with several substeps, in the following sections.

Recording (Journalizing) Transactions

Recall that a source document (invoice, check) is the business record from which a company obtains the information for each transaction. The company uses this information to record each transaction in a journal, after which it transfers the information to its accounts. A **general journal** includes the following information about each transaction: the date of the transaction, the accounts to be debited and credited, the amounts of the debit and credit entries, and an explanation of each transaction. In a manual system, the general journal is a book of columnar pages.

A company can use a general journal to record all types of transactions. The general journal is the kind of journal we will discuss in this appendix. However, many companies have a number of *special journals*, each of which is used to record a particular type of transaction. The common special journals are the sales (for recording credit sales), purchases (for credit purchases), cash receipts (for cash inflows), and cash payments (for cash outflows) journals. We do not discuss these special journals.

A general journal consists of a date column, a column to list the accounts affected by each transaction (and an explanation of the transaction), a column to list the account numbers of the affected accounts, and debit and credit columns to list the amount to be recorded in each account. **Journalizing** is the process of recording a transaction in a company's general journal. A **journal entry** is the recorded information for each transaction. We show an example of transactions and how they are recorded in a general journal in Exhibits B-2 and B-3 later in this appendix.

A company gains several advantages by using a general journal for initially recording its transactions. First, this process helps prevent errors. Since the company initially records the accounts and the debit and credit amounts for each transaction on a single journal page rather than directly in the many accounts, this method makes it easier to prove that the debits and the credits are equal, thus keeping the accounting equation in balance. Second, all the information about each transaction (including the explanation) is recorded in one place, thereby providing a complete "picture" of the transaction. This is useful in the auditing process, or if an error is discovered, because it is easy to review all of the transaction information. Third, the company records the transactions chronologically (day to day), so that the journal provides a "history" of its financial transactions.

Key Procedures in Journalizing

The following list outlines the journalizing procedures for each column of the general journal. Study it carefully, referring to the completed general journal in Exhibit B-3.

1. Enter the month, day, and year of the first transaction in the "Date" column. It is not necessary to repeat the month and year of later transactions until the beginning of a new journal page, a new month, or a new year.

2. Enter the title of the account to be debited at the far left of the column entitled "Account Titles and Explanations." Enter the amount of the debit to this account in the "Debit" column on the same line as the account title. Dollar signs typically are not used in the debit (or credit) columns.

3. Enter the title of the account to be credited on the next line below the title of the debited account. Indent the title of the credit account slightly to the right so that a reader looking at the journal page can easily identify which account titles are

debited and which are credited. Enter the amount of the credit to this account on the same line in the "Credit" column.

4. Some transactions involve two or more debits, two or more credits, or both. (Remember that for each transaction, the *total* amount of the debit entries must equal the *total* amount of the credit entries.) In this case, the type of journal entry a company uses is called a *compound entry*. When recording a compound entry, first list all the accounts and amounts to be debited (list each account on a separate line), followed by all the accounts to be credited (indent and list each account on a separate line). The December 29, 1999 journal entry in Exhibit B-3 is an example of a compound journal entry.

5. Enter a brief explanation of the transaction on the line below the last credit entry of the transaction. Write the explanation at the far left of the column entitled "Account Titles and Explanations." Leave a blank line before beginning another journal entry, to set off each entry.

6. During the process of journalizing, do *not* record a number in the column entitled "Acct. No." (Account Number). You will enter a number in this column during the "posting" process, which we will discuss later. (When you are referring to Exhibit B-3, note that this is what the general journal page looks like *after* the posting process is complete.)

After journalizing the debit and credit entries of a transaction, journalize the next transaction for the day, and continue the process until all the transactions have been recorded. *By strictly following these journalizing procedures, you will minimize the chance of error.*

Illustration of Journal Entries

Recall from Chapter 5 that Anna Cox started Sweet Temptations, a retail candy store, by investing $15,000 on December 15, 1999. During the remainder of December, the store engaged in several transactions to get ready to open for customers on January 2, 2000. Also recall that Sweet Temptations is a retail candy store that uses a perpetual inventory system[2] and leases store space in Westwood Mall.

We have prepared Exhibit B-2 to help you remember the December transactions of Sweet Temptations. This exhibit summarizes the six transactions and analyzes the debit and credit entries for each transaction.

To illustrate the general journal and the journalizing process, Exhibit B-3 shows the journal entries for these six transactions. In studying Exhibit B-3, you should do the following: (1) review each transaction listed in Exhibit B-2, (2) think of the source documents for the transaction, (3) understand the impact of the transactions on the accounting equation, (4) determine the debit and credit entries, (5) think of the journalizing procedures, and (6) compare these procedures with the journal entries that we made in Exhibit B-3.

To understand the journalizing process, look at the December 20, 1999 transaction in which Sweet Temptations purchased $1,620 of inventory on credit from Unlimited Decadence Corporation. The source document for the transaction is the invoice that Sweet Temptations received from Unlimited Decadence Corporation. The effect of this purchase on the accounting equation is that both an asset (Inventory) and a liability (Accounts Payable) are increased by $1,620. To record the transaction in the general journal, Sweet Temptations skipped a line after the previous transaction. It then entered the date and the account title (Inventory) and amount ($1,620) of the account to be debited. It indented the next line and

---

[2]Alternatively, a company could use a *periodic inventory system,* as we discussed in Chapter 10. Under this system, the company does not keep a continuous record of the inventory on hand and sold. Instead, it determines its inventory by taking a physical inventory at the end of the period. The company derives its cost of goods sold by adding its purchases to the beginning inventory and then subtracting the ending inventory.

Exhibit B-2 Sweet Temptations' December 1999 Transactions and Analysis

Date	Transaction	Analysis
12/15	A. Cox makes initial investment in Sweet Temptations of $15,000.	Asset account Cash is increased (debited) by $15,000; owner's equity account A. Cox, Capital is increased (credited) by $15,000.
12/16	Sweet Temptations pays $6,000 for six months of rent in advance to Westwood Mall.	Asset account Prepaid Rent is increased (debited) by $6,000; asset account Cash is decreased (credited) by $6,000.
12/17	Sweet Temptations pays $700 for the purchase of supplies from City Supply Company.	Asset account Supplies is increased (debited) by $700; asset account Cash is decreased (credited) by $700.
12/20	Sweet Temptations purchases $1,620 of inventory (candy) on credit from Unlimited Decadence Corporation.	Asset account Inventory is increased (debited) by $1,620; liability account Accounts Payable is increased (credited) by $1,620.
12/29	Sweet Temptations purchases store equipment for $2,200, paying $1,000 cash and signing a three-month note to Ace Equipment Company for $1,200.	Asset account Store Equipment is increased (debited) by $2,200; asset account Cash is decreased (credited) by $1,000; liability account Notes Payable is increased (credited) by $1,200.
12/30	Sweet Temptations sells $400 of unneeded store equipment on account to The Hardware Store.	Asset account Accounts Receivable is increased (debited) by $400; asset account Store Equipment is decreased (credited) by $400.

Exhibit B-3 Sweet Temptations' General Journal Entries: December 1999

Date	Account Titles and Explanations	Acct. No.	Debit	Credit
1999 Dec. 15	Cash	101	15,000	
	A. Cox, Capital	301		15,000
	Made initial investment in Sweet Temptations.			
16	Prepaid Rent	107	6,000	
	Cash	101		6,000
	Paid 6 months' rent in advance to Westwood Mall.			
17	Supplies	106	700	
	Cash	101		700
	Purchased office supplies from City Supply Company.			
20	Inventory	105	1,620	
	Accounts Payable	201		1,620
	Purchased inventory on credit from Unlimited Decadence Corporation.			
29	Store Equipment	123	2,200	
	Cash	101		1,000
	Notes Payable	204		1,200
	Purchased store equipment from Ace Equipment Company, making cash down payment and signing 3-month note.			
30	Accounts Receivable	103	400	
	Store Equipment	123		400
	Sold unneeded store equipment (desk) on credit to The Hardware Store.			

entered the account title (Accounts Payable) and amount ($1,620) to be credited. On the next line it wrote a brief explanation of the journal entry. After following this process for each transaction, Sweet Temptations stored all the source documents in its files.

After a company records the journal entries, it transfers the amounts (posts them) to the related accounts. It records the number (which we discuss later) of each of these accounts in the "Acct. No." column of the general journal. To save space, we do not illustrate this posting process for Exhibit B-3. Instead, we continue our illustration of journalizing in Exhibits B-4 and B-5. Exhibit B-4 summarizes and analyzes the transactions of Sweet Temptations for January 2000. These include revenue and expense transactions, along with various other transactions.[3]

Exhibit B-5 illustrates the journal entries that Sweet Temptations made to record the January transactions. In studying this exhibit, you should review Exhibit B-4 and think through the steps of the journalizing process. Once again, note that Sweet Temptations did not enter the account numbers at the time it recorded the journal entries; it entered them during the posting process, which we will discuss next.

Exhibit B-4   Sweet Temptations' January 2000 Transactions and Analysis

Date	Transaction	Analysis
1/02	Sweet Temptations sells inventory (candy) at total cash selling price of $300.	Asset account Cash is increased (debited) by $300; revenue account Sales Revenue is increased (credited) by $300.
1/02	Sweet Temptations records cost of goods sold of $135 on cash sale.	Expense account Cost of Goods Sold is increased (debited) by $135; asset account Inventory is decreased (credited) by $135.
1/03	Sweet Temptations pays $1,620 to Unlimited Decadence Corporation for inventory purchased on 12/20/99.	Liability account Accounts Payable is decreased (debited) by $1,620; asset account Cash is decreased (credited) by $1,620.
1/04	Sweet Temptations purchases $4,320 of inventory (candy) on credit from Unlimited Decadence Corporation.	Asset account Inventory is increased (debited) by $4,320; liability account Accounts Payable is increased (credited) by $4,320.
1/06	Sweet Temptations made credit sale of $100.	Asset account Accounts Receivable is increased (debited) by $100; revenue account Sales Revenue is increased (credited) by $100.
1/06	Sweet Temptations records cost of goods sold of $45 on credit sale.	Expense account Cost of Goods Sold is increased (debited) by $45; asset account Inventory is decreased (credited) by $45.
1/07	Sweet Temptations collects $400 of accounts receivable from The Hardware Store.	Asset account Cash is increased (debited) by $400; asset account Accounts Receivable is decreased (credited) by $400.
1/20	A. Cox withdraws $50 for personal use.	Owner's equity account A. Cox, Withdrawals is increased (debited) by $50; asset account Cash is decreased (credited) by $50.
1/25	Sweet Temptations pays $200 to a consultant for promotion coordination.	Expense account Consulting Expense is increased (debited) by $200; asset account Cash is decreased (credited) by $200.
1/25	Sweet Temptations pays $300 for advertising in promotional flyer.	Expense account Advertising Expense is increased (debited) by $300; asset account Cash is decreased (credited) by $300.
1/29	Sweet Temptations purchases store equipment for $200 cash.	Asset account Store Equipment is increased (debited) by $200; asset account Cash is decreased (credited) by $200.
1/31	Sweet Temptations pays salaries totaling $2,050 to employees.	Expense account Salaries Expense is increased (debited) by $2,050; asset account Cash is decreased (credited) by $2,050.
1/31	Sweet Temptations pays telephone bill of $60.	Expense account Telephone Expense is increased (debited) by $60; asset account Cash is decreased (credited) by $60.
1/31	Sweet Temptations pays utilities bill of $190.	Expense account Utilities Expense is increased (debited) by $190; asset account Cash is decreased (credited) by $190.
1/31	Sweet Temptations records $7,700 of cash sales for 1/3/00 through 1/31/00.	Asset account Cash is increased (debited) by $7,700; revenue account Sales Revenue is increased (credited) by $7,700.
1/31	Sweet Temptations records cost of goods sold of $3,465 on cash sales.	Expense account Cost of Goods Sold is increased (debited) by $3,465; asset account Inventory is decreased (credited) by $3,465.

[3]For simplicity, on January 31 we recorded the sum ($7,700) of Sweet Temptations' January 3 through January 31 cash sales. Normally, a company records its cash sales each day.

Exhibit B-5 Sweet Temptations' General Journal Entries: January 2000

Date	Account Titles and Explanations	Acct. No.	Debit	Credit
2000 Jan. 2	Cash Sales Revenue Made cash sales.	101 401	300	 300
2	Cost of Goods Sold Inventory To record cost of goods sold on cash sales.	501 105	135	 135
3	Accounts Payable Cash Paid Unlimited Decadence Corporation for inventory purchased on 12/20/99.	201 101	1,620	 1,620
4	Inventory Accounts Payable Purchased inventory on credit from Unlimited Decadence Corporation.	105 201	4,320	 4,320
6	Accounts Receivable Sales Revenue Made credit sale.	103 401	100	 100
6	Cost of Goods Sold Inventory To record cost of goods sold on credit sale.	501 105	45	 45
7	Cash Accounts Receivable Collected amount owed from The Hardware Store for desk sold on 12/30/99.	101 103	400	 400
20	A. Cox, Withdrawals Cash Withdrew cash for personal use.	304 101	50	 50
25	Consulting Expense Cash Paid consultant for promotion coordination.	502 101	200	 200
25	Advertising Expense Cash Paid for advertising in promotional flyer.	503 101	300	 300
29	Store Equipment Cash Purchased store equipment.	123 101	200	 200
31	Salaries Expense Cash Paid employees' salaries.	504 101	2,050	 2,050
31	Telephone Expense Cash Paid telephone bill.	505 101	60	 60
31	Utilities Expense Cash Paid utilities bill.	506 101	190	 190
31	Cash Sales Revenue To record cash sales for 1/3/00 through 1/31/00.	101 401	7,700	 7,700
31	Cost of Goods Sold Inventory To record cost of goods sold on cash sales.	501 105	3,465	 3,465

Posting to the Accounts

5 *What is the difference between journalizing and posting?*

In the journalizing process, a company records each transaction in its general journal. However, at this point it has not yet recorded the accounting information from each transaction in the accounts, the "storage units" for the company's accounting information. To do so, the company must *post* the amounts from the general journal to the related accounts. **Posting** is the process of transferring the debit and credit information for each journal entry to the accounts in a company's general ledger.

Account Numbers and Chart of Accounts

To help in the accounting process, a company assigns a number to each of its accounts and lists that number to the right of the account title on a T-account. The company obtains the account number from its chart of accounts. A **chart of accounts** is a numbering system designed to organize a company's accounts efficiently and to reduce errors in the recording and accumulating process. A company usually sets up its chart of accounts so that the Cash account is assigned the lowest number, followed in order by all the other asset accounts, all the liability accounts, the permanent owner's equity (capital) account, the withdrawals account, the income summary account (discussed later), the revenue accounts, and the expense accounts. The company then includes the accounts in its general ledger in the order in which they are listed in the chart of accounts. As you will see shortly, ordering the accounts in the general ledger in this way helps in preparing the financial statements.

Exhibit B-6 lists Sweet Temptations' chart of accounts. Notice that the asset account numbers begin at 101, the liabilities at 201, the owner's equity at 301, the revenues at 401, and the expenses at 501. A company uses a numbering system such as this to help identify and classify its accounts. (Some large corporations use numbers as high as six digits for classifying their accounts and even use decimals to further subclassify their accounts.)

Exhibit B-6   Sweet Temptations' Chart of Accounts

Account Titles	Account Numbers
Cash	101
Accounts Receivable	103
Inventory	105
Supplies	106
Prepaid Rent	107
Store Equipment	123
Accumulated Depreciation	124
Accounts Payable	201
Notes Payable	204
Interest Payable	205
A. Cox, Capital	301
A. Cox, Withdrawals	304
Income Summary	306
Sales Revenue	401
Cost of Goods Sold	501
Consulting Expense	502
Advertising Expense	503
Salaries Expense	504
Telephone Expense	505
Utilities Expense	506
Supplies Expense	507
Rent Expense	508
Interest Expense	509
Depreciation Expense	510

Note also that the accounts are not consecutively numbered. Sweet Temptations follows this procedure so that it can insert any new accounts into its chart of accounts (and general ledger) later and still assign account numbers in their proper order.

Key Procedures in Posting

A company with a manual accounting system usually posts at the end of each day. As with the journalizing process, the company follows a set of procedures for posting to the individual accounts. The following list outlines these procedures:

1. In the general ledger, locate the first account of the first transaction to be posted from the general journal.

2. Enter the month, day, and year of the transaction and the debit amount (as listed in the general journal) in the debit (left) side of the account.

3. Go back to the general journal and, on the same line as the account title, enter in the "Acct. No." (Account Number) column the number of the account in which the debit amount was posted. A number in the Acct. No. column indicates that the posting process has been completed for that *line* of the general journal. It also indicates to which account that amount was posted. This is the last step before continuing with the posting of the next line. (*Caution*: Remember that the company completes this procedure *after* it posts the amount in the account.)

4. For the next line of the transaction in the general journal (usually the credit entry, unless a compound entry is involved), repeat steps 2 and 3, except that the date and amount are posted to the credit (right) side of the appropriate account.

After posting the debit and credit entries for the first transaction to the related accounts, post the next journal entry for the day and continue the process until the daily postings are completed. *By strictly following these posting procedures, you will minimize the chance of error.*

Illustration of Posting Process

Exhibit B-7 illustrates the posting process for the January 2, 2000 sales transaction of Sweet Temptations. The arrows from the general journal to the general ledger indicate the debit

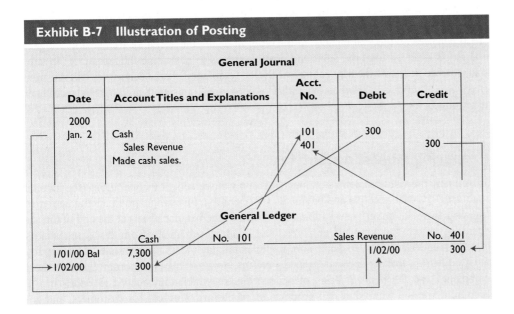

Exhibit B-7   Illustration of Posting

and credit postings. Note that Sweet Temptations transferred the date of the transaction from the general journal to each ledger account. It posted the amount of the debit ($300) in the debit column of the Cash account, and the amount of the credit ($300) in the credit column of the Sales Revenue account in the general ledger. It then listed the account numbers (101 and 401) on the respective lines in the Acct. No. column of the general journal, as we indicate by the arrows from the general ledger to the general journal.

Note in Exhibit B-7 that the Cash account has a beginning (1/01/00) balance of $7,300. This was the ending balance from December 1999, after Sweet Temptations posted the December transactions listed in Exhibit B-3. Note also that the Sales Revenue account did not have a beginning balance. Later in this appendix, we will discuss the computation of account balances and why some accounts have beginning balances and some accounts do not have beginning balances.

Sweet Temptations completes the posting process at the end of each day in January. Exhibit B-8 shows all of the general ledger accounts of Sweet Temptations at the end of January (*before* it makes its adjusting and closing entries). They are listed according to the chart of accounts shown in Exhibit B-6. You should study the postings to the accounts, referring to the journal entries listed in Exhibit B-5. Again, note that in Exhibit B-5, the Acct. No. column had not been completed when the journal entry was made but was completed during the posting process. You should think of the account numbers that would be listed in this column based on the chart of accounts in Exhibit B-6.

Trial Balance

In discussing the journalizing and posting process, we set up procedures so that the double entry rule is followed. That is, the total amount of the debit entries equals the total amount of the credit entries in both the general journal and the general ledger accounts. By following these procedures the accounting equation remains in balance and errors are minimized.

People can make mistakes, however. Therefore, it is helpful to set up a procedure that will help to detect a journalizing or posting error. This procedure involves proving the equality of the debit and credit balances in the accounts by preparing a trial balance.

A **trial balance** is a schedule that lists the titles of all the accounts in a company's general ledger, the debit or credit balance of each account, and the totals of the debit and credit balances. Normally, a company prepares a trial balance at the end of the accounting period, before proceeding with the adjusting entries (which we discuss next). To prepare a trial balance, first compute the balance of each account and list it (along with the date on which it is computed) on the appropriate side of the account. Next, list the account titles and debit or credit balances on the trial balance in the order in which the accounts are listed in the general ledger. Finally, total the debit and credit columns to determine their equality. To save space, we do not show the trial balance of Sweet Temptations here because we will illustrate an adjusted trial balance (which is similar to, but more extensive than, a trial balance) later in Exhibit B-11.

Preparing Adjusting Entries

6 *What are adjusting entries, and what are the three types of adjusting entries?*

A company prepares financial statements to report the results of its operations (the income statement), its cash receipts and payments for operating, investing, and financing activities (the cash flow statement), and its financial position (the balance sheet) at the end of the accounting period. The company prepares these financial statements from the balances in its general ledger accounts. To make sure its financial statements are accurate, the company must be certain that its account balances are up-to-date. This is important because most companies use the *accrual* basis of accounting, in which they record revenues in the accounting period when they sell products to, or perform services for customers, and not

Exhibit B-8 Sweet Temptations' General Ledger (January 2000)

Cash   No. 101

Date		Debit	Date	Credit
1/01/00	Bal	7,300	1/03/00	1,620
1/02/00		300	1/20/00	50
1/07/00		400	1/25/00	200
1/31/00		7,700	1/25/00	300
			1/29/00	200
			1/31/00	2,050
			1/31/00	60
			1/31/00	190
1/31/00	Bal	11,030		

Accounts Receivable   No. 103

Date		Debit	Date	Credit
1/01/00	Bal	400	1/07/00	400
1/06/00		100		
1/31/00	Bal	100		

Inventory   No. 105

Date		Debit	Date	Credit
1/01/00	Bal	1,620	1/02/00	135
1/04/00		4,320	1/06/00	45
			1/31/00	3,465
1/31/00	Bal	2,295		

Supplies   No. 106

Date		Debit	Date	Credit
1/01/00	Bal	700		

Prepaid Rent   No. 107

Date		Debit	Date	Credit
1/01/00	Bal	6,000		

Store Equipment   No. 123

Date		Debit	Date	Credit
1/01/00	Bal	1,800		
1/29/00		200		
1/31/00	Bal	2,000		

Accumulated Depreciation   No. 124

Debit	Credit

Accounts Payable   No. 201

Date	Debit	Date		Credit
1/03/00	1,620	1/01/00	Bal	1,620
		1/04/00		4,320
		1/31/00	Bal	4,320

Notes Payable   No. 204

Debit	Date		Credit
	1/01/00	Bal	1,200

Interest Payable   No. 205

Debit	Credit

A. Cox, Capital   No. 301

Debit	Date		Credit
	1/01/00	Bal	15,000

A. Cox, Withdrawals   No. 304

Date	Debit	Credit
1/20/00	50	

Income Summary   No. 306

Debit	Credit

Sales Revenue   No. 401

Debit	Date		Credit
	1/02/00		300
	1/06/00		100
	1/31/00		7,700
	1/31/00	Bal	8,100

Cost of Goods Sold   No. 501

Date	Debit	Credit
1/02/00	135	
1/06/00	45	
1/31/00	3,465	
1/31/00	Bal 3,645	

Consulting Expense   No. 502

Date	Debit	Credit
1/25/00	200	

Advertising Expense   No. 503

Date	Debit	Credit
1/25/00	300	

Salaries Expense   No. 504

Date	Debit	Credit
1/31/00	2,050	

Telephone Expense   No. 505

Date	Debit	Credit
1/31/00	60	

Utilities Expense   No. 506

Date	Debit	Credit
1/31/00	190	

Supplies Expense   No. 507

Debit	Credit

Rent Expense   No. 508

Debit	Credit

Interest Expense   No. 509

Debit	Credit

Depreciation Expense   No. 510

Debit	Credit

necessarily when they collect cash. Then they *match* all the related expenses against these revenues, regardless of whether they have paid cash. In many cases, not all of a company's revenue and expense account balances are up-to-date at the end of the accounting period. In these cases, the company must *adjust* certain amounts so that it can report the correct net income on its income statement and the correct ending financial position on its balance sheet. The company makes these adjustments by preparing adjusting entries.

Adjusting entries are journal entries that a company makes at the end of its accounting period to bring the company's revenue and expense account balances up-to-date and to show the correct ending balances in its asset and liability accounts. An adjusting entry usually affects both a permanent (balance sheet) account and a temporary (income statement) account. Adjusting entries may be grouped into three types:

1. Apportionment of prepaid items and unearned revenues

2. Recording of accrued items

3. Recording or apportionment of estimated items

We will discuss the adjusting entries for each type in the following sections.

Apportionment of Prepaid Items and Unearned Revenues

This category of adjusting entries includes adjustments of prepaid items and unearned revenues. A **prepaid item** (sometimes called a *prepaid expense*) is an economic resource for which a company has paid cash and that the company expects to use in its operating activities in the near future. When a company purchases goods or services involving a prepaid item, it records the *cost* as an asset. By the end of the accounting period, the company has used a part of the goods or services to earn revenues. Therefore, it must record the "expired" part of the cost as an *expense* to be matched against the revenues on its income statement while retaining the unexpired part of the cost as an asset on its ending balance sheet. Examples of prepaid items are supplies, prepaid rent, and prepaid insurance.

A company records the apportionment (allocation) of the cost of each prepaid item between an expense and an asset in an adjusting entry in its general journal. The adjusting entry involves a debit (increase) to an appropriately titled expense account (e.g., Rent Expense, obtained from the company's chart of accounts) and a credit (decrease) to the asset account (e.g., Prepaid Rent). The calculation of the amount of the adjusting entry depends on the type of prepaid item. For instance, in the case of supplies, the company takes a physical count of the supplies on hand (and related costs) at the end of the accounting period. In the case of prepaid rent or insurance, the company apportions the total cost evenly over the number of months of the rent agreement or insurance coverage.

For example, recall that Sweet Temptations purchased $700 of office and store supplies on December 17, 1999, and recorded an asset—Supplies—for that amount. This was the amount of supplies that was available for operations at the beginning of January 2000. At the end of January, by counting the supplies, the company determined that it had $670 of supplies on hand. Based on this information, the company must have used $30 ($700 − $670) of supplies during January. To record this expense, on January 31, 2000 Sweet Temptations debits (increases) Supplies Expense for $30 and credits (decreases) the asset Supplies for $30 in the general journal, as we show in Exhibit B-9. Note in Exhibit B-10 (which we show later) that after Sweet Temptations posts this adjusting journal entry to its general ledger accounts (as indicated by an *Adj* in the account), the Supplies Expense account has a debit balance of $30. Also note that the Supplies account has a debit balance of $670.

Sweet Temptations records its rent expense in a similar manner. Recall that Sweet Temptations paid $6,000 for six months' rent in advance on December 16, 1999, and recorded this amount as an asset, Prepaid Rent. The rental agreement stated that rent would not be charged for the last half of December. Therefore, at the end of January 2000, one month's rent has expired, and the company has incurred rent expense of $1,000 ($6,000 ÷ 6). To record this expense, on January 31 the company debits (increases) Rent Expense for $1,000 and credits (decreases) Prepaid Rent for $1,000, as we show in Exhibit B-9. After posting, the Rent Expense account has a debit balance of $1,000 and the Prepaid Rent account has a debit balance of $5,000, as we show later in Exhibit B-10.

In some cases, customers may make an advance payment to a company for goods or services to be provided in the future. At the time of the advance receipt, even though the company's asset Cash has increased, the company has not earned revenue because it has not yet provided the goods or services. Instead, the company has incurred a liability because it has an *obligation* to provide the future goods or services. An **unearned revenue** is an obligation of a company to provide goods or services in the future, and results from an advance receipt of cash. A company records an unearned revenue as a liability when it receives the cash. At the end of the accounting period, the company examines all such

Exhibit B-9 Sweet Temptations'Adjusting Entries: January 31, 2000

Date	Account Titles and Explanations	Acct. No.	Debit	Credit
	Adjusting Entries			
2000 Jan. 31	Supplies Expense	507	30	
	Supplies	106		30
	Supplies used during January.			
31	Rent Expense	508	1,000	
	Prepaid Rent	107		1,000
	Expiration of one-month's rent paid in advance on 12/16/99.			
31	Interest Expense	509	8	
	Interest Payable	205		8
	Interest accrued on note payable.			
31	Depreciation Expense	510	15	
	Accumulated Depreciation	124		15
	Depreciation on store equipment for January.			

liabilities and related source documents to determine whether it has provided the goods or services. If it has, the company makes an adjusting entry to reduce the liability and increase its revenues of the period. The adjusting entry involves a debit (decrease) to the liability account and a credit (increase) to a related revenue account.

Sweet Temptations does not have any unearned revenues at the end of January. Therefore, to illustrate, we will use a different example. Recall that Westwood Mall collected $6,000 from Sweet Temptations on December 16, 1999 for six months' rent in advance. At that time, Westwood Mall debited (increased) an asset—Cash—for $6,000 and credited (increased) a liability—Unearned Rent—for $6,000. On January 31, 2000, since Westwood Mall earned one month of rent by providing store space to Sweet Temptations during January, Westwood Mall makes an adjusting entry to reduce the liability and increase its revenue. The journal entry is a debit (decrease) to Unearned Rent and a credit (increase) to Rent Revenue for $1,000, as follows (note that for simplicity, we do not show the "Acct. No." column in the general journal):

Date	Account Titles and Explanations	Debit	Credit
Jan. 31	Unearned Rent	1,000	
	Rent Revenue		1,000
	To record rent earned from Sweet Temptations.		

The remaining $5,000 ($6,000 − $1,000) balance in Westwood Mall's Unearned Rent account represents the obligation to provide store space to Sweet Temptations for five more months.

Accrued Items

This category of adjusting entries includes adjustments for accrued expenses and accrued revenues. A company records most of its expenses when it pays for them. At the end of an accounting period, however, it has not paid some expenses. An **accrued expense** is an expense that a company has incurred during the accounting period but that it has not paid or recorded.

(Sometimes accrued expenses are called *accrued liabilities,* as we did in Chapter 14 when we discussed current liabilities.) A common type of accrued expense is unpaid employees' salaries. Other common accrued expenses include unpaid interest, taxes, and utility bills. To *match* all expenses against revenues and to report all the liabilities at the end of the period, a company makes an adjusting entry to record each accrued expense. The journal entry involves a debit (increase) to an appropriately titled expense account and a credit (increase) to the related liability account.

Recall that on December 29, 1999, Sweet Temptations signed a $1,200, 3-month note payable. It agreed to pay $24 total interest, so that at the end of three months it will repay $1,224 ($1,000 + $24). Since Sweet Temptations owed the note during all of January, one month of interest, or $8 ($24 ÷ 3 months), has accrued and is an expense of doing business during January. To record this expense, on January 31, 2000 Sweet Temptations debits (increases) Interest Expense and credits (increases) the liability account Interest Payable for $8, as we show in Exhibit B-9. It would record other accrued expenses in a similar way.

A company records most revenues at the time it provides goods or services to a customer. At the end of an accounting period, however, it may not have recorded a few revenues. An **accrued revenue** is a revenue that a company has earned during the accounting period but that it has neither collected nor recorded. To report all the revenues of the period and all the assets at the end of the period, a company makes an adjusting entry for each accrued revenue. The journal entry is a debit (increase) to an asset account and a credit (increase) to a related revenue account.

There are not many types of accrued revenues, and Sweet Temptations has none. However, one common accrued revenue is the interest that has accumulated on a note *received* by a company. Recall that the $1,200, 3-month note of Sweet Temptations was issued to Ace Equipment Company. On January 31, 2000, Ace Equipment Company would record accrued interest revenue of $8. The journal entry would be a debit (increase) to the asset account Interest Receivable and a credit (increase) to the revenue account Interest Revenue for $8, as follows:

Date	Account Titles and Explanations	Debit	Credit
Jan. 31	Interest Receivable	8	
	Interest Revenue		8
	To record accrued interest revenue on note earned from Sweet Temptations.		

A company would record other accrued revenues similarly.

Estimated Items

A few other adjusting entries involve estimated amounts because they are based, in part, on expected future events. Adjusting entries involving estimated amounts include the recording of (1) depreciation on buildings and equipment, (2) amortization of intangible assets, and (3) recognition of uncollectible accounts receivable. We discussed the different methods for computing the estimated amounts of depreciation and amortization in Chapter 21. We discussed the alternative ways of computing the estimated amount of uncollectible accounts receivable (bad debts) in Chapter 13.

The adjusting entry for depreciation is a debit (increase) to the expense account Depreciation Expense and a credit (increase) to the contra asset account Accumulated Depreciation. Recall from Chapter 21 that an increase in the Accumulated Depreciation account decreases the book value of the related depreciable asset account because the amount of accumulated depreciation to date is subtracted from the cost of the depreciable asset. The adjusting entry for amortization is a debit (increase) to the expense account Amortization Expense and a credit (decrease) directly to the related intangible asset account (e.g., Patents).

The adjusting entry for uncollectible accounts receivable is a debit (increase) to the expense account Bad Debts Expense and a credit (increase) to the contra asset account Allowance for Bad Debts. The balance of the Allowance for Bad Debts account is subtracted from the balance of the Accounts Receivable account to determine the net realizable value of the accounts receivable, as we discussed in Chapter 13.

To understand the adjustment process for an estimated item, recall that at the end of December, Sweet Temptations purchased store equipment that cost $1,800 and that it used in its operations during January.[4] Sweet Temptations estimates that this equipment will have a life of 10 years (120 months; 12 × 10), with no residual value. Using straight-line depreciation, the monthly depreciation expense is $15 ($1,800 ÷ 120 months). On January 31, 2000, Sweet Temptations records its depreciation expense for January as we show in Exhibit B-9.

Posting the Adjusting Entries

After a company prepares its adjusting entries, the company posts these entries from its general journal to the accounts in its general ledger. Sweet Temptations posts the adjusting entries that it recorded in Exhibit B-9 to its general ledger, as we show in Exhibit B-10. Note that Exhibit B-10 is similar to Exhibit B-8, except that the adjusting entries (as indicated by an *Adj*) are included. This completes the adjusting entry process for Sweet Temptations.

Adjusted Trial Balance

After a company journalizes and posts its adjusting entries, the company balances its accounts and all the account balances are up-to-date for the accounting period. But before preparing the company's financial statements, it is useful to prepare an adjusted trial balance. An **adjusted trial balance** is a schedule prepared to prove the equality of the debit and credit balances in a company's general ledger accounts after it has made the adjusting entries. An adjusted trial balance is similar to a trial balance except that it also includes *all* the revenue and expense accounts. An adjusted trial balance is an accountant's *working paper* and is not a financial statement. It is used to (1) help prevent the company from including debit and credit errors in its financial statements and (2) make preparing the financial statements easier, as you will see shortly.

Exhibit B-11 shows the adjusted trial balance of Sweet Temptations on January 31, 2000. The account balances listed were taken from the general ledger in Exhibit B-10. Note that the $28,643 total of the debits is equal to the total of the credits.

If an adjusted trial balance (or a trial balance) does not balance (i.e., the total debits do not equal the total credits), the company has made an error. To find the error, the company should re-add the debit and credit columns of the adjusted trial balance. If the column totals still do not agree, the company should check the amounts in the debit and credit columns to be sure that it did not mistakenly list a debit or credit account balance in the wrong column.

If it still does not find the error, the company should compute the difference in the column totals and divide it by 9. When the difference is evenly divisible by 9, there is a good chance that a transposition or a slide has occurred. A **transposition** occurs when two digits in a number are mistakenly reversed. For instance, if the $11,030 Cash balance in Exhibit B-11 had been listed as $11,300, the debit column would have totaled $28,913 instead of $28,643. The difference, $270, is evenly divisible by 9. A **slide** occurs when the

---

[4]Sweet Temptations purchased $200 of store equipment at the end of January. Since Sweet Temptations did not use this store equipment in January, it did not depreciate the equipment for that month. Sweet Temptations will include the depreciation on this store equipment as an expense in later months when it uses the equipment.

Exhibit B-10   Sweet Temptations' General Ledger After Adjusting Entries (January 31, 2000)

Cash				No. 101
1/01/00	Bal 7,300	1/03/00		1,620
1/02/00	300	1/20/00		50
1/07/00	400	1/25/00		200
1/31/00	7,700	1/25/00		300
		1/29/00		200
		1/30/00		2,050
		1/31/00		60
		1/31/00		190
1/31/00	Bal 11,030			

Accounts Receivable				No. 103
1/01/00	Bal 400	1/07/00		400
1/06/00	100			
1/31/00	Bal 100			

Inventory				No. 105
1/01/00	Bal 1,620	1/02/00		135
1/04/00	4,320	1/06/00		45
		1/31/00		3,465
1/31/00	Bal 2,295			

Supplies				No. 106
1/01/00	Bal 700	1/31/00	Adj	30
1/31/00	Bal 670			

Prepaid Rent				No. 107
1/01/00	Bal 6,000	1/31/00	Adj	1,000
1/31/00	Bal 5,000			

Store Equipment			No. 123
1/01/00	Bal 1,800		
1/29/00	200		
1/31/00	Bal 2,000		

Accumulated Depreciation				No. 124
		1/31/00	Adj	15

Accounts Payable				No. 201
1/03/00	1,620	1/01/00	Bal	1,620
		1/04/00		4,320
		1/31/00	Bal	4,320

Notes Payable				No. 204
		1/01/00	Bal	1,200

Interest Payable				No. 205
		1/31/00	Adj	8

A. Cox, Capital				No. 301
		1/01/00	Bal	15,000

A. Cox, Withdrawals			No. 304
1/20/00	50		

Income Summary			No. 306

Sales Revenue				No. 401
		1/02/00		300
		1/06/00		100
		1/31/00		7,700
		1/31/00	Bal	8,100

Cost of Goods Sold			No. 501
1/02/00	135		
1/06/00	45		
1/31/00	3,465		
1/31/00	Bal 3,645		

Consulting Expense			No. 502
1/25/00	200		

Advertising Expense			No. 503
1/25/00	300		

Salaries Expense			No. 504
1/31/00	2,050		

Telephone Expense			No. 505
1/31/00	60		

Utilities Expense			No. 506
1/31/00	190		

Supplies Expense			No. 507
1/31/00	Adj	30	

Rent Expense			No. 508
1/31/00	Adj 1,000		

Interest Expense			No. 509
1/31/00	Adj	8	

Depreciation Expense			No. 510
1/31/00	Adj	15	

digits are listed in the correct order but are mistakenly moved one decimal place to the left or right. For instance, if the $1,200 Notes Payable balance in Exhibit B-11 had been listed as $120, the credit column would have totaled $27,563 instead of $28,643. The $1,080 difference is evenly divisible by 9.

A transposition or slide may have occurred when the company transferred the account balances from the accounts to the adjusted trial balance or when it initially computed the account balances. Thus, the company should compare the account balances listed on the

Exhibit B-11 Adjusted Trial Balance

SWEET TEMPTATIONS
Adjusted Trial Balance
January 31, 2000

Account Titles	Debits	Credits
Cash	$11,030	
Accounts receivable	100	
Inventory	2,295	
Supplies	670	
Prepaid rent	5,000	
Store equipment	2,000	
Accumulated depreciation		$ 15
Accounts payable		4,320
Notes payable		1,200
Interest payable		8
A. Cox, capital		15,000
A. Cox, withdrawals	50	
Sales revenue		8,100
Cost of goods sold	3,645	
Consulting expense	200	
Advertising expense	300	
Salaries expense	2,050	
Telephone expense	60	
Utilities expense	190	
Supplies expense	30	
Rent expense	1,000	
Interest expense	8	
Depreciation expense	15	
Totals	$28,643	$28,643

adjusted trial balance with the account balances listed in the general ledger. If it properly transferred the balances, then it should recompute the ledger account balances, and if it finds no error, it should double-check the postings. Finally, if the company still does not find the error, it should review the journal entries for accuracy. As you can imagine, detecting where an error has been made is time-consuming and frustrating. That is why it is very important to follow the set procedures in the journalizing and posting process.

Preparing the Financial Statements

A company prepares its financial statements for the accounting period after it completes the adjusted trial balance. It prepares the income statement first because the amount of net income (or net loss) affects the owner's capital account on the balance sheet. A sole proprietorship prepares the statement of changes in owner's equity (a supporting schedule for the balance sheet) next. Then, it prepares the balance sheet. Finally, the company completes its cash flow statement.[5]

Income Statement

An income statement is the financial statement that summarizes the results of a company's earnings activities (i.e., revenues, expenses, and net income) for its accounting period.

---

[5]For simplicity, in this appendix we do not prepare a cash flow statement. Refer to Chapter 8 and Chapter 19 for an in-depth discussion of the cash flow statement.

Exhibit B-12   Income Statement

SWEET TEMPTATIONS
Income Statement
For Month Ended January 31, 2000

Sales revenue		$8,100
Cost of goods sold		(3,645)
Gross profit		$4,455
Operating Expenses:		
Consulting expense	$ 200	
Advertising expense	300	
Salaries expense	2,050	
Telephone expense	60	
Utilities expense	190	
Supplies expense	30	
Rent expense	1,000	
Depreciation expense	15	
Total expenses		(3,845)
Operating income		$ 610
Other item:		
Interest expense		(8)
Net Income		$ 602

Exhibit B-12 shows Sweet Temptations' income statement for January 2000. Sweet Temptations prepared its income statement from the accounts listed on the lower part of the adjusted trial balance in Exhibit B-11. Because the revenue and expense accounts are listed at the end of each company's chart of accounts (and, therefore, its general ledger), these accounts are always listed in the lower portion of each company's adjusted trial balance. This procedure simplifies preparation of the income statement.

Statement of Changes in Owner's Equity

A statement of changes in owner's equity is a schedule that shows the impact on owner's equity of any additional investments by the owner in the company, the company's net income, and owner withdrawals during the accounting period. A company presents this statement as a supporting schedule to the owner's capital account balance listed on the balance sheet. Exhibit B-13 shows Sweet Temptations' statement of owner's equity for January 2000. A. Cox made no additional investments during January. Sweet Temptations obtained the beginning balance of the A. Cox, Capital account and the amount of the withdrawals from the middle portion of the adjusted trial balance in Exhibit B-11. It obtained the net income from the income statement in Exhibit B-12.

Exhibit B-13   Statement of Changes in Owner's Equity

SWEET TEMPTATIONS
Statement of Changes in Owner's Equity
For Month Ending January 31, 2000

A. Cox, capital, January 1, 2000	$15,000
Add: Net income for January	602
	$15,602
Less: Withdrawals for January	(50)
A. Cox, capital, January 31, 2000	$15,552

Exhibit B-14   Balance Sheet

SWEET TEMPTATIONS
Balance Sheet
January 31, 2000

Assets

Current Assets:
Cash		$11,030
Accounts receivable		100
Inventory		2,295
Supplies		670
Prepaid rent		5,000
Total Current Assets		$19,095

Property and Equipment:
Store equipment	$ 2,000	
Less: Accumulated depreciation	(15)	1,985
Total Assets		$21,080

Liabilities

Current Liabilities:
Accounts payable	$ 4,320
Notes payable	1,200
Interest payable	8
Total Current Liabilities	$ 5,528

Owner's Equity

A. Cox, capital	$15,552
Total Liabilities and Owner's Equity	$21,080

Balance Sheet

A balance sheet is the financial statement that reports the financial position (i.e., assets, liabilities, and owner's equity) of a company on a particular date. Exhibit B-14 shows Sweet Temptations' balance sheet on January 31, 2000. The company prepared the balance sheet from the accounts listed on the upper portion of the adjusted trial balance in Exhibit B-11. Use of the adjusted trial balance makes the preparation of the balance sheet very easy. The assets, liabilities, and owner's capital accounts are the first accounts in a company's chart of accounts and its general ledger. Therefore, these accounts are always listed in the upper portion of the company's adjusted trial balance. Note, however, that the amount listed as the owner's capital on the adjusted trial balance is *not* the amount the company lists on the ending balance sheet because the amount has not been updated for the company's net income or withdrawals. Instead, the company obtains the ending owner's capital account balance from the statement of changes in owner's equity. Sweet Temptations obtained the owner's capital account balance in Exhibit B-14 from the statement in Exhibit B-13.

Preparation of Closing Entries

Earlier we made two points that are relevant to our discussion of closing entries. First, the revenue, expense, and withdrawals accounts are *temporary* accounts. A company uses these accounts to determine the changes in its owner's equity in the current accounting period resulting from its net income (or net loss) and from owner's withdrawals. Second, a company does *not* use the owner's capital account listed on the adjusted trial balance in preparing its balance sheet because this account balance is not up-to-date for the net income and withdrawals of the period.

7 *What are closing entries, and how do they relate to the Income Summary account?*

To begin the next accounting period, the company needs to (1) update the balance in the owner's capital account and (2) show zero balances in the revenue, expense, and withdrawals accounts. The owner's capital account balance should be up-to-date to show the owner's current investment in the assets of the company. The company will use the revenue, expense, and withdrawals accounts in the next accounting period to accumulate the company's net income and any of the owner's withdrawals *for that period*. Therefore, it is important to start with a zero balance in each of these accounts at the beginning of the period so that at the end of the period, the balances in the accounts will show the revenue, expense, and withdrawal amounts for only that period.

As we discussed in Chapter 6, **closing entries** are journal entries that a company makes at the end of its accounting period to create a zero balance in each revenue, expense, and withdrawals account and to transfer these account balances to the owner's permanent capital account. It makes closing entries after preparing the financial statements. Like other journal entries, a company records closing entries in the general journal and then posts them to the respective accounts. It does *not* close the revenue and expense accounts directly to the owner's capital account. Instead, it first transfers these account balances to an account entitled Income Summary. The **Income Summary** account is a temporary account a company uses in the closing process to accumulate the amount of the company's net income (or net loss) before it transfers this amount to the owner's capital account.

Closing the Revenue Accounts

Recall that each revenue account has a credit balance (prior to closing). To reduce this credit balance to zero, the company makes a debit entry in the revenue account for an amount *equal* to that of the credit balance. At the same time, it transfers the revenue amount to the Income Summary account by a credit entry to that account. It first records these debit and credit entries in the general journal. We show Sweet Temptations' closing entries in Exhibit B-15. The $8,100 journal entry of Sweet Temptations to close its revenue account is the first closing entry in Exhibit B-15. Sweet Temptations obtained the amount of the sales revenue from the adjusted trial balance in Exhibit B-11. It obtained the account number of the Income Summary account from the chart of accounts in Exhibit B-6. In this illustration, Sweet Temptations has only one revenue account. When a company has more than one revenue account, it makes a compound entry in which it first debits each revenue account for the amount of the balance in the account and then credits the total of the revenues to the Income Summary account.

Closing the Expense Accounts

Each expense account has a debit balance (prior to closing). To reduce each debit balance to zero, the company makes a credit entry in each expense account for an amount *equal* to that of the debit balance. It transfers this expense amount to the Income Summary account by a debit entry to that account. A company typically has many expense accounts, so it usually closes all the expense accounts by making a compound entry in the general journal in which it credits each expense account for the amount of the balance in the account and debits the Income Summary account for the *total* amount of the expenses. (Remember, however, that it always lists the debit entry first in the general journal.) The $7,498 journal entry of Sweet Temptations to close its expense accounts is the second closing entry at the end of Exhibit B-15. Sweet Temptations obtained the amounts of the various expenses from the adjusted trial balance in Exhibit B-11. (Remember that Cost of Goods Sold is an expense account.)

Closing the Income Summary Account

After a company closes the revenue and expense accounts to the Income Summary account, the balance in the account is the amount of the net income (or net loss). A credit balance indicates that the company earned a net income for the period because revenues exceeded expenses. A debit balance indicates a net loss because expenses exceeded revenues.

Exhibit B-15   Sweet Temptations' Closing Entries: January 31, 2000

Date	Account Titles and Explanations	Acct. No.	Debit	Credit
	Closing Entries			
2000				
Jan. 31	Sales Revenue	401	8,100	
	Income Summary	306		8,100
	To close revenue account.			
31	Income Summary	306	7,498	
	Cost of Goods Sold	501		3,645
	Consulting Expense	502		200
	Advertising Expense	503		300
	Salaries Expense	504		2,050
	Telephone Expense	505		60
	Utilities Expense	506		190
	Supplies Expense	507		30
	Rent Expense	508		1,000
	Interest Expense	509		8
	Depreciation Expense	510		15
	To close expense accounts.			
31	Income Summary	306	602	
	A. Cox, Capital	301		602
	To close net income to owner's capital account.			
31	A. Cox, Capital	301	50	
	A. Cox, Withdrawals	304		50
	To close withdrawals to owner's capital account.			

A company transfers the amount of its net income (or net loss) to the owner's permanent capital account in the third closing entry. In the case of net income, the journal entry is a debit to the Income Summary account for an amount equal to its balance and a credit to the owner's capital account for the same amount. The credit to the owner's capital account increases that account by the amount of the net income. (The company would handle a net loss in the opposite way, with a debit to the owner's capital account and a credit to the Income Summary account.) The $602 journal entry of Sweet Temptations to close the Income Summary account to the A. Cox, Capital account is the third closing entry at the end of Exhibit B-15.

Closing the Withdrawals Account

A company closes the debit balance of the withdrawals account *directly* to the owner's permanent capital account, since withdrawals are *disinvestments* by the owner. The closing entry in the general journal is a debit to the owner's permanent capital account and a credit to the withdrawals account for the amount of the total withdrawals of the period. The debit entry brings the owner's capital account balance up-to-date at the end of the period. The credit entry to the withdrawals account reduces the account balance to zero so that it can accumulate the withdrawals of the next period. A company *never* closes the withdrawals account to the Income Summary account because withdrawals are *not* part of net income. The $50 journal entry to close the A. Cox, Withdrawals account balance to the A. Cox, Capital account is the last closing entry at the end of Exhibit B-15. Sweet Temptations obtained the amount of the withdrawals from the adjusted trial balance in Exhibit B-11.

Posting the Closing Entries

After a company records its closing entries, the company posts these entries from its general journal to the accounts in its general ledger. Sweet Temptations posts the closing entries that it prepared in Exhibit B-15 to the appropriate accounts in its general ledger, as we show in Exhibit B-16. Note that Exhibit B-16 is similar to the right side of Exhibit B-10, except that the closing entries (as indicated by a *Cl*) are included. Also note that after the closing entries are posted, all the revenue, expense, and withdrawals accounts have zero balances. The A. Cox, Capital account has a balance of $15,552, the amount Sweet Temptations listed as the owner's equity on its January 31, 2000 balance sheet in Exhibit B-14. This completes the closing entry process for Sweet Temptations.

Post-Closing Trial Balance

After a company journalizes and posts its closing entries, the only accounts with nonzero balances should be the permanent accounts—that is, the assets, liabilities, and owner's capital accounts. As a check to make sure that no debit or credit errors were made during the closing entries, a company prepares a post-closing trial balance. A **post-closing trial balance** is a schedule a company prepares after making the closing entries to prove the equality of the debit and credit balances in its asset, liability, and owner's capital accounts. The post-closing trial balance includes only permanent accounts because all the temporary accounts have zero balances due to the closing process. After the company prepares the post-closing trial balance, the accounting cycle for the current period is complete. The company then begins the accounting cycle for its next accounting period. To save space, we do not show the post-closing trial balance of Sweet Temptations here.

Exhibit B-16 Sweet Temptations' Postings of Closing Entries (January 31, 2000)

A. Cox, Capital No. 301

1/31/00	Cl	50	1/01/00	Bal	15,000
			1/31/00	Cl	602
			1/31/00	Bal	15,552

A. Cox, Withdrawals No. 304

1/20/00		50	1/31/00	Cl	50
1/31/00	Bal	0			

Income Summary No. 306

1/31/00	Cl	7,498	1/31/00	Cl	8,100
1/31/00	Cl	602			
			1/31/00	Bal	0

Sales Revenue No. 401

1/31/00	Cl	8,100	1/31/00		8,100
			1/31/00	Bal	0

Cost of Goods Sold No. 501

1/31/00	Bal	3,645	1/31/00	Cl	3,645
1/31/00	Bal	0			

Consulting Expense No. 502

1/25/00		200	1/31/00	Cl	200
1/31/00	Bal	0			

Advertising Expense No. 503

1/25/00		300	1/31/00	Cl	300
1/31/00	Bal	0			

Salaries Expense No. 504

1/30/00		2,050	1/31/00	Cl	2,050
1/31/00	Bal	0			

Telephone Expense No. 505

1/31/00		60	1/31/00	Cl	60
1/31/00	Bal	0			

Utilities Expense No. 506

1/31/00		190	1/31/00	Cl	190
1/31/00	Bal	0			

Supplies Expense No. 507

1/31/00	Adj	30	1/31/00	Cl	30
1/31/00	Bal	0			

Rent Expense No. 508

1/31/00	Adj	1,000	1/31/00	Cl	1,000
1/31/00	Bal	0			

Interest Expense No. 509

1/31/00	Adj	8	1/31/00	Cl	8
1/31/00	Bal	0			

Depreciation Expense No. 510

1/31/00	Adj	15	1/31/00	Cl	15
1/31/00	Bal	0			

Modifications for Corporations

For simplicity, earlier we discussed and illustrated the procedures in the accounting cycle of a sole proprietorship (Sweet Temptations). However, many companies are corporations, and you also should be familiar with the accounting procedures for corporations. Fortunately, the procedures we discussed for sole proprietorships have to be modified only slightly for corporations. The modifications involve differences in how a corporation records and reports investments by owners, distributions to owners, and some income statement items and balance sheet items. To illustrate, we will modify the Sweet Temptations example by assuming the company is a corporation instead of a sole proprietorship.

8 *How are accounting procedures modified for corporations?*

Investments by Owners

One difference between the accounting for corporations and that for sole proprietorships involves investments in the company by owners (stockholders). Assume that on December 15, 1999, Sweet Temptations was incorporated and issued 1,000 shares of $10 par value common stock to A. Cox for $15 per share. Sweet Temptations would make the following journal entry to record this transaction:

Date	Account Titles and Explanations	Debit	Credit

1999
Dec. 15
	Cash
	    Common Stock, $10 par
	    Additional Paid-in Capital
	    Issued 1,000 shares of common stock for
	    $15 per share.
		15,000	10,000
			5,000

As we discussed in Chapter 24, the total amount received by a corporation when it issues stock is allocated between the legal capital (par value) and additional paid-in capital. Thus, a corporation has both a Common Stock account and an Additional Paid-in Capital account to record investments (contributed capital) by stockholders. Also, a corporation has a Retained Earnings account, which lists its total lifetime earnings (net income or net loss) that have not been distributed to stockholders as dividends.

Distributions to Owners

The payment of dividends to stockholders by a corporation is recorded differently than are the owner's withdrawals from a sole proprietorship. Since the Retained Earnings account includes total earnings not distributed to stockholders as dividends, a corporation records any dividend payments directly as a reduction in retained earnings by a debit (decrease) to Retained Earnings and a credit (decrease) to Cash. For example, assume that on January 20, 2000, Sweet Temptations Corporation declared and paid a dividend of $0.05 per share. Sweet Temptations Corporation makes the following journal entry to record the dividend of $50 (1,000 shares × $0.05):

Date	Account Titles and Explanations	Debit	Credit

2000
Jan. 20
	Retained Earnings
	    Cash
	    Declared and paid dividends.
		50	50

Sweet Temptations Corporation reports the dividends as a reduction of retained earnings in the statement of retained earnings (which we discussed in Chapter 24).

Income Statement Items

Another difference between a corporation and a sole proprietorship is that a corporation must pay income taxes on its earnings. These income taxes are considered an expense of doing business. Normally, a corporation *pays* its income taxes early in the next quarter after the income is earned. However, since income taxes are an expense, they should be matched against the income in the period the income is earned. Thus, in addition to the adjusting entries described earlier, a corporation also makes an adjusting entry for *accrued* income taxes at the end of each period.

Because, in this example, Sweet Temptations is a corporation, it must pay income taxes. Therefore, at the end of January 2000, Sweet Temptations Corporation must make an adjusting entry for the income taxes that it will pay early next quarter based on its January earnings. During January 2000, Sweet Temptations Corporation earned $602 of income before income taxes. If we assume a 40% tax rate, then it records the $241 ($602 × 0.40, rounded) income taxes in the following adjusting entry:

Date	Account Titles and Explanations	Debit	Credit
2000 Jan. 31	Income Tax Expense Income Taxes Payable To record income taxes for January.	241	241

Sweet Temptations Corporation reports the income tax expense on its income statement for January, and reports the income taxes payable as a current liability on its January 31, 2000 balance sheet.

A corporation's income statement is similar to that of a sole proprietorship, with two exceptions. First, the income tax expense is deducted from income before income taxes to determine net income. Second, earnings per share is shown directly below net income. The income statement of Sweet Temptations Corporation for January 2000 would look exactly like Exhibit B-12, except for the lower portion, which would appear as follows:

Income before income taxes	$602
Income tax expense	(241)
Net income	$361
Earnings per share (1,000 shares)	$0.36

Balance Sheet Items

The balance sheet of a corporation is similar to that of a sole proprietorship, with two exceptions. In addition to including income taxes payable as a current liability, a corporation's balance sheet also has a modified owners' equity section. The owners' equity of a corporation is called **stockholders' equity** and consists of two parts: contributed capital and retained earnings. The contributed capital includes both the Common Stock and the Additional Paid-in Capital account balances from the adjusted trial balance. The corporation obtains the Retained Earnings amount from the statement of retained earnings. This statement is very similar to the statement of changes in owner's equity, which we discussed earlier in this appendix. The balance sheet of Sweet Temptations Corporation on January 31, 2000 would look like Exhibit B-14, except that the liabilities and the stockholders' equity sections would appear as follows:

Liabilities

Current Liabilities:		
Accounts payable		$ 4,320
Notes payable		1,200
Interest payable		8
Income taxes payable		241
Total Liabilities		$ 5,769

Stockholders' Equity

Contributed capital:		
Common stock, $10 par		$10,000
Additional paid-in capital		5,000
Total contributed capital		$15,000
Retained earnings		311
Total Stockholders' Equity		$15,311
Total Liabilities and Stockholders' Equity		$21,080

Sweet Temptations Corporation would have obtained the income taxes payable, common stock, and additional paid-in capital amounts from its adjusted trial balance. It would have obtained the $311 retained earnings amount ($0 beginning retained earnings + $361 net income − $50 dividends) from its statement of retained earnings.

There is also a slight difference in the closing entries of a corporation as compared with those of a sole proprietorship. A corporation closes the balance of the Income Summary account to the Retained Earnings account. Furthermore, since it recorded any dividends during the period directly as a reduction of retained earnings, there is no closing entry at the end of the period for dividends.

Other Journal Entries

Earlier in the appendix, we discussed the journal entries made by Sweet Temptations. As we noted in various chapters of the book, other companies may record journal entries for transactions such as sales discounts, purchases discounts, sales returns and allowances, and purchases returns and allowances. The way a company records these transactions depends on the company's accounting system and whether it uses a perpetual or a periodic inventory system. However, Exhibit B-17 shows a general framework for recording these types

Exhibit B-17 Illustrations of Additional Journal Entries

Sales Discounts

Cash (net)	x	
Sales Discounts Taken	x	
Accounts Receivable (gross)		x

Purchases Discounts

Accounts Payable (gross)	x	
Inventory (or Purchases Discounts Taken*)		x
Cash (net)		x

Sales Returns and Allowances

Sales Returns and Allowances	x	
Accounts Receivable (or Cash		x
Inventory (at cost)	x	
Cost of Goods Sold		x

Purchases Returns and Allowances

Accounts Payable (or Cash)	x	
Inventory		
(or Purchases Returns and Allowances*)		x

*Accounts used under periodic inventory system

of transactions. We show only a few transactions in Exhibit B-17. However, by using your knowledge of the accounting equation, debit and credit rules, revenues and expenses, and assets, liabilities, and owner's equity, you can develop the correct journal entries for recording other transactions.

Summary

At the beginning of the appendix we asked you several questions. Below are the questions from the beginning of the appendix, with a brief summary of the key points relating to the answers. Use your creative and critical thinking skills to expand on these key points to develop more complete answers to the questions and to determine what other questions you have that might lead you to learn more about the issues.

1 What is a debit entry, and what is a credit entry?

A debit entry is a monetary amount recorded (debited) in the left side of an account. A credit entry is a monetary amount recorded (credited) in the right side of an account.

2 What are the rules for recording increases and decreases in asset and liability accounts?

Asset accounts (accounts on the left side of the accounting equation) are increased by debit entries (i.e., amounts recorded on the left side) and decreased by credit entries. Liability accounts (accounts on the right side of the equation) are increased by credit entries (i.e., amounts recorded on the right side) and decreased by debit entries.

3 What are the rules for recording increases and decreases in owner's equity accounts?

Permanent owner's equity, or capital, accounts (accounts on the right side of the equation) are increased by credit entries and decreased by debit entries. *Temporary* owner's equity accounts have the following rules: (a) withdrawal accounts are increased by debit entries and decreased by credit entries, (b) revenue accounts are increased by credit entries and decreased by debit entries, and (c) expense accounts are increased by debit entries and decreased by credit entries.

4 What are the major steps in a company's accounting cycle?

The major steps in a company's accounting cycle include (1) recording (journalizing) the transactions in the general journal, (2) posting the journal entries to the accounts in the general ledger (3) recording (and posting) adjusting entries, (4) preparing the financial statements, and (5) recording (and posting) closing entries.

5 What is the difference between journalizing and posting?

Journalizing is the process of recording a transaction in a company's general journal. A journal entry is the recorded information for each transaction. Posting is the process of transferring the debit and credit information for each journal entry to the accounts in a company's general ledger.

6 What are adjusting entries, and what are the three types of adjusting entries?

Adjusting entries are journal entries that a company makes at the end of its accounting period to bring the company's revenue and expense account balances up-to-date and to show the correct ending balances in its asset and liability accounts. Adjusting entries may be grouped into three types: (1) apportionment of prepaid and unearned items, (2) recording of accrued items, and (3) recording or apportionment of estimated items.

7 What are closing entries, and how do they relate to the Income Summary account?

Closing entries are journal entries that a company makes at the end of its accounting period to create a zero balance in each revenue, expense, and withdrawals account and to transfer these account balances to the owner's permanent capital account. The Income Summary account is a temporary account used in the closing process to accumulate the amount of the company's net income (or net loss) before transferring this amount to the owner's capital account.

8 **How are accounting procedures modified for corporations?**

Accounting procedures are modified for corporations as follows: (1) investments by owners (stockholders) are recorded in capital stock and additional paid-in capital accounts, (2) distributions (dividends) to stockholders are recorded as a decrease in the retained earnings account, (3) the income statement includes income tax expense and earnings per share, and (4) the balance sheet includes income taxes payable in the current liabilities section, and contributed capital and retained earnings in the stockholders' equity section.

Key Terms

accounts (p. 934)	**general ledger** (p. 934)
accounting cycle (p. 937)	**income summary** (p. 954)
accrued expense (p. 947)	**journal entry** (p. 937)
accrued revenue (p. 948)	**journalizing** (p. 937)
adjusted trial balance (p. 949)	**prepaid item** (p. 946)
adjusting entries (p. 945)	**post-closing trial balance** (p. 956)
balance of an account (p. 935)	**posting** (p. 942)
chart of accounts (p. 942)	**slide** (p. 950)
closing entries (p. 954)	**stockholders' equity** (p. 958)
credit entry (p. 934, 935)	**transposition** (p. 949)
debit entry (p. 934, 935)	**trial balance** (p. 944)
double entry rule (p. 935)	**unearned revenue** (p. 946)
general journal (p. 937)	

QUESTIONS

QB-1 Define an account. What are the parts of a T-account? What is a set of accounts for a company called?

QB-2 What is a debit entry? a credit entry?

QB-3 What are the debit and credit rules? How do these rules relate to the accounting equation?

QB-4 Explain the double entry rule. How (if at all) does this rule change in the case of a compound entry?

QB-5 What is a general journal (in a manual accounting system)? List the advantages of initially recording a company's transactions in a general journal.

QB-6 What is journalizing? Briefly describe the journalizing process.

QB-7 What is posting? Briefly describe the posting process.

QB-8 What are adjusting entries? Why are they necessary?

QB-9 What is an adjusted trial balance? Why is it used?

QB-10 What are closing entries? Describe how (a) revenue accounts, (b) expense accounts, and (c) the withdrawals account are closed.

QB-11 How does the lower portion of the income statement for a corporation differ from that of a sole proprietorship? Where does a corporation report its income taxes payable on its financial statements?

QB-12 How is the owners' equity of a corporation shown on its balance sheet?

EXERCISES

EB-1 During the month of July, Sands Insurance Company entered into the following transactions:

Date	Transaction
July 1	Nancy Sands deposited a $40,000 personal check in the company's checking account
10	Purchased land and an office building at a cost of $2,000 and $21,000, respectively, paying $8,000 down and signing a $15,000 note due at the end of the year

    25   Purchased office supplies costing $800 on credit

Required: (1) Prepare journal entries to record the preceding transactions.

              (2) List the source documents normally used in recording each of these transactions.

EB-2   Albert Mitchell started Worldwide Travel Service on April 1 of the current year, and the company engaged in the following transactions during the month of April:

Date	Transaction
Apr. 1	Albert Mitchell opened the business by depositing a $35,000 personal check in the new company's checking account
3	Purchased land and a small office building for $2,500 and $28,000, respectively, paying $10,500 down and signing a 1-year note for $20,000
20	Purchased office equipment at a cost of $6,000. Half of the cost was paid in cash, and the remainder is due at the end of May

Required: (1) Prepare journal entries to record the preceding transactions.

              (2) List the source documents normally used in recording each of these transactions.

EB-3   Both Plumbing Company entered into the following transactions during the month of May:

Date	Transaction
May 4	Installed plumbing in new house under construction; contractor agreed to pay contract price of $1,700 in 30 days
15	Made plumbing repairs for customer and collected $85 for services performed
28	Paid $79 for May telephone bill
31	Paid $800 to employees for May salaries
31	Received $100 utility bill, to be paid in early June

Required: (1) Prepare journal entries to record the preceding transactions.

              (2) List the source documents normally used to record these transactions.

EB-4   Aline Taxi Service entered into the following transactions during the month of September:

Date	Transaction
Sept. 1	Paid $450 rent on garage for the month of September
15	Cash receipts for taxi fares for the first half of the month totaled $1,640.
23	Paid $980 for September fuel bill from Wildcat Oil Company
29	P. L. Aline withdrew $400 for personal use.
30	Paid salaries amounting to $1,200 to employees
30	Cash receipts for taxi fares for the second half of the month totaled $1,340.

Required: (1) Prepare journal entries to record the preceding transactions.

              (2) List the source documents normally used to record these transactions.

EB-5   Nomura Sales, a medical supplies wholesaler, entered into the following transactions (the company uses the perpetual inventory system):

Date	Transaction
Aug 1	Purchased $5,300 of medical supplies on credit from Nead Company
3	Returned $200 of defective medical supplies purchased on August 1 from Nead Company for credit
5	Sold $2,000 of medical supplies on credit to P & H Drugs. The cost of the inventory sold was $1,200.
8	Granted $300 credit to P & H Drugs for return of medical supplies purchased on August 5. The cost of the inventory returned was $180.
9	Purchased $1,000 of medical supplies for cash
10	Paid balance due to Nead Company for purchase of August 1
15	Received balance due from P & H Drugs for medical supplies purchased on August 5
30	Sold $800 of merchandise to customers for cash. The cost of the inventory sold was $500.

Required: Prepare journal entries to record the preceding transactions.

EB-6 Taylor Art Supplies Company sells various art supplies to local artists. The company uses a perpetual inventory system, and the cost of its inventory of art supplies at the beginning of August was $2,500. Its cash balance was $800 at the beginning of August, and it entered into the following transactions during August:

Date	Transaction
Aug. 1	Purchased $400 of art supplies for cash
4	Made a $900 sale of art supplies on credit to P. Marks, with terms of n/15. The cost of the inventory sold was $550.
6	Purchased $700 of art supplies on credit from Tott Company, with terms of n/20
10	Returned, for credit to its account, $100 of defective art supplies purchased on August 6 from Tott Company
12	Made cash sales of $250 to customers. The cost of the inventory sold was $160.
13	Granted a $25 allowance to a customer for damaged inventory sold on August 12
15	Received payment from P. Marks of the amount due for inventory sold on credit on August 4
25	Paid balance due to Rony Company for purchase on August 6

Required: (1) Prepare journal entries to record the preceding transactions.
(2) Set up appropriate T-accounts, post the journal entries to the accounts (for simplicity, it is not necessary to assign numbers to the accounts), and determine the ending account balances.

EB-7 At the end of the current year, Rulem Hair Styling provides you with the following information:
(a) Depreciation expense on styling equipment totals $1,240 for the current year.
(b) Accrued interest on a note payable issued on October 1 amounts to $850 at year-end.
(c) Unearned rent in the amount of $1,000 has been earned (the company records all receipts in advance in an Unearned Rent account).
(d) Hair styling supplies used during the year total $210 (the company records all purchases of supplies in an asset account).

Required: Prepare adjusting entries at the end of the current year based on the preceding information.

EB-8 On June 30 of the current year, Washington Background Music Company showed the following trial balance:

Account Titles	Debits	Credits
Cash	$10,150	
Office supplies	368	
Sound system	6,500	
Accounts payable		$ 295
D. L. Washington, capital		15,000
Music system revenues		3,198
Salary expense	1,000	
Rent expense	300	
General expenses	175	
Totals	$18,493	$18,493

The following adjustments are needed:

(a) Office supplies used during the month of June totaled $58.
(b) Depreciation expense for the month of June on the sound system totaled $75.

June was the first month of operations for Washington Background Music Company.

Required: (1) Prepare adjusting entries to record the preceding adjustments.
(2) Prepare the June 30 adjusted trial balance for Washington Background Music Company.

EB-9 On October 1 of the current year, Bourdon Company paid $480 for a two-year comprehensive insurance policy on the company's building.

Required: (1) Prepare the journal entry to record each of the following:
  (a) The purchase of this insurance policy
  (b) The adjusting entry at the end of the year
  (2) If the adjusting entry had *not* been made in (1)(b), discuss what effect this error would have on the accounts and totals listed on the income statement and balance sheet.

EB-10 On October 1 of the current year, Sagir Appraisal Company received $1,500 in advance from the Land-Ho Real Estate Agency for 6 months' rent of office space.

Required: (1) Prepare the Sagir Appraisal Company journal entries to record the following:
  (a) The receipt of the payment
  (b) The adjustment for rent revenue at the end of the current year
  (2) If the adjusting entry had *not* been made in (1)(b), discuss what effect this error would have on the accounts and totals listed on the income statement and balance sheet.

EB-11 The Cobbler Company shows the following revenue, expense, and withdrawals account balances on December 31 of the current year, before closing:

Account Titles	Debits	Credits
A. B. Cobbler, withdrawals	$1,750	
Shoe service revenues		$ 4,720
Salaries expense	2,300	
Utilities expense	226	
Supplies expense	147	
Rent expense	550	
Depreciation expense	28	

Required: Prepare closing entries.

EB-12 The following are various accounts related to the income statement and owner's equity of Lynn Company (a sole proprietorship) for the current year:

P. Lynn, withdrawals	$ 30,000
Salaries expense	31,400
Delivery expense	9,300
Utilities expense	14,700
Sales	189,500
Depreciation expense	5,600
Cost of goods sold	73,800

Required: From the information given, prepare the December 31 closing entries.

EB-13 For the year ended December 31, 2000, Newhard Corporation had sales revenues of $100,000, operating expenses of $68,000, and other revenue of $2,800. The corporation is subject to a 40% income tax rate and currently has 10,000 shares of common stock held the entire year by stockholders.

Required: (1) Prepare the journal entry on December 31, 2000 to record Newhard Corporation's 2000 income taxes.
  (2) Prepare a 2000 income statement for Newhard Corporation.

EB-14 On January 1, 2000, ACE Corporation showed the following account balances:

Common stock ($10 par)	$100,000
Additional paid-in capital	120,000
Retained earnings	69,700

During 2000, the following events occurred:
(a) The corporation issued 1,000 shares of additional common stock for $30,000.
(b) Net income for the year was $39,000.
(c) Dividends in the amount of $12,000 were declared and paid to stockholders.

Required: Prepare the stockholders' equity section of ACE Corporation's balance sheet on December 31, 2000.

PROBLEMS

PB-1 The Cameron Copy-Quick Company was recently set up by Joseph Cameron. The company's transactions during October, the first month of operations, were as follows:

Date	Transaction
Oct. 3	Joseph Cameron deposited $32,000 in the company's checking account.
4	Acquired land and a building for $3,000 and $42,000, respectively, paying $5,000 cash and signing a five-year mortgage for the remaining balance
15	Copy equipment costing $8,000 was purchased on credit from Tailor Equipment Company.
20	Office supplies costing $1,600 were purchased for cash.
24	Purchased office furniture costing $2,300 from Freddy's Furniture, paying $300 cash. The balance of $2,000 is due in 30 days.
28	Purchased a three-year insurance policy for $900 cash
31	Paid balance due to Tailor Equipment Company for copy equipment purchased on October 15

Required: (1) Set up the following general ledger T-accounts (and account numbers): Cash (101), Office Supplies (105), Prepaid Insurance (106), Land (110), Building (112), Copy Equipment (114), Office Furniture (118), Accounts Payable (201), Mortgage Payable (220), and J. Cameron, Capital (301).

(2) Record the preceding transactions in a general journal.

(3) Post the journal entries to the general ledger accounts and determine the ending account balances.

PB-2 The Foster Tax Services Company was established on January 2 of the current year to help clients with tax planning and preparation of their tax returns. The company engaged in the following transactions during January:

Date	Transaction
Jan. 2	R. Foster set up the company by investing $29,000 cash in the company's checking account.
3	Acquired land and a building at a cost of $3,000 and $21,000, respectively. A $6,000 down payment was made, and a mortgage was signed for the remaining balance.
4	Purchased office equipment costing $7,000 by signing a note due in one year
10	Office supplies costing $735 were purchased for cash.
21	Performed tax planning services for customer and collected $3,020
31	Paid $1,450 for employee's salary
31	Paid utilities bill of $88 for January
31	R. Foster withdrew $850 cash for personal use.

Required: (1) Set up the following T-accounts (and account numbers): Cash (101), Office Supplies (105), Land (110), Building (112), Office Equipment (115), Notes Payable (220), Mortgage Payable (221), R. Foster, Capital (301), R. Foster, Withdrawals (302), Tax Service Revenues (401), Salary Expense (501), Utilities Expense (502).

(2) Prepare journal entries to record the preceding transactions.

(3) Post the journal entries to the accounts.

(4) Prepare a trial balance at January 31.

PB-3 The Ryan Landscaping Service entered into the following transactions during March:

Date	Transaction
Mar. 1	Provided landscaping service for customer, collecting $575 cash
2	Paid three months' rent in advance at $270 per month on storage/office building
5	Purchased $50 of repair parts on credit from JR's, a small-engine service company; the parts are to be used immediately in repairing several of the company's mowers
6-10	Provided landscaping service for a customer; customer agreed to pay the contract price of $2,450 in 15 days
15	Paid $50 due to JR's for repair parts purchased on March 5
25	Collected $2,450 from customer for service provided on March 6-10

31	Paid $40 for March utilities bill
31	Paid $1,800 to employees for March salaries
31	Received $82 March telephone bill, to be paid in early April

Required: (1) Prepare journal entries to record the preceding transactions.
(2) List the source documents normally used to record these transactions.

PB-4   Watson Heater Company sells portable heaters and related equipment. The company uses a perpetual inventory system, and the cost of its inventory at the beginning of November was $2,600. Its cash balance was $1,500 at the beginning of November, and it entered into the following transactions during November:

Date	Transaction
Nov. 1	Made $480 cash sales to customers; the cost of the inventory sold was $280
3	Purchased $1,700 of heaters for cash from Tyler Supply Company
5	Received $250 cash allowance from Tyler Supply Company for defective inventory purchased on November 3
6	Paid $210 for parts and repaired defective heaters purchased from Tyler Supply Company on November 3
8	Made $1,500 sale of heaters on credit to Nate Nursing Home, with terms of 2/10, n/20. The cost of the inventory sold was $850.
15	Purchased $1,100 of heaters on credit from Miller Supplies, with terms of n/15
18	Received amount owed by Nate Nursing Home for heaters purchased on November 8, less the cash discount
30	Paid for the inventory purchased from Duwell Supplies on November 15

Required: Prepare journal entries to record the preceding transactions.

PB-5   Morg Building Supplies sells building supplies and small tools to retail customers. It entered into the following transactions (the company uses the perpetual inventory system) during September:

Date	Transaction
Sept. 1	Purchased $2,000 of building supplies on credit from Doe Company, with terms 2/10, n/30
2	Returned $150 of defective building supplies purchased on September 1 from Doe Company for credit
5	Sold $800 of small tools (which cost $500) to customers for cash
6	Purchased $350 of small tools for cash
6	Granted $70 cash allowance to customer for minor defects found in small tools sold on September 5
10	Paid balance due to Doe Company for purchase of September 1
21	Sold $1,500 of building supplies (which cost $1,000) on credit to R. Bailey, with terms 1/10, n/30
30	Received balance due from R. Bailey for building supplies purchased on September 21

Required: (1) Prepare journal entries to record these transactions.
(2) What were the net sales for the month?

PB-6   The trial balance of Halsey Architectural Consultants on December 31 of the current year (the end of its annual accounting period), included the following account balances before adjustments:

Note receivable...	$14,000 debit
Prepaid insurance..	1,560 debit
Building	92,000 debit
Drafting equipment...	12,000 debit
Unearned rent...	6,240 credit
Note payable...	10,000 credit
Supplies..	1,500 debit

In reviewing the company's recorded transactions and accounting records for the current year, you find the following information pertaining to the December 31 adjustments:

(a) On July 1, the company had accepted a $14,000, 1-year, 10% note receivable from a customer. The interest is to be collected when the note is collected.

(b) On October 1, the company had paid $1,560 for a three-year insurance policy.

(c) The building was acquired several years ago and is being depreciated using the straight-line method over a 20-year life with no residual value.

(d) The drafting equipment was purchased on December 1. It is to be depreciated using the straight-line method over an 8-year life with no residual value.

(e) On July 1, the company had received $6,240 for two years' rent in advance for a portion of its building rented to Shields Company.

(f) On November 1, the company had issued a $10,000, 3-month, 9% note payable to a supplier. The $225 total interest is to be paid when the note is paid.

(g) On January 1, the company had $200 of supplies on hand. During the year the company purchased $1,300 of supplies. A count on December 31 determined that $90 of supplies are still on hand.

Required: Prepare the adjusting entries that are necessary to bring the Halsey Architectural Consultants accounts up-to-date on December 31. Each journal entry explanation should summarize your calculations.

PB-7 Paribus Janitorial Services engaged in the following transactions during the current year and recorded them in its balance sheet accounts:

Date	Transaction
Jan. 1	Purchased cleaning equipment for $12,000, paying $3,000 down and issuing a 2-year, 12% note payable for the $9,000 balance. The equipment has an estimated life of 10 years and no residual value; straight-line depreciation is appropriate. The interest on the note will be paid on the maturity date.
May 24	Purchased $340 of office supplies. The office supplies on hand at the beginning of the year totaled $145.
June 1	Purchased a two-year comprehensive insurance policy for $960
Sept. 1	Received six months' rent in advance at $350 per month and recorded the $2,100 receipt as unearned rent.
Oct. 1	Accepted a $3,000, 6-month, 10% note receivable from a customer. The $150 total interest is to be collected when the note is collected.

Additional Information

(a) On December 31, the office supplies on hand totaled $58.

(b) All employees work Monday through Friday. The weekly payroll of Paribus Janitorial Services amounts to $6,000. All employees are paid at the close of business each Friday for the previous five working days (including Friday). December 31 falls on a Thursday.

Required: On the basis of the preceding information, prepare journal entries to record whatever adjustments are necessary on December 31. Each journal entry explanation should show any related computations.

PB-8 The adjusted trial balance for Swire Interior Decorating Company on November 30, 2000 (the end of its monthly accounting period) is as follows:

Account Titles	Debits	Credits
Cash	$ 7,082	
Accounts receivable	4,394	
Office supplies	1,074	
Prepaid insurance	1,540	
Land	6,000	
Building	29,400	
Accumulated depreciation: building		$ 130
Office equipment	2,880	
Accumulated depreciation: office equipment		40
Accounts payable		1,580
Mortgage payable		10,000
A. Swire, capital		40,000
A. Swire, withdrawals	800	
Interior decorating revenues		3,145
Salaries expense	850	
Insurance expense	140	
Telephone expense	177	*continued*

Utilities expense	276	
Office supplies expense	112	
Depreciation expense: building	130	
Depreciation expense: office equipment	40	
Totals	$54,895	$54,895

Required: (1) Prepare a November income statement, statement of changes in owner's equity, and a November 30, 2000 balance sheet (account form) for Swire Interior Decorating Company.
(2) Prepare the closing entries on November 30, 2000.
(3) Prepare a post-closing trial balance.

PB-9 On May 31, 2000, the bookkeeper of Marina Boat Storage prepared the following closing entries for the month of May:

(a) Storage Revenues	4,060	
Income Summary		4,060
(b) Income Summary	2,724	
Depreciation Expense: Building		140
Depreciation Expense: Equipment		110
Supplies Expense		233
Salaries Expense		1,650
Telephone Expense		92
Utilities Expense		264
Insurance Expense		235
(c) Income Summary	1,336	
L. Marina, Capital		1,336
(d) L. Marina, Capital	830	
L. Marina, Withdrawals		830

In addition, the following *post-closing* trial balance was prepared:

Account Titles	Debits	Credits
Cash	$ 6,120	
Accounts receivable	4,989	
Supplies	1,117	
Land	16,000	
Building	25,200	
Accumulated depreciation: building		$ 140
Equipment	10,560	
Accumulated depreciation: equipment		110
Accounts payable		2,350
Notes payable (due 5/1/02)		7,000
Mortgage payable		20,000
L. Marina, capital		34,386
Totals	$63,986	$63,986

Required: (1) Prepare an income statement for the month ended May 31, 2000.
(2) Prepare a statement of changes in owner's equity for the month ended May 31, 2000.
(3) Prepare a May 31, 2000 balance sheet (report form).

PB-10 Finestein Corporation showed the following balances on January 1, 2000:

Common stock (5,000 shares, $10 par)	$50,000
Additional paid-in capital	95,000
Retained earnings	64,000

On January 4, 2000, the company issued 1,000 shares of common stock for $40,000. For the year ended December 31, 2000, the company had sales revenues of $102,000, cost of goods sold of $48,000, operating expenses of $17,000, and other revenues of $3,000. In addition, the company declared and paid dividends of $6,000 on December 31.

Finestein Corporation is subject to a 40% income tax rate and uses a perpetual inventory system.

Required: (1) Prepare journal entries to record the issuance of common stock on January 4, 2000, and the declaration and payment of the cash dividends on December 31, 2000. (Assume that the company appropriately recorded the journal entries for the other transactions during the year.)

(2) Prepare the journal entry on December 31, 2000 to record the 2000 income taxes of Finestein Corporation.

(3) Prepare an income statement for the year ended December 31, 2000.

(4) Prepare the stockholders' equity section of the December 31, 2000 balance sheet.

(5) Prepare the December 31, 2000 closing entries.

APPENDIX C

General Mills 1998 Annual Report: Financial Section

MANAGEMENT'S DISCUSSION AND ANALYSIS

We believe the keys to delivering increased value for General Mills' shareholders are profit growth, high returns on the capital employed in our businesses, and financial strength. This section of the annual report discusses the recent results of our operations, our financial position and our risk management.

RESULTS OF OPERATIONS – 1998 VS. 1997

Our record financial results in fiscal 1998 were driven by strong growth in worldwide unit volumes and continued productivity gains. For the 53-week period ended May 31, 1998, reported sales grew 8 percent to $6.03 billion. Earnings after tax grew 10 percent to reach $522 million before unusual items. Basic earnings per share of $3.30 and fully diluted earnings per share of $3.22 before unusual items also were up 10 percent from prior-year results.

In the United States, unit volume grew 8 percent, and each one of our domestic operating divisions posted earnings growth of 10 percent or better. The unit volume increase included broad-based gains by established businesses, and strong contributions from the branded cereal and snacks businesses acquired from Ralcorp on Jan. 31, 1997. Excluding incremental volume contributed by these acquired brands in the first eight months of fiscal 1998, domestic unit volume grew 3 percent.

Big G cereals led U.S. performance, with sales up 11 percent to $2.44 billion and total unit volume up 8 percent. This volume gain reflected good growth by several key established brands including *Cheerios*, along with strong contributions from new *Team Cheerios* and *Cinnamon Grahams* plus the acquired *Cookie Crisp* and *Chex* cereals. Excluding incremental volume from acquired brands, Big G unit volume grew nearly 1 percent in 1998.

U.S. convenience foods volume grew 16 percent, with double-digit gains recorded by both the snacks business and by our Yoplait-Colombo yogurt operations. Excluding the eight-month incremental volume provided by the *Chex Mix* snack line, convenience foods volume was up 8 percent for the year. Combined unit volume for *Betty Crocker* baking and dessert products, dinner mixes and side dishes grew 2 percent. Foodservice volume was up 6 percent for the year.

International unit volume, including our proportionate share of joint-venture results, grew 15 percent in 1998. International earnings increased 35 percent to exceed $15 million after tax. Cereal Partners Worldwide (CPW), our joint venture with Nestlé, led international performance, posting 19 percent unit volume growth and strong profit progress. CPW operations in the four initial markets entered in 1991 reached profitability in 1994, and the venture is expected to reach operating profitability overall in calendar 1999. Snack Ventures Europe (SVE), our joint venture with PepsiCo, recorded an 11 percent unit volume gain in 1998, led by strong performance in Spain and Russia. Unit volume grew 4 percent for International Dessert Partners (IDP), our joint venture in Latin America with Bestfoods.

The stronger operating leverage created by our unit volume growth, along with productivity gains and favorable raw material costs, combined to reduce 1998 cost of goods sold to 39.6 percent of sales, nearly 2 percentage points lower than 1997 levels. Selling, general and administrative expense was 1.5 points higher as a percentage of sales in 1998. That increase was consistent with our plans to restore a balanced level of marketing support under our brands, following spending reductions made in the previous year to partially offset lower cereal prices. Despite this increase in expense for brand-building, earnings before interest and taxes grew nearly 11 percent in 1998 to 15.7 percent of sales, a margin improvement of .4 points from the prior year.

Our good earnings growth was coupled with a strong return on invested capital. Return on average invested capital (ROC) before unusual items was 23.9 percent in 1998. This was down slightly from 24.6 percent in 1997, reflecting the full-year impact of the Ralcorp acquisition, but it still ranks among the highest returns on capital in U.S. industry. Our financial goals include a targeted minimum ROC of 25 percent, and we expect to meet that objective in 1999.

Net earnings for 1998 included restructuring charges of 63 cents per share, which primarily related to improving the cost structure of our North American cereal operations. We shut down one cereal line at our Lodi, Calif., facility and closed our two smallest plants, located in Chicago, Ill., and Etobicoke, Ontario. Annual ongoing cost savings from these actions are estimated at 14 cents per share. Net earnings in 1997 included a noncash charge of 18 cents per share for the adoption of SFAS No. 121 (accounting for the impairment of long-lived assets.) Including these unusual items in both years, basic earnings per share were $2.67 in 1998 and $2.82 in 1997. Diluted earnings per share after unusual items were $2.60 in 1998 and $2.76 in 1997.

Net interest expense totaled $117.2 million in 1998, up from $100.5 million in 1997 and $101.4 million in 1996 due to increased borrowings associated with the Ralcorp acquisition and our ongoing share repurchase program. Given our continuing share repurchases and other investment activities, we expect somewhat higher net interest expense in 1999.

The effective income tax rate on earnings as reported in 1998 was 36.3 percent. Excluding the unusual items described above, our effective tax rate was 37.0 percent in 1998, compared to 36.6 percent in 1997 and 36.8 percent in 1996.

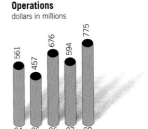

Cash Flow From Operations
dollars in millions

561 — 94
457 — 95
676 — 96
594 — 97
775 — 98

15

It is our view that changes in the rate of inflation have not had a significant effect on profitability from continuing operations over the three most recent years. We attempt to minimize the effects of inflation through appropriate planning and operating practices. Our market risk management practices are discussed later in this section.

For a discussion of new accounting rules effective in future fiscal years, see Note One to the consolidated financial statements.

1997 COMPARED TO 1996

For the year ended May 25, 1997, earnings before unusual items totaled $474.6 million and basic earnings per share were $3.00. These results were essentially flat compared to 1996, when earnings totaled $476.4 million and basic earnings per share were $3.00.

Three primary factors hindered 1997 earnings progress. The most significant of these was price deflation in the U.S. ready-to-eat cereal market, as the major competitors lowered prices. Big G's actions reduced prices an average 11 percent on cereal brands accounting for 42 percent of volume. The second factor to affect 1997 earnings was lower-than-expected unit volume growth in the second half of the year. This shortfall was largely related to Big G volume declines in the second half, when reductions in marketing spending made to partially offset the price declines interrupted momentum. And finally, 1997 earnings were reduced approximately 5 cents per share as anticipated by the acquisition of the Ralcorp branded cereal and snacks businesses.

Total domestic unit volume for established businesses grew 3 percent in 1997 and, including the acquired Ralcorp brands for the final four months of the year, total U.S. volume was up more than 4 percent. Market shares were even or up for nearly all of our major retail businesses. In addition, foodservice operations posted a 6 percent volume gain. International unit volumes, including our share of joint venture results, grew 7 percent. Total international earnings were below the prior year's, however, as a result of development spending for the IDP joint venture with Bestfoods, and lower sales and unit volumes for the SVE joint venture with PepsiCo.

Fiscal 1996 basic earnings per share of $3.00 represented a 28 percent increase from prior-year results. In the United States, unit volume grew 7 percent, led by 10 percent growth in Big G cereal volume. International results included overall unit volume growth of 13 percent and a more than 50 percent improvement in earnings.

FINANCIAL CONDITION

We continue to believe that the ratios of fixed charge coverage and cash flow to debt are the most important measures of our financial strength. The fixed charge coverage ratio measures the number of times each year that we earn enough to cover fixed charges. The cash flow to debt ratio measures the amount of cash we generate each year as a percentage of our total debt. Fiscal 1998 fixed charge coverage of 6.8 times excluding

unusual items remains very strong. Our cash flow to debt declined slightly to 34.6 percent, due to increased debt levels associated with the Ralcorp acquisition and share repurchase activity. We expect this ratio to increase in 1999.

Our balance sheet reflects the impact of several recent transactions. At the end of fiscal 1995, we spun off our restaurant operations, reducing shareholders' equity by approximately $1.2 billion. In January 1997, we acquired the branded ready-to-eat cereal and snack businesses from Ralcorp. For this transaction, we issued approximately $355 million in General Mills common stock (approximately 5.4 million shares) to Ralcorp shareholders and assumed about $215 million of Ralcorp public debt and related accrued interest. This acquisition has been accounted for using the purchase method of accounting. Acquired goodwill totals approximately $550 million and will be amortized on a straight line basis over 40 years. Under our ongoing share repurchase program, we made open-market purchases totaling 6.2 million shares in fiscal 1997 and 7.5 million shares in 1998. These purchases totaled nearly $900 million and reduced stockholders' equity. As a result, stockholders' equity represents $190.2 million of our $2,491.9 million in total capital for 1998.

The company's capital structure is shown in the table below.

CAPITAL STRUCTURE

In Millions	May 31, 1998	May 25, 1997
Notes payable	$ 264.1	$ 204.3
Current portion of long-term debt	153.2	139.0
Long-term debt	1,640.4	1,530.4
Deferred income taxes – tax leases	129.1	143.7
Total debt	2,186.8	2,017.4
Debt adjustments:		
Leases – debt equivalent	218.1	184.4
Marketable investment, at cost	(103.2)	(132.7)
Adjusted debt	2,301.7	2,069.1
Stockholders' equity	190.2	494.6
Total capital	$2,491.9	$2,563.7

We intend to manage our businesses and financial ratios so as to maintain an "A" bond rating, which allows access to financing at reasonable costs. Currently, General Mills' publicly issued long-term debt carries ratings of "A2" (Moody's Investors Services, Inc.) and "A+" (Standard and Poor's Corporation). Our commercial paper has ratings of "P-1" (Moody's) and "A-1" (Standard and Poor's) in the United States and "R-1 (middle)" in Canada (Dominion Bond Rating Service).

The debt equivalent of our leases and deferred income taxes related to tax leases are both fixed-rate obligations. The accompanying table, when reviewed in conjunction with the capital structure table above, shows the composition of our debt structure including the impact of derivatives.

DEBT STRUCTURE

Dollars in Millions	May 31, 1998		May 25, 1997	
Floating-rate debt	$ 819.3	36%	$ 706.0	34%
Fixed-rate debt	1,135.2	49	1,035.0	50
Leases – debt equivalent	218.1	9	184.4	9
Deferred income taxes – tax leases	129.1	6	143.7	7
Total debt	$2,301.7	100%	$2,069.1	100%

Commercial paper is a continuing source of short-term financing. We can isssue commercial paper in the United States and Canada, and subsequent to year end, we established a European commercial paper program. Bank credit lines are maintained to ensure availability of short-term funds on an as-needed basis. As of May 31, 1998, we had fee-paid credit lines of $700 million.

Our shelf registration statement permits us to issue up to $232 million net proceeds in unsecured debt securities. The shelf registration authorizes a medium-term note program that provides additional flexibility in quickly accessing the debt markets.

Sources and uses of cash in the past three years are shown in the accompanying table.

CASH SOURCES (USES)

In Millions	1998	1997	1996
From continuing operations	$ 775.3	$ 594.1	$ 676.4
From discontinued operations	(5.8)	(6.8)	(16.6)
Fixed assets and other investments, net – continuing	(233.0)	(231.8)	(173.9)
Change in marketable securities	29.7	39.7	.9
Proceeds from disposition of businesses	–	6.5	–
Increase (decrease) in outstanding debt – net	198.9	221.9	(164.8)
Common stock issued	92.5	60.5	38.0
Treasury stock purchases	(524.9)	(361.8)	(35.6)
Dividends paid	(336.3)	(320.7)	(303.6)
Other	(2.8)	(9.4)	(13.2)
Increase (decrease) in cash and cash equivalents	$ (6.4)	$ (7.8)	$ 7.6

Continuing operations generated $181.2 million more cash in 1998 than in 1997, primarily due to strong earnings growth recorded by domestic operations and a positive impact from the change in working capital.

Capital investment for fixed assets and joint venture development totaled approximately $211 million in 1998, compared with $209 million in 1997. For fiscal 1999 through 2001, we currently expect our capital investment needs to average about $225 million annually.

MARKET RISK MANAGEMENT

General Mills is exposed to market risk stemming from changes in interest rates, foreign exchange rates and commodity prices. Changes in these factors could cause fluctuations in our earnings and cash flows. In the normal course of business, we actively manage our exposure to these market risks by entering into various hedging transactions, authorized under company policies that place clear controls on these activities. Our hedging transactions involve the use of a variety of derivative financial instruments. We use derivatives only where there is an underlying exposure; we do not use them for trading or speculative purposes. Additional information regarding our use of financial instruments is included in Note Seven to the consolidated financial statements.

Interest rates – We manage our debt structure and our interest-rate risk through the use of fixed- and floating-rate debt, and through the use of derivatives. We use interest-rate swaps to hedge our exposure to interest rate changes, and also to lower our financing costs. Generally under these swaps, we agree with a counterparty to exchange the difference between fixed-rate and floating-rate interest amounts based on an agreed notional principal amount. Our primary exposure is to U.S. interest rates.

Foreign currency rates – Foreign currency fluctuations can affect our net investments and earnings denominated in foreign currencies. We primarily use foreign currency forward contracts and option contracts to selectively hedge our exposure to changes in exchange rates. These contracts function as hedges since they change in value inversely to the change created in the underlying exposure as foreign exchange rates fluctuate. Our primary exchange rate exposure is with various European currencies and the Canadian dollar against the U.S. dollar.

Commodities – Certain ingredients used in our products are exposed to commodity price changes. We manage this risk through an integrated set of financial instruments, including purchase orders, non-cancelable contracts, futures contracts, futures options and swaps. Our primary commodity price exposures are with cereal grains, sugar, fruits, other agricultural products, vegetable oils, packaging materials and energy costs.

Value at risk – These estimates are intended to measure the maximum potential fair value or earnings General Mills could lose in one day from adverse changes in market interest rates, foreign exchange rates or commodity prices, under normal market conditions. A variance/co-variance value at risk (VAR) methodology was used to quantify the market risk for our exposures. The models assumed normal market conditions and used a 95 percent confidence level.

The VAR calculation used historical interest rates, foreign exchange rates and commodity prices from the past year to estimate the potential volatility and correlation of these rates in the future. For interest rate and foreign exchange rate market factors, the data were drawn from the JP Morgan RiskMetrics™ dataset. The calculations are not intended to represent actual losses in fair value or pre-tax earnings that we expect to incur.

17

The model does not consider favorable changes in market rates. Further, since the hedging instrument (the derivative) inversely correlates with the underlying exposure, we would expect that any loss or gain in the fair value of our derivatives would be generally offset by an increase or decrease in the fair value of our underlying exposures. The positions included in the calculations were: debt, investments, interest rate swaps, foreign exchange forwards and commodity swaps, futures and options. The calculations do not include the underlying foreign exchange and commodities-related positions that are hedged by these market-risk sensitive instruments.

The table below presents the estimated maximum potential one-day loss in fair value or pre-tax earnings for our interest rate, foreign currency, and commodity market-risk sensitive instruments outstanding at May 31, 1998, calculated using the VAR methodology described above.

In Millions	Fair Value Impact	Pre-tax Earnings Impact
Value at risk amounts		
Interest rate instruments	$5.3	$ .2
Foreign exchange rate instruments	.6	.2
Commodity instruments	1.5	1.5

YEAR 2000

18

The year 2000 issue is the result of computer programs written using two digits (rather than four) to define years. Computers or other equipment with date-sensitive software may recognize "00" as 1900 rather than 2000. This could result in system failures or miscalculations. If we, or our significant customers or suppliers, fail to correct year 2000 issues, our ability to operate our businesses could be affected.

We have assessed the impact of year 2000 issues on the processing of date-related information for all of our information systems infrastructure and non-technical assets (e.g., plant production equipment). All systems and assets have been inventoried and classified as to their compliance with year 2000 data processing. Any systems found year 2000 deficient will be modified, upgraded or replaced. Project plans anticipate all existing, critical information systems infrastructure to be year 2000 compliant by the end of calendar 1998 and all plant production equipment to be year 2000 compliant by the middle of calendar 1999. Contingency plans will be in place to address any failures resulting from relationships with customers, suppliers or other third parties. We cannot guarantee that circumstances beyond our control will not have an adverse impact on us. However, based on assessments and testing to date, we do not expect the financial impact of addressing any potential internal system issues to be material to our financial position, results of operations or cash flows.

CAUTIONARY STATEMENTS

Here and elsewhere in this report to shareholders, we discuss some of our expectations regarding General Mills' future performance. These forward-looking statements are based on our current views and assumptions. Actual results could differ materially from these current expectations and projections, and from historical performance. For example, our future results could be affected by such factors as: the competitive dynamics in the U.S. ready-to-eat cereal market, including competitive promotional spending levels; the rate of our unit volume growth and our product mix; fluctuations in the cost and availability of supply-chain resources; currency rate fluctuations; and the effect of stock market conditions on our share repurchase activity. Our 1998 Form 10-K contains further discussion of these matters.

REPORT OF MANAGEMENT RESPONSIBILITIES

The management of General Mills, Inc. is responsible for the fairness and accuracy of the consolidated financial statements. The consolidated financial statements have been prepared in accordance with generally accepted accounting principles, using management's best estimates and judgments where appropriate. The financial information throughout this report is consistent with our consolidated financial statements.

Management has established a system of internal controls that provides reasonable assurance that assets are adequately safeguarded and transactions are recorded accurately in all material respects, in accordance with management's authorization. We maintain a strong audit program that independently evaluates the adequacy and effectiveness of internal controls. Our internal controls provide for appropriate separation of duties and responsibilities, and there are documented policies regarding utilization of Company assets and proper financial reporting. These formally stated and regularly communicated policies demand highly ethical conduct from all employees.

The Audit Committee of the Board of Directors meets regularly to determine that management, internal auditors and independent auditors are properly discharging their duties regarding internal control and financial reporting. The independent auditors, internal auditors and employees have full and free access to the Audit Committee at any time.

The independent auditors KPMG Peat Marwick LLP were retained to audit our consolidated financial statements. Their report follows.

S.W. Sanger
Chairman of the Board and
Chief Executive Officer

C.W. Gaillard
President

R.G. Viault
Vice Chairman

REPORT OF THE AUDIT COMMITTEE

The Audit Committee of the Board of Directors is composed of six outside directors. Its primary function is to oversee the Company's system of internal controls, financial reporting practices and audits to ensure that their quality, integrity and objectivity are sufficient to protect stockholder interests.

The Audit Committee met three times during 1998 to review the overall audit scope, plans and results of the internal auditors and independent auditors, the Company's internal controls, emerging accounting issues, officer and director expenses, audit fees, goodwill and other intangible values, and the audits of the employee benefit plans. The Committee also met separately without management present and with the independent auditors to discuss the audit. The Committee also reviewed the

Company's annual financial statements and, acting with other Board members, approved them before issuance. Audit Committee meeting results were reported to the full Board of Directors. The Audit Committee recommended to the Board that KPMG Peat Marwick LLP be reappointed for 1999, subject to the ratification of stockholders at the annual meeting.

The Audit Committee is satisfied that the internal control system is adequate and that the Company employs appropriate accounting and auditing procedures.

M.D. Rose
Chairman, Audit Committee

19

INDEPENDENT AUDITORS' REPORT

The Stockholders and the Board of Directors of
General Mills, Inc.:

We have audited the accompanying consolidated balance sheets of General Mills, Inc. and subsidiaries as of May 31, 1998 and May 25, 1997, and the related consolidated statements of earnings, stockholders' equity and cash flows for each of the fiscal years in the three-year period ended May 31, 1998. These consolidated financial statements are the responsibility of the Company's management. Our responsibility is to express an opinion on these consolidated financial statements based on our audits.

We conducted our audits in accordance with generally accepted auditing standards. Those standards require that we plan and perform the audit to obtain reasonable assurance about whether the financial statements are free of material misstatement. An audit includes examining, on a test basis, evidence supporting the amounts and disclosures in the financial statements. An audit also includes assessing the accounting principles used and significant estimates made by management,

as well as evaluating the overall financial statement presentation. We believe that our audits provide a reasonable basis for our opinion.

In our opinion, the consolidated financial statements referred to above present fairly, in all material respects, the financial position of General Mills, Inc. and subsidiaries as of May 31, 1998 and May 25, 1997, and the results of their operations and their cash flows for each of the fiscal years in the three-year period ended May 31, 1998 in conformity with generally accepted accounting principles.

As discussed in Note Three to the consolidated financial statements, the Company adopted the provisions of the Financial Accounting Standards Board's Statement No. 121, "Accounting for the Impairment of Long-Lived Assets and for Long-Lived Assets to Be Disposed Of," in fiscal 1997.

KPMG Peat Marwick LLP

Minneapolis, Minnesota
June 30, 1998

CONSOLIDATED STATEMENTS OF EARNINGS

In Millions, Except per Share Data, Fiscal Year Ended	May 31, 1998	May 25, 1997	May 26, 1996
Sales	$6,033.0	$5,609.3	$5,416.0
Costs and Expenses:			
Cost of sales	2,389.3	2,328.4	2,241.0
Selling, general and administrative	2,498.6	2,239.2	2,128.3
Depreciation and amortization	194.9	182.8	186.7
Interest, net	117.2	100.5	101.4
Unusual items	166.4	48.4	–
Total Costs and Expenses	5,366.4	4,899.3	4,657.4
Earnings before Taxes and Earnings (Losses) from Joint Ventures	666.6	710.0	758.6
Income Taxes	241.9	258.3	279.4
Earnings (Losses) from Joint Ventures	(2.9)	(6.3)	(2.8)
Net Earnings	$ 421.8	$ 445.4	$ 476.4
Earnings per Share	$ 2.67	$ 2.82	$ 3.00
Average Number of Common Shares	158.1	158.2	158.9
Earnings per Share – Assuming Dilution	$ 2.60	$ 2.76	$ 2.94
Average Number of Common Shares – Assuming Dilution	162.3	161.6	162.0

See accompanying notes to consolidated financial statements.

20

CONSOLIDATED BALANCE SHEETS

In Millions	May 31, 1998	May 25, 1997
Assets		
Current Assets:		
Cash and cash equivalents	$ 6.4	$ 12.8
Receivables, less allowance for doubtful accounts of $4.2 in 1998 and $4.1 in 1997	395.1	419.1
Inventories	389.7	364.4
Prepaid expenses and other current assets	107.2	107.3
Deferred income taxes	136.9	107.7
Total Current Assets	1,035.3	1,011.3
Land, Buildings and Equipment at cost, net	1,186.3	1,279.4
Other Assets	1,639.8	1,611.7
Total Assets	$3,861.4	$3,902.4
Liabilities and Equity		
Current Liabilities:		
Accounts payable	$ 593.1	$ 599.7
Current portion of long-term debt	153.2	139.0
Notes payable	264.1	204.3
Accrued taxes	148.5	97.0
Accrued payroll	129.7	129.4
Other current liabilities	155.1	123.1
Total Current Liabilities	1,443.7	1,292.5
Long-term Debt	1,640.4	1,530.4
Deferred Income Taxes	284.8	272.1
Deferred Income Taxes – Tax Leases	129.1	143.7
Other Liabilities	173.2	169.1
Total Liabilities	3,671.2	3,407.8
Stockholders' Equity:		
Cumulative preference stock, none issued	–	–
Common stock, 204.2 shares issued	619.6	578.0
Retained earnings	1,622.8	1,535.4
Less common stock in treasury, at cost, shares of 49.4 in 1998 and 44.3 in 1997	(1,935.7)	(1,501.9)
Unearned compensation and other	(48.1)	(58.0)
Cumulative foreign currency adjustment	(68.4)	(58.9)
Total Stockholders' Equity	190.2	494.6
Total Liabilities and Equity	$3,861.4	$3,902.4

See accompanying notes to consolidated financial statements.

21

CONSOLIDATED STATEMENTS OF CASH FLOWS

In Millions, Fiscal Year Ended	May 31, 1998	May 25, 1997	May 26, 1996
Cash Flows – Operating Activities:			
Net earnings	$ 421.8	$ 445.4	$ 476.4
Adjustments to reconcile net earnings to cash flow:			
Depreciation and amortization	194.9	182.8	186.7
Deferred income taxes	(29.3)	20.9	42.4
Change in current assets and liabilities, net of effects			
from business acquired	54.5	(86.4)	(25.9)
Unusual items	166.4	48.4	–
Other, net	(33.0)	(17.0)	(3.2)
Cash provided by continuing operations	775.3	594.1	676.4
Cash used by discontinued operations	(5.8)	(6.8)	(16.6)
Net Cash Provided by Operating Activities	769.5	587.3	659.8
Cash Flows – Investment Activities:			
Purchases of land, buildings and equipment	(183.6)	(162.5)	(128.8)
Investments in businesses, intangibles and affiliates,			
net of investment returns and dividends	(9.5)	(42.0)	(40.0)
Purchases of marketable securities	(10.6)	(8.0)	(21.6)
Proceeds from sale of marketable securities	40.3	47.7	22.5
Proceeds from disposal of land, buildings and equipment	2.1	2.6	6.2
Proceeds from disposition of businesses	–	6.5	–
Other, net	(42.0)	(29.9)	(11.3)
Net Cash Used by Investment Activities	(203.3)	(185.6)	(173.0)
Cash Flows – Financing Activities:			
Change in notes payable	63.9	312.7	(42.4)
Issuance of long-term debt	286.6	76.2	42.3
Payment of long-term debt	(151.6)	(167.0)	(164.7)
Common stock issued	92.5	60.5	38.0
Purchases of common stock for treasury	(524.9)	(361.8)	(35.6)
Dividends paid	(336.3)	(320.7)	(303.6)
Other, net	(2.8)	(9.4)	(13.2)
Net Cash Used by Financing Activities	(572.6)	(409.5)	(479.2)
Increase (Decrease) in Cash and Cash Equivalents	(6.4)	(7.8)	7.6
Cash and Cash Equivalents – Beginning of Year	12.8	20.6	13.0
Cash and Cash Equivalents – End of Year	$ 6.4	$ 12.8	$ 20.6
Cash Flow from Changes in Current Assets and Liabilities:			
Receivables	$ 23.7	$ (80.0)	$ (59.5)
Inventories	(26.4)	45.0	(23.7)
Prepaid expenses and other current assets	1.6	2.5	(6.3)
Accounts payable	4.0	(27.8)	93.2
Other current liabilities	51.6	(26.1)	(29.6)
Change in Current Assets and Liabilities	$ 54.5	$ (86.4)	$ (25.9)

22

See accompanying notes to consolidated financial statements.

CONSOLIDATED STATEMENTS OF STOCKHOLDERS' EQUITY

In Millions, Except per Share Data	$.10 Par Value Common Stock (One Billion Shares Authorized) Issued Shares	Amount	Treasury Shares	Amount	Retained Earnings	Unearned Compensation and Other	Cumulative Foreign Currency Adjustment	Total
Balance at May 28, 1995	204.2	$379.5	(46.3)	$(1,372.1)	$1,233.3	$(57.9)	$(41.8)	$ 141.0
Net earnings					476.4			476.4
Cash dividends declared ($1.91 per share), net of income taxes of $2.5					(301.1)			(301.1)
Stock option, profit sharing and ESOP plans	–	4.6	1.7	40.3				44.9
Shares purchased on open market			(.6)	(35.6)				(35.6)
Put option premium/settlements, net	–	.2						.2
Unearned compensation related to restricted stock awards						(6.5)		(6.5)
Earned compensation and other						7.1		7.1
Change in unrealized gain, net of income taxes of $2.0, on available-for-sale securities						(3.1)		(3.1)
Minimum pension liability adjustment						(.8)		(.8)
Translation adjustments, net of income tax benefit of $.2							(14.8)	(14.8)
Balance at May 26, 1996	204.2	384.3	(45.2)	(1,367.4)	1,408.6	(61.2)	(56.6)	307.7
Net earnings					445.4			445.4
Cash dividends declared ($2.03 per share), net of income taxes of $2.1					(318.6)			(318.6)
Shares issued in acquisition	–	181.4	5.4	173.0				354.4
Stock option, profit sharing and ESOP plans	–	9.3	1.7	57.4				66.7
Shares purchased via puts, or on open market			(6.2)	(368.0)				(368.0)
Put and call option premium/settlements, net	–	3.0	–	3.1				6.1
Unearned compensation related to restricted stock awards						(7.9)		(7.9)
Earned compensation and other						13.1		13.1
Change in unrealized gain, net of income taxes of $.1, on available-for-sale securities						(.1)		(.1)
Minimum pension liability adjustment						(1.9)		(1.9)
Amount removed on disposition of foreign operation							6.1	6.1
Translation adjustments							(8.4)	(8.4)
Balance at May 25, 1997	204.2	578.0	(44.3)	(1,501.9)	1,535.4	(58.0)	(58.9)	494.6
Net earnings					421.8			421.8
Cash dividends declared ($2.12 per share), net of income taxes of $1.9					(334.4)			(334.4)
Stock option, profit sharing and ESOP plans	–	29.3	2.4	83.9				113.2
Shares purchased via puts, or on open market			(7.5)	(518.7)				(518.7)
Put and call option premium/settlements, net	–	12.3	–	1.0				13.3
Unearned compensation related to restricted stock awards						(7.3)		(7.3)
Earned compensation and other						11.9		11.9
Change in unrealized gain, net of income taxes of $5.2, on available-for-sale securities						8.2		8.2
Minimum pension liability adjustment						(2.9)		(2.9)
Translation adjustments							(9.5)	(9.5)
Balance at May 31, 1998	**204.2**	**$619.6**	**(49.4)**	**$(1,935.7)**	**$1,622.8**	**$(48.1)**	**$(68.4)**	**$ 190.2**

See accompanying notes to consolidated financial statements.

23

NOTES TO CONSOLIDATED FINANCIAL STATEMENTS

1 SUMMARY OF SIGNIFICANT ACCOUNTING POLICIES

The preparation of the Consolidated Financial Statements in conformity with generally accepted accounting principles requires management to make estimates and assumptions that affect reported amounts of assets and liabilities and disclosure of contingent assets and liabilities at the date of the financial statements, and the reported amounts of revenues and expenses during the reporting period. Actual results could differ from those estimates.

(A) Principles of Consolidation – The consolidated financial statements include the following domestic and foreign operations: parent company and 100% owned subsidiaries, and General Mills' investment in and share of net earnings or losses of 20–50% owned companies.

Our fiscal year ends on the last Sunday in May. Years 1997 and 1996 each consisted of 52 weeks and 1998 consisted of 53 weeks.

(B) Land, Buildings, Equipment and Depreciation – Buildings and equipment are depreciated over estimated useful lives, primarily using the straight-line method. Buildings are usually depreciated over 40 to 50 years and equipment over three to 15 years. Accelerated depreciation methods are generally used for income tax purposes.

When an item is sold or retired, the accounts are relieved of its cost and related accumulated depreciation; the resulting gains and losses, if any, are recognized.

(C) Inventories – Inventories are valued at the lower of cost or market. Certain domestic inventories are valued using the LIFO method, while other inventories are generally valued using the FIFO method.

(D) Intangible Assets – Goodwill represents the difference between the purchase price of acquired companies and the related fair value of net assets acquired and accounted for by the purchase method of accounting. Goodwill is amortized on a straight-line basis over 40 years or less.

Intangible assets include an amount that offsets a minimum liability recorded for a pension plan with assets less than accumulated benefits.

The costs of patents, copyrights and other intangible assets are amortized evenly over their estimated useful lives.

The Audit Committee of the Board of Directors annually reviews goodwill and other intangibles. At its meeting on April 27, 1998, the Audit Committee affirmed that the remaining amounts of these assets have continuing value based upon a return on capital analysis.

(E) Recoverability of Long-Lived Assets – We review long-lived assets, including identifiable intangibles and associated goodwill, for impairment when events or changes in circumstances indicate that the carrying amount of an asset may not be recoverable. An asset is deemed impaired and written down to its fair value if estimated related future cash flows are less than its carrying amount.

(F) Foreign Currency Translation – For most foreign operations, local currencies are considered the functional currency. Assets and liabilities are translated using the exchange rates in effect at the balance sheet date. Results of operations are translated using the average exchange rates prevailing throughout the period. Translation effects are accumulated in the foreign currency adjustment in stockholders' equity.

(G) Financial Instruments – See Note Seven for a description of the accounting policies related to financial instruments.

(H) Research and Development – All expenditures for research and development are charged against earnings in the year incurred. The charges for 1998, 1997 and 1996 were $66.3 million, $61.4 million and $60.1 million, respectively.

(I) Advertising Costs – Advertising expense (including production and communication costs) for 1998, 1997 and 1996 was $366.1 million, $306.5 million and $319.7 million, respectively. Prepaid advertising costs (including syndication properties) of $25.5 million and $22.6 million were reported as assets at May 31, 1998 and May 25, 1997, respectively. We expense the production costs of advertising the first time that the advertising takes place.

(J) Stock-based Compensation – We use the "intrinsic value-based method" for measuring the cost of compensation paid in Company common stock. This method defines our cost as the excess of the stock's market value at the time of the grant over the amount that the employee is required to pay. Our stock option plans require that the employee's payment (i.e., exercise price) is the market value as of the grant date.

(K) Earnings per Share – We adopted Statement of Financial Accounting Standards (SFAS) No. 128, "Earnings per Share" in our third quarter of fiscal 1998. SFAS No. 128 requires dual presentation of basic and diluted earnings per share (EPS) on the statement of earnings. Basic EPS is computed by dividing net earnings by the weighted average number of common shares outstanding. Diluted EPS includes the effect of all dilutive potential common shares (primarily related to outstanding stock options). All prior periods have been restated.

(L) Segment Information – We operate exclusively in the consumer foods industry.

(M) Statements of Cash Flows – For purposes of the statement of cash flows, we consider all investments purchased with an original maturity of three months or less to be cash equivalents.

(N) New Accounting Rules – During 1998, the Financial Accounting Standards Board (FASB) issued SFAS No. 130, "Reporting Comprehensive Income," SFAS No. 131, "Disclosures about Segments of an Enterprise and Related Information," and SFAS No. 132, "Employers' Disclosures about Pensions and Other Postretirement Benefits." These standards, which are all effective in our 1999, revise related disclosures. There will be no impact on our financial position, results of operations, or cash flows from adoption of these standards.

In March 1998, the American Institute of Certified Public Accountants issued Statement of Position (SOP) 98-1, "Accounting for the Costs of Computer Software Developed or Obtained for Internal Use." SOP 98-1 is effective for fiscal years beginning after December 15, 1998 and provides guidance on accounting for the described costs. SOP 98-1 should not have a material impact on our financial position, results of operations, or cash flows when adopted.

In June 1998, the FASB issued SFAS No. 133, "Accounting for Derivative Instruments and Hedging Activities." SFAS 133 is effective for us in our fiscal 2001. We have not yet determined the impact of adoption on our financial statements; however, we do not expect the impact to be material.

2 ACQUISITION

On January 31, 1997, we acquired the branded ready-to-eat cereal and snack mix businesses of Ralcorp Holdings, Inc., including its *Chex* and *Cookie Crisp* brands. This acquisition included a Cincinnati, Ohio, manufacturing facility, and trademark and technology rights for the branded products in the Americas. The purchase price of $570 million involved the issuance of about $355 million in General Mills common stock (approximately 5.4 million shares) to Ralcorp shareholders and the assumption of about $215 million of Ralcorp public debt and accrued interest. This acquisition has been accounted for using the purchase method of accounting. The purchase price was allocated based on fair values at date of acquisition and resulted in acquired goodwill of approximately $550 million, which is being amortized on a straight-line basis over 40 years. The results of the acquired businesses have been included in the consolidated financial statements since the acquisition date. 1997 earnings were reduced approximately $.05 per share by the acquisition.

The following unaudited pro forma information presents a summary of our consolidated results of operations and the acquired branded ready-to-eat cereal and snack mix businesses of Ralcorp as if the acquisition had occurred on May 29, 1995.

	Fiscal Year	
In Millions, Except per Share Data	**1997**	1996
Sales	**$5,892.0**	$5,809.6
Net earnings	**459.4**	487.7
Net earnings per share	**2.84**	2.97

These unaudited pro forma results have been prepared for comparative purposes only and include certain adjustments, such as additional amortization expense as a result of goodwill and an increased interest expense on acquisition debt. They do not purport to be indicative of the results of operations that actually would have resulted had the combination occurred on May 29, 1995, or of future results of operations of the consolidated entities.

3 UNUSUAL ITEMS

In 1998, we recorded a net charge of $166.4 million pre-tax, $100.2 million after tax ($.63 per share) primarily related to shutting down one cereal system at our Lodi, California, facility and closing our two smallest cereal plants based in Chicago, Illinois, and Etobicoke, Ontario. We also received an insurance settlement from one of our carriers related to costs incurred in fiscal 1995 and 1996 (charged against fiscal 1994) from the improper use of a pesticide by an independent contractor in treating some of the Company's oat supplies. Snack Ventures

Europe (SVE), our joint venture with PepsiCo, recorded restructuring charges for productivity initiatives primarily related to production consolidation. We also recorded charges associated with restructuring our sales regions and our trade and promotion organization. The charges include approximately $147 million in non-cash items primarily related to asset write-offs and approximately $19 million of net cash outflows, primarily related to disposal of assets, severance costs and the insurance settlement. These restructuring activities will be substantially completed in fiscal 1999 and there has been no adjustment to the original reserve. At May 31, 1998, there was a remaining reserve of $30.5 million.

In 1997, we adopted SFAS No. 121, "Accounting for the Impairment of Long-Lived Assets and for Long-Lived Assets to Be Disposed Of." The initial, non-cash charge upon adoption of SFAS 121 was $48.4 million pre-tax, $29.2 million after tax ($.18 per share). The charge represented a reduction in the carrying amounts of certain impaired assets to their estimated fair value, determined on the basis of estimated cash flows or net realizable value. The impairments related to assets not currently in use, assets significantly underutilized, and assets with limited planned future use.

4 INVESTMENTS IN JOINT VENTURES

We are involved in four joint ventures. We have a 50% equity interest in Cereal Partners Worldwide (CPW), our joint venture with Nestlé, which manufactures and markets ready-to-eat cereals outside North America. We have a 40.5% equity interest in Snack Ventures Europe, our joint venture with PepsiCo, which manufactures and markets snack foods in continental Europe. We have a 50% equity interest in International Dessert Partners (IDP), our joint venture with Bestfoods, which manufactures and markets baking mixes and desserts in Latin America. We have a 50% equity interest in Tong Want, a new joint venture formed in 1998 with Want Want Holdings Ltd. This venture has a goal of developing a savory snacks business in China, but is not yet operating.

The joint ventures are reflected in our financial statements on an equity accounting basis. We record our share of the earnings or (losses) of these joint ventures. (The table that follows in this footnote reflects the joint ventures on a 100% basis.) We also receive royalty income from these joint ventures, incur various expenses (primarily research and development), and record the tax impact of certain of the joint venture operations that are structured as partnerships. Including all these factors, and excluding the impact of SVE restructuring charges which are included in unusual items, the effect on our net income related to the joint ventures was a charge of $2.9 million, $6.3 million and $2.8 million in 1998, 1997 and 1996, respectively.

Our cumulative investment in these joint ventures (including our share of earnings and losses) was $214.3 million, $234.6 million and $229.8 million at the end of 1998, 1997 and 1996, respectively. We made aggregate investments in the joint ventures of $6.8 million (net of a $20.9 million loan repayment), $46.5 million and $45.3 million in 1998, 1997 and 1996, respectively. We received aggregate dividends from the joint

25

ventures of $.9 million, $7.5 million and $8.2 million in 1998, 1997 and 1996, respectively.

Summary combined financial information for the joint ventures on a 100% basis follows. Since we record our share of CPW and IDP results on a two-month lag, their information is included as of and for the twelve months ended March 31. The SVE information is consistent with our May year end.

**COMBINED FINANCIAL INFORMATION –
JOINT VENTURES – 100% BASIS**

	Fiscal Year Ended		
In Millions	**May 31, 1998**	May 25, 1997	May 26, 1996
Sales	**$1,732.5**	$1,627.6	$1,599.5
Gross Profit	**907.7**	843.5	838.1
Earnings (losses) before Taxes	**20.1**	(7.3)	12.1
Earnings (losses) after Taxes	**(6.3)**	(24.7)	(13.1)

In Millions	**May 31, 1998**	May 25, 1997
Current Assets	**$432.4**	$419.6
Non-current Assets	**675.6**	602.4
Current Liabilities	**609.0**	488.8
Non-current Liabilities	**47.6**	106.1

Our proportionate share of the sales of the joint ventures was $780.7 million, $728.2 million and $705.7 million for 1998, 1997 and 1996, respectively.

5 BALANCE SHEET INFORMATION

The components of certain balance sheet accounts are as follows:

In Millions	**May 31, 1998**	May 25, 1997
Land, Buildings and Equipment:		
Land	**$ 17.8**	$ 17.5
Buildings	**539.9**	526.7
Equipment	**1,790.4**	1,911.2
Construction in progress	**140.9**	116.2
Total land, buildings and equipment	**2,489.0**	2,571.6
Less accumulated depreciation	**(1,302.7)**	(1,292.2)
Net land, buildings and equipment	**$1,186.3**	$1,279.4
Other Assets:		
Prepaid pension	**$ 471.8**	$ 402.5
Marketable securities, at market	**142.1**	158.0
Investments in and advances to affiliates	**201.9**	221.8
Net intangible assets, primarily goodwill	**630.4**	655.2
Miscellaneous	**193.6**	174.2
Total other assets	**$1,639.8**	$1,611.7

Accumulated amortization included in net intangible assets was $62.7 million and $39.8 million at May 31, 1998 and May 25, 1997, respectively.

As of May 31, 1998, a comparison of cost and market values of our marketable securities (all of which are debt securities and considered available-for-sale) was as follows:

In Millions	Cost	Market Value	Gross Gain	Gross Loss
In "Other Current Assets"	$ 14.6	$ 14.6	$ –	$ –
In "Other Assets"	88.6	142.1	53.5	–
Total marketable securities	$103.2	$156.7	$53.5	$ –

Realized gains from sales of marketable securities were $.1 million, $.6 million and $3.8 million in 1998, 1997 and 1996, respectively. In addition, realized losses from purchases of our related debt (see Note Nine) were $.9 million and $2.3 million in 1997 and 1996, respectively. The aggregate unrealized gains and losses on available-for-sale securities, net of tax effects, are accumulated in the "unearned compensation and other" account within stockholders' equity.

Scheduled maturities of our marketable securities are as follows:

In Millions	Cost	Market Value
Under one year (current)	$ 14.6	$ 14.6
From 1 to 3 years	4.2	4.2
From 4 to 7 years	30.9	45.4
Over 7 years	53.5	92.5
Totals	$103.2	$156.7

6 INVENTORIES

The components of inventories are as follows:

In Millions	**May 31, 1998**	May 25, 1997
Raw materials, work in process and supplies	**$ 83.3**	$ 77.4
Finished goods	**262.5**	270.5
Grain	**83.0**	64.0
Reserve for LIFO valuation method	**(39.1)**	(47.5)
Total inventories	**$389.7**	$364.4

At May 31, 1998 and May 25, 1997, respectively, inventories of $221.4 million and $208.5 million were valued at LIFO. The impact of LIFO accounting increased 1998 and 1997 earnings by $.03 and $.03 per share, respectively, and reduced 1996 earnings by $.01 per share.

7 FINANCIAL INSTRUMENTS AND RISK MANAGEMENT

Most of our financial instruments are recorded on the balance sheet. A few (known as "derivatives") are off-balance-sheet items. Derivatives are financial instruments whose value is derived from one or more underlying financial instruments. Examples of such underlying instruments are currencies, equities, commodities and interest rates. The carrying amount and fair value (based on current market quotes and interest rates) of our financial instruments at the balance-sheet dates are as follows:

In Millions	May 31, 1998 Carrying Amount	May 31, 1998 Fair Value	May 25, 1997 Carrying Amount	May 25, 1997 Fair Value
Assets:				
Cash and cash equivalents	$ 6.4	$ 6.4	$ 12.8	$ 12.8
Receivables	395.1	395.1	419.1	419.1
Marketable securities	156.8	156.8	174.8	174.8
Liabilities:				
Accounts payable	593.1	593.1	599.7	599.7
Debt	2,057.7	2,180.1	1,873.7	1,932.3
Derivatives relating to:				
Marketable securities	(.1)	(.1)	(1.8)	(1.8)
Debt	–	19.2	–	9.2
Commodities	–	(.4)	–	–

Each derivative we enter into and hold is designated at inception as a hedge of risks associated with specific assets, liabilities or future commitments and is monitored to determine if it remains an effective hedge. The effectiveness of the derivative as a hedge is based on changes in its market value being highly correlated with changes in market value of the underlying hedged item. We do not enter into or hold derivatives for trading or speculative purposes.

We use derivative instruments to reduce financial risk in three areas: interest rates, foreign currency and commodities. The notional amounts of derivatives do not represent actual amounts exchanged by the parties and, thus, are not a measure of the exposure of the Company through its use of derivatives. Interest rate swap, foreign exchange, and commodity swap agreements are made with a diversified group of highly rated financial institutions, while commodities futures are entered into through various regulated exchanges. These transactions expose the Company to credit risk to the extent that the instruments have a positive fair value, but we do not anticipate any losses. The Company does not have a significant concentration of risk with any single party or group of parties in any of its financial instruments.

(1) Interest Rate Risk Management – We use interest rate swaps to hedge and/or lower financing costs, to adjust our floating- and fixed-rate debt positions, and to lock in a positive interest rate spread between certain assets and liabilities. An interest rate swap used in conjunction with a debt financing may allow the Company to create fixed or floating-rate financing at a lower cost than with stand-alone financing. Generally, under interest rate swaps, the Company agrees with a counterparty to exchange the difference between fixed-rate and floating-rate interest amounts calculated by reference to an agreed notional principal amount.

The following table indicates the types of swaps used to hedge various assets and liabilities, and their weighted average interest rates. Average variable rates are based on rates as of the end of the reporting period. The swap contracts mature during time periods ranging from 1999 to 2023.

Dollars in Millions	May 31, 1998 Asset	May 31, 1998 Liability	May 25, 1997 Asset	May 25, 1997 Liability
Receive fixed swaps – notional amount	$ –	$118.3	$ –	$99.9
Average receive rate	–	5.9%	–	6.5%
Average pay rate	–	5.4%	–	5.4%
Pay fixed swaps – notional amount	$ 14.3	$116.5	$34.2	$16.5
Average receive rate	5.5%	5.6%	5.9%	5.6%
Average pay rate	7.1%	5.8%	8.9%	8.2%

The interest rate differential on interest rate swaps used to hedge existing assets and liabilities is recognized as an adjustment of interest expense or income over the term of the agreement.

The Company uses interest rate options and cap agreements primarily to reduce the impact of interest rate changes on its floating-rate debt, as well as to hedge the value of call options contained in long-term debt issued by the Company in earlier periods. In return for an upfront payment, an interest rate swap option grants the purchaser the right to receive (pay) the fixed rate interest amount in an interest rate swap. In return for an upfront payment, a cap agreement entitles the purchaser to receive the amount, if any, by which an agreed upon floating rate index exceeds the cap interest rate. At May 31, 1998, we had no interest rate options outstanding.

(2) Foreign-Currency Exposure – We are exposed to potential losses from foreign currency fluctuations affecting net investments and earnings denominated in foreign currencies. We selectively hedge the potential effect of these foreign currency fluctuations related to operating activities and net investments in foreign operations by entering into foreign exchange contracts with highly rated financial institutions. Realized and unrealized gains and losses on hedges of firm commitments are included in the cost basis of the asset being hedged and are recognized as the asset is expensed through cost of goods sold or depreciation. Realized and unrealized gains and losses on contracts that hedge other operating activities are recognized currently in net earnings. Realized and unrealized gains and losses on contracts that hedge net investments are recognized in the cumulative foreign currency adjustment in stockholders' equity.

27

The components of our net foreign investment exposure by geographic region are as follows:

In Millions	May 31, 1998	May 25, 1997
Europe	$140.1	$153.8
North/South America	28.5	40.2
Asia	1.5	2.3
Total exposure	$170.1	$196.3

At May 31, 1998, we had forward and option contracts maturing in 1999 to sell $37.8 million of foreign currencies. The fair value of these contracts is based on third-party quotes and was immaterial at May 31, 1998.

(3) Commodities – The Company uses an integrated set of financial instruments in its purchasing cycle, including purchase orders, noncancelable contracts, futures contracts, futures options and swaps. Except as described below, these instruments are all used to manage purchase prices and inventory values as practical for the Company's production needs. All futures contracts and futures options are exchange-based instruments with ready liquidity and determinable market values. Unrealized gains and losses are recorded monthly and deferred until the production flows through cost of goods sold. The net gains and losses deferred and expensed are immaterial. At May 31, 1998 and May 25, 1997, the aggregate fair value of our ingredient derivatives position was $156.7 million and $92.9 million, respectively.

The Company also has a grain-merchandising operation, which uses cash contracts, futures contracts and futures options. All futures contracts and futures options are exchange-based instruments with ready liquidity and determinable market values. Neither results of operations nor the year-end positions from our grain-merchandising operations was material to the Company's overall results.

8 NOTES PAYABLE

The components of notes payable and their respective weighted average interest rates at the end of the periods are as follows:

	May 31, 1998		May 25, 1997	
Dollars in Millions	Notes Payable	Weighted Average Interest Rate	Notes Payable	Weighted Average Interest Rate
U.S. commercial paper	$428.2	5.5%	$379.0	5.5%
Canadian commercial paper	20.4	5.0	32.2	3.2
Financial institutions	295.5	5.2	273.1	5.1
Amounts reclassified to long-term debt	(480.0)	–	(480.0)	–
Total notes payable	$264.1		$204.3	

See Note Seven for a description of related interest rate derivative instruments.

To ensure availability of funds, we maintain bank credit lines sufficient to cover our outstanding short-term borrowings.

As of May 31, 1998, we had $700.0 million fee-paid lines and $63.8 million uncommitted, no-fee lines available in the U.S. and Canada. In addition, we had foreign no-fee lines of $70.4 million, of which $14.9 million are unused.

We have a revolving credit agreement expiring in January 2002 covering the fee-paid credit lines that provides us with the ability to refinance short-term borrowings on a long-term basis. Therefore we have reclassified a portion of our notes payable to long-term debt.

9 LONG-TERM DEBT

In Millions	May 31, 1998	May 25, 1997
Medium-term notes, 5.1% to 9.1%, due 1998 to 2033	$ 997.6	$ 877.9
Zero coupon notes, yield 11.1%, $278.8 due August 15, 2013	54.3	48.7
8.2% ESOP loan guaranty, due through June 30, 2007	57.7	63.5
7.0% Notes due September 15, 2004	163.0	165.1
Zero coupon notes, yield 11.7%, $64.2 due August 15, 2004	31.8	28.3
Notes payable, reclassified	480.0	480.0
Other	9.2	5.9
	1,793.6	1,669.4
Less amounts due within one year	(153.2)	(139.0)
Total long-term debt	$1,640.4	$1,530.4

See Note Seven for a description of related interest rate derivative instruments.

As of May 31, 1998 our debt shelf registration permits the issuance of up to $232.0 million net proceeds in unsecured debt securities to reduce short-term debt and for other general corporate purposes, and includes a medium-term note program that allows us to issue debt quickly for selected amounts, rates and maturities.

In 1998, we issued $268.0 million of debt under our medium-term note program with maturities varying from one to 25 years and interest rates from 5.1% to 5.8%. In 1997, $62.0 million of debt was issued under this program with maturities from one to 12 years and interest rates from 5.6% to 7.5%.

The Company has guaranteed the debt of the Employee Stock Ownership Plan; therefore, the loan is reflected on our consolidated balance sheets as long-term debt with a related offset in stockholders' equity, "unearned compensation and other."

The sinking fund and principal payments due on long-term debt are (in millions) $153.2, $90.6, $62.8, $47.9 and $96.6 in 1999, 2000, 2001, 2002 and 2003, respectively. The notes payable that are reclassified under our revolving credit agreement are not included in these principal payments.

Our marketable securities (see Note Five) include zero coupon U.S. Treasury securities. These investments are intended to provide the funds for the payment of principal and interest for the zero coupon notes due August 15, 2004, and 2013.

STOCKHOLDERS' EQUITY

Cumulative preference stock of 5.0 million shares, without par value, is authorized but unissued.

We have a shareholder rights plan that entitles each outstanding share of common stock to one right. Each right entitles the holder to purchase one one-hundredth of a share of cumulative preference stock (or, in certain circumstances, common stock or other securities), exercisable upon the occurrence of certain events. The rights are not transferable apart from the common stock until a person or group has acquired 20 percent or more, or makes a tender offer for 20 percent or more, of the common stock in which case each right will entitle the holder (other than the acquiror) to receive, upon exercise, common stock of either the Company or the acquiring company having a market value equal to two times the exercise price of the right. The initial exercise price is $240 per right. The rights are redeemable by the Board at any time prior to the acquisition of 20 percent or more of the outstanding common stock. The rights expire on February 1, 2006. On May 31, 1998, there were 154.8 million rights issued and outstanding.

The Board of Directors has authorized the repurchase, from time to time, of common stock for our treasury, provided that the number of shares held in treasury shall not exceed 60.0 million.

Through private transactions in fiscal 1998 and 1997 that are a part of our stock repurchase program, we issued put options that entitle the holder to sell shares of our common stock to us, at a specified price, if the holder exercises the option. In 1998 and 1997, we issued put options for 6.8 million and 4.5 million shares for $12.7 million and $7.4 million in premiums paid to the Company, respectively. As of May 31, 1998, put options for 2.8 million shares remain outstanding at exercise prices ranging from $67.00 to $70.00 per share with exercise dates from June 1998 to December 1998.

STOCK PLANS

A total of 7,109,367 shares (including 5,290,430 shares for salary replacement options, 69,273 shares for restricted stock, and 173,537 shares for non-employee directors) are available for grant of options, restricted stock, or restricted stock units under our 1993, 1995 and 1996 stock plans through October 1, 1998, September 30, 2000, and September 30, 2001, respectively. Options may be granted at a price not less than 100 percent of the fair market value on the date of grant. Options now outstanding include some granted under the 1984, 1988 and 1990 option plans, under which no further rights may be granted. All options expire within 10 years and one month after the date of grant. The stock plans provide for full vesting of options upon completion of specified service periods, or in the event there is a change of control.

Stock subject to a restricted period and a purchase price, if any, as determined by the Compensation Committee of the

Board of Directors may be granted to key employees under the 1993 plan and the Executive Incentive Plan. Most of the employee restricted stock awards require the employee to deposit personally owned shares (on a one-for-one basis) with the Company during the restricted period. The 1996 plan allows non-employee directors to annually choose to receive either 500 shares of stock restricted for one year or 500 restricted stock units convertible to common stock after his or her term of service on the Board is completed. The 1990 plan also allowed grants of restricted stock to directors. In 1998, 1997 and 1996, grants of 128,466, 176,955 and 132,092 shares of restricted stock and units were made, with weighted average values at grant of $65.59, $59.29 and $54.32 per share, respectively. On May 31, 1998, a total of 467,896 restricted shares and units were outstanding.

The 1988 plan permitted the granting of performance units corresponding to stock options granted. The value of performance units was determined by return on equity and growth in earnings per share measured against preset goals over three-year performance periods. For seven years after a performance period holders may elect to receive the value of performance units (with interest) as an alternative to exercising corresponding stock options. On May 31, 1998, there were 936,875 outstanding options with corresponding performance unit accounts. The value of the outstanding options exceeds the value of the performance unit accounts.

The following table contains information on stock option activity:

29

	Options Exercisable	Weighted Average Exercise Price Per Share	Options Outstanding	Weighted Average Exercise Price Per Share
Balance at May 28, 1995	12,576,580	$33.37	21,974,796	$41.60
Granted			4,127,602	52.55
Exercised			(1,778,823)	25.87
Expired			(730,343)	49.40
Balance at May 26, 1996	11,315,131	37.70	23,593,232	44.46
Granted			3,973,277	59.33
Exercised			(2,335,956)	31.74
Expired			(429,898)	51.84
Balance at May 25, 1997	11,949,600	42.53	24,800,655	47.91
Granted			3,185,783	73.10
Exercised			(2,730,311)	31.92
Expired			(236,524)	52.51
Balance at May 31, 1998	**12,044,170**	**$47.63**	**25,019,603**	**$52.82**

The following table provides information regarding exercisable and outstanding options as of May 31, 1998.

Range of Exercise Price per Share	Options Exercisable	Weighted Average Exercise Price per Share	Options Outstanding	Weighted Average Exercise Price per Share	Weighted Average Remaining Contractual Life (years)
Under $40	2,751,418	$31.90	2,751,418	$31.90	1.67
$40–$50	2,622,387	46.60	5,181,816	45.82	5.14
$50–$60	6,165,398	53.78	11,259,079	53.26	5.83
$60–$70	504,967	63.60	3,797,213	63.93	8.62
Over $70	–	–	2,030,077	75.78	9.46
	12,044,170	$47.63	25,019,603	$52.82	5.95

Stock-based compensation expense related to restricted stock for 1998, 1997 and 1996 was $6.0 million, $4.8 million and $3.0 million, respectively, using the "intrinsic value-based method" of accounting for stock-based compensation plans. Effective with 1997, we adopted the disclosure requirements of SFAS No. 123, "Accounting for Stock-Based Compensation." SFAS No. 123 allows either a fair value based method or an intrinsic value-based method of accounting for such compensation plans. Had compensation expense for our stock option plan grants been determined using the fair value based method, net earnings, basic earnings per share and diluted earnings per share would have been approximately $406.1 million, $2.57 and $2.52, respectively, for 1998; $435.2 million, $2.75 and $2.71, respectively, for 1997; and $470.3 million, $2.96 and $2.92, respectively, for 1996. These pro forma amounts are not likely to be representative of the difference between the two methods in future years, because many of our options require service over periods longer than three years for full vesting. The weighted average fair values at grant date of the options granted in 1998, 1997 and 1996 were estimated as $16.59, $11.76 and $9.39, respectively, using the Black-Scholes option-pricing model with the following weighted average assumptions:

	1998	1997	1996
Risk-free interest rate	6.1%	6.5%	6.1%
Expected life	7 years	7 years	7 years
Expected volatility	18%	18%	18%
Expected dividend growth rate	8%	8%	8%

The Black-Scholes model requires the input of highly subjective assumptions and may not necessarily provide a reliable measure of fair value.

 EARNINGS PER SHARE

Basic and diluted earnings per share (EPS) were calculated using the following:

	Fiscal Year		
In Millions	**1998**	1997	1996
Net Earnings	**$421.8**	$445.4	$476.4
Average number of common shares – basic EPS	**158.1**	158.2	158.9
Incremental share effect from: Stock options	**4.1**	3.4	3.1
Restricted stock, stock rights and puts	**.1**	–	–
Average number of common shares – diluted EPS	**162.3**	161.6	162.0

 INTEREST EXPENSE

The components of net interest expense are as follows:

	Fiscal Year		
In Millions	**1998**	1997	1996
Interest expense	**$130.3**	$115.7	$117.2
Capitalized interest	**(.7)**	(1.1)	(.6)
Interest income	**(12.4)**	(14.1)	(15.2)
Interest expense, net	**$117.2**	$100.5	$101.4

During 1998, 1997 and 1996, we paid interest (net of amount capitalized) of $117.2 million, $103.6 million and $103.8 million, respectively.

 RETIREMENT PLANS

We have defined-benefit plans covering most employees. Benefits for salaried employees are based on length of service and final average compensation. The hourly plans include various monthly amounts for each year of credited service. Our funding policy is consistent with the funding requirements of federal law. Our principal plan covering salaried employees has a provision that any excess pension assets would vest in plan participants if the plan is terminated within five years of a change in control. Plan assets consist principally of listed equity securities, corporate obligations and U.S. government securities.

30

Components of net pension income are as follows:

Expense (Income) in Millions	Fiscal Year		
	1998	1997	1996
Service cost – benefits earned	**$ 14.7**	$ 14.3	$ 14.1
Interest cost on projected benefit obligation	**62.4**	59.0	56.7
Actual return on plan assets	**(230.2)**	(168.7)	(162.3)
Net amortization and deferral	**107.0**	59.2	61.4
Curtailment loss and special termination benefits expense	**6.1**	–	–
Net pension income	**$ (40.0)**	$ (36.2)	$ (30.1)

The curtailment loss and special termination benefits expense of $6.1 million was recorded in fiscal 1998 as part of the restructuring charge described in Note Three.

The weighted-average discount rate and rate of increase in future compensation levels used in determining the actuarial present value of the benefit obligations were 7.0% and 4.4% in 1998, and 8.3% and 4.4% in 1997, respectively. The expected long-term rate of return on assets was 10.4%.

The funded status of the plans and the amount recognized on the consolidated balance sheets (determined as of May 31, 1998 and 1997) are as follows:

In Millions	May 31, 1998		May 25, 1997	
	Assets Exceed Accumulated Benefits	**Accumulated Benefits Exceed Assets**	Assets Exceed Accumulated Benefits	Accumulated Benefits Exceed Assets
Actuarial present value of benefit obligations:				
Vested benefits	**$ 807.6**	**$ 25.7**	$ 668.0	$ 20.2
Nonvested benefits	**52.4**	**1.1**	41.9	.8
Accumulated benefit obligations	**860.0**	**26.8**	709.9	21.0
Projected benefit obligation	**921.7**	**29.8**	751.3	22.4
Plan assets at fair value	**1,384.6**	**–**	1,184.1	–
Plan assets in excess of (less than) the projected benefit obligation	**462.9**	**(29.8)**	432.8	(22.4)
Unrecognized prior service cost	**34.1**	**1.8**	39.3	2.2
Unrecognized net loss	**39.1**	**12.1**	10.8	5.8
Recognition minimum liability	**–**	**(13.3)**	–	(10.0)
Unrecognized transition (asset) liability	**(64.3)**	**2.4**	(80.4)	3.4
Prepaid (accrued) pension cost	**$ 471.8**	**$(26.8)**	$ 402.5	$(21.0)

The General Mills Savings Plan is a defined contribution plan that covers our salaried and non-union employees. It had net assets of $876.2 million at May 31, 1998 and $768.2 million at May 25, 1997. This plan is a 401(k) savings plan that includes several investment funds and an Employee Stock Ownership Plan (ESOP). The ESOP's only assets are Company common stock and temporary cash balances. Expense recognized in 1998, 1997 and 1996 was $4.9 million, $3.2 million and $6.9 million, respectively. The ESOP's share of this expense was $4.5 million, $2.7 million and $6.6 million, respectively. The ESOP's expense is calculated by the "shares allocated" method.

The ESOP uses Company common stock to convey benefits to employees and, through increased stock ownership, to further align employee interests with those of shareholders. The Company matches a percentage of employee contributions with a base match plus a variable year-end match that depends on annual results. Employees receive the Company match in the form of common stock.

The ESOP originally purchased Company common stock principally with funds borrowed from third parties (and guaranteed by the Company). The ESOP shares are included in net shares outstanding for the purposes of calculating earnings per share. The ESOP's third-party debt is described in Note Nine.

The Company treats cash dividends paid to the ESOP the same as other dividends. Dividends received on leveraged shares (i.e., all shares originally purchased with the debt proceeds) are used for debt service, while dividends received on unleveraged shares are passed through to participants.

The Company's cash contribution to the ESOP is calculated so as to pay off enough debt to release sufficient shares to make the Company match. The ESOP uses the Company's cash contributions to the plan, plus the dividends received on the ESOP's leveraged shares, to make principal and interest payments on the ESOP's debt. As loan payments are made, shares become unencumbered by debt and committed to be allocated. The ESOP allocates shares to individual employee accounts on the basis of the match of employee payroll savings (contributions), plus reinvested dividends received on previously allocated shares. In 1998, 1997 and 1996, the ESOP incurred interest expense of $5.3 million, $5.7 million and $6.3 million, respectively. The ESOP used dividends of $9.4 million, $8.1 million and $9.1 million, along with Company contributions of $4.4 million, $2.7 million and $6.7 million to make interest and principal payments in the respective years.

The number of shares of Company common stock in the ESOP are summarized as follows:

Number of Shares	May 31, 1998	May 25, 1997
Unreleased shares	**1,873,000**	2,164,000
Committed to be allocated	**19,000**	29,000
Allocated to participants	**2,329,000**	2,185,000
Total shares	**4,221,000**	4,378,000

31

15 OTHER POSTRETIREMENT BENEFITS

We sponsor plans that provide health care benefits to the majority of our retirees. The salaried plan is contributory, with retiree contributions based on years of service.

We fund related trusts for certain employees and retirees on an annual basis. In 1998, 1997 and 1996 we contributed $9.8 million, $8.1 million and $14.0 million, respectively. Trust assets consist principally of listed equity securities and U.S. government securities.

Components of the postretirement health care expense are as follows:

	Fiscal Year		
Expense (Income) in Millions	**1998**	1997	1996
Service cost – benefits earned	**$ 4.5**	$ 4.6	$ 4.9
Interest cost on accumulated benefit obligation	**14.4**	14.2	14.2
Actual return on plan assets	**(34.0)**	(27.4)	(18.7)
Net amortization and deferral	**15.8**	12.2	6.9
Curtailment loss	**4.3**	–	–
Net postretirement expense	**$ 5.0**	$ 3.6	$ 7.3

The curtailment loss of $4.3 million was recorded in fiscal 1998 as part of the restructuring charge described in Note Three.

The funded status of the plans and the amount recognized on our consolidated balance sheets are as follows:

	May 31, 1998		May 25, 1997	
In Millions	**Assets Exceed Accumulated Benefits**	**Accumulated Benefits Exceed Assets**	Assets Exceed Accumulated Benefits	Accumulated Benefits Exceed Assets
Accumulated benefit obligations:				
Retirees	**$ 51.6**	**$ 61.8**	$ 40.4	$ 54.8
Fully eligible active employees	**13.4**	**11.6**	13.8	6.1
Other active employees	**40.5**	**42.7**	33.2	34.0
Accumulated benefit obligations	**105.5**	**116.1**	87.4	94.9
Plan assets at fair value	**169.8**	**24.9**	142.9	18.2
Plan assets in excess of (less than) accumulated benefit obligations	**64.3**	**(91.2)**	55.5	(76.7)
Unrecognized prior service credits	**–**	**(9.3)**	–	(11.5)
Unrecognized net (gain) loss	**(13.5)**	**26.3**	(6.1)	12.2
Prepaid (accrued) post-retirement benefits	**$ 50.8**	**$ (74.2)**	$ 49.4	$(76.0)

The discount rates used in determining the actuarial present value of the benefit obligations were 7.0% and 8.3% in 1998 and 1997, respectively. The expected long-term rate of return on assets was 10%.

The assumed health care cost trend-rate increase in the per capita charges for benefits ranged from 5.4% to 8.1% for 1999 depending on the medical service category. The rates gradually decrease to a range of 4.4% to 5.7% for 2007 and remain at that level thereafter. If the health care cost trend rate were to increase by one percentage point in each future year, the aggregate of the service and interest cost components of postretirement expense would increase for 1998 by $2.8 million and the accumulated benefit obligation as of May 31, 1998 would increase by $27.2 million.

16 PROFIT-SHARING PLAN

The Executive Incentive Plan provides incentives to key individuals who have the greatest potential to contribute to current earnings and successful future operations. These awards are approved by the Board of Directors Compensation Committee, which consists solely of outside directors, and they depend on profit performance in relation to pre-established goals approved by the Committee. Profit-sharing expense was $6.7 million, $4.5 million and $7.0 million in 1998, 1997 and 1996, respectively.

17 INCOME TAXES

The components of earnings before income taxes and earnings (losses) of joint ventures and the income taxes thereon are as follows:

	Fiscal Year		
In Millions	**1998**	1997	1996
Earnings before income taxes:			
U.S.	**$688.1**	$698.5	$744.0
Foreign	**(21.5)**	11.5	14.6
Total earnings before income taxes	**$666.6**	$710.0	$758.6
Income taxes:			
Current:			
Federal	**$242.8**	$208.2	$206.5
State and local	**31.0**	25.7	28.5
Foreign	**(2.6)**	3.5	2.0
Total current	**271.2**	237.4	237.0
Deferred:			
Federal	**(17.1)**	17.1	33.7
State and local	**(3.3)**	3.9	7.1
Foreign	**(8.9)**	(.1)	1.6
Total deferred	**(29.3)**	20.9	42.4
Total income taxes	**$241.9**	$258.3	$279.4

During 1998 and 1997, net income tax benefits of $36.0 million and $28.0 million, respectively, were allocated to stockholders' equity. These benefits were attributable to the exercise of employee stock options, dividends paid on unallocated ESOP shares, translation adjustments and unrealized gain on marketable securities.

32

During 1998, 1997 and 1996, we paid income taxes of $185.6 million, $230.3 million and $194.0 million, respectively.

In prior years we purchased certain income-tax items from other companies through tax lease transactions. Total current income taxes charged to earnings reflect the amounts attributable to operations and have not been materially affected by these tax leases. Actual current taxes payable relating to 1998, 1997 and 1996 operations were increased by approximately $16 million, $16 million and $15 million, respectively, due to the current effect of tax leases. These tax payments do not affect taxes for statement of earnings purposes since they repay tax benefits realized in prior years. The repayment liability is classified as "deferred income taxes – tax leases."

The following table reconciles the U.S. statutory income tax rate with the effective income tax rate:

In Millions	Fiscal Year		
	1998	1997	1996
U.S. statutory rate	**35.0%**	35.0%	35.0%
State and local income taxes, net of federal tax benefits	**2.7**	2.7	3.0
Other, net	**(1.4)**	(1.3)	(1.2)
Effective income tax rate	**36.3%**	36.4%	36.8%

The tax effects of temporary differences that give rise to deferred tax assets and liabilities are as follows:

In Millions	**May 31, 1998**	May 25, 1997
Accrued liabilities	**$112.5**	$ 90.5
Unusual charges	**18.2**	6.6
Compensation and employee benefits	**58.2**	50.7
Disposition liabilities	**9.2**	11.3
Foreign tax loss carryforward	**4.1**	8.6
Other	**14.3**	25.7
Gross deferred tax assets	**216.5**	193.4
Depreciation	**122.5**	127.7
Prepaid pension asset	**185.3**	166.5
Intangible assets	**1.8**	10.2
Other	**44.5**	42.2
Gross deferred tax liabilities	**354.1**	346.6
Valuation allowance	**10.3**	11.2
Net deferred tax liability	**$147.9**	$164.4

As of May 31, 1998, we have a foreign operating loss carryover for tax purposes of $9.2 million, which will expire in 2001 if not offset against future taxable income.

We have not recognized a deferred tax liability for unremitted earnings of $69.7 million for our foreign operations because we do not expect those earnings to become taxable to us in the foreseeable future. A determination of the potential liability is not practicable. If a portion were to be remitted, we believe income tax credits would substantially offset any resulting tax liability.

 LEASES AND OTHER COMMITMENTS

An analysis of rent expense by property leased follows:

In Millions	Fiscal Year		
	1998	1997	1996
Warehouse space	**$20.9**	$17.6	$14.9
Equipment	**8.2**	7.1	7.3
Other	**5.8**	4.8	3.3
Total rent expense	**$34.9**	$29.5	$25.5

Some leases require payment of property taxes, insurance and maintenance costs in addition to the rent payments. Contingent and escalation rent in excess of minimum rent payments and sublease income netted in rent expense were insignificant.

Noncancelable future lease commitments are (in millions) $29.9 in 1999, $28.9 in 2000, $27.0 in 2001, $16.8 in 2002, $7.0 in 2003 and $4.5 after 2003, with a cumulative total of $114.1.

We are contingently liable under guaranties and comfort letters for $48.3 million. The guaranties and comfort letters are principally issued to support borrowing arrangements, primarily for our joint ventures. We remain the guarantor on certain leases and other obligations of Darden Restaurants, Inc. (Darden), an entity we spun-off as of May 28, 1995. However, Darden has indemnified us against any loss.

 GEOGRAPHIC INFORMATION

In Millions	U.S.A.	Foreign	Unallocated Corporate Items[a]	Consolidated Total
Sales				
1998	**$5,793.9**	**$239.1**	**$ –**	**$6,033.0**
1997	5,376.4	232.9	–	5,609.3
1996	5,204.5	211.5	–	5,416.0
Operating Profits				
1998	**842.7**[b]	**(22.6)**[b]	**(153.5)**[b]	**666.6**
1997	806.4[c]	24.1	(120.5)	710.0
1996	862.7	24.0	(128.1)	758.6
Identifiable Assets				
1998	**3,095.6**	**254.3**	**511.5**	**3,861.4**
1997	3,106.8	306.5	489.1	3,902.4
1996	2,509.1	293.2	492.4	3,294.7

(a) Corporate expenses reported here include net interest expense and general corporate expenses.
(b) U.S.A., Foreign and Corporate operating profits are net of charges of $113.6 million, $49.3 million and $3.5 million, respectively, for the unusual items described in Note Three.
(c) U.S.A. operating profits are net of a $48.4 million charge for the unusual item described in Note Three.

The foreign sales reflected above were made primarily by our Canadian subsidiary. Our proportionate share of the joint ventures' sales (not shown above) was $780.7 million, $728.2 million and $705.7 million for 1998, 1997 and 1996, respectively. The foreign operating profits above also exclude our share of the results from the joint ventures. See Note Four.

33

20 **QUARTERLY DATA (UNAUDITED)**

Summarized quarterly data for 1998 and 1997 follows:

In Millions, Except per Share and Market Price Amounts	First Quarter		Second Quarter		Third Quarter		Fourth Quarter		Total Year	
	1998	1997	**1998**	1997	**1998**	1997	**1998**	1997	**1998**	1997
Sales	**$1,416.5**	$1,315.6	**$1,638.3**	$1,560.1	**$1,424.7**	$1,289.6	**$1,553.5**	$1,444.0	**$6,033.0**	$5,609.3
Gross profit (a)	**872.6**	779.8	**984.6**	900.7	**872.3**	741.3	**914.2**	859.1	**3,643.7**	3,280.9
Net earnings	**134.3**(b)	97.7(c)	**64.6**(b)	156.7	**131.1**	122.8	**91.8**(d)	68.2(d)	**421.8**	445.4
Net earnings per share	**.84**	.62	**.41**	1.00	**.83**	.78	**.59**	.42	**2.67**	2.82
Net earnings per share-assuming dilution	**.82**	.61	**.40**	.98	**.81**	.76	**.57**	.41	**2.60**	2.76
Dividends per share	**.53**	.50	**.53**	.50	**.53**	.50	**.53**	.53	**2.12**	2.03
Market price of common stock:										
High	**71 1/2**	58 1/4	**75 7/16**	60 5/8	**78 1/4**	68 3/4	**76 1/16**	67 3/4	**78 1/4**	68 3/4
Low	**60**	52	**63 3/8**	54 3/8	**69 9/16**	60 7/8	**66 7/16**	57 3/4	**60**	52

(a) Before charges for depreciation.

(b) Includes an after tax loss of $.1 million in the first quarter and $100.1 million ($.63 per share) in the second quarter for unusual items described in Note Three.

(c) Includes an after-tax loss of $29.2 million ($.18 per share) in the first quarter related to the adoption of SFAS No. 121.

(d) The earnings impacts of LIFO reserve adjustments were not material to any quarter except the fourth quarter of 1997, when an after-tax credit of $7.2 million ($.05 per share) was recorded.

ELEVEN-YEAR FINANCIAL SUMMARY

In Millions, Except per Share Data	May 31, 1998	May 25, 1997	May 26, 1996	May 28, 1995	May 29, 1994	May 30, 1993	May 31, 1992	May 26, 1991	May 27, 1990	May 28, 1989	May 29, 1988
Financial Results											
Net earnings per share[a]	$2.67	$2.82	$3.00	$2.33	$2.95	$3.10	$2.99	$2.87	$2.32	$2.53	$1.63
Net earnings per share – assuming dilution[a]	2.60	2.76	2.94	2.29	2.91	3.04	2.93	2.83	2.29	2.50	1.61
Continuing operations earnings per share[a]	2.67	2.82	3.00	1.64	2.14	2.52	2.39	2.26	1.71	1.42	1.22
Continuing operations earnings per share – assuming dilution[a]	2.60	2.76	2.94	1.62	2.11	2.47	2.34	2.23	1.69	1.41	1.21
Return on average equity	123.2%	111.0%	212.3%	52.0%	37.7%	39.1%	39.9%	49.2%	49.5%	60.0%	41.1%
Dividends per share[a]	2.12	2.03	1.91	1.88	1.88	1.68	1.48	1.28	1.10	.94	.80
Sales	6,033	5,609	5,416	5,027	5,327	5,138	4,964	4,657	4,242	3,703	3,323
Costs and expenses:											
Cost of sales	2,389	2,328	2,241	2,123	2,012	2,003	1,967	1,819	1,817	1,665	1,451
Selling, general and administrative	2,499	2,239	2,128	2,008	2,351	2,191	2,126	2,075	1,819	1,546	1,413
Depreciation and amortization	195	183	187	192	174	153	143	134	112	97	84
Interest, net	117	101	101	101	79	56	45	51	24	15	24
Unusual expenses (income)	166	48	–	183	147	36	(12)	(48)	–	(4)	(8)
Total costs and expenses	5,366	4,899	4,657	4,607	4,763	4,439	4,269	4,031	3,772	3,319	2,964
Earnings from continuing operations before taxes and earnings (losses) of joint ventures	667	710	759	420	564	699	695	626	470	384	359
Income taxes	242	259	280	153	217	276	283	245	184	151	146
Earnings (losses) of joint ventures	(3)	(6)	(3)	(7)	(7)	(12)	(16)	(9)	(4)	–	–
Earnings from continuing operations	422	445	476	260	340	411	396	372	282	233	213
Discontinued operations after taxes	–	–	–	107	134	95	100	101	99	251	70
Accounting changes	–	–	–	–	(4)	–	–	–	–	(70)	–
Net earnings	422	445	476	367	470	506	496	473	381	414	283
Earnings from continuing operations as a percent of sales	7.0%	7.9%	8.8%	5.2%	6.4%	8.0%	8.0%	8.0%	6.6%	6.3%	6.4%
Average common shares outstanding[a]:											
Basic	158	158	159	158	159	163	166	165	164	164	174
Diluted	162	162	162	160	162	166	169	167	166	165	176
Taxes (income, payroll, property, etc.) per share[a]	1.93	2.00	2.11	1.30	1.68	1.98	2.08	1.86	1.51	1.30	1.19
Financial Position											
Total assets	3,861	3,902	3,295	3,358	4,804	4,310	3,997	3,561	2,990	2,648	2,422
Land, buildings and equipment, net	1,186	1,279	1,312	1,457	1,503	1,463	1,398	1,168	1,048	876	747
Working capital at year end	(408)	(281)	(197)	(324)	(630)	(386)	(238)	(142)	(214)	(242)	(426)
Long-term debt, excluding current portion	1,640	1,530	1,221	1,401	1,413	1,264	916	875	685	532	357
Stockholders' equity	190	495	308	141	1,151	1,219	1,371	1,114	810	732	649
Stockholders' equity per share[a]	1.23	3.09	1.94	.89	7.26	7.59	8.28	6.74	4.96	4.54	3.88
Other Statistics											
Total dividends	336	321	304	297	299	275	245	211	181	154	139
Gross capital expenditures	184	163	129	157	213	317	396	279	292	248	181
Research and development	66	61	60	60	59	56	55	52	45	42	41
Advertising media expenditures	366	306	320	324	292	283	309	314	296	252	254
Wages, salaries and employee benefits	608	564	541	538	558	556	598	633	579	491	461
Number of employees (actual)	10,228	10,200	9,790	9,882	10,616	10,577	12,195	12,521	12,787	12,491	12,722
Accumulated LIFO reserve	39	48	56	53	43	47	50	54	56	52	36
Common stock price range[a][b]:											
High	78 1/4	68 3/4	60 1/2	63 3/4	68 3/4	74 1/8	75 7/8	60 7/8	39 5/8	33 7/8	31
Low	60	52	50	49 3/8	49 7/8	62	54 1/4	37 7/8	31 3/8	22 3/8	20 3/8
Close	68 1/4	64 1/4	58 1/4	60 5/8	54 1/2	65 1/4	63 1/2	58	39	33 3/4	22 7/8

(a) Years prior to 1991 have been adjusted for the two-for-one stock split in November 1990.

(b) Prices shown prior to 1996 are before the spin-off of our former restaurant operations. The closing prices on May 26, 1995 of the two common stocks on a when-issued basis were $49 7/8 for General Mills and $10 7/8 for Darden Restaurants.

Note: Excluding return on equity, amounts presented in this summary have been restated to a continuing operations basis.

35

Glossary

Parentheses indicate page references.

Accelerated depreciation method Records the highest depreciation in the first year of an asset's service life and lower depreciation in subsequent years (747)

Accounting cycle Steps that a company completes during each accounting period to record, retain, and report the monetary information from its transactions (937)

Accounting equation Assets = Liabilities + Owner's Equity (124, 203)

Accounting period Time span for which a company reports its revenues and expenses (132)

Accounting system Process used to identify, measure, record, and retain information about a company's activities so that the company can prepare its financial statements (122)

Accounts Documents used to record and retain the monetary information from a company's transactions (934)

Accounts payable Amounts owed to suppliers for credit purchases (123, 286)

Accounts payable management Setting and following policies for authorizing and making purchases and for processing credit purchases (418)

Accounts payable subsidiary ledger Contains the individual accounts of all the suppliers that sell to the company on credit (461)

Accounts receivable Amounts owed by customers to the company (123, 279)

Accounts receivable management Setting and following policies for granting credit and processing credit sales (418)

Accounts receivable subsidiary ledger Contains the individual accounts of all the customers that purchase from the company on credit (420)

Accounts receivable turnover Net credit sales divided by average accounts receivable (218)

Accrual accounting Recording revenues and related expense transactions in the same accounting period that goods or services are provided, regardless of when cash is received or paid (134, 245)

Accrued expense Incurred by a company during the accounting period but not paid or recorded (947)

Accrued liabilities Short-term obligations (other than accounts payable) that a company owes at the end of an accounting period and that result from the company's operating activities during the period (468)

Accrued revenue Earned by a company during the accounting period but neither collected nor recorded (948)

Accumulated depreciation Total amount of depreciation expense recorded over the life of an asset to date (206, 741)

Activity pool Grouping of related activities involving factory overhead (629)

Activity-based costing (ABC) System which allocates factory overhead to units of product; first allocates factory overhead costs to activity pools, then assigns costs in each activity pool to jobs based on the relative number of activities needed to complete the jobs, and finally assigns the total factory overhead costs allocated to each job equally to the individual units of product in the job (629)

Additional paid-in capital Difference between the selling price and the par value in each stock transaction (313, 880)

Adjusted trial balance Schedule prepared to prove the equality of the debit and credit balances in a company's general ledger accounts after it has made the adjusting entries (949)

Adjusting entries Journal entries that a company makes at the end of its accounting period to bring the company's revenue and expense account balances up-to-date and to show the correct ending balances in its asset and liability accounts (177, 945)

Agent Person who has the authority to act for another (304)

Aging method Estimates the amount of bad debts based on the age of the individual amounts included in the ending balance of accounts receivable (430)

Amortization expense Portion of the acquisition cost of an intangible asset that a company allocates as an expense to each accounting period over the asset's service life (769, 773)

Amount (single future) One-time future cash flow (713)

Annual report Document that includes a company's income statement, balance sheet, and cash flow statement, along with other related financial accounting information (20, 316, 928)

Annuity Series of equal periodic future cash flows (714)

Appraisal costs Costs of catching product defects inside the company (620)

Articles of incorporation State-approved documents required to obtain permission to act as a corporation (307)

Assets A company's economic resources that it expects will provide future benefits to the company (19,122, 204)

Assets of a pension plan Assets that will be used to pay retirement benefits and are under the control of the funding agency (822)

Attribute listing Listing the characteristics of an object or idea to gain insights into its possible usefulness (35)

Auditing Examination of a company's accounting records and financial statements by an independent certified public accountant (317, 928)

Audit report Report issued by an auditor stating that an audit was performed for a company which expresses an opinion as to how well the company's financial statements comply with GAAP (317)

Authorized capital stock Number of shares of capital stock that a corporation may legally issue (882)

Available-for-sale securities Investments in common stocks where the investor does not have significant influence over the investee or bonds that the investor does not expect to hold until their maturity date (844)

Average cost flow assumption Allocates the average cost per unit for the period to both the ending inventory and the cost of goods sold (662)

Average cost method Assigns the total costs of direct materials and conversion separately to products at the average costs per equivalent unit by adding the amount of each type of cost in the beginning inventory to the amount of that cost type incurred during the month (561)

Average rate of return on investment Average return on the investment per year, per dollar invested for a capital expenditure proposal (720)

Avoidable costs Costs that must be incurred to perform an activity at a given level, but that can be avoided if that activity is reduced or discontinued (508)

Back-flush costing System of costing where a company records its product costs directly in cost of goods sold and then "backs out" the costs of the finished goods still on hand at the end of an accounting period (623)

Bad debts expense Expense that represents the estimated cost, for the accounting period, of the eventual noncollection of accounts receivable (426)

Balance of an account Difference between the total increases and the total decreases recorded in the account (935)

Balance sheet Accounting report that summarizes a company's financial position (assets, liabilities, and owner's equity) on a given date (19, 203)

Bank reconciliation Schedule used to analyze the difference between the ending cash balance in a company's accounting records and the ending cash balance reported by the bank on the company's bank statement (272)

Bank statement Statement which summarizes a company's banking activities during the month (272)

Basic earnings per share Corporation's net income per share available to its common stockholders (896)

Board of directors Group of individuals that has the responsibility and authority to supervise a corporation's ordinary business activities, make future plans, and take whatever action is necessary in managing the corporation (879)

Bond certificate Serially numbered legal document that specifies the face value, the annual interest rate, and the maturity date (799)

Bond Type of note in which a company agrees to pay the holder the face value on the maturity date and to pay interest on the face value periodically at a specified rate (799, 842)

Book value Asset's original cost minus the related accumulated depreciation (206, 741, 798)

Brainstorming Process where members of a group try to generate as many solutions as possible to a particular problem (34)

Break-even point Unit sales volume at which a company earns zero profit (69)

Budget Report that gives a financial description of one part of a company's planned activity (86)

Budgeting Process of quantifying manager's plans and showing the impact of these plans on a company's operating activities (15, 86)

Business plan Describes a company's goals and its plans for achieving those goals (56)

Callable bonds Have a provision that allows the issuer to purchase them (809)

Callable preferred stock Corporation claims the right to recall (or retire) at its option (884)

Capital Funds a company uses to operate or expand its operations (6, 60)

Capital expenditure Cost that increases the benefits a company will obtain from an asset (751)

Capital expenditure decision Long-term decision in which a company determines whether or not to make an investment at the time of the decision in order to obtain future net cash receipts totaling more than the investment (706)

Capital expenditures budget Set of schedules that shows the effects that each new project to be undertaken is expected to have on the other master budget schedules (385)

Capital lease Transfers the risks and benefits of ownership from the lessor to the lessee (814)

Capital rationing Occurs when a company cannot obtain sufficient cash to make all of the investments that it would like to make, and thus must choose in which of the acceptable proposals to invest (722)

Capital stock Units of ownership in a corporation that are given to owners in exchange for capital (312, 879)

Carrying costs Costs per unit of keeping an inventory item on hand (511)

Cash Money on hand, deposits in checking and savings accounts, and checks and credit card invoices that a company has received from its customers but not yet deposited (269)

Cash balance management Setting and following policies for maintaining an optimal amount of cash (418)

Cash budget Budget showing a company's expected cash receipts and payments and how they affect the company's cash balance (100)

Cash discount Percentage reduction of the invoice price if the customer pays the invoice within a specified period (170)

Cash equivalents Investments that are short-term, are highly liquid, and involve very little risk (446)

Cash flow return Company's cash flows divided by the dollar amount of its assets or owner's equity (250)

Cash flow statement Accounting report that summarizes a company's cash receipts, cash payments, and net change in cash for a specific time period (19, 234)

Cash payments management Setting and following policies for paying for cash or credit purchases and processing cash payments (418)

Cash receipts management Setting and following policies for collecting cash from credit or cash sales (418)

Certified public accountant Public accountant who has met the requirements of the state and who holds a license to practice accounting (927)

Chart of accounts Numbering system designed to organize a company's accounts efficiently and to reduce errors in the recording and accumulating process (942)

Classified balance sheet Balance sheet which shows subtotals for assets, liabilities, and owner's equity in related groupings (204)

Closely-held corporation Corporation owned by a small number of investors (307)

Closing entries Entries made by a company at the end of an accounting period to create a zero balance in each revenue, expense, and withdrawals T-account, and to update the owner's equity by transferring the balances in the revenue, expense, and withdrawals T-accounts to the T-account for owner's capital (184, 954)

Common stock Ownership unit of a corporation (312, 842, 880)

Comparative financial statements Financial statements from previous years included in a company's annual report to help external users in their analyses (316)

Compensatory stock options Options to buy stock; intended to provide additional compensation to employees (889)

Complex capital structure Structure of a corporation that has issued stock options and convertible securities (898)

Compound interest Interest that accrues on both the principal and the past (unpaid) interest (712)

Conceptual framework Set of concepts that provides a logical structure for financial accounting and reporting (310)

Conservatism principle Holds that a company should apply GAAP in such a way that there is little chance that it will overstate assets or income (674)

Consolidated financial statements Combined financial statements of the parent company and all other companies over which it has control (856)

Contingency Existing condition that will lead to a gain or loss if a future event occurs (479)

Contra account Account that has the effect of reducing the balance in another account (425)

Contract rate Rate at which the issuer of a bond pays interest on the face value each period until the maturity date (799)

Contributed capital Total investments made by stockholders in the corporation (312)

Contribution margin per unit Difference between the sales revenue per unit and the variable costs per unit (70)

Control account General ledger account that takes the place of the individual accounts in the subsidiary ledger (420, 461)

Control over investee More than 50% ownership of the common stock of another company (842)

Controller High-level management accountant who coordinates a company's internal (management) accounting activities and the preparation of its financial reports (926)

Conversion costs Direct labor and factory overhead costs necessary to convert raw materials into a finished product (555)

Convertible preferred stock Exchangeable into common stock at the option of the individual stockholders (884)

Copyright Exclusive right granted by the U.S. government to publish or sell literary or artistic products for the life of the author plus an additional 70 years (770)

Corporation Company organized as a separate legal entity, or body (separate from its owners), according to the laws of a particular state (9, 305)

Cost accounting (Cost analysis) Process of determining and evaluating the costs of specific products or activities of a company (16, 538)

Cost of an asset All the costs a company incurs to acquire an asset and to get it ready for use (743)

Cost center Responsibility center in which the manager who is responsible for its activities can control only the level of costs it incurs (393)

Cost driver Activities on which a company bases activity pools (629)

Cost of capital Weighted average cost (rate of return) a company must pay to all sources of capital (710)

Cost of ending inventory Dollar amount of merchandise on hand, based on a physical count, at the end of the accounting period (176)

Cost of goods sold Major expense of a retail company consisting of the cost of the goods (merchandise) that it sells during the accounting period (173, 656)

Cost report Report showing a comparison between a company's budgeted and actual expenses for an accounting period (103)

Cost-volume-profit (C-V-P) analysis Shows how profit is affected by changes in sales volume, selling prices of products, and the various costs of a company (63)

Creative thinking Process of actively generating new ideas to discover solutions to a problem (33)

Credit entry Monetary amount recorded (credited) on the right side of an account (934, 935)

Credit memo Business document that lists the information for a sales return or allowance (172)

Creditors External parties to whom a company owes debts (123)

Creditors' equity Claims by creditors against the assets of a company (123)

Critical thinking Process that evaluates the ideas generated by creative thinking (35)

Cumulative preferred stock Must receive all dividends of current period and the accumulated unpaid dividends of past periods before any common stockholders receive any dividends (902)

Current assets Cash and other assets that a company expects to convert into cash, sell, or use up within one year (205)

Current liabilities Obligations that a company expects to pay within one year by using current assets (207)

Current ratio Current assets divided by current liabilities (209)

Date of declaration Date that a corporation's board of directors declares that a dividend will be paid to stockholders of record on a specified future date (900)

Date of payment Date that a corporation mails the dividend checks (900)

Date of record Only investors listed as stockholders of the corporation on this date can participate in dividends (900)

Debit entry Monetary amount recorded (debited) on the left side of an account (934, 935)

Debt capital Money that a company borrows from creditors (388)

Debt ratio Total liabilities divided by total assets (211)

Deductive logic Reasoning that moves from general to specific (38)

Deferred tax asset Account that a corporation uses to report on its balance sheet the amount by which its future income will be reduced by deductible temporary differences (820)

Deferred tax liability Account a corporation uses to report on its balance sheet the amount of its future additional income taxes resulting from taxable temporary differences (819)

Defined-benefit plan Pension plan that specifies the amount that a company must pay to its employees each year during their retirement (821)

Defined-contribution plan Specifies the amount that a company must contribute to a pension plan each year while its employees work (821)

Depletion expense Portion of the cost (less the estimated residual value) of a natural resource asset that a company allocates as an expense to each accounting period over the asset's service life (777)

Depreciable cost Cost of a physical asset less its residual value (744)

Depreciation expense Part of the cost of property, plant, and equipment (physical asset) that a company allocates as an expense to each accounting period in which the company uses the asset (141, 741)

Development Translation of research into a plan or design for a new or improved product or process (769)

Diluted earnings per share Includes the effects of all potential common shares that would reduce earnings per share (898)

Direct labor Labor of the employees who work with direct materials to convert or assemble them into a finished product (339)

Direct labor budget Schedule that shows the hours and the cost of the direct labor required to meet the budgeted production (380)

Direct labor efficiency variance Difference between the standard cost of the direct labor hours that a company should have used for the actual number of units produced and the standard cost of the direct labor hours that it did use to produce those units (588)

Direct labor price standard Current wage rate that a company should incur per hour for a specific type of direct labor employed in production (586)

Direct labor price variance Difference between the cost that a company should have incurred for the actual labor hours worked and the actual direct labor cost it did incur for the number of actual labor hours worked (587)

Direct labor quantity standard Amount of direct labor time that a company should use to produce one unit of product (587)

Direct materials Raw materials that physically become part of a manufactured product (339)

Direct materials price standard Cost that a company should incur to acquire one unit of a direct material for production (580)

Direct materials price variance Difference between the standard cost that a company should have incurred to acquire the direct materials and the actual cost it did incur to acquire the direct materials (582)

Direct materials quantity standard Amount of a direct material that a company should use to produce one unit of product (581)

Direct materials quantity variance Difference between the standard cost of the quantity of direct materials that a company should have used for the actual number of units produced and the standard cost of the quantity of direct materials that it did use to produce those units (583)

Direct materials purchases budget Schedule that shows the number of direct material units that must be purchased in each budget period to meet production and ending direct materials inventory requirements (378)

Direct method Subtracting the operating cash outflows from the operating cash inflows to determine the net cash provided by (or used in) operating activities on the cash flow statement (240, 681)

Discount rate Rate used to convert a future amount to a present value (714)

Distribution function Making products available to customers through physical distribution systems (309)

Dividend preference Right of preferred stockholders to receive a dividend before a corporation pays a dividend to common stockholders (901)

Dividends in arrears Accumulated unpaid dividends of past periods on cumulative preferred stock (902)

Double entry rule In the recording of a transaction, the total amount of the debit entries must be equal to the total amount of the credit entries for the transaction (935)

Double-declining-balance method Computes depreciation expense by multiplying the book value of an asset at the beginning of the period by twice the straight-line rate (747)

Double taxation Occurs when a corporation is taxed on its taxable income and then its stockholders are taxed on the dividends they receive from the corporation (306)

Drawing analogies Making connections among facts, ideas, or experiences that are normally considered separately (35)

Dual effect of transactions A company must make at least two changes in its assets, liabilities, or owner's equity when it records each transaction (124)

Earning process Purchasing (or producing) inventory, selling the inventory (or services), delivering the inventory (or services), and collecting and paying cash (133)

Earnings per share (EPS) Amount of net income earned for each share of common stock (315)

Effective interest method Computing annual interest expense by multiplying the annual yield by the book value of the bonds at the beginning of the year (807)

Enterprise resource planning (ERP) system Information system involving computer software that records and stores many different types of data in a data warehouse (309)

Entity concept Separation of accounting records of a company from the records of the company's owner or owners (120)

Entrepreneur Individual who is willing to risk the uncertainty of starting a company in exchange for the reward of earning a profit (and the personal reward of seeing the company succeed) (7)

Equity Claims by creditors and owner(s) against the assets of a company (123)

Equity capital Money that a corporation brings in through the sale of the corporation's own stock (388)

Equivalent units Physical products multiplied by their average percentage of completion (558)

Estimated residual value Cash a company estimates it will receive from the sale or disposal of an asset at the end of its estimated service life (743)

Estimated service life Life over which a company expects an asset to be useful (743)

Evaluating Management activity that measures a company's actual operations and progress against standards or benchmarks (13)

Exchange gain or loss Caused by a change in the exchange rate between the date that a company records a credit sale (purchase) and the date that the company collects (pays) the cash (434, 466)

Exchange rate Measures the value of one currency in terms of another currency (433)

Expected inflation rate Additional interest rate paid by the borrower to compensate for the expected inflation over the life of the borrowing (803)

Expenses Costs a company incurs to provide goods or services to its customers during an accounting period (18, 132)

External failure costs Costs to a company of flaws in products that reach the company's customers (620)

External users Individuals outside of a company who use the company's information for decision-making (11)

Extraordinary item Event or transaction that is unusual in nature and infrequent in occurrence (894)

Face value Stated value on a note (or bond) that must be paid on the maturity date (438, 799)

Factor (decimal fraction) Decimal amount in a present value table (713)

Factory overhead All items, other than direct materials and direct labor, that are necessary for the manufacture of a product (341)

Factory overhead budget Schedule showing estimates of all factory overhead costs and their related cash payments for each budget period (381)

Finance function Plans a company's capital requirements for both the short and the long term (309)

Financial accounting Identification, measurement, recording, accumulation, and communication of economic information about a company for external users to use in their various decisions (16)

Financial flexibility Company's ability to adapt to change (179, 211, 810)

Financial statements Accounting reports used to summarize and communicate financial information about a company (18)

Financing activities Obtaining capital from the owner and providing the owner with a return on investment, as well as obtaining capital from creditors and repaying the amounts borrowed (239)

Financing activities section Section of a company's cash flow statement (or cash budget) that shows the cash receipts and payments from its actual (or planned) financing activities (100, 239, 386)

Finished goods inventory Finished products that are ready to be sold (339)

First-in, first-out (FIFO) Earliest (first) costs incurred are included in cost of goods sold as the products are sold, leaving the latest costs incurred in ending inventory (659)

Fixed costs Costs that are constant in total and that are not affected by changes in volume (64)

Fixed overhead volume variance Difference between the amount of applied fixed overhead and the amount of budgeted fixed overhead (594)

Flexibility Spectrum of ideas generated (34)

Flexible budget Cost or expense budget that shows expected costs or expenses at various activity levels (394)

Flexible manufacturing system Computerized networks of automated equipment that use computer software to control such tasks as machine setups, direct materials and parts selection, and product assembly (625)

Fluency Measure of the number of ideas generated or solutions proposed by the problem solver (34)

FOB destination Selling company transfers ownership to the buyer at the place of delivery (after transit is completed) (657)

FOB shipping point Selling company transfers ownership to the buyer at the place of sale (shipping point), that is, before the inventory is in transit (657)

Franchise Agreement entered into by two parties where, for a fee, one party gives the other party rights to perform certain functions or sell certain products or services over the legal life of the franchise (771)

Functional causes of depreciation Limit the life of the asset, even though the physical life is not exhausted (742)

General accounting Duty of a management accountant to design and operate a company's integrated accounting system (927)

General and administrative expenses Operating expenses related to the general management of a company (177)

General and administrative expenses budget Budget showing the expenses and related cash payments associated with expected activities other than selling (98)

General journal Includes the following information about each transaction: the date of the transaction, the accounts to be debited and credited, the amounts of the debit and credit entries, and an explanation of each transaction (937)

General ledger Entire set of accounts for a company (165, 934)

Generally accepted accounting principles (GAAP) Currently accepted principles, procedures, and practices that are used for financial accounting in the United States (17)

Goal congruence Situation where department, division, or team goals support the company's goals (398)

Goods-in-process inventory Products that a company has started manufacturing but that are not yet complete (339)

Goodwill Difference between the total price a company paid to buy another company and the market value of the identifiable net assets it acquired (773)

Gross pay The amount of an employee's earnings before payroll taxes are deducted (472)

Gross profit Net sales minus cost of goods sold (174)

Gross profit method Used to estimate the cost of ending inventory by multiplying the net sales by the historic gross profit percentage and subtracting this amount from net sales to determine the estimated cost of goods sold, and then subtracting this amount from the cost of goods available for sale (677)

Gross profit percentage Gross profit divided by net sales (180)

High-low method Method that allows a decision-maker to quickly estimate the fixed and variable components of a mixed cost (348)

Historical cost concept Concept that a company records its transactions based on the dollars exchanged at the time the transaction occurred (122)

Holding gain (inventory profit) Artificial profit that results when a company records cost of goods sold at an historical cost that is lower than the replacement cost of the units sold (666)

Horizontal analysis Shows the changes in a company's operating results over time in percentages as well as in dollar amounts (321)

Human resources function Managing the company's employee-related activities, such as recruiting, hiring, training, and compensating employees, as well as providing a safe workplace (309)

Impairment Occurs when the expected future cash flows from an asset are less than the book value of that asset (752)

In transit A freight company is in the process of delivering inventory from the selling company to the buying company (656)

Income from continuing operations Reports a corporation's revenues and expenses that resulted from its ongoing operations (314)

Income statement Accounting report that summarizes the results of a company's operating activities for a specific time period (18)

Income summary account Temporary account used in the closing process to accumulate the amount of net income (or net loss) before transferring it to the T-account for owner's capital (184, 954)

Income tax expense Income taxes that a corporation must pay on its earnings (315)

Incorporation Process of filing the required documents and obtaining permission from a state to operate as a corporation (307)

Incremental costs Cost increases resulting from the performance of an additional activity (508)

Independent thinking In the process of evaluating ideas, relying on one's own conclusions rather than relying on the conclusions of others (35)

Indirect labor Labor that is not traceable to individual products (341)

Indirect materials Raw materials that are not traceable to individual products (341)

Indirect method Adjusting net income to compute net cash provided by operating activities on the cash flow statement (240, 683)

Inductive logic Reasoning that moves from the specific to the general (38)

Initial cost Expected cash payment to put a capital expenditure proposal into operation (707)

Initial public offering (IPO) Corporation's first sale of its common stock to the public, after which the stock begins to trade in a secondary market (307)

Intangible assets Company's long-term assets that do not have a physical substance (766)

Integrated accounting system Means by which accounting information about a company's activities is identified, measured, recorded, and retained so it can be communicated in an accounting report (11)

Intercompany analysis Comparing a company's performance with that of competing companies, industry averages, or averages in related industries (321)

Interest expense Cost to a company of borrowing money for a period (797)

Internal failure costs Costs of reworking defective products, replacement parts and materials, and time that the factory is "down" while employees trace and fix the cause of the defects (621)

Interim financial statements Financial statements prepared for a period of less than one year (320)

Internal control Procedures needed to safeguard a company's economic resources and to promote the efficient and effective operation of its accounting system (927)

Internal control structure Set of policies and procedures that directs how employees should perform a company's activities (268)

Internal users Managers within a company who use information about the company for decision-making (11)

Intracompany analysis Comparing a company's current operations and financial position with its past results or with its expected results (320)

Inventory Merchandise a retail company is holding for resale (173, 282, 654)

Inventory turnover Cost of goods sold divided by average inventory (217)

Investing activities Include lending money and collecting on loans, investing in other companies, and buying and selling property and equipment (239)

Investing activities section Section of a company's cash flow statement (or cash budget) that shows the cash receipts and payments from its actual (or planned) investing activities (100, 239, 386)

Investment center Responsibility center in which the manager has decision-making authority over costs, revenues, and the level of investment in property, plant, and equipment the center uses in its operations (393)

Investments portfolio All of a company's investments in securities of other companies (846)

ISO 9000 Set of quality standards set up by the International Organization for Standardization (619)

Issued capital stock Number of shares of capital stock that a corporation has legally issued to its stockholders as of the balance sheet date (882)

Job order Unique product or group of products being manufactured (543)

Job order cost accounting Keeps track of the costs applied to each job order (544)

Joint ownership Characteristic of a partnership that all partners jointly own all the assets of the partnership (304)

Journal entry Recorded information for each transaction (937)

Journalizing Process of recording a transaction in a company's general journal (937)

Just-in-time strategies Reducing or eliminating inventories, streamlining the factory and increasing operational efficiencies, and controlling quality (622)

Large stock dividend Stock dividend greater than 20% of the previously outstanding common shares (904)

Last-in, first-out (LIFO) Latest costs incurred before a sale are included in cost of goods sold and the earliest costs incurred are included in ending inventory (660)

Lease Agreement giving the right to use property, plant, or equipment without transferring legal ownership of the item (814)

Legal capital Amount of stockholder's equity of a corporation that it cannot distribute to stockholders (312, 879)

Lessee Company that acquires the right to use a leased item (814)

Lessor Company that gives up the use of a leased item (814)

Letter of credit Letter written by a customer's bank ensuring that payment to the selling company will occur when that company presents the bank with documents that show that it has met the conditions of the sale (423)

Leverage Use of borrowing by a corporation to increase the return to common stockholders (800)

Liabilities A company's economic obligations (debts) owed to its creditors (19,123, 206)

LIFO liquidation Occurs when a company reduces the physical quantity of inventory from the beginning of the year to the end of the year (674)

LIFO liquidation profit Extra profit that results from reporting a lower cost of goods sold than would have been reported if a LIFO liquidation had not occurred (674)

LIFO reserve Difference between LIFO and non-LIFO ending inventory amounts (671)

Limited life Occurs when a company's life is linked directly to the operating intentions of its owner (303, 304)

Line of credit Amount of money a company is allowed to borrow with a prearranged, agreed-upon interest rate and a specific payback schedule (62)

Liquidity Measure of how quickly an asset can be converted into cash or a liability can be paid (209, 415)

Liquidity management A company's policies and activities that control its liquidity position (415)

Lockbox system Cash-collection method in which customers mail their payments to the company's post office box, which is monitored by the bank (444)

Long-term capital Capital which will be repaid to creditors or returned to investors after more than one year (62)

Long-term investments Items such as notes receivable, government bonds, bonds and capital stock of corporations, and other securities which a company intends to hold for more than one year (205)

Long-term liquidity Relates to the amount of cash a company will generate over the long run to pay off its liabilities as they become due (810)

Lower-of-cost-or-market (LCM) method When the market value of a company's inventory falls below its cost, the company is required to reduce, or "write down," the inventory to that market value (674)

Maker Company that made and signed a note (438)

Management accounting Identification, measurement, recording, accumulation, and communication of economic information about a company for internal users in management decision-making (14)

Management by exception Management principle where an entrepreneur (or manager) focuses on improving the activities that show significant differences between budgeted and actual results (87)

Management discussion and analysis (MD&A) Portion of the annual report where managers comment on how well (or poorly) the corporation performed over the past year, specifically in regard to its liquidity, capital, and results of operations (318)

Manufacturing company Company that makes its products and then sells these products to its customers (6)

Margin of safety Amount that sales (in units) can decrease without a loss; the difference between the estimated sales volume and the break-even sales volume (358)

Marketing function Identifies consumer needs, analyzes consumer behavior, evaluates customer satisfaction, and promotes a company's products (309)

Master budget Set of interrelated reports showing the relationships among a company's goals to be met, activities to be performed, resources to be used, and expected financial results (89)

Matching principle To determine its net income for an accounting period, a company computes and deducts the total expenses from the total revenues earned during the period (134)

Materiality Occurs when a monetary amount is large enough to make a difference in a user's decision (311)

Maturity date Specific day when a company that issued a bond (or note) promises to pay the principal (and interest) amounts to the bond (or note) holder (438, 799)

Maturity value The amount (principal plus interest) the maker of a note must pay the payee on the maturity date (438)

Merchandising company Company that purchases goods (sometimes referred to as merchandise or products) for resale to its customers (5)

Mixed costs Costs which have elements of both variable and fixed costs (346)

Modified Accelerated Cost Recovery System (MACRS) Accelerated depreciation method acceptable under the Internal Revenue Code and used by companies for income tax purposes (750)

Monetary unit concept Concept that transactions are to be recorded in terms of money (121)

Mortgage payable Long-term liability for which the lender has a specific claim against an asset of the borrower (819)

Moving average cost flow assumption Average cost per unit is calculated after each purchase and this new average cost is assigned to items sold or held in inventory until the next purchase (when another average cost is computed) (660)

Mutually exclusive capital expenditure proposals Proposals that accomplish the same thing, so that when one proposal is selected, the others are not (721)

Natural resource assets Assets that are used up as they are extracted, mined, dug up, or chopped down (777)

Net assets Assets minus liabilities (124)

Net asset value Cost of an asset less its accumulated depreciation (741)

Net income Excess of a company's revenues over its expenses from providing goods or services to its customers during a specific time period (18,132)

Net loss Excess of a company's expenses over its revenues from providing goods or services to its customers during a specific time period (18)

Net pay The amount of earnings after payroll taxes have been deducted (472)

Net present value Present value of the expected future net cash receipts and payments minus the initial cash payment for a capital expenditure proposal (717)

Net purchases Amount of merchandise purchases adjusted for purchase returns, allowances, and discounts (176)

Net sales Total sales minus the sales discounts and sales returns and allowances for an accounting period (424)

No-par capital stock Does not have a par value (880)

Noncurrent liabilities Obligations that a company does not expect to pay within one year (207)

Non-LIFO Costs of ending inventories under an alternative to the LIFO cost flow assumption, such as FIFO, average, current, or replacement cost (671)

Normal activity Average of a company's expected future annual production volumes (591)

Note payable A legal document promising to pay a given amount on a given future date (60)

Note receivable A note for which a selling company expects to receive cash from its customer on a specified future date (419)

Note Written legal document in which the maker of the note makes an unconditional promise to pay another party a certain amount of money on an agreed future date (419)

Notes to the financial statements Inform external users of a company's annual report about its accounting policies and of important financial information that is not reported in the company's financial statements (316)

Number of days in collection period Number of days in a company's business year divided by its accounts receivable turnover (218)

Number of days in selling period Number of days in a company's business year divided by its inventory turnover (217)

Objectivity Quality of being unbiased in critical thinking (35)

Operating Management activity that enables a company to conduct its business according to its plan (12)

Operating activities Include the primary activities of buying, selling, and delivering goods for sale, as well as providing services (239)

Operating activities section Section of a company's cash flow statement (or cash budget) that summarizes the cash receipts and payments from its actual (or planned) operating activities (100, 239, 386)

Operating capability Company's ability to continue a given level of operations (179, 216, 757)

Operating cycle Average time it takes a company to use cash to buy or produce goods (or services) for sale, to sell these goods (or services) to customers, and to collect cash from its customers (87, 88, 374, 680)

Operating efficiency How well a company uses its assets to generate revenue (757)

Operating expenditure Cost that only maintains the benefits that a company originally expected from an asset (751)

Operating expenses Expenses (other than cost of goods sold) that a company incurs in its day-to-day operations (176)

Operating income All the revenues earned less the expenses incurred in the primary operating activities of a company (168, 178, 314)

Operating lease Does not transfer the risks and benefits of ownership (815)

Operating segment Component of a company that earns revenues and incurs expenses, whose performance is reviewed regularly by the company's top executive, and for which financial information is available (857)

Opportunity costs Profits that a company forgoes by following a particular course of action (508)

Ordering costs Costs of placing and receiving each inventory order (512)

Other items Revenues and expenses that are not directly related to the primary operations of a company (168, 178, 315)

Outsourcing Occurs when a company turns over the management of a function to an outside specialist (446)

Outstanding capital stock Number of shares that a corporation has issued to stockholders and that the stockholders still hold as of a specific date (886)

Overhead budget variance Difference between the total overhead budgeted and the total overhead incurred (593)

Owner's equity Owner's current investment in the assets of a company (19,124, 207)

Par value Monetary amount per share that must be kept in a corporation as legal capital (312, 880)

Parent company Investor company that has control over the investee company (856)

Participative budgeting Budgeting in which department and division managers or teams participate with upper-level managers in the planning decisions to determine the goals and resource commitments for the activities of their departments, divisions, or teams (398)

Partners' equity The partners' current investment in the assets of the company (124)

Partnership Company owned by two or more individuals who each invest capital, time, and/or talent into the company and share in its profits and losses (8, 303)

Partnership agreement Contract signed by partners of a partnership before the company begins operations (8, 304)

Patent Exclusive right granted by the U.S. government giving the owner of an invention the control of its manufacture or sale for 20 years from the date of the patent application (770)

Payback period Length of time required for a return of the initial investment in a capital expenditure proposal (719)

Payee Holder of a note receivable (438)

Pension plan Agreement by a company to provide income to its employees after they retire (821)

Percentage analysis Financial analysis in which financial statement information is converted from dollars to percentages (321)

Percentage of sales method Estimates bad debts expense by multiplying the net credit sales of the period by the percentage of these sales that is estimated to be uncollectible (431)

Periodic inventory system System that does not keep a continuous record of the inventory on hand and sold, but determines the inventory at the end of each accounting period by physically counting it (175, 654)

Perpetual inventory system System that keeps a continuous record of the cost of inventory on hand and the cost of inventory sold (173, 654)

Petty cash fund Specified amount of money that is under the control of one employee and that is used for making small cash payments for a company (275)

Physical causes of depreciation Include wear and tear due to use, deterioration and decay caused by the passage of time, and damage and destruction (742)

Piggybacking Process of generating ideas from other ideas (34)

Planning Management activity that establishes a company's goals and the means of achieving these goals (12)

Post-closing trial balance Schedule a company prepares after making its closing entries to prove the equality of the debit and credit balances in its asset, liability, and owners' equity accounts (956)

Posting Process of transferring the debit and credit information for each journal entry to the accounts in a company's general ledger (942)

Potential common shares Securities that can be used by the holder to acquire common stock (898)

Practical capacity Volume of activity at which the company's manufacturing facilities are capable of operating per year under practical conditions, allowing for usual levels of efficiency (592)

Predetermined overhead rate Budgeted factory overhead cost divided by budgeted total volume of manufacturing activity for the year (550)

Preemptive right Right to maintain a proportionate (pro rata) share of additional capital stock if it is issued (879)

Preferred stock Type of capital stock issued for which stockholders receive certain additional rights in exchange for giving up some of the usual stockholders' rights (312, 881)

Prepaid insurance Cost paid for the right to insurance protection (123)

Prepaid item Current asset (economic resource) that a company records when it pays for goods or services before using them (478, 946)

Present value Value today of a certain amount of dollars to be paid or received in the future (712)

Prevention costs Costs to a company of preventing flaws and defects in its products (621)

Price/earnings ratio Market price per share divided by earnings per share (898)

Price standard Cost that a company should incur to acquire one unit of input for its manufacturing process (345, 579)

Price standard for factory overhead Standard predetermined overhead rate (690)

Principal Stated value on a note that must be paid on the maturity date (438)

Process cost accounting system Keeps track of the costs applied to identical units of a product as they move through one or more manufacturing processes (554)

Procurement card Similar to a credit card, permits employees responsible for keeping supplies in stock to purchase directly from suppliers (467)

Production budget Schedule showing how many units a company should produce during each budget period both to satisfy expected sales for that period and to end each period with a desired finished goods inventory level (375)

Production function Manufacturing activity that uses people and equipment to convert materials, components, and parts into products that the company will sell to customers (309)

Product defect rates Percentage of defective products manufactured (624)

Product sales mix Relative proportion of units of the different products that a company sells (352)

Profit Difference between the total revenues of a company and the total costs (expenses) of the company during a specific time period (18)

Profit center Responsibility center in which the manager has decision-making authority over both costs and revenues (393)

Profit margin Net income divided by net sales (180)

Projected balance sheet Statement summarizing a company's expected financial position (assets, liabilities, and owner's equity) at the end of a budget period (103)

Projected benefit obligation Obligation of a company to its employees in regard to its pension plan for the work they have done to date (822)

Projected income statement Statement summarizing a company's expected revenues and expenses for the budget period (102)

Property, plant, and equipment All of the physical (tangible), long-term assets a company uses in its operations (206, 738)

Prospectus Corporation's financial reports and other information which must be provided to potential investors when the corporation offers stock for public sale (319)

Publicly available information Any information released to the public; it may come directly from a corporation or from secondary sources (316)

Publicly-held corporation Sells its stock to the general public (307)

Pull-through production Customers' orders "pull" products through a company's production process, from the customers' orders backward through the production process to the purchase of raw materials (623)

Purchase order Document authorizing a supplier to ship the items listed on the document at a specific price (282, 462)

Purchases allowance Occurs when a company keeps damaged goods that it previously recorded as a purchase, and later receives a refund of a portion of the purchase price (465)

Purchases budget Budget showing the purchases (in units) required in each month to make the expected sales in that month (from the sales budget) and to keep inventory at desired levels (94)

Purchases discount Reduction in the invoice price because the purchaser pays within the discount period (445, 462)

Purchases return Occurs when a company returns goods that it previously recorded as a purchase and receives a refund in exchange for the goods (465)

Push-through production Sales forecast "pushes" the products through a company's production process (623)

Quantity discount (Trade discount) Reduction in the sales price of a good or service because of the number of items purchased or because of a sales promotion (170)

Quantity standard Amount of an input that a company should use to produce a unit of product in its manufacturing process (344, 579)

Quantity standard for factory overhead Volume of production activity (direct labor hours, machine hours, or other measure of activity) that should be used to produce one unit of product (590)

Quick ratio Quick assets divided by current liabilities (210)

Ratio analysis Computations made in financial analysis in which an item on a company's financial statements is divided by another related item (180, 321)

Rational A characteristic of depreciation that relates it to the benefits an asset produces in any period (744)

Raw materials Materials, ingredients, and parts that make up a company's manufactured products (335)

Raw materials inventory Raw materials a company uses either directly or indirectly in manufacturing its products (339)

Receiving report Documents the type, quantity, and condition of goods received by a company (462)

Redeemable preferred stock Subject to mandatory retirement at a specified maturity date and price or at the option of the owner (885)

Reengineering Process of analyzing and redesigning an activity to make it more effective and efficient (429)

Relevant accounting information Having the capacity to influence a user's decision (310)

Relevant cash flows Future cash flows that differ, either in amount or in timing, as a result of accepting a capital expenditure proposal (708)

Relevant range Range of volumes over which cost estimates are needed for a particular use and over which observed cost behaviors are expected to remain stable (350)

Reliable accounting information Having the capability of being verified (311)

Replacement cost Cost that a company would have to pay at the balance sheet date to purchase (replace) an item of inventory (664)

Required rate of return Cutoff rate used to distinguish between acceptable and unacceptable capital expenditure proposals (710)

Research Activity aimed at the discovery of new knowledge intended for use in developing a new or improved product or process (769)

Residual equity Term that is used to refer to owner's equity because creditors have first legal claim to a company's assets (124)

Residual value Estimated cash to be received from the sale or disposal of an asset at the end of its estimated service life (743)

Responsibility center Identifiable portion or segment of a company's operations, the activities of which are the responsibility of a particular manager (393)

Retail inventory method Used to estimate the cost of ending inventory by multiplying the retail value of the ending inventory by the cost-to-retail ratio of the current period (678)

Retained earnings A corporation's total lifetime net income that has been reinvested in the corporation and not distributed to stockholders as dividends (312, 314)

Return Money received from investment and credit decisions (57)

Return on owner's equity Net income divided by average owner's equity (215)

Return on total assets Net income and interest expense are added together and then divided by average total assets (214)

Revenues Prices charged to a company's customers for the goods or services the company provides to them (18, 132)

Risk Amount of uncertainty that exists about the future operations of a company (57, 179, 810)

Risk premium Additional interest that a borrower, such as a company, pays when there is a possibility that it will default (803)

Risk-free rate Interest rate that a borrower would pay, and a lender would receive, when there is no risk of default by the borrower and when no inflation is expected (803)

Sales allowance When a customer agrees to keep damaged merchandise and the company refunds a portion of the original sales price (172, 424)

Sales budget Budget showing the number of units of inventory that a company expects to sell each month, the related monthly sales revenue, and in which months the company expects to collect cash from these sales (91, 375)

Sales-determined expenses Result from selling activities that are necessary to support the volume of budgeted sales (382)

Sales-determining expenses Result from selling activities that affect the sales volume (382)

Sales discount Percentage reduction of the invoice price if the customer pays the invoice within a specified period (170, 424)

Sales order Source document (either on paper or in a computer file) that includes specific information about a sale (421)

Sales return When a customer returns previously purchased merchandise and receives a refund (171, 424)

Scatter diagram Pattern of points on a graph that allow the approximation of a straight line (347)

Secondary equity market Where investors buy the stock of corporations from other investors rather than from the corporations (307)

Segment Separate major line of business whose assets, results of operations, and activities can clearly be separated from the rest of the corporation (893)

Segment report Provides financial information about a company's operating segments (857)

Selling expenses Operating expenses related to the sales activities of a company (177)

Selling expenses budget Budget showing the expenses and related cash payments associated with planned selling activities (97)

Service company Company that performs services or activities that benefit individuals or business customers (5)

Service life Life over which a company expects an asset to be useful (749)

Short-term capital Capital which will be repaid within a year or less (61)

Significant influence over investee When an investor company owns between 20% and 50% of another company's common stock (842)

Slide Occurs when the digits are listed in the correct order but are mistakenly moved one decimal place to the left or right (949)

Small stock dividend Dividend of 20% or less of the previously outstanding common shares (903)

Software production cost Costs of designing, coding, testing, and preparing documentation and training materials (772)

Sole proprietorship Company owned by one individual who is the sole investor of capital into the company (8, 303)

Solvency Company's long-term ability to pay its debts as they come due (18)

Source document Business record used as evidence that a transaction has occurred (121)

Specific identification method Allocates costs to cost of goods sold and to ending inventory by assigning to each unit sold and to each unit in ending inventory the cost to a company of purchasing that particular unit (284, 654)

Standard costs Costs that a company should incur in performing an activity or producing a product under a given set of planned operating conditions (343, 578)

Standard costs of an input Quantity standard of an input multiplied by its price standard (579)

Standard cost system Assigns standard costs rather than actual costs to each inventory account (578)

Standard direct labor hours budgeted Number of direct labor hours that should be used for the company's actual production level (588)

Standard direct materials quantity budgeted Amount of direct materials that should be used for the company's actual production level (583)

Stated value Legal capital per share of no-par stock (880)

Statement of changes in owner's equity Statement that summarizes the transactions that affected owner's equity during the accounting period (182)

Statement of changes in stockholders' equity Supporting schedule that shows the changes in all the accounts in the stockholders' equity section of a corporation's balance sheet (906)

Statement of retained earnings Schedule that starts with the beginning balance in retained earnings, adds the amount of net income, and subtracts the amount of dividends to determine the ending balance of retained earnings (906)

Stock certificate Serially numbered legal document that indicates the number of shares of capital stock owned by a stockholder (879)

Stock dividend Proportional (pro rata) distribution of additional shares of a corporation's own stock to its stockholders (902)

Stock split Decrease in the par value per share of a corporation's common stock and a proportional increase in the number or shares authorized and issued (905)

Stockbroker Person or company that buys and sells (trades) stocks and bonds for other people or companies (843)

Stockholders (Shareholders) Owners of a corporation who hold shares of the corporation's capital stock (305, 879)

Stockholders' equity Owners' equity of a corporation, consisting of contributed capital and retained earnings (19, 124, 312, 878, 958)

Straight-line method Computes depreciation expense by allocating the cost of an asset, less its estimated residual value, equally to each period of the asset's estimated service life (744)

Subsidiary company Investee company that has more than 50% of its common stock owned by an investor company (856)

Sum-of-the-years'-digits method Computes depreciation expense by multiplying the depreciable cost of an asset by a fraction that declines each year (748)

Systematic Following a formula for the calculation of depreciation (744)

T-account Accounts used to record transactions for individual types of assets, liabilities, and owner's equity, as well as revenues and expenses (163)

Tax Amount of money that a government requires a taxable entity to pay (471)

Temporary difference Occurs when a corporation records an expense (or a revenue) for financial reporting in a period different from that used for income tax reporting, but the total lifetime expense (or revenue) is the same for both (819)

10-K report Report filed with the SEC including a corporation's annual report and other information such as officers' names, salaries, and stock ownership (319)

Total contribution margin Difference between the total sales revenue and the total variable costs (70)

Total cost Sum of the fixed costs and variable costs at a given volume (66)

Total equity Total of the liabilities and owner's equity (124)

Total overhead variance Difference between total factory overhead cost applied and total factory overhead cost incurred in a standard cost system (592)

Total quality management Management philosophy or approach that focuses on a company's customers to foster continuous improvement (619)

Trading securities Investments in securities that a company holds for a very short time to earn profits from short-term differences in the selling prices of the securities (842)

Trademark (Tradename) Exclusive right granted by the U.S. government (or the government of another country) to use a name or symbol for product identification (771)

Transaction Exchange of property or service by a company with another entity (120)

Transposition Occurs when two digits in a number are mistakenly reversed (949)

Treasury stock Corporation's own capital stock that stockholders fully paid for and the corporation issued, the corporation later reacquired, and the corporation currently holds (886)

Trial balance Schedule that lists the titles of all accounts in a company's general ledger, the debit or credit balance of each account, and the totals of the debit and credit balances (944)

Unearned revenue Obligation of a company to provide goods or services in the future, resulting from an advance receipt of cash (436, 946)

Units-of-production method Used to compute depletion (or depreciation) based on the level of an asset's physical activity (777)

Unlimited liability Owners of a sole proprietorship or partnership must assume personal responsibility for the debts incurred by their company (303, 304)

Valid accounting information Showing a realistic picture of what is meant to be represented by the information (311)

Variable cost Cost that is constant per unit and that changes in total in direct proportion to changes in volume (65)

Variable manufacturing cost Constant for each unit produced but varies in total in direct proportion to the volume produced (345)

Variance Difference between a standard cost and an actual cost (344)

Vertical analysis Shows each item in a financial statement of a given period or date both as a percentage of another item on the statement and as a dollar amount (321)

Volume Activity level in a company (64)

Wages and salaries payable Amounts owed to employees for work they have done (123, 469)

Withdrawals Payments from the company to the owner (137)

Working capital A company's current assets minus its current liabilities (209, 266)

Yield Market rate at which bonds are issued (804)

Zero-coupon bonds Bonds that do not pay interest each period, but pay the interest on the maturity date (807, 860)

Credits

P. 13	© Clint Clemens/International Stock
P. 29	Photo courtesy of Photopia
P. 61	© Mark Bolster/International Stock
P. 90	Photo courtesy of Photopia
P. 105	Photo courtesy of Photopia
P. 121	© Sebastian Lasse/Plus 49
P. 140	© John Michael/International Stock
P. 175	© Robert Fried, 1998
P. 201	© PhotoDisc
P. 209	© PhotoDisc
P. 234	© Dana M. Cunningham, 1998
P. 249	© Patrick Ramsey/International Stock
P. 283	© Robert Fried, 1998
P. 308	Photo used with permission of the New York Stock Exchange
P. 338	© Gregory Edwards/International Stock
P. 341	© Photofest
P. 415	Photo courtesy of Photopia
P. 433	© International Stock
P. 460	Photo courtesy of Photopia
P. 476	Photo courtesy of Photopia
P. 506 (left)	© PhotoDisc
P. 506 (right)	© Super Stock
P. 517	© Rob Johns/Liason International
P. 543	© Sally Industries, Inc.
P. 557	© PhotoDisc
P. 582	© 1998 Don Couch Photography
P. 602	© Digital Stock
P. 618	© 1998 Madame Alexander® Alexander Doll Company, Inc.
P. 627	Photo courtesy of Tellabs, Inc.
P. 654	© 1998 Don Couch Photography
P. 657	© Ernest H. Robl
P. 677	© J. L. Bulcao/Liason International
P. 723	© Paul Venning/Leo de Wys, Inc.
P. 738	© 1999 Don Couch Photography
P. 753	Photo courtesy of American Airlines
P. 794	© 1998 Don Couch Photography
P. 821	© Dick Luria/FPG International
P. 884	© Weststock
P. 902	© PhotoDisc

Index